ENCYCLOPEDIA OF
RELIGION AND
SOCIETY

ENCYCLOPEDIA OF RELIGION AND SOCIETY

WILLIAM H. SWATOS, JR.
EDITOR

PETER KIVISTO
ASSOCIATE EDITOR

BARBARA J. DENISON
JAMES MCCLENON
ASSISTANT EDITORS

ALTAMIRA
P R E S S
A Division of Sage Publications
Walnut Creek London New Delhi

For information:

AltaMira Press
A Division of Sage Publications, Inc.
1630 North Main Street, Suite 367
Walnut Creek, CA 94596
E-mail: explore@altamira.sagepub.com

SAGE Publications Ltd.
6 Bonhill Street
London EC2A 4PU
United Kingdom

SAGE Publications India Pvt. Ltd.
M-32 Market
Greater Kailash I
New Delhi 110 048 India

Printed in the United States of America

Library of Congress Cataloging-in-Publication Data

Main entry under title:

Encyclopedia of religion and society / edited by William H. Swatos, Jr.
    p. cm.
    Includes bibliographical references and index.
    ISBN 0-7619-8956-0 (alk. paper)
    1. Religion and sociology—Encyclopedia. I. Swatos, William H.
BL60.E53   1998
306.6′03—dc21   97-33724

This book is printed on acid-free paper.

98 99 00 01 02 03 10 9 8 7 6 5 4 3 2 1

Editorial Management:	Erik Hanson
Production Editor:	Astrid Virding
Production Assistant:	Karen Wiley
Designer/Typesetter:	Janelle LeMaster
Cover Designer:	Ravi Balasuriya
Print Buyer:	Anna Chin

Editors and Editorial Board

Editor-in-Chief

William H. Swatos, Jr., Executive Officer, Association for the Sociology of Religion and Religious Research Association. Coauthor, *Icelandic Spiritualism: Mediumship and Modernity* and *For Democracy*; editor or coeditor of numerous volumes in the sociology of religion. Editor of the journal *Sociological Analysis* (1989-1992), *Sociology of Religion* (1993-1994).

Associate Editor

Peter Kivisto, Professor and Chair of Sociology, Augustana College of Illinois. Author, *Key Ideas in Sociology, Illuminating Social Life* and *Americans All* as well as other books and articles in ethnicity, theory, and political sociology. Secretary-Treasurer of the Theory Section of the American Sociological Association, Executive Board Member of the Immigration History Society.

Assistant Editors

James McClenon, Associate Professor of Sociology, Elizabeth City State University of North Carolina. Author, *Deviant Science: The Case of Parapsychology* and *Wondrous Events: Foundations of Religious Belief.*

Barbara J. Denison, Director of Continuing and Distance Education, Penn State Harrisburg-Capital College. Executive Officer, Association for the Sociology of Religion, 1988-1995; North Central Sociological Association, 1985-1993.

Editorial Board

David G. Bromley, Professor of Sociology and Religious Studies, Virginia Commonwealth University. Coauthor and coeditor of books and articles in the area of new religious movements, including *The Handbook of Cults and Sects*. President, Association for the Sociology of Religion (1994). Editor, *Journal for the Scientific Study of Religion* (1993-1995).

Roberto Cipriani, Professor of Sociology, Third University of Rome. Author of *Sociology of Legitimation, La religione dei valori,* and numerous articles on a variety of topics within the sociology of religion. President, Research Committee 22, International Sociological Association (1990-1994). Editor-in-Chief of the journal *International Sociology* (1994-1998).

James D. Davidson, Professor of Sociology and Anthropology, Purdue University. Coauthor, *American Catholic Laity in a Changing Church* and *Laity: American and Catholic.* President, Religious Research Asso-

ciation (1989-1990). Executive Officer, Society for the Scientific Study of Religion (1988-1993). Editor, *Review of Religious Research* (1977-1980).

Grace Davie, Senior Lecturer in Sociology, University of Exeter. Author, *Religion in Britain Since 1945: Believing Without Belonging*; coeditor, *Identités religieuses en Europe*. Secretary General, International Society for the Sociology of Religion (1993-1997).

Doyle Paul Johnson, Professor of Sociology and Chair of Sociology, Anthropology, and Social Work, Texas Tech University, Lubbock, Texas. Author, *Sociological Theory: Classical Founders and Contemporary Perspectives* plus journal articles in sociology of religion and gerontology. Editor, *Review of Religious Research* (1990-1999).

Edward C. Lehman, Distinguished Teaching Professor Emeritus, State University College of New York at Brockport. Author, *Gender and Work, Women in Ministry: Receptivity and Resistance,* and *Women Clergy: Breaking Through Gender Barriers.* President, Association for the Sociology of Religion (1992); Religious Research Association (1999-2000). Editor, *Review of Religious Research* (1984-1990).

Armand L. Mauss, Professor of Sociology and Religious Studies, Washington State University. Author, *The Angel and the Beehive: The Mormon Struggle with Assimilation* and other works in Mormon studies. Editor, *Journal for the Scientific Study of Religion* (1989-1992).

Joseph B. Tamney, Professor of Sociology, Ball State University. Author, *American Society in the Buddhist Mirror, The Resilience of Christianity,* and *The Struggle for Singapore's Soul.* Editor of the journal *Sociology of Religion* (1995-2000).

Contributors

Hans A. Baer
University of Arkansas—Little Rock
Little Rock, Arkansas

Edward I. Bailey
Network for the Study of Implicit Religion
Bristol, England

Eileen Barker
London School of Economics
London, England

Peter Beyer
University of Ottawa
Ottawa, Ontario, Canada

Anthony J. Blasi
Tennessee State University
Nashville, Tennessee

Edward F. Breschel
Morehead State University
Morehead, Kentucky

David G. Bromley
Virginia Commonwealth University
Richmond, Virginia

Steve Bruce
University of Aberdeen
Aberdeen, Scotland

Joseph M. Bryant
University of New Brunswick
Fredericton, New Brunswick, Canada

Colin Campbell
University of York
Heslington, York, England

Melodie Campbell
University of Alberta
Edmonton, Alberta, Canada

Jackson W. Carroll
Duke University
Durham, North Carolina

Kevin J. Christiano
University of Notre Dame
Notre Dame, Indiana

Roberto Cipriani
Third University of Rome
Rome, Italy

Kevin J. Corn
Indiana University
Indianapolis, Indiana

Madeleine R. Cousineau
Mount Ida College
Newton Centre, Massachusetts

M. Herbert Danzger
*Lehman College and the Graduate
Center, City University of New York*
New York, New York

Arnold M. Dashefsky
University of Connecticut
Storrs, Connecticut

James D. Davidson
Purdue University
West Lafayette, Indiana

Grace Davie
University of Exeter
Exeter, England

Lorne Dawson
University of Waterloo
Waterloo, Ontario, Canada

Barbara J. Denison
Penn State Harrisburg-Capital College
Middletown, Pennsylvania

Frederick M. Denny
University of Colorado
Boulder, Colorado

Karel Dobbelaere
Katholieke Universiteit Leuven
Leuven, Belgium

Michael J. Donahue
Donahue Research Associates
Minneapolis, Minnesota

Helen Rose Ebaugh
University of Houston
Houston, Texas

Joel Elliott
University of North Carolina
Chapel Hill, North Carolina

Kieran Flanagan
University of Bristol
Bristol, England

Razelle Frankl
Rowan University
Glassboro, New Jersey

William R. Garrett
St. Michael's College
Colchester, Vermont

Peter Gee
Overseas Development Institute
London, England

Robin Gill
Darwin College, The University of Kent
Canterbury, Kent, England

Stephen D. Glazier
University of Nebraska
Kearney, Nebraska

Charles Y. Glock
*University of California—Berkeley
(Emeritus)*
Berkeley, California

John C. Green
University of Akron
Akron, Ohio

Paul M. Gustafson
Hiram College (Emeritus)
Hiram, Ohio

James L. Guth
Furman University
Greenville, South Carolina

Durk H. Hak
University of Groningen
Groningen, The Netherlands

John Hannigan
University of Toronto
Toronto, Ontario, Canada

W. E. Hewitt
University of Western Ontario
London, Ontario, Canada

Ralph W. Hood, Jr.
University of Tennessee—Chattanooga
Chattanooga, Tennessee

Julie Ingersoll
Millsaps College
Jackson, Mississippi

Larry Ingram
University of Tennessee—Martin
Martin, Tennessee

Janet Jacobs
University of Colorado
Boulder, Colorado

Ted G. Jelen
University of Nevada—Las Vegas
Las Vegas, Nevada

Doyle Paul Johnson
Texas Tech University
Lubbock, Texas

Steven M. Kane
University of Rhode Island—Providence
Providence, Rhode Island

Bruce Karlenzig
Saskatoon, Saskatchewan, Canada

Lyman B. Kellstedt
Wheaton College
Wheaton, Illinois

James R. Kelly
Fordham University
Bronx, New York

Stephen A. Kent
University of Alberta
Edmonton, Alberta, Canada

David A. Kingma
Gonzaga University
Spokane, Washington

Aaron Kivisto
Rock Island, Illinois

Peter Kivisto
Augustana College
Rock Island, Illinois

Jerome Koch
Texas Tech University
Lubbock, Texas

Frank J. Lechner
Emory University
Atlanta, Georgia

Gary Mann
Augustana College
Rock Island, Illinois

Martin E. Marty
University of Chicago (Emeritus)
Chicago, Illinois

Armand L. Mauss
Washington State University
Pullman, Washington

Ronald McAllister
Elizabethtown College
Elizabethtown, Pennsylvania

James McClenon
Elizabeth City State University
Elizabeth City, North Carolina

William McKinney
Pacific School of Religion
Berkeley, California

Hugo Meynell
University of Calgary
Calgary, Alberta, Canada

David O. Moberg
Marquette University (Emeritus)
Milwaukee, Wisconsin

Matthew C. Moen
University of Maine
Orono, Maine

Robert L. Montgomery
Ridgewood, New York

Loretta M. Morris
Loyola Marymount University
Los Angeles, California

Nancy Nason-Clark
University of New Brunswick
Fredericton, New Brunswick, Canada

André Nauta
University of North Texas
Denton, Texas

Mary Jo Neitz
University of Missouri
Columbia, Missouri

Hart M. Nelsen
Penn State University
State College, Pennsylvania

Paula D. Nesbitt
University of Denver
Denver, Colorado

William M. Newman
University of Connecticut
Storrs, Connecticut

Donald A. Nielsen
*State University of New York College
    at Oneonta*
Oneonta, New York

Roger O'Toole
University of Toronto
Toronto, Ontario, Canada

Enzo Pace
University of Trieste
Trieste, Italy

Susan J. Palmer
Dawson College
Montréal, Québec, Canada

Michael H. Peckham
University of Alberta
Edmonton, Alberta, Canada

Everett L. Perry
Presbyterian Church (U.S.A.)
Glenwood, Florida

Ralph E. Pyle
Michigan State University
East Lansing, Michigan

Edward B. Reeves
Morehead State University
Morehead, Kentucky

James T. Richardson
University of Nevada—Reno
Reno, Nevada

Thomas Robbins
Rochester, Minnesota

Keith A. Roberts
Hanover College
Hanover, Indiana

David A. Roozen
Hartford Seminary
Hartford, Connecticut

Barry Sandywell
University of York
Heslington, York, England

Ross P. Scherer
Loyola University Chicago (Emeritus)
Chicago, Illinois

Eugen Schoenfeld
Georgia State University (Emeritus)
Atlanta, Georgia

Robert Segal
Lancaster University
Lancaster, England

Mark A. Shibley
Loyola University Chicago
Chicago, Illinois

Anson Shupe
Indiana University/Purdue University—
Fort Wayne
Fort Wayne, Indiana

William Silverman
Hicksville, New York

John H. Simpson
University of Toronto
Toronto, Ontario, Canada

Corwin Smidt
Calvin College
Grand Rapids, Michigan

James V. Spickard
University of Redlands
Redlands, California

Phillip Stanworth
University of York
Heslington, York, England

Peter Staples
University of Utrecht
Utrecht, The Netherlands

William H. Swatos, Jr.
Association for the Sociology of Religion
and Religious Research Association
Holiday, Florida

Joseph B. Tamney
Ball State University
Muncie, Indiana

Robert Tessier
Université du Québec à Montréal
Montréal, Québec, Canada

Luigi Tomasi
Università degli Studi di Trento
Trento, Italy

C. N. Venugopal
Jawaharlal Nehru University
New Delhi, India

James K. Wellman, Jr.
Bainbridge Island, Washington

Rhys H. Williams
Southern Illinois University
Carbondale, Illinois

Ronald C. Wimberley
North Carolina State University
Raleigh, North Carolina

J. Alan Winter
Connecticut College
New London, Connecticut

Richard L. Wood
University of New Mexico
Albuquerque, New Mexico

David Yamane
University of Wisconsin
Madison, Wisconsin

Susan Zickmund
University of Iowa
Iowa City, Iowa

Introduction

The social scientific study of religion began in earnest a scant century ago. Although precedents for a "scientific attitude" toward religion may be found at least as far back as the pre-Socratics of ancient Greece, it is principally with the works of Émile Durkheim, Max Weber, and Sigmund Freud that we can begin to chart something of the development of today's insights into the "phenomenon" of religion.

The Encyclopedia of Religion and Society marks a unique venture in that it attempts to bring together in a single-volume compendium a state-of-the-art summary of the insights gained by the principal social sciences of religion: anthropology, psychology, and sociology. To do so is to take, admittedly, a "one-sided" approach to the religion-and-society nexus. One could perhaps consider an alternative posture, more ethical in nature—namely, one that considers what religions think about society. This would really be an encyclopedia of religious social ethics, and it is not within the scope of this project.

We have tried to assemble entries, both lengthy and brief, that survey as broadly as possible the different theoretical traditions and research styles that have emerged over the century. Although more heavily oriented toward North America, the scope is global, and an effort has been made to address the major traditions of world religious experience.

We also have attempted to provide a historical reference tool particularly with regard to the major professional societies in the social scientific study of religion: the Association for the Sociology of Religion, the Religious Research Association, the Society for the Scientific Study of Religion, and the Société Internationale de Sociologie des Religions—and as much as possible the Association for the Social Scientific Study of Jewry and Research Committee 22 (sociology of religion) of the International Sociological Association. Entries are also provided for the sections of the major professional organizations, the American Psychological Association and the American Sociological Association. This resource is intended to aid each of these organizations in historical retrieval, and we hope that subsequent editions of this work may increase the detail that can be provided.

The encyclopedia began its course initially in the spring of 1993, more in earnest from 1994 to the present. Charting new ground called for a number of decisions to be made about inclusion and exclusion; some of the decisions were purely practical, but for most at least an attempt was made at rationality. The work began with an extensive citation study of various journal indexes, texts, and bibliographies in the field. These generated a quantitative measure from which decisions about initial subject inclusion and the length of subsequent entries were determined. To these were added the names of those persons who had been elected president of any one of the major societies mentioned above, even if the individual did not qualify by the quantitative index. Subsequently, the publisher and editors consulted about modifications based upon more subjective criteria.

We have not taken up the philosophical background to the social sciences. There are no entries for Plato or Aristotle, Thomas Aquinas or Ibn Khaldūn, or Hobbes, Locke, Hume, or Kant. We pick up with brief entries for Rousseau in the French tradition and Hegel in the German. One could say the American tradition actually begins with the Frenchman Tocqueville, but more so H. Richard Niebuhr, on the one hand, and H. Paul Douglass, on the other.

Similarly, we have not taken up religion "in itself." Neither the great religious founders nor subsequent generations of theologians are to be found here. When an exception is made to this rule, it is because of a unique encounter with the social sciences, as in the case of Paul Tillich or Gayraud Wilmore. There are certainly great encyclopedias of both philosophy and theology for those who wish to pursue these lines. The index to this volume will provide the names of those figures in both philosophy and theology of whose work the social scientific study of religion has taken account.

A word on usage: The actual commissioning of entries had to depend on the persons with time available and how things could be conceived by them. In some cases, topics are taken up under biographical entries; in others, there are separate entries for both a topic and an individual closely associated with that topic. In general, topics associated with a single individual are taken up in his or her biography only. For example, the "dilemmas of institutionalization" are almost uniquely associated with Thomas O'Dea, hence they are discussed there; "civil religion," by contrast, although certainly given new birth by Robert Bellah, has also taken on a life quite its own—a separate entry is called for.

Also with regard to usage, the word *religious* normally should be presumed as a modifier. With the exception of the professions of religious education and religious studies, there are no entries under "religious." Readers interested in religious roles, for example, should refer to the entry on "roles"; those interested in religious evolution should refer to *evolution*; and so on. There is also no entry on "religion." Depending on one's interest, this topic will be treated either in the "definition of religion" entry or that for "religious studies." There is similarly no entry for "society"; the reader should consult that aspect of the social structure that is of interest—for example, attitudes, status, stratification, values.

This encyclopedia owes much to the goodwill of the contributors, none of whom was paid for his or her work. All have contributed from a sense of professional responsibility and dedication. Those of us who have worked closely over the years with the men and women who keep the social scientific study of religion alive and vital recognize a great esprit de corps among them, and this project has certainly benefitted from that. A total of 109 authors have contributed. These individuals range from some exceptionally talented students to world-renowned senior and emeritus professors. Most of the members of the editorial board also have contributed entries; all have worked enormously hard to bring out the best in the entries they have reviewed. For myself, mindful that Samuel Johnson ended the entry on "lexicographer" in his pioneering *Dictionary* (1755) with the words "a harmless drudge," I hope I have been perhaps a helpful drudge in bringing it all together.

It is the case, nevertheless, that in breaking new ground as we are, there is a moment of trial and error. And that is about to come upon us. So we share with you our hope that what you find here is readable, meets your needs, and is also a bit inspirational, that you might join with us in a vocation that challenges humanity's highest hopes and greatest dreams.

To that end, finally, we also invite you to become a participant in this project. If there are entries you think should be included in a future edition, entries you would like to see expanded, or entries you found particularly helpful, contact us at swatos@microd.com through the end of 1999.

—*William H. Swatos, Jr.*

AA *see* Alcoholics Anonymous

AAR *see* American Academy of Religion

ABORTION In current usage: the practice of intentionally terminating a pregnancy prior to childbirth; historically, any termination of pregnancy prior to childbirth.

Abortion has occasioned a great deal of religious rhetoric and activity in the United States since the landmark case of *Roe v. Wade* in 1973. As such, the topic has attracted considerable attention from sociologists of religion.

There have been three general approaches to the study of abortion within the scientific study of religion. Much of the earliest work on abortion has been focused on the discourse of elites: journalists, physicians, governmental officials, judges, and lay activists. In this branch of abortion research, several different themes have merged. Because access to legal abortion has been provided by court decisions rather than acts of legislatures, both sides of the abortion controversy have invoked the language of *rights*. Because rights are, by definition, basic prerogatives, the casting of abortion discourse in terms of opposing rights (a "right to choose" versus a "right to life") has rendered abortion rhetoric artificially polarized. Moreover, activist-level discourse has emphasized competing notions of women's social roles and alternative worldviews concerning sexuality and sexual morality. At the

activist level, the abortion controversy has come to crystalize a number of different basic values. Finally, activist-level rhetoric on the pro-life side has become steadily less religious and more secular over time. Arguments about natural law and the meaning of specific scriptural passages have tended to give way to arguments about the humanity of the fetus and the nature of rights and obligations. This secularization of abortion rhetoric may have enhanced the possibility of ecumenical cooperation on this issue, because early abortion activists may have been divided between the Catholic "natural law" rationale for opposition to legal abortion and the evangelical tendency to invoke specific biblical passages. Pro-life activists are less likely to fragment over theological particularism if the abortion debate is cast in the liberal democratic language of competing rights.

A second research tradition on abortion has been concerned with mass-level opinion. This research has suggested that the opinions of ordinary citizens differ qualitatively from those of abortion activists. At the level of the mass public, relatively few American citizens are either unequivocally "pro-choice" or "pro-life" but tend to take varying intermediate positions on the abortion issue. Unlike other issues, this apparent ambivalence does not indicate a lack of sophistication about the issue but reflects the fact that Americans tend to value *both* the privacy rights of women *and* the value of the potential life of the fetus. In another contrast with activist-level debate, the relationship between abortion

1

attitudes and attitudes toward women's societal roles tends to be quite weak at the mass level. Also, both religious orthodoxy and religiosity are related to pro-life attitudes, regardless of respondents' denominational affiliation. This relationship poses an interesting agenda for future research, because the same relationship between religious observance and antiabortion attitudes pertains across diverse socialization experiences. Some denominations attempt direct religious teaching about abortion (with such observances as "Human Life Sundays" and so on), others tend to downplay the issue, and a few emphasize the right of a woman to make the final decision about abortion. Some research has suggested that religious socialization has a strong effect on denominational members (particularly Roman Catholics), but that such religious activity tends to stimulate pro-choice countermobilization.

The political effects of the abortion issue have varied over time. For most of the period following *Roe v. Wade,* the abortion issue was much more salient to those who preferred restrictive policies toward abortion. This asymmetry ended with the case of *Webster v. Missouri Reproductive Services* in 1989, which permitted states considerably greater latitude in regulating the delivery of abortion services (while retaining abortion as a constitutionally protected right). This ruling was interpreted by both pro-life and pro-choice activists as a clear victory for the pro-life side, and appears to have led to the electoral mobilization of pro-choice citizens. Several studies have suggested that a number of senatorial and gubernatorial races in 1989 and 1990 were decided, in large part, by the abortion issue, with pro-choice candidates faring significantly better than might otherwise have been expected.

One similarity exists between activist-level and mass-level understandings of the abortion issue. In both cases, there has been a convergence of rationales on the pro-life side. Early in the post-*Roe* period, Catholics who opposed abortion tended to do so because of a respect for the human status of the fetus, while "pro-life" evangelicals tended to emphasize the effects of legal abortion on reducing the risks of nonmarital sexual activity or on increasing the incidence of premarital sex. By the 1980s, both groups had assimilated both rationales, with "respect for life" being a somewhat stronger predictor than sexual conservatism. Again, this reduction of religious differences in pro-life rationales has made ecumenical antiabortion activity considerably easier.

Finally, a third approach to the study of the abortion issue has focused on the causes and consequences of "direct action." In recent years, some abortion activists (especially on the "pro-life" side) have engaged in unconventional, sometimes illegal, and occasionally violent activities. These practices have included picketing, "sidewalk counseling," physically obstructing entrances to abortion clinics ("sitting in"), vandalizing the property of abortion clinics, and occasionally murdering or attempting to murder abortion providers. A number of general explanations of such activities have been offered by social scientists. Some have emphasized the role of individual psychological pathologies in accounting for unconventional protest activities. Protesters are thought to be compensating for some personal deficiency (downward economic mobility, individual feelings of inferiority, and so on). Other analysts have focused on the effects of religious beliefs on unconventional activism, arguing that abortion violence is a natural (if not necessarily inevitable) consequence of particular religious commitments. In this style of analysis, it is often argued that people who hold an image of a vengeful, punishing God are much more likely to engage in pro-life violence than are other people. Finally, some have argued that unconventional pro-life activism is an understandable response to an inhospitable political environment. In the aftermath of the pro-choice mobilization that followed *Webster,* and the election of pro-choice President Bill Clinton (with the probable consequence of preserving a pro-choice majority on the Supreme Court), conventional political activity (voting, lobbying, public education, and the like) has seemed futile to many pro-life activists. Given the very high theological and moral stakes of the abortion controversy, some have elected to take drastic action to limit the incidence of legal abortion. Indeed, several studies have suggested that fewer physicians are willing to provide abortion services since the murders of abortion doctors in 1993 and 1994.

—*Ted G. Jelen*

REFERENCES

D. A. Blanchard, *The Anti-Abortion Movement and the Rise of the Religious Right* (New York: Twayne, 1994); D. A. Blanchard and T. J. Prewitt, *Religious Violence and Abortion* (Gainesville: University Press of Florida, 1993); P. E. Converse and G. Markus, " 'Plus ca Change . . . ,' " *American Political Science Review* 73(1979):32-49; E. A. Cook et al., *Between Two Absolutes* (Boulder, Colo.: Westview, 1992); A. Fried, "Abortion Politics as Symbolic Politics," *Social Science Quarterly* 69(1988):137-154; F. Ginsburg, *Contested Lives* (Berkeley: University of California Press, 1989); M.A. Glendon, *Abortion and Divorce in Western Law* (Cambridge: Harvard University Press, 1987); T. G. Jelen, "Respect for Life, Sexual Morality, and Opposition to Abortion," *Review of Religious Research* 25(1984):220-231; T. G. Jelen, *The Political World of the Clergy* (Westport, Conn.: Praeger, 1993); T. G. Jelen (ed.), *Perspectives on the Politics of Abortion* (Westport, Conn.: Praeger, 1995); T. G. Jelen and M. A. Chandler (eds.), *Abortion Politics in the United States and Canada* (Westport,

Conn.: Praeger, 1994); K. Luker, *Abortion and the Politics of Motherhood* (Berkeley: University of California Press, 1984); G. Wills, *Under God* (New York: Simon & Schuster, 1990).

ACQUAVIVA, SABINO (1927–) Professor of Sociology, University of Padua. President, SISR 1969-1971.

Acquaviva is most well known for his hypothesis concerning the eclipse of the sacred, first published as *L'eclissi del sacro nella civiltà industriale* (Comunità 1961; Eng. trans., *The Decline of the Sacred in Industrial Society*, Blackwell 1971), prior to Harvey Cox's *The Secular City* (Macmillan 1965). Based primarily on statistics related to the drop in religious observance, his idea of a progressive disappearance of the sacred—later refuted by developments recorded in subsequent decades—gradually dwindled in his writings to the point of becoming a more limited concept, the "end of the magical use of the sacred" (in *Fine di un'ideologia: la secolarizzazione,* coauthored with R. Stella, Borla 1989). In such more recent works as *Eros, morte ed esperienza religiosa* (Laterza 1990) and the Preface to E. Pace's *Sociologia delle religioni* (Nuova Italia Scientifica 1992), he refers to the biopsychological and anthropological bases of religion, said to arise in the first instance from the "essential needs" of human beings.

—*Roberto Cipriani*

ACSR/ACSS see American Catholic Sociological Society, Association for the Sociology of Religion, *Sociology of Religion: A Quarterly Review*

ADAMS, JAMES LUTHER (1901-1994) Unitarian theologian-ethicist who was a founding member of the Society for the Scientific Study of Religion and the Society of Christian Ethics. Adams graduated from the University of Minnesota (1924) and Harvard Divinity School (S.T.B., 1927; M.A., 1930). He was ordained by the American Unitarian Association and served as pastor in Salem (1927-1934) and Wellesley Hills (1934-1935), Massachusetts. After study in Europe, he assumed a position as instructor in psychology and philosophy of religion at Meadville Theological Seminary before moving, in 1943, to the Federated Theological Faculties at the University of Chicago, where his doctoral thesis was completed in 1945. In 1957, he became the Edward Mallinckrodt, Jr., Profes-

sor of Divinity at Harvard Divinity School, and in 1968, the Distinguished Professor of Social Ethics at Andover Newton Theological Seminary, retiring in 1972. Throughout his career, Adams was recognized as a leading scholar on Paul Tillich, Ernst Troeltsch, and liberal Protestant ethical thought, especially in relation to modern culture.

—*William R. Garrett*

REFERENCES

J. L. Adams, *Paul Tillich's Philosophy of Culture, Science, and Religion,* Thesis, University of Chicago, 1945; J. L. Adams et al., *The Thought of Paul Tillich* (New York: Harper, 1985); M. Stackhouse (ed.), *On Being Human Religiously* (Boston: Beacon, 1976).

ADAPTATION Religion's role in adaptation consists largely of providing an ultimate meaning system that helps individuals deal with life's inevitable contingencies and frustrations. Although religion may not offer tangible resources to solve problems, all religions incorporate a theodicy that helps provide emotional and psychological support and assures individuals of the ultimate value and significance of their lives, despite the problems they face—illness, poverty, oppression, and even death itself—and ultimate release from these problems. At the collective level, the specific role of religion in adaptation varies in different societies. However, its meaning system and collective rituals typically help promote social integration and solidarity, at least for members of a religious in-group. At the same time, religion also may help support conflict between groups, which may decrease optimal adaptation.

—*Doyle Paul Johnson*

REFERENCES

P. Berger, *The Sacred Canopy* (Garden City, N.Y.: Doubleday, 1964); T. O'Dea and J. Aviada, *Sociology of Religion,* 2nd ed. (Englewood Cliffs, N.J.: Prentice Hall, 1983).

ADOLESCENCE/YOUTH CULTURE The word *adolescence* came to indicate an age group in the twentieth century, and many theories have been developed on the subject. In the past, primitive societies had initiation rites to mark the abrupt transition from childhood to adulthood, and the initiated would gradually take their place in adult society, but this social rite has now weakened. In today's society, adolescence marks the transition from a childhood stage that has not yet finished to a mature adult stage that has not yet been acquired, from "pre-sociality" to "socialization."

The term *adolescence* was innovated into the social scientific literature by G. Stanley Hall in 1904. In general, the term indicates this period of development in the life of the individual between childhood and adulthood. It is a phase that goes from age 13 to age 19—the "teens"—and is characterized by a series of physiological, psychological, and social transformations. In this period, the social personality is not yet formed, and teenagers are often regarded as searching for themselves as they move toward their adult identity. (The word *teenager* was coined in 1939.)

A discussion of adolescence can be approached in many different ways and, similarly, there are numerous methods of interpreting it. In general, it is the product of attempts to adapt to the new conditions in which teenagers find themselves. The process of adolescence is often accompanied by feelings of isolation, solitude, and disorientation. It rarely follows a linear path or a uniform rhythm. In contrast, the psychic progress and developmental process that characterize the various phases of adolescence vary for different people.

In "early adolescence," individuals are faced with a series of difficulties linked to object relations, and the chances of reaching adulthood depend in a real or apparent way on how these relations are resolved. True adolescence is the stage in which the processes of social differences start, which in "late adolescence" take on a definite structure.

A typical aspect of adolescence is "rebellion." Young people turn against their first objects of love, seeking to distance themselves from the vision of reality and morality that has been shown to them up until that moment. Adolescent rebellion can be channeled into very different routes. Teenagers may struggle to acquire as soon as possible certain privileges that belong to adults, or they may fight because they do not accept the system of values associated with these privileges and wish to be different. According to the majority of scholars studying adolescence, the direction along which the rebellion is channeled depends on the type of defensive mechanisms that the ego has developed to protect itself from anxiety during the early stages of adolescence.

Broadly speaking, we can say that in early childhood individuals learn control over their bodies, and then control over their environment, and in adolescence, control over their emotions. The stabilization of these achievements, however, is subject to physical maturity and the orderly development of the functions of the ego; only then can there be a balanced development.

The most important aspect of the hierarchical organization of the interests of the ego comes about during "late" adolescence, according to Peter Blos in his book *On Adolescence: A Psychoanalytic Interpretation* (1962). Certain interests are taken further during this phase and others are stratified; the ego is integrative and adaptive rather than defensive in its actions. It restricts itself to a few specific interests, and its identity slowly takes on a definite character.

During adolescence, there is also a process of differentiation between the image of oneself now and the self-image one had as a child; the identity that adolescents develop is above all based on their peer group. Because early adolescence is also a critical period linked to the search for a new identity, psychological and social factors relative to the modification of the role of individuals in relations with their family and the outside world are just as important as physical factors in this period.

According to Iärbel Inhelder and Jean Piaget, in *The Growth of Logical Thinking from Childhood to Adolescence: An Essay on the Construction of Formal Operational Structures* (1958), between the ages of 11 and 12 there is a decisive transition from "concrete" logical operations based on manipulable objects to "formal" operations in which the subject is able to formulate clear propositions. At this stage, adolescents begin to construct systems and theories and also seek to incorporate external reality into their cognitive frameworks.

A further important aspect for teenagers is the "paternal model," which at a certain point is perceived as being inadequate. This leads to the attitude of diminishing the father and all that he represents; teenagers belittle their fathers to establish their own identities. The diminishing of the paternal model, the slow detachment of the adolescent from emotional ties to the family, and his or her shy and exhilarating entrance into the new life constitute one of the most significant experiences in human existence.

Marked anxiety is intrinsic to adolescence. There is an urgency to the search for a specific identity on the part of adolescents through the acquisition of a model that can reassure them regarding their maturity. Teenagers see the need to find their identities to help them with adult decisions such as choosing a profession, getting married, having a family, and adopting acceptable political and social stances. The gap between the welcome that young people are expecting and the way in which they actually are welcomed into adult society is sometimes responsible for the "drama" of adolescence.

Teenagers are unable to complete the process of adolescence if they do not achieve a stable organization of the *self.* Failure to do this may lead to deviant behavior in the postadolescent phase, in which it is impossible to hold the doors to many possible life-choice options permanently open.

Exploring the problems of adolescence in current society means seeking to clarify the place and role claimed by the adolescent state in the social system. Modern society offers adolescents a large range of models, many of which conflict with one another, from which teenagers must make their choices. Placed before this high social differentiation, teenagers today, more than in the past, appear to be exposed to the acquisition of an identity that is not immune to deviant and pathological developments.

Youth Culture To discuss the culture (or subculture) of young people, it is essential to look at what is meant by the word *young,* which dates back to ancient times. The Romans called people aged between 30 and 45 *iuventa,* while people older than this were classed as *senectus.* The Greeks, by contrast, placed youth between the ages of 17 and 30. On the one hand, these two examples show that in different periods there has always been an age group defined as "young," but on the other, it shows that the age of the group in question has constantly changed. For the most part, sociology defines people up to the age of 29 as "young."

The definition of youth remained somewhat fluid until the nineteenth and twentieth centuries, when the various psychological theories regarding the development of the personality appeared along with philosophical theories regarding youth education. Toward the 1950s, youth was generally seen as a transitory phase from childhood to adulthood, characterized by the discovery of individualism, the development of a life plan, and the formation of a personal system of values.

Several authors have explored the concept of "youth culture," and it is still the object of discussion. Talcott Parsons, for example, in "Age and Sex in the Social Structure of the United States" (1942), maintained that the intense parent-children affective relations in a nuclear family are not broken off immediately but require a period of transition before being severed. "The youth culture has important positive functions in easing the transition from the security of childhood in the family of orientation to that of full adult in marriage and occupational status." In another work, *Essays in Sociological Theory: Pure and Applied* (1949), Parsons stated that

the youth culture is not only, as is true of the curricular aspects of formal education, a matter of age status as such but also shows signs of being a product of tensions in the relationship of younger people and adults.

This concept of "youth culture" was later taken further by James S. Coleman. In *The Adolescent Society: The Social Life of the Teenagers and Its Impact on Education* (1961), he stated that the characteristic aspects of youth culture were loyalty to one's peers and the gratuitousness of behavior, contrasting with the responsible behavior of adults.

It can be seen that youth culture arises from a series of behaviors and ways of acting that are typical of young people and that include limitation of economic activities to consumption rather than productive activities, in contrast to the high involvement in productive economic activities by adults; a strong individual search for identity that evolves with strong identification with the peer group; and, on the basis of one's experience of reality, an attempt to adapt to the cultural models transmitted by adults. These specific aspects have been exaggerated and prolonged since the 1930s, because the youth of this period can be seen to have suffered from deep tensions.

This slow formation of youth culture has its roots in the answer to how to be young in today's society; this means that the youth culture is not objectively identified with young people but with the position of being young in a certain social system and context.

In this sense, it is possible to talk of a "youth culture," in other words, of the group rebellion on the part of gangs of young delinquents who were studied by sociologists in Chicago in the 1920s, especially by Frederick Thrasher in *The Gang: A Study of 1,313 Gangs in Chicago* (1927). A further example is the "hippie generation" of the 1960s, which was characterized by a highly euphoric and erotic culture that rejected the values of individualistic competition and any idealization or rationalization of violence and aggression (Rositi 1969).

From here to the "era of challenge" of society was but a short step. This idea of the challenge not only placed itself against the adult system, it actually was intended to have consequences for the system: a period that, passing through the Beat Generation of the 1950s and the hippie movement of the 1960s, modified all the components of society, bringing to the fore the need and the decision on the part of young people to be the protagonists in society (Tomasi 1987).

It is precisely in terms of this wish to be the "protagonists" that the cultural behavior of young people should be interpreted; their behavior tells us that they experience not only a state of uneasiness that stems from the position in which the entire social fabric places them but also a condition of restlessness, already latent, in the collective culture. Given that culture consists of values, norms, beliefs, and expressive symbols, it is certainly possible to speak of a youth culture, in other words, of a period in which a system of values, norms, beliefs, and symbolic expressions (behavior and lifestyles) are different from those of adult society.

Youth culture forms around the most varied interests, which can range from wearing clothes that are "in" to listening to music that is "in," but it also can arise from the inconsistencies that young people perceive in adult society between "acclaimed values" and "visible results." From their assessment of the "culture of society," young people develop norms that enable them both to challenge society and to spread their rebellion. In general, what starts as a revolt ends up as "a style"—in other words, with a "culture" that has "expressive symbols," "norms," and "elements" of particular values. From this particular way of perceiving and living, young people maintain their relations with society.

To distinguish the specific nature of young people, the terms *subculture* and *counterculture* (Yinger 1960) often have been used and are still in use today. Although attempts have been made to find differences between the two terms, it can be said that the underlying concept is more or less the same—in other words, they indicate groups with particular "value systems" that are different from the surrounding dominant culture. But there are differences between these two terms that it probably would be useful to note.

At the turn of the twenty-first century, the term *youth culture* no longer has the meaning that it has had in the past. It no longer indicates rebellion, abstention from, or rejection of the social system; it does not even mean experimenting directly with alternative lifestyles that are outside a given social system. Instead, *youth culture* means the intrinsic capacity that young people have to define themselves in their value behaviors in the society to which they belong and in their projection toward the future.

—*Luigi Tomasi*

REFERENCES

A. Baldwin, *Teoria dello sviluppo infantile* (Milan: Angeli, 1971); P. Blos, *The Adolescent Personality* (New York: Appleton, 1941); P. Blos, *On Adolescence* (New York: Free Press, 1962); M. Brake, *Youth Culture* (London: Routledge, 1985); A. Cohen, *Delinquent Boys* (Glencoe, Ill.: Free Press, 1955); J. S. Coleman, *The Adolescent Society* (Glencoe, Ill.: Free Press, 1961); F. Elkin and A. Westley, "The Myth of Adolescent Culture," *American Sociological Review* 20(1955):680-684; E. H. Erikson, *Childhood and Society* (New York: Norton, 1950); O. Galland, *Sociologie de la jeunesse* (Paris: Colin, 1991); G. S. Hall, *Adolescence* (New York: Appleton, 1904); D. Hebdige, *Subculture* (London: Methuen, 1979); B. Inhelder and J. Piaget, *The Growth of Logical Thinking from Childhood to Adolescence* (New York: Basic Books, 1958); I. M. Jousselyn, *L'adolescente e il suo mondo* (Florence: Giusti-Barbera, 1964); A. Kroeber, *The Nature of Culture* (Chicago: University of Chicago Press, 1952); D. A. Lenzen, "Perpetuated Youth and Self-Sanctification," *Social Compass* 37(1991):345-356; E. Morin, *L'esprit du temps* (Paris: Grasset, 1962); T. Parsons, "Age and Sex in the Social Structure of the United States," *American Sociological Review* 7(1942):604-616; T. Parsons, *Essays in Sociological Theory* (Glencoe, Ill.: Free Press, 1949); R. Rivier, *Lo sviluppo sociale del bambino e dell'adolescente* (Florence: La Nuova Italia, 1970); F. Rositi, "Studio sull'ambivalenza culturale," *Studi di Sociologia* 4(1969):366-388; F. Thrasher, *The Gang* (Chicago: University of Chicago Press, 1927); L. Tomasi, "Contestazione," in *Nuovo Dizionario di Sociologia,* ed. F. Demarchi et al. (Cinisello Balsamo: Paoline, 1987):568-574; J. M. Yinger, "Contraculture and Subculture," *American Sociological Review* 25(1960):625-635.

ADVENTISM From the Latin *adventus* (coming), the concept of adventism has been an aspect of Christianity since its inception, and prophecies predicting the imminent and literal second coming of Christ have been strongly emphasized by certain groups at various periods throughout Christian history. In Christianity, the biblical books of Daniel and Revelation plus passages from some of the Gospels are used most frequently as sources for apocalyptic prophecies. Europe and America during the nineteenth century saw a wide variety of religious groups teaching the imminent return of Christ and the establishment of the Millennium (a thousand-year reign of Christ on Earth). In the United States during the "Second Great Awakening," as the religious movement that emerged in the first half of the nineteenth century has come to be known, William Miller (1782-1849) prophesied the second coming of Christ in 1843. The organizational results of his preaching are generally known as the Millerite movement or Millerite Christians.

"God's everlasting kingdom" failed to materialize, and neither did it come in 1844, the year of "the Great Disappointment." Yet this nonevent was itself turned into a meaningful event by some of Miller's followers: The Seventh-day Adventists, by far the largest adventist sect nowadays, may be looked upon as an outcome of the teachings of William Miller and Ellen Gould White (née Harmon, 1827-1915), the latter of whom was a very prolific writer on every aspect of adventism. Every now and again, extreme outbursts of millennialistic expectations (among adventist groups) can be witnessed. In 1993, the Branch Davidian adventists under the leadership of David Koresh found their apocalypse after a monthlong siege of their "Mount Carmel" headquarters in Waco, Texas, when their headquarters was subjected to a paramilitary governmental raid and subsequent apparent murder-suicide group self-immolation by the Davidians.

See also David Koresh

—*Durk H. Hak*

REFERENCES

M. Bull and K. Lockhart, *Seeking a Sanctuary* (San Francisco: Harper, 1989); N. Cohn, *Pursuit of the Millennium* (Oxford: Oxford University Press, 1970 [1957]); M. Pearson, *Millennial Dreams and Moral Dilemmas* (Cambridge: Cambridge University Press, 1990).

AFFECTIVE COMMITMENT Emotional attraction that encourages affiliation with a group, idea, or cause. Affective commitment is an important component in the recruitment and retention process in religious movements. It involves detachment, or renunciation, of former bonds with other groups and a severing of ties with those who might oppose the convert's association with the group. It also entails intense interaction within the new group that leads to the development and consolidation of strong relationships with organization members.

For example, converts to the Hare Krishna movement are expected to give up the company of anyone who is not a devotee. They cite "warmth and friendship among the devotees" as a major feature attracting them to the movement. The affective commitment process occurs not only within new religious movements but also among more conservative churches. Studies of the spread of Mormonism and of the charismatic movement among American Roman Catholics have found that interpersonal bonds play a significant role in recruitment. Affective commitment may be more important, in many cases, than reduction of deprivation through ideological beliefs. With increases in the size of a denomination, a group may become less able to induce a sense of belonging among its members, and then affective commitment must be supplemented with instrumental and moral commitments for the organization to prosper. Affective commitment is governed by

factors similar to those that influence interpersonal attraction.

—*James McClenon*

REFERENCES

S. L. Franzio, *Social Psychology* (Madison, Wis.: Brown and Benchmark, 1995); J. S. Judah, *Hare Krishna and the Counterculture* (New York: Wiley, 1974); K. A. Roberts, *Religion in Sociological Perspective* (Belmont, Calif.: Wadsworth, 1995); R. Stark and W. S. Bainbridge, "Networks of Faith," *American Journal of Sociology* 85(1980):1376-1395.

AFFILIATION *see* Belonging

AFRICAN AMERICAN RELIGIOUS EXPERIENCE Scholars from a variety of disciplines have recognized the central significance of religion in African American culture. Scholarly studies on African American religion in the United States can be traced to W. E. B. Du Bois's *The Negro Church* (1903). In addition to exemplifying the richness of the African American experience, black religion provides us with significant insights into the social condition of black people in U.S. society. E. Franklin Frazier (1974) argues that African American religion historically has functioned as a "refuge in a hostile white world." At another level, however, it has served as a form of cultural identity and resistance to a white-dominated society. The development of African American religion, particularly during the twentieth century, took a multiplicity of interrelated streams, which makes it a variegated phenomenon that has only begun to be more fully explored in recent decades (Nelsen et al. 1971, Murphy et al. 1993).

Many scholars have debated the extent to which African American religion draws upon African religion in its diverse forms. Despite the presence of Africanisms in African American religion, such as the call-and-response pattern characteristic of black preaching, it is evident that no single African culture or religion could have been diffused intact to North America. African religious concepts and rituals, such as ancestor worship, initiation rites, spirit possession, healing and funeral rituals, magical rituals for obtaining spiritual power, and ecstatic ceremonies enlivened by rhythmic dancing, drumming, and singing, are found in African American religion but generally in syncretized ways, blended with diverse European American elements.

Prior to the American Revolution, very few slaves were Christian, other than in a nominal sense. Most planters initially were reluctant to foster the conversion of their slaves to Christianity because they feared that it might provide them with notions of equality and freedom. Eventually, however, they became convinced that a selective interpretation of the Gospel would foster docility in their subjects. Indeed, as Eugene Genovese (1974) demonstrates in his application of Gramsci's notion of hegemony, the slave owner's paternalistic ideology relied heavily upon religious themes. That the slaves internalized portions of their masters' ideology is manifested by their belief that Jesus Christ was a meek, humble, and compassionate figure with whom they could converse about their earthly tribulations. A few exceptions aside, they did not picture Jesus as a messiah-king bearing a sword and mounted on a horse ready to lead them in battle against their oppressors. As a hegemonic system, paternalism encouraged the slaves to accept the slave masters as brothers in Christ. Conversely, it is important to note that Christianity served as an inspiration in the three best known slave rebellions in U.S. history, namely, those led by Gabriel Proesser, Denmark Vesey, and Nat Turner.

Some blacks joined the evangelical churches—Methodist, Baptist, and Presbyterian—during the Great Awakening (1720-1740). The Second Awakening (1790-1815), with its camp meetings, attracted many slaves and free black people to evangelical Protestantism. The Methodists emerged as leaders in the development of religious instruction among slaves. Following its creation in 1845, the Southern Baptist Convention also initiated missionary work among slaves. The Baptists in particular may have been able to make inroads among the slaves because baptism by immersion resembled initiation rites associated with West African cults. The slaves worshiped in a wide variety of congregations, including with whites, with free blacks, exclusively by themselves, and in private. Slave masters often took house slaves to religious services at white churches, where they were required to sit in separate galleries or in balconies. Although white ministers presided over these services for slaves, the latter often chose instead to hold meetings in their quarters, in "praise houses" or "hush arbors," or even deep in the woods, swamps, and caverns.

Although black people in North America never enjoyed complete religious autonomy during the antebellum period, relatively independent African American congregations and religious associations emerged at this time. Scholars debate whether a slave congregation established in 1758 near Mecklenberg, Virginia, or the Silver Bluff Church in South Carolina established sometime between 1773 and 1775 constituted the first independent black church in North America. Early northern

Baptist churches, such as the Joy Street Baptist Church in Boston (established in 1805) and the Abyssinian Baptist Church in New York (established in 1808), appear to have emerged as protests to discrimination in racially mixed congregations. Black Baptist congregations in the Midwest formed the first separate regional associations beginning in the 1850s. The first of the National Baptist associations, the National Baptist Convention, U.S.A., was formed in 1895.

Black Methodists also established independent congregations and associations during the antebellum period, although primarily in the North. A group of free blacks belonging to the Free African Society, a mutual aid society within St. George's Methodist Episcopal Church in Philadelphia, severed ties with its parent body sometime between 1787 and 1792 in response to the discriminatory practices of the church's white members. The majority of the schismatics formed St. Thomas's African Episcopal Church in 1794, under the leadership of Absalom Jones. Richard Allen led a minority contingent to establish the Bethel African Methodist Episcopal Church. Mother Bethel became the founding congregation of the African Methodist Episcopal Church, the largest of the black Methodist denominations. The racially mixed St. John's Street Church in New York City served as the focal point for the development of what became the second major black Methodist denomination, the African Methodist Episcopal Zion Church.

Because the vast majority of blacks resided in rural areas of the South prior to 1910, the black rural church became the prototype for much of organized African American religion. Most black churches in the countryside relied on circuit preachers or on deacons as ceremonial leaders when their pastors were not present. Most black rural churches were and still are either Missionary Baptist or Methodist, but black Primitive Baptist and Holiness churches began to appear in the countryside in the late nineteenth century. Revivals constitute an important part of the annual ritual cycle and often serve as a homecoming. Funerals are extremely significant religious occasions that often prompt more ecstatic behavior than do preaching services or even revivals. Particularly during the Jim Crow era, black rural churches often played an accommodative role by providing their adherents with a cathartic outlet for coping with the vagaries of racism and the frustrations associated with poverty and economic exploitation. Although the civil rights movement was based primarily in urban churches, some rural churches played a supportive role in it.

African American religion underwent a process of further diversification in the early twentieth century as an increasing number of blacks began to migrate from the rural South to the cities of both the North and the South. By this time, two National Baptist associations and three black Methodist denominations had become the mainstream churches in black urban communities. Congregations affiliated with these denominations were mass churches in that they often crosscut class lines. Conversely, black congregations affiliated with white-controlled Episcopalian, Presbyterian, and Congregational churches catered primarily to elite African Americans.

Although the mainstream churches often valiantly attempted to cater to the social needs of the migrants, their middle-class orientation often made the migrants ill at ease. As a consequence, many migrants established and joined storefront and house churches, many of which eventually became affiliated with one of the black-controlled mainstream denominations. Often, however, the migrants were attracted to a wide array of Holiness-Pentecostal or Sanctified, Spiritual, Islamic, Judaic, and other syncretistic sects, such as Father Divine's Peace Mission and Daddy Grace's United House of Prayer for All People. During its zenith in the 1920s and 1930s, the Peace Mission movement catered to the unmet social and psychic needs of working-class blacks, who elevated their leader to the status of God. Indeed, the Depression accelerated the process of religious diversification. As Gayraud Wilmore observes (1983), the African American community by the end of the 1930s was literally glutted with churches of every variety.

African American Religious Organization Most African American religious groups fit into one of several types: *mainstream denominations, messianic-nationalist sects, conversionist sects,* and *thaumaturgic sects* (Baer and Singer 1992).

The *mainstream denominations* are committed, at least in theory, to a reformist strategy of social action that will enable black people to become better integrated into the American political economy. Although many of their congregations conduct expressive religious services, churches affiliated with mainstream denominations often exhibit a strong commitment to instrumental activities, such as supporting mass actions, social uplift programs, and church-related colleges. Members of mainstream denominations tend to accept the cultural patterns of the larger society and seek to share in the American Dream. Institutional racism, however, historically has been viewed as an impediment to this goal but one that can be overcome through social reform. Most mainstream congregations are affiliated with three National Baptist conventions, the AME, the AME Zion, and the Christian Methodist Episcopal churches. Approximately 90% of churchgoing African

Americans belong to black-controlled religious organizations. The remaining 10% or so belong to white-controlled religious bodies, including various liberal Protestant denominations, the Mormon Church, the Southern Baptist Convention, and various sects such as the Jehovah's Witnesses, Unity, and the Seventh-day Adventists. Black Roman Catholics in the United States numbered close to 2 million in 1990, a figure that resulted in large part from Caribbean immigrants and upwardly mobile African Americans who had children in parochial schools (McDonough 1993).

Messianic-nationalist sects generally are founded by charismatic individuals who are regarded as messiahs who will deliver black people from white oppression. In their early stages, messianic-nationalist sects often repudiate "Negro identity" and define blacks as the original human beings. They express strong criticism of white racism and create alternative communities, businesses, and schools. African American messianic nationalism has exhibited Judaic, Islamic, and Christian streams. Black Judaic or Hebraic sects include the Church of the Living God, the Pillar Ground of Truth for All Nations, the Church of God and Saints of Christ, and the Original Hebrew Israelite Nation.

The best known of the messianic-nationalist sects subscribe to Islam. Noble Drew Ali established the first of these, the Moorish Science Temple, in Newark, New Jersey, around 1913. Its main thrust was picked up by the Nation of Islam, initially under the leadership of Wallace D. Fard during the early 1930s in Detroit and subsequently under Elijah Muhammad. The Nation of Islam grew rapidly, in part due to the militant preaching of Malcolm X during the early 1960s. Rapid growth did not check schismatic tendencies that led to the appearance of numerous splinter groups, including the Ahmadiya Moslem movement of Chicago, the Hanafis of Washington, D.C., and the Ansaru Allah community of Brooklyn. Following the assassination of Malcolm X and the death of Elijah Muhammad, Wallace D. Muhammad led the transformation of the Nation into the American Muslim Mission. To counter the Mission's shift to orthodox Islam, Louis Farrakhan established a reconstituted Nation of Islam.

The smallest wing of messianic nationalism remained within the Christian fold. George McGuire, a former Anglican priest from Jamaica, established the African Orthodox Church as the religious arm of Marcus Garvey's Universal Negro Association. Albert B. Cleage, a former United Church of Christ minister, began to assert in the 1960s that Jesus had been a revolutionary who came to free peoples of color from white oppression, and established the Black Christian Nationalist Church.

Conversionist sects characteristically adopt expressive forms of religious behavior, such as shouting, ecstatic dancing, and glossolalia as outward manifes- tations of "sanctification." They stress a puritanical morality and often are other-worldly and apolitical, although some congregations have been known to participate in social activism. Conversionist sects encompass a multitude of Holiness-Pentecostal (or Sanctified) sects and smaller Baptist organizations. The Church of God in Christ (COGIC) is the largest African American Pentecostal body. Although it still manifests many conversionist elements, the church began a process of denominationalizing and mainstreaming in the middle of the twentieth century. Other conversionist bodies include the Church of Christ (Holiness) U.S.A., Christ's Sanctified Holy Church (Holiness), the Pentecostal Assemblies of the World, and the National Primitive Baptist Convention as well as numerous independent congregations. Although the more established conversionist bodies prohibit women from serving as bishops and pastors, many others have female pastors and even overseers of associations.

Thaumaturgic sects maintain that the most direct means of achieving socially desired objectives, such as financial prosperity, prestige, love, and health, is to engage in various rituals or to obtain esoteric knowledge and develop a positive attitude. These groups generally accept the cultural patterns, values, and beliefs of the larger society but tend to eschew social activism. Spiritual churches constitute the foremost example of the thaumaturgic sect (Baer 1984). These groups blend elements from American Spiritualism, Roman Catholicism, African American Protestantism, and Voodoo as well as other religious traditions, including New Thought, Judaism, and Islam. Spiritual churches often urge their members and clients to obtain salvation in this life by burning candles before images of Jesus, the Virgin Mary, or the saints, obtaining messages from prophets and mediums, and taking ritual baths. Most Spiritual churches are small and cater primarily to lower-class people, but some are housed in substantial edifices and cater to relatively affluent working-class and middle-class people. Even more so than Sanctified churches, Spiritual churches provide women with a vehicle for obtaining religious leadership. Although not a part of the Spiritual movement per se, the United Church and Science of Living Institute, founded by the Reverend Frederik Eikenrenkoetter (better known as Rev. Ike), constitutes the best known of the black thaumaturgic sects in the United States.

African American Religious Music   In addition to their status as houses of worship, black churches func- tion as centers of social life, ethnic identity, and cultural expression in the African American community. While African American music is derived from a variety of sources, religion has historically served as one of its major inspirations. As Lincoln and Mamiya (1990: 347) observe,

> In the Black Church singing together is not so much an effort to find, or to establish, a transitory community as it is the affirmation of a common bond that, while inviolate, has suffered the pain of separation since the last occasion of physical togetherness.

Eileen Southern (1983) traces the "spiritual" to the camp meetings of the Second Awakening where blacks continued singing in their segregated quarters after the whites had retired for the night. Conversely, the spiritual also appears to have had its roots in the "preacher's chanted declamation and the intervening congregational responses" (Lincoln and Mamiya 1990:348). The "ring shout" in which "shouters" danced in a circle to the accompaniment of a favorite spiritual sung by spectators standing on the sidelines was a common practice in many nineteenth-century black churches. By 1830, many black urban congregations had introduced choral singing into their services. Praying and Singing Bands became a regular feature of religious life in many black urban churches. Despite the opposition of African Methodist and other religious leaders to the intrusion of "cornfield ditties," folk musical styles became an integral part of African American sacred music. After the Civil War, the Fisk Jubilee Singers, a student ensemble at the newly established Fisk University in Nashville, did much to contribute to the dissemination of African American spirituals on tours both at home and abroad.

According to Southern (1983:402), black gospel music emerged as an urban phenomenon in revivals conducted in tents, football stadiums, and huge tabernacles. Although Charles Albert Tindley, a black Methodist minister, composed religious songs that drew upon the urban experiences of African Americans around 1900, Thomas A. Dorsey is usually credited as having been the "Father of Gospel Music." Beginning around 1927, he promoted what he called "gospel songs" in churches in Chicago, the Midwest, and the South. At a time when many Baptist and Methodist churches rejected gospel music, Sanctified churches in both urban and rural areas embraced it wholeheartedly. The Church of God in Christ in particular has served as a prime mover in the development of contemporary gospel music. Spiritual churches also accepted gospel music and, in the case of New Orleans, jazz as an integral feature of their worship services. In time, many mainstream congregations incorporated gospel music into their musical repertoire. Based upon their fieldwork, Lincoln and Mamiya (1990:381) conclude "that among young people, teenagers and young adults, gospel music programs constitute the major drawing card."

Interpreting the African American Heritage From its beginnings, African American religion has exhibited a contradictory nature. One of the major themes in the social scientific and historical literature poses the question of whether African American religious movements have served primarily as vehicles of protest or of accommodation. In his classic study of civil rights militancy among churchgoing blacks, Gary Marx (1967:67) made the following observations:

It can be seen that those belonging to sects are the least likely to be militant; they are followed by those in predominantly Negro denominations. Ironically, those individuals in largely white denominations (Episcopalian, Presbyterian, United Church of Christ, and Roman Catholic) are those most likely to be militant, in spite of the perhaps greater civil rights activism of the Negro denominations. This pattern emerged even when social class was held constant.

In a reexamination of Marx's data on religiously inspired civil rights militancy, Hunt and Hunt (1977) argue that Marx failed to differentiate between "conventional militancy" and "corporate militancy." Whereas the items used to measure "conventional militancy" focus upon "structural awareness" of racial inequality in U.S. society, those items from Marx's data measuring what Hunt and Hunt term "corporate militancy" focus upon the advocacy of collective forms of protest. In assessing research on the sociopolitical attitudes of black Catholics, Peck (1982) suggests that Catholicism may have played a more accommodative role in African American history than has black Protestantism. Furthermore, like various other scholars, Marx fails to recognize variations of political attitudes and behavior of unconventional religious groups. One might, for example, expect a member of a messianic-nationalist sect, such as the original Nation of Islam or its reconstituted variant, to be much more militant than a member of a conversionist sect, such as a small Sanctified storefront congregation. Perhaps more than any other institution, religion illustrates the diversity of strategies that African Americans have adopted in attempting to address racism and class inequality. As in the past, African American religion no doubt will continue to manifest both accommodative and activist qualities, but its more progressive expressions hold the potential of being a part of efforts for radical social transformation emanating from the black community.

See also Civil Rights, W. E. B. Du Bois, E. Franklin Frazier, Nation of Islam, Racism

—*Hans A. Baer*

REFERENCES

H. A. Baer, *The Black Spiritual Movement* (Knoxville: University of Tennessee Press, 1984); H. A. Baer and M. Singer, *African-American Religion in the Twentieth Century* (Knoxville: University of Tennessee Press, 1992); W. E. B. Du Bois, *The Negro Church in America* (Atlanta: Atlanta University Press, 1903); E. F. Frazier, *The Negro Church in America* (New York: Schocken, 1974); E. D. Genovese, *Roll Jordan, Roll* (New York: Vintage, 1974); L. L. Hunt and J. G. Hunt, "Religious Affiliation and Militancy among Urban Blacks," *Social Science Quarterly* 57(1977):821-834; C. E. Lincoln and L. H. Mamiya, *The Black Church in the African American Experience* (Durham, N.C.: Duke University Press, 1990); G. T. Marx, "Religion: Opiate or Inspiration of Civil Rights Militancy Among Negroes," *American Sociological Review* 32(1967):64-72; G. W. McDonough, *Black and Catholic in Savannah Georgia* (Knoxville: University of Tennessee Press, 1993); L. G. Murphy et al. (eds.), *Encyclopedia of African-American Religions* (Hamden, Conn.: Garland, 1993); H. M. Nelsen et al., *The Black Church in America* (New York: Basic Books, 1971); G. R. Peck, "Black Radical Consciousness and Black Christian Experience," *Sociological Analysis* 43 (1982):153-169; E. Southern, *The Music of Black Americans* (New York: Norton, 1983); G. S. Wilmore, *Black Religion and Black Radicalism* (Maryknoll, N.Y.: Orbis, 1983).

AGE Maturation process. Age is typically included in survey research as a demographic correlate of religiosity, even in the absence of any specific theory of its effects. By contrast, developmental psychologists such as Erikson (1950, 1959, 1982) focus explicitly on age-related developmental stages even though certain aspects of the more advanced stages of development are not necessarily connected with chronological age. Psychologists vary in terms of whether or not developmental stages are related to religious development. Those influenced by Freud most typically regard maturation as eliminating the need for religious illusions. However, not all developmental psychologists are this negative toward religion, and in fact, psychologists such as Kohlberg (1981) and Maslow (1964, 1968) emphasize the process of growth and development in terms of morality and meaning in life in a way that overlaps with religious and spiritual growth. Fowler (1981) provides an explicit focus on the religious or spiritual dimension of human life in a theory of specific stages of faith development (see also Fowler et al. 1991).

Both sociologists and psychologists emphasize parental influence on religious development and also growing independence from parents and expanding peer group influence in adolescence (see Benson et al. 1989 for a review). Most religious groups provide religious education and some form of rite of passage during adolescence to mark the transition to adulthood. Although young people in mainstream U.S. churches often drop out of organized religion during their adolescent and young adult years, some of them resume involvement in the religious group of their choice when they start their own families. In any case, the maturation process involves the development of one's own unique identity, a certain level of autonomy, and a sense of meaning and purpose in life, and this process generally includes a religious and/or moral orientation, whether or not it is expressed in institutional forms of religious group involvement. Moreover, the stages of moral development identified by Kohlberg (1981), for example, may be regarded as roughly parallel to alternative types or stages of religious development in terms of whether they reflect primarily a self-serving or egocentric orientation, conventional conformity, or commitment to abstract universal principles. In such theories, the highest stage of maturation would be consistent with the ideals of a universalistic religious orientation.

See also Faith Development, Carol Gilligan, Moral Development

—*Doyle Paul Johnson*

REFERENCES

P. L. Benson et al., "Adolescence and Religion," pp. 153-181 in *Research in the Social Scientific Study of Religion* 1 (Greenwich, Conn.: JAI, 1989); E. H. Erikson, *Childhood and Society* (New York: Norton, 1950); E. H. Erikson, *Identity and the Life Cycle* (New York: International Universities Press, 1959); E. H. Erikson, *The Life Cycle Completed* (New York: Norton, 1982); J. W. Fowler, *Stages of Faith* (San Francisco: Harper, 1981); J. W. Fowler et al. (eds.), *Stages of Faith and Religious Development* (New York: Crossroad, 1991); L. Kohlberg, *The Philosophy of Moral Development* (San Francisco: Harper, 1981); A. H. Maslow, *Religions, Values, and Peak-Experiences* (Columbus: Ohio State University Press, 1964); A. H. Maslow, *Toward a Psychology of Being* (New York: Van Nostrand, 1968).

AGED   *see* Gerontology

ALCOHOLICS ANONYMOUS (AA)   Perhaps the most famous of all "self-help" programs for dealing with alcohol and drug abuse, AA began in 1935 in Akron, Ohio. Started by an alcoholic stockbroker named Bill Wilson, AA was strongly influenced by the Oxford Group movement (see Eister 1950). AA has grown into a worldwide movement with over 1 million participants in nearly 50,000 groups in over 100 countries.

The AA "twelve step" program of rehabilitation, which involves a major focus on a Higher Power or God, begins as a first step with persons admitting to a group of fellow alcoholics that they cannot control themselves concerning alcohol and that their lives are out of their hands. The twelve step program has become the model for many different types of self-help programs since the inception of AA. A number of scholars have noted the heavily religious dimension of AA and derivative programs, and such programs have been studied as religions and as ways to develop commitment and meaning in individual lives.

See also Quasi-Religions

—*James T. Richardson*

REFERENCES

Alcoholics Anonymous (New York: AA World Services, 1955); L. Blumberg, "The Ideology of a Therapeutic Social Movement," *Journal of Studies in Alcohol* 38(1977):2122-2143; A. W. Eister, *Drawing Room Conversion* (Durham, N.C.: Duke University Press, 1950); A. Greil and D. Rudy, "Conversion to the World View of Alcoholics Anonymous," *Qualitative Sociology* 6(1983):5-28; M. Maxwell, *The Alcoholics Anonymous Experience* (New York: McGraw-Hill, 1984); D. Rudy and A. Greil, "Taking the Pledge," *Sociological Focus* 20(1987):45-59.

ALIENATION   A state of estrangement of individuals and societies from God, each other, and themselves. The Gnostics viewed estrangement from God as a necessary precondition to rebirth. Plotinus, Augustine, and Aquinas also propose alienation as the proving ground for the true life. More pessimistic accounts include Calvin's, in which original sin threatens separation from God in perpetuity, and Rousseau's secular vision of humanity estranged from its own original nature by society. In Hegel's work, overcoming alienation—the unfolding of self-consciousness—is the principal force in historical development. In contrast,

Feuerbach stated that God (Absolute Spirit) is the estranged essence of humanity, and thus religion is an alienated search for self-awareness. Seizing on this point, the young Karl Marx conceptualized alienation as a pervasive social process inherent in the capitalist mode of production in which workers are estranged from their product, work itself, their human qualities, and each other. Religion expresses real suffering and desires in an alienated form. The writings of Paul Tillich and Karl Barth each carry the analysis of alienation into the present century with special reference to theology. Alienation is often used as a variable in survey research, usually in a social psychological sense, with regard to analyses of the disaffection of youth, work experience, and religiosity.

—*Philip Stanworth*

REFERENCES

L. Feuer, "What Is Alienation?" in *Sociology on Trial,* ed. M. Stein and A. Vidich (Englewood Cliffs, N.J.: Prentice Hall, 1963): 127-147; P. Ludz, "A Forgotten Intellectual Tradition of the Alienation Concept," in *Alienation,* ed. R. F. Geyer and D. Schweitzer (London: Routledge, 1981): 21-35; I. Meszaros, *Marx's Theory of Alienation* (London: Merlin, 1970).

ALLPORT, GORDON W. (1897-1967)

Psychologist who influenced empirical study in the psychology of religion more than any person other than William James. His early work focused upon the study of values, including a popular measure to translate Eduard Spranger's personality types (from his *Types of Man* [Halle 1928]) into a standardized questionnaire, the *Study of Values.* Of Spranger's six types operationalized in this scale, one is the religious type (R scale). This led to early empirical work on the correlates of the religiously oriented person. Frequently, Allport's value-laden views of mature religiosity failed to be supported in empirical studies of correlates of the R scale.

Allport then developed the highly influential *Religious Orientation Scale,* a more sophisticated psychometric measure of religiosity that measured *extrinsic* to *intrinsic* religiosity along a hypothesized single continuum. It also permitted the identification of two indiscriminate religious types, one pro- and one antireligious. Using this measure, Allport was satisfied that undesirable correlates of religiosity held for extrinsic but not intrinsic religion. Subsequent research has focused upon numerous modifications of this scale, treating extrinsic and intrinsic as independent types or dimensions.

Allport's belief that the religious sentiment can best be studied through personal documents and an idiographic approach has been far less influential than the scales he developed and the measurement-based nomothetic studies they encouraged. The *Study of Values* remains one of the most frequently cited standardized personality scales, and measures of intrinsic-extrinsic religiosity are the most frequently used scales in the empirical psychology of religion. This is an unanticipated and somewhat ironic legacy for Allport. His measurement scales have been used largely independently of his theoretical concerns. Allport's theoretical views on religion are expressed in *The Individual and His Religion* (1950), a text that has become one of the classics of the psychology of religion.

—*Ralph W. Hood, Jr.*

REFERENCES

G. W. Allport, *The Use of Personal Documents in Psychological Science* (New York: Social Science Research Council, 1942); G. W. Allport, *The Individual and His Religion* (New York: Macmillan, 1950); G. W. Allport, "Religion and Prejudice," *Crane Review* 2(1959):1-10; G. W. Allport and J. M. Ross, "Personal Religious Orientation and Prejudice," *Journal of Personality and Social Psychology* 5(1967):432-443; G. W. Allport et al., *Manual, Study of Values,* 3rd ed. rev. (Boston: Houghton Mifflin, 1970).

ALTERNATION   The effects upon an individual's identity as a result of his or her changing meaning systems. William James's studies of the psychology of religious experience, and specifically of the conversion process, represent an early exploration of this concept. Drawing upon Alfred Schutz's phenomenology, Peter L. Berger coined this term to describe the near total transformation of identity resulting from the internalization of a different meaning system. The conversion process, religious or secular, is one example. The radical changes in an individual's biography and self-concept that typify this experience are usually accompanied by a shift from one social world to another. Alternation may be more commonplace in modern, pluralistic societies where individuals are exposed to a broader range of meaning systems through communication technology or because of social and geographic mobility.

—*Bruce Karlenzig*

REFERENCES

P. L. Berger, *The Precarious Vision* (Garden City, N.Y.: Doubleday, 1961); P. L. Berger, *Invitation to Sociology* (Garden City, N.Y.: Doubleday, 1963); P. L. Berger and T. Luckmann, *The Social Construction of Reality* (Garden City, N.Y.: Doubleday, 1966); W. James, *The Varieties of Religious Experience* (New York: New American Library, 1958 [1902]).

AMERICAN ACADEMY OF RELIGION (AAR)

The AAR is the largest learned society and professional association of teachers and scholars in the field of religion. It cooperates with the Society of Biblical Literature in its annual meetings and some regional meetings, operating facilities, and publishing program. The AAR has a membership of over 7,500; jointly the societies claim over 12,000 members. "The Academy is dedicated to furthering knowledge of religion and religious institutions in all their forms and manifestations." The offices of the AAR/SBL are permanently located in Atlanta, Georgia.

With origins among college teachers of religion, the AAR now maintains small sections studying religion and society, although its major focus continues to be on such more traditional religious disciplines as texts, liturgy, theology, and history.

The publications program of the AAR is particularly ambitious. It includes not only the quarterly *Journal of the American Academy of Religion* but a variety of book and electronic series under the Scholars Press label. The AAR also has endeavored to facilitate greater public understanding of the role of religion, particularly in American society, through working with the press and through efforts to articulate more clearly methods through which religion can be taught in the public schools without violating Supreme Court interpretations of church-state separation. In addition to its own publishing programs, the AAR presents a variety of awards to scholars for outstanding publications, public service, and teaching.

—*William H. Swatos, Jr.*

AMERICAN CATHOLIC SOCIOLOGICAL REVIEW (ACSR)   *see Sociology of Religion: A Quarterly Review*

AMERICAN CATHOLIC SOCIOLOGICAL SOCIETY (ACSS)   In the late 1930s, the American sociological establishment suspected that *anyone* committed to a specific set of religious beliefs and a specific religious institution would be ideologically incapable of scientifically objective research. During the 1937 annual meeting of the American Sociological Society (now the American Sociological Association), a small group of Catholic sociologists met to share their frustrations at the atmosphere and content of the meeting. As they saw it, scientific sociology on the model of the natural sciences was becoming a vehicle for amoral and antireligious attitudes of secular sociologists. The illogicality of value-neutral research was also an irritation: "Don't ask me how they could even talk about delinquency, crime, poverty, etc., without seeing some kind of norm. We were pretty much satiated with that sort of attitude" (Francis Friedel letter, 1948). In addition to Friedel of Dayton University, the group included Ralph Gallagher, S.J., of Loyola University (Chicago), Louis Weitzman, S.J., of John Carroll University, and Marguerite Reuss of Marquette University.

The outcome of this exchange of views was an organizational meeting at Chicago's Loyola University in 1938 attended by 31 representatives from 30 Catholic colleges and universities. The participants forthwith drafted a constitution and elected Ralph Gallagher the first president of the American Catholic Sociological Society. The founding ethos was one of loyalty to the Catholic Church, even as one pursued sociological research in the interest of social change. Although the scope of papers read at ACSS meetings and published in the quarterly *American Catholic Sociological Review* displayed the varied interests of Catholic sociologists, there was a deep, fractious, and ultimately unresolved debate about the legitimacy of a "Catholic" sociology. In time, this issue was displaced by questions of professional specialization, and 1963 saw the last meeting with a focus on matters generally sociological. In 1964, the annual meeting was devoted to the sociology of the Catholic Church.

Reflecting the pressures of professional specialization, the ACSS journal was in 1963 renamed *Sociological Analysis* (now *Sociology of Religion*), and the society in 1970 became the Association for the Sociology of Religion.

See also Association for the Sociology of Religion

—*Loretta M. Morris*

REFERENCES

R. Rosenfelder, *A History of the American Catholic Sociological Society from 1938-1948*, Dissertation, Loyola University, Chicago, 1948; *Sociological Analysis* 50(1989):319-418.

AMERICAN PSYCHOLOGICAL ASSOCIATION (APA), DIVISION ON THE PSYCHOLOGY OF RELIGION (Division 36)

One of numerous divisions of the APA concerned with specialty interests of psychologists. Its origins lie in the efforts of the American Catholic Psychological Association to reduce Catholic bias against psychology and to encourage Catholics to pursue the science and profession of psychology. In 1968, this organization was disbanded only to be reorganized in 1971 as an ecumenical group, Psychologists Interested in Religious Issues (PIRI). In 1974, it sought divisional status in the APA. Its initial attempts foiled, it finally achieved divisional status in August 1975. Virginia Sexton was its first president. In 1993, its name was changed to Psychology of Religion.

The division's aim is to foster both research and practice related to psychology of religion. Members need have no religious identification. One can become an affiliate member without being a member of the APA. It meets during the annual meeting of the APA and is part of the annual program. Its program accepts submissions relevant to religious issues, including quantitative and qualitative research in the psychology of religion. Each year it presents an award for scholarly contribution in the psychology of religion that is named after William C. Bier, who was influential both in the American Catholic Psychological Association and in the early years of PIRI. Less frequently, the division presents the William James award for research in the psychology of religion. The *Psychology of Religion Newsletter* is the official publication of the Psychology of Religion division.

—Ralph W. Hood, Jr.

AMERICAN RELIGION

Whether there is an "American religion" is a matter of some dispute. The United States has a legal disestablishment that prevents a state church. Also, the country is perhaps the most religiously pluralistic in the world. As a nation of immigrants, many of whom brought distinctive religious traditions with them, the United States is a potpourri of faiths, from the international to the extremely privatized. Thus religion in America is, and historically has been, too fragmented to speak of in terms of an "American religion."

Nonetheless, a persuasive argument can be made that an American religion exists as a cultural reality that is distinct from the evangelical impulses to "Christianize" the continent (see Handy 1984) as well as from the cultural themes known as "civil religion" (Bellah 1967). The importance of religion in the founding of the European colonies, the experience of settling a frontier society with waves of immigrants, the powerful social and political impulses toward Anglo-conformity, and the continued centrality of religious cultures in contemporary politics, all speak to an "American" experience that has produced some distinctive religious forms.

Scholars have used two generally distinct conceptions, or "schemata," to describe the generic organizational forms of religion in the United States. One conception stresses the "denomination" as the quintessential organizational form, while the second schema understands the "congregation" as the heart of American religion. At the cultural level, the first conception stresses religion's role in integrating the American national community, either through support for a diffuse civil religion or through a system of denominational accommodation. By way of contrast, the second schema puts pluralism and processes of group competition and conflict at the center. Although both accommodation and conflict occur at both the denominational and the congregational levels, scholars have tended to focus on one or the other schema.

Despite divergent views on the appropriate interpretive conception, there is general agreement on other characteristics of American religion. For example, "revivalism" as a technique of evangelization has become a cultural and organizational form that has spread far beyond its Protestant origins (e.g., Dolan 1992). Revivalism's effects on the development of mass politics and the structure of the national economy also have been documented (e.g., Hammond 1979, Howe 1990, Thomas 1989). Also, the ideological themes of individualism, voluntarism, and an emphasis on morality over theology are all recognizable among many different faiths as practiced in the United States. Thus something of an irony emerges. Legal disestablishment and religious pluralism have transformed the "New Jerusalem" of the Puritans into a diverse society they neither would have recognized nor would have sanctioned; simultaneously, the American experience has helped produce "Americanized" versions of Catholicism (e.g., Appleby 1992), Judaism (e.g., Lipset 1990), Islam (e.g., Haddad and Smith 1994), and, more recently, Asian-based faiths (e.g., R. B. Williams 1988).

Cultural Consensus and Mainline Denominationalism The most forceful argument for an American religion was Will Herberg's famous essay *Protestant, Catholic, Jew* (1955). Writing during the booming fortunes of the "mainline" religious groups in the U.S. postwar prosperity, Herberg claimed that the central tripartite distinctions of American religion (Protestant, Catholic, Jew) had become mostly variations on a central theme—the celebration of the "American way of life." A comfortable denominational pluralism offered a judicious balance between identity and group membership while supporting civic order in the public sphere.

Other scholars have noted the development of an American religion but questioned Herberg's rosy assessment of the situation. Niebuhr's (1929) classic account of denominational pluralism was a *critique* of American religion. He located the social sources of denominations in ethnic, regional, and class identities. Niebuhr saw such divisions as an ethical failure, because they were divisions within Christ's church. Niebuhr's work also offered an important formulation of the "church-sect" dynamic that had the perhaps unintended effect of demonstrating empirically how "American religion" was created. Niebuhr noted that established churches spawned sectarian schisms, based on dissatisfactions with the institution's worldly "compromises." But forces such as the necessities of organizational survival, the challenge of keeping the second generation within the faith, and general American social mobility led many sects to develop the institutional trappings of "established" religions.

Thus were *denominations* born—reasonably open, "world-accommodating," large-scale organizations, co-existing with other similar organizations, eschewing claims to have the only valid interpretation of absolute truth. They are less encompassing than European-style "churches" but less exclusive than "sects." This very accommodation, of course, leads to yet another round of sectarian schism. One consequence of this cycle has been the increasing organizational and cultural similarity of the surviving denominations and their increasing similarity to nonreligious, formal organizations (see Scherer 1980).

Writing 20 years after Herberg, Cuddihy (1978) charged that the polite civility required for Herberg's version of American religion robbed religions of their distinct traditions and historical authenticity. Cuddihy merged Herberg's Eisenhower-era convergence with an ironic reading of Bellah's "civil" religion and produced a stinging rebuke of a too-easy ecumenical unity. He noted that this civil faith was particularly disastrous for religious minorities. Cuddihy, however, did not deny the reality of American religion.

Wuthnow's (1988) influential assessment of contemporary American religion noted that Herberg's essay appeared just as the putative consensus of the 1950s was crashing on the ideological reefs of the 1960s. Driven by conflicts over civil rights and foreign military adventures, there was a restructuring of religious cleavages from denominational loyalties to ideological divisions. Further, the organizational bases for public involvement shifted from denominational bureaucracies to small, ideologically driven "special purpose groups."

This is not to say that denominations were not part of the 1960s social conflicts. Hadden (1969) demonstrated how clergy working within denominational agencies were deeply involved in antiwar, civil rights, and social justice activism. This involvement helped polarize the "restructured" religious scene and contributed to the declining significance of denominationalism (Wuthnow 1988).

Thus an important body of work accounts for "American religion" in terms of a denominational pluralism that in the nineteenth century helped in the successful assimilation of many European immigrants and in the twentieth century played a major role in shaping the societal consensus so central to civil society. Eisenstadt (1991) goes so far as to claim that the denomination, as such, is a U.S. creation and only truly exists within the American context. Denominationalism's integrating functions reached their zenith in postwar society just before the major challenges of the late 1960s emerged, and the U.S. religious scene and American culture in general began its transition to a more pluralist and ideologically charged landscape.

Religious Pluralism and Social Conflict   An alternative (but not completely incompatible) view of American religious development is to reframe it, deemphasizing the formation and dissolution of consensus and focusing instead on religion as a consistent source of social differentiation and a tool of social conflict. American religious history thus becomes a series of political and cultural challenges to white, male, Anglo-Saxon, mainline Protestant hegemony.

One version of this narrative is to describe American religion as a series of "disestablishments." The first, of course, was the legal disestablishment of the colonial churches. The First Amendment of the Constitution prevented a federal establishment; state governments varied in their religious establishments, some maintaining state churches until early in the nineteenth century. As Murrin (1990) noted, at times in some American colonies there were fewer legitimate religious options than at the same time in England. Those viewing the New World as their opportunity to build a "New Jerusalem" did not have religious tolerance—as we now think of the term—as one of their goals.

Colonial society could not sustain established churches, and a de facto Protestant pluralism developed. Effective control of institutional religious life was undermined by a consistent influx of new immigrants, many with different religious loyalties (e.g., Fischer 1989, Hackett 1991), and the expansion of the frontier (e.g., Finke and Stark 1992, Innes 1983). Also, among seaboard elites, Enlightenment ideas of individual rights, freedom from government intervention, and the historical march of progress gave ideological justification to a right to freedom of expression (Bailyn 1967).

After the legal institutional separation of church and state, however, a Protestant cultural hegemony continued. If one takes church-state cases decided by the U.S. Supreme Court as a measure of conflict over religion, Protestant hegemony was relatively uncontested until the middle of the twentieth century (Demerath and Williams 1984). Certainly there was religious conflict over the waves of Catholic and Jewish immigrants that came to America in the 1840s-1850s and then again in the 1890s-1920. But well into the twentieth century, Protestantism asserted itself successfully, restricting immigration, prohibiting alcohol production and consumption, and fostering assimilation (Anglo-conformity) as a social ideal. Whether nativist or progressive, public discourse was still dominated by Protestant voices.

The second disestablishment was the shattering of this cultural hegemony following World War II. There was a large-scale movement of American Catholics out of urban ethnic neighborhoods into middle-class suburbs and, after 1965's immigration law reform, a new wave of immigration from Latin America and Asia. Protestant control of public life was increasingly eroded, symbolized by conflict over schools and education. Particularly in urban politics, a Catholic ethnoreligious "establishment" emerged (Demerath and Williams 1992).

Increasing socioreligious diversity, combined with the countercultural challenges of the 1960s and early 1970s, has produced a third disestablishment—one that undermines all traditional institutionalized forms of religion in favor of a variety of syncretic, ideologically polarized, grassroots, feminist, and often relatively privatized forms of spirituality (e.g., Hammond 1992, Wessinger 1993, Wuthnow 1988).

The fragmenting of religious, cultural, and even political authority represented by successive disestablishments has been abetted by tendencies that have always been present in American religion but were perhaps minor chords until institutional and social structural changes provided the opportunities to flourish.

The Reformed Calvinist orthodoxy of Puritan New England was intermittently, but repeatedly, challenged by versions of Protestantism that focused on individualized, ecstatic religious expression, emphasizing spirit over intellect, and containing significant components of Arminianism and "perfectionism." These challenges included the "Great Awakening" in western New England in the mid-eighteenth century (e.g., Stout 1986), the growth of evangelizing denominations such as the Baptists and Methodists (Hatch 1989), the "feminization" of American religion (Welter 1976), and a host of less formally organized, popular forms of charismatic faith (P. Williams 1980).

At various times, major political and social divisions have centered on the differences between established, "respectable" forms of religion and pietistic, grassroots forms. For example, Howe (1990) and Carwardine (1993) discuss this very conflict in the antebellum North. Kleppner (1970) and Hammond (1979) demonstrate religion's importance to political conflict by concluding that religious differences influenced voting patterns as much as class or party differences in the Midwest and the "burned over" district of New York, respectively, in the late nineteenth century.

Studying the twentieth century, Marty's (1970) interpretation of American Protestantism holds that religious conflict was centered in a basic disagreement over strategy for the church's work in the world—whether it should save souls or reform social institutions. This conflict emanated from strictly theological differences into issues shaping the public sphere, such as the efficacy of social reform. Relatedly, Pope (1965) connected conflict over religious ideology and cultural styles to labor and class struggles.

Finke and Stark (1992) chart a long history of conflict in American religion between those groups whose strategy for institutional preservation was to relax their opposition to the "world" for the purposes of inclusion, and those groups who retain a sectarian separation and sense of election as a compensation for their doctrinal and behavioral discipline. Thus in many ways American religion has been an arena of social conflict and succession.

Related to this "conflict" approach to American religion is an emphasis on the ubiquity of the "congregation" as the central organizational form for many religions. Wind and Lewis's (1994) recent two-volume work makes this point with a variety of empirical and conceptual arguments. R. S. Warner (1994) argued that the congregation is *the* distinctive form of American religion and that there is a general convergence toward a de facto congregationalism. While the model of congregational life comes from reformed Protestantism's reappropriation of the Jewish synagogue tradition, other faiths have freely adopted and adapted it. As an organizational form, the congregation is neither liberal nor conservative necessarily; bulwarks of liberal Protestantism such as the United Church of Christ or the Unitarian-Universalists share many organizational characteristics with Independent Baptists and the Assemblies of God.

"Local" concerns and local identities have had the preeminent place in American life in religion as in politics. Denominational bureaucracies are often distant, both geographically and socially. Coupled with an anti-institutional cultural theme, and a recurring pattern of distrust of doctrinal knowledge in favor of an emotional immanentism, local congregations may be regarded as the organizational unit that ultimately matters. Even internationally organized religions, such as Catholicism or Islam, have felt this pressure toward congregational autonomy in the United States.

Practical and Cultural Similarities in American Religion Despite the differences among the many religious groups who have arrived in the United States, and the scholarly assessments of what constitutes "American religion," some similarities have arisen in both the practice and the study of religion in America. As mentioned earlier, revivalism began as a technique for energizing new religious converts but became a more general method of persuasion used subsequently in the development of mass politics. Ryan (1981) delineated the ways in which revivals shaped both the private and the public spheres, affected the ideas of what constituted the proper middle-class family, and gave women a significant role in societal-level change as well.

Even the organizational forms of religions in America, whether denominational or congregational, are examples of convergence. Processes of "institutional isomorphism" (DiMaggio and Powell 1983) push different organizations toward similar structural forms. The same legal and social forces that encourage pluralism in religious identification also promote an organizational isomorphism among different groups. Groups look alike organizationally even if they differ theologically, politically, and socially. The American experience has been the stage for both diversity and convergence.

At the cultural level, several themes have become common to American religion. Disestablishment and pluralism have produced an ethos of religious voluntarism. For many groups, beginning with evangelical and Holiness traditions but spreading widely, "real" religion involves voluntary submission of the individual will to the "free grace" of God. The "community of saints" was still filled by the elect, but not necessarily a "predestined" elect. Rather, humans must use their free will to come voluntarily to a Godly humility. This worldview placed a primacy on the individual believer. Thus religious requirements for salvation and the individualism implicit in a rationalizing capitalist economy and a mass political democracy all shared an "elective affinity" (Thomas 1989).

Without legal compulsion holding communicants, disaffected church members can leave. Additionally, the variety of acceptable options offered by increasing religious diversity have forced American religious groups to respond to what is essentially a "religious market" to recruit and maintain members (Berger 1979, Finke and Stark 1992). As ethnicity became submerged by geographic and social mobility (especially for European Americans), church switching became easier, more acceptable, and more common. Indeed, from the early nineteenth century to the late twentieth century, a religious populism became firmly ingrained in American religious culture.

This cultural individualism and religious voluntarism also led to a widely shared emphasis on morality over theology. In a diverse society, an often-shared morality allowed a certain ecumenical and interfaith tolerance that glossed theological differences. This "shared" morality was not a neutral, consensual product of an egalitarian society. Practical and public morality has often been the cornerstone of religious conflict as well as civility. Nonetheless, in American life the idea resonates that a shared sense of the moral is not dependent on specific theological underpinnings (Demerath and Williams 1985).

The case for an American religion also resonates with an argument concerning "American exceptionalism." Exceptionalism has both political and religious dimensions that may be related to efforts to answer such questions as these: Why has there not been a serious socialist challenge in American politics? Why are there continued high levels of religious activity, despite the society's thorough modernization? Why does religion have the political influence that it does despite disestablishment and pluralism? While debates continue over the details of answers to such questions, there is widespread agreement that the United States is distinct from other industrialized, (post)modern societies. The nation's religious profile is one aspect of that distinctiveness; America is what it is in large part because of the development of "American religion."

Americanism Central to U.S. religious culture is the conception of the nation as divinely blessed and Americans as a "chosen people" with a special covenant with God. The Puritans' "errand into the wilderness" (Miller 1956) to create a new Jerusalem (Cherry 1971) is one obvious example, but the notion has spread far beyond that tradition. Indeed, even in Judaism there has been some debate over the special place America holds for Jews (e.g., Lipset 1990). In Weberian terms, Americanism has often been the "priestly" form of U.S.

civil religion (Richey and Jones 1974), a celebratory, often self-congratulatory, and occasionally sentimental form.

Americanism, however, is more a cultural theme than a coherent doctrine. It can be both inclusive and exclusionist, for example, exalting our common history of immigration while opposing the newest arrivals. There is a nostalgic cast to this, celebrating the nation's idealized past while lamenting a confusing present. Often this past is "remembered" as pastoral, agricultural, and ethnically homogenous, made up of people like Jefferson's yeoman farmers—rugged, virtuous, neighborly yet self-reliant—quintessentially American.

This image contrasts sharply with the historical reality of waves of immigrants filling American cities and factories (see Handy 1984) and stimulating extensive social conflicts. An exclusionist nativism has been one reaction; other efforts have attempted to turn immigrants into "good Americans," that is, culturally similar to Anglo-Saxon Protestants. The cultural mystique of the "heartland"—meaning the traditionally WASP Midwest—continues to reflect this Americanism in current culture and politics. Note that Iowa and New Hampshire get the first cracks at picking the candidates for president.

Americanism also has been an important cultural backdrop to U.S. foreign relations. In this venue, it has been both isolationist and interventionist. America's uniquely "chosen" status has allowed the nation to act as though the "old world's" problems had no relevance to it. On the other hand, America's call to be a "city on a hill" has produced a sense of responsibility for leading the world into a better future. The results are sometimes benign, such as the nation's charitable giving and foreign aid.

But Americanism also has been manifested as an aggressive assertion of national privilege. For example, the Monroe Doctrine staked out the entire Western hemisphere as the U.S. sphere of influence, and the doctrine of "manifest destiny" legitimated the expansion of the nation's boundaries from coast to coast. Somewhere in between benign and militant has been the country's conviction, particularly in the twentieth century, that it had the responsibility to spread "democracy" throughout the world. The religious roots of Americanism's "mission to the world" may be given a secular facade, but they do not disappear (e.g., Tiryakian 1982).

A noted analysis of religious themes in the celebration of America is W. L. Warner's (1959) examination of Memorial Day observances in "Yankee City." His symbolic anthropology demonstrates the extent to which the nation's past, present, and future, through its living and its dead, are brought together within a common transcendent plan.

Americanism has been, in sum, both a source of national unity and a tool for social conflict.

—*Rhys H. Williams*

REFERENCES

R. S. Appleby, *Church and Age Unite!* (Notre Dame, Ind.: University of Notre Dame Press, 1992); B. Bailyn, *The Ideological Origins of the American Revolution* (Cambridge: Harvard Belknap Press, 1967); R. N. Bellah, "Civil Religion in America," *Daedalus* 96(1967):1-21; P. L. Berger, *The Heretical Imperative* (Garden City, N.Y.: Doubleday, 1979); R. J. Carwardine, *Evangelical Protestants and Politics in Antebellum America, 1840-1861* (New Haven, Conn.: Yale University Press, 1993); C. Cherry (ed.), *God's New Israel* (Englewood Cliffs, N.J.: Prentice Hall, 1971); J. M. Cuddihy, *No Offense* (New York: Seabury, 1978); N. J. Demerath III and R. H. Williams, "Separation of Church and State?" *Society* 21(May/June 1984):3-10; N. J. Demerath III and R. H. Williams, "Civil Religion in an Uncivil Society," *Annals* 480(1985):154-166; N. J. Demerath III and R. H. Williams, *A Bridging of Faiths* (Princeton, N.J.: Princeton University Press, 1992); P. J. DiMaggio and W. W. Powell, "The Iron Cage Revisited," *American Sociological Review* 48(1983):147-160; J. P. Dolan, *The American Catholic Experience* (Notre Dame, Ind.: University of Notre Dame Press, 1992); S. N. Eisenstadt, "The Expansion of Religions," in *Comparative Social Research* 13 (Greenwich, Conn.: JAI, 1991): 45-74; R. Finke and R. Stark, *The Churching of America* (New Brunswick, N.J.: Rutgers University Press, 1992); D. H. Fischer, *Albion's Seed* (New York: Oxford University Press, 1989); D. G. Hackett, *The Rude Hand of Innovation* (New York: Oxford University Press, 1991); Y. Y. Haddad and J. I. Smith (eds.), *Muslim Communities in North America* (Albany: SUNY Press, 1994); J. K. Hadden, *The Gathering Storm in the Churches* (Garden City, N.Y.: Doubleday, 1969); J. Hammond, *The Politics of Benevolence* (Norwood, N.J.: Ablex, 1979); P. E. Hammond, *Religion and Personal Autonomy* (Columbia: University of South Carolina Press, 1992); R. T. Handy, *A Christian America*, 2nd ed. (New York: Oxford University Press, 1984); N. O. Hatch, *The Democratization of American Christianity* (New Haven, Conn.: Yale University Press, 1989); W. Herberg, *Protestant, Catholic, Jew* (Garden City, N.Y.: Doubleday, 1955); D. W. Howe, "Religion and Politics in the Antebellum North," in *Religion and American Politics*, ed. M. A. Noll (New York: Oxford University Press, 1990): 121-145; S. Innes, *Labor in a New Land* (Princeton, N.J.: Princeton University Press, 1983); P. Kleppner, *The Cross of Culture* (New York: Free Press, 1970); S. M. Lipset (ed.), *American Pluralism and the Jewish Community* (New Brunswick, N.J.: Transaction, 1990); M. E. Marty, *Righteous Empire* (New York: Dial, 1970); P. Miller, *Errand into the Wilderness* (Cambridge: Harvard Belknap Press, 1956); J. M. Murrin, "Religion and Politics in America from the First Settlements to the Civil War," in *Religion and American Politics*, ed. M. A. Noll (New York: Oxford University Press, 1990):

19-45; H. R. Niebuhr, *The Social Sources of Denominationalism* (New York: Holt, 1929); L. Pope, *Millhands and Preachers* (New Haven, Conn.: Yale University Press, 1965); R. E. Richey and D. G. Jones (eds.), *American Civil Religion* (New York: Harper, 1974); M. P. Ryan, *Cradle of the Middle Class* (New York: Cambridge University Press, 1981); R. P. Scherer (ed.), *American Denominational Organization* (Pasadena, Calif.: Carey Library, 1980); H. S. Stout, *The New England Soul* (New York: Oxford University Press, 1986); G. M. Thomas, *Revivalism and Cultural Change* (Chicago: University of Chicago Press, 1989); E. A. Tiryakian, "Puritan America in the Modern World," *Sociological Analysis,* 43(1982):351-368; R. S. Warner, "The Place of the Congregation in the Contemporary American Religious Configuration," in *American Congregations,* Vol. 2, ed. J. P. Wind and J. W. Lewis, q.v. (1994): 54-99; W. L. Warner, *The Living and the Dead* (New Haven, Conn.: Yale University Press, 1959); B. Welter, *Dimity Convictions* (Athens: Ohio University Press, 1976); C. Wessinger (ed.), *Women's Leadership in Marginal Religions* (Urbana: University of Illinois Press, 1993); P. W. Williams, *Popular Religion in America* (Urbana: University of Illinois Press, 1989); R. B. Williams, *Religions of Immigrants from India and Pakistan* (New York: Cambridge University Press, 1988); J. Wind and J. W. Lewis (eds.), *American Congregations* (Chicago: University of Chicago Press, 1994); R. Wuthnow, *The Restructuring of American Religion* (Princeton, N.J.: Princeton University Press, 1988).

AMERICAN SOCIOLOGICAL ASSOCIATION, SOCIOLOGY OF RELIGION SECTION

Begun in August 1994, the purpose of the Sociology of Religion section of ASA as stated in the section bylaws is "to encourage and enhance research, teaching and other professional concerns in the study of religion and society" by promoting "communication, collaboration, and consultation among scholars" in this field.

More than 400 people joined the section during its first year. Two factors likely contributed to the late arrival of this section in the ASA. The first was the belief among many sociologists in the earlier part of the twentieth century that religion had lost its relevance as a social force. This belief led to the isolation of sociologists of religion, who founded separate associations. This created the second factor: Many members of these associations opposed the creation of an ASA section out of a concern that it would lead to the demise of the smaller groups. Others believed that the sociology of religion was growing so rapidly that it could support numerous organizations and that it was time to move it into the mainstream of the profession. Research on the membership growth and meeting attendance of the separate associations thus far has borne out the latter view.

Helen Rose Ebaugh, who was a major leader in the creation of the section, was elected to be its first chair, succeeded by Robert Wuthnow, Rodney Stark, and Ruth Wallace. Initial activities of the section have included, in addition to writing bylaws and preparing slates of officers, the organizing of sessions at the ASA annual meeting, the publication of a newsletter, the setting up of an electronic network, and a program of awards.

—*Madeleine R. Cousineau*

AMISH　A subset of groups of the larger Anabaptist movement. By the 1690s, Anabaptists had migrated from Switzerland into the Alsace region in present-day France. A quarrel between these Alsatian Anabaptists and those remaining in Switzerland erupted.

Named for their founder, Jacob Ammann, the Alsatian "Amish" began holding communion twice a year rather than annually, incorporating foot-washing into the communion service. These innovative religious practices were contrary to the practices of those remaining in Switzerland.

The biggest divisive issue, however, was the practice of what is called *meidung* or "shunning." Swiss Anabaptists excommunicated wayward members from communion and church but maintained social relationships. Ammann ordered his followers to shun even social relations or interaction with those banned from the church and religious services. This practice of shunning irrevocably split the Swiss Anabaptists and the Alsatians, now known as "Amish," in 1693.

The first large group of Amish settlers to North America arrived in Philadelphia in 1737. This group settled in eastern Pennsylvania. Settlements were planted over the next century, and Amish now reside in rural areas across 20 states and the province of Ontario in Canada. The states with the largest Amish populations, accounting for more than 70%, are Indiana, Ohio, and Pennsylvania. More than two dozen branches, or divisions, of Amish have been identified by John Hostetler, Donald Kraybill, and other scholars. There are no Amish outside North America today.

Amish beliefs stress the separateness of God's believers from this world. Connectedness to the outside world is forbidden. Amish do not participate in Social Security or Medicare. They refuse to have high-wire electricity, natural gas, or telephones connected in their houses. Usually it is the strictest group, the Old Order Amish, who represent the image of Amish to many people. Old Order Amish worship every other Sunday in members' homes. They own no automobiles, practice no birth control, and send their children to Amish-run schools (and only through eighth grade). Amish use horses in the field and for transportation with buggies. Gas or kerosene lights their homes and may cook their food. Despite the austerity of this lifestyle in society's eyes, four out of five (80%) Amish teenagers join the church and remain within the group, marrying an Amish spouse. Thus, with a high birthrate and high retention of offspring, the Amish population has grown tremendously.

With this growth, the traditional Amish lifestyle of the family farm is threatened by higher land values, commercialization, and industrial takeovers of areas typically inhabited by Amish farmers and their families (notably, Lancaster County, Pennsylvania) as well as declining farm incomes. Kraybill and Nolt have commented that in the last generation of Amish in the twentieth century, studied extensively in the oldest settlement area of Lancaster County, Pennsylvania, Amish-owned and operated microenterprises have grown and flourished. The future of Amish separateness and their distinct culture and beliefs may be in jeopardy as more and more Amish engage in nonfarming enterprises in response to the need to support more families with less and less farmland available.

—*Barbara J. Denison*

REFERENCES

J. Hostetler, *Amish Society* (Baltimore: Johns Hopkins University Press, 1980); D. Kraybill, *The Riddle of Amish Culture* (Baltimore: Johns Hopkins Press, 1989); D. Kraybill and S. Nolt, *Amish Enterprises* (Baltimore: Johns Hopkins Press, 1995).

AMMERMAN, NANCY TATOM (1950–)

Ph.D. Yale University. After spending more than a decade at Candler School of Theology at Emory University, Ammerman became Professor of Sociology of Religion at Hartford Seminary in July 1995, and President of the Association for the Sociology of Religion in 1996. She also has been recognized by being selected as the Religious Research Association's H. Paul Douglass lecturer.

One of the most highly productive and well-known women in the sociology of religion, Ammerman has focused her research upon Christian fundamentalism and congregational studies. Her two best known books, *Bible Believers: Fundamentalists in the Modern World* (Rutgers University Press 1987) and *Baptist Battles: Social Change and Religious Conflict in the Southern Baptist Convention* (Rutgers 1990), analyze the far-reaching changes that are occurring within one funda-

mentalist denomination. A third book, *Southern Baptists Observed: Multiple Perspectives on a Changing Denomination* (University of Tennessee Press 1993), is less well known and more theoretical than the first two, but it is equally as important for understanding the dynamics of change within a fundamentalist denomination. The books, however, are more than case studies of change and conflict within one group; Ammerman places her analysis within the larger context of what happens when fundamentalist groups grapple with the effects of modern history and intraorganizational tensions between moderates and conservatives. In addition to her work on the Southern Baptists, she has contributed as both editor and author to *Accounting for Christian Fundamentalisms* (University of Chicago Press 1994), a part of the Fundamentalism Project under the direction of Martin E. Marty and R. Scott Appleby, and has written chapters in other volumes produced in this series.

After completing her work on the Southern Baptists, Ammerman turned her attention to the broader study of congregations in changing communities. Funded by the Lilly Endowment, she has been involved with colleagues in a large national research project whose goal is to understand what happens to religious congregations as they confront the myriad changes occurring within American society. This resulted in her book *Congregation and Community* (Rutgers 1997).

—*Helen Rose Ebaugh*

ANABAPTISTS

ANABAPTISTS A part of the legacy of Martin Luther's protests that led to the Protestant Reformation in sixteenth-century Europe. Church leaders and reformers such as Luther in Germany and Zwingli in Switzerland were dependent upon government sanctions at the city or state level to enact their religious reforms. Some, however, did not feel that waiting for political action to gain state approval was in their best interests. Specifically, these young students, artisans, and members of the merchant classes wanted to discard such rituals as infant baptism and the Mass. In 1525, the radicals broke with the state church in Zurich and rebaptized each other in a member's home.

Labeled "anabaptists," meaning "rebaptizers," this group founded a church based not on state sanctions but on voluntary choice. Anabaptists rejected the authority of civil government over religious affairs. They stressed living apart from worldly society and thus rejected military service, violence, the taking of oaths, or the bringing of legal suits.

More important, the anabaptist challenge to the unity of church and state, with the latter controlling much in the former, was a threat to the social order. Like members of the many diverse religious nonconformist groups in Europe at the same time, Anabaptists were threatened, arrested, persecuted, and executed by the thousands in subsequent decades. A book, *The Martyrs' Mirror*, found in anabaptist homes today, records many of these events. This persecution drove Anabaptists farther south into more rural and more tolerant areas of Europe. There, leaders such as Menno Simons encountered and converted the peasant and rural populace to break with Rome.

Anabaptists today include such groups as Mennonites and Amish; some scholars would include also the Quakers and Moravians, even though there are discrepancies between their belief systems and those of traditional Anabaptism. Some of these differences include infant baptism, church-style architecture, and an educated clergy for Moravians, and a unique vision of the nature of God for Quakers. Anabaptists are noted for their pacifism (which they share with the Quakers), and many worked in voluntary service as conscientious objectors during the world wars.

—*Barbara J. Denison*

REFERENCES

L. Driedger and L. Harder (eds.), *Anabaptist-Mennonite Identities in Ferment* (Elkhart, Ind.: Institute of Mennonite Studies, 1990); J. H. Kauffman and L. Harder, *Anabaptists Four Centuries Later* (Scottsdale, Pa.: Herald, 1975).

ANCESTOR WORSHIP   Beliefs and rites concerned with the spirits of one's ancestors. Rituals may be intended to honor the ancestors, to help the ancestors in the other world, or to seek help (guidance, power) from the ancestors. The spiritual world of the ancestors is usually thought to be similar to the life they experienced prior to death. Morality is concerned with pleasing the ancestors.

Ancestor worship is not itself a religion but exists as a part of many groups' religious systems. It fits societies in which the authority of elders is an important component. While ancestor worship is most important within traditional groups or folk religions, practices associated with ancestors linger on in the world religions (e.g., having Catholic Masses said for the dead).

Ancestor worship has been affected by the scientific challenge to magic, by the diffusion of universal religions, and by changes in family life. In East Asia, worship of ancestors is being replaced by simple acts of remembrance (Morioka 1986). A similar process may be occurring in all modernizing societies. In Western societies, the tendency to preserve deceased loved ones in memory conflicts with changes such as multiple marriages; new religious and secular grieving practices emphasize letting go of old relationships in preparation for forming new ones.

—*Joseph B. Tamney*

REFERENCES

M. Freedman, *Chinese Family and Marriage in Singapore* (London: HMSO, 1957); K. Morioka, "Ancestor Worship in Contemporary Japan," in *Religion and the Family in East Asia*, ed. G. A. DeVos and T. Sofue (Berkeley: University of California Press, 1986): 201-213.

ANGLICANISM, ANGLICANS   *see*   Episcopal Church

ANIMISM   A form of religion centered on relating to spiritual powers or beings who permeate the world. The spiritual power may be conceived as an impersonal force running through everything and capable of being used for good or evil. The unseen power also may be understood as numerous spirits, some of whom are friendly, some "tricksters," and some dangerous. Spirits and humans are interdependent parts of a single cosmos. Animist groups have no elaborate religious organization and no required creed. Individuals may be recognized as vehicles for communicating directly with spirits (shamans, spirit-mediums). These religious specialists also may be healers or diviners. Fasting is common as a way of preparing for the bodily reception of the sacred or for allowing the sacral power within to emerge. Ritual activity tends to be magical. Rituals attempt to control spiritual powers or beings for the benefit of oneself or groups with whom one is identified.

Edward Tylor (1832-1917) defined religion as the belief in spiritual beings or animism; that is, he considered the essential element of all religions to be a belief in souls and/or a belief in spirits. Tylor argued that these beliefs were reasonable given experiences such as dreams and trances. The universality of these experiences explains why religion exists everywhere. Monotheism is the "animism of civilized man" (see Morris 1987:98-102).

While animists can be found in almost all Asian countries, they are more than 5% of the population only in Laos. Animists are between 1% and 5% of the population in Burma, India, Indonesia, Kampuchea, Malaysia, and Vietnam.

—*Joseph B. Tamney*

REFERENCES

B. Morris, *Anthropological Studies of Religion* (Cambridge: Cambridge University Press, 1987).

ANOMIE Sociological concept, developed especially by Émile Durkheim; refers to a state of deregulation *(déréglement)* of normative standards and accompanying derangement of individual experience. The term in its modern meaning has ancient roots. Thucydides contrasts Pericles's expression of Athenian "civil religion," in his funeral oration, with the lawlessness *(anomias)* of Athenian conduct under the subsequent plague. Ancient Jewish and early Christian writers refer to sin as *anomia,* but in the sense of iniquity, not lawlessness.

Durkheim discusses the abnormal, anomic division of labor. He also links anomie to the dislocation and excessive inflation or frustration of desires experienced under rapidly fluctuating social and economic circumstances. Less frequently, he ties anomie to the failure of religious constraints on the individual, preferring to conceptualize the influence of religious groups in terms of egoism and altruism. Marcel Mauss applied the concept to religion by studying the physical influence on the individual of collective ideas about death (e.g., "voodoo death").

Robert Merton saw anomie as a disjunctive condition of overemphasis on the cultural value of success at the expense of norms of conduct (e.g., the "work ethic"). This generates deviant adaptations such as innovation, or use of illegitimate means to achieve values, and ritualistic "acting out" of norms in the absence of commitment to social goals. His theory shares as much with Weber's "Protestant ethic" thesis as with Durkheim's thought and touches on traditional issues of religious meaning in its emphasis on the effort-merit-reward complex.

Peter Berger renewed Durkheim's emphasis on the integrative functions of religion by arguing that ideas of "the sacred" establish an orderly cosmos that prevents anomie, while Robert Bellah's analysis of "civil religion" also suggests its possible anomic disintegration under conditions of a "broken covenant."

The concept of anomie is closely related to the ideas of cognitive dissonance and mazeway disintegration, which have been used in the study of millenarianism. Dissonance between millennial prophecies and actual events is overcome through increased proselytizing, which redeems failure. Natural disasters and cultural collapse, frequently both occurring together among tribal peoples, rip apart the thread of meaning woven by the cultural mazeway. Revitalization movements seek to reestablish "the way" by reaffirming traditions, forging syncretisms, or creating new prophecies.

—*Donald A. Nielsen*

REFERENCES

L. Festinger et al., *When Prophecy Fails* (New York: Harper, 1956); R. K. Merton, *Social Theory and Social Structure,* rev. ed. (New York: Free Press, 1968 [1949]); M. Orrù, *Anomie* (Boston: Allen & Unwin, 1987); A. Wallace, "Revitalization Movements," *American Anthropologist* 589(1956):264-281.

ANTHROPOLOGY OF RELIGION

Anthropological studies of religion had their beginnings in the late nineteenth century with the seminal works of Max Müller, W. Robertson Smith, Edward B. Tylor, and Sir James G. Frazer. These scholars, of course, were not the first to take an interest in the comparative study of religion, nor were they the first to speculate on the religions of preliterate and tribal peoples. What set these men apart is that they were the first to suggest that tribal religions might be amenable to study following the rules of the scientific method, and the first to posit specific methodological procedures for the comparative analysis of religious beliefs and practices.

All four of these scholars have been characterized as "armchair theorists" and dilettantes (although Müller was an expert in Sanskrit, Smith had a command of Semitic languages, Tylor had spent time studying the antiquities of Mexico, and Frazer had a strong background in classics). Additionally, all four scholars conducted their research from the center of the far-flung British empire and thereby had access to a wider range of comparative data than had been previously available.

Müller, Smith, Tylor, and Frazer formulated theories that have been characterized as "intellectualistic" (Evans-Pritchard 1965). They were primarily interested in human thought. All sought to understand religious belief and practice at its most fundamental, basic level. Frazer argued, for example, that human thought is best understood as a progression from magic, to religion, to science. Magic—which Frazer contended was based either on the principle of contagion or on "sympathy" (the idea that if two objects are associated they will continue to influence one another even after they are separated) or the notion of imitation (the idea that like influences like)—was said to be the earliest form. In more advanced societies, Frazer contended, magic eventually is replaced by religion, and both are finally replaced by science.

The nineteenth-century anthropologists—like other social scientists of their day—derived assumptions about religion from the Judeo-Christian heritage and from their own religious experiences within that tradition. Müller and Frazer were agnostics, while Tylor and Smith considered themselves devout Christians. Another source of bias is that "armchair anthropologists" such as Tylor and Frazer tested their theories on the basis of the highly suspect reports provided by missionaries and European travelers. It was the rare Western observer who was able to report on non-Western religions objectively and with firsthand data. Indeed, evolutionary models current at the time would have precluded such objective reportage. Given such substantial constraints, it is amazing that the nineteenth-century interpretations of tribal religions are as sympathetic and insightful as they sometimes are. Despite their evolutionary assumptions and their overwhelming Eurocentric biases, Müller, Smith, Tylor, and Frazer made valuable contributions to the study of religion and can profitably be read today.

It is not surprising that many of the leading minds of the nineteenth century would turn their attention to religion. It has never been difficult to make a case for the significance of religion in human life. Religion has been found in all societies studied by anthropologists. It is highly visible and, in the words of Raymond T. Firth (1995:214), represents "a massive output of human enterprise." Religious beliefs and practices are an enduring tribute to humankind's nearly infinite resourcefulness and adaptability in coping with the problems of daily life. As William W. Howells (1948:16) astutely observed, "Man's life is hard, very hard. And he knows it, poor soul; that is the thing. He knows that he is forever confronted with the Four Horsemen—death, famine, disease, and the malice of other men."

Defining the Scope of Religion Despite a keen and enduring interest in religion, there is no single, uniform anthropological theory of religion or a common methodology for the study of religious beliefs and rituals. Researchers in the area cannot agree as to exactly how "religion" should be defined or what the term *religion*

should encompass. Efforts at defining religion—ranging from Tylor's 1871 definition of religion as "the belief in spirit beings" to the more complex definitions offered by Clifford Geertz and Melford E. Spiro—have met with considerable resistance (Morris 1987, Klass 1995, Saler 1993). Nevertheless, Geertz's definition by far has been the most influential anthropological definition of religion in the twentieth century.

Geertz (1973:90) defined religion as (1) a system of symbols which acts to (2) establish powerful, pervasive, and long-lasting moods and motivations in men [and women] by (3) formulating conceptions of a general order of existence and (4) clothing these conceptions with such an aura of factuality that (5) the moods and motivations seem uniquely realistic.

Although his definition may be useful in elaborating what religion is like conceptually and what it does psychologically and socially, Geertz has been criticized for failing to explain specifically how a researcher might identify religion when encountered in the field. A major stumbling block to all definitions of religion, of course, is that religion is not a "thing" but an abstraction.

Other twentieth-century definitions of religion (e.g., Spiro, Jacob Pandian, E. E. Evans-Pritchard) follow Émile Durkheim (1912) in positing a rigid dichotomy between the so-called supernatural and natural, or sacred and profane orders. These alternative definitions have proved no more satisfactory than Geertz's because distinctions between *supernatural* and *natural* are seldom obvious and may vary dramatically from individual to individual and from society to society.

In the later twentieth century, debate has arisen concerning the scope of the anthropology of religion. Do anthropologists of religion only study religions in tribal settings? Is it exclusively the study of non-Western religions? Is it to be limited to the study of religion among oppressed and marginalized people? The focus of anthropological study has shifted from the study of tribal to modern religions. A number of well-received studies have analyzed religion in developing societies, Europe, and the United States. Many of the leading contemporary exponents of anthropology of religion —Geertz, Spiro, Vincent Crapanzano, Victor Turner, James W. Fernandez, Sherry B. Ortner, Mary Douglas, James Boon, and Stanley J. Tambiah—have devoted the bulk of their attentions to local variants of major world religions (Hinduism, Islam, Buddhism, and Christianity) and/or the impact of world religions in developing countries (Java, Indonesia, Morocco, Sri Lanka, South Africa, Nepal, and Burma) instead of the religions of isolated tribal groups. Contemporary ethnographers concentrate on examining religious diversity in complex societies rather than providing further documentation for uniformity in tribal religions.

An unresolved issue facing the anthropology of religion is the nature and problem of religious belief itself. "Belief" is *the* central focus of Protestant Christianity but is clearly of less concern in tribal religions, in which questions of orthodoxy seldom arise. There has been protracted debate among scholars as to whether it is possible for a nonbeliever to make definitive pronouncements concerning the religious beliefs of others. Can a religion be understood fully only from the perspective of the believer? While a number of leading psychologists and sociologists of religion are themselves adherents to the faiths they study, the overwhelming majority of anthropologists are skeptics. Most anthropologists are materialists and reductionists. They would find themselves in strong agreement with Firth (1995:215), who contends that "there is truth in every religion. But it is a human not a divine truth." Belief presents special problems for anthropologists because conversion is seldom an option for outsiders. Nevertheless, a number of anthropologists have insisted that religions can be grasped only from "within." Ethnographers who conduct research among pentecostalists and fundamentalists are often themselves members of these groups, and many younger anthropologists who specialize in new religious movements such as neo- and core shamanism are themselves avid practitioners.

The hallmark of twentieth-century anthropology has been the advocacy of firsthand, participant observation and/or fieldwork. This has altered the character and scope of research on religion and forced anthropologists to become more modest in their goals and less sweeping in their generalizations. Contemporary anthropological assertions are more likely to concern the manifestation of a particular belief in a particular place and time rather than speculate on "religion" in the abstract. Researchers focus on a single aspect of a religion (a specific myth, a specific ritual, or an aspect of a ritual such as divination, sacrifice, spirit possession, and so on) but refuse to examine an entire religious complex. This has had both positive and negative consequences for the anthropological study of religion. Twentieth-century anthropologists of religion have been left with the choice of "saying more with less authority" or "saying less with more authority." Most have chosen the latter path. This is a far cry from the imperious stance taken by Müller, Tylor, and Frazer, and cannot help but have far-reaching consequences for the anthropological study of religion in the next century.

The Study of Ritual and Myth Theories developed in other subfields of anthropology (linguistics, economics, kinship, ecology) have been applied—with varying degrees of success—to the anthropological study of religion. As a result, religions have been analyzed from a variety of perspectives: functional, psychological, ecological, structural, cross-cultural, cognitive, and symbolic. Of these new perspectives, variants of functionalism have been the most enduring, but cognitive and symbolic studies are likely to dominate in the next century.

A number of promising studies have focused on ritual and ritual forms. From this perspective, rituals are seen as the fundamental unit of religious expression and the building blocks for all religions. Earlier studies (Durkheim 1912, Radcliffe-Brown 1961) underscored the role of ritual in mirroring the defining central features of society and culture, worldviews, identities, political forms, and social arrangements. More recently, scholars have argued that ritual not only mirrors these defining features but challenges them as well. Greater attention has been given to so-called ritual inversions and to what Max Gluckman has termed "rituals of rebellion."

In the nineteenth century, scholars such as Lady Jane Harrison argued valiantly for the primacy of ritual over myth. All mythology, they argued, has its roots in ritual activity. The myth-ritual debate raged for more than 60 years until 1942, when Clyde Kluckhohn offered a satisfactory compromise by recounting multiple instances in which a myth clearly began as a ritual and other instances in which a ritual clearly began as a myth.

Anthropological studies of ritual distinguish between calendrical and crisis rituals and between individual and collective rites (Durkheim 1912, Radcliffe-Brown 1961). For Durkheim, rituals both reflect and support the moral framework underlying social arrangements. Radcliffe-Brown improved on Durkheim's theory by attempting to explain why some rituals are chosen over others. Ultimately, Radcliffe-Brown suggested, rituals directly related to the collective and material well-being of a society are elevated to having spiritual, "ritual value" as well.

Perhaps the most influential study of the ritual process was provided by Arnold van Gennep in *The Rites of Passage* (1908), where he argued for the significance of rites of transition, which he categorized as an immutable tripartite sequence: separation, liminality, and reaggregation. Victor Turner's *The Ritual Process* (1969) advanced van Gennep's concept of "liminality" by advocating its applicability for the study of ritual in both tribal (Ndembu) and modern European societies. Roy A. Rappaport's *Pigs for the Ancestors* (1968) skillfully demonstrated how rituals regulate environmental relations. Rappaport's is the best known study linking religious ritual and ecology (Reynolds and Tanner 1995).

Within the anthropological tradition, myth has been understood primarily as an encapsulation of sacred truth. Functional theorists such as Bronislaw Malinowski (1926) argued that myth promotes social cohesion and serves as a "charter" for human behavior. Myth, in short, legitimates human activities. Other theorists have treated mythology separately from religion. The twentieth-century study of mythology has received its greatest proponent in the seminal work of the French structural anthropologist Claude Lévi-Strauss, who finds in myth a key to the underlying structures of the human mind. Myth, for Lévi-Strauss, reveals how the mind functions.

Anthropologists have long noted that religions are highly dynamic, and the role of religion in fostering social change has been extensively explored. An interest in religious change is discernable in the evolutionary theories of Tylor and Frazer as well as the twentieth-century diffussionist studies of Leslie Spier and A. L. Kroeber. Anthony F. C. Wallace (1966) identified a five-stage progression to account for attitudinal and organizational changes that occur within religious movements: prophetic, utopian, messianic, millennial, or millenarian. Wallace is best known for his conception of "revitalization movements" and his application of this concept to the Plains Indian Ghost Dance and cargo cults in Melanesia.

Cognitive, Biological, and Symbolic Approaches
Much recent work in the anthropology of religion focuses on symbols and cognition, as exemplified in the writings of Geertz, Turner, Fernandez, Boon, Ortner, and Douglas. Still other approaches focus on biological and experiential models of religion (Laughlin et al. 1993). Cognitive and neurological sciences have produced great insights into the biology of behavior, and many of these insights have been extended to the study of religion. Organizations such as the Society for the Anthropology of Consciousness are devoted to the rigorous, scientific exploration of religious experience, including the religious use of hallucinogens, altered states of consciousness, shamanism, trance states, and the cross-cultural study of spirit possession. Naturalistic theories of religion have experienced a revival in the writings of Stewart E. Guthrie (1993) and Pascal Boyer (1994).

Other scholars (Morris 1987, Horton 1993, Klass 1995, Saler 1993, Pals 1995) have devoted attention to the reassessment of previous research. They have argued that contemporary anthropologists of religion are constrained by inadequate and outmoded categories and conceptions. Their frustration is eloquently expressed by Morton Klass (1995:xi), who laments that anthropologists of religion continue to embrace "theoretical perceptions and assumptions that have long since been jettisoned in most other areas of anthropological concern and activity." Not all anthropologists would agree. Such critical assessments often fail to do justice to the tremendous amount that can be learned from the excellent textbooks of Lowie (1924), Norbeck (1974), Wallace (1966), Radin (1937), and de Waal Malefijt (1968) as well as more recent texts by Pandian (1991) and Child and Child (1993).

In conclusion, functional, cognitive, and symbolic approaches have dominated the anthropological study of religion in the late twentieth century as researchers have become increasingly concerned with the concept of meaning. Biological, neurological, and cognitive approaches undoubtedly will assume greater importance in the next century. Anthropology of religion is no longer confined to the study of religion in tribal societies. Since the late 1970s, a majority of anthropological studies have dealt with religion in the developed or developing world.

—*Stephen D. Glazier*

REFERENCES

P. Boyer, *The Naturalness of Religious Ideas* (Berkeley: University of California Press, 1994); A. B. Child and I. L. Child, *Religion and Magic in the Life of Traditional Peoples* (Englewood Cliffs, N.J.: Prentice Hall, 1993); É. Durkheim, *The Elementary Forms of Religious Life* (New York: Free Press, 1995 [1912]); E. E. Evans-Pritchard, *Theories of Primitive Religion* (Oxford: Clarendon, 1965); R. T. Firth, *Religion* (New York: Routledge, 1995); J. G. Frazer, *The Golden Bough* (New York: Macmillan, 1935 [1890]); C. Geertz, *The Interpretation of Culture* (New York: Basic Books, 1973); S. D. Glazier (ed.), *Anthropology of Religion* (Westport, Conn.: Greenwood, 1997); S. E. Guthrie, *Faces in the Cloud* (New York: Oxford University Press, 1993); R. Horton, *Patterns of Thought in Africa and the West* (New York: Cambridge University Press, 1993); W. W. Howells, *The Heathens* (Garden City, N.Y.: Doubleday, 1948); M. Klass, *Ordered Universes* (Boulder, Colo.: Westview, 1995); C. D. Laughlin et al., *Brain, Symbol and Experience* (New York: Columbia University Press, 1993); R. H. Lowie, *Primitive Religion* (New York: Liveright, 1924); B. Malinowski, *Myth in Primitive Psychology* (New York: Norton, 1926); B. Morris, *Anthropological Studies of Religion* (New York: Cambridge University Press, 1987); E. Norbeck, *Religion in Human Life* (New York: Holt, 1974); D. L. Pals, *Seven Theories of Religion* (New York: Oxford University Press, 1995); J. Pandian, *Culture, Religion, and the Sacred Self* (Englewood Cliffs, N.J.: Prentice Hall, 1991); A. R. Radcliffe-Brown, *Structure and Function in Primitive Society* (Glencoe, Ill.: Free Press, 1961); P. Radin,

Primitive Religion (New York: Viking, 1937); R. A. Rappaport, *Pigs for the Ancestors* (New Haven, Conn.: Yale University Press, 1968); V. Reynolds and R. Tanner, *The Social Ecology of Religion* (New York: Oxford University Press, 1995); B. Saler, *Conceptualizing Religion* (Leiden, Neth.: Brill, 1993); M. E. Spiro, *Culture and Human Nature,* new ed. (New Brunswick, N.J.: Transaction, 1994); S. J. Tambiah, *Magic, Science, Religion and the Scope of Rationality* (New York: Cambridge University Press, 1990); V. Turner, *The Ritual Process* (Hawthorne, N.Y.: Aldine, 1969); E. B. Tylor, *Primitive Culture* (London: Murray, 1873); A. van Gennep, *The Rites of Passage* (Chicago: University of Chicago Press, 1960 [1908]); A. de Waal Malefijt, *Religion and Culture* (New York: Macmillan, 1968); A. F. C. Wallace, *Religion* (New York: Random House, 1966).

ANTI-CULT MOVEMENT Countermovements opposing new or growing churches and religious movements have a long history in American society. In the nineteenth century, movements opposing Mormonism and Catholicism were particularly well organized and influential. During the 1970s, a new countermovement, the anti-cult movement (ACM), emerged to target the increased numbers of new religious movements (NRMs) that gained adherents in the wake of the declining 1960s counterculture.

The ACM consists of a loosely linked network of countermovement organizations with both religious and secular components. The ACM's religious wing is made up primarily of conservative Christian organizations that oppose NRMs on theological grounds through church networks and printed literature. The first organization in the activist, secular wing of the ACM was Free the Children of God (FREECOG), which was established in 1971 in response to the recruitment of young adults by the Children of God (a group later renamed "The Family"). Dozens of local and regional ACM groups subsequently formed; these coalesced in 1974 into the first national umbrella organization, Citizens Freedom Foundation (CFF), which in 1985 became the Cult Awareness Network (CAN). In 1979, a second national organization, the American Family Foundation (AFF), was established. CAN functioned as the public relations/activist arm and AFF as the intellectual arm of the ACM.

Alongside these two organizations exist several other ACM components: (1) a small but highly visible group of deprogrammers/exit counselors, who most often act as entrepreneurial agents for families of NRM members with the objective of achieving renunciation of NRM membership, (2) a network of mental health professionals who offer counseling/rehabilitation services to exiting NRM members, and (3) small, usually short-lived voluntary associations of former NRM members that serve as transition support groups. The common element linking these ACM components are varying versions of a coercive mind control ideology that interprets NRM membership as the product of manipulative practices that undermine individual capacity for voluntarism, autonomy, and rationality. The central issue that has divided scholars studying NRMs and ACM activists has been the debate over coercive persuasion (or "brainwashing").

The secular ACM began as a grassroots, activist network composed principally of NRM family members and former NRM members. Over time, the ACM added a coterie of mental health and legal professionals to its ranks, generated greater financial stability, and expanded its definitional umbrella to include a broader range of religious groups as "cults." ACM strategy has shifted away from (but has not entirely abandoned) entrepreneurial coercive deprogramming toward more institutionally compatible legal and mental health-based measures. Primary organizational effort has been directed toward achieving informal regulatory agency status. Failure to achieve this status can be attributed to the ACM's inability to forge an alliance with religious-based opposition to NRMs, a failure to gain a basis for invoking state sanctions against NRMs, and, most significantly, rejection of its brainwashing ideology by most members of the scholarly and legal communities. The ACM thus remains an active but relatively marginalized countermovement. In fact, CAN—the most active of secular ACM groups—was successfully sued into bankruptcy in 1995 by a Pentecostal adult through a CAN referral. Its name and logo, ironically, were purchased by its archnemesis, the Church of Scientology.

See also Brainwashing, New Religious Movements

—*Anson Shupe and David G. Bromley*

REFERENCES

R. Billington, *The Protestant Crusade* (Gloucester, Mass.: Smith, 1961); D. G. Bromley and J. T. Richardson (eds.), *The Brainwashing/Deprogramming Controversy* (Lewiston, N.Y.: Mellen, 1984); D. G. Bromley and A. Shupe, "New Religions and Countermovements," in *Handbook on Cults and Sects in America,* ed. D. G. Bromley and J. K. Hadden (Greenwich, Conn.: JAI, 1993): 177-198; D. B. Davis, "Some Themes of Counter-Subversion," *Mississippi Valley Historical Review* 67(1960):205-224; A. Shupe and D. G. Bromley, *The New Vigilantes* (Beverly Hills, Calif.: Sage, 1980); A. Shupe and D. G. Bromley, *The Anti-Cult Movement in America* (New York: Garland, 1984); A. Shupe and D. G. Bromley (eds.), *Anti-Cult Movements in Cross Cultural Perspective* (New York: Garland,

1994); M. Singer and J. Lalich, *Cults in Our Midst* (San Francisco: Jossey-Bass, 1995).

ANTIQUITY   *see* Greek and Roman Religions

ANTI-SEMITISM   *see* Jewish-Christian Relations and Anti-Semitism

APOCALYPTIC   A literary style that employs vivid imagery, symbolism, numerology, and portrayals of cosmic struggle (Armageddon) to distinguish a present age from a future one. It is often stilted in language, exaggerated, and even grotesque—evidently to indicate that it is to be taken as myth, although there never seems to be a shortage of theological futurists who would prefer to treat it as next year's news in code.

The term *apocalyptic,* based on the Greek expression for "revelation," is taken from the New Testament book, The Revelation to John (also called The Apocalypse), which uses the literary device of the author recounting a series of visions. The literary form seems to have emerged in the postexilic period of Jewish history, when writers in the subordinate Jewish nation borrowed Persian imagery for use in a cultural resistance against assimilation into a wider Hellenistic, and later Roman, cultural area. Prophetic literature, which was based on oral preaching against Israelite and Judean rulers, was no longer being written. Beginning with the Book of Daniel, the new literature was written to be read rather than proclaimed, and its critique was directed against foreign-based governing powers.

In addition to Daniel, Jewish works that are considered apocalyptic include the Book of Jubilees, the Apocalypse of Ezra (4 Ezra, or second part of 2 Esdras), the Syrian Apocalypse of Baruch, the Greek Apocalypse of Baruch, and the Genesis Apocryphon (Apocalypse of Lamech). Of these, only Daniel is recognized as a biblical book by Christians, and only part of it by Jews; the Apocalypse of Ezra is often appended to Christian Bibles. The Book of Jubilees is historically important because it uses a solar calendar rather than a lunar one, thereby countering both Hellenism and official Judaism; the Christian Gospel of John seems also to use the solar calendar. In addition to the Revelation to John, Christian apocalyptic literature includes the Apocalypse of Peter, the Apocalypse of Paul, and the Apocalypse of Thomas; only the Revelation to John is recognized as biblical (or "canonical"). Its acceptance was controversial and occurred in the Eastern churches only reluctantly.

From a social science perspective, apocalyptic literature seemed to mark times of severe testing for Jews (Hanson 1976, Riddle 1927), and later Christians (deSilva 1992, Riddle 1927), under Hellenistic and Roman governments. It therefore is analogous to millenarian and messianic revitalization movements that emerged in later colonial empires. Occasionally, sectarian movements in modern settings predict the end of the world as we know it, to be brought about by cataclysms, on the basis of the biblical and near-biblical apocalyptic works. Traces of apocalyptic influences can be found in the rhetoric of diverse modern movements (see Prandi 1984, Léger 1982) in an effort to escape secular (Fenn 1991) as well as religious anxiety.

See also Eschatology

—*Anthony J. Blasi*

REFERENCES

D. A. deSilva, "The Revelation to John," *Sociological Analysis* 53(1992):375-395; R. K. Fenn, "The Secularization of Dread and Despair," *Religion and the Social Order* 1 (Greenwich, Conn.: JAI, 1991): 53-72; P.D. Hanson, *The Dawn of Apocalyptic* (Philadelphia: Fortress, 1976); D. Léger, "Charisma, Utopia and Communal Life," *Social Compass* 29(1982):41-58; C. Prandi, "Le catholicisme italien à l'époque de l'unité," *Archives de sciences sociales des religions* 58(1984):67-83; D. W. Riddle, "From Apocalypse to Martyrology," *Anglican Theological Review* 9(1927):260-280.

APOSTASY AND DEFECTION   *Defection* is the process of abandoning, deserting, or becoming disentangled from a valued relationship. *Apostasy* usually refers to defection from both (1) belief and (2) group identification and participation, although it is possible cognitively to doubt a group's beliefs without abandoning participation, and also to drop group participation while still holding to the group's beliefs. In a pure sense, apostasy and defection imply leaving groups that are normative or imply ties of loyalty, even indelibility —such as religious, patriotic-military, or ideological. Modern American society, however, has so reduced the social stigma applied to noninvolvement in organized religion that it is mainly family-parent example that is left to promote religiosity in children.

Hirschman holds that, ideally, the hallmark of ideological groups is that those who leave tend to be stigmatized, branded, or labeled as defectors upon leaving (e.g., this was the case at one time for those leaving the ordained ministry, priesthood, or convent). Some who disagree with group policy will stifle themselves and remain; others who disagree will openly "voice" their opposition; still others, when voicing fails, will "exit" the group. It should be noted that "switching" denominational church membership in pluralistic societies today is quite common and accepted, but changing group affiliation (e.g., at marriage to the faith with stronger restrictions) does not necessarily connote change in belief. Research has shown that church attenders and nonattenders do not differ that much in belief.

In the modern world, the most important force for doubt is participation in broadened higher education and the personal mobility that results. The rise of modern philosophy and science (including behavioral science) has put dogmatic faiths on the defensive and raised the level of doubt. It is quite common for young people reared in ultraconservative religious traditions to undergo doubt from approximately ages 18 to 30. Rebellion against and taking a "leave of absence" from formal religion during this period is quite common, and there are few "costs" and stigmas for doing so—unless the attack on religion is public and overt (which it seldom is). The nonpractice of youth is frequently followed by a "return to faith" during the years of parenthood. Evidence shows that church nonattenders can include both the socially successful as well as the sidetracked. Even "irreligious traditionalists" generally are older, not countercultural, generally conservative in outlook, and seldom overtly vent antagonism to persons of faith.

Few (7%) in the United States admit to having "no religion." True apostates are rare, but their number may be increasing. True "converts" are also rare, and they should not be confused with those who switch. Research shows that Roman Catholics find it more difficult to switch groups than do Protestants. True apostates and switchers express more doubts than those who "stay," but those who have doubted and switched tend to become stronger believers in their newly adopted denominations. Those who have undergone some doubt but later find cognitive peace tend to be happier, more satisfied, and more confident in the long run versus true apostates, who are the opposite. The strongest force for ensuring conventional belief is the example of parents and the absence of parent-child conflict. Because of the decline of stigma, many so-called religious nones can become religious "returnees."

—*Ross P. Scherer*

REFERENCES

M. B. Brinkerhoff and M. M. Mackie, "Casting Off the Bonds of Organized Religion," *Review of Religious Research* 34(1993):235-257; H. R. F. Ebaugh, *Becoming an Ex* (Chicago: University of Chicago Press, 1988); C. K. Hadaway, "Identifying American Apostates," *Journal for the Scientific Study of Religion* 28(1989):201-215; A. O. Hirschman, *Exit, Voice, Loyalty* (Cambridge: Harvard University Press, 1970); J. B. Tamney et al., "Innovation Theory and Religious Nones," *Journal for the Scientific Study of Religion* 28(1989):216-229.

APPALACHIA   Often defined geographically by the Appalachian mountains, with their general north-south orientation and limited east-west access that create a series of hollows. Containing most of America's anthracite and a significant amount of bituminous coal, the region has long been economically defined by the vagaries of coal production. Agriculture is limited to small farms on steep slopes or small areas of "bottom" lands. With inhabitants of largely Anglo-Saxon origin, and little in-migration, the region has long been dominated by extreme class divisions. Those failing to seek out-migration or enhanced employment opportunities in the urban centers of Appalachia are often characterized as part of an assumed culture of poverty in a region long stereotyped by its presumed economic and cultural backwardness and "otherness."

Many argue that Appalachian religion, especially outside the urban centers, is unique in both the breadth and the scope of its influence. Appalachian religion is often associated with fiercely independent Holiness sects and their rejection of an educated clergy. This is but part of a pattern of persistent forms of rejection of the authority of educated professionals in areas such as education and medicine as well as in religion. Appalachian Studies programs contribute to the maintenance of a sense of "otherness" to this region and its peoples insofar as they have been made into a topic of specialized study. Yet social scientists have failed to establish that Appalachia, its peoples, or their religious practices are unique. Exaggerated emphasis upon some religious practices such as serpent-handling and the drinking of poisons, including both strychnine and lye, often are discussed outside the broader religious context within which both are rationalized and functional. Much religious diversity exists within this region. Many of the nonfundamentalist groups demonstrate similar patterns of religious persistence and change that characterize the culture at large.

Perhaps most significant have been recent analyses of Appalachian fundamentalism in light of theories that explore patterns and mechanisms that illuminate a conscious rejection of modernity. In these analyses, the stereotypical image of an illiterate and impoverished member of a Holiness sect gives way to a description of a person who has maintained a functional identity within a subculture that has resisted at least some of the major defining characteristics of modernism. These include the demonstrative nature of much of Appalachian religion and the rejection of the near universality of a technical rationality integral to capitalism. It is rural Appalachia that most dominates the media coverage and to a large extent the study of Appalachia in academia as well. The emphasis is typically on those aspects of Appalachia defined by their divergence from mainstream American culture. Most likely, specialty studies tend to select the most divergent aspects of this region for study and in so doing serve to foster the maintenance of these divergences. Those studied paradoxically gain affirmation for their lifestyles from the interest of those who would see them as exhibiting a problematic otherness in need of explanation.

See also Snake-Handling Sects

—*Ralph W. Hood, Jr.*

REFERENCES

A. Batteau (ed.), *Appalachia and America* (Lexington: University Press of Kentucky, 1983); D. Billings, "Culture and Poverty in Appalachia," *Social Problems* 53(1974):315-323; J. D. Photiadis (ed.), *Religion in Appalachia* (Morgantown: West Virginia University, 1978); J. E. Weller, *Yesterday's People* (Lexington: University of Kentucky Press, 1966).

APPARITIONS (GHOSTS)   *Apparition* (from Latin *apparere,* to appear) is an anomalous perception of seemingly paranormal nature. Apparitions may be of persons, animals, or inanimate objects and can be perceived through any of the five senses. The term *ghost* generally refers to visual apparitions of deceased humans or animals.

Apparitions of deceased people inevitably suggest to those perceiving them that the deceased has qualities surviving bodily death. Hallucinations, a concept parallel to apparitions, are perceptions arising without external stimuli. It is not certain that all apparitions are hallucinations because some apparitional events are experienced by two or more people simultaneously. Apparitions sometimes correspond, temporally, to real events such as a death or crisis. Although many scholars assume that apparitional episodes are created by the perceiver's mind, and consequently are an outgrowth of cultural conditioning, comparison of apparitional accounts from many societies indicate that these episodes have universal features. Apparitional experiences have the capacity to produce religious beliefs rather than being fully products of them. Apparitions contribute to belief in spirits, souls, and life after death.

—*James McClenon*

REFERENCES

R. C. Finucane, *Appearances of the Dead* (Buffalo, N.Y.: Prometheus, 1984); E. Gurney et al., *Phantasms of the Living* (London: Tubner, 1986 [1918]); J. McClenon, *Wondrous Events* (Philadelphia: University of Pennsylvania Press, 1994); H. Sidgwick et al., "Report on the Census of Hallucinations," *Proceedings of the Society for Psychical Research* 10(1894):25-422.

ARCHIVES DE SCIENCES SOCIALES DES RELIGIONS   Quarterly journal publishing two full-length thematic issues a year and two issues with thematic articles plus extensive book reviews and book notes. The journal was started in 1956 as *Archives de sociologie des religions.* To stress the pluralistic scientific approach to religious phenomena with sociology as its pivot, which had, however, characterized it from the beginning, its name was changed to the current one in 1973. This does not imply that the other human sciences such as anthropology, ethnology, history, and psychology are treated as "auxiliary sciences." In the earlier issues of the journal, sociographic studies had an important place; more recently, theoretical questions and comparative analysis have occupied a more central place. Sociographic studies continue to appear, but the balance between them and comparative and theoretical studies has shifted over the years.

The *Archives* is a French journal that also publishes translations of major contributions to the field in English or other languages. Occasionally an original English article is published. The extensive review sections, written in French, introduce readers to publications on religious phenomena written in all western European languages.

—*Karel Dobbelaere*

ARMAGEDDON   *see* Apocalyptic, Eschatology

ASCETICISM   A system of self-denial or discipline in pursuit of religious values. Archaic purification, initiation, and other rites contain ascetic elements, but more systematic asceticism emerges in Hindu world renunciation, Buddhism, and early religious brotherhoods such as the Jewish Essenes. Opposition to Roman luxury gave early Christianity an ascetic cast, as hermits, pillar saints, and small isolated cadres of monks urged rigorous limitations on dress, diet, sleep, sexuality, and possessions. Extremes of self-mortification reappear in later groups such as the fourteenth-century Flagellants and the Russian Skoptsy ("castrators").

More influential were organized communities of medieval monks under the Benedictine type of rule. Vowing poverty, chastity, and obedience, they were devoted to systematic labor, prayer, the expiation of sins, and religious scholarship. Conflicts over religion and wealth were revived by the mendicant orders (e.g., Franciscans and Dominicans), who insisted on salvation through apostolic poverty and criticized wealthy church officials and worldly monks. Intransigence over the issue of poverty led the Franciscan Spirituals to be persecuted during the Inquisition.

Asceticism has been variously assessed. Nietzsche traced the genealogy of ascetic ideals and saw their origin in the priestly will to power. Weber's more sociologically influential view emphasized self-disciplined conduct and asceticism's socially transformative power, and distinguished other-worldly from inner-worldly asceticism. Material success threatened to undermine medieval monasticism's other-worldly, ascetic quest for salvation. Protestantism opposed monastic other-worldliness as a sin against brotherliness yet carried the spirit of asceticism into everyday life. It demanded that everyone serve God, and thereby the wider community, by leading the life of a monk in devotion to a worldly calling, thus enhancing moral discipline and revolutionizing society.

Although ascetic ideals are less central in recent history, they continue to influence social change in, for example, Gandhi's nonviolent campaigns and the "Puritan" cast of movements such as the Russian Bolsheviks and the Nation of Islam.

See also Self-Denial, Virtuoso

—*Donald A. Nielsen*

REFERENCE

V. L. Wimbush and R. Valantasis (eds.), *Asceticism* (New York: Oxford University Press, 1995).

ASIAN POPULAR RELIGIONS The countries from Afghanistan to Japan have been influenced by Buddhism, Islam, and to a lesser extent Christianity. The region also has small numbers of Baha'is, Jews, and Parsees. At the same time, regional religions that have gained international prominence remain significant in Asia: Jainism, Shintoism, Sikhism, and Taoism. In addition, however, Asia has been noted among social scientists for its popular religiosity, sometimes called "little traditions."

Folk Traditions Folk religions take two forms: as distinct religions (East Asia) and as popularized versions of world religions (South and Southeast Asia). Chinese Folk Religion, in its present form dating back to the Sung Dynasty (960-1279), includes elements traceable to prehistoric times (ancestor worship, shamanism, divination, a belief in ghosts, and sacrificial rituals to the spirits of sacred objects and places) as well as aspects of Buddhism, Confucianism, and Taoism. Buddhist elements include believing in karma and rebirth, accepting Buddha and other bodhisattvas as gods, and using Buddhist meditational techniques. The Confucian influence is the concept of filial piety and associated practices. The numerous gods are organized into a hierarchy headed by the Jade Emperor, a deity borrowed from Taoism. Important annual rituals reflect their origin in an agrarian way of life (e.g., a harvest-time festival) but have been given new or additional meaning to accord with the ancestral cult or Buddhism. The religion is not centrally organized and lacks a formal canon. Rituals take place before home altars or at temples, which have no fixed congregations. Adherents vary considerably in belief and practice. Generally, folk religionists are fatalistic yet believe that one's luck can be affected by pleasing ancestors or gods, by locating graves and buildings in places where vital natural forces are located (geomancy), and by balancing opposing forces (yin, yang) within one's body (Wee 1977, Freedman 1974).

In Korea, Buddhism, Confucianism, and Taoism have influenced the elite, while a folk religion has existed among the common people that resembles Chinese Folk Religion. However, unlike the Chinese case, most Korean spirit mediums are women, a vestige from a time when female deities dominated the folk religion. The Japanese have been influenced by Shintoism, Buddhism, and Confucianism. Buddhism and Shintoism have separate organizations, buildings, festivals, and religious specialists. Thus one can speak of Japanese religions that individuals blend in different ways but not of a distinct Japanese folk religion (Smith 1974).

Indonesia is an example of Asian countries where syncretic religions have been dominant. On Java, nearly everyone identifies with Islam, but most people practice *Agama Jawa,* Javanese religion, or Javanese Islam (Geertz 1960). This form of religion is a mixture of animistic, Islamic, and to a lesser extent Hindu elements (at one time, Java was under the control of local Hindu rulers). Those who practice Javanese religion call themselves Muslims. The label is not meaningless. Such people, among other things, will believe in Allah, accept Muhammad as a prophet, and believe in heaven and hell. In addition, Javanese religionists employ animistic rituals, such as ceremonial meals commemorating a person's transition to a new stage in the life cycle or important moments in the life of the village (*slametan,* the rituals of which reflect animistic beliefs), consult *dukun* (magicians capable of controlling the impersonal force that exists in all things), and use their own numerology to ensure that actions are synchronized with natural processes. The counterpart to Javanese Islam in southern Asia is "popular Islam" (Hassan 1987). In a somewhat similar manner, one can speak of Burmese, Sri Lankan, and Thai Buddhism.

New Religious Movements   The "new religions" of Asia are syncretic forms that include elements from the local folk tradition and may include elements from non-Asian religions but are dominated by the major Asian traditions—Buddhism, Confucianism, Shintoism, Sufism, and Taoism. While such religions are quite visible in Indonesia (e.g., Subud), Singapore (e.g., the Red Swastika Society), South Korea (e.g., Tonghak, the Unification Church), Taiwan, and Vietnam (e.g., Cao Dai), they are numerically significant only in Japan (e.g., Tenrikyo, Soka Gakkai), where perhaps a quarter of the population belong to new religions (Ellwood 1987).

The Japanese groups include religions dating as far back as the early part of the nineteenth century. Unlike more traditional groups, the new religions evangelize and focus on the individual rather than the household or the community. However, new religions retain features of the folk tradition; each group is identified with a shamanesque figure, and rituals are meant to help practitioners attain this-worldly goals such as health and wealth. Depending on the group, elements of Confucianism, Buddhism, or Shintoism will be part of a new religion.

As far as can be determined, adherence to animistic and folk religions are declining everywhere, while new religions are holding their own or growing (Barrett 1982). The syncretic forms of the world religions, such as Javanese Islam, are being replaced by purified versions of these same religions (see, e.g., Tamney 1980). Davis (1991) has suggested that new religions are evolving into purely modern forms of religion. These changes result from the less frequent use of magic in modernizing societies. The decline of folk and syncretic religions also may reflect the desire to belong to a universal religion, which is competitive in global society—a desire that leads to preferring a form of religion that is not culture-bound in any specific sense. An intriguing question is why new religions in Korean and Chinese societies have been relatively unpopular.

See also Buddhism, Islam

—*Joseph B. Tamney*

REFERENCES

D. Barrett, *World Christian Encyclopedia* (Nairobi: Oxford University Press, 1982); W. Davis, "Fundamentalism in Japan," in *Fundamentalisms Observed,* ed. M. E. Marty and R. S. Appleby (Chicago: University of Chicago Press, 1991): 814-824; R. S. Ellwood, "New Religions in Japan," in *The Encyclopedia of Religion,* ed. M. Eliade (New York: Macmillan, 1987): 410-414; M. Freedman, "On the Sociological Study of Chinese Religion," in *Religion and Ritual in Chinese Society,* ed. A. P. Wolf (Stanford: Stanford University Press, 1974): 19-42; C. Geertz, *The Religion of Java* (Glencoe, Ill.: Free Press, 1960); R. Hassan, "Religion, Society, and the State in Pakistan," *Asian Survey* 27(1987):552-565; R. J. Smith, "Afterword," *Religion and Ritual in Chinese Society,* ed. A. P. Wolf (Stanford: Stanford University Press, 1974): 337-348; J. B. Tamney, "Modernization and Religious Purification," *Review of Religious Research* 22(1980):208-218; V. Wee, *Religion and Ritual Among the Chinese in Singapore,* Master's thesis, Department of Sociology, National University of Singapore, 1977.

ASR   *see* Association for the Sociology of Religion

ASSEMBLIES OF GOD   *see* Pentecostalism

ASSOCIATIONAL INVOLVEMENT   *see* Communal Involvement

ASSOCIATION FOR RESEARCH AND ENLIGHTENMENT   *see* Psychic Phenomena

ASSOCIATION FOR THE SOCIAL SCIENTIFIC STUDY OF JEWRY (ASSJ)   Founded in 1971 as the Association for the Sociological Study of Jewry, the ASSJ is a professional association of over 200 members from the fields of anthropology, demography, economics, geography, history, political science, and psychology, as well as sociology and other fields, who have an interest in the social scientific study of Jewry. Friedman (1986) noted that the formal founding of the association was preceded by a formative period, 1966-1970.

ASSJ has organized and cosponsored academic sessions at such professional associations as the American Sociological Association, Association for Jewish Studies, Association for the Sociology of Religion, and Society for the Scientific Study of Religion, among others, and bestows annually the Marshall Sklare Memorial Award, honoring a distinguished scholar of the social scientific study of Jewry. Winners of the Sklare award include Seymour Martin Lipset (1993), Daniel Elazar (1994), Celia Heller (1995), Samuel Klausner (1996), and Walter Zenner (1997). Prior to the Sklare Award, Sidney Goldstein received an award from the ASSJ in 1992.

Publications include a scholarly journal, currently published annually, *Contemporary Jewry,* which was initiated in 1974, first as a *Newsletter* in 1974-1975 (volume 1), then as a journal-newsletter (volume 2) in 1975-1976 (called *Jewish Sociology and Social Research*), with volume 3 in 1976-1977 the first to bear the current name. A new series *Newsletter,* published semiannually, began in 1979.

Presidents include Mervin Verbit (1971-1973), Marshall Sklare (1973-1975), Samuel Klausner (1975-1977), Celia Heller (1977-1979), Chaim Waxman (1979-1981), Harold Himmelfarb (1981-1983), Egon Mayer (1983-1988), Rela Mintz Geffen (1988-1990), Arnold Dashefsky (1990-1996), and Allen Glicksman (1996-1998).

—*Arnold M. Dashefsky*

REFERENCE

N. L. Friedman, "Conception and Birth of the Association for the Sociological Study of Jewry," *Ethnic Forum* 6(1986):98-111.

ASSOCIATION FOR THE SOCIOLOGY OF RELIGION (ASR)

The ASR began life as the American Catholic Sociological Society (ACSS) at a 1938 meeting in Chicago. In its infancy, the ACSS provided a haven for Catholic sociologists who felt professionally isolated by the then American Sociological Society. The secular sociologists of the ASS (now ASA) approached sociology in a way that was supposed to be objective and scientific. For Catholic sociologists, this created an environment that was "for all practical purposes anti-moral and anti-religious" (Morris 1989). Thus a plan to recognize Catholic sociology and organize its adherents nationally was implemented, and the ACSS began to meet concurrently with ASS.

In March 1940, the first issue of the *American Catholic Sociological Review* appeared; questions of finances and editorship remained intermittently problematic until the early 1960s. By 1963, the journal had become *Sociological Analysis* and the content focused increasingly on the sociological study of religion with a particular, but not exclusive, interest in Catholicism. The subtitle *A Journal in the Sociology of Religion* was formally added in 1967, replacing *A Publication of the American Catholic Sociological Society.*

Changing the journal's name and emphasis did not suit everyone; many longtime members left the ACSS. At the same time, however, changes in Catholicism as a result of Vatican II encouraged greater openness to non-Catholics. In 1970, the organization's name became the Association for the Sociology of Religion, reflecting the changes that had already taken place in the association's publication. This finalized a divorce from the social problems/social action aspects that were part of the ACSS's earliest concerns (Kivisto 1989). Religious research and religious commitment in the ASR were bracketed from each other.

Today, the ASR's journal (renamed *Sociology of Religion: A Quarterly Review* in 1993) remains the only English-language journal devoted exclusively to the sociology of religion. With more than 700 members worldwide, the ASR continues to hold annual meetings at the same time and place as the ASA, with a full program of thematic and regular sessions covering current scholarship and research into a wide range of sociologically relevant topics. As in the era of the ACSS, a spirit of *gemeinschaft* pervades these meetings, where many sociologists of religion get their first chance to interact with the leading scholars of the field. Plenary speakers, including an annual Paul Hanly Furfey lectureship, often reflect on a lifetime of research or on the main controversy of the day. In spite of the addition in 1995 of a section on the sociology of religion to the American Sociological Association, separate from the ASR, the ASR-ASA connection remains a part of the ASR's organizational meeting strategy, to the apparent advantage of both groups.

In addition to its journal, the ASR publishes a quarterly newsletter and copublishes an annual series, *Religion and the Social Order.* It also annually provides Joseph H. Fichter research grants competitively to members, a Robert J. McNamara student paper award, and Ralph A. Gallagher travel grants to assist graduate students and non-North American members to attend its meetings.

See also American Catholic Sociological Society, *Sociology of Religion: A Quarterly Review*

—*Barbara J. Denison and William H. Swatos, Jr.*

REFERENCES

P. Kivisto, "The Brief Career of Catholic Sociology," *Sociological Analysis* 50(1989):351-361; L. Morris, "Secular Transcendence," *Sociological Analysis* 50(1989):323-349.

ASTROLOGY   The study of the impact that celestial bodies—the moon, the sun, the planets, and the stars—are presumed to have upon events on the earth. There are three broadly distinct branches of study. One form of astrology is concerned with relating the situation of the heavens at the moment of an individual's birth to all aspects of his or her life. A second relates the situation in the heavens at particularly significant moments, such as eclipses or equinoxes, to events affecting whole classes of people or indeed the world in general, while a third tries to determine the most auspicious time for the commencement of a particular act.

Astrology appears to have been an important ingredient in most early civilizations, being especially prominent in Egypt, India, and China. It was principally through the teachings of the Babylonians, however, that astrological knowledge entered the Greco-Roman world and hence the culture of the West.

Astrology remained a significant element in the civilization of western Europe, even intermingling successfully with Christian teaching and practice (Thomas 1971) throughout the Middle Ages. It is only in modern times that astrology has become separated from the science of astronomy and labeled deviant or occult knowledge. Until the sixteenth and early seventeenth centuries, there was nothing esoteric about astrology, and its doctrines were part of the educated person's picture of the universe and its workings.

Today astrology occupies a somewhat ambiguous position in contemporary culture. Although excluded from the sciences on the grounds that it lacks any empirical support or theoretical credibility (despite efforts to demonstrate its validity; see Gauquelin 1983), it has nevertheless gained widespread popular, although often skeptical, acceptance. A general, if superficial, acquaintance with astrology is almost universal in contemporary society; for example, surveys show that virtually everyone knows what a horoscope is and also knows his or her own birth sign. On the other hand, only a minority of people admit to taking astrology seriously—that is, using astrology to help them make decisions—although major world leaders such as Adolf Hitler and Ronald Reagan (or his wife) would come into this category. Astrology grew considerably in popularity as a consequence of the counterculture movement of the 1960s (the "Age of Aquarius") and can be seen as part of the broader growth in interest in unconventional forms of religion such as mysticism, the occult, and some new religious movements. Robert Wuthnow (1978) found that astrology is most likely to appeal to the less privileged sections of society, for whom it may offer a basically fatalistic theodicy.

—*Colin Campbell*

REFERENCES

M. Gauquelin, *Birth-Times* (New York: Hill & Wang, 1983); K. Thomas, *Religion and the Decline of Magic* (Harmondsworth, U.K.: Penguin, 1971); R. Wuthnow, *Experimentation in American Religion* (Berkeley: University of California Press, 1978).

ATHEISM   Conventionally assumed to refer to disbelief in a supreme being, or to belief in the nonexistence of God or gods. However, as the famous Victorian atheist Charles Bradlaugh noted, it is rather illogical to use the term *atheist* to refer to someone who believes in the nonexistence of something. His position was that, because theistic claims were either contradictory or incomprehensible, they were necessarily to be rejected. This meant that an a-theist was one who was "without" a belief in God rather than someone who "believed" in anything. This point has not always been carefully noted in discussions of atheism, with the result that *atheism* is still used to refer to disbelief. Conventional distinctions in forms of atheism reflect this, with dogmatic atheism—which is seen as positive in its assertion—distinguished from skeptical or critical atheism—both of which resemble agnosticism in assuming that the question cannot be resolved. Atheism is usually employed with reference to matters of belief, although it can be noted that the Romans called Jews atheists because they did not pay honor to the emperor. This suggests not only that the term has a long history but that it also may have different meanings. Atheism was certainly a concept present in the ancient world—it being the charge leveled against Socrates.

It would be wrong to assume that atheism is always and everywhere at odds with religion, as there is a strong atheistic strand in such major world religions as Hinduism, Buddhism, and Jainism. Even within Christianity, atheism has been incorporated into modern theological developments such as the "New Theology" and "Death of God" movements of the 1960s.

In many societies, atheism has been equated with immorality and—labeled as "blasphemy"—treated as a criminal offence, while atheists themselves have suffered both civil and political discrimination. Although in western Europe and North America, the laws against atheists that still exist are rarely invoked (the last person to be imprisoned for blasphemy in England was John Jacob Holyoake in 1841), it is noticeable that few individuals who aspire to public office are prepared to identify themselves as atheists.

Methodological atheism is a term coined by Peter Berger (1967) to describe a sociological approach that seeks to understand religion as a human creation and deliberately leaves open the question of the truth of religious beliefs.

—*Colin Campbell*

REFERENCES

P. L. Berger, *The Sacred Canopy* (Garden City, N.Y.: Doubleday, 1967); J. Thrower, *A Short History of Western Atheism* (London: Pemberton, 1971).

ATTITUDE The readiness to respond to a certain object in a favorable or unfavorable fashion; every attitude has both an intrinsic belief and a behavioral disposition. Attitudes are a permanent system of evaluations, emotions, and direct behavioral tendencies for or against an object.

Individuals develop their attitudes through a continuous process of adaptation to the social environment. Attitudes are organized ways of thinking and acting in relation to facts and people in our environment, and they help influence our overall way of life.

To understand the development of attitudes in the individual, it is necessary to study the latter's membership in groups and his or her self-identifications. At the basis of attitudes lie evaluative convictions, and when these change, so do the attitudes. Attitudes connect individuals to other individuals, groups, and institutions. Each person has hundreds of attitudes, presumably one for each object in his or her environment; for example, there are attitudes toward work, school, the church, and various types of groups. Socialization through one's parents, religious and educational instruction, and relations with friends are important sources of attitudes.

Social institutions influence attitudes in different ways. For example, membership in religious organizations or ethnic groups influences the attitudes that adults adopt toward their children. Instruction received at school influences attitudes toward the economic and political institutions of society.

In sociology, a substantial contribution to the concept of attitude and its study was made by William I. Thomas and Florian Znaniecki in *The Polish Peasant in Europe and America* (1918-1920). They introduced an element of cognitive and emotional intermediation between a person's situation and his or her behavior. They used the concept of *personality* as a locution referring to a "structured attitude." Attitudes are not innate but stem from a process of acculturation. According to Thomas and Znaniecki, the terms needed to explain an action that has social importance are (1) the objective situation within which the subject has to act and (2) his or her attitude as a manifestation of previous social and cultural experience. However, the distinction between the two terms proposed by Thomas and Znaniecki do not always seem clear because, according to them, the situation includes the preexisting attitudes of the individual or group as well as the objective conditions that the individual encounters. The terms are based on the "four wishes" of Thomas's theory, which he developed before *The Polish Peasant*; these four wishes are the desire for new experiences, the desire for recognition, the desire for domination, and the desire for security. Combined with the values of a preexisting situation, the four wishes give rise to certain attitudes.

The root of new attitudes is to be sought in the establishment of new relationships between the person and the world outside the community. The emergence of economics as an independent sphere reflects the tendency to reduce quality to a quantity that typifies the productive technology, of which the clearest representative is, of course, money.

Of all the methods of measuring attitudes, the most widely used are "attitudes scales," which differ from one another mainly in their type and method of construction and in the attitude "objects" that are the focus of study. An attitude scale consists of a series of statements to which subjects typically respond in terms of fixed-choice options, and their answers enable sociologists to make inferences about the subjects' attitudes. The objective typically is to assign to each respondent a numerical score along a continuum, a score that is taken to measure the valence of an attitude toward a particular object. The most important scales include those developed by Emory Bogardus (1925) and Louis Thurstone (Thurstone and Chave 1929).

Today a further source for attitudes is the mass media. Television in particular with its varied programs influences, often in a decisive manner, individuals' attitudes, which may be affected by various events and social groups on a large-scale basis throughout society. As time passes, the influence of the flow of information may bring about a change in individuals' attitudes.

However, the earlier that attitudes are learned, the more they are resistant to change—and this is particularly true if their internalization has come about in the first years of life and if they contribute to the satisfaction of basic needs.

Attitudes toward various aspects of religion also may be analyzed by this line of reasoning; while they reflect one's personal beliefs and experiences, they are always subject to influence by one's immediate social environment as well as by the larger climate of opinion that results from the mass media as they reflect the social processes of a complex society undergoing continuous change.

—*Luigi Tomasi*

REFERENCES

L. Allen, *Techniques of Attitude Scale Construction* (New York: Appleton-Century, 1957); E. S. Bogardus, "Measuring Social Distance" *Journal of Applied Sociology* 9(1925):299-308; M. L. DeFleur and R. W. Catton, Jr., "The Limits of Determinacy in Attitude Measurement," *Social Forces* 4(1957):295-300; M. L. DeFleur and F. R. Westie, "Attitude as a Scientific Concept," *Social Forces* 3(1963):17-31; J. D. Delamater, "Attitude," *Encyclopedia of Sociology*, ed. E. F. Borgatta and M. L. Borgatta (New York: Macmillan, 1992): 117-124; L. Festinger, *A Theory of Cognitive Dissonance* (Stanford, Calif.: Stanford University Press, 1962); K. J. Kiecolt, "Recent Developments in Attitudes and Social Structure," *Annual Review of Sociology* 14(1988):381-403; M. Rosenberg et al., *Attitude Organization* (New Haven, Conn.: Yale University Press, 1960); W. I. Thomas and F. Znaniecki, *The Polish Peasant in Europe and America* (Chicago: University of Chicago Press, 1918-1920); L. L. Thurstone and E. J. Chave, *The Measurement of Attitude* (Chicago: University of Chicago Press, 1929); W. W. Torgeson, *Theory and Methods of Scaling* (New York: Wiley, 1958).

ATTRIBUTION THEORY   A group of social psychological orientations that seek to portray people's efforts to understand the causal structure of events. The founder of attribution theory, Fritz Heider, suggested that people logically attempt to uncover connections between causes and effects. Edward Jones, Harold Kelley, and others analyzed the processes by which people infer others' intentions and dispositions —and explain events in terms of being caused by self or others or God or luck.

Daryl J. Bem theorized that people come to know their own attitudes, emotions, and other internal states partially by inferring them from observations of their own overt behavior. For example, people who attend church regularly come to perceive themselves as reli-

gious. Bem hypothesizes that self-attribution occurs in the same way that we learn about others' attitudes and dispositions. People's emotions are self-labeled according to the characteristics of the situation. If certain actions are perceived as rewarding, people tend to conclude that, because they enjoyed the behavior, they must be a certain type of person. People who partake in religious rituals, for example, come to perceive of themselves as religious.

Attribution theory also has allowed a better understanding of spontaneous religious experiences. Environmental and cultural factors affect the degree that an experience is interpreted as "religious." A person's predisposition and setting shape his or her attribution of an unusual experience to brain chemical states, God, or fate.

See also Mysticism

—*James McClenon*

REFERENCES

D. J. Bem, "Self-Perception Theory," in *Cognitive Theories in Social Psychology*, ed. L. Berkowitz (New York: Academic Press, 1978): 221-282; J. H. Harvey and W. P. Smith, *Social Psychology* (Saint Louis: Mosby, 1977); F. Heider, *The Psychology of Interpersonal Relations* (New York: Wiley, 1958); H. H. Kelley, "Attribution Theory in Social Psychology," *Nebraska Symposium on Motivation*, ed. D. Levine (Lincoln: University of Nebraska Press, 1967); B. Spilka and D. N. McIntosh, "Attribution Theory and Religious Experience," in *Handbook of Religious Experience* (Birmingham, Ala.: Religious Education Press, 1995): 421-455.

AUTHORITARIANISM   Personality trait defined using such terms as *dogmatic, rigid, low tolerance for ambiguity,* and *high regard for structural hierarchy*. It is considered the antithesis of egalitarianism. The term *authoritarianism* became one of the most famous in social psychology through a huge research effort on the part of T. W. Adorno and others (1950) after World War II that focused on explaining how the German people could have allowed and participated in the Holocaust that killed over 6 million Jews.

Efforts to explain virulent anti-Semitism focused on the concept of authoritarianism, and a measure of authoritarianism called the "F-scale" came to be perhaps the most used such instrument in all of personality research. Authoritarianism was thought to be related to general prejudice and ethnocentrism as well as to certain lifestyles and belief systems. Specifically, considerable research using the F-scale and related measures has revealed that political and social conservatives and traditionally religious people generally score relatively high on such instruments. Many, including especially Milton Rokeach (1960), criticized the concept of authoritarianism as being too limited and ideologically based. Rokeach developed a more general term—*dogmatism*—that he claimed encompasses authoritarians on both the left and the right of the political spectrum.

The consistent finding of a positive correlation between religiosity and authoritarianism has provoked considerable efforts at explication as well as critiques of the initial work in this area (Altemeyer 1988). The debate has contributed to the development of general notions of intrinsic versus extrinsic religiosity and of such concepts as "religious maturity." Leak and Randall (1995) have shown, for instance, that although authoritarianism is positively correlated with traditional measures of religiosity, it is inversely related to a number of measures of "religious maturity." Such findings offer some solace to religionists and demand further research on the troubling relationship between religiousness and authoritarianism.

See also Ethnocentrism, Faith Development, Fundamentalism, Intrinsic-Extrinsic Religion, Milton Rokeach

—*James T. Richardson*

REFERENCES

T. W. Adorno et al., *The Authoritarian Personality* (New York: Harper, 1950); B. Altemeyer, *Enemies of Freedom* (San Francisco: Jossey-Bass, 1988); B. Altemeyer and B. Hunsberger, "Authoritarianism, Religious Fundamentalism, Quest, and Prejudice," *International Journal for the Psychology of Religion* 2(1992):113-133; G. Leak and B. Randall, "Clarification of the Link Between Right-wing Authoritarianism and Religiousness," *Journal for the Scientific Study of Religion* 34(1995):245-252; M. Rokeach, *The Open and Closed Mind* (New York: Basic Books, 1960).

BAHA'I Syncretistic religion founded in Iraq in 1863 around the teachings of a Persian named Bahú'u'lláh, who is viewed by believers to be the latest in a line of prophets that includes Abraham, Moses, Jesus, and Muhammad. The coming of a new prophet had been predicted by Siyyid 'Alí Muhammad in Persia in the 1840s. Authorities executed him for his teachings in 1850. A monotheistic religion, Baha'i promotes the idea of a united social order and a federated system of international relations. The faith encourages religious tolerance and opposes racial and sexual discrimination. There are approximately 17,000 congregations, or Local Spiritual Assemblies, worldwide, including approximately 1,000 in the United States, where the National Spiritual Assembly is located in Wilmette, Illinois. The world headquarters is in Haifa, Israel. Baha'is have suffered religious persecution, particularly in Iran in the past two decades.

—*Peter Kivisto*

BAILEY, EDWARD I(AN) (1935–) Rector of Winterbourne Parish, Bristol, England (1970–); Convener, Network for the Study of Implicit Religion (NSIR, 1978–); Founder and Chair, Centre for the Study of Implicit Religion and Contemporary Spirituality.

Bailey's doctoral thesis, *Emergent Mandalas: The Implicit Religion of Contemporary Society,* at the University of Bristol was supervised by F. B. Welbourn and marked the start of Bailey's energetic promotion of the study of the religion implicit in contemporary society but increasingly outside the confines of conventional institutional religion. With its affinity to the sociological concepts of common religion, civil religion, and invisible religion, in its focus on the empirical reality of the religious in everyday life, the notion of implicit religion has received widespread recognition and acceptance on an international basis, largely through Bailey's efforts—a remarkable achievement in the absence of significant institutional backing or a cadre of graduate students' output. Since 1978, Bailey has organized an annual "implicit religion" academic conference at Denton, North Yorkshire, as well as many courses and study days for religious professionals and religious educators. The NSIR has formed an important link between academics, religious professionals, and all interested in empirical studies of popular contemporary religion.

—*Peter Gee*

REFERENCE

E. I. Bailey, *Implicit Religion in Contemporary Society* (Kampen, Neth.: Kok Pharos, 1997).

BAKKER, JIM   *see* Televangelism

BAPTISTS   Despite a persistent claim that Baptists can trace their heritage to the New Testament period, scholars place Baptist origins in the English Separatist movement of the 1600s. Early Baptists earned a reputation as advocates for religious freedom; their leaders were frequently jailed but not often silenced. The movement grew, and by 1650 there were three main branches under the Baptist label: General Baptists, who proclaimed a universal opportunity for salvation; Particular Baptists, who preached an atonement limited to certain groups; and the Seventh Day Baptists, distinguished by their insistence upon the keeping of the Sabbath. The three groups were united by their belief in baptism only for adult believers and in their defense of religious liberty. Later, they demanded baptism by immersion (Torbet 1963).

History   Baptist history is filled with controversy, the result of regional, doctrinal, and personality conflicts (Shurden 1972), and the label covers a variety of organizations. Of at least 27 different Baptist groups or denominations (Mead 1990), three may be selected for special mention: Southern Baptists, Northern (American) Baptists, and National Baptists.

Baptist work began and grew initially in the northern states, where coordination of missionary activity and publication was left in the hands of separate societies. There was no overall governing structure for religious activity until the establishment of the Southern Baptist Convention in 1845 in response to the slavery issue (Torbet 1963).

Growth among Southern Baptists was consistent. In 1845, the 351,951 members included 130,000 blacks, who left shortly after the Civil War; by 1990, there were more than 15 million Southern Baptists located in all 50 states (Torbet 1963, Jacquet 1991). Today, the SBC is the largest non-Catholic denomination in the United States.

Southern Baptists have traditionally emphasized evangelism and are theologically conservative, decidedly more so in recent years. In 1963, the SBC adopted the Baptist Faith and Message as a (noncreedal) guide to the beliefs of the Convention. Since 1979, when a conservative-fundamentalist coalition began to dominate the group's meetings, this document has been used to define eligibility for appointment to committees and employment in SBC agencies (Ammerman 1990). In 1995, a plan for reorganizing and centralizing the SBC was put forth.

When the southern churches left to form the SBC, Northern Baptists continued their efforts under three societies: the American Baptist Home Mission Society, the American Baptist Missionary Union (later changed to the American Baptist Foreign Mission Society), and the American Baptist Publication Society. These separate corporations competed for funds but often met together. Eventually they merged to form the Northern Baptist Convention (1907); the name was changed to the American Baptist Convention in 1950 (now American Baptist Churches of the USA).

American Baptists have pursued activities similar to the SBC, but since 1963 have moved toward a more connectional church organization. Also, they are typically less conservative theologically, and consequently more open to ecumenical initiatives, being affiliated with both the National and the World Council of Churches (Brackney 1988). The northern convention has been less evangelistic than its southern counterpart and is now only about one-eighth the size of the SBC (Jacquet 1991). Also, since the 1960s, white membership in the ABC has declined by about one-third, while African American membership has almost doubled (Green and Light 1993).

Relations between the ABC and the SBC have not been harmonious. SBC home missionaries have moved aggressively into northern states and established local churches, associations, and state conventions, creating resentment among northern Baptists (Brackney 1988). A major cooperative effort, the Baptist Joint Committee on Public Affairs, fell victim to fundamentalist tendencies when the SBC withdrew its support in 1988 (Ammerman 1990).

By the end of the Civil War, there were perhaps a million black Baptists in the South. Freed from slavery, they sought to establish their own institutions. In 1895, three groups met in Atlanta to form the National Baptist Convention of America. A dispute over adoption of the charter in 1915 led to a split and formation of the National Baptist Convention, USA (Torbet 1963). These two organizations account for about one-third of all church membership among African Americans.

During the days of segregation, National Baptists contributed significantly to the moral uplift, spiritual comfort, and material progress of their members. More recently, they have become more active politically, recapturing some membership losses of the 1950s and 1960s (Nelsen and Nelsen 1975). Civil rights leaders Martin Luther King, Jr., Ralph Abernathy, and Jesse Jackson were National Baptist ministers.

The organization of National Baptist bodies has paralleled that of the white groups, but they are more Calvinistic in their theology and are more oriented to social issues than Southern Baptists (Mead 1990). All three major bodies recognize different levels of organization that are in principle independent from one another (Brackney 1988).

Social Organization Despite numerous histories of Baptists, until recently social scientists have been rather inattentive. Nevertheless, significant studies do exist in the areas of church growth, denominational polity, race and gender, and—cutting across the others—the fundamentalist controversy since 1979.

Southern Baptists have long been considered among the most successful of denominations in terms of church growth. Jones (1979) has shown that between 1900 and 1977, most growth occurred in the South but that the highest percentage gains were outside the South. Furthermore, much of the growth came from new churches. Hadaway (1990), using data from the 1980s, found that new churches are more efficient in producing new members than older churches; the result of adding no new churches to the SBC during the period would have been to cut growth rates in half. Nevertheless, both Jones (1979) and Finke (1994) demonstrate that the average size of SBC churches has increased dramatically over time.

Among Baptists, the denominational body has no power to control the local church. Denominational leaders are given tasks to perform but lack formal authority to accomplish them. In a classic study of American Baptist polity, Harrison (1959) has shown how this situation forces the denominational executives to operate according to rational-pragmatic principles of leadership. Using case study materials, Ingram (1980, 1981) argued that this model applies also to the local church, where the pastor lacks formal authority over the congregation. Nevertheless, Wood (1970) demonstrated that churches with congregational polity tend to take weaker stands on civil rights issues (see also Campbell and Pettigrew 1959).

Various researchers have studied the neglect of prophetic ministry among Southern Baptists. A pioneering study by Eighmy (1972) argued that the churches reflected the surrounding culture rather than challenging it. More recently, Rosenberg (1989) has shown that Baptists are both numerically dominant and hold positions of political power in many parts of the South yet do little to eliminate racism from the region. Former SBC editor Walker Knight (in Ammerman 1993) documented the reluctance of the denomination to deal with racial problems, but in 1995 the SBC adopted a resolution apologizing and asking forgiveness for their history of racial prejudice and discrimination. National Baptists have been more active in addressing social problems, especially minority issues (Nelsen and Nelsen 1975).

American Baptists clearly have been more open to women in ministry than have Southern Baptists (Carroll et al. 1983, Lehman 1985). By 1991, there were some 800 ordained women in the SBC but only 38 local church pastors, a much smaller proportion than in most mainline denominations (Anders and Metcalf-Whittaker in Ammerman 1993).

The fundamentalist controversy stimulated social science interests in the SBC. A five-year project resulted in *Baptist Battles: Social Change and Religious Conflict in the Southern Baptist Convention* in which Ammerman (1990) documented the dissatisfaction of Baptists with their agencies. Dissatisfaction was associated with a number of social factors, especially amount and type of education. More significantly, Ammerman showed that although fundamentalists were not a majority in the SBC, they gained control by attaching their agenda to the inerrancy of the Bible, a position endorsed by 85% of her survey respondents. The difficulty experienced by denominational moderates in explaining and defending their views contributed to fundamentalist success.

Ammerman's edited collection of articles *Southern Baptists Observed: Multiple Perspectives on a Changing Denomination* (1993) demonstrated both the scope of the conflict and the uncertain future of the denomination. In that volume, political scientist James Guth supplemented Ammerman's earlier findings by showing that it was not clear whether theological or political conservatism was more important among those who favored the fundamentalist agenda.

—Larry Ingram

REFERENCES

N. T. Ammerman, *Baptist Battles* (New Brunswick, N.J.: Rutgers University Press, 1990); N. T. Ammerman (ed.), *Southern Baptists Observed* (Knoxville: University of Tennessee Press, 1993); W. H. Brackney, *The Baptists* (Westport, Conn.: Greenwood, 1988); E. Q. Campbell and T. F. Pettigrew, "Racial and Moral Crisis," *American Journal of Sociology* 64(1959):509-516; J. W. Carroll et al., *Women of the Cloth* (San Francisco: Harper, 1983); J. L. Eighmy, *Churches in Cultural Captivity* (Knoxville: University of Tennessee Press, 1972); R. Finke, "The Quiet Transformation," *Review of Religious Research* 36(1994):3-22; N. M. Green and P. W. Light, "Growth and Decline in an Inclusive Denomination," *Church and Denominational Growth*, ed. D. A. Roozen and C. K. Hadaway (Nashville: Abingdon, 1993): 112-126; C. K. Hadaway, "The Impact of New Church Development on Southern Baptist Growth," *Review of Religious Research* 31(1990):370-379; P. M. Harrison, *Authority and Power in the Free Church Tradition* (Princeton, N.J.: Princeton University Press, 1959); L. C. Ingram, "Notes on Pastoral Power in the Congregational Tradition," *Journal for the Scientific Study of Religion* 19(1980):40-48; L. C. Ingram, "Leadership, Democracy, and Religion," *Journal for the Scientific Study of Religion* 20(1981):119-129; C. H. Jacquet, Jr., *Yearbook of American and Canadian Churches* (Nashville: Abingdon, 1991); P. B. Jones, "An Explanation of the Statistical Growth of the Southern Baptist Convention," *Understanding Church Growth and Decline*, ed. D. R. Hoge and D. A. Roozen (New York: Pilgrim, 1979): 160-178; E. C. Lehman, Jr., *Women Clergy* (New Brunswick, N.J.: Transaction, 1985); F. S. Mead, *Handbook of Denominations*, 9th ed. (Nashville: Abingdon, 1990); H. M. Nelsen and A. K. Nelsen, *Black Church in the Sixties* (Lexington: University of Kentucky Press, 1975); E. M. Rosenberg, *The Southern Baptists* (Knoxville: University of Tennessee Press, 1989); W. B. Shurden, *Not a Silent People* (Nashville: Broadman, 1972); R. G. Torbet, *A History of the Baptists*, rev. ed. (Valley Forge, Pa.: Judson, 1963); J. R. Wood, "Authority and Controversial Policy," *American Sociological Review* 35(1970):1057-1069.

BARKER, EILEEN (VARTAN) (1938–)

Professor of Sociology (with special reference to the Study of Religion), and Convener of the Department of Sociology, London School of Economics and Political Science; Vice-Dean of the Faculty of Economics, University of London; Past Academic Governor of the LSE (1988-1992). Founded INFORM (Information Network Focus on Religious Movements) in 1988 and now serves as the Chair of its Board of Governors. Many elected positions in professional associations, including President, Society for the Scientific Study of Religion (1991-1993); Chair of the British Sociological Association, Sociology of Religion Study Group (1985-1990); Executive Committee, Conférence (now Société) Internationale de Sociologie des Religions (1985-1989); Vice President, International Sociological Association Research Committee 22 (1985-1993); Executive Council, Association for the Sociology of Religion (1987-1991); Nominating Committee, Religious Research Association (1989-1991); President, London Society for the Study of Religion (1994-1996).

Author of two books, including the award-winning *The Making of a Moonie: Brainwashing or Choice?* (Blackwell 1984), and editor of seven collections, including *Of Gods and Men: New Religious Movements in the West* (Mercer University Press 1984). A leading scholar in the sociology of new religious movements, Eileen Barker has published more than 100 articles in journals or chapters in books. Her work has been translated into 15 languages. She has been awarded

research funds from both government and foundation sources. Over the last 20 years, she has delivered in excess of 500 guest lectures in universities in North America, East and West Europe, Australasia, and Asia.

—*Nancy Nason-Clark*

BARRETT, DONALD N. (1927-1987)

Member of the sociology faculty at the University of Notre Dame from 1966 until his death; 1948-1965, sociology faculty, LaSalle College; President, American Catholic Sociological Society, 1967.

Barrett's principal substantive interests were in the social demography of marriage and the family, particularly as related to fertility. In 1961, he published *Values in America* (University of Notre Dame Press). Between 1964 and 1966, Barrett served as one of eight American members of the International Commission on Fertility Control and Population convened by Pope Paul VI in anticipation of an encyclical on contraception—what emerged in 1968 as *Humanae vitae*. In 1964, he edited the volume *The Problem of Population: Moral and Theological Considerations* (University of Notre Dame Press), which was a part of the ICFCP study process. He was also a Vatican delegate to the World Population Conference in Bucharest in 1974.

—*Kevin J. Christiano*

BASE CHRISTIAN COMMUNITIES or BASE ECCLESIAL COMMUNITIES   *see* Preferential Option for the Poor

BATSON, C. DANIEL (1943–)   Professor of
Psychology at the University of Kansas and a leader in the use of the experimental method within the social psychology of religion.

Batson's studies regarding religiosity, altruism, and religious experience span three decades. Batson built on Gordon Allport's theories regarding extrinsic (means) and intrinsic (ends) dimensions of religiosity. Allport suggested that extrinsically motivated people use their religion as a means to gain security, solace, sociability, distraction, status, and self-justification. Allport hypothesized that, for individuals with intrinsic religiosity, religion is an ultimate end in itself, a motive for living that was more important than other concerns. Intrinsically motivated people internalize their religion, following it more fully—a practice that makes them less prejudiced than those who are externally religious.

Batson explored and extended the explanatory power of this orientation through empirical research. He suggested adding a *quest* element within explanations of religiosity. Quest components include a readiness to face existential questions without reducing their complexity, a perception of religious doubts as positive, and an openness to future change in one's religious views. Batson devised a scale for measuring "quest" and found that it reflected a parameter that differed from intrinsic and extrinsic dimensions. This allowed him to fill in gaps in Allport's formulations regarding altruism: "The Quest orientation was found to relate to more tentative, situationally responsive helping [while] the End orientation related to more persistent helping that was less attuned to the expressed needs of the person seeking aid" (Batson 1976:29). Those who responded high on the Quest orientation seemed more sensitive and showed greater cognition complexity when dealing with existential concerns (Batson and Raynor-Prince 1983:38). Batson noted that religious belief can act as a form of "double agent," pretending to be one thing but sometimes shaping behavior in dysfunctional directions.

The Religious Experience: A Social-Psychological Perspective (Oxford University Press 1982), with coauthor W. Larry Ventis, focused on cultural impacts on religious experience and ways that meditation, drugs, and language facilitate such episodes. Batson and Ventis hypothesized that creative experiences are psychologically close to religious revelations because both artistic and scientific creativity involve profound inspiration. They argued that the psychodynamics of creative/religious experiences follow certain principles. People create the "reality" regarding such episodes using hierarchically arranged cognitive structures. The process involves an improvement in one's cognitive organization and has identifiable stages (preparation, incubation, illumination, and verification). Religious experiences involve cognitive restructuring to deal with existential questions. When a religious experience is creative, it allows the individual to deal more effectively with a wider range of experiences and people.

In *The Altruism Question: Toward a Social-Psychological Answer* (Erlbaum 1991), Batson reviews the history of altruism, tracing beliefs about human nature from the Greek era through modern times. He reveals the influence of these formulations on the early schools of psychology and argues that psychologists often assume that people are social egoists, caring only about themselves. Such thinking about cognition and social psychology uses a computer analogy, overlooking the fact that people care about each other. Batson reviews the empirical support for a empathy-altruism hypothesis that suggests a different orientation. Not only do people care, they also feel empathy for others. They care not just for their own sakes but in an altruistic manner. Although Batson is aware of the limitations of this formulation, he elaborates upon a "Galilean" model and evaluates the published scientific research in this domain using his altruistic definition as a reference point.

Religion and the Individual: A Social-Psychological Perspective (with Patricia Schoenrade and L. Ventis, Oxford University Press 1993) extends this work by discussing the sources, nature, consequences, and implications of individual religion. Not all aspects of religious belief are beneficial; religion has intrinsic, extrinsic, and quest dimensions that interact in a complex manner affecting behavior in both prosocial and antisocial directions.

—*James McClenon*

REFERENCES

C. D. Batson, "Religion as Prosocial," *Journal for the Scientific Study of Religion* 15(1976):29-45; C. D. Batson and Lynn Raynor-Prince, "Religious Orientation and Complexity of Thought About Existential Concern," *Journal for the Scientific Study of Religion* 22(1983):38-50.

BECKER, ERNEST (1925-1974)   American social psychiatrist, prominent figure in "existential psychiatry."

Becker's many writings went beyond disciplinary boundaries and merged motifs from sociology, anthropology, history, psychiatry, and religion into a unique philosophical anthropology. He especially criticized the failure of the specialized social sciences to address central problems of meaning in human existence. He attempted to remedy this situation in a series of works that extended and synthesized the insights of a varied group of writers, including Rousseau, Marx, Freud, and Otto Rank, whose work on heroes and hero worship was particularly central for Becker.

In a trilogy of volumes—*The Birth and Death of Meaning* (Free Press 1962), *The Revolution in Psychiatry* (Free Press 1963), and *The Structure of Evil* (Braziller 1968)—Becker established a unified perspective on human behavior rooted in a comprehensive theory of human alienation and a new valorization of scientific progress. *The Denial of Death* (Free Press 1973) studied the establishment of standardized cultural symbol systems and heroic images as activities precipitated by the need to overcome the terror of death. The posthumously published companion volume, *Escape from Evil* (Free Press 1975), traced evil in human existence to these very efforts to deny mortality and create heroic self-images.

—*Donald A. Nielsen*

BECKFORD, JAMES A(RTHUR) (1942–)

Sociologist of religion; Professor of Sociology, University of Warwick (England). Founder of the British Sociological Association's Study Group for the Sociology of Religion (1975) and its Chairman from 1978 to 1983; President, International Sociological Association Research Committee 22 (1982-1986); President, Association for the Sociology of Religion (1989); Acting Chairman of INFORM (1994-1995); Vice-President for Publications, International Sociological Association (1994-1998); Editor, *Current Sociology*, 1980-1987; President, Société Internationale de Sociologie des Religions, 1999-2002.

Beckford's work in the sociology of religion began with a doctoral thesis that was the first major study to provide a sociological understanding of the Jehovah's Witnesses, *The Trumpet of Prophecy* (Blackwell 1975), which remains to this day a standard work on the subject. He then turned to what is perhaps the research for which he has become best known, providing an analysis of the new religious movements (NRMs) and, in particular, the varieties of reactions that they have elicited from the wider society. His empirical studies of the anti-cult movement in Britain, France, and Germany, complemented by his research into media coverage of the movements, provide the basic data to substantiate his contention that the ways in which the movements are received can tell us as much, if not more, about a society as the study of the movements themselves.

In *Cult Controversies: Societal Responses to New Religious Movements* (Tavistock 1985), one of the more readable and informative texts on the subject, Beckford has proposed a new framework for the classification of NRMs on the basis of the manner in which they are "inserted" in society, or, as Beckford puts it more formally, "What is distinctive about the way in which members of NRMs are individually and collectively related to other people, groups, institutions, and social processes?" His model highlights the dynamic association between, on the one hand, those relationships that link persons associated with a movement with each other (apostates, patrons, clients, adepts, and devotees) and, on the other hand, the relationships that exist between the collectivity of members and nonmembers.

A recurrent *cri de cœur* in Beckford's work has been that the sociology of religion should reverse its isolation from neighboring subdisciplines, as much is to be learned by adopting some of the latter's new theoretical texts. Such an exercise might, Beckford argues in *Religion and Advanced Industrial Society* (Unwin-Hyman 1989), return the study of religion to the central position it held in the days of the founding fathers. Beckford himself is a fine example of one who does indeed practice what he preaches; not only does he explore ideas to be found in other areas of sociology for himself, but he takes his readers into unfamiliar territories. Apart from his impressive familiarity with both classical and emerging trends in theoretical perspectives, his interests carry him into a number of adjacent areas such as deviancy, social movements, and environmental concerns. His familiarity with the literature of continental Europe as well as that of Japan enables him to make an unusually broad contribution to English-speaking scholarship, which is particularly evidenced in such collected works as *New Religious Movements and Rapid Social Change* (Sage 1986) and *The Changing Face of Religion* (with Thomas Luckmann, Sage 1989).

Beckford previously has been a faculty member at the universities of Reading and Durham, England, and Loyola University Chicago. He has published around 70 articles or book chapters.

—*Eileen Barker*

BEIT-HALLAHMI, BENJAMIN (1943–)

Trained as a clinical psychologist at the University of Michigan; Professor of Psychology at the University of Haifa (Israel).

Widely known as a social psychologist of religion, he is thus inextricably associated with a topic manifestly marginal to the dominant "tough-minded" model of academic psychology. Viewing the study of religion as central to his own more flexible and humanistic conception of the discipline, he asserts his fundamentally interrelated and interdisciplinary convictions that (1) there are no purely psychological questions or answers concerning religion and (2) study of the religious factor must be embedded in a broader psychology of culture focused on the diverse products of the human imagination. Evident in his general treatises, these insights are astutely infused into Beit-Hallahmi's perceptive empirical investigations of various contemporary routes to salvation, most notably in the Israeli context. They also underlie his poignantly prophetic assessment of the interwoven fates of Judaism and the Zionist dream in the twentieth century.

—*Roger O'Toole*

REFERENCES

M. Argyle and B. Beit-Hallahmi, *The Social Psychology of Religion* (London: Routledge, 1975); B. Beit-Hallahmi (ed.), *Research in Religious Behavior* (Belmont, Calif.: Wadsworth, 1973); B. Beit-Hallahmi, *Prolegomena to the Psychological Study of Religion* (London: Associated University Press, 1989); B. Beit-Hallahmi, *Despair and Deliverance* (Albany: SUNY Press, 1992); B. Beit-Hallahmi, *Original Sins* (London: Pluto, 1992); B. Beit-Hallahmi (ed.), *The Illustrated Encyclopedia of Active New Religions, Sects, and Cults* (New York: Rosen, 1993); Z. Sobel and B. Beit-Hallahmi (eds.), *Tradition, Innovation, Conflict* (Albany: SUNY Press, 1991).

BELIEF/BELIEFS   The idea of religion is perhaps inseparable from a distinctive cognitive, or belief, dimension. Yet the social scientific study of religious belief has long struggled with an adequate definition of this dimension. There are two basic, long-standing schools of thought. One, the substantivist, argues that religion is fundamentally a belief in supernatural agents or forces (Goody 1961). This conceptualization has a strong intuitive appeal to social scientists, who for the most part are directly influenced by Judeo-Christian traditions, but there are drawbacks to the use of this definition in comparative studies.

In any religious culture where there exists a set of beliefs clearly demarcating a supernatural order from the natural world, little difficulty occurs in applying the term *religious* to beliefs about the supernatural. Christianity and Islam, objectified as they are in dogma that denigrates our present, mundane existence and looks forward to a transcendent, spiritual existence after death, yield familiar examples. But in some religious traditions, the dividing line between the natural world and the supernatural is not plainly distinguished by believers. In the traditional culture of Bali, for example, every venue of human worldly activity is tinged with spiritual understandings. Therefore, in religious cultures such as Bali's, belief in the supernatural blends with naturalistic beliefs in a smooth continuum so that the two cannot be separated without distorting the understandings of the believers.

The second school of thought, the functionalist, defines religious belief to consist of understandings about a transcendental reality, the experience of which is an ultimate concern to human beings (Luckmann 1991). This perspective may owe its origins to Plato, who insisted that we ought not be beguiled by or place our trust in the world of appearances but instead should seek that which is most true and permanent that lies hidden beyond. Although gods and spirits—seen as inhabitants of the transcendental realm—can be accommodated in this approach, the supernatural premise is not deemed essential.

This second definition of religious belief easily stretches to incorporate antidogmatic mysticisms that make a virtue of being ambiguous about the supernatural. Philosophical Buddhism, which is rather atheistic, is also easily encompassed using this perspective. The second approach defines religious belief so broadly that scientific humanism, Marxism, nationalism, and psychotherapy are all conceivably religious because they deal with deep, nonobvious realities that are an ultimate concern to at least some people.

Clearly, each school has its own strengths and weaknesses. Social scientists who advocate the supernatural premise usually sidestep the difficulty of separating the natural from the supernatural by confining their research to religious cultures where the distinction is unambiguous. When required to draw comparisons to religious cultures where the distinction is blurred, they generally do this by adopting a secularization argument. In traditional societies, religion is a "sacred canopy" (Berger 1967) that constructs and maintains an entire "world" of social experience. The natural and the supernatural meld seamlessly. As societies approach the modern, all features of social life, including religion, become more specialized and differentiated. Religious belief becomes dogma, a codified creed under the care of a professionalized corps of religious specialists. Under the influence of religious specialists, the plethora of spirits and deities is systematized into a hierarchy with a supreme god at its head. Eventually, religious professionals may declare the lesser deities and spirits to be alternative manifestations of the one deity, or they may expunge them altogether as superstitions or heterodox beliefs. Once an abstract and hierarchical conception of supernatural agents has become dogma, the separation in believers' minds between the natural world and the supernatural has been accomplished. Then, as society modernizes, even more belief in supernatural agents and forces atrophies. Increasing human control of nature as well as the spread of scientific understanding of natural processes obviates the need and desire to believe in the supernatural.

By defining religion as a belief in a transcendental reality that is of ultimate human concern and thereby diminishing the importance of the supernatural premise, advocates of the second school escape one dilemma but must cope with an embarrassment of riches in contemporary societies where traditional religions, upstart cults, civil creeds, quasi-religions, and secular "faiths" coexist in profusion while individual believers eclectically construct their personal belief systems drawing from these numerous sources. Perhaps the real strength of the second definition is that it leads to an exploration of the functional substitutes for religious belief (Luckmann 1967, 1991).

The Origin of Religious Beliefs During the past century and a half, there have been various attempts by social scientists to explain the origin of religious beliefs. The anthropologist Edward B. Tylor (1873) represents an early attempt. To him, belief in spirit beings, or animism, constitutes the minimum definition of religion. Tylor went on to speculate that animism developed from early humanity's attempts to explain puzzling experiences. First, he finds the concept of the soul to be universal in simple societies; then he asks how people came to create the concept of the soul, and finds the answer in people's attempts to explain dreams, hallucinations, and other psychic experiences that puzzle them. From this, it is only a reasonable step that early humanity would extend the idea of the soul to other animals, and then to plants. Continuing to reason by analogy, Tylor says, early humanity would in due course come to attribute spiritual qualities to stones, water sources, weapons, food, and ornaments.

Sigmund Freud (1961) proposed an equally distinctive theory of the origin of religious belief. According to him, the religious experience was most like the experience of complete dependency that an infant feels for the parent. A belief in supernatural beings was therefore an adult projection of infantile dependency and should be interpreted as a desire to return to the security of early childhood. Freud concluded that religious beliefs are collective neuroses that save people from developing more severe individual neuroses.

Émile Durkheim (1965) argued that because all human beings are creatures of society and dependent upon it, religious beliefs should therefore be interpreted as "collective representations" that express this dependent relationship between the individual and the collectivity. When we worship the gods or other sacred symbols, we are actually worshiping our social collectivity, whether we realize this or not. Durkheim's theory entailed an important innovation because he considered religiosity to be an attribute of the collective experience rather than a product of individual intellectual speculation or wish fulfillment. As long as human beings remained social creatures, they would have need of religious beliefs and representations, but the character of these beliefs and representations would change radically under the influence of science.

A more recent effort to explain the origin of religious beliefs was made by Talcott Parsons (1972), whose explanation was grounded in certain social psychological universals of the human condition. In addition to setting forth a definition of religion as a universal feature of human society, Parsons stated that religion consisted of a more or less integrated set of beliefs concerning entities that are supernatural or sacred, and thus set apart from the ordinary objects and events that have utilitarian or instrumental importance. Further, Parsons declared that meaning in human life is fundamentally dependent on religious belief because of the universal presence of frustrating experiences that humans cannot avoid.

According to Parsons, two main types of frustration in the human situation provide the focal points for the development of religious beliefs. One of these is that people are "hit" by events that they cannot foresee, prepare for, or control, such as the occurrence of premature death. The second type is present where there is a strong emotional investment in accomplishing some goal, yet despite the greatest energy and skill brought to bear in this effort, success remains uncertain. Frustrations arising from the discrepancy between expectations and what actually occurs pose "problems of meaning," in the sense that Max Weber wrote about. That is, we can explain why an automobile accident caused a premature death, but we cannot explain why it had to happen to a person we loved. Why do the innocent suffer while "the wicked flourish like a green bay tree"? We have no practical answers to such dilemmas. Hence the significance of religious belief is that it is made up of those aspects of the life situation to which people cannot remain indifferent, which they cannot in the long run evade, but which they cannot control or adjust to with every practical means available.

The difficulty with all such attempts to explain the origins of religious beliefs is that the results are speculative and can never be adequately tested. Hence, in recent decades, social scientists have been less motivated to explain the origin of religious belief. Instead, more attention has been devoted to elucidating how religious beliefs articulate with societies and social groups. Social scientists have attempted to grapple with the social consequences of religious beliefs—to see them either as social cement or as social control (Thompson 1986). The first perspective derives from

Durkheim, the second from Karl Marx and Friedrich Engels. Yet a third perspective has been to interpret religious beliefs as cultural models. This approach derives partly from Durkheim and Weber via Parsons, and partly from cultural anthropology.

Religious Beliefs as Social Cement or Social Control
The idea that religious beliefs can provide an integrating focus for relatively homogeneous collectivities and, under the right circumstances, even for complex societies is indisputably one of the main findings of twentieth-century social science. The entire corpus of cultural anthropological studies of simple societies demonstrates the first point. The second point has been the contention of the civil religion thesis. Civil religion is the expression of the cohesion of the society or nation. Sacred beliefs transcend ethnic, denominational, geographic, and class distinctions. In the United States, for example, historical figures (George Washington, Abraham Lincoln, Martin Luther King, Jr.) have been elevated to a quasi-mythical status and are venerated as champions of American ideals and values. Although there have been many debates over the civil religion thesis, it does appear to grasp a reality: Many Americans regardless of their background do say that they feel drawn together by these unifying sacred beliefs.

Noting that religious beliefs may serve as social cement is only half the picture, however. It is also useful to consider religious ideas as weapons in an ongoing struggle within society between social classes or between other groups with divergent interests (e.g., children versus adults, women versus men, immigrants versus long-established residents). Religious beliefs may be seen to serve the ends of one group or section of society attempting to control another. One kind of social control engendered by religious beliefs falls under the rubric of the dominant ideology thesis, originated by Marx and Engels (1970). In their view, the dominant faction in society not only controls the production of wealth, it also controls the production of sacred beliefs. Thus orthodox religious dogmas are supported by the dominant class because they legitimate its lifestyle and roles in society.

However, the social control function of religious beliefs is usually not so transparent. It can refer to the efforts of a dominant class or group (1) to legitimate itself in its own eyes and/or (2) to suppress—without resorting to threats and physical coercion—rebellious behavior by the subordinate class or group. In the classic Marxian formulation, (2) is accomplished because religion is "the opium of the people." On the other hand, social control can have a contrary meaning: the use of religious beliefs by the weak to constrain or modify the behavior of power holders. Thus religious belief is potentially one of the "weapons of the weak" employed to obtain concessions or favors from those with privilege and power. It is also conceivable that religious beliefs constitute an arena in which social control is attempted in both directions. The weak attempt to constrain the behavior of the strong by appealing to religious precepts, while the strong legitimate their privileged positions in public display of their conformity with these precepts. Each party has an interest in ascribing to and supporting the beliefs, but for different reasons. The situation resembles a positive-sum game (Reeves 1995).

Religious Beliefs as Cultural Models Émile Durkheim was an early proponent of the idea that religious beliefs are cultural models. This point was explicated in a seminal article written by Talcott Parsons (1978) in which Durkheim's classic, *The Elementary Forms of the Religious Life,* was reassessed. According to Parsons, Durkheim was well in advance of his contemporaries when he grasped that religious beliefs embody a cultural code for social action. Operating in a manner that is analogous to the genetic code in the organic sphere and to syntax in language, the cultural code made up of religious beliefs allows variation to occur within a predetermined structure of action. Stated differently, the possibility of variation is built into the expression of the code in concrete situations, just as a language speaker is partially constrained by grammar in forming statements but is free nevertheless to express an endless variety of ideas.

Parsons's student, the anthropologist Clifford Geertz (1973), wrote the manifesto for this perspective. Geertz made an enormous impact on the social sciences when he argued that, unlike other animal species, *Homo sapiens* is not constitutionally whole without extragenetic, cultural models to channel perceptions, behavior, beliefs, and evaluations. The peculiar, incomplete nature of human biology necessitates the existence of a complex system of meanings represented in symbols to give human life direction and purpose. Because of their transcendence, religious beliefs objectified as symbols are often the most comprehensive and profound cultural models. At present, this perspective probably remains the dominant approach to religious beliefs in the social sciences (see Greeley 1995).

The historian Bernard Lewis's brief book, *The Political Language of Islam* (1988), provides an excellent example of what is possible with a cultural model perspective. Referring to Arabic, Persian, and Turkish sources, Lewis shows how political theory and practice in the Muslim countries were informed by Islamic beliefs and encapsulated in Islamic terminology. In the United States, the "civil religion" thesis also has been strongly influenced by the cultural model concept. India has long been a favorite subject for scholars interested in how religious beliefs model extreme social inequality in the caste system (Dumont 1980, Milner 1994).

—*Edward B. Reeves*

REFERENCES

R. N. Bellah, "Civil Religion in America," *Daedalus* 96 (1967):1-21; P. L. Berger, *The Sacred Canopy* (Garden City, N.Y.: Doubleday, 1967); L. Dumont, *Homo Hierarchicus* (Chicago: University of Chicago Press, 1980); É. Durkheim, *The Elementary Forms of the Religious Life* (New York: Free Press, 1965 [1912]); S. Freud, *The Future of an Illusion* (New York: Norton, 1961 [1927]); C. Geertz, *The Interpretation of Cultures* (New York: Basic Books, 1973); J. Goody, "Religion and Ritual," *British Journal of Sociology* 12(1961):142-164; A. M. Greeley, *Religion as Poetry* (New Brunswick, N.J.: Transaction, 1995); B. Lewis, *The Political Language of Islam* (Chicago: University of Chicago Press, 1988); T. Luckmann, *The Invisible Religion* (New York: Macmillan, 1967); T. Luckmann, "The New and the Old in Religion," in *Social Theory for a Changing Society*, ed. P. Bourdieu and J. S. Coleman (Boulder, Colo.: Westview, 1991): 167-182; K. Marx and F. Engels, *The German Ideology* (London: Lawrence & Wishart, 1970 [c. 1845]); M. Milner, Jr., *Status and Sacredness* (New York: Oxford University Press, 1994); T. Parsons, "Religious Perspectives in Sociology and Social Psychology," in W. A. Lessa and E. Z. Vogt, *Reader in Comparative Religion*, 3rd ed. (New York: Harper, 1972): 88-93; T. Parsons, "Durkheim on Religion Revisited," in *Action Theory and the Human Condition* (New York: Free Press, 1978): 213-232; E. B. Reeves, "Power, Resistance, and the Cult of Muslim Saints in a Northern Egyptian Town," *American Ethnologist* 22(1995):306-323; K. Thompson, *Beliefs and Ideology* (London: Tavistock, 1986); E. B. Tylor, *Primitive Culture*, 2nd ed. (London: Murray, 1873).

BELLAH, ROBERT N. (1927–) Elliott Professor of Sociology at the University of California, Berkeley, where he has been on the faculty since 1967, chairing the Center for Japanese and Korean Studies from 1968 to 1974 and the Department of Sociology from 1979 to 1985.

One of the most distinguished sociologists of the post-World War II era, a "public intellectual" seeking to address a wide audience, Bellah is conversant with sociologists, anthropologists, and political scientists as well as ethicists and philosophers, theologians, and the general public. (Significantly, although he is widely known, Bellah has not held a major office in any professional association.) At Harvard, where he earned a joint Ph.D. in sociology and Far Eastern languages in 1955, Bellah was a student of Talcott Parsons. Although Parsons's influence on Bellah's thinking is evident, during his career Bellah has worked within several theoretical traditions.

Although his later work increasingly manifests a Weberian ambivalence toward rationalization, his early work exemplifies the "modernization theory" of the 1950s and is clearly and self-consciously structural-functionalist. A Durkheimian concern for shared symbols and the obligations they articulate runs through many of his writings. Bellah's more recent work also has been informed by the critical functionalism of Habermas, especially the idea that economic and political "systems"—wherein the primary media of communication are money and power, respectively— invade and "colonize" the "life-world"—in which the medium of communication is linguistic and ideally oriented toward mutual understanding.

Religious Evolution Bellah's dissertation, published as *Tokugawa Religion: The Cultural Roots of Modern Japan* (Free Press 1957, second edition 1985), provides a Weber-like analysis of Japanese development, explaining the role of premodern cultural values in modernization. Against a Parsonian theoretical background, Bellah identifies the indigenous equivalent of the Protestant ethic in the motivational ethic of inner-worldly asceticism fostered by certain religious movements in the Tokugawa period (1542-1868). This early work and Bellah's later contributions to the study of religion can be characterized as variations on a theme most clearly articulated in his essay "Religious Evolution" (1964), which he developed in a course on social evolution cotaught with Parsons and S. N. Eisenstadt at Harvard.

Bellah begins by defining *religion* as "a set of symbolic forms and acts that relate man to the ultimate conditions of his existence." He argues that beginning with the single cosmos of the undifferentiated primitive religious worldview in which life is a "one possibility thing," evolution in the religious sphere is toward the increasing differentiation and complexity of symbol systems. His evolutionary religious taxonomy specifies five stages: primitive (e.g., Australian Aborigines), archaic (e.g., Native American), historic (e.g., ancient Judaism, Confucianism, Buddhism, Islam, early Palestinian Christianity), early modern (e.g., Protestant Christianity), and modern (religious individualism). In the modern stage of religious evolution, the hierarchic dualistic religious symbol system that emerged in the historic epoch is collapsed and the symbol system that results is "infinitely multiplex." In this posttraditional situation, the individual confronts life as an "infinite possibility thing," and is "capable, within limits, of continual self-transformation and capable, again within limits, of remaking the world, including the very symbolic forms with which he deals with it, even the forms that state the unalterable conditions of his own existence."

This argument foresaw the reflexive individualism that characterizes both the intellectual culture of postmodernism and the "new religious consciousness" of the 1960s and 1970s. With Charles Glock, Bellah undertook a project in the early 1970s to investigate the latter, the results of which were published as *The New Religious Consciousness* (University of California Press 1976). In his concluding remarks, Bellah foreshadows the argument of *Habits of the Heart: Individualism and Commitment in American Life*—written with Richard Madsen, William M. Sullivan, Ann Swidler, and Steven M. Tipton (University of California Press 1985 [second edition 1995], hereafter *Habits*)—in arguing that the deepest cause of the 1960s counterculture was "the inability of utilitarian individualism to provide a meaningful pattern of personal and social existence." The crisis of the 1960s therefore was "above all a religious crisis." As a response to the sterility of the utilitarian worldview, the counterculture turned to the American tradition of expressive individualism in the form of a spirituality grounded in the primacy of individual experience and the belief in nonduality, exemplified by the appropriation of Zen Buddhist practices. Again foreshadowing the argument in *Habits,* Bellah highlights the danger that expressive individualism may come to articulate with utilitarian individualism, to which it was originally a response. When expressive individualist-inspired religious symbols and practices "become mere techniques for 'self-realization,' then once again we see utilitarian individualism reborn from its own ashes."

Thus, by the 1970s, Bellah's positive embrace of the "wide-open chaos of the post-Protestant, postmodern era" in *Beyond Belief: Essays on Religion in a Post-Traditional World* (Harper 1970) had grown more cautious as the full consequences of the "modern" religious epoch became more evident. By the 1980s, the relationship is clearly strained. Understanding that the treatment of religion in *Habits* is an elaboration of the fifth "modern" stage of religious evolution makes clear that the "infinite possibility thing" he lauds in "Reli-

gious Evolution" has become the hyperprivatized "Sheilaism" ("my own religion") he laments in *Habits*. Particularly troubling about the personalized and privatized modern religion examined in *Habits* is that it is underwritten by what Alasdair MacIntyre in *After Virtue* (1981) calls an "emotivist" view of ethics that reduces the foundation of moral claims to the subjective feelings of individuals and renders the development of common moral understandings difficult if not impossible.

Civil Religion Bellah's strong position that "any coherent and viable society rests on a common set of moral understandings" is a Durkheimian thread that runs throughout his work and draws attention back to his work in the 1960s. While his guiding theoretical framework is encapsulated in the "Religious Evolution" paper, Bellah is best known for his landmark "Civil Religion in America" (1967), an essay that, according to Bellah, he has "never been allowed to forget" and that "in important respects changed" his life. Alongside church religion and distinct from it, Bellah argued, is an elaborate and well-organized *civil religion*. It is actually a religious "dimension" of society, characteristic of the American republic since its founding. It is not Judeo-Christianity but grows out of the American historical experience, which is heavily influenced by Protestantism. Civil religion is "an understanding of the American experience in the light of ultimate and universal reality" and can be found in presidential inaugural addresses from Washington to Kennedy, sacred texts (the Declaration of Independence) and places (Gettysburg), and community rituals (Memorial Day parades). It is especially evident in times of trial for the nation such as the Revolution and Civil War.

In *Varieties of Civil Religion* (coedited with Phillip Hammond, Harper 1980), Bellah ties this argument to the religious evolution framework, arguing that every society has a "religio-political" problem, and that in premodern phases the solution consists either in a fusion of the two realms (archaic) or in a differentiation but not separation (historic and early modern). Civil religion proper comes into existence only in modern society, where church and state are separated as well as differentiated. A civil religion that is differentiated from *both* church and state is possible only in a modern society.

Although Bellah concludes his 1967 essay by declaring American civil religion to be "still very much alive," he also warns that the nation is facing a third time of trial centered on "the problem of responsible action in a revolutionary world." Decrying U.S. involvement in Vietnam, Bellah claimed America to be "at the edge of a chasm the depth of which no man knows." Just as his hope in "Religious Evolution" became more cautious in *Habits,* so too does his concern at the conclusion of "Civil Religion" turn somewhat despairing in his American Sociological Association Sorokin Award-winning book, *The Broken Covenant: American Civil Religion in Time of Trial* (Seabury 1975 [second edition, University of Chicago Press 1992]) in which he famously declares American civil religion to be "an empty and broken shell." Written at the time of Watergate and the continuation of the Vietnam War, there was little to temper Bellah's pessimism in the mid-1970s. By the 1980s, however, some hope began to emerge once again.

Although he never uses the term *civil religion* in *Habits,* the "biblical and republican traditions" championed in *Habits* are a new and more dynamic conceptual response to the same substantive issues. A public focus on commitment to the common good as opposed to the excesses of utilitarian and expressive individualism is possible, for Bellah, if the once-dominant cultural language of the biblical and republican traditions—relegated in contemporary America to the status of "second languages"—are reappropriated by citizens actively pursuing the good society in common. The obstacles to forging a national community based on common moral understandings are considerable—they are institutional as well as cultural, as Bellah states in *The Good Society* (Knopf 1991)—but as any Durkheimian would argue, surmounting them is essential.

Symbolic Realism　As should be evident, Bellah has always been a cultural sociologist, taking seriously the causal efficacy of values, the centrality of meaning, and the sui generis reality of symbols. His famous definition of religion in "Religious Evolution" is unmistakably cultural. This perspective on religion is also evident in his major methodological statement on behalf of a nonreductionist perspective in the social scientific study of religion, the perspective of "symbolic realism."

In the essay "Between Religion and Social Science," Bellah criticizes the "Enlightenment myth of secularization . . . the view that there is only a mechanical relation between science and religion, namely, the more of one the less of the other." He argues that the theories of Marx, Freud, Durkheim, and Weber contribute to this myth because of their *reductionist* view of religion. Even when they correctly see the symbolic (nonrational, noncognitive) dimensions of human life and hence religion (Freud's unconscious, Durkheim's collective effervescence, and Weber's charisma), they end up explaining religious symbols away as expressing some other more fundamental "reality." Bellah, in contrast,

advocates a position he calls *symbolic realism* in which religious symbols are seen to express a nonreducible reality, a reality sui generis. While not denying that rationalistic and reductionistic approaches have something to tell us about religion, he refuses to allow them to be the only voices.

Social Science as Moral Inquiry　That the social sciences regardless of their empirical focus must have a moral voice is a point Bellah has made in various essays, but nowhere more clearly than in the Appendix to *Habits,* "Social Science as Public Philosophy." Against those who would place social science firmly on the former side of the allegedly unbridgeable divide between "is" and "ought," Bellah argues for a reappropriation of the larger, synoptic view of a social science that is at once philosophical, historical, and sociological. Such an approach would embrace the ethical aims of social inquiry: holding a mirror up to society, being a form of social self-understanding, discerning the good society from actually existing societies, or, as any good Durkheimian would say, distilling the ideal from the real. A social science that ignores its ethical meaning not only fails to live up to its highest calling but also can more easily be put in service of manipulative ends by those with political and economic power. For Bellah, then, the social sciences must always be *moral* sciences.

In conclusion, it must be said that the meaning of Robert Bellah's work cannot be fully understood without recognizing that he is a man of faith (see 1991). At Harvard, he came under the influence of the Lutheran theologian Paul Tillich during the period when Bellah was "reappropriating" his Presbyterian religious upbringing on his own terms. Indeed, there are as many references to Tillich in *Beyond Belief* as to Durkheim and Parsons. The question Tillich posed in *The Theology of Culture* (1959) is the one with which Bellah seems to be wrestling: "How can the radicalism of prophetic criticism which is implied in the principles of genuine Protestantism be united with the classical tradition of dogma, sacred law, sacraments, hierarchy, cult, as preserved in the Catholic churches?" As Bellah himself has said, "Discipleship and citizenship and the relation between them have been my enduring preoccupations."

—David Yamane

REFERENCES

R. Bellah, "Religious Evolution," *American Sociological Review* 29(1964):358-374; R. Bellah, "Civil Religion in America," *Daedalus* 96(1967):1-21; R. Bellah, "Between Religion and Social Science," in *Beyond Belief* (New York: Harper, 1970): 237-259; R. Bellah, "Comment," *Sociological Analy-*

sis 50(1989):147; R. Bellah, "Finding the Church," in *How My Mind Has Changed*, ed. J. Wall and D. Heim (Grand Rapids, Mich.: Eerdmans, 1991): 113-122; A. MacIntyre, *After Virtue* (Notre Dame, Ind.: University of Notre Dame Press, 1981); P. Tillich, *The Theology of Culture* (London: Oxford University Press, 1959).

BELONGING

BELONGING   People sharing the same representations of the sacred (beliefs and rituals) feel like being members of the same society and are concerned by what is happening in their society. According to Émile Durkheim (1912), their belonging is not only the result of this sharing, it is also the source of it.

Religious people are aware of being part of something that goes beyond themselves: the sacred. With respect to belonging, the sacred is the semantic function that regulates the social tension of human life by forging links of solidarity between individuals, groups, and societies through symbolic representations of their respective identities. The symbol of "God," for example, conveys a sense of belonging to something greater, the identity of which is close enough to their own that they act on its behalf. This is the sacred: the representation of a moral power that tells people to act in a certain way; it is not wholly they because it transcends them. Such a normative representation responds to one of the exigencies of being human, that of life in society, because of the de facto interdependence linking human beings. This is why Durkheim perceived the origins of all manifestations of the sacred in the "moral power" of society: Belonging is first, and religion is a functional way to maintain it.

See also Beliefs, Émile Durkheim, Moral Community, Ritual, Sacred

—*Robert Tessier*

REFERENCES

É. Durkheim, *Les formes élémentaires de la vie religieuse* (Paris: Alcan, 1912); *The Elementary Forms of the Religious Life* (New York: Free Press, 1965).

BENDIX, REINHARD (1916-1990)

German-born sociologist, fled Nazi rule to America and later did his doctoral work at the University of Chicago; his father, Ludwig, was a lawyer in Weimar Germany and influenced the young Reinhard's involvement in ethical and sociological questions.

Bendix's early interest in the relationships between truth, politics, and society, and in the problems of rationality and irrationality, led him to engage critically Marxian and other theories of ideology and examine the historical role of knowledge elites in modern societies.

Bendix spent most of his career at the University of California, Berkeley, and became one of the major interpreters of Max Weber's writings in America. His book *Max Weber: An Intellectual Portrait* (Doubleday 1960), once unrivaled as a comprehensive treatment of Weber, remains a balanced and compelling synthesis of his comparative, historical sociology. In contrast to Talcott Parsons's development of Weber's social action theory, Bendix emphasized Weber's work on status groups, political and administrative organization, and types of legitimacy but also examined Weber's treatment of the world religions and their civilizations. His distinctive combination of Weber with perspectives drawn from writers such as Tocqueville, Otto Hintze, and others resulted in a series of books marked by conceptual clarity and global breadth. *Work and Authority in Industry* (Wiley 1956) compared managerial ideologies of industrialization in England, America, and Russia, while *Nation-Building and Citizenship* (Wiley 1964) examined the changing balance of private and public authority and of tradition and modernity in the transformation of societies, including western Europe, Germany, Japan, and India. The deeper historical and cultural roots of modernity in earlier struggles in East and West around the problem of kingship were explored in his volume *Kings and People: Power and the Mandate to Rule* (University of California Press 1978).

Bendix's interpretation of Weber and his explorations in comparative sociology influenced several generations of students, among them Guenther Roth, whose English edition of Weber's *Economy and Society* (with Claus Wittich) made available for the first time large and previously untranslated portions of this landmark work. Roth also has written extensively about Weber's work, both in collaboration with Bendix as well as independently (e.g., *Scholarship and Partisanship*, University of California Press 1971).

—*Donald A. Nielsen*

REFERENCE

R. Bendix, "What Max Weber Means to Me?" in *Max Weber's Political Sociology*, ed. R. M. Glassman and V. Murvar (Westport, Conn.: Greenwood, 1984): 13-24.

BERGER, PETER L. (1929–) Professor, Boston University; Director, Institute for the Study of Economic Culture, Boston. Leading scholar in the sociology of religion and the sociology of knowledge. Lay Lutheran theologian. Frequent contributor to public policy debate. Education: Wagner College, New School for Social Research. Has held faculty positions at Evangelical Academy (Bad Boll, West Germany), University of North Carolina, Hartford Theological Seminary, New School for Social Research, Rutgers University, Boston College. Honorary doctorates from Loyola University, Wagner College, University of Notre Dame. President, Society for the Scientific Study of Religion, 1966-1967.

Berger's work in sociology and theology is notable for the scope and depth of his analysis, the lucidity of his style, and the consistency of his efforts in facing some of the basic dilemmas posed by the modern age. Much of his work may be understood as a systematic attempt to understand modernity's characteristics and its implications for individuals and sociocultural institutions.

Developing a Sociology of Religion Berger first gained a national profile in the United States with the publication of two books in 1961. In *The Noise of Solemn Assemblies* and *The Precarious Vision* (both Doubleday), he strongly criticized contemporary Protestant theology and religious institutions. He accused Protestant clergy of failing to meet the challenge of offering individuals in modern America a means for understanding and living in accordance with Christian beliefs. In attacking what many saw as the smug conservatism and spiritual emptiness of the Protestant establishment, Berger also drew attention to the social control functions it willingly performed. He viewed the church as giving legitimacy to the social fictions and injustices of the time. The power of a Christian faith rooted in transcendent experience and meanings was not being called upon in offering individual believers a more authentic existence. Although not without its detractors, Berger's polemic was applauded by many within the upcoming generation of Protestant clergy. He had captured their concerns about the direction of mainstream Christianity in a rapidly changing world.

Although he would later question the neo-orthodox content and "stern, quasi-Barthian" style of the theological perspective advocated in these early books, Berger nevertheless had begun expressing a number of important themes that would become central to his later works: the development of a sociological critique of modernity, the tensions between sociological and theological paradigms, the implications of modernity for

institutions, beliefs, and personal identity, and the quest for an ethic of responsibility in a social context characterized by moral relativism. Underlying all of these efforts was what would eventually become a highly influential theoretical perspective. During the first half of the 1960s, Berger had begun to identify and integrate, in collaboration with Thomas Luckmann, among others, the key elements of this approach. Drawing upon influences as diverse as Marx, Durkheim, Weber, Gehlen, and Pareto, and heavily indebted to members of the growing school of phenomenologists, most notably Alfred Schutz, this sociology of knowledge framework focused upon the meanings and social processes through which individuals construct reality in everyday life.

Berger soon began applying this perspective to the sociological study of religion and, more specifically, to the analysis of modernity's impact on religious institutions and beliefs. In *The Sacred Canopy* (Doubleday 1967), he argued that, from a sociological perspective, religion must be understood as a social construction, a human projection of a sacred cosmos. Throughout history, these projections or "externalizations" (to use the more technical language of Berger and Luckmann's sociology of knowledge) have played a crucial role in constructing and maintaining social institutions and processes. Key to religion's significance is the legitimation of social realities through its claims of accessibility to nonhuman or transcendent powers.

Much of the book's argument was an encounter with the Durkheimian legacy. Yet Berger characteristically reached beyond what might otherwise have been a strictly functionalist interpretation of religion to explore its social psychological implications. Religion, according to Berger, is essentially a set of alienated and alienating realities that become "internalized" within individual identity. Through religion, believers are offered crucial explanations and ultimate meanings needed for making sense of their lives and the surrounding universe, especially during times of personal or social crisis. Religion is a kind of "canopy" that shields individuals and, by implication, society from the ultimately destructive consequences of a seemingly chaotic, purposeless existence.

Methodological and Theoretical Positions With *Sacred Canopy,* Berger outlined the analytical framework that would guide many of his subsequent efforts in the sociology of religion. He also identified some of the central methodological and theoretical questions and issues facing the discipline. On the level of methodology, Berger encouraged fellow sociologists to draw upon Weber when designing their overall research strategy, to examine the full significance of *Verstehen* and systematically understand religion from the believer's perspective, that is, "from within." He was convinced that sociologists of religion should demonstrate a "methodological atheism" whereby, in the course of studying religious phenomena from a social scientific perspective, they would maintain a strict detachment from personal theological leanings. Religious truth claims must always be "bracketed" in the sense that they cannot be verified using the tools of the social scientist. Berger has consistently maintained his commitment to these methodological principles in explaining and promoting his understanding of an interpretive sociology.

On the level of theory, however, Berger has changed his views somewhat. *Sacred Canopy,* like many of his publications in the mid- to late 1960s, examined in depth the challenges posed to religion in the modern world by secularization and pluralism. Berger focused on the dialectical relationship between these two phenomena. Secularization generates pluralism by undermining the plausibility structure of monopolistic religious institutions and beliefs. Pluralism, on the other hand, relativizes the taken-for-granted or "objective" nature of religious meaning systems, thereby encouraging secularization. Partly because of the Western bias then prevalent in sociological circles in the United States, secularization was seen by many sociologists, including Berger, as representing the more serious problem for religion. Beliefs and symbols had apparently become hollowed out, stripped of their former religious significance. The canopy that protected individuals and societies from the terrors of a chaotic, anomic cosmos no longer appeared so sacred or intact.

Through the years, Berger has shifted much of his attention away from the secularization thesis to the study of pluralism. In the late 1960s and early 1970s, travel to non-Western religious cultures led him to question the inevitability of secularization. Even in the most "modern" societies, there was strong evidence of countersecular developments. Although secularization was not a spent force, it was less pervasive than once thought. Pluralism, however, seems to have raised critical problems for religion. The coexistence within a pluralistic society of multiple meaning systems, each with its own truth claims, has weakened the plausibility or certainty of religious traditions and beliefs. In many modern societies, religion has receded or been pushed almost entirely into the private sphere. For individuals living in those societies, religious commitment has become a highly personal choice (what Berger has called "the heretical imperative") and subject to revisions

resulting from ever changing sociocultural and biographical factors.

Concerned that *Sacred Canopy* seemed to have been misunderstood by some readers as an atheistic treatise that left little hope for religion's future, Berger responded with the largely theological *A Rumor of Angels* (Doubleday 1969). Applying the sociological perspective with which he had analyzed religion, he now "relativized the relativizers" of religious beliefs by examining the socially constructed nature of modern consciousness. Modernity has not, Berger argued, negated the possibility of the supernatural. Rather, the secularism and pluralism of the modern age have made the theological task of uncovering religious truths more difficult. Berger proposed an "inductive approach," a return to the spirit of the liberal theology initiated by Friedrich Schleiermacher and his followers. With the benefit of phenomenological theory, this strategy would seek out "signals of transcendence" within modern human experience.

Developing a Critique of Modernity   Scholars disagree about whether Berger is correct in his analysis of pluralism's extent and consequences. Some question whether pluralism is a particularly new phenomenon in human history. Others believe that he has exaggerated its supposed unsettling effects on modern consciousness. Berger himself has not disputed the existence of pluralism in earlier eras. His argument has been that the scope and intensity of modern pluralism are historically unprecedented. Like any other social construction, however, pluralism (and modernity itself) is not inevitable. Even while speaking metaphorically about the "homeless mind" of modern individuals, Berger has consistently pointed to evidence of countermodern trends and the need for a critique of modernity that is informed by a multidisciplinary approach.

For Berger, an important goal for both sociologists and theologians in this regard is to understand modern pluralism's characteristics, limitations, and likely impact on religious institutions and faith. In carrying out these tasks, they should avoid repeating their earlier failure to recognize countersecular developments and other indications of religious resurgence throughout the world. Theologians especially must not allow themselves to become conceptually or methodologically blinded to signals of transcendence. Berger's own contributions in this area include the further exploration, in *The Heretical Imperative* (Doubleday 1979) and *A Far Glory* (Free Press 1992), among other publications, of the inductive method outlined in *A Rumor of Angels.*

Berger's overall impact on sociological and theological thinking has been enormous. And, as one of the most frequently cited authors of the twentieth century, his influence has now extended far beyond the social sciences and religion. Perhaps a key reason for this phenomenon lies in the accessibility of his writing and the ultimately hopeful message in his thought. With a skillful and seemingly effortless style, he has applied a complex analytical framework to the core questions and dilemmas facing modern individuals and institutions. Unlike those of his contemporaries who see little of value in modernity, Berger has tempered his criticisms of modern excesses with an informed awareness that this age also brings with it significant human and spiritual possibilities.

—*Bruce Karlenzig*

REFERENCES

P. L. Berger and T. Luckmann, *The Social Construction of Reality* (Garden City, N.Y.: Doubleday, 1966); J. D. Hunter and S. C. Ainlay (eds.), *Making Sense of Modern Times* (New York: Routledge, 1986).

BERGSON, HENRI (1859-1941)   Held the prestigious chair of modern philosophy at the College de France from 1900 to 1921; awarded the Nobel Prize in 1927.

Around the turn of the century, Bergson wrote a number of influential philosophical works on the role of time (*Time and Free Will,* Harper 1910 [1889]), memory (*Matter and Memory,* Swan Sonnenschein 1919 [1896]), and evolutionary creativity (*Creative Evolution,* Holt 1911 [1907]) in human experience. His philosophy generally emphasized the opposition between human creativity, rooted in life and the inner stream of consciousness, and the spatial objectifications of experience in stable cultural forms and institutions. He later supplemented these ideas with a philosophy of religion (*The Two Sources of Morality and Religion,* Holt 1935 [1932]), which, among its other features, offered an alternative to the sociological, especially the Durkheimian, view of religion's origins and historical role.

Bergson's theory of two types of religion also reflects his distinction between a measurable, spatially based time, and real duration, the inner flow of the individual's temporal experience. Static religion, through myth and ritual, promotes closed societies and automatism in thought and action, yet defends humanity against the corrosive powers of reason and paralyzing thoughts about death. Dynamic religion involves God's love and desire with multiply creative beings, who advance an open society, and appears in mystical visions.

—*Donald A. Nielsen*

BHAGWAN   *see* Rajneesh Movement

BIBBY, REGINALD W. (1943–)   Beginning his career as a Baptist minister, Bibby completed his Ph.D. in sociology under Armand Mauss at the University of Washington with a study of a skid road mission in Seattle. Since 1975, he has held a position in the Department of Sociology at the University of Lethbridge, Alberta.

A major and a minor direction have dominated his research and publications: Since 1975, he has conducted quinquennial national social surveys of Canadian social and religious trends under the heading *Project Canada*; and, with its roots in his master's research at the University of Calgary, he has addressed (in collaboration with Merlin B. Brinkerhoff) the question of why conservative Christian churches are growing through the idea of the "circulation of the saints."

The importance of the *Project Canada* longitudinal studies for the sociology of Canadian religion is considerable. They represent the hitherto only national surveys of Canadian religious attitudes and behaviors beyond the limited data emanating from the governmental Statistics Canada and from the Gallup poll. As well, during the two decades since its beginning, Bibby has extended this core research into various related directions, which include studies of Canadian teenagers (in collaboration with Donald C. Posterski), the United Church of Canada, and the Anglican Church of Canada.

The religious trends that this research has revealed are quite consistent. Canadians, much like the people of other Western countries, are still overwhelmingly Christian by identification; they still believe in God and even in the divinity of Jesus. Yet fewer and fewer of them are members of religious organizations or participate regularly in religious rituals. In two volumes, *Fragmented Gods: The Poverty and Potential of Religion in Canada* (Irwin 1987) and *Unknown Gods: The Ongoing Story of Religion in Canada* (Stoddard 1993), Bibby analyzes these trends, pointing out how Canadians pick and choose "fragments" of religious items (e.g., rites of passage, specific beliefs) or treat religion like a consumer item, partaking of it "à la carte" rather than remaining full practicing members of their traditional denominations. In this, his work tends to confirm the view of religion in the modern world that Thomas Luckmann represents in *The Invisible Religion* (Macmillan 1967).

The work on the "circulation of the saints" shows a related manifestation. Although the conservative Christian churches in Canada are recruiting some new members from the liberal mainline churches, largely their growth has come from a greater ability to keep more existing members and their children. They are growing as religious organizations but have had little success in halting or reversing the more general fragmentation and decline. The early and recent versions of the thesis are in Bibby and Brinkerhoff, "The Circulation of the Saints: A Study of People Who Join Conservative Churches" (1973) and "Circulation of the Saints, 1966-1990: New Data, New Reflections" (1994).

Bibby has not viewed the trends his research shows with indifference. Increasingly since the publication of *Fragmented Gods,* he has explicitly lamented what is happening. As a cultural parallel, Bibby also decries the cultural fragmentation of late-twentieth-century Canadian society. Here as well, he uses the data from his *Project Canada* series to make his points. These two aspects of Bibby's work are most clear in *Mosaic Madness: The Poverty and Potential of Life in Canada* (Stoddard 1990) and *There's Got to Be More: Connecting Churches and Canadians* (Wood Lake Books 1995).

—*Peter Beyer*

REFERENCES

R. W. Bibby and M. B. Brinkerhoff, "The Circulation of the Saints," *Journal for the Scientific Study of Religion,* 12(1973):273-283; R. W. Bibby and M. B. Brinkerhoff, "Circulation of the Saints, 1966-1990," *Journal for the Scientific Study of Religion,* 33(1994):273-280.

BIBLICAL STUDIES Social scientific interest in Hebrew, early Jewish, and early Christian social organization stems from the fact that the modern world has been affected greatly by the religions that originated in ancient Israel. It is also true that biblical scholars and social historians find social scientific theories suggestive of interpretations of ancient data, although obviously one cannot mechanically apply modern models in such unmodern settings.

Although archaeological findings and ancient histories are helpful, most of the relevant knowledge comes from the Bible and other religious writings. These texts are often reworkings of earlier material, applying traditions to new circumstances and making them comprehensible to new groupings of people. The social scientist cannot ignore the literary history of such works. Every time an ancient editor has refashioned a text, there are resultant clues in it about the audience that the editor had in mind as well as a resultant set of interpolations that do not reflect an earlier point in time. Thus, much that is in Deuteronomy provides us with information about the social world of the Deuteronomist, not about the world of Moses, who is depicted as the speaker in Deuteronomy; much that is in the Gospel of Matthew provides us with information about the social world of the Matthean writer, not about the world of Jesus of Nazareth. It would certainly be naive to portray the personalities of Moses or Jesus on the basis of reedited legends and discourses. Rather, one should look at the histories or "trajectories" of the editing of the texts, develop portrayals of intended audiences, and focus on the reception of works as scripture; these can tell us something about specific historical societies.

Hebrew and Early Jewish Societies Hebrew and early Jewish societies are reflected in the Hebrew Bible or Christian Old Testament, the "apocrypha," and the New Testament. The first explicitly sociological study of Hebrew religion seems to be that by Louis Wallis (1905), who read the history of Hebrew religion as a series of efforts to make collective responses to other nations. Wallis described his model of human action as "indirect egoism," wherein people would form motives from the perspective of others. Such an approach reminds one of "Chicago School" social psychology. In a series of articles in the *American Journal of Sociology* from 1907 to 1911, which he edited into the book, *The Sociological Study of the Bible* (University of Chicago Press 1912), Wallis formulated accounts of Hebrew ethnic identity, kinship systems, industrial institutions, the Covenant, the settlement in Canaan, hostility toward other nations and their religions, sanctuaries, centralization of the cult, law, and national unity. These are all matters that would be taken up by subsequent writers. After his 1912 book, there does not seem to have been much further interest in the sociology of Hebrew society among the Chicago scholars.

Within a few years, the German sociologist Max Weber was also investigating ancient Hebrew society. His *Antike Judentum* (Mohr 1921 [*Ancient Judaism,* Free Press 1952]) reveals a thorough knowledge of the source criticism and other aspects of Old Testament scholarship of the day. Weber was particularly interested in contrasting Hebrew to Hindu and Confucian developments and in exploring the contribution that the Hebrew prophetic tradition made to the promotion of rationalism over magic in Western culture. Following the mid-nineteenth-century work of the historian Eduard Meyer, he was interested in the accretion of traits in the tradition through the centuries. He therefore pays particular attention to the social location of the prophets and others, and to the different sources of charisma in ancient Israel. Despite some minor errors that he probably would have caught had he lived to complete the work, *Ancient Judaism* reads very well three-quarters of a century later.

The one major aspect of the study that has not stood the test of time is Weber's application of the "pariah people" concept from Indian caste society to the Jews; his effort to explain how a nation became a "pariah people" uncritically retrojects a nineteenth-century European phenomenon back into history, although the Dead Sea materials do show that ritual separations did occur in ancient Palestine. Weber's use of such types as the city-state, the oath community, and kingdom remains valid, although ancient Judaism was more heterogeneous than Weber knew. Weber also seems to have underestimated the popularity of monotheism among the populace of Israel and the importance of the priesthood in maintaining it, and accorded the prophets too great a preservative role (Zeitlin 1984). Weber's impact on Old Testament scholarship has been largely mediated through Albrecht Alt and Martin Noth.

The Durkheimian tradition of social science took up the study of the Hebrews in the person of Antonin Causse, who wanted to apply the developmental scheme of Durkheim's student, Lucien Lévy-Bruhl, to Hebrew history. Lévy-Bruhl maintained that primitive and prehistorical people were pre-logical and corporative in their thinking while moderns are logical and individualist. Causse (1937) believed that the Hebrews marked a transition between these two mentalities.

Other studies of the ancient Hebrews by social scientists have been scattered in time, place, and topic. A few studies have explored Hebrew family structures and a few (Martindale 1962, Berger 1963) have addressed Weber's old question of the social location of the prophets. Berger's review of the biblical scholars' literature on prophets convinced him that the prophets were not as opposed to priests as Weber thought, while Martindale's independent analysis parallels Weber's depiction. Winter (1983) associates the Hebrew belief in a high god with the monarchical regime of David transcending local interests.

The last quarter of the twentieth century has seen an explosion of sociologically informed studies of the Hebrews conducted by biblical scholars. Norman Gottwald's *The Tribes of Yahweh* (Orbis 1979) made a considerable impact; citing Karl Marx but proceeding in a largely Durkheimian manner, Gottwald portrays the emergence of Israel in Canaan as a heterogeneous, classless, decentralized association of tribes that came to conceive of themselves as an egalitarian brotherhood under the symbolism of the Israelite deity. One study (Dutcher-Walls 1991) seeks to find the social location of the Deuteronomist. Major works on prophecy applied social psychological cognitive dissonance theory to them (Carroll 1979), depicted prophets as marginalized religionists who gained prominence by providing an explanation for Israel's catastrophes (Wilson 1980), and applied the personal charisma model of Max Weber to them. The charisma model also has been used in careful studies of the premonarchy leaders, or "judges" (Malamat 1976, Munch 1990). That the premonarchy legends pertain to small groupings of people who resemble the tribes studied by anthropologists rather than the societies studied by most sociologists is not lost on some; Wilson (1984) and Malamat (1973) compare the biblical tribal genealogies to those of other tribal peoples, noting the function of genealogies in legal and military matters. Studies of the postexilic Jewish period include a major survey by Kippenberg (1978) and Saldarini's careful analysis of Pharisees, Scribes, and Sadducees in first-century Palestine (1988).

Early Christianity   The initial uses of social science to understand early Christianity appeared early in the twentieth century at the University of Chicago. The general approach was to describe the broad social environment of the first-century Roman Empire. Biblical scholars do that anyway, but in Chicago, Shirley Jackson Case (1923) proposed doing it with the help of sociological sensitizing concepts. Today some works continue in much the same way, drawing parallels with extra-Christian phenomena—such as miracles (Kee 1983) and women's religion (Kraemer 1992)—or treating such broad subjects as ancient slavery and city-states.

There was considerable discussion early on about whether the early Christians were proletarian activists, but only the argument by Lohmeyer (1921) that the movement drew on the same strata of craftsmen and professionals as did the Pharisees—although adding a few upper-strata members, especially women—has stood the test of time. Advances in New Testament critical techniques as well as the refinement of sociological conceptualizations have led to further explorations of the middle-strata, and even interstitial-strata, character of early Christianity (e.g., Esler 1987, Holmberg 1990, Malherbe 1977, Meeks 1983, Stark 1986).

It is necessary to distinguish between a sociology of the Jesus movement, led by Jesus of Nazareth in Palestine, and subsequent early Christianity. The literary evidence we have about the former was written from within the latter. The clues a scholar can use to establish the social world of the writer and audience pertain to early Christianity, not to the Jesus movement. Consequently, students of the Jesus movement need to rest satisfied with identifying whatever seems historically accurate in the Gospels and interpreting it in terms of depictions of the social context of early-first-century Palestine, using such concepts as relative deprivation, the millenarian movement, and the charismatic prophet (Gager 1975), wandering charismatics, social rootlessness, city-countryside tension, status inequality, and intensification and relaxation of norms (Theissen 1977), the religious virtuoso within the Jewish framework (Zeitlin 1988), the social movement and imperial systems (Horsley 1989), the precarious legitimacy heritage (Fenn 1992), Jewish-Christian relations (Sanders 1993), and stigma—including the embracing of stigmatized traits in a countercurrent against status coordinates (Ebertz 1992).

The social scientific study of the early Christian movement, that is, the movement after the time of Jesus, can use the literary evidence of the New Testament much more readily. The various New Testament books were written for purposes; they themselves represent social acts that we can observe and interpret. We can see Paul asserting authoritative claims on the basis of apostolic charisma, and we can see the original charisma of Jesus being routinized in an institutionalization process (Bendix 1985); various stages in the process emerge visibly when the New Testament books are read in chronological order (Blasi 1991). We can also see the logic of cognitive dissonance following upon the execution of Jesus and the absence of any visible kingdom (Gager 1975), and we can see it at work in the thinking of Paul after his break with the Antiochene church (Taylor 1992).

It is useful not only to use source criticism to help arrange the data temporally to see such processes at work but also to arrange the material geographically. A number of studies have focused on particular communities, such as those for whom Luke (Esler 1987) and Matthew (Saldarini 1991, Stark 1991a) wrote, and that in Corinth (Theissen 1982, Meeks 1983). These locality-based studies have occasioned the use of the perspectives of urban sociology, stratification, and deviance perspectives, respectively.

Social scientific perspectives have supplied numerous sensitizing concepts and their attendant vocabularies to the study of early Christianity—gender roles (Funk 1981, Corley 1993), group (Schreiber 1977), household (Malherbe 1977), role sets (Funk 1981), social movement (Blasi 1988), sect (Watson 1986), and the stranger (Elliott 1981). Such concepts can and have made their appearance apart from any explicit social scientific intent, but with such an intent they have come to be elaborated and evaluated. Together with such conceptualizations have come new analytical methodologies and perspectives—population analyses (Stark 1991b), content analysis (Funk 1981), sociolinguistics, the sociology of knowledge (Blasi 1991, Holmberg 1990). Consequently, it has become difficult to take any discussion of biblical studies seriously that does not have a social scientific dimension. Moreover, once the social phenomena rather than theologically privileged texts are taken as the matter of inquiry, scholars are led beyond the biblical materials to other early works (see Edwards 1919, Riddle 1931).

See also Greek and Roman Religions, Judaism

—*Anthony J. Blasi*

REFERENCES

R. Bendix, "Umbildungen des persönlichen Charismas," in *Max Webers Sicht des antiken Christentums,* ed. W. Schluchter (Frankfurt: Suhrkamp 1985): 404-443; P. L. Berger, "Charisma and Religious Innovation," *American Sociological Review* 28(1963):940-950; A. J. Blasi, *Early Christianity as a Social Movement* (Bern: Lang, 1988); A. J. Blasi, *Making Charisma* (New Brunswick, N.J.: Transaction, 1991); R. P. Carroll, *When Prophecy Failed* (New York: Seabury, 1979); S. J. Case, *The Social Origins of Christianity* (Chicago: University of Chicago Press, 1923); A. Causse, *Du groupe ethnique à la communauté religieuse* (Paris: Alcan, 1937); K. E. Corley, *Private Women, Public Meals* (Peabody, Mass.: Hendrickson, 1993); P. Dutcher-Walls, "The Social Location of the Deuteronomists," *Journal for the Study of the Old Testament* 52(1991):77-94; M. N. Ebertz, "Le stigmate du mouvement charismatique autour de Jésus de Nazareth," *Social Compass* 39(1992):255-273; L. P. Edwards, *The Transformation of Early Christianity* (Menashe, Wis.: Banta, 1919); J. H. Elliott, *A Home for the Homeless* (Philadelphia: Fortress, 1981); P. F. Esler, *Community and Gospel in Luke-Acts* (Cambridge: Cambridge University Press, 1987); R. K. Fenn, *The Death of Herod* (Cambridge: Cambridge University Press, 1992); A. Funk, *Status und Rollen in der Paulusbriefen* (Innsbruck: Tyrolia, 1981); J. G. Gager, *Kingdom and Community* (Englewood Cliffs, N.J.: Prentice Hall, 1975); N. K. Gottwald, *The Tribes of Yahweh* (Maryknoll, N.Y.: Orbis, 1979); B. Holmberg, *Sociology and the New Testament* (Minneapolis: Fortress, 1990); R. A. Horsley, *Sociology and the Jesus Movement* (New York: Crossroad, 1989); H. C. Kee, *Miracle in the Early Christian World* (New Haven, Conn.: Yale University Press, 1983); H. G. Kippenberg, *Religion und Klassenbildung im antiken Judäa* (Göttingen: Vandenhoeck & Ruprecht, 1978); R. S. Kraemer, *Her Share of the Blessings* (New York: Oxford

University Press, 1992); E. Lohmeyer, *Soziale Fragen im Urchristentum* (Leipzig: Quelle & Meyer, 1921); A. Malamat, "Tribal Societies," *Archives européennes de sociologie* 14(1973):126-136; A. Malamat, "Charismatic Leadership in the Book of Judges," in *Magnalia Dei*, ed. F. Cross et al. (Garden City, N.Y.: Doubleday, 1976): 152-168; A. J. Malherbe, *Social Aspects of Early Christianity* (Baton Rouge: Louisiana State University Press, 1977); D. Martindale, "Priests and Prophets in Palestine," in *Social Life and Cultural Change* (Princeton, N.J.: Van Nostrand, 1962): 239-307; W. A. Meeks, *The First Urban Christians* (New Haven, Conn.: Yale University Press, 1983); P. A. Munch, "The 'Judges' of Ancient Israel," in *Time, Place, and Circumstance*, ed. W. H. Swatos, Jr. (New York: Greenwood, 1990): 57-69; D. W. Riddle, *The Martyrs* (Chicago: University of Chicago Press, 1931); A. J. Saldarini, *Pharisees, Scribes and Sadducees in Palestinian Society* (Wilmington, Del.: Glazier, 1988); A. J. Saldarini, "The Gospel of Matthew and Jewish-Christian Conflict," in *Social History of the Matthean Community* ed. D. L. Balch (Minneapolis: Fortress, 1991): 38-61; J. T. Sanders, *Schismatics, Sectarians, Dissidents, Deviants* (Valley Forge, Pa.: Trinity, 1993); A. Schreiber, *Die Gemeinde in Korinth* (Münster: Aschendorff, 1977); R. Stark, "The Class Basis of Early Christianity," *Sociological Analysis* 47(1986):216-225; R. Stark, "Antioch as the Social Situation for Matthew's Gospel," in *Social History of the Matthean Community*, ed. D. L. Balch (Minneapolis: Fortress, 1991a): 189-210; R. Stark, "Christianizing the Urban Empire," *Sociological Analysis* 52(1991b):77-88; N. Taylor, *Paul, Antioch and Jerusalem* (Sheffield: JSOT Press, 1992); G. Theissen, *Soziologie der Jesusbewegung* (München: Kaiser, 1977); G. Theissen, *The Social Setting of Pauline Christianity* (Philadelphia: Fortress, 1982); L. Wallis, *Egoism* (Chicago: University of Chicago Press, 1905); F. Watson, *Paul, Judaism and the Gentiles* (Cambridge: Cambridge University Press, 1986); R. R. Wilson, *Prophecy and Society in Ancient Israel* (Philadelphia: Fortress, 1980); R. R. Wilson, *Sociological Approaches to the Old Testament* (Philadelphia: Fortress, 1984); J. A. Winter, "Immanence and Regime in the Kingdom of Judah," *Sociological Analysis* 44(1983):147-162; I. M. Zeitlin, *Ancient Judaism* (Cambridge: Polity Press, 1984); I. M. Zeitlin, *Jesus and the Judaism of His Time* (Cambridge: Polity Press, 1988).

BLACK CHURCH *see* African American Religious Experience

BLACK MUSLIMS *see* Nation of Islam, African American Religious Experience

BLASI, ANTHONY J. (1946–) Associate Professor of Sociology, Tennessee State University; previous appointments include the universities of Alabama, Louisville, and Hawaii, and Muskingum College, where he received the William Rainey Harper award in 1992.

Doctorates from Regis College, Toronto (theology, 1986), and the University of Notre Dame (sociology and anthropology, 1974). President, International Society for the Study of Human Ideas on Ultimate Reality and Meaning (URAM), 1996-1998.

Blasi's earliest interests were rooted in Thomistic theology and history, but he turned to sociology when confronted by Karl Mannheim's *Ideology and Utopia* (Harcourt 1955 [1929]). This explains his interest in the linkages between religious and political symbol systems and patterns of everyday life. At an early stage in his sociological development, he became a pupil of Louis Schneider at the University of Texas, who taught sociology of religion from an explicitly functionalist perspective. Rejecting functionalism, Blasi went to the University of Notre Dame to work under Fabio Dasilva and Andrew Weigert. Dasilva introduced him to the work of Gurvitch, neo-Marxist social analysis, and the phenomenology of Husserl, while Weigert introduced him to the symbolic interactionism of G. H. Mead and Alfred Schutz (on the "life-world"). His mentors in Toronto encouraged him to work on the sociology of early Christianity. Together with Richard Fenn (Princeton) and Peter Staples (Utrecht), he founded what is now the Sociology of Early Christianity Workshop in 1992.

His publications reflect not only a wide range of interests but also his attempts to find the right match between theories and cases. He also produces computerized bibliographies that are an invaluable asset to the profession.

—*Peter Staples*

REFERENCES

A. J. Blasi, *A Phenomenological Transformation of the Social Scientific Study of Religion* (Bern: Lang, 1985); A. J. Blasi, *Early Christianity as a Social Movement* (Bern: Lang, 1989); A. J. Blasi, *Making Charisma* (New Brunswick, N.J.: Transaction, 1991); A. J. Blasi (ed.), "Giudaismo e cristianesimio delle origini in prospettiva sociologica," *Religioni e Società* 24(1996):6-62.

BLIZZARD, SAMUEL W. (1914-1975) With his undergraduate work done at Maryville College (Tennessee), seminary degrees from Princeton Theological Seminary and Hartford Seminary and his Ph.D. in rural sociology from Cornell (1946), Blizzard served as a pastor (1939-1943), taught at Wooster and Penn State, and was on seminary faculties, first at Union (New York) and then Princeton.

Blizzard conducted a significant research project on the ministry, funded by the Russell Sage Foundation. He was as intent to inform seminary faculty and clergy about societal contexts affecting the ministry as he was to add this occupational knowledge to sociology. His most important articles were in professional or theological rather than sociological journals. His book *The Protestant Parish Minister: A Behavioral Science Interpretation* (Society for the Scientific Study of Religion 1985) was published after his death and includes an introduction detailing how researchers built on his framework.

Blizzard saw the ministry as a status, or set of statuses, with appropriate (normative) behaviors. He developed three concepts, from more general, or abstract, to most specific. The "master role" was how clergy perceived their ministry as alike or different from other occupations; for example, the clergy person might see her- or himself as a servant of God (a theological view). The "integrative roles" had to do with how clergy specifically saw themselves—for example, as a believer-saint, scholar, or evangelist. "Practitioner roles" dealt with specific tasks, from teacher and priest to administrator and organizer.

He reported on "the minister's dilemma," or how the minister wanted to do one thing (perhaps be a scholar) but was functionally doing another (spending considerable time on church administration, for example). Changes in society had brought considerable stress to the clergy.

—*Hart M. Nelsen*

REFERENCES

S. W. Blizzard, "The Minister's Dilemma," *Christian Century* 73(1956a):508-509; S. W. Blizzard, "Role Conflicts of the Urban Protestant Parish Ministry," *The City* 7(1956b):13-15; S. W. Blizzard, "The Protestant Parish Minister's Integrating Roles," *Religious Education* 53(1958):374-380; S. W. Blizzard, "The Parish Minister's Self-Image of His Master Roles," *Pastoral Psychology* 10(1959):27-36; J. W. Carroll and J. E. Wallace (eds.), "Special Issue in Memory of Samuel W. Blizzard," *Review of Religious Research* 23(1981):97-218 (includes complete Blizzard bibliography); H. M. Nelsen, "Why Do Pastors Preach on Social Issues?" *Theology Today* 32(1975):56-73.

BOGARDUS, EMORY S(TEPHEN) (1882-1973)

Sociologist; awarded B.A. (1908) and M.A. degrees (1909) by Northwestern University and his Ph.D. (1911) by the University of Chicago. From 1911 to 1946, he taught at the University of Southern California, and for 31 years he was Chairman of the Department of Sociology at USC, where he made an enormous contribution to the development of sociology. He founded the journal *Sociology and Social Research* and went on to edit it for more than 45 years. In 1931, he was elected President of the American Sociological Association.

With the assistance and encouragement of Robert E. Park, Bogardus produced the "Bogardus Social Distance Scale," which was widely used in social research on prejudice, including religious prejudice. The term *social distance* attempts to measure degrees of tolerance or prejudice between social groups, including religious groups (e.g., Would you want to live next to a Catholic? Would you have a Catholic into your home? Would you want your son or daughter to marry a Catholic?). The scale is assumed to be cumulative and has had the longest period of usage of any special research device developed by sociologists. This research was developed during the 1920s, when Bogardus was the Director of the Pacific Coast Race Relations Survey.

—*Luigi Tomasi*

REFERENCES

E. S. Bogardus, "A Social Distance Scale," *Sociology and Social Research* 3(1933):265-271; M. N. Neumayer, "Dr. Emory Bogardus, 1882-1973," *Sociology and Social Research* 43(1973):1-5.

BOOK OF MORMON

First published in 1830. Regarded by the Church of Jesus Christ of Latter-day Saints (Mormons) as a volume of scripture (521 pages in English) equal in authority to the Holy Bible; source of the nickname "Mormon" for the Church.

Joseph Smith, founding Mormon prophet, claimed to have translated the text into English from an original in Hebraic Egyptian engraved on golden sheets and given him temporarily by an angel. The book recounts the religious history of Semitic peoples (ancestors of today's aborigines or Indians) who had migrated to the western hemisphere and recorded a visit to ancient America by the resurrected Christ (thus the subtitle on recent editions of the book, *Another Testament of Jesus Christ*). It was first published in 1830, when Smith was only 24.

In sheer size and complexity, it is a formidable book, now translated into many languages, and not readily dismissed as the sheer fabrication of an unlettered youth. Yet, understandably, it has never been taken seriously as a work of ancient scripture by non-Mormon scholars, who have usually explained it as the product of hidden authorship or of sheer plagiarism (perhaps based on *View of the Hebrews* by Ethan Smith, no relation to Joseph). Accordingly, no exegetical or hermeneutical treatment of the book has been undertaken by non-Mormon scholars, although in more recent years they have started to take the book more seriously as a legitimate, if rather imaginative, nineteenth-century American religious treatise (e.g., O'Dea 1957, Stendahl 1984).

For Mormons, the book provides the most convincing and palpable testimony to Smith's divine calling, and much effort has been expended to vindicate it through scientific scholarship, including Meso-American archaeological explorations and research, textual analyses searching for Hebraisms and other links with ancient Semitic literature, and statistical analyses of "word-prints" or stylistic differences among the various ancient American prophets and scribes named as authors of the various sections within the book (to refute non-Mormon claims of single authorship by Smith). Archaeological and geographic support for the book generally has been lacking, the most sophisticated effort being that of Sorenson (1985).

Despite the obvious Mormon bias in the various kinds of textual analysis, the scholarship in recent years has been formidable if not incontrovertible. The best examples have been collected and published by the Foundation for Ancient Research and Mormon Studies (FARMS) at Brigham Young University, beginning with the work of Hugh Nibley, a seasoned scholar of ancient languages. Other Mormon scholars have been critical of such church-sponsored research and have produced a counterliterature akin to that which might be expected from non-Mormon critics (see, e.g., Metcalf 1993, Larson 1977). Less heterodox Mormon scholars (but not church sponsored) have explored the human elements and uses of the book in ways that do not necessarily question its ultimately supernatural origins (e.g., Van Wagoner and Walker 1982, Ostler 1987, Underwood 1984).

See also Mormonism, Joseph Smith

—*Armand L. Mauss*

REFERENCES

S. Larson, "Textual Variants in Book of Mormon Manuscripts," *Dialogue* 10(1977):8-30; D. H. Ludlow (ed.), *Encyclopedia of Mormonism* (New York: Macmillan, 1992 [various entries on Book of Mormon]); B. L. Metcalf (ed.), *New Approaches to the Book of Mormon* (Salt Lake City: Signature Books, 1993); H. Nibley, *The Collected Works of Hugh Nibley*, vols. 5-8 (Salt Lake City: Deseret, 1989); T. F. O'Dea, *The Mormons* (Chicago: University of Chicago Press, 1957); B. T. Ostler, "The Book of Mormon as a Modern Expansion of an Ancient Source," *Dialogue* 20(1987):66-124; B. H. Roberts, *Studies of the Book of Mormon* (Urbana: University of Illinois Press, 1985); J. L. Sorenson, *An Ancient American Setting for the Book of Mormon* (Salt Lake City: Deseret, 1985); K. Stendahl, "The Sermon on the Mount and Third Nephi in the Book of Mormon," in *Meanings*, ed. K. Stendahl (Philadelphia: Fortress, 1984): 99-113; G. Underwood, "Book of Mormon usage in early L.D.S. theology," *Dialogue* 17(1984):35-74; R. Van Wagoner and S. Walker, "Joseph Smith," *Dialogue* 15(1982):49-68.

BORN AGAIN   *see* Evangelicalism

BOUMA, GARY D. (1942–)   American-born sociologist, now resident in Australia; Ph.D., Cornell University, 1970.

A second-generation sociologist, Bouma also has been a Presbyterian minister and is a priest in the Anglican Church of Australia. He has maintained both academic and ecclesiastical involvement throughout his career, serving a variety of parishes and teaching in seminaries as well as sustaining a full role in the two departments he has served. After 10 years at Dalhousie University in Nova Scotia, he moved to Monash University in 1979, where he now holds a Personal Chair of Sociology in the Department of Anthropology and Sociology, which is a rare honor for academics in Australia and indicates the high regard of his colleagues and university. He also has had a visiting four-year fellowship at the Australian National University with the Reshaping Australian Institutions Project.

His main interests include the sociology of religion in Australia, sociology of the family, and social science research methodology. He is the author of 16 books and many articles and chapters widely ranging over the sociology of religion, sociology of ministry, and sociology of theology. His research has primarily focused on the interaction between religion and society in Western societies including Canada, the United States, Australia, New Zealand, and Europe. These comparisons have been made quite real by extended periods of residence and serving parishes in a variety of countries. The insights gained by hands-on involvement in ministry and the opportunity to stand back and reflect is an important part of his personal sociological methodology.

Bouma's major research projects have included a sociology of conservative Calvinism, several studies of clergy, religion, and migration, and ongoing work on a sociology of theology. Following the publication of his *Mosques and Muslim Settlement in Australia* (AGPS 1994), he has begun a study of Buddhist settlement in Australia, and the role and place of Japanese religions (focusing on Mahikari and Zen). His current work includes a major study of religious plurality in multicultural Australia, the theory of institutions, and postmodernity as a context for doing theology.

—*James T. Richardson*

REFERENCES

G. Bouma, *The Religious Factor in Australian Life* (Melbourne: Marc, 1986); G. Bouma, *Religion* (Melbourne: Longmans, 1992); G. Bouma, "The Emergence of Religious Plurality in Australia," *Sociology of Religion* 56(1995):285-302.

BOURDIEU, PIERRE (1930–)   Social science professor at the Collège de France.

Bourdieu's sociological approach may be described as "structural constructivism," starting from the objectivity of social structures but taking the subjective experience of these structures into account. This is expressed in his core concepts, *habitus* and *fields,* which stress the objectivity of dispositions, practices, and spaces of positions but allow for recombinations and innovations. He critically analyzed Weber's theory of religious power using his notion of field, that is, differentiating categories of laypersons in relation to various religious agents. He also analyzed the domestication of those dominated by religion, and in the field of symbolic power, he made a study of the French bishops.

—*Karel Dobbelaere*

REFERENCES

P. Bourdieu, "Une interpretation de la théorie de la religion selon Max Weber," *Archives Européennes de Sociologie* 12(1971a):3-21; P. Bourdieu, "Genèse et structure du champ religieux," *Revue Française de Sociologie* 12(1971b):295-334; P. Bourdieu and M. de Saint Martin, "La sainte famille," *Actes de la recherche en sciences sociales* 44-45(1982):2-53.

BOURG, CARROLL JULIAN (1928–)   Then Jesuit Carroll Bourg earned the Ph.D. at Brandeis University in 1967, writing on the contrast between the critical and historical tradition of sociological thought, on the one hand, and contemporary theory, on the other. His examination of the 1960s civil rights and ecumenical movements showed the relevance of a critical sensitivity and historical vision. He advocated the latter for sociology using the term *sociology as participation.*

Bourg taught briefly at Boston College and Woodstock College, left the Jesuit order, married, and took up a position at Fisk University, where he worked until retirement in 1996. He served as editor of *Sociological Analysis* (1973-1980), in many respects defining the character of that journal, which holds under its current title, *Sociology of Religion.* He was President of the Association for the Sociology of Religion in 1980.

Bourg's thoughtful and conceptually oriented writings reveal a continuing interest in a participatory sociology, the Jesuits, the participatory endeavors of youth, the compass of sociology as a discipline, religion, and the well-being of the elderly. The social scientific study of religion has benefitted from a series of his book reviews (some 17 between 1981 and 1996), which reflect an insightful and broadly informed intellect, and from his participation in published symposia on civil religion and on the work of theologian Harvey Cox.

—*Anthony J. Blasi*

BRAHMINS   *see* Hinduism

BRAINWASHING   A term, first coined and introduced into popular use in 1953 by CIA-connected journalist Edward Hunter, that refers to a putative psychotechnology capable of subverting the free will and mentally enslaving persons subjected to its effects.

In its original Chinese usage, "to cleanse [or wash clean] thoughts," the term was an ideological concept referring to sociopolitical attitude "correction." However, the subsequent American literature transformed the concept into a sometimes coercive, sometimes subtle seductive and hypnotic process of mind control against which the average person is helpless. A post-Korean War literature (predominantly based on either thought reform seminars employed in "Revolutionary Colleges" or the harsh treatment of American POWs during the Korean War) produced primarily by clinical psychologists and psychiatrists elaborated these claims.

The term *brainwashing* (and related terms such as *menticide, mind control, coercive persuasion, thought control, spiritual hypnosis*) was resurrected in the early 1970s by the modern American anti-cult movement (ACM), and its use spread during the 1980s to Europe, Australia, and other regions of the world. Anti-cult groups seized on the post-Korean War literature as evidence that the unconventional lifestyle/spiritual choices their loved ones apparently made were not in fact freewill decisions. Rather, they alleged, new religious movement (NRM) leaders had perfected potent brainwashing mechanisms that superficially resembled spiritual conversion but in fact rested on coercive mind control techniques. The concept allowed the ACM to distinguish between legitimate religious groups and those that they labeled "cults." For families with relatives involved in any one of a wide range of NRMs, brainwashing functioned to conceal conflicts and deflect feelings of guilt and blame experienced by both family members and former NRM adherents.

Behavioral scientists who were sympathetic with the ACM's goals and became spokespersons for its viewpoint developed more sophisticated versions of the brainwashing concept, adding terms such as *cult-imposed thought patterns, cult-imposed personality syndromes,* and *dissociative states.* The most sophisticated formulation of the ACM perspective has been developed by Margaret Singer in her "systematic manipulation of social influence" model (SMSI), and the most articulate critique of the ACM perspective has been formulated by Dick Anthony and Thomas Robbins. It was the distinction between cultic and legitimate groups, resting on various versions of the brainwashing concept, that was the focal point of the cult controversy beginning in the 1970s. The ACM sought to legitimate its brainwashing argument in legislative and judicial forums but met with sufficient opposition from NRMs and most social scientists who conducted field studies on these movements that these concepts were not accorded official standing in state regulatory agencies.

See also Anti-Cult Movement, New Religious Movements

—*Anson Shupe and David G. Bromley*

REFERENCES

D. Anthony, "Religious Movements and 'Brainwashing' Litigation," in *In Gods We Trust*, ed. T. Robbins and D. Anthony (New Brunswick, N.J.: Transaction, 1990): 295-344; D. Anthony and T. Robbins, "The 'Brainwashing' Exception to the First Amendment," *Behavioral Sciences and the Law* 10(1992):5-30; D. G. Bromley and J. T. Richardson (eds.), *The Brainwashing/Deprogramming Controversy* (Lewiston, N.Y.: Mellen, 1984); E. Hunter, *Brainwashing in Red China* (New York: Vanguard, 1953); E. Hunter, *Brainwashing from Pavlov to Powers* (New York: Bookmailer, 1962); R. J. Lifton, *Thought Reform and the Psychology of Totalism* (New York: Norton, 1963); J. Meerlo, *The Rape of the Mind* (New York: World, 1956); W. Sargent, *Battle for the Mind* (New York: Doubleday, 1957); A. Shupe and D. G. Bromley, *The New Vigilantes* (Beverly Hills, Calif.: Sage, 1980); M. Singer and J. Lalich, *Cults in Our Midst* (San Francisco: Jossey-Bass, 1995).

BRANCH DAVIDIAN　　*see* David Koresh

BREWER, EARL D. C. (1914-1993)　　Among other degrees, awarded the B.D. from Candler School of Theology (1941) and the Ph.D. from the University of North Carolina (1951). He was Professor of Sociology and Religion at Emory University and served as the Director of Research of the National Council of Churches (1967-1969). President, Religious Research Association, 1974-1975.

Brewer's publications reflected a wide spectrum of interests and concerns: adaptation of theological schools in modern society, religion in Southern Appalachia, attitudes toward racially mixed church memberships, the employment of women in church executive positions, religion and the ministry, and aging. Perhaps his classic work was a surprisingly brief but effective essay titled "Sect and Church in Methodism" (1952) in which he traces the movement of American Methodism from sect to church, from poverty to a well-developed religious (and economic) institution with a growing acceptance of the American normative order.

—*Hart M. Nelsen*

REFERENCES

E. D. C. Brewer, "Sect and Church in Methodism," *Social Forces* 30(1952):400-408; E. D. C. Brewer, "Religion and the Churches," in *The Southern Appalachian Region*, ed. T. R. Ford (Lexington: University of Kentucky Press, 1962): 201-218.

BRICOLAGE　　Concept coined by Claude Lévi-Strauss, first used in the sociology of religion by Thomas Luckmann. It signals the individualization of religion: People "pick and choose" what to believe, selecting their preferred religious practices and ethical options. This phenomenon has been called "religion à la carte" because people disregard the set church "menu": In their religious outlook, they mix elements from different religions and incorporate folk-religious practices, superstitions, and ideas typical of psychoanalysis and group dynamics. As a consequence, one may allude to religious recomposition or refer to a patchwork: different elements integrated in a personal religious system.

—*Karel Dobbelaere*

REFERENCES

R. W. Bibby, *Fragmented Gods* (Toronto: Irwin Publishing, 1987); T. Luckmann, "The Structural Conditions of Religious Consciousness in Modern Societies," *Japanese Journal of Religious Studies* 6(1979):121-137; L. Voyé, "From Institutional Catholicism to Christian Inspiration," in *The Post-War Generation and Establishment Religion,* ed. W. C. Roof et al. (Boulder, Colo.: Westview, 1995): 191-206.

BROMLEY, DAVID G. (1941–) Professor of Sociology and Religious Studies at Virginia Commonwealth University. Bromley received his B.A. degree in sociology from Colby College in 1963 and his M.A. (1966) and Ph.D. degrees (1971) in sociology from Duke University. He has served on the faculties of the University of Virginia, University of Texas at Arlington, and the University of Hartford. President, Association for the Sociology of Religion, 1994.

Bromley's early work was concentrated in deviant behavior as well as political sociology and urban sociology. His extensive work in religion reflects his interests in political organization and processes, conflict theory, and the social construction of deviance. One line of work has taken an organizational perspective on religious movements. In his early book on the Unificationist Movement, *"Moonies" in America: Cult, Church and Crusade* (with Anson Shupe, Sage 1979), Bromley employed resource mobilization theory to interpret the growth and development of that movement. He has continued to pursue related organizational issues such as movement economic structure (1985) and movement success, particularly in *The Future of New Religious Movements* (with Phillip Hammond, Mercer University Press 1987). Bromley's interests in politics and deviance are reflected in a second line of work analyzing the interactive relationship between new religious movements and countermovements, treating movement and countermovement as the unit of analysis. This approach to the study of controversial "cults" initially entailed a trio of books: *"Moonies" in America, The New Vigilantes* (with Shupe, Sage 1980), and *Strange Gods: The Great American Cult Scare* (with Shupe, Beacon 1981). It continues with his contribution to *The Handbook on Cults and Sects in America* (with Jeffrey Hadden, JAI 1993). In the process of analyzing religious movement mobilization and antimovement social control efforts, Bromley has examined a diverse array of issues. These include the narratives constructed to discredit new religions such as "brainwashing accounts" (with James Richardson, 1984) and "atrocity tales" (with Shupe, 1979), the "deprogramming" process of forcibly extricating members of new religions from those groups (1988), and governmental regulations aimed at controlling a variety of organizational practices by new religions (with Thomas Robbins, 1992). Bromley also has extensively researched the "anti-cult movement" as an integral part of treating movement and countermovement as an analytic unit.

Following *The New Vigilantes,* Bromley and Anson Shupe have become the primary social science interpreters of that countermovement in a series of books and articles. The most recent examines anti-cultism on an international level (Shupe and Bromley 1994). Finally, Bromley has compared the moral panic surrounding religious "cults" with the related agitation positing the existence of a widespread conspiratorial network of satanic cults engaged in pervasive ritual abuse of children (Richardson et al. 1991). Bromley's work connects both anti-cult and antisatanist crusades to structural tensions involving deepening contradictions between contractual and covenantal forms of social relations. Bromley is currently broadening his focus to include institutional as well as social movement forms of religion, arguing that reactions to historic contractual-covenantal tensions may be observed in movements and organizational innovations within mainstream churches as well as the formation of more marginal religious movements (1997).

Bromley has provided significant leadership in professional associations of social scientists dedicated to the study of religion. He has been elected to the Executive Councils of both the Association for the Sociology of Religion (ASR) and the Society for the Scientific Study of Religion (SSSR). He is the founding editor of the ASR series, Religion and the Social Order (JAI), which produces volumes annually examining new developments and perspectives in the social scientific study of religion. In the SSSR, he has served as Editor of the *Journal for the Scientific Study of Religion*.

—*Thomas Robbins*

REFERENCES

D. G. Bromley, "The Economic Structure of the Unificationist Movement," *Journal for the Scientific Study of Religion* 24(1985):253-274; D. G. Bromley, "Deprogramming as a Mode of Exit from New Religious Movements," in *Falling from the Faith* (Newbury Park, Calif.: Sage, 1988): 166-184; D. G. Bromley, "A Sociological Narrative of Crisis Episodes, Collective Action, Culture Workers, and Countermovements," *Sociology of Religion* 58(1997):105-140; D. G. Bromley and J. T. Richardson (eds.), *The Brainwashing/Deprogramming Controversy* (Lewiston, N.Y.: Mellen, 1984); D. G. Bromley and T. Robbins, "The Role of Government in Regulating New and Unconventional Religions," in *Governmental Monitoring of Religion,* ed. J. Wood (Waco, Texas: Baylor University Press, 1992): 101-137; D. G. Bromley and A. Shupe, "Atrocity Tales, the Unification Church, and the Social Construction of Evil," *Journal of Communication* 29(1979):42-53; J. T. Richardson et al. (eds.), *The Satanism Scare* (Hawthorne, N.Y.: Aldine de Gruyter, 1991); A. Shupe and D. G. Bromley (eds.), *Anti-Cult Movements in Cross-Cultural Perspective* (New York: Garland, 1994).

BROPHY, MARY LIGUORI (1901-1982)

Already possessing a law degree from DePaul University before entering the Sisters of Charity (B.V.M.) in 1926 (in 1965 she was the only Catholic nun to be a member of the Illinois State Bar), Sister M. Liguori later earned an M.A. in sociology and economics from the University of Notre Dame, adding in 1943 a Ph.D. in sociology from Catholic University of America. Melvin Williams, in his *Catholic Social Thought* (1950:92), considered her doctoral dissertation among "the most important research by American Catholics on social thought that has been produced." Professor and Chair of Sociology at Mundelein College (Chicago), Sister M. Liguori served until 1980 as teacher, attorney/scholar, social justice advocate, and researcher. In 1971, she was appointed Assistant Dean and Professor at Saints Junior College in Mississippi.

Sister M. Liguori was one of the early organizers of the American Catholic Sociological Society, helping Ralph Gallagher S.J. in the first organizational meeting of March 1938. Hers was a moderating and supportive voice, frequently interpreting for others Gallagher's decisions in his early years as Executive Secretary. She served as the organization's Treasurer until the position was joined to that of the Executive Secretary. She also

served in various capacities on the executive committee of ACSS for a number of years.

Sister M. Liguori's research interests were within the fields of sociology and economics, and they centered upon changing neighborhoods and social justice. She published little, because her emphasis was on the applied aspects of the social sciences.

—*Loretta M. Morris*

BRUNNER, EDMUND DE S(CHWINITZ) (1889-1973)

Receiving his B.A., Ph.D., and B.D. degrees from Moravian College and Seminary, Edmund de S. Brunner was, in order, a pastor, Moravian church representative on the Rural Church Commission of the Federal Council of Churches, Director of Rural Investigations of the Institute for Social and Religious Research, and professor at Columbia University Teachers College (retiring in 1955). He lectured in rural sociology and also taught in Australia and New Zealand and at Western Connecticut State College (1957-1967). He held numerous appointed assignments, some at the federal level. He is best known for his study of the role of the church in the rural community. He wrote or cowrote many books, including *The Protestant Church as a Social Institution* (Harper 1935, with H. Paul Douglass), *American Society: Urban and Rural Patterns* (Harper 1955, with Wilbur C. Hallenbeck), *The Study of Rural Society* (Houghton Mifflin 1935, with John H. Kolb [reprinted 1952]). He was president of the Rural Sociological Society (1945). He delivered the first of the Religious Research Association series of lectures in honor of H. Paul Douglass (*Review of Religious Research* 1[1959]:3-16, 63-75).

—*Hart M. Nelsen*

BUBER, MARTIN (1878-1965)

Philosopher, theologian, Zionist thinker and leader, born in Vienna. As a child, Buber lived with his grandfather, a noted midrash scholar.

Buber was an active Zionist who emphasized education, dialogue, and the establishment of a joint Arab-Israeli state. His earliest works retold Hasidic tales (e.g., *Tales of Rabbi Nachman* and *The Legend of the Baal Shem,* 1906, 1908, in German). His *I and Thou* (first German edition, 1923) set forth his philosophical position and won lasting acclaim. In this work he distinguishes "I-it," or instrumental relations, from "I-Thou" relations, which he describes in humanistic terms. The I-Thou relationship leads to his notion of God as the Eternal Thou.

Buber was the first head of the Department of Social Relations at Hebrew University (Jerusalem), joining it as Professor of Social Philosophy in 1938 after the Gestapo forbade his lectures in Germany. He taught there until his retirement in 1951.

—*M. Herbert Danzger*

REFERENCE

M. A. Beek and S. Weiland, *Martin Buber* (Westminster, Md.: Newman, 1968).

BUDDHISM The founder of Buddhism is a Hindu, Sakyamuni (also: Siddhartha Gautama), meaning "the sage of the Shake tribe," a group that lived in what is today Nepal. His followers called him "the Buddha" or "enlightened one." Gautama lived from 563 to 483 B.C.E.

His life is a model for Buddhists to follow. Gautama was the son of an Indian ruler and was expected to follow in his father's footsteps. The father feared his son would become an ascetic, so he tried to shield him from all suffering. But Gautama

saw four visions: the first was a man weakened with age, utterly helpless; the second was the sight of a man mere skin and bones, supremely unhappy and forlorn, smitten with some pest; the third was the sight of a band of lamenting kinsmen bearing on their shoulders the corpse of one beloved for cremation. These woeful signs deeply moved him. The fourth vision, however, made a lasting impression. He saw a recluse, calm and serene. (Piyadassi 1964:12)

These encounters with suffering deeply affected Gautama. At the age of 29, on the day his wife was to give birth to a son, he renounced wife, child, father, and crown. Gautama tried to find peace by practicing rigorous self-mortification. This failed. Finally, Gautama discovered the middle way between sensual indulgence and self-mortification and began a life of meditation, the true path. Thereafter he was a teacher and lived as a mendicant peripatetic. Because of the emphasis on self-help, Buddhism has been called "a true warrior's religion" (Piyadassi 1964:168).

Buddhism originated as part of a *chromatic* movement, that is, a movement centered on wandering ascetics. Some 2,500 years ago, the region that included Nepal was undergoing social change as a result of new technologies and urbanization. The old social order based on kinship groups was crumbling. The power and privileges of the Brahmans were being challenged. The chromatic movement was both a religious movement and a protest against the existing caste system (Gómez 1989).

The Jewels of Buddhism The Buddhist laity take refuge in, that is, confess faith in, "the three jewels": the Buddha, his teachings (the *dharma*), and the *shanghai* (the monks, or, more broadly, the living and dead enlightened ones). The basic social structural element is the master-disciple relationship. Buddhists are not required to attend the temple rituals, which are based on the lunar calendar. "The holy days occur at the new moon, the full moon, and eight days after each, making them about a week apart" (Corbett 1994:264). Buddhists may have a shrine in their homes with a statue of Buddha, or a statue representing an aspect of Buddha, or a statue of some other enlightened one. Buddhists who reside temporarily or permanently in a monastery lead a highly structured, ritualized life. (For a detailed description of life in a Korean monastery, see Bushel 1992; in an American Zen Center, see Preston 1988.) The monk's life involves solitude, poverty, and moderation.

Central to Buddhism are the Four Noble Truths: "Suffering . . . i.e., the illness; craving . . . is . . . the root cause of the illness . . . [T]hrough the removal of craving the illness is removed and that is the cure . . . . The Eightfold Path . . . i.e., the remedy" (Piyadassi 1964:39). The cravings that must be given up include longings for money, revenge, affection, household love, and success. The Path involves being virtuous, which allows concentration, which results in wisdom.

Within Buddhism it is said that reality is empty. Reality is an unbroken flow, which we divide up into some things causing other things (the doctrine of "dependent arising"). Nothing is permanent or nothing exists. One of the earliest texts, for example, contains this statement:

Purity is not [attained] by views, or learning,
   by knowledge, or by moral rules, and rites.
Nor is it [attained] by the absence of views,
   learning, knowledge, rules or rites.
Abandoning all these, not grasping at them,
   he is at peace; not relying, he would not
   hanker for becoming.
   (quoted in Gómez 1989:47-48)

Even Buddhism is empty.

Wisdom produces *nibbana* (the word in Pali, which is used in the Theravada tradition) or *nirvana* (the word in Sanskrit, which is used in the Mahayana tradition). This condition is essentially a mystery. It is living beyond good and evil, and actions have no consequences for the actor. In nirvana a person has experiences but remains attached to nothing. Giving up craving is natural to a wise person because he or she knows that all is transient; all is becoming and therefore impossible to cling to. Ultimately, one realizes there is no self, no "I," who might possess something. Signs of having achieved nirvana in one's lifetime would be a lack of dissatisfaction, a lack of attachments, and peacefulness.

Karma is the belief that suffering is caused by former acts of evil and that people are born into the social status they earned in previous lives. It is the Buddhist attempt to explain injustice in the world. Nirvana is the transcendence of the karmic principle. However, if wisdom includes realizing there is no self, the existence of karma seems challenged.

> This leads to a reinterpretation of reincarnation, because nothing goes through the rebirth process. Buddhists simply say that each lifetime is connected to the ones before it, and will be connected to those that come after it, in a chain of causation. The analogy of lighting the wick of one candle from the flame of another is often used. Nothing is transmitted from candle to candle, but the flame of the second is unarguably connected to the flame of the first. (Corbett 1994:259)

The emphasis given wisdom is balanced, perhaps, by the importance of compassion *(metta)*. This attitude has been described as love without a desire to possess, without lust, without profit-seeking.

Although monks aspire for wisdom and nirvana, most people settle for virtue and a good rebirth. Virtue for the common person means obeying five precepts—to abstain from killing anything that breathes, from stealing, from sexual misconduct, from lying, and from using intoxicants. Folk Buddhism, that is, the form of Buddhism among the nonliterate people, involves making merit—for example, by supporting monks or by listening to the chanting of Buddhist texts, even if one does not understand them, as long as the listening has a spiritually uplifting effect. Folk Buddhists also emphasize transferring merit to the dead, believing in a future saviorlike Buddha *(Maitre)*, and a belief in paradise. The images of paradise "are entirely sensuous, offering the worldly pleasures so rarely encountered in the real social life of a peasant community. Women, music, dancing, and 'wish-fulfilling trees,' which give the individual whatever he wants, characterize the sensual delights of heaven" (Obeyesekere 1968:29).

For Buddhists, then, there are a variety of focal points—Buddha himself, the attainment of wisdom by meditation, and being virtuous to have a good rebirth.

The Types of Buddhism　The three major divisions of Buddhism are *Theravada, Mahayana,* and *Vajrayana.* The first school is dominant in South and Southeast Asia. Mahayana Buddhism is most influential in the Chinese and Japanese versions of this religion. Theravada and Mahayana coexist in Malaysia and Singapore. Vajrayana is most influential in Tibet and wherever Tibetan monks have gained influence. In the Theravada world, Buddhism tended to be the religion of elites; in the Mahayana world, it coexisted with other religions (e.g., Taoism, Shinto) and, among the masses, became part of the folk religions.

Vajrayana Buddhism (also called esoteric Buddhism or Tantric Buddhism) is strongest within Tibetan Buddhism but has influenced the entire Mahayana world (e.g., the Japanese Swinging school). Vajrayana Buddhists use texts (called *Tantras*) based on deliberately obscure symbolism. They incorporate magical techniques and a rich supply of symbols originating in folk traditions. *Mantras* (i.e., magical speech) and visualization techniques are used. More than in the other traditions, sense experience, sexual imagery, and the imagination are means to achieve spiritual progress. In some schools, the ritual performance of sexual acts is a spiritual technique.

Theravada Buddhism "has a fixed body of canonical literature, a relatively unified orthodox teaching, a clearly structured institutional distinction between the monastic order and laity, and a long history as the established 'church' of the various Southeast Asian states" (Poured 1968:165). Theravadins use a statement attributed to Buddha: "He who would be an *arhat* [an enlightened one] should not do good deeds." To reach a point at which a meditative life is a realistic option, one must have been good. However, after that point, Theravadins believe one must withdraw because involvement with others inevitably results in good and bad karma. "Salvation must therefore ultimately be sought in a total renunciation of society and of the world" (Obeyesekere 1968:20). Within Theravada Buddhism, hermit monks epitomize this ideal.

Mahayana Buddhism is less centralized and is more diverse than the Theravada tradition. Mahayana Buddhism is also less dependent on the state than its Theravada counterpart. Moreover, the Mahayana laity are perceived to be able to reach a higher spiritual level than in the Theravada tradition. Finally, the Mahayana tradition attaches great prestige to being a *Bodhisattva*. This is a person "who, although worthy of nirvana, sacrifices this ultimate satisfaction in order to help all sentient creatures with acts of love and compassion" (Poured 1968:171).

There are two distinct strands of Chinese Buddhism popular today: Pure Land (Japanese: Jodo) and Ch'an (Japanese: Zen). Pure Land asserts that people can be saved by having faith in Amitabha, a Buddha. The ritual developed to help people achieve this faith involves the countless repetitions of Amitabha's name. Amitabha resides in the "Western Paradise," which is a place of beautiful music, jewels, and gardens. Although Pure Land Buddhism condemns worldly attachment, more than Ch'an it is solicitous about mundane problems. Prominent in Pure Land Buddhism is the Bodhisattva Kuan Yin, goddess of mercy, who is concerned about this world. So, for instance, Chinese pray to her for children.

According to Ch'an Buddhism, our nature is Buddha. The task is to strip away conceptualizations and to calm our passions. This can be done in a monastery, at work, or in the home. Meditation is important as is a form of study based on asking paradoxical questions (in Japanese: *koans*) meant to make us aware of the artificiality of language and therefore culture.

> "I have no peace of mind," said Hui-K'o. "Please pacify my mind."
>
> "Bring out your mind here before me," replied Bohdidharma, "and I will pacify it."
>
> "But when I seek my mind," said Hui-K'o, "I cannot find it."
>
> "There!" snapped Bohdidharma, "I have pacified your mind." (quoted in Watts 1959:92)

The enlightened person is nonattached (neither indifferent nor attached), spontaneous, and compassionate. The focus is on the here and now, not a future paradise. More than Pure Land Buddhism, the Ch'an version is a "warrior's religion."

Social Organization Within Buddhism These two versions of Buddhism, along with tantric influences, exist throughout the Mahayana world. The actual social organization is complex, as Mahayana Buddhism is divided into a variety of schools. Whereas in China various schools may be followed by monks in the same monastery, in Japan each monastery is affiliated with just one school. The Nichiren school, which gives preeminence to the Lotus sutra and emphasizes the desirability of close ties with the state, is specifically Japanese. The best known such group is Nichiren

Shoshu. Distinctive of Japan is that monks who belong to some branches of the Pure Land school may be married.

Based on a study of a Korean monastery, Bushel (1992) has questioned some shibboleths about Zen-type Buddhism. First, monks do not spend a lot of time studying texts. Second, a majority of residents at the monastery do not meditate; the crucial aspect of the monk's life is leading a disciplined life (see also King 1980, Finney 1991). Third, the meditative practice followed by the monks does not require the monastic life; that is, the monk's Buddhism is not only for an elite.

Buddhism does not have a strong organizational base. In South Asia, the *shanghai* has depended on state support, which makes the shanghai vulnerable. In East Asia, there is no widely accepted authority able to define orthodoxy or to lead a process of adaptation to modernity; moreover, East Asian states have used Confucianism more than Buddhism to form civic moralities (Tamney 1993). In the communist-controlled countries, Buddhism has been weakened by public policies, such as the confiscation of Buddhist land and buildings by the state.

Modernization and Buddhism At least since the beginning of the twentieth century, Buddhists have been transforming their religion in response to modernization (e.g., on China, see Welch 1968). Traditional cultures have declined in importance. For instance, in South Asia modernization ended the dominance of the "traditional Buddhist-Brahmanic-animistic synthesis." Reformed doctrines have the following characteristics:

> an emphasis on the ethical dimensions of the tradition at the expense of the supernatural and mythical; a rejection of magical elements of popular thought and practice as incompatible with the authentic tradition; and a rationalization of Buddhist thought in terms of Western categories, along with an apologetic interest in depicting Buddhism as scientific. (Swearer 1989:134)

Other changes include more influence for laypeople and the political involvement of monks and laity. To accommodate the needs of laypeople, the meditation techniques taught by monks have been simplified (King 1980). Buddhists are more involved in community education and charitable endeavors, some of which are modeled on Christian programs. At the same time, Buddhist cults led by charismatic monks are a new form of Buddhism.

Buddhism has gained popular attention, and perhaps popularity, by becoming political, especially in South Asia. In India, a neo-Buddhist movement that presents Buddhism as a social gospel has led a protest against the caste system (Ling 1980). In Burma and Sri Lanka, Buddhism was an aspect of nationalist movements for independence (Smith 1965, Houtart 1980). During the 1980s, many monks were actively involved in politicking and even political violence in Sri Lanka (Tambiah 1993).

Buddhism is also being influenced by the women's movement. Traditionally, women played an inferior role in Buddhism, although there have always been orders of nuns (Paul 1985). Probably women have influenced Buddhism most in the United States. Where American women practitioners are influential, they shape Buddhism in distinctive ways:

(1) minimizing power differences and bringing warmth to all relationships, (2) working with emotions and the body, (3) group activity that promotes sharing experiences and open communication; "effort" and "striving" are being replaced by "healing" and "openness," and (4) an activist orientation based on a vision that the essential fact about the universe is interrelatedness. (Tamney 1992:95)

As Buddhism adapts to modernity, its appeal and influence seem to be growing. Buddhists have developed elaborate schemes for describing the inner working of human beings and various methods for training the mind that result in "liberation." The psychological insights of Buddhism have attracted self-conscious, educated people. Meditation has become widely valued for medical and spiritual reasons. Among Westerners, the Buddhism they encounter is appealing because it is not puritanical, is not dogmatic, and emphasizes religious experience, not religious beliefs. Moreover, Westerners are interested in Buddhism as part of New Age multiculturalism or because this religion seems con- sonant with the detachment accompanying postmodernism (Tamney 1992). As Asians modernize, some of them will likely discover, and be attracted to, a form of Buddhism that is taking shape in the Western world.

See also Compassion, Hinduism, Jainism, Shinto, Taoism

—*Joseph B. Tamney*

REFERENCES

R. E. Buswell, Jr., *The Zen Monastic Experience* (Princeton, N.J.: Princeton University Press, 1992); J. M. Corbett, *Religion in America*, 2nd ed. (Englewood Cliffs, N.J.: Prentice Hall, 1994); H. C. Finney, "American Zen's 'Japan Connection,' " *Sociological Analysis* 52(1991):379-396; L. O. Gómez, "Buddhism in India," in *The Religious Traditions of Asia*, ed. J. Kitagawa (New York: Macmillan, 1989): 41-96; F. Houtart, *Religion and Ideology in Sri Lanka* (Maryknoll, N.Y.: Orbis, 1980); W. L. King, *Theravada Meditation* (University Park: Pennsylvania State University Press, 1980); T. Ling, *Buddhist Revival in India* (New York: St. Martin's, 1980); G. Obeyesekere, "Theodicy, Sin, and Salvation in a Sociology of Buddhism," in *Dialectic in Practical Religion*, ed. E. R. Leach (Cambridge: Cambridge University Press, 1968): 7-40; P. A. Pardue, "Buddhism," in *International Encyclopedia of the Social Sciences*, ed. D. Sills (New York: Macmillan, 1968): 196-184; D. Y. Paul, *Women in Buddhism*, 2nd ed. (Berkeley: University of California Press, 1985); T. Piyadassi, *The Buddha's Ancient Path* (London: Rider, 1964); D. L. Preston, *The Social Organization of Zen Practice* (Cambridge: Cambridge University Press, 1988); D. E. Smith, *Religion and Politics in Burma* (Princeton, N.J.: Princeton University Press, 1965); D. K. Swearer, "Buddhism in Southeast Asia," in *The Religious Traditions of Asia*, ed. J. Kitagawa (New York: Macmillan, 1989): 119-142; S. J. Tambiah, "Buddhism, Politics, and Violence in Sri Lanka," in *Fundamentalisms and the State*, ed. M. E. Marty and R. S. Appleby (Chicago: University of Chicago Press, 1993): 589-619; J. B. Tamney, *American Society in the Buddhist Mirror* (New York: Garland, 1992): J. B. Tamney, "Religion in Capitalist East Asia," in *A Future for Religion?* ed. W. H. Swatos, Jr. (Newbury Park, Calif.: Sage, 1993): 55-72; A. W. Watts, *The Way of Zen* (New York: New American Library, 1959); H. Welch, *The Buddhist Revival in China* (Cambridge: Harvard University Press, 1968).

BURHOE, RALPH W. (1911-1997) Harvard College, 1928-1932; Andover-Newton Theological School, 1934-1936. Sc.D., Meadville-Lombard Theological School, 1975; L.H.D., Rollins College, 1979. Professor Emeritus of Theology and Science, Meadville-Lombard Theological School; founding member of the Society for the Scientific Study of Religion (SSSR).

Burhoe was an advocate in the SSSR for including the natural, as well as the social, sciences in its purview. Failing in that endeavor, he created, in 1954, the Institute for Religion in the Age of Science (IRIS). In 1980, he was the first American recipient of the Templeton Prize for progress in religion. Founder of the journal *Zygon*, Burhoe served as its Editor from 1966 to 1979. In 1984, he was presented with the SSSR's first Distinguished Career Award.

—*Charles Y. Glock*

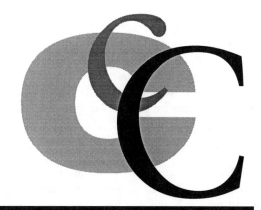

CALVINISM   As a theological system and framework for church doctrine, Calvinism is above all a spiritual tradition. Tracing its roots to the writings and teachings of John Calvin (1509-1564), Calvinist tradition conceives itself as faithful to the Christian scriptures, always seeking to illuminate the manner in which the Divine God initiates and maintains a communal relationship with human creation.

Calvinism is essentially a theology of redemption. The fall of humanity has necessitated God's intervention; this is accomplished by the ongoing revelation of God's will through the mediating presence of the Holy Spirit. The bond between God and humanity, which was first made manifest in the birth, death, and resurrection of the Christ, continues to be revealed as the Holy Spirit works through the institutional church. Thus God is the initiator of creation; God has provided the means for ultimate redemption; the Holy Spirit reveals God's will through inspired church teaching.

Calvinism is often noted as the tradition that teaches the doctrine of (double) predestination. That is, God has preordained those who will inherit eternal life and, derivatively, those who will be eternally damned; hence human actions are of no soteriological consequence. However, Calvin himself articulated this principle not as a doctrine or even inspired scriptural interpretation; rather, understanding salvation to be God's work and God's work alone is a human response to a faithful understanding of God's providence and power.

Max Weber (1864-1920) appropriated the concept of predestination to explain the rise of capitalism as an economic system. Because no one knows exactly who will be saved, one can look only to temporal conditions as evidence of God's favor. Thus the most faithful response to the life one is given is to care prudently for one's resources and work diligently to show further evidence of humility and sobriety. If one accumulates wealth and property in the process of careful management of earthly resources, one can live more hopefully—and thus more faithfully. Randall Collins (1996) writes:

> If one does this, turning one's life into a calling, restricting any impulse to frivolous pleasure, one comes to experience a feeling of assurance that one is a member of the Elect. The puritan, ascetic lifestyle thus emerges as a response to the doctrine of predestination. Its effects, in turn, are to bring worldly economic activity under religious control and to harness religious motivation to a new spirit of capitalism.

Weber argues, finally, that the Protestant ethic arises from a spiritual interpretation of the relationship between God and humanity. It then produces a cultural "spirit" that values, promotes, and ultimately reproduces rational capitalism.

In very general terms, the American Puritans were Calvinists, if only because they carried a Calvinist understanding of the relationship between God and humankind, and they adopted a worldview similar to Calvin's. However, by the early seventeenth century, Calvinist thought had undergone refinement and specification by Dutch and Scottish theologians. By the time Calvinist principles were appropriated into the Congregational Church, the human will and human behavior were injected into the process by which God decided who would be saved. The Puritan doctrine of salvation was God centered, but human good works made it happen.

The Calvinist tradition continues in the modern Presbyterian Church, the hallmarks of which are congregational "connectedness" and a rational, representative form of church government. In addition to the epic *Institutes,* setting forth Calvin's spirituality and doctrinal theology, his *Ecclesiastical Ordinances* set forth the organization of the church and are the roots from which the Presbyterian *Book of Order* has emerged.

See also Presbyterianism, Protestant Ethic Thesis, Max Weber

—*Jerry Koch*

REFERENCES

R. Collins, *A New Introduction: The Protestant Ethic and the Spirit of Capitalism* (Los Angeles: Roxbury, 1996); T. George (ed.), *John Calvin and the Church* (Louisville: Westminster/Knox, 1990); P. Miller, *Errand into Wilderness* (New York: Harper, 1956).

CAMPBELL, JOSEPH (1904-1987)   Professor at Sarah Lawrence College (1934-1972), author, and editor.

Campbell's work focused on the functions of mythology, portraying archetypes through comparative study of a wide range of literatures. His work was popularized through a series of interviews with Bill Moyers that aired as public television specials during the 1980s. Notable books were *The Hero with a Thousand Faces* (Princeton University Press 1949), which examined the archetype of the hero; *The Masks of God* (four volumes, Viking 1959-1968), a vast study of world mythology; and a collection of his essays, *Myths to Live By* (Bantam 1984).

—*James McClenon*

REFERENCE

J. Campbell (with B. Moyers), *The Power of Myth* (Garden City, N.Y.: Doubleday, 1988).

CAMPICHE, ROLAND J. (1937–)   Associate Professor of Sociology of Religion at the University of Lausanne (Switzerland) and Director of the French-speaking section of the Institut d'éthique sociale de la Fédération des Eglises Protestantes de la Suisse. Secretary General (1985-1989) and President (1991-1995) of the International Society for the Sociology of Religion (SISR).

He has studied the role of values in a changing social environment—with a special interest in urbanization, the family, youth, and energy consumption. His interests include the reconceptualization of the sociological approach of religion, and he has undertaken research on authority and power in Protestantism, the changing role of the clerics, and voluntary work.

—*Karel Dobbelaere*

REFERENCES

R. J. Campiche et al., *L'Exercice du pouvoir dans le protestantisme* (Geneva: Labor et Fides, 1990); R. J. Campiche et al., *Croire en Suisse(s)* (Lausanne: L'Age d'Homme, 1992); C. Dovay et al., *Bénévolat* (Lausanne: Réalités Sociales, 1994).

CANADIAN STUDY OF RELIGION   In theory, method, and often substance, Canadian sociology of religion is quite similar to that produced in other Western countries. Thus, for example, Weber and Durkheim have exerted a strong influence; the question of secularization has often dominated; quantitative and, to a lesser extent, qualitative empirical studies are the most common; and topics cover a wide range from institutional, denominational, and ethnic studies to investigations of the relation between religion and various social and personal variables.

The distinctive features of Canadian efforts, by contrast, owe much to peculiarities of the country. Here two factors stand out. The French-English divide in Canada has led, in effect, to the establishment of two separate academic enclaves, each with its own literature and, to some degree, characteristic questions. And the relatively recent but precipitous pan-Canadian decline in religious authority and practice has lent the much-attacked secularization thesis a certain self-evidence that few have questioned.

Among the seminal figures on the English-speaking side, none stands out more than Samuel D. Clark. In what amounts to a classic similar in influence to H. Richard Niebuhr's *Social Sources of Denominationalism* (Holt 1929) in the study of American religion, Clark's 1948 work, *Church and Sect in Canada* (University of Toronto Press) uses Niebuhr and Frederick Jackson Turner's frontier thesis to show English Canadian religious history as a continuing saga of sectarian innovation followed by denominational routinization. Clark's effort yielded an important sequel in William F. Mann's similarly titled *Sect, Cult and Church in Alberta* (University of Toronto Press 1955) and established the respectability of historical sociology in Canadian circles. Reflecting a prewar focus, however, this work has yielded in recent decades to the dominance of perspectives charting and assuming secularization and to ethnic, regional, and denominational studies.

Of the latter, perhaps the best developed in the post-1960s period have been studies on religion and ethnicity, especially on Mennonites/Hutterites and Jews in Canada. Important authors are Leo Driedger and Karl Peter for the former and Evelyn Kallen and William Shaffir for the latter. The two largest Protestant denominations, the United Church of Canada and the Anglican Church of Canada, have received the most attention, notably through works by Stewart Crysdale, W. S. F. Pickering, and Reginald Bibby.

What is largely missing in the Canadian literature is overarching studies of the role of religion in Canadian society. There are some partial exceptions: the edited volume by Stewart Crysdale and Les Wheatcroft, *Religion in Canadian Society* (Macmillan 1977), gives a sense of the range of work done in the Canadian field at that time, and Reginald Bibby's recent volumes provide the first quantitative survey overview and documentation of post-1960 secularization. Probably the most influential more general work in the postwar period, however, has been John Porter's *The Vertical Mosaic* (University of Toronto 1965), which, in a broader context, argues for the pivotal role played by above all the Anglican and Roman Catholic Churches in historical Canadian power stratification.

If the historical denominationalism of English-speaking Canada is well reflected in Clark's work, the near-monopolistic stature of Roman Catholicism in pre-1960s French Canada received its early sociological expression in Horace Miner's *St. Denis: A French-Canadian Parish* (University of Chicago Press 1939) and Everett Hughes's *French Canada in Transition* (University of Chicago Press 1943). Even more than in the rest of Canada, however, most postwar French Canadian sociology of religion has been preoccupied with the sharp decline in the status of religion as part of what is generally known as Québec's "Quiet Revolution." Building on important earlier work by Jean-Charles Falardeau, Marcel Rioux, and Louis- Edmond Hamelin, numerous scholars have focused on, above all, the transformations in French Canadian Roman Catholic institutions and the question of a surviving explicit or implicit Catholicism often tied to contemporary, decidedly secular Québec nationalism. Important works include Colette Moreux's *Fin d'une religion?* (Université de Montréal 1969), Jacques Grand'-Maison's *Nationalisme et religion* (Beauchemin 1970), and, more recently, Raymond Lemieux and Micheline Milot's *Les Croyances des Québécois* (Université Laval 1990). A particularly productive research center among Québécois has been social scientists at Laval University, notably Jean-Paul Rouleau, Paul Stryckman, and Jacques Zylberberg. Overall, the work of these and many other French speakers in recent decades has been sufficiently rich that those without a reading knowledge of French will be unable to appreciate the full diversity of Canadian sociology of religion.

—*Peter Beyer*

REFERENCES

R. W. Bibby, *Anglitrends* (Toronto: Anglican Diocese of Toronto, 1986); R. W. Bibby, *Unitrends* (Toronto: United Church, 1994); S. Crysdale, *The Changing Church in Canada* (Toronto: United Church, 1965); L. Driedger, *Mennonite Identity in Conflict* (Lewiston, N.Y.: Mellen, 1988); J. Falardeau, "The Role and Importance of the Church in French Canada," in *French Canadian Society*, ed. M. Rioux and Y. Martin (Toronto: McClelland and Stewart, 1964): 342-357; L. Hamelin and C. Hamelin, *Queleues matériaux de sociologie religieuse canadienne* (Montréal: Lévrier, 1956); E. Kallen, *Spanning the Generations* (Toronto: Longmans, 1977); K. A. Peter, *The Dynamics of Hutterite Society* (Edmonton: University of Alberta Press, 1987); W. S. F. Pickering and J. L. Blanchard, *Taken for Granted* (Toronto: Anglican Church, 1967); J-P. Rouleau, *Le prêtre, le frère et la religieuse vus par des étudiants des collèges* (Québec: Université Laval, 1971); W. Shaffir, *Life in a Religious Community* (Toronto: Holt, 1974); P. Stryckman, *Les prêtres du Québec d'aujourd'hui* (Québec: Université Laval, 1970-1973 [2 vols]); J. Zylberberg and P. Côté, "Les balises étatiques de la religion au Canada," *Social Compass* 40(1993):529-553.

CAPPS, DONALD E(RIC) (1939–)   William Harte Felmeth Professor of Pastoral Theology at Princeton Theological Seminary; honorary doctorate from the University of Uppsala, Sweden, 1989. Editor, *Journal for the Scientific Study of Religion,* 1983-1988; President of the Society for the Scientific Study of Religion, 1990-1992. Received the William Bier award for the scholarly study of religion from Division 36 of the American Psychological Association, 1994.

Donald Capps is widely recognized for his innovative application of dynamic psychology to personalities and issues in the psychology of religion. He has both edited and written works involving analysis and commentary on such notable religious personalities as St. Augustine and John Henry Newman. He has been particularly influential in advocating the relevance of poetry and biography for both pastoral care and the psychology of religion. He also has championed idiographic methods, employing a variety of theoretical viewpoints, in a field dominated by nomothetic approaches. In addition, he has argued for the relevance of certain religious beliefs to the phenomenon of child and sexual abuse, suggesting that certain religious beliefs may in fact foster such abuse practices.

—*Ralph W. Hood, Jr.*

REFERENCES

D. E. Capps, "Religion and Child Abuse," *Journal for the Scientific Study of Religion* 31(1992):1-14; D. E. Capps, *The Poet's Gift* (Louisville: Westminster/Knox, 1993); D. E. Capps, "Sex in the Parish," *Journal of Pastoral Care* 47(1993):350-361; D. E. Capps, "An Allportian Analysis of Augustine," *International Journal for the Psychology of Religion* 4(1994):205-228; D. E. Capps and J. E. Dittes (eds.), *The Hunger of the Heart* (Washington, D.C.: Society for the Scientific Study of Religion, 1990); D. E. Capps and R. K. Fenn (eds.), *The Endangered Self* (Princeton, N.J.: Center for Religion, Self, and Society, 1992).

CARGO CULTS   Large-scale millenarian movements centered in Melanesia.

In the language of the peoples of Papua New Guinea, *cargo* is the word for the trade goods and supplies—such as tinned meat, steel tools, military equipment, cotton, and motor vehicles—brought by missionaries, traders, planters, and colonial administrators. Members of cargo cults await the arrival of an abundance of goods as well as the restoration of power of their ancestors. Cargo cults proliferated at the time of initial contact with Europeans (1860-1970), when as many as 200 separate cults were reported. Peter Worsley (1957) suggested that cargo cults represented an embryonic form of class struggle against economic and political oppression and gave expression to anticolonial sentiments, while Kenelm Burridge (1969) stressed the importance of cargo cults in maintaining the dignity and equality of Melanesians in their encounters with Europeans. Peter Lawrence (1964) provided a balanced intellectual analysis of cargo cults with attention to the natives' point of view, and his study is by far the most sophisticated.

Although some revitalization of the cults took place during World War II, when planes often "dumped cargo," the number of cargo cults has declined dramatically since the 1960s. The meaning of *cargo* has gradually expanded to encompass all good things that people want and in some societies has come to signify the establishment of a utopia.

—*Stephen D. Glazier*

REFERENCES

K. Burridge, *New Heaven, New Earth* (New York: Schocken, 1969); P. Lawrence, *Road Belong Cargo* (Manchester, U.K.: University of Manchester Press, 1964); P. Worsley, *The Trumpet Shall Sound* (New York: MacGibbon and Kee, 1957).

CARIBBEAN RELIGIONS   Largely a product of forced migrations and the dramatic encounter between the Old World and the New World, the best documented Caribbean religions—such as Haitian voodoo, Rastafarianism, Cuban Santeria, and the Spiritual Baptists in Trinidad—are prime examples of creativity and change in this dynamic region that has become a fertile ground for the development of new religious admixtures and syncretisms.

Almost everyone in the Caribbean is from someplace else, and Caribbean religions have been greatly affected by the presence of Europeans, Africans, and, to a somewhat lesser extent, by Asian peoples as well. A majority of these religions have either an African or a Christian base, but Caribbean peoples have modified selected aspects of these traditions, added to them, and made them their own. While much attention has been given to African influences, one cannot completely understand religious developments in the region solely in terms of an African past, which is but a piece—albeit a large piece—of a more complex whole. Syncretisms of Hinduism and Christianity abound, and one can never underestimate the potential impact of Islam.

Rastafari is perhaps the most widely known of Caribbean religions. It is difficult to estimate the exact number of Rastafarians ("Rastas"), but the religion's influence vastly exceeds its numbers in its original Jamaica or even elsewhere in the Caribbean, to include persons in Europe (particularly the United Kingdom), Latin America, and the United States. The movement traces its history to a number of indigenous preacher-leaders in the 1930s, most notably Leonard Howell, Joseph Hibbert, Archibald Dunkley, Paul Earlington, Vernal Davis, Ferdinand Richetts, and Robert Hinds. The influence of Jamaican-born North American black leader Marcus Garvey is also apparent. Each of these leaders—working in isolation from the others—came to the conclusion that Haile Selassie, then enthroned as Ethiopian emperor, was the "Lion of Judah," who would lead all peoples of African heritage back to the Promised Land of Africa. While Rastafarianism is by no means a homogeneous movement, Rastas share seven basic tenets: (1) Black people were exiled to the West Indies because of their moral transgressions; (2) the wicked white man is inferior to black people; (3) the Caribbean situation is hopeless; (4) Ethiopia is Heaven; (5) Haile Selassie is the Living God; (6) the Emperor of Ethiopia will arrange for all expatriated persons of African descent to return to their true Homeland; and (7) black people will get revenge by compelling white people to serve them. Among contemporary Rastas, different subgroups stress different elements of the original creed; for example, the alleged death of Haile Selassie has raised significant questions regarding Selassie's place in the movement.

Cuban Santeria combines European and African beliefs and practices, but, unlike voodoo, Santeria is inspired mainly by one African tradition—the Yoruba. In Santeria, the Yoruba influence is marked in music, chants, foodstuffs, and by animal sacrifice. During major ceremonies, fresh blood—the food of the deities—flows onto sacred stones belonging to the cult leader. These stones are believed to be the objects through which the gods are fed and in which their power resides. A significant religious development in North America has been the large-scale transfer of Cuban Santeria to urban centers, notably New York, Miami, Los Angeles, and Toronto. It is estimated that there are currently more than 100,000 Santeria dev-otees in New York City alone. In 1993, the U.S. Supreme Court, in response to an appeal by Santeristas of a Florida ruling, upheld the constitutional right of Santeristas to practice ceremonial animal sacrifice (*Lukumi Babalu Aye, Inc., v. City of Hialeah*, 113 S.Ct. 2217, 1993).

The Spiritual Baptists are an international religious movement with congregations in St. Vincent (where some of their followers claim the faith originated), Trinidad and Tobago, Grenada, Guyana, Venezuela, Toronto, Los Angeles, and New York City. Membership is predominantly black, but in recent years congregations in Trinidad have attracted membership among wealthy East Indians and Chinese. A central ritual among the Spiritual Baptists is the *mourning rite*. This is an elaborate ceremony involving fasting, lying on a dirt floor, and other deprivations. A major component of the mourning rite is to discover one's true rank within the church hierarchy.

A critical issue in the study of Caribbean religions is the selection of a unit of analysis. Because syncretism plays such a prominent role in the development of religions in the region, it is often difficult to separate indigenous and foreign elements. Because there has been so much outreach, it is often difficult to discover the "true" origin of any single religious group. Because most of these religions lack a denominational chain of command, one cannot make statements about them as one might make statements about the Roman Catholic Church or Presbyterianism. The most accurate assessments refer to individual congregations and their leaders. To examine movements such as Rastafarianism, Santeria, voodoo, or the Spiritual Baptists as if they were unified denominations on the European and North American model is to present an overly coherent picture of an incredibly fragmented and volatile religious situation.

See also Voodoo

—*Stephen D. Glazier*

REFERENCES

G. F. Brandon, *Santeria from Africa to the New World* (New Brunswick, N.J.: Rutgers University Press, 1993); S. D. Glazier, *Marchin' the Pilgrims Home* (Salem, Wis.: Sheffield, 1991); M. Kremser (ed.), *Av Bobo* (Vienna: Institute fur Volkerkunde, 1994).

CARROLL, JACKSON W. (1932–) Ruth W. and A. Morris Williams, Jr., Professor of Religion and Society and Director of the J. M. Ormond Center for Research, Planning and Development in the Divinity School of Duke University. President, Religious Research Association, 1983.

Following pastoral assignments in Scotland and South Carolina and four years as Methodist chaplain at Duke, Carroll completed his Ph.D. at Princeton University in 1970, where he studied with Samuel Blizzard. From 1968 to 1974, he was on the faculty of Candler School of Theology, Emory University, before moving to Hartford Seminary in 1974. At Hartford Seminary, he founded the Center for Social and Religious Research and served in a variety of administrative positions, including a year as acting president. He was instrumental in establishing the center as a leader in applied social research in religion relied upon by religious institutions, foundations, and the press for fairminded studies of religious change in America. In 1992, he returned to Duke University as a member of the faculty and director of its Ormond Center.

Congregations and ministry have been dominant themes in Carroll's scholarly research and publication. His writing on congregations includes books on small churches (*Small Churches Are Beautiful,* Harper 1977); congregations and public life; varieties of religious presence (in a book with the same name, with William McKinney and David Roozen, Pilgrim 1985); and understanding congregational life (*Handbook for Congregational Studies,* with William McKinney and Carl S. Dudley, Abingdon 1986). With respect to ministry, he has published on clergy supply-and-demand issues (*Too Many Pastors?* with Robert L. Wilson, Pilgrim 1980), women in ministry (*Women of the Cloth,* with Barbara Hargrove and Adair Lummis, Harper 1982), and clergy authority (*As One with Authority,* Westminster/John Knox 1991). The latter combines Carroll's interests in sociology and theology.

With Carl S. Dudley, James Hopewell, Loren B. Mead, and Barbara Wheeler, Carroll was a founder of the Project Team for Congregational Studies, an informal coalition of individuals and institutions committed to disciplined inquiry into the dynamics of congregational life.

—*William McKinney*

CASUISTRY   The study of cases, especially those of conscience, or doubtful situations where it is not easy to distinguish the good from the bad, and where it is insufficiently clear to which rules or principles one should refer. For several centuries in the Roman Catholic Church, priests have been trained to deal with hypothetical cases so as to be able later on to resolve them in reality, especially in administering the sacrament of reconciliation (or "confession") and generally in spiritual guidance. The word *jesuitical* is sometimes used in a pejorative sense for this practice. Currently, casuistry is widely used in the field of birth control and in bioethics—for example, in relation to artificial insemination, donation of organs, and euthanasia.

—*Roberto Cipriani*

CATHOLICISM   *see* Roman Catholicism

CEBs   *see* Preferential Option for the Poor

CELIBACY   *see* Asceticism, Clergy, Self-Denial

CHALFANT, H. PAUL (1929-1994)   Professor of Sociology at Texas Tech University, 1974-1994, Chair 1974-1990; first Executive Officer of the Religious Research Association, 1991-1994; Ph.D., University of Notre Dame, 1970; M.Div., McCormick Theological Seminary, 1954; Presbyterian pastor prior to graduate work in sociology.

Chalfant's scholarly publications are concentrated in the sociology of religion plus medical sociology and social problems, particularly poverty and alcoholism. He is well known for his sociology of religion textbook, *Religion in Contemporary Society* (with Robert Beckley and Eddie Palmer, third edition, Peacock 1994) and for numerous regional, national, and international professional association activities, including presidency of the Mid-South Sociological Association (1977-1978) and the Southwestern Sociological Association (1991-1992) and membership on the Association for the Sociology of Religion Executive Council.

—*Doyle Paul Johnson*

CHANGE   Although its demise has been long predicted by social scientists, religion today—far from being driven out by the combined forces of industrialization, materialistic values, sociotechnological specialization, and science, in short, the forces of secularization—shows remarkable vitality. This fact is an embarrassment to modern social theory. If we accept the hypothesis that secularization inexorably results from the growth of specialization, science, and so on, then we would expect the United States to be one of the most secularized countries in the world. Instead, it is among the most God-believing and religion-adhering nations. It is also the seedbed for an enormous number of new religious movements. The picture that is unfolding not only in the United States but in many of the advanced industrial societies as well is one of mainline traditionalism in religious devotion competing with a somewhat militant fundamentalism and a panoply of highly personalized and syncretistic forms of religious expression (Roof and McKinney 1987). The personalized forms of religion include occultism (Luhrmann 1989), self-discovery and support groups (Westley 1983, Wuthnow 1994), and small communities where charismatic leaders preach varying degrees of separation from society and, in extreme cases, suicidal confrontation (Moore and McGehee 1989, Zablocki 1980).

Much of what is new in this picture is the result of the general privatization of individual life in modern societies (Luckmann 1991). The "private sphere" is enhanced by the phantasmagoric character of modern mass media and consumer markets—talk-show personalities espousing the spiritual benefits of body massage, pocketbooks sold at supermarket checkout lines that promise new self-awareness obtained from special diets, astrological advice in newspaper columns, and the like; the list seems endless. Because the present state of religious institutions and religiosity is extremely diverse and in flux, any attempt to predict what changes may come about even in the next few decades is problematic. Here, we will focus instead on general models of religious change that have been employed in the social sciences.

The social sciences have devised a number of general approaches to the problem of religion and change. One perspective stresses that religion is a cause of macrohistorical changes in social, political, and economic institutions. A second emphasizes that religions themselves undergo change in response to forces emanating from nonreligious spheres of social and personal experience. A third argues that, viewed long term and on a global scale, religious change is evolutionary. Fourth, an influential initiative has explored the connection between modernization and secularization. Finally, it has been argued that religious change can have an oscillating pattern.

Although it is heuristic to classify social scientific approaches to religion and change in this manner, it is important to recognize that these several perspectives overlap in practice. Moreover, there are other ways to categorize the different research perspectives in this arena. For example, some students of religion and change take an interest in large-scale, historical processes while others focus on small-scale, localized, and comparatively ephemeral changes. As we proceed, an important caveat to keep in mind is that all theories of religion and change remain tentative at this writing. As quantitative analyses of religious phenomena become increasingly sophisticated, social scientists grow ever more impressed with the fact that statistical models in which religious variables are either the cause or the effect yield only modest relationships. Religion, although connected with society and social conditions, remains a somewhat autonomous sphere.

Religion as a Cause of Institutional Change Christianity has provided the focus for two major theses regarding the impact of religion on other institutions. The first of these studies was Edward Gibbons's analysis of the decay of the Roman Empire under the dissipating influence of Christianization. An even more influential study was that by Max Weber. His *Protestant Ethic and the Spirit of Capitalism* (Scribner 1958 [1904-1905]) spawned a tireless debate concerning the possibility that religion lies behind the development of rational, capitalist economies in Europe. In Weber's original thesis, it was the "worldly asceticism" of Protestantism that formed the basis for capitalist business practices of savings and investment. The idealist thrust of the Protestant ethic thesis invited much criticism for failing to take into account a host of technological and institutional innovations that accompanied or, in many cases, preceded the Protestant Reformation. Recent Weberian scholarship has shown that later in his career Weber had substantially revised his original thesis to suggest that the Roman Catholic Church of the High Middle Ages, which itself had become rational-bureaucratic and entrepreneurial, laid the institutional foundations for the development of capitalist enterprises in Europe (Collins 1986).

Religious Change in Response to External Forces One of Émile Durkheim's (1984 [1912]) most seminal contributions to the sociology of religion was to suggest that religious beliefs and practices change in accordance with changes in the morphology or structure of the social group adhering to these beliefs and practices. Followed rigidly, this leads to a crude reductionism. The basic concept, however, has exerted an enormous influence on the social sciences. Anthropologists, for example, have found the idea useful for comparing the religious systems of preindustrial societies. (Swanson [1960], in an empirical cross-cultural study, demonstrates that specific religious beliefs correspond to the number and variety of "sovereign groups" in societies.)

Predictably, Weber, with his greater sensitivity to social inequality and differentiation *within* societies, offers an alternative inspiration to sociologists of religion. He argued that social classes have different experiences and needs, and so tend to acquire and support quite different forms of religious orientation. Prophetic, moralistic religions come into existence with the rise of urban, commercial classes. Emotional, salvationist religion has an elective affinity with the urban poor, while rural populations, subject to the whims of nature, use magic in the attempt to control these forces, and elites prefer an intellectualist religion that confirms their right to high status.

On a less grand historical stage, there have been countless studies of cult formation and the development of new religious movements. Although it is generally conceded that new religions often appeal to marginalized members of society, this doesn't mean that new recruits are necessarily limited to the poor and downtrodden. Many of the new religious movements in the United States have successfully appealed to the well educated and affluent. Stark and Bainbridge (1985) suggest that what often distinguishes these recruits is that they come from family backgrounds where more conventional religion was given little or no emphasis. On the other hand, anthropologists have shown that new religious movements, particularly of a nativistic or millenarian sort, tend to proliferate when small societies come into contact with large, dominating societies (Wallace 1966).

Religious Evolution The idea that religion has undergone a fairly steady, unilinear process of differentiation and development was accepted by many thinkers of the late nineteenth and early twentieth centuries, including Durkheim and Weber (although Weber did not see the process as inevitably unilinear). Modern proponents of this model of change (Bellah 1964, Luckmann 1991, Wallace 1966) have refined it with better data supplied by recent ethnographic, historical, and archeological research.

A rough outline of religious evolution can now be given with some confidence. Prior to the late modern period of present-day industrial societies, the social forms of religion were of three basic types, and these types directly corresponded to the complexity of the societies in which they were embedded. In hunting-gathering and simple horticultural societies, the social form of religion appears diffused throughout the social structure and is virtually homologous with society itself. The second social form of religion developed with the advent of the first state organized societies of the Middle East and was characterized by a differentiation of religious functions and their coalescence in institutions that were in close proximity to, or partial identity with, political institutions. The third social form of religion—a highly differentiated and specialized institutional sphere—became prevalent in the agrarian societies of Europe and Asia but most notably in western European Christianity. The most recent, modern phase of evolutionary religious development is still unfolding and is thus hard to define accurately. Nevertheless, modernity seems to be characterized by multitudinous religious institutions and bountiful forms of privatized religious expression (Luckmann 1991).

Secularization The term *secularization* suggests that religious culture, religious institutions, and religious beliefs tend to atrophy under conditions of advanced industrialization and modernization. Although several distinct lines of theory spring from this basic idea (Tschannen 1991), the secularization thesis was one of the major assumptions of the social sciences until only a couple of decades ago. Now, with conservative religious movements thriving in advanced industrial countries such as the United States and religious revivals occurring in western Europe and the former Soviet Union, it is no longer certain that the secularization thesis has validity.

One recently proposed theory disputes the secularization thesis entirely (Stark and Iannaccone 1994). When public expression of religion is monopolized by the state, people will in time grow apathetic and feel less inclined to practice the prescribed religion. The resulting ebb in public religious enthusiasm is what is normally taken to indicate secularization. According to the advocates of this theory, however, religious expression has not actually disappeared. It has gone underground and finds expression in unofficial ways. This situation can be contrasted to the one when there is no state monopoly of religion and instead there exists an "open market" of freely competing faiths. Now, religious organizations zealously promote their products, and public religious participation is enthusiastic. Such a theory naturally lends itself to the idea that religious change can fluctuate over periods of time as the market of religious "suppliers" changes.

Oscillating Change Ages of faith alternate with ages of apathy and disbelief; periods dominated by vibrant religious symbolism and healthy religious organizations alternate with periods when symbolism pales and the organizations teeter; periods in which there is only one accepted church give way to periods rife with sectarian revival and religious pluralism. These are all examples of oscillating religious change.

The grand historical schemes of oscillating change that Pitirim Sorokin advocated are no longer favored by most social scientists, but more limited employment of the oscillating change model is still quite viable. Church-sect theory, to cite what is perhaps the most notable example of this, finds ample historical evidence for cycles of church development followed by sectarian division (Finke and Stark 1992). A much older and often neglected version of the oscillation model was put forward by a fourteenth-century Arab historian credited with being a forerunner of social science, Ibn Khaldūn. His classic theory of religious revival and the circulation of political elites in the Muslim societies of the Middle East is a prototype of oscillating change theory and has been recently used to understand the relation between Islam and society (Gellner 1981).

—*Edward B. Reeves*

REFERENCES

R. N. Bellah, "Religious Evolution," *American Sociological Review* 29(1964):358-374; R. Collins, *Weberian Sociological Theory* (New York: Cambridge University Press, 1986); É. Durkheim, *The Elementary Forms of the Religious Life* (New York: Free Press, 1965); É. Durkheim, *The Division of Labor in Society* (New York: Free Press, 1984[1912]); R. Finke and R. Stark, *The Churching of America* (New Brunswick: Rutgers University Press, 1992); E. Gellner, *Muslim Societies* (New York: Cambridge University Press, 1981); T. Luckmann, "The New and the Old in Religion," in *Social Theory for a Changing Society*, ed. P. Bourdieu and J. S. Coleman (Boulder, Colo.: Westview, 1991): 167-182; T. M. Luhrmann, *Persuasions of the Witch's Craft* (Cambridge: Harvard University Press, 1989); R. Moore and F. McGehee III (eds.), *New Religious Movements, Mass Suicide, and Peoples Temple* (Lewiston, N.Y.: Mellen, 1989); W. C. Roof and W. McKinney, *American Mainline Religion* (New Brunswick, N.J.: Rutgers University Press, 1987); R. Stark and W. S. Bainbridge, *The Future of Religion* (Berkeley: University of California Press, 1985); R. Stark and L. R. Iannaccone, "A Supply-Side Reinterpretation of the 'Secularization' of Europe," *Journal for the Scientific Study of Religion* 33(1994):230-252; G. E. Swanson, *The Birth of the Gods* (Ann Arbor: University of Michigan Press, 1960); O. Tschannen, "The Secularization Paradigm," *Journal for the Scientific Study of Religion* 30(1991):396-415; A. F. C. Wallace, *Religion* (New York: Random House, 1966); F. Westley, *The Complex Forms of the Religious Life* (Chico, Calif.: Scholars Press, 1983); R. Wuthnow, *Sharing the Journey* (New York: Free Press, 1994); B. Zablocki, *Alienation and Charisma* (New York: Free Press, 1980).

CHANGE MOVEMENTS To initiate change, a religious group must mobilize resources—including financial assets and personal commitments of time and energy from the membership. An issue in mobilizing these resources is legitimacy within the society. Groups with different kinds of change strategies therefore face different kinds of opposition and will develop different issues in trying to initiate change. Using two variables—extent of change and level of change—four types of groups, each with its own set of strategic problems, can be identified.

Alterative religious groups focus on partial change within individuals. Members are expected to change their worldview and behavior relative to one particular aspect of life, but change in larger political or economic structures is unnecessary. Such groups usually experience low levels of organizational opposition, as they do not threaten the self-interests of many other established groups. They seldom need to demand total and unqualified commitment of members because their access to resources is unlikely to be severely limited by stigmatization and open hostility. Without external opposition, a problem of these groups may be that of stimulating enough commitment and group solidarity.

Redemptive religious groups seek sweeping change of values, attitudes, and behaviors of individuals, but modifications in the social structure are deemed insignificant. Such groups are opposed mostly by individuals, especially family members, who have emotional ties to the devotees. Because opposition to these groups is not from powerful institutions, access to resources for survival is less problematic for redemptive groups than for those trying to transform the entire society. Social stigmatization is usually moderate. If family members themselves are sympathetic to the group, opposition may be nonexistent. Cooperation with other organizations is possible, and intense indoctrination of members becomes unnecessary.

Reformative religious groups seek partial change in the social structure. Change in individuals is believed to be insufficient; the society itself must be reformed. However, the society and culture are not viewed as totally depraved; they simply need refinement. Reformative groups encounter opposition from institutions and persons with vested interests, but the opposition is not usually as widespread as occurs with groups demanding total change of society and total commitment of members. Levels of opposition to reformative groups are moderate and come from specific segments of society whose self-interests are threatened. Cooperation with other organizations in society is usually possible.

Transformative religious groups seek total change of all aspects of social structure and culture. They usually experience great resistance from those with a vested interest in the status quo and are likely to be labeled "subversive." Because these groups are small, they cannot use coercion to bring change; cooperation or bargaining with other social agencies would compromise the group's purity. Thus intense sense of mission, alienation from the larger society, and limited access to resources often lead to a membership requirement of total commitment of resources, time, and energy. This, in turn, creates conflict with other people and other institutions seeking access to members or their resources. These organizational conflicts often mean these groups are short lived.

There are other ways to conceptualize religious social movements. Roy Wallis, for example, distinguishes three types of new religious movements: world-rejecting, world-affirming, and world-accommodating. Those interested in religious change may also want to explore the literature on "sects" (including Bryan Wilson's typology of sects) and "cults" (including Stark and Bainbridge's typology of cults).

—*Keith A. Roberts*

REFERENCES

D. Aberle, *The Peyote Religion Among the Navaho* (Chicago: Aldine, 1966); D. G. Bromley and A. D. Shupe, Jr., *Moonies in America* (Beverly Hills, Calif.: Sage, 1979); R. Stark and W. S. Bainbridge, *The Future of Religion* (Berkeley: University of California Press, 1985); R. Wallis, *The Elementary Forms of the New Religious Life* (London: Routledge, 1984); B. R. Wilson, *Religious Sects* (New York: McGraw Hill, 1970).

CHANTING   May have been the original form of speech. In ancient times, epic poetry was chanted. Chanting occurs in animistic religions (by shamans), Judaism, Hinduism, Buddhism, Christianity, Islam—indeed perhaps in all religions. The repetitive nature of chanting helps to quiet mind and body.

Gregorian chant, the traditional music of the Catholic Church, was fully developed by the seventh century and was modeled on Jewish practices. During 1994, a compact disc containing Gregorian chant by contemporary Spanish monks became an international best-seller, no doubt reflecting the appeal of New Age music, a genre meant to create a relaxed meditative mood.

—*Joseph B. Tamney*

CHARISMA   Theoretical concept of a mode of authority in human groups. Innovated in sociology by Max Weber, the idea of charisma or charismatic authority is becoming increasingly important to the sociology of religion, in part because leadership in proliferating (and sometimes highly controversial) new religious movements (NRMs) "has almost wholly assumed a personal charismatic form" (Bird 1993:76). Charismatic leadership is often associated with dynamic and volatile religious phenomena and with profound and sudden transformations of a spiritual milieu.

In *Economy and Society* (University of California Press 1985 [1922]), Max Weber distinguished between traditional, rational-legal, and charismatic modes of authority. The third is based upon the perception of

believers that a particular individual possesses extraordinary qualities. Charisma thus denotes a *relationship* rather than an individual personality attribute (Wilson 1975). Charismatic authority nevertheless represents personal and noninstitutionalized leadership, although Weber employed the term *routinized charisma* to refer to the partial institutionalization of charisma through the establishment of specified positions open exclusively to persons who demonstrate personal specialty. Institutionalized charisma is also represented by *charisma of office,* which pertains to beliefs that certain officeholders, by virtue of occupying a sacred office (e.g., priesthood), acquire certain special powers or qualities. In contrast, the *pure* personal charisma of prophets and sages resists institutional influences. It is antithetical to stable authority lodged in fixed codes and customs. "Charisma, then, represents the extraordinary, the non-routine aspects of life and reality" (Hamilton 1995:142).

Priests and other representatives of institutionalized charisma are generally associated with received spiritual and normative ideas derived from existing traditions. "In contrast, personal charismatic leaders such as sages and prophets communicate normative messages for which they are the primary authors" (Bird 1993:76). Weber saw the charismatic prophet as a vital "agent of religious change and of the development of new and more complete solutions to the problem of salvation" (Hamilton 1995:142). On the other hand, some scholars have criticized this view as reflecting an idealistic "Great Man" theory of history (Worsley 1970). In any case, charismatic leaders generally are said to arise in unsettled times suffused with disorienting sociocultural change. In such periods, unconventional sects arise "composed of people who are fearful of the future, who hope that by placing their faith in some charismatic leader they will eradicate the past and protect their lives against unknown and unseen dangers" (Fogerty 1993:486).

Instability of Charisma   The *volatility* of charismatic authority and of groups manifesting charismatic leadership has been a persistent theme (Johnson 1979, Robbins and Anthony 1995, Wallis 1984, Wallis and Bruce 1986). In essence, charismatic leadership is unstable because it lacks *both* institutional restraints and institutional supports (Robbins and Anthony 1995).

By definition, charismatic leaders are not tied to institutional means that define and structure their accountability (Bird 1993). "Aside from existing legal constraints, few structures have been established or inherited to control the conduct of charismatic [NRM] founders" such as the Rev. Moon, Bhagwan Rajneesh, or Moses David Berg (Bird 1993:85). The absence of routinized structures of accountability fosters corruption in charismatically led "cults" (Balch 1988) and perhaps also in televangelical operations. In conjunction with the "deification of idiosyncrasy" (Lifton 1979), or tendency for believers to rationalize the whimsical behavior of revered leaders, the lack of institutional restraints also can facilitate other forms of deviant or extreme behavior, including violence. Wallis and Bruce see charismatic leadership as the enabling context for the sexual deviance and/or violence that appeared in movements such as the Peoples Temple, Synanon, and the Children of God (now "The Family"). The dynamics of charismatic leadership can thus "provide opportunities for charismatic leaders to indulge the darker forces of their subconscious" (Wallis and Bruce 1986:117).

The absence of institutional restraints upon charismatic leaders interfaces with the lack of institutional supports available to sustain leaders' authority. "Charismatic authority," notes Wallis (1993:176) "is a fundamentally precarious status" because leaders' claims to authority rest "purely on subjective factors." Followers' perception of the leader's extraordinary qualities may be situated and ephemeral. The charismatic leader must continually face the prospect that his special "gift of grace" will no longer be perceived and his authority will fade. Johnson (1979) analyzes a spiraling process whereby the steps that Jim Jones took in response to challenges to his charismatic authority brought into play new factors that potentially undermined his authority, and that in turn required new defensive responses. The leader's increasingly frantic defensive measures to shore up his authority and the unanticipated consequences of his responses contributed to the cataclysmic end of the Peoples Temple settlement at Jonestown, Guyana.

Charismatic leaders must continually be on the alert for threats to their authority from outsiders, dissidents, and rivals within the movement as well as from their administrative staff. The latter is generally oriented toward expanding the scope of its authority and rationalizing administrative procedures to the detriment of the leader's freedom of action (and sometimes leading to his or her actual deposition). As noted by Johnson (1992), leaders may opt to ignore this conflict, support institutionalization and the consequent shrinkage of their role, or act to resist staff encroachments. The latter strategy tends to maximize volatility, as the leader may engage in persistent "crisis-mongering" to keep the movement in constant turmoil such that stable institutional structures cannot be consolidated, hence the leader's indispensability is underlined. "Routinization may be resisted by perpetual environmental change and the shifting of goals" (Hiller 1975:344). A variation of this approach entails ratcheting up tension at the group's boundary to enhance internal solidarity. In the process, conflict with persons and groups in the environment is heightened. The lynching of the founding Mormon prophet Joseph Smith demonstrates that this can be a risky strategy. In any case, internal and boundary turmoil often tends to force out of the group persons who are not entirely loyal to the leader or who may be disinclined to endorse extreme (e.g., violent) measures in support of the leader's vision.

Lacking both immediate restraints and long-term supports, a charismatic leader will be inclined to protect his or her position by attempting to "simplify" the group's internal environment to eliminate sources of dissension, normative diversity, and alternative leadership. To the degree that the leader succeeds, one consequence will be the attenuation of the cross-pressures that inhibit group members from accepting extreme demands made upon them by an eccentric authoritarian leader (Mills 1982). The absence of both restraints and supports also may provide the context for extreme acts promoted by a leader who perceives his or her authority threatened. This may have been a factor in the 1994 murder-suicides in Québec and Switzerland associated with the Order of the Solar Temple (Palmer 1996).

An additional consequence of the lack of institutional supports for charismatic leadership involves the absence of regularized procedures for the transfer of authority, that is, the problem of *succession*. Thus, failure to effectively institutionalize the charisma of the founding prophet led to intensifying factionalism and ultimately to lethal violence in the Hare Krishna movement (Rochford 1985; Huber and Gruson 1987).

Roy Wallis (1984) has posited a connection between charismatic leadership and "world-rejecting" movements, which often have apocalyptic worldviews and envision themselves "as islands of sanity or righteousness in a hostile and degenerate world." But, "so great a break with prevailing society can only be justified by the authority of someone perceived to be truly extraordinary" (Wallis and Bruce 1986:122). Such movements tend to be founded and led by charismatic leaders, who will often resist tendencies toward institutionalization, as the latter threatens the leader's authority and will likely lead to a mitigation of the movement's apocalyptic vision and world-rejecting posture.

When an older movement, such as the Seventh-day Adventist Church (SDA), remains committed to apocalyptic prophecy while simultaneously becoming more accommodative in its practical stance to the larger society, schisms may develop whereby aspiring charismatic leaders develop their own movements based upon revisions of the original prophecy and linked to their claimed prophetic or messianic role. Such groups are also prone to schisms and conflicts between rival prophets. The notorious David Koresh (née Vernon Howell) rose to the leadership of the Branch Davidians, an offshoot of the earlier schismatic Davidian offshoot of the SDA Church (Bromley-and Silver 1995, Pitts 1995). Koresh "identified himself as the Lord's anointed and saw the standoff at Waco as the literal fulfillment of an intensifying campaign by demonic earthly rulers to destroy the righteous remnant" (Boyer 1993:30). It is arguable, then, that the most potentially volatile form of personal charismatic leadership is the *messianic* pattern in which charismatic leaders "identify the millennial destiny of humankind with their own personal vicissitudes and demonize any opposition to their aspirations and personal aggrandizement" (Robbins and Anthony 1995:244). "Messianic" leadership combines the instability of charismatic authority with the potential for volatility and tension inherent in apocalyptic world-rejecting movements.

Charisma and Social Explanation The precariousness and instability of charismatic leadership and its consequences in terms of group volatility, factionalism, and possible violent episodes represent instances in which the concept of charisma can facilitate the explanation of sociohistorical events. Wallis (1993) partly accepts the views of Worsley (1970) and Wilson (1973) that charisma is basically a descriptive concept that labels rather than explains the power of leaders and the submission of believers. Nevertheless, an explanatory role for charisma may be salvaged when violence or other kinds of deviance (e.g., sexual deviance) emerge within movements. Wallis (1993:177) suggests "that charisma has a greater role as an explanation of a *leader's* actions and their consequences than . . . as an attempted explanation of the behavior of his *followers*."

It has been suggested above that the development of controversial new movements and noninstitutionalized spiritual ferment in contemporary society is enhancing the importance of charisma to the sociology of religion. Yet charismatic authority and its concomitants in terms of the tendency to view social relationships and organization in personal terms and to envision messianic termination of present evils is generally thought to be associated more with primitive rather than complex modern societies (Wilson 1975). Indeed, the controversiality of contemporary NRMs is due in part to the lack of legitimacy accorded to charismatic authority in modern society, where it is widely seen as primarily appropriate to the "unserious" realms of sports and entertainment (Wilson 1987).

—*Thomas Robbins*

REFERENCES

R. P. Balch, "Money and Power in Utopia," in *Money and Power in New Religions,* ed. J. Richardson (Lewiston, N.Y.: Mellen, 1988): 185-222; F. B. Bird, "Charisma and Leadership in New Religious Movements," in *Handbook of Cults and Sects in America,* Vol. B, ed. D. G. Bromley and J. K. Hadden (Greenwich, Conn.: JAI, 1993): 75-92; P. Boyer, "A Brief History of the End of Time," *New Republic* (May 17, 1993): 30-33; D. G. Bromley and E. Silver, "The Davidian Tradition," in *Armageddon at Waco,* ed. S. Wright (Chicago: University of Chicago Press, 1995): 43-72; R. Fogerty, "Sects and Violence," *The Nation* (April 12, 1993): 485-487; M. B. Hamilton, *The Sociology of Religion* (London: Routledge, 1995); H. Hiller, "A Reconceptualization of the Development of Social Movement Development," *Pacific Sociological Review* 17(1975):342-359; J. Huber and L. Gruson, "Dial 'OM' for Murder," *Rolling Stone* 497(1987):53-59; B. Johnson, "Of Founders and Followers," *Sociological Analysis* 53(1992):S1-S13; D. P. Johnson, "Dilemmas of Charismatic Leadership," *Sociological Analysis* 40(1979):315-323; R. Lifton, "The Appeal of the Death Trip," *New York Times Sunday Magazine* (Jan. 7, 1979): 26; E. Mills, "Cult Extremism," in *Violence and Religious Commitment,* ed. K. Levi (University Park: Penn State University Press, 1982): 75-102; M. J. Neitz, *Charisma and Christianity* (New Brunswick, N.J.: Transaction, 1987); S. Palmer, "Purity and Danger in the Solar Temple," *Journal of Contemporary Religion* 11(1996):303-318; W. R. Pitts, "Davidians and Branch Davidians," in *Armageddon in Waco,* ed. S. Wright (Chicago: University of Chicago Press, 1995): 20-42; T. Robbins and D. Anthony, "Sects and Violence," *Armageddon in Waco,* ed. S. Wright (Chicago: University of Chicago Press, 1995): 236-259; E. B. Rochford, *Hare Krishna in America* (New Brunswick, N.J.: Rutgers University Press, 1985); R. Wallis, *The Elementary Forms of the New Religious Life* (London: Routledge, 1984); R. Wallis, "Charisma and Explanation," *Secularism, Rationalism and Sectarianism,* ed. E. Barker et al. (Oxford: Clarendon, 1993): 167-179; R. Wallis and S. Bruce, "Sex, Violence and Religion," in *Sociological Theory, Religion and Collective Action,* ed. R. Wallis and S. Bruce (Belfast: Queens University, 1986): 115-127; M. Weber, *Economy and Society* (Berkeley: University of California Press, 1978); B. Wilson, *Magic and the Millennium* (London: Heinemann, 1973); B. Wilson, *The Noble Savage* (Berkeley: University of California Press, 1975); B. Wilson, "Factors in the Failure of New Religious Movements," in *The Future of New Religious Movements,* ed. D. G. Bromley and P. E. Hammond (Macon, Ga.: Mercer University Press, 1987): 30-45; P. Worsley, *The Trumpet Shall Sound* (St. Albans, U.K.: Paladin, 1970).

CHARISMATIC MOVEMENT Also called neo-Pentecostalism, this movement emerged in the 1960s and caught fire in the 1970s, although the fires have since cooled. Following in the American tradition of revivalism, it is concretely linked with and shares "classical" pentecostalism's enthusiastic and experiential approach to religious practice. In particular, charismatics share with their pentecostal cousins a belief in "baptism of the Holy Spirit" and the related "gifts of the Spirit" such as speaking in tongues (glossolalia), healing, and prophecy (*charismatic* is from the Greek *charismata*, meaning "gifts"; see Acts 2 and 1 Corinthians 12-14). However, while pentecostalism is a group of independent sects formed by schism, the charismatic movement remains a revitalization movement within established churches, seeking to integrate Spirit baptism and gifts into the organization and practices of mainline Protestant denominations as well as the Roman Catholic Church. Although initially there was some experimentation with independent "covenant communities," the predominant organizational form currently is the parish-based prayer group.

History A notable aspect of the charismatic movement is that it surfaced early in the two churches that are the most hierarchically and sacramentally organized, churches in which priests have traditionally monopolized the "technologies of grace": the Episcopal Church in 1960 and the Roman Catholic Church in 1967. The roots of this infusion of pentecostal spirituality into mainline churches are complex, but one important source can be traced to 1952, when Southern California dairyman Demos Shakarian's Full Gospel Business Men's Fellowship International held its first meeting (at which then pentecostal faith healer Oral Roberts was the guest speaker) and began providing a space for mainline clergy to interact with pentecostals.

Wider recognition of neo-pentecostalism is associated with Dennis Bennett, who, while rector of St. Mark's Episcopal Church in Van Nuys, California, received Spirit baptism and spoke in tongues while worshiping with a group of charismatic laypersons in 1959. His resignation in 1960 under pressure from his superiors gained national attention for the charismatic movement, including coverage in *Time* magazine. Bennett was appointed to a stagnant congregation in Seattle, Washington, where he continued to encourage baptism of the Spirit and assisted thousands in receiving the charismata (Poloma 1982:14).

The birth of Catholic neo-pentecostalism is dated to 1967 when a group of faculty—who had been involved with the Cursillo movement—and students at Duquesne University in Pittsburgh experienced baptism of the Spirit while on a retreat. The movement quickly spread to Notre Dame and the University of Michigan, and at its peak the "Catholic Charismatic Renewal" (CCR) encompassed hundreds of thousands of Roman Catholics and had made contact with perhaps as many

as 4 to 7 million more. The movement generally embraces orthodox Christian teachings, stressing particularly Christ's divinity, and the church hierarchy up to and including Pope John Paul II has been supportive of the CCR—or has co-opted it, depending on one's perspective.

Sources of Neo-Pentecostalism Although Pentecostalism has been analyzed in terms of classical deprivation theory—Pentecostals being drawn from "the disinherited" economic classes—the social sources of the charismatic movement within mainline churches do not suggest a similar explanation. Early pentecostals were indeed predominantly marginalized in the new, urban, industrial social order; neo-pentecostals, in contrast, are typically white, suburban, well educated, and of middling socioeconomic status. In this sense, it might be said that the charismatic movement is pentecostalism for the middle classes. Some have suggested, following Charles Glock, that the deprivation that leads people to enthusiastic religion such as neo-pentecostalism need not be exclusively socioeconomic but can also be psychic, ethical, or health related. Neitz (1987:251), by contrast, argues that conversion to the charismatic renewal is based less on deprivation—unless *deprivation* is defined so broadly as to lose its explanatory power—than on "a practical and rational process of assessing the claims of competing belief systems in the light of daily experience with an eye toward particular goals." Neitz suggests that the renewal movement emerged as a result of the same "cultural crises" that produced the "self-awareness" movement of the 1970s: It is a reaction to the "iron cage" of modern, rationalized life experienced by those middle-class Americans most exposed to its sterility.

Moral, Social, and Political Views Morally, charismatics see society as being in a state of crisis to which spiritual activities such as prayer and worship are the appropriate response. While they bear a surface resemblance to classical pentecostals in this respect, they differ considerably in the details. Charismatics diverge from pentecostals in their liberalism on issues such as abortion, divorce, premarital sex, and homosexuality; they are, however, more conservative than Americans generally on these same issues.

Although charismatics seem to be apolitical, even narcissistic (Neitz 1987), it simply may be the case that social factors other than religious affiliation explain charismatic political opinions better than religious beliefs and practices. That is, in the political sphere, they may simply mirror those who fit their demographic profile (Poloma 1982:222). More research is needed if this issue is to be addressed adequately.

—David Yamane

REFERENCES

M. B. McGuire, *Pentecostal Catholics* (Philadelphia: Temple University Press, 1982); M. J. Neitz, *Charisma and Community* (New Brunswick, N.J.: Transaction, 1987); M. M. Poloma, *The Charismatic Movement* (Boston: Twayne, 1982).

CHILDREN OF GOD   *see* The Family

CHRISTIANITY   Like marriage, for instance, Christianity can be regarded as a social phenomenon, for such it is, but it is only that among other things. If cognizance is to be taken of what it is, in itself and as a whole, then it must be recognized as being, in the first place, what is called a *religion* (as marriage is, primarily, a *relationship*).

As a *belief system,* Christianity may be defined as the existential recognition that (in the New Testament phrase) "Jesus is Lord," or, in the theological formulations of the Councils of Nicea, Constantinople, and Chalcedon (325, 381, and 451 C.E.), that the Divinity is a unity with three particular faces (the Father, Son, and Spirit), and that Jesus is "God incarnate" (both fully Divine and fully human).

As an *ethical ideal,* Christianity may be described as the practical recognition that (in Jesus's words, in the four Gospels) "the Kingdom [of God, or of heaven] has come [or, is here, in the midst]," meaning, in *him,* and in the attempt to extend its boundaries, in the life of the disciple and of the world.

As a *social institution,* Christianity may be delineated by the dominical sacraments of Baptism and the Eucharist as well as by the spiritual and organizational "fellowship" (to use St. Paul's expression in his Epistles) to which they give entrance and sustenance.

These three customary approaches to the phenomenon of religion correspond to Paul's "abiding" trio: faith, hope, and charity (love), of which "the greatest" is the last (1 Cor. 13:13). This early description of the spirituality at the heart of the new religion represents the classic analysis, based upon participant observation.

However, seen historically rather than structurally, Christianity began as one of a number of Jewish movements that thought it had found the Messiah ("anointed with the Spirit [of God]"; Greek, *Christos*). The hope was as utterly dashed, religiously, as it was politically, by the death of Jesus through the accursed method of crucifixion. The hope was revived by his (equally unexpected) postresurrection appearances; but its content and its consequences demanded immediate and continuing transformation on the part of members of his "Body." Those who "followed [participated in] the Way," and that which united them, were quickly contextualized by contemporary pluralism, respectively, as "Christians" and as "Christianity." Indeed, *Christ* soon came to be used as a proper name, rather than an honorific title or cosmological value judgment, even by Christians themselves.

With the spread of the faith, the meanings subsequently given to the concept were increasingly influenced by the direct and indirect experience of those who "profess[ed] and call[ed] themselves Christians." In the millennium (500-1500) following the decline of the Roman Empire in the West, *Christianity* primarily meant that sphere (those aspects) of life in which the writ of Christ ran. Although measured largely in terms of canon law, it was nevertheless comparable to Jesus's own nongeographic use of *Kingdom* (and to a similar understanding of *Islam*). This spiritual (or Spiritual) emphasis was facilitated by the contrasting use of *religion* as the way of life *(religio)* of those following a particular Rule *(regula),* such as that of St. Benedict (d. 550).

During the last half millennium, the concept of Christianity has wobbled uneasily (depending upon users' own evaluations of the phenomenon itself and of life in general) between a theological system, seen as a variety of ontological or historical hypotheses (a "philosophy"), on the one hand, and, on the other, a (functional or dysfunctional) support for the lifestyles of particular individuals or groups (a "prop"); or between a shorthand term for a somewhat utopian love of the neighbor ("toleration"), on the one hand, and, on the other, a passionate zeal for the honor due uniquely to the Christ ("fundamentalism").

Recent scholarship has tended to place Christianity within a category of "world religions." Precise definition of what is meant by "religion," "a religion," and each particular religion may never be possible, either for adherents or for those who seek an alternative viewpoint. Judaism and Islam have, however, long had their own understandings of the Christianity that was common to Christians. To the Jews, they were "the sect of the Nazarenes" (Acts 24:5, 28:22; Hebrew, *Nozerim*); thus they were described in terms of their leader's hometown. To Moslems in the Arab world, they continue to be *Nasrani,* a word that is used 15 times in the Qur'ān and is also derived from the locality of Nazareth.

Indeed, the preference continues for communal expressions that denote (for instance) Nestorians or Melkites or Jacobites, or Copts or Abyssinians or Armenians, or Greeks or Romans or "Christians" (i.e., Protestants), in the Moslem world, as in Asia and as in popular usage generally. Representing a "Middle Eastern" viewpoint, such a list usefully puts Westerners in mind of the churches to the east even of the Orthodox Patriarchate of Constantinople. Their history is less well known but at least comparable with that of those churches originating from within the Roman Empire. The Armenians became the first Christian "nation" in 301, for instance—a dozen years before the Roman Emperor Constantine's Edict of Milan (313).

Such items also demonstrate an exemplary care in the bestowal of accolades—and a matching attention to empirical observation. Indeed, when the eschatological concepts of Christ and Christianity (the Anointed, the Kingdom) are given their validity as ultimate value judgments, then concurrent social realities, such as tribal identities, also can be given their due recognition in this way.

—*Edward I. Bailey*

REFERENCES

The Gospels, especially *St Mark*; the Epistles, especially *I & II Corinthians* and *Philemon*; the *Oxford English Dictionary*; K. S. Latourette, *A History of the Expansion of Christianity* (New York: Harper, 1937); T. R. Morton, *The Twelve Together* (Glasgow: Iona Community, 1956); J. E. L. Newbigin, *A South India Diary* (London: SCM, 1951); local ephemera (many Christian fellowships publish a monthly magazine).

CHRISTIAN RIGHT Also known as the *New Christian Right* (NCR) or the *Religious Right,* this label was first used in the late 1970s to describe the surge in political activity among Protestant fundamentalists and evangelicals. Its usage has since been flexible, sometimes referring to the broad community of religious conservatives and other times referring to a small subset of institutionalized organizations pursuing cultural and economic conservatism.

The Christian Right arose in the late 1970s in response to such broad concerns as moral decline and secularization of American life as well as such narrow concerns as the attempt of federal regulatory agencies to intrude into the operations of evangelical and fundamentalist institutions. The Christian Right was embodied by the Rev. Jerry Falwell and his organization, the Moral Majority, in the early 1980s; more recently, Pat Robertson and his Christian Coalition have assumed that status.

Although social scientists use the term *Christian Right,* those who are involved in the movement sometimes consider it a pejorative phrase. They prefer such terms as *religious conservatives* or *pro-family conservatives* to describe their place in the American political system.

The scholarly literature on the Christian Right is vast. It has reflected that maturation of the movement. In the late 1970s and early 1980s, sociologists focused heavily on the rise of the Christian Right, seeking to explain its emergence through frameworks emphasizing perceived threats to the social status of the movement's members; political scientists focused on estimating the movement's electoral contribution to the Republican Party; scholars of religious studies explored the theological underpinnings of the movement and undertook cross-national comparisons to other fundamentalist movements.

By the mid-1980s, scholars began offering widely divergent interpretations of the Christian Right's progress and prospects. Those applying secularization theories believed it was in sharp decline and doomed to fail, while those applying social movement theories argued that the Christian Right was successfully institutionalizing itself. More recently, as the Christian Right has focused on exercising influence in state and local arenas, as one part of a much broader devolution of political power promoted by Republicans in Congress, scholars have conducted examinations of the impact of the Christian Right in subnational settings. Although the clarity and consistency of scholarship on the Christian Right was uneven in its early years, it too has matured over time. Many excellent treatments exist on different facets of the movement.

See also Evangelicalism, Politics, Televangelism

—*Matthew C. Moen*

REFERENCES

S. Bruce et al. (eds.), *The Rapture of Politics* (New Brunswick, N.J.: Transaction, 1995); M. Lienesch, *Redeeming America* (Chapel Hill: University of North Carolina Press, 1993); M. C. Moen, *The Transformation of the Christian Right* (Tuscaloosa: University of Alabama Press, 1992); D. Oldfield, *The Right and the Righteous* (Lanham, Md.: Rowman & Littlefield, 1996); M. J. Rozell and C. Wilcox, *Second Coming* (Baltimore: Johns Hopkins University Press, 1996); C. Wilcox, *God's Warriors* (Baltimore: Johns Hopkins University Press, 1992).

CHRISTIAN SCHOOL MOVEMENT Refers specifically to conservative Protestant evangelical and fundamentalist schools, and generally does not include Catholic parochial schools or those sponsored by mainline Protestant denominations. Tremendous growth has occurred in the "Christian School Movement" since the late 1970s.

Although some of the original impetus for the earliest schools was to avoid federally mandated racial integration, by the late 1980s significant racial integration was common. Moreover, by that time, most of the schools had policies specifically forbidding discrimination. In 1983, the Supreme Court ruled in *Bob Jones University v. U.S.* that the Internal Revenue Service could revoke the tax-exempt status of any private religious school engaged in discriminatory practices.

The Christian School Movement was one catalyst for the rise of the New Christian Right, as parents organized to protect their schools' autonomy from federal and state regulation. The National Christian Action Coalition—the first identifiable Christian-right lobby—organized on that basis. Parents also have fought regulations dealing with zoning and general hiring practices.

Given that regulation of private schools is a state prerogative, disparities exist in the level of control. The more restrictive states set curricular guidelines and accreditation standards and require teacher certification, going so far as jailing parents who send their children to schools violating those guidelines; other states grant the schools virtual autonomy, believing that education is a protected religious activity. Many schools not subject to state regulation voluntarily submit to nongovernmental accreditation from organizations such as the Association for Christian Schools International.

Christian Schools vary widely in their conservatism. Some schools have a distinctly fundamentalist orientation, replete with strict dress codes, while others are more relaxed. In contrast, the small number of publishers producing the curricula for a cross section of schools gives them an underlying similarity.

—*Julie Ingersoll and Matthew C. Moen*

REFERENCES

J. Ingersoll, *Train Up a Child,* Master's thesis, George Washington University, 1990; A. Peshkin, *God's Choice* (Chicago: University of Chicago Press, 1990); S. Rose, *Keeping Them Out of the Hands of Satan* (New York: Routledge, 1988); M. B. Wagner, *God's Schools* (New Brunswick, N.J.: Rutgers University Press, 1990).

CHRISTIAN SCIENCE The most organized manifestation of the New Thought movement, which stressed mind cure or metaphysical healing (Gottschalk 1973). Phineas Parkhurst Quimby, a magnetic healer in the Portland, Maine, area, served as the pivotal figure in the development of New Thought. After noticing that some of his patients responded well to simple remedies, he concluded that healing was mental and decided to give up hypnotism for mental suggestion or mesmerism.

Mary Baker Eddy (1821-1910), one of Quimby's patients, announced in 1866 that God had revealed to her the "key" by which to heal herself of an injury that physicians had declared incurable. She suffered from nervous disorders and a variety of physical ailments that eventually found relief through the belief, based upon her reading of the scriptures, that illness is an illusion and the recognition of such results in the restoration of health. Based upon the teachings in her book *Science and Health with Key to the Scriptures* (1875), Eddy established the Church of Christ, Scientist, in 1879. Christian Science denies the existence of matter, sin, death, and sickness, and asserts that all is mind, God, and good (Christian Science Publishing Society 1990). It is a religious healing system that claims to eradicate all manner of disease through spiritual power. In addition to drawing upon Quimby's work, Eddy incorporated ideas from transcendentalism, Swedenborgianism, and spiritualism. Christian Science recast God the Father of traditional Christianity into a father-mother god.

By 1900, the Church of Christ, Scientist, with its "Mother Church" in Boston, claimed to encompass nearly 500 congregations in North America and Europe. Because the church does not publicize membership figures, it is difficult to determine the size of the group. Estimates indicate that the membership may have reached 400,000 during the 1960s, but recent reports suggest a decline in the United States, Britain, and elsewhere. Studies of Christian Science suggest that its appeal has been mainly to the urban upper middle class, particularly to middle-aged and elderly women. Christian Science does not have a clergy but has its own professional body of teachers and practitioners. The board of directors has complete authority over the governing and doctrinal context of the Church of Christ, Scientist. Although branch churches elect their own officers, all officers are accountable to the board of directors.

Historians and journalists have given more attention to Christian Science than have social scientists. In contrast to the former, who have tended to focus on the life of Mary Baker Eddy and the organizational development of the church that she established, social scientists have expressed an interest in Christian Science as a religious healing system. Female practitioners reportedly outnumbered men by five to one by the 1890s and eight to one by the early 1980s (Schoepflin 1988). In contrast, men predominate in the more prestigious, higher paying administrative jobs in the organization (Fox 1989). Despite its religious orientation, Singer (1982:8) argues that Christian Science approaches to treatment for alcoholism function in much the same manner as conventional psychotherapeutic programs in that both "express a shared assumption: alcoholism is an individual problem rather than a reflection of more general structural contradictions in the larger society." This observation confirms DeHood's (1937:175) assertion that Christian Science constitutes "an opiate for those whose lives are already sheltered."

In the social scientific literature, Christian Science formed one of the four core groups upon which Bryan Wilson centered his pioneering work in church-sect theory (1961).

—*Hans A. Baer*

REFERENCES

Christian Science (Boston: Christian Science Publishing Society, 1990); S. Gottschalk, *The Emergence of Christian Science in American Medicine* (Berkeley: University of California Press, 1973); N. B. DeHood, *The Diffusion of a System of Belief,* Doctoral dissertation, Harvard University, 1937; M. Fox, "The Socioreligious Role of the Christian Science Practitioner," in *Women as Healers,* ed. C. Shepherd (New Brunswick, N.J.: Rutgers University Press, 1989): 98-113; R. B. Schoepflin, "Christian Science Healing in America," in *Other Healers,* ed. N. Gevitz (Baltimore: Johns Hopkins University Press, 1988): 192-214; M. Singer, "Christian Science Healing and Alcoholism," *Journal of Operational Psychiatry* 13(1982):2-12; B. Wilson, *Sects and Society* (London: Heinemann, 1961).

CHRISTIAN SOCIAL THOUGHT Social scientists bring their assumptions as well as their particular scientific theories to their work. The fact that many social scientists have lived and still do live in generally Christian societies leads us to expect that unspoken Christian tenets shape their research questions and interpretations. For example, the very idea of religion as a worship-centered supernaturalism comes from the Jewish-Christian heritage. The distinctness of religious from political organization and from ethnic identity is predicated on the circumstances in which Christianity first flourished as an alternative to the Roman imperial cult and as a competitor to the Jewish ethnic religion.

By the time sociology developed as an academic discipline in the universities, Christian thinkers as well as their secular counterparts found good reason to be critical of the capitalist social order. The exploitation of child labor by industry undermined the family as an institution; the prevailing low wages dehumanized the general workforce; the fast-paced materialism among the prosperous classes left only token space for religious pursuits. In the nineteenth and early twentieth centuries, what was termed the *social question* generated a reformist impulse in both the social sciences and Christianity.

In Europe and Latin America, official Christian church organizations were identified with social classes that were not the disprivileged or exploited sectors of society, and the churches often also were identified with regimes that were unfriendly toward reformist movements. In a few notable instances, European social scientific thinkers brought religious perspectives into analyses of social conditions—Frédéric Le Play in France, Thomas Masaryk in Czechoslovakia, and Luigi Sturzo in Italy—but it was in North America that religious reformism thrived. In early American sociology, reformism paralleled but did not stem from the Protestant Social Gospel movement (Swatos 1983). A number of early University of Chicago sociological theses and dissertations treated religion as an ethnic cultural resource for social betterment (Tomasi 1993). Parallels between early sociology and the tenets of the Social Gospel movement made sociology an acceptable course of study in many of the American denominational colleges (Morgan 1969). The Social Gospel movement itself became an object of inquiry for some social scientists (Horton 1940, Crysdale 1975) well after a post-World War I pessimism marked the end of the movement's heyday.

Meanwhile, the presence of Catholic working-class immigrants in the United States and Canada gave that denomination a class identity that it had lacked in Europe. *Rerum novarum* and subsequent papal encyclicals that criticized both unchecked capitalism and secular socialism were used by "labor priests" as a charter for providing intellectual leadership to the mainstream North American labor movement. Msgr. John A. Ryan was the most influential spokesman for this "social Catholicism"; he drafted a significant 1919 statement on social reconstruction that was published by the American bishops, and he provided the broad framework for the program of social legislation adopted by the Franklin Roosevelt administration in the 1930s and 1940s. Social Catholicism was also the ethical perspective of the generations of American Catholic sociologists who founded the American Catholic Sociological Society and then transformed it into the Association for the Sociology of Religion. Some of these sociologists, such as Eva Ross, Gerald Schnepp, Paul Hanley Furfey, Franz H. Mueller, and Marie Augusta Neal, wrote treatises in or about the social Catholic tradition as well as strictly sociological works, while others such as Joseph H. Fichter, Thomas P. Imse, and Joseph P. Fitzpatrick predicated their personal perspectives on it, while not generally mentioning it in their writings.

Both the Social Gospel movement and social Catholicism were concerned about economic justice. Children were not to be required to work for a living but were to experience a childhood that allowed for self-development and were to attend schools that would prepare them to be productive citizens. Work was to be compensated at rates that would afford one-wage families a reasonable standard of living as well as medical insurance and retirement plans. The state was to provide for the disabled with programs that would be funded by a progressive tax system. Labor would have the right to migrate across national boundaries and to organize in unions. There would be freedom of religion, opportunities for cultural pursuits, and protection from unsafe and unwholesome consumer products. Both the Social Gospel and social Catholicism defined social justice in terms of class issues but failed to foresee the importance of racial, gender, and other status group issues.

—*Anthony J. Blasi*

REFERENCES

S. Crysdale, "The Sociology of the Social Gospel," in *The Social Gospel in Canada*, ed. R. Allen (Ottawa: National Museums of Canada, 1975): 263-285; P. B. Horton, "The Social Orientation of the Church," *Sociology and Social Research* 24(1940):423-432; J. G. Morgan, "The Development of Sociology and the Social Gospel in America," *Sociological Analysis* 30(1969):42-53; W. H. Swatos, Jr., "The Faith of the Fathers," *Sociological Analysis* 44(1983):33-52; L. Tomasi, "The Influence of Religion on the Chicago School of Sociology," *Clinical Sociology Review* 11(1993):17-34.

CHRISTIAN SOCIOLOGY A phrase used in two distinct, although not unconnected, ways to refer to developments within the field of sociology since the late 1800s.

The older context of use was a movement, largely centered in liberal Protestant circles, that reflected a general quest to "make Christianity relevant to modern society." J. W. H. Stuckenberg can probably be credited with introducing the phrase in his book by that title published in 1880. The 1890s saw two Institutes of Christian Sociology formed—one under the leadership of George Herron of Iowa College (Grinnell), the other founded as an alternative to the first, under the leadership of Z. Swift Holbrook (with the imprimatur of Social Gospel leader Washington Gladden) at Oberlin College—neither of which lasted any length of time or made a significant impact upon subsequent sociology. Hartford Seminary also began a Summer School of Sociology, first inserting and then dropping *Christian* from its title. The journal *Bibliotheca Sacra,* of which Holbrook was coeditor, originally included sociology in its subtitle. A survey conducted by Holbrook in 1895 demonstrated that the phrase had a variety of meanings to both its supporters and its detractors, although there was some consensus that Christian *sociology* should be distinguished from Christian socialism, and that *Christian* sociology should be distinguished from the high-priestly new religion of Auguste Comte's sociology. *Christian sociology* from these roots has been a long-standing heading in the Library of Congress classification system.

A Christian approach to sociology began a process of revivification with the publication of essays by William L. Kolb in the 1960s. An organizational network began later with the Christian Sociologists prayer group, largely as an effort by George A. Hillery, Jr., but with support from others, including David O. Moberg, Margaret Poloma, Patricia Kirby, Thomas C. Hood, and Jack O. Balswick, which subsequently became the Christian Sociological Society, as well as ACTS, the Association of Christians Teaching Sociology, both of which meet annually. Leadership in the recent movement has come from evangelical and charismatic traditions, has tended to be primarily outside of the hands of the clergy, and has been rather cool toward sociologists from the liberal traditions, even if professing Christians, who treat sociology as a "value-free" discipline. The CSS initially published an occasional *Newsletter* that has now become a quarterly.

—*William H. Swatos, Jr.*

REFERENCES

G. A. Hillery, Jr., *A Research Odyssey* (New Brunswick, N.J.: Transaction, 1982); Z. S. Holbrook, "What Is Sociology," *Bibliotheca Sacra* 52(1895):458-504; W. L. Kolb, "Sociology and the Christian Doctrine of Man," in *Religion and Contemporary Western Culture*, ed. E. Cell (Nashville: Abingdon, 1967): 360-369; J. W. H. Stuckenberg, *Christian Sociology* (New York: Funk, 1880); W. H. Swatos, Jr., *Faith of the Fathers* (Bristol, Ind.: Wyndham Hall, 1984); W. H. Swatos, Jr., "Religious Sociology and the Sociology of Religion in America at the Turn of the Twentieth Century," *Sociological Analysis* 50(1989):363-375; issues of the CSS *Newsletter*.

CHURCH-AND-STATE ISSUES IN THE UNITED STATES

Church-state relations in the United States are currently undergoing a significant and highly conflicted transformation. Substantial revisions are being made in the seminal church-state jurisprudence of the midcentury decades in which both the "no establishment" and the "free exercise" clauses of the First Amendment were interpreted more broadly than previously and, moreover, became enshrined in elaborate constitutional "balancing tests." The midcentury judicial interpretive structures are now being disassembled while church-state tension, conflict, and litigation are increasing (Robbins 1993).

The "no establishment" (or simply "establishment") clause of the First Amendment has in recent decades been interpreted as mandating governmental neutrality not only between or among religions but also, implicitly, between religion and irreligion; that is, the state cannot support religion in any manner. This was not always the case. Indeed, the First Amendment's prohibition on Congress from making any law "respecting an establishment of religion" initially may have been intended to "protect the state religious establishments from disestablishment by the federal government" (Carter 1993:118). For many decades, courts perceived little or no conflict between the establishment clause and a de facto Protestant establishment (Demerath and Williams 1987).

In the twentieth century, the notion of a broad "separation of church and state" linked to an expansive conception of the "no establishment" norm became more attractive to Protestant churches in part as a response to the mainstreaming of Catholicism. It was feared that the latter, increasingly powerful and reputable, might conceivably "establish" itself in those cities in which it predominated (Demerath and Williams 1987). Separationism thus became Protestantism's compensation for loss of hegemony. More recently, however, Southern Baptists and other evangelical groups have somewhat reversed their position on church-state separation and now see the latter as associated with the insidious modern "establishment" of secular humanism.

The American combination of a formal separation of religious and public spheres and a culture pervaded by religion is somewhat of an anomaly that produces a periodic eruption of quasi-religious puritanical movements such as abolitionism, temperance, or McCarthy-ism, which impinge on the political realm (Tiryakian 1993). Research by Williams and Demerath (1991) indicates that the idea of separation enjoys broad support among Americans, as does a partly conflicting notion of "civil religion," or the sacredness of American society and the moral and spiritual unity of the nation. According to the authors, there are three modes of popular and intellectual rationalizations that mitigate the tension between the values of separation and civil religion: (1) A *selective* resolution manipulates narrow and convenient definitions of "religion" and "politics"; (2) a *contingent* resolution stresses the mutually reinforcing interdependence of civil religion and church-state separation; and (3) a *majoritarian* resolution implicitly redefines the separation of church and state as pertaining mainly to deviant sects who alone are to be kept out of the public sphere or denied full legal protection.

Midcentury Balancing Tests In a line of Supreme Court cases between the late 1940s and the early 1970s, the purpose-effect-entanglement criteria, or "Lemon Test" (from *Lemon v. Kurtzman* 1971), evolved to adjudicate "separation" claims under the establishment clause. The First Amendment was held to be violated if a public measure did not have a "secular purpose," if it tended to promote or inhibit religion, or if it unduly "entangled" the state with a religion. In the context of evangelical religious revival and politicization plus conservative political and judicial ascendancy, the Lemon Test is losing support and is strongly criticized (e.g., Carter 1993:109-115). More permissive alternatives have been suggested (McConnel 1992:155-168) such as a "coercion test," merely prohibiting the government from coercing anyone to accept or relinquish a faith. At this writing, there does not seem to be any judicial consensus on what should replace the Lemon Test or how the latter might be modified. Souring on the Lemon Test but uncertain as to how to improve or transcend it, the Supreme Court seems to be marking time by redefining cases that seem to raise establishment clause issues as essentially *free speech* cases. Religious litigants can thus be vindicated without formally redefining the scope of the establishment clause or explicitly revising or repudiating the Lemon Test (e.g., the 1995 decision in *Rosenberger v. U. Virginia* compelling the university to subsidize a religious magazine out of funds collected from students). The Lemon Test thus languishes from not-so-benign neglect, while an indirect approach to weakening the separation of church and state evolves (Bradley et al. 1995).

The free exercise clause of the First Amendment remained more or less of a dead letter for many decades.

"The nation's consensus on core religious beliefs made it unlikely that many 'free exercise' cases would arise" (Demerath and Williams 1987:78). For many decades, the controlling precedent was the 1878 Mormon polygamy case, *Reynolds v. U.S.,* which ordained that the First Amendment's guarantee of religious "free exercise" protects mainly religious *belief* and that "conduct, however religiously motivated, must conform to valid secular laws" (Way and Burt 1983:660). Midcentury cases in the 1960s and 1970s modified this dictum and established the rule that if a regulation "burdens" religious practice, it must be supported by a demonstration of a "compelling state interest" (CSI) on behalf of intervention. This test appears to have been recently overturned by Justice Scalia's majority opinion in *Employment Div. v. Smith* (1990), which proclaimed that uniform, across-the-board (i.e., nondiscriminatory) regulations are not to be viewed as presumptively invalid and do not require a showing of a CSI. An ambiguous loophole involves "hybrid cases" in which free speech as well as free exercise is implicated; that is, religious *speech* acts may possibly still receive "substantive" (CSI) protection (Laycock 1991). In 1994, Congress passed the Religious Freedom Restoration Act (RFRA), which was supposed to restore the CSI test, but interpretations of the scope and effect of the RFRA vary markedly, and one federal judge has already declared RFRA unconstitutional. At this writing, the Supreme Court is considering the constitutionality of RFRA.

Problems of Religious Minorities   Powerful, reputable churches can forfend against burdensome regulations by nonjudicial means, therefore the effect of *Smith* will fall mainly on minority sects (Finke and Iannaccone 1993). The ruling "entrenches patterns of de facto discrimination against minority religions" (Sullivan 1992:216). Of interest, the CSI balancing test may actually have had a slight operational bias in favor of minority religions (Way and Burt 1983). A widespread perception that deviant sects were becoming the primary clientele of modern free exercise jurisprudence may have made it easier for conservative jurists to dispense with substantive (CSI) free exercise (Carmella 1992), although conventional churches also may need First Amendment protection. "In an increasingly secular society, churches begin to play sectarian roles and the notion of mainstream religion becomes oxymoronic" (Demerath and Williams 1987:81).

Religious minorities are on the cutting point of free exercise litigation because regulatory initiatives may be "tested" first on politically weak or disreputable groups before becoming integrated into church-state law (Robbins 1985). Scholars in religious studies and the sociology of religion have been particularly concerned with church-state issues involving minority religions (Bromley and Robbins 1992, Pfeiffer and Ogloff 1992, Robbins and Beckford 1993), and most particularly with issues involving *conversion processes,* that is, "brainwashing" claims (Anthony and Robbins 1995, Richardson 1993, Shinn 1992). Because "new religious movements" (NRMs) generally lack a large membership base for internal donative funding, they often become commercially diversified; hence state regulation of their economic activities also has been a concern (Passas 1994, Richardson 1988a), as have legal issues regarding violent confrontations with authorities (Gaffney 1995). Nevertheless, the overwhelming majority of scholarly contributions in the area of NRMs and the law have dealt with "mind control" issues, perhaps because litigants' claims and state intervention in this area implicate religious *beliefs* (Anthony and Robbins, 1992), as well as *free speech,* and raise the specter of state regulation of *subjective consciousness.* Although the evolving legal situation with respect to "cults" and psychological coercion claims remains ambiguous (Anthony and Robbins 1992), the spate of recent episodes of large-scale violence involving American, Euro-Canadian, and Japanese "cults" (1993-1995) may shift public opinion against the defense of the First Amendment rights of sectarian minorities.

There is some dissensus over whether the rights of religious minorities will be protected better under conditions of a strict separation of church and state, in which majoritarian discrimination might be minimized, or whether minority rights are more safely entrusted to (antiseparationist) "accommodationists" who believe in weak state regulatory claims and strong free exercise protections. "Accommodation," however, is often primarily accommodation to powerful and reputable churches at the expense of dissident or minority movements (Richardson 1988b). More generally, there is conflict over whether the establishment and free exercise clauses of the First Amendment are coequal such that religion is protected from state interference while the public realm is simultaneously protected from religious interference. Alternatively, the protection of religious freedom is seen as the first priority such that "separation" becomes merely instrumental (Carter 1993). In this view, secularization and religious exclusion from "the naked public square" now have become excessive (Carter 1993, Neuhaus 1984). The degree of "separation" that should exist between church and state is thus currently controversial among religious intelligentsia. There is greater consensus, at least among writers and scholars focusing on religion, on the need for broad constitutional protection of free exercise.

Nevertheless, Hammond and Mazur (1995) suggest that free exercise should be more narrowly defined in terms of individual *conscience,* an approach that favors individual commitments over what a writer with a different view has called the "corporate free exercise" of churches (Worthing 1985). However, Carter (1993:129-132) sees the *reduction* of protected free exercise to individual (as opposed to collective-institutional) commitments, or to verbal communicative acts (as opposed to ritual acts and physical acts of worship), as trivializing religion and denying its collective and behavioral nature.

Growing Church-State Tension Various factors may be identified as contributing to the current growth of church-state tension. The increase in religious pluralism represents a key factor because a disproportionate amount of free exercise and general church-state litigation now involves religious minorities (Wood 1985). The growth of government in connection with the increasing dependence of religious and other service groups on direct or indirect state support to pursue their missions accentuates conflict as the state hungrily eyes tax-exempt church revenues while churches seek non-discriminatory public support for their social programs as integral to their free exercise. It is frequently maintained that in the context of the "welfare-regulatory state," there are simply too many inexorable points of contact between the state and religious organizations for the "benign neglect" ideal of strict separation to remain viable (Carter 1993:136-155, McConnel 1992).

The presently enhanced politicization of some forms of American religion and the associated decline of moral consensus and rise of "cultural politics" clearly form part of the context of heightened church-state tension. Increasingly, "moral disputes must be referred to the political process and the courts" (Berger 1982:18). The litigation and legislation of moral issues "entangles" both the state in the religio-moral realm and the religio-moral interests in political and legal processes. Religious groups and leaders are thus increasingly encouraged to put forward claims in the public sphere; that is, the "politicization of religion" comes to entail the "religionization of the state" (Robertson and Chirico 1985). According to Cochran et al. (1987:612), under the impact of various social, technological, political, and cultural changes, the hallowed liberal dichotomies of public-private, religious-secular, and church-state are becoming blurred; church-state tension proliferates in the growing ambiguity, as "changes in the activity and scope of government are likely to continue to stimulate religious politics."

It may be ironic that the current increase in church-state conflict and litigation, to which religious revival and religious politicization are contributing, may conceivably result in a curtailment of the traditionally *deregulated* quality of American religion, which some scholars view as a key source of its vitality (Finke and Iannaccone 1993).

—*Thomas Robbins*

REFERENCES

D. Anthony and T. Robbins, "Law, Social Science and the 'Brainwashing' Exception to the First Amendment," *Behavioral Sciences and the Law* 10(1992):5-30; P. Berger, "From the Crisis of Religion to the Crisis of Secularity," in *Religion and America,* ed. M. Douglas and S. Tipton (Boston: Beacon, 1982): 14-24; D. G. Bromley and J. K. Hadden (eds.), *Handbook of Cults and Sects in America* (Greenwich, Conn.: JAI, 1993); D. G. Bromley and T. Robbins, "The Role of Government in Regulating New and Unconventional Religions," in *Government Monitoring of Religions,* ed. J. Wood (Waco, Tex.: Baylor University Press, 1993): 101-137; A. Carmella, "A Theological Critique of Free Exercise Jurisprudence," *George Washington Law Review* 60(1993):782-808; S. Carter, *The Culture of Disbelief* (New York: Basic Books, 1993); C. Cochran, "Public/Private—Secular/Sacred," *Journal of Church and State* 29(1987):113-125; C. Cochran et al., "Public Policies and the Emergence of Religious Politics," *Polity* 19(1987):595-612; N. J. Demerath III and R. Williams, "A Mythical Past and Uncertain Future," in T. Robbins and R. Robertson (eds.), *q.v.* (1987): 77-90; R. Finke and L. Iannaccone, "Supply-Side Explanations for Religious Change," *Annals* 527(1993):27-39; E. M. Gaffney, "The Waco Tragedy," in *Armageddon in Waco,* ed. S. Wright (Chicago: University of Chicago Press, 1995): 323-358; P. E. Hammond and E. M. Mazur, "Church, State and the Dilemma of Conscience," *Journal of Church and State* 37(1995):555-572; D. Laycock, "The Remnants of Free Exercise," *Supreme Court Review 1990* (Chicago: University of Chicago Press, 1991): 1-58; M. W. McConnel, "Religious Freedom at a Crossroads," in *The Bill of Rights in the Modern State,* ed. G. Stone et al. (Chicago: University of Chicago Press, 1992): 115-194; R. Neuhaus, *The Naked Public Square* (Grand Rapids, Mich.: Eerdmans, 1984); N. Passas, "The Market for Gods and Services," in *Between Sacred and Secular,* ed. A. Greil and T. Robbins (Greenwich, Conn.: JAI, 1994): 217-240; J. Pfeiffer and J. Ogloff (eds.), "Cults and the Law," *Behavioral Sciences and the Law* 10, 1(1992); J. T. Richardson, "Changing Times," *Sociological Analysis* 49(1988a):S1-S14; J. T. Richardson (ed.), *Money and Power in the New Religions* (Toronto: Mellen, 1988b); J. T. Richardson, "A Social Psychological Critique of 'Brainwashing' Claims About Recruitment to New Religions," in D. G. Bromley and J. K. Hadden (eds.), Vol. B, *q.v.* (1993): 75-97; T. Robbins, "Government Regulatory Powers over Religious Movements," *Journal for the Scientific Study of Religion* 24(1985):237-251; T. Robbins, "The Intensification of Church-state Tensions in the United States," *Social Compass* 40 (1993):505-527; T. Robbins and J. Beckford,

"Religious Movements and Church-State Issues," in D. G. Bromley and J. K. Hadden (eds.), Vol. A, *q.v.* (1993): 199-218; T. Robbins and R. Robertson (eds.), *Church-State Relations* (New Brunswick, N.J.: Transaction, 1987); R. Robertson and J. A. Chirico, "Humanity, Globalization and Worldwide Religious Resurgence," *Sociological Analysis* 46(1985):219-242; L. D. Shinn, "Cult Conversions and the Courts," *Sociological Analysis* 53(1992):273-285; K. Sullivan, "Religion and Liberal Democracy," in *The Bill of Rights and the Modern State,* ed. G. Stone (Chicago: University of Chicago Press, 1992): 195-224; E. Tiryakian, "American Religious Exceptionalism," *Annals* 527(1993):40-54; F. Way and B. Burt, "Religious Marginality and the Free Exercise Clause," *American Political Science Review* 77(1983):654-665; R. Williams and N. J. Demerath III, "Religion and Political Process in an American City," *American Sociological Review* 56(1991): 417-431; S. Worthing, "Corporate Free Exercise," in *Religion and the State,* ed J. Wood, Jr. (Waco, Tex.: Baylor University Press, 1985): 167-184.

CHURCH OF JESUS CHRIST OF LATTER-DAY SAINTS   *see* Mormonism

CHURCH-SECT THEORY   In its many permutations and combinations as an explanation of religious organization and religiosity, church-sect theory may be the most important middle-range theory that the sociology of religion has to offer.

Although the terms *church* and *sect* have a long heritage in the writings of church historians, credit for their first attachment to sociological concepts belongs to Max Weber. Their first popularization among students of religion in the modern sense, however, was through H. Richard Niebuhr's adaptation of the work of Weber's sometime associate Ernst Troeltsch. To understand some of the confusion and debate in contemporary sociological usage, it is helpful to review how the concepts fit into Weber's sociology of religion and how Troeltsch's work modified them.

Weberian Sociology and Troeltschian Syndrome Weber's sociology is united by the overarching thematic element of the process of the rationalization of action. Weber was attempting to answer the question of why the universal-historical rationalization-disenchantment process had come to fruition most completely in the Anglo-American spirit of capitalism. As a part of this project, Weber also had to develop an analytical method that would permit him to resolve the dilemma of his commitment to the principle that sociology was a scientific discipline, on the one hand, and on the other, the difficulty in supplementing empathic *verstehende Soziologie* with anything even approximating experi-

mental accuracy. Weber's answer was a comparative methodology using the tool of the *ideal-type*—a hypothetically concrete reality, a mental construct based upon relevant empirical components, formed and explicitly delineated by the researcher to facilitate precise comparisons on specific points of interest. Like the "inch" in measurement, the conceptualizations of "church" and "sect" serve to enable two or more religious organizations to be compared with each other; church-sect theory in Weber's usage was *not* a standard *to* which religious organizations were compared but *by* which they were compared. The critical differentiating variable for Weber was "mode of membership"—that is, whether the normal method of membership recruitment of the organization was by "birth" (church) or "decision" (sect).

In the transition from Weber to Troeltsch's *The Social Teachings of the Christian Churches,* the church-sect typology underwent significant alterations. Troeltsch was not a social scientist but a theologian attempting to relate types of religious experience to the varieties of social teachings with which they might be correlated. In so doing, he departed from Weber on two critical points. First, he shifted the emphasis of the type from organization to behavior. Second, he stressed the notion of "accommodation" or "compromise" as differentiating between the different religious styles. The first departure is most clearly seen in Troeltsch's positing of *three* types of religious behavior: churchly, sectarian, and mystical. The third of these is now generally dropped from consideration by church-sect theorists; in Weber's conceptualization, it occurs in a separate bipolar typology, namely, that of asceticism-mysticism. Nevertheless, the presence of the mystical type at the outset of Troeltsch's discussion suggests that he was actually using the terms in a conceptually different operation from that to which *church-sect* is usually put in organizational analysis. The "dichotomy" of church-sect that has been attributed to Troeltsch—whatever its value—must be understood within his three-way scheme and within the instrumental context of the Weberian ideal-type as well. Troeltsch shared with Weber primarily method, partially content, and peripherally project. Weber and Troeltsch were working on different, although related, questions; Troeltsch understood Weber's concept of the ideal-type, capitalized on what Weber termed its "transiency," and hence made church, sect, and mysticism work for his own purposes.

Subsequent church-sect arguments have largely revolved around an overemphasis upon the Weber-Troeltsch association that assumes that because Troeltsch used Weber's method and to some extent his content, the *intention* of Troeltsch's work was the same as Weber's, which it was not. *What Troeltsch himself calls a "sociological formulation" of a theological question has been misidentified with Weber's attempt to solve a sociological problem.* We see the difference between the two projects clearly in the critical distinguishing elements that form the focus for each one's work. Whereas Weber uses mode of membership, Troeltsch adopts accommodation or compromise. While mode of membership can be ascertained relatively directly, accommodation has a more mediated character: What is and is not accommodation is more perspectival. A theological rather than organizational focus comes to frame the theory.

The basis for the shift in usage lies in the way in which the theory was introduced to English-speaking audiences, with the corresponding void created in German scholarship as a result of the two world wars. The first major American publication to use the types was the work of another sociologically inclined theologian, H. Richard Niebuhr, *The Social Sources of Denominationalism* (1929). Although at times possessed by a rather naive evolutionism and narrow perspective, Niebuhr's work contributed a significant element that was lacking in earlier treatments. He used church and sect as poles of a continuum, rather than simply as discrete categories. Niebuhr did not merely classify groups in relation to their relative sect-likeness or church-likeness but analyzed the dynamic process of religious history as groups moved along this continuum. An unfortunate result of Niebuhr's work, however, was that taken by itself it tended toward the reification of the types and the hypothetical continuum that he in turn posited. It thus contained further seeds for church-sect theory to develop into an evaluative device, quite outside the sociological frame of reference in which it was conceived. This disjuncture was compounded by the fact that Troeltsch's *Social Teachings* was translated in 1931, whereas Weber's methodological work was not available in translation until 1949. Many of the subsequent difficulties that have attended church-sect theory may be traced to the strange movements of this framework and its methodological base across the Atlantic.

Elaboration, Reaction, and Revision Subsequent elaborations of church-sect theory have been clearly dependent upon the work of Troeltsch and Niebuhr. The original "church-sect dichotomy" became generally interpreted as a continuum having a multicriteria basis for its analyses. Howard Becker (1932) was the first American trained as a sociologist to use and extend church-sect theory. Attempting to facilitate increased specificity, Becker delineated two types within each of the original two types, resulting in a cult-sect-denomination-ecclesia model. In thus developing the typology, Becker abandoned the ideal-type method for that of "abstract collectivities," ideal realities rather than constructs.

J. Milton Yinger in *Religion and the Struggle for Power* (1946) increased the limitations for specific points along the continuum, extending Becker's four types to six: cult, sect, established sect, class church/ denomination, ecclesia, and universal church—the latter most clearly evidencing the increasingly theological focus of the usage. Yinger went further in his specification, however, by subtyping sects in terms of their relationship to the social order—whether they were accepting, avoiding, or aggressive. This development began a wave of interest in the sect type within church-sect theorizing, with numerous writers offering contributions on the best way of treating this possibility, the most lasting of which has been that of Bryan Wilson (1959). The result of this strategy was to shift the focus of church-sect theory from a tool for comparative analysis toward a classificatory system to apply sociological jargon to religious organization.

An exception to this general tendency to focus on religious organizations (first "sects," later "cults") that were increasingly more marginal to mainstream society was the publication of a seminal essay on the *denomination* by David Martin (1962). Although it did little to stem the tide of interest in marginal groups at the time, Martin's article would bear fruit in various ways in new typologies that appeared in the late 1970s. The action sociology models of both Wallis and Swatos as well as the rational choice models of Stark and his colleagues emphasize the importance of denominational religiosity as the typological alternative to sectarianism (and cultic forms).

On the heels of these developments came criticism of the framework. A number of critics denounced the orientation as meaningless or, at best, woefully inadequate to systematic investigation of the empirical world. Church-sect theorizing has been criticized as ambiguous and vague, lacking precise definitions, unsuited to tests for validity and reliability, merely descriptive rather than explanatory, less informative than other possible approaches, historically and geographically restricted, and unrelated to the rest of sociological theory. Despite all of these criticisms, however, the theoretical framework into which church-sect has evolved has allowed a tremendous amount of data to be organized and reported.

In response to these criticisms, a number of scholars have made revisions within the church-sect framework, making it a more viable theoretical orientation for the sociology of religion. Yinger (1970), Paul Gustafson

	Self-Conceived Basis of Legitimacy	
	Pluralistically legitimate	*Uniquely legitimate*
Exclusive	Institutionalized sect	Sect
Inclusive	Denomination	Church

Membership Principle

Figure C.1. Robertson's Church-Sect Model

(1967, 1973), Roland Robertson (1970), Roy Wallis (1975), and William Swatos (1979), for example, each have suggested the value of an explicit visual scheme for modeling and analysis. (The Robertson and Swatos models are illustrated in this entry; Yinger's model appears in his entry.) Bryan Wilson, whose work on sects has now spanned almost 40 years, has come increasingly to accept a Weberian approach. Stark and Bainbridge (1979) have reached back into earlier work by Glock and Stark to use pieces of church-sect theorizing in their "rational choice" modeling.

Neo-Weberian Analyses   Particularly significant to this process of rethinking church-sect theory was the work of Benton Johnson. Early in his career, Johnson (1957) critiqued the Troeltschian approach to church-sect. In Johnson's subsequent work (1963, 1971), he returned to Weber, not directly to his discussion of church-sect but to Weber's distinction between emissary and exemplary prophets. From this perspective, Johnson focuses upon the single universal variable property of a group's relationship to the social environment in which it exists. "Church" is employed as the polar type of *acceptance* of the social environment, whereas "sect" is the polar type of its *rejection*. This conceptualization is similar to an earlier one proposed by Peter Berger (1954), in which the more-difficult-to-operationalize variable "nearness of the spirit" was the central focus. In later work, Bryan Wilson (1973) also embraced "response to the world" as the principal basis for classification of sects in an ideal-typical (rather than taxonomic) way. Johnson contends that the sociologist should strive toward the discovery of universal properties at a high level of generality that vary in such ways that typologies might be constructed. He sees "acceptance/rejection of the social environment" as a single variable around which empirical church-sect distinctions may be grouped and asserts that this typological approach is superior to one that simply adds types as historical circumstances alter. Johnson's work has significantly affected such differing streams as Swatos's situationalism as well as the rational choice modeling of Stark and his colleagues.

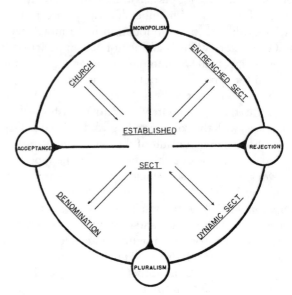

Figure C.2. Swatos's Church-Sect Model

Although Johnson's distinction possesses definite advantages in terms of conceptual parsimony, its lack of integration of the historical differences in the basic social structures and cultural systems in which religious organizations function produces potential difficulties in macrosociological analyses. Whereas the microsociologically based rational choice model focuses primarily on the effects of the organizational experience of the decision maker and only secondarily on the organization-system component, a more culturally oriented analysis would note that different system contexts produce different styles of organizational response that cannot be entirely comprehended by a single, universal variable component. Thus Swatos crosscuts Johnson's acceptance-rejection dichotomy with the sociocultural system polarity of monopolism-pluralism. Following upon the work of both Peter Berger (1969) and David Little (1969), Swatos contends that the nature of the sociocultural system shapes the patterns of acceptance and rejection that become expressed in specific religious organizational forms and rationales. In related work, Swatos (1981), following up leads from Martin and Wallis, has criticized the use of "cult" in Stark's church-sect modeling; Swatos argues that from the

Weberian point of view out of which church-sect theorizing sprang, "cult" is properly contrasted to "order" as organizational manifestations of the mysticism-asceticism typology, rather than incorporated into church-sect itself.

See also Denominationalism, H. Richard Niebuhr, Ernst Troeltsch, Max Weber

—*William H. Swatos, Jr.*

REFERENCES

H. Becker, *Systematic Sociology* (New York: Wiley, 1932); P. L. Berger, "The Sociological Study of Sectarianism," *Social Research* 21(1954):467-485; P. L. Berger, *The Sacred Canopy* (Garden City, N.Y.: Doubleday, 1969); A. W. Eister, "H. Richard Niebuhr and the Paradox of Religious Organization," in *Beyond the Classics?* ed. C. Y. Glock and P. E. Hammond (New York: Harper, 1973): 355-408; W. R. Garrett, "Maligned Mysticism," *Sociological Analysis* 36(1975):205-223; P. Gustafson, "UO-US-PS-PO," *Journal for the Scientific Study of Religion* 6(1967):64-68; P. Gustafson, "Exegesis on the Gospel According to St. Max," *Sociological Analysis* 34(1973):12-25; P. Gustafson, "The Missing Member of Troeltsch's Trinity," *Sociological Analysis* 36(1975):224-226; B. Johnson, "A Critical Appraisal of Church-Sect Typology," *American Sociological Review* 22(1957):88-92; B. Johnson, "On Church and Sect," *American Sociological Review* 28(1963):539-549; B. Johnson, "Church and Sect Revisited," *Journal for the Scientific Study of Religion* 10(1971):124-137; D. Little, *Religion, Order, and Law* (New York: Harper, 1969); D. Martin, "The Denomination," *British Journal of Sociology* 13(1962):1-14; H. R. Niebuhr, *The Social Sources of Denominationalism* (New York: Holt, 1929); R. Robertson, *The Sociological Interpretation of Religion* (New York: Schocken, 1970); R. Robertson, "On the Analysis of Mysticism," *Sociological Analysis* 36(1970):241-266; R. Stark and W. S. Bainbridge, "Of Churches, Sects, and Cults," *Journal for the Scientific Study of Religion* 18(1979):117-131; W. H. Swatos, Jr., *Into Denominationalism* (Storrs, Conn.: Society for the Scientific Study of Religion, 1979); W. H. Swatos, Jr., "Church-Sect and Cult," *Sociological Analysis* 42(1981):17-26; E. Troeltsch, *The Social Teachings of the Christian Churches*, Vol. 1 (New York: Macmillan, 1931); R. Wallis, "Scientology," *Sociology* 9 1975):89-100; M. Weber, *The Methodology of the Social Sciences* (New York: Free Press, 1949); M. Weber, "On Church, Sect, and Mysticism," *Sociological Analysis* 34(1973):140-149; M. Weber, *Economy and Society* (Berkeley: University of California Press, 1978); B. Wilson, "An Analysis of Sect Development," *American Sociological Review* 24(1959):3-15; B. Wilson, *Magic and the Millennium* (New York: Harper, 1973); J. M. Yinger, *Religion and the Struggle for Power* (Durham, N.C.: Duke University Press, 1946); J. M. Yinger, *The Scientific Study of Religion* (New York: Macmillan, 1970).

CIPRIANI, ROBERTO (1945–) Professor of Sociology of Religion, Third University of Rome. Successively Secretary and President of the Research Committee 22 (Sociology of Religion), International Sociological Association (1986-1994).

Cipriani has written or edited more than 20 books and more than 200 articles. He has written extensively on popular religion, the sacred and secularization, and has coined the concept of "diffused religion"—a pervasive and persistent religiosity diffused throughout the population by primary and secondary socialization, which is periodically revitalized by the cycle of the Christian calendar. Recently, he has been especially interested in the persistence of values traditionally linked to Christianity that are becoming increasingly independent of it.

—*Karel Dobbelaere*

REFERENCES

Il Cristo rosso (Roma: Ianua, 1985); " 'Diffused Religion' and New Values in Italy," in *The Changing Face of Religion*, ed. J. A. Beckford and T. Luckmann (London: Sage, 1989): 24-48; *La religione dei valori* (Caltanissetta-Roma: Sciascia, 1992).

CISR *see* Société Internationale de Sociologie des Religions

CIVIL DISOBEDIENCE A tactic used in the pursuit of social change, often connected with religiously based activism. Current use is rooted in the writings of Mohandas Gandhi and Martin Luther King, Jr., and is usually related to commitments to nonviolence.

Civil disobedient actions deliberately violate existing laws to demonstrate conditions of injustice. For example, African Americans in the U.S. civil rights movement protested legal segregation by sitting in "whites only" sections of lunch counters and public buses. Antinuclear demonstrators have deliberately "occupied" nuclear power and weapons sites. Participants allow themselves to be arrested, further reinforcing the message that the laws, not their actions, are immoral.

—*Rhys H. Williams*

REFERENCES

B. Epstein, *Political Protest and Cultural Revolution* (Berkeley: University of California Press, 1991); M. L. King, Jr., *Letter from the Birmingham Jail* (San Francisco: Harper,

1994); A. Morris, *The Origins of the Civil Rights Movement* (New York: Free Press, 1984).

CIVIL RELIGION Originating in the work of Rousseau, with echoes in Tocqueville, this concept made its major impact on the social scientific study of religion with the publication of an essay titled "Civil Religion in America," written by Robert Bellah in *Daedalus* in 1967. The article caused an almost unprecedented burst of excitement among sociologists and other scholars of religion. Soon the topic became the major focus at professional conferences in the social scientific study of religion, and numerous articles and books—most being conceptual and historical, some being empirically based—began to appear.

In social scientific usage, cultural institutions are usually matched by certain kinds of social groups. Religion, for example, is socially embodied in associations called churches, education in schools, the economy in businesses, and so on. Civil religion is unique in U.S. culture—and arguably in other cultures as well—in that it does not claim an identifiable social group short of the entire society itself.

Definition The concept refers to a "transcendent universal religion of the nation" and resonates well with the functional sociology of Émile Durkheim and Bellah's mentor, Talcott Parsons. Indeed, it was Parsons who was originally intended to write the *Daedalus* article (Bellah 1989).

Bellah's article claimed that most Americans share common religious characteristics expressed through civil religious beliefs, symbols, and rituals that provide a religious dimension to the entirety of American life. Later, he adds that civil religious principles transcend the nation and represent a "higher standard" by which the nation should be judged (Bellah 1970:168, 1974:255). Therefore, civil religiosity is posited to be a common, if not socially integrative, set of beliefs in transcendent principles and reality against which the historical experience and actions of the nation should be evaluated.

Bellah's definition of American civil religion is that it is "an institutionalized collection of sacred beliefs about the American nation," which he sees symbolically expressed in America's founding documents and presidential inaugural addresses. It includes a belief in the existence of a transcendent being called "God," an idea that the American nation is subject to God's laws, and an assurance that God will guide and protect the United States. Bellah sees these beliefs in the values of liberty, justice, charity, and personal virtue and concretized in,

for example, the words *In God We Trust* on both national emblems and on the currency used in daily economic transactions. Although American civil religion shares much with the religion of Judeo-Christian denominations, Bellah claims that it is distinct from denominational religion. Crucial to Bellah's Durkheimian emphasis is the claim that civil religion is definitionally an "objective social fact."

Although other American scholars had articulated civil religion types of ideas (for example, Martin Marty's "religion-in-general" [1959] and Sidney Mead's "religion of the republic" [1963]), the publication of Bellah's essay at the height of national soul-searching during the Vietnam War occasioned Bellah's place as a major interpreter of American religion in the second half of the twentieth century and caused an enormous and prolonged outpouring of scholarly activity. The nature and extent of this work may be examined best through the Russell Richey and Donald Jones anthology *American Civil Religion* (Harper 1974), a bibliographic essay by Phillip Hammond (1976), Gail Gehrig's monograph *American Civil Religion: An Assessment* (Society for the Scientific Study of Religion 1981), and James Mathisen's 20-year review essay (1989).

Finding Civil Religion A subsequent "civil religion debate" began that focused on several interrelated issues at the heart of which, however, was a definitional question: In other words, what really qualified as both *civil* and *religion* in the concept? For example, W. Lloyd Warner (1961) had previously delineated a dynamic in the United States that he called *Americanism*: How did civil religion differ from this? Did people have to know they were civil religious to be civil religious? Was civil religion in America more than "an idolatrous worship of the American nation"? (see Mathisen 1989:130). Some general tendencies may be noted here.

First, there was a systematic critique of the concept of civil religion qua *religion,* principally from the historian John F. Wilson (e.g., 1979). This was partially offset, on the other hand, by a shift in Bellah's own work, wherein civil religion became an increasingly evaluative concept, as in his bicentennial volume *The Broken Covenant* (Seabury 1975). No doubt, the U.S. bicentennial provided a major impetus to civil religion discussion, so much so that Mathisen refers to the period 1974-1977 as the "Golden Age" of civil religion discussion.

Although the civil religion thesis claims that civil religion exists *symbolically* in American culture, such symbols must be perceived and believed by actual people if the symbols are to be said to have meaning. Several studies by Ronald Wimberley (1976) and others (Wimberley et al. 1976) developed statements on civil religious beliefs and obtained responses on them from various public samples. The findings show that people do affirm civil religious beliefs, although most would not know what the term *civil religion* means. Examples of civil religious beliefs are reflected in statements used in this research such as these: "America is God's chosen nation today." "Holidays like the Fourth of July are religious as well as patriotic." "A president's authority . . . is from God." "Social justice cannot only be based on laws; it must also come from religion." "God can be known through the experiences of the American people." These large surveys and factor analytic studies helped to give empirical credence to Bellah's conceptual argument that civil religion is a distinct cultural component within American society that is not captured either by American politics or by denominational religiosity.

Further research sought to determine the locus and incidence of civil religion in the population: "Who is civil religious?" (Christenson and Wimberley 1978). These studies found that, indeed, a wide cross section of citizens do share such civil religious beliefs. In general, however, college graduates and political or religious liberals appear to be somewhat less civil religious. People identifying with major Protestant denominations and Catholicism show similar levels of civil religiosity. Groups having denominational roots within the United States—Mormons, Adventists, and Pentecostalists—score the highest on an index used to measure civil religiosity, while Jews, Unitarians, and those with no religious preference tend to score the lowest. Despite individual variation on the measures, the "great majority" are found to share the types of civil religious beliefs Bellah suggested.

Still further research evidence suggests that civil religion plays a role in people's preferences for political candidates and policy positions. For example, Wimberley (1980) found that civil religious beliefs were more important than political party loyalties in predicting support for Nixon over McGovern among a sample of Sunday morning church attenders surveyed near the election date. The same was the case for a general representation of residents from the same community. In a statewide survey, Wimberley and Christenson (1982) found no social indicators to be especially strong in showing people's public policy preferences, but civil religiosity was second only to occupational status in predicting one's policy outlooks. Another analysis of these data shows that civil religious beliefs do not conflict with the principle of church and state separation (Wimberley and Christenson 1980).

Regrettably, there has not been a consistent, sustained attempt to measure the civil religious dimension in American culture through time or to determine its effects on, say, American politics through time. The reaction that greeted the original publication of Bellah's essay can hardly be detached from concern over the politics of Vietnam and its aftermath. The switching of attention in the study of the religion-and-politics area from civil religion to the "New Christian Right" that has been evident over the last two decades may obscure the role of civil religion in the processes of selective agenda successes and failures on the part of the Christian right as well as the secular left (see Williams and Alexander 1994). Not to be ignored either is John Murray Cuddihy's earlier, provocative work, *No Offense: Civil Religion and Protestant Taste* (Seabury 1978), wherein the case is made that civil religion constitutes a set of platitudes that substitute for either serious religious or serious political action.

The Larger Scene Various studies—some quantitative but more of them qualitative—attempted to test the civil religion hypothesis cross-nationally. These studies were largely uncoordinated; hence their effects are difficult to assess. Some took the view that because civil religion in the Durkheimian perspective is an "objective social fact," then every nation should have some form of civil religion; therefore any particular nation's civil religion should be able to be detailed by an observant social scientist. Others took the point of view that "civil religion in America" might be a unique phenomenon, hence comparative studies should show how other societies are or are not like the United States, and hence do or do not have a civil religious component. Particular interest focused on the Canadian case—why it seemed as though Canada lacked a civil religion, and whether or not, if it lacked a civil religion, Canada were a "true" nation. Relatively little attention in these cross-national studies as a whole, on the other hand, was paid to the French intellectual tradition out of which the civil religion concept emerged.

The civil religious inquiry has also spawned a number of related concepts as more or less direct responses to civil religion. These include civic religion, diffused religion, and implicit religion, among others. In this context, the publication of the English translation of Thomas Luckmann's book *The Invisible Religion* (Macmillan 1967) in the same year as Bellah's essay is not an insignificant coincidence. Both works received considerable attention, and they provided fertile soil for the growth of an extensive conceptual apparatus for studying religion in contemporary society and culture. The two works also provide new frameworks for the classical sociological debate over public versus private religion.

By the mid-1980s, the concept of civil religion itself had become institutionalized within social scientific and other scholarly work. Bellah himself consciously chose to drop the use of the term in his magisterial collaborative assessment of American public morality and American individualism *Habits of the Heart* (University of California Press 1985; see Bellah 1989). But recent publications indicate that the wind has not gone from civil religion's sails (see Linder 1996, Marvin and Ingle 1996). There now seems to be a firm consensus among social scientists that there is a component of Americanism that is especially religious in nature, which may be termed *civil religion,* but that, at the same time, this component is markedly less in its significance than the "transcendent *universal* religion of the nation" that late-eighteenth-century French intellectuals envisioned.

Overall, the available social scientific research finds that civil religious beliefs do exist in people's minds in the United States, that these beliefs are widely shared and provide a basis for pluralistic social integration across the society, and that civil religious beliefs may be a relatively important factor in making a difference in public preferences for presidential candidates and social policies.

See also Robert N. Bellah, Public Religion

—*Ronald C. Wimberley and William H. Swatos, Jr.*

REFERENCES

R. N. Bellah, "Civil Religion in America," *Daedalus* 96 (1967):1-21; R. N. Bellah, *Beyond Belief* (New York: Harper, 1970); R. N. Bellah, "American Civil Religion," in *American Civil Religion,* ed. R. E. Richey and D. G. Jones (New York: Harper, 1974): 255-272; R. N. Bellah, "Comment," *Sociological Analysis* 50(1989):147; J. A. Christenson and R. C. Wimberley, "Who Is Civil Religious?" *Sociological Analysis* 39(1978):77-83; P. E. Hammond, "The Sociology of American Civil Religion," *Sociological Analysis* 37(1976):169-182; R. D. Linder, "Universal Pastor," *Journal of Church and State* 38(1996):733-749; M. E. Marty, *The New Shape of American Religion* (New York: Harper, 1959); C. Marvin and D. W. Ingle, "Blood Sacrifice and the Nation," *Journal of the American Academy of Religion* 64(1996):767-780; J. A. Mathisen, "Twenty Years After Bellah," *Sociological Analysis* 50(1989):129-146; S. E. Mead, *The Lively Experiment* (New York: Harper, 1963); W. L. Warner, *The Family of God* (New Haven, Conn.: Yale University Press, 1961); R. H. Williams and S. M. Alexander, "Religious Rhetoric in American Populism," *Journal for the Scientific Study of Religion* 33(1994): 1-15; J. F. Wilson, *Public Religion in American Culture* (Philadelphia: Temple University Press, 1979); R. C. Wimberley, "Testing the Civil Religion Hypothesis," *Sociological Analysis* 37(1976):341-352; R. C. Wimberley, "Civil Religion and the Choice for President," *Social Forces* 59 (1980):44-61; R. C. Wimberley and J. A. Christenson, "Civil Religion and Church and State," *Sociological Quarterly* 21(1980):35-40; R. C. Wimberley and J. A. Christenson, "Civil Religion, Social Indicators, and Public Policy," *Social Indicators Research* 10(1982):211-213; R. C. Wimberley et al., "The Civil Religious Dimension," *Social Forces* 54(1976):890-900.

CIVIL RIGHTS   Broadly, the relationships between civil rights and the churches and religion in the United States are at least threefold: (1) behaviors and attitudes of church members of majority, predominantly white churches and denominations relative to inclusive membership; (2) the attitudes of these members to social activism, especially by the clergy; and (3) African American religion and the black church as helping or hindering civil rights advances.

Early studies on racial inclusiveness often focused on white attitudes. In 1965, Earl D. C. Brewer reported on data from delegates to the white United Methodist Southeastern Jurisdictional Conference. Clergy held more inclusive attitudes than laity. Also more inclusive were younger respondents, those exhibiting geographic mobility, residents of larger cities, and those with more education.

Some researchers have examined the degree to which inclusiveness actually occurs and in what contexts. C. Kirk Hadaway and colleagues (1984), using national sample data, report that about a third of whites do attend churches with at least a few blacks. Factors associated with this include education and income levels, region, and place of residence. Most important in predicting inclusiveness was living in urban areas and *not* living in the South and Midwest. For blacks, it is noted, the "fear of assimilation into 'white culture,' while certainly not new, may now overshadow concern with segregation in the church environment" (p. 217). For earlier studies on racial inclusiveness, with some data, see the references given by Nelsen (1975).

Half a century earlier, the classic study by H. Richard Niebuhr, *The Social Sources of Denominationalism* (Holt 1929), had a chapter titled "Denominationalism and the Color Line," which emphasized the social source (racism) as the cause of racial schism. Niebuhr held out little hope for the union of white and black denominations that were so divided (see Hill [1967] for a later analysis). Hadaway et al. (1984) observe that "a surprisingly large proportion of whites do attend churches with blacks" and that levels have increased since the 1960s.

The 1950s and 1960s saw the clergy increasingly involved in civil rights activism. The African American churches provided leadership, places to meet, and, especially, a network of members within the churches that could be counted upon for resources (especially see Morris 1984, also McAdam 1982; for an overview of Martin Luther King, Jr., and his ministry and leadership, Fairclough 1995). The white churches and leaders (ministers) were also involved but less so (and more in the 1960s than the 1950s). White clergy were more favorable to civil rights activism and were more likely to be involved than their laity (see Hadden 1969). Earlier, Hadden and Rymph studied clergy from several denominations attending an urban training program in Chicago. Half of these clergy chose to participate in a civil rights demonstration and to be arrested. Those arrested were younger, were from denominations taking pro-integration stands, were themselves not responsible to all-white congregations, and had roommates at this program who also chose to be arrested.

Perhaps the classic study on (mostly the lack of) civil rights activism in (southern) white churches was by Campbell and Pettigrew, who examined the relationship between attitude and behavior on the part of Little Rock ministers relative to the crisis over the admission of black students to Central High School in the fall of 1957. For the Little Rock ministers, there existed three reference systems relating to the final outcome of behavior (two of four ministers escorting the black students, along with numerous black leaders, were local white clergy). Of 29 local clergy interviewed, sixteen were "inactive integrationists," eight were active integrationists (most of whom experienced "serious difficulty with their members"), and five were segregationists not active in defending that position. The three reference systems were self (ministers' own views), membership (already noted), and professional (other ministers and church bureaucrats, who did not impose sanctions, in part because local clergy were not expected to lose their churches or their members). Campbell and Pettigrew saw inaction as a "typical response to conflicting pressures." (On social justice and power, and for an introduction to the Campbell and Pettigrew study, see Neal 1984.) Campbell and Pettigrew did not see clergy roles centering on social action as existing (but see Nelsen et al. 1973, Quinley 1974).

From his study of 28 denominations, James R. Wood (1970) found that the strength of the church's policy on civil rights is positively related to the degree of leadership authority, with the more hierarchical churches being more in favor and the congregational type less so. The denomination's stand could range from commending integrated services and citizens having equal access to public accommodation, to providing sanctions against local units (churches) refusing to integrate and not approving interracial marriage. The continuing importance of the liberal Protestant denominations relative to social action has been discussed by Wood as recently as 1990.

—*Hart M. Nelsen*

REFERENCES

E. D. C. Brewer, "Attitudes Toward Inclusive Practices in the Methodist Church in the Southeast," *Review of Religious Research* 6(1965):82-89; E. Q. Campbell and T. F. Pettigrew, *Christians in Racial Crisis* (Washington, D.C.: Public Affairs Press, 1959a); E. Q. Campbell and T. F. Pettigrew, "Racial and Moral Crisis," *American Journal of Sociology* 64(1959b):509-516; A. Fairclough, *Martin Luther King, Jr.* (Athens: University of Georgia Press, 1995); C. K. Hadaway et al., "The Most Segregated Institution," *Review of Religious Research* 23(1984):204-219; J. K. Hadden, *The Gathering Storm in the Churches* (Garden City, N.Y.: Doubleday, 1969); J. K. Hadden and R. C. Rymph, "Social Structure and Civil Rights Involvement," *Social Forces* 45(1966):51-61; S. S. Hill, *Southern Churches in Crisis* (New York: Holt, 1967); D. McAdam, *Political Process and the Development of Black Insurgency* (Chicago: University of Chicago Press, 1982); A. Morris, *The Origins of the Civil Rights Movement* (New York: Free Press, 1984); M. A. Neal, "Social Justice and the Right to Use Power," *Journal for the Scientific Study of Religion* 23(1984):329-340; H. M. Nelsen, "Why Do Pastors Preach on Social Issues?" *Theology Today* 32(1975):56-73; H. M. Nelsen et al., "Ministerial Roles and Social Actionist Stance," *American Sociological Review* 38(1973):375-386; H. E. Quinley, *The Prophetic Clergy* (New York: Wiley, 1974); J. R. Wood, "Authority and Controversial Policy," *American Sociological Review* 35(1970):1057-1069; J. R. Wood, "Liberal Protestant Social Action in a Period of Decline," in *Faith and Philanthropy in America*, ed. R. Wuthnow and V. Hodgkinson (San Francisco: Jossey-Bass, 1990): 164-186.

CLARK, WALTER HOUSTON (1902–) A major figure in the middle years of the psychology of religion as a Professor of Psychology at Andover-Newton Theological Seminary, he was a student of Gordon Allport at Harvard. His understanding of religion was profoundly shaped by Allport as well as by William James.

Allport's influence can be seen in Clark's 1958 textbook, *The Psychology of Religion* (Macmillan), especially in his distinction between primary, secondary, and tertiary religious behavior—reminiscent of Allport's intrinsic-extrinsic dichotomy. *Primary* religious behavior is at the heart of Clark's definition of religion: "the inner experience of the individual when he senses a

Beyond, especially as evidenced by the effect of this experience on his behavior when he actively attempts to harmonize his life with the Beyond." *Secondary* behavior is a "pale approximation" of primary behavior, being habitual or obligatory (e.g., routine church attendance). *Tertiary* behavior, even further removed, having nothing to do with firsthand experience, is conventional, accepted on the authority of others (e.g., children's behavior).

Clark's steadfast maintenance of the centrality of mysticism to understanding religion is markedly Jamesian. His interest in mysticism flowered in the 1960s as a result of an encounter with then Harvard psychologist Timothy Leary, after which Clark focused his attention on psychedelic drugs and religion. His 1969 book *Chemical Ecstasy* (Sheed & Ward) is a guardedly optimistic defense of the importance of psychedelic drugs for religion. Although he argues that psychedelics provide access to mystical consciousness, he sees drugs not as a *cause* but as a *trigger,* facilitating the realization of what is already inside the person. Clark also claims that he learned as much about religion from his six "trips" as he had from all his "plodding study" of the psychology of religion.

—*David Yamane*

CLASS   *see* Karl Marx, Status, Stratification

CLEMENS, ALPHONSE (HENRY) (1905-1977)

Holding undergraduate and doctoral degrees from St. Louis University, Clemens directed the university's Department of Sociology and Economics from 1936 to 1946, when he moved to the Catholic University of America, where he taught until retirement in 1970. Ninth President of the American Catholic Sociological Society (1946).

In his ACSS presidential address, Clemens urged the application of sociology to solving social problems. In that speech, Clemens also warned of "the constant danger of Catholic sociologists becoming exclusively empirical and positivistic, or exclusively social philosophers"—reflecting a fear current in the ACSS. He contended that in tackling social problems, Catholic sociologists had the uniquely important responsibility of synthesizing not only the social sciences and social philosophy but "even theology" (*American Catholic Sociological Review,* 1947). His primary interests and publications were concerned with marriage counseling and family: *Design for Successful Marriage, Marriage and Family: An Integrated Approach, Survey of the Cana Movement in the U.S.* He promoted the Catholic Family

Life movement, both as a member of its associations and as an editor for its publications.

—*Loretta M. Morris*

CLERGY   Ordained as public, authorized functionaries for their religious organizations, clergy have constituted the occupational class responsible for formulating, interpreting, and preserving tradition, scriptures, and doctrines, and presiding over the worship and pastoral concerns of their religious communities. For religious groups that ordain, clergy typically have held top leadership roles, often serving concurrently as religious visionary, authoritative spokesperson for their tradition, professional pastor, and organizational administrator overseeing the demographic growth and viability of the religious community. Occasionally, clergy leaders come into social tension with their congregation, their denomination, or the wider community, particularly where they hold prophetic commitments rather than a primary interest in tradition maintenance. U.S. clergy, working across denominational and racial boundaries, have been at the forefront of abolitionist, Social Gospel, and civil rights movements. Similarly, clergy have held prophetic roles in inspiring social change for justice and human rights in South Africa, Latin America, and elsewhere.

Social scientific approaches to studying clergy have focused on ministerial roles and role conflicts, changes in prestige and occupational self-understanding, politicization as a leadership force for social change in contrast to tradition maintenance, clericalist and anticlericalist movements, and demographic changes in clergy composition including occupational recruitment, shifts in clergy supply and demand, age, gender and racial effects, and related implications for their religious organizations.

While clergy traditionally have borne the primary roles of authoritative religious teacher, preacher, worship leader, or sacramentalist for their religious communities, the emphasis upon certain roles over others varies by religion. The teaching role of ordained religious leaders has been particularly important in rabbinical Judaism. In sacramental traditions, only the clergy may be allowed certain worship and ritual roles, such as the celebration of Christian holy communion. The preaching role gained ascendancy in post-Reformation Christianity, notably in emergent Protestant sects, and has remained central for Protestant clergy. It also has been the motivational force behind much Protestant evangelism and effort toward widespread social change.

Preaching Preaching and teaching roles for clergy in most religious traditions have been closely linked. Preaching, the major ritual activity in those Protestant denominations in which sacraments are not emphasized, historically has served as a means of religious commentary on social and political issues. Especially where clergy have been well educated in relation to the membership, preaching has served as a form of religiomoral education and inspiration, giving clergy opportunities to shape ethical values and discourse both within the religious community and to some extent within wider society.

Protestant puritan, evangelical, and black church traditions have had especially strong preaching legacies responsible for inspiring and mobilizing various socioreligious movements. The European American preaching tradition has been split between a pietistic perspective, tending to shun political engagement, and a social action outlook, which has called for direct transformative action to achieve social reform. Compared with puritan reflectivity and interpretation, the evangelical preaching style has tended more toward proclamation. In Pentecostal preaching, emphasis on the word has been less important than the reception of spiritual gifts, such as speaking in tongues (glossolalia) or faith healing. Both evangelical and Pentecostal preaching, emphasizing a personalized relationship with Jesus Christ through conversion or receipt of spiritual gifts, attributes social problems to the breakdown of personal morality.

Revival preaching, inspired by German pietism and using a spontaneous and emotional preaching style, undergirded the eighteenth-century Great Awakening and the westward European American expansion. Methodist circuit riders and other frontier evangelists conducted open air or tent revival meetings as well as camp meetings, and temporarily filled empty pulpits. The explicit use of psychological techniques for persuasion or audience manipulation was first popularized by nineteenth-century revivalist preacher Charles Grandison Finney. Other noted preachers in Finney's tradition include Dwight Moody, Billy Sunday, and Billy Graham.

In the twentieth century, Harry Emerson Fosdick was responsible for the advent of a preaching movement using psychological theory as a means of pastoral guidance around a basic human issue or concern. Fosdick also became the first well-known national radio preacher. Radio and television preaching, subsequently known as the "electronic church," reached its zenith in the televangelism movement during the 1980s, where enormous earnings resulted from large viewership audiences and successful marketing of religious products or prayer services prior to the moral and financial scandals that rocked televangelist empires during the latter years of the decade. The movement subsequently shifted from an emphasis on preaching to integrated discussion and prayer, the most well-known broadcast being Pat Robertson's *700 Club*. Such a format also minimizes denominational differences in the use of scripture and worship style, thus appealing to a wider audience. Discussion forums, prayer chains, and written text appear on the World Wide Web, although the Web's potential for mass media preaching has not yet been technologically fully developed.

The Liberal Protestant preaching tradition, characteristically attributing the source of social inequality and injustice to systemic problems that foster institutionalized racism, sexism, or classism, has emphasized a call to individual and collective action undergirded by scriptural and moral argument. Preaching consequently has resulted in both a public and a politically charged role for the clergy, inciting substantial conflict, particularly between European American clergy and laity within their respective denominations. Where laity disagree with activist preaching, pressure often has been applied to redirect clergy to the privatized realm of piety, spirituality, and pastoral care.

Preaching has been particularly central to the African American church tradition, serving as both a religious and a political nucleus for community cohesion. Where denominational schisms formed over slavery and segregation, particularly in Methodist-Episcopal and Baptist traditions, the new African American groups departed from European American styles of preaching, developing a passionate oratorical style, interactive responses between preacher and congregation, and an emphasis upon biblical narratives related to freedom, martyrdom, and resurrection. From slavery days, the "preacher" had been the only public role according African Americans any leadership opportunities or prestige, a position that also often served as intermediary with European Americans. African American preachers have continued to retain high prestige within their religious organizations and surrounding communities, with many seeking to maintain the legacy of working collaboratively for political and socioeconomic betterment, exemplified in the Rev. Martin Luther King, Jr.'s merger of preaching and social activism during the civil rights movement.

Clergy advocating social action and political involvement, doing so from conservative as well as liberal perspectives, have risked the erosion of lay participation and financial support, particularly in European American congregations. The Rev. Jerry Falwell, leader of the 1980s Moral Majority movement, and Pat Robertson, as head of the 1990s Christian Coalition movement, have developed comprehensive political action programs seeking to legislate perspectives on morality issues based on conservative Christian religious tradition. Falwell, facing an erosion of public and financial backing, stepped down from the Moral Majority leadership in 1987, and the Christian Coalition, faced with the financial investigation of its youthful strategist and previous leader, Ralph Reed, has declined in political clout since the early 1990s. Alternatively, clergy leaders in mainline denominations, working either internally or ecumenically, have taken social and public policy stances on racial, gender, and justice-related issues that have generated open conflict between conservative local congregations and their national religious organizations. Such dissension has resulted in reduced congregational giving for denominationwide operations and in renewed movements for decentralization. Jeffrey Hadden's foundational study *The Gathering Storm in the Churches* (Doubleday 1969) identified a growing rift between mainline Protestant clergy and laity stemming from clergy political involvement in the civil rights movement and other areas of liberal social action. Finding that clergy were leading their churches in directions not supported by the laity, Hadden contended that they would be increasingly likely to challenge clergy authority for denominational direction. By the 1990s, both laity and conservative clergy have challenged denominational leadership through increased financial and political pressure for congregational autonomy in protest over progressive social perspectives, particularly those related to gender and human sexuality.

Clericalism and Anticlericalism Conversely, the conflict over clergy authority has fueled *anticlericalist* movements, which have emerged throughout Christian history. Typically these movements have surfaced in strife over the abuse of the church's political power, most often when it has been in alliance with the government or ruling elite. Successive anticlerical struggles in Europe between the twelfth and sixteenth centuries led to the Protestant Reformation. At the heart of the anticlericalist movement during the European Enlightenment were the French principles of 1789—liberty, equality, and fraternity—and the replacement of religious belief by humanism and science as primary guiding social forces. Anticlericalism also represented widespread opposition to the Roman Catholic Church's dominance in Europe in the wake of the secularist notion of the separation of church and state over matters pertaining to politics and education. The movement sought to ensure freedom of conscience as part of the democratic movement un-

dergirded by the rise of liberalism in government, economics, and public expression during that period, modeled by the newly emergent U.S. republic. Anticlericalism forms the core of Rousseauean and Marxian thought on religion, in which clergy were perceived to collude with the ruling class to create, according to Marx, *an opiate of the masses,* which effectively maintained social control to ensure little interference with their class interests. Contemporary manifestations of anticlericalism have occurred in liberation theology movements, where lay-led base communities have responded to authoritarian support within the Roman Catholic Church of various repressive political regimes. Black, feminist, and other liberation theology movements similarly have responded to the hegemonic dominance of European American male clergy in defining and interpreting what of Christian religious tradition should be considered normative or appropriate for all believers.

Anticlericalism has become manifest in movements for greater congregational control, which have effectively eroded financial support for denominational programs and commitments, particularly those tied to ecumenism, racial, gender, and sexual orientation issues. This trend instead has pressed for congregationalist decentralization where local laity, with or without support of their clergy, maintain control of financial support for programs and outreach ministries. In this respect, Berger (1981) intimated that clergy-laity class conflict may be a political struggle between two elite groups: the business elite and a *new elite,* highly educated clergy, intellectuals, and other professionals who oversee ideas. Antiecumenism is also essentially an anticlericalist trend, reacting in part to clergy across religious traditions developing professional networks and building alliances on controversial political issues, especially given that ecumenical perspectives have tended to be more liberal than parochial outlooks.

Demographic Changes In addition to resurgent anticlericalist movements affecting the financial stability of large mainline denominations, the changing demographic picture of the clergy since 1970 suggests that major occupational as well as organizational shifts are likely to ensue during the opening decades of the twenty-first century. Dislocations of clergy supply and demand have sharply affected both Roman Catholic and Protestant denominations, although in different ways. The number of Roman Catholic priests in the United States has been moderately estimated to decline about 40% between 1966 and 2005 (Schoenherr and Young 1993). Concerns over supply have been related to mandatory celibacy and the Roman Catholic

Church's position against ordaining women. Clergy shortages were projected for Protestant churches in the late 1980s, based upon high rates of the retiring clergy ordained after World War II, although they have not materialized for reasons such as the proliferation of women seeking ordination since the late 1970s, the increased frequency of men being ordained as a second or third career, the licensing or ordination of laity for a specific congregation or geographic locale, and the deployment of retired clergy for part-time and interim work. Some denominations have experienced sizable clergy oversupply, for instance, the Episcopal Church, with more than a 60% increase in clergy ordained between 1960 and 1990 while confirmed communicants decreased by 20% during that period.

In the late 1960s, substantial attention became focused on Roman Catholic and Protestant clergy leaving the occupation. Resignation of Roman Catholic priests peaked between 1968 and 1973, a period that Schoenherr and Young (1993) call the "mass exodus" years for primarily young priests who, based upon NORC and other research data, typically were concerned over loneliness, celibacy, or conservatism in church doctrine and values. Studies of Protestant clergy during that period were more inconclusive in identifying common reasons for occupational exodus, although more recent research has suggested role ambiguity as a primary basis for departure (e.g., Hoge et al. 1981). Since the mid-1980s, some concern has been raised over the increased attrition of women clergy.

The most consistent demographic decline across Roman Catholic, most Protestant, and Jewish religious traditions during the 1980s and 1990s has been in the ratio of young, first-career men seeking ordination. Concurrently, the rising age of both female and male seminarians during this period has been well documented (e.g., Larsen 1995), resulting in a sharp influx of second-career clergy, which, combined with retiring clergy continuing to work on an interim or part-time basis, has created an overall *graying* of the occupation. While male clergy ordained as young adults tend to retain an edge in attaining leadership positions, studies have shown that ordination at an older age does not present a significant barrier to opportunities for ministry (e.g., Zikmund et al. 1997, Nesbitt 1997), although denominational size and structure as well as supply relative to demand can affect age-related prospects.

Women Clergy   The most dramatic trend affecting nearly all mainline religious organizations has been the ordination and proliferation of women clergy. Although there is some evidence that women may have served as clergy in very early Christian communities, the practice died out with Christianity's consolidation and development as a church during its early centuries. Following the Protestant Reformation, women developed a lay preaching presence in Europe, England, and subsequently in North America. In the United States, women were represented among nineteenth-century Quaker, Universalist, and revivalist preachers, but ordination as clergy, with opportunities for the same tasks, responsibilities, and positions as men, began only during the mid-nineteenth century.

Antoinette Brown was the first woman ordained in a U.S. denomination, as a Congregational minister in 1853 following graduation from Oberlin seminary three years earlier and a protracted struggle over the legitimacy of ordaining a woman. The first woman ordained with denominationwide recognition was Olympia Brown, in 1863, as a Universalist minister. By the end of the nineteenth century, more than 1,000 women had been ordained, representing at least a dozen denominations. Many of the earliest women clergy had been active in social reform, particularly abolition and women's rights, and as clergy they continued to work for political and social change. Other women perceived their clergy status as offering more pragmatic advantages, such as in assisting domestic or foreign missionary work, in copastoring with their ordained husbands, or in securing clergy discounts when traveling with their husbands. Resistance to women clergy increased, toward the end of the nineteenth century, and women experienced both greater difficulty in finding placements and decreased support by denominational leaders.

During the opening decades of the twentieth century, the number of women clergy began to grow, primarily because of the receptivity they found in pentecostalism. Through the depression years, mainline and evangelical denominations remained overtly resistant to women, either to the female clergy in their midst or to the prospect of opening their ordination processes to women. Following World War II and facing an expanding need for clergy during the 1950s, several religious organizations opened full ordination to women, primarily in American Methodist, Presbyterian, and European Lutheran traditions, to the extent that by 1958, 48 denominational members of the World Council of Churches ordained women on the same basis as men. Another wave of religious organizations granting women full ordination began in 1970, primarily within American Lutheran, Mennonite, British Methodist, Anglican (Episcopal), and Jewish traditions. By 1995, women represented about 11% of all ordained U.S. clergy. The presence of women clergy has increased in

Asia and Africa over the last two decades, as more denominations locally opened ordination to them. At least three women were secretly ordained to the Roman Catholic priesthood in Czechoslovakia during the communist regime, although the Vatican has refused to recognize them.

Occupationally, studies consistently have shown that women clergy have not had opportunities equivalent to those of men. Traditionally, opportunities for women clergy have been primarily in small, poorer congregations that have been unsuccessful in attracting men, often in rural locations. In response, women clergy have developed a legacy for building up congregational membership and financial resources—the two criteria traditionally considered by male clergy as measures of occupational "success"—but often have found themselves replaced by men, either by congregations newly able to afford a man or through denominational reappointment. Women clergy in more hierarchically stratified denominations have disproportionately remained in staff positions, as assistants or associates, while their male counterparts move into higher level placements.

The most widely known multidenominational study on women clergy, by Jackson Carroll, Barbara Hargrove, and Adair Lummis, *Women of the Cloth* (Harper 1983), found that female and male clergy held similar entry-level placements, but that sharp gender differences appeared when they moved to midlevel positions, with men tending to move upward while women moved laterally. They attributed the differences to a variety of influences from passive socialization to tendencies by congregational search committees not to generalize positive experience with women clergy into receptivity toward subsequent female candidates. A comparative update of this research by Zikmund et al. (1997), as well as other recent studies, shows that these earlier trends have remained consistent across denominations, resulting in a "glass ceiling" effect for women clergy interested in the senior leadership of a large congregation or denominational leadership. Women's ongoing difficulties with male clergy colleagues, their frustration with limitations placed upon their opportunities, and a concurrent desire for occupational growth have been evident in other multidenominational studies (e.g., Clark and Anderson 1990). Although these have been predominantly European American denominations, similar trends have been identified for women rabbis. Women clergy in African American denominations have reported comparable difficulties in finding opportunities to pastor congregations and in terms of resistance to their efforts by laity and male clergy (Lincoln and Mamiya 1990). Similar patterns have been found in studies on women clergy in Canada, England, Sweden, Australia, and elsewhere.

Women's ordination to the episcopate, as denominational leaders with authority over male as well as female clergy, has been an even more difficult struggle. The first female bishop, Marjorie Matthews, was consecrated by the United Methodist Church in 1980, a denomination that subsequently has consecrated seven more female bishops. The first woman consecrated in a denomination claiming apostolic succession (an unbroken chain of the laying on of hands since apostolic times) was Barbara Harris in the U.S. Episcopal Church (1989). Anglican and Lutheran female bishops have since been consecrated in New Zealand, Germany, Norway, the United States, and Canada.

Occupational Feminization   Across denominations, the ratio of women to men ordained annually had remained at token levels until the late 1970s. The first denomination to have more women than men ordained annually was the Unitarian Universalist Association—a gender shift that occurred in 1978. The annual ratios of women being ordained have increased more slowly in other denominations. Throughout the 1990s, the gender ratio of Association of Theological Schools (A.T.S.) institutions has averaged 30% female, although more liberal seminaries have averaged two-thirds female or higher.

One consequence of the proliferation of women clergy has been a rise in the number of clergy couples and in ensuing complications for dual-clergy careers. In addition to "fishbowl" pressures of clergy life within the congregation, Rallings and Pratto's (1984) multidenominational study on clergy couples found that wives tend to hold positions subordinate to husbands and, where husbands and wives share a single position and salary, wives typically encounter subordinate role expectations from the congregation. Other, more recent studies have affirmed that these patterns persist.

A second consequence of the increase in women clergy has been denominational concern over the likelihood that the clergy as an occupation will become primarily female. Such concerns have risen from comparative trends in secular occupations, in which prestige and compensation decline as the ratio of women increases, fewer young men are attracted to the occupation, and women become disproportionately gender segregated into lower level jobs as the rate of feminization increases. Some concerns have been distinctive to religious organizations, in that the majority of lay participants in congregations are female and in that, if clergy become primarily female, women will effectively "take over the church" and men will retreat from participation. The increasing presence of women clergy has been associated, however, not only with occupational trends that disproportionately advantage men but with a resurgent resistance to deploying women in advantageous placements. Conservative Protestant denominations have eroded opportunities for women clergy through lack of support or, in some cases, reversal of policies toward women's ordination. Consequently, the prospect that women clergy will dominate organized religion seems unlikely.

Despite changing age and gender demographic factors, the opportunities for clergy to offer visible leadership toward liberal or conservative social change, and the denominational conflicts likely to ensue, clergy will remain viable so long as religion continues to provide foundational meaning to support or challenge trends and practices in the wider society.

See also Feminization Thesis, Charles Grandison Finney, Ministry, Ordination, Televangelism

—*Paula D. Nesbitt*

REFERENCES

C. H. Barfoot and G. T. Sheppard, "Prophetic vs. Priestly Religion," *Review of Religious Research* 22(1980):2-17; P. L. Berger, "The Class Struggle in American Religion," *Christian Century* 86(1981):194-199; J. N. Clark and G. Anderson, "A Study of Women in Ministry," in *Yearbook of American and Canadian Churches*, ed. C. H. Jacquet, Jr. (Nashville: Abingdon, 1990): 271-278; D. Hoge et al., "Organizational and Situational Influences on Vocational Commitment of Protestant Ministers," *Review of Religious Research* 23 (1981):133-149; D. T. Holland, *The Preaching Tradition* (Nashville: Abingdon, 1980); T. G. Jelen, *The Political World of the Clergy* (Westport, Conn.: Praeger, 1993); E. L. Larsen, "A Profile of Contemporary Seminarians Revisited," *Theological Education* 31(Suppl., 1995):1-118; E. L. Larsen and J. M. Shopshire, "A Profile of Contemporary Seminarians," *Theological Education* 24(1988):10-136; E. C. Lehman, Jr., *Women Clergy in England* (Lewiston, N.Y.: Mellen, 1987); E. C. Lehman, Jr., *Gender and Work* (Albany: SUNY Press, 1993); E. C. Lehman, Jr., *Women in Ministry* (Melbourne: Joint Board of Christian Education, 1994); C. E. Lincoln and L. H. Mamiya, *The Black Church in the African American Experience* (Durham: Duke University Press, 1990); P. D. Nesbitt, *Feminization of the Clergy in America* (New York: Oxford University Press, 1997): 152-171; E. M. Rallings and D. J. Pratto, *Two-Clergy Marriages* (Lanham, Md.: University Press of America, 1984); S. Ranson et al., *Clergy, Ministers and Priests* (London: Routledge, 1977); J. Sanchez, *Anticlericalism* (Notre Dame, Ind.: University of Notre Dame Press, 1972); F. W. Schmidt, *A Still Small Voice* (Syracuse, N.Y.: Syracuse University Press, 1996); R. A. Schoenherr and L. A. Young, *Full Pews and Empty Altars* (Madison: University of Wisconsin Press, 1993); R. Simon et al., "Rabbis and Ministers," in *Gender and Religion*, ed. W. H. Swatos, Jr. (New Brunswick, N.J.: Transaction, 1993): 45-54; B. Stendahl, *The Force of Tradition* (Philadelphia: Fortress, 1985); B. B. Zikmund, "Winning Ordination for Women in Mainstream Protestant Churches," in *Women and Religion in America*, ed. R. R. Ruether and R. S. Keller (San Francisco: Harper, 1986): 339-383; B. B. Zikmund et al., *An Uphill Calling* (Louisville: Westminster, 1997).

COGNITIVE DISSONANCE   Leon Festinger directed a field study of a flying saucer "cult" that has become a classic, both in the social scientific study of religion and in social psychology (Festinger et al. 1956). The study also contributed to the discussion of ethical issues of field research on religious groups, being cited by some as research with serious ethical problems (Richardson 1991). The theory of cognitive dissonance dominated the social psychology journals from the late 1950s to early 1970s and is still an important theoretical idea that appears in virtually all psychology and social psychology texts (Jones 1985).

The basic theory of cognitive dissonance is simple: People prefer a situation in which their cognitions are consistent with each other and their cognitions are consistent with their behaviors. If there are inconsistencies among a person's cognitions, or between cognitions and behaviors, these will cause disquiet in the person, leading him or her to seek some resolution of the discomfort. Research on this basic idea has led to some interesting and counterintuitive results, including those from the *When Prophecy Fails* study. In that research, the expectation that flying saucers would come to remove all believers at a specific time and place was disproved, but this did not lead to the immediate dissolution of the group. Instead, Festinger et al.'s predictions that the group would seek other explanations that were consistent with the failure to appear, and that they would promote those alternative ideas energetically through proselytizing, were supported. This result made the research an instant classic that aroused great interest and controversy.

—*James T. Richardson*

REFERENCES

L. Festinger et al., *When Prophecy Fails* (New York: Harper, 1956); E. Jones, "Major Developments in Social Psychology During the Past Five Decades," in *The Handbook of Social Psychology*, 3rd ed., Vol. 1, ed. G. Lindzey and E. Aronson (New York: Random House, 1985): 47-107; J. T. Richardson, "Experiencing Research on New Religions and 'Cults,' " in *Ex-*

periencing Fieldwork, ed. W. Shaffir and R. Stebbins (Newbury Park, Calif.: Sage, 1991): 62-71; R. Wallis, "Reflections on *When Prophecy Fails* in *Salvation and Protest,* ed. R. Wallis (New York: St Martin's, 1979): 44-50.

COGNITIVE MODELS   Models of religious experience and religious conversions that focus on the way people process information. These theories are rooted in the field of social psychology, focusing on intellectual processes in forming and sustaining a worldview or on stages of intellectual development. Broadly speaking, there are two main approaches: cognitive structuralism and cognitive re-creation theory.

The theoretical perspective of *cognitive structuralism* posits an innate developmental structure in the intellectual maturation of humans—irrespective of cultural or religious background. Also known as cognitive developmentalism, structural developmentalism, developmental epistemology, or developmental constructionism, this perspective evolved from the work of Jean Piaget. Because each stage represents a kind of worldview, scholars believe there are implications for religious education, moral thinking, faith maturation, and the process of conversion.

Lawrence Kohlberg (1981, 1984) identified three levels of moral thinking with two stages at each level— six stages in all. The key to his schema is increased capacity to role-take. James Fowler followed Kohlberg's work with a six-stage model of faith development, emphasizing sophistication in understanding symbolism and in perception of authority. All six stages may occur within any religion; the stages refer to the cognitive processing of symbols and myths, not to the specific content of a faith.

Some structuralists insist that change of stage is as important in transforming one's worldview as a change of one's specific beliefs. Thus each change of stage can be seen as a kind of conversion experience in itself.

Cognitive re-creation theory is based on the premise that an intense reality-transforming experience of conversion or inspiration is closely analogous to the process of artistic or scientific creativity. Developed by Daniel Batson and Larry Ventis (1982), the model focuses on psychological research on the processes of creativity, suggesting four distinctive steps in the formation of an entirely new religious worldview or of an innovative interpretation of a religious tradition: preparation, incubation, illumination, and verification. The theory

includes analysis of the possible role of specialization in right and left brain hemispheres in religious inspiration.

See also Faith Development, Moral Development, Jean Piaget

—*Keith A. Roberts*

REFERENCES

C. D. Batson and W. L. Ventis, *The Religious Experience* (New York: Oxford University Press, 1982); J. W. Fowler, *Stages of Faith* (San Francisco: Harper, 1981); L. Kohlberg, *Essays on Moral Development* (New York: Harper, 1981, 1984 [2 vols.]); J. Piaget, *The Psychology of Intelligence* (London: Routledge, 1950); J. Piaget, *The Construction of Reality in the Child* (New York: Basic Books, 1954); J. Piaget, *The Moral Judgement of the Child* (New York: Free Press, 1965 [1932]); M. M. Wilcox, *Developmental Journey* (Nashville, Tenn.: Abingdon, 1979).

COMMITMENT   The concept of commitment can be generalized to apply to any type of disposition, behavior, or attribute. Commitment is a process that begins when an alternative is voluntarily decided upon by oneself or is selected and imposed by others. This process of attachment to the alternative is maintained with some degree of commitment strength through pertinent situations until that decision or selection is terminated or replaced by another alternative (Wimberley 1972, 1978).

How do people become committed? The sociology and social psychology of religion have played an important role in developing what we know about the concept of commitment. Today, the concept is used in many studies of religion and continues to spread to research on other topics.

A computer search for research on *commitment* will readily produce more than 100 recent applications of the term to one topic or another. Theoretically, many studies of commitment use the symbolic interactionist perspective (e.g., Heimer and Matsueda 1994), while many others use an exchange perspective (e.g., Mottaz 1988, Kollock 1994). Much of the research, however, focuses on applying the concept to such practical matters as commitment to organizations (e.g., Mottaz 1988, Morrow 1992), to family and work (e.g., Gerson 1993), or to interpersonal friendships (e.g., Cox et al. 1997).

Here we examine commitment mainly from the exchange and symbolic interactionist perspectives and with special attention to religious commitment. In the 1960s, the concept of commitment was introduced into the sociology of religion primarily by Gerhard Lenski (*The Religious Factor,* Doubleday 1961), who delineated several dimensions of religious orientation, and by Rodney Stark and Charles Glock, who likewise conceptualized several dimensions of religiosity (Glock and Stark 1965, Stark and Glock 1968). This multidimensional approach to studying religious commitment was rather different from the way religiosity had been studied earlier. Most previous research measured religiosity by asking only about one's church membership or attendance.

Of course, there is more to religious commitment than can be asked in a single question. People are committed to religion along such dimensions as belief, behavior, feelings of religious experience, and religious knowledge. There is also a dimension of interacting with others who are religious. Interacting with other people makes a difference in the ways we perceive things, and human interactions with one another are the essence of sociology.

Commitment as a General Concept Religious commitments provide a springboard for looking at commitments in general. Consequently, the term can be applied to any kind of thinking or activity. The same concept of commitment that describes how people are religious has been used to describe how people are deviant. Some may ask, "Is there any difference?" And, to some people, there may not be, for deviance depends upon one's perspective. If strange or unusual behaviors are defined as deviant, many religious ways that are considered unusual could be defined as deviant.

Commitment also has been applied to such topics as dating, marriage, and family; to occupations, careers, and organizations; and to educational pursuits. For instance, one may begin a college program without having chosen a major and not having definite career plans. Or, one may make definite plans but change them before even taking a class in that subject.

Depending upon the commitments one makes initially, there will be repercussions for the commitments made later. These later commitments may develop rather slowly. Although we make commitments without fully realizing the implications they are going to have in the future, we are still making important commitments whether or not we fully intend them.

Small children make many commitments and terminate them very quickly. They can shift from one thing to the next—no great problem. But when children become adults and develop career specialties, their earlier commitments become more binding on their current choices. Given earlier commitments to certain lines of action that identify one's self and roles, there

are fewer options from which to choose freely. This not only applies to educational or occupational commitments but to commitments to tastes, habits, ideas, friendships, and other aspects of one's life course.

Interpersonal Commitments: A special type of commitment is the kind we make to other persons—commitments to relationships that we share and trade with others. Social exchange theory, as seen in an early book by Peter Blau, Power and Exchange in Social Life (Wiley 1964), uses the concept of commitment in regard to interpersonal commitments. In fact, in a section called "Excursus on Love," he tells how to make commitments and fall in love according to exchange theory.

Blau suggests that as one begins to commit oneself to another person—an acquaintance, a friend, or potential spouse—the more one invests in the other. As more time and activities are invested in a particular person, the more the possibilities are closed to relationships with alternative persons. In other words, the more time that is spent with one person as a friend, the less time there is to invest in friendships with anyone else. The same is the case for the friend. Furthermore, the more one invests in another, the more one becomes obligated to that person due to the closing of other interpersonal alternatives. Therefore, we make investments in others; we become committed to others. According to social scientific theory, the rewards received from personal relationships with others are extremely important to us.

Commitment and Commitment Strength Commitments, then, can result from decisions. All commitments do not have to be long or enduring or deal with major events in life. One can be committed, say, to wearing a certain pair of shoes. A decision is made to buy them; a commitment is made to them. One can be committed to eating certain types and amounts of food at breakfast tomorrow. Although some commitments become very important and fairly permanent, they often begin as very transitory, trivial decisions.

Commitment is a process. In this process, one decides among the alternatives of which he or she is aware, or has alternatives selected by others. After the decision or selection is made, the commitment is pursued with some degree of commitment strength, through pertinent situations, and until that commitment is dropped.

Commitment strength is not the same thing as the commitment itself. Consider a commitment to a certain religious belief. The belief to which one is committed may be conservative, moderate, or liberal. But regardless of the commitment position, the strength of the commitment may vary from weak to strong. The belief

Alternatives in the Situation	Types of Alternatives in Situations			Decision or Selection of an Alternative	Commitment Stages		
	1. Objectively realistic, but not subjectively perceived (noncognitive)	2. Subjectively perceived but not objectively realistic (cognitive but misperceived)	3. Subjectively perceived and objectively realistic (cognitive and accurately perceived)		Stage 1. Latent	Stage 2. Active	Stage 3. Passive
A B C D E	A B	C	D E	E	E	E	E

Figure C.3 The Process of Initiating and Maintaining a Commitment

to which the commitment is made may be a strong commitment at first, then weaken, and then grow strong again. In other words, the strength of a commitment may vary while the underlying commitment position does not change. Commitment strength therefore is more or less painted over the basic, underlying commitment. However, commitment and commitment strength are related. The strength of a commitment to a political party, for example, can be seen to be important for whether one stays with the same political party in the future. High or low commitment strength is an important predictor of whether one keeps or drops a commitment over time.

Situations and Alternatives To understand better the concept of commitment, it is helpful to understand commitment alternatives. Alternatives come to us in situations, and situations provide the contexts in which to evaluate alternatives. Some alternatives can be defined or perceived in everyday situations; others are not so clear. This and the ensuing steps of the process of commitment are shown in Figure C.3.

When we consider viable alternatives in a situation, we consider only the ones we can recognize. For example, when looking for a job, it is possible to consider only those of which we are aware. We cannot knowingly commit ourselves to any of those unknown alternatives unless we find out about them. It is as simple as that. If there are good jobs out there—commitment alternatives—they can be considered only when their existence is discovered.

Sociologist William Cole once said that education is the process of increasing one's awareness of alternatives. By expanding the known alternatives, more desirable commitment decisions may be made. Theoreti-

cally, an educated person should have a larger repertoire or arsenal of commitment alternatives as resources from which to choose.

Alternatives exist in situations. Situations constantly surround us. We are in a situation now; five minutes from now we shall be in a situation. Situations, like dreams, blend one into another. We are always in situations that contain alternatives. Some of these alternatives are recognized and some are not. When one chooses an alternative, a commitment begins.

Decisions and Selections: When we choose for ourselves, we prefer to choose from desirable, rewarding alternatives. Sometimes all alternatives appear rewarding, and the objective is to take the most rewarding. But in other situations, nothing we can choose is a good choice or will make us feel better. Still, we have to sort things out and pick something that is thought to hurt the least or to be the least costly.

On the other hand, there are situations where the alternatives are severely restricted by the social structure. Others make selections for us. Parents restrict and guide children; teachers instruct students; a community exerts influence over its members. The social structure limits the choice of what is proper and acceptable. Due to the process of socialization, those who were once coerced into certain behaviors, such as brushing one's teeth or studying, may now find these acts to be daily habits—ongoing commitments. These are socially acceptable behaviors. And as noted earlier, social approval is a very important reward and force in life.

Commitment as a Process The selection of alternatives in situations often takes place as a gradual process rather than with an instantaneous decision. An

A. Acute commitment-making; immediately recognizable to the actor.

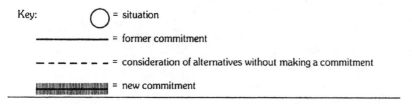

B. Progressive commitment-making; gradually recognizable to the actor.

Key: ◯ = situation

———————— = former commitment

– – – – – – = consideration of alternatives without making a commitment

▮▮▮▮▮▮▮▮▮ = new commitment

Figure C.4 Acute and Gradual Commitment-Making

example is religious conversion (compare Kox et al. 1991, Wimberley 1974a, Wimberley et al. 1975). Religious conversions often have been thought to occur all of a sudden: Zap, and there is instant change. At least, that is the way many people report religious conversions.

But if one were to observe closely persons undergoing religious conversions, it would be found that many conversions are not so instantaneous. More often, conversions are lengthy processes. Conversion is a process of interacting with other people, acquiring alternative commitment choices that are learned through interactions with others, and adjusting choices to avoid disturbing others whose approval is most important to us.

The acute versus gradual processes of commitment-making are illustrated in Figure C.4. Consider the following situation: Suppose a Baptist is converting to Catholicism. The Baptist may have married a Catholic and moved into a new community where most acquaintances are Catholics. The process may unfold across a series of encounters in social situations something like the following. The Baptist defines his commitment along the following lines, "I am a Baptist . . . I am a Baptist . . . I am a Baptist . . . I am a Baptist . . . well, you know there's something to Catholicism al-

though I am a Baptist . . . I am a Baptist . . . maybe Catholicism is a satisfactory alternative . . . I am a Baptist . . . I am a Baptist . . . I am a Baptist . . . maybe I'm a Catholic . . . maybe I'm a Catholic . . . no, I'm a Baptist . . . no, I'm a Baptist . . . I'm a Catholic . . . I'm a Baptist . . . I'm a Catholic . . . I'm a Catholic . . . I'm a Catholic." Through these situations, the individual finally comes out committed to the Catholic alternative and will probably continue to remain Catholic as long as the individual stays in the same set of social relationships.

This suggests that if one is to convert others to a particular religious identity—to make a new commitment—social interactions with the potential convert are very important. The on-the-spot conversion may be highly desired by those seeking converts because it takes so little time and requires such a small social investment by the evangelist. But in studies of sudden conversions, it is found that the conversion's effects tend to wear off and the convert is likely to change back unless he or she is sustained by significant social interactions with other committed persons at the expense of relationships with the convert's former associates.

On the other hand, those who are converted through a process of interactions with others and remain in the social interaction network are not as new commitments. Alternatives for commitments, other than the one to which the individual has converted, cannot easily enter his or her social situations. Like friendships, one's network of social interactions closes out other such alternatives.

Scientifically, it is useful to know how different types of commitments operate in the same, basic ways. Although conversions are not usually thought to be like marital choices, research suggests that the marriage decisions that are made very quickly are likely to be the first broken. Also, educational choices made on the spur of the moment, such as "I'm going to major in history rather than economics," are the most likely commitments—or conversions to a major—to be changed.

Because the concept of commitment is fairly abstract, the conversion analogy may be widely generalizable. If so, any type of quick, acute, turnabout commitments are not as likely to last.

When considering situations and alternatives, decisions and selections, and quick decisions versus drawn-out decisions, a couple of points may be emphasized. First, every decision begins a commitment. Second, decision alternatives often come through social interaction. That is, they come primarily through the others with whom we relate. Friends and associates serve as major resources for commitment alternatives whether, at first, we want them or not.

Stages of a Commitment: Once a decision or a selection of alternatives has been made, as noted in Figure C.3, several stages of a commitment follow. First comes the latent stage. A latent commitment is one that has been decided upon by the individual or selected by the social structure, but it has not yet been put into effect. For instance, when a voter decides to vote for a particular candidate, the commitment has been made in his or her mind even though there has not yet been an actual opportunity to cast the vote.

Next comes the active stage. Here, a latent commitment is transformed into action. This is the actual voting behavior.

The final, passive stage switches back and forth with the active stage. It covers situations in which the previously activated commitment lies dormant. Therefore, the stages proceed as latent, active, and passive and then oscillate between the active and passive stages for the duration of the commitment. One walks across the street or reads a book. But none of these behaviors is involved with voting for the candidate. However, the next time there is an opportunity to vote for that candidate, it will be done—assuming that, meanwhile, a new commitment has not been made to an alternative candidate.

Breaking Commitments: Some commitments are broken because the person simply chooses to give them up. Certainly, commitments that are painful may be readily dropped in opportune situations where pleasurable or, at least, less painful alternatives are defined. In some cases, commitments are fulfilled when their goals are reached. When one graduates from school, one may remain committed to continuing to educate oneself, but it is inappropriate to stay and work further on the degree. That goal is completed, and the commitment is ended. In other cases, new alternatives enter the picture and give rise to a change of commitments. Job opportunities arise, and some students quit their educational commitments for more immediate career rewards.

In still other cases, commitments are terminated against one's personal choice. The person is forced to discontinue the commitment. The social structure takes the choice away and imposes a new selection.

Of the commitments that terminate with relationships with other persons, one type is ultimately traumatic. This is the death of a friend. A friend is a source of rewards. In exchange, there are feelings of obligation to the friend. But upon the friend's death, these mutual obligations cannot be repaid in a direct way. When a friend dies, the trauma is that a commitment is terminated involuntarily, and a set of rewarding exchanges is broken. This causes grief.

Conclusion   In brief, commitment is a process applicable to an individual's dispositions and behaviors. Commitments can be made to religion, politics, deviance, jobs, friends, a spouse, or to any disposition or behavior. Commitments may be weak or strong. Situations present alternatives for commitments. An individual either personally decides what commitment to make, or some part of the social structure selects and imposes a commitment. A latent commitment may go through active and passive stages until it is terminated. Reasons for terminating a commitment result from coercion, learning of preferable alternatives, or finishing the course of a commitment. Your commitment to reading this article is about to become passive.

See also Religiosity, Salience, Social Psychology

—*Ronald C. Wimberley*

REFERENCES

C. L. Cox et al., "Prescriptive Support and Commitment Processes in Close Relationships," *Social Psychology Quarterly* 60(March 1997):79-90; K. Gerson, *No Man's Land* (New York: Basic Books, 1993); C. Y. Glock and R. Stark, *Religion and Society in Tension* (Chicago: Rand McNally, 1965); K. Heimer and R. L. Matsueda, "Role-Taking, Role Commitment, and Delinquency," *American Sociological Review* 59(1994):365-390; P. Kollock, "The Emergence of Exchange

Structures," *American Journal of Sociology* 100(1994):313-345; W. Kox et al., "Religious Conversion of Adolescents," *Sociological Analysis* 52(1991):227-240; P. Morrow, *The Theory and Measurement of Work Commitment* (Greenwich, Conn.: JAI, 1992); C. J. Mottaz, "Determinants of Organizational Commitment," *Human Relations* 41(1988):467-482; R. Stark and C. Y. Glock, *American Piety* (Berkeley: University of California Press, 1968); R. C. Wimberley, *Commitment and Commitment Strength with Application to Political Parties,* Doctoral dissertation, University of Tennessee, Knoxville, 1972; R. C. Wimberley, "Conversion and Commitment," *Border States* 1, 2(1974a):30-41; R. C. Wimberley, "Toward the Measurement of Commitment Strength," *Sociological Analysis* 35(1974b):211-215; R. C. Wimberley, "Dimensions of Commitment," *Journal for the Scientific Study of Religion* 17(1978):225-240; R. C. Wimberley et al., "Conversion at a Billy Graham Crusade," *Sociological Quarterly* 16(1975):162-170.

COMMUNAL GROUPS/RELIGIOUS COMMUNITY

Community has two meanings: (1) the way people feel about groups in which they are members that is expressed in group morale, cohesion, commitment, or love and (2) a form of social organization that enables people voluntarily to live together (Hillery 1992). The second definition, which emphasizes a type of social structure established to facilitate cohesion and commitment, has generated most of the social scientific research on community and will be the focus of this discussion.

Communal groups differ from highly institutionalized formal organizations in that they do not give primacy to specific goals; rather, they exist for the well-being of members and the achievement of more general goals such as prayer, rearing families, welfare of the group, sharing values, and so forth. Membership in the group is usually voluntary, and group survival depends on the commitment of members to group goals.

The most stable and widely occurring type of community is the village or city, which is based on families cooperating in a localized setting. Maintenance of the communal group relies on natural replacement through the biosocial family. As Kanter (1972) demonstrates, however, in groups in which communal ideology is strongly emphasized, the nuclear family is usually weak or nonexistent. Such communes that rely on voluntary recruits tend to be fragile structures and many do not last. The one exception is Christian monasteries, communal groups that have been in existence for almost 2,000 years. Although these groups exclude the biosocial family by requiring celibacy of their members, love known as *agapé* (i.e., one that transcends affection for any individual and is rooted in religious ideology) compensates for the usual sentiments and ties among biological family and kin members. In a brilliant work, Hillery (1992) describes the kind of love and commitment that has sustained communal monastic life for centuries.

A parallel to religious monasteries are Catholic religious orders of women. While the majority of these orders, at least in the West, are active orders in which members combine lives of prayer with apostolate service, celibacy is required, recruitment is voluntary, and agapé love compensates for the biological family. A number of recent studies (Neal 1990, Nygren and Ukeritis 1993, Ebaugh 1993, Wittberg 1994) describe the changes that are occurring within these orders that parallel a rapid decline in membership. While Hillery suggests that the recent changes occurring in monasteries may result in their demise, Ebaugh (1993) predicts that religious orders of women in the West will either become extinct or radically changed in terms of size and structure. The explanation offered in each case relates to changes occurring in the mechanisms of commitment that have sustained these institutions for centuries. As Kanter (1972) demonstrated, there is a strong relationship in communal groups between the sacrificial demands made of members and the degree of membership commitment; that is, the more renunciation and discipline required of members, the higher the degree of commitment that is generated. The types of changes occurring both in monasteries and in Catholic religious orders as a response to modernization and renewal are the relaxation of lifestyle demands in favor of greater personal freedom. The challenge facing these groups today is to achieve communal commitment while responding to demands, both internal and external, for renewal and increased individual autonomy.

The vast amount of social scientific research on communes and cults in the past two decades has also contributed to the analysis of communal groups. Through numerous case studies of specific groups, social scientists have illuminated many of the structures and processes that operate to generate group commitment, group harmony and conflict, recruitment, and longevity. The myriad recent studies on communal groups demonstrate that a major issue for each of them is the tension between group ideology and commitment, on the one hand, and the desire for individual freedom, on the other.

—Helen Rose Ebaugh

REFERENCES

H. R. Ebaugh, *Women in the Vanishing Cloister* (New Brunswick, N.J.: Rutgers University Press, 1993); G. A. Hillery, Jr., *The Monastery* (Westport, Conn.: Praeger, 1992); R. M. Kanter, *Commitment and Community* (Cambridge: Harvard University Press, 1972); M. A. Neal, *From Nuns to Sisters* (Mystic, Conn.: Twenty-Third Publications, 1990); D. Nygren and M. Ukeritis, *The Future of Religious Orders in the United States* (Westport, Conn.: Praeger, 1993); P. Wittberg, *The Rise and Fall of Catholic Religious Orders* (Albany: SUNY Press, 1994).

COMMUNAL INVOLVEMENT By developing the concept of communal involvement at length in a landmark study of religious communities in Detroit, Michigan, Gerhard Lenski (1961) set out to address a central issue in the sociology of the United States. The classical theory of urbanism had suggested that religion becomes a highly specialized aspect of social life in the modern metropolis. Churches themselves became highly specialized formal associations that cease to be nuclei around which a variety of social relationships are organized, as was typical of agrarian communities. Nevertheless, the impersonality of urban life stimulates in individuals the need for communal relationships, broader than the family yet narrower than the entire society.

Earlier in American history, ethnic groups served this function, and individuals achieved a sense of community by identifying with German, Polish, Italian, or other ethnic heritages of their immigrant forebears. By the 1950s, the ethnic communities were disintegrating. A problem that Lenski set for himself was to determine whether involvement in religious communities was taking the place of the older identification with ethnic groups. Did the specialization and compartmentalization inherent in an urban way of life compel people to transform their religious groups from narrow, specialized associations into groups that are more communal in character?

Lenski's research found considerable evidence that this was indeed the case, despite the many differences among religious communities in Detroit. To investigate this matter, he made a conceptual distinction between *associational involvement* in religion and *communal involvement* in religion. Associational involvement meant participation in church activities, and frequency of church attendance was Lenski's prime indicator of this. Communal involvement, on the other hand, meant the degree to which the primary relationships of the individual (i.e., marriage, kinship, and friendship) are confined to persons in the same socioreligious group. The distinction was important empirically as well as theoretically, Lenski discovered, because the correlation between associational involvement and communal involvement was quite low.

In Detroit, socioreligious groups exhibited distinct patterns of associational and communal involvement. The strong communal involvement of Jews was attributable to the norm of religious endogamy that was very prominent in this group. The strong communal bond among black Protestants appeared less internally generated and more a result of prejudice and segregation of blacks by the white population as a whole.

Lenski went on to demonstrate that endogamy (rather than same-group friendships) was the backbone of communal involvement and that socioreligious group endogamy became more frequent with each generation after immigration. Not only endogamy but the conversion of a marital partner to the other's faith became increasingly common as well. Lenski was also able to establish that communal involvement correlated with a number of attitudes. For instance, he found high communal involvement to be associated with a provincial outlook, a lessened interest in world affairs, negative assessments of other socioreligious groups, and diminished concern with the problems faced by their members. Communal involvement was also related to attitudes on numerous moral issues and correlated with a high valuation of kinship ties and obedience rather than personal autonomy. These many findings led Lenski to conclude that socioreligious groups had indeed

Socioreligious Group	Strength of Bonds	
	Associational	Communal
Jews	weak	strong
White Catholic	strong	medium
White Protestant	medium	medium
Black Protestant	medium	strong

Figure C.5. Structures and Dynamics of Associational and Communal Involvement

replaced ethnic groups as the anchorage in the contemporary urban society of the United States.

Communal involvement is not a term that has been used widely in the literature in recent years. But the 1990s has seen a renaissance of the communitarian perspective in sociology (Etzioni 1994), and this may well reawaken interest in Lenski's landmark study.

See also Gerhard Lenski

—*Edward B. Reeves*

REFERENCES

A. Etzioni, *The Spirit of Community* (New York: Touchstone, 1994); G. Lenski, *The Religious Factor* (Garden City, N.Y.: Doubleday, 1961).

COMMUNITARIANISM A philosophy associated with thinkers such as Burke and Rousseau, which opposes the individualism of liberal political theory embodied in such thinkers as Hobbes and Locke. Whereas liberals stress the primacy of the "unencumbered" self and individual rights, communitarians see individual identity as socially embedded and stress responsibility for the common good. *Habits of the Heart* (1985), by Robert Bellah and his colleagues, is an exemplary sociological study based on communitarian premises. Walzer (1990:6) notes that historically the communitarian critique of liberalism has been "like the pleating of trousers: transient but certain to return." Led by the George Washington University sociologist Amitai Etzioni, communitarianism was formally organized as the "Communitarian Network" in 1990 with the goal of shoring up the moral, social, and political environments of America by strengthening the family, putting character building at the center of schools, and rebuilding local communities.

—*David Yamane*

REFERENCES

R. Bellah et al., *Habits of the Heart* (Berkeley: University of California Press, 1985); A. Etzioni, *The Spirit of Community* (New York: Touchstone, 1994); M. Walzer, "The Communitarian Critique of Liberalism," *Political Theory* 18(1990): 6-23.

COMMUNITY ORGANIZATION Broadly used to refer to any nonprofit organization of civil society.

Often used more specifically to refer to nonprofit groups intended to serve or represent the interests of a "grassroots" constituency, especially when such organizations are controlled by local residents.

Much attention to community organizations derives from the "community organizing" work of Saul Alinsky (e.g., 1969, 1971, see Horwitt 1989). Alinsky's work from the 1930s to the 1970s focused on linking community organizations into an alliance that could project sufficient political power to influence city policies. These alliances included religious congregations, trade unions, neighborhood groups, ethnic associations, schools, and other community organizations.

Contemporary community organizing largely descends from Alinsky's work and can be divided into four types: Faith-based or church-based organizing has built strong institutional ties to local religious congregations, with a political vision informed by a socioreligious worldview. Race-based or multiracial organizing emphasizes racial identity and the construction of a multiracial culture. Issue-based organizing revolves around generating commitment to specific issues affecting the community. Neighborhood organizing focuses more narrowly on local concerns.

All four may receive a substantial portion of their funding from religious institutions, with the goal of reinvigorating democracy by representing marginalized constituencies that are ethnically, economically, and religiously diverse. Church-based community organizing is the most widespread of the four models, present in some 120 metropolitan areas throughout the United States. Typically, such efforts draw together multiple religious congregations from various traditions to address issues affecting local residents: funding and standards for public education, deteriorating public safety, minimum wage levels, housing programs, police reform, parks and recreation, economic development, bank lending practices, and so on. Working through preexisting networks within congregations, they draw participants to organization-sponsored efforts to change local, regional, or state policies. Typically, they appeal both to participants' economic, political, and social needs ("self-interest") and to their religiously based ethical traditions.

Church-based community organizing has also been extended internationally, primarily to Europe and Latin America. Four national networks sponsor most of the U.S.-based efforts: the Industrial Areas Foundation (based in Chicago), the Pacific Institute for Community Organization (Oakland, California), Gamaliel (Milwaukee and Chicago), and Dart (Florida).

—*Richard L. Wood*

REFERENCES

S. D. Alinsky, *Reveille for Radicals* (New York: Vintage, 1969 [1946]); S. D. Alinsky, *Rules for Radicals* (New York: Vintage, 1971); H. Boyte, *Commonwealth* (New York: Free Press, 1989); E. Cortes, Jr., "Reweaving the Fabric," in *Interwoven Destinies*, ed. H. Cisneros (New York: Norton, 1993); W. Greider, *Who Will Tell the People* (New York: Simon & Schuster, 1992); S. Horwitt, *Let Them Call Me Rebel* (New York: Knopf, 1989).

COMPASSION   Sorrow for the troubles of another, accompanied by an urge to help. Although this attitude is encouraged probably in all religions (certainly in all the world religions), compassion is not equally important in all of them nor does it have the same meaning in all of them.

Within Islam, compassion is expressed as charity. One of the "five pillars" of Islam is payment of the *zakat,* that is, alms for the poor. In this way, income is redistributed to create a more just community.

In the Chinese tradition, Mo Tzu and Confucius offer two contrasting approaches to compassion. Mo Tzu favored a universalistic approach; that is, the degree of compassion should be determined by the extent of the other's suffering; it matters not whether the other is a stranger or a member of one's family. Confucius gave more importance to the degree of relationship, with priority given to family members (Wong 1989). The Confucian approach has been more influential.

Within Buddhism, one is to show concern for all living things; for example, compassion can be shown by feeding the homeless or by releasing caged birds. Buddhist practices are supposed to reduce egotism and lead to wisdom (the realization of "emptiness"). Insight results in nonattachment to everything, which is supposed not only to allow but somehow also to require compassion for all beings. Buddhist compassion is not passionate but "cool" (Piyadassi 1964).

The Christian notion of compassion is often expressed as love, in the agapic sense. The primary meaning has been a willingness to sacrifice for others. However, the understanding of whom one is to love as well as the meaning of love has changed over time. As evidenced by their interpretation of Deuteronomy 23:19-20, which forbade taking interest from a "brother" but allowed it in relation to a "stranger," Christian leaders slowly changed their interpretation of *brother* to mean a fellow townsman, fellow countryman, and then all Christians, until finally an unequivocally universalist treatment of the word *brother* was established during the twelfth and thirteenth centuries (Nelson 1969). Similarly, Christian love is now interpreted universalistically. For example: "For agape enjoins one to attribute to everyone alike an irreducible worth and dignity, to rule out comparisons at the most basic level, to refuse to defer to the particular social and ethnic groups to which an individual happens to belong" (Outka 1972:269).

The nature of love is still debated. For some, it is akin to duty (e.g., Kant's "practical love") and can be directed to an aggregate of people (e.g., humanity); for others, love is a spontaneous identity with another rooted in the immediate experience of a particular person (Tamney 1992). Moreover, the equating of love and sacrifice is being reexamined; some Christians argue that caring for others should not mean disregard for the self; rather, they say, people should have more or less equal regard for themselves and others (Outka 1972).

—*Joseph B. Tamney*

REFERENCES

B. Nelson, *The Idea of Usury*, 2nd ed. (Chicago: University of Chicago Press, 1969); G. Outka, *Agape* (New Haven, Conn.: Yale University Press, 1972); T. Piyadassi, *The Buddha's Ancient Path* (London: Rider, 1964); J. B. Tamney, *American Society in the Buddhist Mirror* (New York: Garland, 1992); D. B. Wong, "Universalism Versus Love with Distinctions," *Journal of Chinese Philosophy* 16(1989):251-272.

COMPENSATORS (GENERAL AND SPECIFIC COMPENSATORS)   One of the key concepts in the formal theory of religion developed by the U.S. sociologists Rodney Stark and William Sims Bainbridge (e.g., 1987). According to this theory, people seek rewards and try to acquire them at low costs. Rewards are anything people *desire,* material and or immaterial. The things people desire depend both on their personal preferences and on the sociocultural context in which they are embedded.

Rewards are unequally distributed: Some are scarcer than others, and some even seem to be attainable only in the distant future or in an "other world," such as life eternal. This is why substitutes or *compensators* have been invented for these rewards, and they are treated as if they were rewards. Two types of compensators can be discerned: general and specific. *General* refers to "a great array of rewards or rewards of vast scope," whereas a *specific* compensator is the opposite. As a rule, general compensators are found in religion, whereas magicians are the providers of specific compensators par excellence.

See also Rational Choice Theory

—*Durk H. Hak*

REFERENCE

R. Stark and W. S. Bainbridge, *A Theory of Religion* (New York: Lang, 1987).

CONFLICT   Sociologists of religion tend to emphasize the prevalence of order in society and in social organizations. They stress the importance of common values as the basis of societal and organizational stability. They view conflict and other forms of deviation as problematic. Their analyses imply the need to resocialize deviants and restore order. This research tradition tends to see religion as a cultural institution that brings people together for common purposes and, except for temporary disruptions, contributes to the overall well-being and orderliness of society.

However, the sociology of religion also includes a subordinate strand of theory and research stressing the prevalence of disorder in society and social organizations. Groups in society generally, and in the religious arena particularly, are prone to in-group/out-group distinctions: superior versus inferior, saved versus unsaved. Division and turmoil are natural extensions of such conflicting values and interests. Analyses in this tradition stress the normalcy of conflict between religious groups, the prevalence of conflict within religious groups, and the relationship between religion and societal conflict (Raab 1964, Menendez 1985).

Conflict Between Religious Groups   There is a considerable body of literature on historic conflicts between Protestant groups. Studies document late-nineteenth-century and early-twentieth conflicts between "mainline" supporters of the "Social Gospel," who felt religion should address social concerns such as urban poverty, and "fundamentalists," who insisted that religion's focus should be on spiritual matters. Studies also record struggles in the 1920s and 1930s between "modernists," who wanted religion to embrace modern science, and "conservatives," who stressed the importance of scriptural literalism and religious tradition. Finke and Stark (1992) document conflicts between mainline denominations and evangelicals over control of American radio waves in the 1930s and 1940s. These tensions persist in present-day "culture wars" between liberal mainline denominations and conservative evangelical groups (Liebman and Wuthnow 1983, Hunter 1983, 1991).

The history of conflict between American Protestants and Catholics also is well documented (Kane 1955). Protestant nativism was directed at eighteenth-century Catholic colonists and nineteenth- and early-twentieth-century Catholic immigrants. The Know Nothing Party, the Ku Klux Klan, the Anti-Saloon League, and the temperance movement depicted Catholics as intellectually inferior and morally depraved. Protestants feared that, following orders from Rome, "papists" might try to supplant American democracy with an authoritarian state based on Catholic beliefs (Ray 1936, Billington 1938, Higham 1965). Catholics responded by establishing parallel institutions of their own (e.g., parochial schools, professional associations). Catholics' so-called ghetto mentality engendered prejudice against Protestants, who were seen as "separated brethren" and "holy rollers" who preached religious falsehoods.

Protestant-Catholic conflict also has been a prominent part of religious history in Northern Ireland. Religious differences are at the root of the tensions between the more affluent and politically powerful Protestant community against the economically and politically disenfranchised Catholic minority (Moore 1972). In Latin America, the Catholic Church has been dominant, often aligning itself with economic and political elites. Increasingly, Catholics have come into conflict with evangelical Protestants, who have sought the allegiance of working-class peasants who feel they have been abandoned by the Catholic Church. Liberation theology is the Catholic Church's attempt to realign itself with peasants and, in the process, stifle evangelical gains in the competition for Latin American souls (Burns 1992).

There is a long history of Christian anti-Semitism. Researchers have documented many forms of Christian discrimination against Jews in early-twentieth-century America, such as Ivy League universities' use of quotas to exclude Jewish students (Zweigenhaft and Domhoff 1982, Pyle 1996). Neighborhood and housing discrimination against Jews persisted well into the 1960s. Some evidence suggests that prejudice toward Jews is based on Christian particularism—the tendency to judge others in terms of Christian beliefs, including the tendency to see Jews as responsible for the crucifixion of Christ (Glock and Stark 1966).

Religious groups also have locked horns over issues such as religious truth, abortion, sex roles, and church-state relations. Religious truth has been at the root of numerous tensions between "mainline" religions and new religious groups, especially ones with cultlike qualities and unconventional religious practices. Legal challenges to Mormon theology and polygamous marital practices during the late-nineteenth and early-twentieth centuries are but one example (O'Dea 1957). More recently, cults have been seen as "brainwashing" their followers (Robbins and Anthony 1978, Shupe and Bromley 1979, Melton 1986). Liberal religious groups have tended to favor a pro-choice view on abortion, sexual equality (including the ordination of women clergy), the separation of church and state, and religious unity (ecumenism). Conservative groups have advocated "respect for life," traditional sex roles, prayer in schools, and doctrinal purity. These incompatibilities have taken the form of political, as well as religious, conflicts.

Conflict Within Religious Groups   In addition to these intergroup conflicts, there also have been very intense intragroup struggles. Protestantism has known its share of intradenominational conflicts. Acrimonious conflict between denominational officials and seminary faculty led to a major schism within the Lutheran Church-Missouri Synod in the 1970s (Scherer 1990). In the 1980s and 1990s, "fundamentalists" and "moderates" have struggled for control over national offices, publishing houses, and denominational seminaries in the Southern Baptist Convention (Barnhart 1986, Ammerman 1990).

Wood (1970) has demonstrated that high-ranking denominational officials often take liberal stands on controversial issues such as racial integration, against the more conservative wishes and interests of church members. Hadden (1969) and Hoge (1976), among others, have documented major differences between Protestant clergy and laity with regard to parish priorities and social issues.

There also are well-documented conflicts within Catholicism. Several analysts have described conflicts between "integrationist" or "Americanist" Catholics, who have wanted to assimilate into American culture, and "anti-Americanists" or "restorationists," who have wanted to perpetuate the Catholic Church's distinctive traditions and its goal of transforming American society (Greeley 1967, D'Antonio et al. 1996). Others (Seidler and Meyer 1988, Burns 1992) have provided a vivid account of how conflict between clergy with competing theological models of the Catholic Church precipitated the Second Vatican Council (1962-1965). They also have documented the extent of clergy conflict in the wake of Vatican II.

There have been fewer studies of conflict in Judaism, but the divisions among Orthodox, Conservative, and Reform Judaism indicate the significance of theological pluralism. Class and ethnic differences have compounded the religious tensions among these Jewish "denominations" (Wertheimer 1990).

In addition to these studies of conflict within particular faith groups, there have been numerous studies of conflict at the congregational or parish level. Davidson and Koch (1997) use a political framework to explain conflicts over congregations' "inward [mutual benefit] and outward [public benefit] orientations." Wood (1981) has shown that, from time to time, congregational leaders are able to transcend parishioners' priorities and institutionalize social action programs oriented toward helping nonmembers. They do so by calling members' attention to superordinate religious values and gaining permission to engage in actions that individual members might not endorse. Hadden and Longino (1974) documented the fragility of an outward-oriented Presbyterian congregation that was unable to sustain its prophetic mission in the face of conflict within the organization and between the church and the larger community. Long (1991) has shown how clergy-laity conflict in Lutheranism devolved into a lose-lose situation in the 1970s and 1980s.

Religion and Societal Conflict   Religion is both a product and a source of social conflict (Maduro 1982). Societal conflicts often lead to bitter conflicts within churches. Several scholars have argued that conflict between the old capitalist class and "new class" of knowledge elites is at the root of today's conflicts between religious liberals and conservatives (Hunter 1980, Hargrove 1986).

Racial inequality—from the time of slavery to the present—has fostered racial divisions in denominations and local congregations. Race was at the base of nineteenth-century regional schisms in several Protestant denominations. In the 1960s, the gap between black and white churches grew as blacks formed new congregations based on "black theology" and as white churches opposed black demands for financial reparations for white churches' complicity in America's history of slavery and racial segregation (Lincoln and Mamiya 1990).

The women's movement of the 1960s-1990s has spawned religious debates over the roles of women in churches. Battle lines have been drawn between religious liberals who favor greater participation (including ordination) of women and religious conservatives who prefer patriarchal models of church life (Carroll et al. 1983, Lehman, 1985, 1993).

More recently, the gay and lesbian movement has led to sharp divisions in churches. Church leaders, in groups such as Dignity, have proposed an end to prejudice based on sexual orientation and insisted that homosexuals have a right to be ordained. They have been opposed by others who feel that scriptures portray homosexuality as a serious sin that should preclude ordination.

But religion also is a source of societal conflict. In addition to the religious bases of macro-level conflicts in Northern Ireland and the Middle East, churches initiate political agendas that often produce conflict. Black churches, and some white churches, took the lead in advocating racial justice in the United States during the civil rights era of the 1950s and 1960s (Morris 1984). The Catholic Church, some mainline Protestant denominations, and some evangelicals have taken prophetic positions against the increased concentration of wealth and power in America (Davidson et al., 1990). Peace churches (e.g., the Brethren) vigorously opposed the arms race and the Vietnam War. Evangelical Protestants have opposed the Supreme Court's ruling against prayer in public schools. Catholics and evangelicals have found themselves on the same side of the pro-life movement against abortion. These prophetic stands—both left and right—have precipitated prolonged debates, volatile rallies, political battles, and even violence between opposing forces.

—James D. Davidson and Ralph E. Pyle

REFERENCES

N. T. Ammerman, *Baptist Battles* (New Brunswick, N.J.: Rutgers University Press, 1990); J. E. Barnhart, *Baptist Holy Wars* (Austin: Texas Monthly Press, 1986); R. A. Billington, *The Protestant Crusade* (New York: Rinehart, 1938); G. Burns, *The Frontiers of Catholicism* (Berkeley: University of California Press, 1992); J. W. Carroll et al., *Women of the Cloth* (New York: Harper, 1983); W. V. D'Antonio et al., *American Catholic Laity in a Changing Church* (Kansas City, Mo.: Sheed & Ward, 1989); W. V. D'Antonio et al., *American Catholic Laity* (Kansas City, Mo.: Sheed & Ward, 1996); J. D. Davidson and J. R. Koch, "Beyond Mutual and Public Benefits," in *Sacred Companies*, ed. N. J. Demerath et al. (New York: Oxford University Press, 1997); J. D. Davidson et al., *Faith and Social Ministry* (Chicago: Loyola University Press, 1990); R. Finke and R. Stark, *The Churching of America* (New Brunswick, N.J.: Rutgers University Press, 1992); C. Y. Glock and R. Stark, *Christian Beliefs and Anti-Semitism* (New York: Harper, 1966); A. M. Greeley, *The Catholic Experience* (Garden City, N.Y.: Doubleday, 1967); A. M. Greeley, *The Ugly Little Secret* (Kansas City, Mo.: Sheed Andrews and McMeel, 1974); "Grosse Pointe's Gross Points," *Time* (Apr. 25, 1960): 25; J. K. Hadden, *The Gathering Storm in the Churches* (Garden City, N.Y.: Doubleday, 1969); J. K. Hadden and Charles Longino, *Gideon's Gang* (New York: Pilgrim Press, 1974); B. Hargrove, *The Emerging New Class* (New York: Pilgrim, 1986); J. Higham, *Strangers in Our Land* (New Brunswick, N.J.: Rutgers University Press, 1965); D. R. Hoge, *Division in the Protestant House* (Phila-delphia: Westminster, 1976); J. D. Hunter, "The New Class and Young Evangelicals," *Review of Religious Research* 24(1980): 155-169; J. D. Hunter, *American Evangelicalism* (New Brunswick, N.J.: Rutgers University Press, 1983); J. D. Hunter, *Culture Wars* (New York: Basic Books, 1991); J. J. Kane, *Catholic-Protestant Conflicts in America* (Chicago: Regnery, 1955); E. C. Lehman, Jr., *Women Clergy* (New Brunswick, N.J.: Rutgers University Press, 1985); E. C. Lehman, Jr., *Gender and Work* (Albany: SUNY Press, 1993); R. Liebman and R. Wuthnow, *The New Christian Right* (New York: Aldine, 1983); C. E. Lincoln and L. Mamiya, *The Black Church in the African American Experience* (Durham, N.C.: Duke University Press, 1990); T. E. Long, "To Reconcile Prophet and Priest," *Sociological Focus* 23(1991):251-265; O. Maduro, *Religion and Social Conflicts* (Maryknoll, N.Y.: Orbis, 1982); M. N. Marger, *Race and Ethnic Relations* (Belmont, Calif.: Wadsworth, 1991); J. G. Melton, *Encyclopedic Handbook of Cults in America* (New York: Garland, 1986); A. J. Menendez, *Religious Conflict in America* (New York: Garland, 1985); R. Moore, "Race Relations in the Six Counties," *Race* 14(1972):21-42; A. Morris, *The Origins of the Civil Rights Movement* (New York: Free Press, 1984); T. O'Dea, *The Mormons* (Chicago: University of Chicago Press, 1957); R. E. Pyle, *Persistence and Change in the Protestant Establishment* (Westport, Conn.: Praeger, 1996); E. Raab (ed.), *Religious Conflict in America* (New York: Doubleday, 1964); M. A. Ray, *American Opinion of Roman Catholicism in the Eighteenth Century* (New York: Columbia University Press, 1936); T. Robbins and D. Anthony, "New Religions, Families, and Brainwashing," *Society* 15(May-June 1978): 77-83; R. P. Scherer, "Faith and Social Ministry," in Davidson et al., *q.v.* (1990): 97-121; J. Seidler and K. Meyer, *Conflict and Change in the Catholic Church* (New Brunswick, N.J.: Rutgers University Press, 1988); A. Shupe and D. Bromley, "The Moonies and the Anti-Cultists," *Sociological Analysis* 40(1979):325-334; J. Wertheimer, *A People Divided* (New York: Basic Books, 1993); J. R. Wood, "Authority and Controversial Policy," *American Sociological Review* 35(1970):1057-1069; J. R. Wood, *Leadership in Voluntary Associations* (New Brunswick, N.J.: Rutgers University Press, 1981); R. L. Zweigenhaft and G. W. Domhoff, *Jews in the Protestant Establishment* (New York: Praeger, 1982).

CONFUCIANISM The name given by Westerners to a large body of Chinese scholarly works. The Chinese refer to "the scholarly tradition." *Confucius* is the latinized version of Kung Fu-tzu (i.e., Master Kung), who was a teacher in China (c. 551 B.C.E.-479 B.C.E.). The Analects, which is a collection of sayings attributed to Confucius, are the roots for a large literature that comments and embellishes on the principles set forth in the Analects. These supposed sayings of Confucius were written down 70 to 80 years after his death. Confucianism also includes the Five Classics: stories about Ancient China, poetry, ritual rules, and court records. As the classics exist today, they were written after Confucius's time, but some version of them probably predated Confucius and influenced his thinking. Through the centuries, scholars have selected preferred ideas from the vast canon, sometimes combining them with notions from competing ideologies such as Taoism or Buddhism, and called their selections "Confucianism."

During the second century B.C.E., Confucianism became the basis of China's civil morality. Until 1911, an applicant's knowledge of Confucian classics was used for selecting state bureaucrats. Throughout China, state-supported Confucian temples were established. Although deified by the state, Confucius was never a popular deity, and among the elite the acceptance of Confucius as a god steadily declined.

The ordinary people, until the late twentieth century, did not know Confucianism; however, aspects of this ideology, especially filial piety and all it implies, are part of Chinese Folk Religion. Confucianism has been an important influence on Korean, Japanese, and Vietnamese cultures.

Confucius valued self-cultivation. Each person must continually improve by learning how to carry out duties better so as to advance society. By and large, Confucianists do not consider human nature as inclined to evil; rather, each of us needs the right education to achieve wisdom, then we will spontaneously enact *jen* or humaneness. Although religious beliefs were accepted by Confucius, they remained in the background. Self-cultivation does not depend on divine grace but on self-disciplined study. The reward for good behavior is not living in heaven after death; goodness is its own reward: We feel fulfilled, and society is harmonious. The good person is courteous, considerate, avoids extremes (such as by neither craving luxury nor practicing asceticism), and follows the "golden rule": "Do not inflict on others what you yourself would not wish done to you" (Analects 15:24).

Confucianism presents the individual not as a detached entity but always as part of human relationships. Five such relationships are addressed specifically: father and son, elder and younger brothers, husband and wife, friend and friend, as well as sovereign and subject. In each relationship, both parties have obligations. For instance, the father should be kind, furnish security, and provide education. The son should be respectful, obedient, and care for his father in old age.

As Asian societies have modernized, Confucianism has been criticized for inhibiting democracy, being an obstacle to economic development, and justifying the subjugation of women. Regarding democracy, Creel (1960) noted aspects of Confucianism that are compatible with democracy: instruction to political leaders to maximize the wealth and happiness of the people, a preference for persuasion rather than force, and the elevation of faithfulness to principles over loyalty to persons. At the same time, three crucial aspects of Confucianism inhibit the development of democracy. First, the ideal political situation is a society ruled by a sage-emperor, that is, someone who has both wisdom and power. Confucius believed that the elite should control the common people. However, gaining political office should not be a hereditary right; leaders should be chosen because they are intelligent and morally upright. Second, the ideal society is in a constant state of harmony; in contrast, democracy assumes that some degree of conflict advances the common good. Third, Confucianism does not contain the idea of human rights; the ideology offers no basis for legitimating such principles as freedom of speech or a zone of privacy.

Scholars, in praising harmony, have implied a preference for social order and continuity. Ideally, everyone remains in the same status and is committed to retaining the traditional relationships among existing statuses. Order is maintained by *li*, that is, by each person acting with propriety. Confucianism is oriented toward the past, which attitude conflicts with the most basic aspects of a modern society: the orientation to the future and the expectation of continual change (Weber 1951, Jenner 1992).

Regarding economic development, Confucianism has valued being a gentleman or a sage higher than being a merchant. In the Analects, we read: "The Master said, 'The gentleman is familiar with what is right, just as the small man is familiar with profit'" (4:16). However, because of the economic success of Confucian-influenced societies such as Taiwan, the argument is now made that once economic development is under way, the process is reinforced by certain aspects of the Confucian tradition: support for a strong state, the value given to education, and a model of the family that encourages adult children to care for their parents and that discourages divorce.

Confucianism conflicts with modern familial norms. Gender equality is inconsistent with the preeminence of the father-son relationship in Confucianism. This attitude means that sons are valued more than daughters, and the father-son relationship is more important that the husband-wife relationship; appropriately, the proper role of a wife is to be obedient and look after her family. Moreover, modern children expect some independence, whereas Confucianism stresses obedience. Finally, modern couples want marriage to bring happiness, whereas Confucianism emphasizes harmony and the endurance of the relationship.

In capitalist East Asian societies, there is a revival movement, as scholars work to define a form of Confucianism that is modern but distinctive from Western culture (Rozman 1991, Tu 1991).

See also Taoism.

—*Joseph B. Tamney*

REFERENCES

H. G. Creel, *Confucius and the Chinese Way* (New York: Harper, 1960); W. B. F. Jenner, *The Tyranny of History* (London: Lane, 1992); G. Rozman (ed.), *The East Asian Region* (Princeton, N.J.: Princeton University Press, 1991); L. Kam, *Critiques of Confucius in Contemporary China* (Hong Kong: Chinese University Press, 1980); J. B. Tamney, "Modernizing Confucianism," in *Twentieth-Century World Religious Movements in Neo-Weberian Perspective,* ed. W. H Swatos, Jr. (Lewiston, NY: Mellen, 1992): 31-44; W. Tu, "The Search for Roots in Industrial East Asia," in *Fundamentalisms Observed,* ed. M. E. Marty and R. S. Appleby (Chicago: University of Chicago Press, 1991): 740-781; M. Weber, *The Religion of China* (New York: Free Press, 1951).

CONGREGATIONALISM   Used in three interrelated ways, this term emphasizes the role of the *laity* within the church (as contrasted to the "ordained," set-apart clergy). It is especially important to understanding religion in America, although it is characteristic of Western religious traditions in general.

One use of *congregationalism* is to refer to the American religious denomination once called the Congregational Church, now formally titled (since a 1950s merger with the Evangelical and Reformed Church) the United Church of Christ (UCC). This body is the inheritor of the established church of New England formed through a Puritan-Pilgrim alliance in the early seventeenth century, shortly after immigration from England. (The name "Congregational Church" is still used in England; in Canada, most Congregational churches merged into the United Church of Canada in the 1920s.) New England Congregationalism spawned a number of offshoots, including Unitarianism.

The name "Congregational Church" is taken from the fact that this denomination theoretically vests authority in the *local congregation;* that is, it has a *congregational polity* (other forms of polity, or organization, are "presbyterian" and "episcopal," although neither of these polities has had the same impact on American religious life as congregationalism, and in U.S. practice both are modified by congre-

gationalism). In strict usage, the local congregation *is* "the church." It "calls" (hires) its own minister (and can "fire" him or her as well). It also decides acceptable forms of doctrinal profession, liturgy, and so on, and decides on what forms of "fellowship" it will accept with other churches—for example, whether it will allow members who belong to a different congregation to come to receive various sacramental ministrations, particularly the Holy Communion, and the terms on which it will allow members of some other congregation to join its congregation. The congregation also normally owns the property on which any facilities it uses are located (e.g., the worship building, education facilities, offices).

As a form of polity, *congregationalism* descends from the Jewish synagogue tradition (from the Greek for "a gathering together") in which, in Orthodox practice, a synagogue is created whenever 10 men gather together for prayer. In its modern usage, however, which is quintessentially American, *congregationalism* has come to symbolize a greater principle—namely, religious *voluntarism.* The upshot of American religio-political ideology is that religion is an entirely voluntary activity: One not only may go to whatever church one chooses, but one may also go or stay home whenever one chooses, and one does not have to go to any church at all. Thus, the church is largely seen as serving the "needs" of its congregation, rather than the reverse. By establishing the voluntary basis of financial support for the church, furthermore, the role of the congregation is considerably more magnified than it is even in other countries where "freedom of religion" is the norm. In this sense, all American churches are congregationalist in a radical way: Unless a church has been extremely well endowed by prior generations, if the congregation leaves, the church must be closed. (This is very different, for example, from Scandinavian churches, where state support ensures that a regular program of activities will go on, even though only a tiny percentage of the population attends church; by the same token, some Scandinavians, and others, will find the American religious practice of passing of an offering—"collection"—plate or basket during worship offensive.)

Steeped in the Pilgrim myth, the voluntaristic principle that is inherent in congregationalism colors all American religion, not simply the Congregational Church or even Protestantism or even Judeo-Christianity. American Buddhist, Islamic, Roman Catholic, and national Orthodox groups must all adjust to aspects of this organizational worldview to survive. Americans can and do worship as well as vote with their feet and their pocketbooks. A degree of accommodation to this aspect of the "American way of life" is inherent in all religious practice. By the same token, Americans are more likely to see "religion," positively or negatively, as a congregational activity ("belonging to a church," or sometimes "organized religion"), and in recent usage distinguish this from personal religiosity by referring to the latter as *spirituality*.

See also Parish, Public Religion

—*William H. Swatos, Jr.*

REFERENCE

J. P. Wind and J. W. Lewis, *American Congregations,* 2 vols. (Chicago: University of Chicago Press, 1994).

CONSCIENCE   The consciousness of what is right or wrong according to certain principles of reference. It either produces peace of mind or guilt as a result of the action performed. The Western understanding of conscience was particularly influenced by Thomas Aquinas. It is a sentiment that may have a social dimension beyond the individual one. Indeed, for Durkheim, the "collective conscience" (*conscience collective*) is the "total of the beliefs and sentiments common to the mean of members of the same society." There is often confusion between consciousness and conscience. The latter concept is older and refers to aspects of a moral nature, whereas the former has a more sociological dimension—for example, in "class consciousness," a context where the religious dimension may also be studied.

—*Roberto Cipriani*

REFERENCES

É. Durkheim, *Division of Labor in Society* (London: Macmillan, 1933); P. E. Hammond, "Conscience and the Establishment Clause," *Journal for the Scientific Study of Religion* 35(1996):356-367.

CONTEMPORARY JEWRY   The official journal of the Association for the Social Scientific Study of Jewry, began publishing in 1974 as *Jewish Sociology and Social Research,* taking its present name in 1976. It has appeared in various formats but is now an annual devoted to the multidisciplinary study of Jewry, publishing theoretical and empirical works of interest to social scientists studying Jews and Judaism in Israel, North America, and elsewhere. It typically includes research articles, book reviews, a bibliography of recent works in the social scientific study of Jewry, and the Marshall Sklare Distinguished Scholar address given at the association's annual meeting.

—*J. Alan Winter*

CONTINGENCY   A philosophical/theological term, from *contingentia,* originally introduced by Greek philosophers, which designates that which is actual or accidental in contrast to that which is logically necessary and in accordance with law.

Scholastic scholars revived the term when Aristotelian categories were appropriated for the development of medieval theological systems. The Nature philosophers of the Renaissance, followed by pure Rationalists such as Spinoza, attempted to eliminate the notion of contingency, but the Empiricists Locke and Hume, along with the later Leibniz and Kant, insisted on the fact of contingency. Social scientists and comparative religionists rarely use the term today, preferring instead to refer to *individuality, freedom,* and the emergence of *anomalies* in relation to analytical systems. The relationship between law and necessity, on the one hand, and freedom and anomaly, on the other, is an issue that no theorists or comparative religion scholars can ignore.

—*William R. Garrett*

REFERENCE

E. Troeltsch, "Contingency," in *Encyclopedia of Religion and Ethics* Vol. 4, ed. J. Hastings (Edinburgh: Clark, 1911): 87-89.

CONTRIBUTIONS   Historically, religions have derived a substantial amount of their financial revenue through some arrangement with the political system in which they function (now generally termed the *state*). This has taken place through direct grants or through a tax either collected or enforced by the state with proceeds passed to religious leaders (although in most of these settings, there was also a tradition of religious begging on the part of individual religious virtuosi).

Since the American Revolution, however, the principle of the separation of church and state has resulted in a decrease of state-supported religious establishments and an increase in the dependence of religions on voluntary *contributions.* In various Anglo-American traditions, these are known as *tithes, pledges, dues,* or *offerings,* while the process of fund-raising may be placed into a larger context as *stewardship.* Regardless of the term, the nature of the voluntary contributory system means that religious organizations are dependent upon their members for the organization's ongoing maintenance. Either direct contributions or endowments provide the primary material resources for all organized religion in the United States.

Social scientists recently have become interested in the processes that lead people to contribute and that build successful contributory systems for religious institutions. Paramount in this research is Dean Hoge et al.s' *Money Matters: Personal Giving in American Churches* (Westminster 1996) and an issue of the *Review of Religious Research* guest edited by Hoge, "Patterns of Financial Contributions to Churches" (Vol. 36, No. 2, Dec. 1994).

—William H. Swatos, Jr.

CONVERSION Conversion research has been a dominant theme in the sociology and social psychology of religion for several decades, especially in studies of the "new religions." Much of the early work on the new religions such as Jesus Movement groups, the Unification Church, Hare Krishna, Divine Light Mission, and other unusual religions focused on explaining why and how people were recruited to such groups, and how and why they decided to participate. This process is discussed under the rubric of *conversion* in the religious literature, a term with a more cognitive and emotional meaning and referring more to beliefs. Those who study social movements, including new religious movements, more often use terms such as *recruitment,* which has more of a behavioral connotation focused on participation.

The research on joining the new religions was initially derived from literature in sociology and psychology of religion that shared a common assumption of something being wrong with a person who would seek religion—what Stark (1965) called the "psychopathological" explanation of religious participation. The early literature in this psychopathological vein assumed that a person must be suffering some major deprivation or have had some major trauma in his or her life to be interested in religion—a "religion as crutch" perspective. Bainbridge (1992) uses the term *strain theories* to refer to such ideas within the sociological realm. This broad perspective also assumed a high degree of passivity on the part of the person being converted—he or she was defined almost as an object to be acted upon by external or internal forces—and the power to bring about a conversion was posited elsewhere than with the subject of the conversion/recruitment (Richardson 1985a, Machalek and Snow 1993).

Two Approaches to Conversion Almost from the beginning of research on participation in new religions, that research and scholarly writing took on a dramatically bifurcated perspective. Some extended the deprivation- or strain-oriented tradition from the psychology and sociology of religion, integrating those ideas with results of studies on radical resocialization of Chinese after the communist takeover as well as research on U.S. soldiers who were Korean POWs and on the Russian purge trial under Stalin (Singer 1979). This amalgam was used to develop the "brainwashing" or "mind control" perspective that has come to dominate popular conceptions of how people are recruited to the newer religions (see discussion in Richardson and Kilbourne 1983, and critiques in Anthony 1990, Kilbourne and Richardson 1989, Richardson 1991).

The integration of the psychopathological tradition with these newer ideas focused on mysterious psychotechnologies allegedly being used by leaders of the newer religions. Supposedly, these new religious leaders had taken the ideas of the communists and were applying them to the youth of America (Solomon 1983). Those youth were assumed to be relatively helpless against such techniques, and thus were joining the new groups by the thousands.

This perception of powerful psychotechniques being used against young people has fueled much of the animosity toward the new and exotic religions and their recruitment processes. Such views also have been essential to the many legal attacks that have been launched against the newer religions (Anthony 1990, Richardson 1991).

A sharply contrasted view of conversion/recruitment phenomena, and one with important implications for understanding past research on conversion as well as for general theory on social movement participation, has been fostered through the works of a number of scholars doing studies on participation in the new religions (Barker 1984, Kilbourne and Richardson 1989, Richardson 1985a, Rochford 1985, Straus 1976, 1979). This research has led to questioning of some basic assumptions of the psychopathology model described above, especially the idea that potential recruits are being forced to do something by pressures beyond their control.

Instead, this empirical work has revealed that recruits are usually acting on their own volition, making decisions about participation based on a sometimes quite systematic and thorough analysis of alternatives, and engaged in negotiations about what must be done and believed to become a member in good standing. This more subject-centered and volitional model assumes that the person is in control of the situation, not the other way around (Kilbourne and Richardson 1989).

The battle over which paradigm to adopt in conversion/recruitment studies has been intense and has been carried on in many forums, including professional meetings, scholarly publications, legislative halls, and the legal system (see Bromley and Robbins 1992, Richardson 1991, Anthony and Robbins 1995, for updates on legal and political conflicts involving recruitment tactics).

The "World-Saver" Model Within the scholarly arena, the issue often has been couched in terms of empirical assessments of the recruitment/conversion process used by religious groups. This work has frequently been focused on tests or applications of the famous "world-saver" conversion/recruitment model deriving from John Lofland's dissertation research on the beginnings of the Unification Church presented in two publications (Lofland and Stark 1965, Lofland 1966) and revised dramatically in later publications (Lofland 1978, Lofland and Skonovd 1981).

The world-saver model was unique in its combination of traditional ideas with more contemporary issues in this area of research. The basic elements of the model include three *predisposing characteristics* (perception of long-term tension, strain, and so on; possession of a religious rhetoric and problem-solving perspective; self-definition as a "religious seeker") and four *situational factors* (reaching a "turning point" when old lines of action no longer work, development of affective ties between preconvert and group members, weakening affective ties with nongroup members, intensive interaction with group members).

The Lofland-Stark model was important in developing an alternative paradigm because it served as a bridge between the old and the new, containing a logically complete statement of the traditional psychological predisposition perspective focused on forces that might "push" a person into conversion, but also including elements explaining why a movement might be attractive to potential recruits. This latter aspect spoke to the future of research on conversion by focusing on the *process of conversion,* recognizing that conversion has a definite organizational aspect and is a *social* event.

One other key aspect of the model was the incorporation of subjects who would *self-define* themselves as religious *seekers* and take action to change by interacting with selected people and by allowing affective ties to develop with them.

Thus the Lofland-Stark model contained an implicit focus on a volitional subject, along with more traditional deterministic elements. The seminal quality of this work is shown by its being a starting point for those working in both the old and the new traditions of research on conversion. Those researchers more oriented toward predispositions have used this aspect of the model, while others find support for a more sociological and even *activist* starting point in the interactionist elements of the situational part of the model.

This creative eclecticism is perhaps the genius of the model and helps explain why it is the most often cited model in the history of conversion/recruitment research (see, for instance, Heirich 1977, Richardson and Stewart 1978, Snow and Phillips 1980, Greil and Rudy 1984, Richardson 1985a). Tests of the model have revealed that it has some serious empirical problems, especially in the more deterministic predisposition elements.

Lofland himself modified the model in significant ways later by stressing the volitional aspects of the process. He said (1978:22), "I have lately encouraged students of conversion to turn the process on its head and to scrutinize how people go about converting themselves." Roger Straus (1976, 1979), one of Lofland's doctoral students, has taken his advice most seriously, and his work has influenced others (such as Richardson).

Another publication of Lofland (with Skonovd 1981) also moved far beyond the initial conversion model and instead focused on basic "motifs" that seem to characterize conversions in a given time period. This view, coupled with that of a basic paradigm shift (Richardson 1985a, Kilbourne and Richardson 1989) or "drift" of conversion research interpretations (Long and Hadden 1983), has moved this area of scholarly research far beyond the more psychological and deterministic perspective dominant just a few decades ago. Now such research is likely to be more sociological in orientation (e.g., Stark and Bainbridge 1980, Bromley and Shupe 1979, Beckford 1978) and to be done from a more humanistic and interactionist perspective (Gordon 1974; Straus 1976, 1979; Downton 1980; Pilarzyk 1983; Richardson 1980, 1985a, 1985b). This latter line of research has been most succinctly presented in Dawson's (1990) discussion of the "active" conversion.

—*James T. Richardson*

REFERENCES

D. Anthony, "Religious Movements and Brainwashing Litigation," in *In Gods We Trust,* 2nd ed., ed. T. Robbins and D. Anthony (New Brunswick, N.J.: Transaction, 1990): 295-344; D. Anthony and T. Robbins, "Negligence, Coercion, and the Protection of Religious Belief," *Journal of Church and State* 37(1995):509-536; W. Bainbridge, "The Sociology of Conversion," in Malony and Southard, *q.v.* (1992): 178-191; E. Barker, *The Making of a Moonie* (Oxford: Blackwell, 1984); J. A. Beckford, "Accounting for Conversion," *British Journal of Sociology* 29(1978):235-245; D. G. Bromley and T. Robbins, "The Role of Government in Regulating New and Unconventional Religions," in *Government Monitoring of Religions,* ed. J. Wood (Waco, Tex.: Baylor University Press, 1992): 101-137; D. G. Bromley and A. Shupe, "Just a Few Years Seem Like a Lifetime," in *Research in Social Movements, Conflicts, and Change,* ed. L. Krisberg (Greenwich, Conn.: JAI, 1979): 159-186; L. Dawson, "Self-Affirmation, Freedom, and Rationality," *Journal for the Scientific Study of Religion* 29(1990):141-163; J. Downton, "Spiritual Conversion and Commitment," *Journal for the Scientific Study of Religion* 19(1980):381-396; D. Gordon, "The Jesus People," *Urban Life and Culture* 3(1974):159-179; A. L. Greil and D. Rudy, "What Have We Learned from Process Models of Conversion?" *Sociological Focus* 17(1984):305-323; M. Heirich, "Change of Heart," *American Journal of Sociology* 83(1977):653-680; B. Kilbourne and J. T. Richardson, "Paradigm Conflict, Types of Conversion, and Conversion Theories," *Sociological Analysis* 50(1989):1-21; J. Lofland, *Doomsday Cult* (Englewood Cliffs, N.J.: Prentice Hall, 1966); J. Lofland, "Becoming a World-Saver Revisited," in *Conversion Careers,* ed. J. T. Richardson (Beverly Hills, Calif.: Sage, 1978): 1-23; J. Lofland and N. Skonovd, "Conversion Motifs," *Journal for the Scientific Study of Religion* 20(1981):373-385; J. Lofland and R. Stark, "Becoming a World-Saver," *American Sociological Review* 30(1965):863-874; T. E. Long and J. K. Hadden (eds.), *Religion and Religiosity in America* (New York: Crossroad, 1983); R. Machalek and D. Snow, "Conversion to New Religious Movements," in *Handbook of Cults and Sects in America,* Vol. B, ed. D. G. Bromley and J. K. Hadden (Greenwich, Conn.: JAI, 1993): 53-74; H. N. Malony and S. Southard (eds.), *Handbook of Religious Conversion* (Birmingham, Ala.: Religious Education Press, 1992); T. Pilarzyk, "Conversion and Alternation Processes in the Youth Culture," in *The Brainwashing/Deprogramming Controversy,* ed. D. G. Bromley and J. T. Richardson (Lewiston, N.Y.: Mellen, 1983): 51-72; J. T. Richardson (ed.), *Conversion Careers* (Beverly Hills, Calif.: Sage, 1978); J. T. Richardson, "Conversion Careers," *Society* 17, 3(1980): 47-50; J. T. Richardson, "The Active Versus Passive Convert," *Journal for the Scientific Study of Religion* 24(1985a): 163-179; J. T. Richardson, "Studies of Conversion," in *The Sacred in a Secular Age,* ed. P. Hammond (Berkeley, University of California Press, 1985b): 104-121; J. T. Richardson, "Cult/Brainwashing Cases and the Freedom of Religion," *Journal of Church and State* 33(1991):55-74; J. T. Richardson and B. Kilbourne, "Classical and Contemporary Applications of Brainwashing Models," in *The Brainwashing/Deprogramming Controversy,* ed. D. G. Bromley and J. T. Richardson (Lewiston, N.Y.: Mellen, 1983): 29-45; J. T. Richardson and M. W. Stewart, "Conversion Process Models and the Jesus Movement," in Richardson, *q.v.* (1978): 24-42; E. B. Rochford, *Hare Krishna in America* (New Brunswick, N.J.: Rutgers University Press, 1985); M. Singer, "Coming out of the Cults," *Psychology Today* 12(Jan. 1979): 72-82; D. Snow and C. L. Phillips, "The Lofland-Stark Conversion Model," *Social Problems* 27(1980):430-437; T. Solomon, "Programming and Deprogramming the Moonies," in *The Brainwashing/Deprogramming Controversy,* ed. D. G. Bromley and J. T. Richardson (New York: Mellen, 1983): 163-182; R. Stark, "Psychopathology and Religious Commitment," *Review of Religious Research* 12(1965):165-176; R. Stark and W. S. Bainbridge, "Networks of Faith," *American Journal of Sociology* 85(1980):1376-1395; R. Straus, "Changing Oneself," in *Doing Social Life,* ed. J. Lofland (New York: Wiley, 1976): 252-273; R. Straus, "Religious Conversion as a Personal and Collective Accomplishment," *Sociological Analysis* 40(1979):158-165.

COUNTERREFORMATION   *see* Reformation

CREATION/CREATIONISM   *see* Science and Religion

CRIMES   Defined as violations of law, religious crimes vary according to societies' positions on church-state relations in addition to the general expectations about civil behavior. In democracies, religious belief remains unregulated, but religious action can be criminal. (For example, late-nineteenth-century American Mormons realized that they risked prosecution if they acted on their polygamous beliefs.) Authorities in repressive regimes, however, likely will criminalize any religious beliefs or activities that they fear will undermine the control of the state.

Paralleling what occurs in the political realm, crime in a religious context takes multiple forms. First, *crimes against religions* involve individuals or groups committing criminal acts against religious organizations for personal or ideological gain. Examples include theft of organizational funds or anti-Semitic slogans painted on synagogue walls. Second, *religious crimes* or *crimes for religions* involve acts performed in accordance with groups' operational goals. These crimes may be against (1) other religions (e.g., Islamic extremist group FUQRA's probable involvement in bombings against Hare Krishna temples); (2) governments (i.e., the Church of Scientology of Toronto's 1992 conviction on breach of trust charges resulting from its spy operations against police forces); (3) employees (the Tony and Susan Alamo Foundation refusing to pay its workers minimum wage and overtime compensation); (4) congregants (e.g., clerical child abuse and the conviction of former PTL Ministries' Jim Bakker for conspiring to defraud his flock by overselling lifetime partnerships in his Heritage Grand Towers hotel); or (5) the public (e.g., Rajneeshees' poisoning of approximately 750 citizens, possibly as a test of plans to influence an upcoming election).

Finally, *criminal religious organizations* have basic goals or purposes that require the perpetration of illegal acts. Evidence is mounting, for example, that Japan's Aum Shinri Kyo religious sect will classify as such a criminal religious organization because of its probable poison gas murders along with criminal investigations into confinement, kidnapping, manslaughter, theft, counterfeiting and using stamped documents, wiretapping, and agricultural land law violations.

—*Stephen A. Kent*

REFERENCES

J. Berry, *Lead Us Not into Temptation* (Toronto: Image, 1992); A. Carnahan, "Sect Suspected in Crimes Across U.S.," *Rocky Mountain News* [Denver, Colorado] (Oct. 18, 1992): 6, 21; L. Carter, *Charisma and Control in Rajneeshpuram* (New York: Cambridge University Press, 1990); T. Claridge, "Church Guilty in Spy Case," *Globe and Mail* [Canada] (June 27, 1992): A7; J. S. Conway, *The Nazi Persecution of the Churches* (New York: Basic Books, 1968); J. M. Day and W. S. Laufer (eds.), *Crime, Values, and Religion* (Norwood, N.J.: Ablex, 1987); "Raymond J. Donovan, Secretary of Labor, United States Department of Labor, Plaintiff v. Tony and Susan Alamo Foundation et al, Defendants," *United States District Court,* Western District of Arkansas, Fort Smith Division. No. Civ 77-2183 (Dec. 13, 1982): 34, 317; "Raymond J. Donovan, Secretary of Labor, United States Department of Labor, Plaintiff v. Tony and Susan Alamo Foundation et al, Defendants," *United States District Court,* Western District of Arkansas, Fort Smith Division. No. Civ 77-2183 (Feb. 7, 1983): 34, 326; J. L. Embry, *Mormon Polygamous Families* (Salt Lake City: University of Utah Press, 1987); S. P. Freedberg, *Brother Love* (New York: Pantheon, 1994): J. Hubner and L. Gruson, *Monkey on a Stick* (New York: Harcourt, 1988); D. E. Kaplan and A. Marshall, *The Cult at the End of the World* (New York: Crown, 1996); M. Kleg, *Hate, Prejudice and Racism* (Albany: SUNY Press, 1993); C. E. Shepard, *Forgiven* (New York: Atlantic Monthly Press, 1991).

CULT There are two rather different uses of the term *cult*. General usage, as well as that common among anthropologists, implies a body of religious beliefs and practices associated with a particular god or set of gods, or even an individual saint or spiritually enlightened person, that constitutes a specialized part of the religious institutions of a society. It is in this sense of the word that one would refer to the Marian cult within Roman Catholicism or to the Krishna cult within Hinduism.

There is also a distinct sociological usage of the term that, although related to this general one, has developed a more specialized meaning. Here the influential figures are Ernst Troeltsch and Howard Becker. In *The Social Teaching of the Christian Churches* (1931), Troeltsch distinguished three main types of Christian thought and traced both their interconnections and their implications for social life up to the eighteenth century. His three types were church religion, sect religion, and mysticism, or, more properly, "spiritual and mystical religion." The first two he identified with the dichotomous forms of religious organization, the church and the sect, while he described the third type as a form of antiassociational individualism that, although it did not lead to the formation of religious organizations in the conventional sense, might be the occasion for small, informal, and transient groups. Troeltsch emphasized that this form of religion was extremely individualistic, and that it usually did not lead to organizations, its adherents being bound together by an "invisible church."

The Introduction of "Cult" in Sociology It was to these small and transient groups, however, that Howard Becker (1932) subsequently attached the label of "cult," stressing the private, personal character of the adherents' beliefs and the amorphous nature of the organization. Becker's usage found favor, with the result that through time sociologists came to employ the term without reference to Troeltsch's original tripartite typology of religious responses; rather, it was used simply to refer to a group whose beliefs and practices were merely deviant from the perspective of religious or secular orthodoxy, and that was characterized by a very loose organizational structure. Typically, such groups are short lived, as small numbers of like-minded seekers gather round some common interest, or charismatic spiritual leaders, before moving on to explore some other area of the cultic milieu.

The term *cultic milieu* was coined by Colin Campbell to refer to a society's deviant belief systems and practices and their associated collectivities, institutions, individuals, and media of communication. He described it as including "the worlds of the occult and the magical, of spiritualism and psychic phenomena, of mysticism and new thought, of alien intelligences and lost civilizations, of faith healing and nature cure" (Campbell 1972:122), and it can be seen, more generally, to be the point at which deviant science meets deviant religion. What unifies these diverse elements, apart from a consciousness of their deviant status and an ensuing sense of common cause, is an overlapping communication structure of magazines, pamphlets, lectures, and informal meetings, together with the common ideology of *seekership.*

Seekers Among Religious Alternatives   The concept of seekership was originally proposed by Lofland and Stark in 1965. They defined it as a "floundering among religious alternatives, an openness to a variety of religious views, frequently esoteric, combined with failure to embrace the specific ideology and fellowship of some set of believers" (p. 870). This rather negative definition betrays the influence of Judeo-Christian assumptions concerning the nature of religious belief, suggesting as it does that seekership represents an inability to decide between alternatives. In reality, the seeker is someone who is likely to see some truth in all alternatives, while regarding the movement from one doctrine or practice to the next as a genuine advancement in spiritual understanding and enlightenment.

In fact, the concept of seekership is at the heart of Troeltsch's original formulation of spiritual and mystical religion. What he had in mind was not simply the phenomenon of mysticism, which could be an ingredient in any religious tradition, but a religion in its own right, with its own system of beliefs. This form of religion regards religious experience as a valid expression of that universal religious consciousness that is based in the ultimate divine ground, a view that leads to an acceptance of religious relativity as far as all specific forms of belief are concerned as well as to the doctrine of polymorphism, in which the truth of all religions is recognized. Hence not only are the widely differing views of the central truths of Christianity tolerated but all forms of religion are regarded as identical. Nevertheless, its own teachings, which emphasize the truths obtained through mystic and spiritual experience, are regarded as representing the "purest" form of religion. It is because they hold to beliefs of this kind that seekers are able to regard movement from one cult to another as part of a process of spiritual enlightenment rather than as evidence of their own confusion or uncertainty, let alone as a "floundering among religious alternatives."

Cults have proliferated in Europe and the Far East in the postwar period. Often associated with the 1960s counterculture and new religious movements, their increase in numbers has brought into question claims concerning progressive secularization. Indeed, it is possible to see their growth as evidence of the spread of that form of spiritual and mystical religion that Troeltsch judged to be most likely to flourish in the modern world. At the same time, the careless application of the cult concept by both the media and opponents of specific groups has made the social scientific use of the cult concept increasingly difficult (see Richardson 1993).

—*Colin Campbell*

REFERENCES

H. Becker, *Systematic Sociology* (New York: Wiley, 1932); D. G. Bromley and J. K. Hadden (eds.), *The Handbook on Cults and Sects in America* (Greenwich, Conn.: JAI, 1993); C. Campbell, "The Cult, the Cultic Milieu and Secularization," in *A Sociological Yearbook of Religion in Britain 5* (London: SCM Press, 1972): 119-136: C. Campbell, "The Secret Religion of the Educated Classes," *Sociological Analysis* 39(1978):146-156; J. Lofland and R. Stark, "Becoming a World-Saver," *American Sociological Review* 30(1965):862-875; J. T. Richardson, "Definitions of Cult," *Review of Religious Research* 34(1993):348-356; E. Troeltsch, *The Social Teaching of the Christian Churches* (London: Allen and Unwin, 1931).

CURTIS, JACK H(OMER) (1921–)   After receiving a Ph.D. from Stanford in 1954, Curtis taught at St. Louis University, Canisius College, Marquette University, and the University of San Francisco, which saw his retirement in 1986. President, American Catholic Sociological Society, 1961.

Curtis's early work in the sociology of religion was concerned with group marginality and religious practices; he also received a Ford Foundation grant to study urban parishes as social areas (1956). His later areas of research and publication were in medical sociology.

Considered by some in the ACSS as a "young Turk," he was one of the members seeking to break a ghettolike mentality among Catholic sociologists in the society. This came to a head in 1964 when the society restricted the focus of the *American Catholic Sociological Review* to the sociological study of religion and American Catholicism, and changed the publication's name to *Sociological Analysis,* a title it retained until 1993 when it became *Sociology of Religion.*

—*Loretta M. Morris*

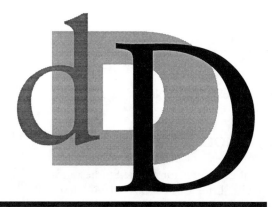

D'ANTONIO, WILLIAM V. (1926–) Born and reared in New Haven, Connecticut, D'Antonio received his undergraduate degree from Yale University, 1948; M.A., University of Wisconsin, 1953; Ph.D., Michigan State, 1958. Assistant to Full Professor and Chair, Department of Sociology, University of Notre Dame, 1959-1971; Professor and head (1971-1976), Department of Sociology, University of Connecticut, 1971-1982; executive officer, American Sociological Association, 1982-1991; Adjunct Research Professor, Catholic University of America, 1991–. President, Society for the Scientific Study of Religion, 1978-1979; Association for the Sociology of Religion, 1993; International Institute of Sociology, 1992-1993.

D'Antonio's scholarly contributions to the social scientific study of religion express his special interest in the relationship between authority and individual freedom, particularly with regard to sexual and reproductive norms in his Roman Catholic tradition. He also has written extensively on the link between religion and family life as well as religion's connection to ethnicity (especially his Italian heritage). He is the author of several books on religion, including *Religion, Revolution, and Reform* (with Frederick Pike, Praeger 1964), *Families and Religions* (with Joan Aldous, Sage 1983); *American Catholic Laity in a Changing Church* and *Laity: American and Catholic* (with James D. Davidson, Dean Hoge, and Ruth Wallace, Sheed & Ward 1989, 1996). He also has published articles on these subjects in all the major journals in the social scientific study of religion and elsewhere. D'Antonio's other interests include political sociology, in which he has been a leader in the study of community power (e.g., *Power and Democracy in America,* with Howard Ehrlich, University of Notre Dame 1961, and articles in the *American Sociological Review,* c. 1960). He also has been coauthor of a leading textbook, *Sociology* (with Melvin DeFleur and Lois DeFleur, Scott Foresman 1972) and a book on gender and sexuality, *Female and Male* (with Elaine C. Pierson, Lippincott 1974).

D'Antonio has been a leader in professional associations. Prior to his presidency of the SSSR, he served as its executive secretary from 1970 to 1976. In this work, particularly, he was assisted by his wife, Lorraine, who at one point simultaneously served as business manager of the SSSR, ASR, and Religious Research Association. He also has held offices and board positions in the North Central Sociological Association, American Council of Learned Societies, District of Columbia Sociological Society, Consortium of Social Science Associations, among others. His special honors and awards include the Aida Tomeh Distinguished Service Award from the NCSA and the Stuart A. Rice Merit Award from the DCSS.

As a central spokesperson for American sociology for a decade, D'Antonio has made many appearances on television, lectured at numerous colleges and universities, and been asked to evaluate sociology programs on more than a dozen campuses. In addition, he has been actively involved in progressive movements to foster academic freedom, improve the quality of undergraduate education, and promote change in the Roman Catholic Church.

—*James D. Davidson*

DARWIN, CHARLES/DARWINISM   *see* Science and Religion

DASHEFSKY, ARNOLD (1942–)   Professor of Sociology at the University of Connecticut, Storrs campus, and Director of its Center for Judaic Studies and Contemporary Jewish Life; earned B.A. (1964) and M.A. (1966) degrees at Temple University, and a University of Minnesota Ph.D. (1969) in sociology.

Dashefsky's major works focus on Jewish identity formation, Jewish communal organizations, and the emigration of American Jews to Israel. These include *Ethnic Identification Among American Jews: Socialization and Social Structure* (with Howard Shapiro, 2nd ed, University Press of America 1993) and *Americans Abroad: A Comparative Study of Emigrants from the United States* (with Jan DeAmicis, Bernard Lazerwitz, and Ephraim Tabory, Plenum 1992).

He served as (1986-1987) Editor of *Contemporary Jewry,* the journal of the Association for the Social Scientific Study of Jewry, and President (1990-1996) of the association.

—*J. Alan Winter*

DAVIDSON, JAMES D. (1942–)   Professor of Sociology, Purdue University; Ph.D., Notre Dame (1969). Editor, *Review of Religious Research,* 1977-1980; President of the Religious Research Association, 1989-1990. Executive Secretary, Society for the Scientific Study of Religion, 1988-1993. President, North Central Sociological Association, 1984-1985.

Davidson has pursued a wide range of religious research projects, including studies that analyze the link between faith and social concern, the changing face of contemporary American Catholicism, the religious affiliation of America's elites, and other issues. He also has played an important role in ensuring the vitality of the social scientific study of religion through his development of a large graduate program in the sociology of religion at Purdue.

Davidson has spent much of his professional career exploring the relationship between religious faith and concern for the poor and the powerless. In 1985, he published *Mobilizing Social Movement Organizations* (Society for the Scientific Study of Religion monograph series), a study of an interfaith urban ministry located in Lafayette, Indiana. Davidson used a resource mobilization approach to analyze the formation of this social service organization and its subsequent effectiveness in promoting church involvement in social support programs. In 1990, he edited, with Lincoln Johnson and Alan Mock, *Faith and Social Ministry: Ten Christian Perspectives* (Loyola University Press), a cross-denominational analysis of faith and social concern that featured religious leaders discussing how their organizations promote social outreach programs. In several studies, Davidson has noted that despite church teachings that emphasize that there ought to be a close relationship between love of God and love of neighbor, there is virtually no relationship between faith and social concern. Religion plays a larger role in comforting church members than inspiring their social participation in the community (Davidson 1972, 1986).

Davidson has written extensively about American Catholics. He served as coauthor (with William V. D'Antonio, Dean Hoge, and Ruth Wallace) of *American Catholic Laity in a Changing Church* (Sheed & Ward 1989) and *Laity: American and Catholic* (Sheed & Ward 1996). These two volumes have documented changes in Catholics' religious orientations as they have moved into America's middle class and been assimilated into the cultural mainstream. Davidson also headed the Catholic Pluralism Project, a large-scale study that has explored the social bases of increasing theological pluralism among Catholics. The research has highlighted important differences in the beliefs and practices of pre-Vatican II and post-Vatican II Catholics. Davidson notes that although Catholics born before World War II were taught a respect for authority as they learned to support "the one true church," those born after Vatican II have cultivated a more privatized faith. Davidson and others involved in his pluralism project have prepared a book for scholars and church leaders titled *The Search for Common Ground: What Unites and Divides Catholic Americans* (Our Sunday Visitor Press 1997).

Some of Davidson's other studies have analyzed the multiple dimensions of religious commitment (Davidson 1972, 1975), religion and the meaning of work (Davidson and Caddell 1994), and the nature and sources of religious involvement (Roberts and Davidson 1984). He has contributed an insightful article that examines different theories and measures of poverty (Davidson 1985). Additionally, he has conducted studies that analyze the religious affiliations of American elites between the 1930s and the 1990s (Davidson

1994, Davidson et al. 1995). His research suggests that despite an increasing proportion of society's leaders with Catholic or Jewish affiliations, Episcopalians, Presbyterians, and members of the United Church of Christ continue to be disproportionately represented among Americans with power, position, and prestige. Consequently, disestablishment theories (those stressing that America's Protestant establishment has been replaced by a religiously pluralistic elite) are only partly correct. Davidson has argued that we have not yet entered a post-Protestant age in American life.

—*Ralph E. Pyle*

REFERENCES

J. D. Davidson, "Religious Belief as an Independent Variable," *Journal for the Scientific Study of Religion* 11(1972):65-75; J. D. Davidson, "Glock's Model of Religious Commitment," *Review of Religious Research* 16(1975):83-93; J. D. Davidson, "Theories and Measures of Poverty," *Sociological Focus* 18(1985):177-198; J. D. Davidson, "Captive Congregations," in *The Political Role of Religion in the United States,* ed. S. D. Johnson and J. B. Tamney (Boulder, Colo.: Westview, 1986): 239-261; J. D. Davidson, "Religion Among America's Elite," *Sociology of Religion* 55(1994):419-440; J. D. Davidson and D. P. Caddell, "Religion and the Meaning of Work," *Journal for the Scientific Study of Religion* 33(1994):135-147; J. D. Davidson et al., "Persistence and Change in the Protestant Establishment," *Social Forces* 74(1995):157-175; M. K. Roberts and J. D. Davidson, "The Nature and Sources of Religious Involvement," *Review of Religious Research* 25(1984):334-350.

DEATH AND DYING Responses to death demonstrate and dramatize, not least by their variety, human responses to life. The contrast between a common traditional view and a common contemporary view is epitomized in the story of the mother who, at the beginning of this century, asked the clerical headmaster of England's best-known independent school (Eton), "What, in a word, are you educating the children for?" and received the reply, "In a word, madame: death." Such an answer would hardly be forthcoming today.

Religion can be held responsible for the emphasis placed upon death in Western culture in the last century, and in the seventeenth century, and in the later Middle Ages. Alternatively, it can be held to have been responsive to the human needs of those periods. (Parallels may be suggested with the development of medicine or counseling in the twentieth century.) In either case, it may be praised for helping people to come to grips with death, its ubiquity, inevitability, and significance, or else it may be blamed for diverting resources of time and energy and *matériel* from more immediate, soluble, and secular concerns. Certainly, the consequent Western silence about death earlier in this century has now been broken.

Typical of the "traditional" view (that is, of "early modern" society) was the retention, from earlier forms of society, of an awareness of the continued presence of the dead, who were less "departed" than simply "lost to sight" (the Africanists' "living dead"). They were, however, dichotomized into denizens of either heaven or hell, in both Buddhist and Catholic wall paintings and Moslem and Protestant literature. It would be facile to assume that such displays induced exactly comparable motivation, any more automatically than contemporary allusions to "tropical paradises" or "infernal swamps," yet the representations cannot have been totally counterintuitive. Individual human lives were seen as capable of moral summation and of subsequent division: Somehow and sometime, the righteous would be rewarded, and the unrighteous would receive their "comeuppance." Yet, both in Catholic Christianity, and in Hinduism and Buddhism, where iconography made the dichotomy vividly graphic, its implementation could only be maintained by its almost infinite postponement, beyond ordinary death: through the development of doctrines of purgatory and reincarnation and, in the Christian case, of the extensive institutionalization of prayers for the departed.

Traditionally, the moment of dying was similarly dichotomous. If only because of the relative universality, both of baptism and of cultural faith, the medieval church stressed two prophetic elements in Christ's teaching that were subversive of its own order. On the one hand, based upon Jesus's preaching of the Kingdom, even the foulest of sinners could, by a deathbed repentance, be saved from the natural and otherwise inevitable consequences of their own past misdeeds. On the other hand, based upon his teaching about the Last Judgment, mercy would be shown to those "anonymous Christians" who had shown mercy to others in their own hour of need. The moment of death being as inevitable, but unknowable, as the condition of life after death, it also became as momentous as well as momentary. "Praying for a good death" therefore meant attending to and preparing for it, in the same way as the semieternity of purgatory was serviced by prayers for the dead.

Contemporary culture may be equally conscious of the dichotomy between righteous and unrighteous behavior, but it is less sanguine about even the divine ability to reach a simple verdict about the individual's overall achievement and personal responsibility. The newly bereaved widow or parent may confidently assert (partly for reassurance), "He's all right now, he's with Jesus [wherever He is]," but that is as far as traditional society feels able to pontificate or speculate, in the contemporary climate, about life after death. Such ruminations have been privatized. ("Spiritualist" activities are as much an instance of, as an exception to, the rule.) Thus *postmortem,* in contemporary culture, is a medical term referring to the body, to the cause of its death, and, if necessary, to its dissection, not to life after death.

Current concern, which is at least as driven by fear as any past concern, among all ages from adolescence onward, has been transferred to what happens before death. The nub of the matter is what is assessed as the loss of personal dignity: beginning with the diminution of mobility, continuing with the restriction of speech and memory, and concluding with incontinence. "Hell," in connection with death, is now a premortem senility, which is virtually a matter of biological chance but can be very prolonged. Indeed, before the process is finished, the dying may empathically live through the bereavement of those who are losing the person while still tending his or her body. Thus the hospice movement can be seen as the answer to the (unspoken) prayer for a "good death," which, if not "holy," is at least humane.

As far as the moment of death is concerned, attention has switched from prayer for the appropriate spiritual attitude to analysis of the process into its component parts: social, spiritual, mental, biological, legal, organic, and so on. Yet "near-death experiences" now seem to echo elements in traditional descriptions of life after death.

—*Edward I. Bailey*

REFERENCE

R. Grainger, *The Unburied* (Worthing, U.K.: Churchman, 1988).

DECISION MAKING Most religious institutions emerged in traditional societies where actions were largely and automatically determined by precedent and custom without much need for rational calculation. Societies were held together by "natural" institutions like the family, and role assignments were largely prescribed by traditions of age and gender. Religious groups tended to be monopolistic and supported by the community-at-large. In the modern world, however, religious groups are voluntary associations, governed by written constitutions and operated as parliamentary assemblies. Their support is not automatic, and congregations as well as denominational bodies must attend to raising budgets, developing pay scales, and handling housekeeping and maintenance.

Decision making involves the processes of making explicit major values (assumptions), prioritizing objectives (goals), adopting larger means (strategies), and smaller means (tactics). The preceding are all essentials in what administrators term the organization's *policy.* John Dewey outlined the basic steps in the idealized model of rational problem solving—diagnosing the break in habit/routine; "defining the problem"; determining the immediate goal(s), the means (resources under your control), and the limits (circumstances not under your control such as the law, funds); evaluating the possible alternative choices to control the problem; and, finally, prioritizing and applying alternative solutions to the problem one by one. (A new stage, evaluating outcomes, has recently been added.) Lindblom, however, says this ideal model is seldom used, because there seldom are time or resources to formulate ideal solutions. Furthermore, traditions, "sunk costs" (previous investments of time, effort, "human resources," money), lack of expertise and/or information, and human fallibilities prevent ideal solutions. Thus most committees "muddle through" as best they can.

Thompson proposed a fourfold typology of decision models involving the agreement or disagreement on available ends and means. (1) *Computational* decisions are those involving agreement on both ends and means—engineering or bureaucratic situations where technical knowledge (space exploration) or a manual of rules (tax solutions by the Internal Revenue Service) determine outcomes. (2) *Political-compromising* decisions are those in which the means is agreed upon (voting) but the ends are not always clear—representative assemblies or councils run by negotiation and voting. (3) *Judgmental* decisions are those in which the goal is agreed to but the best means may not be—medical and other professional decisions. (4) *Inspirational* decisions are those in which there is little agreement on either ends or means (termed the *garbage can* model), such as devising an entirely new social policy for health care, welfare, evangelism, governing a country, or inventing an electric car; religious and utopian movements and "think tanks" would seem to operate by this model.

Sometimes particular decisions can combine two or more of the above models (e.g., 2 and 3). Probably most religious groups will decide via "muddling through," because religious groups are more encumbered with traditions, sentiments, and loyalties than business or community groups. Usually church groups can little tolerate conflict, and decisions tend to be unanimous. Probably most decisions by denominational assemblies and congregational councils tend to be of the computational and political varieties (replacing an organ, expanding or repairing the building). More complex decisions (adopting new liturgies) will begin with recommendations by the clergy followed by ratification by a representative assembly. The "inspirational" decision strategy is rare but can be peculiarly religious, as when a denominational or congregational assembly decides to venture to adopt a new policy involving, for example, ethnic-gender quotas in staff hiring or an interracial evangelism campaign. Although most modern voluntary associations have adopted parliamentary voting as the dominant decision strategy, congregational groups have difficulty operating other than by unanimous vote. This means that if pastors are to lead their congregations in prophetic ways, they must be astute not only in theology but also in the political dynamics of voluntary organizations.

See also Organization Theory, Evaluation Research

—*Ross P. Scherer*

REFERENCES

R. L. Daft, *Organization Theory and Design* (St. Paul, Minn.: West, 1983); C. E. Lindblom, "The Science of Muddling Through," in *Readings on Modern Organizations*, ed. A. Etzioni (Englewood Cliffs, N.J.: Prentice Hall, 1969): 154-166; J. D. Thompson and A. Tuden, "Strategies, Structures, and Processes of Organizational Decision," in *Comparative Studies in Administration*, ed. J. D. Thompson et al. (Pittsburgh: University of Pittsburgh Press, 1959): 195-216.

DECLINE OF RELIGION   *see* Secularization

DEFECTION   *see* Apostasy

DEFERRED GRATIFICATION   Delay of want satisfaction is a common feature of choices; that is, individuals make choices in which both costs and benefits are spread over time. It used to be received knowledge that the lower socioeconomic strata were less concerned with the future and had low achievement orientation, whereas the higher classes knew of deferred or delayed gratification and were highly achievement oriented. Max Weber (1930) argued that the monastic way of life in the Occident had become "a systematic method of rational conduct with the purpose of overcoming the *status naturae*" by not yielding to

emotional impulses. With the Reformation, this form of active asceticism was no longer restricted to religious virtuosi, and the devout had to be "monks" all their lives. The ethics of particular Protestant groups (e.g., puritanism) were one long exercise in imposing self-control and delay of gratification. Weber also pointed out the significance of this inner-worldly asceticism or the extreme delay in consumption of the Protestants for the rise of capitalism.

See also Protestant Ethic, Max Weber

—*Durk H. Hak*

REFERENCES

G. Loewenstein and J. Elster (eds.), *Choice over Time* (New York: Russell Sage, 1992); M. Weber, *The Protestant Ethic and the Spirit of Capitalism* (New York: Scribner, 1930).

DEFINITION OF RELIGION   Defining *religion* is problematic, with some definitions threatening to drive theories and determine conclusions. Some writers recommend proceeding with study and fashioning definitions only afterward (Harrison 1912, Weber 1922).

With new religions, revitalization movements, and quasi-religious pursuits coming to the fore in modern societies, the definitional issue takes on renewed importance (Hervieu-Léger 1987; see Greil and Rudy 1990 on "quasi-religion"), and the more aspects of the social world that are deemed religious, the less one can see any secularization process taking place.

One does not know if certain conduct is religious unless one begins with a concept of religion, and one cannot conceptualize it unless one already is familiar with cases. Moreover, participants in religion, and their critics, *already* have working definitions of religion. As the *Verstehen* school social scientists point out, a depiction that does not reflect such definitions would distort rather than report (Horton 1960).

Whether and when to define *religion* also raises "how" questions. Should one set up sharp lines around religion, to ascertain certainly whether a phenomenon is religious? Or should it have ambiguous boundaries, allowing for the unfamiliar and surprising? Should a definition be broad, including all that might be religious, or narrow so that religion serves as a variable? Should one have a preliminary definition that is fuzzy-edged and broad, and a later one that is sharply cut and narrow? Or does scientific progress begin with narrowly defined, clear cases and proceed to broad, diffuse categories? Should a definition be based primarily on the conceptions held by religious participants, or should it be based on concepts in detached minds?

The definitional literature can be organized around four approaches: substantive, functional, *verstehende,* and formal.

Substantive Definitions   Early in the history of social science, Tylor (1871) wanted a minimum definition that would prevent categorizing primitive religions with spiritualism, which was in disrepute in Europe. The primitives, he proposed, were explaining the difference between life and death, and they conceived of life as animation by spirits. Tylor used *religion,* which had favorable connotations, to refer to a "belief in spiritual beings" with this in mind; such beliefs were primitives' equivalents of today's life sciences. Tylor's definition is often cited as the first *substantive* one.

Substantive definitions are often used in otherwise functionalist analyses. Ross (1901:197) saw religion as something that would exert a certain social control, but he defined it as belief about the Unseen, with such attendant feelings as fear, wonder, reverence, gratitude, and love, and such institutions as prayer, worship, and sacrifice. Similarly, Parsons's early work (1937:665 ff.) developed functionalism while using a substantive concept of religion. He gave Weber's writings about charisma a functional reading: Charisma would be that which functioned to legitimate power by associating governance with teleological meanings. Religious beliefs, defined by their reference to the supernatural, would characterize a particular kind of charisma. Later commentators, not interpreting Weber as a functionalist, would still see him implicitly taking religion to be a patterning of social relationships around beliefs in supernatural powers, creating ethical consequences (Swatos and Gustafson 1992).

Sorokin (1947:225) straddles the formal and substantive approaches. Taken literally, his definition is formal: a set of ultimate values expressed in a credo, objectified by vehicles of a cult, and socialized by conduct complying with religious norms that unite members into one religious group. However, his examples suggest that he had the supernatural in mind as the religious content. Nevertheless, he had a functionalist concern; his reference to uniting members into one religious group echoes the functional portion of Durkheim's (1912) definition.

Substantive definitions often appear in critiques of functionalism. Horton (1960:211) argued that people reject as not genuine religiouslike conduct done for (functional) reasons of social symbolism. He modeled his own definition after Tylor's: an extension of the field of people's social relationships beyond the confines of purely human society.

Glock and Stark (1965:4) also used a substantive definition in preparing for their influential questionnaire studies. Their key term was *ultimate meaning,* and they felt obliged to explain that belief systems of ultimate meaning that had supernatural referents were religious.

Berger (1967:175-177) at first merely noted his own preference for a substantive definition. He cited the concept of the holy as described by Otto (1923), but saw it all as a matter of personal preference having little scientific import. Revealingly, Otto's phenomenology of the holy rests upon the experiences of social actors, and it was this fact (rather than culturally distant allusions by anthropologists to beliefs in supernatural beings) that appealed to Berger. Later he spelled out his methodological preference for the *Verstehen* approach in social science that grounded scientists' definitions in those of social actors, but he still called his definitional preference "substantive" (Berger 1974; see Weigert 1974). Meanwhile, Garrett (1974) also revived interest in the substantive approach, similarly referring to Otto and expressing concern about giving adequate accounts of religious participants' experiences. He found concepts analogous to Otto's in the works of Simmel, Weber, and Troeltsch, and citations of Otto in those of Wach, Scheler, and Schutz. Significantly, it is the effects of the religious rather than the transcendent itself that was being described in all these works—an inherently "troublesome" circumstance. The implication was that even the substantive definitions falter.

James did not develop a general definition but merely pointed to his topic. There could be a list of features, and any several could serve as criteria for considering something religious but need not all appear in any one religion (1902:39). James was interested in personal religion: feelings, acts, and experiences of individuals in their solitude, so far as they apprehend themselves to stand in relation to whatever they may consider the divine (1902:42). As he defined *divine,* it was quite broad: "only such a primal reality as the individual feels impelled to respond to solemnly and gravely" (1902:47).

Substantive definitions are sometimes thought to resist a certain ideological, passive image of humans. If religion defined functionally would benefit society, the social actor takes no directive role in the process. If religion seems to bring some cognizance of society itself into the consciousness of the adherent, religion itself is a transmitter of charisma or legitimacy to a passive social actor. But if religion is defined substantively, the religious person is seen as the active agent maintaining a particular viewpoint.

Functional Definitions Featuring what religions do rather than their contents, functional definitions enjoy the advantage of dodging the issue of the truth-value of beliefs. Kidd (1894), influential in his day, wrote in the social evolution tradition, with a focus on conflict. Societies having features that gave them advantages in conflict survived; he called such features "functions." Religion was a function; it was any belief that provided an ultrarational sanction for the prosocial whenever individual interests and those of the social organism were antagonistic. Although similar to Comte's concept, this seemed acceptable to scholars because it was not associated, as was Comte's, with any religious program. Kidd's approach was readily incorporated into the far different sociologies of Small and Vincent (1894), Ward (1898), and Ross (1901). Only Ward made such a function definitive of religion; for him, religion would be a substitute in the rational world for instinct in the subrational world. Cooley defined religion in terms of a microfunction: a need of human nature, centering in a craving to make life seem rational and good (1909:372).

The functionalist element of Durkheim's definition—"beliefs and practices that unite into a single moral community called a Church all those who adhere to them" (1912)—was macrofunctional, too much so because it identified the religious group with the total society (Dobbelaere and Lauwers 1973). Updated applications of Durkheim's macrofunctionalism in the "civil religion" literature give that aspect of his definition a continuing relevance. Some functionalists would distinguish religion from magic, with religion serving latent functions in public activity and magic serving manifest instrumental purposes in private activity (Malinowski 1925 [1954]). Parsons, who thought religion central to "the integration of cognitive systems in their implications for action," defined religious ideas as answers to problems of meaning (1951:367 ff.).

Definitional functionalists would generally phrase religion's benefits in individualist terms in the manner of Cooley, given that evidence contradicted the macrofunctional theories (Friedrichs 1985). For Luckmann (1967), religion would be the transcending of human biological nature and the formation of a self—an inevitable occurrence that all societies effect in individuals. For Yinger (1970), religion is social but relativizes evils and desires for individuals; he defines religion as a system of beliefs and practices with which a group struggles with ultimate problems of human life. For Geertz (1966:4), religion is a system of symbols that

establishes powerful, pervasive, and long-lasting moods and motivations by formulating conceptions of a general order of existence and by clothing those conceptions with an aura of factuality.

No doubt, various human phenomena could be "religious" in the functionalist manner. If functional definitions did not specify identifiable functions, one would want to label the definitions *formal* rather than *functional.* Schneider (1970) saw a potential for theoretical development in the sociology of religion in functionally examining all kinds of conduct as if it were religion, and vice versa.

Stark and Bainbridge (1979), like Durkheim, used a two-part definition when they introduced the idea of *compensators,* postulations of reward according to explanations that are hard to evaluate. Religion would be a system of general compensators based on supernatural assumptions. The "compensator" part is microfunctional, and the "supernatural" part, substantive.

The turn to the micro level lends an entirely different flavor to functionalism. Suddenly religion embodies the utopian spaces that the major institutions of society neglect. Religion comes to be defined as an imaginative enterprise that addresses the unfulfilled promises of life (Hervieu-Léger 1989:73).

Verstehende Definitions *Verstehen* approaches to definition have not often emerged in theoretical statements in the study of religion. Searching for understandings within particular social worlds is implicit in ethnographic and participant observation methodology. Runciman (1969) criticized both substantive and functional definitions by pointing out that social actors decide such matters as whether there is a sacred-profane divide or an empirical-nonempirical distinction in their world, and that, moreover, any two members of a society might disagree (see Weigert 1974).

Again, how can we recognize the social actors' definitions as defining *religion?* Swatos (1990) advocates beginning with a very minimal substantive definition, a sensitizing concept we might call it, and then using the *verstehen* or "definition of the situation" approach to find out what the social actors do with what had been tentatively identified as religious. The preliminary definition could use the supernatural as its criterion, with either the transcendent or the immanent being supernatural.

Formal Definitions Formal definitions have a long history in the study of religion, but they have received little attention. Writers often cite Durkheim's *Elementary Forms of the Religious Life,* written late in his career (1912), as the locus of a definition that has both substantive and functional elements (Dobbelaere and Lauwers 1973), but his earlier definition (1899) exemplifies the formal approach. One seeks to find how religious facts can be grouped, even on the basis of secondary traits. Whatever is not found in all cases could not be definitive; consequently, he ruled out the unknowable as a criterion, because primitives have no such category, as well as belief in gods, because Buddhists do not have them. Durkheim ended up with a definition that he later judged valid but too formal and hard to use: obligatory beliefs connected with clearly defined practices that are related to the beliefs' objects.

Simmel, the founder of formal sociology, related religion to a moral imperative rather than to knowledge. By distinguishing such forms as moral imperative and knowledge from their contents, he was able to argue that "the religious state of the soul produces no logically necessary, pre-determined content" and that "no content possesses in itself the logical necessity to become religion" (Simmel 1984 [1903]: 69). He observed that religion, like morality, resided in the person's response to an object, and this was key to the religious form as he saw it.

Wach (1951) specified the religious response—elicited by an experience of ultimate reality, response by the whole person and not merely a cognitive or affective response, an experience having the potential of becoming the most intense of all, and leading to an urge to act. He maintained that such religion was a human universal. So long as religion would be a response, any particular content, such as the holy, would be a secondary, nondefining feature.

Formal definitions can be used with other kinds of theoretical problematics (Problemstellungen). We have already observed that Durkheim deemed his earlier, formal definition compatible with his later functional theory, and O'Dea (1966:1) used a formal concept of religion in a functionalist presentation.

The formal strategy often looks for a structure that resembles known cases. Zeldin (1969) points to the narrative structure of a fall from and return to an ideal state—a structure she sees in Soviet Marxism and in world religions. Lemert (1975) and Blasi (1980) take the structure of related discontinuity between an empirical, mundane order and a superempirical, cosmic-level order as definitive of religion. Richard (1978) observed that this can lead to an analytical program of seeing the cosmic Otherness being domesticated (e.g., Berger 1974) or a domestic signaling of the relevance of the Other. Turner (1976) accepted the basic structure of a discontinuous relatedness but rejected the empirical-superempirical phraseology. Maduro (1982:6) shows

religion's role at the nexus of two kinds of consciousness in social critique and transformation.

—Anthony J. Blasi

REFERENCES

P. L. Berger, The Sacred Canopy (Garden City, N.Y.: Doubleday, 1967); P. L. Berger, "Some Second Thoughts on Substantive Versus Functional Definitions of Religion," Journal for the Scientific Study of Religion 13(1974):125-133; A. J. Blasi, "Definition of Religion and Phenomenological Approach Towards a Problematic," Cahiers du centre des recherches en sociologie religieuse 3(1980):55-70; C. H. Cooley, Social Organization (New York: Scribner, 1909); K. Dobbelaere and J. Lauwers, "Definition of Religion," Social Compass 20(1973):535-551; É. Durkheim, "De la définition des phénomènes religieux," Année sociologique 2(1899):1-28; É. Durkheim, Les formes élémentaires de la vie religieux (Paris: Alcan, 1912); R. W. Friedrichs, "The Uniquely Religious," Sociological Analysis 46(1985):361-366; W. Garrett, "Troublesome Transcendence," Sociological Analysis 35(1974): 167-180; C. Geertz, "Religion as a Cultural System," in Anthropological Approaches to the Study of Religion, ed. M. Banton (New York: Praeger, 1966): 1-46; C. Y. Glock and R. Stark, Religion and Society in Tension (Chicago: Rand McNally, 1965); A. L. Greil and D. R. Rudy, "On the Margins of the Sacred," in In Gods We Trust, 2nd ed., ed. T. Robbins and D. Anthony (New Brunswick, N.J.: Transaction, 1990): 219-232; J. Harrison, Themis (Cambridge: Cambridge University Press, 1912); D. Hervieu-Léger, "Faut-il définir la religion?" Archives de sciences sociales des religions 63(1987): 11-20; D. Hervieu-Léger, "Tradition, Innovation and Modernity," Social Compass 36(1989):71-81; R. Horton, "A Definition of Religion, and Its Uses," Journal of the Royal Anthropological Institute 90(1960):201-226; W. James, The Varieties of Religious Experience (New York: Modern Library, 1902); B. Kidd, Social Evolution (London: Macmillan, 1894); C. C. Lemert, "Defining Non-church Religion," Review of Religious Research 16(1975):186-198; T. Luckmann, The Invisible Religion (New York: Macmillan, 1967); O. Maduro, Religion and Social Conflicts (Maryknoll, N.Y.: Orbis, 1982); B. Malinowski, Magic, Science and Religion and Other Essays (Garden City, N.Y.: Doubleday, 1954 [1925]); T. F. O'Dea, The Sociology of Religion (Englewood Cliffs, N.J.: Prentice Hall, 1966); R. Otto, The Idea of the Holy (London: Oxford University Press, 1923); T. Parsons, The Structure of Social Action, vol. 2 (New York: Free Press, 1937); T. Parsons, The Social System (New York: Free Press, 1951); R. Richard, "Le concept de religion," Cahiers de centre des recherches en sociologie religieuse 2(1978):3-17; E. A. Ross, Social Control (New York: Macmillan, 1901); W. G. Runciman, "The Sociological Explanation of 'Religious' Beliefs," Archives européennes de sociologie 10(1969):149-191; L. Schneider, "The Sociology of Religion," Sociological Analysis 31(1970):131-144; G. Simmel, "On Religion from the Point of View of the Theory of Knowledge," New England Sociologist 5(1984 [1903]):66-77; A. W. Small and G. E. Vincent, *An Introduction to the Study of Society* (New York: American Book Company, 1894); P. A. Sorokin, *Society, Culture, and Personality* (New York: Harper, 1947); R. Stark and W. S. Bainbridge, "Of Churches, Sects, and Cults," *Journal for the Scientific Study of Religion* 18(1979):117-133; W. H. Swatos, Jr., "Renewing 'Religion' for Sociology," *Sociological Focus* 23(1990):141-153; W. H. Swatos, Jr., and P. M. Gustafson, "Meaning, Continuity, and Change," in *Twentieth-Century World Religious Movements in Neo-Weberian Perspective*, ed. W. H. Swatos, Jr. (Lewiston, N.Y.: Mellen, 1992): 1-20; R. G. Turner, "Consciousness, Valuation, and Religion," *Review of Religious Research* 18(1976):25-35; E. B. Tylor, *Primitive Culture* (London: Murray, 1871); J. Wach, *Types of Religious Experience* (Chicago: University of Chicago Press, 1951); L. F. Ward, "The Essential Nature of Religion," *International Journal of Ethics* 8(1898):169-192; M. Weber, *Economy and Society* (Berkeley: University of California Press, 1978 [1922, original German edition]); A. J. Weigert, "Functional, Substantive, or Political?" *Journal for the Scientific Study of Religion* 13(1974):483-486; J. M. Yinger, *The Scientific Study of Religion* (New York: Macmillan, 1970); M. Zeldin, "The Religious Nature of Russian Marxism," *Journal for the Scientific Study of Religion* 8(1969):100-111.

DEMERATH, N(ICHOLAS) JAY, III (1936–)

Professor of Sociology at the University of Massachusetts in Amherst; his academic career has been spent at two institutions, the University of Wisconsin (1962-1972) and the University of Massachusetts (1972–). He has served as Executive Officer of the American Sociological Association (1970-1972), Vice-President of the Eastern Sociological Society (1975-1976), and President of the Society for the Scientific Study of Religion (1998-1999). He has been Book Review Editor of the *American Sociological Review* (1965-1968) and was the founding Editor of ASA *Footnotes* (1970-1972).

Jay Demerath is a second-generation sociologist who has earned a solid reputation on the merits of his own work in both the sociology of religion and in the general field of sociology. In addition to the sociology of religion, his writings span the subfields of sociological theory, social policy issues, the sociology of politics, and the sociology of science.

Upon graduating magna cum laude from Harvard College (1958), he enrolled in graduate studies at the University of California at Berkeley, where he earned his M.A. (1962) and Ph.D. (1964). While at Berkeley, he developed a close association with Charles Y. Glock, who was then director of the Survey Research Center at Berkeley and was developing a survey research program in the sociology of religion. Demerath's dissertation, published under the title *Social Class in American Protestantism* (Rand McNally 1965), would become a benchmark study during an era when empirical studies of religion based on survey research were only first beginning to be produced. Similarly, Demerath's text with coauthor sociologist Philip Hammond, *Religion in Social Context* (Random House 1968), was one of the first textbook treatments of the field designed for undergraduate readers. His other book-length treatments of religion include *A Tottering Transcendence: Civil vs. Cultic Aspects of the Sacred* (Bobbs-Merrill 1973), *A Bridging of Faiths: Religion and Politics in a New England City* (with Rhys Williams, Princeton University Press 1992), and a coedited volume titled *Sacred Companies* (Oxford University Press 1997).

Demerath's extensive journal publications in the sociology of religion span at least five concerns: why some people are more religious than others, the social factors connected to varieties of religious expression (social class), the forms of religious organizations (church and sect), the intersection of religions and politics, and what it is that religion teaches about the human condition. While Demerath has been a major figure among that generation of sociologists who welcomed the sociology of religion into the age of survey research, his diverse writings in the sociology of religion have not been limited to that methodology.

—*William M. Newman*

DEMOCRACY

DEMOCRACY Originally, a form of direct governance by the citizens of a city *(polis)* in ancient Greece. In modern times, governance based upon representative institutions with officeholders chosen through popular election.

Attention to the relationship between religion and democracy has focused on, first, the historical role of religion in directly generating, opposing, and sustaining democratic nation-states and movements; second, the study of religious organizations as mediating institutions that strengthen civil society and thus reinforce democracy; third, the influence of democratic political authority upon religious traditions founded on other modes of legitimate authority; fourth, democratic and nondemocratic forms of governance within religious organizations; fifth, the long-term viability of religion and religious belief in modern democracies characterized by high levels of religious pluralism.

Many writers have focused on this last area, under the themes of secularization and the role of religion in the public realm. The former debate revolves around whether or not religious pluralism necessarily leads to a loss of religious social authority, the privatization of religious belief, and the erosion of religious faith. The latter debate asks what public role religions and religious language can appropriately play within religiously pluralistic democracies.

Thus the advent of democracy as the dominant form of governance in the world has raised a host of new problems, questions, and opportunities for religious leaders and social scientists alike.

See also American Religion, Politics and Religion

—*Richard L. Wood*

REFERENCES

R. N. Bellah, *The Broken Covenant* (New York: Seabury, 1975); J. T. Duke and B. L. Johnson, "Protestantism and the Spirit of Democracy," in *Religious Politics in Global and Comparative Perspective,* ed. W. H. Swatos, Jr. (New York: Greenwood, 1989): 131-146; R. M. Glassman et al., *For Democracy* (Westport, Conn.: Greenwood, 1993); M. E. Marty, *Righteous Empire* (New York: Dial, 1970); A. de Tocqueville, *Democracy in America* (Garden City, N.Y.: Doubleday: 1969 [1835]).

DEMONOLOGY   *See* Satanism

DEMYTHOLOGIZING   An approach to religious imagery advocated in the mid-twentieth century by Rudolf Bultmann (1953), who was concerned that the Christian Bible was written in a way that obscured rather than revealed Christianity to modern people. He believed that existentialism described the universal in the human condition, and that translating biblical imagery into existential terms would more effectively communicate the biblical message. Although biblical literalists objected to the very ideas of myth and interpretation, others granted the need for a demythologizing hermeneutic but disagreed with Bultmann over exactly what required demythologizing and what did not.

The comprehension of any text where there is a cultural chasm between author and reader will involve some inevitable hermeneutics, or "translation," from one myth system into another. Demythologizing assumes that the reader's perspective is less mythical than the author's. It reflects the empiricist and rationalist nature of modern culture.

—*Anthony J. Blasi*

REFERENCE

R. Bultmann, "The New Testament and Mythology," in *Kerygma and Myth,* vol. 1, ed. H. W. Bartsch (London: SPCK, 1953 [1941]): 1-44.

DENOMINATION/DENOMINATIONALISM

The term *denomination* was innovated in the late seventeenth century by those groups of Christians in England who dissented from the established Church of England but considered themselves to be entirely loyal to the British state and recognized the monarch as having rights with respect to the Church of England. In 1702, specifically, the Presbyterians, Baptists, and Congregationalists formed "the body of the Dissenting Ministers of the Three Denominations in and about the City of London." The term was introduced to counter the pejorative term *sect,* which in popular usage had the sense of deviant or undesirable practices. The term is now used in pluralist societies for those forms of organized religious expression that generally support the established social order and are mutually tolerant of each other's practices.

Typology   The term *denominationalism* was significantly introduced into the subsequent literature of the sociology of religion by H. Richard Niebuhr in his book *The Social Sources of Denominationalism* (Holt 1929). The central thesis of this work was that new religious organizations ("sects") begin among the socially "disinherited," but in the United States, as these groups attain higher social status, their religious expressions become more "respectable" or socially accepted; thus there is a movement across generations from sectarian to denominational religious life—or else the sectarian group dies out. This strongly evolutionary view has been considerably modified today. A particularly important contribution to the study of denominationalism was David Martin's seminal article "The Denomination," published in 1962, where he forced a reconsideration of this organizational form as a historically specific type sui generis, rather than as a stage on a quasi-evolutionary continuum.

A standard current definition of the denomination would be that of Bryan Wilson (1959:4-5), who writes that the denomination is "a voluntary association" that "accepts adherents without imposition of traditional prerequisites of entry," such as belonging to a particular ethnic or national group, or sectarian testimonies of spiritual regeneration.

Breadth and tolerance are emphasized. . . . Its self-conception is unclear and its doctrinal position unstressed. . . . One movement among many . . . it accepts the standards and values of the prevailing culture. . . . Individual commitment is not very intense; the denomination accepts the values of the secular society and the state.

The association between denominationalism and pluralism is crucial. In pluralism, one may belong to any denomination—or none at all! Religion is pigeonholed and privatized. It is a voluntary activity to be undertaken or dismissed at the discretion of the individual. The denomination is thus marked perhaps most significantly by this voluntarism of support coupled to mutual respect and forbearance of all other competing religious groups. It is, indeed, this quality of *competition* that is the unique hallmark of the pluralistic religious situation; acceptance of the "free market" situation in religious ideas is the critical operating principle of denominationalism. Denominations are the structural-functional forms that dominant religious traditions assume in a pluralistic culture. The distinction between monopolistic and pluralistic societies in typological differentiation between the church and the denomination was drawn particularly in Swatos's church-sect model (1979; see Figure C.2).

Although denominationalism is now characteristic of virtually all Western societies, it reaches its quintessential expression in the United States; that is, American denominationalism has been the model for religious pluralism throughout the world. (Andrew Greeley, for example, titled a text on American religious life *The Denominational Society* [Scott Foresman 1972].) The particular effect this had on American development up to the 1950s was chronicled in Will Herberg's benchmark volume *Protestant-Catholic-Jew* (Doubleday 1955). Although, strictly speaking, denominationalism is a Protestant dynamic, it has become fully accepted in principle by all major religious groups in the United States; in fact, one could say that the denominationalizing process represents the *Americanizing* of a religious tradition, which is at the same time and in the same measure a *relativizing* process. Religious groups that too strongly resist this process will probably eventually face run-ins with the legal system. Since the 1940s, social scientists have been particularly interested in the relationship between denomination and both social stratification and sociopolitical variables; the term *class church* was first applied as an equivalent to denomination by J. Milton Yinger in the 1940s.

Although some religious groups have made specific efforts to eschew the term as a label, *denomination* nevertheless has been the most neutral and general term used to identify religious organizations in the United States. *Organized religion* or *church affiliation* both anticipate the denomination as the dominant religious expression in society. Religious belief and action "work together" with the sociocultural system to develop a legitimation system as a result of a mutual interdependence. The cultural significance of denominationalism in the United States particularly is that it provided a structural-functional form for organizing communal relationships relating to the transcendent realm in a pluralistic sociocultural system that itself had a specific civilizational history.

Denominations Today Since the 1980s, and particularly with the publication of Robert Wuthnow's *The Restructuring of American Religion* (Princeton University Press) in 1987, there has been considerable debate within the sociology of religion over the current significance of denominationalism in American society. This debate was presaged by a distinction drawn by the church historian Martin Marty in *Righteous Empire* (Dial 1970) between two "parties" in American religion. According to Wuthnow's elaboration of this view, each denomination is now divided between the two parties (roughly, "liberal" and "conservative" Christians) on critical sociopolitical issues—reflecting in turn the relative rise in importance of "the State" as a sociocultural actor since the 1940s. The ecclesiastical "party" with which people identify is more important to both their spiritual and their moral lives than is a particular denominational label, according to this theory. The growth of "nondenominational" and "parachurch" organizations is seen as part of this process.

Others argue that this view is historically short-sighted and needs modification. Swatos (1981, 1994), for example, uses the local-cosmopolitan distinction elaborated in the sociology of religion by W. C. Roof (1972) to argue that denominationalism in the context of American voluntarism is preeminently a *local* dynamic, providing people "place" in a specific setting, and that this dynamic operates as much as it ever did, to the extent that cosmopolitan elaborations (e.g., denominational agency structures) can be discounted from analyses. Denominational bureaucracies are not, according to this thesis, the crucial social dynamic of the typology but a specific, transitory development. In addition, intradenominational debates have created more internally consistent denominational worldviews—conservatives now dominate the Southern Baptists, while liberals have won the day among Episcopalians. Davidson and colleagues (1995) also have shown that the various denominations continue to remain significantly disproportionately represented among American elites across the twentieth century, with corrections required only to accommodate specific immigration effects. Reform Jews, for example, are now significantly overrepresented among elites, along with Episcopalians, Unitarians, and Presbyterians; Roman Catholics have achieved approximate parity with their share of the general population. On the other hand, conservative Protestants generally remain significantly underrepresented, which may explain their attempt to achieve greater political visibility.

An often overlooked historical dimension of American denominationalism is the role women played in maintaining the life of the different denominations and in the social ranking system that they may have implied. The decline of membership in some mainline denominations (e.g., Methodists, Presbyterians, Episcopalians, Congregationalists [United Church of Christ]) is at least partially due to the increased presence of women in the workforce, which has resulted in a corresponding absence of women to undertake volunteer activities. Women in these denominations also are more likely to be in the professional classes and thus to have job responsibilities that do not end with the workday. Denominations that have declined in membership directly correspond to those that have most endorsed gender equality, while those that have gained membership are more gender differentiated. They also tend to attract membership from the working stratum, where even women working outside the home are, relatively speaking, more likely to be able to devote more "free" time to church activities and are less likely to experience role redefinition in the home.

See also American Religion, Church-Sect Theory, Two-Party Thesis

—*William H. Swatos, Jr.*

REFERENCES

J. D. Davidson et al., "Persistence and Change in the Protestant Establishment," *Social Forces* 74(1995):157-175; D. Martin, "The Denomination," *British Journal of Sociology* 13(1962):1-14; W. C. Roof, "The Local-Cosmopolitan Orientation and Traditional Religious Commitment," *Sociological Analysis* 33(1972):1-15; W. H. Swatos, Jr., *Into Denominationalism* (Storrs, Conn.: Society for the Scientific Study of Religion, 1979); W. H. Swatos, Jr., "Beyond Denominationalism?" *Journal for the Scientific Study of Religion* 20(1981):217-227; W. H. Swatos, Jr., "Western Hemisphere Protestantism in Global Perspective," pp. 180-196 in R. Cipriani (ed.), *Religions sans frontières?* (Rome: Presidenza del Consiglio dei Ministri, 1994); B. Wilson, "An Analysis of Sect Development," *American Sociological Review* 24(1959):3-15; J. M. Yinger, *Religion and the Struggle for Power* (Durham, N.C.: Duke University Press, 1946).

DEPRIVATION THEORY   Deprivation is distinguishable into relative and absolute deprivation. Physical abuse, starvation, and poverty are seen as forms of absolute deprivation, whereas relative deprivation can be defined as the discrepancy between what one expects in life and what one gets. Both absolute and relative deprivation are causes of the deprived one's receptivity to particular (religious) messages: "Come to me, all you who labor and are heavy laden, and I will give you rest" (St Matthew 11:28).

Deprivation was seen by generations of scholars, not necessarily Marxists, as the cause of both personal religious commitment and sect and cult formation. The German scholars Max Weber and Ernst Troeltsch were pioneers with regard to the relationships between sect and church membership, and social class and status group. In *The Social Sources of Denominationalism* (Holt 1929), H. Richard Niebuhr saw sects as the "churches of the disinherited"; because of their lack of economic and political power, the less privileged needed religion most, and sects and cults could provide their members with compensation for the lack of social and personal success.

In the 1950s and 1960s, much theorizing centered on the construction of typologies. This was also the case in deprivation theory. For example, Charles Glock (1964, Glock and Stark 1965) distinguished five types of deprivation, depending on the kinds of strain felt: economic, social, organismic, ethical, and psychic deprivation. Every type gave rise to a particular type of religious group, respectively: sect, church, healing movement, reform movement, or cult. According to the class into which it fell, Glock could predict the "career" of the particular religious group. According to Bryan Wilson (1973), most new religious movements in the Third World were either thaumaturgic—that is, they responded to very specific and acute forms of deprivation—or revolutionist—to the strain felt by the putative imminent destruction of the world.

Since the 1970s, deprivation theory has been criticized by various scholars. Its main defect is that, although the ideology component in the recruitment of members is rightly stressed, class is but one of the many factors that affect religious commitment. Another serious defect is the absence of any social network consideration. These shortcomings can be met when deprivation theory is integrated into a more full-fledged theory. This can be done, as was demonstrated by Stark and Bainbridge (1987), for example, in their formal, rational choice theory on religious behavior.

See also Compensators, Rational Choice Theory.

—*Durk H. Hak*

REFERENCES

C. Y. Glock, "The Role of Deprivation in the Origin and Evolution of Religious Groups," in *Religion and Social Conflict,* ed. R. Lee and M. E. Marty (New York: Oxford University Press, 1964): 24-36; C. Y. Glock and R. Stark, *Religion and Society in Tension* (Chicago: Rand McNally, 1965); R. Stark and W. S. Bainbridge, *A Theory of Religion* (New York: Lang, 1987); B. Wilson, *Magic and the Millennium* (London: Heinemann, 1973).

DESACRALIZATION   *see* Secularization

DESROCHE, HENRI (1914-1994)   For many years a Dominican priest. After leaving the order, he studied Marxism at length, evidenced in his books *Marxisme et religions* (P.U.F. 1962) and *Socialismes et sociologie religieuse* (Cujas 1965), without ever becoming a Marxist. His work is not completely systematic, due to his manifold interests, although these do examine particularly the development of religious movements of the innovative-utopian kind, for example, *The American Shakers* (University of Massachusetts Press 1974 [1955]), *Sociology of Hope* (Routledge 1979 [1973]), *Les religions de contrebande* (Mame 1974), *La société festive* (Seuil 1975). Aware of the interdisciplinary slant of the study of religious phenomena (see *Introduction aux sciences humaines des religions,* with coauthor J. Séguy [Cujas 1970], *L'homme et ses religions* [Cerf 1972]), he inspired, together with others, the *Archives des sciences sociales des religions,* a journal of primary importance at the international level.

His analysis of the historical development of the sociology of religion in *Jacob and the Angel* (University of Massachusetts Press 1973; originally *Sociologies religieuses,* P.U.F. 1968) distinguishes between a sociologized theology (also called sociotheology) and an atheological sociology (the latter more closely tied to writers considered as classics in the field). Having studied a multitude of collective religious experiences in depth in his *Dieux d'hommes* (1969), he often stressed the relations between Christianity and socialism. He complemented his research with commitment at the practical level in the areas of cooperation and development, especially in the context of the Intergroupe Religion-Développement (IRD) at the Centre de Recherches Coopératives de l'École Pratique des Hautes Études (Vie section) in Paris. He also founded the Collège Coopératif, a cultural foundation for the Third World.

—*Roberto Cipriani*

REFERENCE

J. Séguy, "In Memoriam," *Archives des sciences sociales des religions* 87(1994):5-12.

DEVIANCE   Defined most basically as normative violations, deviance occurs in a wide range of religious settings. As with analyses of other types of deviance, social scientists examine issues on both social psychological (micro) and social structural/institutional (macro) levels. Deviant activities occur within normative religions, within interactions between nontraditional religions and societally normative bodies, in social debates involving contesting parties over religious tolerance versus unacceptability, and within nontraditional religions as they attempt to control their members.

No social group can escape deviance, so the appearance of deviance within normative or mainstream religious organizations is not, in and of itself, noteworthy. Of considerable research interest, however, is the manner in which mainstream groups either cause deviance to occur or respond to it in socially unacceptable ways.

For example, discussion continues about the extent to which the celibacy rules for Catholic priests may relate to social psychological and personality factors among some sexual deviants who are members of religious orders. More certain, however, is the extent to which some Catholic authorities on an institutional level have facilitated priestly pedophiliac behavior. Authorities have done so through such activities as transferring accused clerics to other parishes, neglecting to report allegations against priests to proper investigating authorities, sending suspected abusers to church-run treatment centers whose success rates are uncertain, buying victim silence through out-of-court financial settlements, and shifting blame onto either the victims themselves or the general sexual ethos of society. These same patterns of denial, avoidance, and blame-shifting have taken place in other denominations. In essence, the institutional behavior of some mainstream religious denominations unintentionally facilitated the perpetration of deviant acts by some of their members.

By and large, pluralistic societies have transcended definitions of religious deviance based upon practices that differ from the majority because countless denominations, ethnic religions, and sects flourish within any geographic locale. Nonetheless, charges of unacceptable religious deviance still occur as previously dominant groups feel threatened by the religious requirements of others. For example, male Sikhs living in Western societies occasionally encounter societal restrictions (often involving employment) because of their turbans. Likewise, some Western countries have debated the possibility of banning Moslem head coverings on women in public schools. Finally, members of minority religions often must fight for the right of their members to observe their religious holidays without suffering employment penalties.

Problems such as these—involving religions having to defend their practices as acceptable behavior—become accentuated when at least one of the religious disputants is not representative of a major world faith. Various parties in these disputes call such disputing groups *sects, cults, alternative religions,* or *new religious movements.* Labeling groups in this manner becomes a political issue because each of the terms carries potentially significant societal implications regarding public images of acceptability.

In essence, the process of labeling religions as deviant is a highly charged social dynamic involving struggles for limited societal resources (such as status, influence, tax benefits, denominational cooperation). Consequently, religious groups aspire to have society define them as morally normative or, at the very least, acceptably deviant new or alternative religions. Critics and opponents, however, strive to have these same groups defined as unacceptably deviant cults and hence worthy of societal sanctions. Occasionally, entire communities get embroiled in these debates, as occurs when noticeable numbers of religious followers quickly move into a new locale and alarm longtime residents.

A strategy that many groups use in societal debates involves attempts to control the labels by which others identify them. They put forward a *demanded designation* about themselves that simultaneously emphasizes morally normative or tolerably deviant qualities while ignoring all other, and often less tolerable, aspects of their organizations.

A crucial part of this debate among societal contenders involves allegations that many "new religions/cults" impose unacceptable constraints and demands upon members. Critics (often from the so-called anti-cult movement) charge that "cults" violate the "core selves" of members through harsh systems intended to maintain loyalty at the expense of personal well-being, financial security, and informed decision making.

While these charges overlook the complexities of conversions, membership, and defections, they nonetheless identify patterns of disempowerment that differ from mainstream religions. In extreme cases, "deviant" religions superempower leaders at the same time that they diminish members' self-worth, self-control, and critical capacities. Indeed, adult members relate to group leaders as children do to demanding parents and, by doing so, often undergo forms of abuse similar to what dysfunctional families and abused spouses suffer.

It is not surprising, therefore, that parents of young adults who joined controversial religions in the 1970s were instrumental in founding so-called countercult groups in countries around the world. Some countercult members actively engaged in forcible removals of group members, followed by intense efforts to convince or pressure (i.e., "deprogram") these detainees to renounce their newly adopted faiths. In turn, these new faiths responded by labeling their "countercult" opponents as antireligious bigots in an effort to portray the critics (and not the groups themselves) as intolerably deviant.

The high demands of commitment that some groups require increases the likelihood that their members will experience group sanctions. Consequently, some groups develop formal systems of sanctions against members who reputedly deviate from doctrines or prescribed behaviors. Some groups (e.g., Synanon) use structured situations of verbal aggression as a means to punish deviance and elicit conformity. Others (e.g., The Family/Children of God and Scientology) developed special penal systems for delinquents. Because of the intensity and harshness of many sanctions, these groups may achieve conformity among members while heightening their public image as deviant religious organizations.

By no means has all research on deviance and religion concentrated on dysfunction. Various studies have shown how participation in some nontraditional or deviant faiths has created functional benefits to both individuals and society. On a micro level, members of some groups gained freedom from substance abuse, developed a work ethic, and felt a sense of community. On a macro level, these same groups allow for social experimentation that could not occur within traditional social settings. Finally, they can be vehicles for social change because they can introject into societies sets of ideas and projects that are not likely to arise within ordinary social constraints.

See also Cult, New Religious Movements

—*Stephen A. Kent*

REFERENCES

J. Atack, *A Piece of Blue Sky* (New York: Lyle Stuart, 1990); J. A. Beckford, *Cult Controversies* (London: Tavistock, 1985); J. Berry, *Lead Us Not into Temptation* (Toronto: Image, 1994); R. H. Cartwright and S. A. Kent, "Social Control in Alternative Religions," *Sociological Analysis* 53(1992): 345-361; A. P. Hampshire and J. A. Beckford, "Religious Sects and the Concept of Deviance," *British Journal of Sociology* 34(1983):208-229; C. L. Harper and B. F. Le Beau, "The Social Adaptation of Marginal Religious Movements in America," *Sociology of Religion* 54(1993):171-192; B. Johnson, "Do Holiness Sects Socialize in Dominant Values," *Social Forces* 39(1961):309-316; B. Johnson, "On Founders and Followers," *Sociological Analysis* 53(1992):S1-S13; S. A. Kent, "Deviance Labelling and Normative Strategies in the Canadian 'New Religions/Countercult' Debate," *Canadian Journal of Sociology* 15(1990):393-416; S. A. Kent, "Misattribution and Social Control in the Children of God," *Journal of Religion and Health* 33(1994):29-43; K. S. Khalsa, "New Religious Movements Turn to Worldly Success," *Journal for the Scientific Study of Religion* 25(1986):233-247; D. Nielsen, "Charles Manson's Family of Love," *Sociological Analysis* 45(1984):315-337; R. Ofshe, "The Social Development of the Synanon Cult," *Sociological Analysis* 41(1980):109-127; R. Ofshe and M. Singer, "Attacks on Peripheral Versus Central Elements of Self and the Impact of Thought Reforming Techniques," *Cultic Studies Journal* 3(1986):2-24; T. Robbins, *Cults, Converts and Charisma* (London: Sage, 1988); T. Robbins and D. Anthony, "Getting Straight with Meher Baba," *Journal for the Scientific Study of Religion* 11(1972):122-140.

DEVIL WORSHIP (DIABOLISM)   *see* Satanism

DIALECTICS   Originating in ancient Greece, *dialektike*—or the art of argumentative conversation—derives from *dialektos* (from *legein* or *logos,* discourse, speech, reason, measure). *Dialegein* literally involves two participants who enter the play of discourse (logos).

For the ancient Sophists, dialectic was the art of disputation *(eristic),* the *dissoi logoi* or "Twofold Arguments" that could be developed on any topic. At one level, as Aristotle later observed, *dialektos* is simply "everyday talk," the language of common life or the common medium of articulation (*Poetics* 1458b32), although in more technical works he gives a specific definition of *dialectic* as "a process of criticism wherein lies the path to the principles of all inquiries/methods" (*Topics* I 2, 101b 3-4). In the latter sense, *dialectic* becomes for both Plato and Aristotle the central philosophical method and queen of the sciences.

Following the lead of the church fathers, Scholastic theology made dialectics subservient to Logic (as part of the *trivium* of Grammar, Rhetoric, and Logic "proper") as the "science of discourse" or, more narrowly understood, as the "science of reason," teaching the forms and procedures of valid reasoning (e.g., Robert Kilwardby [c. 1250] in his *De ortu scientiarum* speaks of Logic as "a ratiocinative science, or science of reason, because it teaches one how to use the process of reasoning systematically, and a science of discourse because it teaches one how to put it into discourse systematically").

The modern conception of dialectics derives from the German philosopher G.W.F. Hegel who, in effect, revived the ancient art of dialogue and transformed it into a substantial principle of historical change. In Hegel's conception of *Geist,* or Spirit, the manifestation of the "world-process" proceeds as a dialectical process (although not necessarily restricted to the famous "thesis-antithesis-synthesis" pattern commonly associated with Hegelian logic). The Hegelian image of history as a realm of negativity, contradiction, and developmental changes enters into social theory when Karl Marx "inverted" the "philosophy of Spirit" to interpret the "real movement" of history as a dialectical struggle of groups and classes. It can be said that the tradition of "historical materialism" both revives the ancient theory of dialectic but transforms the "spirit of contradiction" into a real process—setting the scene for a continuing debate concerning the role of contradictions in history, the "laws" of society (as in Soviet "dialectical materialism"), and alternative and nondialectical views of history. In this way, the quest to think dialectically or to elaborate a non- or postdialectical method of inquiry continues to the present day as a vital source of modern philosophy and social inquiry.

—*Berry Sandywell*

REFERENCES

Aristotle, *On Sophistical Refutations*; N. Kretzmann et al., *The Cambridge History of Later Medieval Philosophy* (Cambridge: Cambridge University Press, 1952); G. E. R. Lloyd, *Magic, Reason, and Experience* (Cambridge: Cambridge University Press, 1979); G. E. McCarthy, *Marx and Aristotle* (Savage, Md.: Rowman & Littlefield, 1992); Plato, *Republic* (510-511, 530-534, 537-539), *Sophist* (217-225), *Gorgias*.

DIANETICS   *see* Scientology

DILEMMAS OF INSTITUTIONALIZATION
see Thomas O'Dea

DIMENSIONS OF RELIGIOSITY   *see* Religiosity

DISCIPLES OF CHRIST   Protestant denomination, one of several known as "the Christian Church"; began in the early 1800s through the work of three ex-Presbyterian ministers (Thomas and Alexander Campbell and Barton Stone). In 1832, their congregations joined together to form the Christian Church. Initially strongly congregational in polity, the Disciples more recently assumed a strong national body. The general assembly meets biennially. It elects a general board, which then elects those to serve on the administrative committee, which is in charge of implementing programs between assemblies. The Disciples practice baptism of believers by immersion and celebrate the Lord's Supper every Sunday as a memorial meal.

The Disciples has been subjected to church-sect analyses by Whitley (1955) and, more thoroughly, the Stone-Campbell movement generally, by Bungard (1985). Recently, the Disciples engaged in a major self-study, which relied heavily on research by social scientists.

—*André Nauta*

REFERENCES

J. E. Bungard, *Becoming a Denomination,* Doctoral dissertation, University of Kansas, 1985; O. R. Whitley, "The Sect to Denomination Process in an American Religious Movement," *Southwestern Social Science Quarterly* 36(1955): 275-282.

DISENCHANTMENT   Received English translation of the German *Entzauberung,* a concept preeminently introduced to social scientific discourse by Max Weber to describe the character of modern, secularized society. Such literal renderings as "de-magi-fication" or "de-mysteri-zation" probably more accurately render the meaning in current American usage. At one point, Weber described the condition as a world "robbed of gods." Disenchantment does not mean simply that the world is no longer seen as filled with angels and demons, but that the category "mystery" is negatively valued: Mysteries are to be solved by science, technology, or other this-worldly efforts. Modern people do not wish to "enter into" mysteries but to conquer them;

moderns similarly are pleased when they can say, for example, that a particular event or condition is "no longer mysterious." The term *reenchantment* is a spinoff from disenchantment.

See also Modernism, Secularization, Max Weber

—*William H. Swatos, Jr.*

DITTES, JAMES E. (1926–)   Professor of Pastoral Psychology and Psychology at Yale University. He is a former Executive Secretary (1959-1965) and President (1971-1972) of the Society for the Scientific Study of Religion. He also served as editor of the *Journal for the Scientific Study of Religion* (1966-1971).

Dittes wrote one of the first contemporary critical reviews of the empirical literature in the psychology of religion. He has contributed to studies in religious biography, including works on St. Augustine and an authoritative analysis of William James. He also has written on mainstream psychology of religion topics, including religion and prejudice and intrinsic/extrinsic religion. In addition, he has written extensively on characteristics of religious professionals and the psychological assessment and testing of ministerial candidates.

—*Ralph W. Hood, Jr.*

REFERENCES

D. E. Capps and J. E. Dittes (eds.), *Hunger of the Heart* (Washington, D.C.: Society for the Scientific Study of Religion, 1990); J. E. Dittes, "Psychology of Religion," in *Handbook of Social Psychology* 5, ed. G. Lindsey and E. Aronson (New York: Addison-Wesley, 1969): 602-659; J. E. Dittes, "Some Basic Questions About Testing Ministerial Candidates," in *Psychological Testing for Ministerial Selection,* ed. W. Biers (New York: Fordham University Press, 1970): 3-26; J. E. Dittes, "Psychological Characteristics of Religious Professionals," in *Research in Religious Development,* ed. M. P. Strommen (New York: Hawthorn, 1971a): 355-390; J. E. Dittes, "Typing the Typologies," *Journal for the Scientific Study of Religion,* 10(1971b):375-383; J. E. Dittes, "Beyond William James," in *Beyond the Classics?* ed. C. Y. Glock and P. E. Hammond (New York: Harper, 1973a): 291-354; J. E. Dittes, *Bias and the Pious* (Minneapolis: Augsburg, 1973b).

DIVINE LIGHT MISSION   Movement founded in India in 1960 by Sri Hans Ji Maharaj, who died shortly afterward and was succeeded by his 8-year-old son, Maharaj Ji. In 1971, Guru Maharaj Ji came to the

United States to proclaim the dawning of a new era. He gained considerable attention and many followers after arriving in the United States, including Rennie Davis, one of the "Chicago Seven" political radicals who became a devotee. Initiates, called "premies," were shown how to obtain "the Knowledge" as a part of their initiation.

The DLM was said to have developed some 500 centers, or *ashrams,* in nearly 40 different countries for several million followers, although these figures are impossible to verify. In 1973, a disastrous rally at the Houston Astrodome left the movement in the United States in dire financial straits and bereft of credibility. Also, the guru married his Caucasian secretary in 1974 when he was 17, shocking many of his followers (he had championed celibacy until his marriage) and leading to many defections. The movement has faded into relative obscurity since then.

—*James T. Richardson*

REFERENCES

C. Cameron (ed.), *Who Is Guru Maharaj Ji?* (New York: Bantam, 1973); J. Downton, *Sacred Journeys* (New York: Columbia University Press, 1979); M. Galanter and P. Buckley, "Psychological Consequences of Charismatic Religious Experience and Meditation," in *The Brainwashing/Deprogramming Controversy,* ed. D. G. Bromley and J. T. Richardson (New York: Mellen, 1983): 194-199. J. Messer, "Guru Maharaj Ji and the Divine Light Mission," in *The New Religious Consciousness,* ed. C. Y. Glock and R. N. Bellah (Berkeley: University of California Press, 1976): 52-72.

other, and he therefore suggests a study of the different meaning systems that direct behavior.

Author/editor of 15 books and author/coauthor of some 150 articles, Dobbelaere's research interests run from the role of the hospital in a predominantly Christian society (with M. Ghesquière-Waelkens and J. Lauwers, *La dimension chrétienne d'une institution hospitalière,* Part 3, Licap 1975) to the spread of Buddhism in the United Kingdom (with B. Wilson, *A Time to Chant,* Clarendon 1994) as well as a number of quantitative studies of religiosity (collaborative volumes, *La Belgique et ses Dieux,* Cabay 1985; *Belges, heureux et satisfaits,* De Boeck Université 1992).

Starting with the metaphor of the Catholic "pillar" in Belgian society in different forms (schools, cooperatives, trade unions, hospitals, banking, newspapers, political parties), Dobbelaere demonstrates how important changes occurred during the 1960s in the "pillarized structure of Belgian society." There appeared to be no weakening of ties with a Catholic inspiration corresponding to changes in doctrinal belief or liturgical observance; indeed, these organizations appear to retain their capacity to attract (e.g., 1978, 1988).

—*Roberto Cipriani*

REFERENCES

K. Dobbelaere, "Secularization, Pillarization, Religious Involvement, and Religious Change in the Low Countries," in *World Catholicism in Transition,* ed. T. Gannon (New York, Macmillan, 1988): 80-115; K. Dobbelaere et al., "Secularization and Pillarization," *Annual Review of the Social Sciences of Religion* 2(1978):97-123.

DIVORCE *see* Marriage

DOBBELAERE, KAREL (1933–) Professor of Sociology and Sociology of Religion at the Catholic University of Leuven (Belgium). President, International Sociological Association Research Committee 22, 1978-1982; International Society for the Sociology of Religion (SISR), 1983-1991. ASR Furfey lecturer, 1986.

His most well-known work to English-speaking readers is the volume *Secularization: A Multidimensional Concept* (Sage 1982, originally published as an issue of the journal *Current Sociology*). He considers secularization in three dimensions: as laicisation of social institutions, as weakening of religious integration, and as a specifically religious phenomenon. These dimensions do not always appear distinct from each

DOGMATISM In *The Open and Closed Mind,* published in 1960 (Basic Books), the psychologist Milton Rokeach developed the Dogmatism Scale. Its purpose is to "measure individual differences in openness or closedness of belief systems." The development of the scale is set within a more broadly based theoretical argument that suggests the Dogmatism Scale is useful in identifying "general authoritarianism and general intolerance."

The scale comprises 66 items, to which respondents are asked to quantify their level of agreement or disagreement, ranging from +3 (I agree very much) to –3 (I disagree very much). Intermediate opinions are expressed by agreeing or disagreeing "on the whole" (+2) or "a little" (+1).

Categories within the Dogmatism Scale identify openness or closedness of belief systems across several continua. These include the following:

- isolation between belief and disbelief systems
- degrees of differentiation of belief and disbelief systems
- specific content of primitive belief
- formal content of intermediate belief
- interrelations among primitive, intermediate, and peripheral beliefs
- attitudes toward the past, present, and future

Research using this scale (by Rokeach and others) suggests that Catholics are more dogmatic than other religious groups (except in the American South), and that dogmatism emerges in specific religious groups because dogmatic attitudes carry social rewards in those groups.

—*Jerry Koch*

DONOVAN, JOHN D. (1918–)   With B.A. and M.A. degrees from Boston College and a Ph.D. from Harvard, Donovan was a faculty member at Fordham University until 1952, when he joined the Boston College faculty, where he taught until his retirement in 1988. He was President of the American Catholic Sociological Society in 1958 and served as Associate Editor of *American Catholic Sociological Review, Sociological Analysis,* and *Sociology of Education.*

Donovan is best known for *The Academic Man in the Catholic College* (Sheed & Ward 1964), which received very positive reviews at the time of publication. He received the Best Book Award from ACSS in 1965. His books, monographs, and contributed book chapters have focused primarily on issues in Catholic education, sociology of American Catholicism, issues of the Catholic parish, dilemmas of the priesthood, social profiles of the American hierarchy, and Catholic intellectuals. His current research is concerned with issues of institutional religious identity at Catholic universities and colleges, and with the hypothesis that outstanding Catholic graduates are increasingly less likely to enter the ranks of Catholic academe.

—*Loretta M. Morris*

DOOMSDAY CULT   Name of first book dealing with what have come to be called "the new religions" or contemporary "cults."

This book by John Lofland (Prentice Hall 1966), which described the early beginnings of the Unification Church in America, has become a classic for several reasons, including its sociological perspective, its presentation of the most-cited "conversion model" in the social sciences (see Lofland and Stark 1965), and the information contained about the early UC. The book was republished in 1977 (Irvington) with a lengthy "epilogue" updating developments in the UC as well as the theoretical work contained in the first edition. The term *doomsday cult* has become a part of everyday parlance, being used regularly in the media to refer to apocalyptic religious groups.

—*James T. Richardson*

REFERENCES

J. Lofland, "Becoming a World-Saver Revisited," in *Conversion Careers,* ed. J. T. Richardson (Beverly Hills, Calif.: Sage, 1978): 10-23; J. Lofland and R. Stark, "Becoming a World-Saver," *American Sociological Review* 30(1965):862-874.

DOUGLAS, MARY (TEW) (1921–)   British anthropologist; professor emerita of University College, London, where she worked from 1951 to 1977. She has subsequently served as Research Director of the Russell Sage Foundation, as Avalon Professor of Humanities at Northwestern University, and in various visiting appointments. Born in Italy, Douglas graduated from Oxford, where she studied under E. E. Evans-Pritchard. Originally an Africanist—her fieldwork was among the Lele in present-day Zaire—she soon became interested in comparative social life and gradually turned toward an anthropology of modern industrial society. Throughout her career, she has insisted that there is no great divide between "primitives" and "moderns": The same social processes are at work in all societies. Cultural patterns, however, can be quite different. The core of Douglas's work has been an attempt to specify what causes these differences and similarities—particularly on the level of belief.

Purity and Danger (Routledge 1966) was Douglas's first book to attract wide attention from scholars of religion. In it, she asked why some religions emphasize rules and others do not. She demonstrated that modernity is not the cause and that there is no necessary split between ritualism and theologizing. Indeed, ritualism can be seen as concrete thinking: as overt symbolism that both creates and expresses a meaningful universe. Her next book *Natural Symbols,* first published in

1970, tied ritualism and antiritualism to particular kinds of social structure and introduced the grid-group schema. (The 1970, Pantheon, and 1973, Vintage, editions are radically different from one another; the 1970 edition was reprinted in the 1980s.) "High-grid, high-group" societies were prone to ritualism; "low-grid, low-group" societies were prone to shun it. "Low-grid, high-group" societies were prone to witchcraft accusations and sectarianism. Douglas and others applied the resulting "grid-group" analysis to a series of religious, scientific, and other beliefs in *Essays in the Sociology of Perception* (Routledge 1982). Scholars of religion will also be interested in the essay collection *Implicit Meanings* (Routledge 1976).

Douglas's later work has continued these interests, although with less of a focus on religion. *Risk and Culture* (with Aaron Wildavsky, University of California Press 1982) used the grid-group schema to explain environmental groups' heightened concern over environmental risks. *The World of Goods* (with Baron Isherwood, Norton 1979) used a generalized version of it to reintroduce culture and choice to economics. Various essays in *In the Active Voice* (Routledge 1982) gave the theory an ethnomethodological turn. *How Institutions Think* (Syracuse University Press 1986) generalized the theory into a neofunctionalist account of the social origin of ideas—a topic that should be of particular interest to sociologists of religion. *Risk and Blame* (Routledge 1992) focuses on the social variability of risk avoidance.

—*James V. Spickard*

REFERENCES

M. Douglas, "The Background of the Grid Dimension," *Sociological Analysis* 50(1989):171-176; J. V. Spickard, "A Guide to Mary Douglas's Three Versions of 'Grid/Group' Theory," *Sociological Analysis* 50(1989):151-170; J. V. Spickard, "A Revised Functionalism in the Sociology of Religion," *Religion* 21(1991):141-164.

DOUGLASS, H(ARLAN) PAUL (1871-1953)

Church researcher. Graduate courses in sociology at the University of Chicago and Columbia University; several pastorates (Congregational); psychology and philosophy instructor; missions administrator; journal editor. His church research appointments included the Interchurch World Movement (1919-1921), Research Director of the Institute of Social and Religious Research (1921-1933) and of the Committee for Cooperative Field Research (CCFR, 1944-1950).

Douglass had broad interests and abilities; was an indefatigable researcher and writer, sociologically perceptive, always looking for new ways to categorize and generalize; used massive hand-manipulated statistical data sets; was driven by an overarching commitment to use empirical data as a basis for recommended actions to strengthen churches and promote interchurch cooperation.

His work, mostly focused on the local church, ranged from town and country to urban and suburban, to factors that relate to antipathy and affinity between churches. He is best known for the study of city churches, based on the hypothesis that city churches evolved from rural predecessors through adaptation. The degree of adaptation was measured by the number and scope of their programs. This provided the basis for a typology. He recognized multiple factors—particularly financial, theological/historical, ethnic, and environmental—to be of importance in adaptation. Parish areas were usually analyzed by compactness and balance on a four-segment circular grid (see *1,000 City Churches,* Doran 1926; *The Church in the Changing City,* Doran 1927).

During the 13 years of the existence of the Institute of Social and Religious Research, it published 78 volumes of applied religious research. An inventory of the Harlan Paul Douglass Collection of Religious Research Reports, housed in the Department of Research, Office of Planning and Program, National Council of Churches in New York, contains several thousand "fugitive" studies, primarily from the 1950s to the present, that rarely found their way into published format. A microfiche edition of 2,270 of those produced before 1970 is now available under the title *Social Problems and the Churches* (Brewer and Johnson 1970).

For the Committee for Cooperative Field Research, Douglass coordinated work of denominational researchers, under the sponsorship of local councils of churches, to make metropolitan and local/regional studies. These were aimed at adaptation to change, consolidation, and application of comity principles to guide new church development. The urban church studies made by the CCFR were summarized by Douglass in an article titled "Some Protestant Churches in Urban America" (*Information Service,* vol. 29, no. 3, January 21, 1950). As a pioneer church researcher, he contributed greatly to the early literature and stimulated denominations and metropolitan- and state-level church councils to develop research capabilities. He brought together a group of the next-generation researchers who later established the Religious Research Association, developed closer involvement with academically based sociologists of religion, and used more sophisticated research methods. The H. Paul Douglass Lecture of the Religious Research Association is given biennially and published in the *Review of Religious Research* as a continuing reminder of his legacy to religious research. (A complete list of the Douglass lecturers appears annually in the September issue of the *Review.*)

—*Everett L. Perry*

REFERENCES

E. D. C. Brewer and W. D. Johnson, *An Inventory of the Harlan Paul Douglass Collection . . .* (Woodbridge, Conn.: Research Publications, 1970; microfiche edition, complete holdings titled *Social Problems and the Churches*); E. deS. Brunner, "Harlan Paul Douglass," *Review of Religious Research* 1(1959):3-16, 63-75; H. P. Douglass and E. deS. Brunner, *The Protestant Church as a Social Institution* (New York: Harper, 1935).

DRUGS   Many religious traditions have used "mind-altering" substances in their ritual celebrations. The intoxicating *soma* has been venerated in hymns in the Rig Veda of ancient India. A violent Moslem sect in the eleventh century is known to have used hashish. And the ingestion of mushrooms *(teonanactl)* and cactus buttons *(peyote)* by Mesoamerican Indians, especially Aztecs (who called the substance "flesh of the gods"), is also well documented.

Existing underground after being repressed by Spanish priests in the sixteenth century, the use of peyote—the active ingredient of which is synthesized as mescaline—was brought north to the American Plains Indians in the mid-1900s. Peyotism would later be institutionalized in the loosely organized Native American Church, which claims some 100,000 adherents from more than 50 tribes.

The bulk of social scientific attention has been directed to the relationship between "psychedelic" ("mind-manifesting") drugs and mysticism in the Anglo-North American context. Interest can be traced to the nineteenth century, when William James experimented with nitrous oxide (reported in *The Varieties of Religious Experience,* Longman 1902), and especially to 1954, when novelist Aldous Huxley published an account of his personal experiment with mescaline, *The Doors of Perception* (Harper). Huxley's assessment of the religious import of the experience is implicit in the passage from William Blake's (1757-1827) poem from which Huxley took his title: "If the doors of perception were cleansed, everything would appear to man as it really is, infinite."

James's and Huxley's speculations about the religious implications of drugs based on their personal experiences were most rigorously tested by Pahnke (1963) in his famous "Good Friday Experiment" (also known as the "Miracle at Marsh Chapel"). Pahnke used a double-blind design, assigning 10 subjects each to control and treatment groups. After giving 30 milligrams of psilocybin to the treatment groups, Pahnke had all the subjects listen to a Good Friday service. With nine purportedly universal elements of mysticism as his criteria—derived largely from the philosopher Walter Stace's 1960 book, *Mysticism and Philosophy* (Lippincott)—Pahnke found that there were statistically significant differences between the groups, with the treatment group scoring higher on each element of the mysticism scale.

This experiment supported psychologist Timothy ("turn on, tune in, drop out") Leary's claim (1964) that 40% to 90% of those taking psychedelics had mystical experiences when the set and setting were appropriate. Unfortunately, interactions between treatment and control subjects during the experiment may have tainted the data, so that a simple inference that the drugs made the difference is impossible. Even more unfortunate is the fact that further studies of the connection between drugs and mysticism were halted by the criminalization of psychedelics in the 1960s. While Clark's (1969) contention that psychedelics *trigger* but do not *cause* mystical experiences seems sensible enough, the precise relationship between drugs and mysticism may never be established.

—*David Yamane*

REFERENCES

W. H. Clark, *Chemical Ecstasy* (New York: Sheed and Ward, 1969); T. Leary, "The Religious Experience," *Psychedelic Review* 1(1964):324-346; W. N. Pahnke, *Drugs and Mysticism,* Doctoral dissertation, Harvard University, 1963.

DU BOIS, W(ILLIAM) E(DWARD) B(URGHARDT) (1868-1963)   As part of his effort to comprehend the complexity of African American social life, W. E. B. Du Bois, a renowned scholar and radical activist based for most of his career at Atlanta University, examined various aspects of black religion in American society.

In his *The Philadelphia Negro* (Schocken 1962 [1899]), he presented the first social survey of black congregations in an urban community. Du Bois's classic *The Negro Church* (Atlanta University Press 1903) serves as the baseline for the social scientific study of African American religion in the United States. Although a critic of specific black denominational practices, early in his career he viewed the "black church" as an important vehicle for African American liberation.

—*Hans A. Baer*

REFERENCE

M. Marable, *Du Bois* (Boston: Twayne, 1986).

DUDLEY, CARL S. (1932–)   Professor of Church and Community at Hartford Seminary. Dudley is known for an emphasis on congregations and their mission in local communities. President, Religious Research Association, 1997-1998.

After serving as a Presbyterian pastor, Dudley taught for 20 years at McCormick Seminary and founded the Center for Church and Community Ministries. He is author or editor of 10 books, including an important work on small congregations, *Making the Small Church Effective* (Abingdon 1978). A large-scale church and community action research project that Dudley directed led to publication of *Basic Steps in Community Ministry* (Alban Institute 1991) and *Energizing the Congregation* (with Sally A. Johnson, Westminster 1993).

—*Jackson W. Carroll*

DURKHEIM, ÉMILE (1858-1917)   French sociologist, and guiding figure in the influential French or "Durkheim school" of sociology. Born to Jewish parents in Epinal, in the Eastern part of France, his father was a prominent rabbi in the region, while his grandfather and great-grandfather had been rabbis before him. As a youth, Durkheim himself was apparently destined for the rabbinate but instead entered on a course of secular education. At the École Normale Superieure in Paris, he concentrated on philosophy but also explored a wider range of political and social issues. Among his eminent classmates were Henri Bergson, Jean Jaurès, and Pierre Janet. After a year of study in Germany (1885-1886), Durkheim secured a position at Bordeaux in 1887. There he taught pedagogy and social sciences until 1902, when he was called to a professorship of education (later changed to include sociology) at the Sorbonne in Paris, where he remained until his death in 1917. Although he had already emerged to prominence at Bordeaux, Durkheim became a leading figure in French intellectual life during his years in Paris, and his work exercised a strong influence in official educational circles as well as the social sciences.

Although Durkheim was not actively involved in politics, he and most of the members of his school were socialists of an idealistic, state-oriented, non-Marxian type, like Jaurès. He remained a partisan of liberal Republicanism during the political crises faced by France during his lifetime and spoke out publicly on several important occasions in defense of such ideals. During the Dreyfus affair, at a pivotal time for the development of his sociology (i.e., the latter half of the 1890s), Durkheim stood with the defenders of Dreyfus, not primarily to combat anti-Semitism but to support the ideal of a secular republic, rooted in morality and justice. Indeed, his sustained interest in the sociology of religion and morality was motivated, in part, by the hope of providing the scientific basis for a new moral order.

Durkheim's sociology of religion reflects his engagement with the ideas of many thinkers. His teacher, Fustel de Coulanges, helped to mold his view of religion as a social force. The efforts of Saint-Simon and Comte at moral and social regeneration inspired him, and he found Rousseau's notion of the general will congenial. His sociology was partially shaped by contemporary neo-Kantianism, including the philosophies of Renouvier, Boutroux, and Hamelin. However, his work reverberates strongly with the thought of other major figures in the philosophical tradition, including Plato, Descartes, Pascal, and Spinoza. He returned from Germany with an admiration for Wundt's teachings about morality and society and, in his own day, was already thought (erroneously) to be entirely under the sway of German ideas. He criticized Guyau's work on the "irreligion of the future" and also engaged Spencer's theories, including his study of ecclesiastical institutions. He later became increasingly open to English-language speculations about religion. Indeed, in light of Durkheim's broad cultivation and capacity for intellectual synthesis, it would be unwise to insist upon any exclusive influence on his thought.

Durkheim's Early Sociology of Religion   Durkheim's efforts in the sociology of religion are best divided into two phases. Although religion is frequently mentioned and some of his major ideas on the subject are already evident in his early writings, Durkheim's central focus on religion emerged after about 1895. In his own view, it was only then, due to the influence of English writers, such as Tylor, Frazer, and, especially,

William Robertson Smith, that he came to appreciate the centrality of religion and recast his earlier work in light of this new discovery. Although this somewhat exaggerates the discontinuity in his thinking, it is true that Durkheim did emphasize religion and its importance, and wrote about it more directly, after 1895 than he had during his formative period. Indeed, the sociology of religion, or *sociologie religieuse,* as it was more frequently named by Durkheim, along with the so-called sociology of knowledge, became his and his school's main preoccupation.

Durkheim published three books while at Bordeaux and another during his time at Paris. His first book, *The Division of Labor in Society* (1893), and his third one, *Suicide* (1897), contain significant and mutually congruent analyses of religion in the context of a focus on other sociological problems. His final book, *The Elementary Forms of the Religious Life* (1912), develops his full and widely influential theory of religion. Although his second book, *The Rules of Sociological Method* (1895), does not treat religion directly, it presents Durkheim's distinctive sociological approach, with its emphasis on the reality of society (versus the individual level), the need to study social facts as things *(choses),* and the comparative, analytical method.

In his book on the division of labor, Durkheim argued that religion plays an important role in uniting members of segmentary (i.e., clan-based) societies through the creation of a common conscience or consciousness *(conscience collective).* The contents of each individual's consciousness largely coincide with those of others, and such a society is therefore integrated by mechanical solidarity, or the mutual likeness of its members. As societies become more differentiated and individuated, the division of labor increasingly requires a new morality of specialized service. Organic solidarity, based on a "categorical imperative" of specialized, yet mutually supportive social performances, displaces the need for a collective consciousness.

In his later work, Durkheim noted that modern rates of suicide varied decisively with religious conditions. Protestants regularly had higher suicide rates than Catholics because the latter religion integrated the individual into a set of social practices (confession, penances, obligatory doctrine, church hierarchy, and so on) that blunted the tendencies toward egoistic suicide. Protestant emphasis on salvation by faith alone, as well as its diminished forms of religious support, enhanced egoistic withdrawal. Finally, Durkheim noted that some traditional religions (e.g., Hinduism) encouraged distinctive obligatory forms of altruistic suicide (e.g., *suttee)* through their insistence on the intense integration of the individual into the group. Although Durkheim's study contains varied observations on the relationship of religion to the different types of suicide, the central emphasis is now placed on the freer reign provided for social pathologies because of religion's diminished influence. Indeed, both of his early books envision a decreased role for religion in modern society and aim at creating new, sociological remedies for this situation (e.g., social integration through occupational groups and morality).

One of Durkheim's first direct explorations of religion was the essay "Concerning the Definition of Religious Phenomena" (1897-1898). There he defined religious facts in terms of obligatory beliefs and the practices related to those beliefs. This definition hardly represented a new point of departure and is quite congruent with the emphases already found in his earlier books, where constraint is said to characterize social facts in general. Moreover, little is said about the sacred-profane distinction or about the socially integrative functions of religion, both of which became central to his later analysis of religion. Finally, the notion that our key categories of experience grow out of religion and society appears only briefly in this essay. These emphases began to emerge more fully when he had begun to incorporate new research findings into his thinking during the first decade of the century.

Durkheim founded the journal *L'Année Sociologique* in 1896, and its first volume appeared in 1898. The large yearbook volumes contained monographic essays as well as reviews by the Durkheimians of prominent literature in sociology. A major section was devoted to the sociology of religion. Its first series ran until 1913, when publication was suspended due to World War I. (A second series, edited after Durkheim's death by Marcel Mauss, was begun in 1923-1924 but was soon discontinued.) More than a mere publication outlet, *L'Année Sociologique* was an important "laboratory" for the critique and further development of sociological ideas. The common intellectual spirit of its contributors marked it as a distinctively Durkheimian enterprise.

Durkheim assembled a group of investigators around the journal. Marcel Mauss, Henri Hubert, Celestin Bouglé, Georges Davy, and Paul Fauconnet were some major early figures in the school who wrote about religion and morality. The group came to include a large number of others including Maurice Halbwachs and Robert Hertz. Several of the younger ones, including Hertz and Durkheim's own son David, a budding linguistic scholar, perished in fighting during World War I. Hertz was perhaps the most promising student of religion among this ill-fated cohort. He published several important monographs, one on the collective representation of death and another on right and left, or religious polarity. The latter has exercised a widespread influence on the study of systems of dual classification.

Hertz had also projected a study of sin and expiation in religion, the introduction to which was published posthumously by Mauss in the *Revue d'Histoire des Religions* in 1922.

Durkheim's Later Sociology of Religion and the Durkheim School   Despite the continuity between his early writings and his final work, *The Elementary Forms of the Religious Life* (1912), it is clear that this book emerged gradually from research done by him (and members of his school) after 1895. Durkheim reviewed large numbers of publications about the theory and history of religion, primitive social organization (especially family and kinship), and totemism in *L'Année Sociologique*—and thus laid the foundation for his later book. In particular, Durkheim read the new Australian ethnography, especially the works of Spencer and Gillen. Durkheim also began to theorize more explicitly about the nature and origin of religion, critically engaging the varied ideas about religion of Spencer, Tylor, Max Müller, J. G. Frazer, the Protestant theologian Auguste Sabatier, William James, and others. He opposed the individualistic presuppositions that he found in their work as well as their tendency to explain away religion as an illusion based on the misinterpretation of primitive experiences (e.g., dreams, natural phenomena).

In *The Elementary Forms of the Religious Life*, Durkheim rejected any definition of religion in terms of the supernatural and opposed both "naturism" and "animism" as inadequate accounts of religion. Instead, he defined religion as a system of beliefs and practices relative to the sacred, ones that united their followers into a moral community. Although he was very interested in religion as a system of "representations," he generally placed rites at the heart of primitive religion, in this respect following the precedent of Robertson Smith. Religious beliefs, and states of common consciousness generally, are themselves revivified periodically by a variety of rites, which are focused around the central objects of religion, those things held "sacred" by the community. These rituals communicate between mankind and the gods, commemorate mythical beings and events, expiate sins, transport the individual through the life course, and function in a variety of other ways to enhance the sense of participation in a symbolically rich social environment. These rites are highly emotional collective experiences, states of "collective effervescence," which overcome the divisions among individuals and subgroups. They forge a collective identity that sustains members of society during periods of dispersion into routine ("profane") activities. Durkheim thought that these periods of collective fervor more generally corresponded to the periods of great

historical rebirth and transformation of cultures (e.g., during the Renaissance of the twelfth-century era and the French Revolution). While he studied these phenomena primarily in the setting of clan and tribal societies (i.e., Australia and Native America), he illustrated his arguments by repeated references to other religious settings, ancient and modern.

Durkheim insisted on the idea that the universal sentiment of religious belief could not be a mere illusion but must have its roots in some real force in reality. Religious rituals gestate experiences of a reality beyond individuals and enhance their sense of dependence on a higher power and authority existing above them. In Durkheim's view, this power is none other than society itself. Society provides the object to which our experiences of "divinity" correspond.

Religion also molds our central categories of understanding (time, space, cause, substance, the soul, and so on) through its representations about reality as well as its ritual organization of existence. Because religion is primarily a social affair, the categories themselves are social in both form and content. Taken together, they define the "totality" of our experience. Indeed, the notions of Divinity, Totality, and Society are three modes of a single reality.

Durkheim argued for the "dualism of human nature." He thought that only a sociological theory could account for the dualism frequently noted but left unexplained by philosophers from Plato to Kant. The limitations imposed on individual representations could be transcended only by higher ideals rooted in collective processes. He was by no means uninterested in the religion of the individual. However, the idea of the soul itself was born in collective rites, which were of primary significance. The individual cult was only slowly disengaged from collective practices. The important, even "sacred," role played by the individual in modern religion and society was itself the result of a long history and could not be the starting point for an adequate study of religion.

The turn toward "primitive" society as the appropriate research site for Durkheim's study of religion suggests both the continuity and the discontinuity in his thinking. The idea that aboriginal Australian clan organization is the simplest form of society and its totemic religion the most elementary one echoes the emphasis on the segmentary organization, mechanical solidarity, and collective consciousness of archaic society analyzed in his first book. However, the new emphasis on a crucial test case based on recent ethnography contrasts with the diffuse evidence from primitive and archaic societies used to illustrate mechanical solidarity in his earlier work. This reflects the research done after 1895, which led him to recast his sociologies of religion and knowledge into one unified theory. Moreover, the idea of a transformation in religion and culture toward more international or universal forms recapitulates, yet revises, the evolutionary argument of his first book as well as parts of his 1895 lectures on socialism. However, Durkheim now emphasizes the parallel transformation of societal and religious structures, suggesting a modified version of Fustel de Coulanges's theory of ancient history and also a move toward what later became "structuralist" theory. Perhaps the greatest departures from his early work (if not that of his school) are his dualism of the sacred and the profane, his insistence on the mutually immanent character of religion and society, and his radical willingness to trace much of human culture ultimately to religious and social sources.

In discussing the development of Durkheim's ideas, it is important to recall that the members of the Durkheim school worked together closely on the topic of religion after 1895. During this period, Henri Hubert and Marcel Mauss wrote important monographs on sacrifice (1898) and magic (1902-1903); Durkheim and Mauss wrote on primitive classification (1903); and Robert Hertz analyzed the problem of religious polarity (1909). Many of the central ideas discussed in Durkheim's *Elementary Forms* already were being collaboratively developed. The early analysis of sacrifice introduces an institution central to the later discussion. The essay on magic distinguishes magic (individual rites) and religion (collective ones), treats the problem of mana, or religious force, and analyzes the category of causality. The essay on classification discusses the social origins and structuring of reason. The pathbreaking work on religious polarity treats key aspects of the opposition between the sacred and profane, especially in relation to the social and religious definition of space, and may be the first place where this set of ideas is given a precise, thorough treatment by any Durkheimian. While differences in perspective and emphasis can be found among these writings, their mutual congruence is striking. Any account of Durkheim's evolving view of religion that neglected them would be incomplete.

Critiques and Influence   Durkheim's sociology of religion was attacked when it first appeared and has been criticized frequently since. He has been accused of "reductionism" for his identification of religion as a symbolic expression of social experience, while his general emphasis on society as a reality sui generis, one that transcends the individual, has led to the accusation of "social realism," a "group mind" theory, and even "scholasticism." Other critics question the validity of

his evidence or the logic of his argument. The ethnography of his day (e.g., the work of Spencer and Gillen on Australia) is now viewed as inadequate. Durkheim's own (admittedly brilliant) use of the evidence also has been questioned, in particular his heavy reliance on the (probably untypical) Australian test case and his tendency to explain empirical deviations from his theory of primitive totemism by reference to allegedly later evolutionary developments in the societies under examination. Durkheim's logical method is criticized for often assuming the antecedent validity of the theory he is attempting to demonstrate and proving his own theory's validity by critically eliminating its competitors. It is also not clear that he resolved the tensions between the established dualistic and the newly emerging monistic elements in his theory of religion and society.

Despite such criticisms, Durkheim's ideas about religion have had a positive influence on scholars from various specialized fields, for example, Marcel Granet on Chinese religion and mentality, Jacques Soustelle on the representation of time and space among the ancient Aztecs, Stefan Czarnowski on the hero cult of St. Patrick, Claude Lévi-Strauss on the "savage mind," and Louis Dumont on the Indian caste system. In England, classics scholars Jane Ellen Harrison and Francis M. Cornford wrote studies of Greek religion and philosophy under Durkheim's influence, while social anthropology also absorbed Durkheim's perspectives and subsequently extended the Durkheimian orbit of influence to such American figures as W. Lloyd Warner and Erving Goffman.

Many of Durkheim's central ideas remain fruitful: his emphasis on the sociologically explicable dualism of human nature and the social nature of religion (and morality); the idea that the roots of human reason, cognition, and culture, generally, are to be found in religion (and therefore in society); his notion that religious symbolism expresses, yet transfigures social experience; his emphasis on the function of religious ritual in the creation of social solidarity; his emphasis on the sacred (versus the profane) as a defining feature of religion; his and his school's focus on sacrifice as a central religious rite and their distinction between magic and religion. Durkheim's uncompromising insistence on the social dimension of religion has helped create and sustain a field otherwise too easily divided between history and psychology. These and other aspects of his work provoked valuable debate when they appeared and continue to inspire sociological reflection about religion.

—Donald A. Nielsen

REFERENCES

É. Durkheim, *Les formes élémentaires de la vie religieuse* (Paris: Alcan, 1912); É. Durkheim, *The Elementary Forms of the Religious Life* (London: Allen & Unwin, 1915); É. Durkheim and M. Mauss, *Primitive Classification* (Chicago: University of Chicago Press, 1963 [1903]); R. Hertz, *Death and the Right Hand* (Glencoe, Ill.: Free Press, 1960 [1907-1909]); H. Hubert and M. Mauss, *Sacrifice* (Chicago: University of Chicago Press, 1964 [1898]); H. Hubert and M. Mauss, *A General Theory of Magic* (London: Routledge, 1972 [1902-1903]); S. Lukes, *Emile Durkheim* (London: Penguin, 1973); D. A. Nielsen, "Robert Hertz and the Sociological Study of Sin, Expiation and Religion," in *Structures of Knowing,* ed. R. Monk (Lanham, Md.: University Press of America, 1986): 7-50; W. S. F. Pickering (ed.), *Durkheim on Religion* (London: Routledge, 1975); W. S. F. Pickering, *Durkheim's Sociology of Religion* (London: Routledge, 1984).

DYSFUNCTIONS OF RELIGION   *see* Functionalism

EASTERN ORTHODOXY Embodies an aesthetic theology that stresses tradition, ritual, and hierarchy. A resistance to modernization has meant that the Greek or Russian Christian churches, unlike Roman Catholicism and Protestantism, have had little significant impact on Western social science. Differing in style, discipline, and doctrine from Catholicism, the cultural influences of these churches are great. Orthodoxy's concern with icons and symbols makes it a rich resource for reference in current debates on culture and postmodernity. Pitirim Sorokin, the emigré Russian sociologist, drew from an Orthodox background in his writings. Since 1989, the Russian Orthodox Church has had to cope with a religious market of sects and new religious movements where its resistance to modernization has come into question. Orthodoxy has had an important monastic revival since the late 1960s in Russian, Greek, and Coptic traditions.

—Kieran Flanagan

REFERENCES

C. Lane, *Christian Religion in the Soviet Union* (London: Allen & Unwin, 1978); D. Martindale, *Personality and Milieu* (Houston, Texas: Cap & Gown, 1982); P. A. Sorokin, *The Long Journey* (New Haven, Conn.: College and University Press, 1963).

EBAUGH, HELEN ROSE (FUCHS) (1942–)
Professor and former Chair of the Department of Sociology, University of Houston; Ph.D. in sociology, Columbia University, 1975. President, Association for the Sociology of Religion, 1990.

Ebaugh's books include *Out of the Cloister: A Study of Organizational Dilemmas* (University of Texas Press 1977), *Becoming an Ex: The Process of Role Exit* (University of Chicago Press 1988), the edited volume *Vatican II and United States Catholicism* (JAI 1992), and *Women in the Vanishing Cloister: Organizational Decline in Catholic Religious Orders* (Rutgers University Press 1993). She has also published numerous chapters in edited volumes and articles in scholarly journals. In addition to her presidency of the ASR, she has served in a variety of capacities in all the American professional societies devoted to the social scientific study of religion. She was instrumental in organizing the American Sociological Association Section on the Sociology of Religion and was elected its first Chair.

—Madeleine R. Cousineau

ECOLOGY MOVEMENT Formed in the early 1970s as a fusion of a scientific model for understanding plant and animal communities with the alternative consciousness of the 1960s, it is now closely identified with "deep ecology"—a holistic ecophilosophy that stresses the organic interrelatedness, value, and equal rights of all living things. The ecology movement has strong religious underpinnings in Asian religions, in the nature religion of North American indigenous peoples, in the creation-centered spirituality of the medieval Catholic mystics, and in the transcendentalist musings of the turn-of-the-century American conservationist and environmental crusader John Muir.

Along with theologian Matthew Fox, Thomas Berry is the foremost proponent of a "creation-centered spirituality" in which the creation story is reinterpreted according to the tenets of deep ecology. Weaving together strands from the "new physics" and medieval mysticism, Berry rejects the stewardship role conferred on humans in the Genesis account of creation in favor of a more holistic ethic that accords other inhabitants of the Earth (plants, animals) an equal place with humans. Berry's biocentric vision has been a touchstone for the ecospiritual movement for whom he is a prominent spokesperson.

European "new social movement" (NSM) theorist Klaus Eder (1993) has argued that environmentalism has the capacity to replace socialism as the first genuinely modern form of religion. Eder believes that the "environmental crisis" elevates ecological counterculture movements to a unique historical position from which they are tasked with the responsibility of establishing a new current of moral progress in our social relation with nature. In so doing, class action will be fundamentally reorganized, because the "new middle class" constitutes the primary carrier of this revised, spiritually charged vision of modernity.

—*John Hannigan*

REFERENCES

C. Albanese, *Nature Religion in America* (Chicago: University of Chicago Press, 1990); T. Berry, *The Dream of the Earth* (San Francisco: Sierra Club, 1988); T. Berry and B. Swimme, *The Universe Story* (San Francisco: Harper, 1992); B. Devall and G. Sessions, *Deep Ecology* (Salt Lake City: Smith, 1985); K. Eder, *The New Politics of Class* (London: Sage, 1993); D. Hervieu-Léger (ed.), *Religion et écologie* (Paris: Cerf, 1993); J. Muir, *A Thousand Mile Walk to the Gulf* (New York: Houghton Mifflin, 1916); A. Naess, *Ecology, Community and Lifestyle* (Cambridge: Cambridge University Press, 1989).

ECOLOGY OF RELIGION All religions appear and develop in some specific geohistorical context. Contingent historico-environmental factors may encourage this development in certain areas and hinder it in others. Even in the same area over time, conditions may ripen to favor or inhibit the growth of a religious confession. Therefore, localization of religious beliefs, attitudes, and behavior has a decisive weight regarding the inception and continuation of every religious form or its burgeoning from "nothing."

Sacred Places It is significant that particular geographic sites are defined and identified as sacred. They function as spaces for the celebration of ritual, becoming a reference point of convergence and presence to create around themselves urban centers of practical significance. This is the story, for example, of Jerusalem, growing upon Mt. Oria, where Abraham is supposed to have been about to sacrifice Isaac—an event recalled by Solomon with the building of the Temple (2 Chron. 3:1). *Madinat an nabawi,* the prophet's city, became the most beloved place for Muslims because in that complex of villages known as Yathrib, the Prophet Mohammed took refuge on July 16, 622, the day of the beginning of the Muslim era. Another example is provided by the foundation of the Shinto sanctuary of Ise, of considerable religious importance in the national religious culture of Japan, located at the spot where the goddess Amaterasu landed on Earth.

The link between religion and locality was quite clear to Émile Durkheim in *The Elementary Forms of the Religious Life* (1912), where he stressed that the totem is not connected to persons or groups of persons that are well defined but instead to places. Each totem is therefore placed in a precise environment where it is believed that the souls of the forefathers constituting the totemic group at its formation were installed. The *churinga* are also kept in the same place; these are pieces of wood or fragments of stone worked into an oval or elongated form, bearing a carving that represents the group totem. The churinga are placed in a secret spot that also becomes sacred, radiating its sacredness all around. This is a real sanctuary, where the cult is celebrated. The same geographic distribution of the totems defines clan membership. On the other hand, the festival of the *Intichiuma* is typical for each totemic group. If the general characteristics are the same, there is nonetheless some aspect that varies. In each tribe too there are ritual differences between the various clans. A detail insignificant in one context becomes basic for another: The Aruntas's Intichiuma is not that of the Warramungas. One might be able to apply here as elsewhere the expression *cuius regio, eius religio* to mark out the localistic dimensions of religious forms.

As sacred places exercise remarkable influence on the human and social environment that surrounds them, so specific religious confessions have an increased ability to condition and control in their areas of influence. In other words, it is not easy to postulate that around the centers of the most important cults, other religious practices different from the dominant one might thrive, or that new beliefs might easily take off where a long-practiced religious faith of widespread character has been observed (see Kniss 1989).

Exceptions are certainly not rare, but at times one is allowed to identify the ongoing variables that permit multiple religious presences in an area already broadly infused with a specific religious culture. Indeed, it is not surprising that, with the independent variable of the phenomenon of emigration from countries of the Muslim faith, Islam should have become from the nineteenth century onward the second religion by numbers of adherents in Rome, the capital of world Catholicism, where for a long time other religions, both formal and otherwise, also have been at work.

A rigid ecological determinism does not thus let us fully grasp certain facets of complex modern societies. This is so in the presumed relation between the success of cults where Christianity is weak and the success of sects where Christianity is sound (Stark and Bainbridge 1985). Yet it also may occur that sects, especially if they are revolutionist rather than conversionist, are able to break through where one would expect a good result for cults. Thus there seems no break between revolutionist sects and cults. Furthermore, "not all sects will be negatively correlated with cults and regions high in no religious affiliation" (Nock 1989:245). The same distinction between cults and sects must be set alongside the characteristics of the societies to which it is proposed to be applied, if the cult-sect distinction holds here at all.

Urban and Rural Contexts   Another commonplace idea that deserves refutation concerns the differences between city and countryside. Usually it is believed that the rural environment is more attached to orthodox kinds of behavior regarding institutional religions, generally providing high rates of religious observance, whereas a dynamic of secularization is presumed to attack the habits of urban subjects to a greater degree. It is no accident that in the 1960s, there was a long discussion of the end of the sacred and of the secular city (e.g., Cox 1965). At one stage, it was remarked that there was a recovery of the sacred—its reawakening or, more correctly, its persistence. In fact, many recent studies have set in crisis the once-accepted reading of raging secularization. Meanwhile, one notices that in several cases, religiosity lodges better in the city than the countryside. It is in a rural setting that the impact of the global village of information and television entertainments finds little resistance and easily wins out

over weak affiliations and traditional kinds of belief held with little awareness (see Francis 1985; Finke and Stark 1992).

In fact, this discussion cannot be generalized, especially if one considers that the city is not a homogeneous conglomerate either in terms of social classes or in sociocultural terms. It manifests stratifications that make its periphery markedly similar to many rural situations. Nor is it necessarily true that big cities are less religiously inclined than the small ones; it is not the territorial dimensions, the number of inhabitants, or the importance of the urban center that determine a lesser concern with the religious factor. Much depends on the development of the cities; to the extent to which this rhythm is orderly, gradual, and controlled, it allows an efficient integration and adaptation without too many upheavals regarding a possibly peasant past, with a consequent tendency to continuity on the religious plane also. Precarious employment, difficulties in making ends meet, and social marginality all increase uneasiness and leave little room for attendance at temples and services. At the same time, the city provides exceptional opportunities for deeper analysis of the problematics of faith and for religious activism committed overall to the social. Rural and urban religion may experience the same difficulties in a state of impasse, without finding referents or leaders who are capable and ready for interpersonal interaction. One may be lost in the country as in the city, with no meaningful religious affiliation.

In reality, there are stratified, differentiated religious attitudes and behaviors both in the city and in the countryside. A discernable difference in religiosity largely depends on the circumstances, on the cultural traditions, and on the type of religiosity. In countries where folk religion is still strong, the difference is, indeed, small or even negligible. Of course, the specific conditions in the United States make that society unique; although it is not by chance that one speaks of the "Bible belt." Thus one could assume that regionalism in the United States, and maybe elsewhere too, prevails over the city-countryside dichotomy.

Perhaps the comparison between sociocultural areas and urban-rural homogeneous zones is more analytical, but that does not prevent one from observing islands of "deviance" with a greater or lesser religiosity in relation to the overall regional territory (Boulard and Rémy 1968). It is not, however, the case that the geographic factor is the independent variable every time; one also ought to mention the different cultural traditions in different geographic areas. Among other things, we must ask what criteria are used to constitute cultural regions, not forgetting that the religious variable too has its own intrinsic weight.

There are no easy solutions to this problem in light of the methodological difficulties of definition and especially of delimiting cultural regions connected with religious phenomenology. In other words, how do we constitute a cultural region apart from religion in such a way as to take religion seriously while, at the same time, how do we take religion as lived experience apart from a cultural area?

The attempt made by Liliane Voyé (1973) in Belgium to join the level of religious practice with the use of the territory by the residents of certain regions is interesting in this respect. The differentiation by class and socioanthropological culture seems to pass through participation in Sunday services on the basis of territorial characteristics; these are depicted on an accurate topographical map, accompanied by numerous statistics that show the degree of urbanization and ruralization, the "regional" and "ordinary" cities, the eponymous communities in a region and the peripheral ones. In sum, the regionalization of religion is largely confirmed.

Communal Religion   Moreover, as Betty Scharf observes (1970:42),

communal religion . . . is not confined to preliterate societies. . . . The city-states of the Greek world and of Babylonian civilization each had their protecting deity, and to be a citizen was to participate in his worship. Confucianism, taken as that group of cults of which Confucian philosophers approved, was a communal religion in which participation in cults of family, city and empire was part of the duty of the subject and the mark of acceptance of paternal and imperial authority. Even the other worldly religions have sometimes taken on this aspect of communalism. To the Russian, baptism in the Orthodox church was a rite of membership in the Russian nation. To the majority of Poles the Catholic faith is an inseparable part of their nationhood. . . . The alliance between the Presbyterian form of Protestantism and the Scottish sense of nationhood was once very strong, and even now still lives, as does the link between Catholic Christianity and Irish nationhood. Anglicans, at least up to the nineteenth century, looked upon membership in their church as the religious aspect of membership in the English nation.

The link with the community becomes very close in cases where ethnic-religious identity itself runs the risk of being extinguished, hence arises the strong solidarity typical of Jewish ghettoes or the strenuous defense by groups such as the Mormons and Sikhs, literally encircled by other dominant religious customs. (Nevertheless, most of the Jews in Bohemia and Moravia, Hungary, Austria, Germany, and western Europe generally became urbanized and assimilated—and even looked down upon the nonassimilated, "ghetto" Jews.)

However, the countryside can also represent a kind of refuge for religious confessions. That is what, with a wealth of data regarding North American denominationalism, H. Richard Niebuhr remarked (1929:183-187), returning to the beginning of the twentieth century, when

the unusually rapid growth of industry quickened the growth of cities in an unprecedented manner, eighty-eight per cent of all Baptists lived outside of the principal cities; eighty-six per cent of all Methodists, almost eighty-nine per cent of the Disciples and ninety-two of the United Brethren belonged to this class. On the other hand, less than fifty percent of the communicants of the Episcopal Church, fifty-four percent of the Unitarians, sixty-nine percent of the Congregationalists, seventy-two percent of the Presbyterians, and seventy-five percent of the Lutherans were classified in this category. Yet the religious conservatism and religious simplicity, the greater emotional interest, the individualism and continued sectarian organization of the rural churches evidently distinguish them from the urban group.   . . . [It should also be remembered that] rural religion, however, is subject to further transition. The influence of rapid and frequent communication, the increasing dependence of the farm, as of industry, on the human devices of trade and commerce, the extension of urban education to the district schools, the migration of the members of rural denominations to the cities, where they remain loyal to their churches—these and many other influences, which are obvious to everyone, involve the rural churches of the West in a new process of accommodation. Passing through the median state of agricultural life the churches of the frontier become churches of the city and take on in rapidly increasing measure the character of urban and established culture.

In such a manner, the continuum between country and city, religious and social, becomes manifest. A similar phenomenon in French Protestantism, radically transformed in the last years of this century, has been discussed by Lambert and Willaime (1986). The rural exodus has emptied the typically Protestant lands, such as the Cévennes and Vivarais, promoting dispersal into urban settings and widespread recourse to mixed marriages (on average more than one in two Protestants marries a non-Protestant). The changes in religious practice and discussions are profound. Nonetheless, the relations between the religious and localistic dimensions remain solid, even though ethnicity becomes an ever more important factor.

It is no accident that very often a locality is identified with a religious building, and especially its bell tower (indeed, one speaks of *campanilismo* [bell towerism] in reference to identification with a place), not to mention the minister of religion, the real "officiator of the locality" (Lambert and Willaime 1986:183), able to give meaning and coherence to a whole series of local phenomena. According to Wach (1944), it is the spatial element that gives the local community its religious dimension. Thus, in Hindu culture, a united family also has a community of cult. The Yoruba family has a double bond of religion, with the divinity of the clan and that of the tribe. From the time that gave birth to the epic of Gilgamesh, there has been discussion of the difference between city dwellers and inhabitants of the desert: From this contrast Arab religion is said to be derived. Hebrew culture is also said to be based, according to a dominant interpretation, on the contrast between city and countryside. A Chinese village, especially in the south, may evolve in such a way that it becomes a center of cultural and symbolic significance at the intertribal level. The same thing occurred in ancient Egypt, where certain lesser residential areas became real, quite autonomous, states, which helped the autochthonous development of theological systems. Among the Hittites too, cities were organized theocratically.

Complexity and Differences Today the problem of the manifest difference between urban centers with a wealth of cult centers, even an excess of them, and urban peripheries almost completely devoid of them, presents itself. The situation of the countryside seems ambivalent: There are sacred places left to fend for themselves, with no attendance, and others whose very isolation has led them to acquire and maintain a sacral aura of the first order, making them privileged points of reference (i.e., sanctuaries and the pilgrimages directed toward them).

This multiple form of the relation between sacred place and the outspreading and/or aggregating capacity of religion may explain many dynamics and suggest interpretations consistent with both the historical and the sociological aspects. Take the case of Palestine: It is the perennial "promised land," the goal to achieve after the traumatic experience of the Jewish people in the Egypt of the Pharaohs or the Europe of Nazism. But it is also an occasion for strife, charged as it is with meanings for the great religions of the written word. To enter into possession of the holy places is a way of confirming one's own faith. To go there on a pilgrimage is a unique, unforgettable experience. Basically, religion seems above all a link with a place, a space, a temple, a land, a building. Establishing its boundaries is itself an object of sacral legitimation that is translated into political contests and even military conflict. Liminality is reduced to a minimum; it is hard to maintain a no-man's-land for long, as the events of the last days of the second millennium dramatically demonstrate. Nor is it only the case of the Israeli-Palestinian dispute but also that between Indians and Pakistanis (or Hindus and Muslims), not to mention the Sikhs, who practice and defend a religion halfway between Hinduism and Islam (especially in a temple, that of Amritsar, protected to the extent of a massacre). In this instance, it is no accident that the Sikhs attribute the greatest importance to the territorial dimension of their religion, to the point of viewing the Sikh state as a real article of faith. If the Jews repeat "next year in Jerusalem" (at the end of the Passover meal), the Sikhs wish each other that "the Khalsa shall rule."

A variation of the relation between place and religion is exhaustively described by Jean Pouillon (1975), who introduces it with a quotation from Fritz Zorn (in *Mars*, p. 254): It is "really regionality which grants beauty and efficiency to God." Pouillon (1981) dwells especially on the example of a people in Chad, the Kenga, about 20,000 subjects, who in every village divide into two clans, of which one, religious in nature, is called "of the land," whereas the other has a more political character. The "chief of the land" *(garnang)* looks after the sector of natural forces whose benevolent support depends on the cult of the genii of the soil and the mountain of the locality. However, the religious dignitary is also chief of his clan, which he represents before the political leader, who is in turn the clan delegate to the religious leader. In short, the two powers, religious and political, are balanced with each other.

The legitimation of the difference occurs, as often happens in explanatory processes of an existing reality, through a mythological tale: The clan of the land, led by the religious leader, is said to be the indigenous one, whereas the other clan is said to be composed of immigrants. Thus the people longest on the spot know better the genii of the place and how to deal with them. It is the task of the head of the clan of the land to preside over the cult, but the ceremonial witnesses, above all, the participation of the "mountain chief" *(garkwa)*, who oversees the sacrifice, and the person who serves as interpreter *(dalige)* of the local genie; both belong to the clan of the land whose chief they obey on the political level, whereas on the religious plane they are autonomous. Moreover, in every village there is a mound with a hole from which it is said the forefathers of the clan of the land emerged. In short, the religion is autochthonous, endogenous, and strictly linked to the place. Pouillon (1981:175), specializing in the analysis of myths, undertook a sophisticated interpretation in this instance, which may be summarized thus: "The cult defines the territorial community, outlines the geographic limits of the authority of the 'chief of the people' and as it were localises it." Pouillon notes furthermore that the situation of Christianity and Islam is quite different, in that these are religions of a universal nature, exogenous, imported and importable, which cross politico-territorial boundaries, assuming the character of a conquest. The local genii of the Kenga, on the contrary, are like people—only of one place and not elsewhere.

Localization and Delocalization Precisely the delocalization of religion is at the basis of the phenomenon of secularization, insofar as, according to Dobbelaere (1981:39), "modern society does not need religion for its integration." Furthermore, according to Wilson (1976:20, 102),

> The basic locus of operation is not the local community any more, but the societal system, which is organically integrated on the basis of impersonal roles. Consequently, the traditional, moral and religious culture is no longer the basis for legitimated control. In a societal system control is impersonal, technical, legal and bureaucratic; not local, human and moral as it was; it is increasingly mechanical, technical, computerized and electronized.

Indeed, in the last decades there have been no significant changes regarding what was previously written about the fact that "various studies confirm the negative influence of urbanization on religious behaviour. One should not therefore conclude that there is an identity between metropolis and secularization, or between metropolis and irreligion. The factors in play are many and vary from place to place" (Ferrarotti and Cipriani 1974:180).

The context of these variations is specific and gives rise to an equivalent number of interpretations that take their lead from the work of Cox (1965), who saw in urbanization the "context" in which the emancipation of man took place—secularization, that is—and hence arrived at Robert Bellah's "civil religion" (1967), a mode typical of the United States—the "promised land" and "new Jerusalem" seen as allusive, orientating symbols that relocalize the religious aspect.

However, there are also situations where the overall territorial dimension does not correspond to a precise religious design. This is the case in the former Yugoslavia, with its 16 major and 10 lesser religious confessions, all having in common their being rooted primarily in specific areas. The Orthodox believers are in Serbia, although there are more in Macedonia and still others in Vojvodina; Roman Catholics are in Croatia and Slovenija; Muslims in Bosnia-Hercegovina and Montenegro; Slovak Evangelicals in Novi Sad, Slovenian in Lendava, Croat in Zagreb, and Serbian in Subotica; Calvinists are in the regions of Bačka, Banat, Baranya, and Slavonija; Baptists in Vojvodina, Kosovo, and Serbia; Adventists in Novi Sad, Zagreb, Niš, and Sarajevo; Old Catholics in Zagreb, Belgrade, and Ljubljana; Methodists in Skopje and Novi Sad; Jews in Belgrade (headquarters of a league of 36 communities); Pentecostal Christians are in Zagreb; members of the church of the Christian Brethren in Bački Petrovac and Zagreb; Jehovah's Witnesses operate in several regions, with over 100 communities; the Nazarene Christians are at Novi Sad. Among the groups with a lesser diffusion, there are Christians of the Evangelical Brothers at Belgrade, the Holy Church of Saints in Zagreb, Seventh-day Adventists in Belgrade, the "Less Baptized" in Subotica, the Christians with "Washed Feet" in Vrdnik, Free Catholics in Zagreb, members of the Esoteric University in Zagreb, the Seventh Day Church of God at Gložan, the Church of God at Vinkovci, that of the "Late Rain" in Osijek (Ceranić 1971).

However, the complexity of ex-Yugoslavia is also encountered at the global level. Fifteen religions have a truly global nature, because they occur in approximately 80 countries, hence in many nations religious complexity has become a constant. The link with the local dimension is important but not indispensable. In other words, there always has to be a source, a starting point, but subsequent diffusion, proselytism, and intercultural mobility do the rest. One may thus speak of a new geography of world religions (Dory 1993), their distributive relations and overlay, their influence on and from territory; but the ties with the past remain, especially that with the motherland, the country of origin. This is the case with Greek Orthodoxy, resting on autonomous parishes and autocephalous churches but also on a strong democracy from below, whose origin is to be dated to the ancient *polis*, the city-state of classical Greece (Bruneau 1993). Of a different kind is the process of gentrification, defined as the return of the middle-upper social classes from the suburbs to city centers. This postindustrial type of change is accompanied by an increase of nonbelief and "religious disaffiliation" in the core of urban centers. However, this is not supposed to mean "the completion of the secularization process in the gentrified inner city, for alongside the demise of the traditional church is a more hidden landscape of alternative movements, pursuing self-actualization, psychic awareness and spiritual exploration of many kinds" (Ley and Martin 1993:230).

Natural Areas of Religiosity Nonetheless, cities have been and still are important religious centers and places where new religious movements or movements of religious rebirth arise. Cities would thus seem to favor religious practice, which may be as true in São Paulo as in Mexico City, Dakar as Guatemala City. In Iran and Turkey too, the process of urbanization in the previous decades has given renewed stimulus to religious initiatives. In Teheran, there were 293 mosques in 1961-1962, but by 1975-1976 there were already 1,140; whereas the population had increased by 100%, the mosque rate outdistanced the population threefold (as Arjomand reports, 1984; see also Gill 1993 on the rate of church building in nineteenth-century England). The same is true of Djakarta: 460 mosques in 1965, 1,186 in 1978-1979. In the more urbanized regions of Turkey too, an increase of visible religiosity has been recorded, thanks to numerous associations of a socioreligious nature. In fact, urbanization and religious revitalization may go hand in hand; Islamization is reinforced in the passage from rural to urban environments. Similarly in the West, cities are historically important religious centers like bishoprics and other seats of power—religious, secular, or an admixture of the two. But what about New York, London, Stockholm, Budapest, or Prague: Are they also centers of religion?

However, one should not forget the historico-territorial continuity of religious roots (Gaustad 1962: 159): "In 1650 American Religion displayed a high degree of geographical unity, with Congregationalists in New England, Baptists in Rhode Island, Dutch Reformed in New York, Presbyterians on Long Island, Lutherans in Delaware, Roman Catholics in Maryland and Anglicans in Virginia." Some portions of this regionalism remain three centuries later, while others are quite different. One can see, however, that as waves of migration took place across the United States—for example, from New England to Northwestern Illinois to the Willamette Valley—the New England religious traditions moved out and on with the settlers, as more recent migration patterns effected for at least a period

a "southernization" of American religion (see Shibley 1996).

Rural areas also present a religious continuum, especially in Japan. It is because of tradition and culture:

Rissho Koseikai developed before the period of industrialisation and still maintains a hold on the rural middle class, appealing only to the relatively well-to-do small business groups in cities. The *Soka Gakkai,* on the other hand, is a post-industrialisation phenomenon appealing specifically to the lower middle class or young, labouring class. Buddhism and Tenrikyo still maintain a strong foundation in traditional rural areas. The majority of the "new religions" are, however, predominantly urban in character. Thus . . . , the rural-urban factor appears to exert a profound influence of religiosity in most industrial societies. This rural-urban difference does not necessarily exhaust the range of variation uncovered by sociographic analysis, and some evidence has been discovered to suggest the possible presence of "natural areas" of religiosity or "areas with religious personalities" which relate to geographical rather than local factors. Certainly such possibilities are relatively well established and should be incorporated into theories of the secularisation process. (Glasner 1977:86)

The problem of the *definition* of these "natural" areas of religiosity, however, remains open. The concept seems acceptable to the extent that the naturalness is given by a local, native, indigenous, but *historically contextualized* origin of every religious phenomenon.

A typical example of historical contextualization is that of American civil religion as described by Bellah (1967). For Italy, one may instead speak of a *diffused religion* in relation to Catholicism (Cipriani 1989): People's orienting principles, both personally and socially, definitely do not neglect the religious education that is received in the phases of primary and secondary socialization but that, in fact, often arise from them. In this way, their capillary nature and their interrelatedness substantiate and testify to diffused religion. It is not expressed in the familiar form of church religion but through the continual reorientation of attitudes and conduct that deal with everyday circumstances of various kinds: moral, political, economic, or juridical. Furthermore, the characteristic factors in church religion seem more constant. The variables in diffused religion are, by contrast, more changeable according to the syntheses that it produces from time to time and naturally from *place to place*. In fact, the new way of seeing reality, the different *Weltanschauung,* is the result of the collision-encounter between what already exists and what is still in the process of becoming.

Diffused religion therefore becomes dominant precisely where there is a preexisting, dominant, fideistic type of religion. If this were not the case, the outcome of social interactions would produce quite different sedimentations that could be typical of multicultural and therefore pluriconfessional situations. It is important, above all, to distinguish clearly between the manifold contents of diffused religion. The Catholicism of Italians, for example, is in fact crisscrossed horizontally and vertically by quite heterogeneous strands that reflect regional and territorial backgrounds, social stratification, and contingent historical events. Hence it is impossible to simplify matters. The space-time differences are noteworthy and certainly not generic in character.

New Movements   It is equally true that irreligious, secularist, and atheistic movements find a way to develop in the urban environment as a particularly fertile and welcoming terrain.

> The "decline of religion" hypothesis, for example, may or may not be associated with a rise of irreligion. On the other hand, there are good grounds for assuming that the rise of irreligion will be associated with secularisation. This is because the political aim of most irreligious movements has been the realization of a secular society. Free thought, secular, ethical, rationalist and humanist organisations have all worked in different ways and different contexts to achieve the complete separation of Church and State, the abolition of privileges granted to religious bodies, the repeal of religiously-based legislation, and a completely secular system of education, as components in a complete programme for secularisation. (Campbell 1971:6-7)

But the results of these acts have been ambiguous. There have been some results in France and in England, but in the United States the effect has been minimal, after an initial flurry of results at the beginning of the nineteenth century:

> Ironically it was the very same conditions which appeared to favour the growth of secularism in America which in fact worked against a strong and influential movement. One feels that in the long run the secularists would have benefitted from the sort of official persecution and opposition which

they experienced in Britain, and they would certainly have benefitted from the existence of a state Church in that there would have been a real possibility of uniting radical, political and theological opinion. (Campbell 1971:61)

On the contrary, it was religious freedom in the United States that prevented the birth of a strong antistatist and antiecclesial movement.

Nor can the ecological aspect be excluded in phenomena of intraecclesial and, afterward, extraecclesial dissent. The movement of "traditionalist" Archbishop Lefèbvre, who ultimately bolted from the structure of the Roman Church, analyzed by Isabelle Raboud (1983), is emblematic in this sense: She hypothesized that the involvement of residents of Valais in religious traditionalism was motivated by dissatisfaction with recent changes in that part of Switzerland, where the conservative bishop had installed his seminary (at Ecône). Lefèbvre's movement was supposed thus to have provided again a familiar, emotionally rich environment above all to elderly people who believed certain values and lifestyles were forever lost (their catechism told them, among other things, to "pay taxes, defend the homeland and vote according to conscience"; the priest was a key figure; services had a basic importance). The creation of dams and the development of an industrialized agriculture had upset the system of local life, which now became marked by a new way of economic thinking. Many were marginalized. The ground was thus ready for the sprouting of the seed of the gospel of traditionalist salvation sown by Lefèbvre.

For many areas, there is a shortage of adequate probing data that might help us understand current trends. For example, regarding the situation in Bulgaria, there are no broad representative scientific data on the religious phenomenon. The gaps cannot be filled in by the occasional study-visit, thinking that one can avoid in this way elaborating mere impressionistic observations (Martin 1969:131-152). However, some analysis of the countries of central and eastern Europe is starting to become available (Swatos 1994), and there emerges the importance as a strategic symbol of a place such as the Catholic sanctuary of Medjugorje (formerly in Hercegovina, now in Croatia), which has sociopolitical, mysticotheological, and medical value —like Lourdes). In fact,

> it is often presented as a simple story, a devotional beginning with the vision of six peasant children and ending with the pilgrimage of millions of faithful. But nothing is simple in Yugo-

slavia: to Croats the apparition is a reaffirmation of faith but also a "focal point for [nationalistic] solidarity"; to the Serbs *Gospa Ustasha* recalls a nightmare but a generation removed. So the Medjugorje narrative needs to be placed in a sociohistorical context of ethnic and religious disagreement, strife and conflict. The village of Medjugorje is part of the complex and tortured Yugoslav history. (Markle and McCrea 1994: 206)

Once again, the local factor has its religious weight (but not that alone).

Mobility and Religions A last relevant phenomenon should not be neglected: that of increasing social and territorial mobility, which also means new occasions for encounters and conflicts among different cultures and religions, possibly outside their places of origin. However, cultural geography plays an important role not only in the rural-urban complex but also in cultural differences. Thus

East Asia is an ideological market dominated by folk religion, Buddhism, Christianity, Confucianism (or Confucianism-nationalism), the new religions, and communism. The strength of any one is partially dependent on the weakness of all the others. As a world view, folk religions are losing their usefulness, legitimacy, and integrity. Folk rituals are being transformed into artistic ethnic markers. Folk beliefs and practices are being coopted by charismatic Christianity and the new religions. (Tamney 1993:67)

Meanwhile, however, why do some religious modes not seem fitted to easy mobility? Why has liberation theology, typically Latin American, not been exported to other contexts, save with limited exceptions? Why did this theology develop particularly in Brazil? There clearly exist conditions that promote or prevent the outcome of a vast social and religious enterprise. These are the ecological, temporal, and human contingencies that orient the action of subjects from one minute to the next, and from place to place. If one does not grasp this dynamic, it is impossible to understand the importance of the ecology of religion that explains (or attempts to explain) the emergence of Mecca or Medjugorje, the defense of Jerusalem or Amritsar, the sacral legitimation of the Ise complex or of a mountain near a Kenga village. In all these cases, as others, the religion-locality nexus is as much taken for granted as it is obvious, but the tendentiously free action of individuals

is what lets them establish and calculate what advantage to derive from the sacrality of a space, a temple, or a soil.

See also Geographic Mobility, Pilgrimage

—*Roberto Cipriani*

REFERENCES

S. A. Arjomand, *From Nationalism to Revolutionary Islam* (Albany: SUNY Press, 1984); R. Bellah, "Civil Religion in America," *Daedalus* 96(1967):1-21; F. Boulard and J. Rémy, *Pratique religieuse et régions culturelles* (Paris: Éditions Ouvrières, 1968); M. Bruneau, "L'église orthodoxe et la diaspora hellénique," *Social Compass* 40(1993):199-216; C. Campbell, *Toward a Sociology of Irreligion* (London: Macmillan, 1971); I. Ceranić, "Communautés confessionnelles en République Socialiste Fédérative de Yougoslavie," in *Les Religions en Yougoslavie*, ed. Z. Frid (Zagreb: Binoza, 1971): 1-37; R. Cipriani, " 'Diffused Religion' and New Values in Italy," in *The Changing Face of Religion*, ed. J. A. Beckford and T. Luckmann (London: Sage, 1989): 24-48; R. Cipriani, "Immagini della religiosità in Italia," in *Immagini della religiosità*, ed. S. Burgalassi et al. (Milan: Angeli, 1993): 199-212; R. Cipriani (ed.), *"Religions sans frontières?"* (Rome: Presidenza del Consiglio dei Ministri, 1994); H. Cox, *The Secular City* (New York: Macmillan, 1965); K. Dobbelaere, *Secularization* (London: Sage, 1981); D. Dory (ed.), "The Geography of Religions," *Social Compass* 40, 2(1993); É. Durkheim, *Les formes élémentaires de la vie religieuse* (Paris: Alcan, 1912); F. Ferrarotti and R. Cipriani, *Sociologia del fenomeno religioso* (Rome: Bulzoni, 1974); R. Finke and R. Stark, *The Churching of America* (New Brunswick, N.J.: Rutgers University Press, 1992); L. J. Francis, *Rural Anglicanism* (London: Collins, 1985); E. Gaustad, *Historical Atlas of Religion in America* (New York: Harper, 1962); *Geographia Religionum* (Berlin: Reimer, 1985-1990), 7 vols.; R. Gill, *The Myth of the Empty Church* (London: SPCK, 1993); P. E. Glasner, *The Sociology of Secularization* (Boston: Routledge, 1977); F. Kniss, "Toward a Theory of Ideological Change," in *Time, Place and Circumstance*, ed. W. H. Swatos, Jr. (New York: Greenwood, 1989): 151-161; Y. Lambert and J.-P. Willaime, "La vie religieuse," in *L'esprit des lieux* (Paris: CNRS, 1986): 177-208; D. Ley and R. B. Martin, "Gentrification as Secularization," *Social Compass* 40(1993):217-232; G. E. Markle and F. B. McCrea, "Medjugorje and the Crisis in Yugoslavia," in W. H. Swatos, Jr. (ed.), *q.v.* (1994): 197-207; D. Martin, *The Religious and the Secular* (London: Routledge, 1969); H. R. Niebuhr, *The Social Sources of Denominationalism* (New York: Holt, 1929); D. A. Nock, "Differential Ecological Receptivity of Conversionist and Revolutionist Sects," *Sociological Analysis* 50(1989):229-246; J. Pouillon, *Fétiches sans fétichisme* (Paris: Maspero, 1975); J. Pouillon, "Des dieux et des lieux," *Le temps de la réflexion* 2(1981):171-181; I. Raboud, "Mgr Lefèbvre et ses fidèles Valaisans," *Schweizerische Zeitschrift für Soziologie* 9(1983):617-638; B. R. Scharf, *The Sociological Study of Religion* (London: Hutchinson, 1970); M. A. Shibley, *Resurgent Evangelicalism* (Columbia: University of South Carolina Press, 1996); R. Stark and W. S. Bainbridge, *The Future of Religion* (Berkeley: University of California Press, 1985); W. H. Swatos, Jr. (ed.), *Politics and Religion in Central and Eastern Europe* (Westport, Conn.: Greenwood, 1994); J. Tamney, "Religion in Capitalist East Asia," in *A Future for Religion?* ed. W. H. Swatos, Jr. (London: Sage, 1993): 55-72; L. Voyé, *Sociologie du geste religieux* (Brussels: Les Éditions Vie Ouvrière, 1973); J. Wach, *Sociology of Religion* (Chicago: University of Chicago Press, 1944); B. R. Wilson, *Contemporary Transformations of Religion* (Oxford: Oxford University Press, 1976).

ECUMENISM   Ecumenics developed into an academic discipline in the 1960s after the Second Vatican Council (1962-1965) when Catholic and Protestant universities in Europe began to appoint ecumenical specialists. The World Council of Churches (WCC) founded an Ecumenical Institute in 1946 (affiliated to University of Geneva, 1952). Disciplinary institutionalization is lower in Britain and North America than continental Europe, so ecumenics is often combined with theology (occasionally sociology). Ecumenists tend to be recruited from history, dogmatics, and biblical studies, which explains why sociology of ecumenism is still underrepresented in the academy. Neither the catalogues of the WCC nor Lossky's *Dictionary of the Ecumenical Movement* (Eerdmans 1991) has entries on "sociology of ecumenism." Currie's sociological study *Methodism Divided* (Faber 1968) appears under "Methodist positions in the Ecumenical Movement," Wilson's *Religion in Secular Society* (Watts 1966) under "Social Theology," Berger's "market model" (1963) is not even mentioned. Sociology of ecumenism is still a blind spot, although Towler (1974:165) argues that "an ideology as strong and persuasive as ecumenism deserves careful study."

The first scholar to examine the sociological aspects of denominationalism and ecumenicalism was H. Richard Niebuhr. In *The Social Sources of Denominationalism* (Holt 1929), he identified such "sociological factors" as race and social class in explaining the tendency toward schism and the persistence of denominationalism—hence the report "The Non-theological Factors in the Making and Unmaking of Church Unity" presented to the Conference on Faith and Order in 1937. F&O reopened the discussion in 1952 after C. H. Dodd sent a letter on "Unavowed Motives" to the Central Committee. Ehrenström and Muelder's report (1963) is the only sociological analysis commissioned by the WCC.

It is a moot point whether Niebuhr's *Social Sources* is full-fledged sociology of religion (although it is often excerpted in sociological readers). He treated nontheological factors as the independent variable in 1929 and "the power of theology" in *The Kingdom of God in America* (Harper) in 1937. So it is still not clear what the independent variable is in the complex ecumenical equation (a problem now compounded by the division of labor that relegates theological factors to theologians and nontheological factors to sociologists). Mixed motivations are not uncommon. The Winnipeg Call to Union of 1902 preceding the Canadian union of 1925 is a good example. Theological statements can be used to legitimate nontheological motivations such as the quest for greater economic efficiency (see Lee 1960, Thompson 1978).

Turner (1972:242) noted that ecumenists do not define their concepts consistently. It is not always clear what they mean when they use terms such as *ecumenism, ecumenicalism, ecumenicity, ecumenicality,* the *ecumene,* the *Ecumenical Movement,* and *Ecumenics. Ecumenism* and *ecumenics* are often treated as synonyms, whereas the *Ecumenical Movement* or the *ecumene* are treated as blanket terms to cover the whole of the ecumenical enterprise. "Ecumenism" and "ecumenicalism" are best treated as an "ideology." Its basic form is the ideal "that all should be one" (John 17). It is elaborated in the form of Models of Unity: Organic Unity, Federal Unity, Reconciled Diversity, a Communion of Communions, Conciliar Ecumenism, Secular Ecumenism, and Spiritual Ecumenism (Lossky 1991). "Ecumenicity" is an "attitude": that is, the "affective" dimension of the processes of ecumenical dedifferentiation. It (1) denotes positive perceptions of other Christian denominations and their members and (2) presupposes commitment to ecumenical goals.

Durkheimians might object that we are dealing with psychology (i.e., the attitudes of *individuals*); in practice, however, much sociology of ecumenism consists of surveys of the ecumenical and antiecumenical attitudes of affiliates, the clergy, and denominational leaders (examples in Black 1983:94 ff.; Ranson et al. 1977:76 ff.). "Ecumenism" (an ideology) presupposes "ecumenicity" (an attitude). "Ecumenics" denotes an academic discipline. It should ideally be based on the best that historical, sociological, and theological scholarship have to offer. It should also avoid the extremes of sociological and theological "reductionism." Ecumenics (like the law and medicine) is also a practical discipline, because it is relevant to the task of uniting Christian denominations. The "ecumenical elite" is distributed over such sites as (1) ecumenical bureaucracies in the network of Councils of Churches, (2) denominational "boards," (3) ecumenical negotiations, (4) universities and ecumenical institutes. (These are analytical distinctions because ecumenists often work in two or more of these sites.) Its main tasks are (1) to produce and evaluate "consensus texts" (the "diplomatic dialogue of experts"; Willaime 1989:15); and (2) to describe and explain processes of "denominational differentiation" and "ecumenical dedifferentiation" (Staples 1992). Ecumenics should not be reduced to studies of texts produced by the elite.

The "Ecumenical Movement" denotes nonofficial groups of Christians that organized themselves in the nineteenth century into "social movements" to propagate ecumenism and pursue ecumenical goals. They recruited mostly from the ranks of like-minded Protestants such as Anglo-Saxon Evangelicals and Lutheran Pietists (together with liberals) and joined forces to provide education, to found interdenominational missionary societies, to provide services for young people (YMCA and YWCA) and college students (e.g., the Student Christian Movements affiliated to the World's Student Christian Fellowship in 1895), and to struggle for peace and social justice. The International Missionary Council (1921), the Life and Work Movement (1925), and the Faith and Order Movement (1927) became departments of the WCC in 1961 and 1948. All were founded by charismatic leaders or "ecumenical pioneers" (Willaime 1989:15) who emerged from the ranks of the earlier social movements.

The Ecumenical Movement is a complex cluster of "social movements" that was gradually "officialized" in the form of a network of councils of churches from the local to the global level as denominations obtained the right to appoint official delegations to the classical ecumenical conferences and to the assemblies and "boards" of the WCC (from 1948). Like the United Nations, multinational corporations, and the world economic system, it is now a "global" phenomenon; so ecumenical studies must be inserted into globalization studies. The "ecumenical process" is a sociohistorical phenomenon that subsumes all those features denoted by terms such as *ecumenism, ecumenicity,* and the *Ecumenical Movement* and also subsumes the individual and concerted actions of "ecumenicals" and "antiecumenicals" (and interactions between them) in the interlocking processes of "denominational differentiation" and "ecumenical dedifferentiation." The ecumenical process could now be treated as a "living laboratory" in which to describe, explain, and theorize a number of macro-to-micro linkages from the local to the global level such as "processes of reception" (Rusch 1988). If theologians, historians, and sociologists can learn to work together in one "interdiscipline," it could also be used as a laboratory in which to test theories that link "ideas," individual and concerted ecumenical actions ("agency"), and processes of ecumenical "structuration" (described by Giddens [1984] as that which both "enables" and "constrains"; for inherent "constraints" in the ecumenical process, see Staples 1995, Black 1993).

The "ecumene" (*oikoumene*) means the "inhabited world" in Greek. It can now be analytically divided into the "little ecumene" (Christian denominations) and the "great ecumene" (all the world's religions and the interfaith dialogue among them). This raises the question of whether their members perceive each other in ways that are positive, negative, or hostile. The full range of reactions runs from religious wars and persecutions to syncretism and mergers with "peaceful coexistence," "mutual cooperation," and "federal constructions" as the middle terms (see Turner 1972:242 f). Ecumenical dialogue is the means for shifting the balance toward the positive end of the spectrum. In the "little ecumene," one aim of dialogue is to correct misperceptions.

Attitude surveys, identity studies, and inculturation studies (Lossky 1991:506 f) shed light on such perceptions. Attitudes of Jews, Christians, Muslims to each other are regularly featured in the *Journal of Ecumenical Studies.* The applicability of Mol's account of religious identity is limited because he did not ask how religionists with the same denominational identity interact with others in the ecumenical process. His claim that only "invasion from outer space" can unite divided denominations (Mol 1976:85) explains neither "Objective Progress" toward Christian unity nor the network of councils of churches, while he prefers group identities with firm identity boundaries buttressed by "prejudice" (1976:86 ff). A better understanding of "we-feeling" can be found in Gilbert's essay *On Social Facts* (Princeton University Press 1992). Mol also overlooks the possible emergence of "a powerful cultural consensus" (Turner calls this "homogenization," 1972:239 ff). A good example is Protestantism in nineteenth-century Canada (Westfall 1989). This explains why union efforts did not fail in Canada, even if they failed in the United States (Finke and Stark 1992; but they did not always fail in the United States, see Douglass 1937).

—*Peter Staples*

REFERENCES

P. Berger, "A Market Model for the Analysis of Ecumenicity," *Social Research* 30(1963):77-93; A. W. Black "Ironies of Ecumenism," *Ecumenical Review* 45(1993):469-481; A. W.

Black, "The Sociology of Ecumenism," in *Practice and Belief,* ed. A. W. Black and P. E. Glasner (Sydney: Allen & Unwin, 1983): 86-107; H. P. Douglass, *A Decade of Objective Progress in Church Unity 1927-1936* (New York: Harper, 1937); N. Ehrenström and W. G. Muelder, *Institutionalism and Church Unity* (New York: Association, 1963); R. Finke and R. Stark, *The Churching of America 1776-1990* (New Brunswick, N.J.: Rutgers University Press, 1992); A. Giddens, *The Constitution of Society* (Cambridge: Polity, 1984); R. Lee, *The Social Sources of Church Unity* (New York: Abingdon, 1960); N. Lossky (ed.), *Dictionary of the Ecumenical Movement* (Grand Rapids, Mich.: Eerdmans, 1991); H. Mol, *Identity and the Sacred* (Oxford: Blackwell, 1976); S. Ranson et al. (eds.), *Clergy, Ministers and Priests* (London: Routledge, 1977); W. G. Rusch, *Reception* (Philadelphia: Fortress, 1988); P. Staples, "Theory and Method in Ecumenical Science," pp. 139-173 in *Ekumeniken och forskningen,* ed. Sigurd Bergmann et al. (Uppsala: Nordiska Ekumeniska Rådet, 1992); P. Staples, "Ultimates as Paradoxical Limits in Christian Ecumenical Science," *URAM Journal* 18(1995): 139-150; D. M. Thompson, "Theological and Sociological Approaches to the Motivation of the Ecumenical Movement," in *Religious Motivation,* ed. D. Baker (Oxford: Blackwell, 1978): 467-479; R. Towler, *Homo Religiosus* (London: Constable, 1974); B. S. Turner, "The Sociological Expla- nation of Ecumenicalism," pp. 231-245 in *The Social Sciences and the Churches,* ed. C. L. Mitton (Edinburgh: Clark, 1972): 231-245; W. Westfall, *Two Worlds* (Montreal: McGill-Queen's University Press, 1989); J. Willaime (ed.), *Vers de nouveaux oecuménismes* (Latour-Maubourg: Cerf, 1989).

EDUCATION   *see* Religious Education

EDWARDS, JONATHAN (1703-1758)

American Congregationalist minister and theologian.

After graduating from Yale College (1720), Edwards joined his grandfather Solomon Stoddard in Northampton, Massachusetts (1727). Alarmed at the moral laxity and emotional poverty of the town's religious life, Edwards stressed an experiential religion that still acknowledged God's autonomous grace. He reformulated puritanism's predestination doctrine to accommodate personal conversion and missionary outreach. Edwards's intellectual leadership and George Whitefield's preaching are credited with the "Great Awakening" of the 1740s (also known as the "First Great Awakening"). However, Edwards did not endorse the Arminian tendencies of the awakening. He remained convinced that only a combination of head and heart brought authentic faith.

Edwards was a quintessentially American religious figure. He reformulated Calvinism, pushing it away from formalistic academic theology toward experien-

tial faith and more inclusive membership. The combination of rational philosophy and intuitive faith created an "evangelical liberalism." Edwards was committed to the institution of the church and its traditions, yet his reforms set the stage for a thorough democratization of American Protestantism—both spiritually and institutionally.

—*Rhys H. Williams*

REFERENCES

N. Fiering, *Jonathan Edwards's Moral Thought and Its British Context* (Chapel Hill: University of North Carolina Press, 1981); N. O. Hatch and H. S. Stout (eds.), *Jonathan Edwards and the American Experience* (New York: Oxford University Press, 1988); P. Miller, *Jonathan Edwards* (New York: Meridian, 1959); D. B. Shea, "Jonathan Edwards," *Journal of American Studies* 14(1980):181-197; D. Weber, "The Figure of Jonathan Edwards," *American Quarterly* 35(1983):556-564.

EISTER, ALLAN W. (1915-1979)

Professor and Chair, Department of Sociology and Anthropology, Wellesley College, Wellesley, Massachusetts.

A native of Upper Sandusky, Ohio, Eister studied at DePauw University (B.A., 1936), American University (M.A., 1937), and the University of Wisconsin (Ph.D., 1945). Prior to his arrival at Wellesley in 1953, he served on the faculties of Hood College (1944-1946) and Southern Methodist University (1946-1952). His distinguished academic career included a Ford Foundation fellowship at Harvard (1952-1953), a Fulbright lectureship at the University of Karachi (1959-1960), and a fellowship at All Souls College, Oxford (1966-1967).

Eister was a critical figure in the formalization of the social scientific study of religion. His long involvement in the Committee for the Scientific Study of Religion, the forebear of the Society for the Scientific Study of Religion (SSSR), began in 1950. He later served on the Executive Council of the SSSR (1957 to 1966), was Secretary of that organization (1964 to 1967), and was the founding Editor of the book review section of the *Journal for the Scientific Study of Religion.* In 1962, he coedited (with Lauris Whitman and Constant Jacquet) *Sociology and Religion: Proceedings of the Hazen International Conference on the Sociology of Religion,* and in 1968, he edited a special issue of the Religious Research Association's journal, *Review of Religious Research.* In 1971, Eister was program chair of the annual meetings of the Society for the Scientific Study of Religion, and he later edited a collection of papers from those meetings titled *Changing Perspectives in the Scientific Study of Religion* (Wiley 1974).

The emergence and development of new religious movements was an abiding interest of Allan Eister long before the topic became fashionable among sociologists of religion in the 1970s. It was the focus of his earliest work, *Drawing Room Conversion: A Sociological Account of the Oxford Movement* (Duke University Press 1950). Eister's critical abilities especially shine in two of his widely read essays. The first, published in the *American Sociological Review* in 1957, is titled "Religion in Complex Societies: Difficulties in the Specification of Functions." The second, which appears in Glock and Hammond's *Beyond the Classics* (Harper 1973), is "H. Richard Niebuhr and the Paradox of Organizations: A Radical Critique." Allan Eister was an academic of the *old school* in the good senses of that term. Even upon issues about which he felt deeply, his discourse always was as reserved and polite as it was clear. He was an outgoing person who constantly offered encouragement to younger scholars.

—*William M. Newman*

ELAZAR, DANIEL J. (1934–)   Senator N. M. Patterson Professor, Bar Ilan University (Israel), and Director, Center for the Study of Federalism, Temple University.

Born in Minneapolis, Elazar received his M.A. and Ph.D. in political science from the University of Chicago. Recognized as an expert on Jewish community organization worldwide and Jewish political thought, he is an authority on Israel and world Jewry and founding President of the Jerusalem Center for Public Affairs, a major independent Jewish "think tank" concerned with analyzing and solving key problems facing Israel and world Jewry. He is the author of more than 60 books, including *Community and Polity* (Jewish Publication Society 1995 [1976]), a classic in-depth study of the American Jewish community, and many other publications. Moreover, he is author or editor of several books exploring practical solutions to the Israeli-Palestinian conflict based on federal principles found in the Jewish political tradition; these works include *Two Peoples-One Land: Federal Solutions for Israel, the Palestinians and Jordan* (University Press of America 1991) and *Israel: Building a New Society* (Indiana University Press 1986).

As editor of the Jerusalem Letter/Viewpoints series, he has analyzed such topics as Sephardic Jewry and religious politics in Israel. Among his other books are *Covenant and Commonwealth* (Transaction 1996) and *Covenant and Polity in Biblical Israel* (Transaction 1994). In addition, he has published widely on federalism, for example, *American Partnership* (University of Chicago Press 1962), *American Federalism: A View from the States* (Crowell 1972), *Cities of the Prairie* (Basic Books 1970), *Exploring Federalism* (University of Alabama Press 1987), *Federal Systems of the World* (Longman 1994), and *The American Mosaic* (Westview 1994). Elazar has been awarded many honorary degrees, including those from Hebrew Union College-Jewish Institute of Religion and Gratz College as well as the Sklare Memorial Award from the Association for the Social Scientific Study of Jewry.

—*Arnold M. Dashefsky*

ELECTIVE AFFINITY   Innovated by Max Weber to conceptualize in nondeterministic fashion the coincident interaction of components from different sociocultural systems in comparative analysis. The specific case study that is the quintessential example in Weber's work is *The Protestant Ethic and the Spirit of Capitalism* (Scribner 1930 [1904-1905]). According to Weber, there was an *elective affinity* between Puritan ethical norms and emerging capitalist business practices in seventeenth-century England; later theorists have extended this to include the political position of Puritan partisans. In other words, a particular economic status along with a particular political status along with a particular religious practice all coincide in such a way that each is especially favorable to the other, and the whole form a culture complex (or civilizational complex) that is especially powerful for the advancement of all of these sociocultural spheres combined—this is what Weber means by the *spirit* of capitalism. Elective affinity is not restricted to the single case, however, and can be considered a general theory of social change; that is, when this favorable coincidence of sociocultural spheres occurs, there can be a quantum leap forward (or backward) on the part of a sociocultural system.

—*William H. Swatos, Jr.*

ELIADE, MIRCEA (1907-1986)   At the time of his death, Eliade was Sewell L. Avery Distinguished Professor Emeritus of History of Religions at the University of Chicago Divinity School, to which he had come from his native Romania as Visiting Professor in 1956.

The crowning achievement of Eliade's scholarly work appeared posthumously; he is Editor-in-Chief of the 16-volume *Encyclopedia of Religions,* published by Macmillan in 1987.

According to one biographer (Olson 1992), Eliade

interpreted his own life as a paradox: an attempt to live in history and beyond it; to be involved in current events yet withdrawn from them; to be Rumanian and live in a foreign land; to be a literary figure and a scholar of religion.

Among the myriad insights offered in the more than 150 scholarly books and novels Eliade has written is a paradoxical intertwining of *the sacred and the profane* (also the title of one of his most important books, a development upon a fundamental notion of Émile Durkheim). Rather than dichotomous categories, Eliade argues that these two concepts are modes of being that are embedded in a singular human experience. One discerns the manifestations of the sacred within ordinary human objects, myths, and rituals. Moreover, this discernment emerges from the cosmos and comes to the individual as a form of revelation (heirophany): "Something sacred shows itself to us."

See also Religious Studies

—*Jerry Koch*

REFERENCES

M. Eliade, *The Sacred and the Profane* (New York: Harcourt, 1959); C. Olson, *The Theology and Philosophy of Eliade* (New York: St. Martin's, 1992).

ENCYCLICAL At its simplest, "a letter circulated by the pope."

The term is importantly connected with the Roman Catholic understanding, shared both by liberals, who stress dialogue, and by conservatives, who stress authority, that the papacy is a primary means of maintaining and creating unity within the church and for the world. At first, these letters were mostly about matters internal to the church, and included letters written by archbishops and bishops to their dioceses or to other bishops. But since the eighteenth century, these more intramural letters have been called *pastoral letters,* and the term *encyclical* is reserved for documents of some major importance for worldwide

Catholicism, such as the great poverty associated with unregulated capitalism, the topic of Pope Leo XIII's 1891 encyclical *Rerum novarum* (Of New Things), which gave special prominence to the social teaching of Catholicism. Since then this has become the most common meaning of *encyclical* and the one of primary interest to sociologists.

Since Pope John XXIII (see his 1963 *Pacem in Terris,* or Peace in the World), these letters are often now addressed not merely to Catholics but to men and women of "goodwill." While their vision is clearly grounded in biblical and theological insights, their analysis is in terms of reason and the best models of empirical inquiry. Their conclusions are offered as "prudent," that is, as directions suggested by practical reason for contingent applications of grounding principles of the good society. Since Paul VI's 1964 *Ecclesiam Suam* (On the Church), social encyclicals have stressed the importance of culture, historical differences, and the centrality of dialogue. The church itself, in the spirit of Vatican II, is presented as a "pilgrim" in dialogue with the world. Although the models and metaphors used in encyclicals vary over time (Schuck 1991), scholars can identify primary affirmations (the common good, the dignity of each person, the importance of the family, the responsibility of governments for justice, subsidiarity, and that economic development must first be social development). These communitarian themes, retrieved from precapitalist orientations of thought and sensibility, were a major reason for the formation of the American Catholic Sociological Society, as American sociology at the time remained wedded to scientist methodologies that precluded an overt ethical concern or explicit social criticism.

It should be noted that the papal encyclical tradition is but one of many sources of Catholic social thought, neither the most radical (see, for example, *The Catholic Worker* or Pax Christi) or the most conservative (see, for example, Michael Novak, *The Spirit of Democratic Capitalism,* Simon & Schuster 1982).

—*James R. Kelly*

REFERENCE

M. J. Schuck, *That They Be One* (Washington, D.C.: Georgetown University Press, 1991).

ENGELS, FRIEDRICH (1822-1895) German social theorist, born to a Pietist family of industrialists.

Influenced by David Strauss's radical critique of early Christian lives of Jesus, he became a convert to left Hegelianism but retained an interest in religion. From 1850 through 1869, he worked for his family's manufacturing firm in Manchester, in part, to help support his financially dependent, lifelong friend Karl Marx. With no doctoral training, Engels was an autodidact who wrote on many subjects, including primitive religion, early Christianity, and religion's role in early modern European historical conflicts. His later writings, especially his correspondence, allow for the possible influence of religious ideas on the economic structure and lay the basis for both mechanical Marxism as well as multifactor sociological theories of sociocultural change.

Although Engels relied too heavily on a limited number of secondary sources of evidence, his writings about religion and society are frequently insightful. He compared early Christianity's place in antiquity with the role of socialist movements in the modern capitalist state and likened the spirit of the communist movement to early Christian brotherliness. *The Peasant War in Germany* (1850) located the Reformation teachings of Luther as well as the millenarian religiosity of Münzer in their social class settings.

Engels's emphasis on the peasant and plebeian origins of the radical sects has been widely accepted and has encouraged the recent revival neo-Marxian Reformation historiography. His attempts to correlate specific religious doctrines with social class interests have been less enthusiastically received.

—*Donald A. Nielsen*

REFERENCE

D. McLellan, *Marxism and Religion* (New York: Harper, 1987).

ENVIRONMENTALISM   *see* Ecology Movement

EPISCOPAL CHURCH   The Christian denomination in the United States that formally traces its heritage to the Church of England and is recognized by the Church of England as being its legitimate associate in the United States as a part of the worldwide "Anglican Communion."

Formally founded in 1789, there was a Church of England presence in North America from the earliest English merchant adventurers. The name "episcopal" is derived from the NT Greek *episkopos,* normally translated "bishop." At the time of its founding in the United States, the church took the title Protestant Episcopal, although in recent decades the modifier has been dropped to an alternate title in everything but legal documents. Strictly speaking, however, only the "General Convention" of the church exists as a body, since the Episcopal Church is actually a confederation of approximately 100 local judicatories (dioceses), each of which remains technically independent and legally capable of withdrawing from the confederation, which is modeled structurally on the Articles of Confederation of the United States. The first bishop consecrated for the United States was Samuel Seabury, in 1784, through the Scottish Nonjuror succession; two additional bishops, Provoost and White, were consecrated in the English succession in 1785.

Episcopalian expansion was slow relative to other denominational traditions. In the 1820s, for example, when U.S. Supreme Court Chief Justice John Marshall was approached for a subscription for the Virginia Theological Seminary, he replied that it was "almost unkind to induce young Virginians to enter the Episcopal ministry," because he thought the church "too far gone ever to be revived." Church growth was hindered by lack of experience with the church as a voluntary society, insistence on a classically trained ministry, and adherence to fixed liturgical forms all based on a model of parish life from sixteenth-century England. The church grew fastest in New England and the Mid-Atlantic states, where it had already had to face the consequences of disestablishment, but growth was much slower in the South. Westward expansion was spotty, especially outside of major urban areas. On the other hand, the Episcopal Church was among the least fractured denominations during the Civil War, and the "high church" or Anglo-Catholic movement that budded in England in the 1830s gradually had a strengthening effect, particularly in westward mission development. As the nineteenth century wore on, some Episcopalians became leaders in progressive social movements, even though the denomination as a whole was identified with commercial-industrial leaders.

The Episcopal Church benefitted numerically from the churchgoing "revival" in the 1950s but in the 1980s experienced a significant loss of membership and now stands at about 2 million. The Episcopal Church was a leading force in the civil rights movement of the 1960s and in other causes of social justice, but in recent years the church has been wracked by controversies surrounding the ordination of women, gay/lesbian issues, clergy sexual misconduct, and fiscal mismanagement.

The Episcopal Church has not directly been the subject of extensive social scientific investigation (see Swatos 1979), but its major American offshoot, Methodism, has been. Additionally, the extensive body of research on puritanism and the Protestant ethic is largely to be juxtaposed with the Anglican worldview (see Little 1969). Recent research has focused primarily on the ordination of women controversy (see, e.g., Nesbitt 1997).

More general sociological research on social status has consistently found Episcopalians to be significantly overrepresented among American elites (see Davidson et al., 1995). This finding occurs whether the measures are relatively "hard" data such as income and wealth or such things as proportionate numbers of members of Congress or listees in volumes such as *Who's Who*. Although the Episcopal Church is often considered part of the U.S. "Protestant establishment," a study of moral valuing across a national sample (Wood and Hughes 1984) found that Episcopalians formed a constellation with Unitarians and Reform Jews that stood separate from any other group of Christians. Because these two groups share with Episcopalians significant overrepresentation among elites today, this strongly suggests that the social status component operates in shaping life values.

—*William H. Swatos, Jr.*

REFERENCES

J. D. Davidson et al., "Persistence and Change in the Protestant Establishment," *Social Forces* 74(1995):157-175; D. Little, *Religion, Order, and Law* (New York: Harper, 1969); P. D. Nesbitt, *The Femininization of the Clergy* (New York: Oxford University Press, 1997); W. H. Swatos, Jr., *Into Denominationalism* (Storrs, Conn.: Society for the Scientific Study of Religion, 1979); M. Wood and M. Hughes, "The Moral Basis of Moral Reform," *American Sociological Review* 49(1984):86-99.

EQUAL RIGHTS AMENDMENT   First proposed in 1923, the Equal Rights Amendment (ERA) to the U.S. Constitution was intended to assure equality of rights at the federal and state levels without regard to sex. It was passed by Congress on March 22, 1972, but failed to be ratified by a necessary 38 states prior to an extended deadline of June 6, 1982. Phyllis Schafly, the Rev. Jerry Falwell, and the Moral Majority were key to mobilizing opposition. Church leaders supporting the ERA justified their perspective on the belief that God had created people as a single class, while religious opponents argued that it violated the divine order of creation, abrogating a husband's rightful dominance over his wife.

—*Paula D. Nesbitt*

REFERENCES

D. G. Mathews, "Spiritual Warfare," *Religion and American Culture* 3(1993):129-154; D. G. Mathews and J. S. DeHart, *Sex, Gender, and the Politics of ERA* (New York: Oxford University Press, 1990).

ERHARD, WERNER   *see* est

ERIKSON, ERIK H. (1902-1994)   Developed an influential life span developmental theory in which *identity* is a central concept.

Erikson adopted from embryology the epigenetic principle that potentialities can only develop in a proper sequence. As part of the revisionist psychoanalytic movement, Erikson applied the epigenetic principle to the psychodynamic process of ego development throughout the life cycle. He postulated eight stages of development, each characterized by a dichotomous tension between two opposing potentialities. Each stage represents a psychosocial crisis, the outcomes of which prepare the way for the next stage of development. Furthermore, positively, each stage is associated with the potential to develop a unique strength or virtue, or, negatively, a pathology, defined as the antipathy of a virtue.

In the first stage of development, infancy, the tension between basic trust and mistrust are paralleled by the tendency to develop the virtue of hope or its antipathy, withdrawal. Early childhood is characterized by tendencies toward autonomy or shame and doubt, with the associated possibilities of either will (a virtue) or compulsion (a pathology). Initiative and guilt are the dichotomies characteristic of late childhood and are associated with the virtue of purpose or its antipathy, inhibition. School-age children develop the virtue of competence or its pathology, inertia, based upon the tension between industry and inferiority at this stage. Adolescence can lead to either fidelity (a virtue) or repudiation (pathology), based upon Erikson's highly influential discussion of the tension between identity and confusion that characterizes adolescence. In young adulthood, intimacy and isolation are the dichotomies that lead to the development of either love or its pathological counterpart, exclusivity. Adulthood leads to the challenge between generativity or rejectivity and is associated with either care (a virtue) or stagnation.

Finally, the last stage of development, old age, can lead to disdain or the virtue of wisdom, as one struggles with the tendencies toward the virtue of integrity or the pathology of despair and disgust at this final stage of the life cycle.

Erikson argues that faith traditions often have been the cultural guardians of virtues associated with stages of ego development. His overt sympathy to religion is reflected in his widely acclaimed studies of Luther and Gandhi and in his psychohistorical works. While Erikson's stages of development were not generated by systematic empirical research, nor have they been systematically tested, their influence remains immense and part of the literate culture of Western civilization.

—*Ralph W. Hood, Jr.*

REFERENCES

E. H. Erikson, *Childhood and Society,* 2nd ed. (New York: Norton, 1963 [1950]); E. H. Erikson, *Young Man Luther* (New York: Norton, 1958); E. H. Erikson, *Gandhi's Truth* (New York: Norton, 1968); E. H. Erikson, *Toys and Reason* (New York: Norton, 1977).

EROTICISM   *see* Sexuality and Fertility

ESCHATOLOGY   The term has a diversity of sociological implications and usages encompassing millennarianism, utopian studies, teleology, the secularization of thought since the Enlightenment, and religious movements and sects concerned with the end of time (or the end of the world, sometimes referred to as "end time"). The term also has a significance in relation to New Age religions.

Eschatology refers to the study of the ultimate, of last things, and to prophecies of judgment and the restoration of a kingdom (e.g., of Judah, of Israel, of Christ, of God). The term relates to the inevitability of the future, the Apocalypse, and to the unveiling of a final truth. Its most important biblical reference is in the Book of Revelation.

Since the nineteenth century, the term has come to exemplify the tension between religion and revelation over ideas and understandings of progress. Eschatology has particular importance in relation to treatments of the secularization of modernity (Blumenberg 1985, Falk 1988, Tiryakian 1978). The term has had a revival of interest in the context of liberation theology and Vatican II. The change can be related to contrasting approaches to the issue of hope and redemption between theology and politics (Bloch 1985, Moltmann 1967, 1977).

Concerns with the fin-de-siècle and the chaos of postmodernity also have led to a stress on enchantment and issues of hope (Flanagan 1996). This stress emerges from a sense of unsettlement at the end of the millennium. It also reflects a response to issues of Armageddon. Eschatology has arisen in the case of sects such as the Jehovah's Witnesses (Beckford 1975) but also has emerged in response to the happenings at Waco, where millennial expectations and American federal law collided with tragic consequences (Tabor and Gallagher 1995, Wright 1995).

See also Apocalyptic

—*Kieran Flanagan*

REFERENCES

J. A. Beckford, *The Trumpet of Prophecy* (Oxford: Blackwell, 1975); M. Bloch, *The Principle of Hope* (Oxford: Blackwell, 1985); H. Blumenberg, *The Legitimacy of the Modern Age* (Cambridge: MIT Press, 1985); P. Falk, "The Past to Come," *Economy and Society* 17(1988):374-394; K. Flanagan, *The Enchantment of Sociology* (New York: St. Martin's, 1996); J. Moltmann, *Theologies of Hope* (London: SCM, 1967); J. Moltmann, *The Church in the Power of the Spirit* (London: SCM, 1977); J. A. Tabor and E. V. Gallagher, *Why Waco Cults* (Berkeley: University of California Press, 1995); E. A. Tiryakian, "The Time Perspectives of Modernity," *Society and Leisure* 1(1978):125-156; S. A. Wright (ed.), *Armageddon in Waco* (Chicago: University of Chicago Press, 1995).

---

est (THE FORUM)   Founded in 1971 by Werner Erhard, a former encyclopedia salesman who had experimented with Zen through reading Alan Watts, Silva Mind Control, Scientology, humanistic psychology, and many other self-actualizing techniques, *est* (Erhard Seminars Training, always written in lowercase) was one of many popular therapeutic or "human potential" movements that developed around this time in the United States. These movements, of which est was one of the most successful, shared several characteristics, including a focus on individual well-being and a sense of optimism about human possibilities. est was developed from the beginning as a well-organized business enterprise, structured to maximize profits and minimize tax liabilities. Its major corporate arm, Transformational Technologies, is an extreme example of the rationality that pervades some such movements that have as a major goal the maximizing of profit (Tipton 1988). By 1988, it had trained nearly 400,000 people, all of whom had taken the two-weekend, 60-hour training session, paying a sizable fee ($400 per person) for so doing. est grossed some $30 million dollars in 1981, and it was claimed that one of every nine San Francisco Bay Area college-educated young people had gone through the training.

Erhard has become a controversial figure, with many lawsuits against him, mostly by the Internal Revenue Service but including some by his own family members. The controversies have contributed to Erhard reestablishing his enterprise under a new name—The Forum—which is the organizational form under which he operates currently.

—*James T. Richardson*

REFERENCES

A. Bry, *60 Hours That Transform Your Life* (New York: Avon, 1976); H. Clinewell, "Popular Therapeutic Movements and Psychologies," in *Dictionary of Pastoral Care and Counseling*, ed. R. Hunter (Nashville: Abingdon, 1990): 928-929; S. Tipton, *Getting Saved from the Sixties* (Berkeley: University of California Press, 1982); S. Tipton, "Rationalizing Religion as a Corporate Enterprise," in *Money and Power in the New Religions*, ed. J. T. Richardson (Lewiston, N.Y.: Mellen, 1988): 223-240.

ETHICS, PROFESSIONAL   One may distinguish morality, which is a practical matter of acting rightly, from ethics, a general matter of how to seek clarity in difficult moral cases. The social scientists who study religion have no code of ethics of their own, but their several disciplines have such codes.

The study of religion raises some ethical questions that do not often arise in other areas. One's identification with a religion and the level of commitment represented by that identification are matters proper to the person and to the person's mode of living. It is relatively easy for academics to do symbolic violence to consciences that may be tender, to persons who may have but a limited verbal apparatus at hand to articulate subtle nuances of belief, or to communities that may enshrine important values in religions. One person's atheism may play an instrumental role in establishing intellectual autonomy. Another person's conversion may have prevented despair and suicide. For another person yet, a tradition may invoke all goodness that lies beyond instrumental reason.

Ethical questions need to mediate among several kinds of objects that may bear moral value. First, there are norms, the content of which may be morally neutral but the authority of which may not be. For example, wearing a veil, hat, or yarmulke in a given place may be morally neutral, except for being prescribed or proscribed in a given society. Second, there are acts that themselves are morally weighted; most people do not utter falsehoods, for example, without having qualms. Third, there is the matter of identity; some moral obligations need be met by particular persons, not just anybody (e.g., disciplining a child). Fourth, there are the consequences of a deed; a given action may be innocent enough (e.g., revealing a source to whom no promise of anonymity had been given), but foreseeable consequences may lead one to refrain from doing so.

Norms   Norms relevant to the social scientific study of religion include the wider norms of the society in which one lives, the norms of the religious groupings under study, and the professional norms of the social scientists themselves. Norms are relative; they are engendered by social groupings. The norms of religions have at times been foundational to the cultures of whole civilizations; however, they change as they come to be applied in new situations. Historians and historical sociologists of religion have the power to affect the course of normative developments by reaching into the past and finding new relevances in a heritage. There is consequently an ethical duty not only to be respectful of normative heritages but also to be critical of them in the light of present social needs (see Séguy 1984).

Social scientists informally follow many professional norms. They cooperate with colleagues irrespective of their religions. They report technical shortcomings and problems that arise in the course of their research, which in the study of something as elusive as religion are common. They report findings that, because of their own persuasions, they wish were otherwise. They exercise caution in citation practices, crediting another whose work is helpful but avoiding attributing to another stances that the other has not publicly expressed. Moreover, social scientists are not cited with any religious modifiers attached to their identities; doing so would imply that there are confessional motives rather than scientific ideas or findings under review. Finally, social scientists acknowledge relevant funding sources, the contexts in which research opportunities arise, and any policy questions that may have led to the formulation of research questions.

Activities   Activities of social scientists who study religion are often value-relevant. Because people in general need information upon which to base their moral judgments, the social scientific activities of collecting, analyzing, interpreting, and disseminating information have moral importance. This brings to bear on the scientist the imperative to provide accurate, sufficiently complete as to be adequate, and fair portrayals of various religions, practices, and adherents.

Conducting inquiry raises many issues and has led to developing ethical standards in research (Babbie 1995). If a project might place people at risk of civil or criminal liability, financial cost, or damaged employment prospects, one seeks advice and permission from institutional review boards, which universities routinely empanel. The participation of individuals as subjects in interviews or as respondents to questionnaires needs to be voluntary; prisons, training facilities, and even university classrooms may not leave potential subjects feeling free not to participate. Surreptitious observation of people's private lives or the use of deception is deemed unethical because it infringes on this principle of voluntary participation (for a case of qualms developing during research, see Alfred 1976). In the cases of interviews, questionnaires, and participant observation, guarantees of anonymity are usually given and kept. In some instances where potential controversial information is obtained, it may be advisable to destroy as soon as possible information that may be used to establish identities, lest files be subpoenaed and put to uses that would violate guarantees that the researcher has given. Sometimes it is necessary to conceal the specific purpose of a study, lest people artificially do or say things so as to affect the findings; in such cases, there is often a broad statement of purpose and sometimes a "debriefing" during which people can withdraw permission to use data they have given.

Denominational officials and even publishers sometimes attempt to keep studies of religious phenomena from being published. Because of the contingencies of research funds and publishing rights, proprietary claims may exist that can be used to inhibit the dissemination of information. Threats of litigation and the filing of suits against scholars are by no means unknown. In general, proprietary claims can be valid with respect to particular interview or questionnaire data or to particular accumulations of field notes as well as to creative literary texts; they are not valid with respect to general findings, public domain information, or new literary texts that are created differently in concept and structure from ones to which proprietary rights apply.

Scholars have debated presenting studies of controversial religions in conferences funded by and organized under the auspices of the controversial religions themselves. The concern is that the scientists might be co-opted by a religion under study, and subtly, if not blatantly, lose their objectivity (Horowitz 1978). In informal discussions, concern has been expressed about whether scientists should accept invitations for expense-paid trips to such conferences, whether they should publish their findings in volumes subsidized by the religious bodies, whether compromised individuals might form a powerful scholarly network, and

whether work in the whole field would lose credibility because of the appearance of being compromised. Journal editors have declined offers even from non-controversial religions for special subsidized issues because of these discussions. Editor Roger O'Toole of *Sociological Analy- sis* (now *Sociology of Religion*) published a symposium in 1983 designed to bring the discussion into the open; there was general agreement on principles but disagreement over whether co-optation had taken place. One view, expressed by Irving Louis Horowitz, was that if a religion were pursuing a pernicious objective, there would be an ethical obligation to study not merely its workings and the backgrounds of its members but also its wider purposes. This concern is analogous to one expressed by Marie Augusta Neal (1972: 129), that sociological analyses that serve a prophetic purpose are criminalized by some regimes while those that do not are made required reading. The distribution of disposable resources in a society can affect the balanced or imbalanced nature of social scientific inquiry and publication, and the study of religion is not immune to this possibility.

Among the personal stratagems described in the 1983 *Sociological Analysis* symposium was that of Bryan Wilson, who made his participation in any conference conditional upon, inter alia, his being free to say what he chose and not be subjected to any propagandistic addresses; he did not want to be co-opted and did not want to lend his reputation to any campaign of advocacy. Eileen Barker found the conferences useful for obtaining some information for her studies, but she declined honoraria and accepted only travel reimbursements that would have been covered anyway from other sources; she did not want her own financial position affected by the group she was studying.

Beyond conducting research and reporting it, there is another kind of relevant activity—serving as experts. Scholars know that there are multiple explanations of events in social life, religious events included; but the superficiality of the media and the quest for one-sided decisions in litigation do not allow for an honest circumspection regarding multiple explanations. The expert is left in the quandary of how to give "yes" and "no" answers when truthfulness demands greater nuance. Moreover, there seems to be no shortage of perpetrators of such pseudoscientific notions as "brainwashing" and "snapping" to give media operatives and attorneys the simplistic testimony they want (Shinn 1992).

Identity   The identity of the social scientist, as an ethical matter, pertains to what the scientist should or should not do by virtue of being a scientist. The scientist is someone who needs to maintain access to information that may be private or sensitive in nature. Because of the wider social significance of knowledge, it is important in the social world for people to be able to talk to scientists, answer questionnaires, and share their experiences with observers, without having their privacy violated. Thus the social scientist not only needs to protect the anonymity of sources as a promise to be kept, as discussed above, but also by virtue of being a member of a profession that plays a significant role in society. Moreover, it is incumbent on others not to attempt to compromise the privacy of social scientists' sources, save for the gravest of reasons.

The identity of the social scientist also involves responsibilities regarding the accurate and adequate dissemination of information. The scientist is the custodian of certain kinds of information. Publishing is not a mere stratagem for personal career advancement but an obligation. Many social scientists present lectures on a pro bono basis; others conduct research for groups that cannot pay anything; and still others serve as consultants for a variety of community organizations. The scientist who studies religion not only consults on matters involving information about religion but also, because of having gained the confidence of religious officials, is asked to serve in various other capacities for religious organizations.

Consequences Consequences of the research and publication activities of social scientists of religion vary from the relatively immediate to the remote. The concern that no harm come to the subjects of research pertains to relatively immediate consequences; the process itself should not occasion an attack on respondents' self-concepts or affect their levels of religiosity. Such possibilities are more relevant to participant observation research than questionnaire surveys, but even in the latter the researcher needs to be careful when delegating data collection to others. Religious officials who have distributed questionnaires for researchers have been known to lecture groups of respondents about what were supposed to be confidential responses (Babbie 1995:450). The concern over maintaining professional confidences is a traditional one in ethics and takes the form in the contemporary world of the right to privacy (Hurley 1982:53).

In general, the social scientific study of religion has revealed the extent of the variety of religious and moral systems; this is particularly true of cultural anthropology and comparative studies. The remote but inevitable result of this is that it becomes increasingly difficult for educated people to condemn actions that violate their own standards but appear to work no harm on anyone. For better or for worse, social science furthers broad-mindedness and thereby is value-relevant. The remoteness of such consequences often makes adequate foresight difficult if not impossible in this regard. Consequently, the ethics of scientific pursuits rarely takes the form of applying a priori principles to projected actions but, instead, takes the form of finding oneself in an activity that engenders, furthers, or inhibits some social change and intellectually evaluating one's own contribution well after having begun a line of inquiry (see Caceres 1990).

—*Anthony J. Blasi*

REFERENCES

R. Alfred, "The Church of Satan," in *The New Religious Consciousness,* ed. C. Y. Glock and R. N. Bellah (Berkeley: University of California Press, 1976): 180-202; E. Babbie, *The Practice of Social Research,* 7th ed. (Belmont, Calif.: Wadsworth, 1995); M. Caceres, "Gramsci et l'éthique," *Social Compass* 37(1990):353-366; I. L. Horowitz, *Science, Sin and Scholarship* (Cambridge: MIT Press, 1978); M. Hurley, *The Church and Science* (Boston: Daughters of St. Paul, 1982); M. A. Neal, "How Prophecy Lives," *Sociological Analysis* 33(1972):125-141; R. O'Toole (ed.), "Symposium on Scholarship and Sponsorship," *Sociological Analysis* 44(1983):179-225; J. Séguy, "Ernst Troeltsch," *Social Compass* 31(1984):169-183; L. D. Shinn, "Cult Conversions and the Courts," *Sociological Analysis* 53(1992):273-285.

ETHNICITY Most definitions of *ethnicity* include two central elements: a shared culture and a real or putative common ancestry. E. K. Francis (1947) defined the ethnic group as a subtype of *Gemeinschaft* groups, which was a secondary group with some of the features of a primary group. The term *ethnicity* was first used by W. Lloyd Warner in his community studies, particularly in the work on "Yankee City" (Sollors 1981:259 f.). The use of the term *ethnic* dates to a century earlier but was not widely employed prior to the publication of William Graham Sumner's *Folkways* (1906). Since midcentury, both *ethnicity* and *ethnic* have been used widely to describe certain types of identity and group affiliation, although without consensus about what they mean.

Some scholars have sought to define the ethnic group in the broadest terms possible. This can be seen in the case of the editors of the *Harvard Encyclopedia of American Ethnic Groups* (Thernstrom et al. 1980:vi), when, in seeking to define ethnic groups, they offered the following list of features that they contended tend to coexist in various and differing combinations: common geographic origin; migratory status; race; language or dialect; religious faith or faiths; ties that transcend kinship, neighborhood, and community boundaries; shared traditions, values, and symbols; literature, folklore, and music; food preferences; settlement and employment patterns; special interests in regard to politics; institutions that specifically serve and maintain the group; an internal sense of distinctiveness; and an external perception of distinctiveness.

By contrast, other scholars have sought to construct far more parsimonious definitions. Wsevold Isajiw (1979:25), for example, defined the ethnic group as "an involuntary group of people who share the same culture or the descendants of such people who might identify themselves and/or are identified by others as belonging to the same involuntary group." He explicitly argued for the need to differentiate religious groups from ethnic groups.

However, most scholars have argued that religion and ethnicity are often intertwined and frequently mutually reinforcing. Indeed, like language, traditions, and values, religion is often one of the key building blocks of ethnic cultures (see Gordon 1964, Schermerhorn 1978).

Ethnic America   Given the sheer diversity of ethnic America, there is considerable variation in the relationships between ethnicity and religion among its constituent peoples. Historically, British settlers played a hegemonic role in constructing a white, Anglo-Saxon, Protestant culture. However, immigrants from the British Isles were not as religiously or culturally homogeneous as many commentators assume. While Cavaliers were traditionalists who remained loyal to the Church of England, Puritans and Quakers represented important dissenting religious groups that reflected distinctive constellations of cultural values. For example, while the Cavaliers were a central element among the slaveholding class in the South, the Quakers' antipathy toward slavery led to the establishment from within their ranks of the first antislavery society in the Western world. In the case of the Scots-Irish, a fusion of an ethnic identity defined as separate from the English and an allegiance to Presbyterianism set this group apart (Fischer 1989, Bailyn 1986).

In the case of Germans, the second largest European immigrant group after the British, Lutherans exhibited differences with both Reformed church bodies and Pietist sects. However, the differences within German America extended beyond Protestantism, as the ethnic community also included Roman Catholics and Enlightenment-inspired political radicals (e.g., the Forty-Eighters) who were outspoken opponents of religion.

By contrast, the Irish were clearly identified with Catholicism, and here religion played a crucial role in forging ethnic group identity and creating ethnic boundaries. The Irish quickly came to dominate the development of Roman Catholicism in the nineteenth century. Investing heavily in the institutional development of Catholicism, the Irish viewed it as a bulwark against absorption into the Anglo-American mainstream. Thus parochial schools were seen as an alternative to the public schools, which were perceived to be in the hands of Protestant elites who were hostile to Catholicism.

The Irish were the first voluntary immigrant group to confront intense nativist hostility, which achieved an organizational presence in such anti-Irish groups as the Order of the Star-Spangled Banner and the Know-Nothing Party. Anti-Irish sentiment had three components. First, the Irish were seen as a social problem, manifested in high levels of alcoholism, criminal activity, and other antisocial behavior. Second, they were accused of undermining democracy because of their propensity to align themselves with urban political machines. Finally, they were criticized because of their Catholicism, which was depicted as authoritarian and antidemocratic, and thus a potential threat to political freedom (Higham 1970).

This conflict would set the stage for the cultural wars that ensued during the period of the Great Migration—from 1880 to 1930—when the sheer volume of immigration transformed the ethnic character of the nation. During this period, immigrants from eastern and southern Europe outnumbered those from western Europe. Christians among these new immigrants were more likely to be Roman Catholic or Eastern Orthodox rather than Protestant. Two of the largest immigrant groups, Italians and Poles, were overwhelmingly identified with Roman Catholicism, while Greek immigrants constituted the largest group among the Eastern Orthodox. During the same time, approximately 3 million Jews from eastern Europe emigrated to the United States.

Religion and Ethnicity   The relationship between ethnicity and religion for these new arrivals varied. For example, religion and its institutional manifestations played a less significant role in the Italian community than it did in either the Irish or the Polish community. Italians had a long history of hostility to the Catholic Church, due to the impact of secular ideals, the continuing impact of magic in the place of religion, and a tradition of anticlericism. Added to these transplanted negative orientations toward Roman Catholicism, Italians in America were often suspicious of the Irish dominance of the Catholic Church in America; the

Italian aversion to parochial education was partly due to a desire to protect their children from "Irishization" (Kivisto 1995).

By contrast, the central institution of the Polish American community was the Roman Catholic Church. Polish religiosity was high, in no small part because religion and nationalism were intertwined in Poland, given that religion was a key ideological source of resistance to external domination. Not a surprise, in the United States, Poles reacted differently from Italians to Irish domination of the church. They demanded Polish-speaking priests in their parishes and sought representation in the ranks of the church hierarchy. In a conflict with the established church, the excommunication of a Polish priest led in 1904 to the establishment by the dissidents of an independent church body, the Polish National Church (Greene 1975), which was subsequently transported back to Poland (although relatively insignificant in its numbers).

For some groups, religion and ethnicity are integrally connected. Among these "religio-ethnic groups," we include Jews, Greeks, Amish, and Hutterites. Jews are the largest and most complicated of these religio-ethnic groups. The Jewish community was divided along several intersecting cleavages. First, as a diaspora people, Jews in America arrived from different geographic origins: Sephardic Jews from Spain and Portugal, the earliest arrivals; Ashkenazic Jews from Germany, whose arrival began in the first half of the nineteenth century; and eastern European Jews, who arrived en masse after 1880. Jews were divided between secularists and religious practitioners. They were divided between those urging assimilation and those intent on remaining apart from the larger society. Within the world of religious Jewry, three major religious expressions emerged. Orthodox Jews represented the forces of traditionalism, with a demand for the strict observance of Jewish law *(halach)*. Reform Judaism was an assimilative response to Orthodox traditionalism. Reform Jews sought accommodation with the outside world and were receptive to modernization and Enlightenment thought. Between these poles, Conservative Jews sought to find a middle ground by seeking to balance the demands of traditionalism against the benefits of modernity.

Religious differences between the host society and the wave of new arrivals—Christians and Jews—were compounded by cultural and linguistic differences and by the generally impoverished state of the new immigrants. Nativist hostility intensified during the first two decades of the twentieth century. Racialist thought during the era tended to convolute biology and culture, the net result being the depiction of unbridled immigration leading to a degeneration of American culture—a culture seen as defined by "Nordic" peoples—due to the presence of large numbers of intellectual and moral inferiors. This presumed debasement of the culture meant that the righteous Protestant empire was under assault by papists, Christ-killers, and others seen as hostile to the religious worldview of the dominant culture.

Assimilation Versus Pluralism   On the other hand, those with a more optimistic view about the transformative capacity of American society urged on the immigrants Americanization campaigns. These campaigns were intended to eradicate the cultural heritages of the immigrants, instilling in them what were deemed to be genuinely American cultural values. Advocates of the melting pot in the popular media and scholarly exponents of assimilationist theories—and these included most of the prominent sociologists associated with the Chicago School of sociology, such as William I. Thomas and Robert E. Park—thought this would be the inevitable outcome of intergroup relations over time. They did not specifically address what this meant in terms of the religious identities of the new immigrants: Although nobody suggested that a large-scale conversion to Protestantism was likely, they tended to assume either increased secularization, and with it the growing irrelevance of religious institutions, or the transformation of immigrant religions into modified forms modeled more or less closely after Protestantism.

An influential critique of the melting pot thesis came from philosopher Horace Kallen (1924 [1915]) in an article in *The Nation* titled "Democracy *Versus* the Melting Pot." He contended that the demand to repudiate ethnic cultures was antithetical to democratic ideals. Moreover, he claimed that self-identity was partially based on an identification with one's ancestral background. In calling for what he termed "cultural pluralism," Kallen urged the preservation and strengthening of ethnic ties, with the end being to ensure the perpetuation of distinctive and separate subcultures.

In a different fashion, cultural critic Randolph Bourne (1977[1916]) criticized the "100% Americanization" campaigns of the era, urging instead the emergence of what he referred to as a "trans-national America," which not merely implied the preservation of immigrant cultures but also saw their progressive integration into the culture as contributing to a transformation of American culture itself. This was seen as a way of rejuvenating the national culture, which would occur in a dialectical process in which both immigrant cultures and the national culture would be receptive to the other. The result would be a new culture, different from the heretofore hegemonic WASP culture.

Anti-immigration forces won out and in 1924 legislation was passed that effectively ended mass immigration for the next four decades. During that time, considerable assimilation occurred among the second- and third-generation offspring of the new immigrants. Ethnic communal institutions declined in numbers and influence, and members exited ethnic enclaves, frequently moving from central cities to the suburbs. In short, European-origin ethnic groups experienced considerable cultural and structural assimilation.

However, according to sociologist Ruby Jo Reeves Kennedy (1944), when looking at intermarriage, a crucial indicator of assimilation, one could detect a shift in which religion began to replace ethnicity as a barrier to intermarriage. In a study of New Haven, Connecticut, from 1870 to 1940, she contended that ethnic intermarriages increased for all groups except Jews, but that they did not occur randomly. British, German, and Scandinavians intermarried mutually, based on the common link of Protestantism. A similar pattern emerged among the Catholic groups in the city: Irish, Italians, and Poles. Among Jews, she detected movement across the lines of the three major religious expressions within the religio-ethnic community. Kennedy referred to this as the "triple melting pot." While Cheri Peach (1980) has reexamined Kennedy's findings and questioned whether or not religion actually did replace ethnicity as a determinant in mate selection, the notion of the triple melting pot had larger cultural implications.

These implications were made explicit in Will Herberg's highly influential *Protestant-Catholic-Jew* (Doubleday 1955). Herberg contended, parallel to Kennedy's thesis, that the salience of ethnicity would progressively erode, to be replaced by a heightened affiliative salience of the three religious traditions. Herberg argued, in effect, that the religious character of the nation has changed. America was by the middle of the twentieth century no longer a Protestant empire but defined itself as a Judeo-Christian land in which each of these three religious expressions was accorded a place in the nation's religious pantheon. This was, not surprisingly, an era in which anti-Catholic and anti-Semitic prejudice declined considerably and the ecumenical movement was at its peak. It was a period that stressed religious tolerance and the mutual appreciation of these major religions expressions, each of which was accorded a prominent place under the sacred canopy of the American civil religion.

The New Immigrants   In 1965, a reformulation of existing immigration laws established the basis for a new wave of mass immigration, which has been occurring since 1968, when the new law took effect. Three consequences of the Hart-Cellar Act are of particular importance: It made possible a sizable increase in the volume of immigration; by ending racist-inspired national quotas, it facilitated a dramatic increase in the number of immigrants from Asia and Latin America; and it encouraged professionals (an instance of the "brain drain" from the less developed countries) to migrate, thereby increasing the number of middle-class immigrants (Takaki 1993).

As a consequence of the recommencement of mass immigration, the ethnic landscape has changed in significant ways. In the first place, the newcomers are overwhelmingly from places other than Europe. Asians account for 37% of the total number of immigrants arriving between 1960 and 1989, with the largest Asian groups being Filipino, Chinese, Korean, and Vietnamese. Hispanics from various Latin American nations account for 39% of immigrants during the same period. They have come primarily from Mexico, Puerto Rico (these are not strictly speaking immigrants given the island's territorial status), and Cuba. Although their numbers are much smaller than the above-noted groups, immigrants from the Middle East have had an impact on certain regional areas, such as the Syrian and Lebanese populations in metropolitan Detroit. In addition, a number of smaller groups have arrived. These include such diverse peoples as Jews (from Russia, Israel, and elsewhere in the Middle East), Haitians, Dominicans, Jamaicans, Salvadorans, Colombians, and Cambodians.

Among the changes that are in process is the infusion of new coreligionists within Protestantism, Catholicism, and Judaism. The largest infusion is from Catholic immigrants, with the result being that Catholics are now a higher percentage of the total population than before. This is primarily due to the fact that most Latin American and Filipino immigrants are Catholic. At the same time, new Protestants have arrived, especially from Korea (although South Korea is predominantly Buddhist, most immigrants are Protestants) and from Latin America, which is witnessing inroads by evangelical Protestants. For Jews, many of the new arrivals come from cultures quite different from those rooted in Europe, and this has led to problems of mutual accommodation.

The second change brought about by recent immigration is the rise in the numbers of people who are neither Christian nor Jewish. While a wide range of new religions are represented among the new immigrants, including Jamaican Rastafarians, Caribbean practitioners of Santeria, and Sikhs and Jains from India, of particular consequence is the rise in the number of adherents to the major world religious traditions: Islam, Hinduism, and Buddhism. Although it is difficult to determine precise numbers of adherents to these traditions, it is clear that Islam, with an estimated 2-3 million members in America today, has the largest presence among these traditions. It is also clear that, particularly in major metropolitan areas where new immigrants are concentrated, an institutional presence is being created, with an expanding number of mosques and temples. The result, as R. Stephen Warner (1993:1061) posed it, is that "the purely religious boundaries of American religious pluralism have expanded." It is this expansion of pluralism that has become a focal point of the recent cultural "wars," as those on the political right have voiced concerns about the impact of new religious traditions on American culture, while multiculturalists (the era's cultural pluralists) argue for the need for inclusiveness.

—*Peter Kivisto*

REFERENCES

B. Bailyn, *The Peopling of North America* (New York: Knopf, 1986); R. Bourne, *The Radical Will* (New York: Urizen, 1977); D. Fischer, *Albion's Seed* (New York: Oxford University Press, 1989); E. K. Francis, "The Nature of the Ethnic Group," *American Journal of Sociology* 52(1947):393-400; M. Gordon, *Assimilation in American Life* (New York: Oxford University Press, 1964); V. Greene, *For God and Country* (Madison: Wisconsin Historical Society, 1975); J. Higham, *Strangers in the Land* (New York: Atheneum, 1970); W. Isajiw, *Definitions of Ethnicity* (Toronto: Multicultural History Society, 1979); H. Kallen, *Culture and Democracy in the United States* (Salem, N.H.: Ayer, 1924); R. Kennedy, "Single or Triple Melting Pot?" *American Journal of Sociology* 49(1944):331-339; P. Kivisto, *Americans All* (Belmont, Calif.: Wadsworth, 1995); C. Peach, "Which Triple Melting Pot?" *Ethnic and Racial Studies* 3(1980):1-16; R. A. Schermerhorn, *Comparative Ethnic Relations* (New York: Random House, 1978); W. Sollors, "Theories of Ethnicity," *American Quarterly* 33(1981):257-283; W. G. Sumner, *Folkways* (Boston: Ginn, 1906); R. Takaki, *A Different Mirror* (Boston: Little, Brown, 1993); S. Thernstrom et al., *Harvard Encyclopedia of American Ethnic Groups* (Cambridge: Harvard Belknap Press, 1980); R. S. Warner, "Toward a New Paradigm," *American Journal of Sociology* 98(1993):1044-1093.

ETHNOCENTRISM   The use of one's own culture as a basis for judging other cultures. Generally, ethnocentrism assumes the superiority of one's own culture and is an inevitability, given that most people are reared in and are familiar with only one culture. Ethnocentrism may serve positive functions for society; for example, it encourages and reinforces group solidarity. But it also can have a negative impact. Ethnocentrism discourages rapid assimilation into another culture and, in its most negative aspects, can contribute to racial and ethnic prejudices, foster conflict, and provide a rationale for suspicion and hostility in dealings with outsiders.

—*Steven D. Glazier*

ETHOS   The general spirit or collective sentiment informing a people's activities or institutions; used in this sense already by Aristotle *(Rhetoric)*, the term's sociological bearings were developed especially in William Graham Sumner's *Folkways*. He emphasized that the ethos of a people represented the totality of cultural traits that individualized them and differentiated them from other groups. This included especially the folkways and mores. The folkways emerged from repeated actions serving the common needs or interests of a group in the struggle for existence. The addition of philosophical or ethical reflection concerning the contribution of the folkways to the public welfare led to the emergence of mores. Religion emerges in this latter context in response to the "aleatory" element in life, that is, good or bad fortune, the fact that expedient practices often fail to produce the desired results. The group's ethos is, in part, expressed in its distinctive response to the aleatory interest, that is, in its religion.

The problems of national character, cultural relativism, ethnocentrism, and in-group/out-group relations all emerge from this matrix of social life, including religion. Group ethos is generally opposed to cosmopolitanism, although Sumner also recognized that a transnational ethos (or "civilization") existed for larger unities such as Europe, China, the Hindus, and others. The ethos thus separates groups and provides the standpoint from which one group criticizes another.

These concepts have become the stock in trade of sociology. Although the idea of "national character" has lost much of its appeal, the notions of cultural relativism, ethnocentrism, and in-group/out-group relations remain central to current controversies over culture.

—*Donald A. Nielsen*

REFERENCES

A. Inkeles, *National Character* (New Brunswick, N.J.: Transaction, 1997); W. G. Sumner, *Folkways* (New York: Ginn, 1906).

EVALUATION RESEARCH   The application of scientific method to determining the overall benefits (or detriments) of practical, program implementations of "public policies." Interest in such research has been spurred by national legislators who desire to learn whether alternative, remedial programs in, for example, education, health care, criminal justice, and welfare have "paid off"—that is, whether they have met the criteria of efficiency (costs) and/or effectiveness (projected goals). *Church policy* refers to all programs and activities, including goals and implementations, carried on by denominations and congregations. *Evaluation* employs the basic tools of rational problem-solving, concentrating on determining the clarity of stated program objectives and the adequacy of program means used to reach such goals as well as uncovering undesired "side effects." Unfortunately, however, religious groups often adopt unstated, conflicting, or ambiguous goals, making evaluation difficult or impossible. Some authorities even term religious groups *goalless.*

The following are examples of current "policy" controversies in the churches that need elucidation by evaluation research: whether and to what extent numerical growth should be the prime goal of denominations and their congregational units; whether and to what extent worship services should be based upon so-called entertainment models; whether and to what extent monetary contributing should be based on "tithing" models; whether and to what extent the traditional homily (versus alternate communication modes) should be the main pastoral vehicle for teaching and motivating; whether and to what extent the building of "small groups" within large congregations increases solidarity.

See also Decision Making, Organization Theory

—*Ross P. Scherer*

REFERENCES

T. R. Dye, *Understanding Public Policy* (Englewood Cliffs, N.J.: Prentice Hall, 1992); P. H. Rossi and H. E. Freeman, *Evaluation* (Beverly Hills, Calif.: Sage, 1985).

EVANGELICALISM   The word *evangelical* comes from the Greek word *euangelion,* used in the New Testament to describe the "good news" of salvation through Jesus Christ, and often translated as the "evangel" (see Hill 1989). From the Greek root, we get the verb *to evangelize,* the nouns *evangelist* and *evangelicalism,* and the adjective *evangelical.* Prior to the Reformation, the word *evangelical* described all of Christianity and meant believing and proclaiming the evangel, but following Luther the word took on more specific meanings as well as emphases on the authority of Scripture (the source of the evangel) and on salvation by grace through faith (the message of the evangel). This pattern would repeat itself many times throughout the centuries: the rise of a sectarian movement charging established churches with diluting the evangel and accommodating the culture. As a result, the very meaning of the word *evangelical* has changed over the years. These changes have caused enough confusion to lead one scholar to suggest that the term be abandoned (Dayton 1991).

R. Stephen Warner (1975) and James Davison Hunter (1982, 1983) began the social scientific effort to clarify the meaning and measurement of contemporary American evangelicalism. Using survey data collected by the Gallup organization, Hunter (1983:141) devised criteria for identifying "evangelicals": Protestant affiliation, belief in the inerrancy of Scripture and the divinity of Christ, and either belief that Christ is the only way to salvation or the "experience" of conversion, or both. Building upon this, we can explore the meaning and measurement of evangelicalism, focusing on (1) doctrinal essentials or "distinctives," (2) religious movements closely associated with these doctrines, and (3) religious tradition, churches, and denominations associated with these doctrines and movements.

Doctrinal Distinctives   Every religion has a belief component or a series of doctrinal essentials. Evangelicalism is no different. We developed a small number of criteria that would cover the "minimal" essentials for

Table E.1 Various Operational Measures of Evangelicalism

A	B	C
Doctrinal Distinctives	*Movement Criteria*	*Religious Traditions*
Bible "True," 44%	Fundamentalist, 5%	Evangelical Protestant, 26%
Jesus Only, 46%	Charismatic or	Roman Catholic, 23%
Witness, 37%	Pentecostal, 8%	Mainline Protestant, 17%
Born Again, 31%	Evangelical, 4%	Secular, 20%
All Four, 14%		Black Protestant, 8%
		All Others, 7%

NOTE: Percentages of the U.S. population identified as "evangelical" by doctrinal distinctives, movements, and religious tradition.

adequate conceptualization but few enough so that space would not be a problem in most surveys. Four criteria were used: (a) salvation only through faith in Jesus Christ (the mechanism of the evangel); (b) an experience of personal conversion, commonly called being "born again" (the mechanics of the evangel); (c) the importance of missions and evangelism (sharing the message of the evangel); and (d) the truth or inerrancy of Scripture (the source of the evangel). These distinctives capture the minimal essence of the term *evangelical* in its contemporary American manifestation (see also Babbington 1989, Kellstedt and Green 1996).

The results of a large national survey ($N = 4,001$) show that from 31% to 46% of the U.S. population affirm these evangelical distinctives (see Table E.1, section A). Does that mean that the size of the evangelical population in the United States is somewhere between 31% to 46%? The answer is *yes* if a *single* measure of evangelical doctrine is used. If all four of the distinctives are employed, however, only 14% of the population meet these criteria.

Religious Movement Evangelicalism is more than a set of doctrinal distinctives. These distinctives get embodied in social institutions or in movements dedicated to reforming and revitalizing existing institutions. Americans are famous for sectlike movements, some operating today such as fundamentalism, pentecostalism, the charismatic movement, and "evangelicalism" (not to be confused with "evangelical" doctrines or tradition). In contrast to the affirmation of the doctrinal distinctives, movement affiliation is much smaller, with just under one-twentieth of the population affiliating with evangelicalism and fundamentalism and about twice as many with the "spirit-filled" movements, pentecostalism and the charismatic (see Table E.1, section B). By this approach, 17% of the population can be

classified as "evangelical." They are the "card-carrying" members of the evangelical community.

Religious Tradition Evangelicalism is more than doctrinal distinctives and religious movements, it is also an aggregate of local churches and denominations, or what we call a religious "tradition." The "evangelical" tradition affirms the doctrinal essentials and/or is part of the religious movements. It includes large "subtraditions" such as the Baptist, Pentecostal, Holiness churches and the growing number of nondenominational churches. "Evangelical" as religious tradition presumes careful measurement of denominational affiliation, a care rarely taken in surveys. To illustrate, the answer "Presbyterian" to a survey question does not permit differentiation between the moderate to liberal Presbyterian Church USA (PCUSA) and the conservative Presbyterian Church in America (PCA). To surmount these difficulties, specific affiliation was obtained through detailed probes. Then doctrinal stands and institutional histories were examined to assign denominations to distinct religious traditions using the work of scholars such as Melton (1991) to assist in the process. We can identify four relatively large religious traditions in addition to the evangelical Protestant: mainline Protestant, black Protestant, Roman Catholic, and an unaffiliated group that may be called "seculars." (Assigning denominations to the three Protestant traditions is, of course, subject to error. This is particularly the case for smaller, lesser known denominations. Still, defensible assignments can be made; see Kellstedt and Green 1993:70 f)

By this method, roughly one-fourth of the American population is "evangelical" (see Table E.1, section C), slightly fewer are Roman Catholic, somewhat less than one-fifth are mainline Protestant, with about one-fifth "secular" and 8% black Protestant. Smaller traditions

Table E.2 Pro-Life Attitudes* on Abortion for Groups Based on Combinations of Doctrinal Distinctives, Religious Movements, and Traditions

Combinations	Percentage of Population	Percentage Pro-Life
4 Doctrines, Evangelical Tradition, + Movement	5.1	81
3 Doctrines, Evangelical Tradition, + Movement	3.8	70
4 Doctrines, Evangelical Tradition, No Movement	3.2	65
3 or 4 Doctrines, Catholic	4.0	56
3 or 4 Doctrines, Black, + Movement	1.9	56
3 or 4 Doctrines, Mainline, + Movement	1.5	55
3 Doctrines, Evangelical Tradition, No Movement	4.0	50
3 or 4 Doctrines, Mainline, No Movement	5.1	46
1 or 2 Doctrines, Evangelical Tradition, + Movement	3.2	36
0 to 2 Doctrines, Evangelical Tradition, No Movement	8.3	28
National Average	100.0	38

*Pro-life attitudes on abortion include respondents who oppose abortion in all circumstances or would permit abortion only in extreme circumstances, for example, when the life of the mother was at stake.

such as Jews, Eastern Orthodoxy, Muslims, and others account for the remaining 7% of the population.

Table E.1 shows that a simple question, "What is an Evangelical?" produces varied answers. It becomes even more complicated if we combine these various measures of evangelicalism (see Table E.2). The first entry identifies "true-blue" evangelicals who hold all four doctrinal distinctives, affiliate with an evangelical movement, and belong to a church or denomination in the evangelical tradition. This group numbers about 5% of the adult population—small but still significant, outnumbering Jews and Episcopalians two to one. If the second entry is added (those holding three doctrinal essentials plus movement and tradition affiliation), the 5% figure jumps to almost 9%. These findings suggest that the core of evangelicalism is small but intense. If mainline and black Protestants with three or four doctrinal distinctives and movement identification, as well as Roman Catholics who meet the doctrinal criteria (few Catholics identify with evangelical movements), are added to the 9% figure, about one-sixth of the population is "distinctively evangelical." This figure jumps to almost three of ten if the movement criterion is ignored. Mobilizing such a disparate group is not easy, but its size makes it an important force in the society.

Do the combinations in Table E.2 make a difference? The answer is a resounding "yes" if just one issue, abortion, is examined. Research has shown that evangelicals are strongly pro-life on abortion (Kellstedt et al. 1994), but the data in the second column of Table E.2 show that the degree of pro-life support depends on how one defines and measures evangelicalism. The combination of all four doctrinal essentials and affiliation with an evangelical tradition and movement has the strongest effect. There is dramatic falloff for pro-life positions on abortion as one moves down the column. Indeed, those who do not hold at least three of the four distinctive evangelical doctrines actually fall *below* the national average pro-life position.

To conclude, the size of the evangelical population depends on how evangelicalism is conceptualized and measured. It ranges from a high of 46%, if only one doctrinal essential is considered, to a low of 5% if a "fine-tuned" definition that includes doctrine, tradition, and movement is used. Understanding religion in America—and its links to politics, for example—calls for this more complex conceptualization and measurement. This is likely to hold true in other societies as well, although not necessarily in reference to the same issues.

—*Lyman Kellstedt, John Green, James Guth, and Corwin Smidt*

REFERENCES

D. Babbington, *Evangelicalism in Modern Britain* (London: Unwin Hyman, 1989); D. W. Dayton, "Some Doubts About the Usefulness of the Category 'Evangelical," in *The Variety of American Evangelicalism,* ed. D. W. Dayton and R. K. Johnson (Knoxville: University of Tennessee Press, 1991): 245-251; S. S. Hill, "What's in a Name?" in *Handbook of Denominations in the United States,* 9th ed., ed. F. S. Mead and S. S. Hill (Nashville: Abingdon, 1989): 251-262; J. D. Hunter, "Operationalizing Evangelicalism," *Sociological Analysis* 42(1982):363-372; J. D. Hunter, *American Evangelicalism* (New Brunswick, N.J.: Rutgers University Press,

1983); L. Kellstedt and J. Green, "The Mismeasure of Evangelicals," *Books and Culture* (Jan.-Feb. 1996): 14-15; L. Kellstedt and J. Green, "Knowing God's Many People," in *Rediscovering the Religious Factor in American Politics*, ed. D. Leege and L. Kellstedt (Armonk, N.Y.: Sharpe, 1993): 53-71; L. Kellstedt, J. Green, J. Guth, and C. Smidt, "Religious Voting Blocs in the 1992 Election," *Sociology of Religion* 55(1994):307-326; J. G. Melton, *The Encyclopedia of American Religions* (Tarrytown, N.Y.: Triumph Books, 1991); R. S. Warner, "Theoretical Barriers to the Understanding of Evangelical Christianity," *Sociological Analysis* 49(1975):1-9.

EVANS-PRITCHARD, E(DWARD) E. (1902-1973)

British social anthropologist who conducted extensive fieldwork on the Azande and the Nuer of the Sudan, including the religious dimensions of their respective cultures. Although E. E. Evans-Pritchard initially wrote in the functionalist tradition of Bronislaw Malinowski, his mentor, he eventually adopted an approach that Morris (1987:189) characterizes as "at once hermeneutic, structural, comparative, and historical."

Witchcraft, Oracles, and Magic Among the Azande (Clarendon 1937) represents a work that marks a shift between these two theoretical orientations. According to Evans-Pritchard, witchcraft beliefs enable people to feel that their misfortunes are not due to their own ignorance, incompetence, or bad luck but are due to people who can be identified and then influenced. Since the accused witch is someone who is perceived to exhibit antisocial behavior, the witchcraft beliefs function to uphold the moral standards of Zande society. Evans-Pritchard argues that Lévy-Bruhl's argument that indigenous people exhibit a "pre-logical" mentality was mistaken. Evans-Pritchard also argues that Zande thought integrated mystical and natural conceptions of causation.

Nuer Religion (Clarendon 1956) fully represents the interpretive approach that Evans-Pritchard's work took in the latter part of his academic career. Evans-Pritchard maintains that religious ideas are sui generis and that the essence of Nuer religion cannot be understood by reference to the functions it performs in relation to larger society. He critiques writers such as Radcliffe-Brown and Durkheim who regarded religion as illusion and whose theories attempted to account for this illusion.

In many ways, *Nuer Religion* constituted a study of religious symbolism that anticipated the development of symbolic anthropology, particularly as it came to be expressed in the works of Victor Turner, Mary Douglas, and Clifford Geertz. Evans-Pritchard gives considerable attention to sacrifice among a cattle pastoral people. In his view, the nature of this rite expresses the great importance of cattle in Nuer society, especially as the rite exists in the relationship between men and their herds, because, ideally, the sacrificial victim is an ox.

—*Hans A. Baer*

REFERENCES

M. Douglas, *Edward Evans-Pritchard* (New York: Penguin, 1980); B. Morris, *Anthropologies of Religion* (Cambridge: Cambridge University Press, 1987).

EVOLUTION OF RELIGION   A framework for understanding the changes in religious systems over long-scale historical time. Robert Bellah's oft-cited statement on religious evolution (1964) treated evolution as "a process of increasing differentiation and complexity of organization," giving some religious systems greater adaptive capacity. This schema focuses attention on how religion as a symbolic system evolves toward "more differentiated, comprehensive, and rationalized formulations," accompanied by changes in conceptions of religious action, religious organization, and the social implications of religion. It traces five stages: primitive, archaic, historical, early modern, and modern religion.

Primitive religious symbolism focuses on mythical beings deeply implicated in all aspects of human life. Religious action is "participation," the ritual enactment of mythical events and the fusing of participants' self-identities with those of mythical beings. A differentiated religious organization does not exist at this stage, or exists only minimally. Durkheim had already identified the social implications of this kind of religious system: socialization of the young and cementing of social solidarity. Primitive religion thus provides little leverage for changing its surrounding world.

Archaic religion exists wherever primitive religion becomes systematized into true cultic worship, usually with the rise of a two-class system of domination made possible by agriculture. Archaic religious symbolism develops when a specialized religious caste reworks and elaborates mythical figures more fully, making them more objectified, definitive, and separate from the human world. This leads to a far more hierarchical conceptualization of the world, although the world is still conceived as a unified whole encompassing this hierarchy. Archaic religious action emphasizes communication through worship—particularly sacrificial worship.

Archaic religious organization remains largely fused with its surrounding social structure, with elite status groups monopolizing religious authority, either directly or through subordinated priesthoods. The social implications are essentially static; religion reinforces social conformity because current arrangements are seen as rooted in the will of divine beings.

The rise of *historic religion* represents a critical turn in human history, occurring sometime during the first millennium B.C.E. in ancient Greece, Confucian China, Buddhist India, and ancient Israel, which itself spawned the later historic religions of Christianity and Islam. The key common denominator among these historic religions is their differentiated conception of some other realm of reality transcending this-worldly life and hierarchically superior to it.

The crucial characteristic of historic religious symbolism is the symbolic dualism generated by this transcendental thrust and rejection/devaluation of this world. *Salvation* becomes the critical goal of religious action, with a new "clearly structured conception of the self" who can be saved. Symbolic dualism leads to a split in the realm of religious organization, as explicitly religiously organized groups gain religious legitimation at least partially autonomous from political authority. The social implications are that these developments gave the historic religions new leverage with which to strive to reform the world, a fulcrum point from which to change a world heretofore all-encompassing. This leverage resulted from the *combination* of a symbolic vantage point from which to judge current social arrangements as moral or immoral and a partially autonomous organizational vantage point from which to work to change those arrangements.

Early modern religion involves dedifferentiating the hierarchical structuring of historic religion. Many of the historic religions generated efforts at this kind of dedifferentiation, but it was originally only institutionalized for the long term in Protestantism. Instead of separation from the world, early modern religion demands engagement in this-worldly action to achieve salvation. Religious symbolism now focuses on individual believers' direct access to the divine, and all worldly life becomes important religious action, through what Weber called ethical striving in a vocation. Religious organization was also dedifferentiated through rejection of the concept of salvation mediated by religious specialists, in favor of direct salvation of individuals. The key social implication of early modern religion was its contribution to the flourishing of voluntary association as the basis for social action in all spheres of life—with results ranging from the development of modern democracy and science to the rise of revolutionary vanguards.

The character of *modern religion* remains hotly debated. The best discussions characterize modern religion critically (Bellah et al. 1985) or sympathetically (Bloom 1990) as locating the divine symbolically within the self. Bellah originally characterized modern religion as involving a collapse of symbolic dualism and a deemphasis on religious organization. This now appears to be moving forward in some settings but also to be refuted by new religious movements and revitalization movements in the modern descendants of the historic religions. Both typically combine close identification of the divine with the self and a strong emphasis on symbolic dualism and religious organization.

The best recent work on this topic has come from Peter Beyer (1994), drawing primarily on work by Luhmann and Robertson.

—*Richard L. Wood*

REFERENCES

R. N. Bellah, "Religious Evolution," *American Sociological Review* 29(1964):358-374; R. N. Bellah et al., *Habits of the Heart* (Berkeley: University of California Press, 1985); P. Beyer, *Religion and Globalization* (London: Sage, 1994); H. Bloom, *The American Religion* (New York: Simon & Schuster, 1992); J. Habermas, *Communication and the Evolution of Society* (Boston: Beacon, 1979); N. Luhmann, *Religious Dogmatics and the Evolution of Societies* (Lewiston, N.Y.: Mellen, 1984); T. Parsons, *The Evolution of Societies* (Englewood Cliffs, N.J.: Prentice Hall, 1977); J. Peacock and A. T. Kirsch, *The Human Direction* (Englewood Cliffs, N.J.: Prentice Hall, 1973); M. Weber, *The Sociology of Religion* (Boston: Beacon, 1993 [1920]).

EXPERIENCE While "religious experience" is commonly named as a central aspect of religion and as a core dimension of religiosity, it has been studied far less frequently than such other aspects as beliefs and practices. This is due at least in part to the fact that the precise referent of "religious experience" is elusive. In addition to being variously defined, it often simply goes undefined, and varieties of it appear under a host of other labels including mystical, ecstatic, numinous, born-again, anomalous, paranormal, out-of-body, flow, transcendental, and conversion experiences.

As there seems not to be any use of the phrase *religious experience* as a technical term prior to William James's *The Varieties of Religious Experience* (VRE: 1902:xiii, n. 6), this discussion necessarily begins with his usage. Although James never defines *religious expe-*

rience as succinctly as he defines *religion,* he does suggest that any experience that combines religious (sacred, Godlike) objects with appropriate emotions (joyfulness, seriousness) constitutes a variety of religious experience (*VRE:* 31).

While James sought the "essence of religious experience . . . in those religious experiences which are most one-sided, exaggerated, and intense" (*VRE:* 44), it is not clear that he intended to limit the study of religious experience only to *extraordinary* experiences. Unfortunately, James's own work, while not equating mysticism and religious experience, does seem to conflate them in arguing that "personal religious experience has its root and centre in mystical states of consciousness." (*VRE:* 301) Thus James's notion that there are a *variety* of religious experiences often has been narrowed to one type: *mysticism.* While mysticism is certainly one variety of religious experience, and while other varieties of religious experience have some of the same characteristics as mysticism, the two are not identical. Mysticism is but one species of the genus religious experience.

Even when scholars have not exclusively studied mysticism under the rubric of religious experience, they have still tended to focus (with James) on the more dramatic, intense types, to the exclusion of more ordinary or mundane experiences. Although James and other early psychologists of religion (e.g., Starbuck, Lueba) pioneered the social scientific study of religious experience near the turn of the twentieth century, it was not until the 1960s that rigorous methods of social scientific inquiry were commonly applied to religious experience. This contemporary period is of interest here.

Empirical Studies of Religious Experience Recalling Ludwig Wittgenstein's dictum that the meaning of a word is in its usage, it will be helpful to review how *religious experience* has been used in contemporary research. While this strategy avoids the question of what religious experience *actually is,* it is a practical way to approach so varied a collection of phenomena. In examining how social scientists have treated religious experience when they have chosen to study it, various aspects of religious experience emerge that, taken together, constitute a partial, although still incomplete, definition of the phenomenon.

The most common operationalization of *religious experience* is in terms of *the sense, feeling, or perception of being in the presence of the sacred, holy, or supernatural.* Stark (1965), in one of the earliest rigorously empirical studies of religious experience, used the following question to get at the phenomenon: "Have you ever as an adult had the feeling that you were somehow

in the presence of God?" He found a high positive response rate, 71.6%, although it should be noted that his sample consisted of church members. A more diverse sample was surveyed by Robert Wuthnow and the Berkeley New Religious Consciousness project directed by Charles Glock and Robert Bellah in the early 1970s. Wuthnow (1978) used the question, "Have you ever felt you were in close contact with something holy or sacred?" to measure religious experience among a San Francisco Bay Area sample, 50% of whom answered affirmatively.

This line of inquiry has not been limited to the United States. A group of researchers organized as the Religious Experience Research Unit (RERU) in Oxford, England, also have contributed to the scholarship in this area (Hay and Morisy 1978). In a national survey of Britons in 1976, these researchers asked: "Have you ever been aware of or influenced by a presence or a power, whether you call it God or not, which is different from your everyday self?" and 36.4% of respondents indicated they had, with half of these aving had such experiences "several times" or more frequently.

Often related to being in the presence of the supernatural are out-of-body experiences. Andrew Greeley (1975) developed a question to measure this aspect of religious experience, which was subsequently asked of a representative sample of Americans in 1974. Of that sample, 35% responded affirmatively to the question: "Have you ever felt as though you were close to a powerful, spiritual force which seemed to lift you out of yourself?" Greeley calls this *ecstasy,* recalling the term's origin in the Greek *ekstasis,* "to be placed outside." This same question subsequently has been included several times in NORC's annual General Social Survey. It also has been used by researchers at the RERU, who found 30.4% of their British sample also reported such ecstatic religious experiences.

These out-of-body experiences have been explained by some as "altered states of consciousness." Most often, these altered states are not simply seen as different but are considered higher forms of consciousness, often called self-transcending consciousness. In the first study based on a nationally representative sample, Bourque (1969:154) defined religious experience as "an expansion of consciousness, or the entrance into the new level of consciousness." This understanding is reminiscent of Abraham Maslow's generic category of dramatic experiences, "peak experiences," which are a form of "hyperconsciousness" that he called "Being-cognition." Using data gathered by the Gallup Organization in 1966, Bourque found that 31.8% of the sample responded affirmatively to the question: "Would you say that you ever had a 'religious or mystical experience'—that is, a moment of sudden religious insight or awakening?"

Focusing also on the cognitive dimension, Greeley (1974) has argued, with the Gnostics, that religious experience is a "way of knowing"—a direct apprehension of ultimate reality. In the literature on mysticism, this is referred to as its "noetic" quality: The experience is seen to be a valid source of knowledge. The importance of experience has long been recognized in Western philosophy, notably among the British empiricists who saw experience as the only reliable source of knowledge. Religious experience, at least in the West, has therefore been invoked frequently as evidence for the existence of God or other supernatural entities (Davis 1989).

Facilitators and Consequences of Religious Experience   Considerable effort has been put into determining the individual and environmental conditions that facilitate religious experience as well as the psychological and behavioral consequences of religious experiencing. While dozens of antecedents and consequences have been identified (Greeley 1975, Hardy 1979, Laski 1961), there are some consistently named factors in the literature.

Psychological facilitators: The most common antecedents seem to operate in the same way as facilitators of religious experience. Meditation and other forms of prayer, sensory deprivation, psychedelic drugs, and music all disrupt everyday patterns of perception, loosen the grip of the normal mental construction of reality, and thereby facilitate a heightened awareness of alternative models of reality, modes of perception, and states of consciousness.

Looking at the issue more broadly, Batson and his colleagues (1993:106) argue that "religious experience involves cognitive restructuring in an attempt to deal with one or more existential questions." Thus, in addition to the perceptual processes above, they find a key antecedent to be an existential crisis. They find precedent for this conceptualization of religious experience in William James, who found "an uneasiness and its solution" to characterize all religious experiences. Empirical support for this idea can be found in Hardy's (1979) large collection of cases in which the most frequently cited antecedents of religious experience are depression, despair, and death.

Social facilitators: Despite the suggestion of many psychologists that religious experience is a profoundly individual accomplishment, and that involvement in religious organization stifles rather than supports such experiences (see James 1902, Maslow 1964), accounts of religious experience reveal one of the most frequently cited antecedents to be "participation in religious worship" (Hardy 1979). This anecdotal finding has been corroborated by statistical analyses of national survey data (Yamane and Polzer 1994).

A few attempts have been made to explain this consistent relationship from a sociological perspective, the best of which is that of Neitz and Spickard (1990:22), who argue that religious groups structure activities in ways conducive to what Csikszentmihalyi (1975) calls "flow experiences," especially in ritual practices that "manipulate sensory stimuli to focus their participants' concentration," which facilitates religious experiences. Building upon this insight, Yamane and Polzer (1994:11) have argued that "religious traditions provide symbolic resources for the construction of alternative realities and promote actions directed at breaking through to those realities," and therefore involvement in religious traditions—especially in prayer and religious services—is conducive to religious experience.

Consequences: There is much to suggest that the primary consequence of religious experience is satisfaction with one's life. Maslow found "peak experiences" common among his "self-actualized" individuals and Csikszentmihalyi finds "flow experiences" to be related to individual happiness. In a national survey sample, Greeley (1975) found "ecstasy" to be strongly and positively correlated with Bradburn's happiness scale, and Hardy (1979) found "a sense of purpose or new meaning to life" to be far and away the most frequently named consequence of religious experience in the self-reports he collected. If we recall James's assertion that religious experience is characterized most generally by prior discontent and its resolution, it should not surprise us that religious experience is consistently found to be positively related to individual well-being.

Other positive consequences of religious experience include being less authoritarian and racist, less materialistic and status conscious, and showing more social concern and more self-assurance (Greeley 1975, Wuthnow 1978). In fact, it is in large part because of such consequences that scholars continue to acknowledge the importance of the experiential dimension of religion, even if not many study it.

The Road Less Traveled   According to Michael Oakeshott (1933:xxi), " 'Experience', of all the words in the philosophic vocabulary, . . . [is] the most difficult to manage; and it must be the ambition of every writer reckless enough to use the word to escape the ambiguities it contains." The same can be said of social scientists who attempt to study the experiential dimension of religion. As we have seen, most have avoided the ambiguities by focusing on the most extraordinary of experiences, as did William James—this despite the fact that a persistent criticism of *The Varieties* is precisely that its focus on extreme cases neglected more mundane aspects of religious experience. Common experiences such as quiet devotion or ordinary piety fall outside the purview of James and those influenced by him. Even Batson and his colleagues, who claim an interest not only in "dramatic" experiences but also in *"religion as experienced by the individual,"* follow James's suggestion "to focus on the most dramatic and intense experiences."

Thus, while James and others claim that the focus on dramatic experiences is strictly for practical purposes, according to John E. Smith, "It seems clear . . . that James believed the epic and heroic experiences to be not only especially instructive but more *authentic*" (*VRE:* xviii). Davis (1989:30), for one, is explicit about her belief that certain experiences are more genuine than others, arguing that

> not all experiences in a religious context are "religious experiences"—an itch during communion is unlikely to be, for instance! Similarly, the perception of religious texts and works of art and the participation in religious rituals, though experiences with religious content, do not in themselves constitute "religious experiences."

While the one-sided focus on "those religious experiences that are most one-sided" dominates the area, there is an alternative, if less traveled, road that scholars might take in approaching religious experience. It is a path cut by the most sustained and ambitious attempt to study religious experience empirically yet undertaken. Founded in 1969 by the zoologist Sir Alister Hardy, the aforementioned Religious Experience Research Unit has gathered thousands of self-reports of religious experiences, largely by publishing requests for self-reports in newspapers. In contrast to the Jamesian tradition, Hardy (1979:18 f.) and his colleagues have been interested in religious experience as "a continuing feeling of transcendental reality or of a divine presence," not simply dramatic experiences but also "seemingly more ordinary but deeply felt experiences."

For Hardy, *all* of an individual's lived experience is a candidate for study under the broad umbrella of religious experience. Religious experience in this view refers to all of the individual's subjective involvement with the sacred: the sense of peace and awe, mysticism and conversion, the presence of God, absorbing ritual experience, and on and on. Thus it is Hardy, not James and his descendants, who has truly begun cataloging the *varieties* of religious experience.

—*David Yamane*

REFERENCES

C. D. Batson et al., *Religion and the Individual* (New York: Oxford University Press, 1993); L. B. Bourque, "Social Correlates of Transcendental Experiences," *Sociological Analysis* 30(1969):151-163; M. Csikszentmihalyi, *Beyond Boredom and Anxiety* (San Francisco: Jossey Bass, 1975); C. F. Davis, *The Evidential Force of Religious Experience* (Oxford: Clarendon, 1989); A. Greeley, *Ecstasy* (Englewood Cliffs, NJ: Prentice Hall, 1974); A. Greeley, *The Sociology of the Paranormal* (Beverly Hills, Calif.: Sage, 1975); A. Hardy, *The Spiritual Nature of Man* (Oxford: Clarendon, 1979); D. Hay and A. Morisy, "Reports of Ecstatic, Paranormal, or Religious Experience in Great Britain and the United States," *Journal for the Scientific Study of Religion* 17(1978):255-268; W. James, *The Varieties of Religious Experience* (Cambridge: Harvard University Press, 1985 [1902]); M. Laski, *Ecstasy* (London: Cresset, 1961); A. Maslow, *Religions, Values, and Peak Experiences* (New York: Penguin, 1964); M. J. Neitz and J. V. Spickard, "Steps Toward a Sociology of Religious Experience," *Sociological Analysis* 51(1990):15-33; M. Oakeshott, *Experience and Its Modes* (Cambridge: Cambridge University Press, 1933); R. Stark, "Social Contexts and Religious Experience," *Review of Religious Research* 6(1965): 17-28; R. Wuthnow, "Peak Experiences," *Journal of Humanistic Psychology* 18(1978):59-75; D. Yamane and M. Polzer, "Ways of Seeing Ecstasy in Modern Society," *Sociology of Religion* 55(1994):1-25.

EXTRINSIC RELIGIOSITY *see* Intrinsic-Extrinsic Religiosity

FACEY, PAUL W. (1909-1994)　Roman Catholic priest of the Society of Jesus (Jesuits); Ph.D. Fordham University, 1945; sociology faculty, College of the Holy Cross, 1936-1967; President, American Catholic Sociological Society, 1964.

Facey collaborated with his Fordham mentor Nicholas Timasheff on an introductory text in 1949. In 1974, his 1945 doctoral dissertation, *The Legion of Decency: A Sociological Study of the Emergence and Development of a Social Pressure Group,* was reissued by Arno Press in its cinema publications program.

—*William H. Swatos, Jr.*

FAITH DEVELOPMENT　A developmental model of religious thinking in the tradition of Piaget and Kohlberg.

The best known model, by James Fowler (1981, 1991), posits six stages in the maturation of faith. Increased sophistication in understanding of symbolism and of authority are the key elements in coding each stage. All six stages may occur within any religion; the stages refer to the cognitive processing of symbols and myths, not to the specific content of a faith.

In the *intuitive-projective* stage, the world is a magical place, the line between reality and fantasy being indistinct. At this stage, children are not able to understand abstractions. God is viewed most frequently as an elderly man with a long beard.

In the *mythic-literal* stage, the person tends to be oriented toward acceptance of whatever authority figures say and is extremely literal in acceptance of anything in print. Belief itself is believed to carry sufficient power to obliterate the laws of nature in certain cases. Also characteristic of this stage is a concept of one's relationship with God as being reciprocal. Acts of praise toward God are sometimes done so that God will "owe" the person later on.

Stage 3 religiosity is *conventional,* with the primary focus on group conformity. Authority is external to the self, residing in the reference group. Faith is not rationally scrutinized, remaining more implicit or unexamined. Symbols are believed to have intrinsic power rather than being abstractions that stand for something else.

In the *individuative-reflective* stage, the symbol is understood as separable from its meaning. The individual understands that meaning is "constructed" or arbitrarily assigned to symbols. There may even be interest in "demythologizing" the myths of the faith to reduce symbols to logical propositions detached from a carrier. Authority for determination of what is true or false is transferred to an evaluation process occurring *within* oneself.

At Stage 5—*conjunctive faith*—a new openness to nonrational experience allows the individual to affirm the imagery and fantasy that a symbol stimulates. Myths and symbols are appreciated as carriers of truth and wisdom, but, unlike earlier stages, those truths are viewed as relative and as less than complete. Both the myths and the symbols of one's own tradition and those of other traditions are affirmed as carrying wisdom.

Universalizing faith is very difficult to describe briefly, for it occurs in so many diverse forms. The element that Stage 6 persons have in common is that they are driven by a vision of *justice* that supersedes the normal boundaries between groups and nations. The commitment to one's vision of Truth becomes complete (not compromised by the feeling that one's vision is relativistic). But even though the commitment is uncompromising, it is not exclusive or particularistic.

James W. Fowler III, the first theorist to develop a cognitive theory of faith development, was born in 1940, the son of a Methodist minister. He received his Ph.D. from Harvard University in 1971 and currently teaches at Candler School of Theology of Emory University, Atlanta.

See also Moral Development

—*Keith A. Roberts*

REFERENCES

J. W. Fowler, *Stages of Faith* (San Francisco: Harper, 1981); J. W. Fowler, *Weaving the New Creation* (San Francisco: Harper, 1991); M. M. Wilcox, *Developmental Journey* (Nashville: Abingdon, 1979).

FALWELL, JERRY   *see* Christian Right, Televangelism

FAMILY   *see* Marriage and Divorce, Sexuality and Fertility

THE FAMILY/CHILDREN OF GOD   "The Family" is the current name used by one of the more controversial of the "new religions," a group best known by the name Children of God (COG).

This group developed as a part of the Jesus Movement (JM) in the late 1960s, and quickly, through mergers and aggressive recruitment, became the largest of the JM groups. The COG spread across the world and has had outposts in well over 100 countries. It is best known for its "litnessing," which refers to the production and distribution of thousands of different publications, many known as "Mo Letters," after the name Moses, which was assumed by the founder David Berg.

A recruitment tactic know as "flirty fishing," or "ffing," which was practiced for a number of years by the COG, also gained it notoriety because it involved young women using sexual favors to attract potential recruits. That practice, and the accompanying COG literature, has caused this group to be controversial, even though the practice of ffing has been discontinued for years.

In recent times, The Family has attracted considerable attention as the focus of a number of government-initiated legal actions in several different countries to take away children of the group on grounds that they were being abused (including sexual abuse), and that being reared in Family communal living situations with home schooling itself constituted abuse or neglect. All of these efforts to take away Family children have ultimately failed, although the battles and controversy have been very demanding and costly. The Family currently has between 8,000 and 9,000 members, with about 5,000 of those being children of early recruits.

—*James T. Richardson*

REFERENCES

R. Davis and J. T. Richardson, "Organization and Functioning of the COG," *Sociological Analysis* 37(1976):321-339; J. Lewis (ed.), *Sex, Slander, and Salvation* (Stanford, Calif.: Center for Academic Publication, 1994); J. T. Richardson and R. Davis, "Experiential Fundamentalism," *Journal of the American Academy of Religion* 51(1983):397-425; D. Van Zandt, *Living in the Children of God* (Princeton, N.J.: Princeton University Press, 1991); R. Wallis (ed.), *Salvation and Protest* (New York: St. Martin's, 1979).

FEMINIST RESEARCH AND THEORY
Religion has been seen as a major institution for the social control of women. It has been the focus of feminist attacks in both first and second wave feminism. Elizabeth Cady Stanton's last work, *The Woman's Bible*, in 1895 (1972), and Mary Daly's first work, *The Church and the Second Sex* in 1975 (1985), were attacks on institutionalized religion and its treatment of women. Yet women have also found ways of using religious ideologies to argue for egalitarian treatment or demand that men change their behavior. Women have sometimes found space in religious institutions to organize on their own behalf; at other times they have created female-based religious groups.

Women, Ministry, and Oppression   A number of sociologists have designed research projects that attempted to identify the extent to which organized religion and religious ideologies fostered sexism (e.g., Himmelstein 1986).

Some of this research was tied to resistance to the ordination of women in particular. Changes in society regarding women in the professions, as well as the pressures inside the denominations from women in the seminaries, spurred research on the topic of women in the ministry. Most of the research on women clergy has been conducted within mainline Protestant denominations. These denominations have been most affected by second wave feminism. The portion of clergy that was female doubled from 2.1% in the 1950s to 4.2% by 1980. Additionally, by 1980, half the M.Div. students at mainline seminaries were female. In *Women of the Cloth* (Harper 1983), Jackson Carroll, Barbara Hargrove, and Adair Lummis offered the first broad look at the impact of growing numbers of women in the ministry. Another major direction was the examination of resistance to women in ministry, both in denominations where ordination occurred and in denominations where it has not been sanctioned (e.g., Lehman 1985, Nason-Clark 1987).

Although most of this research examines mainstream Protestant denominations, there is some material on the rather different situations of women leaders within pentecostal churches (e.g., Kwilecki 1987, Lawless 1988, Poloma 1989) and in Roman Catholicism. Ruth Wallace (1992) suggests that women as well as men benefitted from the increased official enthusiasm for lay participation in governance of the Catholic Church following the Second Vatican Council. Although power remained in the hands of the male clergy, changes in canon law allowed women to participate in public ministry in many ways, including acting as eucharistic ministers, lectors, and even chancellors of dioceses. Involvement in the women's movement mobilized Catholic women to seek changes in their church, including ordination. In the early 1980s, the Woman-Church movement emerged from a coalition of Catholic feminist organizations to keep the issue of ordination under discussion within the Catholic Church.

Gendered Experience Within Abrahamic Religious Traditions When fundamentalism began to attract scholarly attention in the 1970s, feminist writers became interested as participants in the new Christian Right mobilized against the Equal Rights Amendment (ERA) and abortion rights. Analysis of the public writings, especially of male conservatives, stressed official positions on traditional family values, "male headship," antifeminist positions on abortion and the ERA, as well as opposition to the welfare state (e.g., Eisenstein 1982); yet this work left unanswered questions about why women would be attracted to fundamentalist reli-

gion, and the extent to which evangelical women endorsed the official views. Early research on fundamentalist women, based on women who had joined religious communal groups, argued that in a period of time when cultural values seemed to be in flux, part of the appeal for women was the certainty of traditional roles (Aidala 1985, Harder et al. 1976). Other studies of charismatics, evangelicals, and the New Christian Right have suggested that women as well as men see themselves as having something to gain from the pro-family stance articulated by these groups (Ginsburg 1989, Luker 1984, Neitz 1987, Rose 1987). The pro-family ideology dictates that both males and females make family life a top priority. Younger married women, some of whom had seen themselves as feminists prior to joining the movement, saw it as a way to solve problems in their marriages; they traded formal authority for their husbands' emotional expressiveness and involvement in family life.

Feminist scholars studying women newly converted to Orthodox Judaism face a similar puzzle: Why would modern women embrace such an apparently restrictive religiosity? Recent research suggests that the answer to the question depends in part on the population one is studying (see Davidman 1991, Kaufman 1991).

Women-Centered Religious Groups and Practices In addition to various sorts of accommodations and resistances by women within Abrahamic religions, women also have created women-centered religions outside of the dominant cultural tradition. These are often relatively small and relatively unorganized—by their very nature hard to research. Yet they are important sites for investigating theories about gender and alternative structures of authority.

The women's spirituality movement embraces a number of women-centered ritual groups that offer ideologies explicitly supportive of women's authority. Coming out of both the neopaganism of the counterculture and the feminist movement, these groups are oriented primarily to immanent female deities and the celebration of seasonal rituals (Neitz 1990). Several authors are exploring how these woman-affirming beliefs, symbols, and rituals may be empowering to women.

Claiming the identity of witch can itself be empowering to women. Participation in inverting a cultural stereotype and identifying with those midwives and healers of another time, who were persecuted by male authorities, is seen as affirming an alternative construction of gender, religion, and self. Rituals offer settings in which women who have been marginalized and alienated can be healed (see Jacobs 1990).

Both feminists and nonfeminists have questioned what such empowerment means. Rather than power being seen primarily in terms of the ability to get someone else to do as one wants, empowerment for these women may be an attempt to gain legitimacy for their desires to act on their own behalf.

New Directions for Research   While the question, "Where are the women?" has been attributed to the first stage of feminist research, it remains a necessary question for sociologists who study religion. In part, this is because some religious organizations are making a transition between being male-dominated and letting women in, and that change must be assessed (see Hargrove 1987). It is also because other religious organizations continue as highly sex-segregated institutions.

The feminist project of asking how any given experience is gendered also continues to be important. Individuals participate in religious organizations and movements as males and females. Organizations and movements create and maintain structures that continue to reproduce gendered relations. The strand of contemporary feminist theory coming out of the work of Nancy Chodorow (1978) and Carol Gilligan (1982) posits a model of the self that is connected to others. Gilligan's work on moral development showed girls with "connected selves" working through moral choices in ways that are markedly different from the prevailing models developed with male subjects.

Another area to be explored concerns sociological treatments of the body. A related topic is that of sexuality. In Judeo-Christian cultures, sexual norms have often denied women their sexuality while permitting male sexual abuse of women. Alternative religious movements also create norms of sexual conduct.

Perspectives in the sociology of emotion also suggest a number of yet unexplored avenues for feminist analysis in the sociology of religion. Perhaps because religious behaviors were dismissed as being "merely emotional," sociologists have favored organizational analysis; yet Hochschild's (1983) concept of "emotion work" suggests a new, sociological way to think about emotion.

See also Sexism, Sexuality and Fertility

—*Mary Jo Neitz*

REFERENCES

A. Aidala, "Social Change, Gender Roles, and New Religious Movements," *Sociological Analysis* 46(1985):287-314; N. Chodorow, *The Reproduction of Mothering* (Berkeley: University of California Press, 1978); M. Daly, *The Church and the Second Sex* (Boston: Beacon, 1985 [1975]); L. Davidman, *Tradition in a Rootless World* (Berkeley: University of California Press, 1991); Z. Eisenstein, "The Sexual Politics of the New Right," *Signs* 7(1982):567-588; C. Gilligan, *In a Different Voice* (Cambridge, Mass.: Harvard University Press, 1982); F. Ginsburg, *Contested Lives* (Berkeley: University of California Press, 1989); M. W. Harder et al., "Life Style, Courtship, Marriage and Family in a Changing Jesus Movement Organization," *International Review of Modern Sociology* 6(1976):155-177; B. J. Hargrove, "On Digging, Dialogue, and Decision-Making," *Review of Religious Research* 28(1987):395-401; J. Himmelstein, "The Social Basis of Antifeminism," *Journal for the Scientific Study of Religion* 25 (1986):1-15; A. Hochschild, *The Managed Heart* (Berkeley: University of California Press, 1983); J. Jacobs, "Women-Centered Healing Rites," in *In Gods We Trust,* 2nd ed., ed. T. Robbins and D. Anthony (New Brunswick, N.J.: Transaction, 1990); D. Kaufman, *Rachel's Daughters* (New Brunswick, N.J.: Rutgers University Press, 1991); S. Kwilecki, "Contemporary Pentecostal Clergywomen," *Journal of Feminist Studies in Religion* 3(1987):57-75; E. Lawless, *Handmaidens of the Lord* (Philadelphia: University of Pennsylvania Press, 1988); E. C. Lehman, Jr., *Women Clergy* (New Brunswick, N.J.: Transaction, 1985); K. Luker, *Abortion and the Politics of Motherhood* (Berkeley: University of California Press, 1984); N. Nason-Clark, "Are Women Changing the Image of the Ministry?" *Review of Religious Research* 28 (1987):330-340; M. J. Neitz, *Charisma and Community* (New Brunswick, N.J.: Transaction, 1987); M. J. Neitz, "In Goddess We Trust," in *In Gods We Trust,* 2nd ed., ed. T. Robbins and D. Anthony (New Brunswick, N.J.: Transaction, 1990): 353-371; M. Poloma, *Assemblies of God at the Crossroads* (Knoxville: University of Tennessee Press, 1989); S. Rose, "Woman Warriors," *Sociological Analysis* 48(1987): 245-258; E. C. Stanton, *The Woman's Bible* (Salem, N.H.: Ayer, 1972 [1895]); R. Wallace, *They Call Her Pastor* (Albany: SUNY Press, 1992).

FEMINIST THEOLOGY   A theology grounded in the promotion of the full equality of women with men in church and society. As the second wave of feminism was introduced throughout the 1960s and 1970s in the Western world, women theologians began to incorporate their growing feminist consciousness into their religious practice and scholarship. Theologian Elisabeth Schüssler Fiorenza in *But She Said: Feminist Practices of Biblical Interpretation* (Beacon 1992), *Bread Not Stone: The Challenge of Feminist Biblical Interpretation* (Beacon 1984), and *In Memory of Her: A Feminist Theological Reconstruction of Christian Origins* (Crossroads 1985) as well as Rosemary Radford Ruether in *Women-Church: Theology and Practice* (Harper 1985), *Womanguides: Readings Toward a Feminist Theology* (Beacon 1985), and *Sexism and God-Talk: Toward a Feminist Theology* (Beacon 1983) were instrumental in creating, nurturing, and developing feminist theology.

In their recent sociological book *Defecting in Place: Women Claiming Responsibility for Their Own Spiritual Lives* (Crossroad 1994), Therese Winter, Adair Lummis, and Allison Stokes argue that most feminist and alienated women have not left the church but are "defecting in place," challenging the institution from within and supplementing their faith journey by contact with women's spirituality groups. At a very broad level, this is but one indication of the impact of feminist theology on contemporary religion.

—*Nancy Nason-Clark*

FEMINIZATION THESIS   A view introduced more or less coincidentally by several comparative-historical social scientists that religion in the West, and particularly in the United States, has been undergoing a process of fundamental orientational change in which feminine (rather than masculine) images of the nature of deity and the role of the clergy come to predominate. God is seen as loving and consoling, rather than as authoritarian and judgmental; similarly, members of the clergy are seen as "helping professionals" rather than as representatives of God's justice. These changes have been related to both cultural (e.g., Welter 1976, Swatos 1992) and sociostructural variables (e.g., Schoenfeld and Mestrovic 1991), both as "cause" and as "effect." The feminization thesis is particularly powerful in explaining shifts in the practices of organized religions that have opened the ordained ministry to women (see Nesbitt 1997). Recently, the feminization thesis has also been applied to politics.

—*William H. Swatos, Jr.*

REFERENCES

P. D. Nesbitt, *The Feminization of the Clergy in America* (New York: Oxford University Press, 1997); E. Schoenfeld and S. Mestrovic, "With Justice and Mercy," *Journal for the Scientific Study of Religion* 30(1991):363-380; W. H. Swatos, Jr., "The Feminization of God and the Priesting of Women," in *Twentieth-Century World Religious Movements in Neo-Weberian Perspective* (Lewiston, N.Y.: Mellen, 1992); B. Welter, "The Feminization of American Religion," *Dimity Convictions* (Athens: Ohio University Press, 1976).

FERRAROTTI, FRANCO (1926–)
Distinguished Professor of Sociology at the University of Rome "La Sapienza," he is widely regarded as the father of postwar Italian sociology, occupying the first chair of sociology in an Italian university in 1961. He wrote his dissertation at Torino on Thorstein Veblen. Ferrarotti has held numerous visiting appointments, including the New School for Social Research, New York.

By criticizing Benedetto Croce's idealistic approach, which effectively reduced sociology to a pseudoscience, Ferrarotti restored its scientific status both in the academic field and in the wider cultural debate. In particular, he introduced the work of Thorstein Veblen, Max Weber (particularly his *Sociology of Religion*), and Vilfredo Pareto into Italian sociology. Ferrarotti's theoretical approach to sociology combines the empirical observation of social reality with "ideal tension," that is, social and political commitment.

Ferrarotti's major works are devoted to working-class movements, social marginality, power stratification and conflict, and the social dimensions of the sacred in contemporary society. Ferrarotti develops a theory of the sacred as a metautilitarian social dimension of reality in opposition to institutionalized religion. A number of his books have been translated into English, the most well-known of which in the scientific study of religion is *Faith Without Dogma: The Place of Religion in Post Modern Societies* (Transaction 1993). Since 1967, Ferrarotti has been the founding editor of *La Critica sociologica.*

—*Enzo Pace*

REFERENCES

F. Ferrarotti, *Max Weber and the Destiny of Reason* (Armonk, N.Y.: Sharpe, 1982); F. Ferrarotti, *Il paradosso del sacro* (Rome: Laterza, 1983), excerpted as "The Paradox of the Sacred," *International Journal of Sociology* 14(1984); F. Ferrarotti, *A Theology for Non-believers* (Millwood, N.Y.: Associated Faculty Press, 1985); F. Ferrarotti, *Max Weber and the Crisis of Western Civilization* (Millwood, N.Y.: Associated Faculty Press, 1987).

FERTILITY   *see* Sexuality and Fertility

FEUERBACH, LUDWIG (1804-1872)   German philosopher, a student of Hegel and associated with the "idealist" school of philosophy (with whom he subsequently broke); one of the first of whose work is centered in an anthropological criticism of religion.

In 1840, Feuerbach published his major work, a criticism of Christianity, under the title *The Essence of Christianity*. Although his criticism is of Christian belief and its theology, his views are also relevant to the sociological study of religion in general, not only Christianity.

Feuerbach's contribution to the sociology of religion ·can be summarized in two propositions. His first proposition states: The development of religion, central to which was the creation of God, has led to believers' self-alienation. If God is to be real and thus to have effect on us, we therefore must endow Him with a personality. The qualities with which we seek to endow the deity must be ones that give God a divine nature—a nature that expresses no limitations and no defects—and are qualities perceived by us as most desirable. However, by endowing God with all that is positive, we divest ourselves from all that can make us good. "To enrich God," he writes, "man must become poor; that God may be all, man must become nothing." This postulate has been empirically examined by Schoenfeld (1987), who found that attributing a positive quality to God does not automatically lead to attributing negative qualities to people.

In the second proposition, Feuerbach postulates that faith, which by its very nature is highly particularistic, leads to interpersonal alienation. Feuerbach suggests five reasons that religious faiths cannot lead to universal human integration: First, religion is particularistic. Monotheistic faiths stress the ideas that they alone have a monopoly on truth and they alone have a true conception of God. All other descriptions of God are false. The believer feels that his faith alone distinguishes and exalts him above other men; he alone is in the possession of special privileges. Second, faith is arrogant: That is, faith endows its adherents with a sense of superiority and pride stemming from the belief that they were singled out, chosen by God to be objects of particular favor. Third, faith is essentially determinate, specific; that is, faith is imperative—it changes its beliefs into dogma, into a set of principles of belief that cannot be altered or challenged. Faith is essentially illiberal—it is concerned not only with individual salvation but, most important, with the honor of God. Fourth, faith blinds: Faith is unwilling to accept any truth that exists outside itself. It is unwilling to accept the perspective that lies outside its own God. Fifth and finally, faith necessarily, Feuerbach proposes, passes into hatred, and hatred into persecution.

Feuerbach's work had a great influence on Karl Marx's view of alienation as well as such existentialist writers as Martin Buber, Erich Fromm, and Jean-Paul Sartre. Feuerbach's views are also incorporated in Troeltsch's (1931) and Wilson's (1982) analyses of religious sects.

—*Eugen Schoenfeld*

REFERENCES

L. Feuerbach, *The Essence of Christianity* (New York: Harper, 1957); E. Schoenfeld, "Images of God and Man," *Review of Religious Research* 28(1987):224-235; E. Troeltsch, *The Social Teaching of the Christian Churches* (New York: Macmillan, 1931); B. Wilson, *Religion in Sociological Perspective* (Oxford: Oxford University Press, 1982).

FICHTER, JOSEPH H(ENRY) (1908-1994)   A member of the Society of Jesus (Jesuits), Fichter received a Ph.D. in sociology from Harvard University and became a member of the Department of Sociology at Loyola University of New Orleans, Louisiana, where he remained until his death. He held visiting faculty appointments at various universities and was the Chauncey Stillman Professor of Catholic studies at Harvard (1965-1970). President, Society for the Scientific Study of Religion, 1970-1971; Southern Sociological Society, 1982-1983.

One of the most prolific researchers and published authors in the sociology of religion, most of Fichter's work was what he called "one-man research." As Paul Roman suggested in his Preface to Fichter's autobiographical *Sociology of Good Works* (Loyola University Press 1993), Fichter's primary focus on issues concerning the Catholic Church placed him in the outsider-insider dilemma. This is well illustrated by the ecclesiastical suppression of *Southern Parish,* a projected four-volume work reporting a yearlong survey in 1948 of a New Orleans Catholic parish. Volume 1, *Dynamics of a City Parish* (1951), had already been published by the University of Chicago Press, and Volume 2, accepted by the Press, was making its way through the censorship process mandated by the church's canon law, when the pastor of the surveyed parish, irate at perceived slights and improprieties, by various means pressured Fichter's local Jesuit superior into denying publication approval for the remaining volumes. The completed and revised manuscripts of Volumes 2 and 3 of this work, together with the material for Volume 4, remain unpublished to this day.

As Fichter indicated in *One-Man Research* (Wiley 1973), the "great awakening to the need for sociological research occurred among the American bishops several years after the close of the Second Vatican Council." In his later work, Fichter continued to probe sensitive areas in Catholic life: the transmission of values in Catholic secondary schools and colleges; Catholic school desegregation in New Orleans; research on Catholic clergy as a profession (*Religion as an*

Occupation, University of Notre Dame Press 1961); problems experienced by some priests (alcoholism, health, married priests and their wives); Catholic charismatics; organizational shortcomings of the Catholic Church. Toward the end of his life, Fichter's research on the Unification Church and his sympathy with it was a source of comment among some sociologists of religion. What they may have overlooked in Fichter was something admirably caught by Ralph Lane in his review of *The Sociology of Good Works* in the *Journal for the Scientific Study of Religion* (Vol. 33, p. 300):

> At times, one detects a note of impatience, indeed exasperation at the reluctance he encountered in his colleagues within the Catholic Church to change and to accept the good in others. At no time did he give up on them, and he wanted his research to advance, in as loving a way as possible, the plight of the suffering.

Joseph H. Fichter Grants given annually by the Association for the Sociology of Religion for research in the area of gender and religion honor Fichter's career contributions.

—*Loretta M. Morris*

REFERENCES

J. K. Hadden and T. E. Long (eds.), *Religion and Religiosity in America* (New York: Crossroad, 1983, [festschrift]); R. Lane, Jr. (ed.), "Symposium on Joseph H. Fichter, S.J.," *Sociology of Religion* 57(1996):337-377.

FINNEY, CHARLES GRANDISON (1792-1875)

American revivalist, educator, and reformer, known as the "Father of Modern Revivalism." After a religious conversion experience in 1824, he rejected his training as a lawyer to become a Presbyterian minister (later he joined the Congregationalists). In 1835, Finney published *Lectures on Revivals of Religion,* which has remained the principal text of revivalists into the twentieth century. A professor of theology, he became President of Oberlin College in 1851, leaving in 1865 and continuing revival efforts at his Broadway Tabernacle in New York City. Finney's revivalistic travels took him throughout the East Coast and Great Britain.

Finney's legacy to urban revivalism was an ethos "to use any means to stir religious enthusiasms" as well as know-how for conducting a revival *(Lectures).* He be-

lieved that the primary calling of the revivalist was to win souls for the Lord, hence new means were more than justified. These included setting aside a period of days for protracted meetings, using the "anxious bench" (where those wishing to be saved would sit during a meeting), praying for sinners by name, and prayer meetings lasting all night. His church also permitted women to offer prayer publicly. Most important, he rejected formalistic preaching discourse for a colloquial and dramatic appeal to believers' enthusiasms. Sermons were injected with common sense and examples based on cause and effect. Signaling a shift toward religious volunteerism, individuals were free to choose salvation. His personal success with spirit-led preaching and the new revivalist practices were criticized by his Presbyterian Church for permitting fanaticism and spiritual wildfire. As his theology developed, he rejected both old school and new school Presbyterian precepts to rely on personal Bible study and his own experiences, probably shaped by the philosophy of Common Sense Realism influential in nineteenth-century America.

See also Televangelism

—*Razelle Frankl*

REFERENCES

C. Finney, *Memoirs* (New York: Barnes, 1876); R. Frankl, *Televangelism* (Carbondale: Southern Illinois University Press, 1987); J. Hadden, "Religious Broadcasting and the New Christian Right," *Journal for the Scientific Study of Religion* 26(1987):1-24; K. J. Hardman, *Charles Grandison Finney* (Syracuse, N.Y.: Syracuse University Press, 1987); G. A. Hewitt, *Regeneration and Morality* (Brooklyn, N.Y.: Carlson, 1991); W. McLoughlin, *Modern Revivalism* (New York: Ronald Press, 1959); W. McLoughlin, *Revivals, Awakenings, and Reform* (Chicago: University of Chicago Press, 1978); H. C. Trumbull, *My Four Religious Teachers* (Philadelphia: Sunday School Times, 1903).

FITZPATRICK, JOSEPH P. (1913-1995)

Jesuit sociologist, Ph.D. Harvard (1949); President of the American Catholic Sociological Society (1953); founder of the Fordham University Department of Sociology.

Fitzpatrick pioneered bringing sociology to autonomous departmental status in American Catholic university life. He compared his sociology to a medical school model of testing theory by the criterion of human betterment. His unifying scholarly theme was the primary importance of understanding culture. During the late 1930s, he directed the New York City Xavier

Institute of Industrial Relations. In the 1950s, he became a pioneer scholar of the Puerto Rican migration and served as adviser to such boards as the Puerto Rican Legal Defense and Education Fund. The next decade, he studied juvenile delinquency and programs of intervention. In 1979, he was named "Puerto Rican Man of the Year," and his later work emphasized the problems and prospects of diversity and multiculturalism in both American society and the Catholic Church.

The Fitzpatrick Archive is located in Faber Hall on the Bronx campus of Fordham University. In addition to his many publications and vast correspondence, the archive contains information about Puerto Rican community organizations from the 1950s until his death.

—James R. Kelly

REFERENCES

J. P. Fitzpatrick, "Catholics in the Scientific Study of Society," *American Catholic Sociological Review* 15(1954):2-6; J. P. Fitzpatrick, *One Church, Many Cultures* (Mahwah, N.J.: Paulist Press, 1987a); J. P. Fitzpatrick, *Puerto Rican Americans,* 2nd ed. (Englewood Cliffs, N.J.: Prentice Hall, 1987b); J. P. Fitzpatrick and J. Martin, *Delinquent Behavior* (New York: Random House, 1969).

FLYING SAUCER CULTS   *see* UFO/Flying Saucer Cults

FOLK RELIGION   The concept of "folk religion" has at least four possible emphases, reflecting the place of origin of its use.

Most frequent scholarly usage probably occurs in northern Europe. As the *Volk* refers to the ethnic nationality, and draws upon its corporate memory of tribal invasion (unsubjugated by Rome), so *folk religion* in this context refers to a traditional, and largely continuing, widespread and public acceptance of the Christian religion. In Scandinavia, the Baltic states, and Nordic countries generally, as well as in many of the German *Länder* and Swiss cantons, it allows minimal churchgoing to be combined with maximal infant Baptism, adolescent confirmation, and adult payment of the church tax. This "social anthropological" approach is particularly appropriate for the study of religion, not least in Europe, where identity may be voluntary but is inherited. Persons who express this form of religiosity are sometimes referred to as "sociological Christians."

In Japan, the meaning of folk religion is similarly basic but is more individualistic or, at most, familial. It refers to that congeries of private beliefs or, more accurately, actions that individuals perform, which may be seen either as attempts to manipulate the course of events or as "enacted prayers" in connection with them. Scholars elsewhere may dismiss such activities as magic, intended to coerce the divinities, or as superstitions, wasting resources, but Japanese students credit them as religious *in nuce*: neither more, nor less. This history, or phenomenology of religion approach, can be seen as a Japanese contribution toward the nonnormative study of the wider religious spectrum.

North American scholars, when discussing folk religion, seem to have in mind either those customs imported by eastern European immigrants or the customs of post-Columbian Latin America. In either case, the emphasis is initially upon their survival. However, it increasingly acknowledges the possibility of their revival—although as cultural, rather than either as dynamically religious or as holistic, phenomena. Such a "cultural anthropological" approach has the potential of relativizing not only cultures but also culture.

In Britain, the term *folk religion* was used in the 1970s, mainly by Church of England clergy, to refer to members of the population who made "occasional" use of the Offices (baptisms, weddings, funerals) of the Church, in connection with such "occasions" as birth, marriage, and death. A disparaging attitude was sometimes shocked to discover that the request for such Offices was nonetheless serious for being singular. The dismissive attitude, however, was often adopted as a defensive stratagem: to obtain a place on the corporate agenda for that which, at that time, was belittled by both cleric and academic. When this approach is properly pastoral, it allows for the vicariousness of both events and persons: for the "coinherence" of that which is also distinct.

Certain common elements can be discerned behind these four emphases. Thus *folk religion* refers to the ways in which people within socioreligious groupings and traditions, especially at the level of the household, relate to their local and immediate environment, both natural and social. Indeed, a sea change in the study of religion (and society) can be gleaned from the place occupied by "folk religion," both in general and in its particular forms, in Eliade's 1987 *Encyclopedia of Religion,* compared with its complete absence as an entry in Hastings's 1918 *Encyclopedia of Religion and Ethics.*

—Edward I. Bailey

REFERENCES

D. Clark, *Between Pulpit and Pew* (Cambridge: Cambridge University Press, 1982); I. Hori, *Folk Religion in Japan* (Chicago: University of Chicago Press, 1969); G. Mensching, *Structures and Patterns of Religion* (Delhi: Motilal Banarsidass, 1976); F. Musgrove, *Ecstasy and Holiness* (London: Methuen, 1974).

FORUM, THE   *see* est

FOWLER, JAMES W.   *see* Faith Development

FRAZER, JAMES G. (1854-1941)   Classical scholar and prolific compiler of ethnographic information, long associated with Cambridge University.

Although Frazer wrote extensively on a variety of topics, he is best remembered for his 12-volume *The Golden Bough*, a compendium on magic and religion, originally published in two volumes in 1890 and later expanded (St. Martin's 1990). The aim of this treatise is to explain the ancient Roman ritual murder of the priest of Diana at Nemi, the site of a sacred grove with a golden bough. According to this custom, the priesthood went to the person who could break off the bough and kill the incumbent priest. Although *The Golden Bough* never answers the central question posed, it provides a veritable series of intellectual trails and detours that have fascinated many students of comparative religion.

Following Edward B. Tylor's conceptual division between magic, religion, and science, Frazer delineated a schema of the evolution of thought. Magic preceded religion and represented a pseudoscientific worldview that operated on the assumption that it was possible to control nature by coercing supernatural entities. It assumed two basic forms: (1) homeopathic or imitative magic based on the "law of similarity" and (2) contagious magic based on the "law of contact." Religion entailed the recognition that spells and incantations do not produce the effects desired and that natural forces are regulated by greater beings. It constituted a more mature stage that prepared the way for the emergence of a scientific worldview. Science represents the culmination of mental development that would over time supersede religion. Like other Eurocentric evolutionary theoreticians, Frazer failed to realize that the magician's manipulation of sacred symbols is based on a phenomenological understanding of processes that may produce certain kinds of mental states. Furthermore, various scholars, such as W. E. H. Stanner, have demonstrated that the Australian Aborigines, a foraging society, exhibit a highly complex religious system.

In his four-volume *Totemism and Exogamy* (Macmillan 1910), Frazer examined totemism as both religion (an indigenous system of worshiping animals, plants, and inanimate objects) and a system of kinship classification that identifies individuals and groups as having descended from a lineal mythological ancestor. Frazer initially argued that consumption of the totemic species was prohibited and that clan exogamy was the fundamental principle of totemism. He later maintained that the ban on the eating of totemic animals was intended for the clan descended from the totemic species and not for the entire group.

Frazer also contributed to critical biblical studies with a three-volume compendium, *Folklore in the Old Testament* (Macmillan 1918).

—*Hans A. Baer*

REFERENCE

E. Hatch, *Theories of Man and Culture* (New York: Columbia University Press).

FRAZIER, E. FRANKLIN (1894-1963) Prominent African American sociologist who studied with Robert E. Park at the University of Chicago and went on to become a major student of race relations, the black family, and the black middle class in the United States. Although Frazier was not a specialist on religion, his *The Negro Church in America* (Schocken 1963) has served as a classic overview of African American religion. In his view, the "black church" historically functioned as an institution of accommodation and refuge in a racist society but was being called upon to respond to processes of secularization and modernization.

—*Hans A. Baer*

FREUD, SIGMUND (1856-1939) Creator of psychoanalysis. Born in Freiburg, Moravia, to Jewish parents who moved to Vienna when he was 4, Freud entered the University of Vienna in 1873, where he studied for a career in medical research, and worked in Paris in 1885-1886 with Jean-Marie Charcot. His ideas on the psychosexual etiology of neurosis appeared in *Studies in Hysteria* (with Josef Breuer) in 1895, while his full psychoanalytic theory of mental processes emerged in his masterpiece, *The Interpretation of Dreams* (1900). His analysis of the unconscious dynamics behind dreams and his idea that the dream is the disguised expression of an unfulfilled wish laid the theoretical foundation for his later cultural studies.

Freud maintained a strong Jewish ethnic identity, yet from an early date he was also an atheist. He wrote psychoanalytic studies of religious topics, yet viewed religion with suspicion. His work on *The Psychopathology of Everyday Life* (1901) already contained illuminating discussions of popular superstitions. The essays collected in *Totem and Taboo* (1912) developed a fuller theory of religion and its origins. He argued that sacrifice emerged from the collective guilt of the primitive horde over the murder of its patriarchal leader. He also analyzed the relationships among religious rituals, obsessive neuroses, and childhood practices. The emphasis on the role of guilt in the gestation of religious and moral ideals (later called the *superego*) remained central to his writings. These essays contain some of Freud's most suggestive, yet disputed, speculations and make for interesting comparison with Durkheim's contemporaneous treatment of religious beliefs and practices.

The circle around Freud evolved into the Vienna Psychoanalytical Society (1908) and soon the International Psychoanalytic Association (1910). Early associates included Alfred Adler, Hans Sachs, Otto Rank, Ernest Jones, and Carl Jung, although personal disagreements, and divisions over theory and practice, soon led Adler, Jung, and Freud to pursue separate paths. The latter two developed widely divergent views of religion. Freud emphasized the sublimation of libidinal energies into cultural forms, including religion, and tended to see religion as comparable to neurosis. For instance, his *Group Psychology and the Analysis of the Ego* (1921) showed how libidinal identification with real or symbolic leaders helped to solidify organizations such as the church. By contrast, Jung wrote extensively on religion and rejected Freud's pansexualism, emphasized the role of spiritual quests in personal development, and focused on the autonomous significance of archetypes, symbols, and myths.

Freud attacked religion more generally in *The Future of an Illusion* (1927). This work exhibits Freud's Enlightenment rationalism and bears comparison with Feuerbach's humanistic theory of religion. Religion is an infantile wish projection and an illusion. It is rooted in the wish for immortality and the return to the guidance of a powerful father in an imagined primary family. It is a consolation for suffering. Science, creative work, and a stoic attitude toward suffering are superior to the false consolations of religion. In *Civilization and Its Discontents* (1930), Freud noted that the suffering caused us by external nature, our physical frailties, and the actions of fellow human beings helped gestate soteriological responses. He also examined mystical experiences in terms of intrapsychic dynamics, in particular,

the recreation of the sense of undividedness experienced in infancy. While Freud was a rationalist, his own theories suggest mythical and religious parallels. His dualistic view of existence as a struggle between *eros* and *thanatos,* life and death instincts, first developed in *Beyond the Pleasure Principle* (1920), as well as his revival of the Oedipus myth for the explanation of religion and society, are examples.

In his last book, *Moses and Monotheism* (1938), Freud psychoanalytically dissected the Moses story and argued that Moses had been an Egyptian who propagated a monotheistic cult. He had been killed by his own discontented followers, who, in a guilty reaction, set him up as a founding religious hero. The return of this repressed memory also helped account for the origins of Christianity, especially the work of Paul. Although severely criticized at the time, Freud's psychoanalytic theory of Judaism has recently been revived in modified form.

Freud's psychoanalytic approach, including his focus on primary family experiences, his analysis of unconscious mental dynamics, his emphasis on symbolisms, and his explorations of primitive society encouraged many valuable psychoanalytic investigations of religion and culture. Notable books ultimately indebted to Freud include Otto Rank's work on the myth of the birth of the hero, Erich Fromm's analysis of early Christian doctrine, Geza Roheim's studies of primitive religious symbolisms, Erik Erikson's psychoanalytic biography of Luther, Phillip Slater's analysis of Greek mythology, and others.

Freud left Nazi-occupied Vienna with difficulty in 1938 and emigrated to England, where in 1939 an overdose of morphine released him from the painful cancer with which he had suffered stoically for over 15 years. Although critics of varying persuasions have extensively deconstructed Freud's life and work, his theories, including his ideas about religion, continue to provoke fruitful discussion.

—*Donald A. Nielsen*

REFERENCES

J. Dittes, "Biographical/Theological Exegesis on Psychological Texts," in *Religion and the Social Order* 1 (Greenwich, Conn.: JAI, 1991): 37-51; S. Freud, *Standard Edition of the Complete Psychological Works of Sigmund Freud* (New York: Norton, 1955); P. Gay, *A Godless Jew* (New Haven, Conn.: Yale University Press, 1987); P. Pruyser, "Sigmund Freud and His Legacy," in *Beyond the Classics?* ed. C. Y. Glock and P. E. Hammond (New York: Harper, 1973): 243-290.

FRIEDEL, FRANCIS J. (1897-1959) A member of the Society of Mary, Friedel received an S.T.D. from the University of Freiburg (1926) and a Ph.D. in sociology from the University of Pittsburgh (1950). He began his teaching career in philosophy and history at the University of Dayton in 1927. In 1937, he was made Professor of Sociology, and in 1938, Dean of Arts and Science. From 1943 to 1949, he was President of Trinity College, Iowa. He was third President of the American Catholic Sociological Society (1940). His published scholarly sociological works were textbooks in social problems and in marriage and family.

Friedel was one of the four sociologists who, while attending the 1937 convention of the American Sociological Society in Atlantic City, and frustrated by the profession's positivistic atmosphere, set in motion the events resulting in the establishment of ACSS. Although he questioned the existence of a "Catholic" sociology and insisted on distinctions among sociology, social philosophy, and social action, Friedel argued for uniting all three in the role of the Catholic sociologist.

—*Loretta M. Morris*

FRIENDS, SOCIETY OF *see* Quakers

FRIESS, HORACE L. (1900-1975) Professor of Philosophy at Columbia University, where with H. Richard Niebuhr and Paul Tillich, Friess helped develop the University's graduate program in religion and the establishment of its Department of Religion. He was Chairman of that Department from 1962 to 1964. Friess also served as Editor of the *Review of Religion* from 1942 to 1958 and was a prominent member and leader of the New York Society for Ethical Culture. Active in the Society for the Scientific Study of Religion, he served as its President in 1962-1963 and was a member of the committee that brought about the establishment of the society's journal.

—*Charles Y. Glock*

FUKUYAMA, YOSHIO (1921-1995) Professor emeritus, Chicago Theological Seminary. Prior to his seminary faculty and deanship positions, Fukuyama was a researcher for the United Church Board for Homeland Ministries and an influential member of the Religious Research Fellowship, which evolved into the Religious Research Association. He was the circulation manager of the *Review of Religious Research* from 1961 to 1966.

Fukuyama's most widely known publications are *The Fragmented Layman: An Empirical Study of Lay Attitudes* (with Thomas Campbell, Pilgrim 1970), based on a survey of 8,549 members of the United Church of Christ, and *The Ministry in Transition: A Case Study of Theological Education* (Penn State University Press 1973), which analyzes and interprets data from 1,283 seminary students and 1,191 recently ordained clergy in the United Church of Christ. He also pioneered the concept of the multidimensional character of religiosity.

—*David O. Moberg*

REFERENCE

Y. Fukuyama, "The Major Dimensions of Church Membership," *Review of Religious Research* 2(1961):154-161.

FUNCTIONALISM A theoretical approach that explains the existence of social institutions such as religion in terms of the needs that the institutions would meet.

Early Functionalism At first, functionalists likened societies to higher organisms; as one would understand animal lungs and livers by what those organs do for the whole animal body, one would understand institutions by what they do for whole societies. Because the intelligence embodied in the arrangement of traditional institutions transcended any calculative ratiocination on the part of individuals in society, this kind of theory appealed to early-nineteenth-century thinkers who reacted against Enlightenment rationalism. Auguste Comte incorporated functionalism into his early-nineteenth-century amalgam of conservatism and science. Émile Durkheim had a similar insight in his concept of "organic solidarity" at the end of the century; societies held together because their dissimilar parts made unique contributions toward collective life. In emphasizing the needs of the society, and benefits to collective life, Comte and Durkheim conceived societal or macro-level realities that were not reducible to the wants or impulses of individuals or even groups. Their macro-functionalism was adopted in anthropology by A. R. Radcliffe-Brown.

Meanwhile, an individualist, or microfunctionalist, approach was developed by Herbert Spencer. In the tradition of Adam Smith, who saw the wider society profiting from individuals pursuing their own interests,

Spencer believed individual needs to be foundational to social functions and structural change. He spoke of an evolution away from populations of similar people paralleling one another, toward societies of different kinds of persons performing different functions. The differentiated societies were more competitive than undifferentiated ones in a struggle for survival. Because Spencer's sociology provided a rationale for disparities of power and wealth in society, it gained popularity in the gilded age and was suspect in the eyes of people concerned about impartial science. It did bring individual needs and aims into view, and that emphasis was taken up by the anthropologist Bronislaw Malinowski in a functionalism that rivaled the macro approach of Radcliffe-Brown. The sociologist Vilfredo Pareto similarly saw individual dispositions as the motor of social life; patterns in society were states of equilibrium among individual people's impulses.

Religion had a prominent position in early functionalism. According to Comte, the macrofunctionalist, it prompted simple folk to serve unseen purposes that even clever scholars could barely detect. Durkheim (1912) proposed that religion sacralized social life itself and, because the perspective of society was implicit in all cognition, religion thus served as the foundation of all knowledge. The microfunctionalist Malinowski (1948 [1925]) observed that religion established, fixed, and enhanced individual attitudes that were valuable to the collective existence and survival of societies—attitudes such as reverence for tradition, harmony with the environment, and courage in the struggle with difficulties and at the prospect of death.

Functionalism remained viable in anthropology, which studies small societies that can be conceived as systems, but by 1920 it seemed to have run its course in sociology. Durkheim (1982 [1895]) had described a function as such an odd process that not many later sociologists wanted to make functional analyses. According to Durkheim, a function could not be intended by people because they would use multitudinous means rather than common institutions to accomplish intended ends; rather, a function would be an effect that somehow revitalized its causes, much as punishment revitalized the collective feeling for laws. The famous German sociologist Max Weber (1921 [1978]: 15) dismissed functions as merely preliminary heuristic devices and saw the whole point of sociology to be the uncovering of typical intentions in the conduct of people.

Harvard Functionalism   Talcott Parsons (1951) revived sociological functionalism in the mid-twentieth century and, together with his students, most notably Robert K. Merton, made it a dominant paradigm in

American sociology in the 1950s and 1960s. He met Weber halfway by dwelling on the attitudes, if not intentions, that somehow enhanced the workings of society. These attitudes would reflect the beliefs and values proper to the cultures of societies. Moreover, he would specify what the needs of a social system are ("functional requisites") and what institutions served which functions. Religion would function to reconcile personality systems with social systems. In a step away from nineteenth-century analogies with animal bodies, he looked for "systems," interactions that formed patterns of relative equilibrium. According to the contemporary neofunctionalist Jeffrey C. Alexander (1985), functionalism views society as composed of elements whose interaction forms a pattern that is distinct from an environment; the elements are symbiotically interconnected without any directive or governing force. Functionalism is concerned with the degree to which ends succeed in regulating and stimulating means.

Criticisms of Functionalism   There is a serious logical problem in functionalism that social scientists have debated for decades. Functionalism seems to be a teleology, an explanatory scheme that assumes some great intelligence exists that designs features of societies to serve large purposes. The more functionalists propose unobvious functions—the more they emphasize what Robert Merton (1957) termed "latent" functions—the greater this logical problem becomes. As Pitirim Sorokin (1969:339) once put it, functionalists would say, "Birds have wings in order to fly" rather than "Birds have wings and therefore they can fly." It is difficult to explain functions apart from conscious purpose, and conscious purposes require intelligent beings with purposes. Religion often focuses on other-worldly concerns and hence has latent functions proposed for it.

Functionalism also tended to justify social arrangements as found at hand by showing some system-maintaining benefit they brought about. Many functionalists have in fact been humane thinkers who favored conscious efforts at social amelioration; so, rather than defend the conservative aspect of older functionalist thought, they have revised the approach to make it politically acceptable. Merton proposed paying attention to system-disturbing consequences of social features—"dysfunctions," as opposed to "eufunctions." Parsons added an emphasis on social change, with increasing levels of system complexity and differentiation emerging over time. Merton, again, noted that abstracting institutions from their value-laden traditions and assessing them in terms of hardheaded system benefits can be a radical rather than conservative exercise. Nevertheless, as Marie Augusta Neal noted (1979), functionalism fails to analyze important aspects of societies if it neglects asking in whose *interest* systems function and who are the victims of social arrangements, and if it neglects issues of class and power in nongovernmental and noneconomic institutions such as religion.

There was also a problem of functionalism dwelling too much on the largest possible systems—whole societies. Parsons actually helped overcome this difficulty by specifying smaller systems, such as personalities and organizations, within the larger, but the more interesting functional statements about religion actually pertained to the relationships between personalities and the functioning of whole societies. One could question whether modern life actually operates as a more or less closed pattern of interaction ("system") at all. Merton and other functionalists of the mid-twentieth century proposed that system units be specified explicitly, and that functional analyses be made of small groups and of organizations as well as of macro-level systems.

Finally, there seemed to be some confusion over just what kind of question was actually a functionalist one. Were functionalists trying to explain, for example, the origins of religions, the reasons that religions persisted, or the reasons that societies that had religions survived? The question of origins was a concern largely in nineteenth-century anthropology, but late-twentieth-century sociologists took to studying the emergence of new religions in the youth culture. The persistence of religion came to be studied in terms of some individuals in society being more religious than others, but this created problems for those who saw universal functional needs being served by religion; functionalists often defined *religion* broadly so that individuals would be differently religious rather than more or less so. The question of the survival of systems came to be applied to religious identity groups rather than to societies.

Applications and Potential For all the importance placed on functionalism in general sociological textbooks and in major works of social theory, it has inspired relatively little actual research. What research there is has focused on religion. Thus studies of premodern societies, such as Karl-Heinz Messelken's (1977) examination of the late Roman Empire and Kai Erikson's (1966) study of the Massachusetts Bay Colony, saw religion as functional for the coherence and identity, respectively, of whole societies.

Modern societies do not seem to be amenable to such analyses. For example, Richard Sykes (1969) observed that American churches typically focus on matters other than those relevant to the functioning of the wider society. John L. Thomas (1962) noted that a minority religion, such as mid-twentieth-century American Catholicism, could not succeed in providing the function needed by its host society without losing its own internal coherence; the societal and organizational systems were mutually dysfunctional. Not only minority status but also social change creates the same dilemma, as Jean-Paul Rouleau (1990) observes in regard to Catholicism in Québec. In a few studies, the finding that religious questionnaire respondents are happier at work and more likely to endorse generous helping behavior norms are given macrofunctionalist interpretations. More often surrogates for religion—political ideologies and public education, for example—are found to serve some function in lieu of religion doing so. Sometimes different religions have been conceived as functional substitutes for one another. In between religions being societally functional and surrogates for religion being so, one finds the *civil religion* school of thought.

Functionalist studies that have specified religious organizations as the systems having needs have tended to focus on small entities that have well-defined boundaries—a particular Quaker meeting group, a communal sect such as the Hutterites, Catholic orders of sisters. Occasionally the system in question may be a large denomination, or some commonly encountered feature such as ritual or myth is hypothesized to be functional for any subsocietal religious system.

The greater part of late-twentieth-century functionalist sociology of religion has taken a social psychological, or alternatively a sociology of knowledge, approach. Involvement in society transforms individuals, born as largely biological systems, into socialized selves, persons. However, once the person manages to develop a coherent biography, further social involvements raise problems, and additionally there are always the dilemmas of suffering and death that intrude upon life. The system having needs, especially a need for "meaning," is the socialized self in its everyday life, and external factors, ranging from the biological to the political, cause problems that can be addressed through religion. These problems, according to J. Milton Yinger (1963), become particularly critical when individuals experience social changes that place them in new, unfamiliar social lives. The functioning of religion moves from public churches, which have become marginal to societal workings anyway, and into the sphere of everyday life, in a process that Thomas Luckmann (1967 [1963]) calls "privatization." Thus many activities and experiences that have nothing to do with religion as defined in traditional institutional settings are "religious" insofar as people work out suprabiological, meaningful biographies, according to Luckmann. In a variation on this kind of thought, Volker Drehsen (1980) distinguishes personal-level functions (meaning, value integration, the ordering of emotions), interpersonal-level functions (identity security, religious construction of social reality), and transpersonal-level functions (coping with authority and contingency).

There have been a number of efforts to expand the functionalist paradigm in the study of religion. Hans Mol (1977) spoke of individual, group, and national identities that integrate lines of conduct in a dialectic with processes of adaptive differentiation. For him, religion is the process of sacralizing identity; it bolsters the personal and social forces that tend toward wholeness, and thereby compensates for the numerous fragmentary facets of human existence (Mol 1982). This approach solves the logical problem of individuals not being cognizant of functional requisites; they need only be cognizant of their identities. Niklas Luhmann (1977) developed a very similar approach, but with a more abstract and inclusive systems theory model; subsystems would define both themselves and their environmental systems through a process of selection. For Luhmann, religion manages contingency experiences brought upon personality systems by society at large; religion does this by reformulating the conditions for insecurity in religious terms, interpreting them, and making them more acceptable.

The problem of consciousness, of who is aware of system needs and responds in such a way as to occasion functions, is at the center of both the logical difficulties and the promise of functional analysis. When Mol uses the concept of identity, and when Luhmann points to the constitution of selectivity of small and environmental systems, they are locating consciousness within the functional model. This goes beyond Parsons, who saw subjectivity *in* the functional system but only as a recipient of functional beliefs, values, and norms. It even goes beyond the Merton-inspired analysis of inspirational religious literature conducted by Louis Schneider and Sanford Dornbusch (1958), who wondered whether a latent function could still "work" if it became too manifest, whether the inspirational writers were not blowing their cover when they promised inner peace and worldly success. Robert Stauffer (1973) noted that different sectors of a society could be differently conscious, with elites sharing in a rationally functional religious consciousness and nonelites inoculated against such instrumental reason by preoccupations with sacralized identities and nationalisms. Frank Lechner (1985) noted conscious resistance against the rationalist functioning of the wider society, a resistance that took the form of "fundamentalist" religious movements.

When taking up the study of religious consciousness, it is important to give an adequate assessment and portrayal of the subjective phenomenon of religion. If a religious experience or subcultural worldview largely concerns matters that have little to do with the functioning of a large system, if it works more or less on its own or is likely to be put consciously to a variety of personal purposes, as James Beckford (1989) suggests, it will hardly do to set out on a functional analysis. This is simply to suggest that functionalism should not be a procrustean bed. Thomas O'Dea (1954) followed up an excellent exposition of Parsons's functionalist analysis of religion with an eloquent critique that argued, in effect, that a functional analysis that led to an understanding of too little of what a religion is about hardly provides an understanding at all. The problem with functionalism was that it presupposed too positivistic a model of the human, leaving too little allowance for the human as a symbolizing and myth-evolving being. To fit the human person and religious interest into a closed conceptual construct concerned with social structures and functions is to commit the logical error of including the whole in a part.

There remains much promise in functionalism, however. Let us take up where O'Dea left off, with symbol, myth, and other forms in which humans manifest to one another and to themselves vague or at least nonconceptual awarenesses of life in society. Durkheim, for example, proposed that humans externalized the authority of society in religious form. However one defines religion, it occurs in the human biography after and as a consequence of socialization. The individual is aware of society and uses that awareness to shape the contents of religious symbols; social forms are imported into the imagination. It is difficult to conceive of society not being affected by the fact that its members are often aware of it through indirection and implication, whether or not in the manner Durkheim described this occurs.

—*Anthony J. Blasi*

REFERENCES

M. Abrahamson, *Functionalism* (Englewood Cliffs, N.J.: Prentice Hall, 1978); J. C. Alexander (ed.), *Neofunctionalism* (Beverly Hills, Calif.: Sage, 1985); J. A. Beckford, *Religion and Advanced Industrial Society* (London: Unwin Hyman, 1989); V. Drehsen, "Dimensions of Religiosity in Modern Society," *Social Compass* 27(1980):51-62; É. Durkheim, *Les Formes élémentaires de la vie religieuse* (Paris: Alcan, 1912 [*The Elementary Forms of the Religious Life*, Free Press, 1952]); É. Durkheim, *The Rules of Sociological Method* (New York: Free Press, 1982 [1985]); K. T. Erikson, *Wayward Puritans* (New York: Wiley, 1966); F. J. Lechner, "Modernity and Its Discontents," in *Neofunctionalism*, ed. J. C. Alexander q.v.: 157-176; T. Luckmann, *The Invisible Religion* (New York: Macmillan, 1967 [1963 original German edition]); N. Luhmann, *Religious Dogmatics and the Evolution of Societies* (Lewiston, N.Y.: Mellen, 1984); B. Malinowski, *Magic, Science and Religion* (Garden City, N.Y.: Doubleday, 1948 [1925]); R. K. Merton, *Social Theory and Social Structure* (New York: Free Press, 1957); K. Messelken, "Zur Durchsetzung des Christentums in der Spätantike," *Kölner Zeitschrift für Soziologie und Sozialpsychologie* 29(1977):261-294; H. Mol, *Identity and the Sacred* (Oxford: Blackwell, 1977); H. Mol, "Time and Transcendence in a Dialectical Sociology of Religion," *Sociological Analysis* 42(1982):317-324; M. A. Neal, "The Comparative Implications of Functional and Conflict Theory as Theoretical Framework for Religious Research and Religious Decision Making," *Review of Religious Research* 21(1979):24-50; T. F. O'Dea, "The Sociology of Religion," *American Catholic Sociological Review* 15(1954):73-92; T. Parsons, *The Social System* (New York: Free Press, 1951); J. Rouleau, "Le catholicisme, vingt-cinq ans après Vatican II," *Sociologie et Sociétés* 22(1990):33-48; L. Schneider and S. M. Dornbusch, "Inspirational Religious Literature," *American Journal of Sociology* 62(1958):476-481; P. A. Sorokin, *Society, Culture, and Personality* (New York: Cooper Square, 1969); R. E. Stauffer, "Civil Religion, Technocracy, and the Private Sphere," *Journal for the Scientific Study of Religion* 12(1973):415-425; R. E. Sykes, "An Appraisal of the Theory of Functional-Structural Differentiation of Religious Collectivities," *Journal for the Scientific Study of Religion* 8(1969):289-299; J. L. Thomas, "Family Values in a Pluralistic Society," *American Catholic Sociological Review* 23(1962):30-40; J. H. Turner and A. Maryanski, *Functionalism* (Menlo Park, Calif.: Benjamin/Cummings, 1979); M. Weber, *Economy and Society* (Berkeley: University of California Press, 1978 [1921]); J. M. Yinger, "Religion and Social Change," *Review of Religious Research* 4(1963):65-84.

FUNDAMENTALISM   Term derived from series of publications on "The Fundamentals" of the (Christian) faith (1910-1915) that served as a point of reference for groups of conservative American Protestants early in the twentieth century, now commonly used to describe attempts inspired by a religious vision or sacred text to resist or turn back liberal or secular tendencies in theology, culture, and society, regardless of historical religio-cultural origin; has drawn increased public and scholarly attention in the late twentieth century in efforts to understand groups ranging from the American Christian Right to Shī'ites establishing the Islamic Republic of Iran.

Definitions   In scholarly discussion, three types of definition prevail. The *subjective* definition relies on what believers or movement participants themselves mean by the term. In the American context, this identifies as fundamentalist either, narrowly speaking, those who identify themselves as such or, more broadly, those who profess adherence to certain fundamentals of Protestant Christianity, such as the inerrancy of the Bible. This approach facilitates making useful distinctions, in the American case notably between *fundamentalists* and *evangelicals,* but limits analysis to societies where the term has been used and to groups that use it, ignoring factors that influence the self-perception of groups and resistance to use of the label.

The variable historical meanings and political content of fundamentalism are the concern of those favoring a *sociohistorical* approach. They are interested in the renewed use of religious symbols for what actors claim to be conservative political purposes. Focusing on public action and the consequences of religion, they have a sound basis for comparative analysis but discount the actual experience of religiously inspired groups.

A third *analytical* type of definition derives from a theoretical interest in fundamentalism as one type of antimodernism characterized by value-oriented dedifferentiation. *Fundamentalism* here refers to those engaged in reintegrating a social order under the canopy of one all-encompassing sacred tradition. This approach facilitates systematic explanation of fundamentalism as a type of movement and stresses its significance in the context of modernization, but engages in reinterpretation of subjectively understood terms and symbols, and cannot account for variable uses of the concept of fundamentalism. These three ways of studying fundamentalism serve different purposes and are often combined in the work of individual scholars, as illustrated in the volumes of *The Fundamentalism Project,* which itself is guided by an inductive definition stressing family resemblances among various groups of religious conservatives with partially overlapping aims.

Origin and Meaning   The main substantive trend in social analyses of fundamentalism is the emergence of an account of the rise and role of fundamentalism that debunks misconceptions, specifically the view of fundamentalism as an archaic form of religiosity of the culturally backward who seek to bring about a moral cleansing of societies that have lost their traditional bearings. In this view, fundamentalists offer certainty in periods of social crisis, through antimodern means and goals, and thus represent a real threat for liberal modernists.

Fundamentalism may seem archaic to those who think cultural certainty is something not to be achieved in this world. Yet many of the themes in fundamentalist thought derive from recent intellectual developments, such as the individualist premises and post-Newtonian commonsense philosophy that American evangelicals shared with other religious groups. Moreover, adhering to tradition is different from traditionalism, a deliberate effort to regenerate tradition and make it socially significant again. The latter is a form of engagement with the modern world. In fact, the activist thrust of certain fundamentalists involves important changes in the "tradition" they claim to represent; their traditionalism is in some ways bound to be revolutionary, as the actions taken by the Ayatollah Khomeini in merging political and religious leadership demonstrate. Is fundamentalism nevertheless religious activism of the culturally backward? Few present-day fundamentalists can claim elite status. At the same time, it is now well known that early American fundamentalist leaders were by and large highly educated urbanites, several from elite institutions, and that in Iran students and merchants played a crucial role in the Islamic Revolution of 1978-1979. In many instances, those experiencing a kind of social transition, moving into closer contact with "modernjty," are more likely to respond to this in a fundamentalist fashion.

Are fundamentalists antimodern in their worldview? The orientation of ordinary fundamentalists partly fits this element of many scholarly approaches: The opposition to the evils of modernity is real; its plural and inclusive world is to be replaced by a highly integrated and closed one. Yet the very antimodernism of fundamentalists is problematic, due to the ways in which even self-styled fundamentalists are implicated in the culture of modernity. American fundamentalists, for example, come from a tradition that used to value religious pluralism and separation of church and state; the differentiating rationality of modern times is by no means alien to them.

The fundamentalist predicament stems even more from the very pressures to which any kind of antimodernism is exposed in a minimally liberal environment. Modernity is a corrosive force, by making religious traditions less and less significant in social affairs and by making the very idea of a return to certainty and homogeneity implausible. With few exceptions, fundamentalists wanting to make a case for change must appeal to modern principles for legitimation; in the process, the radical implications of the fundamentalist stance are moderated. This means that the certainty offered by fundamentalist leaders is at best a temporary solution. Not only does fundamentalism have its origins in a sense of uncertainty, of a tradition under siege, the envisioned center cannot hold. Applying a presumably old tradition to new problems invariably rekindles dilemmas the fundamentalist project intended to resolve. As a result, the influence of fundamentalism is also easily overstated. In any recognizably full-fledged form, it is a rare phenomenon. Even where conditions seem fertile, often only small minorities of potential activists become deeply involved in public action. The influence of fundamentalism is limited, at the very least, by the cognitive bargaining with modernity in which fundamentalists must engage. Beyond this general limitation, there are many local conditions that determine the fortunes of fundamentalist efforts. Only occasionally do these conditions help to make fundamentalists flourish and gain great influence; the Islamic Republic of Iran in the 1980s was the prototypical (but still exceptional) case.

Interpretations Apart from some work on non-Islamic fundamentalism in Asia, most scholarly analysis has focused on a limited number of fundamentalist manifestations in Christianity, Islam, and Judaism—traditions concerned with shaping the world according to a religious vision based on textual fundamentals. Lawrence (1989) views fundamentalism in the context of a struggle with modernism and modernity. In accounting for fundamentalism, the impact of the Great Western Transformation comes first. Although the variant force of this impact explains the emergence of fundamentalism in the form of self-conscious groups, it is a necessary, not a sufficient, condition. To clarify the active "defense of God" from the inside, Lawrence further examines how actors bring the resources of their tradition to bear on problems they encounter. When those resources include precedent for sectarian action and a scripture that can serve as script, fundamentalist modes of dealing with social crisis become more likely. In particular instances, fundamentalism also is fueled by doctrinal debates that may have little societal relevance (such as those in America over millennnialism and evolutionism). When this symbolic fuel mixes with the structural inequities prevalent in countries that experience modernization as a relatively alien imposition, fundamentalism becomes a plausible vehicle for resistance.

Riesebrodt (1993) conceptualizes fundamentalism as one kind of radically traditionalist movement, which typically has its origin not so much in a grand ideological struggle between modernity and tradition but, instead, in the increasing inability of traditional cultural milieux to reproduce themselves under modern (concretely: urban) conditions. Central to this reproduction is an overriding concern with maintaining or restoring a patriarchal structure. Finding variations on this general theme becomes a matter of identifying the factors aiding in the mobilization of protest movements that hark back to an original community, albeit for highly contemporary purposes. In the case of turn-of-the-century American fundamentalism, he emphasizes both internal stimuli, such as the resistance against church bureaucratization, and external conditions, such as the sociocultural differentiation of major cities. In the case of Iran, he highlights not only the impact of modernizing structural change in society at large but also such factors as the actual threat from state action experienced by traditional milieux and the pervasive influence of new, Western cultural conceptions.

Lechner (1985) has incorporated variables like those employed by Lawrence and Riesebrodt but focuses comparisons more clearly on an analytically derived question. He treats fundamentalism, like Lawrence, as a form of antimodernism in the analytical manner, and modernity more broadly as a particular, relatively recent form of social order characterized by structural differentiation, cultural pluralism, social inclusion, and world mastery. Emphasizing antimodernism serves to show the many ways in which fundamentalism is implicated in and co-opted by the culture it opposes. Treating relevant variables more abstractly and regarding the patriarchal thrust of some fundamentalist movements as part of a larger process, Lechner proposes the following pattern: Religious movements are more likely to become a significant fundamentalist force in a particular society if they have at their disposal a tradition that can easily be interpreted as legitimation for dedifferentiation, if modernizing change represents a special problem for religiously constituted groups, if a fundamentalist program is the most effective and most plausible way to define and resolve multiple discontents, if there are historic precedents in the society for religious attempts at significant social change, if the society in question is not inherently culturally pluralistic or socially differentiated, and if the main concerns of an emerging fundamentalist movement cannot be channeled or deflected by existing institutions. Tracing this pattern in different times and places shows not only how fundamentalist movements can emerge but also why in most cases their influence is severely circumscribed. Theoretical contributions to *The Fundamentalism Project* build on such analyses linking the dynamics and ideology of movements to their context, and confirm the movements' likely limitations.

Fundamentalism as a Global Phenomenon As many students of fundamentalism have recognized, it is no longer a phenomenon affecting only some societies but has acquired a new global meaning. The predicament addressed by fundamentalist movements is a global one. Modernity is no longer a "societal" phenomenon, if it ever was. A reaction *against* modernity therefore necessarily has global implications; it entails a worldview in the literal sense of advocating a distinct view of the world. For Islamic fundamentalists, this includes an obligation to spread the Islamic revolution and defeat the dominant Western Satan. A global culture becomes the target of fundamentalist movements. The defenders of God aspire to bring the kingdom of God to the Earth as a whole, and in this sense they become important actors on the global scene. As global antisystemic movements, they attempt to resolve worldwide problems in global fashion—changing both the actual balance of power in the world and the cultural terms on which global actors operate.

The changing global condition not only becomes context and target of fundamentalism but also serves as its primary precipitating factor. Apart from globally induced variations in the strength of fundamentalism, the very attempt to restore a sacred tradition as a basis for a meaningful social order is globally significant, as one effort among others to preserve or achieve a certain cultural authenticity in the face of a greedy, universalizing global culture. It is a particular, albeit radical and problematic, form of striving for communal and societal identity under circumstances that make such deliberate identification a global expectation. Indeed, fundamentalism itself has become a global category, part of the global repertoire of collective action available to discontented groups but also a symbol in a global discourse about the shape of the world. In the process, the term has become contested everywhere, leading to concern about its use as a way to denigrate the aspirations of some movements. Yet seeing fundamentalists locked in a struggle about the shape of the world is to recognize part of their actual predicament, not to deny their particularity in imperialist fashion. Studying such particularity as such has become difficult in any case; fundamentalism is inevitably contaminated by the culture it opposes. No fundamentalist can simply reappropriate the sacred and live by its divine lights. The very reappropriation is a modern, global phenomenon.

Influence and Future The global turn in the study of fundamentalism was partly inspired by widespread concern about the possible public influence of fundamentalism. The scholarly and the public interest in fundamentalism converge on the question about the likely extent of this influence. There are grounds for judging this influence to be relatively minor and for skepticism about the overall future of fundamentalism. Fundamentalism is a quintessentially modern phenomenon. It actively strives to reorder society; it reasserts the validity of a tradition and uses it in new ways; it operates in a context that sets nontraditional standards; where it does not take decisive control, it reproduces the dilemmas it sets out to resolve; as one active force among others, it affirms the depth of modern pluralism; it takes on the tensions produced by the clash between a universalizing global culture and particular local conditions; it expresses fundamental uncertainty in a crisis setting, not traditional confidence about taken-for-granted truths; by defending God, who formerly needed no defense, it creates and recreates difference as part of a global cultural struggle. So compromised, fundamentalism becomes part of the fabric of modernity.

Being thus compromised portends a problematic future for fundamentalism, seen from a fundamentalist point of view. It indicates one of the ways in which fundamentalism, like any other cultural movement, engages and must engage in creolization, juxtaposing the seemingly alien and the seemingly indigenous into a worldview and identity that combine both in new seamless wholes. The hybrid results become a normal feature of globalization, which robs cultures of easy authenticity while making the search for the authentic a virtual obligation. If the point of fundamentalism is to restore an authentic sacred tradition, this means that fundamentalism must fail.

This failure is exacerbated by the modern circumstances fundamentalism must confront. In some respects, modernity does act as a solvent, undermining the thrust of fundamentalist movements. Insofar as a society becomes structurally differentiated, religion loses social significance; once that happens, restoration is difficult if not impossible. In differentiated, specialized institutions engaged in technical control of the world, religious distinctions have little role in any case; the very conception of infusing a perceived iron cage with religious meaning necessarily remains nebulous. If a culture becomes pluralistic and tears down its sacred canopy, those who would restore it are themselves only one group among others. Making claims for a fundamentalist project requires wider legitimation, except where there is overwhelming popular support; such wider legitimation entails diluting the message. Trying to act globally with some effectiveness presupposes the use of global means— technological and institutional—but satellite dishes and nation-states draw the would-be opposition farther into the culture it claims to disdain. Although its relative success varies according to the conditions sketched above, fundamentalism is inevitably co-opted. Being modern and becoming co-opted presupposes that there is a viable modern order to be co-opted into. The future of fundamentalism is thus closely linked to the future of liberal modernity.

—*Frank J. Lechner*

REFERENCES

N. T. Ammerman, *Bible Believers* (New Brunswick, N.J.: Rutgers University Press, 1987); S. A. Arjomand, *The Turban for the Crown* (Oxford: Oxford University Press, 1988); S. Bruce, *The Rise and Fall of the New Christian Right* (Oxford: Clarendon, 1989); J. D. Hunter, *American Evangelicalism* (New Brunswick, N.J.: Rutgers University Press, 1983); G. Kepel, *Muslim Extremism in Egypt* (Berkeley: University of California Press, 1985); B. Lawrence, *Defenders of God* (San Francisco: Harper, 1989); F. Lechner, "Fundamentalism and Sociocultural Revitalization," *Sociological Analysis* 46 (1985):243-260; G. Marsden, *Fundamentalism and American Culture* (New York: Oxford University Press, 1980); M. E. Marty and R. S. Appleby (eds.), *The Fundamentalism Project* (Chicago: University of Chicago Press, 1991-1995); M. Riesebrodt, *Pious Passion* (Berkeley: University of California Press, 1993); M. Watt, *Islamic Fundamentalism and Modernity* (London: Routledge, 1988).

FUNERALS   Human bodies could be disposed of without any form of ceremony. Foetuses in some societies, and bodies in such emergencies as war and famine, often are. Usually, however, a person is given more apparent honor at the time of death than during life: This is the last chance to "do" him or her "justice."

Although many other motives also may be present (sorrow, guilt, anxiety, initiation into new roles, and so on), this apparently more altruistic motive should not be overlooked, especially in contemporary, atomistic culture. Consonant with this is a growing desire on the part of the bereaved to take a creative part in the shaping of what is seen as "their" funeral. Unconsciously perhaps, they are asserting that "man does not die by biology alone." Indeed, the very fact of a funeral achieves some kind of (spiritual) resurrection.

—*Edward I. Bailey*

REFERENCE

T. Walter, *Funerals* (London: Hodder and Stoughton, 1990).

FURFEY, PAUL HANLY (1896-1992)   Roman Catholic priest-scholar; received a Ph.D. in sociology from Catholic University of America and in 1922 joined its Department of Sociology, where he spent the rest of his academic life until his retirement in 1967. President, American Catholic Sociological Society, 1944.

He published 17 books and many articles; his last book, *Love and the Urban Ghetto* (Orbis 1978), was written at the age of 82. As late as 1987, he still firmly believed and wrote that sociology could be "Catholic." He maintained that sociologists not only could make value judgments in their work but frequently did— even as they proclaimed their value-neutrality. As basic a move as conceptualizing a "social problem" required that one had to decide that something is *bad* for society: clearly, a value judgment. In broader sociological circles, Furfey is noted for a debate on this question with the American positivist George Lundberg; he is also recognized for his conceptual innovation of *metatheory*.

Adequately defined, "social problems" were in fact "social evils," and Furfey confronted them in his published works: slavery, the Holocaust, the slow but inexorable "murder" of the American population locked below the poverty level, the U.S. involvement in the Vietnam War. His writings, inspiration, and support helped some returning World War II conscientious objectors become sociologists.

Furfey's conception of culture was both broad and deep, embracing not only the material preconditions for human association but also those moral and spiritual, artistic and ethical qualities and activities that make for human progress. Considered by many an outstanding methodologist, Furfey believed in using empirical evidence as the fulcrum on which religion could apply leverage to culture. In consequence, many of his books, beginning with *Fire on the Earth* (Macmillan 1936), strongly advocated cultural engagement. He urged his students to become involved in social action as part of their understanding of what it meant to be a sociologist and a Christian. In keeping with this philosophy, with two CUA colleagues he cofounded Fides Neighborhood House and El Poverello House. The Association for the Sociology of Religion has honored him by maintaining an annual lecture in his name.

—*Loretta M. Morris*

REFERENCES

P. H. Furfey, *Social Problems of Childhood* (New York: Macmillan, 1929); P. H. Furfey, *The Scope and Method of Sociology* (New York: Harper, 1953); G. A. Lundberg and P. H. Furfey, "Letters and Rejoinders," *American Catholic Sociological Review* 7(1946):203-205, 8(1947):47-48; G. Ritzer, "Sociological Metatheory," *Sociological Theory* 6(1988):187-200.

GALLAGHER, RALPH A. (1896-1965) Jesuit priest and sociologist; founder of the American Catholic Sociological Society.

After earning a B.A. and an M.A. in psychology from Gonzaga University, Ralph Gallagher completed his theological studies at St. Louis University. There he entered the doctoral program in sociology, gaining his Ph.D. in 1932 and going on to study social work at Fordham University. He became a member of the sociology faculty at John Carroll University in 1933, and in 1936 became the first Chairman of the Department of Sociology at Loyola University Chicago, where he remained as Chair until 1963. He established Loyola's Institute of Industrial Relations in 1941, retaining his title of Director until his death.

Gallagher's areas of primary interest were criminology and penology. He led efforts to reform and professionalize the Chicago Police Department, holding intensive in-service seminars and training programs for police officers, correctional, probation, and parole workers. Gallagher believed social principles could not be divorced from social practice. From the beginning of his professional career when such ideas were not fashionable, Gallagher's sociological perspective was value oriented.

With three other sociologists, Francis Friedel, Louis Weitzman, and Marguerite Reuss, Gallagher was responsible for founding the American Catholic Sociological Society and quickly became its moving spirit. It would, he hoped, be a haven for Catholic sociologists alienated by the positivistic and antireligious climate he and his colleagues perceived in the American Sociological Society. More than that, it would show that one could be loyal both to a church and to scientific objectivity. The outcome was the March 1938 meeting that would lead to the formation of the American Catholic Sociological Society. He served as the first President of the society, then as Executive Secretary from 1938 to 1962, wielding considerable influence over the existence and progress of the organization. In 1940, Gallagher established the ACSS journal, *American Catholic Sociological Review,* and served as its editor for over a decade. In the 1960s, the focus of the review and of the organization shifted from the general field of sociology to the sociology of religion.

—*Loretta Morris*

REFERENCES

P. Kivisto, "The Brief Career of Catholic Sociology," *Sociological Analysis* 50(1989):351-361; L. Morris, "Secular Transcendence," *Sociological Analysis* 50(1989):329-350.

GALLUP, GEORGE, Jr./GALLUP POLLS *see* Public Opinion Polling

GANDHI, MOHANDAS K. (1875-1949)
Indian sociopolitical leader.

Trained as a barrister in London, Gandhi practiced law for some years in South Africa. On his return to India in 1917, he led the National Congress in its fight for India's freedom. Drawing upon India's religion and culture, Gandhi inspired many groups, including youth, women, urban professionals, and rural peasants, to employ the method of *nonviolence* in resisting British rule. He urged people to lead simple and truthful lives, and set an example for others in this respect. He also sponsored cottage industries for India's economic self-reliance and is widely regarded as a great leader of the masses in India, with an influence well beyond that country's borders (e.g., the civil rights movement in the United States). He was assassinated by a right-wing Hindu.

—*C. N. Venugopal*

REFERENCE

M. K. Gandhi, *The Story of My Experiences with Truth* (Ahmedabad: Navajivan, 1940).

GANNON, THOMAS M. (1936–) A member of the Society of Jesus (Jesuits), Gannon gained an undergraduate degree in classics, a Ph.L. and M.A. at Loyola University Chicago; he received an S.T.L. from Chicago's Jesuit School of Theology and a Ph.D. in sociology from the University of Chicago. He was a member of the Sociology Department at Loyola University Chicago, 1971-1983, and later engaged full time in a number of research-oriented activities. He has held numerous visiting professorships, lectureships, and fellowships, both in the United States and at institutions in Asia and Europe. Gannon has served as President of the Religious Research Association (1971-1973) and of the Association for the Sociology of Religion (1978). He was a member of the Executive Council of the Society for the Scientific Study of Religion (1984-1988) and Associate Editor, *Review of Religious Research* (1980-1988).

Gannon has published several books, two of which are concerned with the Catholic Church: *The Catholic Challenge to the American Economy* (Macmillan 1987) and *World Catholicism in Transition* (Macmillan 1988). He has written numerous articles, their topics encompassing religion and delinquency, church-related education, Catholic religious clergy, Catholic religious orders, intellectual and religious values, religion and urban community, social organization and belief systems among clergy, and the Christian right.

—*Loretta M. Morris*

GARRETT, WILLIAM R. (1940–) Professor of Sociology at St. Michael's College (Vermont), obtained his undergraduate degree from William Jewell College, the M. Div. degree from Yale, and the Ph.D. in sociology of religion from Drew University. President, Association for the Sociology of Religion, 1985.

An ordained minister recognized in both American and Southern Baptist Conventions, Garrett has enjoyed a multifaceted career that includes being a productive scholar; the editor of *Sociological Analysis,* the official journal of the Association for the Sociology of Religion, and several associate editorships; an academic administrator; a pastor; a chaplain; president of his state chapter of AAUP; board member of several organizations; and college professor. He has also served as town moderator for his Vermont community.

Although Garrett has done significant work in family sociology, the main thrust of his scholarly contributions has been in the area of historical and comparative sociology. His studies of religion and society are typically focused at the societal or macro level. In his presidential address to the ASR, he traced the emergence of the notion of "God-given rights" from the development of canon law in the Catholic Church, through the Enlightenment period in France, and into the modern world by way of Roger Williams, the Levellers, and Isaac Backus. Since then, he has enlarged his interest to consider the relation of religion and human rights to globalization theory, often in collaboration with Roland Robertson. Also, Garrett has recently been involved in comparative studies of Eastern and Western family systems.

Throughout his career, Garrett has demonstrated a personal and professional interest in ecumenical issues, in recent years through extensive participation in conferences and programs sponsored by the Unification Church.

—*Larry C. Ingram*

REFERENCES

W. R. Garrett, "Religion, Law, and the Human Condition," *Sociological Analysis* 47S(1987):1-34; W. R. Garrett, "Thinking Religion in the Global Circumstance," *Journal for the Scientific Study of Religion* 31(1992):297-303; W. R. Garrett and

R. Robertson (eds.), *Religion and Global Order* (New York: Paragon House, 1991).

GEERTZ, CLIFFORD J. (1926–)   One of the leading American anthropologists of the twentieth century, best known for his focus on the meaning of religious symbols and for his extensive ethnographic studies of religion in complex societies; since 1970, Professor of Social Science at the Institute for Advanced Study in Princeton, New Jersey.

Geertz received his Ph.D. in Human Relations from Harvard University in 1956 and taught anthropology at the University of Chicago from 1960 to 1970. He is a fellow of the National Academy of Science and the American Academy of Arts and Sciences, and author of a number of seminal studies focusing on his fieldwork in Indonesia, Java, Bali, and Morocco. Among his most significant publications dealing with religion are *The Religion of Java* (Free Press 1960), *Islam Observed* (Yale University Press 1968), *The Interpretation of Cultures* (Basic Books 1973), *Local Knowledge* (Basic Books 1983), and *Works and Lives* (Stanford University Press 1988).

Geertz advocates an interpretive approach to religious beliefs and institutions, and suggests that a major task of anthropology is to "make sense" of cultural systems. Symbols, Geertz cogently argues, play a double role. They simultaneously express images of reality and shape that reality. Religious symbols thus provide a representation of the way things are (what Geertz calls "models *of*") as well as guides or programs directing human activity (what he calls "models *for*"). Religion, for Geertz, consists of a cluster of symbols that make up an ordered whole and provide a charter for the ideas, values, and lifestyles of a society.

In a classic 1966 article, "Religion as a Cultural System," he asserted that the study of religion should be a two-stage operation. The first stage concentrates on an analysis of the system of meanings embodied within religious symbols. The second stage is primarily concerned with relating these systems to social structures and psychological processes. Critics point out that he has devoted considerably more attention to the first stage than to the latter. But there is general agreement that Geertz's approach allows for a more dynamic perspective on religion than did earlier functionalists (A. R. Radcliffe-Brown and Bronislaw Malinowski). This is especially apparent in *The Religion of Java*, where Geertz outlines three distinctive opposing worldviews and religious traditions—the village *(Aban-gan)*, the market *(Santri)*, and the government bureaucracy *(Prijaji)*—and successfully establishes an association between specific religious traditions and specific social strata.

For Geertz, religion is understood as a social—not an individual—product, and while religion arises to serve the individual, it also ends up serving society. All of Geertz's publications are ultimately concerned with religion's consequences. Sometimes he focuses on the consequences of religion for the individual; at other times he focuses on religion's social consequences. His perspective changes slightly from study to study and from year to year. As Robert Segal (1998) correctly points out, books such as *Islam Observed* and *Local Knowledge* give greater attention to the impact of religion on the individual, while books such as *Religion of Java* stress its social functions. But Geertz's abiding interest in the consequences of religion is a consistent thread in his many and varied studies of religious institutions and rituals throughout the world.

—*Stephen D. Glazier*

REFERENCES

H. Munson, Jr., "Geertz on Religion," *Religion* 16(1986):19-32; R. Segal, "Clifford Geertz's Interpretive Approach to Religion," in *Selected Essays in the Anthropology of Religion*, ed. S. D. Glazier (Westport, Conn.: Greenwood, 1998): 124-139; P. Shankman, "The Thick and the Thin," *Current Anthropology* 25(1984):261-279.

GEFFEN, RELA MINTZ (1943–)   President of the Association for the Social Scientific Study of Jewry, 1988-1990; member of the editorial board of its journal, *Contemporary Jewry* (1985–), of which she assumed the editorship in 1997. Graduate of a joint bachelor's program of Columbia University and the Jewish Theological Seminary, 1965; M.A. Columbia University, 1967; Ph.D., University of Florida, 1972.

Geffen's major research interest within the sociology of religion is the sociology of American Jewry with particular attention to Jewish communal associations, gender roles, the family, and rites of passage as evidenced in her edited volume, *Celebration and Renewal: Rites of Passage in Judaism* (Jewish Publication Society 1993).

—*J. Alan Winter*

GELLNER, ERNEST (1925-1995) Born in Paris and educated at Prague and at Balliol College, Oxford, Gellner was Professor of Social Anthropology at Cambridge University from 1984 to 1992.

Gellner has produced almost 20 books and numerous articles covering a very wide range of philosophical, ethnographic, historical, and anthropological interests. His main specializations have been in Arab, Mediterranean, and Islamic studies, theory and explanation in anthropology, and the place of reason in characterizing primitive societies. He has made notable contributions to debates on nationalism, characterized in terms of the tension between reason and passion, which form part of a wider concern with the study of beliefs. A continual theme in his writings has been the defense of the place of reason in human affairs. Writing in a punchy, provocative, and witty style, Gellner's versatility in so many areas, combined with the richness of his insights, have given him a unique place in British anthropology.

His recent work, *Postmodernism, Reason and Religion* (Routledge 1992), embodies many of his characteristics as a thinker, first displayed in his *Words and Things* (Oxford University Press 1959). The fashion of postmodernism is lambasted in his characteristic style. Gellner dislikes anything that smacks of relativism in human affairs. His notion of a constitutional religion in this work marks debts to Durkheim but also characterizes a defense of a mild rationalist fundamentalism, where reason holds sway over revelation.

—*Kieran Flanagan*

GENDER The study of religion that challenges the concept of universality as an assumption of scholarly inquiry. The tendency toward universalism, which governed religious studies through the mid-twentieth century, equates the masculine with the universal (Cook and Fonow 1990). The inclusion of gender as a category of analysis challenges this bias by recognizing women as legitimate subjects of research and gender as an important lens through which to interpret the meaning and symbol systems of religious cultures. By focusing on the significance of women and women's experience, the study of gender transforms the androcentric paradigms of traditional research.

The development of gender scholarship within the study of religion has created a more inclusive scholarship. Drawing on a number of different disciplines, including sociology and psychology, a gender perspective contributes to an understanding of religious phenomena and social trends. For example, as gender is brought to bear on the study of mystical experience, differences emerge between women and men that can be explained through an analysis of female development and the importance of attachment and connection. Within the gender paradigm, differences among women are highlighted as well. Segura and Pierce (1993), for example, discuss the relationship among political identity, religious culture, and motherhood within the Chicana/o family.

The subjects of gender scholarship are varied and diverse. Since the 1960s, a number of key areas in the study of religion have emerged. Among these are the impact of religious ideology on the development of patriarchy and misogyny (Daly 1968, Plaskow 1990); the study of reform movements that have expanded the roles of women in traditional religious institutions (Carroll et al. 1983, Ruether 1985); the relationship among gender, race, and religious activism (Isasi-Diaz 1993, Higginbotham 1993); the creation of alternative spiritual practices (Northup 1993); the development of goddess-centered spirituality (Neitz 1990); and the study of abuse and exploitation within new religions (Jacobs 1989).

See also Feminist Research and Theory, Sexism

—*Janet L. Jacobs*

REFERENCES

J. Carroll et al., *Women of the Cloth* (San Francisco: Harper, 1983); J. Cook and M. Fonow, "Knowledge and Women's Interests," in *Feminist Research Methods*, ed. J. Nielsen (Boulder, Colo.: Westview, 1990): 69-93; M. Daly, *The Church and the Second Sex* (San Francisco: Harper, 1968); E. B. Higginbotham, *Righteous Discontent* (Cambridge: Harvard University Press, 1993); A. M. Isasi-Diaz, *En la Lucha* (Minneapolis: Fortress, 1993); J. L. Jacobs, *Divine Disenchantment* (Bloomington: Indiana University Press, 1989); M. J. Neitz, "In Goddess We Trust," in *In Gods We Trust*, 2nd ed., ed. T. Robbins and D. Anthony (New Brunswick, N.J.: Transaction, 1990): 353-371; L. A. Northup (ed.), *Women and Religious Ritual* (Washington, D.C.: Pastoral Press, 1993); J. Plaskow, *Standing Again at Sinai* (San Francisco: Harper, 1990); R. R. Ruether, *Woman-Church* (San Francisco: Harper, 1985); D. A. Segura and J. L. Pierce, "Chicana/o Family Structure and Gender Personality," *Signs* 19(1993):62-91.

GEOGRAPHIC MOBILITY The effect of geographic mobility on religiosity is commonly understood as leading to a decline. However, from empirical research, its effects appear to be very much dependent on the migrants' preferences and on the sociocultural context of both the old and the new residence.

As an individual's preferences depend to a great extent on past experiences, they are not stable and do vary over time. Geographic mobility is consequently seen to lead to both a decline and a rise in religious commitment (as measured by church attendance). More private dimensions of religiosity, such as private prayer, are less prone to change because of migration.

In addition to individual mobility, there is group migration (including family migration). Historically, the migration of "deviant" religious groups occurred to preserve the faith (and physical safety) when actual or potential suppression threatened (Mennonites, Mormons, and Quakers). Sometimes strict denominational groups or families have been known to migrate due to the threat of eroding religiosity in the face of the nearing of the "world" (Amish). Others are known to break up, because the group grows too large, and the exertion of social control on the observance of the communal and private religious practices becomes very difficult. In research on contemporary religious groups, less attention is paid to the effects of geographic mobility on religiosity.

Atlases of religious geography in the United States, principally under the editorship of Peter L. Halvorson and William M. Newman, are produced and distributed by the Glenmary Research Center in Atlanta; these are the standard reference works on the social geography of religious denominations in America. A unique single-nation, single-tradition study is Isambert and Terrenoire's *Atlas de la pratatique religieuse de catholiques en France* (FNSP-CNRS 1980). The irregular serial *Geographia Religionum* is published in Germany by Reimer.

See also Ecology of Religion, Pilgrimage

—*Durk H. Hak*

REFERENCES

R. W. Stump, "Regional Migration and Religious Commitment in the United States," *Journal for the Scientific Study of Religion* 23(1984):292-303; M. R. Welch and J. Baltzell, "Geographic Mobility, Social Integration, and Church Attendance," *Journal for the Scientific Study of Religion* 23(1984):75-91.

GERONTOLOGY The aging process as a focus of academic study. As an interdisciplinary area with a strong practical focus, gerontology draws from both the social and the medical sciences, and has expanded greatly in the last few decades.

Specific topics of concern range from the mental and emotional well-being of older persons living alone to public policy debates regarding health care. Many issues that concern gerontologists also interest sociologists of religion. These include, for example, emotional well-being and facing the inevitability of death. Although some research in the sociology of religion has focused explicitly on older persons, particularly the work of Moberg (1965), the linkage between the two areas of study is limited. In 1972, Heenan indicated the "empirical lacunae" between these two areas. Since then, however, work has been done to bridge the gap. At least one journal now is devoted explicitly to the area where religious studies and gerontology overlap: the *Journal of Religious Gerontology* (initiated in 1984). In addition, edited volumes by Koenig et al. (1988) and Thomas and Eisenhandler (1994), which include contributions representing a variety of perspectives, illustrate a convergence between the two specialties. On the other hand, the specialized journals within each field probably inadvertently help maintain the distance between them.

One basic question sociologists have investigated is whether people become more religious as they get older. Given that religion deals with life-and-death issues, a strong theoretical argument can be made that as individuals approach their own death, they are likely to become more religious. However, an alternative argument, which is supported by much empirical research, is that older people are not likely to change the basic orientation established earlier in their lives. The answer may depend on how religious older people were in earlier stages of their lives. Some research suggests that persons who have been religious throughout their lives find their religious faith becoming subjectively more important as they grow older. However, as health and mobility deteriorate, the range of public religious activities such as church attendance often declines. This pattern is consistent with the once popular, but frequently criticized, disengagement theory (Bahr 1970). At the same time, however, for those who are religious, private activities such as viewing religious TV programs or personal prayer often show an increase. In general, the increased subjective importance of religion for those who are religious applies particularly to those with a strong *intrinsic* religious orientation, for whom religion is important in achieving the highest and final stage of psychological development and in alleviating fear of death. In any case, sociologists would emphasize the importance of specifying which dimensions of religion may increase, which ones decrease, and which ones remain stable among older persons (Blazer and Palmore 1976, Mindel and Vaughan 1978).

Gerontologists and sociologists of religion also have overlapping interests in the role of churches and clergy in providing support services to the elderly, both social and spiritual, as well as to primary caregivers (Gray and Moberg 1977). Although this area is probably not as thoroughly researched as the individual-level relationship between religion and aging, studies of the clergy role recognize the importance of counseling individuals with life transitions and problems of various kinds, and this would include dealing with the spiritual dimension of bereavement and acute health problems, both of which are likely to increase in frequency with increasing age. Some religious organizations provide worship and social services in nursing homes or retirement centers, and some provide transportation to religious services.

—*Doyle Paul Johnson*

REFERENCES

H. M. Bahr, "Aging and Religious Disaffiliation," *Social Forces* 49(1970):59-71; G. Blazer and E. Palmore, "Religion and Aging in a Longitudinal Panel," *Gerontologist* 16(1976): 82-85; R. Gray and D. O. Moberg, *The Church and the Older Person* (Grand Rapids, Mich.: Eerdmans, 1977); E. F. Heenan, "Sociology of Religion and the Aged," *Journal for the Scientific Study of Religion* 11(1972):171-176; *Journal of Religious Gerontology* (1984–); H. G. Koenig et al. (eds.), *Religion, Aging, and Health* (New York: Greenwood, 1988); C. H. Mindel and C. E. Vaughan, "A Multidimensional Approach to Religiosity and Disengagement," *Journal of Gerontology* 33(1978):103-108; D. O. Moberg, "Religion in Old Age," *Gerontologist* 5(1965):78-87, 111-112; L. E. Thomas and S. A. Eisenhandler (eds.), *Aging and the Religious Dimension* (Westport, Conn.: Greenwood, 1994).

GHOSTS　*see* Apparitions

GILLIGAN, CAROL (1936–)　Psychologist at Harvard University. Has written on differential views of morality between men and women.

Gilligan's most well-known statement of her views is *In a Different Voice* (Harvard University Press 1982). There she argues that, unlike men, women in our society tend to regard moral questions in terms of responsibilities and potential harm to others rather than in terms of abstract ethical principles. Gilligan takes issue with moral development theorists, such as Lawrence Kohlberg, who posit a progression through moral stages culminating in an ability to make moral judgments from universalistic moral principles. She maintains that women's moral development goes through similar stages that involve increasingly comprehensive, differentiated and reflective forms of

moral thought. However, women tend to construct moral problems in terms of care and responsibility rather than rights and rules. She maintains that the male-centered focus on abstract ethical principles ignores important aspects of women's moral development and leads to unfairly categorizing many women as being less morally developed because of their failure to fit a male model of morality. Gilligan emphasizes an elucidation of the dynamics of women's moral development without any detailed examination of the cultural roots and dynamics of differential female moral development.

Named "Woman of the Year" in 1984 by *Ms. Magazine,* Gilligan has received numerous honorary degrees.

See also Moral Development

—*Edward F. Breschel*

REFERENCES

K. Davis, "Toward a Feminist Rhetoric," *Women's Studies International Forum* 15(1992):219-231; C. Gilligan, "Moral Development in the College Years," in *The Modern American College,* ed. A. Chickering (San Francisco: Jossey-Bass, 1981): 139-157; C. Gilligan et al. (eds.), *Mapping the Moral Domain* (Cambridge: Harvard University Press, 1988); A. Mason, "The Gilligan Conception of Moral Maturity," *Journal for the Theory of Social Behavior* 20(1990):167-179; V. A. Sharpe, "Justice and Care," *Theoretical Medicine* 13(1992):295-318.

GLOBALIZATION　Processes that bring about a single worldwide sociocultural system, or the development of the modern world system, not exhausted by specific trends in marketing, finance, and politics, are sometimes described with this term. In sociology of religion, globalization is associated above all with the work of Roland Robertson (1992), who has offered one of several contending interpretations of the phenomenon.

Traditionally, social scientists thought of modernizing change as those things nation-states had to do, the phases they had to go through, to become modern. More recently, many scholars have come to see modernization as itself a transnational process. Economic growth, state formation, the rise of national cultures, changes in the place of religion around the world—all are processes affected by relations between societies and in turn create new economic, political, and cultural relations not contained by societal boundaries. *Globalization,* then, refers to those aspects of long-term historical processes that help to form new patterns of global interaction, new global institutions, and new ways of thinking about the world as such. How one views the role and future of religion in the expanding world system depends on how one accounts for that process generally.

If one thinks of the world system as a world market linking units differentiated by geography and history, in which some (core countries) have vastly greater control over economic resources than others (periphery), religion is bound to appear of little consequence. Thus, in the work of Immanuel Wallerstein (e.g., 1983), Christianity may have served as at best one source for the universalism and rationality that serve as a supporting ideology for the capitalist world system. Yet because there is no possibility of class solidarity across the globe, and because this dominant ideology is a powerful tool of exploitation, religion can become a vehicle for the resistance of exploited peripheral groups. Religion may inspire antisystemic movements. Fundamentalist Islam is a case in point.

If one thinks of the world system as consisting of institutionalized sets of rules (a world polity that steers local state action), religion may be assigned a more important historical role. For example, to support his argument that there is a world polity that specifies what a society must look like and strive for, John Meyer (1989) looks to classic Christendom as a model of how such a polity can work. Christianity not only contained values that have been transposed to the global level, it also linked a particular worldview to a powerful form of organization. Although some global norms may acquire quasi-sacred status, the world polity is unlikely to legitimate a public role for religion in any conventional sense.

If one thinks of the world system as a new global culture in which different actors debate the nature and direction of the expanded relations between them, religion becomes crucial in several respects. As Robertson has argued, the direction of global change is uncertain; new global relations call into question the identities of societies and individuals; globalization brings different civilizations into one public square. Under these circumstances, religious traditions are powerful sources of new images of world order. At least some groups will respond to new identity demands by reinterpreting their religious heritage. In each society, new tensions will emerge between political and religious institutions. Religious leaders become global actors, engaged in global debates. All this is not to say that religion somehow determines the direction of globalization. It is to say

that religion, in its many forms, will help to influence definitions of the global situation.

But how can it do that? A study by Peter Beyer (1994) addresses the issue. Following Robertson, he distinguishes between religious movements that defend sociocultural particularism and those that support change toward a pluralistic world order in which different traditions coexist. Conservative antisystemic movements, such as Islamic fundamentalism, react against global trends that threaten old identities. However, their desired public impact usually remains limited and localized. Liberal movements, such as some kinds of religious environmentalism, aim to infuse world culture itself with ultimate meaning. They may contribute resources for dealing with residual problems that secular systems cannot address, but they are unlikely to determine the ways secular institutions actually operate. From Beyer's work, we may infer that religious actors and beliefs will be more prominent in discourse about the globe than in the institutions shaping actual global relations. He holds out the prospect of many contending versions of a global civil religion but envisions the traditional religions as cultures that primarily serve individuals.

In the study of religion, globalization has come to indicate both a set of substantive issues and a change in perspective. The issues concern the historical role of religious values and institutions in fostering a new global system, the actual religious content of current debates about world order, and the future role of religiously inspired actors as significant players in globalization. Apart from this emerging agenda, the change in perspective suggests a new way of thinking about religion. It questions notions of secularization as something that affects individual societies. It suggests that seemingly ethnocentric conservatives also are engaged in a global discourse. It undermines attempts to link religion to a cohesive national culture that bolsters solidarity. Perhaps most important, it assigns the sociology of religion the role of interpreting global cultural change.

—*Frank J. Lechner*

REFERENCES

P. Beyer, *Religion and Globalization* (London: Sage, 1994); M. Featherstone (ed.), *Global Culture* (London: Sage, 1990); J. Meyer, "Conceptions of Christendom," in *Cross-National Research in Sociology*, ed. M. Kohn (Newbury Park, Calif.: Sage, 1988): 395-413; R. Robertson, *Globalization* (London: Sage, 1992); R. Robertson and W. Garrett (eds.), *Religion and Global Order* (New York: Paragon House, 1991); W. Swatos (ed.), *Religious Politics in Global and Comparative Perspective* (New York: Greenwood, 1989); I. Wallerstein, "Crisis," in

Crises in the World System, ed. A. Bergesen (Beverly Hills, Calif.: Sage, 1983): 21-36.

GLOCK, CHARLES YOUNG (1919–)

Sociologist of religion and expert in survey research. Attended public schools in the Bronx, New York, where he was born; earned B.S. degree in marketing at New York University (1940), M.B.A. at Boston University (1941), and after four years of military service, a Ph.D. in sociology at Columbia (1952). Closely associated with research projects under Paul Lazarsfeld and others at the Bureau of Applied Social Research at Columbia, 1946-1957, and Managing Director and then Director of that bureau, 1948-1957. Then, after a year at the Center for Advanced Study in the Behavioral Sciences (Stanford, California), 1957-1958, Glock joined the faculty of the Department of Sociology, University of California, Berkeley, from 1958 until his retirement in 1979; was Director of the Survey Research Center there, 1958-1967, and also Director of the Program in Religion and Society at that center, 1967-1979. During the 1967-1968 school year, and again in 1969-1971, he chaired the Department of Sociology at Berkeley. He was also Adjunct Professor at Berkeley's Graduate Theological Union, 1965-1979. Active in various professional societies, Glock was a council member in the Religious Research Association in the early 1950s; president, American Association of Public Opinion Research, 1963-1964; one of the earliest members of the Society for the Scientific Study of Religion, and its President, 1967-1968. During 1978-1979, he served as Vice-President of the American Sociological Association.

Glock is author, coauthor, or coeditor of 14 books and numerous articles reflecting his interests in survey research methodology, in the sociology of religion, and in religious and racial prejudice. Survey research was the empirical basis for most of his books and articles. As a disciple of Lazarsfeld and the Columbia school of survey methods, Glock favored a straightforward additive approach to scaling and measurement, and a multivariate tabular presentation of the data, over more abstract and mathematically sophisticated statistical methods. His work thus communicated successfully, regardless of the degree of quantitative sophistication on the parts of his readers, although he was sometimes criticized for the inadequacy of this approach in appropriately weighting causal variables.

Glock's accomplishments and prominence in the sociology of religion have tended to obscure somewhat his important work in the social and cognitive (as opposed to psychopathological) sources of racial and ethnic *prejudice*. His 1966 *Christian Beliefs and Anti-Semitism* (with Rodney Stark, Harper), based on a national survey and on a survey of Protestant and Catholic parishioners in northern California, was the first work ever to marshal empirical, quantitative data in support of a theory tying anti-Semitism to selective elements in Christian indoctrination. Later works (e.g., Stark et al. 1971, Glock et al. 1975, Quinley and Glock 1979, Apostle et al. 1983) both verified and expanded the theoretical orientation of the 1966 book. In particular, these later works demonstrated the importance not only of religious beliefs per se but also of more general outlooks or worldviews in giving rise to prejudice of various kinds (not just anti-Semitism).

Yet it is indeed in the sociology of religion that Glock's most prominent contributions are to be found. He was interested especially in three aspects of religious commitment (or "religiosity"), as he categorized them: *nature, sources, and consequences.* With his early collaborator Stark, he originally envisioned one volume on each of those three aspects, based primarily on data from the northern California survey; but only the first volume, on the *nature* of religious commitment, was ever published. Nevertheless, much of Glock's other work dealt, in one way or another, with the other two aspects. For example, *To Comfort and to Challenge* (with Benjamin Ringer and Earl Babbie, University of California Press 1967), based on Episcopalian survey data gathered during Glock's Columbia days, found the *sources* of religiosity partly in forms of deprivation associated with demographic traits such as age, gender, and family status. An early theoretical essay on deprivation as a source of religiosity (more fully developed in Glock 1973) identified five different forms of deprivation as central to the origin and etiology of religious and also secular institutions and movements. As for *consequences,* the third aspect of religiosity, certainly all of Glock's work on prejudice could be understood in large part as a series of investigations of at least one of religiosity's potential consequences.

Aside from his work on prejudice, Glock is probably best known for his five-dimensional scheme of the nature of religious commitment (Glock 1962). In their final form (Stark and Glock 1968), these dimensions consisted of *belief, knowledge, experience, practice* (sometimes subdivided into private and public ritual), and *consequences.* The last of these is qualitatively different than the other four, because it is by definition always a dependent variable, more complicated to isolate, and less clear in conceptualization. Glock's other four dimensions, however, have proved widely useful in research, because they are generally simple to measure and to distinguish one from another.

Relatively late in his career, Glock collaborated with Robert Bellah and with many doctoral and postdoctoral students in a series of studies resulting in *The New Religious Consciousness* (University of California Press 1976), a phenomenon expressed in a variety of new movements during the 1960s and 1970s, particularly in places like Berkeley. In this project, as well as in his various roles at Columbia and at UC Berkeley, Glock was mentor to at least three dozen students in various disciplines. Those who have subsequently gained some national prominence mainly in the sociology of religion include N. J. Demerath III, Phillip Hammond, Steven Hart, Armand Mauss, Rodney Stark, Ruth Wallace, and Robert Wuthnow.

—*Armand L. Mauss*

REFERENCES

R. Apostle et al., *The Anatomy of Racial Attitudes* (Berkeley: University of California Press, 1983); C. Y. Glock, "On the Study of Religious Commitment," *Review of Recent Research on Religion and Character Formation* (research supplement to *Religious Education,* July-August 1962): 98-110; C. Y. Glock (ed.), *Religion in Sociological Perspective* (Belmont, Calif.: Wadsworth, 1973); C. Y. Glock and R. Stark, *Religion and Society in Tension* (Chicago: Rand McNally, 1965); C. Y. Glock et al., *Adolescent Prejudice* (New York: Harper, 1975); H. Quinley and C. Y. Glock, *Anti-Semitism in America* (New York: Free Press, 1979); R. Stark and C. Y. Glock, *American Piety* (Berkeley: University of California Press, 1968); R. Stark et al., *Wayward Shepherds* (New York: Harper, 1971).

GLOSSOLALIA Also known as "speaking in tongues" (from the Greek *glossai,* "tongues, languages," and *lalein,* "to speak"), this term traditionally describes the expression of profound religious experiences in words or languages unknown to the speaker. It is a historical and contemporary practice found in Christian and non-Christian religious communities worldwide.

Psychologists initially held to a "pathology model" of glossolalia, seeing it as caused by mental illnesses such as hysteria or schizophrenia, although evidence has since refuted this position. In fact, glossolalics seem to exhibit lower levels of anxiety, depression, and hostility than nonglossolalics, although they also display higher levels of suggestibility, passivity, and dependence.

There has been considerable debate over whether glossolalia is the result of an altered state of consciousness or whether it is simply acquired and maintained through social learning. Samarin (1972), a linguist, argues that glossolalia is essentially a reduction and simplification of one's native language, and is therefore something that anyone with normal linguistic capacities can produce given the proper training, set, and setting. In contrast, Goodman (1972), a psychological anthropologist, finds cross-cultural similarity in the structure of glossolalic utterances, and suggests that there are universal neurophysiological changes that cause it. Specifically, she argues that glossolalia is the outward manifestation of a "trance" state. To date, no conclusive evidence has been offered to adjudicate between these two positions, although it is likely that both explain important aspects of the complex event.

Sociologists have been especially concerned with the function of glossolalia in the process of conversion and commitment to pentecostal and charismatic movements, which are distinguished by the centrality of the practice to their worship and in which glossolalia is seen as a sign of membership by virtue of "baptism in the Spirit." Communities in which tongues-speaking is normative are among the fastest growing in the world (e.g., the Assemblies of God), and Poloma (1989) has argued that the growth can be explained in part by the motivation and empowerment felt by glossolalics, which lead to successful evangelism.

See also Pentecostalism

—*David Yamane*

REFERENCES

F. D. Goodman, *Speaking in Tongues* (Chicago: University of Chicago Press, 1972); M. Poloma, *The Assemblies of God at the Crossroads* (Knoxville: University of Tennessee Press, 1989); W. J. Samarin, *Tongues of Men and Angels* (New York: Macmillan, 1972).

GOLDSTEIN, SIDNEY (1927–) George Hazard Crooker University Professor of Demography and Sociology (Emeritus), Brown University.

Having completed his B.A. and M.A. at the University of Connecticut, Goldstein received his Ph.D. from the University of Pennsylvania. Generally recognized as the "Dean of Demographers of American Jewry," Goldstein's international acclaim led to his appointment as visiting scholar in Denmark, Thailand, Hawaii, Australia, China, Italy, and Israel. He served as the President of the Population Association of America (1975-1976) and as a consultant to the Ford Foundation, United Nations, NIH, and the Council of Jewish Federations. The author of 38 books and monographs, about 150 articles, and 200 professional papers and lectures, he is especially well known as coauthor of *Jewish Americans* (with Calvin Goldscheider, Prentice Hall 1968) and *Jews on the Move* (with Alice Goldstein, SUNY Press 1996), based on the 1990 Jewish Population Survey. In recognition of his contribution to the Social Scientific Study of Jewry, Goldstein received the first award for Distinguished Scholarship in the Study of Jewry from ASSJ in 1992.

—*Arnold M. Dashefsky*

GORSUCH, RICHARD L. (1937–)   Professor of Psychology and Director of Research at the Graduate School of Psychology, Fuller Theological Seminary. He is past President of Division 36 of the American Psychological Association and a recipient of its William James award for outstanding and sustained contribution to the psychology of religion. He also edited (1975-1978) the *Journal for the Scientific Study of Religion.*

Gorsuch is widely recognized as an expert in psychometrics. He continues to publish productive research in the areas of personality and social psychology, methodology, and substance abuse as well as the psychology of religion. He advocates that rigorous scientific methods be employed in the psychological study of religion. He also emphasizes that psychology of religion is a part of mainstream psychology using identical methods and assessment procedures. His major research contributions in the psychology of religion include analyses of prejudice, intrinsic/extrinsic religion, and the relationship between change in religiousness and a decrease in substance abuse. He is widely recognized for his authoritative reviews of research in the psychology of religion. His major theoretical contribution is in the ongoing development of a nonreductionistic model for the psychology of religion based upon beliefs, attitudes, and values (the BAV model). In this model, each component is independently measured and their contributions to differentially predicting behaviors determined by multivariate methods.

—*Ralph W. Hood, Jr.*

REFERENCES

R. L. Gorsuch, *Factor Analysis,* 2nd ed. (Hillsdale, N.J.: Lawrence Erlbaum, 1983); R. L. Gorsuch, "Measurement," *American Psychologist* 39(1984):228-236; R. L. Gorsuch, "The Psychology of Religion," *Annual Review of Psychology* 39(1988):201-221; R. L. Gorsuch, "Religion and Prejudice," *International Journal for the Psychology of Religion* 3(1993):

20-31; R. L. Gorsuch and M. Butler, "Initial Drug Abuse," *Psychological Bulletin* 83(1976):120-137.

GRAHAM, (WILLIAM FRANKLIN) BILLY (1918–)   Southern Baptist minister; American mass-crusade evangelist.

Graham began his formal career as an evangelist working in the Youth for Christ movement in 1944, with his 1949 Los Angeles crusade gaining him national attention and popular recognition. Although following in a revivalist pattern set by figures like Billy Sunday and Dwight L. Moody, Graham's ministry coincided with the advent of television. As his reputation grew, Graham's crusades around the world became standard television fare through the 1950s and 1960s and continue to have some airtime presence. Graham was frequently listed among the 10 most admired men in America or the world, although his image was somewhat tarnished through too close an association with the Nixon White House.

Graham's crusades were also the first studied by direct social science research, and a body of knowledge has developed around them. This work provides important insights not only into the crusade event itself but also into the larger dynamics of the conversion and mobilization processes.

See also Conversion, Charles G. Finney, Televangelism

—*William H. Swatos, Jr.*

REFERENCES

D. L. Altheide and J. M. Johnson, "Counting Souls," *Pacific Sociological Review* 20(1977):323-348; D. A. Clelland et al., "In the Company of the Converted," *Sociological Analysis* 35(1974):45-56; N. R. Johnson et al., "Attendance at a Billy Graham Crusade," *Sociological Analysis* 45(1984):383-392; W. T. Johnson, "The Religious Crusade," *American Journal of Sociology* 76(1971):873-890; F. L. Whitlam, "Revivalism as Institutionalized Behavior," *Social Science Quarterly* 1(1968):115-127; R. C. Wimberley et al., "Conversion in a Billy Graham Crusade," *Sociological Quarterly* 16(1975): 162-170.

GRAMSCI, ANTONIO (1891-1937)   Marxist intellectual and a founder of the Italian Communist Party who died in prison during Mussolini's rule. His social theory is found in his *Prison Notebooks.*

Among the concepts of Gramsci that are useful to the social scientific study of religion are the historical bloc, which refers to the complex set of changing cultural and material forces that characterize a society, and organic intellectuals, who assist an oppressed class in articulating a revolutionary consciousness. These concepts have been used by scholars who study the role of the Roman Catholic Church in supporting efforts toward social change in Latin America.

See also Marxism, Radicalism

—*Madeleine R. Cousineau*

REFERENCES

L. A. Gómez de Souza, *Classes Populares e Igreja nos Caminhos da História* (Petrópolis, Brazil: Vozes, 1982); O. Maduro, "New Marxist Approaches to the Relative Autonomy of Religion," *Sociological Analysis* 38(1977):359-367; H. Portelli, *Gramsci et le Bloc Historique* (Paris: Presses Universitaires de France, 1972).

GREAT AWAKENINGS   American Protestantism has been marked historically by "revivals"—practices that sponsor and reinforce an enthusiastic, emotional, and evangelistic faith. Revivals have been the quintessential American religious practice, even spreading to American Catholicism (Dolan 1978).

However, scholars disagree as to whether revivals have been a more or less steady phenomenon (Butler 1990) or whether there have been periodic waves of revivalism. The latter idea is generally termed the "great awakenings" thesis. In this account, awakenings are periods of intense religious fervor, spreading over entire geographic regions. Large numbers of revivals renew the faith among the formally churched as well as gain new converts. Awakenings produce an emotion-based, experiential, immanentist faith. Many have credited awakenings with helping to foster religious pluralism, advance ideas sympathetic to political democracy and social reform, and forge an American national identity (e.g., Ahlstrom 1972, Hammond 1979, Hatch 1989, Mathews 1969, Smith 1980, Stout 1986).

More contentious is the claim that awakenings are cyclical, representing a religious response to social and cultural change. They help believers come to terms with the stress that change produces and adjust the culture to new modes of societal organization (e.g., Gordon-McCutchan 1981, Huntington 1981, McLoughlin 1978).

The first Great Awakening is generally placed in the 1740s, originating in western New England; Jonathan Edwards and George Whitefield were the major figures. The second Great Awakening occurred in approximately 1800-1830, spreading from the "burned over district" of upstate New York throughout the frontier and moving back again to the seaboard; the major figure was Charles G. Finney. A third Great Awakening is occasionally associated with the years 1890-1920.

The journal *Sociological Analysis* (now *Sociology of Religion*) had a symposium on religious awakenings (Vol. 44, No. 2, 1983).

—*Rhys H. Williams*

REFERENCES

S. E. Ahlstrom, *A Religious History of the American People* (New Haven, Conn.: Yale University Press, 1972); J. Butler, *Awash in a Sea of Faith* (Cambridge: Harvard University Press, 1990); J. P. Dolan, *Catholic Revivalism* (Notre Dame, Ind.: University of Notre Dame Press, 1978); R. C. Gordon-McCutchan, "The Irony of Evangelical History," *Journal for the Scientific Study of Religion* 20(1981):309-326; J. Hammond, *The Politics of Benevolence* (Norwood, N.J.: Ablex, 1979); N. O. Hatch, *The Democratization of American Christianity* (New Haven, Conn.: Yale University Press, 1989); S. P. Huntington, *American Politics* (Cambridge: Belknap Press, 1981); D. Mathews, "The Second Great Awakening as an Organizing Process," *American Quarterly* 21(1969):23-43; W. G. McLoughlin, *Revivals, Awakenings and Reform* (Chicago: University of Chicago Press, 1978); T. L. Smith, *Revivalism and Social Reform in Mid-Nineteenth Century America,* rev. ed. (Baltimore: Johns Hopkins University Press, 1980); H. S. Stout, *The New England Soul* (New York: Oxford University Press, 1986).

GREEK AND ROMAN RELIGIONS   The religious beliefs and practices of the ancient Greeks and Romans have not attracted social scientific investigation to the extent accorded either the major world faiths or the religions of band and tribal peoples. Notwithstanding that one would be hard-pressed to find a living devotee of Zeus or Athena, Janus or Mars, that imbalance in scholarly attention is somewhat surprising, not only in consideration of the formative impact of classical civilization upon world religious history but also given the early dependence of sociological and anthropological "theory" upon evidence drawn from Greco-Roman sources. Comte, Tylor, Marx, Weber, Freud, Durkheim, Frazer, and other celebrated "founding fathers" of social science typically passed through an educational crucible featuring immersion in Greek and Latin, and their writings display easy familiarity—and at times even professional competence—with classical materials. Indeed, much of the theoretical armature of early social science discourse—evolutionary and developmental schemata, models of social organization, ideal-types, and concepts—derives from that engagement.

A true analytical dialogue between historians and social scientists on the subject of religion commences with Fustel de Coulanges's *The Ancient City,* published in 1864 (Johns Hopkins University Press 1980). Fustel's central thesis—that the primordial religious beliefs of the Greeks and Romans provided organizing frames for their advanced social institutions (family, law, property, politics)—would encourage his former pupil, Émile Durkheim, to explore the connections between religion and society more comprehensively. In two seminal works, *Primitive Classification* (University of Chicago Press 1963 [1903]), with Marcel Mauss, and *The Elementary Forms of the Religious Life* (Free Press 1952 [1912]), Durkheim sought to establish that the sacred beliefs and practices of a people constitute a symbolic and ritual representation of their social order; in venerating imaginary spirits and deities, they are honoring the actual powers and structures of their own collective life. Those postulates—mingled with insights from J. G. Frazer's *The Golden Bough* (St. Martin's 1990 [1890])—would stimulate new approaches to the study of classical antiquity, pioneered by leaders of the Cambridge school. Exemplary yields from that interdisciplinary ferment include Jane Harrison's (1903, 1912) attempts to document the dependence of various myths and rituals upon social institutions and customs, and F. M. Cornford's (1912) efforts to trace the origins of Hellenic rationalism to key collective representations—*moira, physis, nomos*—that were grounded in the primitive religious notion of *mana,* the impersonal ordering power of life. Important later contributions by H. J. Rose (1948), Martin Nilsson (1955, 1961), and George Dumézil (1970), although differing significantly on points of interpretation, all owe various debts to the creative exchanges between the Durkheimian and Cambridge schools. The anthropological structuralism of Claude Lévi-Strauss likewise builds on that legacy, and his views—eclectically spiced with Marx, Weber, and Foucault—have exerted considerable influence on the circle of French classicists led by Jean-Pierre Vernant (1974), Marcel Detienne (1972, 1977), and Pierre Vidal-Naquet (1986).

Two other prominent traditions in social science—those founded by Marx and Freud—have also furnished analytical principles for work on ancient religion by classical specialists. Alban Winspear's (1940) pioneering exploration into the social origins of Plato's thought offers a religion-as-ideology line, while G. Thomson (1949, 1955) employs the categories of class and false

consciousness to address issues ranging from the cultural consequences of slavery to the politics of the pantheon. In E. R. Dodds's highly influential *The Greeks and the Irrational* (University of California Press 1951), key developments in the history of Hellenic religiosity are explicated with the aid of psychoanalytic principles and anthropological insights on such matters as dream states and the shame-culture/guilt-culture polarity.

Max Weber's comparative studies in sociological world history are commonly buttressed by the author's interpretive mastery of the source materials of Greco-Roman antiquity. In his wide-ranging explorations in *Religionssoziologie,* Weber strategically uses aspects of Hellenic spiritual culture and practice to draw out parallels and contrasts with other religious traditions of historic consequence: Judaism, Confucianism, Taoism, Hinduism, Buddhism, and Christianity. More directly, in the major section of *Economy and Society* (University of California Press 1978 [1921]) devoted to religious matters, Weber grounds many of his ideal-type categories and propositions in Greek and Roman experiences. Ancestor cults, ideas regarding the soul and afterlife beliefs, anthropomorphization and pantheon formation, the fundamental role of poets and philosophers in providing cognitive order for the divine in the absence of corporate priesthoods and canonical texts, the political religiosity of the classical city-state, Roman religious "legalism," the rise of personal or individualistic spirituality in the form of mystery cults promising both worldly and afterlife rewards to their ritual adherents and the congregational-soteriological faiths of Orphism and Pythagorianism, the religious life of women, the consequences of civic depoliticization under Roman imperium for the growth of Christianity—these are among the many topics illuminated by Weber's comparative-sociological analysis.

Although current scholarly fashion favors eclectic and more "middle-range" applications over "grand theorizing," social science perspectives continue to inform the researches of ancient historians and classicists. The historian Keith Hopkins (1978, 1983), in a manner befitting his formal sociological training, has examined the religious dimensions of gladiatorial contests, the emperor cult, and the complex of beliefs and practices regarding death in Roman society. An anthropologically framed focus on gender and religion is featured in the pathbreaking studies of Sarah Pomeroy (1975) and Sally Humphreys (1983). S. R. F. Price (1984) draws upon Geertz and Bourdieu to show how emperor worship functioned both as a cognitive system and as a vehicle of symbolic power in consolidating Rome's expanding suzerainty in the Mediterranean world. Ramsay

MacMullen (1981), with a social historian's attention to context, provides an invaluable and variegated portrait of how paganism actually "worked" in the daily lives of inhabitants of the Roman empire. The classical scholar Walter Burkert (1983, 1985, 1987) has produced several authoritative studies that display a deep learning in the social sciences and in biology, shedding light on virtually all aspects of Greek religion. The complex and tension-ridden interfacial contacts between Greco-Roman paganism, Judaism, and Christianity have preoccupied scholars since the time of Gibbon, but few have matched the analytical rigor and mastery over empirical detail displayed by either Arthur Darby Nock (1933, 1972) or Arnaldo Momigliano (1977, 1987). In the ongoing, multilingual series, *Aufstieg und Niedergang der römischen Welt* (de Gruyter), volumes II.16, II.17, II.19, and II.23 explore diverse facets of Greek and Roman religion, with varying degrees of social science sophistication; particularly valuable treatments are offered of the mystery cults, demonic powers, the Sibylline oracles, magical practices, and the histories and functions of principal deities of the Roman pantheon.

Religions have generally proved to be among the more durable—if endlessly adaptive—of social phenomena; once institutionalized and culturally elaborated, they are seldom eradicated or abandoned altogether. The fate of Greek and Roman "paganism" provides a striking exception to that tendency, for the triumph of Christianity—although accompanied by selective "borrowings" and syncretic fusions in both thought and ritual—did entail the eclipse of a polytheistic religious order that had reigned for more than a millennium. The sociological issues raised by that fact alone provide sufficient warrant for renewed attention by social scientists in a field that so captivated the founders of their disciplines.

—*Joseph M. Bryant*

REFERENCES

W. Burkert, *Homo Necans* (Berkeley: University of California Press, 1983); W. Burkert, *Greek Religion* (Cambridge: Harvard University Press, 1985); W. Burkert, *Ancient Mystery Cults* (Cambridge: Harvard University Press, 1987); F. M. Cornford, *From Religion to Philosophy* (London: Arnold, 1912); M. Detienne, *Les jardins d'Adonis* (Paris: Gallimard, 1972); M. Detienne, *Dionysos mis à mort* (Paris: Gallimard, 1977); G. Dumézil, *Archaic Roman Religion* (Chicago: University of Chicago Press, 1970); J. Harrison, *Prolegomena to the Study of Greek Religion* (London: Merlin, 1962 [1903]); J. Harrison, *Themis* (Cambridge: Cambridge University Press, 1912); K. Hopkins, *Conquerors and Slaves* (Cambridge: Cambridge University Press, 1978); K. Hopkins, *Death and Renewal* (Cambridge: Cambridge University

Press, 1983); S. Humphreys, *Family, Women and Death* (London: Routledge, 1983); R. MacMullen, *Paganism in the Roman Empire* (New Haven, Conn.: Yale University Press, 1981); A. Momigliano, *Essays in Ancient and Modern Historiography* (Oxford: Blackwell, 1977); A. Momigliano, *On Pagans, Jews, and Christians* (Hanover, N.H.: Wesleyan University Press, 1987); M. Nilsson, *Geschichte der griechischen Religion* (Munich: Beck, 1955, 1961); A. D. Nock, *Conversion* (Oxford: Clarendon, 1933); A. D. Nock, *Essays on Religion and the Ancient World* (Oxford: Clarendon, 1972); S. Pomeroy, *Goddesses, Whores, Wives, and Slaves* (New York: Schocken, 1975); S. R. F. Price, *Rituals and Power* (Cambridge: Cambridge University Press, 1984); H. J. Rose, *Ancient Roman Religion* (New York: Hillary House, 1948); G. Thomson, *The Prehistoric Aegean* (London: Lawrence & Wishart, 1949); G. Thomson, *The First Philosophers* (London: Lawrence & Wishart, 1955); J. Vernant, *Mythe et société en Grèce ancienne* (Paris: Maspero, 1974); P. Vidal-Naquet, *The Black Hunter* (Baltimore: Johns Hopkins University Press, 1986); A. Winspear, *The Genesis of Plato's Thought* (New York: Dryden, 1940).

GREELEY, ANDREW M. (1928–)   Priest of the Roman Catholic Archdiocese of Chicago; S.T.L., St. Mary of the Lake Seminary, 1954; ordained priest the same year and assigned as curate to Christ the King parish, Chicago. While engaged in parish work, he was directed in 1960 to part-time study at the University of Chicago, where he received an M.A. (1961) and Ph.D. (1962) in sociology. In 1965, Greeley was assigned to full-time work at the National Opinion Research Center (NORC), Chicago, where he holds an appointment as Research Associate. Lecturer, University of Chicago, 1963-1972; Professor of Sociology at the University of Arizona, 1979–, and concurrently Professor of Social Science, University of Chicago, 1991–. President, American Catholic Sociological Society, 1966. Recipient of several honorary degrees.

A bibliography of Greeley's work (Harrison 1994) lists 3,715 items encompassing his activities as a sociologist, novelist, teacher, religious writer, commentator, syndicated newspaper columnist, media personality, poet, opera librettist, and photographer. His sociological publications include research monographs on the sociology of ecstasy (1974), the sociology of the paranormal (1975), ethnic stratification and mobility in the United States (1976), and ethnicity and drinking (Greeley et al. 1980). *The Sociology of Andrew M. Greeley* (Scholars Press 1994) contains 48 reprinted journal articles representing the core of his publications on the sociology of religion. An autobiography, *Confes-*

sions of a Parish Priest (Simon and Schuster), appeared in 1986.

Greeley is a social scientist in the survey research tradition. He eschews extensive theoretical abstraction and data-free discourse in favor of testable hypotheses anchored in a covering perspective and assessed in probability samples of population. During the course of his career as a sociologist, he has consistently analyzed religion as a differentiated, irreducible phenomenon that provides meaning and organizes belonging in ways that are independent of the expression of instrumental and adaptive activity in modern societies.

Greeley's accomplishments as a successful novelist of religious sensibility are a pastoral application of his theory of religion. In his view, religion is root images that are embedded in rituals and narratives that enable individuals to tell and enact salutary stories in their own lives—witnessed, for example, in his *Religion as Poetry* (Transaction 1995).

Early Sociological Work   Greeley's early work was a response to questions stimulated by developments in American society from the end of World War II to about the mid-1960s. The decline of WASP hegemony, the identification of the categories of Protestant, Catholic, and Jew as the major elements of American pluralism, the incorporation of the offspring of immigrant subpopulations into the middle classes, and suburbanization led to questions regarding ethnic assimilation and the nature of religious meaning and belonging in America.

Greeley's study (1962) of an upper-middle-class parish in the Beverly area of Chicago adduced evidence of Will Herberg's triple-melting-pot thesis advanced in *Protestant-Catholic-Jew* (Doubleday 1955). The upwardly mobile offspring of immigrants (largely Irish in Beverly) were not assimilated to a single standard identity. They were Americans within the confines of religious categories that downplayed ethnic origins. Ethnic exogamy and religious endogamy underwrote the categories.

Notwithstanding the homogeneity of Beverly's citizens on the standard socioeconomic indicators, the Catholic-Protestant distinction divided the community into two endogamous solitudes. Adults of both faiths shared the common recreational ground of the country club, where friendly competition occurred but informal social interaction was limited. Protestant and Catholic youth never mixed in the community. Greeley's analysis (1970) of data from the 1957 *Current Population Survey of the United States* indicated that the endogamous religious marriage patterns that he found in Beverly

held among Catholics and Jews in the general population and within Protestant denominations as well.

The Education, Values, and Careers of American Catholics   The American educational system became a focus of intense public concern after the Soviet Union orbited the space capsule *Sputnik* in 1957. The post-*Sputnik* public malaise coincided with criticism of the American Roman Catholic educational system and the ethos that was deemed to be the foundation of the system. Catholic intellectuals and critics pointed to the absence of a scholarly American Catholic tradition, fear of modern science, and the failure of Catholic colleges and universities to produce significant numbers of research-oriented graduates. On the basis of data gathered in the Detroit metropolitan area, Gerhard Lenski, in his widely acclaimed book *The Religious Factor* (Doubleday 1960), reported that Catholics were not disposed to make choices that led to economic achievement (the "Protestant ethic thesis"), and that they exhibited antiscientific attitudes. Lenski speculated that Catholicism's stress on obedience and the high value it placed on close family and kin ties rather than on secondary relationships were responsible for inhibiting the choice of scientific careers and lowering the level of orientation to economic achievement among Catholics.

Greeley responded to Lenski and to those Catholics whom he called "the self-critics" (Thomas O'Dea, Gustave Weigel, John Tracey Ellis) in *Religion and Career* (Sheed & Ward 1963) and in a series of articles (reprinted in *The Sociology of Andrew M. Greeley*). Using data gathered by NORC from a national sample of 1961 college graduates, he showed that Catholics did not differ from Protestants and in some cases Jews too in terms of academic experiences, career plans, and occupational values. Catholics were no less interested in science or mathematics than Protestants or Jews and no less desirous of success than Protestants. Greeley's findings destroyed the widely held stereotype that all American Catholics were anti-intellectual, feared science, and rejected the core values of American society: autonomy, achievement, and material success.

Greeley's conclusions differed from Lenski's because, as Greeley pointed out, he had used a national sample, whereas Detroit still had a lot of recent immigrants when Lenski gathered his data in the late 1950s. Recent immigrants often were not able to afford higher education. For that reason, many Catholics in Detroit were less likely than the average American Catholic to attend college and acquire the values associated with higher education, including autonomy and achievement. What held in Detroit in the 1950s had held in

America earlier in the century. Recent Catholic immigrants and their children formed a substantially higher fraction of the American population in 1910 than they did after World War II. The criticisms voiced by the Catholic intellectuals in the 1950s were based on old facts that did not apply to many Catholics after World War II. By the mid-1970s, Catholics exceeded Protestants on standard measures of education, income, and occupational achievement. Irish, Italian, and Polish Catholics living in the North had higher annual incomes than white Episcopalians (Greeley 1976).

Religiosity, Ethnicity, and Secularity While Greeley destroyed the stereotype that American Catholics were generally anti-intellectual and had values and career plans that set them apart from most Americans even after exposure to higher education, questions remained regarding the effects of religion and religiosity versus nonreligious factors on behavior, attitudes, and adaptation to American society. Greeley's work points to a complex relationship between sources of behavior that are fundamentally religious (for example, Catholic norms regarding birth control), the nonreligious aspects of culture that immigrants brought with them to America (for example, a taste for *cannoli* versus *Wurst*), residential patterns of settlement (urban versus suburban versus rural), and the dominant secularized Protestant culture of America (the "American Way of Life").

Greeley realized earlier than most intellectuals that the triple-melting-pot thesis—that is, assimilation to the categories of Protestant, Catholic, or Jew—oversimplified the realities of adjustment in America. There were persistent nonreligious differences among groups. Greeley argued that many of the effects that Lenski attributed to religion and religiosity could be traced to the development of secular norms and roles formed in the segregated communication networks of groups that were marked in the first instance by distinctive religious boundaries. According to Greeley, group characteristics such as voting behavior (for example, the loyalty of the Celtic Irish to the Democratic Party) did not flow from religious ideology but from nonreligious constraints and secular action within religiously homogeneous communities (1963). Ethnicity, in other words, was alive and well in America!

Although he sensed the aptness of ethnicity as an analytical tool and underwrote it in his own work, Greeley was not willing to concede the religious question to the secularization theorists either by conflating ethnicity and religion—thereby reducing religiosity to ethnicity—or by accepting as true the popular decline-of-religion-in-modernity thesis. Long before many academics and opinion makers realized that religion was not irrelevant to either private or public life in America (the presidential elections of 1976 and, especially, 1980 marked the turn), Greeley marshaled data and arguments against the secularization thesis in *Unsecular Man: The Persistence of Religion* (Schocken 1972). His analysis of social surveys—some predating World War II—later led him to conclude in *Religious Change in America* (Harvard University Press 1989) that Americans' religious behavior had changed little from 1940 to 1985; there was always more than less of it.

***Humanae Vitae* and the Religious Imagination** The high level of aggregate religious practice and behavior in America over the course of the twentieth century does not support the secularization thesis. However, there have been some "ups and downs." Between 1968 and 1975, American Catholics reduced their weekly church attendance by one-third, marking an unprecedented decline in Catholic religious observance. Although lower than the Catholic rate (as usual), the weekly attendance rate for Protestants in the same period was unchanged (Greeley et al. 1976, Hout and Greeley 1987).

A popular interpretation of the decline linked it to changes in the Catholic Church as a result of Vatican II. Having analyzed a variety of databases, Greeley and his colleagues concluded that it was not the actions of the council that caused the decline. Rather, it was the 1968 papal encyclical on birth control, *Humanae Vitae*. They noted that there was little change in Catholic observance between the end of the council in 1964 and 1968. The decline in observance began in 1968 and leveled off in 1975.

Analysis of data gathered from representative samples of the U.S. Catholic population showed that about half of American Catholics accepted the birth control teaching in 1963, but the figure declined to 15% by 1974. A similar change occurred in the acceptance of papal authority. The change in weekly observance was accounted for by the decline in the acceptance of both the birth control teaching and papal authority. It could not be explained by age-related lifestyle factors, changes in the demography of American Catholics, or secularization.

The decline in observance stabilized in the mid-1970s at about 50%. However, among those who attended church weekly, there were still many who did not accept the birth control teaching and questioned papal authority. Why did they remain observant Catholics? Greeley showed in *The Young Catholic Family: Religious Images and Marital Fulfillment* (Thomas More Press 1980) that the key variable was how people imagine God. Those who reject the church's sexual ethic and nonetheless have an image of God as kind, gentle, and loving are the ones who are most likely to go to weekly Mass and Communion. The laity justify the reception of the sacraments by appealing in their minds to an image of God who understands the importance of sex in marriage.

The insight that images of God have an important impact on religious behavior has been expanded into a theory of religion in such books as *The Religious Imagination* (Sadlier 1981), *Religion: A Secular Theory* (Free Press 1982), and *Religion as Poetry* (see also Greeley 1989). The theory elaborates the work of Rudolph Otto and William James (religion as experience), Talcott Parsons and Clifford Geertz (religion as powerful symbols), and Roger Schank (religion as stories). Experience, symbols, and stories are entwined and mutually encoded.

Adapting an approach from David Tracey's *The Analogical Imagination* (Crossroad 1981) on the dialectical (Protestant) and analogical (Catholic) imaginations, Greeley has formulated in *Religion as Poetry* a specification of his theory that incorporates the fundamental Protestant and Catholic images of God. In scale form, the specification forces choices between images of God as Mother/Father, Master/Spouse, Judge/Lover, and Friend/King. Respondents' choices—the items have been administered to thousands of subjects—are explained by a single factor. These factor scores account for a wide variety of behaviors and attitudes, including prayer, political attitudes, attitudes toward the environment, attitudes toward AIDS, and differences between U.S. Catholics and Southern Baptists.

See also Gerhard Lenski, Protestant Ethic Thesis, Roman Catholicism

—*John H. Simpson*

REFERENCES

A. M. Greeley, "Some Aspects of Interaction Between Religious Groups in an Upper Middle Class Roman Catholic Parish," *Social Compass* 9(1962):39-61; A. M. Greeley, "A Note on the Origins of Religious Differences," *Journal for the Scientific Study of Religion* 3(1963):21-31; A. M. Greeley, "Religious Intermarriage in a Denominational Society," *American Journal of Sociology* 75(1970):949-952; A. M. Greeley, *Ecstasy* (Englewood Cliffs, N.J.: Prentice Hall, 1974); A. M. Greeley, *The Sociology of the Paranormal* (Beverly Hills, Calif.: Sage, 1975); A. M. Greeley, *Ethnicity, Denomination and Inequality* (Beverly Hills, Calif.: Sage, 1976); A. M. Greeley, "The Sociology of American Catholics," *Annual Review of Sociology* 5(1979):91-111; A. M. Greeley, "Protestant and Catholic," *American Sociological Review* 54(1989):485-502; A. M. Greeley et al., *Catholic Schools in a Declining Church* (Kansas City, Mo.: Sheed and Ward, 1976); A. M. Greeley et al., *Ethnic Drinking Subcultures* (New York: Praeger, 1980); E. Harrison, *Andrew M. Greeley* (Metuchen, N.J.: Scarecrow, 1994); M. Hout and A. M. Greeley, "The Center Doesn't Hold," *American Sociological Review* 52(1987):325-345.

GREENS   *see* Ecology Movement

GROUPS   A group, whether human or otherwise, is distinguished by its members' possession of an interrelationship of some kind; the members of groups, properly speaking, each have something "in common," if only their relationship to each other. A category, by way of contrast, is the "grouping" by an outside agent of a number of otherwise discrete phenomena. Thus groupings are aggregates that are distinguished by a common attribute.

The student of *religion* (especially if understood in the broadest sense: of "spirituality") will be universally concerned with *groups* in the stricter sense (their identities, spirit)—whether "religious" or "secular." The social scientist, on the other hand, is equally concerned with formulating categories.

This distinction is reflected in the classification of groups. Thus Cooley distinguished "primary" from "nucleated" groups; Tönnies distinguished *Gemeinschaft* from *Gesellschaft;* Redfield, folk from urban society; Maine, societies of status and of contract; Durkheim (with unhappy appellations), mechanical solidarity from organic solidarity. The greater cohesion, content, and specificity of the type cases clustered at the first end of the spectrum, compared with the need to impose the grouping at the other end of the spectrum, echoes the common distinction between that which is of the *esse* of human life (and therefore religious) and that which is comparatively accidental or contingent (and therefore secular).

—*Edward I. Bailey*

REFERENCE

C. H. Cooley, *Social Organization* (Chicago: Free Press, 1956 [1902]).

GRUESSER, JEANINE (1917–)   A member of the Sisters of St. Francis of Assisi, Gruesser received a Ph.D. in sociology from the Catholic University of America (1950) and thereafter spent her academic career at Cardinal Stritch College, Milwaukee. When she was elected President of the American Catholic Sociological Society in 1955, Sister Jeanine was the first Catholic nun to head a professional organization of sociologists.

Sister Jeanine's early research studies concerned differences between school-age Jewish and Catholic children in the Bronx and Manhattan. Her later studies included research on the permanent diaconate program in Milwaukee. Strongly social action oriented, Sister Jeanine responded to the denial of civil rights to African Americans by joining Dr. Martin Luther King, Jr., in his 1964 march on Selma, Alabama. Her ACSS presidential address broke new ground by calling on the society to make Catholicism itself an object of study. She focused in that address on how Catholics "define a given social situation with reference to Catholic beliefs and externalize that definition in their actions in a given situation" (*American Catholic Sociological Review,* Vol. 17, p. 2).

—*Loretta M. Morris*

GUILT   Central construct in psychoanalytic studies of religion. Freud argued that a heightened sense of guilt, originating in the fear of loss of love, is a necessary correlate of civilization. The dynamics of guilt include both submission to authority and an unconscious desire to be punished. Thus religious traditions are seen as analogous to developmental neuroses. Contemporary empirical studies of guilt are more restricted to what can be justified empirically. However, reliable scales to measure theoretically meaningful dimensions of guilt are rare, contributing to a lack of consensus on relationships between guilt and religion among empirical psychologists.

—*Ralph W. Hood, Jr.*

REFERENCES

S. Freud, *Civilization and Its Discontents* (New York: Norton, 1961 [1930]); D. H. Harder and A. Zalma, "The Assessment of Shame and Guilt," in *Advances in Personality Assessment,* Vol. 6 (Hillsdale, N.J.: Lawrence Erlbaum, 1990): 89-114; R. W. Hood, Jr., "Sin and Guilt in Faith Traditions," in *Religion and Mental Health,* ed. J. F. Shumaker (New York: Oxford University Press, 1992): 110-121.

HADDEN, JEFFREY K. (1936–) Professor of Sociology at the University of Virginia in Charlottesville.

Hadden received his B.A. degree in psychology in 1959 and his M.A. in 1960 in sociology from the University of Kansas; he was awarded a Ph.D. in sociology from the University of Wisconsin in 1963. The interdisciplinary nature of his interests is reflected in his appointments as Associate Professor of Sociology and Associate Director of the Civil Violence Research Center at Case Western Reserve University, Professor of Sociology and Urban Studies at Tulane University, and Visiting Professor in the Department of Medicine at the Baylor College of Medicine.

Hadden has provided sustained leadership in professional societies. He has been appointed to the editorial boards or as associate editor for a number of journals, including *Social Forces, Sociological Inquiry, Sociological Focus,* and *Second Opinion.* On two occasions (1973-1979 and 1992-1995), he served as Book Review Editor for the *Journal for the Scientific Study of Religion.* He was elected to the executive councils of the Society for the Scientific Study of Religion, Association for the Sociology of Religion, Religious Research Association, Southern Sociological Society, and American Association for the Advancement of Science. In 1979, he gave the H. Paul Douglass Lecture to the Religious Research Association. He served as President of Association for the Sociology of Religion (1979), both Vice-President (1981-1982) and President (1983-1984) of the Society for the Scientific Study of Religion, and Vice-President (1982) and President (1986) of the Southern Sociological Society. He is a Fellow of the American Association for the Advancement of Science.

Throughout Hadden's career, he has pursued a diverse program of research. His work in the area of sociology of the family has focused on the relationship between social status and interpersonal patterns of address. In the area of urban sociology, Hadden has written on issues ranging from typologies of urban communities, the process of suburbanization, civil violence in urban areas, the demography of nuclear war, and urban social problems. The most important thrust of his work in urban sociology was the development of a classificatory system identifying a common set of variables that could be used at a variety of levels of ecological analysis. The book that best exemplifies this line of work is *American Cities: Their Social Characteristics* (with Edgar Borgatta, Rand McNally 1965). Another major focus of his work in this area has been the process of suburbanization, which he explored in a series of books such as *Suburbia in Transition* (coedited with L. H. Masotti, New Viewpoints 1974) and *The Urbanization of the Suburbs* (coedited with L. Masotti, Sage 1973). Finally, Hadden has analyzed the roots of urban racial violence during the 1960s, most notably in *A Time to Burn?* (with Masotti and others, Rand McNally 1969).

During the last two decades, Hadden's primary corpus of work has been in the sociology of religion. The general theme unifying the dozen books and 70 journal articles and book chapters he has published in this area is the relationship between religion and politics. His early work focused on more institutionalized forms of religion. Most notable is his book *The Gathering Storm in the Churches* (Doubleday 1969). As with the early work of Glock and Stark, this interdenominational study of Protestant clergy revealed wide diversity of theological, social, and political beliefs both within and between denominations. It also analyzed tension between clergy and laity over the appropriate posture of churches toward social and political issues.

When Hadden moved to the University of Virginia in 1972, he became aware of an important parachurch phenomenon in America, religious broadcasting. He has written several books in this area, most notably *Televangelism, Power and Politics* (with Anson Shupe, Holt 1988) and *Prime Time Preachers* (with Charles Swann, Addison-Wesley 1981). These books are analyses of the political movement that gave rise to religious broadcasting, the nature and size of the audience, the broadcasters and the nature of their messages, and the link between their theologies and political programs. He has also written extensively on religious fundamentalism and pentecostalism, which he argues are the most successful sectarian religious movements of the twentieth century. This theme along with his conceptualization of fundamentalism as a global phenomenon are explored in three books coedited with Anson Shupe: *Prophetic Religions and Politics* (Paragon House 1986), *The Politics of Religion and Social Change* (Paragon House 1988), and *Secularization and Fundamentalism Reconsidered* (Paragon House 1989).

Most recently, Hadden has worked in the area of new religious movements. His two-volume work *Handbook on Cults and Sects in America* (coedited with David Bromley, JAI 1993), cosponsored by the Association for the Sociology of Religion and the Society for the Scientific Study of Religion, compiles more than two decades of research by leading scholars in this area.

Hadden's Southern Sociological Society Presidential Address (*Social Forces*, Vol. 65, 1987) raised significant questions about the tenability of the secularization thesis and remains a crucial contribution to that debate.

—*David G. Bromley*

HALÉVY, ÉLIE/HALÉVY THESIS   *see* Methodism, Protestantism

HAMMOND, PHILLIP E. (1931–)   D. Mackenzie Brown Professor of Religious Studies and Sociology, University of California at Santa Barbara.

Hammond was a student of Paul Lazarsfeld in the Bureau of Applied Social Research at Columbia University in the late 1950s, completing his Ph.D. in 1960. He taught sociology at Yale, Wisconsin, and Arizona before joining the Department of Religious Studies at UCSB in 1979. During his Santa Barbara tenure, Hammond cultivated one of the premier graduate programs for the social scientific study of religion. Hammond's distinguished teaching and research career includes visiting appointments at Berkeley, Stanford, the London School of Economics, and the University of Copenhagen. Beyond his scholarly contributions to the sociology of religion, Hammond has been a devoted member of the Society for the Scientific Study of Religion. He edited the *Journal for the Scientific Study of Religion* (1978-1982) and was elected President of SSSR in 1985. He also served as President of the Western Region of the American Academy of Religion (1986-1987).

Hammond established himself in the discipline of sociology with the publication of the edited volume *Sociologists at Work* (Basic Books 1964), a benchmark study of how social research is done. He also published an introductory sociology textbook; but, the son of three generations of Methodist clergymen, Hammond is foremost a sociologist of religion. Distinguishing his scholarly career is an intellectual preoccupation with the changing role of religion in the modern world and the strengths and limitations of the nineteenth-century theories that tried to explain it as a sociological and historical phenomenon. That concern was explored explicitly in the publication of two widely used essay collections, *Beyond the Classics? Essays in the Scientific Study of Religion* (with Charles Y. Glock, Harper 1973) and *The Sacred in a Secular Age: Toward Revision in the Scientific Study of Religion* (University of California Press 1985). Hammond has written extensively on a wide range of topics in the social scientific study of religion—from prayer in public schools and the New Christian Right to religious identity and the rise of new religious movements—but is perhaps best known for his long-standing work on civil religion in America, exemplified by the volume *Varieties of Civil Religion* (with Robert Bellah, Harper 1980).

The monograph *Religion and Personal Autonomy: The Third Disestablishment in America* (University of South Carolina Press 1992) is a comparative study of regional religious subcultures in America. In it Hammond shows how social changes in the 1960s accelerated fundamental change in the religion-culture relationship in the United States. Moral authority is shifting, Hammond argues, from churches to autonomous individuals. Therefore, while church membership and attendance remain relatively high in the United States, the social meaning of religious participation has changed. Thus the book makes a major contribution to the secularization debate and is perhaps the crowning achievement of Hammond's prolific career.

—*Mark A. Shibley*

HARE KRISHNA   *see* International Society for Krishna Consciousness

HARGROVE, BARBARA J(UNE WATTS)
(1924-1988)   Sociologist of religion whose scholarly contributions focused on the effects of social change on institutional religion. Specific concerns involved the rural environment, the impact of new religious movements of the 1970s and 1980s, and women entering the ministry. Her prolific scholarship, which included being author, coauthor, or editor of 7 books and 52 articles or chapters in books within a career span of 20 years, was particularly unusual for a second-career scholar who began her academic professional life after age 40.

After "raising chickens and kids and gardens," and intrigued by the dynamics of conflict within rural congregations and communities between those eager for change and those resistant to it, she returned to college in 1960 and, as a single parent following the death of her husband, earned the first Ph.D. in sociology at Colorado State University. Teaching and chairing the Sociology Department at Hollins College (Virginia), her first monograph, *The Reformation of the Holy: A Sociology of Religion* (Davis 1971), attracted the attention of sociologist Rodney Stark, resulting in a postdoctoral appointment at the University of California at Berkeley with Charles Glock and Robert Bellah (1972-1973). There, her study of the effects of new religious movements on mainline churches, through research on youth and campus ministries, transformed her ensuing research commitments. Her subsequent academic appointments were at the University of North Florida (1973-1975), where she founded and chaired the Department of Sociology and Social Welfare, Yale Divinity School (1975-1979), and finally as Professor of Sociology of Religion at Iliff School of Theology (Denver) from 1979 until her death.

Following her Berkeley experience, Hargrove's scholarship focused on the nexus of new religious movements and mainline denominationalism. Prominent in the sociology of religion academy, she edited *Sociological Analysis* (now *Sociology of Religion*), the official journal of the Association for the Sociology of Religion, from 1985 until her death. She also served as President of the Religious Research Association (1978-1979) and Vice President of the Association for the Sociology of Religion (1984). Illness and death prevented her delivery of the Religious Research Association's H. Paul Douglass lecture for which she had been selected in 1989 (see Long et al. 1989). Hargrove was widely known for her mentorship of junior colleagues and graduate students, and acclaimed as a role model for women scholars starting their careers. As a committed Presbyterian, she was widely known for her denominational and ecumenical activity, including work with the National Council of Churches.

Immediately prior to her death, Hargrove had been researching religion's role in U.S. rural communities facing the farm crisis, and had planned to examine the diversity of socioeconomic issues in the rural West for which theological education needed to prepare future ministers, a research interest integrating her sociological expertise, religious commitment, and passion for the rural environment.

—*Paula D. Nesbitt*

REFERENCES

R. Fernandez-Calienes, "Bibliography of the Works of Barbara J. W. Hargrove," *Sociological Analysis* 51(1990):315-329; B. J. W. Hargrove, *Religion for a Dislocated Generation* (Valley Forge, Pa.: Judson, 1980); B. J. W. Hargrove, "Free to Be Me," in *A Time to Weep, A Time to Sing,* ed. M. J. Meadow and C. A. Rayburn (Minneapolis: Winston, 1985): 64-78; B. J. W. Hargrove, *The Emerging New Class* (New York: Pilgrim, 1986); B. J. W. Hargrove, *The Sociology of Religion,* 2nd ed. (Arlington, Ill.: Harlan Davidson, 1989); R. S. Jarles, "Barbara June Watts Hargrove," in *An Intellectual History of the Iliff School of Theology,* ed. J. A. Templin (Denver: Iliff School of Theology, 1992): 359-373; T. E. Long et al., "In Memoriam," *Review of Religious Research* 30(1989):321-328.

HARTE, THOMAS J. (1914-1974)   Born in Ireland and orphaned by the age of 11, Harte moved to New Jersey at the age of 14 to live with an uncle. He joined the Redemptorist order (C.SS.R.) in 1937 and was ordained a priest in 1942. He received both an M.A. and a Ph.D. in sociology from Catholic University of America. He was a member of the Department of Sociology at Catholic University of America from 1947 until his death. He was also Research Consultant and

Chief Investigator for the Council on Applied Research in the Apostolate (CARA), Hagerstown, Maryland. President, American Catholic Sociological Society, 1951.

One of his published books in the sociology of religion was coedited with C. Joseph Nuesse, *The Sociology of the Parish* (Bruce 1951). His ACSS presidential address focused on the evidence of research among Catholic sociologists, particularly in Catholic institutions of higher education. He asked, "Do Catholic sociologists measure up to what may be reasonably expected of them as scholars and as scientists?" Based on a recent survey of members of the American Catholic Sociological Society, his answer was a resounding "No!" and he deplored the state of scholarship as demonstrated by the membership's paucity of publication.

—*Loretta M. Morris*

HEALING   *see* Wellness

HEALY, MARY EDWARD (1906-1991)

A member of the Sisters of St. Joseph of Carondelet, Healy received a Ph.D. in sociology from the Catholic University of America in 1948. She was a member of the faculty of the College of St. Catherine, St. Paul, later its president, and then became provincial superior of her religious order. President, American Catholic Sociological Society, 1959.

Her research and publications were on social change, which was the subject of her presidential address to the ACSS. Echoing two of her predecessors in the ACSS presidency, Sister Mary Edward called for the study of Catholicism itself. Specifically, she recommended the study of Catholic universities and colleges, their students, the milieu, and the influence of values in their lives. She placed this within the wider scope of social change and Catholic education.

—*Loretta M. Morris*

HEGEL, G(EORG) W(ILHELM) F(RIEDRICH) (1770-1831)   German philosopher; taught at the University of Jena, where his *Phenomenology of Spirit* was completed the night before Napoleon's victorious battle there; later appointed to Berlin.

The categories of Spirit *(Geist)* and history are central to his philosophy. Spirit realizes itself in the whole of history. Its alienations form an expanding circle, from subjective spirit (individual interests and psychology) to objective spirit (economics, politics, moral community) to absolute spirit (art, religion, philosophy). Religion and philosophy are humanity's highest attainments. They have the same content, the knowledge of God, but employ different forms. Religion is a totality of feeling, cult, and symbolic representation in tangible images. Philosophy is "worship" in conceptual form and its scientific system is a more complete manifestation of divine knowledge.

Hegel's *Early Theological Writings,* unpublished in his lifetime, sound a protoexistentialist note, while his mature system emphasizes the historical diversity and transformations of religions, especially the movement from Judaism and Greek philosophy to Christianity, whose concrete trinity is superseded, yet preserved in the dialectical movement of philosophy. Hegel decisively influenced modern thought, including Marxism, existentialism, phenomenology, the philosophy of history, and the human sciences.

—*Donald A. Nielsen*

REFERENCES

E. L. Fackenheim, *The Religious Dimension in Hegel's Thought* (Boston: Beacon, 1967); G. W. F. Hegel, *The Phenomenology of Spirit* (Oxford: Clarendon, 1977 [1807]); G. W. F. Hegel, *Lectures on the Philosophy of Religion,* 3 vols. (Berkeley: University of California Press, 1984-1987 [1827]).

HELLER, CELIA STOPNICKA (1927–)   Born in Poland, received a B.A. from Brooklyn College (1950), M.A. (1952) and Ph.D. from Columbia University (1962), and rose from the rank of Assistant Professor (1964) to Professor (1971) at Hunter College, CUNY. President, Association of the Social Scientific Study of Jewry, 1977-1979.

Her major work in the sociology of religion is *On the Edge of Destruction: Jews in Poland Between the Two World Wars* (Columbia University Press 1977), which has been twice reprinted. In addition, she has written on the attitudes of African Americans toward Jews and contributed to *Commonweal* and *Commentary.*

—*J. Alan Winter*

HERBERG, WILL (1901-1977)   Russian-born Jewish author, Herberg never completed an academic

degree in course. He received three honorary doctorates, the first in 1956; Graduate Professor, Drew University, 1956-1974.

Herberg's early work and writing was associated with the far left of the American labor movement, but he later came to reject the Marxist program, particularly as a result of reading the work of Reinhold Niebuhr. Convinced of the essential sinfulness of human nature, Herberg turned toward theology and published his first major work, *Judaism and Modern Man* in 1951 (Farrar Straus).

Herberg made his lasting mark on the study of American religion and society, however, with the publication of *Protestant-Catholic-Jew: An Essay in American Religious Sociology* in 1955 (Doubleday). The thesis of this work was that waves of immigrants to the United States became integrated into a larger societal community, "the American Way of Life," that provided an overarching value system of which the three principal religions had become subdivisions, distinguishing among but not dividing a common core rooted in the Judeo-Christian heritage. *Protestant-Catholic-Jew* laid much of the intellectual groundwork for the introduction of the "civil religion" thesis a decade later.

Herberg's later works reflect a continued interest in both religion and in labor, but in the latter case, he adopted the position of a staunch anticommunist, basing his labor theory on a combination of a relatively conservative biblicalism as well as more conservative political economics.

See also American Religion, Andrew M. Greeley

—*William H. Swatos, Jr.*

REFERENCE

H. J. Ausmus, *Will Herberg* (Westport, Conn.: Greenwood, 1986).

HERSKOVITS, MELVILLE (1895-1963)

Professor of Anthropology at Northwestern University who conducted extensive fieldwork in Dahomey, Dutch Guinea, Haiti, Trinidad, and, to a lesser degree, Brazil. His *Life in a Haitian Valley* (Knopf 1931) illustrates Herskovits's awareness of the African contributions to family organization, economics, and religion in the New World. In his classic *The Myth of the Negro Past* (Harper 1941), he argued that African American religions and cultures have retained numerous practices surviving from Africa, or "Africanisms." For example, he found that in such areas as Brazil, Haiti, Cuba, and

the American Deep South, Catholic saints and African deities had merged to produce a new set of spirits.

—*Hans A. Baer*

HERVIEU-LÉGER, DANIÈLE (1947–)

Directeur d'Études at the École des Hautes Études of the Centre d'Études Interdisciplinaires des Faits Religieux (CEIFR) in Paris, Editor-in-Chief of the journal *Archives de Sciences sociales des Religions.*

Beginning with research on Catholic students (Hervieu and Léger 1973) and then on the utopian reformulation of beliefs in the context of anti-institutional and communitarian movements (1983), Hervieu-Léger critically reviews the notion of *secularization,* which she understands not only as a loss of influence by religious institutions but also as the production of new forms of religion by modern societies, particularly through the possibilities for sociability provided by new religious movements (1986, Champion and Hervieu-Léger 1990). In this perspective, religion appears as a particular mode of believing in relation to the authority of a tradition and to the continuity of belief. It is conceived as a form of *collective memory* (1993a).

—*Roberto Cipriani*

REFERENCES

F. Champion and D. Hervieu-Léger, *De l'émotion en religion* (Paris: Centurion, 1990); D. Léger, *De la mission à la protestation* (Paris: Cerf, 1973); B. Hervieu and D. Hervieu-Léger, *Des communautés pour des temps difficiles* (Paris: Centurion, 1983); D. Hervieu-Léger, *Vers un nouveau christianisme?* (Paris: Cerf, 1986); D. Hervieu-Léger, *La religion pour mémoire* (Paris: Cerf, 1993a); D. Hervieu-Léger (ed.), *Religion et écologie* (Paris: Cerf, 1993b).

HIMMELFARB, HAROLD S. (1944–)

B.A., UCLA (1966); master's (1968) and doctorate (1974), University of Chicago. President, Association for the Social Scientific Study of Jewry (1981-1983).

His study (1979) of the long-term impact of childhood Jewish education on adult Jewish religious involvement was among the first to use multivariate analyses, and pointed to the threshold of cumulative hours necessary to have lasting effects. He also has examined the dimensions of Jewish identity (Himmelfarb and Loar 1984) and the methodological advisability of using distinctive Jewish names (DJN) to locate a study population.

—*J. Alan Winter*

REFERENCES

H. S. Himmelfarb, "Agents of Religious Socialization Among American Jews," *Sociological Quarterly* 20(1979):477-494; H. S. Himmelfarb and R. M. Loar, "National Trends in Jewish Ethnicity: A Test of the Polarization Hypothesis," *Journal for the Scientific Study of Religion* 23(1984):140-154.

HINDUISM   The dominant religious expression of the Indian subcontinent. Its salient characteristics include a hoary mythology, an absence of recorded history (or "founder"), a cyclical notion of time, a pantheism that infuses divinity into the world around, an immanentist relationship between people and divinity, a priestly class, and a tolerance of diverse paths to the ultimate ("god"). Its sacral language is Sanskrit, which came to India about 5,000 years ago along with the Aryans, who came from Central Asia.

Texts   The following are the Hindu sacred texts: (1) Vedas, which are four in number (Rig, Yajur, Sama, and Atharva; 1500 to 1200 B.C.E.); (2) Upanishads (some traced back to the sixth century B.C.E.); (3) Dharma Shastras (sixth and third centuries B.C.E.); (4) Ramayana and Mahabharata (third century B.C.E. and first century C.E.); (5) Puranas (first and tenth centuries C.E.); and (6) Tantras (sixth-seventh centuries C.E.).

The Vedas are mythopoeic compositions that celebrate the divine guardians of earth (Aditi), sky (Varuna, Indra, and Surya), and fire (Agni). The fire sacrifices were conducted by kings and their priests to acquire prosperity in work, success in warfare, and felicity in domestic life. The Upanishads were collectively called Vedanta. These texts often contain mystical discourses between a *virtuoso* and his disciples. They are less ritualistic and more introspective in orientation. Many of them impart esoteric knowledge to the aspirant who seeks illumination. The Dharma Shastras are canonical treatises that enjoin upon Hindus observance of ritual and normative regulations. They uphold a hierarchic social order in which the higher and lower castes are ranked according to the level of their ritual purity. For centuries they have been accepted as the compendia of norms for the social behavior of the Hindu.

The Ramayana and Mahabharata are records of ancient dynastic struggles. They delineate the heroic deeds of men and women who were pitted against court intrigue, warfare, and turbulence. The themes drawn from them are put into plays, songs, and ballads; up to the present, they have inspired creativity in literary and other cultural outputs. The Puranas are records of theophany that aim at the destruction of evil (symbolized by demons) and the recovery of good (symbolized by suffering people). The Puranas center on the principal deities of the post-Vedic era: Shiva, Shakti, and Vishnu. Tantras are a body of formulae and techniques that eliminate the mechanical rituals to seek a direct access to superconsciousness.

Beliefs   The three central tenets of Hinduism on the transcendent level are Dharma, Karma, and Moksha. *Dharma* is the basic moral force that holds the universe (composed of all sentient beings) together. By contrast, *Karma* is individualized. A man or woman's present status in life is a consequence of good or evil deeds in past lives. Likewise, present conduct holds the key to future existence. Fatalism and free will are two faces of the same synergy. Individuals can cross over metaphysical and social obstacles through sustained effort. Hagiographic accounts of India reveal the success of esteemed men and women who overcame their limitations through determination. *Moksha* is the transcendence of karmic bondage: the cessation of births and deaths. Even in the present life, one can attain liberation from worldly ensnarements and attain mental peace. The Bhagavad Gita (Divine Song) shows the path through which an individual finds detachment in the midst of occupational commitments.

For the numerous householders who constitute the bulk of Hindu society, there are three social pursuits that are normatively defined. These are *dharma* (ritual and legal obligations), *artha* (attainment of prosperous life), and *kama* (satisfaction of sexual and procreative needs). These tenets show that Hinduism did not lack commitment to this world. The virtuosi have mainly pursued the transcendent ends; the laity have usually operated on a normative level. Popular Hinduism has centered on fasts and feasts, pilgrimage to temple towns, and so on. It provides scope for the religiously minded people to reach emotional catharsis through collective participation in rituals.

Organization   Brahmins are, in ritual terms, at the top of the caste system. They are the literati safeguarding the sacred traditions of Hindus. They are mostly householders who are often aligned with sectarian or monastic centers. Brahmins are not monolithic; only a few of them are priests catering to people's sacramental needs. Many of them have been engaged in secular pursuits both in the past and at present. Although not landed or wealthy, they have retained a high ritual position. Their social exclusiveness and inflexibility have often made them targets of attack by Hindu reformers; however, a number of Brahmin individuals were absorbed into the heterodox sects because of their intellectual acumen. This was a paradoxical element in the development of Hinduism.

Although there is no central church in Hinduism, sects have arisen within it from time to time to reform, innovate, and provide a more concise interpretation of spirituality. Hindu orthodoxy has often been challenged by heterodox sects, but Hinduism and its sects have always retained links with each other. The main inspiration to innovate has come from orthogenetic sources. Buddhism and Jainism were the early sects that devalued priestly liturgy; they protested against the ascriptive constraints (caste and status) and promoted a new ethicospiritual order. Buddhism made compassion to all living entities (man, animal, and plant) religiously significant; Jainism forbade killing of animals and birds for food. Both these groups made monasticism a more important factor than worship at the temple.

Subsequently, the bhakti (devotional) sects emerged in south India during the sixth to eleventh centuries C.E. and in north India during the fourteenth to seventeenth centuries. These sects propagated a liberalism that freed people from ritual and social inhibitions and made them all equal before god. These bhakti sects mediated between the Marga (Sanskrit tradition) and the Desi (folk tradition) and reached out to the common people. Through their literary compositions, they greatly enriched the regional languages, such as Punjabi, Hindi, Bengali, Marathi, Tamil, Kannada, and so on.

In the wake of colonial rule, new reformist trends emerged in Indian society. Hindu reformism had three well-known figures: Ram Mohan Roy, Dayananda Saraswati, and Vivekananda. Drawing upon the Vedantic tradition, they staunchly supported a *cultural nationalism*. The political awakening came in the early part of the twentieth century. Aurobindo, Tilak, and Gandhi were among the notables who launched the struggle for freedom from foreign rule. All of them made attempts to redefine Hinduism and make it more adaptable to modern times. In the meantime, the colonial policies of the British rulers engendered a feeling of separateness between Hindus and non-Hindus (especially Muslims). Amity had persisted between the two communities up to the colonial period, in spite of the political rivalries of Hindu and Muslim rulers. The

Partition of India (1948) estranged the two groups on a large scale; it was the culmination of a political process that had begun some decades earlier. A careful study of Hinduism will reveal that the phrase *Hindu communalism* is an oxymoron: Hinduism has been tolerant, while communalism has been overzealous. Despite its traumatic impact on the plural society of India at present, it will weaken or fade out in the near future.

Social Scientific Study of Hinduism The pioneer sociologist to study India on a comparative basis was Max Weber, who inquired into Hinduism and its sects; he drew upon the Indological literature that was available in Germany. More recent studies have taken a social anthropological approach. Bose (1975) has described the religious ties that exist between India's tribes and castes; an index of these ties is the participation of Hindu men and women across the country in celebrations at places of pilgrimage. Ghurye (1969) has shown that the major gods and goddesses of Hinduism are symbols of ethnic integration; the complex process of assimilating minor, local deities into the all-India pantheon of major deities—namely, Shiva, Vishnu, and Shakti—has lent unity to an extremely heterogeneous society. Srinivas (1952) has depicted the Hinduization of an indigenous group in a hill area of south India; this study has enabled him to develop the concept of "Sanskritization" for the analysis of wider aspects of Hindu society. Dumont (1970) has traced the worship of a folk deity of south India to the interactions between Aryan and Dravidian liturgical forms. Marriott (1955) has studied the encounter between the Great Tradition (derived from Sanskrit scriptures) and the Little Tradition (derived from folk beliefs and practices) in a village in north India. Singer (1972) has highlighted the adaptability of the Great Tradition to modern times in spite of its religiosity and hieratic structure.

Beyond these social anthropological works, economic and psychological aspects have been considered. Mishra (1962) has examined economic growth in Hindu society with an emphasis on diachronic aspects. Kakar (1982) has referred to the roles of shamans and mystics in the treatment of certain mental illnesses that have afflicted Hindus. Pocock (1973) has analyzed the social impact of a Vaishnavite sect on the beliefs and rituals of a village in western India. Ishwaran (1983) has explored the rise of a Shaivite sect in south India that, inter alia, contributed to an indigenous model of modernization. Babb (in Madan 1991) and Haraldsson (1987) have analyzed different aspects of the cult surrounding the south Indian mystic Sathya Sai Baba. Vidyarthi (1961) has studied the ritual interdependence between the Brahmin priests of a sacred center in north India and the pilgrims of various castes. Oommen (1986, 1994) has referred to the dominant cultural mainstream (derived from Hinduism and caste hierarchy) that has tended to treat religious minorities as outsiders. Venugopal (1990) has shown that the reformist sects in India have contributed to a sociopolitical ordering of Indian society. In addition to these, there are also studies of temple dancers, ritual specialists, and ascetic groups who belong to Hindu society.

—*C. N. Venugopal*

REFERENCES

N. K. Bose, *The Structure of Hindu Society* (Delhi: Orient Longman, 1975); L. Dumont, *Religion, Politics and History in India* (Paris: Mouton, 1970); G. S. Ghurye, *Caste and Race in India* (Bombay: Popular, 1969); E. Haraldsson, *Modern Miracles* (New York: Fawcett, 1987); K. Ishwaran, *Religion and Society Among the Lingayats of South India* (New Delhi: Vikas, 1983); S. Kakar, *Shamans, Mystics and Doctors* (New York: Knopf, 1982); T. N. Madan (ed.), *Religion in India* (New York: Oxford University Press, 1991); M. Marriott (ed.), *Village India* (Chicago: University of Chicago Press, 1955); V. Mishra, *Hinduism and Economic Growth* (Bombay: Oxford University Press, 1962); T. K. Oommen, "Insiders and Outsiders," *International Journal of Sociology* 1(1986):53-74; T. K. Oommen, "Religious Nationalism and Democratic Polity," *Sociology of Religion* 55(1994):455-479; D. F. Pocock, *Mind, Body and Wealth* (Oxford: Blackwell, 1973); L. Renou, *Hinduism* (Englewood Cliffs, N.J.: Prentice Hall, 1961); M. Singer, *When a Great Tradition Modernizes* (New York: Praeger, 1972); M. N. Srinivas, *Religion and Society Among the Coorgs of South India* (Oxford: Clarendon, 1952); C. N. Venugopal, "Reformist Sects and the Sociology of Religion in India," *Sociological Analysis* 51(1990):S77-S88; L. P. Vidyarthi, *The Sacred Complex of Hindu Gaya* (Bombay: Asia, 1961); M. Weber, *The Religion of India* (Glencoe, Ill.: Free Press, 1958).

HISTORY OF RELIGIONS   *see* Religious Studies

HOGE, DEAN R. (1937–)   Studied architecture at Ohio State University, where he received the Bachelor of Architecture degree summa cum laude in June 1960. During 1961, he was an exchange student at the University of Bonn, Germany, and in September he enrolled at Harvard Divinity school with a Rockefeller Trial Year Fellowship. During seminary, he studied with Talcott Parsons, Robert Bellah, and James Luther Adams, which turned his interests toward social ethics and sociology of religion. After finishing a divinity baccalaureate in 1964, he entered doctoral study in sociology, completing it in 1970. His dissertation examined trends in college students' attitudes and behaviors and later appeared as *Commitment on Campus* (Westminster 1974). Hoge served as Assistant Professor of Christianity and Society at Princeton Theological Seminary from 1969 to 1974. He then joined the faculty of the Catholic University of America, where he remains Professor and Chair of the Sociology Department. At Catholic University, he also serves as a member of the Life Cycle Institute, a social science research center. President, Religious Research Association, 1980, he also has given the Douglass distinguished lecture of the RRA.

During his tenure at Princeton Theological Seminary, Hoge began the research that was later to be published as *Division in the Protestant House* (Westminster 1976). He then joined with Jackson Carroll and David A. Roozen in a broad study of Protestant church trends, published as *Understanding Church Growth and Decline* (Pilgrim 1979).

Hoge's position at Catholic University was as a sociologist of youth, and he published several studies in this area (e.g., Hoge et al. 1979). In 1979, he conducted research for the American Catholic Bishops' Committee on Evangelization. This research investigated the determinants of Catholic affiliation and was published as *Converts, Dropouts, Returnees: A Study of Religious Change Among Catholics* (with Kenneth McGuire, Bernard F. Stratman, and Alvin A. Illig, Pilgrim 1981). His attention then turned to the Catholic priest shortage: *The Future of Catholic Leadership* (Sheed & Ward 1987, awarded "Best Professional Book" by the Catholic Press Association) and *Patterns of Parish Leadership* (with Joseph Shields and Francis Sheets, Sheed & Ward 1988). He also examined the attitudes of seminarians and young priests in *Seminary Life and Visions of the Priesthood* (with Eugene Hemrick, National Catholic Educational Association 1987) and *A Survey of Priests Ordained Five to Nine Years* (NCEA 1991).

Turning his attention back to the Protestant tradition, he collaborated on an interview study of Protestant "baby boomers" titled *Vanishing Boundaries* (Westminster, with Benton Johnson and Donald Luidens), which received the 1994 Distinguished Book Award from the Society for the Scientific Study of Religion.

His most recent research has involved heading an extensive survey of church-related giving, examining giving patterns among Catholics and four Protestant denominations, *Money Matters* (with Charles Zech, Patrick McNamara, and Michael Donahue, Westminster 1996; see Hoge 1994). Thus his research career has been marked with a singular emphasis and a singular productivity in practical and applied issues in the sociology of religion.

—*Michael J. Donahue*

REFERENCES

D. R. Hoge (ed.), "Patterns of Financial Contributions to Churches," *Review of Religious Research* 36(1994):101-244; D. R. Hoge et al., "Youth and the Church," *Religious Education* 74(1979):305-313.

HOLINESS CHURCHES   *see* Pentecostalism

HOLY SPIRIT   *see* Pentecostalism, Christianity

HOLY SPIRIT CHURCH FOR THE UNIFICATION OF WORLD CHRISTIANITY   *see* Unification Church

HOMANS, GEORGE C(ASPAR) (1910-1989)

Professor of Sociology at Harvard University. Homans is best known for his *The Human Group* (Harcourt 1950), although he himself preferred *Social Behavior* (Harcourt 1961) because it was "a work of deduction." Homans (1964, 1967) criticized functionalist theory for its failure both to meet scientific aims and to explain human behavior. To make the structure of society comprehensible, social scientists, according to Homans, had up to now put forward concepts concerning the characteristics of societies, such as norms and roles, that could not explain anything but were in need of explanation themselves. Instead, they should have put forward propositions based on the presupposition that human nature is universal, and that individuals act purposively in seeking social approval.

Homans's impact on sociology has been considerable: In the work of the sociologists Stark and Bainbridge (e.g., 1987) on religion, his influence is clear, although other rational choice theorists criticize him for the psychological basis of his theory. There can be no doubt, however, that his work has given direction and impetus to the development of the rational choice paradigm.

See also Rational Choice Theory, Rodney Stark

—*Durk H. Hak*

REFERENCES

G. C. Homans, "Bringing Men Back In," *American Sociological Review* 29(1964):809-818; G. C. Homans, *The Nature of Social Science* (New York: Harcourt, 1967); G. C. Homans, *Coming to My Senses* (New Brunswick, N.J.: Transaction, 1984); R. R. Lee, "Religious Practice as Social Exchange," *Sociological Analysis* 53(1992):1-35; R. Stark and W. S. Bainbridge, *A Theory of Religion* (New York: Lang, 1987).

HOMOSEXUALITY/BISEXUALITY   Sexuality, as Kinsey stated more than 50 years ago, is a spectrum of human experience, not an either-or proposition. Homosexuality and bisexuality therefore are points along the continuum at varying distances from heterosexuality. Homosexuality attracts much controversy, much of it grounded in religious objection. Moderate, mainstream Christian and Jewish groups tend to create policy and practice informed by the work of social scientists and historians who argue that Western religions have not always condemned homosexuals. The moderate-to-liberal religious stance is to recognize homo/bisexuals, gay men and lesbians, as persons of worth like any other, needing God's grace and the congregation's care. Bisexuality, involving one person in both homosexual and heterosexual emotional and erotic relationships (not necessarily simultaneously), is even less understood by religious bodies and teachings.

Many religious organizations struggle with admitting homo/bisexuals to the ordained ministry. Despite the care for souls this position putatively encourages, the essence of homosexuality is understood as a flawed (perhaps even sinful) expression of human sexual nature by most laity belonging to mainstream religious groups. Questions surrounding civil rights and protections for homo/bisexuals are, however, troublesome for those who maintain a "hate the sin and love the sinner" dichotomy in dealing with the vexing questions surrounding homosexuality.

More liberal and even radical religious teachings would affirm the homosexual's right to be fully human and fully homosexual. Openly gay and lesbian pastors may lead congregations who embrace this ideology. Unions of same sex people may be blessed in appropriate ceremonies. Gay/lesbian/bisexual activism is promoted in these congregations.

By contrast, the growing number of religious conservatives reject homosexuality and homo/bisexuals. God's creation of man and woman means homosexuals have no existence except as sinful and sick individuals who will be saved and cured by God if the desire is present. Scientific evidence suggesting biological, genetic, and social psychological explanations for homosexuality has no meaning in this worldview. Antihomosexual political campaigns are usually rooted in this type of fundamentalist religiosity.

See also Sexuality and Fertility

—*Barbara J. Denison*

REFERENCES

J. Boswell, *Christianity, Social Tolerance and Homosexuality* (Chicago: University of Chicago Press, 1980); G. D. Comstock, *Gay Theology Without Apology* (Cleveland: Pilgrim, 1993); D. Greenberg, *The Construction of Homosexuality* (Chicago: University of Chicago Press, 1988); R. Hasbany (ed.), *Homosexuality and Religion* (New York: Harrington, 1989); R. R. Troiden, *Gay and Lesbian Identity* (Dix Hills, N.Y.: General Hall, 1988).

HOOD, RALPH W., JR. (1942–) Professor of Social Psychology at the University of Tennessee at Chattanooga; Ph.D., University of Nevada at Reno, 1968. He has taught at the University of Tennessee at Chattanooga since 1970.

Hood was a founding Editor and is currently Co-editor of the *International Journal for the Psychology of Religion* and, beginning in 1995, Editor of the *Journal for the Scientific Study of Religion*. He is a coauthor of *The Psychology of Religion: An Empirical Approach* (with Bernard Spilka and Richard Gorsuch, Prentice Hall 1988), a popular psychology of religion textbook, and Editor of the *Handbook of Religious Experience* (Religious Education Press 1994), a major volume pertaining to this topic. He is a fellow of the American Psychological Association, past President of the Division on Psychology of Religion of the American Psychological Association, and recipient of its William James Award.

Hood's (1975) mystical experience scale is the most widely used measure in the field. The scale has allowed Hood to analyze mysticism in relation to a variety of domains such as church participation, self-actualization, nature experiences, personality correlates, gender, knowledge and experience criteria, death, the paranormal, the psychology of religion, the Freudian critique of religion, and the self.

Hood and Morris (1983) devised scales to measure five cognitive modes of death transcendence (creative, nature, biosocial, religious, and mysticism), the use of which provided the foundation for a preliminary theory of death transcendence. Their orientation opposes "denial" theories.

Much of Hood's work deals with intrinsic-extrinsic (I-E) religious orientations, as hypothesized by Gordon Allport, who argued that extrinsically motivated people use their religion as a means to gain security, solace, sociability, distraction, status, and self-justification. Those with intrinsic religiosity use their faith as an ultimate end in itself, a motive for living more important than other concerns. The intrinsically motivated people internalize their religion, following it more fully. C. Daniel Batson added a quest dimension to this scheme, attempting to increase its explanatory power. Hood (1985) elicited reports of mystical experiences from intrinsic and extrinsic participants in a wide variety of contexts and noted that the indiscriminately pro-religious type is likely to be sensitive to normative pressures to appear appropriately religious. In an example of more recent research, Hood et al. (1990) subjected subjects to an isolation tank experience under religious and nonreligious conditions. As predicted, indiscriminately pro-religious participants used religious interpretations under the religious set conditions, and intrinsic types used religious interpretations to a greater degree than did extrinsic types. The findings support Allport's contention that truly intrinsic persons live their religion, while indiscriminately pro-religious people are more likely to report religious experiences only in contexts cued as "religious."

Although they have contributed much to the understanding of intrinsic-extrinsic religious orientation, Kirkpatrick and Hood (1990) argue that research in this tradition suffers from serious limitations. They provide a variety of theoretical and methodological criticisms of contemporary I-E research and appear uncertain whether the I-E paradigm is a "boon or bane" for the contemporary psychology of religion. They argue that much work in this domain is theoretically impoverished, teaching very little about the psychology of religion.

—*James McClenon*

REFERENCES

R. W. Hood, Jr., "The Construction and Preliminary Validation of a Measure of Reported Mystical Experience," *Journal for the Scientific Study of Religion* 14(1975):29-41; R. W. Hood, Jr., "Extrinsic, Quest and Intrinsic," *Journal for the Scientific Study of Religion* 25(1985):413-417; R. W. Hood, Jr., and R. J. Morris, "Toward a Theory of Death Transcendence," *Journal for the Scientific Study of Religion* 22(1983): 353-365; R. W. Hood, Jr., et al., "Personality Correlates of the Report of Mystical Experience," *Psychological Reports* 44(1979):804-806; R. W. Hood, Jr., et al., "Quasi-Experimental Elicitation of the Differential Report of Religious Experience Among Intrinsic and Indiscriminately Pro-Religious Types," *Journal for the Scientific Study of Religion* 29(1990):164-172; L. A. Kirkpatrick and R. W. Hood, Jr., "Intrinsic-Extrinsic Religious Orientation," *Journal for the Scientific Study of Religion* 29(1990):442-462.

HOUR OF POWER   see Televangelism

HUGHES, JOHN E. (1922-1995)   Sociologist; Ph.D., University of Pennsylvania (1960). Hughes taught at the University of Notre Dame (1955-1961) and at Villanova University, where he ended his teaching career in 1986. President, American Catholic Sociological Society, 1963.

As president of the ACSS, Hughes reiterated a major concern voiced by the previous five presidents in their presidential addresses: the scientific quality of the work of American Catholic sociologists and the (in)adequacy of their empirical approach. Hughes argued that their religion did not bar Catholics from being scientists. He closed his 1963 presidential address by stating that what Catholics "can offer our discipline by way of sound scientific work is more important than how we are viewed" (*ACSR*, 1963, p. 301). It was during his presidency that a poll of ACSS members resulted in changing the name of the *American Catholic Sociological Review* to *Sociological Analysis,* reflecting a change in editorial focus from the generalities of sociology to the sociological particularities of religion, especially those of Catholicism.

—*Loretta M. Morris*

HUMAN RIGHTS   Principally political and economic rights based on the notion that all human beings have inherent dignity and worth as individuals, and that such qualities are entitled to societal protection. The concept has been subject to controversy within the religious community, as it seems to promote the rights of individuals over the community, especially the religious community, where rights and privileges are often not extended equally to all believers. The position of women within many religious organizations often has been cited as a case in point and has generated considerable conflict within and between religious organizations, and between religious organizations and their critics within the secular realm. For example, while the

Roman Catholic Church has upheld and sought to justify different sets of religious and administrative roles for women and men on biblical or other grounds, critics note that this practice historically has excluded the former from the clergy (and higher office), in contravention of their "human rights." In Islam, the wearing of the *hijab* is seen by its detractors as a form of discrimination and of arbitrary subjugation of women believers.

Where many of the world's religious organizations and human rights advocates are coming to agree, however, is on the inviolability of universal economic and political rights. This is especially true of the Christian churches, which, in the past, either had actively supported or had turned a blind eye to systemic economic inequity (often resulting in abject poverty) and to arbitrary rule of political elites (often designed to retain and promote economic privilege for the few). In North America, early involvement in economic and political rights arose with the spread of the Social Gospel movement (1865-1915), which saw a number of religious organizations, primarily Protestant, begin to concern themselves with the welfare of the weakest members of society: farmers, factory workers, the poor, and so on. In Canada, the Social Gospel is credited with forming a major plank in the platform of the continent's first viable socialist political party, the Cooperative Commonwealth Federation (CCF), later the New Democratic Party (NDP), which has formed the government in several Canadian provinces since 1930.

Since 1970, Christian churches have become increasingly active in the promotion of economic and political rights on a global scale. In Latin America, for example, national church organizations officially adopted a "preferential option for the poor" after the 1968 Medellín meeting of the region's bishops, as a direct response to the economic policies and political repression orchestrated by a growing number of dictatorial (often military) regimes in the region. Members of the hierarchy wrote missives condemning the abuses of arbitrary government, calling for more just economic arrangements and a return to civilian rule. Activists within both the hierarchy and the laity worked directly with the poor to assist them in organizing against repression through lower class, self-help associations such as the *comunidades eclesiales/eclesiais de base* (CEBs). For their efforts, many members of the Catholic Church were expelled, jailed, tortured, and sometimes killed by security forces or clandestine organizations working in their service. At the same time, the drive for human rights, which was ultimately joined by a large number of other religious organizations, is credited with mobilizing popular support against repressive regimes in Latin America, which gradually began to dissolve after the late 1970s.

—*W. E. Hewitt*

REFERENCES

W. L. Holleman, *The Human Rights Movement* (New York: Praeger, 1987); L. S. Rouner (ed.), *Human Rights and the World's Religions* (Notre Dame, Ind.: University of Notre Dame Press, 1988).

HUMBARD, REX   *see* Televangelism

HYMNS   Corporately sung songs of religious praise.

Facing declining membership and financial stress, American Lutherans stand firm at their national convention and sing "A Mighty Fortress Is Our God." A new congregation opens its doors, and "All Glory, Laud and Honor" guides the inaugural procession. A few friends sing "Abide with Me, Fast Falls the Eventide" as one who was long-loved is laid to rest. Whether embedded within formal liturgies or simply echoing the pathos of grief, hymns become the stories religious people want to tell each other.

American hymnody traces its roots, in part, to the writings of Martin Luther, John Calvin, and John and Charles Wesley. Lutherans, Presbyterians, and Methodists continue to sing the theology of the Reformation. Less formally constituted, Ira Sankey sang the message that Dwight L. Moody preached, and American revivalism became an international movement of religious style and musical theater.

Although it is widely recognized that African Americans used spirituals to focus their attention away from enslavement toward future freedom in a heavenly promised land, those field hymns carried a more worldly message as well. Certain lyrics of particular songs signaled the impending arrival of a "conductor" for the Underground Railroad. Frederick Douglas has written that "O Canaan, Sweet Canaan, I am bound for the land of Canaan" meant that someone was heading "north." "North was our Canaan," he proclaimed.

Hymns are part of what brings religious people together to celebrate specific religious traditions. Particular hymns serve to provide individuals special comfort in times of grief and need. Hymns also galvanize social movements and become the anthems of social change, as in the civil rights theme "We Shall Overcome."

The social and psychological dynamics of hymnody in the religious life of human beings represent a generally neglected field in the social scientific study of religion.

See also African American Religious Experience

—*Jerry Koch*

REFERENCES

S. S. Sizer, *Gospel Hymns and Social Religion* (Philadelphia: Temple University Press, 1978); E. Southern, *Readings in Black American Music* (New York: Norton, 1972).

IDENTITY Bridge concept shared between intrapersonally oriented psychological approaches and interpersonally oriented sociological traditions in the social sciences. The former are less precisely operationalized and typically investigated by clinical procedures; the latter are more clearly operationalized and investigated by mainstream empirical methodologies of the social sciences.

Popularized by Erik Erikson (1959, 1968) as a central psychoanalytic concept, identity is a characteristic defining one's sense of self. It represents a continuity in the ego's integrating functioning that must be achieved; it is not simply a defining attribute of the ego. A stable identity is deemed to be optimal for psychological health; failure to achieve ego identity results in ego diffusion, a failure in optimal psychological development. Ego identity is largely unconsciously determined and thus difficult to operationalize and measure. In Erikson's theory, the process of identity formation reaches a head in adolescence when identity versus identity confusion is the dichotomous challenge in the fifth of his eight theoretically specified developmental stages. Adolescence is a likely period of identity crisis. The tendency to identify prematurely with cultural heroes or groups in adolescence makes the virtue of fidelity, seen as the cornerstone of healthy identity formation, impossible. While three of Erikson's defining characteristics of identity are largely intrapsychic (a sense of uniqueness, a feeling of continuity over time, and a sense of ego completeness), his fourth characteristic demands identification with the ideals of some group that affirms the sense of self that is the final achievement of a healthy sense of identity. It permits a free and continuous commitment to group values and persons that characterizes fidelity.

In nonpsychoanalytic traditions, interpersonal processes in identity formation are emphasized. Memberships in organizations or collectives that serve as reference groups are typically emphasized as integral to the process of identity formation. These socially based identities provide potential sources of identity for the individual. What factors determine which groups an individual uses as sources of identity formation is an empirical issue variously addressed and tested by these theories. Most findings suggest that identity is seldom restricted to one group. Sources of potential identities are as varied as the ideologies of the groups with which the individual identifies. Thus individuals may have a variety of identities or subidentities, each supported by group memberships.

These identities are often conceived to be hierarchically ordered, merely compartmentalized, or differentially activated based upon situational factors. Yet in all cases, a sense of self or personal continuity is maintained by an awareness of group memberships that helps to define and create the person. This process emphasizes interpersonal dynamics in which individuals reflexively define themselves by the same labels used by the groups with which they identify. Various psychological factors may predispose individuals to accept or reject certain groups as sources of identity. Religions often serve as key reference groups and are particularly likely to provide the claim to a single universal identity or to an identity seen as highest in a hierarchical scheme. In the broadest sense, one can then speak of a collective identity, often seen to be one's true or ultimate identity. Thus identity becomes a crucial concept in linking individuals to both the maintenance and the transmission of cultures, as it is both socially bestowed and sustained.

Beit-Hallahmi (1985) has been most instrumental in linking interpersonal and intrapersonal theories of identity as applied to religion. He identifies three levels of identity. Collective identity is created by religious communities by both conscious and unconscious processes. Social identity in turn may include a religious identity among one of several subidentities formed by conscious commitments to different groups. Finally, a collective religious identity or a religious subidentity may be a source for support and integration of ego identity. Through this three-tiered structure of identity concepts, Beit-Hallahmi links both intrapersonal (psychoanalytic) and interpersonal (social) traditions of identity research in a single theory applicable to religion.

Empirical consequences derived from diverse interpersonally based identity theories largely support the general thesis that religious identity is predictive of many social variables. This is especially true when religious identity is operationalized in terms of denominational affiliation. In addition, if psychological factors such as high and low ego involvement are introduced, the differential effects of religious identity can be empirically assessed with added precision. High ego involvement is often equivalent to making religion highly salient and thus empirically relevant to a variety of predictive situations. Low ego involvement is often equivalent to making religion of minimal salience and hence not predictive in situations where religious factors would otherwise be predictive. In addition, ego involvement and saliency may vary situationally such that religious identities are differentially predictive even with a given individual. Religious socialization attempts through rituals and other means to foster high ego involvement in one's religious identity and thus make religion salient in many situations. This is most effectively achieved when one's collective identity and one's ego identify are united in communities that are able to sacralize identity both in ritual and myth that assure ego involvement and in a sense of the transcendent.

—*Ralph W. Hood, Jr.*

REFERENCES

B. Beit-Hallahmi, *Prolegomena to the Psychological Study of Religion* (Lewisburg, Pa.: Bucknell University Press, 1989); A. Dashefsky, "And the Search Goes On," *Sociological Analysis* 33(1974):239-245; E. H. Erikson, *Identity and the Life Cycle* (New York: International Universities Press, 1959); E. H. Erikson, *Identity* (New York: Norton, 1968); H. J. Mol, *Identity and the Sacred* (Oxford: Blackwell, 1976).

IDENTITY TRANSFORMATION ORGANIZATION   *see* Quasi-Religions

IDEOLOGY   A system of collective representations—concepts, ideas, myths, images embedded in symbols—by which people live their imagined relations to the material conditions of their social existence.

An ideology usually does not mirror the social world exactly but exhibits some transformation of that world. Very often the analysis of this transformed image brings about a deeper sociological understanding of how the distribution of material resources and the relations of power are culturally constructed and legitimized.

The study of the ideological role of religious beliefs and values has gained a steady impetus in recent decades with the confluence of Durkheimian and Weberian traditions with the neo-Marxist theory of Louis Althusser and with feminist social theory. Drawing on the diverse threads of this eclectic mixture, social scientists have explored how religious ideology informs nation building and political crisis (Bellah 1957, Geertz 1960, Hunt 1988). But current research draws most heavily on the feminist perspective. An ambivalent treatment of women is prevalent in many religious traditions. In historical Western religions, for example, the dominant images of women are built on a dualistic symbolization of female sexuality: A dangerous, evil image of woman as a temptress, schemer, and polluter contrasts with a morally approved image of woman as virgin and mother. These ambivalent images have defined women's traditional status in Western societies. In an Islamic context, Janice Boddy (1989) has written a masterful analysis of spirit possession cults in northern Sudan. Boddy shows how women make ideological use of cultic beliefs and practices to interpret their personal crises and to construe their experiences of gender inequality.

—*Edward B. Reeves*

REFERENCES

R. N. Bellah, *Tokugawa Religion* (New York: Free Press, 1957); J. Boddy, *Wombs and Alien Spirits* (Madison: University of Wisconsin Press, 1989); C. Geertz, *The Religion of Java* (Chicago: University of Chicago Press, 1960); L. Hunt, "The Sacred and the French Revolution," in *Durkheimian Sociology*, ed. J. C. Alexander (New York: Cambridge University Press, 1988): 25-43; K. Thompson, *Beliefs and Ideology* (London: Tavistock, 1986).

ILLNESS   *see* Wellness

IMMANENCE   Belief that spiritual powers are present in this world and infuse people, organizations, and objects. Expressions of immanence are found in traditional magical practices, the theologies of ancient Judaism and of Islam, the pantheism of classical Greece and Rome, and the Catholic sacramental tradition as well as in many contemporary "New Age" religions. Immanence is commonly contrasted with the Protestant view of God as exclusively transcendent. In *Religion and Regime* (University of Michigan Press 1967), Guy E. Swanson links the belief to a particular social structure, arguing that the rejection of immanence—indicated by the spread of the Protestantism in Europe—is explained by the prior development of associational forms of governance. The Catholic emphasis on immanence continued where the state was primarily organized as a social system.

—*David Yamane*

IMPLICIT RELIGION   Particularly associated with the "Network for the Study of Implicit Religion" (NSIR), the concept has at least three (nonexclusive) definitions: *commitments* or *integrating foci* or *intensive concerns with extensive effects*. The concept of "implicit religion" counterbalances the tendency to equate "religion" with specialized institutions, with articulated beliefs, and with that which is consciously willed (or specifically intended).

The approach opens up the possibility of discovering the sacred within what might otherwise be dismissed as profane, and of finding an experience of the holy, within an apparently irreligious realm. Above all, in contemporary society it allows for the discovery of some kind of religiosity within what conventionally might be seen as an unrelievedly secular sphere. The concept therefore gives credence to the opinion of the

"person in the street," that while "some who go to church really mean it," others who go to church "really have a different religion altogether"—but that "everybody has a religion of some sort," a faith by which they live, albeit as an unconscious core at the center of their way of life and being.

—*Edward I. Bailey*

REFERENCES

E. Bailey, *Implicit Religion in Contemporary Society* (Kampen, Neth.: Kok Pharos, 1997); M. M. Bell, *Childerley* (Chicago: University of Chicago Press, 1994); P. L. Berger, *A Rumor of Angels* (Garden City, N.Y.: 1971); F. Blum, *The Ethic of Industrial Man* (London: Routledge, 1970); M. ter Borg, *Een Uitgewaaierde Eeuwigheid* (Ten Have, Neth.: Baarn, 1991); P. Halmos, *The Faith of the Counsellors* (London: Constable, 1965); T. Luckmann, *The Invisible Religion* (London: Macmillan, 1967); A. Nesti, *Il Religioso Implicito* (Rome: Ianua, 1985); R. Panikkar, "Time and Sacrifice," in *The Study of Time*, ed. D. Park et al. (New York: Springer, 1978): 637-727.

IMSE, THOMAS P. (1920—)   After receiving a Ph.D. in sociology from the University of Maryland in 1958, Imse taught at the University of Maryland, Canisius College, and College of the Holy Cross, from which he retired in 1988; President, Mount Senario College (Wisconsin), 1995-1996. President, Association for the Sociology of Religion, 1973.

Although his general areas of research have been industrial sociology and population, Imse's concerns have also embraced social problems of the community in both their theoretical and their applied aspects. At professional meetings focusing on the sociology of religion, he has delivered papers on religious conservatism and political conservatism.

—*Loretta M. Morris*

INDIANS   *see* Native American Religions

INDIVIDUALISM   Term coined originally in the nineteenth century by Alexis de Tocqueville in reference to the modern tendency to pursue one's private concerns in isolation from the concerns of others, the common good, or social institutions.

Currently often used to identify various strands within modern cultural patterns (e.g., possessive individualism, expressive and utilitarian individualism, ethical individualism, and aesthetic individualism). Regarding religion, used in reference to the modern tendency to insist on personal choice in matters of morality and faith rather than seeking primary guidance from religious traditions. Also used in reference to social researchers focusing on isolated individuals rather than on social groups, such as "methodological individualism."

—*Richard L. Wood*

REFERENCES

R. N. Bellah et al., *Habits of the Heart* (Berkeley: University of California Press, 1985); E. Fox-Genovese, *Feminism Without Illusions* (Chapel Hill: University of North Carolina Press, 1991); H. J. Gans, *Middle American Individualism* (New York: Free Press, 1988); D. Gelpi (ed.), *Beyond Individualism* (Notre Dame, Ind.: University of Notre Dame Press, 1989); S. R. Gupta et al., *Citizenship Values in India* (Calcutta: Mandira, 1990); K. Miyanaga, *The Creative Edge* (New Brunswick, N.J.: Transaction, 1991); B. A. Shain, *The Myth of American Individualism* (Princeton, N.J.: Princeton University Press, 1994); A. de Tocqueville, *Democracy in America* (Garden City, N.Y. Doubleday, 1969 [1835]); H. Varenne, *Americans Together* (New York: Teachers' College Press, 1977).

INNER-WORLDLY   *see* Other-Worldly

INSTITUTIONALIZATION   *see* Thomas F. O'Dea

INTERNATIONAL SOCIETY FOR KRISHNA CONSCIOUSNESS (ISKCON)

One of the most successful and conspicuous of the new or Eastern-import religions springing out of the counterculture, often known as the "Hare Krishna" movement.

It was brought to the West in 1965 by A. C. Bhaktivedanta Swami Prabhupada Bhaktivedanta (1896-1977), who arrived in New York City and began to attract participants in the *kirtan* of chanting the HARE KRISHNA *mahamantra*. Srila Prabhupada, as he is called by the devotees, was a former manager for a pharmaceutical company in India and a translator of ancient Vedic scriptures into English. Upon his retirement, his guru charged him with bringing Krishna consciousness to the West. The movement attracted youthful members of the counterculture disillusioned with drugs and hippie utopian ideals. Initiates recited four vows—renouncing meat, drugs, illicit sex, and gambling—were given sanskrit names, and promised to chant 16 rounds of the HARE KRISHNA mantra, which requires two and a half hours daily. Members donated their assets to the temple and, until recently, lived communally. By the time of his death, Prabhupada had initiated about 10,000 devotees worldwide and established temples throughout the world.

ISKCON might be described as a sect or denomination of Hinduism, as it is rooted in the *bhakti* tradition and venerates its sixteenth-century founder, Sri Chaitanya Mahaprabhu. Evangelical methods include preaching, distributing books and the *Back to Godhead* magazine, public chanting of the HARE KRISHNA mantra, and offering free feasts on Sundays.

ISKCON is administered by the Governing Body Commissioners, who are responsible for the different geographic zones. Since Prabhupada's death, the spiritual leadership resides in the initiating gurus, who counsel their individual *chelas*. Local parishes are tended by a temple president. Only men can hold leadership positions. The movement has been beset with schisms and controversies since the guru's death, mainly at the large dairy-farming commune in West Virginia, New Vrindavan, where a murder investigation focused on Swami Kirtananda, who claimed to be Prabhpada's successor in the Indian tradition of disciplic succession. Charges were eventually dropped, and ISKCON appears to be adopting a more accommodating stance toward society. The communal structure and monastic life are declining in favor of family-centered communities and neighborhoods.

Social scientific literature focuses on ISKCON's historical roots and beliefs (see Judah 1974, Gelberg 1991); for ISKCON's later history and organizational changes, see Rochford (1985) and Gelberg (1992).

—*Susan J. Palmer*

REFERENCES

D. G. Bromley and L. D. Shinn (eds.), *Krishna Consciousness in the West* (Lewisburg, Pa.: Bucknell University Press, 1989); D. G. Bromley and A. Shupe, Jr., *Strange Gods* (Boston: Beacon, 1981); F. Daner, *American Children of Krishna* (New York: Holt, 1976); S. J. Gelberg, *The Hare Krishna Movement* (New York: Garland, 1991); S. J. Gelberg, "The Call of the Lotus-Eyed Lord," in *When Prophets Die*, ed. T. Miller (Albany: SUNY Press, 1992): 149-164; G. Johnson, "The Hare Krishna in San Francisco," in *The New Religious Consciousness*, ed. C. Glock and R. Bellah (Los Angeles: University of California Press, 1976): 34-51; S. Judah, *Hare Krishna and the Counterculture* (New York: Wiley, 1974); E. B. Rochford, *Hare Krishna in America* (New Brunswick, N.J.: Rutgers University Press, 1985).

INTERNET Most established religions have a presence on the World Wide Web, from the level of worldwide organizations to individual churches. The present American dominance of the Internet means that non-Western religions are underrepresented online, although virtually any belief has some degree of Internet presence. For example, the *Yahoo! Internet Directory* lists 6,951 WWW pages on Christianity, 859 on Judaism, 303 on Islam, and 213 on Buddhism. *USENET News* has more than 150 religion discussion groups.

The Internet provides inexpensive avenues for worldwide proselytization, and small groups or even individuals potentially can reach millions. Well-financed organizations may produce more professional WWW sites, but their potential viewing audience is no larger than that of a fledgling religion. Pluralistic authorship means that any proponent of a particular belief system can offer his or her personal interpretations, often competing with authorized canon.

Opponents to and dissenters from religious groups also can express their views widely, leading to particularly vibrant debates. Through Web pages, an opponent of a particular church can disseminate critical materials as widely as the church. Also, many discussion forums are unmoderated, and a *USENET News* group ostensibly created to provide a meeting place for believers often becomes a forum for confrontation between believers and nonbelievers.

The Internet also has spawned new religions based solely in cyberspace. Some of these movements are amalgamations of other religions, creating global interfaith organizations (e.g., "ORIGIN, the Meeting Place of All Religions"). Some are wholly new creations, usually stressing globalization themes and universal philosophies (e.g., " 'All', the Universal Religion"). Many exclusively on-line religions are based on the transformative or transcendental potential of the Internet itself, borrowing concepts from the science fiction writer/cyberspace theorist William Gibson and memetics (i.e., ideas act as viruses, a notion attributed to the evolutionary theorist Richard Dawkins). Parody religions, such as Kibology, are also popular on the Internet.

—*Michael H. Peckham*

REFERENCES

" 'All', the Universal Religion" <http://www.netzone.com/~dgganon/All1.html>; J. Baker, *Christian Cyberspace Companion* (Grand Rapids, Mich.: Baker, 1995); "Chaplain On-Line Home Page" <http://www.infi.net/~rllewis/ chaplain. html)>; "Church of Perpetual Change(Agere)" <http://www.ceridwyn.com/cpc/>; "Church of Scientology" <http://www.scientology.org>; "Church of Scientology vs. the Net" <http:// www.cybercom.net/~rnewman/scientology/home.html>; "The Church of Virus" <http://www.lucifer.com/virus/>; "First Church of Wintermute" <http:// Gridley.AAACNS.Carleton. edu/harrisws/wintermute/>; T. Geller, "Deux ex Machina," *Net* 1, 7(1995):51-55; W. Grossman, "alt.scientology.war," *Wired*, 3, 12(1995):172-177, 248-252; "Kibology" <http:// www.autobahn.mb.ca/~gary/kibology.html>; "Kibo's Page" <http://www.nutcom.com/~ken/kibo.html>. "ORIGIN, The Meeting Place of Religions" <http://www.rain.org/~origin/>; "Yahoo! Society and Culture/Religion" <http://www.yahoo.com/Society_and_Culture/Religion/>.

INTRINSIC-EXTRINSIC RELIGIOSITY Dominating conceptual paradigm in the empirical psychology of religion during the last three decades.

Based on Gordon Allport's theoretical distinction between mature and immature religion (see Allport and Ross 1967), the construction of an intrinsic-extrinsic scale to measure different religious orientations appeared to clarify the troubling finding that general measures of religion had positively correlated with prejudice. Consistent with Allport's conceptualization of mature religion, it was found that only extrinsic religion, or religion as a means, correlated with prejudice. Intrinsic religion, or religion as an end, characterized the unprejudiced and was compatible with Allport's views of mature religion. The scale to measure religious orientation, initially conceived as a continuum from extrinsic to intrinsic, quickly generated interest among empirical researchers. Numerous studies have been published that relate intrinsic and extrinsic religion to a variety of individual difference variables such as coping styles, narcissism, guilt, fear of death, a wide variety of religious experiences, various cognitive processes, and varieties of prejudice.

Consistent with Allport's view of mature religiosity, extrinsic but not intrinsic religiosity typically correlates with more dysfunctional psychological constructs. Many psychometric critiques and modifications of the scales have been published. The only consensus is that extrinsic and intrinsic must be treated as independent scales, not as a continuum as initially conceived. Major critical reviews have emphasized the lack of theory-driven research, the inadequacies of these scales to operationalize fully Allport's theory, and the failure to clearly define religious orientations in value-neutral terms. The psychometric limitations of the original scales repeatedly have been challenged. An age-universal version of these scales is available. It is a matter of contention whether the scales are best used as independent dimensions or the basis for constructing typologies. Studies using these scales and theoretically linked alternatives continue to provide the major database for the contemporary empirical psychology of religion.

—*Ralph W. Hood, Jr.*

REFERENCES

G. W. Allport and J. M. Ross, "Personal Religious Orientation and Prejudice," *Journal of Personality and Social Psychology,* 5(1967):432-443; C. T. Burris, "Curvilinearity and Religious Types," *International Journal for the Psychology of Religion* 4(1994):245-260; M. J. Donahue, "Intrinsic and Extrinsic Religiousness," *Journal of Personality and Social Psychology* 48(1985):400-419; R. W. Hood, Jr. (ed.), "Symposium on Religious Orientation Typologies," *Journal for the Scientific Study of Religion* 24(1985):407-442; R. A. Hunt and M. King, "The Intrinsic-Extrinsic Concept," *Journal for the Scientific Study of Religion* 10(1971):339-356; L. A. Kirkpatrick and R. W. Hood, Jr., "Intrinsic-Extrinsic Religious Orientation," *Journal for the Scientific Study of Religion* 29(1990):442-462.

INVESTMENTS   Refers, in the theoretical structure of Stark and Bainbridge (1987), to an aspect of the controlling mechanism of human bondage. The other dimensions of social binding, according to Stark and Bainbridge, are attachment, involvement, and belief.

The concept of *investments,* however, marks the most unique contribution of their "rational choice" theory within the social scientific study of religion. Investments are costs borne in lasting relationships that have not yet yielded their rewards fully. The standard example in religion is formed by the person living a righteous life to achieve salvation. Living righteously means that the person forgoes all kinds of short-term rewards (that is, bears costs) for an uncertain long-term reward. Investments form a mechanism of social binding, and, accordingly, high current investments may form a barrier toward exiting the religious group.

—*Durk H. Hak*

REFERENCE

R. Stark and W. S. Bainbridge, *A Theory of Religion* (New York: Lang, 1987).

INVISIBLE RELIGION   A concept introduced through the English title of Thomas Luckmann's first major publication, *The Invisible Religion,* which appeared in 1967 (Macmillan), four years after its publication in German (original title *Das problem der Religion in der modernen Gesellschaft*).

The Invisible Religion has been a highly influential text, and also the concept that its title embodies. The theoretical context of the work provides its point of departure. It forms part of Luckmann's concerted effort to understand the locus of the individual in the modern world. Sociological approaches to religion, deriving from the sociological classics, form a central theme within this quest. Luckmann's essay aims to reestablish this connection, insisting that the problem of individual existence in society is essentially a "religious" one.

It is, precisely, the lack of theoretical reflection within the flourishing subdiscipline of the sociology of religion in the postwar period that concerns Luckmann. The association of religion with church has oriented a whole generation of scholars toward a relatively narrow field, the more so in that church-orientated religion has become a marginal phenomenon in modern societies. To redress this balance, Luckmann opts firmly for a functional definition of religion but differentiates this from the structural-functionalism prevalent in contemporary sociology. Luckmann regards as problematic what is taken for granted in sociological functionalism. His perspective is, essentially, an anthropological one.

The core of the argument can be summarized in the following extract from *The Invisible Religion* (pp. 48 f):

> The organism—in isolation nothing but a separate pole of "meaningless" subjective processes—becomes a Self by embarking with others upon the construction of an "objective" and moral universe of meaning. Thereby the organization transcends its biological nature.
>
> It is in keeping with an elementary sense of the concept of religion to call the transcendence of biological nature by the human organism a religious phenomenon. As we have tried to show, this phenomenon rests upon the functional relation of Self and society. We may, therefore, regard the social processes that lead to the formation of Self as fundamentally religious.

From the narrowly institutional, the notion of religion becomes quite simply part of being human; it is that which transcends biological nature.

The debate between substantive and functional definitions of religion continues within the subdiscipline of the sociology of religion. Hervieu-Léger's *La religion pour mémoire* (Cerf 1993) contains a recent discussion of the issues involved. Within this debate, Luckmann's notion of invisible religion stands at one extreme; it is the most inclusive of all definitions and will be favored by those who find functional approaches more satisfying than substantive ones. Luckmann's analysis itself, however, remains solid apart from the definitional debate: Out of basic human processes emerge the construction of objective worldviews, the articulation of sacred universes, and, in some situations, the institutional specializations of religion. What forms these take and how they emerge pose important *empirical* questions. The *theoretical* position remains, however, unaltered: Religion is present in nonspecific form in all societies and in all socialized individuals. It is part of the human condition.

See also Thomas Luckmann

—*Grace Davie*

IRRELIGION Active rejection of either religion in general or any of its more specific organized forms. It is thus distinct from the *secular,* which simply refers to the absence of religion.

Irreligion is a reaction or alienative response to established religion. More specifically, irreligion is those beliefs and actions that are expressive of attitudes of hostility or indifference toward prevailing religion, together with indications of the rejection of its demands. The term hence covers actions as well as beliefs, such that the desecration of churches or anticlericalism would each come under the heading of *irreligion.* The value of the term is that it draws attention to a sociocultural phenomenon that is distinctive of the modern Western world. For, although atheism and skepticism have a history stretching back to at least Greco-Roman times, the widespread rejection of religion, especially in the form of organizations devoted to its elimination, is unique to modernity.

First appearing at the time of the French Revolution, *irreligion* has become a significant ingredient in such major modern movements as communism, socialism, and anarchism. However, the term is not always used this specifically, often being applied loosely to refer to the absence or rejection of religious belief (Demerath and Theissen 1966). In contemporary usage, it is increasingly employed as a synonym for unbelief, and thus the distinction between the areligious and the antireligious is often glossed, as too is that between those individuals with no religious affiliation and those who are members of organizations actively hostile to religion. For, although irreligion may be individual or

organized, it is most noticeable in its organized form. The principal irreligious organizations are those for humanists, secularists, rationalists, and atheists. Thus the principal irreligious organizations in the United States would be the American Association for the Advancement of Atheism, Freethinkers of America Inc., United Secularists of America, the Rationalist Association Inc., the American Rationalist Federation, the Freethought Society of America, the Secular Society of America, the American Ethical Union, and the American Humanist Association.

—*Colin Campbell*

REFERENCES

C. Campbell, *Toward a Sociology of Irreligion* (London: Macmillan, 1971); N. J. Demerath III and V. Theissen, "On Spitting Against the Wind," *American Journal of Sociology* 6(1966):674-687.

ISA-22 *see* Research Committee 22

ISLAM An Arabic word *(islām)* meaning "submission" (to God). One who submits is a *muslim,* from the same root as *Islam.* A closely related word, also using that root, is *salām,* "peace," a Semitic cognate of the Hebrew *shālôm.* Islam is the youngest of the three major world religions that trace their spiritual lineages back to the biblical patriarchs. Muslims consider Islam to be a fulfillment of Judaism and Christianity and the restoration of a primordial Abrahamic ethical monotheism. The prophet Muhammad (c. 570-632 C.E.) proclaimed Islam to the polytheistic Arabs of Mecca between 610 and 632 C.E. His mission was inspired throughout by the oral revelations he received, cumulatively, in the *Qur'ān* ("recitation") from God through the archangel Gabriel. Because of increasing persecution of the Muslims in the commercial and pagan cultic capital of Mecca, with the Ka'aba temple as its center, Muhammad led his followers to the oasis community of Medina in 622, where he had been called to serve as an outside, impartial arbitrator in that conflict-filled city of warring factions. This *hijra,* or emigration (from Mecca to Medina), marks the beginning of the Islamic lunar calendar. (The Muslim year has 354 days and, because intercalation is not permitted, it recedes approximately 11 days behind each solar year. This permits the Islamic canonical feasts, as well as the fasting and pilgrimage months, to occur—providentially, according to Muslim opinion—in each season over a 33-year period.)

In Medina, the Muslim *umma* ("community") was founded as a theocratic state, eventually extending its authority during the Prophet's lifetime to most of the Arabian peninsula. Mecca was conquered peacefully in 628, its idols destroyed, and the Ka'aba rededicated as the ritual center of Islam. Whereas the Arabs of old had lived in a politically fragmented way according to tribal and clan customs and social patterns, Islam transcended kinship ties by establishing a common faith as the bonding agent of society. Muhammad was both prophet and statesman in Medina. He resembled more than anything else a combination of biblical judge and prophet, charismatic offices that combined political and religious leadership. And, like Judaism, Islam has since its origins emphasized legal orthopraxy far more than theological orthodoxy.

Basic Beliefs and Practices of Islam The Qur'ān, Islam's revealed scripture, contains the essential teachings of Islam, known as *īmān,* "faith." Although there is no canonical creed in Islam in the form of a required statement of beliefs, there are universally agreed upon doctrines. First and most important is the Divine Unity, *tawḥīd.* God is one and his umma should also be unified in belief and practice. The umma is in fact defined by a common pattern of worship that is far more uniform than Christian, or even Jewish, liturgy. The second major doctrine is the belief that God has spoken to prophets for the guidance and correction of human communities. Muhammad is the last in a series of many prophets that includes Adam, Noah, Abraham, Moses, and Jesus. Third is belief in angels, who are God's messengers. Fourth is belief in holy scriptures that God has revealed through some of His prophets. The Qur'ān is the final, definitive scripture, correcting errors that crept into the previous monotheistic scriptures while confirming their enduring truths. The fifth belief is in a Last Judgment ushered in by a trumpet blast, an upsetting of the natural order of things, and a general resurrection of the dead. Each person will stand alone before God's judgment seat; the righteous will be rewarded with a heavenly afterlife, whereas the reprobates will be consigned to hell. The final element of Islamic doctrine is the Divine Decree and Predestination (predetermination). Although this difficult teaching may appear fatalistic, Muslims do not regard it as inconsistent with human responsibility. Rather, it is viewed as an essential dimension of God's power, wisdom, and mercy.

The basic beliefs of Islam are discussed and clarified in numerous advanced theological treatises in the field of dogmatic theology known as *kalām* (literally, "dialectical discourse"). Some Islamic philosophical theologians (e.g., Ibn Rushd/Averroës) influenced medieval Christian scholasticism through their Aristotelian method of relating reason to revelation. Classical Islamic civilization in the Nile-to-Oxus regions, North Africa, and South Asia reached the most advanced levels in the human and natural sciences, including philosophy, mathematics, optics, astronomy, pharmacology, surgery, and geography. The fourteenth- to fifteenth-century scholar Ibn Khaldūn, for example, is sometimes called father of both historiography and sociology. His grand theory of the rise of empires depends on an analysis of the tensions between urban, agricultural folk and pastoral nomads. The latter, among which camel herders are the most excellent, provide the energy, ideals, courage, organization, and endurance needed to conquer and rule. But, over time, the conquerors are themselves overwhelmed, first by their own ease and progressive corruption in cities, then by a new wave of pastoralists that rises to replace them as rulers, only to begin the inevitable cycle anew. Ibn Khaldūn thoroughly and lucidly explicates his—for his times—frankly historicist theory in his *The Muqaddimah: An Introduction to History* (English translation, three volumes, Bollingen 1958).

The "Pillars" of Islam The basic devotional duties of Islam are conventionally classified under five "pillars": (1) *Shahāda* is "witnessing" to the unity of God and the messengerhood of the Prophet Muhammad by declaring, "There is no god but God (Allah); Muhammad is the Messenger of God (Allah)." It is necessary only to declare the shahāda sincerely to become a Muslim. The shahāda is the closest Islam comes to a formal creed. (2) *Ṣalāt* is formal prayer five times daily (at dawn, noon, midafternoon, sunset, and night) either in congregation or alone, while facing the holy Ka'aba shrine, Islam's *axis mundi,* in Mecca. On Friday is an obligatory noonday congregational ṣalāt with a sermon. There are also ṣalāts for funerals, feasts, and the two eclipses. Worshippers must be in a state of ritual purity before the ṣalāt is performed. This is accomplished by either a minor or a major ablution, depending on the degree of impurity experienced. (3) *Zakāt* is annual almsgiving amounting to a set percentage of one's wealth (provided it reaches a minimum level) for the benefit of the poor, new converts in need of assistance, defenders of Islam, debtors, alms administrators, and certain other classes of recipients. The paying of zakāt purifies one's remaining wealth. The profound social-ethical dimension of almsgiving may be discerned, for example, in the regulation that money used to pay for the pilgrimage to Mecca must have been purified first by the paying of zakāt. (4) *Ṣaum* is fasting during the holy month of Ramadan between sunrise and sunset, when no food or drink may be consumed or smoking or sexual relations engaged in. Evenings are spent enjoying a meal, meeting for special litanies in mosques, visiting friends, and resting. Before dawn, a meal is taken to sustain people through the day, when work, school, homemaking, and other occupations con- tinue, usually at a slower pace than normal. (5) *Ḥajj* is the pilgrimage to the holy city of Mecca once in a Muslim's life, if circumstances and resources permit. The ḥajj is the high point in most Muslims' lives, after which the pilgrim is permitted to add the title ḥajji before his or her name. During the ḥajj, pilgrims circumambulate the holy Ka'aba shrine in Mecca and ritually reenact experiences of the holy ancestors Abraham, Ishmael, and Hagar.

Sometimes a sixth pillar is included in the list of required Islamic practices. This is *jihād*, "exertion" in the way of God. Although in the West *jihād* is usually thought to mean holy war, that is only one of the meanings accorded to it by Muslims. A "Greater Jihād," as Muhammad called it, is the struggle each Muslim sustains to overcome evil and to do good.

Sectarian Divisions and Legal Schools The umma does not have denominations in the Christian and Jewish senses. However, there is a basic division in the community between Sunnīs and Shī'īs. The former constitute a majority of about 85% of all Muslims. The division is based on different political philosophies, and not essential theological disagreement or diverse worship practices. Shī'īs hold that Muhammad designated his son-in-law Ali as his successor, with the intention that succeeding leaders of the Muslims would be in that line. The subcommunity of Muslims that eventually called themselves Sunnīs (after the Sunna, or "customary way" of the Prophet Muhammad) hold that any good Muslim with requisite leadership ability, legal knowledge, and membership in the Arabian tribe of Quraysh—Muhammad's own—can be selected as *khalīfa* (caliph), "deputy" of Muhammad. Shī'ism has several subsects, among which the Ismā'īl'īs may be mentioned for their esoteric doctrines and very close community loyalty. The largest Shī'ite community is the Imamī sect, also known as the "Twelvers" because they recognize that number of perfect leaders who lived before the line was interrupted with the disappearance and "occultation" of the Twelfth Imām, who continues to rule through earthly representatives (e.g., Ayatollahs), until he returns again to advent the Last Judgment. Shī'ite rule is charismatic, with the imāms ("leaders") believed to be endowed with supernatural authority and infallible wisdom.

Legal schools: Another set of subcommunities in Islam centers upon which of several legal rites are followed. The Sunnīs recognize four orthodox law schools, all of which emerged in the early centuries. The Ḥanafī rite is rather flexible and predominates in Turkey and India. The Mālikī rite is conservative and found principally in North and West Africa. The Shāfi'ī rite, which features analogical reasoning as a major source of jurisprudence, is preeminent in Egypt and Southeast Asia. The final school is the Ḥanbalī rite, a conservative school that distrusts rational dialectic in reaching legal decisions. Ḥanbalism is dominant in Saudi Arabia. The major Shī'ī legal rite is the Ja'farī school. Shī'īs are most numerous in Iran, southern Lebanon, and Iraq.

No more than the Sunnī and Shī'ī divisions do the different legal schools of Islam constitute denominationlike entities. Although most Muslims follow only one of the allowable schools, it is permissible to seek a legal opinion from any of them. Islamic jurisprudence is known as *fiqh* (literally, "understanding"), and the legal specialists constitute a professional class known as *'ulamā'* (singular, *'ālim*), the "learned" in theological and legal matters. Most legal reasoning relies on four sources of authority: The most important is the Qur'ān; the second is the Sunna—the teaching and example of Muhammad as preserved in the literary reports known as *ḥadīth*. Third is analogical reasoning, known as *qiyās*. Finally, there is, among the Sunnīs, consensus of the learned, called *ijmā'*. Shī'ites depend heavily on their enlightened teachers, whereas Sunnī Islam views the community itself as having charismatic authority. A renowned ḥadīth of Muhammad states that "My umma shall never agree together on an error." Although dissenting views are tolerated, consensus is nevertheless a powerful legitimizing force. Strictly considered, *ijmā'* means broad consensus of the 'ulamā'.

The Contemporary Islamic Revival Although for many centuries Islamic law has been conservative and cautious, modern times have seen a renewal of *ijtihād*, "independent legal decision making," which characterized fiqh's early development. Islam's traditional unification of religion and state is severely challenged by modernity. There are increasing numbers of Muslims now living in Western countries. In North America, for example, where as many as 5 million Muslims now reside, there is a fiqh council that addresses new issues and challenges faced by Muslims living as minorities in a secular, pluralistic society. One of the greatest concerns of Muslims in North America is assimilation/nonassimilation into the larger society.

Recent decades have witnessed a global revival of Islam, accompanied by a great migration of Muslims to Western countries as well as substantial conversions to Islam in sub-Saharan Africa, Europe, and the Americas. The oil crisis of the early 1970s, followed by the Iranian Islamic revolution later in that decade, greatly increased the visibility of Islam and Muslims in the West. Although the media continue to focus on violence and terrorism associated with so-called fundamentalist Islam, the Muslim world is in no way a hostile monolithic entity pitted against the West and modernity. *Islamist* (a term preferred by Muslims to *fundamentalist*) movements vary from place to place, but they tend to agree that the Qur'ān and Muhammad's Sunna should be the ultimate authorities in the challenge of living life Islamically. Modern science and technology are not considered by Islamists to be adverse to Islamization, although Westernization and secularism are rejected as thoroughly un-Islamic.

Among the leading Islamic revivalist movements of the present are the Muslim Brotherhood, founded in Egypt in 1928 by Ḥasan al-Bannā'. That strongly revivalist brotherhood sees itself not so much as an organization but as a community based on Qur'ānic principles. It has had a turbulent career because of its opposition to governments in Egypt, but it is at present unofficially tolerated in its home country with some of its members even serving as elected representatives in the National Assembly. Associated organizations have been formed in neighboring countries. Another movement is the Jamaat-i-Islami, founded in Pakistan by Abū Alā Mawdūdī in the 1940s. That vigorously assertive organization strives to counter Western influences on Islam and pushes a strong program of Islamization of society. A final revivalist organization, and by far the largest in the world, is the Jama'at al-Tablīgh ("Society for the Propagation [of Islam]"), founded in India in 1927. The Tablīgh is nonideological and nonmilitant, sending missionaries throughout the world with a message centering on scrupulous imitation of the Prophet Muhammad, viewing all other ways as sinful and corrupt.

—*Frederick M. Denny*

REFERENCES

A. Ahmed, *Postmodernism and Islam* (New York: Routledge, 1992); L. Ahmed, *Women and Gender in Islam* (New Haven, Conn.: Yale University Press, 1992); *American Journal of Islamic Social Sciences* (Silver Spring, Md.: Association of Muslim Social Scientists and International Institute of Islamic Thought, three issues per year, 1985–); R. Antoun, *Muslim Preacher in the Modern World* (Princeton, N.J.: Princeton University Press, 1989); F. M. Denny, *An Introduction to Islam* (New York: Macmillan, 1994); C. Geertz, *Islam Observed* (New Haven, Conn.: Yale University Press, 1968); M. Gilsenan, *Recognizing Islam* (New York: Pantheon, 1983); Y. Y. Haddad and A. T. Lummis, *Islamic Values in the United States* (New York: Oxford University Press, 1987); M. G. S. Hodgson, *The Venture of Islam* (Chicago: University of Chicago Press, 1974); M. H. Kamali, *Principles of Islamic Jurisprudence* (Kuala Lumpur: Pelanduk, 1989); G. Kepel, *Muslim Extremism in Egypt* (Berkeley: University of California Press, 1986); I. Lapidus, *A History of Islamic Societies* (Cambridge: Cambridge University Press, 1988); F. Mernissi, *The Veil and the Male Elite* (Reading, Mass.: Addison-Wesley, 1991); Y. al-Qaradawi, *The Lawful and the Prohibited in Islam* (Indianapolis: American Trust Publications, n.d.; Arabic original, 1960); A. Schimmel, *Islamic Names* (Edinburgh: Edinburgh University Press, 1989); B. S. Turner, *Weber and Islam* (London: Routledge, 1974); E. H. Waugh et al. (eds.), *Muslim Families in North America* (Edmonton: University of Alberta Press, 1991).

JACKSON, JESSE (1941–)
African American clergyman and political leader.

The Rev. Jesse Jackson began his career as a civil rights activist with the Council on Racial Equity (CORE) in Greensboro, North Carolina, in the early 1960s. He was involved in the Rev. Martin Luther King, Jr.'s Southern Christian Leadership Conference (SCLC) and participated in the protest at Selma, Alabama (1965). He was also National Director of Operation Breadbasket, a group designed to advance black economic autonomy. After King's assassination, Jackson created various organizations to advance civil rights for African Americans. The "Rainbow Coalition" was the most prominent and was intended to mobilize a broad array of minority groups to participate in electoral politics. Others included PUSH (People United to Save Humanity) and PUSH-Excel (PUSH for Excellence), a program designed to keep urban adolescents in school. Jackson ran for president in 1984, as did televangelist Pat Robertson, with moderate success, and again in 1988. Both candidates excelled in early primaries, with Jackson finishing second for the Democratic nomination, with 6.9 million votes from a loose coalition of the more disenfranchised members of society. He focused on a progressive agenda involving voting rights, affirmative action, homelessness, and an overall increase in the social safety net (health/elder care and so on). In 1991, he was elected Senator of the District of Columbia and was hailed as the third most admired man in America.

Yet, in 1992, he lost political influence, as least partially due to his association with Louis Farrakhan, leader of the Nation of Islam, which alienated the liberal Jewish wing of mainstream Democratic support. Now, Jackson faces questions about his ability to defend civil rights legislation. Although he strives to become "part" of the traditional two-party system, Jackson *can* act independently, and appear erratic, as in 1979 when he tried on his own to negotiate relations between the Israelis and the Palestinians. It is this *style* that he may have most in common with Robertson. Thus while Jackson's Rainbow Coalition and Robertson's Christian Coalition may be ideologically antithetical, there is a charismatic and ego involvement driven by the styles of the two leaders that creates an interesting parallel.

—*Susan Zickmund*

REFERENCES

T. Celsi, *Jesse Jackson and the Political Power* (Brookfield, Conn.: Millbrook, 1991); E. O. Colton, *The Jackson Phenomenon* (Garden City, N.Y.: Doubleday, 1989); A. L. Reed, *The Jackson Phenomena* (New Haven, Conn.: Yale University Press, 1987).

JACQUET, CONSTANT ("CONNIE") H(ER-BERT), JR. (1925-1990)   M.Phil., Columbia University; Episcopalian layman; core leader in the founding and maintenance of the Religious Research Association (RRA) and its president, 1985-1986.

Jacquet worked in the National Council of Churches of Christ (NCC) research department from 1952 to 1990; from 1959, he directed its research library, including the H. Paul Douglass collection of church-related field studies. He compiled and edited the *Yearbook of American* (since 1973, *and Canadian*) *Churches*, 1966-1990. By 1990, this included statistics on 306 denominations, an extensive directory of religious organizations, periodicals, other sources of religious research material, interpretive articles, and some special reports, such as his "Women Ministers in 1986 and 1977: A Ten Year Review." Daily, he answered inquiries from the media and others about the use and interpretation of church statistics. As a member and officer of the Association of Statisticians of Religious Bodies, he promoted ways to achieve greater uniformity in statistical reporting by denominations. Jacquet served as President, Secretary, and Archivist of the Religious Research Association and as a contributing editor to its *Review of Religious Research*. The Constant H. Jacquet Research Award of the RRA memorializes his contribution to the field.

—*Everett L. Perry*

JAINISM   Dating from a movement of the sixth century B.C.E., about 3 million Jains now live in their original homeland of northern India. Salvation or liberation can be attained only by monks living an ascetic style of life similar to Brahmanic ascetics and Buddhist monks. A central doctrine is *ahimsa,* nonviolence to living things; this doctrine was crucial to Mohandas Gandhi, who was not a Jain but who grew up among Jains.

See also Buddhism, Gandhi, Hinduism

—*Joseph B. Tamney*

REFERENCE

M. Langley, "Respect for All Life," in *Handbook to the World's Religions,* rev. ed. (Grand Rapids, Mich.: Eerdmans, 1994): 207-216.

JAMES, WILLIAM (1842-1910)   Psychologist and philosopher; considered by some the "father" of American psychology and also of American pragmatism.

Born in New York City, the son of theologian Henry James, Sr. (1811-1882), William James had a wide-ranging education that began with home schooling by his unconventional father and included studies in England, France, Switzerland, and Germany between 1855-1860 (often with his younger brother, Henry, the novelist). After trying his hand as a painter, James studied chemistry, anatomy and physiology, and psychology at Harvard University, where he received his medical degree in 1869. His medical education included a nine-month expedition in Brazil with zoologist Louis Agassiz in 1865-1866. Such a vast array of experience, according to Ralph Barton Perry (1948:71), stimulated and revealed in James "a mind as energetic and acquisitive as it was voracious and incorrigibly vagrant."

James never practiced medicine, becoming instead a professor at Harvard, where he taught from 1872 to 1907 on a variety of topics including anatomy and physiology, psychology, and philosophy. A leading figure in experimental psychology, James established a laboratory at Harvard—one of the first such laboratories in the world—to study the subject. During this period, he befriended the philosopher C. S. Peirce and was greatly influenced by Peirce's pragmatism.

James attained considerable notoriety with the publication, in 1890, of *The Principles of Psychology,* but it was *The Varieties of Religious Experience: A Study in Human Nature*—his Gifford Lectures delivered at Edinburgh in 1901-1902—that established James as one of America's leading philosophers and religious thinkers. Indeed, *The Varieties* has been called "the most famous of all American treatises on religion" (Clebsch 1973:153). Although James called his lectures a "descriptive survey" of the varieties of religious experience, they in fact represent an early defense of his pragmatic view of religion. James sought to articulate a defense of the religious impulse of human beings, arguing against "medical materialism," which would reduce religion to abnormal states of mind rooted in physiology; transcendental idealist and neo-Hegelian philosophies, which threatened to reduce religion to an intellectual exercise; and institutional religions, which sought to place ritual and dogma ahead of individual experience.

Against those who would dismiss religious experience as psychologically or physiologically pathological, James argued for an assessment of its value in terms suggested by his conception of the pragmatic theory of truth: Beliefs or ideas are true if they "work," that is, if they are useful. Thus, in *The Varieties,* James claims that religion should neither be arbitrarily privileged nor dismissed but should be judged according to its usefulness in achieving some valued end. Religious experiences and beliefs, in James's well-known words, should be judged "by their fruits . . . not by their roots."

In James's view, beliefs—like scientific hypotheses—are always conditional, fallible, and subject to experimental testing. This is true of religious beliefs no less than other beliefs. As James succinctly put it in the Preface to *The Will to Believe* (Dover 1959 [1897]: xi-xii),

> If religious hypotheses about the universe be in order at all, then the active faiths of individuals in them, freely expressing themselves in life, are the experimental tests by which they are verified, and the only means by which their truth or falsehood can be wrought out. The truest scientific hypothesis is that which, as we say, "works" best; and it can be no otherwise with religious hypotheses.

This pragmatic view of truth is sometimes referred to as "experimentalism."

In *The Varieties,* James found the greatest "fruits of the religious life," and therefore the greatest justification for religion, in *saintliness.* Typical of the individual "regenerate character" and indicated by charity, modesty, piety, and happiness, saintliness is "present in all religions." Recalling the subtitle of *The Varieties,* James finds in saintliness a key insight into human nature: the possibility that religious experience might regenerate the original "rightness" of human being.

James the psychologist is also amply represented in *The Varieties,* especially in distinctions he made early in the lectures between two types of religious experience: the "religion of healthy-mindedness" and the "sick soul." The religion of healthy-mindedness is exemplified by the "once-born" person who is cheerful and optimistic (James's exemplar was Walt Whitman), while the sick soul possesses a "divided self" characterized by pessimism and anguish (James's exemplar seems to have been himself). The sick soul must be "twice-born," the "divided self" reunified and renewed through a process of conversion to achieve happiness. Although he considers a variety of emotions and interpretations of religious experience in *The Varieties,* the type of religious experience he considers most often is the twice-born conversion of the sick soul—which is not surprising because that best fit his own personal experience.

James is rightfully considered a "founding father" of the psychology of religion. Indeed, he is the most frequently cited individual in the field. Arguably his greatest enduring contribution has been his legitimation of the study of the *experiential dimension* of religion. By invoking James—especially his delineation of the four characteristics of *mysticism* (ineffability, noetic quality, transiency, and passivity)—later scholars could study religious experience with less fear of being dismissed for studying the esoteric or the extreme.

Definitive scholarly editions of James's work have been published by Harvard University Press with the support of the American Council of Learned Societies under the general editorship of Frederick Burkhardt, Fredson Bowers, and Ignas Skrupskelis as *The Works of William James,* including *The Varieties of Religious Experience* (volume 15, 1985, with an introduction by John E. Smith). The text of *The Varieties* has been published by many presses, including editions by the Library of America and the Modern Library. Most frequently cited is the original Longmans, Green edition (1902)—or editions produced from those plates (e.g., the Penguin Classics edition)—which is cross-referenced in the Harvard edition. An exemplary biography of James is Gerald E. Myers's *William James: His Life and Thought* (Yale University Press 1986). For the intellectual context of James's thought, see Bruce Kuklick's *The Rise of American Philosophy, Cambridge, Massachusetts, 1860-1930* (Yale University Press 1977).

See also Experience, Mysticism, Religiosity

—*David Yamane*

REFERENCES

W. Clebsch, *American Religious Thought* (Chicago: University of Chicago Press, 1973); J. E. Dittes, "Beyond William James," in *Beyond the Classics?* ed. C. Y. Glock and P. E. Hammond (New York: Harper, 1973): 291-354; H. S. Levinson, *The Religious Investigations of William James* (Chapel Hill: University of North Carolina Press, 1981); R. B. Perry, *The Thought and Character of William James* (New York: Harper, 1948).

JARRETT, WILLIAM H. (1930–)   Educated at St. Louis University and awarded B.S. and M.S. degrees, Jarrett received a Ph.D. in sociology at Michigan State University in 1961. Since that time, he has been a member of the Department of Sociology at Canisius College, Buffalo, New York, and is currently also Director of the Criminal Justice Program in the same institution. President, Association for the Sociology of Religion, 1974.

Jarrett has pursued research on adolescents, family size, and aging parents. He is currently involved in criminal justice issues and in the health field, serving as a member of a hospital ethics committee since 1987. His ASR presidential address was titled "Sociology and the New Religious Prophets: Is the New Wine Any Better?" (*Sociological Analysis* 1974). Of his published works, this was the closest Jarrett came to dealing with the issue of religion from a sociological perspective. Jarrett was the last president elected to ASR whose specific interest was not in the sociology of religion.

—*Loretta M. Morris*

JEANINE, Sr. MARY   *see* Jeanine Gruesser

JEHOVAH'S WITNESSES   Adventist sect that arose in the United States under the influence of Millerite millennialism in the 1870s. Jehovah's Witnesses (the name adopted in 1931) now claim an international membership of over 5 million, with a significant majority located outside the United States. The group is legally incorporated under the names *Watchtower Bible and Tract Society* (1884, United States) and *International Bible Students Association* (1914, United Kingdom). C. T. Russell served as president of the WTS until his death (1916); the able leadership of Russell and his successors (including J. F. Rutherford, N. Knorr, and F. Franz) has contributed significantly to the organizational stability and expansion of the Witnesses in the twentieth century.

Jehovah's Witnesses are strongly tied to their printed literature. The society's biweekly magazines *The Watchtower* and *Awake!* are important sources of information about Witness beliefs and practices. Witness life is based on a regimen of active proselytizing and participation in weekly meetings at their Kingdom Halls, where they study WTS literature and learn new-member recruiting skills. The society's Bible translation, the *New World Translation* (revised edition 1984), is an important source of Witness doctrine (e.g., John 1:1); the Witnesses' distinct communal argot ("theocratic English") is based in part on the *NWT*'s unique English style. In 1993, the WTS published its most thorough history to date, *Jehovah's Witnesses: Proclaimers of God's Kingdom*. The WTS's *Yearbook* is an important resource for social scientists as it includes thorough membership and growth statistics from the WTS's previous service year.

Some early studies of the Witnesses are still worth consulting (e.g., Stroup 1945, Cohn 1955). But the works of James Beckford (e.g., 1975), Joseph F. Zygmunt (e.g., 1967, 1970), and Bryan Wilson (e.g., 1970) constitute the most significant bodies of literature on the Witnesses from a social scientific perspective. This literature clusters around three principal theoretical foci: the Weber-Troeltsch-Niebuhr model of sect-to-church development, the theory of relative deprivation, and the problem of millennial delay and disconfirmation (see Festinger et al., *When Prophecy Fails*, Harper 1956). It is commonly assumed that the WTS draws its membership principally from the working classes, although Beckford has strongly contested the "neatness" of such an analysis. Sociologists often treat Witnesses as an "established sect." In spite of multiple disappointments and prophetic recalculations (most recently in 1975), Witnesses maintained their sectarian style and apocalyptic fervor. The history of the WTS suggests that its institutional identity and momentum have insulated the organization from the destabilizing potential of the society's eschatology.

Other studies of the Witnesses have explored issues of race, ethnic identity, and migration (e.g., Cooper 1974), cross-cultural dynamics (e.g., Wilson 1974, Long 1968), conversion processes (Beckford 1978), and rhetoric and symbolism (Botting and Botting 1984).

See also Adventism, Cognitive Dissonance, Church-Sect Theory, Deprivation Theory, Millenarianism

—*Joel Elliott*

REFERENCES

J. A. Beckford, *The Trumpet of Prophecy* (New York: Wiley, 1975); J. A. Beckford, "Accounting for Conversion," *British Journal of Sociology* 29(1978):249-262; H. Botting and G. Botting, *The Orwellian World of Jehovah's Witnesses* (Toronto: University of Toronto Press, 1984); W. Cohn, "Jehovah's Witnesses as a Proletarian Movement," *American Scholar* 24(1955):281-298; L. R. Cooper, " 'Publish' or Perish," in *Religious Movements in Contemporary America*, ed. I. I. Zaretsky and M. P. Leone (Princeton, N.J.: Princeton University Press, 1974): 700-721; N. Long, *Social Change and the Individual* (Manchester, U.K.: Manchester University Press, 1968); H. H. Stroup, *The Jehovah's Witnesses* (New York: Russell & Russell, 1945); B. R. Wilson, *Religious Sects* (London: Weidenfeld & Nicolson, 1970); B. R. Wilson, "Jehovah's Witnesses in Kenya," *Journal of Religion in Africa* 5(1974): 128-149; J. F. Zygmunt, *Jehovah's Witnesses*, Doctoral dissertation, University of Chicago, 1967; J. F.

Zygmunt, "Prophetic Failure and Chiliastic Identity," *American Journal of Sociology* 75(1970):926-948.

JESUS PEOPLE (JESUS MOVEMENT/JM)

A generic name given by the media to a number of groups of young people who came together in the late 1960s and early 1970s to live communally and promote an "experiential" version of fundamentalism (Richardson and Davis 1983). The best known of these was the Children of God (now known as The Family), but there were other such groups, including Shiloh Youth Ministries, which was the second largest of the JM groups (Richardson et al. 1979), and many others around the country (Enroth et al. 1972, Ellwood 1973).

The JM groups were made up of young, relatively affluent people, the majority of whom were white males. Most participants had been involved with drug use, and a number had been caught up in the sexual "revolution" of the time as well. The groups proselytized aggressively, promoting the message of fundamentalist Christianity among young people on the streets and highways of America. Most of the groups also practiced glossolalia, and their lifestyle was very casual in terms of dress and living situations. The JM had a heavy emphasis on music, with "Jesus rock" becoming quite popular in part because of the promotion of the JM Christian message to other young people via music. Some of the groups became international and spread their lifestyle and practices around the world.

Jesus People USA is another major JM group, currently centered in the Chicago area. They publish a well-respected Christian periodical called *Cornerstone* as a part of their ministry.

See also The Family

—*James T. Richardson*

REFERENCES

R. Ellwood, *One Way* (Englewood Cliffs, N.J.: Prentice Hall, 1973); R. Enroth et al., *The Jesus People* (Grand Rapids, Mich.: Eerdmans, 1972); J. T. Richardson and R. Davis, "Experiential Fundamentalism," *Journal of the American Academy of Religion* 51(1983):397-425; J. T. Richardson et al., *Organized Miracles* (New Brunswick, N.J.: Transaction, 1979); L. Streiker, *The Jesus Trip* (Nashville, Tenn.: Abingdon, 1971); H. Ward, *The Far-Out Saints of the Jesus Communes* (New York: Association Press, 1972).

JEWISH-CHRISTIAN RELATIONS AND ANTI-SEMITISM

Anti-Semitism, meaning hatred for Jews and attempts to repress them and/or their religion, predates Christianity. The Bible reports attempts by Pharaoh and Haman to annihilate Jews. Greeks not only warred against the Jews but, having conquered them, attempted to impose their culture on Jews by violence. Jews, led by the Macabees, resisted. Cultural competition between these two civilizations resulted in ethnic conflict between Jews and Greeks at many points around the Mediterranean Basin. This led to the emergence of anti-Semitic stereotypes and literature.

With Christianity, hostility toward Jews and Judaism became central to a religion for the first time. The crucifixion of Jesus and Jewish culpability for his death are central to the Gospels. Matthew and John are contemptuous of and hostile to Judaism and Jews. The former (see 27:25) claims that Jews willingly and enthusiastically accepted the label of killers of Jesus Christ for themselves and their descendants (which for Christians is *deicide*); the latter identifies them with the devil (8:44). These bitterly hostile images came to be woven into the liturgy, particularly of Easter, and thus annually reinforced among ordinary Christians. The early church fathers, particularly John Chrysostom, developed these themes with singular vehemence.

Later the church developed the doctrine of itself as the "true church" and Jews as the "witness" condemned to servitude (Augustine). As a result, Jews become Esau to Christians' "Jacob" (see Genesis 25:21-27:46). The Christian claim to have supplanted the Jews as "God's chosen people" goes to the core foundations of both religions. It precipitated an implacable conflict against Jews and Judaism. The Jews' continued adherence to Judaism was a negation of the very essence of the Christian claim to a new chosenness. Jews had to be punished for this rejection.

The Middle Ages and the Catholic Church

Despite clerical polemics, at the beginning of the Middle Ages there was little hostility toward Jews among the laity. The church condemned usury, an economic necessity, but permitted its practice by Jews. At the beginning of the eleventh century, clerical efforts resulted in expulsions from a number of cities. The crucial change occurred with the First Crusade (1096). Crusaders on their way to the Holy Land attacked Jews in German and French towns. Jews were massacred, and numbers of them committed collective suicide to avoid conversion. Each call for a crusade resulted in renewed attacks on Jews.

In the thirteenth century, following the adoption of the doctrine of transubstantiation, blood libels and charges of Host desecration were made against Jews. Jews were required to wear a distinguishing symbol, a hat or a badge. The imposed social distance facilitated the spread of additional myths, such as Jews being physically different from other humans (see Shylock's soliloquy in Shakespeare's *Merchant of Venice*). As trade and money moved into the hands of Christians at the end of the thirteenth century, Jews were no longer as necessary to the nobles. Protection was removed. Numerous expulsions and massacres occurred. Rabbis were required to enter into *disputations* with clergy to defend Judaism's doctrines. Win or lose, the Jewish community would be required to convert or leave. Often the disputations involved passages of the Talmud, and the Talmud was banned and burned. In the fourteenth century the outbreak of the black plague resulted in the myth that the Jews were poisoning the wells, hence further massacres ensued.

On the Iberian Peninsula, when the Christians wrested control from the Muslims, the Inquisition was vigorously promoted. Finally, in 1492 in Spain (1497 in Portugal), Jews were required to choose between conversion and expulsion. Those who converted to Christianity (*anusim,* or "forced converts," in Hebrew; *marranos,* or "pigs," in Spanish) nonetheless remained suspect. They continued to be subject to the Inquisition's tortures and to death by the *auto de fe* (burning at the cross; literally, an "act of faith"). The Spanish developed a notion of purity of blood to keep the *marranos* separate.

The Reformation gave rise to a fracturing of anti-Semitic sentiments. Luther preached extreme hatred and violence, but Calvinists identified with the Old Testament and with Jews. Among Catholics, ghettoes for Jews were introduced.

The Modern Period   In the modern period, while Christianity in eastern Europe continued its open hostility to Jews, elsewhere other forces, particularly nationalism and racism, became the lead forces of anti-Semitic persecution. Churches, retreating from the arena of politics, continued their support of anti-Semitism with their teachings and their influence, although at times opposition to anti-Semitism was also voiced.

The Enlightenment required that Jews be absorbed and disappear, yet society did not permit Jews to do so. A backlash developed against Jews among the new nationalists as well as supporters of prerevolutionary regimes. Political anti-Semitism developed particularly in Germany and France in the latter part of the nineteenth century. Racism was created as a new justifica-

tion for anti-Semitism. This was especially useful where Jews had shed their religious and ethnic behaviors. It was used in much the same way that "pure blood" had been used by the Spanish *hidalgos* against the *marranos.*

Russia and Central Europe: Russia acquired a Jewish population following its annexation of eastern Poland. The czarist regime derived its legitimacy from the Orthodox faith, and anti-Semitism based on Christian religious prejudice remained a powerful political force. Jews were required to remain in the "pale of settlement," and they were forbidden to enter a number of occupations. Boys were drafted to the army for periods of up to 20 years (cantonists). The regime encouraged pogroms against Jews to direct hostility away from itself. In 1905, under the auspices of the secret police, the press of the czar published the fraudulent *Protocols of the Elders of Zion,* a forgery purporting to show the existence of an international Jewish conspiracy bent on world power. Similar anti-Semitic patterns characterized the Ukraine and the Austro-Hungarian Empire.

Western Europe and the United States: Persecution of Jews in Russia led many Jews to flee to the West. The Jewish populations in England, France, and Austria-Germany expanded rapidly, and with this expansion, anti-Semitism increased. There had been little overt anti-Semitism in the United States, but it became manifest at the end of the nineteenth century. There was open discrimination in housing, higher education, and jobs. As other minorities also suffered discrimination in the United States, it was easier for Jews to find allies and to avoid the brutal political repressions by the state that characterized anti-Semitism elsewhere.

The Holocaust and its aftermath: Beginning in the 1930s, the Nazis conducted a war of extermination against Jews and Judaism that came to be known as the Holocaust. The tactics used—armbands to distinguish Jews from others, racial ideology, debasing of Jews and denigration of Judaism, herding Jews into ghettoes, stripping Jews of legal protection, encouraging mobs against them, caricaturing Jews and Judaism, slandering of Jews and their holy books, desecrating synagogues and Torahs—had been used before in the persecution of Jews in the name of religion. This time persecution in the name of nationalism and racism culminated in a campaign of extermination in which 6 million people, including women and children, perished.

This was not an ordinary attempt to vanquish a people, because Jews had no armies and no arms. Neither was it an attempt to take territory, for Jews controlled none. The persecution did not end when Jews had been despoiled of their wealth and their homes and expelled from the countries in which they lived. Stripped of all they owned, they were hunted down to be killed. This war was directed against both Jews and Judaism. The Talmud and other works of Jewish scholarship were slandered and burned. Synagogues were pillaged. The Jews' Torah scrolls were desecrated and made into lamp shades or shoe liners. Frequently the two persecutions came together, as when Jews were herded into synagogues to be burned alive. Nazism's anti-Semitic appeals fell on the fertile ground that had been prepared by religious persecutions. In the late 1930s, before the Nazis had begun their campaign of extermination and were still bent on driving the Jews out of Germany and the areas they had conquered, western Europe and North America closed their doors to refugees, with some minor exceptions. The British "White Paper" of 1939 blocked further immigration to Palestine. As a result, Jews could not flee and were trapped in Europe.

When the Nazi plan for the "liquidation" of the Jewish people came to be known in 1943, the allies refused to make it public, arguing that it would "hinder the war effort." Although the Roman Catholic Church protested Nazi policies (*Mit Brennender Sorge* Encyclical, 1937) and some Protestant pastors (Martin Neimoeller, Dietrich Bonhoeffer) were imprisoned, during the war the Vatican did not openly condemn the atrocities against the Jews.

In the immediate postwar period, as the extent of the atrocities against Jews became known, revulsion at the crimes committed against the Jews led to a reaction against anti-Semitism, particularly in the United States, and to a sympathetic view of the establishment of a homeland for Jews in Israel.

The Soviet Union: Following the Russian Revolution of 1917, religiously driven anti-Semitism abated. From 1948 to his death in 1953, however, Stalin pursued an anti-Semitic policy. Accusations were made of a doctors' plot against Stalin. All Jewish cultural institutions were liquidated. Thousands of Jews were dismissed from their jobs. Jewish artists and writers were arrested and executed.

Under Khrushchev, the executions ceased, but the persecution of Jews continued. Books and pamphlets were printed by government agencies attacking not only Jews and Israel (which was the enemy of the Soviet Union's Arab client states) but also Judaism. Synagogues were closed and attacked as hangouts for criminals. With the fall of the Communist regime in 1989, Soviet Jews were permitted to emigrate in mass numbers. Fearing a revival of anti-Semitism, about 1 million Jews left the Soviet Union in the next five years.

In Islam: Although the Qur'ān attacks Jews for refusing to recognize Mohammed as a prophet, Jews were rarely demonized as in Christianity. Arab anti-Semitism was furthered by the growing Jewish-Arab conflict during the Mandate period and intensified by the birth of the State of Israel in 1948. In the postwar period, its virulence has been unequaled. Arab regimes that published much hate literature show the influence of the Nazi canards and cartoons as well as those of Russian anti-Semites. This literature has been used to support the Arab case against Israel. Anti-Zionism is now used to cloak anti-Semitism. The Arab bloc succeeded in 1975 in having the United Nations adopt a resolution condemning Zionism as racism as part of this anti-Semitic campaign.

Changing Jewish-Christian Relations The failure of the Catholic Church to condemn the atrocities perpetrated against the Jews by the Nazi regime became an embarrassment after the war. The Second Vatican Council, following the intentions of Pope John XXIII (d. 1963), in 1965 undertook a revision of the Easter liturgy to remove "the Jews in our time" from blame for the death of Jesus. Nonetheless, Jews are still damned for not accepting Jesus as the Messiah. The State of Israel is still not officially recognized by the Vatican, although the beginnings of this process are under way. Controversy also still exists over the meaning of the Holocaust and attempts by Catholic groups to define Auschwitz and other death camps primarily as places of martyrdom of Catholics.

The response of Protestant groups to the Holocaust has reflected their divisions. German Lutherans tended to embrace Nazis, but Denmark, also a Lutheran country, following the lead of their king, saved their entire Jewish population, even adopting wearing of the Jewish badge. Following the establishment of the State of Israel, and particularly following the Six Day War and reunification of Jerusalem (1967), fundamentalist Protestant groups, particularly in the United States, tended to embrace Israel and Jews generally, while Protestant mainstream groups and organizations tended to support the Arabs.

Interfaith dialogue developed from efforts to missionize Jews. Christians saw these efforts as sharing the opportunity for personal salvation. Jews saw it as an attempt to undermine their ancestral faith. Following World War II, churches began to recognize that some of the roots of anti-Semitism derived from their own teachings. Nonetheless, the hostile stance of many Protestant churches to Israel following the Six Day War seriously undermined this movement.

Blacks and Jews in the United States were generally close allies throughout the period of the civil rights movement. Since the mid-1960s, conflict has erupted between the two. Black Muslims have been particularly virulent in their attacks on Jews and Judaism, and some of this has affected attitudes of the wider black community.

Defense Organizations   The Anti-Defamation League of B'nai Brith, founded in 1913—the largest and best known of Jewish defense organizations—is an American national organization with offices in Israel and Europe. It engages in research on hate crimes and hate groups in the United States and worldwide, and seeks to combat anti-Semitism through programs of education and legal and political means.

Student Struggle for Soviet Jewry, founded in 1964, gained the support of major Jewish organizations in the 1970s.

The Jewish Defense League, founded in 1967 by Rabbi Meir Kahane, advocated violence in self-defense but has been shunned by major Jewish organizations. Kahane was assassinated in New York in 1990.

Since the 1960s, Israel has been a participant in international Jewish defense. Examples include the capture and trial of Adolf Eichmann, the Entebbe raid rescuing Jewish hostages in Uganda, assistance to various government agencies in countering terrorism against Jews, and the rescue of Jews from regimes where they are threatened, such as Ethiopia.

—*M. Herbert Danzger*

REFERENCES

Anti-Semitism (London: Institute of Jewish Affairs, 1994); *Anti-Semitism Worldwide* (Tel Aviv: Anti-Defamation League, 1996); S. W. Baron, *A Social and Religious History of the Jews* (New York: Columbia University Press, 1952, 14 vols.); L. Dinnerstein, *Antisemitism in America* (New York: Oxford University Press, 1994); C. Y. Glock and R. Stark, *Christian Beliefs and Antisemitism* (New York: Harper, 1966); M. V. Hay, *The Foot of Pride* (Boston: Beacon, 1951); R. Hilberg, *The Destruction of European Jews* (Chicago: Quadrangle, 1961); J. Isaac, *The Teaching of Contempt* (New York: Holt, 1964); J. Katz, *From Prejudice to Destruction* (Cambridge, Mass.: Harvard University Press, 1980); J. W. Parkes, *Conflict of the Church and the Synagogue* (London: Socino, 1934); J. W. Parkes, *Antisemitism* (Chicago: Quadrangle, 1964).

JEWS   From Judah or Judea. In Jewish law *(halakha)*: anyone born of a Jewish mother or converted to Judaism; currently Reform Judaism includes those born of a Jewish father.

Hostility toward Jews has affected the definition of *Jew.* Spaniards in the fifteenth to nineteenth centuries suspected Jewish converts to Christianity *(marranos)* of retaining a Jewish identity. Similarly, Hitler defined anyone with one Jewish grandparent as subject to anti-Jewish decrees. These hostile definitions led to the inclusion of people in the Jewish community who were not halakhic Jews. The State of Israel accepted those persecuted as Jews by the Nazis and permitted them to enter Israel under the "Law of Return."

Since the early nineteenth century, the abandonment of Jewish religious practices led to a search for a new basis for Jewish identity by both Jews and their enemies. Secular Jews have sought to base Jewish identity on culture (including the Yiddish language), on communal ties (such as to Jewish organizations), or on living in a Jewish nation-state (Zionists). Anti-Semites who in earlier periods objected to Jews because of their religious practices, revised their stance and attacked Jewish culture and the Jewish "race," a biological categorization that Jews (even converts!) could not escape. More recently, Jews have been lumped together as "Zionists" and attacked for this.

Populations   A variety of methodological problems make it extremely difficult to estimate the world Jewish population almost into the twentieth century. Some guess that the population of Judah and Israel in 1,000 B.C.E. was about 1.8 million, then falling to 150,000 in 586 B.C.E. with the Babylonian exile. Shortly before the fall of Jerusalem (70 C.E.), the world Jewish population probably exceeded 8 million, and the population in Palestine was about 2.5 million. Following the defeat of Bar Kochba (135 C.E.), the population of what was then known as Palestine dwindled, and the center shifted to Babylon. In the eleventh century, it shifted to the Iberian Peninsula. Expelled from there at the end of the fifteenth century, the Jewish population moved to Poland. The center of Jewish population remained in the Mediterranean basin, and Sephardim (Jews in Arab lands) dominated demographically until the nineteenth century. At that point, a spurt in growth made Europe the population center. In the twentieth century, there has been a major shift in the center of Jewish population from eastern and central Europe to the United States and Israel.

In 1900, the Jewish population worldwide was estimated at 10.6 million, with 8.7 million in Europe and 1 million in the United States. By 1939, the world Jewish population was 16.7 million, with 9.5 million in Europe and 5 million in the United States. The best evidence still suggests that about 6 million Jews were killed by the Nazis during World War II (the Holocaust). In 1993, the total world Jewish population was estimated at 13 million, distributed as follows: United States, 5.7 million; Israel, 4.3 million; France, 530,000; Russia, 410,000; Canada, 358,000; United Kingdom, 296,000; Ukraine, 245,000; Argentina, 210,000; Brazil, 100,000; South Africa, 98,000; Australia, 91,000.

Assimilation and Intermarriage Historically, the "Ten Tribes" driven out of their land (the "Northern Kingdom," called in some biblical accounts "Israel") by Sargon II (722 B.C.E.) apparently assimilated and were lost to Judaism. On the other hand, during the Babylonian exile, Jews developed mechanisms for maintaining group identity in diaspora (dispersion from Judea), not least the *synagogue* as an alternative/adjunct worship experience to the Temple at Jerusalem. Numbers assimilating and intermarrying in premodern societies are not available. Nonetheless, it appears that except for periods of forced conversion, assimilation into and intermarriage with members of the larger societies in which Jews were embedded in the diaspora was almost nonexistent.

Political emancipation changed that by allowing Jews to leave their community (sometimes in Europe called a "ghetto") without requiring a conscious effort to do so. They could simply become part of the religiously "neutral" society. Of the total American population of 3 million in 1790, 2,000 were Jews, and many intermarried. German Jews immigrated to the United States in the nineteenth century. They adopted Reform Judaism and abandoned religious practices that marked them off from the larger Christian society. East European Jews poured into the United States at the beginning of the twentieth century. They too assimilated in the first generation and began to intermarry in the second generation. The rate of intermarriage increased from 4% in 1940 to 52% in 1990.

In western Europe, Jews assimilated into the larger societies and were intermarrying at a high rate prior to World War II. Political emancipation did not reach Jews in the Polish-Russian "pale of settlement" (which includes the Ukraine) until after World War I. Within a short period, the proportion of Orthodox among the Jews dropped from about 80% to about one-third of the population. But with World War II and the Nazi campaign of extermination, two-thirds of the total Jewish population was destroyed.

In Israel, until the latest wave of Russian immigrants, only about 4% of the population were intermarried with non-Jews. This reflects not only the tendency to join the majority but also the migration to Israel of more than 600,000 Jews from Arab lands.

These Jews were traditional in orientation. The present large-scale immigration from the former Soviet Union, which includes about 30% non-Jews, has changed that pattern.

—*M. Herbert Danzger*

REFERENCES

S. W. Baron, *A Social and Religious History of the Jews* (New York: Columbia University Press, 1952); S. W. Baron (New York: NYU Press, 1995); C. Goldscheider, *The Transformation of the Jews* (Chicago: University of Chicago Press, 1984); C. S. Heller, *On the Edge of Destruction* (New York: Columbia University Press, 1977); S. N. Herman, *Jewish Identity* (Beverly Hills, Calif.: Sage, 1977); J. Katz, *Jewish Emancipation and Self-Emancipation* (Philadelphia: Jewish Publication Society, 1986); M. A. Meyer, *Jewish Identity in the Modern World* (Seattle: University of Washington Press, 1990); U. O. Schmelz, "Valuation of Jewish Population Estimates," in *American Jewish Yearbook,* ed. M. Fein and M. Himmelfarb (New York: American Jewish Committee, 1969); U. O. Schmelz, *Studies in Jewish Demography Survey for 1972-1980* (New York: Ktav, 1983); U. O. Schmelz, *Ethnic Differences Among Israeli Jews* (Jerusalem: Institute of Contemporary Jewry, 1991); D. Singer (ed.), *American Jewish Yearbook* (New York: American Jewish Committee, 1995).

JOHNSON, (GUY) BENTON (1928–)

Professor of Sociology, University of Oregon. After completing a B.A. in sociology at the University of North Carolina, Chapel Hill (where both his parents were prominent faculty members in the Department of Sociology), Johnson went to Harvard University for graduate study under the tutelage of Talcott Parsons, receiving a doctorate in sociology in 1952. Following academic appointments at Guilford College and the University of Texas (Austin), Johnson joined the Department of Sociology at the University of Oregon, where he has been on the faculty for almost 40 years, chairing the Sociology Department and the Department of Religious Studies. Unique among his peers, Benton Johnson has served as president of three major organizations in the social scientific study of religion: the Society for the Scientific Study of Religion (1980-1981), the Association for the Sociology of Religion (1987), and the Religious Research Association (1995-1996). He also has been Editor of the *Journal for the Scientific Study of Religion* (1972-1974).

Johnson's contributions to sociology include an undergraduate text on functionalism and Talcott Parsons (1975), but his scholarship has focused almost exclusively on theoretical issues in the sociology of religion and their application to the study of contemporary American Protestantism.

With a series of articles in the late 1950s and early 1960s on the church-sect typology (1957, 1961, 1963), Johnson endeavored to refine those classic sociological concepts while exploring their utility for understanding the fit between various aspects of ascetic Protestantism and American culture more generally. His applications of church-sect theory to twentieth-century Protestantism spawned a career-long interest in the relationship between religion and politics in the United States, in particular the political preferences of persons whose religious background (or orientation) is some form of ascetic Protestantism (1962, 1964, 1966). Together, these bodies of work established Johnson as both a major contributor to key theoretical debates in the sociology of religion and an important empirical researcher on the relationship between religion and politics in the contemporary United States. Johnson's work in the 1960s explored the Weberian thesis that "individuals who adhere strongly to traditional Protestant theologies are inclined to support political movements that emphasize individualism, lim- ited government, and private enterprise" (1966:200). Thirty years later, this would be considered a conservative political outlook, associated with Republican Party voting. In the 1980s when social scientists were surprised by the emergence of a cadre of politically active conservative Protestants, Johnson was prompted to title an article, "How New Is the New Christian Right?" (with Mark Shibley, 1989).

Given this intellectual backdrop and his own affinity for the liberal Protestant tradition, Johnson turned his attention in the mid-1980s to understanding the causes and consequences of membership decline in mainline Protestant denominations in the United States (1985, 1986) rather than focusing—as many sociologists of religion did—on the growth and political activism of evangelical Protestants. This interest in the apparent declining appeal and influence of liberal Protestant churches culminated in the publication of *Vanishing Boundaries: The Religion of Protestant Baby Boomers* (with Dean R. Hoge and Donald A. Luidens, Westminster 1994), a case study of membership decline among Presbyterians. Johnson and his coauthors show how a nonsectarian mainline church fosters an openness to the wider culture that over a generation diffuses commitment among members. *Vanishing Boundaries* won the annual book award given by the Society of the Scientific Study of Religion in 1994 and was praised as a definitive

study of why so many young people left mainline Protestant churches in the latter half of the twentieth century. Johnson's work on liberal Protestantism has drawn the attention and praise of denominational staff struggling to understand the social sources of their membership decline.

—*Mark A. Shibley*

REFERENCES

B. Johnson, "A Critical Appraisal of the Church-Sect Typology," *American Sociological Review* 22(1957):88-92; B. Johnson, "Do Holiness Sects Socialize in Dominant Values?" *Social Forces* 39(1961):309-316; B. Johnson, "Ascetic Protestantism and Political Preference," *Public Opinion Quarterly* 26(1962):35-46; B. Johnson, "On Church and Sect," *American Sociological Review* 28(1963):539-549; B. Johnson, "Ascetic Protestantism and Political Preference in the Deep South," *American Journal of Sociology* 69(1964):359-366; B. Johnson, "Theology and Party Preference Among Protestant Clergymen," *American Sociological Review* 31(1966):200-208; B. Johnson, *Functionalism in Modern Sociology* (Morristown, N.J.: General Learning Press, 1975); B. Johnson, "Liberal Protestantism," *Annals* 480(1985):39-52; B. Johnson, "Winning Lost Sheep," in *Liberal Protestantism*, ed. R. S. Michaelsen and W. C. Roof (New York: Pilgrim, 1986): 220-234; B. Johnson and M. A. Shibley, "How New Is the New Christian Right?" in *Secularization and Fundamentalism Reconsidered*, ed. J. K. Hadden and A. D. Shupe (New York: Paragon House, 1989): 178-198.

JONES, JIM (The Rev.)/JONESTOWN   *see* Peoples Temple

JOURNAL FOR THE SCIENTIFIC STUDY OF RELIGION
The Society for the Scientific Study of Religion (SSSR) was founded in 1949 by scholars of religion and social science. Its purpose is to stimulate and communicate significant scientific research on religious institutions and experience. In 1961, the SSSR inaugurated publication of the *Journal for the Scientific Study of Religion (JSSR)*, which is published quarterly as the SSSR's official scholarly record.

JSSR is committed to publishing scholarly articles that formulate and test social scientific theories of religion. *JSSR* reflects the interdisciplinary character of the SSSR and its membership, publishing manuscripts from scholars in a variety of academic disciplines—sociology, psychology, political science, economics, anthropology, religious studies, and history. *JSSR* ranks as the leading journal in North America dedicated to pursuing the social scientific study of religion, and has a substantial international constituency among both individual scholars and university libraries.

—David G. Bromley

JOURNAL OF CHURCH AND STATE

Published four times a year by the J. M. Dawson Institute of Church-State Studies of Baylor University. From its inception in 1958 through 1994, the editor was the journal's founder, James E. Wood, Jr.

The journal is intended to stimulate interest in and advance research about the subject of church and state. Each issue contains scholarly essays, book reviews, notes on church-state affairs around the world, important texts issued by religious or governmental bodies, and a list of relevant doctoral dissertations. The journal has been an advocate of religious freedom.

—Joseph B. Tamney

JUDAISM The religion of the Jewish people; technically, the religion ascribed to the people of the kingdom of Judah. These included descendants of the tribes of Judah and Benjamin as well as Levites and priests. The ten remaining tribes constituting the "Kingdom of Israel" were conquered by Sargon II (722 B.C.E.) and were lost to Jewish history (the "ten lost tribes").

Social Scientific Study of Judaism Judaism has been the focus of work of some of the major figures in the social sciences, including Max Weber, Sigmund Freud, W. Robertson Smith, and Émile Durkheim. Some points of interest to these theorists will be followed by a survey of normative Judaism, which is the focus of some of these theorists. This discussion describes briefly the development of Judaism from a sociohistorical perspective and also comments on contemporary Judaism in light of contemporary social science.

Karl Marx viewed Judaism with hatred. For Marx, whose family converted to Protestantism when Karl was 6, Judaism was synonymous with bourgeois capitalism (see Marx's essay, *On the Jewish Question,* 1843).

W. Robertson Smith's work focused on the Bible, the prophets, and family relations and culminated in his study *The Religion of the Semites* (1889). This last work examined temple ritual and sacrifice. Analyzing ancient Judaism in his comparative study of Semitic societies, Smith noted the importance of ritual without rationale (1889:3). Smith argued that sacrifice is a communion between the god and his worshipers in the joint participation in eating the flesh and blood of the animal (1889:345). What is directly expressed in the sacrificial meal is that the god and his worshipers are *commensals* (1889:269). The paschal lamb and the laws surrounding it—the requirement that it be eaten as part of a family group, for example, and that no bone may be broken—suggest that this particular sacrifice represented the community, and eating of it joined one with community (1889:345). The participation of the members of the community in the annual paschal sacrifice renews their holiness. Similarly, piacular rites—rites of sorrow, fear, or mourning—restore the connection of the community to its god. They too are an expression of and an intensification of attachment to the sacred.

Émile Durkheim, scion of a distinguished rabbinical family and trained in Jewish scholarship and talmudic study, appears to address Judaism only peripherally. Yet his early education is visible in more than his style of reasoning. His analysis comparing Jewish rates of suicide with rates for Protestants and Catholics is well known among sociologists. Many are also familiar with his discussion of Hebrew law as an example of repressive law (in *The Division of Labor in Society,* 1902). Durkheim's categorization of legal fines as repressive may appear surprising but is fully consonant with the talmudic law with which Durkheim was thoroughly familiar. The distinction Durkheim drew between repressive and restitutive law is identical to the talmudic distinction between *k'nass* (fines) and *mamon* (monetary obligations).

While Durkheim's notion of "collective conscience," which is connected to his idea of the sacred, has no counterpart in Judaism, the connection of the sacred to community clearly does. His distinction between sacred and profane is thoroughly consonant with Judaism's, and possibly rooted in it as well, as Durkheim clearly acknowledges his debt to Robertson Smith (Parsons 1949:401).

Sigmund Freud's *Moses and Monotheism* (1962 [1939]), written at the end of his influential career, tried to account for the origins and special characteristics of the Jewish people. Writing with a disregard for evidence and biblical texts that he himself characterized as "drawing on it [the Bible] for confirmation whenever it is convenient, and dismissing its evidence without scruple when it contradicts my conclusions" (1962:30), he proposed that Moses had been an Egyptian who taught Egyptian monotheism to Israel. Moses was killed when the Jews rebelled against him. This patricide gave rise to a self-perpetuating unconscious guilt feeling passed down in the national consciousness. He argued that Jesus was the resurrected Moses and the primeval father of the horde as well (1962:112 ff). The point of this was that Jews not only killed the primeval god and his reincarnations but *admitted* it.

Freud freely reconstructs other elements of Judaism as well. Circumcision, he argues, is an Egyptian rite and is proof that Moses was an Egyptian. Levites were Egyptian officers recruited by Moses when he became leader of Israel. Other elements of Judaism, including stories drawn from the *midrash,* are introduced when they support Freud's thesis.

The foregoing simply suggests some of the elements of Judaism that attracted the attention of some leading modern social scientists. Marx, Durkheim, and Freud all had Jewish roots, and the former two descended from rabbinical families. Nonetheless, it is Max Weber who showed the greatest interest in Judaism and described aspects of it in positive, if not complimentary, terms.

Weber's Sociology of Judaism For Weber, the world historical importance of Judaism is not exhausted by the fact that it fathered Christianity and Islam. It is a turning point of the whole cultural development of the West and the Middle East. It compares in historical significance with "Hellenic intellectual culture, Roman law, the Roman Catholic church resting on the concept of office, the medieval estates, and Protestantism" (1952 [1921]:5).

Weber found two aspects of Judaism of particular significance: its rationality and its ethicalism. Weber considered that the absolute monotheism of Judaism set it off from all other religions, including Christianity and even Islam (Weber 1963 [1922]:138 ff). When this monotheism and its requirement for rationality confronted the imperfection of the world, it gave rise to the problem of theodicy in its sharpest and most philosophical form. Although magic played a major role in other religions, it was systematically opposed by the Torah teachers (1952:219). Moreover, Weber held that only Judaism and Islam are strictly monotheistic, and he contrasts the universal monotheism of Judaism with the relative monotheism of Zoroastrianism (1963:20-24). In his Introduction to the edition of *The Protestant Ethic and the Spirit of Capitalism* written just before his death in 1920, Weber noted the primacy of rationality in Occidental thought. In place of magical ritual, the Occident has developed rational systems of thought and organization. Weber describes the God of Israel as the "god of intellectuals" as well as god of plebeians, al-though these masses are led and taught by an educated stratum (1952:223).

Ethical prophecy: Weber saw the ritualism of Judaism promoting ethics, and argued that "a ritualistic religion may exert an ethical effect in an indirect way, by requiring that participants be specially schooled. This happened in ancient Judaism, resulting in systematic popular education. Systematic regulation of ritual led to systematic regulation of ethics of everyday living" (1963:154). Weber contends that Judaism requires rational mastery over the world but not strict inner-worldly asceticism (1963:256). This rationalism is heightened by "the immense impact of the absence in Judaism and in ascetic Protestantism of a confessional, the dispensation of grace by a human being" (1963:189 f).

Pariah people: Weber's use of the term *pariah people* with regard to the Jews is well known. Gerth and Martindale consider it an unfortunate term and suggest that Park's concept of the "marginal man" is a better description (in Weber 1952:xxv). Weber uses the term to describe Jews' "guest people" (i.e., minority) status. The term *pariah* resonates with the religious conflict between Christians and Jews, particularly with the notion of the Jews' outcast status resulting from their ostensibly having killed Christ. Weber does not suggest this in his use of the term; as he uses it, it refers either to their minority or marginal status or to aspects of Judaism that set it off from other religions. Some of the latter factors are viewed positively by Weber.

For example, Weber notes the importance of the Sabbath and circumcision in effecting a separation of Jews from other nations (1963:71, 1952:354) and describes in detail the development of ritualistic segregation (1952:336-343). Here Weber is describing the "pariah" community in terms of religious boundary-maintaining mechanisms. Weber argues that the outcome of this "pariah intellectualism" in Judaism resulted in general public schools for the diffusion of literacy and systematic education in critical thinking, the hallmark of Jews (1963:128). Elsewhere Weber connects pariah status to the tenacity with which Jews and pariah Hindus hold to their religion in the face of "murderous humiliation and persecution." Pariah status gives rise to resentment, which is "important in Jewish ethical salvation religion, although completely lacking in all magical and caste religions" (1963:109-110).

Weber's discussion of the religion of nonprivileged classes refers in detail to Judaism and to its pariah status. He contrasts Indian and Jewish pariah status and notes the emergence of congregational religion in Judaism. He concludes that only a congregational religion, especially one of the rational and ethical type, could conceivably win followers easily, particularly among the urban lower middle classes, and then given certain circumstances, exert a lasting influence on the pattern of life of these classes. This is what actually happened. (1963:99)

Pariah status, in the sense of marginality or minority status, also led to Judaism's emphasis on a day when their inferior position would be reversed and they would became masters. This too differed from Hindu pariah notions. In an extended discussion of resentment and retribution, Weber finds some points of agreement with Nietzsche's analysis of *resentiment* but, in contrast to Nietzsche, finds this sentiment is consonant with critical ethical and rational elements of Judaism (1963:110-116)

Werner Sombart (1914) challenged Weber's well-known thesis on the importance of Protestantism for the emergence of capitalism. Sombart argued that the Jews were the principal cause of the disruption of feudalism and its replacement by capitalism. Although it is accepted that Jews had an important role in the early development of capitalism, Sombart's theories provided the Nazis with anti-Semitic material. Weber's discussion of Judaism, Christianity, and the socio-economic order (1963, chap. 15) is a response to Sombart's thesis.

The Faith of Judaism What follows are definitions and descriptions of some of the significant beliefs, rituals, and sacred components of normative Judaism.

The *Torah* is the body of Divine Jewish teaching; narrowly, the term indicates the Five Books of Moses. The term is also used with reference to all the books of the Bible and the oral traditions. Jewish tradition ascribes the origin of the Torah to Moses (Deut. 33:4). The Torah was accepted by the Children of Israel in a covenental ceremony *(b'rit)* at Sinai (Exod. 24:7). Nonetheless, the message of the Torah is for all mankind.

Israel was "chosen" because it accepted the Torah. The Covenant is eternal and nonabrogable. With the rise of Christianity and Islam, which claim to replace both the "Old" Testament and the Jewish people, the nonabrogability of both the Covenant and the chosenness of Israel became crucial.

Moses was teacher, prophet, lawgiver, and leader; known as *Moshe Rabbeinu* (Moses Our Teacher [literally, "master"] in Rabbinic literature, and as "father [greatest] of the prophets." Under him, Israel was shaped into a nation. He led them out of Egypt and for 40 years in the desert. It was he who received the Torah

at Sinai and transmitted it to Israel. Yet he is portrayed as human and mortal and is punished by God for his errors. In contrast to founders of other religions, he was not to be deified or glorified. Moses's authority, although challenged during his lifetime, remained unchallenged after his death. He is the "trusted servant" who spoke to God "mouth to mouth, manifestly and not in riddles" (Num. 12:8).

God is the creator and sustainer of the universe and all the creatures in it (see Gen. 1-3, Psalms, et passim in the OT). The *Sh'ma* declares God's unity; the Ten Commandments, His sole and sovereign rule as creator, sustainer, and savior. He requires moral behavior of His creatures, and particularly of man. He is long suffering, merciful, loving, and just (Exod. 34:6, 7). He is omnipotent, omniscient (Job 28:23, 42:2), and eternal. He is the Father of all mankind yet has a unique covenantal relationship with the Jewish people.

God not only blew life's breath into man but created man in His image. This was understood by the rabbis to refer to man's *soul* (Hebrew, *neshama* or *nefesh*). "The human soul is God's light" (Prov. 20:27). The nature of the soul is nowhere authoritatively defined. The soul exists after death. But where? In *sheol*? In heaven or in *Gehinom* (literally, "valley of Hinom"; in the Talmud, the place of punishment of evildoers)? Do animals too have souls (Ecl. 3:21)? Answers to all these questions are uncertain. Similarly, the afterlife has remained undefined and a source of speculation in Judaism. Emphasis has focused instead on ethical action. Weber also has commented on a number of other concepts including election of Israel, good and evil, free will, Providence, salvation, messiah, redemption, repentance, resurrection, revelation, and reward and punishment.

No single statement of belief or set of practices is universally accepted as containing Judaism's essence. Several traditional formulations are provided below. There is overlap in these various statements.

Sh'ma is the statement, "Hear, O Israel, The Lord [Y-H-W-H] is our God, The Lord [Y-H-W-H] is one" (Deut. 6:5), a central affirmation of God's unity. It has distinguished Judaism from polytheism and from the duality of Zoroastrianism and the trinitarianism of Christianity. This statement and the following verses that command one to "Love God . . . with all your heart and with all your soul" (Deut. 6:6-9) have been understood as the essential credo of Judaism. Rabbinical Judaism has required that the Sh'ma be repeated each evening and morning. The Sh'ma written on parchment is also contained in the *tefillin,* small black leather boxes that traditional Jews place on their arms and their heads during weekday morning prayer. The Sh'ma parchment is also placed on doorposts (called *mezuzot;* singular, *mezuzah*).

The *Decalogue* or Ten Commandments was a covenant between God and Israel (Deut. 4:13) written on stone tablets, by the "finger of God." They were placed in the Ark of the Covenant in the Holy of Holies. The first four commands deal with duties to God; the fifth requires respect for parents. The last five deal with relations to fellow human beings.

The prophet Micah defined the essence of Judaism as "to do justice, to love mercy, and to walk humbly with God" (6:5). The Talmud reports that for Hillel the Elder, its core was the following: "What is hateful to you do not do to your neighbor. The rest is commentary, Go and learn it" (Shab. 31a). The Talmud (Sanhedrin 74a) also sets three rejections as central: A Jew should be martyred rather than (1) commit murder, (2) worship idols, or (3) engage in forbidden sexual relations.

Despite the variations in views of the central beliefs, in the twelfth century Maimonides formulated "13 Principles of Belief" accepted by traditional Jews as authoritative. They include references to the oneness of a personal God, His incorporeality, the immutability of the Torah, ultimate justice, resurrection, and the messiah.

Jewish Religious Practice The *unity* of Judaism and the *community* of Jews emerges primarily from practices rather than from beliefs. Judaism places its major emphasis on behaviors rather than beliefs. While one is a "believing Christian," one is an "observant" or "practicing Jew." Rituals or practices are viewed as holy commandments, or *mitzvot.* They include not only worship behaviors but also those that sanctify ordinary behaviors such as eating (rules of "kosher") or sexual relations (rules regarding incest, modesty, and purity) that transform and sanctify the action.

Halakha is the authoritative laws and rules of Judaism, laws derived from the scriptures as well as from rabbinic traditions and the customs of the Jewish people. It encompasses the life of the individual from awakening in the morning until and including how and where one sleeps—and with whom and when. It provides a detailed set of instructions for all roles of life. Although life everywhere is lived by roles, halakha is unique in that the roles are explicit, articulated, and taught as part of the obligatory behavior of the member of the community. Ethical rules are the core of halakha.

Justice plays a central role and has a uniquely universal quality: "Justice, justice shall ye pursue" (Deut. 16:20). Charity derives from the same Hebrew root word as justice *(zdk).* The principle of equality of all before the law (Lev. 24:22) permeates all of Jewish law. Also emphasized is care of the poor and the less fortunate; charity is regarded as justice. The poor were given a tithe of the crops and in addition were permitted to gather forgotten sheaves of grain *(shikchah)* and to pick up after the harvesters *(leket).* The Talmud created a special fund for the poor *(kupa)* and provided soup kitchens *(tamchoi).* Interest-free loans also are provided for the needy.

Widows and orphans are provided with additional protections. Slavery was permitted but was carefully limited. Girls sold into slavery by their fathers were to be married to their masters or the masters' sons. If not, they were to be set free. They could not be resold. Runaway slaves were not to be returned to their masters. In the year of the jubilee, liberty was to be proclaimed throughout the land, and all slaves were to be freed. Judaism concretized its ethics in laws of contracts, torts, domestic law, marriage and divorce, charity, business and inheritance laws, laws of privacy, of prevention of cruelty to animals, of ecology, and in building regulations. These constitute a major part of the Talmud and the religious codes.

The Religious Calendar: Biblically Mandated Holy Days The seventh day of the week is *shabbat* (sabbath, literally, "rest") to recall that "God created the world in six days and rested on the seventh" (Exod. 20:11) and "so that your slaves may rest as you do, remembering that you were slaves in Egypt" (Deut. 5:14-15). No work may be done or fire lit. Orthodox Jews do not cook, write, travel, or answer the phone on the Sabbath.

Passover is a one-week spring festival celebrating the exodus from slavery in Egypt. *Matzo,* unleavened flat bread, is eaten in remembrance that the Israelites left Egypt hurriedly (Exod. 12:39). In ancient times, families ate a paschal lamb on the first night of Passover. That is recalled in a feast called a *seder* (denoting the order of the ceremonies at the meal) on the Eve of Passover. The seder remains one of the most widely celebrated ceremonies in contemporary Judaism.

For the *Feast of Weeks (Shavuot),* seven weeks are counted from the second evening of Passover; the fiftieth day (Pentecost) is *Shavuot* (literally, weeks). In ancient times, the first "new fruits" were brought to the Temple beginning on the fiftieth day to the end of the harvest season. In Jewish tradition, this is also the day on which God gave the Torah to Israel at Mount Sinai.

New Year, or *Rosh Ha-Shanah* (literally, beginning of the year), is celebrated with the sounding of the *shofar,* a hollowed ram's horn. It marks the beginning of a ten-day period known as "Days of Awe" and "Ten Days of Repentance" ending on *Yom Kippur*. In Jewish tradition, this is a period of judgment for each person and for the entire world.

Yom Kippur (literally, "Day of Atonement") is the holiest day of the year, a day of fasting and prayers of repentance. In ancient times, it was also a day of purification of the Temple. A solemn day, it is nonetheless marked by joy in the certainty of forgiveness.

The *Feast of Booths* (*Succot,* also Feast of Harvest) is a one-week festival during which one "dwells in the booths," a hut roofed with boughs or twigs, taking one's meals there. A joyous holiday, it is celebrated with the singing of psalms of thanks (*Halleluyah*), prayers for the next year's bounty (*Hoshanna*), the taking of the palm branch, citron (*lulav*), myrtle, and willow (*etrog*). It was celebrated during the Second Temple period with particular joy in the Temple courtyard. The annual cycle of reading the Pentateuch is completed on the last day of this holiday known as *Simchat Torah* (the Rejoicing with the Torah). In the 1960s, *Simchat Torah* became a major occasion among Soviet youth seeking to affirm their Jewish identity. On this day, they would gather outside synagogues in the major cities.

The Religious Calendar: Rabbinically Instituted Holy Days *Purim* (literally, "lots") is a reference to the lots cast to determine the date for the annihilation of every Jewish person in the Persian Empire. The threat was overcome through the efforts of Esther and Mordechai. The day is celebrated by reading the *Scroll* (Hebrew, *megillah*) *of Esther* in the synagogue, by the giving of alms to the poor and gifts to friends, and by a festive meal. It is a day for costumes and alcoholic drinks.

Hanukkah (literally, "dedication") is an eight-day festival that celebrates the restoration of the Temple service following the victory of Judah Macabee and his army over the Selucid Greeks in 166 B.C.E. Each day of the holiday, an additional candle is lit in a *menorah,* a candelabrum, until on the eighth day all eight candles are lit. They are placed in the window to publicize the miracle of the victory of the few against many and that the only undefiled cruse of oil that could be found burned for eight days rather than one. Although this is a minor holiday in the Jewish religious calendar, because it is celebrated around Christmas time (the date varies as Jewish holidays follow a lunar-solar calendar), American Jews have given it added significance as a counterweight to Christmas. It has become one of the most widely celebrated Jewish holidays among American Jews.

Life Cycle Celebrations

Circumcision: For *B'rit Milah* (literally, "the covenant of circumcision"), newborn males are circumcised at 8 days old and are thus "brought into the Covenant of Abraham" (Gen. 17:10-14). This b'rit binds the newborn to his people. The b'rit is widely practiced even among Reform Jews, although they questioned it for a period. The ceremony is accompanied by a celebratory meal.

Bar/bat mitzvah: (The literal translation of the term is "son/daughter of commandment.") This ceremony occurs at the age at which persons are considered religiously and legally responsible for their actions and required to perform the commandments (age 13 for a boy and age 12 for a girl). A boy is called to the Torah, which signifies his entry into the religious community. At this age, boys become obligated to wear *tefillin* during the morning weekday prayer service. The bat mitzvah ceremony for girls is a modern innovation, currently accepted even among many Orthodox. In non-Orthodox circles, girls may be called to the Torah. In contemporary America, this religious ceremony is often followed by and sometimes replaced by a party celebrating the occasion.

Wedding and marriage: Marriage is considered a blessed state (Gen. 2:18-24). It is assumed to be monogamous, although polygyny was accepted. Love is a major theme in marriage (e.g., Jacob and Rachel). Marriage provides companionship, joy, blessing, goodness, and peace (Proverbs; Yev. 62b). Marriages can be ended by divorce (Gen. 21:10-15, Deut. 24:1-4). The rabbis see celibacy as unnatural (Kid. 29b). Polygyny was discouraged by the rabbis and finally prohibited among European Jews in medieval times. Although early marriage was strongly encouraged by the rabbis, in modern times Jews have tended to marry later than others. Marital stability also has suffered. These factors appear to reflect the level of education and urbanization of Jewish populations.

Wedding ceremonies are not described in the Bible, although they are implied (Gen. 22:9). Detailed descriptions of the marriage ceremony, and the joyous dancing and feasts in which the rabbis took part, are found in the Talmud. A number of customs, including the groom giving the bride a ring and declaring that "he takes her as his wife according to the laws of Moses and Israel," are still widely practiced.

Death, burial, mourning: The dead are to be buried as soon as possible (Deut. 21:23). Biblical and rabbinic tradition have followed the practice of burial in the ground or in a cave. Reform Jews have permitted cremation and delay of the funeral. *Shiva* is a seven-day mourning period. As described in the Talmud, during this period the mourners sit on the floor (i.e., low chairs in the West). They wear clothes that they rend at the funeral as a sign of grief. Friends come to comfort them during this period. Mourning continues in mitigated form up to 30 days and for parents for a year. Reform Jews have an abbreviated mourning period.

Ritual Constants

Study: Study of the Torah is a central value in Judaism. In mishnaic times (100 B.C.E. to 200 C.E.), public elementary schools for the education of children were developed. Jews are "the people of the Book" not simply because they possess "the Book" (i.e., the [Hebrew] Bible) but because of their concern to study it. The rabbis developed academies for study by the elite (Hebrew, *yeshivot;* Aramaic, *metivtot*) and study halls (Hebrew, *bet midrash*) and were enjoined to "nurture many disciples" (Avot. 1:1). At the same time, the public lectures were widespread in the synagogues on sabbath, and their essence came to be transcribed as the *midrash.* Study of sacred texts, both the Scriptures and the Oral Law, continued to mark traditional Judaism. The religio-legal discussion of the academies came to be embodied in the *Talmud.* The authority of the *rabbi* derives from his knowledge of the law rather than from priestly or charismatic powers.

The requirements for a religious education led to the establishment of schools for the masses for study of the Torah. Day schools providing intensive religious (as well as secular) studies emerged in the early twentieth century. Currently, the overwhelming majority of Orthodox Jews and a noticeable portion of Conservative Jews attend these schools. Some men devote themselves entirely to study for some years after marriage. Study has carried over to other areas as well, and in contemporary times Jews tend to seek formal education to a greater degree than other ethnic or religious groups (Kosmin and Lachman 1993).

Kosher: (The literal translation of the term is "prepared," that is, prepared in accordance with Jewish religious law.) Biblical law forbids the consumption of animals except ruminants that have cloven hooves, and permits consumption of only some fowl, while generally forbidding consumption of raptors and carrion scavengers. Animals may be eaten only when properly slaughtered. Blood must be removed and is strictly forbidden. Meat and milk products may not be cooked together, and even dairy and meat dishes and pots must be separated. One does not eat dairy foods with or immediately following meat dishes. Orthodox Jews tend to follow these laws and currently have developed organizations to certify prepared foods as following kosher standards. These rules, intended to hallow the act of eating, also serve as boundary markers, setting off observant Jews from others. Conservative Jews often have followed the practice of eating kosher at home while being less strict outside the home. Reform Jews have generally abandoned the practice of eating kosher.

Family purity: There is a requirement that the wife separate herself from her husband during her period of menses and for a week following, a "week of purity." On the evening following that week, she bathes and then immerses herself in a *mikvah,* a ritual bath. She is then ritually pure, and husband and wife may have marital relations. This practice is followed by Orthodox women and marks off Orthodoxy from Conservative and Reform Judaism.

Sex roles: Men are obligated to perform the commandments. Women are primarily required to refrain from doing that which is forbidden but are not obligated to perform rituals that are "time related." Thus men are required to pray thrice daily and to wear the *talit* (prayer shawl) and *tefillin.* Women are not (Kid. 29a). Nonetheless, there are complexities in these rules, and women are required to do some things that are time related (e.g., eat matzo at the seder) and not obligated to do others (e.g., religious study). Women's roles have become a major point of contention between the Orthodox on one side and Conservative and Reform Jews on the other. Reform and Conservative Jews now ordain both women rabbis and cantors. Although the Orthodox do not, Orthodox women are now far more educated in religion than in the past. There are also a scattering of women's prayer groups, where women not only pray separately from men but lead the service and read the Torah. These services have encountered strong opposition.

Holy Places

The Temple: Although "the heavens are God's throne and the earth His footstool" (Isaiah 66:1), the Temple at Jerusalem symbolized God's presence. Prayers and sacrifices were offered there. There were two temples. The first, built by King Solomon (973-933 B.C.E.), was destroyed by Nebuchadnezzar in 586 B.C.E. The second, begun 70 years later by Ezra, was destroyed by the Romans in 70 C.E. Ruins of the wall surrounding the Temple courtyard remain in Jerusalem. This is known as the *Kotel HaMa'aravi* (Western Wall) to Jews and the *Wailing Wall* to others, a term Jews consider pejorative. The Muslim *Dome of the Rock* has been built upon the ruins of the Temple, creating a site of religious confrontation in modern times.

Synagogues: (This term is from the Greek "gathering together.") The Talmud ascribes the origin of the synagogue to the period of the Babylonian exile (Meg. 29a). Traditionally, synagogues were built with a separate women's gallery based on the existence of a women's court and women's gallery in the Temple. Orthodox Judaism generally maintains that separation. Conservative and Reform Judaism have abandoned it.

The Land of Israel: Israel is a real territory with clear boundaries (although variously defined). Its significance lies in its being "the promised land." God promised this land to the descendants of Abraham, Isaac, and Jacob (Gen. 12). The land is part of a covenantal agreement between God and the Children of Israel. It is of central importance throughout the Bible and remains so in Jewish theology and theodicy.

Jerusalem: In Jewish tradition, the Temple site is identified with Mount Moriah (Chron. 3:1). Here, Abraham, tested by God, almost offered Isaac as a sacrifice (Gen. 22). David brought to Jerusalem the Holy Ark, making it at once the political and religious capital of the kingdom. So central is Jerusalem to Judaism that it is mentioned 349 times in the Bible, and Zion (another name for Jerusalem, see 2 Sam 5:7-9) is mentioned 108 times.

Jerusalem was sacked in 586 B.C.E., rebuilt, again overrun in 70 C.E., and then razed following the Bar Kochba revolt against the Romans in 135 C.E. However, a Jewish population has continued to live in this city for much of the time since.

With the emergence of the State of Israel in 1948, Jerusalem came under siege by Arab armies and was divided. Jews were forbidden to enter the Arab-held areas or visit their sacred sites until 1967 following the Six Day War. Currently, Jerusalem is the capital of the State of Israel.

Modern Judaism The *Emancipation*—that is, the acceptance of Jews as "citizens of the Mosaic faith" rather than as a separate "nation within a nation" in nineteenth-century western Europe and in America— led to efforts to adjust Judaism to the larger society in which it was embedded. The question of what could be considered "essential" when Judaism was stripped of its practices and adherence to the Torah was subject to various interpretations.

For Reform Judaism, the "ethical core"—the moral ideas, principles of justice, and universalism—are held to be the essence of Judaism. Mosaic and rabbinical laws and customs are rejected (see the Pittsburgh Platform of 1885).

For the Historical School, the center of authority in Judaism is the collective conscience of Israel. This perspective sees flexibility and change in historical and social factors affecting Judaism while maintaining adherence to tradition. This idea is central to Conservative Judaism.

For Orthodox Judaism, the essence is the halakha as embodied in religio-legal codes. Recent research in the social sciences has focused particularly on "returnees" to Orthodoxy from Reform or secular Jewish backgrounds (examples of this trend include studies by Danzger 1989, and Kaufman 1991).

The State of Israel: Modern Israel holds an important place in the religious life of contemporary Jews. Efforts on its behalf are central in synagogue life. It is viewed not only as a covenantal promise and religious homeland but also as a haven for persecuted Jews. Jews attempting to flee from the Nazis were barred entry to Western countries. Trapped, they were caught and exterminated. When Israel became an independent nation in 1948, it passed the "Law of Return," which declared that any Jew had the right to become a citizen of Israel. Within weeks after the declaration of statehood in 1948, 250,000 European "displaced persons" poured into Israel. This was followed by a major exodus to Israel of Jews from Arab lands. When Jews in various countries were threatened, Israel mounted major evacuation efforts to rescue them.

Judaism is the official religion of Israel. Israel's government offices close for Jewish holidays. Jewish symbols are incorporated into government buildings and ceremonies. Nevertheless, five religious communities are recognized and receive government support: Jewish, Moslem, Christian, Druze, and Baha'i. Freedom of religion is guaranteed by law. Jews are the largest group, constituting 81% of the population. Of this group, about 15% to 20% are Orthodox and another 50% have traditional leanings.

According to Israel's Central Bureau of Statistics, the country's population as of September 1995 was 5,570,000: 4,510,000 Jews (81%), 805,000 Moslems (14.4%), 160,000 Christians (2.9%), and 95,000 Druze (1.7%). In raw numbers, however, the United States remains the country with the largest Jewish population in the world.

—*M. Herbert Danzger*

REFERENCES

M. H. Danzger, *Returning to Tradition* (New Haven, Conn: Yale University Press, 1989); H. H. Donin, *To Be a Jew* (New York: Basic Books, 1972); É. Durkheim, *Suicide* (New York, Free Press, 1953 [1897]); É. Durkheim, *The Division of Labor in Society* (New York: Free Press, 1947 [1902]); É. Durkheim,

The Elementary Forms of the Religious Life (New York: Collier, 1961 [1912]); I. Epstein, *Judaism* (Baltimore: Penguin, 1959); S. Freud, *Moses and Monotheism* (New York: Vintage, 1962 [1939]); D. Kaufman, *Rachel's Daughters* (New Brunswick, N.J.: Rutgers University Press, 1991); B. A. Kosmin and S. Lachman, *One Nation Under God* (New York: Harmony, 1993); K. Marx, "On the Jewish Question," in K. Marx and F. Engels, *Collected Works,* vol. 3 (New York: International Publishers, 1975 [1843]); G. F. Moore, *Judaism in the First Centuries of the Christian Era* (New York: Schocken, 1927); T. Parsons, *The Structure of Social Action* (Glencoe, Ill.: Free Press, 1949); A. I. Shiff, *The Jewish Day School in America* (New York: Jewish Education Committee, 1966); W. R. Smith, *The Religion of the Semites* (New York: Meridian, 1959 [1889]); W. Sombart, *The Jews and Capitalism* (Glencoe, Ill.: Free Press, 1951 [1914]); M. Steinberg, *Basic Judaism* (New York: Harcourt, 1947); M. Weber, *Ancient Judaism* (New York: Free Press, 1952 [1921]); M. Weber, *The Protestant Ethic and the Spirit of Capitalism* (New York: Scribner, 1930 [1904-1905, 1920]); M. Weber, *The Sociology of Religion* (Boston: Beacon, 1963 [1922]).

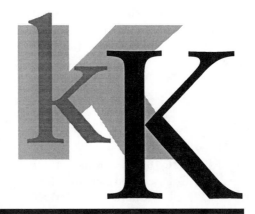

KALLEN, HORACE M(EYER) (1882-1974)

Philosopher-educator. One of the original core faculty of the New School for Social Research in New York City, where he was Professor of Social Philosophy.

Prominent in Zionism and various liberal movements, Kallen was the author of some 30 books, among them *Art and Freedom* (Greenwood 1969 [1942]) and *The Education of Free Men* (Farrar Strauss 1949). He was an early member of the Council of the Society for the Scientific Study of Religion and its President in 1955-1956. He was instrumental in obtaining the grant from the J. A. Kaplan Foundation that enabled the establishment of the *Journal for the Scientific Study of Religion.*

—*Charles Y. Glock*

KANE, JOHN J. (1909-1972)

Sociologist, with principal interest in the family. Educated in Philadelphia at St. Joseph's College (B.A.), Temple University (M.A.), and the University of Pennsylvania (Ph.D.), Kane's academic career took him from St. Joseph's College, Philadelphia, to the University of Notre Dame (1948-1970). He returned to St. Joseph's College as head of the Department of Sociology (1970-1972) while on a two-year leave of absence from Notre Dame. President, American Catholic Sociological Society, 1952.

Kane's ACSS presidential address examined the status of Catholic sociologists as academic professionals and as confessing Catholics, finding it low in both milieux. In Kane's view, most professional sociologists doubted that anyone with a religious affiliation could do genuine sociology while Catholics were disappointed in not hearing Catholic sociologists authoritatively denounce "statements of those non-Catholic sociologists which run counter to Catholic theology and philosophy." He ended his presidential address with the wish that the ACSS would step out of its professional ghetto, becoming instead a bridge that "should extend to non-Catholic colleagues on one side, our Catholic people on the other" (*American Catholic Sociological Review,* Vol. 14, 1953).

—*Loretta M. Morris*

KASLOW, GEORGE W., JR. (1930–)

Methodist clergyman; B.A., Hamline, 1952; M.Div., Drew University, 1956. President, Religious Research Association, 1967-1970.

Kaslow was Research Assistant for the National Council of Churches, 1956-1957; Assistant Director of the Bureau of Research and Planning, Church Federation of Greater Chicago, 1957-1958; organizer for and Director of the Department of Research and Field Survey of the New Jersey Council of Churches, 1958-

1961; Executive Director of the New York Metropolitan Planning Commission of the Methodist Church, 1961-1966; Research Associate at the Board of Missions of the United Methodist Church, 1966-1970; and a local church pastor from 1971 until retirement in 1995. He was Treasurer of the Religious Research Association, 1964-1967.

—*Everett L. Perry*

KELLEY, DEAN M. (1926-1997) From 1990 until his death, served as Counselor on Religious Liberty to the National Council of Churches. Kelley received an A.B. degree from the University of Denver in 1946 and a Th.M. from the Iliff School of Theology in 1949. He pursued graduate work in sociology at Columbia University beginning in 1949. Kelley was ordained as a Methodist minister and served local churches in Colorado and New York.

Throughout his career, Kelley has combined interests in religious liberty and social science, creating a unique blend of academic work and public advocacy. His work in defense of religious liberty began while he was pastor of the Crawford Memorial United Methodist Church in the Bronx, when he organized a three-year study of church and state relations for the denomination. This project led to his being named in 1960 the Executive for Religious Liberty on the staff of the National Council of Churches, a position he held until 1990. In this role, Kelley organized a number of significant projects for the National Council of Churches related to church-state and religious liberty issues: a national study conference on church and state in 1964, a consultation on churches and tax law in 1975, and two conferences on government intervention in religious affairs in 1981 and 1984. His edited book *Government Intervention in Religious Affairs* (Pilgrim 1982) was a product of the first of these conferences. He also organized a Bicentennial Conference on the Religion Clauses at the University of Pennsylvania Law School in 1991. Kelley was instrumental in shaping church-state safeguards in the Elementary and Secondary Education Act of 1965, organizing successful opposition to seven successive efforts to amend the First Amendment to permit prayer in public schools, and working with the National Council of Churches and the U.S. Catholic Conference to gain inclusion in the 1969 Tax Reform Act of provisions ending exemption of churches from tax on unrelated business income.

The more academic aspect of Kelly's career has involved numerous books and articles on church-state

issues and defense of religious diversity and liberty. Perhaps his best known and most widely cited book, *Why Conservative Churches Are Growing: A Study in the Sociology of Religion* (Harper 1972)—which formulated the controversial thesis that "strict churches" were growing because they offered the more meaningful religious experience for which Americans were searching (the "strictness thesis")—has been actively debated in the social science literature for several decades. His book *Why Churches Should Not Pay Taxes* (Harper 1977) offered a defense of economic separation of church and state. With Charles Whelan, S.J., Kelley also directed a three-year Project on Church, State, and Taxation supported by the Eli Lilly Endowment. In 1979, he edited the November issue of the *Annals of the American Academy of Political and Social Science* on the theme, "The Uneasy Boundary: Church and State." At the time of his death, Kelley was working toward completing a five-volume treatise, *The Law of Church and State in America* (Greenwood).

Since the 1970s, Kelley has been an articulate spokesman for protecting the religious liberty of new and unpopular religious groups. Most recently, he has written articles critical of the federal government's role in the confrontation that resulted in the deaths of the Branch Davidian movement near Waco, Texas.

—*David G. Bromley*

KELLY, JAMES R. (1937–) Professor and Chair of Sociology, Fordham University, Bronx, New York, where he has taught since 1970, after completing his Ph.D. in sociology at Harvard. President, Association for the Sociology of Religion, 1998.

Principally an essayist, Kelly's early articles centered on the social and cultural significance of ecumenism and related changes in religion, particularly as a result of the Second Vatican Council in the Roman Catholic Church. His most recent publications in both scholarly journals and such more general periodicals as *America,* *Commonweal,* and *Christian Century* continue a decision to work to link the academy with its appropriate larger publics (e.g., "Why Republican and New Democrat Welfare Changes Both Need Legal Abortion," *America,* 1996). In 1995, he was awarded the Catholic Press Association First Place award for best book review. In addition to writing on these topics, Kelly has been a member of the NYC Ecumenical Commission since 1974 and, soon after its inception, a member of the Board of Advisors of the Common Ground Network for Life and Choice. He has also reviewed major Lilly Endowment grants (and was author of a study of the

Renew Program and *The First Decade of Catholic Grants*) and has recently completed (with Gene Hamrick) a four-phase national study for the U.S. Conference of Catholic Bishops of the restored order of the diaconate.

—*William H. Swatos, Jr.*

KHOMEINI, AYATOLLAH RUHOLLAH (1900-1989)

Revolutionary leader of Iran from 1979 until his death in 1989. From exile in France, Khomeini became a symbol of Shīʿite opposition to the secular shah (ruler, king) during the 1970s. Khomeini was regarded by some as the deputy of the mythical "Twelfth Imām," believed by some Shīʿite Moslems to represent the eventual establishment of a purified Islamic state. Khomeini came to power in 1979, following the departure of the shah. Khomeini established a militant Shīʿite theocracy in Iran and was in power during the "hostage crisis" of 1979-1980 in which more than 50 U.S. diplomats were taken hostage by Islamic university students.

—*Ted G. Jelen*

REFERENCES

M. S. Kimmel and R. Tavakol, "Against Satan," in *Charisma, History, and Social Structure*, ed. R. M. Glassman and W. H. Swatos, Jr. (New York: Greenwood, 1986): 101-112; R. Wright, *In the Name of God* (New York: Simon & Schuster, 1989).

KINCHELOE, SAMUEL C. (1890-1981)

Ph.D., University of Chicago. Ordained clergyman, United Church of Christ. Beginning in 1928, he taught sociology of religion at Chicago Theological Seminary and in addition was recognized (1942) as a member of the Federated Theological Faculty of the University of Chicago.

Through the many student projects that he directed under church auspices, Kincheloe used metropolitan Chicago as a laboratory for teaching as well as for helping churches adjust to the changing city. In such works as *The American City and Its Church* (Friendship 1938) and "The Behavior Sequence of a Dying Church" (*Religious Education*, Vol. 24, No. 4, 1929), he used concepts of the "Chicago School" of sociology such as competition, adaptation, and succession within the concentric circle-and-sector framework of urban devel-

opment; ecology, anthropology, and social interaction were used in developing long-term case studies.

—*Everett L. Perry*

KING, MARTIN LUTHER, JR. (1929-1969)

African American clergyman and one of the most important leaders of the civil rights movement, born in Atlanta, the son of the pastor of Ebenezer Baptist Church. After graduating from Morehouse College (1948), he was ordained to the Baptist ministry; he subsequently studied at Crozer Theological Seminary (B.D., 1951) and Boston University (Ph.D., 1955). While at BU, he became acquainted with the work of Mohandas Gandhi, whose ideas about nonviolent protest King would embrace and apply to the struggle for racial justice in the United States.

His involvement in the civil rights movement commenced after King accepted the pastorate of the Dexter Avenue Baptist Church in Montgomery, Alabama. As part of an effort throughout the South to end segregation in public accommodations, the bus company was targeted in Montgomery, beginning with the legendary refusal of Rosa Parks to take a seat in the back of the bus in 1955. King spearheaded the ad hoc committee that was formed to boycott the bus company. The result of this boycott was the end of segregated public transportation in the city, and the process of this victory catapulted King into national prominence.

He became involved in discussions between influential northern blacks such as A. Philip Randolph, Bayard Rustin, and Ella Baker as well as southern clergy that resulted in the creation, in 1957, of the Southern Christian Leadership Conference (SCLC). King soon became the leader of this organization, which Aldon Morris (1984:77) has described as "the decentralized political arm of the black church." The SCLC became the main vehicle for promoting King's strategy of nonviolent protest. As such, it was more militant than such organizations as the NAACP, which preferred to work through the courts and the legislative system. On the other hand, its commitment to nonviolence was challenged over time by more militant groups associated with the Black Power phase of the civil rights movement.

King led a massive protest in Birmingham, Alabama, where, jailed, he penned his famous "Letter from a Birmingham Jail." This campaign was followed by campaigns focusing on housing, education, and voter registration. He also turned his attention away from a singular focus on the South and initiated campaigns in several northern cities. One of the high points of his career occurred during the 1963 March on Washington, which he led, when he delivered his "I Have a Dream" speech at the Lincoln Memorial.

During King's career as a civil rights activist, he fought for a number of causes that some movement activists viewed as being outside the purview of black civil rights. Most notably, he became increasingly involved in the movement to end the war in Vietnam. His stature was enhanced when he was awarded the Nobel peace prize in 1964, but at the same time, his life was often in jeopardy. His home was bombed, and he received numerous death threats. In addition, he had to endure a protracted effort on the part of FBI head J. Edgar Hoover to destroy his career. While standing on his hotel balcony in Memphis, Tennessee (where he had gone to add his support to striking municipal workers), on April 4, 1968, he was shot and killed. In the years after his death, a symbolic crusade led by his widow, Coretta Scott King, urged the passage of legislation to make his birthday a federal holiday. This became a reality in 1986.

—Aaron Kivisto and Peter Kivisto

REFERENCES

T. Branch, *Parting the Waters* (New York: Simon & Schuster, 1988); D. J. Garrow, *The FBI and Martin Luther King, Jr.* (New York: Penguin, 1981); D. J. Garrow, *Bearing the Cross* (New York: Morrow, 1986); D. L. Lewis, *King* (Urbana: University of Illinois Press, 1978); A. Morris, *The Origins of the Civil Rights Movement* (New York: Free Press, 1984).

KLAUSNER, SAMUEL Z. (1923–)   Professor of Sociology, University of Pennsylvania. Holding two Columbia University doctorates (psychology and sociology), Klausner joined the University of Pennsylvania faculty in 1967, where he has been an associate of the university's Program in Energy Management and Policy, the Middle East Center, and the Jewish Studies Program as well as a member of the graduate group in Religious Studies. Joining the Society for the Scientific Study of Religion in 1957, he served as Executive Secretary (1964-1970), editor of its journal (1966), and Vice President (1971-1973). He has also been chair of the social science section of the American Academy of Religion (1969-1971) and President of the Association for the Social Scientific Study of Jewry (1975-1977).

Klausner's publications have ranged over social theory, social psychology, environmental sociology, and the sociology of religion. In this last area, he has published *Psychiatry and Religion* (Free Press 1964) and, with

Edward Foulkes, *Eskimo Capitalist* (Allanheld 1982). He is currently working on a book on mass religious conversion with special attention to the conversion of American Jews to Christianity.

—Arnold M. Dashefsky

KLOETZLI, WALTER (1921–)   Lutheran church administrator and urban planner who later became a federal housing administrator and, still later, a substance abuse counselor. President, Religious Research Association, 1962-1964. Attended Johns Hopkins University and later graduated successively from Gettysburg College and Gettysburg Lutheran Seminary, the latter in 1950, where he came under the influence of Bertha Paulssen, Professor of Church and Society. He was awarded the Litt.D. from Carthage College in 1961. Fellow in urban studies, University of Chicago, 1965-1967.

After serving in the Army Air Corps in World War II and as a pastor in Paramus, N.J., 1950-1953, he was National Director of Urban Ministries for the National Lutheran Council from 1954 to 1967. Then from 1967 to 1983, he worked for the federal Department of Housing and Urban Development in Chicago, Kansas City, and Washington, D.C. He has since worked as a substance abuse counselor in the Washington area. He also has served on committees for social ministry for the Lutheran Church in America and for the Virginia Association of Alcoholism and Drug Abuse Counselors.

In his *Urban Church Planning* (with coauthor Arthur Hillman, Muhlenberg Press 1958), he produced a widely used training manual for joint self-study by regional groups of urban congregations. He also is the author of *The City Church: Death or Renewal* (Muhlenberg 1961), *Challenge and Response in the City* (Augustana Press 1962), and *Community Organization Today* (HUD 1968).

—Ross P. Scherer

KLUCKHOHN, CLYDE (KAY MAHBEN) (1905-1960)   Harvard anthropologist who argued that religion and myth are central to human existence and suggested that tool making, language, and religion are the three major characteristics that serve to distinguish humans from all other animals.

Kluckhohn's often reprinted essay, "Myths and Rituals: A General Theory" (1942), underscored the importance of context in the study of myth and ritual. Myths and rituals, he contended, will be differently phrased in different societies according to their unique historical experiences. Kluckhohn also stressed the adjustive and integrative functions of religious practices. His classic *Navaho Witchcraft* (Beacon 1944) focused on the implicit function of witchcraft among the Navaho and described the relationship between witchcraft and other aspects of Navaho culture and society. The increase and decrease of witchcraft accusations, he found, relate to Navaho religion and worldview.

—*Stephen D. Glazier*

REFERENCE

C. Kluckhohn, "Myth and Rituals," *Harvard Theological Review* 35(1942):48-79.

KOHLBERG, LAWRENCE   *see* Moral Development

KORESH, DAVID (1959-1993)   Vernon Howell (later "David Koresh") joined the Seventh-day Adventist Church and was inspired by the apocalyptic message of church-sponsored "Revelation Seminars" that featured dramatic images in a multimedia depiction of Armageddon. Howell became fascinated by the premillennial prophetic focus on imminent end times, which in the New Testament Book of Revelation is mystically represented by the "Seven Seals"; Howell came to believe that these could be opened only by a new messiah. In 1981, Howell joined the "Branch Davidians," an offshoot of the schismatic "Davidian Seventh Day Adventists" founded by Victor Houtoff in 1935.

Koresh was "intelligent, mechanically adept, a capable guitarist, and possessor of an immense store of memorized passages of scripture" (Kelley 1995:23). Howell was mentored by Lois Roden, wife of deceased Branch Davidian leader Benjamin Roden, whose son George Roden ousted Howell. In 1987, there was a shootout between Howell's followers and Roden, after which Howell and several Davidians were tried for attempted murder, which resulted in a hung jury for Howell and acquittals for the others. Howell paid the back taxes on the Mt. Carmel estate in Waco, Texas (founded by Houtoff), and took over the Branch Davidian leadership. Mt. Carmel was renamed "Ranch Apocalypse," and Howell became "David Koresh,"

which denoted the messianic House of David and King Cyrus, conqueror of the Babylonians.

In Koresh's dualistic, midtribulationist vision, evil was concentrated in the "Babylonians," who were identified with the U.S. government. An arsenal was established to defend the settlement—an inevitable war with the Babylonians was seen as necessary for the advent of God's Kingdom. The arsenal was expanded in response to the coincidental maneuvers of a local SWAT team in 1992. This expansion brought Koresh and some followers to the attention of the Bureau of Alcohol, Tobacco and Firearms (ATF). Koresh was also being investigated by Texas child protection officials for possible child molestation and statutory rape while "spreading the seed of the Messiah." On February 28, 1993, about 90 ATF agents (some in helicopters) tried to execute a "dynamic entry" into ranch Apocalypse, which produced a shootout (an alleged Davidian "ambush") followed by a 51-day standoff. During this period, two religion scholars, Phillip Arnold and James Tabor, communicated with Koresh and suggested a reinterpretation of the Seven Seals scenario (in the biblical Book of Revelation), which would postpone the final apocalypse. Tabor is certain that Koresh, who appeared to accept the altered scenario, would have given himself up after he completed writing down his new interpretation. FBI agents, who became involved in the case after the failed ATF mission, deny he ever would have come out, and thus justify their apparent assault on April 19 with armored vehicles, rams, and tear gas. Mt. Carmel went up in flames, and most persons therein perished, including Koresh. It is quite possible that Koresh and his followers, interpreting the FBI action as the final murderous assault of the Babylonians, chose to die in a purifying fire ("mass suicide"), but this has not been clearly established.

—*Thomas Robbins*

REFERENCES

D. M. Kelley, "Waco," *First Things* 53(May 1995):22-37; J. Lewis (ed.), *From the Ashes* (Lanham, Md.: Rowman & Littlefield, 1994); D. J. Reavis, *The Ashes of Waco* (New York: Simon & Schuster, 1995); J. D. Tabor and E. Gallagher, *Why Waco* (Berkeley: University of California Press, 1995); S. Wright (ed.), *Armageddon in Waco* (Chicago: University of Chicago Press, 1995).

KU KLUX KLAN   The Ku Klux Klan was born in 1866 amidst the travails of the Confederate loss in the Civil War. Begun as a society club designed to relieve boredom for former Confederate soldiers, it later blossomed into a vigilante group when it was led by General Nathan Forrest the very next year. Retaining the ghoulish costumes donned by its founders, Forrest ushered in a constitution. Within two years, he abolished the organization after it spawned a rash of atrocities so great that President Grant threatened to use government invention to stop it.

Demographic studies have shown that two of the prominent professions in the Klan were Protestant minister and police officer. In the original *Organization and Principles* of the Klan (1868, written by General Forrest), the "Creed" praised the "majesty and supremacy of the Divine Being and recognize[d] the goodness and providence of the same." The "Character and Objects of the Order" also focused heavily on the need to protect the weak and innocent as well as uphold the law.

Since its creation, the Klan has waxed and waned in strength, thriving during times of anxiety and social prejudice. Initially it fed on southern fears of the Republican Party. Klan members sought to frighten newly enfranchised blacks from extending their support to Republicans. Later, during the 1910s and 1920s, the Klan also vilified Catholics, Jews, and immigrants. It experienced sudden popularity after the release of D. W. Griffith's pro-Klan film, *Birth of a Nation* (1915). By the 1920s, the Klan had millions of supporters, including members of Congress. The Depression and American postwar prosperity lessened its ranks, yet the civil rights movement of the 1960s brought new converts.

Recently, the Klan has suffered fragmentation. Members have joined neo-Nazi groups, such as the Aryan Nations. Even leader David Duke could not unify the Klan in the 1970s, when he broke off contact to start his own organization. The Klan was largely separate from Nazi groups from the 1930s through the 1950s. It also opposed such natural allies as the anti-Semitic Father Coughlin (1938-1942 being his most radical period) on the basis that his organization (the "Christian Front") was Catholic. Major connections between the Klan and neo-Nazi groups did not come about until the 1970s, when organizations such as the Aryan Nations and WAR (White Aryan Resistance) began to make inroads into Klan territory. This was due in part to increasingly similar enemy figures between the two groups, dwindling membership on the part of the Klan (which created a need for such mergers), and advancements in telecommunication that made loose connections between organizations easier and more profitable. Thus, while white supremacy continues to rise, the Klan is no longer at its center; nonetheless, its presence persists.

—*Susan Zickmund*

REFERENCES

Annals of America, Vol. 14 (Chicago: Encyclopedia Britannica, 1968); W. L. Katz, *The Invisible Empire* (Seattle: Open Hand, 1986); M. Newton and J. A. Newton (eds.), *The Ku Klux Klan: An Encyclopedia* (New York: Garland, 1991); J. Ridgeway, *Blood in the Face* (New York: Thunder's Mouth Press, 1992).

LABBENS, JEAN (1921–) Studied at the École Pratique des Hautes Études (Paris) and spent a period of study in the United States before becoming Professor of Sociology at the Facultés Catholiques de Lyon and Director of its Institut de Sociologie.

In 1953, he became Secretary General of the Conférence Internationale de Sociologie Religieuse (CISR, now the SISR) and, in 1956, its second president. He was an eminent representative of *sociologie religieuse.* He defended the position that such research was to be undertaken by Catholics whose mode of analysis was necessarily tributary to their transcendent faith and whose observations had to be enlightened by their religious commitment.

—*Karel Dobbelaere*

REFERENCES

J. Labbens, *Les 99 autres*(Paris: Vitte, 1954); J. Labbens, *La sociologie religieuse* (Paris: Fayard, 1960).

LAITY The regular membership of a religious organization.

In hierarchically structured organizations, the laity constitutes the lowest rank and is subject to the authority of appointed or (in rare cases) elected "officials." Some members of the laity may, however, undertake specified religious or administrative tasks. The primary example of such an organization is the Roman Catholic Church, where the laity are subordinate to the regular clergy, the bishops, and, ultimately, the Pope but may form or join religious orders as monks or nuns or hold positions as lay ministers or administrators. In more egalitarian organizations, all members form part of the laity, with some appointed or elected to perform religious or administrative duties on behalf of their peers. Such an arrangement is common within many sectarian organizations of the Protestant faith.

—*W. E. Hewitt*

LANE, RALPH, JR. (1923–) Emeritus Professor of Sociology, University of San Francisco. Receiving A.B. and M.A. degrees from Columbia University and a Ph.D. in sociology from Fordham University, Lane taught at Manhattan College (1949-1950) and at Fordham University (1948-1955). Between 1955 and 1957, he served as cultural affairs officer at the American Embassy in Kabul, Afghanistan. He joined the sociology faculty at the University of San Francisco in 1958, where he remained until his retirement in 1988. President, Association for the Sociology of Religion, 1971.

In the area of sociology of religion, Lane's published materials have been primarily on aspects of Catholicism. His research covered areas of religiosity, Catholics as a status group, Catholic marriage and family life in the United States, Catholic charismatics, and sociology of the parish.

Lane became the first president of the reorganized and renamed Association for the Sociology of Religion. His presidential address critically analyzed the state of research in the sociology of religion, pointing to three elements threatening to become "impediments" to further developments: (1) the focus on social structures of formal religious institutions (parochial focus); (2) replicative studies of survey research, when the survey is not always the best or *only appropriate* technique for getting at dimensions of religiosity; (3) "accepting definitions of the contemporary religious situation that have the ring of plausibility because they are so skillfully developed but that lack any kind of systematic thoughtfulness" (plausibility fallacy).

—*Loretta M. Morris*

LANGUAGE Religious language, especially language about God, is subject to two opposite dangers: that of associating creatures too closely with their Creator and that of stressing so far the difference in sense of the same terms as applied to God and creatures that apparently one might infer that God could as well be called bad as good, impotent as almighty, nonexistent as existent, and so on. When admonished repeatedly by exponents of the "negative way" and other sophisticated theologians, that they do not mean what it seems that they mean by the terms that they apply to God (e.g., How could the reality of divine omnipotence and goodness, in any ordinary senses of these expressions, fail to imply that little girls would *not* die agonizing deaths of throat cancer?), the sincere inquirer may well conclude that religious claims, which once seemed good brash hypotheses, have died the death of the thousand qualifications (Flew 1966). It will not do, in other words, for language to be *equivocal* as applied to God and creatures—as the English word *box* is equivocal as applied to a container, a sort of shrub, and pugilism. On the other hand, it hardly can be *univocal* either—as though knowledge or goodness could be just the same in nature as between God and humanity.

A mediating doctrine of "analogy" has been developed, especially by Thomas Aquinas (*Summa Theologica* I, xiii): The meanings of terms to be predicated of God and creatures may have the same sort of relation as the meanings of the term *healthy* when applied to a human being, on the one hand, and to her food or her complexion, on the other. One may say in this case that the human being is healthy in the primary sense, while food and complexion are healthy in a derivative sense, as causes or signs of such health. However, there is no problem about describing and identifying a human being apart from such analogies, and if *all* terms are to be thus qualified as analogical in their theological as opposed to their ordinary use, it is hard to see how we can really know what we are doing in attributing goodness, knowledge, creativity, or anything else, to God.

To overcome this difficulty, Duns Scotus (*Opus Oxoniense,* I,8,3; I,3,2) maintained that "being" must be understood as univocal in all its applications, but one might protest that matters are not much mended by the invocation of a peculiar property called "being" supposed to belong in just the same sense to God, the Battle of Thermopylae, and a potted shrimp (Kenny 1959). Another possible solution is that certain attributes, for example, understanding and will, are to be conceived as the same in kind but vastly different in degree, as between God and humanity; thus God may be deemed to conceive all possible worlds, and to will the actual one, as the reader may conceive possibilities and will what actually is to be the case within her own limited sphere of influence (Lonergan 1992).

In the middle decades of the twentieth century, the logical positivists were influential in their claim that God-talk violated the rules of meaningful discourse. This they did on the ground that it did not comply with their "verification principle"—which was to the effect that all meaningful statements that were not true by virtue of the definitions of their terms were in principle verifiable or falsifiable by sense experience. But this principle is no longer much in vogue, because it not only makes mincemeat of ethics, and apparently of science in the bargain, as well as of religion, but actually self-destructs. Furthermore, on a more liberal understanding of "verification," religion might well in principle be verified—through postmortem experience (Hick 1971) or, in the case of Christianity, by objective historical inquiry tending to confirm rather than impugn the peculiar claims made by the New Testament writers about Jesus Christ (Crombie 1955). Ludwig Wittgenstein's *Tractatus Logico-Philosophicus* (Routledge 1961) seemed grist to the mill of the logical positivists, owing to the sharp distinction it drew between significant discourse, which could aspire to represent the facts of the world, and that which was not so significant. (The quasi-mystical intimations that form the conclusion to that enigmatic work did not suit their purposes so well.) However, Wittgenstein's later philosophy, expounded most notably in *Philosophical Investigations* (Blackwell 1958), has been interpreted in such a way as to encourage a view of religion and its language as autonomous and self-justifying, to be neither corroborated nor impugned by the different "language games" constitutive of science, ethics, or whatever.

—Hugo Meynell

REFERENCES

W. P. Alston, "Aquinas on Theological Predication," in *Reasoned Faith*, ed. E. Stump (Ithaca, N.Y.: Cornell University Press, 1993): 145-178; A. J. Ayer, *Language, Truth and Logic* (New York: Dover Books, n.d.); C. Barrett, *Wittgenstein on Ethics and Religious Belief* (Oxford: Blackwell, 1991); I. Crombie, "Theology and Falsification," in *New Essays in Philosophical Theology,* ed. A. G. N. Flew and A. C. MacIntyre (London: SCM Press, 1955): 109-130; A. G. N. Flew, *God and Philosophy* (London: Hutchinson, 1966); J. Hick, "Theology and Verification," in *Philosophy of Religion,* ed. B. Mitchell (Oxford: Oxford University Press, 1971): 53-71; D. Hume, *Dialogues Concerning Natural Religion*; A. Kenny, "Aquinas and Wittgenstein," *Downside Review* 77(1959): 368-381; B. J. F. Lonergan, *Insight* (Toronto: University of Toronto Press, 1992); D. Z. Phillips, *Belief, Change and Forms of Life* (London: Macmillan, 1986).

LAST SUPPER　Seen by the Christian Church as Christ's formal institution of the Eucharist (or the Holy Communion, Mass, Divine Liturgy, or Lord's Supper), the central symbolic practice of the Christian faith. The two "commands" given on the occasion were unusually specific and clearly intended as paradigmatic: to wash one another's feet and to bless and share bread and wine in "remembrance" of (to re-"present") himself. However, just as it has been "repeated" ever since, beginning with the breaking of the bread on the evening of Easter day on the road to Emmaus, so it is seen as being "anticipated," in the Feeding of the Four and Five Thousands, in the gift of Manna in the Wilderness—and in all human nourishment.

—Edward I. Bailey

REFERENCE

St. Paul, First Letter to the Corinthians, 11:17-34 (c. 43 C.E.).

LAZERWITZ, BERNARD (1926–)　Born in Clayton, Missouri, trained at the University of Michigan in sociology and survey research, Lazerwitz has taught at Illinois, Brandeis, and Missouri before joining the faculty at Bar-Ilan University in Israel in 1974.

Lazerwitz's work has focused on religion and, in particular, American Jews. His methodological acuity has particularly benefitted survey studies of Jews. His work has integrated survey findings on Jews with equivalent data on Protestants and Catholics, and has located the Jewish community within the larger American religious community.

Lazerwitz's research and publications have centered on the areas of survey research, ethnicity, religious involvement, and urban affairs. His ethnic and religious studies have focused on the components of consequences of religiosity. He is author or coauthor of several books, the most recent of which is *Jewish Choices: American Jewish Denominationalism* (with Arnold Dashefsky, Ephraim Tabory, and J. Alan Winter, SUNY Press 1997), and more than 60 articles, a number of which have appeared in the major journals in sociology and in religion.

—M. Herbert Danzger

LEADERSHIP　Religious leadership, typically studied from the perspectives of organizational stratification or social behavior, has been central to research on religious organizations and movements. Sociological scholarship on religious leadership has been built primarily upon a Weberian foundation, as refinement or critique of typological differences between the notion of *prophet,* one who attracts followers while proclaiming radical reform of a religion's beliefs and practices, or who founds a new religion altogether, and of *priest,* one who holds leadership status by virtue of office in the religious community, functionally maintaining religious tradition through interpretation and control of its authoritative body of scripture or custom. Max Weber identified three forms of religious authority by which the leader's status is collectively legitimated. *Charismatic authority,* based on a leader's exemplary or persuasive power, has characterized prophetic leaders. As religious movements institutionalize, developing differentiated offices and responsibilities for transmitting teachings and emergent tradition, leadership is legitimated by means of *traditional authority,* where leaders are selected on the basis of inheritance or by specific rules for succession grounded in religious tradition, or *rational-legal authority,* where leaders are chosen or elected through governing rules or bylaws that can be legally amended through discursive reason.

Religious leadership typically is ordained in organizations with traditional or rational-legal forms of authority. Among Christian denominations with hierarchically stratified ordination, bishops form the leadership core. Roman Catholic bishops are appointed by and ultimately report to the pope, while in other denominations they are elected by their judicatories. Some traditions consecrate bishops by apostolic succession, a belief in leadership passed down from apostolic times through a continuous laying on of hands. Historically, bishops have been male. The first female bishop of any contemporary denomination, Marjorie Matthews, was elected in 1980 by the United Methodist Church; the first female bishop to claim apostolic succession was Episcopalian Barbara Harris in 1989.

Although women have been well represented among founders and leaders of new religious movements, leadership roles beyond the founding generation disproportionately come to be held by men. Women's ordination has opened some leadership opportunities for women in Protestant and Jewish traditions. The Roman Catholic Church's priest shortage has resulted in new opportunities for women in lay pastoral leadership (Wallace 1992). Gender differences in leadership style have been empirically debated, with little conclusive evidence shown other than at senior levels. Lehman (1993) found racial differences in leadership style to be more marked than gender differences.

Authoritarian leadership has been criticized as a means of social control and maintenance of oppression in both new religious movements and established religious institutions. Erich Fromm characterizes authoritarianism as a deterministic worldview in which human happiness depends upon submission to external forces perceived to govern life. Authoritarianism also has been linked with externalized aggression, prejudice, conservatism, and, in its extreme form, totalitarianism. Extreme authoritarian control by religious leaders has been accused of totalitarian and genocidal outcomes.

See also Charisma, Organization Theory

—*Paula D. Nesbitt*

REFERENCES

J. W. Carroll, *As One with Authority* (Louisville: Westminster, 1991); E. Fromm, *Escape from Freedom* (New York: Avon, 1965 [1941]; R. A. Hutch, *Religious Leadership* (New York: Lang, 1991); E. C. Lehman, Jr., *Gender and Work* (Albany: SUNY Press, 1993); R. A. Wallace, *They Call Her Pastor* (Albany: SUNY Press, 1992); M. Weber, *Economy and Society* (Berkeley: University of California Press, 1978 [1922]); C. Wessinger, *Women's Leadership in Marginal Religions* (Urbana: University of Illinois Press, 1993); C. Wessinger (ed.), *Religious Institutions and Women's Leadership* (Columbia: University of South Carolina Press, 1996).

LE BRAS, GABRIEL (1891-1970)   Member of the Académie des Sciences Morales et Politiques and Professor of Canon Law.

Le Bras's interest was aroused by questions such as these: "Why, for whom, for which society and in what social circumstances were these laws established, and how did this society receive them, apply them, and change them?" Beginning in 1931, and employing anthropological, geographic, and psychological principles, he stimulated empirical and historical studies to evaluate the regional vitality of French Catholicism, establishing a "school" of religious sociology. Later, he extended his field of inquiry to other religions, adopting the term *sociology of religions*.

—*Karel Dobbelaere*

REFERENCES

H. Desroche, "In memoriam Gabriel Le Bras" (followed by G. Le Bras, " 'Discours synthétique' d'un Récipiendaire"), *Archives de sociologie des religions* 27(1970):3-14; F.-A. Isambert, "Développement et dépasssement de l'étude de la pratique religieuse chez Gabriel Le Bras," *Cahiers Internationaux de Sociologie* 20(1956):149-169; G. Le Bras, *Études de sociologie religieuse* (Paris: Presses Universitaires de France, 1955-1956).

LECLERCQ, JACQUES (1891-1971)   Professor of Moral Philosophy and Natural Law at the Catholic University of Louvain, where he introduced sociology (which until 1938 had been prohibited for its so-called positivistic orientation).

In 1948, he founded the Conférence Indernationale de Sociologie Religieuse (CISR, now the SISR) and was its first president. The goal of the society, as he defined it, was to promote methodologically sound socioreligious research for the benefit of those in charge of evangelization. The Vatican immediately warned Leclercq against positivism and the Durkheimian school. As president, he retorted publicly at a CISR conference that "religious sociology" did not need "speculative sociology" like Durkheim's but an American-style sociology, which he characterized as social research into empirical data.

—*Karel Dobbelaere*

REFERENCES

P. de Bie, "Jacques Leclercq et le développement de la sociologie," in *Jacques Leclercq* (Leuven: Société d'Études Politiques et Sociales, 1972): 31-41; J. Leclercq, *Introduction à la sociologie* (Leuven: IRES, 1948).

LEE, (MOTHER) ANN   *see* Shakers

LEHMAN, EDWARD C., JR. (1931–)

Distinguished Teaching Professor Emeritus of Sociology, State University of New York College at Brockport. President, Association for the Sociology of Religion, 1992.

As a pioneer in the study of women clergy, Lehman conducted research not only in the United States but also in England and Australia on the role of women clergy and lay reactions to their ministry. His first book, *Women Clergy: Breaking Through Gender Barriers* (Transaction 1985), was based on a national sample survey of membership in the United Presbyterian Church, U.S.A., and focused on the attitudes and behaviors of both clergy and laity toward clergywomen. His next book, *Women Clergy in England: Sexism, Modern Consciousness, and Church Viability* (Mellen 1987), was a study of Anglican clergywomen and attitudes toward them on the part of both male clergy and laity within the Anglican Church. In 1988, Lehman was awarded a Fulbright Exchange Scholar Grant to spend a year in Australia to study receptivity and resistance to women in ministry in the Anglican Church of Australia and in the Uniting Church of Australia. After a decade and a half studying clergywomen in various countries and denominations, in 1993 Lehman integrated his studies and wrote his influential book *Gender and Work: The Case of the Clergy* (SUNY Press 1993) in which he summarized findings regarding the role of clergywomen and the effects of varying attitudes toward the changing role of women within denominations.

In addition to his scholarly contributions on clergywomen, Lehman has played a central organizational role in three national religious associations. He was an executive council member in both the Association for the Sociology of Religion and the Religious Research Association, and served as Editor of the *Review of Religious Research,* 1984-1990. He also served as executive officer for the Society for the Scientific Study of Religion 1992-1996.

—*Helen Rose Ebaugh*

LENSKI, GERHARD E., JR. (1924–)

Alumni Distinguished Professor, University of North Carolina at Chapel Hill.

A native of Washington, D.C., Gerhard Lenski earned both his B.A. (1947) and Ph.D. (1950) at Yale University. He served on the faculty of the University of Michigan from 1950 to 1963, and on the eve of his advancement to the rank of professor, left Michigan to become Professor of Sociology at the University of North Carolina at Chapel Hill, where he later would serve as department chair (1965-1972) and Chair of the Division of Social Sciences (1976-1978). His accomplishments in the general field of sociology place him among the most widely recognized practitioners of his generation.

Lenski's writings in the sociology of religion were confined to the first two decades of his academic career (e.g., 1953, 1971), largely centering on a single crucial research contribution. Although he would later gain wide recognition for his work in the areas of social stratification and social theory, his 1961 opus *The Religious Factor: A Sociological Study of Religion's Impact on Politics, Economics, and Family Life* (Doubleday) brought him acclaim both as a general sociologist and as a sociologist of religion.

Why was this one publication so important, and especially so for sociologists of religion? First, the empirical research on which the book was based (the 1957-1958 Detroit Area Study) was the first major application of the then emerging techniques of survey research to the subject matter of religion. In this sense, *The Religious Factor* launched the sociology of religion as a field for empirical social scientific research. Second, Lenski's research provided an empirical test of some of the major themes of Max Weber's sociology of religion, the most important of which was his construct of a "Protestant ethic." By empirically investigating and comparing distinct religio-ethnic communities (whites, blacks, Protestants, Catholics, and Jews), Lenski was able to document the apparent social consequences of religious group membership. Finally, Lenski's measurement of religion as a multidimensional phenomenon would open the door to much conceptual innovation within the sociology of religion for the next several decades.

Although today sociologists of religion have moved far beyond the conceptualizations on which Lenski's *The Religious Factor* was based, there is no overstating its importance. This study announced the arrival of the subfield as an empirical branch of sociology, and for a time quieted the long debate over the possibilities for studying religion scientifically.

See also Communal Involvement

—*William M. Newman*

REFERENCES

G. Lenski, "Social Correlates of Religious Interest," *American Sociological Review* 18(1953):533-544; G. Lenski, "The Religious Factor in Detroit Revisited," *American Sociological Review* 36(1971):48-50.

LÉVI-STRAUSS, CLAUDE (1908–)

Professor of Social Anthropology at the College de France; founder and leading exponent of a major twentieth-century intellectual movement known as *French structuralism.*

Lévi-Strauss studied law and philosophy at the University of Paris but became disenchanted with these fields and accepted a teaching post in sociology at the University of São Paulo, Brazil. While in Brazil, he made numerous expeditions to study the indigenous peoples of the interior. He spent the war years teaching at the New School for Social Research in New York City. For Lévi-Strauss, a major goal of anthropology is to seek fundamental, underlying structures or organizing principles of the human mind, which, he argues, are to be found among all peoples in all places at all times. His investigations focus on ways in which the unconscious "orders" cultural phenomena. Lévi-Strauss has applied structuralist principles to the analysis of myth, social organization, ritual, and native systems of thought. Among his publications of relevance to the scientific study of religion are *Totemism* (Penguin 1969), *Structural Anthropology* (Basic Books, 1963), *The Savage Mind* (University of Chicago Press, 1962), *The Raw and the Cooked, From Honey to Ashes,* and *The Origin of Table Manners* (Harper 1964, 1966, 1978).

—*Stephen D. Glazier*

REFERENCES

E. Leach, *Lévi-Strauss* (London: Fontana/Collins, 1970); I. Rossi (ed.), *The Unconscious in Culture* (New York: Dutton, 1974).

LÉVY-BRUHL, LUCIEN (1857-1939)

French anthropologist, trained in philosophy, appointed to the chair of the history of modern philosophy at the Sorbonne in 1904, turned his interest in logic toward the study of "primitive mentality"—the role of emotions in the psychic life of native peoples.

Much of Lévy-Bruhl's work was in opposition to the "rationalism" associated with Durkheimian sociology then dominant in France. Lévy-Bruhl forcefully argued that ways of thinking may vary from society to society. His most important book, *Les Fonctions Mentale dans les sociétés inférieures* (1910 [*How Natives Think,* Allen & Unwin 1926]), argued that primitive thought is "pre-logical" and "mystical." It uses a "law of participation," governing supersensible forces, rather than logical categories; hence, it does not shrink from violating the law of contradiction. He examined missionary reports, ethnographic literature, and travelers' accounts dealing with the mental functions of tribal peoples and concluded that mysticism pervaded all of their perceptions. *La Mentalité Primitive* ([Primitive Mentality] Macmillan 1923) examined the primitive notion of cause, and *L'Âme Primitive* (The "Soul" of the Primitive, Macmillan 1928), the idea of the soul or individual. Later works extended his method to the supernatural, myth, symbols, rituals, and related topics among tribal people. His posthumous *Carnets* (notebooks) express some changes in his main theses, including repudiation of his theory of "primitive mentality." Despite criticisms of his theory (e.g., by Durkheim) and ethnographic evidence, his work remains a suggestive treatment of modes of thought.

—*Donald A. Nielsen and Stephen D. Glazier*

REFERENCE

J. Cazeneuve, *Lucien Lévy-Bruhl* (New York: Harper, 1972).

LEWIS, G. DOUGLASS (1934–)

College teacher and chaplain, 1964-1970; National Council of Churches Project Director, 1967-1971; Director, Institute for Ministry Development, 1971-1974; Coordinator of Parish Development and Director, Doctor of Ministry Program, Hartford Seminary, 1974-1982; President, Wesley Theological Seminary, 1982–. President, Religious Research Association, 1981.

Merging a Ph.D. in systematic theology completed at Duke University in 1965 with organizational development perspectives, Lewis was an early advocate for a parish development focus within doctor of ministry degree programs and a contributor to what subsequently has evolved into the field of congregational studies. He collaborated in the development of the Hartford Seminary Center for Social and Religious Research's *Parish Profile Inventory* questionnaire. The seminary's experimental, pastor-parish track D.Min. program, to which an entire issue of *Theological Education* was devoted (winter 1980), gave concrete expression to his empirically informed approaches to assessment, planning, and contextual leadership. He is a leader in the use of teaching-case pedagogy within theological education (e.g., *Resolving Church Conflicts,* Harper 1981), in the Institute for Theological Education, and in the globalization of theological education.

—*David A. Roozen*

LIBERATION THEOLOGY   *see* Preferential Option for the Poor; Social Justice

LIFE SATISFACTION   Covers numerous domains (community, family, income, occupation, and so on) plus global measures of overall satisfaction or happiness (Campbell et al. 1976). The effect of religion on life satisfaction may vary, depending on specific religious orientation and measurement. To the extent that religion provides meaning and purpose, reinforces belief in the benevolence of a higher power in one's life, and integrates individuals into a supportive group, it should be expected to enhance life satisfaction. On the other hand, religious beliefs themselves may be shaped by satisfaction with life circumstances. Empirical studies generally find at least a modest relationship between religiosity and life satisfaction (Ellison et al. 1989, Hadaway 1978, Hadaway and Roof 1978).

See also Well-Being

—*Doyle Paul Johnson*

REFERENCES

A. Campbell et al., *The Quality of American Life* (New York: Russell Sage, 1976); C. Ellison et al., "Does Religious Commitment Contribute to Individual Life Satisfaction?" *Social Forces* 68(1989):100-123; C. K. Hadaway, "Life Satisfaction and Religion," *Social Forces* 57(1978):636-643; C. K. Hadaway and W. C. Roof, "Religious Commitment and the Quality of Life in American Society," *Review of Religious Research* 19(1978):295-307.

LIGUORI, Sr. MARY   *see* Mary Liguori Brophy

LINCOLN, ABRAHAM (1809-1865)
President of the United States at the time of the American Civil War (1861 to 1865). Important in the study of American religion primarily for his two inaugural addresses and particularly his battlefield speech "The

Gettysburg Address." In the latter, Lincoln reinterpreted the meaning of the Civil War and in the process permanently reshaped American civil religion. Although never referring explicitly to Christianity, Lincoln drew implicitly on Christian religious imagery in a way that instilled meaning into the Civil War's vast death and destruction by linking it to a rebirth of freedom and equality in American life and the world.

—*Richard L. Wood*

REFERENCES

R. N. Bellah, "Civil Religion in America," *Daedalus* 96(1967):1-21; G. Fox, *Abraham Lincoln's Religion* (New York: Exposition Press, 1959); A. Nevins, *Lincoln and the Gettysburg Address* (Urbana: University of Illinois Press, 1964); G. Thurow, *Abraham Lincoln and American Political Religion* (Albany: SUNY Press, 1976); G. Wills, *Lincoln at Gettysburg* (New York: Simon & Schuster, 1992); W. J. Wolf, *The Almost Chosen People* (Garden City, N.Y.: Doubleday, 1959).

LIPSET, SEYMOUR MARTIN (1922–)   One of the most distinguished contemporary social scientists, Lipset is currently Hazel Professor of Public Policy at George Mason University and Emeritus Professor of Sociology at Stanford University. President, American Sociological Association (1993); President, American Political Science Association (1982); member, National Academy of Sciences; recipient of the first Marshall Sklare Award of the ASSJ and numerous other honors.

A political sociologist, Lipset's main concern throughout his career has been the social conditions necessary for stable democracy. In *The First New Nation* (Doubleday 1963), Lipset explores the relationship between the central value system of American society and religion as a social institution. The two basic American values Lipset identifies—equality and achievement—are supported by the Protestant emphases on voluntarism and personal achievement of grace, respectively. The stability of these values during the course of American history is associated with disestablishment and denominationalism in the religious sphere. That religious groups are voluntary organizations competing in a marketplace is central to America's vital civil society, which is in turn supportive of democracy.

Lipset was also an early contributor to understanding the role of "religious factors" in American politics. As Lipset (1964) notes, for many years America's leading pollster, George Gallup, did not inquire regularly into the religious affiliation of survey respondents. In 1940, when Paul Lazarsfeld found that Protestants and Catholics differed in political party preference net of other socioeconomic factors, Gallup expressed disbelief. Lipset explains Catholic support for the Democratic Party and Protestant support for the Republican Party to be an artifact of the late-nineteenth-century position of Catholics as immigrant newcomers to American society who were more welcomed by the Democrats than by Republican supporters of the Protestant status quo.

—*David Yamane*

REFERENCE

S. M. Lipset, "Religion and Politics in the American Past and Present," in *Religion and Social Conflict*, ed. R. Lee and M. E. Marty (New York: Oxford University Press, 1964): 69-126.

LOCAL-COSMOPOLITAN DISTINCTION

First introduced in the sociology of community, the local-cosmopolitan distinction was used to great effect in the sociology of religion by Wade Clark Roof as an explanatory tool for understanding changes in American denominational religiosity.

The distinction suggests that people operate primarily on one of two worldviews: Either they are oriented to their immediate surroundings, or they are oriented to a "larger" culture, centered in a global civilizational complex that has generally been referred to as "modern." The advantage of the local-cosmopolitan distinction is that it avoids the loaded quality of words such as *liberal* and *conservative*, and focuses instead on the subjective experience of participant actors in specific contexts.

Although localism is probably more likely to exist in more isolated areas, and correspondingly cosmopolitanism in more urban areas, *localism/cosmopolitanism* should not be seen as simply a new phraseology for *rural/urban*. It is possible to be cosmopolitan in a rural setting and localistic in an urban setting. Similarly, local/cosmopolitan is not simply a social stratification measure. Relatively speaking, there is local wealth and cosmopolitan poverty, and vice versa. The local-cosmopolitan distinction bridges between spatial location and the concept of "reference group." The localism factor, particularly, has played a significant role in Swatos's estimate (e.g., 1981) of the nature and function of denominational religiosity in the United States and in Robertson's understanding (e.g., 1992) of the dynamics of antiglobal tendencies

and apparent contradictions in the process of globalization.

—*William H. Swatos, Jr.*

REFERENCES

R. Robertson, *Globalization* (Newbury Park, Calif.: Sage, 1992); W. C. Roof, "The Local-Cosmopolitan Orientation and Traditional Religious Commitment," *Sociological Analysis* 33(1972):1-15; W. C. Roof, "Traditional Religion in Contemporary Society," *American Sociological Review* 41(1976): 195-208; W. H. Swatos, Jr., "Beyond Denominationalism?" *Journal for the Scientific Study of Religion* 20(1981):217-227.

LOFLAND, JOHN (1936–)   B.A., Swarthmore, 1958; M.A., Columbia, 1960; Ph.D., University of California, Berkeley (1964); currently Professor Emeritus in the Department of Sociology at the University of California at Davis.

Lofland has published extensively in the social movements literature and on a variety of other topics, often from an interactionist perspective. His most important contributions to the study of religion center on the process of conversion. In the sociology of religion, Lofland is best known for two scholarly works. The first, *Doomsday Cult* (Prentice Hall 1966), is an analysis of proselytization and conversion in what was then a fairly obscure new religious movement with origins in Korea that was brought to the United States in the late 1950s (the Unification Church). The second is a model of conversion developed with Rodney Stark (Lofland and Stark 1965). Others have tried applying the Lofland-Stark model to other types of movements to evaluate the adequacy of the model (e.g., Austin 1977, Snow and Phillips 1980), although Lofland (1978) has maintained that the conversion model was not meant for wider application but was intended as an example of how one might develop a conversion model for a particular movement.

—*Edward F. Breschel*

REFERENCES

R. Austin, "The Empirical Adequacy of Lofland's Conversion Model," *Review of Religious Research* 18(1977):282-287; J. Lofland, "Becoming a World-Saver Revisited," in *Conversion Careers*, ed. J. T. Richardson (Beverly Hills, Calif.: Sage, 1978): 10-23; J. Lofland, "Theory-Bashing and Answer-Improving in the Study of Social Movements," *American Sociologist* 24(1993):37-58; J. Lofland and J. T. Richardson, "Religious Movement Organizations," *Research in Social*

Movements, Conflict and Change 7 (Greenwich, Conn.: JAI, 1984): 29-51; J. Lofland and N. Skonovd, "Conversion Motifs," *Journal for the Scientific Study of Religion* 20(1981):371-385; J. Lofland and R. Stark, "Becoming a World-Saver," *American Sociological Review* 30(1965):862-875; D. Snow and C. L. Phillips, "The Lofland Stark Conversion Model," *Social Problems* 56(1980):598-603.

LONG, THEODORE E(DWARD) (1944–)

Sociologist, academic administrator. Ph.D. in sociology, University of Virginia, 1979, studying particularly with Jeffrey Hadden and Randall Collins. He has taught at George Washington University, Hollins College, and Washington and Jefferson College. From 1989 to 1996, he served as Dean, Vice President, and Provost at Merrimack College, at which time he was elected President of Elizabethtown College, which position he now holds. President, Association for the Sociology of Religion, 1991.

Most of Long's publications deal with theoretical issues. He has updated Weber's analysis of prophetic religion (1986, 1988), analyzed the place of healing in religion (1983), and proposed theories concerning new religious movements (1993, Long and Hadden 1983). He did a comprehensive study of the clergy and union activists who protested against unemployment in the Pittsburgh area from 1983 to 1987. The early stages of these protests were supported by agencies of the Lutheran Church. A preliminary report of his findings has been published (1990).

In addition to his scholarly work, Long has been an active member of professional organizations in the sociology of religion. From 1981 to 1988, he served as committee chair, council member, and executive officer of the Association for the Sociology of Religion. Long made a major contribution to improving the organizational effectiveness and financial solvency of the association. He also collaborated with Jeffrey Hadden in publishing a festschrift in honor of Joseph H. Fichter, *Religion and Religiosity in America* (Crossroad 1983), which began the ASR's Fichter Research Grant fund.

See also Association for the Sociology of Religion

—*William Silverman*

REFERENCES

T. E. Long, "Religion and Therapeutic Action," in *Religion and Religiosity in America*, ed. J. K. Hadden and T. E. Long (New York: Crossroad, 1983): 144-156; T. E. Long, "Prophecy, Charisma, and Politics," in *Prophetic Religions and Politics*, ed. J. K. Hadden and A. Shupe (New York: Paragon House, 1986): 3-17; T. E. Long, "A Theory of Prophetic Religion and Politics," in *The Politics of Religion and Social Change*, ed. A. Shupe and J. K. Hadden (New York: Paragon House, 1988): 3-16; T. E. Long, "To Reconcile Prophet and Priest," *Sociological Focus* 23(1990):251-265; T. E. Long, "New Religions and the Political Order," in *Handbook on Cults and Sects in America*, Vol. A, ed. D. G. Bromley and J. K. Hadden (Greenwich, Conn.: JAI, 1993): 263-276; T. E. Long and J. K. Hadden, "Religious Conversion and the Concept of Socialization," *Journal for the Scientific Study of Religion* 22(1983):1-14.

LUCKMANN, THOMAS (1927–)

Sociologist born in Slovenia, his sociological education took place partly in Europe (at the Universities of Vienna and Innsbruck) and partly in North America (at the New School for Social Research in New York); he has, in addition, honorary doctorates from the Universities of Linköping (Sweden) and Ljubljana (Slovenia). His teaching career has been equally international, with spells in New York State, Frankfurt, Constance, New York, Harvard, and as a fellow at Stanford and at Wollongong (Australia). Thomas Luckmann is a major figure in the postwar development of the social sciences; his influence is by no means confined to the aspects of social science that relate to religion. On the contrary, his name has been associated with major theoretical and methodological developments in both philosophy and sociology.

The Invisible Religion (Macmillan 1967, original title *Das problem der Religion,* 1963), Luckmann's first major publication—although it appeared in English *after* Luckmann's joint work with Peter Berger, *The Social Construction of Reality* (Doubleday 1966), leading to some misunderstandings with respect to the development of his ideas—has become a milestone in sociological thinking. As a systematic treatise in the sociology of knowledge, it is a key text within the subjectivist approach to sociology—a form of sociology in which human beings are not merely acted upon by social facts or social forces but are themselves constantly involved in the shaping and creating of social worlds as they interact with other human beings. Social order exists; it is, however, constructed from below, not imposed from above. The methodological implications follow. If we are to study human processes from a subjective point of view, appropriate methodologies must be put in place that enable the nuances of meaning to emerge. Positivist techniques are unlikely to suffice.

Luckmann's relationship to his former teacher Alfred Schutz (already evident in the Berger and Luckmann text) requires further elaboration. In the preface to the first volume of *The Structures of the Life World* (Northwestern University Press 1973:xii)—published under the names of Schutz and Luckmann—Luckmann explains the genesis of the book:

> The completion of the *Strukturen der Lebenswelt* combined the difficulties of the posthumous editing of the manuscripts of a great teacher by his student with the problems of collaboration between two unequal authors: one dead, the other living; one looking back at the results of many years of singularly concentrated efforts devoted to the resolution of the problems that were to be dealt with in the book, the other the beneficiary of these efforts; one a master, always ready to revise his analyses but now incapable of doing so, the other a pupil, hesitant to revise what the master had written but forced by the exigencies of the analyses that he continued in the direction indicated by the master to go back, occasionally, to the beginning.

The basic problematic of the book concerns the methodological foundations of the social sciences, bringing together Schutz's formation as both philosopher and social scientist. Schutz sought to analyze the structures of everyday life, uncovering those elementary structures that "provide the foundation of social experience, language, and social action, and thus of the complete historical world of human life" (p. xv). Luckmann's preface continues by indicating his own variations from Schutz's original outline; it concludes by announcing the imminent publication of a second volume. This did not in fact appear for more than a decade (1984 in German; 1989 in English, Northwestern University Press).

The themes of this joint work are developed in *Life World and Social Realities* (Heinemann 1983) in which Luckmann gathers together his own essays in social theory. These essays fall into two categories—phenomenological investigations and sociological analyses. There is, however, a common thread between them all (a motif that repeats itself in much of Luckmann's writing), that is, an attempt to minimize the cost of the separation of the new social sciences from the old philosophies. More specifically, Luckmann follows both Schutz and Gurvitch "in the conviction that an accurate phenomenological description of the lifeworld provides a foundation for the social sciences" (p. viii). Phenomenological description uncovers the universal and invariant structures of human existence at all times and in all places; one of these structures (a crucially important one) can be found in the forms of communication that are based on intersubjective production and interpretation of meaning.

In 1978, Luckmann edited a Penguin reader, *Phenomenology and Sociology*. In collecting this set of readings, Luckmann aims once again to elucidate the connections between the two disciplines and to reconcile two modes of human knowledge that have become separate in recent history. The influence of Weber, Husserl, Gurvitch, and, above all, Schutz can be seen clearly. Part One of the reader draws together all those who have illuminated the connections between phenomenology and sociology; Part Two is intended to be a small sample of work in progress within the perspective already outlined. A final edited text (together with James Beckford), *The Changing Face of Religion* (Sage 1989), assembles papers presented at the International Sociological Association in New Delhi in 1996, an appropriate enough place for a discussion of religious change that questions the assumptions of Western—at times triumphalist—thinking about secularization. Such a volume, moreover, brings the reader back to the social scientific study of religion per se. The collection is wide ranging and has two principal objectives: The first is to account for the changing meaning and form of religion in the modern world; the second is to discuss the challenge that changes in religion are continually presenting to social scientists. In so doing, the book invites questions that concern the discipline of sociology in general as well as the sociology of religion, an essential feature of Luckmann's work in this field. The study of religion necessarily involves the study of rapidly changing societies.

See also Invisible Religion

—*Grace Davie*

LUHMANN, NIKLAS (1927–)   After an early career in law and public administration, this German sociologist studied under Talcott Parsons in the early 1960s. Through hundreds of publications, he developed a rather different systems theory that understands social and psychic systems as self-organized and self-referential (autopoetic) entities based on meaning. In this framework, he has analyzed religion particularly in the Western context according to its systemic functions, organizability, and capacity to respond to secularization. He sees religion's future in a somewhat priestly capacity to assure us that it makes sense to continue, as well as in a kind of prophetic countercultural capacity.

—*Peter Beyer*

REFERENCES

N. Luhmann, *Funktion der Religion* (Frankfurt: Suhrkamp, 1977); N. Luhmann, *Essays on Self-Reference* (New York: Columbia University, 1990).

LUTHERANISM   A movement within Protestant Christianity that traces its origins to Martin Luther and its confessional identity to a collection of teachings contained in *The Book of Concord* (1580). Prefacing these teachings with the three major ecumenical creeds—Nicene, Apostles, and Athanasian—Lutherans claim to maintain their connection to the ancient apostolic tradition. Contained in *The Book of Concord* are the *Small and Large Catechisms* of Martin Luther, the *Smalcald Articles* (1537), the *Augsburg Confession* (1530) and its *Apology* (1531), and the *Formula of Concord* (1577). Originating in Germany, Lutheranism had spread into Sweden, Norway, Finland, Denmark, and eastern Europe by the time of Luther's death in 1545. The Lutheran Church was established as the state church in the Scandinavian countries. In 1619, Rasmus Jensen, a Lutheran pastor and one of those founding a colony on Hudson Bay, brought Lutheranism to North America. In the 1740s, German immigrants brought Lutheranism to Nova Scotia. Swedish immigrants to Fort Christina on the Delaware River in 1638 brought Lutheranism to the shores of the United States for the first time. Immigration throughout the nineteenth and twentieth centuries from Germany, Sweden, Norway, Denmark, and Finland, along with the gaining of converts, increased the number of Lutherans in the United States to nearly 10 million by the 1960s. Lutheran missionary societies during the latter part of the 1800s and early part of the 1900s took Lutheranism into Latin America, Australia, the former Soviet Union, Africa, Asia, and the Pacific islands.

Martin Luther (1483-1546)   Luther was a German theologian whose doctrinal conflicts with the papacy led to the Protestant Reformation. His reform of medieval theological anthropology from a body-soul dichotomy toward an individuated person and conscience led to new ways of understanding, as in the following: (1) the equality of secular and sacerdotal orders and a functional understanding of ministry and secular vocation *(Beruf)*, thus "the priesthood of all believers"; (2) salvation (justification) as based on the individual's faith relation to God as opposed to the medieval penitential system; (3) the role of secular order and authority in the providence of God and the individual's obedient

relation to it; (4) the individual conscience before God as the basis of ethical action.

Luther served as a case study for Erik H. Erikson's use of psychoanalysis as a tool in historical research. Erikson's theory proposed that the public data of adult life were expressive of the inner depths of the psyche. His epigenetic theory claimed that not only the childhood stages of Luther's development but also the adult stages were formative in the development of Luther's theological thought. For example, through analysis of the relationship with his father, the corresponding crisis of individuation in the young adult stage, and Luther's struggle with issues of obedience and control in his monastic experiences, Erikson provides a new dimension to understanding Luther's reforming of the Catholic tradition from a corporate authority to individual conscience.

Luther's writings concerning secular authority as well as Judaism have received significant attention regarding their role in the development of the German National Socialists/Nazis (1925-1945). His writings were quoted by Nazi propagandists to justify their position on the Jewish question and encourage the support of the German Evangelical Church for their policies.

Polity and Liturgical Practices   Luther taught that there were two doctrines essential to Christianity: (1) the doctrine of justification by faith through grace *(sola gratia)* and (2) the Scripture as the sole norm of faith and sole authority for doctrine *(sola scriptura)*. All else was nonessential *(adiaphora)*. This character of tolerance and the international character of Lutheranism has led to a diversity of stances taken by different bodies within the movement in terms of theology, polity, liturgical practices, and positions on social issues.

Lutheran polity takes a number of forms. Whereas some Lutheran bodies practice a strong congregational polity in which democratic principles function as authoritative for the particular congregation, the Lutheran Church of Sweden practices a strong episcopal polity based on its tradition of apostolic succession. Other bodies practice a form of presbyterianism in which power is vested in the assembly of congregations in a given geographic area (synod) or in a body of clergy (ministerium).

Luther's reform of the Roman liturgy maintained the basic structure of that liturgy, but his theological focus on the Word led him to emphasize the use of the vernacular in the liturgy, preaching, and hymnody. If the means of God's grace are Word and Sacrament, the people ought to be able to hear and understand that Word. Vestments, music, candles, icons, and such were adiaphorous and therefore optional. Such flexibility in liturgical practice remains today.

American Lutheranism   The diversity of expressions of Lutheranism in America can be attributed to several factors: immigration patterns, geography, and linguistic groups. The Lutheran immigrants who first came to the shores of the United States did not find the small states they were more familiar with in Europe. America was a vast land. So immigration patterns scattered the Lutherans throughout the country. Many of them were farmers and sought out climates and soils similar to those of their homelands in Germany, Sweden, Norway, and Denmark and settled in the Midwest. Others had been primarily fisherman and settled along the eastern seaboard.

The immigrants brought with them various languages. Wherever they settled, they established their own Lutheran church around that language and the particular customs of their native culture. Eventually, German-speaking Lutheran churches joined together in the state or territory to form a synod, an autonomous church. The same occurred with other linguistic groups. Due to these factors and the rapid immigration of the nineteenth century, there were more than 150 separate and autonomous Lutheran church bodies in the United States by 1850. Since then, Lutheranism in America has expended significant energies in efforts to unite by merging different Lutheran bodies into larger synodical entities. By 1988, with the creation of the Evangelical Lutheran Church in America, the largest of the bodies with approximately 5 million members, the 150 separate bodies had merged into 21 Lutheran bodies.

Lutheranism and Weber's Protestant Ethic   In his *Protestant Ethic and the Spirit of Capitalism,* Max Weber claimed that much of Protestantism was integral to the development of capitalism and to a "Protestant" work ethic. Although Weber believed that Luther's concept of vocation (Beruf), linking the performance of one's work with one's faithfulness to God, and the individual conscience as the final seat of one's relationship with God, had an affinity with the spirit of capitalism, he concluded that the concept of vocation entailed a vision of the social order as an organic whole and did not demand the mastering of reality as did the spirit of capitalism. Weber also concluded that the individual conscience as understood by Luther also did not necessitate the domination of reality. Finally, Weber concluded that whereas Calvinism supported the development of a spirit of capitalism, Lutheranism most likely did not. Indeed, the point of the earliest version of the Protestant ethic essays was *not* to contrast Protestantism to Catholicism directly but to contrast Anglo-American Puritanism (the Protestant ethic), deriving from Calvin, to German Lutheranism.

—*Gary Mann*

REFERENCES

I. Asheim and V. Gold (eds.), *Episcopacy in the Lutheran Church* (Philadelphia: Fortress, 1970); H. Bornkamm, *Luther in Mid-Career 1521-1530* (Philadelphia: Fortress, 1983); M. Brecht, *Martin Luther* (Philadelphia: Fortress, 1985); G. Dünnhaupt (ed.), *The Martin Luther Quincentennial* (Detroit: Wayne State University Press, 1985); E. H. Erikson, *Young Man Luther* (New York: Norton, 1962); E. Gritsch and R. Jensen, *Lutheranism* (Philadelphia: Fortress, 1976); M. Luther, "The Babylonian Captivity," "The Freedom of the Christian," "On Temporal Authority," and "To the Christian Nobility of the German Nation Concerning the Reform of the Christian Estate," all in *Martin Luther's Basic Theological Writings,* ed. T. Lull (Minneapolis: Fortress, 1991); *Lutheran Churches of the World* (Minneapolis: Augsburg, 1972); E. C. Nelson (ed.), *The Lutherans in North America* (Philadelphia: Fortress, 1980); E. C. Nelson, *The Rise of World Lutheranism* (Philadelphia: Fortress, 1982); T. Nichol, *All These Lutherans* (Minneapolis: Augsburg, 1986); M. Weber, *The Protestant Ethic and the Spirit of Capitalism* (New York: Scribner, 1930).

M

MAGIC A general term that covers any attempt to control the environment or the self by means that are either untested or untestable, such as charms or spells.

Magical beliefs are those that survive because they have not been subject to any attempt to disprove them. Usually some other explanation—other than that the belief is false—is invoked to account for those occasions when practices based on such beliefs fail to produce the desired result, for example, that countermagic was employed or that there was a failure to recite the spell correctly. If the unwarranted presumption of validity is what distinguishes magical beliefs about the world from scientific ones, then it is the practical aim of gaining control over the environment that principally distinguishes them from religious ones. For, like religion, magic can be said to consist of nonempirical beliefs, but while religion is oriented primarily to the worship of supernatural beings that are either propitiated or worshiped, magic deals primarily with the manipulation of impersonal forces. In addition, magic is usually only employed to achieve the ends of individuals, while religion also usually addresses the needs of communities.

Malinowski's "theory of the gap" is probably the best known and most influential of all theories of magic. He claimed that magic serves to reduce anxiety, to fill the void of the unknown, especially for people at a low level of technological development. Thus, although human beings will employ technology to achieve their aims wherever possible, some situations contain unpredictability and uncertainty. Consequently,

> man, engaged in a series of practical activities, comes to a gap; the hunter is disappointed by his quarry, the sailor misses propitious winds, the canoe builder has to deal with some material which he is never certain that it will stand the strain, or the healthy person suddenly finds his strength failing . . . his anxiety, his fears and hopes, induce tension in his organism which drives him to some sort of activity. . . . His nervous system and his whole organism drive him to some substitute activity. . . . His organism reproduces the acts suggested by the anticipation of hope. (1948 [1925]: 79-81)

It should be observed that although, as Malinowski pointed out, the natives of the Trobriand Islands could distinguish magic from technology, this is not true of all practitioners of magic, and on some occasions magical means may be employed for nonutilitarian ends. Yet, most critically, Malinowski failed to recognize the extent to which believing in magic can create the tension and anxiety that the practice is itself intended to alleviate.

Witchcraft and sorcery are both forms of magic. The term *sorcery* is usually employed to refer to that specialized branch of magic in which the aim is to harm others. *Witchcraft,* on the other hand, once one sets aside the distinctive meanings that this term has acquired within Christian-dominated societies, is commonly used to refer to the possession by individuals of special magical powers—ones that may be used for good or ill.

Very often practitioners assume that, for their magical practices to be effective, the knowledge upon which they are based must be kept secret—in which case, it approximates the occult. Traditionally, *occultism* has referred to theories and practices concerned with the attainment of secret powers of mind and spirit, especially those believed to derive from an essential wisdom that was known to a greater extent among the ancient civilizations of the East than it is today. Sociologists, however, have come to use the term *occult* to refer to deviant, or at least variant, aspects of the religious phenomena that cannot be included under the more conventional "sectarian" banner (Galbreath 1983).

The practice of magic is commonly associated with traditional and nonliterate societies rather than the modern, developed world. Yet most definitions of magic, such as Leech's "believing in the control over objects or events by verbal or nonverbal gestures (words or actions) where there is no empirical . . . connection between the gesture as cause and the object or event as effect" (1964:397), embrace what in contemporary society is known as "superstition." Thus individuals commonly cross their fingers, avoid walking under ladders, knock on wood, or throw salt over their shoulders, all to deflect bad luck or to attract good. Studies show that at least one-third, and possibly between one-half and three-quarters, of adults in contemporary industrial societies admit to engaging in such practices (Abercrombie et al. 1970, Jarvis 1980)—the most common being avoiding walking under ladders, knocking on wood, and throwing salt over one's shoulder—while a majority admit that they would feel uneasy if they failed to do these things in those situations where they deemed such action appropriate. There is no evidence to suggest that these practices are dying out, although there is evidence to suggest that each generation is characterized by a somewhat different pattern of superstition from that which preceded it (Opie and Tatum 1989). The fact that many individuals deny, when questioned, that they "believe" in these practices does not seem a sufficient basis for excluding them from the category of magic.

There are some people, however, even in contemporary society, who not only engage in "superstitious" practices but are prepared to state that they believe in magic. Luhrmann notes that in contemporary England, "several thousand people—possibly far more—practice magic as a serious activity" (1989:4). These people are those who "find magic persuasive," to use Luhrmann's phrase, and, as such, are the exception and not the rule among those who engage in superstitious practices. Unlike the vast majority of people, this small group of dedicated "magicians" not only take magic seriously but are also prepared to defend their beliefs. These defenses are often very sophisticated and bear witness to the time and energy that some individuals, even in the modern world, are prepared to devote to magic.

See also Bronislaw Malinowski

—*Colin Campbell*

REFERENCES

N. Abercrombie et al., "Superstition and Religion," *Sociological Yearbook of Religion in Britain* 3(1970): 93-129; R. Galbreath, "Explaining Modern Occultism," in *The Occult in America,* ed. H. Kerr and C. L. Crow (Urbana: University of Illinois Press, 1983): 11-37; P. Jarvis, "Toward a Sociological Understanding of Superstition," *Social Compass* 27(1980):285-295; E. Leech, "Magic," in *A Dictionary of the Social Sciences,* ed. J. Gould and W. L. Kolb (New York: Free Press, 1964): 388-399; T. M. Luhrmann, *Persuasions of the Witch's Craft* (Oxford: Blackwell, 1989); B. Malinowski, *Magic, Science and Religion* (Garden City, N.Y.: Doubleday, 1948 [1925]); I. Opie and M. Tatum, *A Dictionary of Superstitions* (Oxford: Oxford University Press, 1989).

MAINLINE CHURCHES   In the United States, so-called mainline churches are the large and established denominations that constitute the majority of organized American Christianity. The term, while somewhat inexact, is used informally to refer to the major players in the American religious sector, implying a shared concern for "public ordering" (see Table M.1, from Roof and McKinney 1987).

In the United States, church-state separation produced a pattern of "denominational pluralism," with previously state-established "transplants" (Roman Catholic, Episcopal, Lutheran, Presbyterian) reduced to nonmonopolies (denominations) in competition with and/or accommodation to each other. Denominations that mainly originated in the new world (e.g., Baptists, Disciples, Methodists) originally began with notions of pluralism.

Generally, mainline churches exhibit many or most of the following characteristics: They have their own (or predecessor) origins in the eighteenth or nineteenth centuries; have a million or more members spread widely among the 50 states; are predominantly Caucasian (except for black Baptist or Methodist denomina-

Table M.1 Religious Participation of Religious Groups

Religious Group	Church Attendance			High Denominational Commitment	Member Church Group	Belief in Life after Death
	Low	Moderate	Regular			
National	34	21	46	43	38	77
Liberal Protestants	37	24	39	33	43	82
Episcopalians	39	28	33	32	37	79
United Church of Christ	32	24	44	39	58	80
Presbyterians	37	22	40	32	42	84
Moderate Protestants	35	23	41	36	41	83
Methodists	38	24	38	32	40	83
Lutherans	29	26	45	41	43	81
Christians (Disciples of Christ)	30	19	51	50	49	89
Northern Baptists	44	19	37	34	34	86
Reformed	25	12	64	59	48	77
Black Protestants	20	25	56	52	51	72
Methodists	17	26	57	58	57	77
Northern Baptists	27	27	46	46	43	69
Southern Baptists	15	23	62	55	55	73
Conservative Protestants	24	19	58	53	48	89
Southern Baptists	26	22	52	48	44	90
Churches of Christ	19	19	62	57	51	91
Evangelicals/Fundamentalists	18	5	77	63	64	94
Nazarenes	24	12	64	63	53	91
Pentecostals/Holiness	19	16	65	58	50	89
Assemblies of God	16	11	73	70	56	91
Churches of God	31	12	57	59	49	85
Adventists	24	13	63	59	51	78
Catholics	25	20	55	42	30	75
Jews	48	39	13	42	38	27
Others						
Mormons	27	9	64	59	61	93
Jehovah's Witnesses	13	10	77	58	49	48
Christian Scientists	31	25	44	40	35	69
Unitarian-Universalists	64	14	22	35	31	43
No Religious Preference	91	6	3	—	4	47

tions) but include proportions of African Americans, Hispanics, Asiatics, Native Americans, and others; are governed by elected, parliamentary assemblies, with agency offices and staffs at a central location; sponsor colleges, seminaries/theological schools, and part-time local church schools (sometimes also elementary and high schools); staff their congregations with full-time, professional, seminary-educated, ordained clergy who now increasingly include women; run publishing houses and publish theological journals, denominational magazines, and newspapers; operate program units in domestic and global missions, social action and social welfare, evangelism, and Christian education; issue "social statements" on political, economic, and social issues and sponsor representation (lobbying) to governmental agencies; contribute to and/or cooperate with councils of churches at local, state, national, and world levels.

"Mainline" churches thus may include the following bodies, listed according to denominational "family" and specific self-naming: Baptist (American, National, Southern), Catholic (Roman), Christian Churches-Disciples, Episcopal, Lutheran (Evangelical Lutheran, Missouri Synod), Methodist (African Episcopal, Christian, United), Orthodox (Greek, Russian, some other "Eastern"), Presbyterian, Reformed Church in America, United Church of Christ. Sometimes coordinating associations of Reform and Conservative Jewish groups are also included. (Developing associations of Buddhist, Hindu, and Muslim groups may over time also attain "mainline" status.) A deliberate policy on the part of specific denominations to play a sociopolitical role in the national arena is important in assigning a label of "mainline" for such groups.

There are many exceptions to and/or variations in the qualifying characteristics given above. It should be stressed that differences among conservative, moderate, and liberal *individuals* within any one denomination may be as great as those between the denominations overall themselves. That is, the correlation between denominational "profession" and pastoral and member "practice" may vary a great deal. Also, the degree of democracy in denominational government varies from much grassroots participation to high oligarchy. For the most part, however, mainline churches and their members tend to be "moderate" in degree of theological orthodoxy, personal lifestyle, and official openness to interchurch relations (ecumenism) and exhibit a sense of ethical responsibility toward the "public" sphere (e.g., concern for social justice versus purely individual morality or spirituality).

Regarding exceptions, the Roman Catholic Church does not permit divorce or abortion, the ordination of women, or marriage of its priests, and any policy assemblies are purely advisory. Missouri Lutheran and Southern Baptist bodies officially endorse scriptural "inerrancy" and disapprove abortion, women's ordination, and council memberships, although some clergy may join local ministerial alliances. The United Church of Christ alone approves ordination of active gays and lesbians. Latter-day Saints and Christian Scientists, while fairly prominent in the media and public life, are not considered part of the "mainline churches." Many conservative, established, smaller bodies in the United States, while usually not listed as "mainline," share many of the above characteristics, sometimes forming loose alliances in action groups like the National Association of Evangelicals. So-called evangelical groups often attribute mainline membership losses to allegedly less "strict" theological and moral stands. The Unitarian-Universalist Church, while possessing many "mainline" criteria, is usually excluded from the category because it is not officially Christian.

See also Church-Sect Theory, Denominationalism, Evangelicalism, Organization Theory

—*Ross P. Scherer*

REFERENCES

W. C. Roof and W. McKinney, *American Mainline Religion* (New Brunswick, N.J.: Rutgers University Press, 1987); R. Stark and C. Y. Glock, *American Piety* (Berkeley: University of California Press, 1970); R. Wuthnow, *The Restructuring of American Religion* (Princeton, N.J.: Princeton University Press, 1988).

MALINOWSKI, BRONISLAW (1884-1942)

British social anthropologist instrumental in the development of functionalist theory.

Malinowski is renowned for his meticulously detailed and sympathetic descriptions of Trobriand Island life, although his reputation was diminished somewhat by the unauthorized publication of his personal diary in 1967. His diary contained what many considered to be unflattering racial slurs against native peoples. Nevertheless, Malinowski is still highly regarded as a fieldwork researcher and was among the first to incorporate ethnographic descriptions that included native commentaries concerning their likes and dislikes, daily routines, actions, and beliefs. He was also a preeminent theorist of his day. His ideas concerning functionalism differ somewhat from those of his contemporary A. R. Radcliffe-Brown. Although Radcliffe-Brown used the term *function* in a strictly biological sense, Malinowski used the term with reference to "purposes" and/or societal goals.

Malinowski's most important theoretical contribution to the study of religion is his 1925 essay *Magic, Science and Religion*. Magic, for Malinowski, is always utilitarian, whereas religion lacks all utility. Religion, he contends, must be seen as an end in-and-of-itself. Another distinguishing factor is that while magic can be amoral, religion is essentially moral. Although Malinowski's specific ethnographic examples have been criticized, he was effective in demonstrating that ritual activities are most often performed whenever the outcome of a human undertaking is uncertain. All rituals are performed in times of emotional distress, but—unlike magical rites—religious rituals are not expected to bring about clearly definable or direct results. He cites the example of death rituals, which do not bring about immortality but serve mainly to comfort the bereaved.

—*Stephen D. Glazier*

REFERENCES

B. Malinowski, *Magic, Science and Religion* (Garden City, N.Y.: Doubleday, 1954 [1925]); B. Malinowski, *A Diary in the Strict Sense of the Term* (New York: Harcourt, 1967).

MARRIAGE AND DIVORCE The joining together of persons in a union marked by affective or conjugal intimacies; one of the foundational institutions of society. As such, it affects and is in return affected by the activity of other institutions, such as economy, education, and religion. As the purveyor of meaning and source of legitimation, religion plays a central role in explaining cultural beliefs, values, and prescribed action patterns for marital relationships. Religion provides for boundaries affirming marriage as well as consequences for those who fall short of religion's ideals.

Marriage provides the first functional unit into which peoples divide themselves. Marriage may regulate sexual access, procreation, and membership of offspring into the larger culture as well as claims on resources both present and future. There are clearly well-documented differences between Eastern and Occidental structures governing the role of the conjugal, kin groups and of inheritance structures (see Goody 1983). Nevertheless, animist and folk forms of religious life may depend on the marital unit as a basis for clan membership and its related objects of worship and sacred awe. Marriage can determine one's place in the religious panoply (Orthodox Judaism, for example), or it can be the paradigmatic relationship describing the ineffable bond between a god and the believers (e.g., Christianity). Religion defines, celebrates, and protects marriage with sacred spaces; religion also acts as oppressor and violator when its teachings demand inequity and loss of self-determination in marriage. This entry will survey Western models of religion and marriage using monotheism's traditions from antiquity into modernity; in general, however, analogues for other civilizational complexes across geohistory can be found to complement the principal trajectories of the Western case.

Economics, Contracts, and Conjugal Love In the First Letter to the Corinthians (7:9) of the Christian New Testament, St. Paul writes that "it is better to marry than to burn." Obviously, marriage was not held in high regard in terms of access to the deity. Yet, throughout much of the Greco-Roman world, the monogamous union of the propertied classes was held to be an important social institution for the purposes of property arrangement. Lower classes did not actually "marry" even though their permanent monogamous couplings were held to be similar in function. Marriage was the chief business of the upper classes: It was the difference between dependence on parents and legal independence; it was the full initiation into adulthood for the woman (the man may have achieved that separately and earlier); it provided for satisfactory conjugal relationships and the parenting of children, specifically as legitimate heirs to family wealth.

Ceremonies governing the business transaction of the marriage often were seen as binding at the betrothal stage; religious trappings were added to this economic "handshake" as well as being useful in the symbolic (but usually less important) marriage ceremony itself (Boswell 1994). Roman husbands and wives shared a life that intertwined procreative, parenting, economic, community, and legal responsibilities. But marriage was not necessarily the seat of love; it was left to the industrialized West to develop notions of romantic love. Between the Roman Empire and the romance of the capitalist era, we have the Catholic Church, which as early as the third century defined marriage as "the union of man and wife persevering in a single sharing of life," with emphasis on propagation as the primary goal of marriage. The natural bond of marriage existed before the church; however, the church held that Christ had elevated marriage to a sacrament, for which state the church alone held full responsibility.

The Council of Trent in 1566 defined marriage as that sacrament in which is found the source of educating God's people in the religion and worship of the true God. The pre-Christian Greco-Roman world understood marriage as a business contract; by the sixteenth century, dominant Christian religious culture defined marriage as instituted by God for the sole benefit of his people. Along the way, religion took over as arbiter of the civil component of the relationship, although not without challenges from various secular authorities. Nevertheless, by the fourteenth century, the church held inviolably that the sacredness of the sacrament superseded the secular interests in forming this contract.

This transformation from secular economic partnership to sacred contract creates a backdrop to the development of what is now seen as the Western basis for marriage: romantic love. Ideas from the troubadours of the twelfth and thirteenth centuries, most definitely influenced by the Cathari (a movement the church condemned as heretical), centered on "love" as a model for devotion-from-afar under the heraldic code of chivalry. Stories of unrequited "love" were carried about the Cathari regions by troubadours, whose paradigmatic story is that of *Tristan and Issolde*: Love can lead only to death, the story goes in its earliest form.

By the start of the industrial revolution, the separation from the family unit of production, education, and even the dispersal of kin meant the conjugal unit needed more than an economic contract to maintain the indissoluble bonds made increasingly stringent by church teachings. Love was borrowed from the courtly poems of the troubadours as a way of bonding together, after the fact, the marital pair.

Love, Sex, and Marriage   In *The Natural History of Love* (Doubleday 1994), Morton Hunt describes the movement, throughout the industrial revolution, of marriage away from an arrangement for economic inheritance and property rights toward an arrangement between appropriate families for financial and, perhaps, mutual support and affection. Increasingly, love is idealized and idolized in literature and popular culture. With asides to Jane Austen, many an impoverished young woman was given in marriage to gain financial stability, and not a few heirs of entailed estates searched for purse strings behind coquettish looks. The nouveau riche and the bourgeois middle class, once ignored, were now players on the marriage field.

Throughout these centuries, marriage was considered essentially indissoluble. Unlike the Semitic, nomad cultures whence Western Christian culture was born, a man could not simply put aside a wife by returning the dowry money and sending her away with a writ of divorce. By the eleventh century, Christianity's hold on the civil law of the land created in marriage an indissoluble bond (see Mackin 1982). Relief could come only from papal annulment, decreeing the marriage to have been lacking in sacramental bond from the first. History only need look to the marital problems of England's Henry VIII to discover that not even the rich and powerful could guarantee themselves rid of a legal wife.

By the twentieth century, several forces joined together to slowly open the possibility of divorce. The 1917 revolution in Russia and the socialist movements in many Western countries held women to be equals and divorce to be readily available—although this was more a socialist ideal than a practical reality. Women gained enfranchisement in many countries; universal education for girls was increasing; factory employment for women was readily available (although women's wages were still lower than those of men); notions of romance and emotional attraction were encouraged by both high and popular culture; contraception within marriage was more widely discussed and used (and supported by Protestants of the Social Gospel ilk). Both world wars created an atmosphere of intensity and the feeling that there was no tomorrow; but it was the "make love not war" generation of the 1960s that broke sexuality fully away from its ties to love and marriage, and created of sex a recreational activity.

Today the need for marital stability across a lifetime has dissipated. The need to tie nuclear families together as working units by love and marriage has declined. Women's income has steadily risen. Children reared by one parent, stepparents, or a combination of parenting units are no longer an exception but the norm. Religious bodies now need to recognize to varying degrees that, with increased life expectancies (especially in Western postindustrial countries), we need different partners for the different lifetimes we have. First, lust, passion, and sexual experimentation as young adults lead to multiple partners, childbearing, and perhaps marriage. Stability, economic partnership, and a rediscovery of romance may mark the marriage or remarriage of younger middle age and into the midlife crisis. Relationship, companionship, and sexuality freed from the demands of launching adolescents into the adult world may create partnerships (not necessarily marriages) in the maturing years. Even Max Weber understood the "passionate enthusiasm of youth" to contrast deeply with "the mature love of intellectualism reaffirm[ing] the natural quality of the sexual sphere . . . as an embodied and creative power" (in Kent 1985:319).

Different churches offer reconciliations of divorce, remarriage within the church, and counseling and support groups for ex-spouses and children from divorces (Mackin 1984). Some religious leaders are asked to bless sacral, without creating civil, bonds of the partnerships of those drawing Social Security. A few, notably the Unitarians and the Metropolitan Community churches, offer ceremonies marking the unions of same sex couples.

The growth of worldwide fundamentalism stands in a reactionary position against this view of marriage as, at best, a form of serial polygamy. Fundamentalisms denounce marital breakdown, discourage or disallow remarriage, completely prohibit recognition of a homosexual lifestyle, and seek to promote the "traditional" family as the only viable sacred option socially, economically, and emotionally.

Current Research Trends   While secularization theory suggests religion has become a less important determinant of family behaviors and outcomes, other research emphasizes the growing importance of such factors as women's increasing socioeconomic status and involvement in the workforce in creating today's marriage "marketplace" of serial monogamy, alternative lifestyles, and single parenting (to name a few variations). Organized religions and their formal teachings seem to affect directly neither religious behavior within family units nor women's changing roles and economic contributions. Divorce rates are static but not declining, yet marriage as an institution is healthy, as individuals "try it again."

The future may hold a deeper division between those religious bodies defining marriage and its prescriptions within the context of the here and now, allowing for the replacement of partners "when love dies," to use a phrase popular in the 1970s, and those continuing the tradition of indissoluble and irrevocable marriage vows. People may move from one to another (or to no) religious body depending on life stages. Marriage itself is alive and well, as attested by the high rate of remarriage and divorce. Stigma has all but disappeared from divorce among the baby boomers now entering their middle age (and middle state) of married life. Those younger are reluctant to marry easily but more ready to divorce when the relationship sours. Personal lifestyles and religious ideals may move farther apart as culturally legitimate opportunities grow and persist for sexuality, relationship, and social and economic recognition outside of marriage.

See also Homosexuality, Sexuality and Fertility

—*Barbara J. Denison*

REFERENCES

J. Boswell, *Same Sex Unions* (New York: Villard, 1994); W. D'Antonio and J. Aldous (eds.), *Families and Religions* (Beverly Hills, Calif.: Sage, 1983); B. J. Denison, "Papal Authority," *Social Compass* 37(1990):269-279; J. Goody, *The Development of the Family and Marriage in Europe* (Cambridge: Cambridge University Press, 1983); T. B. Heaton and M. Cornwall, "Religious Group Variation in the Socioeconomic Status and Family Behavior of Women," *Journal for the Scientific Study of Religion* 28(1989):283-299; S. A. Kent, "Weber, Goethe and William Penn," *Sociological Analysis* 46(1985):315-320; T. Mackin, *What Is Marriage?* (Mahwah, N.J.: Paulist Press, 1982); T. Mackin, *Divorce and Remarriage* (Mahwah, N.J.: Paulist Press, 1984).

MARTIN, DAVID (1929–)   First as Lecturer, then as Reader and Professor at the London School of Economics (1962-1989), Martin has been a prolific contributor to public as well as sociological debate about religion. The author of some 20 books, he has established creative lines of thinking both within the sociology of religion and at the interface between sociology and theology. President, International Society for the Sociology of Religion, 1975-1983.

Early books include *Pacifism* (Routledge 1965), *The Sociology of English Religion* (SCM 1967), and *The Religious and the Secular* (Routledge 1969), but Martin is best known for his magisterial *A General Theory of Secularization* (Blackwell 1978), which questioned the inevitability of secularization in modern societies. The secularization issue is complex, contingent, and infinitely variable, requiring detailed comparative analysis. Later work, notably *Tongues of Fire* (Blackwell 1990), elaborates the Latin American case within the "secularization" framework. *Forbidden Revolutions* (SPCK 1996) continues the commitment to comparative sociology, and *Reflections on Sociology and Theology* (Oxford University Press 1996) collects a series of essays on the title theme.

The work on secularization remains, however, not only seminal but central to the continuing debate about religion in the modern world. In Martin's own words some 20 years after the publication of *A General Theory,* this is true not only of his "critique . . . of one-directional theories of secularization in terms of covert philosophical assumptions, selective epiphenomenalism, conceptual incoherence, and indifference to historical complexity" but also of the view that "whether in its hard version as the death of religion or in its soft form as marginalization, secularization should be treated as contingent in particular on the situation in Europe since the Enlightenment." North and South America and the Middle East, "for example, show how things can be otherwise, and even in Europe the hostilities of the last two centuries are over" (*British Journal of Sociology,* Vol. 42, No. 3, 1991).

As a teacher, Martin has initiated at least two generations of scholars into the discipline; organizationally he has promoted the sociology of religion both in Britain, through the British Sociological Association's Sociology of Religion Study Group, and internationally, through the SISR. His distinction can be quantified in numerous invitations to give the most prestigious public lectures in the field and in a variety of academic appointments in both Europe and the United States. In England, Martin is equally well known in church circles, and indeed beyond, for his vigorous defense of the continued use of the (1662) Book of Common Prayer as opposed to more "contemporary" revisions.

—*Grace Davie*

MARTY, MARTIN E(MIL) (1928–)   Fairfax M. Cone Professor Emeritus of Modern Christianity at the University of Chicago and Director of the Public Religion Project; a foremost, objectively historical, and simultaneously scholarly and popular interpreter of American religious pluralism, its institutions, and behavior.

Born in 1928 in West Point, Nebraska, Marty is the son of pious Lutheran parents, his father a Lutheran schoolteacher. After studies at Concordia Seminary–St. Louis and ordination into the Lutheran ministry in 1952, he received his Ph.D. in American religious and intellectual history from the University of Chicago in 1956. After serving as a parish pastor, including seven years in a new Chicago suburb, he joined the University of Chicago Divinity School faculty in 1963, acting as mentor to countless dissertation students. He has written over 45 books (not counting prefaces for books by friends and students) and has had conferred on him more than 50 honorary doctorates. He has served for some 40 years as an editor of *Christian Century* magazine, since 1963 as coeditor of the quarterly *Church History,* and as editor-author of the fortnightly newsletter *Context.* He has pioneered in founding the Park Ridge Center for the Study of Faith, Health, and Ethics (Chicago), for which he has served as editor first of its journal *Second Opinion* and later of its newsletter *Making the Rounds in Health, Faith, and Ethics.*

He has been honored by election to memberships in the American Philosophical Society, the American Academy of Arts and Sciences, the American Antiquarian Association, and the Society of American Historians. He is past President of the American Academy of Religion, American Society of Church History, and the American Catholic Historical Association. He has served as a Douglass lecturer for the Religious Research Association and a Furfey lecturer for the Association for the Sociology of Religion. In 1971, he won the National Book Award for *Righteous Empire* (Dial 1970). In 1996, the Society for the Scientific Study of Religion bestowed upon him its second Career Achievement Award in its half century of existence, and the American Academy of Religion initiated a new award named in his honor.

Lutheran intellectual mentors have included R. R. Caemmerer and O. P. Kretzmann (Missouri Synod) and Joseph Sittler (Lutheran Church in America), and history mentors, Sidney Mead and Daniel Boorstin (University of Chicago). He sees himself as a historian-storyteller who is also a person-of-faith, whereby his "theology forms a *cantus firmus* [of the Christian Gospel] under the melodies that make up our stories." He sees history as the way to do theology but "does not set out to convert while engaging in open-ended conversation."

Marty sees the foci of his theological-historical vocation to be the themes of "pluralism" and "the public" in American life, "second-order themes for first-order stories of real life." He sees socioreligious pluralism as the human condition and "written into the script of history," although he is aware that the Scriptures hardly mention these concepts. He sees the Christian historian's task to be interpreting and relating "radical monotheism and anti-idolatrous faith . . . with the acceptance, enjoyment, and affirmation of pluralism" where "faith, other faith, and nonfaith meet." Accordingly, he also sees the local congregation as "public" and "pluralist," not private and homogeneous.

—*Ross P. Scherer*

REFERENCES

M. E. Marty, *A Short History of Christianity* (Minneapolis: Augsburg, 1980 [1959]); M. E. Marty, *The Infidel* (Cleveland: Meridian, 1961); M. E. Marty, *A Nation of Behavers* (Chicago: University of Chicago Press, 1976); M. E. Marty, *The Public Church* (New York: Crossroad, 1981); M. E. Marty, *Health and Medicine in the Lutheran Tradition* (New York: Crossroad, 1983); M. E. Marty, *Religion and Republic* (Boston: Beacon, 1987); M. E. Marty, *Under God, Indivisible* (Chicago: University of Chicago Press, 1995); M. E. Marty and R. S. Appleby (eds.), *The Fundamentalism Project,* 5 vols. (Chicago: University of Chicago Press, 1991-1995); M. E. Marty and R. S. Appleby, *Modern American Religion* (Chicago: University of Chicago Press, 1991).

MARX, KARL (1818-1883)   Social economist, born in Trier, Germany. Marx's father was a lawyer who, because his Jewish religion caused him to be deprived of social and occupational mobility, decided to convert himself and his children to Protestantism. (His wife converted much later after her mother's death.)

After university studies at Bonn and Berlin, with a doctorate from Jena in 1841, Marx assumed the editorship of the *Reinische Zeitung,* a newspaper opposed to the ruling political system. Because of his socialist perspective, Marx had to flee Germany. For a while he lived in Paris, where in 1848 he and Friedrich Engels published the *Communist Manifesto* and participated in the 1848-1849 revolution. After its defeat, Marx again had to flee and settled in London, where he began his studies in political economy that led to the publication of *Capital*. He lived in London until his death.

Theory of Religion Marx's theory of religion (Marx and Engels 1975:38 f) must be viewed as an aspect of his general theory of society. Like many others in his era, Marx too was critical of religion. Unlike them, however, Marx did not seek to criticize the logic of religion as a set of beliefs. Rather, he proposed that religion reflects society, therefore any criticism of religion must ipso facto be a criticism of society itself. "Thus the criticism of heaven turns into the criticism of earth, the *criticism of religion* into the *criticism of law* and the *criticism of theology* into the *criticism of politics*." Religion for Marx is a human product. "Man makes religion, religion doesn't make man. Religion is the self-consciousness and self-esteem of man who has either not yet found himself or has already lost himself again." In short, what Marx proposes is that religion does not reflect man's true consciousness. Religion, as Marx sees it, is a false consciousness; religion is the product of men, the product of those in power—those who control the productive process.

Religion comes to divert people's attention from their miseries, which are the consequences of exploitation.

> Religious distress is at the same time the expression of real distress and also the protest against real distress. Religion is the sigh of the oppressed creature, the heart of a heartless world, just as it is the spirit of a spiritless condition. It is the opium of the people.
>
> To abolish religion as the illusory happiness of the people is to demand their real happiness. The demand to give up illusions about the existing state of affairs is the demand to give up a state of affairs which needs illusions. The criticism of religion is therefore in embryo the criticism of the vale of tears, the halo of which is religion.

This passage clearly illustrates Marx's view that religion is *not the creation of the bourgeoisie* but the resulting conditions of the historical systems of exploitation. Given that religion has existed long before capitalism, its clear that, even from Marx's view, this is not the product of capitalism. It is the natural consequence of

distress, which includes both transvaluation and *ressentiment*.

Both Marx and Engels renounced the anarchists such as the Blanquists and Dühring who sought to use coercive methods against religion. For Marx and Engels, religion cannot be eliminated until the social and political conditions that foster it are eliminated.

A concomitant factor is the development of religion as a compensatory mechanism. This is achieved through the process of transvaluation (Nietzsche 1927 [1887]). This is the process by which those of the lower class when faced with their powerless conditions redefine them and attribute a positive value to those conditions (see Mannheim 1936: 45 f). This, for instance, is best exemplified in the Christian teachings of meekness, turning the other cheek, and the desirability of poverty.

But are not people aware of their interests? Are not people aware that religion serves the interests of the ruling classes? The answer is obviously—No. It is no because people are socialized into believing that what they know is the truth. Marx proposes that religion internalizes in people a set of beliefs that are contrary to their interest but are in the interest of the ruling class. In short, it teaches obedience to authority as a condition for achieving future happiness through salvation. Both Halévy (1971 [1906]) and Thompson (1966), for instance, suggest that the rise of Methodism in England was a primary force that dissipated political fermentation that, in their opinion, otherwise would have led to revolution. In fact, Marx was even skeptical of Christian socialism's ability to serve the interests of the proletariat. He comments that just "as the parson has ever gone hand in hand with the landlord, so has Clerical Socialism with Feudal Socialism. . . . Christian Socialism is but the holy water with which the priests consecrate the heartburn of the aristocrats" (Marx and Engels 1968 [1848]: 55). In the *Communist Manifesto*, Marx suggests that religion, like morality and philosophy, must be eliminated if we are to achieve a new political and economic existence. "Communism," he and Engels write, "abolishes all religion, and all morality, instead of constituting them on new basis" (1968:52). The reason for this is the historical evidence that regardless of previous changes in the productive systems, religion has always supported the maintenance of the legitimacy of the exploiter and exploited. Thus, to create a truly free society, religion as a tie to the past must be eliminated.

Religion as the Social Superstructure To Marx, religion is one facet of that whole that he called the *superstructure* and that is based on and affected by the *infrastructure.* Differences in religion occur with changes in the infrastructure. Thus Marx and Engels proposed that earlier (precapitalist) religious beliefs arose from primitive man's helplessness in his struggle against nature, while in the class society it is rooted in his struggle against man. In man's quest and struggle against his exploiters, the working masses experience a different form of helplessness—and this experience is what changed religion and introduced the belief in a better life in a hereafter, the alleged reward for his earthly suffering. Moreover, Engels suggests in "Bruno Bauer and Early Christianity" (in Marx and Engels 1975) that Christianity, with its concept of salvation, reflects the outlook of utterly despairing people, of slaves who lost their battles with their masters, of indigent people and Greeks and other nationalities who lost wealth and status.

Religion as a Dominant Ideology

In *The German Ideology,* Marx (Marx and Engels 1976 [c. 1845]: 67) writes,

> The ideas of the ruling class are in every epoch the ruling ideas: i.e., the class which is the ruling material force of society, is at the same time its ruling intellectual force. The class which has the means of material production at its disposal, has control at the same time over the means of mental production, so that thereby, generally speaking, the ideas of those who lack the means of mental production are subject to it. . . . The individuals composing the ruling class possess among other things consciousness, and therefore think. Insofar, therefore, as they rule as a class and determine the extent and compass of an epoch, it is self evident that *they do this in its whole range,* hence among other things rule also as thinkers, as producers of ideas, and regulate the production and distribution of the idea of their age: thus their ideas are the ruling ideas of the epoch.

One apparatus of the transmission of ideas is the church through religion. Religion adds legitimacy to ideas (by making them sacred) that enhance the ruling class's economic position and their hegemony. (This view has been challenged in Abercombie et al. 1980.) The influence religion exerts on the lower classes is only possible to the extent that they constitute a class by itself *(eine Klasse en Sich),* namely, a class that has not developed a class consciousness. However, when a class develops consciousness, becomes aware of its own interests and become a class for itself *(eine Klasse für Sich),* then the consciousness it develops reflects its own interests.

Marx and Judaism

Marx's opposition to Christianity was extremely mild compared with hostility to Judaism. While on the one hand his hostility toward Jews may reflect a general anti-Semitism that pervaded Germany, and in fact made the mid-twentieth-century Holocaust possible, on the other hand it also reflects his hostility to his mother and her family, the Phillips, who were wealthy Dutch manufacturers. His hostile view of Jews and Judaism is expressed in 1843 under the title "On the Jewish Question" (Marx 1977 [1843]). This essay is Marx's criticism of Bruno Bauer's study on the emancipation of Jews in Germany. In the first part of the essay, Marx seeks to solve the problem of the duality of egoistic individualism that can be expressed in the "civil society" and the political individual as a member of the state. In the second section, Marx turns to the question of Jewish emancipation. Here he advocates the need to emancipate the Christian world, which made the civil world possible, from Judaism. The real Jew, in contrast to the abstract Jew, is a selfish huckster whose god is Mammon.

This hostile attitude was not due to his lack of knowledge of Jewish history. Feuer (1969: 36 f.) writes of Marx, "He knew the history of the Spanish and German Jews and their decisions to resist economic determination and to sacrifice their goods for their religious loyalties." Marx's hatred of Jews in general and Dutch Jews in particular is so intense, so dogmatic, that it led him, according to Feuer, to the verge of a conspiracy theory of history that cannot be but a "reaction-formation," an ego-defense mechanism of an insecure person.

In spite of a number of problems with his ideology and personality, Marx's theory of society and of religion, while in many ways controversial, has nonetheless provided great insight into the functioning of society. While one may not accept his political views, his social theory based on the interaction between the social infrastructure and superstructure has been and continues to be an important departing point for the sociological approach to the study of society and religion.

—*Eugen Schoenfeld*

REFERENCES

N. Abercombie et al., *The Dominant Ideology Thesis* (London: Allen & Unwin, 1980); L. S. Feuer, *Marx and the Intellectuals* (Garden City, N.Y.: Doubleday, 1969); É. Halévy, *The Birth of Methodism in England* (Chicago: University of Chicago Press, 1971 [1906]); K. Mannheim, *Ideology and Utopia* (New York: Harcourt, Brace, 1936); K. Marx, "On the Jewish Question," in *Karl Marx,* ed. D. McLellan (Oxford: Oxford University Press, 1977 [1843]): 39-62; K. Marx and F. Engels, "Manifesto of the Communist Party" in *Selected Works* (Moscow: Progress Publishers, 1968 [1848]): 35-71; K. Marx and

F. Engels, *On Religion* (Moscow: Progress Publishers, 1975); K. Marx and F. Engels, *The German Ideology* (Moscow: Progress Publishers, 1976 [c. 1845]); F. Nietzsche, "The Genealogy of Morals," in *The Philosophy of Nietzsche* (New York: Modern Library, 1927 [1887]): 617-807; E. P. Thompson, *The Making of the English Working Class* (New York: Vintage, 1966).

MARXISM   Changes in Marxist attitudes toward religion and the view taken of Marxism's own historical role have influenced Marxist theorizing as well as the quasi-religious uses made of Marxian doctrine. The topic of Marxism and religion can involve either an analysis of Marxian theories of religion or a study of Marxism as a functional equivalent of religion. The two are difficult to disentangle. Moreover, although Marxists have often distinguished between the oppressive role of established churches and the emancipatory possibilities of religious movements, they have historically linked their own worldview to both.

The positivist thrust of German Social Democracy fostered little sympathy for religion, although Eduard Bernstein and Karl Kautsky each wrote books on the role of religion in Reformation and Renaissance Europe, and Kautsky's *Foundations of Christianity* (International Publishers 1925 [1908]) discussed the influence of Roman socioeconomic conditions on early Christianity. The Austro-Marxists were more sympathetic to religion, partly in the hope of attracting the large Roman Catholic working populations. Their neo-Kantianism also encouraged moral theorizing and made greater room for religious speculation.

Lenin wrote little about religion and viewed it primarily as an impediment to political action. However, his book *Materialism and Emperio-Criticism* (Foreign Languages Publishing 1920 [1908]) attacked current "subjectivist" epistemologies and the cover that they provided for the reintroduction of religion. Trotsky approvingly analyzed the parallel, now commonly made, between the disciplined Puritan and Jesuit "parties" and the contemporary Bolsheviks, while other Soviet Marxists either saw a more positive role for religious ideals as a road to Socialism or elevated Scientific Socialism itself into a new "religion."

The Italian Marxist Antonio Gramsci developed a suggestive treatment of religion in his *Prison Notebooks* (Lawrence & Wishart 1971 [1948-1951]). His broad definition of ideological hegemony frequently included reference to religious ideas and elites. The distinction between traditional and organic intellectuals, in his theory of intellectuals, allowed him to discuss both the conservative and the revolutionary roles of religious elites. He analyzed early Medieval and Reformation Christianity, as well as modern Roman Catholicism, especially in their relationships to current Italian conditions. His discussion of the ways in which disaffected members of established religious elites (e.g., Savonarola and Luther) attack hegemonic institutions in the name of new ideals and organizations is particularly interesting.

By contrast, the Frankfurt School produced no sustained analysis of religion. Its members demonstrated a sympathy for religion as a repository of unfulfilled ideals (e.g., Horkheimer) and a source of theological motifs for their writings (e.g., Adorno and Benjamin). Only marginal members, such as Erich Fromm (in *The Dogma of Christ,* Routledge 1963 [1930]) and Franz Borkenau (in his study of feudal and capitalist worldviews), wrote works systematically linking religion to changing societal circumstances.

Among later Marxists, Lucien Goldmann (*The Hidden God,* Routledge 1964) offered a valuable analysis of Pascal's life and thought, one influenced by Lukács's Marxism and modified by categories drawn from Piaget. He established structural homologies between social classes and styles of thought and saw the "tragic vision" of Pascal and the Jansenists as the worldview of an administrative class yoked, yet historically opposed, to the monarchy's increasing power. Goldmann's work stands out among Marxist accounts of religion for its theoretical innovations and its thorough and sensitive treatment of historical texts.

Other Marxian-inspired efforts in the study of religion include those of Houtart and Lemercinier, two Catholic thinkers, who have adapted Marxian ideas effectively to the study of Asian religious traditions, and Bryan Turner, who has offered a "materialist" theory of religion.

The rapprochement of Marxism and Christianity among eastern European intellectuals in the postwar era (e.g., Leszek Kolakowski) and the amalgam of Marxism and Christianity in the social reform efforts of Liberation Theology in Latin America since the 1960s (e.g., Guttiérez) are only two examples of the continuing mutual fertilization of Marxism and religion. With the demise of world communism, Marxism's new, yet not unfamiliar, situation is likely to allow its proponents once again to forge links with religion.

—*Donald A. Nielsen*

REFERENCES

F. Houtart and G. Lemercinier, *The Great Asiatic Religions* (Louvain: Université Catholique, 1980); L. Kolakowski, *Main Currents in Marxism* (New York: Oxford University Press,

1978); D. McLellan, *Marxism and Religion* (New York: Harper, 1987); B. Turner, *Religion and Social Theory* (Atlantic Highlands, N.J.: Humanities Press, 1983).

MASLOW, ABRAHAM (1908-1970)

Psychologist and author at Brandeis University.

Maslow argued that each person has a hierarchy of needs, ranging from basic physiological requirements to love, esteem, and, finally, self-actualization. As lower needs are met, higher levels in the emotional hierarchy demand attention. Those who satisfy their highest needs are "self-actualizers." Such individuals have a propensity for "peak experiences." Maslow argued that such intense, transcendent episodes were at the heart of all religions, and that organized religion seeks to pass on meanings derived from peak experiences to those who lack the ability to attain them. Maslow believed that peak experiences are natural events that need not be cast in religious terms.

See also Experience

—*James McClenon*

REFERENCES

E. Hoffman, *The Right to Be Human* (Los Angeles: Tarcher, 1988); A. H. Maslow, *Toward a Psychology of Being* (Princeton, N.J.: Van Nostrand, 1962); A. H. Maslow, *Religions, Values, and Peak Experiences* (Columbus: Ohio State University Press, 1964).

MASS

The Eucharist, a thanksgiving, a commemoration with an injunction, a sacrificial meal, a sacrament, is a rite of worship of Catholicism and, to a lesser extent, of Anglicanism (Emminghaus 1978, Martimort 1986).

The ritual form and ceremonial shape of the Mass have oscillated from the simple to the complex according to theological preference and cultural circumstances. It can be said publicly or privately. It is rarely said in Latin nowadays, although that was for at least a thousand years the standard form among Western Christians, more usually now being said in the vernacular of the congregation. Embodying horizontal and vertical properties, it is a ritual transaction in community that requires a priest, servers, and sometimes choir; it services four other sacraments covering life stages of a community of believers.

The Mass marks sacred time, the main periods being Advent and Lent, Christmas and the Easter tridium, but also feast days and commemorations in a calendar that is universal in the Catholic Church, with some diocesan variations for local memoria. A variety of musical styles are employed, almost every major classical composer having written settings for the six parts of the Mass that permit choral rendition. In Catholicism, the authority for the recent form of the Mass is derived from the *Roman Missal,* promulgated in 1970. Recent efforts to simplify and to renew have led to much dispute since Vatican II.

—*Kieran Flanagan*

REFERENCES

J. H. Emminghaus, *The Eucharist* (Collegeville, Minn.: Liturgical Press, 1978); A. G. Martimort, *The Church at Prayer,* Vol. 2 (London: Chapman, 1986).

MAUSS, MARCEL (1872-1950)

French sociologist-anthropologist; succeeded his uncle, Émile Durkheim, as editor of *L'Année Sociologique* and leader of the French school. Studied with Sanskritist Sylvain Levi and wrote essays (with Henri Hubert) on sacrifice and magic as well as studies of the person, the influence of collective ideas of death on the individual, the concept of civilization, and an unfinished work on prayer, which focused on collective oral rites. His most influential work, on gift exchange, examines it as "total social phenomenon," integrating economic, legal, religious, magical, and other facts.

—*Donald A. Nielsen*

REFERENCES

C. Lévi-Strauss, *Introduction to the Work of Marcel Mauss* (London: Routledge, 1987); M. Mauss, *Oeuvres,* 3 vols. (Éditions de Minuit, 1969-1975); M. Mauss, *Sociologie et Anthropologie,* 3rd ed. (Paris: Presses Universitaires de France, 1973).

MAYER, EGON (1944–)

Sociologist; born in Switzerland but reared in Budapest, from which he emigrated to the United States during the 1956 Hungarian Revolution. Director of the Center for Jewish Studies of the Graduate School of CUNY and of its Jewish Outreach Institute. B.A., Brooklyn College, 1967; M.A., New School for Social Research, 1970; Ph.D., Rutgers University (1975). President, Association for the Social Scientific Study of Jewry, 1983-1988.

Mayer has completed major studies of Jewish-Gentile courtship, marriage, and child rearing, including *Love and Tradition: Marriage Between Jews and Christians* (Plenum 1985), and has examined Orthodox and Hasidic communities in New York in *From Suburb to Shtetl* (Temple University Press 1979).

—*J. Alan Winter*

McCAFFREY, D. AUGUSTINE (1900-1963)

Earning both an M.A. and a Ph.D. in sociology from the Catholic University of America, McCaffrey spent 45 years as a member of the Institute of Brothers of the Christian Schools (F.C.S.) and 21 years as a faculty member in the Sociology Department of La Salle College, chairing that department for 15 years. President, American Catholic Sociological Society, 1956.

Among Brother Augustine's scholarship and research interests were those concerned with moral education among North American Indians, youth in Catholic parishes, and Catholic college men and race relations. He was Moderator of the National Federation of Catholic College Students. While he served on the faculty of La Salle College, McCaffrey was actively involved in social action projects with the poor and underprivileged in Philadelphia. He served on the Executive Council of the American Catholic Sociological Society. As Program Chair and Local Arrangements person for the 1955 annual ACSS meeting in Philadelphia, McCaffrey was responsible for the largest annual meeting in the society's history: a tribute to his leadership among the city's Catholic universities, colleges, and high schools. In his 1956 presidential address, he—like other ACSS presidents before him—exhorted his members to fear neither sociological science nor the scientific method but to embrace them.

—*Loretta M. Morris*

McGUIRE, MEREDITH B. (1944–)

B.A. degree from Eckerd College, M.A. and Ph.D. (1970) from the New School for Social Research. Professor at Trinity University (San Antonio) since 1988. Rose through the ranks (1970-1978) and was chair of the Department of Sociology at Montclair State College (N.J.); Senior Fulbright Fellow (1977) in Ireland. President, Association for the Sociology of Religion, 1982; Society for the Scientific Study of Religion, 1988-1989.

At the New School, she studied with Thomas Luckmann and Peter Berger; her dissertation focused on the "underground church"—a movement within Catholicism that emphasized peace and justice social activism. She has returned to the social activism theme, as evidenced in the Latino community of San Antonio.

Her text *Religion: The Social Context* (Wadsworth) was first published in 1981 and is now in its fourth edition. It is organized as a series of essays on major theoretical themes or issues, and these are integrated throughout the text. The final chapter focuses on religion in the modern world; it discusses privatization and the individual, with personal identity increasingly found in the private sphere. This promotes personal freedoms, but it can cause problems of meaning for the person. There exists, therefore, a "relatively widespread quest for holistic world views, as expressed by many alternative health movements, agrarian communes, and contemporary religious movements" (3rd ed., p. 265). The chapter closes on a discussion of religion, power, and order in the modern world. She observes that "religion-politics tensions are . . . promoted by global interdependence" (p. 281).

Following her research on social activists, she undertook her first major postdoctoral study, which centered on directions the less activist (but strongly spiritual) families took: gravitating toward the new pentecostal movement in Catholicism. *Pentecostal Catholics,* published in 1982 (Temple University Press), won the Distinguished Book Award of the Society for the Scientific Study of Religion in 1984.

The next project centered on nonmedical healing. Chapters six and seven of *Pentecostal Catholics* had dealt with definitions and issues of health among that population. *Ritual Healing in Suburban America* (with Debra Kantor, Rutgers University Press 1988) is an ambitious and very successful study of 130 different groups in the suburban communities of West Essex County, New Jersey, that have to do with alternative healing, dealing with health and illness as an alternative to the biological (medical) definitions of disease. These groups are diverse, ranging from meditation, metaphysical, and psychic groups to Christian groups concerned with healing. The participants were, for the most part, well-educated, middle-aged suburbanites. Ritual language and nonverbal symbolism are important in these healing movements because they provide "a sense of order and control together with a sense of personal empowerment [that] may indeed be both physically and emotionally healing" (p. 239).

McGuire's two presidential addresses were related to these research projects. Her 1982 address to the ASR set forth an agenda for theory and research on the discovery of religious power; her address to the 1989 meeting of the SSSR focused on the need to incorporate the person *as body* into our research and theory. A volume by Peter E. S. Freund and McGuire, *Health, Illness, and the Social Body* (Prentice Hall 1991), is a text on the sociology of health and illness that goes beyond, but includes, standard topics on medicine and health care systems, by defining health and illness and describing alternative healing systems. Her research and writings on the theoretical and methodological underpinnings for a sociology of mind-body-self are applicable not only to studies of healing but also to an appreciation of the links between religion and sexuality as well as religious experience and other religious loci for the interpenetration of mind and body and self.

—*Hart M. Nelsen*

REFERENCES

M. B. McGuire, "Discovering Religious Power," *Sociological Analysis* 44(1983):1-10; M. B. McGuire, "Religion and the Body," *Journal for the Scientific Study of Religion* 29(1990): 283-296.

MCKINNEY, WILLIAM (1946–) Since 1996, President, Pacific School of Religion; 1985-1996, Professor of American Religion and Dean, Hartford Seminary; 1974-1985, Research Director, United Church Board for Homeland Ministries. Ph.D., Pennsylvania State, 1979. Ordination, United Church of Christ (UCC). President, Religious Research Association, 1984; RRA Douglass lecturer, 1997.

A common thread in McKinney's professional career is the combination of applied research and administration, with the balance shifting more to administration over time. During his years with the United Church Board, he directed a research and evaluation program for the principal domestic mission arm of the UCC, including dozens of research projects on issues of concern to both religious leaders and the general public. During this period, he published, with David Roozen and Jackson Carroll, *Religion's Public Presence* (Alban Institute 1982) and *Varieties of Religious Presence* (Pilgrim 1984).

During his years at Hartford Seminary, an institution with a long tradition of fostering interplay of religion and social science, McKinney's most well-known contributions to the social scientific study of religion appeared: the *Handbook for Congregational Studies* (with Carroll and Carl S. Dudley, Abingdon 1986), *American*

Mainline Religion: Its Changing Shape and Future (with W. Clark Roof, Rutgers University Press 1987), and *Studying Congregations* (with Nancy Ammerman, Carroll and Dudley, Abingdon 1997). Out of a deep commitment to making congregational studies as accessible as possible, McKinney also coproduced a video, *Invitation to Congregational Studies* (Hartford Seminary 1986). And out of his deep concern for enhancing the reflective practice of denominational leadership, McKinney developed a national leadership education program, one product of which was *The Responsibility People: Eighteen Senior Leaders of Protestant Churches and National Ecumenical Agencies Reflect on Church Leadership* (Eerdmans 1994).

Throughout his career, McKinney has been the author or coauthor of dozens of articles for both the religious and the academic press. In addition to his contributions to the Religious Research Association, McKinney is a member of the Board of Trustees of the Alban Institute and has provided consultative and editorial services on both the local and the national levels.

—*William H. Swatos, Jr., and David A. Roozen*

McNAMARA, PATRICK HAYES (1929–)

Sociologist; Ph.D., University of California, Los Angeles. Most of his career has been spent as a member of the sociology faculty at the University of New Mexico. President, Association for the Sociology of Religion, 1984.

McNamara is best known for his research on the Catholic Church in the United States (e.g., 1985). He was one of the first sociologists to study relationships between the Catholic Church and Mexican Americans. He reported on efforts by Catholic priests to empower Chicanos. He discussed the clash of perspectives between the policy of assimilation favored by officials of the Archdiocese of Los Angeles and the policy of preserving separatism favored by some Chicano activists. Early on, McNamara argued that Catholic social thought offers a vision of society that favors human rights and could facilitate democratization in Latin America (1968, 1970, 1979).

McNamara has summarized the available information on changes in the religiosity of young American Catholics. In a longitudinal study of graduates of a Catholic high school, *Conscience First, Tradition Second: A Study of Young American Catholics* (SUNY Press 1992), he has shown how upward mobility of American Catholics has changed the relationship between young people and their religion (see 1991). In a more prescriptive mode of discussion, he has offered practical proposals about how teachers can encourage student reflection on values and spiritual awareness (1994).

In a series of articles written with Arthur St. George, McNamara has explored the possibility of using survey data to develop social indicators for religion. They found that religiosity is a good predictor of psychological well-being. They also tested hypotheses derived from "deprivation theory." They showed that people of low social status are somewhat more likely to be religious, but low-status people in their sample did not use religion to compensate for low status (McNamara and St. George 1978, 1979).

—*William Silverman*

REFERENCES

P. H. McNamara, "Social Action Priests in the Mexican American Community," *Sociological Analysis* 29(1968):177-185; P. H. McNamara, "Dynamics of the Catholic Church," in *The Mexican-American People*, ed. L. Grebler et al. (New York: Free Press, 1970): 449-485; P. H. McNamara, "Conscience, Catholicism and Social Change in Latin America," *Social Research* 46(1979):329-349; P. H. McNamara, "American Catholicism in the Mid-Eighties," *Annals* 480(1985):63-74; P. H. McNamara, "Catholic Youth in the Modern Church," *Religion and the Social Order,* Vol. 2 (Greenwich, Conn.: JAI, 1991): 57-65; P. H. McNamara, "Teaching the Sociology of Religion as a Reflective Enterprise," *Social Compass* 41(1994):329-338; P. H. McNamara and A. St. George, "Blessed Are the Downtrodden?" *Sociological Analysis* 39(1978):303-320; P. H. McNamara and A. St. George, "Measures of Religiosity and the Quality of Life," in *Spiritual Well-Being*, ed. D. O. Moberg (Washington, D.C.: University Press of America, 1979): 229-236.

McNAMARA, ROBERT J. (1926-1985)

Sociologist; Ph.D. Cornell University; a member of the Jesuit order during the 1950s and 1960s. Member of the Sociology Department at Fordham University, 1962-1970 (chair 1968-1970); Professor of Sociology and sometime Dean of the College of Arts and Sciences, Loyola University Chicago, 1970-1985. President, American Catholic Sociological Society, 1969.

McNamara was a crucial figure in the transition of the ACSS to the Association for the Sociology of Religion. He served as book review editor of *Sociological Analysis* from 1964 to 1970 and, after his presidency, returned to serve as Executive Officer of the ASR from 1977 to 1984: "For some time, it almost seemed as if Bob *was* the ASR."

McNamara was keenly interested in his students and in student life. The ASR's annual Robert J. McNamara Award for an outstanding student paper is named in his honor.

—*William H. Swatos, Jr.*

MEANING   One of the most complex problems in social science, with particular significance for the study of religion, is "the problem of meaning." It is of special difficulty because the act of defining meaning ("the meaning of meaning") is self-referential (" 'Meaning' means . . .").

In Max Weber's sociology of religion, *meaning (Sinn)* is given central place. He writes that the task of the sociology of religion is "to study the conditions and effects of a particular type of social action," namely, religious behavior, which can be understood "only from the subjective experiences, ideas, and purposes of the individuals concerned—in short, from the viewpoint of the religious behavior's 'meaning' " (1978: 399). This viewpoint has characterized all subsequent "action" sociologies of religion—that is, all approaches to religion that treat religion as reflecting choice-making behavior, although there have been considerable divergences among action sociologists about the foundational presuppositions of these choices (the relative rationality or nonrationality of action).

See also Max Weber

—*William H. Swatos, Jr.*

REFERENCES

H. G. Blocker, *The Meaning of Meaninglessness* (The Hague: Nijhoff, 1974); C. K. Ogden and I. A. Richards, *The Meaning of Meaning* (New York: Harcourt, 1930); M. Weber, *Economy and Society* (Berkeley: University of California Press, 1978).

MEDIA   *see* Televangelism

MEDITATION   *see* Experience, Mysticism

MENNONITES   The word *Mennonite* is one of several general terms describing various groups around the world that trace their origins to the Anabaptist religio-social movement in sixteenth-century western Europe. *Mennonite* is an elaboration of *Menist,* which evolved into *Mennonist* and finally *Mennonite,* designating followers of Menno Simons, a leading writer and scholar in the Anabaptist movement.

Anabaptists, so called derisively from the beginning by church and state officials alike, were typically peasants, and there are indicators the Anabaptist movement was as much a political rebellion with utopian ideals as a religious protest against the established religions of the day. It is not surprising that major social upheaval and the Peasants' Revolt occurred in Germany simultaneously with the strengthening of the Anabaptist movement. Indeed, Redekop (1989) suggests there is a complex link between the Anabaptist movement and the peasants' sociopolitical revolt. Mennonites, he claims, are just as much a social movement as a religious group.

Mennonite groups, including Amish, Brethren, Hutterites, and others found in North and South America, emigrated to the Americas during the seventeenth and into the eighteenth centuries. Given the strength of Mennonite world missions in the past century or so, non-Germanic origin Mennonites now outnumber Mennonites of Germanic origins or ethnicity and are present in all populated parts of the world. This does create some tensions for a religious tradition bound by ethnic as well as religious and utopian ideals. Mennonite theology is part of the mainstream, clearly a product of Western civilization and the winds of reformation sweeping Europe at that time in history.

Today, Mennonites approach 900,000 baptized adults in world membership. Approximately one-third of these are found in North America. Mennonite faith is characterized by four basic tenets: an emphasis on baptism of the believer (baptism of adults), opposition to war (with a concomitant emphasis on nonviolence and peacemaking), the lordship of Jesus Christ, and the importance of church discipline (Kauffman and Driedger 1991). Mennonites were found among the conscientious objectors to wars and the draft in this century, although some did serve in humanitarian capacities. Mennonites worldwide are today known for providing dispute processing and negotiation services. Mennonites score significantly high on some measures of fundamentalism and general Protestant orthodoxy. Nevertheless, these are the four basic historical areas distinguishing Mennonite groups from other Protestant movements.

Tensions exist in contemporary Mennonite groups, as Mennonites move from their strictly agrarian roots, still dominant as late as the mid-twentieth century, into more urban and suburban settings. Trends of modernization, and, some would say, secularization, have taken their toll on a group originally dedicated to separation from the worldly powers around them. Various Mennonite groups, such as the Amish and Hutterites, have attempted to remain separate from the world; others have accommodated so as to carry out better a mission of evangelization and social justice. Mainstream Mennonite groups collaborate to provide schools, colleges, missions, and relief activities, the latter notably through the Mennonite Central Committee. Other groups in the Mennonite family maintain a separateness from the world and do not participate in these efforts. Both reform and reactionary trends are visible in Mennonite society as its approaches its sixth century.

See also Amish, Anabaptists

—*Barbara J. Denison*

REFERENCES

J. H. Kauffman and L. Driedger, *The Mennonite Mosaic* (Scottsdale, Pa.: Herald Press, 1991); C. Redekop, *Mennonite Society* (Baltimore: Johns Hopkins University Press, 1989).

MENTAL HEALTH   The relationship between mental health and religion has generated contradictory theoretical arguments and inconsistent empirical findings (Bergin 1983, Gartner et al. 1991, Larson et al. 1992, Batson et al. 1993). One basic question is whether religion contributes positively to individuals' mental health or undermines it. Another question concerns the support role of churches and the counseling role of clergy in the mental health system (McCann 1962).

The opposing theoretical perspectives regarding the relation between religion and mental health probably reflect biases in evaluations of religion. The view that religion enhances mental health emphasizes that religious beliefs help fulfill the basic human need for meaning, purpose, and confidence in the face of life's disappointments, frustrations, and exigencies. In addition, church attendance and involvement in religious groups provide reinforcement for these beliefs and also a social support network. The argument that religion undermines mental health emphasizes the notion that religion perpetuates immature dependency needs and unrealistic illusions, and prevents mature adjustment to the exigencies of life. These positive and negative theoretical orientations are reflected in the classical works of Jung and Freud, with Jung recognizing religion's importance in human experience and Freud emphasizing religion as a source of immature illusions. William

James's (1958 [1902]) classic distinction between the religion of "healthy-mindedness" versus the "sick soul," plus his description of the positive effects of a conversion experience for the latter type, have clear implications for mental health.

In the voluminous research literature (Schumaker 1992, Pargament et al. 1993, Brown 1994), the weight of the evidence seems generally to support the notion that religion contributes positively to mental health, but this depends in part on how *religion* and *mental health* are defined and measured. Beyond a minimum definition based on absence of dysfunctional symptoms, mental health may include a sense of well-being and satisfaction with life, appropriate coping skills, a sense of ego integrity, and, optimally, continual growth and development of one's potential. Religiosity measures most often include beliefs, practices, and religious experience as different dimensions. Religious experience is less frequently measured in survey research, except for investigations of a conversion (or "born-again") experience, but may be a major element of case studies. The relationship between religion and mental health is most likely to be positive for persons for whom religion is intrinsically important (as opposed to serving selfish interests); however, a rigid and dogmatic religious orientation may help reinforce irrational and compulsive behaviors reflecting less than optimal mental functioning. It is also plausible that one's religiosity is itself a reflection of one's level of mental health.

—*Doyle Paul Johnson*

REFERENCES

C. D. Batson et al., *Religion and the Individual* (New York: Oxford University Press, 1993); A. E. Bergin, "Religion and Mental Health," *Professional Psychology* 14(1983):170-184; L. B. Brown (ed.), *Religion, Personality, and Mental Health* (New York: Springer-Verlag, 1994); J. Gartner et al., "Religious Commitment and Mental Health," *Journal of Psychology and Theology* 19(1991):6-25; W. James, *The Varieties of Religious Experience* (New York: New American Library, 1958 [1902]); D. B. Larson et al., "Associations Between Dimensions of Religious Commitment and Mental Health Reported in the *American Journal of Psychiatry* and *Archives of General Psychiatry*," *American Journal of Psychiatry* 149(1992):557-559; R. V. McCann, *The Churches and Mental Health* (New York: Basic Books, 1962); K. I. Pargament et al., *Religion and Prevention in Mental Health* (Binghamton, N.Y.: Haworth, 1993); J. F. Schumaker (ed.), *Religion and Mental Health* (New York: Oxford University Press, 1992).

MERTON, ROBERT K(ING) (1910–)

Giddings Professor of Sociology and University Professor Emeritus, Columbia University; Ph.D., Harvard University under Talcott Parsons. President, American Sociological Association, 1957.

Merton made his direct impact on the sociology of religion with the publication of his doctoral dissertation on the coincidence of science and Protestant religion, *Science, Technology and Society in Seventeenth Century England* (Harper 1970 [1938]). Modeled on Max Weber's Protestant ethic thesis, Merton's work suggests a similar value-based dynamic for the rise of British science and the "scientific attitude" in Britain and Anglo-America, hence known (and debated) as the "Merton thesis."

As one of the giants in American sociology, many of Merton's concepts frame not only sociological research but everyday language regarding the social world; examples include the self-fulfilling prophecy, role models, the focused interview, unintended consequences of social action, social structure, role set, middle-range theory. In his best-known exposition of his theories, *Social Theory and Social Structure* (Free Press 1968 [1949]), he established himself as one of the founders of structural-functional analysis. Although he did not continue to write explicitly on religion, throughout his works he recognized religion as one of the influential institutions in society and was the first major functionalist to take issue with the naive neo-Durkheimian view that religion must always and every-where be socially eufunctional.

See also Functionalism, Talcott Parsons, Protestant Ethic Thesis, Max Weber

—*Helen Rose Ebaugh*

METAPHOR   The application of a descriptive word or phrase to something to which it does not literally apply; as when Lenin called intellectuals "insects." That at least *some* biblical language about God is metaphorical could scarcely be denied by any sane person. God cannot literally both be a consuming fire (Hebrews 12:29) and have a strong right arm (Deuteronomy 4:34, 7:19, and so on). And few would take the doctrine of verbal inspiration so far as to follow certain "fanatics" mentioned by Leibniz in his *Theodicy* (1710) in insisting that, when Christ referred to Herod as "that fox" (Luke 13:32), Herod was for an instant miraculously turned into a fox. But for *all* statements about God to be admitted to be metaphorical, and none literally true, would presumably be the end of theism as traditionally understood.

See also Language

—*Hugo Meynell*

REFERENCES

T. Aquinas, *Summa Theologica* I:1,9; H. N. Frye, *The Great Code* (Toronto: Academic Press Canada, 1982); P. D. Neilsen, *Religious Language as Metaphor* (Ottawa: National Library of Canada, 1985): J. Soskice, *Metaphor and Religious Language* (Oxford: Oxford University Press, 1985).

METHODISM Few religious movements can claim the social impact of American Methodism. It began as an evangelical revitalization movement within the Church of England in the early eighteenth century and spread to the American colonies in the 1760s. In both Britain and America, its early membership came mostly from the poorest and most marginal social classes. However, by 1830 the Methodist Episcopal Church had become the largest religious denomination in the United States, and its influence was so great that more than one historian of religion has dubbed the nineteenth as America's "Methodist Century." Although Methodism split into various denominational forms over the years, the Methodist Episcopal Church's most direct successor, the United Methodist Church, is currently the second largest of the Protestant churches in the United States. Taken together, the Methodist family of denominations remains a powerful influence on the nation's religious culture.

The success and popularity of Methodism stems from two mutually reinforcing factors. First, Methodists learned to foster a range of powerful religious experiences that they put at the center of their worship. Second, they learned to channel the religious enthusiasm that came from these experiences into a tightly structured organization. This combination proved peculiarly well suited to reaching out to the newly rising class of British industrial workers, who had been largely ignored by the established church. It also proved effective in evangelizing America's expanding frontier population as well as attracting many people from the established churches in the colonies of the Atlantic seaboard.

John Wesley (1709-1791) Methodism's founder, John Wesley, was an Anglican priest whose own religious experiences spurred him to try to reinvigorate the religious lives of people throughout the English-speaking world. Himself the son of an Anglican clergyman, Wesley first attracted attention to his work in the 1730s as a tutor at Oxford University, where he and his brother Charles brought together a group of pious students and instructors. It was during this period that Wesley and his followers acquired the name "Methodists," a derisive reference to the methodical way they went about their religious devotions. It was in these Oxford years that Wesley became associated with George Whitefield, who would later become one of the leading lights of England's Evangelical Revival. In numerous preaching trips to America, Whitefield also became one of the fathers of America's (first) Great Awakening.

The Wesley brothers attempted to take their message to the American colonies as well, and set sail in 1735. However, the trip was a disappointment for both, and a near disaster for John. After a broken romance with the daughter of a Georgia magistrate degenerated into a flurry of lawsuits, he shipped for England in 1738. Disillusioned, Charles also returned home. But on the trip to England, John fell under the influence of a party of the Moravian Brethren whose emphasis on faith as a total reliance on Christ, rather than as a mode of intellectual assent to revelation, had a great impact on Wesley. He began to attend Moravian meetings in London, where he soon experienced a great conversion, more powerful and thorough than his early experience of "justification." This "Aldersgate Experience" had the effect of energizing Wesley and motivating him to promote his new understanding of Christianity and spread to others the same experience of grace he had.

Wesley began to recruit others to his plans for promoting the kind of religious experience he had at Aldersgate. The year 1738 marked the start of the Evangelical Revival that swept England. For Wesley, furthering the revival meant he had to push the church to reconsider a comfortable posture in society and take the experience of the gospel beyond the upper and middle classes to evangelize among the poor. However, rather than expect the Church of England to bring evangelical religion to the people, he thought the peo- ple could evangelize themselves and eventually transform the institutions of the church. His announced object became to "reform the nation and spread scriptural holiness over the land." John Wesley's great ally in this work was his brother Charles, whose influence on Methodism was chiefly in the hymns that he wrote for the new movement. Among populations with a low rates of literacy and at a time when books were scarce, the hymns of Charles Wesley became primary instruments for the communication of religious ideas as well as a source of inspiration and communal solidarity.

John Wesley also wrote a number of hymns, but his special genius seemed to be organization and evangelization. He developed a formula for recruiting lay preachers from among just those groups he most wanted to reach. They became itinerant circuit riders whose job was to produce conversion experiences among their listeners, and organize those listeners into Methodist societies and class meetings, in which the people engaged in regular group prayer, song, and mutual criticism. Some individuals who could not travel as itinerants were licensed to preach in their local societies in the long periods between visits by the itinerant assigned to them. This organizational formula promoted local organizations that could function with a great deal of independence under the leadership of lay leaders chosen from among themselves, in their own communities. At the same time, these different local "societies" were held together by the network of circuit riders who were shifted around and tightly managed by Wesley himself and, as the organization took off, through the presiding elders Wesley placed over the itinerants. Wesley himself maintained a rigorous regime of travel and constant preaching. The result was a network of industrial laborers and itinerant evangelists dedicated to living life with the sort of austerity and piety that they thought they discerned from the Bible as God's will. It was a self-consciously countercultural position, at odds with the prevailing social values of all classes.

Sociocultural Contexts   The Evangelical Revival in England was largely an affair of the lowest orders of British society. Its profound effect on the customs and values of the British working class has been the subject of great speculation and some important research. At the turn of the last century, French theorist Élie Halévy speculated that the rise of Methodism in England headed off the kind of revolutionary cycle his own countrymen experienced. His 1906 book, *The Birth of Methodism in England* (reprint edition, University of Chicago Press 1971), supported his claim with few facts or historical research. But Halévy's ideas inspired a later generation of Marxist scholars, most notably historian E. P. Thompson, to find just this sort of evidence. Thompson presented his evidence in his 1963 book, *The Making of the English Working Class* (Vintage 1963). In it, he attempted to show how Methodism helped create the conservative character of the British proletariat.

In America, Methodism evolved somewhat differently. The movement hit a snag when the revolution erupted, and Wesley sent a letter admonishing his followers to stay loyal to the king. All but one of the several British-born itinerants sent by Wesley returned to England to ride out the war. Additionally, the Methodists were still technically Anglicans and depended on the Church of England to provide the sacraments. This situation was rendered impossible when much of the Anglican clergy fled the colonies during the war years and made only a very slow return in its aftermath. Wesley and his associates saw they had little choice but to authorize that American Methodists become an independent church, a step Wesley's English followers did not take until his death in 1791.

Wesley decided that there was scriptural precedent for the priests of the church to ordain others as priests and to elevate some from among themselves to the episcopal office. He chose one of his English itinerants, Thomas Coke, to be ordained on both counts and go to America. Coke's mission was to ordain all of the American itinerants as true clergymen, and to elevate one of them, Francis Asbury (the only English itinerant to remain in America during the fighting), as a second superintendent. He also sent over a set of rules by which the new church was to abide. The Methodist Episcopal Church came together at a conference of the itinerant preachers in Baltimore on Christmas Eve, 1784. Asbury asked that the conference vote to confirm him and Coke as superintendents. It was a gesture more symbolic than substantive, for as Wesley's influence over American Methodism began to wane with age and distance, and as Coke eventually returned to England, Asbury would come to exercise a dominant authority over the new church. He was quickly given the title *bishop*, although Wesley opposed it, and exercised a rigid control over the new denomination.

Francis Asbury adapted Wesley's form of organization to the much larger geographic scale of North America and inspired a new generation of itinerants and presiding elders to evangelize every place inhabited by Americans, either white or black. When the Great Revival broke out on the southern frontier in the years bridging the eighteenth and nineteenth centuries, Asbury enthusiastically joined the forces of his church with ministers of other denominations to promote and spread it. The most important institution in spreading the revival, the camp meeting, was eventually abandoned by most other churches as too hard to control and subject to undignified emotional excesses. But Asbury and the Methodists embraced camp meetings and similar revivals with great enthusiasm. Under Methodist control, the meetings became a highly organized ritual dedicated to the mass replication of a certain religious experience. This experience was developed in two parts. In the first part, the sinner was called to acknowledge his or her sorry condition—to be convicted of inherent sinfulness. The second part was to accept Christ as savior from that sinfulness. This *conviction-conversion scheme* of personal religious experience became the standard structure of Methodist religious conversion in the early nineteenth century, and Methodists soon developed a variety of revival forms that produced it in large numbers of people.

Historian Nathan Hatch in *The Democratization of American Christianity* (Yale University Press 1989) has suggested this early evangelical phase of American Methodism was part of a larger democratic revolution in society, and that the Methodists were essentially democratic because they were involved in spreading this experience among the common people, empowering them spiritually, without regard to class or education. The Methodist itinerants were themselves drawn from among the common people of the new nation. On the other hand, the American Methodism that Asbury shaped was hardly democratically run. Even after Asbury died, and his successors to the episcopacy allowed the itinerants a little more leeway in decision making, the business of the church was entirely within the hands of the clergy. Lay Methodists exercised their leadership only at the local level, and even there the decisions they made could be overridden by the itinerant clergy. The more conservative strain in the Methodist character was reinforced by the experience of the denomination as it moved westward with the population. Because Methodist itinerants were willing to travel into the far reaches of the frontier country, they were frequently able to organize their societies long before the educated clergymen of the older denominations ventured beyond the Eastern seaboard. Consequently, Methodist churches became part of the original institutional infrastructure of many Western communities. As the wealth of the frontier population increased with time, so did the Methodist Episcopal Church see itself become identified with a rising middle class.

Fissures and Fusions   Much of the energy of Methodism throughout the nineteenth and twentieth centuries has been taken up in debates over issues of decentralization and democratization. Some Methodists pulled out of the church in the 1790s, upset with Asbury's dominant position. In addition, the opposition of some Methodists even to having the office of bishop led to the 1830 secession of the Methodist Protestant Church. Even the 1845 separation of the southern conferences over the issue of slavery was technically fought over different interpretations of the relationship of the bishops to the General Conference. The result was the proslavery Methodist Episcopal Church South.

Other notable splits in the Methodist fold erupted over the treatment of African American Methodists by their white brethren. In 1816, blacks in Philadelphia set up the African Methodist Episcopal Church (A.M.E. Church) under the leadership of Richard Allen. Similar circumstances led to the formation of the African Methodist Episcopal Zion Church (A.M.E.Z. Church) in New York, in 1821, under the leadership of Peter Williams and James Varick. A third African American Methodist denomination came together in 1870 when the black members of the Methodist Episcopal Church South split away to become the Colored Methodist Episcopal Church, now known as the Christian Methodist Episcopal Church (C.M.E. Church).

As American Methodism became more identified with the American middle class in the nineteenth century, it began to develop more stately and emotionally restrained styles of worship. In response, a revitalization effort rose within the Methodist Episcopal Church to reemphasize personal religious experiences along with the quest to "perfect" the individual. This became known as the Holiness Movement. When it began in the 1840s, it enjoyed the support of many of the bishops; however, by the turn of the century it had acquired a constituency beyond the membership of the Methodist Church and an institutional structure organized around its summer encampments. Many holiness leaders became dissatisfied with the Methodist Episcopal Church and split away to form new denominations. This led to the separation of the Church of the Nazarene in 1908, the Pilgrim Holiness Church in 1897, and the Evangelical Methodist Church in 1946.

Ultimately the Methodist Episcopal Church South and the Methodist Protestant Church reunited with the Methodist Episcopal Church to form the Methodist Church in 1939. In 1968, this body merged with the Evangelical United Brethren (a body formed in 1946 by the merger of the Church of the United Brethren in Christ and the Evangelical Church, two originally German-speaking denominations with Methodist organization and theology). The result is the United Methodist Church, which is currently the largest Methodist denomination.

An American Church   From the middle of the nineteenth century on, the Methodist Episcopal Church moved toward a close identification with the American middle class and its values. Methodist Episcopal Churches of both the North and the South gave enthusiastic support to their respective governments and the war. By the end of that century, Methodist leaders, especially in the North, were deeply committed to notions of progress and improving the human condition. Methodists invested heavily in educational institutions, even as they resisted making a college education a prerequisite for entering the ministry. The church began to see itself as a guardian of "American-ness" and as a bulwark of American virtues threatened by the influx of Catholic and Jewish immigrants. Although it advocated a compassionate and fair treatment of the new industrial workers, church publications and position statements make it clear that it identified most with the managers of the factories rather than the largely immigrant workforce.

From the 1870s on, nearly all Methodist denominations played an active role in the movement to ban alcoholic beverages and cooperated together in the support of such middle-class-based organizations as the Anti-Saloon League, the Women's Christian Temperance Union, and the Prohibition Party. Methodists dominated all these organizations.

At the same time, the nature of Methodist religious experience and activity broadened. The Holiness Movement promoted the older forms of the conviction-conversion experience and found its greatest success among Methodists who had been born in rural settings but who had migrated to the cities. The advocates of the Social Gospel also had a great influence on the church. In 1912, the Methodist Episcopal Church adopted a "Social Creed," which later became the basis for the Social Creed of the Federal Council of Churches.

Theology has rarely been the cause of division or marked enthusiasm among Methodists. The denomination has always been more invested in issues of social behavior and organization. Wesley adopted a theology based on the ability of individuals to accept and reject a universally offered salvation. This "Arminianism" distinguished Methodists from the various Calvinist sects and their predestinationist theologies. But Methodists never made agreement on theological fine points a qualification for membership. More central was the experience of the believer and a basic faith in Christ as Savior. This enabled Methodism to avoid deep involvement in the modernist controversy that rocked many American religious denominations, and it also has made for a relatively free play of ideas in most Methodist colleges and seminaries.

Since the 1960s, the United Methodist Church, along with most of the churches based in the American middle class, has suffered an erosion in its membership base and has fallen to second place behind the Southern Baptist Convention as the largest Protestant denomination in the United States. In *The Churching of America* (Rutgers University Press), sociologists Roger Finke and Rodney Stark have looked at Methodism as a prime example of what happens to any denomination that makes too many accommodations with the larger society. They claim that the Methodists began their decline in the 1850s, about the time they became closely identified with the middle class and the dominant values of society. Finke and Stark contrast Methodists with the Baptists, who began as a movement among the same class of people as the Methodists but who have retained a greater degree of sectarian suspicion of the world. Other scholars dispute this theory and object that the Methodist numbers actually grew relative to other Protestant denominations until the latter half of the twentieth century. Whatever the explanation, in 1996 the United Methodist Church in the United States had 36,559 local churches. There were 8,588,116 full members, and that figure has stabilized in the last 12 years, dropping at an average of 0.5% per annum.

See also Earl D. C. Brewer, Church-Sect Theory

—*Kevin Corn*

REFERENCES

S. M. Blumin, "The Hypothesis of Middle-Class Formation in Nineteenth-Century America," *American Historical Review* 90(1985):299-338; E. S. Bucke (ed.), *The History of American Methodism* (New York: Abingdon, 1964); N. Clark, *Deliver Us from Evil* (New York: Norton, 1976); R. H. Craig, "The Underside of History," *Methodist History* 24(1989):73-88; M. E. Dieter, *The Holiness Revival of the Nineteenth Century* (Metuchen, N.J.: Scarecrow, 1980); E. S. Gaustad, "The Pulpit and the Pews," in W. R. Hutchinson, *q.v.* (1989): 21-47; J. R. Gusfield, *Symbolic Crusade* (Urbana: University of Illinois Press, 1963); N. B. Harmon, *The Organization of the Methodist Church* (Nashville: Methodist Publishing House, 1962); W. R. Hutchinson, *Between the Times* (New York: Cambridge University Press, 1989); C. E. Jones, *The Holiness Movement and American Methodism* (Metuchen, N.J.: Scarecrow, 1974); D. G. Jones, *Perfectionist Persuasion* (Metuchen, N.J.: Scarecrow, 1979); K. A. Kerr, *Organized for Prohibition* (New Haven, Conn.: Yale University Press, 1979); J. W. Lewis, *The Protestant Experience in Gary, Indiana* (Knoxville: University of Tennessee Press, 1992); W. W. Sweet, *The Story of American Methodism* (Nashville: Abingdon Press, 1974); C. I. Wallace, "Wesleyan Heritage," in *Encyclopedia of the American Religious Experience*, ed. C. H. Lippey and P. W. Williams (New York: Scribner, 1988): 525-537; J. Wesley, *The Works of John Wesley* (London: Wesleyan Conference Office, 1872); J. F. White, *Protestant Worship* (Louisville, Ky.: Knox, 1989); C. Yrigoyen, "United Methodism," in *Encyclopedia of the American Religious Experience*, ed. C. H. Lippey and P. W. Williams (New York: Scribner, 1988): 539-553.

MIHANOVICH, CLEMENT S. (1913–)

After receiving undergraduate, A.M., and Ph.D. degrees in sociology at St. Louis University (1935-1939), Mihanovich joined the St. Louis faculty in 1938, becoming Emeritus Professor in 1981. President, American Catholic Sociological Society, 1950.

Mihanovich's contributions to the *American Catholic Sociological Review* were varied. His earliest publication in the *Review* was a study of the geographic mobility of prominent American Catholic laymen; a later article examined the social attitudes of Catholic high school seniors; a study of the legal grounds for divorce also appeared in the *Review*. Mihanovich wrote for a wide variety of publications: professional journals, newsweeklies such as *America,* family-oriented publications such as *Family Digest,* and church-related publications such as *The Missionary Servant*. His areas of later concern continued to be wide ranging, as evidenced by published studies of immigration, teenage criminals, law enforcement, and issues concerning science and technology.

—*Loretta M. Morris*

MILLENARIANISM (MILLENNIALISM)

A set of beliefs concerning end times (the "end of the world"), often including images of an apocalypse or utopian eternity of paradise.

In some versions of Judaism and Islam (especially Shī'a), millenarian expectations include the appearance of a messiah. Specifically, Christian millenarianism is usually called "millennialism" and tied to prophesy concerning the second coming of Jesus and the millennium of peace, prosperity, and righteousness that it entails.

American religion has had two broad versions of millennialism, with differing implications for this-worldly sociopolitical action. "Postmillennialism" generally conceives of the second coming as occurring at the end of the thousand-year period of righteousness; the establishment of the "Kingdom of God on Earth" is a prelude to Jesus's actual return. This vision has an affinity for worldly activism, as believers are religiously obligated to strive for the righteous social reforms that are necessary to establish the millennial period.

"Premillennialism" posits Jesus's physical return as the event that initiates the millennium of righteousness. Thus many premillennialists have eschewed social activism as pointless in affecting the course of the end times. Getting individuals "right with God" is more effective Christian activity than social change. However, comparative studies of religion and politics (Ar-jomand 1993, Fields 1985) have demonstrated that the connections between millenarian beliefs and political action are varied and complex.

Premillennialism's role in modern fundamentalism is discussed elsewhere. However, historians note that a millennialist cast flavors much of American religion, including American civil religion (e.g., Bloch 1985, Hatch 1977, Marty 1970, Miller 1956, Moorhead 1984, Tuveson 1968). Other social scientists have placed millenarian beliefs in the context of modern American culture and the social changes the nation has experienced (e.g., Barkun 1986, Boyer 1992, Hall 1987, Wright 1995, Zamora 1982).

See also Adventism, Premillennialism

—*Rhys H. Williams*

REFERENCES

S. A. Arjomand (ed.), *The Political Dimensions of Religion* (Albany: SUNY Press, 1993); M. Barkun, *Crucible of the Millennium* (Syracuse, N.Y.: Syracuse University Press, 1986); R. Bloch, *Visionary Republic* (New York: Cambridge University Press, 1985); P. Boyer, *When Time Shall Be No More* (Cambridge: Harvard Belknap Press, 1992); K. E. Fields, *Revival and Rebellion in Colonial Central Africa* (Princeton, N.J.: Princeton University Press, 1985); J. R. Hall, *Gone from the Promised Land* (New Brunswick, N.J.: Transaction, 1987); N. O. Hatch, *The Sacred Cause of Liberty* (New Haven, Conn.: Yale University Press, 1977); M. E. Marty, *Righteous Empire* (New York: Dial Press, 1970); P. Miller, *Errand into the Wilderness* (Cambridge: Harvard Belknap Press, 1956); J. H. Moorhead, "Between Progress and Apocalypse," *Journal of American History* 71(1984): 524-542; E. L. Tuveson, *Redeemer Nation* (Chicago: University of Chicago Press, 1968); S. A. Wright (ed.), *Armageddon in Waco* (Chicago: University of Chicago Press, 1995); L. P. Zamora (ed.), *The Apocalyptic Vision in America* (Bowling Green, Ohio: Bowling Green University Popular Press, 1982).

MILLER, WILLIAM/MILLERITES

see Adventism, Jehovah's Witnesses

MILLS, CHARLES WRIGHT (1916-1962)

American sociologist, born in Waco, Texas. Graduated from the Universities of Texas and Wisconsin, and taught at the University of Maryland before becoming full professor at Columbia in 1956.

Mills's most important works are *White Collar: The American Middle Classes* (Oxford University Press 1951), which is a somewhat pessimistic analysis of the changing nature of the American middle class; *The Power Elite* (Oxford University Press 1956), which presents the thesis that the United States was governed by a set of interlocking and self-perpetuating business, military, and political elites; and *The Sociological Imagination* (Oxford University Press 1959), an outline of the humanistic impulse that he considered to be essential to the discipline of sociology. He was also the author (with Hans Gerth) of *Character and Social Structure* (Routledge 1954) and coeditor and translator (with Gerth) of selections in *From Max Weber: Essays in Sociology* (Oxford University Press 1946), a volume that was critical for introducing the larger Weberian corpus to a generation of Anglo-American scholarship.

A radical on the political left who saw sociology as a means of challenging social ideas and prejudices, Mills was an influential critic of the consensus and functionalist perspectives. Although his work has been criticized for lacking a sound empirical base and for being relatively unrelated to general theories of modern society, he was an important figure in American postwar sociology as well as a significant influence on the New Left.

—*Colin Campbell*

REFERENCES

G. W. Domhoff and H. B. Ballard (eds.), *C. Wright Mills and the Power Elite* (Boston: Houghton Mifflin, 1968); J. E. Eldridge, *C. Wright Mills* (New York: Ellis Harwood, 1983).

MINISTRY   Ministry is both an office and a function designated for serving the religious, pastoral, and human needs of a group or community. It can be an individual or corporate effort, practiced intradenominationally or in conjunction with other religious groups through community service associations or coalitions.

Ministry normally takes three different forms: that of the *Word*, which involves preaching, proclamation, teaching, and evangelization; that of the *Sacrament*, or of worship, which concerns leadership of liturgy or collective ritual; and that of *Service*, which entails assisting those in need either by helping individuals or by seeking social change in sources of oppression. Usage of the term *ministry* historically has been distinctive to Christianity, stemming from the Apostle Paul's self-identification as a minister (Rom. 15:16). Luther and others during the Protestant Reformation believed that all people were called to ministry although only some to ordination, which has given rise to an emphasis upon lay as well as ordained ministry, particularly in the form of service. Some congregations or denominations place

a strong emphasis on external ministry such as missionary work, evangelization of nonbelievers, or striving for social justice through education, health care, and political or economic pressure. Others retain an internal focus on the needs of their own membership with more limited outreach activity.

Although ministry in many denominations has been undergirded with a theology of divine call to vocation and servanthood, the ministry as an occupation also has been understood to be a paid career normally beginning in young adulthood. Sociologically, it is considered to be an internal labor market bound within a denomination or tradition. Although some denominational crossover may take place, such situations are not commonplace. There is substantial evidence that ministers have tended to think of their careers in ways similar to secular occupations, such as moving up an informal job ladder to congregations of increasing size and budget and to positions of denominational influence and leadership. In socioeconomically poorer congregations, ministerial tasks and responsibilities have been handled on a part-time or nonstipendiary basis, either by ordained or by lay individuals.

Roles and Role Tension   Ministerial roles have differed in emphasis across time and religious traditions. In the early church, ministry at various points involved prophetic commitment, priestly responsibilities, and pastoral insight. Since the Reformation, Protestantism has put special emphasis on the preaching and pastoral functions. Ministers from mainline denominations emphasizing the pastoral caregiving role have tended to become involved in social reform, although countervailing beliefs in individual autonomy, relativism regarding the rightness of one's own perspective, and hesitancy to generate disagreement and possible membership decline within the congregation have produced some ministerial ambivalence over social action commitments (Jelen 1994). Ministerial roles in the black church tradition have focused primarily on preaching and on leadership for the welfare of the community as well as wider civil rights and social change activism (Harris 1993). Contemporary ministerial issues within the black church include the need for greater formalized training, concern over the persistence of sexism against female ministers, and the need to develop inclusive ministerial models that can encompass a growing diversity within the African American community (Lincoln and Mamiya 1990).

Dual commitment to congregation and family has been a major source of domestic role tension for married ministers. Additionally, marriage has been a valued occupational resource for men in the Protestant ministry, where the minister's wife normatively has been expected to volunteer a considerable amount of labor as a lay leader within the congregation. Such expectations have incurred tension as more women pursue careers or otherwise join the workforce. Expectations also have been challenged with the growing presence of male ministerial spouses, as more women enter the ministry. Blizzard's (1985) multidenominational study on Protestant ministerial roles, duties, and frictions during the 1950s was foundational in identifying a critical ministerial dilemma as one of multiple-role conflict. Subsequent studies have built on Blizzard's work, associating role ambiguity and changes in occupational self-understanding as core occupational concerns of the ministry (see Kleinman 1984, Malony and Hunt 1991). Comparative research on Roman Catholic priests has additionally focused on demographic concerns, namely, high attrition rates and growing shortages of priests.

Prestige and Professional Tensions Historically, while the ministry has offered low income compared with other professions, it has proffered a level of prestige exceeding secular occupations with similar earnings. In the past, selection for monastic or ordained orders often served as a means of upward social mobility, particularly for men otherwise not having access to formal education. Rising literacy and education have facilitated occupational and professional differentiation, which subsequently has infringed upon many traditional ministerial roles and responsibilities, depressing occupational prestige as well as contributing to occupational role tension and conflict. Other long-range factors have contributed to a decline in ministerial prestige as well. According to Douglas (1977), when religion was disenfranchised from state support, ministers became dependent upon local congregations for their subsistence, a relationship that has tended to suppress not only professional authority but also a minister's persuasive power. Conflict over ministerial authority and prestige can be manifested in congregational power struggles between clergy and laity, in disparate expectations over professional autonomy and financial compensation, in consumerist expectations by laity, and in pressure to diminish and renegotiate ministerial roles and responsibilities. Additional trends associated but not necessarily causally linked with a decline in prestige within mainline denominations include a sharp decrease in young men seeking to enter the ministry and a substantial increase in women ministers, resulting in a feminizing and graying of the occupation. Declines in church attendance and real income, and boundary issues between ministers and congregational members evident in increased litigation over sexual abuse, have further eroded occupational autonomy, authority, and prestige.

Deprofessionalization of the ministry is another trend related to declining prestige. While increased secular education and occupational role encroachment have been widely discussed as leading causes of depleting the distinctive nonsacramental functions of the ministry, Kleinman (1984) also argues that a shift in the ministry's self-understanding of professional authority, changing primarily during the 1960s and early 1970s from a traditionally elite clericalist notion of being *set apart* from lay functions by virtue of ordination, to a humanistic perspective of the minister as an enabler or facilitator for developing ministerial skills among all participants, has raised concern over what remains distinctive to the ministry as a professional occupation. Another contributor to deprofessionalization has been the decreased ability for many congregations to support full-time ministers in several denominations. Formalized ministerial pay scales and compensation packages have pressured congregational budgets and denominational willingness to supplement ministerial salaries for non-self-supporting congregations, resulting in increasing use of part-time and nonstipendiary lay pastoral ministers or those ordained only for a particular site. Due to clergy supply shortages, deprofessionalization of Roman Catholic priests' nonsacramental roles to a series of lay administrative and pastoral positions has opened up new ministerial opportunities for laity, particularly for women (Wallace 1992), although the denomination's maintenance of a male priestly class set apart through ordination keeps lay ministers peripheral to denominational leadership and decision making.

Many religious organizations also have upgraded and formalized requirements for ordained and lay ministry offices or licensing as part of a concurrent occupational *reprofessionalization* movement. Ministerial professionalization has been particularly apparent in conservative evangelical and pentecostal Protestant traditions, where ministers increasingly are holding seminary degrees and have developed both professional specializations and technological expertise. Reprofessionalization movements have recast traditional ministerial functions into highly developed concentrations in pastoral counseling, education and supervision, preaching and homiletics, administrative management, urban ministry, fund-raising, agency program development, and specialized chaplaincies for ethnic communities, hospitals and care facilities, colleges, prisons, and the workplace.

The ministry is an occupation in flux, partly owing to widespread demographic change from primarily first-career men to include both women and second-career men, and the varied backgrounds and interests they bring, and partly owing to the way the ministry must rearticulate its traditional roles in contemporary denominational environments of shifting supply and demand, differing professional needs, fresh attention to role boundaries, and increased heterogeneity within many congregations and their communities.

See also Samuel W. Blizzard, Clergy, Ordination, Roles

—*Paula D. Nesbitt*

REFERENCES

S. W. Blizzard, *The Protestant Parish Minister* (Storrs Conn.: Society for the Scientific Study of Religion, 1985); J. W. Carroll, *As One with Authority* (Louisville, Ky.: Westminster, 1991); J. D. Davidson et al., *Faith and Social Ministry* (Chicago: Loyola University Press, 1990); A. Douglas, *The Feminization of American Culture* (New York: Knopf, 1977); L. J. Francis and S. H. Jones (eds.), *Psychological Perspectives on Christian Ministry* (Leominister, U.K.: Gracewing, 1996); F. E. Harris, Sr., *Ministry for Social Crisis* (Macon, Ga.: Mercer University Press, 1993); T. G. Jelen, "Protestant Clergy as Political Leaders," *Review of Religious Research* 36(1994): 23-42; S. Kleinman, *Equals Before God* (Chicago: University of Chicago Press, 1984); C. E. Lincoln and L. H. Mamiya, *The Black Church in the African American Experience* (Durham, N.C.: Duke University Press, 1990); H. N. Malony and R. A. Hunt, *The Psychology of Clergy* (Harrisburg, Pa.: Morehouse, 1991); P. D. Nesbitt, "Marriage, Parenthood and the Ministry," *Sociology of Religion* 56(1995):397-415; H. R. Niebuhr and D. D. Williams (eds.), *The Ministry in Historical Perspectives* (San Francisco: Harper, 1983 [1956]); M. E. Reilly, "Perceptions of the Priest Role," *Sociological Analysis* 35(1975):347-356; R. A. Schoenherr and L. R. Young, *Full Pews and Empty Altars* (Madison: University of Wisconsin Press, 1993); R. A. Wallace, *They Call Her Pastor* (Albany: SUNY Press, 1992).

MISSIONS/MISSIOLOGY   World religions, especially Buddhism, Christianity, and Islam, have diffused widely over the last 2,000 years. The word *mission* comes from the Latin root, meaning "to send," and although religions have spread informally and by migration, these three religions have deliberately sent people across numerous sociocultural borders carrying their faiths to others.

Although Buddhism, along with other eastern religions, and Islam continue to spread in the world,

Christianity, which earlier had diffused northward to Europe, has spread the most dramatically since 1500 in conjunction with an exploratory, economic, political, and cultural expansion from Europe and North America. Today, numerous organizations carry out mission work, either as branches of religious bodies or as independent mission agencies.

In the Enlightenment heritage within academia and in today's religiously pluralistic world, the subject of missions is sensitive, if not viewed negatively. However, mission activity aimed at both religious conversion and the betterment of human life continues unabated. There is considerable debate in religious circles on how the two goals (conversion and human betterment) are related. However, while the debate takes place, large numbers of people change (or resist changing) their religious identities as an immediate or delayed result of missions. Furthermore, mission work not only is partly an accompaniment of social change but has also contributed enormously to social change in numerous societies. In addition to bringing about broad changes in religious identifications, other changes influenced by modern missions are the introduction of modern medicine, education, and science as well as the stirring of nationalistic aspirations and the provision of new organizational experiences.

Missiology is the formal study of missions and is especially prominent in Christianity, although it has not been a central theological discipline. Most missiologists are trained as historians as well as theologians. Some missiologists are anthropologists, and most have received some training in anthropology and many in linguistics. However, there has been considerably less interaction between the disciplines of sociology and missiology than between anthropology and missiology. For example, sociological researchers and theorists in the fields of social change, diffusion, social movements, intergroup relations, globalization, and even religion have paid relatively little attention to the phenomena of missions.

In addition to the histories of various areas and nations that throw light on missions or the diffusion of religions, there are voluminous church and agency archives and records that have been only partially mined. However, the preponderance of church and agency data are related to the sending, rather than the receiving, side of missions. An ongoing project (see Barrett 1982) to maintain statistics on Christianity and other religions in almost all countries adds to the descriptive material showing religious changes since 1900 on a worldwide basis. Case studies abound, but there continues to be relatively little theoretical work of a social scientific nature on the phenomena of missions.

—*Robert L. Montgomery*

REFERENCES

D. Barrett (ed.), *World Christian Encyclopedia* (Nairobi: Oxford University Press, 1982); R. W. Hefner (ed.), *Conversion to Christianity* (Berkeley: University of California, 1993); J. A. B. Jongeneel, *Philosophy, Science, and Theology of Mission in the 19th and 20th Centuries* (Bern, Switzerland: Lang, 1995); K. S. Latourette, *The History of the Expansion of Christianity* (New York: Harper, 1937-1945); D. Martin, *Tongues of Fire* (Oxford: Blackwell, 1990); "Mission Studies," *Missiology* 24, 1(1996); R. L. Montgomery, *The Diffusion of Religions* (Lanham, Md.: University Press of America, 1996).

MOBERG, DAVID O. (1922–)   An enormous contributor to the area of religious studies and social science. Born and reared in Minnesota, Moberg was drafted during World War II and eventually ended up on the West Coast, where he received the A.B. degree from Seattle Pacific College. He earned an M.A. from University of Washington, then returned to the University of Minnesota for a Ph.D. (1952). After 20 years at Bethel College in Minnesota, he became Professor of Sociology at Marquette University until his retirement in 1991. President, Association for the Sociology of Religion, 1977; Religious Research Association, 1982.

Moberg's career goal has been to mediate the exchange between Christianity (especially evangelical Christianity but also other traditions) and the social sciences. In pursuit of this goal, he has done much to facilitate the work of others. He played a role in the founding of the Christian Sociological Society and has been a contributor to and supporter of the Association of Christians Teaching Sociology. He has held important offices in several organizations, including Editor of the *Review of Religious Research* (1969-1973), Editor of the *Journal of the American Scientific Affiliation* (1962-1964), and founding coeditor of the annual *Research in the Social Scientific Study of Religion*. Among the projects that Moberg himself rates most important was the founding of the Association for the Development of Religious Information Systems (ADRIS), an organization dedicated to promoting a global network of religious information exchange.

In addition to his work as a facilitator of others, Moberg has been a prolific scholar in his own right, writing and editing 20 books, more than 200 book chapters and articles, 126 articles in professional journals, and almost 1,200 book reviews. Frequently cited for his research on aging and on spiritual well-being—Moberg's conceptualization of spiritual well-being as a two-dimensional phenomenon is credited by Ellison and Paloutzian as the original idea behind their widely used scale—his books *The Church as a Social Institution: The Sociology of American Religion* (Prentice Hall 1962, 1984) and *The Great Reversal: Evangelism Versus Social Concern* (Lippincott 1972, 1977) are especially highly regarded.

David Moberg has received numerous honors. Among them are two Fulbright Professorships (Netherlands, 1957-1958, and Germany, 1964-1965), the H. Paul Douglass Lecture of the Religious Research Association (1986), Inaugural Kellogg Gerontology Lectures, Southwestern Baptist Theological Seminary (1987), Frederick A. Shippey Lecturer, Drew University (1988), and the inaugural lecture of the Moberg Lectureship on Christianity and Sociology (1992) at Bethel College, plus a number of visiting professorships.

—*Larry C. Ingram*

REFERENCES

D. O. Moberg (ed.), *Spiritual Well-Being* (Washington, D.C.: University Press of America, 1979); D. O. Moberg and R. Gray, *The Church and the Older Person* (Grand Rapids, Mich.: Eerdmans, 1962, 1977).

MOBILITY (SOCIAL)   There is considerable intergenerational and intragenerational mobility in America (Blau and Duncan 1978, Featherman and Hauser 1978). Sons and daughters are more likely to rise above or fall below their parents' social standing than they are to occupy the same social status. Short-range mobility is quite extensive, with offspring being about three times as likely to rise above their parents' social standing as they are to fall below it. Dramatic mobility from the bottom of the occupational ladder to the top, or vice versa, is not common. Religion contributes to this mobility but also is affected by it.

Religion-Mobility Interactions   Several researchers have suggested that some forms of religion contribute to mobility. Johnson (1961) argued that working-class Holiness sects espouse an ascetic Protestantism that encourages a simple lifestyle, denial of luxuries and pleasure, a rational (means-end) approach to life, and economic frugality. These religious values promote planning, saving, the accumulation of disposable income, and upward social mobility (Dearman 1974).

Other researchers have argued that stringent lifestyle demands and opposition to the prevailing culture militate against upward mobility. Lenski (1961), for example, argued that Catholics' reliance on obedience to church authority and their tendency to have larger families stifled upward mobility.

Most research also suggests that social mobility contributes to movement between different religious traditions. As people's life chances improve, their religious beliefs and practices—even their religious affiliations—are likely to change.

The prevailing pattern is for members of lower status faith groups to join religious groups that are associated with more affluent strata. Baltzell (1958: 225) provides the following tongue-in-cheek description of upward switching:

> The average American is born the son of a Baptist or Methodist farmer; after obtaining an education he becomes a businessman in a large city where he joins a suburban, Presbyterian church; finally, upon achieving the acme of economic success, he joins a fashionable Episcopal church in order to satisfy his wife's social ambitions.

This classic pattern of social mobility and religious switching has been widely documented (e.g., Hoge et al. 1994, Roof and McKinney 1987). Switching has been more common among upwardly mobile Protestants than among Catholics and Jews.

Several factors contribute to mobility's tendency to promote religious change. One is the fact that religious groups differ in class, status, and power. The United Church of Christ and the Episcopal and Presbyterian churches are linked with privilege, while Baptists, Nazarenes, and other sectarian groups rank lower in socioeconomic status. As upwardly mobile individuals strive for lifestyles that are more compatible with higher status, some feel socially compelled to switch to a denomination that corresponds with their new station in life.

Another factor linking mobility to denominational switching is interfaith marriage. Upwardly mobile persons often marry persons who belong to higher status religions. The desire to share one's spouse's religious affiliation often leads to switching, even when there is no substantive change in one's religious beliefs and practices.

Upwardly mobile persons also are likely to develop new social relationships at work and in their neighborhoods. Switching to the religion of one's new friends and associates is likely to have this-worldly rewards, such as a wider circle of friends and relationships, which enhances performance on the job.

There have been several recent trends in religious switching (e.g., Hadaway and Marler 1993). First, willingness to switch faith groups seems to be increasing. This willingness reflects increased cultural individualism and religious voluntarism, which are most evident in Protestant denominations but also occur among Catholics and Jews.

Second, while liberal denominations once gained the most and conservative groups lost the most as a result of switching, today's patterns are a bit different. Mainline Protestant denominations (both liberal and moderate) and the Catholic Church are losing members more rapidly, while the net results among conservative Protestants have improved somewhat. One factor that may explain the increased retention rate among conservative Protestants may be increased economic polarization between rich and poor and the growing number of formerly middle-class persons who have lost socioeconomic status. Another factor may be the development of large, nondenominational "megachurches," churches that have sprung up along major highways in recent years. Increased cultural conservatism, sectarian groups' effectiveness in recruiting new members, and the combination of other-worldly and this-worldly rewards they offer downwardly mobile persons also contribute to this trend (Finke and Stark 1992, Perrin and Mauss 1991).

Third, several recent studies dispute the thesis that mobility plays a major role in switching (Nelsen and Snizek 1976, Hadaway 1991, Sherkat 1991, Hadaway and Marler 1993). These studies contend that mobility pales in significance compared with family influences and other social relationships.

Mobility's Effects with Groups: Church and Sect
Mobility often spawns changes within religious groups. As working-class sects evolve into middle-class denominations, they tend to change their religious norms and practices (Finke and Stark 1992). Sectarian beliefs emphasizing absolute truth, the highly emotional expressions of faith associated with revivals, and distinctive practices such as snake-handling or Catholics' use of Latin at Mass often give way to more churchlike emphases on relative and symbolic interpretations, more sedate forms of religious participation, and more culturally acceptable styles of worship. Sectarian emphasis on evangelizing others also may give way to the live-and-let-live approach that seems more compatible with affluent status. These transformations have been especially evident in groups, such as United Methodists and Catholics, that have experienced a great deal of social mobility.

Thus, even when mobility does not produce changes in affiliation, it often fosters changes in what people believe and how they practice their faith. It discourages working-class beliefs and practices and encourages beliefs and practices that are seen as more compatible with a middle- or upper-class lifestyle.

While some members approve of such changes, others do not. Dissidents feel the group has lost its roots, forsaken its original principles, and turned its back on the truth. A frequent step is for dissenters to form their own sect, with the goal of returning to the group's original worldview. Finke and Stark (1992) argue that sect transformation and reformation are at the heart of American religious history.

See also Geographic Mobility, Stratification

—*James D. Davidson and Ralph E. Pyle*

REFERENCES

E. D. Baltzell, *Philadelphia Gentlemen* (Englewood Cliffs, N.J.: Prentice Hall, 1958); P. Blau and O. D. Duncan, *The American Occupational Structure* (New York: Free Press, 1978); M. Dearman, "Christ and Conformity," *Journal for the Scientific Study of Religion* 13(1974):437-453; D. Featherman and R. Hauser, *Opportunity and Change* (New York: Academic Press, 1978); R. Finke and R. Stark, *The Churching of America* (New Brunswick, N.J.: Rutgers University Press, 1992); C. K. Hadaway, "Denominational Switching, Social Mobility, and Membership Trends," in *A Case Study of Mainstream Protestantism*, ed. N. Williams (Grand Rapids, Mich.: Eerdmans, 1991): 491-508; C. K. Hadaway and P. L. Marler, "All in the Family," *Review of Religious Research* 35(1993):97-116; D. Hoge et al., *Vanishing Boundaries* (Louisville, Ky.: Westminster, 1994); B. Johnson, "Do Holiness Sects Socialize in Dominant Values?" *Social Forces* 39(1961):309-316; G. Lenski, *The Religious Factor* (Garden City, N.Y.: Doubleday, 1961); H. M. Nelsen and W. E. Snizek, "Musical Pews," *Sociology and Social Research* 60(1976):279-289; R. D. Perrin and A. L. Mauss, "Saints and Seekers," *Review of Religious Research* 33(1991):97-111; W. C. Roof and W. McKinney, *American Mainline Religion* (New Brunswick, N.J.: Rutgers University Press, 1987); D. E. Sherkat, "Leaving the Faith," *Social Science Research* 20(1991):171-187.

MODERNISM   In social scientific usage, encompasses the distinctive features of modern societies and the distinctive problems associated with social change in the modern era; also used to refer to intellectual discussion of such matters, that is, the discourse of modernity.

Modernism/modernity is the central concern of sociology as a discipline. Many of its classic texts systematically reflect on the differences between "modern" and "traditional" societies. In its early period, sociology aimed to illuminate, with new theoretical tools, the changes that were remaking Europe and America. Concretely, it dealt with the consequences of industrialization and urbanization in leading nation-states. More generally, it was part of a broader debate about the meaning of change, which had long pitted conservatives against more liberal intellectuals. Since at least the French Revolution, the place of religion had been a central issue in these debates, with conservatives arguing for the validity of the Christian faith and its central role in upholding an authoritative hierarchical order. Sociology addressed many problems first raised by conservatives, but generally did not provide support for the conservative position. That position was articulated clearly by the Roman Catholic Church, which resisted the theological implications of the scientific and democratic revolutions at the end of the nineteenth century. Pope Pius X condemned modernism as the "synthesis of all heresies."

Since the nineteenth century, students of modernity have answered five questions, implicitly or explicitly: What is new? How did it come about? Is it viable? Is it valuable? Is it still here? Each of the classic contributions to sociology offers an argument or narrative touching on all five. Each also had specific implications for religion. Marx offered the critical view: Under capitalism, religion is part of the dominant ideology, a relatively insignificant part of the superstructure; it cannot prevent the demise of capitalism and is unlikely to survive the coming revolutionary changes. Weber's stance was more skeptical: Certain Christian ideas historically played a central role in making the rise of Western capitalism possible, but religious faith becomes a matter of hard individual choice in a rationalized world no longer governed by shared tradition. Durkheim's version was progressive: New sacred symbols will arise to express and bolster the more complex solidarity that is typical of modern societies; this maintains a role for religion, although not in any of its traditional forms. For them, as for many nineteenth-century authors, religion was crucially involved in identifying what was new; their arguments about the viability and worth of modernity often presumed a traditional religious foil. By advocating the dispassionate study of religious phenomena, the social scientists already allied themselves with the forces of modernity lamented by religious conservatives. Indeed, sociology itself could reasonably be viewed, then and now, as one agent of secularization.

Much of the subsequent debate about the place of religion in modern societies revolved around the issue of secularization. Extending Durkheim, Talcott Parsons held that at least modern American society had generalized originally Christian values in a manner that could integrate a modern social structure. Peter Berger countered with a more Weberian view of religion as bound to be privatized. Similarly extending Weber, Bryan Wilson came to view religion as the culture of community, no longer viable in a *gesellschaft* context and thus bound to lose its social significance. Critics of the latter two arguments contend that they overestimate the extent to which modernity produces a break with the past, that they assume an untenable golden age of religion, that religion remains a vital presence in the lives of many individuals and groups, and that our overall conceptions of religious modernism remain beholden to misleading nineteenth-century debates. The ongoing debate about secularization in fact reflects broader trends in analyses of modernity.

One of these trends is the growing inclination of scholars to question whether modernity represents a genuinely new historical phase. Historical evidence suggests considerable continuity in many areas, and older interpretations of modernity often imposed simplifying stories on that evidence. To contemporary skeptics, for example, postmodernists, such accounts often aimed uncritically to prove the viability and value of modernity. Whatever features they singled out as characteristic of modernity now appear irrelevant in any case, because all societies are being drastically transformed—or so such postmodernists might hold. But in all these areas, the debate about modernism—its historical status, viability, and value—continues. Contemporary modernists would hold that, taken together, the last two centuries of change have indeed transformed the lives of people in the West. Their societies, democratic-capitalist nation-states, now display a high degree of structural differentiation and cultural pluralism. In this world of rationalized institutions, religion indeed is "deregulated" (Beckford 1989), as one set of institutions and worldviews among many, still providing sustenance to individuals and symbolic tools to the society at large. Although they have not produced a clear consensus, the social sciences themselves have helped to provide a more profound and coherent interpretation of modernizing change. Liberal modernity has demonstrated an unreasonable viability, and so has the scholarly enterprise to make sense of it.

In the now-classic period of sociology, religion was a prominent concern; today this is no longer true for many scholars interested in the viability and value of modernity, however conceived. Secularization has made inroads. This is not to say that the study of religion has lost any connection with the broader study of modernity in all its facets. For example, the debate about secularization continues, although the ambiva-

lence of many participants is telling. The comparative study of religious institutions and movements promises to shed light on the variable role and vitality of religion in different societies. Students of religion also have much to offer with analyses of ostensibly antimodern movements staged by self-professed religious conservatives or fundamentalists, which have repeatedly challenged the premises and consequences of modernity. Indeed, their studies of that subject help to lay bare some critical fault lines in modern societies. Finally, religion remains an important dimension of global conflict. The study of globalization likely will change the conventional understanding of modernity as a property of individual nation-states. Thus the study of religion as a global phenomenon and of religious leaders as global actors will preserve its relevance to the scholarly analysis of modern culture.

See also Postmodernism

—*Frank J. Lechner*

REFERENCES

J. A. Beckford, *Religion and Advanced Industrial Society* (London: Unwin Hyman, 1989); P. L. Berger, *The Sacred Canopy* (Garden City, N.Y.: Doubleday, 1967); A. Giddens, *The Consequences of Modernity* (Stanford, Calif.: Stanford University Press, 1990); H. Haferkamp and N. Smelser (eds.), *Social Change and Modernity* (Berkeley: University of California Press, 1992); L. R. Kurtz, *The Politics of Heresy* (Berkeley: University of California Press, 1986); F. J. Lechner, "The Case Against Secularization," *Social Forces* 69(1991):1103-1119; F. J. Lechner, "Against Modernity," in *The Dynamics of Social Systems*, ed. P. Colomy (London: Sage, 1992): 72-92; B. Turner, *Theories of Modernity and Postmodernity* (London: Sage, 1990); B. Wilson, *Religion in Sociological Perspective* (Oxford: Oxford University, 1982).

MOHAMMED, MOHAMMEDANS   *see* Islam, Nation of Islam

MOL, JOHANNES (HANS) J. (1922–)

Professor in the Department of Religious Studies, McMaster University, Hamilton, Ontario, until his retirement (to Australia) in 1987. Born in the Netherlands, Mol immigrated to Australia and then the United States. He studied theology and worked as a pastor in both countries before completing his Ph.D. in sociology in 1960 at Columbia. Prior to McMaster, he taught at Canterbury University (New Zealand), Australian National University, and briefly at a number of American universities. He served on the Council of the International Sociological Association (1966-1970) and as Secretary (1970-1974) and President (1974-1978) of its Research Committee 22.

The author or editor of a dozen books (e.g., 1969, 1971, 1972) and many articles on aspects of religion in Australia, Canada, and elsewhere, Mol is best known for his neo-functionalist, general social scientific theory of religion focused on the "sacralization of identity" presented in such works as *Identity and the Sacred* (Free Press 1976), the edited volume *Identity and Religion* (Sage 1978), and *The Firm and the Formless* (Wilfrid Laurier University Press 1982). Setting religion against a natural and social dialectic of processes of integration and differentiation, and positing a fundamental human need for secure identity, Mol provides a sophisticated discussion of how religions operate to regulate symbolic and social changes so as to perpetuate personal, group, and social identities. In every instance, Mol stresses, these identities are both congruent and in conflict. The process of sacralizing identities is analyzed in terms of four interrelated "mechanisms": objectification, commitment, ritual, and myth. This perspective leads Mol to be relatively optimistic about the continued relevance of religion to modern societies.

—*Lorne Dawson*

REFERENCES

J. J. Mol, *Christianity in Chains* (Melbourne: Nelson, 1969); J. J. Mol, *Religion in Australia* (Melbourne: Nelson, 1971); J. J. Mol (ed.), *Western Religion* (The Hague: Mouton, 1972).

MONASTICISM   *see* Communal Groups, Orders

MOODY, DWIGHT L. (MOODY BIBLE INSTITUTE)   *see* Televangelism

MOON, SUNG MYUNG (THE REVEREND MOON)   *see* Unification Church

MOONIES   *see* Unification Church

MORAL COMMUNITY   In Émile Durkheim's whole discussion of religion and quite explicitly in his definition, the idea of *moral community* figures prominently.

Durkheim defined *religion* as "a unified system of beliefs and practices relative to sacred things, that is to say set apart and forbidden, beliefs and practices which unite into one single moral community, called a church,

all those who adhere to them" (1965 [1912]: 62). Thus he stated unequivocally that religion is not primarily a false science, nor is a belief in supernatural beings and powers its most distinguishing characteristic. Instead, religion is quintessentially social, a product of the collective life and an embodiment of the moral requisites of human social existence. For Durkheim, humans are religious because they are members of collectivities, and neither individuals nor groups can long exist without religious—that is to say, moral—constraint.

It has been noted that Durkheim's definition of *religion* is more than a definition; it is a theory of the sociological import of religion. Durkheim not only isolates criteria that mark off religion—beliefs and practices centered on the sacred—but goes on to state that because of their peculiar effect on the consciousness and moral sensibility of individuals, these criteria create a moral community, or church. It is also noteworthy that Durkheim equates church with moral community, a conflation that perhaps seems wrong today in an era of sectarian rivalries and violent conflicts. Durkheim's definition leaves open the possibility of inclusion within the general rubric of *religion* various moral communities that would not be considered religious if belief in the supernatural is taken to be definitive. Hence, from the broad Durkheimian perspective, support groups (Wuthnow 1994) espousing broadly varying beliefs and purposes can be said to embrace a religious (meaning *moral*) significance. To avoid this confusion, it is perhaps preferable to treat religious communities as one type of moral community (see, for example, Lenski 1961).

—*Edward B. Reeves*

REFERENCES

É. Durkheim, *The Elementary Forms of the Religious Life* (New York: Free Press, 1965 [1912]); G. Lenski, *The Religious Factor* (Garden City, N.Y.: Doubleday, 1961); R. Wuthnow, *Sharing the Journey* (New York: Free Press, 1994).

MORAL DEVELOPMENT   A developmental model of moral thinking based on Jean Piaget's cognitive development theory. Because religion is closely intertwined with values and morality, this field of research is highly relevant to religion. Additionally, some theorists insist that a change in stage of moral thinking is such a profound transformation that it amounts to a kind of conversion experience.

Lawrence Kohlberg, the foremost scholar associated with this paradigm on morality, maintained that all persons, regardless of religious background or culture, move through the same sequence of stages. Kohlberg's research was conducted by giving children moral dilemmas in which two values are in conflict. Based on longitudinal studies with the same individuals over two decades, he has identified three levels of thinking with two stages at each level, six stages in all. Each stage represents an increased ability to place oneself in a role more removed from oneself.

Preconventional thinking: At this level, the person is entirely *egocentric* in outlook. There are two stages at the preconventional level. In the first of these, punishment-obedience, the child is concerned first and foremost about obeying superiors to avoid punishment. The stage 2 person is more calculating in determining right from wrong, showing willingness to risk the possibility of being caught and punished if the potential reward is great enough. A person at this stage engages in a cost-benefit analysis with his or her own needs and desires as the criteria for evaluation of cost and benefit. The concept of justice or fairness in relationships is guided by reciprocity. The bottom line in any relationship at stage 2 is the question: "What's in it for me?"

Conventional level: Conformity to the social group takes on extreme importance, and values become *ethnocentric* rather than egocentric. Stage 3, interpersonal sharing, is oriented toward pleasing significant others or conforming to a reference group so as to be liked. The stage 3 person wants to conform to the expectations of those with whom she or he has a face-to-face relationship. Stage 4 represents an awareness that survival of a society requires laws, and it requires that the citizens obey the laws. Maintenance of the social order at all costs becomes the criterion for "right." The circle of loyalties has expanded beyond one's immediate acquaintances; one's loyalties now include one's nation or ethnic group.

Principled level: Thinking at this level is more abstract; one considers many more factors to determine a just solution to a problem and attempts to be universalistic in concern. The fifth stage, social contract thinking, involves thinking about how to construct a legal system (a social contract) in which the rights of each individual can be protected. Laws must be fair to all members of that society, and due process is essential. Stage 6, the universal ethical principle orientation, emphasizes respect for human personality as a supreme value. Moral decisions are based on logical, comprehensive, and universalistic ethical principles.

The most serious flaw in Kohlberg's work was that he used only males in his original studies, and the model of stage development was built on the basis of his early data. One former associate of Kohlberg, Carol Gilligan, insists that the stages of development are rather different for girls and women from those for boys and men.

Kohlberg (1927-1987) was Professor of Education and Social Psychology at Harvard University at the time of his death. He received his Ph.D. from the University of Chicago in 1958.

See also Cognitive Models, Carol Gilligan

—*Keith A. Roberts*

REFERENCES

C. Gilligan, *In a Different Voice* (Cambridge: Harvard University Press, 1982); L. Kohlberg, *Essays on Moral Development,* 2 vols. (New York: Harper, 1981, 1984); J. Piaget, *The Moral Judgement of the Child* (New York: Free Press, 1965 [1932]); M. M. Wilcox, *Developmental Journey* (Nashville: Abingdon, 1979).

MORALITY Viewed cross-culturally, religion is second only to kinship in providing a foundation for social solidarity based on ties of interpersonal and collective obligation. Pointing up this close affinity between religion and morality was a central premise of Émile Durkheim's sociology:

Howsoever complex the outward manifestations of the religious life may be, at bottom it is one and simple. It responds everywhere to one and the same need, and is everywhere derived from one and the same mental state. In all its forms, its object is to raise man above himself and to make him lead a life superior to that which he would lead, if he followed his own individual whims: beliefs express this life in representations; rites organize it and regulate its working. (1965 [1912]: 461)

Underlying this and similar discussions was a persistently recurring note, namely, Durkheim's insistence on the separateness of the moral sphere from the appetitive, and the association of the former with the sacred charter of religion and the latter with the profane activities of daily existence. For Durkheim, religion did not simply serve a function of promoting morality; morality was its essential nature. Defining religion in this way caused him to equate religion with the existence of a *moral community.*

Durkheim's essentialist and reductionist position has provoked frequent criticism. Nevertheless, the social sciences have benefitted immensely by following Durkheim's lead and investigating religious beliefs and practices as embodiments of social values and moral precepts that are internalized by individuals through religious socialization. By specifying what the gods want people to do or to avoid doing, religions can be seen to support directly norms of social behavior. Further, religions explain why these norms exist and why they must be obeyed. Murder and theft are not simply violations of human law, they violate commandments laid down by the gods and will be punished by supernatural sanctions, whether or not the culprit is brought to justice by human authorities. As a consequence, religious beliefs and their associated practices can be a major force in legitimating and sanctioning social norms.

Research suggests that religious socialization received early in life has a moderate, continuing ability to influence the individual's conformity with moral values and precepts, but it is far more effective when there exists a community of believers to reinforce the morality so that the individual need not stand up to temptation alone. This capacity of religious community to sustain morality has been demonstrated in the United States by studies that show that cities with high church membership rates have lower rates of crime, suicide, venereal disease, and alcoholism than cities with low church membership rates (Stark et al. 1980, Stark et al. 1982, Stark et al. 1983).

Cross-national survey data also support a close relationship between religion and morality. There are significant correlations of individuals' religious beliefs and practices with their attitudes toward a wide variety of moral issues, including sympathy for AIDS victims, opposition to capital punishment, support for government intervention in favor of the unemployed and the poor, support for environmental preservation, and opposition to cheating on taxes (Greeley 1995).

One implication of the linkage between religion and morality is that moral compassion ends at the boundary of the religious community. In tribal societies and primitive states, religious conceptions of communal belonging and morality are typically ethnocentric; the religion of outsiders is harmful to the interests of one's own community (Clendinnen 1991; Redfield 1953). In agrarian states, different religious systems supporting different moral communities often have coexisted (if somewhat uneasily) under a central political authority. A striking example of this was the millet system of indirect rule adopted during the Ottoman Empire. Religio-ethnic communities of Jews and Christians were permitted to be largely self-governing as long as they paid taxes to the Sultanate and maintained internal order according to the moral code of their respective religious traditions. In contemporary urban-industrial societies, overt conflicts between religious communities are effectively suppressed for the most part, although Protestant-Catholic clashes in Northern Ireland and Christian-Muslim warfare in Bosnia-Herzegovina provide stark evidence to the contrary. And even when overt conflict is suppressed, the prevalence of religious prejudice (Glock and Stark 1966) is testimony to the fact that the moral obligations owed one's coreligionists do not extend to outsiders.

One of the reigning theoretical ideas in the social sciences is that religiously informed morality undergoes change as societies themselves grow more differentiated and complex. Two illustrations of this idea will be cited. First, it was Durkheim's thesis that the extreme division of labor and individualism characteristic of modern industrial societies would result in a broad desacralization of everything except the individual. The prevalence of "cult of man" groups as an increasingly prominent feature of present-day advanced industrial societies has been put forward as evidence that supports Durkheim's thesis (Westley 1983). A related development is the advent of religious fundamentalisms with their vehemently antisecular, antimodernist beliefs and morality. Interviews with American fundamentalists, for instance, suggest strongly that their faith is centered on the restoration of a moral community to stand as a bulwark against the tide of individualism, amorality, and immorality that in the view of fundamentalists is flooding modern secular life (Bellah et al. 1985).

See also Émile Durkheim, Moral Community

—*Edward B. Reeves*

REFERENCES

R. N. Bellah et al., *Habits of the Heart* (New York: Harper, 1985); I. Clendinnen, *Aztecs* (New York: Cambridge University Press, 1991); É. Durkheim, *The Elementary Forms of the Religious Life* (New York: Free Press, 1965 [1912]); C. Y. Glock and R. Stark, *American Piety and Anti-Semitism* (New York: Harper, 1966); A. M. Greeley, *Religion as Poetry* (New Brunswick, N.J.: Transaction, 1995); R. Redfield, *The Primitive World and Its Transformations* (Ithaca, N.Y.: Cornell University Press, 1953); R. Stark et al., "Rediscovering Moral Communities," in *Understanding Crime*, ed. T. Hirschi and M. Gottfredson (Beverly Hills, Calif.: Sage, 1980): 43-52; R. Stark et al., "Religion and Delinquency," *Journal of Research in Crime and Delinquency* 19(1982):2-24; R. Stark et al., "Beyond Durkheim," *Journal for the Scientific Study of Religion* 22(1983):120-131; F. Westley, *The Complex Forms of the Religious Life* (Chico, Calif.: Scholars Press, 1983).

MORAL MAJORITY *see* Christian Right, Tele-vangelism

MORMONISM The popular, colloquial name for the Church of Jesus Christ of Latter-day Saints, founded in upstate New York in 1830 on the basis of revelations claimed by Joseph Smith, the founding prophet. In its Christian primitivism and antinomianism, it was akin to many other "restorationist" movements, such as the Campbellites, which emerged at about the same time in the "burned over district" (Shipps 1985). From the beginning, however, it distinguished itself from cognate movements by its claims of (1) the restoration of exclusive apostolic authority or priesthood to the new prophet and his closest associates; (2) a reopened canon, with many new divine revelations through modern prophets to complement the Holy Bible; and (3) the Book of Mormon, chief among the new revelations, and the obvious source of the church's colloquial name (Arrington and Bitton 1992, O'Dea, 1957).

Historical Overview During the first few years, the theology of Mormonism, while innovative in certain respects, was not remarkably different from that of its sectarian cousins on the "left" of the Christian spectrum of the time, particularly in its theodicy, Christology, soteriology, and eschatology. However, starting especially in the 1840s, Joseph Smith and his successor prophets began to promulgate a series of new revelations and doctrines that moved Mormonism in a sharply heterodox direction relative to the Protestant heritage from which it had emerged. Since then, mainstream Protestantism, especially the more evangelical and fundamentalist varieties, has generally been unwilling to consider Mormons as part of the Christian family, despite the continuing Mormon claims to being the one, true, authentic church of Jesus Christ, restored to usher in a new dispensation of the fullness of the Gospel.

The nineteenth-century history of the Mormon movement is probably the most turbulent of any American-born religion. Between 1830 and 1846, the ever-increasing Mormon flock moved from New York to northern Ohio, then to western Missouri, and then to southwestern Illinois, where they established their own city of Nauvoo with about 10,000 souls, plus a few others in surrounding communities (Flanders 1965). Each move occurred under pressure from severe persecution, including regular mob action, for this period was well before the "equal protection" amendments to the federal constitution passed after the Civil War. The Mormon flight from Missouri in early 1839, indeed, was in response to an order from

the state governor himself that Mormons must either leave or be exterminated. While the Mormon religious claims were themselves the objects of considerable ridicule, and no doubt some indignation as well, the persecution was a reaction less to the Mormons' heterodoxy than to their real and imagined political and economic dominance, as they moved en masse from one location to another, each time claiming God's sanction for possession of their new homeland. The founding prophet Smith was finally assassinated by a mob in 1844 while awaiting trial on a dubious charge in Carthage, near Nauvoo. A year and a half later, in early 1846, the eastern U.S. chapter of Mormon history came to an end with the final Mormon exodus from Nauvoo to the far west in Utah.

Brigham Young emerged from the postassassination turmoil as the successor to Smith and proved an exceptionally able organizer with a somewhat authoritarian style. In Mormon lore, the saga of thousands of emigrants crossing the Great Plains in wagons and afoot rivals the story of the Israelites in the Book of Exodus. The parallel was complete when the "promised land" in Utah, like that of Palestine, proved also to have a salty sea and a fresh-water lake connected by a river. Both geographic separation and the growing North-South strife in the rest of America conspired to provide the Mormons some respite from persecution, so they were free for a while to experiment with certain new institutions (Arrington 1958). Chief among these were theocratic government, communal economic projects, and (most notorious of all) "plural marriage" or polygamy (actually, polygyny), the latter having been already started secretly on a small scale in Nauvoo. It was these experiments, more than anything else, that guaranteed several more decades of hostile relations between the Mormons and the rest of the country, including an episode in 1856-1857 misnamed "the Utah War," in which bloodshed was actually averted by the Mormons' preemptive "commando tactics," on the one hand, and, on the other hand, by their willingness to accept a new non-Mormon territorial governor in place of Young. Nevertheless, after the Civil War, the federal government launched an escalating legislative and judicial campaign against Mormon polygamy that eventually disincorporated the church and threatened a military occupation of Utah.

Only then, in 1890, did the Mormons officially abandon polygamy, although it persisted underground for a few more decades and eventually produced sectarian schisms (Hardy 1992). In 1896, after the Mormons had also replaced their theocratic civil form of government with the regular American two-party system, the new state of Utah was admitted to the federal union (Lyman 1986). During the next century, the Mormons sought conscientiously to "live down" their nineteenth-century disrepute and to accept a more or less complete Americanization (Alexander 1986). The main Mormon preoccupations of the twentieth century were (1) the struggle to maintain a distinctive way of life while still enjoying the advantages of American assimilation and respectability (Gottlieb and Wiley 1984, Mauss 1994, O'Dea 1957, Shepherd and Shepherd 1984) and (2), somewhat paradoxically, a gigantic missionary effort to export around the world a Mormonism free of conspicuous American cultural taints.

Before the end of the century, worldwide Mormon membership had surpassed 10 million, about evenly distributed between North America and the rest of the world, but mostly in Latin America. Nearly half of all the world's Mormons, indeed, were Spanish-speaking by then. Rapid Mormon growth during the second half of the century has suggested to some non-Mormon scholars the prospect that we might be seeing the rise of the first new world religion since Islam (Shipps 1985, Stark 1984). Other non-Mormon scholars (e.g., Bloom 1992, Leone 1979) have been more intrigued by the relationship between Mormonism and American culture itself, seeing in Mormonism not only an authentic new religion but indeed a uniquely American one.

Early Social Science Literature   Very little scholarly literature on the Mormons appeared until the middle of the twentieth century. Publications prior to that time were mostly the work of journalists and travelers, who tended to regard Mormons with contempt and ridicule, usually with special and salacious attention to the institution of polygamy. Even the few publications by scholars tended to carry that same general tone. A definite exception was historian Hubert H. Bancroft's *History of Utah* (1889 [Nevada Publications 1981]), which even now is very useful as a balanced and reliable source on early Utah and the Mormons. Another exception was social economist Richard Ely's article in *Harper's* magazine (1903), which hailed (indeed, exaggerated) Mormon success in communal economic experiments and contained the startling claim that "the organization of the Mormons is the most nearly perfect piece of social mechanism with which I have ever . . . come in contact, excepting alone the German army," a much greater compliment at the end of the nineteenth century than it would have been at the end of the twentieth.

It was, indeed, the rural economic life of the Mormons that constituted the earliest focus of serious scholarly work, according to Arrington (1966), due in part to the influence on American social scientists of German social and economic historians of the fin de siècle, some

of whom themselves even wrote on the Mormons. Ely himself had studied with these German scholars (and had apparently at the same time acquired his admiration for the German army). The work of Arrington and others in midcentury was much informed by the work of these few early economic historians (e.g., Arrington 1958, Nelson 1952). A second prominent theme in studies on Mormons from early on has been family and fertility, starting, understandably, with polygynous families (e.g., Young 1954), a preoccupation that has scarcely abated even in more recent times (Foster 1981, Hardy 1992). One does see, however, a broadening of interest in Mormon family life to more conventional issues later in the twentieth century, such as family governance and socialization, sex and reproduction, and spousal relationships (e.g., Heaton 1994).

Recent Social Science Literature   The relative paucity of work on the Mormons in the first decades of the twentieth century, especially beyond the foci on economy, community, and family, can be attributed partly to the hiatus in the sociology of religion more generally and partly to the shortage of home-grown Mormon social scientists during that period. From midcentury on, however, a great flowering is apparent in social scientific studies on the Mormons, most of it (but by no means all) by scholars of Mormon background. This work has retained to some extent the earlier concerns with family and community but has gone well beyond those to studies of Mormon religiosity and its consequences, Mormon political orientations and influence, Mormon public images and image-making, Mormon interethnic relationships, Mormon women and sex roles, and the general topic of the impact on Mormons of modernization and secularization (see these categories in the bibliographies and bibliographic essays of Arrington 1966, Bahr and Forste 1986, Mauss 1984, Mauss and Reynolds 1998).

The Mormon preoccupation with genealogy and family histories, furthermore, has made available an enormous cache of cross-generational data for historical demographic studies, including the relation between genetics and morbidity, producing several federally financed projects based at the University of Utah (e.g., Bean et al. 1978, 1980). Many other potentially interesting aspects of Mormon culture have, however, been slighted in the social scientific literature. These include anthropological topics such as myth, ritual, values, folk religion, and syncretism. A few works by anthropologists nevertheless have appeared, starting with those derived from Kluckhohn's five-cultures project at Harvard in the 1950s (e.g., Vogt and Albert 1966, O'Dea 1957) and the early work on Mormon folklore by Fife and Fife (1956) as well as a few more recent works (Leone 1979, Wilson 1976). Other neglected topics include organizational governance and control, intellectual history, dissent and defection, education and its impact, crime and deviance among the Mormons, and, perhaps most conspicuous of all in a rapidly growing international religion, any scholarly work to speak of on Mormons outside the United States (in any language). To be sure, there is a smattering of work on these topics, but very little.

Readers wishing to know more about peaks and valleys in Mormon studies might wish to consult the bibliographical works cited earlier. A useful sampling of late-twentieth-century social science research on Mormons will be found in the anthology edited by Cornwall et al. (1994). Those wishing to pursue scholarly studies of the Mormons would also do well to consult several periodicals privately published by Mormon scholars, which are generally well refereed and free of church control: *Brigham Young University Studies* (published since 1959), *Dialogue: A Journal of Mormon Thought* (since 1966), *Journal of Mormon History* (since 1974), and *Sunstone* magazine (since 1975). These publications are quite eclectic and are not devoted exclusively to social science, but they tend to contain many articles in the social science genre. An important general source on a great variety of Mormon topics is the *Encyclopedia of Mormonism,* published in 1992 by the Macmillan Company with the cooperation (and thus the influence) of the Mormon Church.

—*Armand L. Mauss*

REFERENCES

T. S. Alexander, *Mormonism in Transition* (Urbana: University of Illinois Press, 1986); L. J. Arrington, *Great Basin Kingdom* (Cambridge: Harvard University Press, 1958); L. J. Arrington, "Scholarly Studies of Mormonism in the Twentieth Century," *Dialogue* 1(1966):15-132; L. J. Arrington and D. Bitton, *The Mormon Experience*, 2nd ed. (Urbana: University of Illinois Press, 1992); H. M. Bahr and R. T. Forste, "Toward a Social Science of Contemporary Mormondom," *BYU Studies* 26(1986):73-121; L. L. Bean et al., "The Mormon Historical Demography Project," *Historical Methodology* 11(1978):45-53; L. L. Bean et al., "The Genealogical Society of Utah as a Data Resource for Historical Demography," *Population Index* 46(1980):6-19; H. Bloom, *The American Religion* (New York: Simon & Schuster, 1992); M. Cornwall et al. (eds.), *Contemporary Mormonism* (Urbana: University of Illinois Press, 1994); R. T. Ely, "Economic Aspects of Mormonism," *Harper's* 106(1903):667-678; A. Fife and A. Fife, *Saints of Sage and Saddle* (Salt Lake City: University of Utah Press, 1956); R. B. Flanders, *Nauvoo* (Urbana: University of Illinois Press, 1965); L. Foster, *Religion and Sexuality* (New York: Oxford University Press, 1981); R. Gottlieb and P. Wiley, *America's Saints* (New York: Putnam, 1984); B. C. Hardy, *Solemn Covenant* (Urbana: University of Illinois Press, 1992); T. B. Heaton, "In Search of a Peculiar People," in Cornwall et al., *q.v.* (1994): 87-117; M. P. Leone, *Roots of Modern Mormonism* (Cambridge: Harvard University Press, 1979); E. L. Lyman, *Political Deliverance* (Urbana: University of Illinois Press, 1986); A. L. Mauss, "Sociological Perspectives on the Mormon Subculture," *Annual Review of Sociology* 10(1984):437-460; A. L. Mauss, *The Angel and the Beehive* (Urbana: University of Illinois Press, 1994); A. L. Mauss and D. I. Reynolds, "Bibliography of Twentieth-Century Social Science Works on Mormonism," in *Comprehensive Bibliography of Historical Works on Mormonism*, ed. J. B. Allen et al. (Urbana: University of Illinois Press, 1998); L. Nelson, *The Mormon Village* (Salt Lake City: University of Utah Press, 1952); T. F. O'Dea, *The Mormons* (Chicago: University of Chicago Press, 1957); G. Shepherd and G. Shepherd, *A Kingdom Transformed* (Salt Lake City: University of Utah Press, 1984); J. Shipps, *Mormonism* (Urbana: University of Illinois Press, 1985); R. Stark, "The Rise of a New World Faith," *Review of Religious Research* 26(1984):18-27; E. Z. Vogt and E. M. Albert, *The People of Rimrock* (New York: Atheneum, 1966); W. A. Wilson, "A Bibliography of Studies in Mormon Folklore," *Utah Historical Quarterly* 44(1976):389-394; K. Young, *Isn't One Wife Enough?* (New York: Holt, 1954).

MOSLEMS   *see* Islam

MOTIVE (MOTIVATION)   Conventionally considered to refer to any condition or event within an organism that impels or directs behavior toward the attainment of a goal; current sociological usage differs radically from this usage.

For Max Weber, the concept of motive, defined as "a complex of subjective meaning which seems to the actor himself or to the observer an adequate ground for the conduct in question" (1964: 98), was central to *wissenschaftlich* ("scientific") sociology. For, once an individual's action had been identified through a process of direct observation, the sociologist was required to engage in "explanatory" or "motivational" understanding of the act. However, this central role accorded to motive in the sociological analysis of action was not echoed by subsequent generations.

Specifically, C. Wright Mills (1940) radically shifted the focus of attention from an inquiry into motive considered as either an initiating or a maintaining force, or even as the reason or reasons for an action, to the words employed in the process of justifying it to others. Thus Mills (together with Burke 1969) helped to initiate the "vocabulary of motives" tradition of inquiry that has come to predominate within the discipline of sociology, an approach subsequently endorsed by Lyman and Scott (1989 [1964]) and Blum and McHugh (1971).

This approach, which has lasted to the present day, effectively treats human conduct as if it were unmotivated, while focusing instead on the topic of "motive talk" (Semin and Manstead 1983). Contemporary sociologists have largely accepted this approach (although see Campbell [1996] for a strongly dissenting view), espousing a broadly functional theory concerning the way that actors' accounts serve to meet the needs experienced in social situations, and thus serve as "justifications," "excuses," "apologies," or "disclaimers" for their actions. Consequently, the study of motives, in the Weberian sense, is absent from contemporary social science.

Motivation is a psychological term not widely employed in social science. It refers to any organismic state that mobilizes activity that is in some sense selective, or directive, with respect to the environment.

—*Colin Campbell*

REFERENCES

A. F. Blum and P. McHugh, "The Social Ascription of Motives," *American Sociological Review* 36(1971):98-109; K. Burke, *A Rhetoric of Motives* (Berkeley: University of California Press, 1969); C. Campbell, "On the Concept of Motive in Sociology," *Sociology* 30(1996):1-14; S. M. Lyman and M. B. Scott, *A Sociology of the Absurd* (Dix Hills, N.Y.: General Hall, 1989 [1970]); C. W. Mills, "Situated Action and the Vocabulary of Motives," *American Sociological Review* 5(1940):904-913; M. B. Scott and S. M. Lyman, "Accounts," *American Sociological Review* 33(1968):46-62; G. R. Semin and A. S. R. Manstead, *The Accountability of Conduct* (London: Academic Press, 1983); M. Weber, *The Theory of Social and Economic Organization* (New York: Free Press, 1964).

MOVEMENTS   *see* New Religious Movements, Social Movements

MUELLER, FRANZ H(ERMAN JOSEPH) (1900-1994)

Born in Berlin, Germany, Mueller studied at the University of Berlin and the Berlin School of Commerce, where in 1922 he earned his master's degree in business administration, his thesis director being Werner Sombart. He continued his studies at the University of Cologne, writing his Ph.D. dissertation under the direction of Leopold von Wiese. He married Dr. Therese J. Geuer, a member of the Königswinter Study Circle, which did preparatory work for the papal labor encyclical *Quadragesimo*

Anno. Mueller was Assistant Director for Research in Social Sciences at the University of Cologne until he was dismissed by the Nazis in 1934. He went to England and from there, in 1935, to St. Louis University, where he stayed until assuming the post of Professor of Economics at the College of St. Thomas (now St. Thomas University), St. Paul, Minnesota. There he remained until 1968, when he was made Professor Emeritus of Economics. President, American Catholic Sociological Society, 1948.

Mueller was always concerned with Catholic social teaching, and in 1988 he was awarded the Heinrich Pesch Prize for Social Science and Social Action by the Federation of Catholic Student Fraternities in Germany. Contributing many articles to the *American Catholic Sociological Review*, Mueller periodically addressed what was a burning issue in the early history of the society: the possibility of a *Catholic sociology*. He strongly objected to the ideological connotations of the term, calling for rigorous scientific methodology and constant attention to scholarship. Mueller wrote in the Fiftieth Anniversary Special Issue of *Sociological Analysis,*

> I hope and pray that our early endeavors as Catholic sociologists to see to it that sociology be recognized as an empirical science have not been in vain. . . . But I am convinced that there is *no* such thing as Catholic or Christian sociology and that we can serve our highest ideals best if we do a good job as genuine sociologists who stick to what the scholastic philosophers called the formal (or specific) object of each science and strive to provide the actionists with reliable data and, perhaps, even forecasts. (p. 389)

—*Loretta M. Morris*

REFERENCES

F. H. Mueller, "The Formal Object of Sociology," *American Catholic Sociological Review* 1(1940):55-61; F. H. Mueller, *The Church and the Social Question* (Washington, D.C.: American Enterprise Institute, 1984 [1963]).

MÜLLER, (FRIEDRICH) MAX (1823-1900)

German-born scholar of Sanskrit, philology, and comparative religion who worked in England for over half a century.

Max Müller achieved a fame in his day that rivaled that of even his most eminent Victorian contemporaries. Accordingly, the question, "Who now reads

Müller?" darkens any modern assessment of his work. Neglect by sociologists of his vast scholarly outpouring has been an inevitable consequence of Émile Durkheim's devastating critique of "Naturism," while anthropological indifference has even deeper roots in the evolutionism of Andrew Lang and E. B. Tylor.

Although current scholarship is unlikely to subscribe to Müller's version of Nature Mythology (in which historical religion derives from a "disease of language"), it must acknowledge his extraordinary energy and undoubted skill as a writer, researcher, translator, and intellectual popularizer. These qualities are exhibited in such works as *Introduction to the Science of Religion* (1873), *The Origin and Growth of Religion* (1878), and *Contributions to the Science of Mythology* (1897) as well as in his volumes on natural, physical, anthropological, and psychological religion (1889-1993) and his edited multivolume series *Sacred Books of the East* (1879-1994).

Despite his faults and excesses, Müller deserves recognition as one of the pioneers and founders of the social scientific study of religion. Prone to sweeping generalization in the manner of Frazer, Spengler, and Toynbee, he was often charged with superficiality and dilettantism in his highly ambitious *comparative* ventures linking language, thought, and religion. His repeated assertion that "he who knows one, knows none" was not always an adequate defense, but it remains nonetheless a mighty maxim for students of *Religionswissenschaft* in an era of both specialization and globalization.

—*Roger O'Toole*

REFERENCES

N. C. Chaudhuri, *Scholar Extraordinary* (London: Chatto & Windus, 1974); G. A. Müller (ed.), *The Life and Letters of the Rt. Hon. Friedrich Max Müller* (London: Longmans, 1902); J. H. Voigt, *F. Max Müller* (Calcutta: Mukhopadhyay, 1967).

MULVANEY, BERNARD G. (1910-1995)

With an M.A. in sociology from Catholic University of America, a licentiate degree in Political Science from Louvain University, and a Ph.D. in sociology from University of Illinois (1941), Mulvaney taught at the Catholic University of America from 1941 until 1957. Member of the Clerics of St. Viator (Viatorian) religious order.

Mulvaney's areas of interest and his journal publications were in demography and theory. He was one of the members of the American Catholic Sociology Society who insisted on the use of empirical method in sociology at a time when empiricism was often equated in Catholic circles with determinism.

Elected President of the American Catholic Sociological Society for 1957, Mulvaney was prevented from fulfilling his duties by being elected in the summer of that year to the second highest office in his religious order; this required his immediate residence in Rome. At that point, ACSS Executive Secretary Ralph Gallagher, ignoring the candidate slated for nomination by the election committee, placed in nomination Allen Spitzer, a St. Louis University anthropologist. The ensuing controversy failed to derail Spitzer's election as president for 1957.

—*Loretta M. Morris*

MUNDIE, PAUL J. (1904–)

Awarded a Ph.D. in sociology by Georgetown University in 1930, Mundie joined the faculty of social sciences at Marquette University that same year and became department head in 1936. He left Marquette in 1943 to become a consultant in private industry. President, American Catholic Sociological Society, 1940.

Mundie's research interests lay in labor relations and in criminology. He participated in the meeting at Chicago's Loyola University in March 1938, which saw the foundation of the American Catholic Sociological Society, and was elected treasurer at that meeting. His presidential address was concerned with the family in transition.

—*Loretta M. Morris*

MUNDY, PAUL (1920-1995)

Granted a Ph.D. in sociology from Catholic University of America in 1951. President, American Catholic Sociological Society, 1965; Religious Research Association, 1965-1966.

Mundy was Assistant Editor of the *American Catholic Sociological Review* 1951-1955, succeeding as Editor of the *Review* 1955-1960. It was at the end of his editorship that he accepted a paper read by Gordon Zahn at the ACSS convention in 1959, the fruit of Zahn's research on the German Catholic press under the Nazi regime, for publication in the fall 1959 *Review*. The paper received adverse publicity of a clearly biased nature in the Chicago Catholic press. Nonetheless, Mundy proceeded with publication plans, and Zahn's piece was at the galley correction stage when the incoming editor, Sylvester Sieber, S.V.D. (acting, he claimed, on the instructions of Executive Secretary Ralph Gallagher, S.J.), "yanked the article." The violation of academic freedom and censorship was brought before the ACSS Executive Council meeting held at the time of the organization's 1960 convention. The council ordered Sieber to print the article; he refused and resigned his position as editor. Sieber was succeeded ultimately by Paul Reiss, and this marked a major change in the editorial direction of the *Review*.

Mundy spent his entire academic life at Loyola University of Chicago, publishing and teaching primarily in the areas of intergroup relations and criminal justice, and in later years in sociology of health-related fields. Together with two other authors, he wrote and published a short piece on the work of Ralph Gallagher, S.J., titled *Citizen Jesuit*.

—*Loretta M. Morris*

MURRAY, RAYMOND W. (1893-1973)

Roman Catholic priest; L.L.B., Notre Dame, 1918; Ph.D., Catholic University, 1926; sociology faculty, University of Notre Dame, 1926-1968 (professor and founding department head, 1926-1953); awarded L.L.D. upon his retirement. Second President of the American Catholic Sociological Society, 1939.

Murray's interests were divided between anthropology, particularly prehistoric archeology, and social problems, particularly delinquency. He published introductory sociology texts in 1935 and 1950, in addition to *Man's Unknown Ancestors* (Bruce 1943).

—*Kevin J. Christiano*

MUSLIMS   *see* Islam, Nation of Islam

MYSTICISM The doctrine that special mental states or events allow an understanding of ultimate truths. Although it is difficult to differentiate which forms of experience allow such understandings, mental episodes supporting belief in "other kinds of reality" are often labeled *mystical*. Such events include religious, transcendental, and some paranormal experiences. James (1902), Stark (1965), and Hardy (1979) argue that the distinguishing feature of religious experience is a sense of contact with a supernatural being. Definitions of mystical experience often include experiences with nonpersonal or anthropomorphic powers. There seems no reliable way of precisely demarcating religious and mystical experiences because such episodes are often thought incapable of being reduced to words. Mysticism tends to refer to experiences supporting belief in a cosmic unity rather than the advocation of a particular religious ideology.

Religious experiences have been categorized into four basic types (Stark 1965). The most common form, *confirming*, is regarded as intrinsically true. A second type, *responsive*, includes a component of mutual awareness in both the experiencer and the supernatural. The third form, *ecstatic*, includes both the confirming and the responsive types but also entails an intimate relationship with the supernatural. During the least frequent *revelational* form, the experiencer receives a divine message or prophesy for broadcast to others.

Universal features within experiential accounts have stimulated responses from such thinkers as Friedrich Schleiermacher, William James, Rudolph Otto, and Aldous Huxley. Schleiermacher (1958 [1799]) portrayed religious experience as the foundation for all other forms of religious activity. Religious consciousness was thought to be a "sense" or "taste" for the Infinite. James (1902) compiled an important early collection of accounts shedding light on mystical experience. Otto (1950 [1917]) argued that the central feature of "numinous" experience was an element of fearful awe central to the concept of the "holy." Huxley (1970) described a "perennial philosophy" recurring over the ages as a result of mystical experiences.

Stace (1960) provides a traditional theory explaining the nature of mystical experience. According to his model, mystical experiences are "given" to the mystic. Experiences are indubitable and incorrigible, share basic characteristics such as unity and timelessness, and are the objects of idiosyncratic interpretation.

This model has been subject to criticism because much empirical evidence supports the argument that social and psychological events influence the experience itself, not just the interpretation of it. Experiences vary according to mystics' religion, education, experience, and culture, and appear to be a product of the cultural milieu in which they occur. Bourque (1969) found that religious ecstatic-transcendental experiences occur more frequently among poorly educated, older, rural, and black populations while aesthetic ecstatic-transcendental experiences are reported more often by the middle-class, well-educated, white residents of the suburbs.

Triggers of Mystical Experience Spontaneous mystical episodes appear to be stimulated by a variety of "triggers." Examples of triggers include sensory deprivation, frustration, threat, music, prayer, beauty, nature, sex, and joyful events (Hardy 1979, Laski 1961). Experimental studies verify that set and setting determine whether or not people in wilderness solitudes have religious experiences (Rosegrant 1976). Mystical experiences also are activated by a variety of procedures that, through the ages, have been found to be effective. Methods include meditation, pilgrimage, fasting and special diets, sensory restriction or overstimulation, hypnotic motions such as dancing or twirling, and both sexual abstinence and indulgence. A wide variety of trance-induction techniques (chanting, rhythmic singing, drumming, meditation, and other sensory overload and restriction techniques) appear outwardly different but lead to a common state of parasympathetic dominance and a slow wave synchronization of the frontal cortex (Winkelman 1986). This altered state of consciousness seemingly contributes to mystical experience and is central to shamanic performance.

This existence of culturally specific "triggers" for mystical experience coincides with attribution theory. Proudfoot (1985) argues that an apologetic strategy underlies the attempts of many scholars to differentiate religious experience from the normal structures associated with culture and language. He bases his position on the research of Schachter and Singer (1962), who argued that nervous system arousal without apparent reason leads to the attribution of a causal explanation dependant on the environmental factors prevalent at the time. This orientation allows Proudfoot to apply sociological orientations to the understanding of religious perceptions.

Although Proudfoot's work is frequently cited, his formulations have been subject to criticism (Garnard 1992). The basis for many of his arguments, the work of Schachter and Singer (1962), has received only limited support by later researchers. Studies indicate that different physiological sensations are associated with different emotions. Although Proudfoot's orientation does not explain the incidence of some forms of mystical experience (noted by Hay and Morisy 1978, for example), attribution theory continues to provide a valuable means for explaining many of the characteristics of religious experience (Spilka and McIntosh 1995). Environmental and cultural factors shape experiential perception and affect the degree that experiences are interpreted as "religious."

Surveys of Mystical Experience Hood's (1975) construction and validation of a measure of reported mystical experiences allows experimental studies of the factors influencing their induction. His *Mysticism Scale, Research Form D* (M scale) has 32 items, four for each of eight categories of mysticism initially conceptualized by Stace (1960). Factor analysis of the scale indicates two major factors, a general mystical experience factor and a religious interpretation factor. Hood's research (e.g., 1995) has allowed identification of various parameters correlated with mystical experience: commitment, psychological health, self-actualization, intrinsic religious orientation, unexpected stress, and hypnotizability. Survey-based data indicate that religious, paranormal, and mystical experiences are more widespread in Western society than might be assumed. More than one-third of all adults in Britain and the United States claim to have had experiences. Experiences are more likely to be reported by female, younger, better educated, and upper-class respondents (Greeley 1975, Hay and Morisy 1978).

The Religious Experience Research Unit in Oxford has collected and examined accounts of religious experience received as the result of appeals though the mass media (Hardy 1970). Their filter question asks, "Do you feel that you have ever been aware of or influenced by a presence or power, whether referred to as God or not, which was different from your everyday self?" As with other mystical experience questions, about one-third of respondents responded affirmatively. Hay (1979) analyzed qualitative responses to the filter question. Among those providing affirmative response, 23% felt that there was "a power controlling and guiding me," 22% referred to an "awareness of the presence of God," and 19% recalled "a presence in nature." Other forms of response included "answered prayer," "experience of a unity with nature," "ESP, out-of-body, visions, etc.," "awareness of an evil power," and "conversion."

Greeley (1975) used the "mysticism" question: "Have you ever had the feeling of being close to a powerful spiritual force that seemed to lift you out of yourself?" More than a third of respondents in various U.S. national surveys responded positively to this question. The question also has been used in national European surveys. Response is significantly positively correlated with education, social class, and psychological well-being. Unfortunately, positive responders vary greatly in the nature of experiences they recall. Content analysis of open-ended responses to this question indicates that 72% of respondents who answered the question in the affirmative referred to experiences of a psychic or conventional religious nature while only 5% of the responses were judged to be of a mystical nature (Thomas and Cooper 1978).

Paranormal and anomalous experiences, seemingly a subcategory of mystical perception, are often ignored by academics due to scientist bias (Greeley 1975, McClenon 1994). More than half of American national samples report such episodes. The most common forms of experience include apparitions, precognitive dreams, waking extrasensory perceptions, out-of-body experience, sleep paralysis, and contacts with the dead. Cross-cultural comparisons of narrative accounts reveal common features within the observed categories of experience. Such episodes appear to have the capacity to shape culture rather than being totally produced by it. Episodes contribute to folk beliefs in spirits, souls, life after death, and anomalous capacities (McClenon 1994).

Mystical Experience and Physiological Factors
Universal features within mystical experience suggest a physiological basis. Pahnke (1966) found that LSD stimulates mystical experience when administered under suitable conditions. Research also links paranormal, mystical, and religious experiences with temporal lobe processes in the brain. Patients with unilateral temporal epileptic foci differ from patients with neuromuscular disorders with regard to specific psychosocial aspects of behavior. Sensory-affective associations appear to be established within the temporal lobes. Temporal lobe epilepsy is associated with holding deep religious beliefs, sudden and multiple religious conversions, mystical states, and unusual perceptions attributed to spiritual forces. A temporal lobe signs inventory, which includes questionnaire items reflecting mystical and paranormal experiences, has been validated electroencephalographically as related to temporal lobe lability. Studies of normal and clinical populations indicate that the incidence of complex partial epileptic signs occurs as a continuum from normal people to epileptics. Although extreme forms of temporal lobe lability are associated with pathology, more common, moderate levels are linked with creativity (Persinger and Kakarec 1993).

Studies indicate that mystical experience is associated with health benefits. Maslow (1964) identified some religious experiences as "peak experiences," which tend to be associated with good mental health. Greeley (1975) found his "mystical" experience question to be highly correlated to indications of psychological well-being. Hay and Morisy (1978) reported that individuals claiming religious/mystical experiences scored significantly higher on the Bradburn Balanced Affect Scale of psychological well-being than did non-experiencers. Kass et al. (1991) devised an "Index of Core Spiritual Experience," which included both mystical and anomalous perceptions. They found that this index was associated with increased life purpose and satisfaction and decreased frequency of medical symptoms.

Rather than a pathological process, mystical experience might be portrayed as the exercising of a beneficial ability, the skill to experience unitively (Overall 1982). The mystic is one who actively seeks and obtains, through learning and practice, a special unitive state of consciousness. Although mystical experiences are influenced by expectations, education, goals, and beliefs, such episodes reflect a skill that apparently provides psychological and physiological benefits.

Modern social scientific evidence does not refute the possibility that some mystical experiences are associated with scientifically unknown processes. Parapsychologists have accumulated a body of evidence supporting belief in paranormal phenomena (Broughton 1992). Even though their evidence has been criticized, the existence of universal features within collections of mystical experience accounts supports the argument that some forms of these perceptions are not fully cultural products but have important impacts on religious belief (Hufford 1982, McClenon 1994).

The high incidence, recurrent features, and perceived impact on belief of mystical experiences suggest that these episodes warrant greater interest by scholars of religion. Paranormal, religious, and mystical experiences seemingly provide foundations for universal forms of religious belief.

—*James McClenon*

REFERENCES

L. B. Bourque, "Social Correlates of Transcendental Experiences," *Sociological Analysis* 30(1969):151-163; R. S. Broughton, *Parapsychology* (New York: Ballantine, 1992); G. W. Garnard, "Explaining the Unexplainable," *Journal of the American Academy of Religion* 60(1992):231-256; A. M. Greeley, *The Sociology of the Paranormal* (Beverly Hills, Calif.: Sage, 1975); A. C. Hardy, "A Scientist Looks at Religion," *Proceedings of the Royal Institute of Great Britain* 43(1970):201; A. C. Hardy, *The Spiritual Life of Man* (New York: Oxford University Press, 1979); D. Hay, "Religious Experience Amongst a Group of Postgraduate Students," *Journal for the Scientific Study of Religion* 18(1979):164-182; D. Hay and A. Morisy, "Reports of Ecstatic, Paranormal, or Religious Experience in Great Britain and the United States," *Journal for the Scientific Study of Religion* 17(1978): 255-268; R. W. Hood, Jr., "The Construction and Preliminary Validation of a Measure of Reported Mystical Experience," *Journal for the Scientific Study of Religion* 14(1975): 29-41; R. W. Hood, Jr. (ed.), *Handbook of Religious Experience* (Birmingham, Ala.: Religious Education Press, 1995); D. J. Hufford, *The Terror That Comes in the Night* (Philadelphia: University of Pennsylvania Press, 1982); A. Huxley, *The Perennial Philosophy* (New York: Harper, 1970); W. James, *Varieties of Religious Experience* (New York: Longman, 1902); J. D. Kass et al., "Health Outcomes and a New Index of Spiritual Experience," *Journal for the Scientific Study of Religion* 30(1991):203-211; M.

Laski, *Ecstasy* (Bloomington: University of Indiana Press, 1961); A. H. Maslow, *Religions, Values, and Peak-Experiences* (Columbus: Ohio State University Press, 1964); J. McClenon, *Wondrous Events* (Philadelphia: University of Pennsylvania Press, 1994); R. Otto, *The Idea of the Holy,* 2nd ed. (Oxford: Oxford University Press, 1950 [1917]); C. Overall, "The Nature of Religious Experience," *Religious Studies* 18(1982):47-54: W. Pahnke, "Drugs and Mysticism," *International Journal of Parapsychology* 8(1966):295-320; M. A. Persinger and K. Kakarec, "Complex Partial Epileptic Signs as a Continuum from Normals to Epileptics," *Journal of Clinical Psychology* 49(1993):33-45; W. Proudfoot, *Religious Experience* (Berkeley: University of California Press, 1985); J. Rosegrant, "The Impact of Set and Setting on Religious Experience in Nature," *Journal for the Scientific Study of Religion* 15(1976): 301-310; S. Schachter and J. E. Singer, "Cognitive, Social, and Physiological Determinants of Emotional State," *Psychological Review* 69(1962):379-399; F. Schleiermacher, *On Religion* (New York: Harper, 1958 [1799]); B. Spilka and D. N. McIntosh, "Attribution Theory and Religious Experience," in *Handbook of Religious Experience,* ed. R. W. Hood, Jr. (Birmingham, Ala.: Religious Education Press, 1995): 421-455; W. T. Stace, *Mysticism and Philosophy* (Philadelphia: Lippincott, 1960); R. Stark, "A Taxonomy of Religious Experience," *Journal for the Scientific Study of Religion* 5(1965):97-116; L. E. Thomas and P. E. Cooper, "Measurement and Incidence of Mystical Experiences," *Journal for the Scientific Study of Religion* 17(1978):433-437; M. Winkelman, "Trance States," *Ethos* 14(1986):174-203.

NASON-CLARK, NANCY (1956–) Professor of Sociology, University of New Brunswick (Canada), where she has taught since receiving her Ph.D. in 1984 from the London School of Economics under Eileen Barker. President, Association for the Sociology of Religion, 1999.

Nason-Clark's dissertation research and early publications focused on the ordination of women controversy in the Church of England. More recently, her focus has turned to abusive relationships especially within religious contexts, as witnessed, for example, in her book *Shattered Silence: Wife Abuse and Contemporary Christianity* (Westminster 1997). She has held offices in all three North American professional societies in the social scientific study of religion.

—William H. Swatos, Jr.

NATIONAL COUNCIL OF CHURCHES The National Council of Churches of Christ in the United States (NCC) was created in 1950 through a merger of predecessor councils to coordinate Protestant endeavors.

The NCC's organizational roots date to the early twentieth century. Leaders in mainline Protestant denominations were becoming increasingly aware of the need for churches to express more adequately their unity in Christ and to engage more actively in applying the Christian ethic to problems of a rapidly growing and changing industrial society. The Federal Council of Churches of Christ in America, organized in 1908 with initial participation of 33 Protestant denominations, was their answer. Conservatives who consider the Christian Gospel to apply solely to individuals were critical of this and later attempts to implement Social Gospel ideology. Nevertheless, numerous projects, such as an investigation of work conditions in steel plants and the beginning of a major study of the implications of Christian ethics for the conduct of economic life, were accomplished. The Home Missions Council (1908) focused on other aspects of the relation of Protestant churches to changing society, such as comity arrangements to reduce denominational competition in new areas of population growth, reducing duplication of efforts in sparsely populated or declining rural areas, and coordinating efforts to serve new immigrants.

The NCC brought together these two organizations, along with 10 others and their concerns, such as campus ministries, church world service, foreign missions, Protestant films and radio, and religious education. The current NCC provides a wide range of coordinative services for the moderates of American Protestantism. Some research activity was an original dimension of approaching most of these concerns. In the NCC, research was centralized, then reduced in scope, and finally eliminated as a discrete in-house function.

The NCC publishes the *Yearbook of American Churches,* which began in 1916 as the *Federal Council Handbook,* now including Canada. It is the only comprehensive source of church statistics in North America. The Federal Council began publication of *Information Service* in 1921 (terminated in 1969), which summarized and interpreted sociological studies on socioethical issues. Other documents were internally produced with the aid of social science consultants. The heritage of field studies of communities and their churching came through the Home Missions Council to the NCC. Major new approaches were taken later, such as a decennial county church and membership distribution study, beginning in 1956 (now continued under the auspices of the Glenmary Research Center); the mass media study *The Television-Radio Audience and Religion* (1955); the *Unchurched American* study (1978), coordinated with George Gallup and a number of denominations.

—*Everett L. Perry*

REFERENCE

S. M. Cavert, *Church Cooperation and Unity in America* (New York: Association Press, 1970).

NATIONALISM   *see* Pluralism, Politics

NATION OF ISLAM   The exact origin of the Nation of Islam remains shrouded in mystery, as does the character of the sect's founder. Wallace D. Fard, possibly an individual of Middle Eastern extraction, began to proselytize in the ghetto of Detroit around 1930. His followers regarded him as the messiah who had come to lead blacks into the millennium that was to follow the Battle of Armageddon. After Fard mysteriously disappeared in 1933, his mantle fell to Elijah Poole, who renamed himself Elijah Muhammad (Clegg 1997). Muhammad's teaching that Fard had actually been Allah provoked a split in the sect, prompting Elijah and his faction to relocate their headquarters to Chicago.

Like other messianic-nationalist sects, the Nation of Islam under Elijah Muhammad asserted that black people were intentionally kept ignorant of their true origins, history, and religion. Elijah asserted that whereas God had created blacks as the first human beings, an evil black scientist named Yakub created the white race 6,000 years later. He also maintained that Christianity is a "slave religion" that keeps blacks in social and spiritual bondage. Until the millennium, blacks were counseled to abide by puritanical behavioral codes that included a ban on the consumption of pork, tobacco, coffee, and alcohol. The Muslims were to maintain patriarchal households and traditional gender roles. The Nation of Islam also stressed economic independence from white people as well as the creation of a separate nation for blacks consisting of several southern states.

The Black Power movement of the 1960s prompted many young poor blacks, including many prisoners, to join the Nation of Islam. Malcolm X, the charismatic minister of the Harlem temple, developed a national and ultimately international reputation as a fiery orator and uncompromising black leader. Despite the strident image of the Nation of Islam, it had made some significant accommodations with the larger society, including greater acceptance of integrationist leaders in the African American community and decreasing emphasis on racial separatism. While Malcolm X played a role in these changes, he found himself increasingly at odds with Elijah Muhammad in the former's critique of the larger society. Malcolm publicly criticized U.S. military intervention in Southeast Asia and the federal government's lack of commitment toward solving domestic problems among African Americans. He also took offense at Elijah's extramarital involvements. In January 1964, Elijah removed Malcolm from his position as the minister of Temple 7 in Harlem for his remark that the John F. Kennedy's assassination was a "case of chickens coming home to roost."

On March 8, 1964, Malcolm announced his departure from the Nation of Islam and his plans to establish his own organization called the Muslim Mosque Inc., with an associated political body, the Organization of Afro-American Unity. Although his organization did not admit whites, Malcolm expressed a willingness to work with whites against racism and for social justice. On February 21, 1965, an assassin's bullet ended Malcolm's growing influence in the African American community. Three former members of the Nation of Islam were imprisoned for the death of Malcolm X, although controversy continues as to whether the FBI played a part in his assassination.

Following the death of Elijah Muhammad in February 1975, Wallace D. Muhammad, one of his sons, assumed leadership of the Nation of Islam and transformed it into a relatively orthodox Islamic sect now known as the American Muslim Mission. In 1978, Louis Farrakhan created a reorganized Nation of Islam that regards W. D. Fard as Allah incarnate, blacks as the original human beings, and whites as devils (Gardell 1996). As the principal organizer of the Million Man March in Washington, D.C., Farrakhan has emerged as the most provocative and perhaps influential leader in the African American community.

—*Hans A. Baer*

REFERENCES

C. A. Clegg III, *The Life of Elijah Muhammad* (New York: St. Martin's, 1997); E. U. Essien-Udom, *Black Nationalism* (Chicago: University of Chicago Press, 1962); M. Gardell, *In the Name of Elijah Muhammad* (Durham, N.C.: Duke University Press, 1996); M. F. Lee, *The Nation of Islam* (Lewiston, N.Y.: Mellen, 1988); C. E. Lincoln, *The Black Muslims in America*, 3rd ed. (Grand Rapids, Mich.: Eerdmans, 1994); C. E. Marsh, *From Black Muslim to Muslim* (Metuchen, NJ: Scarecrow, 1984).

NATIVE AMERICAN RELIGIONS The serious systematic study of Native American religions may be said to have had its beginning in 1851 with the publication of Lewis Henry Morgan's *League of the Ho-de-no-sau-nee, or Iroquois,* generally regarded as the first scientific account of an American Indian tribe. Morgan devoted a major portion of his monograph to Iroquois religious conceptions, festivals, and modes of worship, focusing special attention on the so-called New Religion of the celebrated prophet, Handsome Lake.

The founding in 1879 of the Bureau of American Ethnology greatly stimulated interest in this area of investigation and led to the production by a variety of researchers of a series of descriptively rich papers on topics ranging from ceremonies of the Zuñi to sacred formulas of the Cherokee. The great classic among these reports is James Mooney's *The Ghost-Dance Religion and the Sioux Outbreak of 1890* (Government Printing Office 1896), the first full-scale field study of a Native American revivalistic movement and the work that opened up messianism as a general cultural phenomenon to social scientific inquiry.

Like Morgan, a lawyer by profession, Mooney and his bureau cohorts were self-educated scholars. By the turn of the century, a new breed of investigators were making the domain of Native American studies its own. These were academically trained ethnologists, students of Franz Boas (1858-1942), the man largely responsible for the professionalization of anthropology in the United States. Distrustful of theorizing and generalizing, Boas insisted that the fundamental task of anthropology was "historical reconstruction" based on meticulous gathering of empirical data on specific cultures and cultural patterns. He sought to endow the discipline with the same rigor of method that characterized the physical sciences.

An outstanding example of a work produced in accordance with Boas's canons of ethnographic research is Leslie Spier's *The Sun Dance of the Plains Indians: Its Development and Diffusion* (American Museum of Natural History 1921). Using all available accounts of this most important of Plains tribal ceremonies, Spier reduced the dance to its component elements and plotted their geographic distribution. His trait-analysis technique enabled him to identify the Arapaho and Cheyenne as originators of the dance and to trace the rite's subsequent dissemination and assimilation. Spier's study was the model for another classic work, Weston La Barre's *The Peyote Cult* (Yale 1938). Other noteworthy monographs in the Boasian tradition include Robert Lowie's *The Religion of the Crow Indians* (American Museum of Natural History 1922), Ruth Benedict's *The Concept of the Guardian Spirit in North America* (American Anthropological Association 1923), and Cora DuBois's *The 1870 Ghost Dance* (University of California Anthropological Records 1939).

Specialists in the study of Native American religions have developed a wide range of fresh theoretical and methodological orientations toward their topic since the days when Boas first outlined his program for a modern anthropology. Some of these approaches were foreshadowed in the work of Boas himself or were introduced by those who trained under him.

Dynamic/Behavioral Analyses The *functionalist* approach examines religion in terms of what it does for individuals and/or their society. In his *The Peyote Religion Among the Navaho* (Aldine 1966), David Aberle analyzed peyotism as a "redemptive movement" that established a "new inner state" in persons suffering from relative deprivation occasioned by forced government livestock reductions. Joseph Jorgensen's *The Sun Dance Religion: Power for the Powerless* (University of Chicago Press 1972) offered similar conclusions regarding the place of the Sun Dance in the lives of Utes and Shoshone. Alexander Lesser in *The Pawnee Ghost Dance Hand Game* (Columbia University Contributions to Anthropology 1933) showed how the Ghost Dance provided the stimulus for a general cultural renaissance among the Pawnee, while Anthony Wallace discussed the Iroquois cultural regeneration provoked by the religion of Handsome Lake in *The Death and Rebirth of the Seneca* (Knopf 1970).

The *psychological* approach is based on application to ethnographic materials of theories and concepts derived, for the most part, from dynamic psychiatry. Easily the most significant contribution of this type is Weston La Barre's *The Ghost Dance: Origins of Religion* (Doubleday 1970). La Barre used the classical Freudian framework, with its emphasis on the Oedipus complex, in an attempt to reach a deeper understanding of Native American ideas about power as well as of the genesis of the successive "crisis cults" that have arisen among these people. Other works in this vein include George Devereux's "Dream Learning and the Individual Ritual Differences in Mohave Shamanism" (*American Anthropologist,* 1957) and Morris Opler's "An Interpretation of Ambivalence of Two American Indian Tribes" (*Journal of Social Psychology,* 1936). George Spindler, as reported in his "Personality and Peyotism in Menomini Indian Acculturation" (*Psychiatry,* 1952), used the Rorschach projective test to discover the psychological characteristics of peyotists, concluding that peyote ritual, symbolism, and ideology work together to produce a "distinctive personality type." More recently, Wolfgang Jilek argued that the guardian spirit ceremony of the Coast Salish of British Columbia embodies several types of well-defined psychohygienic and therapeutic procedures of demonstrable effectiveness in *Salish Indian Mental Health and Culture Change* (Holt 1974).

Historiographic Analyses   The *life-history* approach uses first-person accounts that are the products of intensive collaboration between native informants and ethnographers. While most such narratives do not consider religion in any systematic way or even present sustained analysis of the biographical materials, some are extremely valuable for the data they contain on rituals and ceremonials as they are experienced subjectively by particular individuals. Peter Nabokov's *Two Leggings: The Making of a Crow Warrior* (Crowell 1967) is important for the information it contains on the Sun Dance and the vision quest. Peyotism among the Winnebago receives attention in Paul Radin's *Crashing Thunder* (Appleton 1926) and in Nancy Lurie's *Mountain Wolf Woman* (University of Michigan Press 1961). Leo Simmons's *Sun Chief* (Yale University Press 1942) vividly conveys the spiritual life of the Hopi. Navajo ceremonialism is a principal focus of Charlotte Frisbie and David McAllester's *Navajo Blessingway Singer: The Autobiography of Frank Mitchell, 1881-1967* (University of Arizona Press 1978).

The *historical* approach concentrates on the construction of chronological narratives, emphasizing the ordering of facts and events rather than their interpretation. Omer Stewart's *Peyote Religion: A History* (University of Oklahoma Press 1987) is perhaps the finest report of this kind, a large-scale account that may be regarded as definitive. Still useful, however, is James Slotkin's *The Peyote Religion: A Study in Indian-White Relations* (Free Press 1956).

Descriptive/Conceptual Analyses   The *textual/linguistic* approach takes native texts, as recorded and translated by ethnographers, as its units of analysis. In her *Prayer: The Compulsive Word* (University of Washington Press 1944), Gladys Reichard examined the form and content of Navajo prayers, suggesting that this highly specialized "ceremonial" language contains the key to the ultimate understanding of Navajo belief and practice. A more exhaustive and sophisticated treatment of the subject is Sam Gill's *Sacred Words: A Study of Navajo Religion and Prayer* (Greenwood 1981). Gill explored the "structuring principles" of Navajo prayers to uncover the premises and categories that are at the core of Navajo religion. (Gill is also the author of *Native American Religions: An Introduction,* Wadsworth 1982, which is a good general overview.)

The *phenomenological* approach seeks to achieve an "inside" view of religion, to understand religious behavior in terms of native conceptions and categories of experience. The pioneer of this mode of inquiry was A. Irving Hallowell, a leader in the area of culture-and-personality studies. In a groundbreaking series of papers written over a period of some three decades, he elucidated basic aspects of Ojibwa religion by assuming the perspective of the "culturally constituted Ojibwa self in its culturally constituted behavioral environment." Articles in the series include "Some Empirical Aspects of Northern Saulteaux Religion" (*American Anthropologist,* 1934), "Spirits of the Dead in Saulteaux Life and Thought" (*Journal of the Royal Anthropological Institute,* 1940), and "Ojibwa Ontology, Behavior, and World View" (in Stanley Diamond, ed., *Culture and History* 1960).

The *history-of-religions* (or comparative) approach treats religion substantively, in terms of its believed contents. This approach is associated mainly with Åke Hultkrantz, a Swedish scholar of notable prolificacy. Decrying the tendency of most social scientists to "do away" with religion by reducing it to something else (i.e., social processes, psychological conditions, and so on), Hultkrantz deals with religion "as an entity sui generis," identifying patterns, constructing typologies, and probing meanings. His principal works include *Conceptions of the Soul Among North American Indians* (Ethnological Museum of Sweden 1953), *The Religions of the American Indians* (University of California 1979), *Belief and Worship in Native North America* (Syracuse University Press 1981), and *The Study of American Indian Religions* (Crossroad 1983), an exhaustive bibliographic essay covering both American and European sources.

The study of Native American religions holds a secure place within the social sciences. Interest is currently running very high, as evidenced by the steady production of books and articles on the subject and by the creation, in 1994, of a specialized periodical, *American Indian Religions: An Interdisciplinary Journal*.

—*Steven M. Kane*

REFERENCES

W. La Barre, *The Peyote Cult*, 5th ed. (Norman: University of Oklahoma Press, 1989); L. H. Morgan, *League of the Ho-de-no-sau-nee, or Iroquois* (New York: Citadel Press, 1962 [1851]).

NAVIN, ROBERT B(ERNARD) (1895-1970)

Roman Catholic priest; Ph.D., Catholic University, 1935. Robert Navin was sequentially Dean (1929-1948) and President (1948 until his death) of St. John's College, Cleveland, Ohio (now defunct). He served as President of the American Catholic Sociological Society in 1949, and had interests in social welfare and social action.

—*William H. Swatos, Jr.*

NEAL, MARIE AUGUSTA (1921–)

Sister of Notre Dame de Namur; Ph.D., Harvard University, 1963; Professor Emerita and longtime Chair of the Sociology Department at Emmanuel College, Boston. President, Association for the Sociology of Religion, 1972; Society for the Scientific Study of Religion, 1982-1983.

Sister Marie Augusta is the author of eight books, 31 chapters in collected volumes, and 33 articles, with frequent contributions to the refereed journals in the social science of religion. She is the recipient of several honorary degrees as well as the Isaac Hecker Social Justice Award from the Paulist Center in Boston (1977), the Distinguished Teaching Award from the American Sociological Association (1986), and the Ecumenical Award from Xavier University in Cincinnati (1988). She has given guest lectures in the United States, Canada, and New Zealand and has been a visiting professor at several colleges and universities, including the University of California at Berkeley and Harvard Divinity School.

There are four main components to the work that Sister Marie Augusta has been doing during the past 35 years: (1) survey research on change in the Roman Catholic Church, conducted first with diocesan priests and later with members of women's religious orders; (2) analysis of Catholic social teaching as expressed in the encyclical letters of the popes for the past hundred years; (3) experimentation with a dialogical teaching style adapted from the Brazilian educator Paulo Freire, wherein social issues are discussed by means of critical analysis from the point of view of oppressed peoples; (4) a passion for social justice, with a current emphasis on human rights. In this context, Sister Marie Augusta also has written articles and papers on women's issues, has conducted research on schools in South Africa, and has done a critical analysis of sociobiology. She has served on the Boston Archdiocesan Commission on Human Rights, on the Governor's Commission on the Status of Women in Massachusetts, on the Board of Advisors to the U.S. Catholic Conference of Bishops, on the Board of the Women's Theological Center, on the Educational Policies Commission of the Boston Theological Institute, and on the Advisory Committee of the Massachusetts Civil Liberties Union. The range of her interests may be seen in a sampling of her publications: *Values and Interests in Social Change* (Prentice Hall 1965), *The South African Catholic Education Study* (Catholic Education Council of Durban 1971), *The Just Demands of the Poor* (Paulist Press 1987), *From Nuns to Sisters: An Expanding Vocation* (Twenty-Third Publications 1990).

Sister Marie Augusta's intellectual perspectives have blended elements that some might consider disparate: the structural-functionalism of her mentor, Talcott Parsons; Marxian sociology; quantitative analysis; and the strong religious foundation that has consistently inspired her views on social justice. She has accomplished this synthesis in a credible manner by means of a rigorous research methodology that is grounded in classical and contemporary social theory and the critical use of a wide range of written sources. As a result, her commitment to thorough, painstaking scholarship is evident throughout her published work.

—*Madeleine R. Cousineau*

REFERENCE

M. A. Neal, *Themes of a Lifetime* (Boston: Emmanuel College, 1995).

NEAR-DEATH EXPERIENCE (NDE)

An experience wherein the individual comes close to death but revives and describes perceptions of other worlds.

Researchers find that these experiences have specific stages. According to Kenneth Ring, these are experiencing "a feeling of peace," the sensation of "body separation," "entering the darkness," "seeing the light," and "entering the light." Some people describe events in the real world of which they had no knowledge previously, suggesting that some NDEs have a paranormal component. Universal features within NDE accounts suggest that commonalities within conceptions of heaven, hell, and spiritual beings can be attributed, in part, to these experiences.

—James McClenon

REFERENCES

B. Greyson and C. P. Flynn (eds.), *The Near-Death Experience* (Springfield, Ill.: Thomas, 1985); C. R. Lundahl, *A Collection of Near-Death Research Readings* (Chicago: Nelson-Hall, 1982); J. McClenon, *Wondrous Events* (Philadelphia: University of Pennsylvania Press, 1994); R. A. Moody, Jr., *Life After Life* (Atlanta: Mockingbird, 1975); K. Osis and E. Haraldsson, *At the Hour of Death* (New York: Avon, 1977); K. Ring, *Life at Death* (New York: Coward, McCann and Geoghegan, 1980); K. Ring, *Heading Toward Omega* (New York: Morrow, 1984); M. Sabom, *Recollections of Death* (New York: Simon & Schuster, 1982).

NELSEN, HART M. (1938–)   Ph.D., Vanderbilt University; Professor of Sociology, Pennsylvania State University. President, Association for the Sociology of Religion, 1981; Religious Research Association, 1987-1988.

As a Danish American Presbyterian in a rural community in Minnesota dominated by Lutheran and Catholic interests, Nelsen learned of in-groups and out-groups at an early age. At age 11, he wondered about the effects of cowboy and Indian movies on Native American children from the area. These youthful questions would mature into a distinguished career of teaching and research focused on the sociology of religion, minority status, and ethnic relations.

Nelsen's early academic training was in biology and chemistry, but then his interests in sociology and religion led him to Princeton Theological Seminary (M.Div., 1963), before taking his doctorate in sociology in 1972.

Teaching and research have been Nelsen's enduring commitments, accompanied by significant years in university administration. Nelsen's administrative experience began at Catholic University. Later, he moved to Louisiana State University as chair of sociology and head of rural sociology, answering to two different sets of administrators, which serendipitously served as preparation for accepting the position of Dean of the

College of Liberal Arts at Pennsylvania State University in 1984. Nelsen returned to the classroom as a full professor at Penn State in 1990.

Unswervingly committed to quantitative sociology, Nelsen has produced a stream of articles and books oriented to four topics: (1) sectarianism and southern Appalachian religion and values, (2) clergy and the black church as politicizing agents, (3) development of religious and other attitudes among children and adolescents, and (4) political orientations, religious involvement, and political behavior of evangelicals. He is currently examining black-white differences in religious and political orientations.

Without question, Nelsen's most important work has been on the black church, much of it done in collaboration with his wife, Anne Kusener Nelsen (Ph.D., history, Vanderbilt), and also with R. L. Yokley and Thomas Madron. *The Black Church in America* (coedited with Raytha Yokley and Anne Nelsen, Basic Books 1971) advanced the theses that membership in the black church was almost involuntary and that the black power movement would redirect the church's effort from dependence on a white-determined status quo to a progressive policy of advocacy for its black constituency.

A second volume, *The Black Church in the Sixties* (with Anne Nelsen, University Press of Kentucky 1975), substantiated the earlier argument. In addition to documenting the activism of black ministers, the Nelsens emphasized the importance of the black church in building a sense of ethnic identity and interest. This book also showed that declines in attendance during the 1950s and early 1960s were partially reversed with the emergence of political involvement. However, in later work Nelsen demonstrates a downward trend for black church participation, especially outside the South (Nelsen 1988, Nelsen and Kanagy 1993).

Beyond his work on the black church and its ministers, Nelsen has been interested in the clergy role as such, arising in part from his training under Samuel Blizzard and Ernest Campbell. He laments the lack of attention to the clergy role by current scholars.

A central contribution of Nelsen's career was to challenge Holt's theory that rural migrants to metropolitan areas turn to sectarian religion as a result of culture shock. Using data from the southern Appalachian and Detroit areas, Nelsen and Whitt (1972) not only found a lack of culture shock but also that sectarianism was less prominent among rural migrants than among those remaining in rural areas. In related work with Kanagy and Firebaugh (Nelsen et al. 1994), Nelsen showed that regional differences in church attendance are declining and cannot be explained by migration; rather, the evidence suggests increasing secularization in the South.

Nelsen's work on the religious socialization of children and adolescents, using data from Minnesota, is also significant. He found (1980) that parental religiousness is strongly related to preadolescent religiousness, but parental support is weakly related. Sex of the child has no bearing on the relationship. Also, he was able to demonstrate that factors external to the family, such as denomination and historical developments, interact with gender and birth order to enhance or impede religious transmission (1981).

In addition to organizational presidencies, Nelsen was Executive Secretary of the Society for the Scientific Study of Religion (1983-1987) and Editor of the *Review of Religious Research* (1980-1984); he has also served terms on the editorial boards of *Social Forces* and *Sociological Quarterly* and represented the social scientific study of religion to the American Academy for the Advancement of Science.

—*Larry C. Ingram*

REFERENCES

C. L. Kanagy et al., "The Narrowing Gap in Church Attendance in the United States," *Rural Sociology* 59(1994):515-524; H. M. Nelsen, "Religious Transmission Versus Religious Formation," *Sociological Quarterly* 21(1980):207-218; H. M. Nelsen, "Religious Conformity in an Age of Disbelief," *American Sociological Review* 46(1981):632-640; H. M. Nelsen, "Ministers and Their Milieu," in S. W. Blizzard, *The Protestant Parish Minister* (Storrs, Conn.: Society for the Scientific Study of Religion, 1985): 1-18; H. M. Nelsen, "Unchurched Black Americans," *Review of Religious Research* 29(1988):398-412; H. M. Nelsen and S. Baxter, "Ministers Speak on Watergate," *Review of Religious Research* 23(1981):150-166; H. M. Nelsen and C. L. Kanagy, "Churched and Unchurched Black Americans," in *Church and Denominational Growth*, ed. D. A. Roozen and C. K. Hadaway (Nashville: Abingdon, 1993): 311-323; H. M. Nelsen and H. P. Whitt, "Religion and the Migrant in the City," *Social Forces* 50(1972):379-384.

NELSON, BENJAMIN (1911-1977)

American historian and sociologist; after training as a medievalist at Columbia, taught at several universities, including Chicago, Minnesota, and SUNY–Stony Brook before moving to the Graduate Faculty of the New School for Social Research in 1966.

Nelson merged his studies of usury in the history of religion, law, and literature with sociological perspectives drawn especially from Max Weber. This culminated in 1949 in *The Idea of Usury* (second augmented edition, University of Chicago Press 1969), where he argued that interpretation of the Deuteronomic commandment on usury shifted from a dualistic ethic of "tribal brotherhood" in Ancient Judaism and early Christianity, to an experiment with "universal brotherhood" in the Medieval period, from the twelfth century forward, to a new ethic of "universal otherhood" forged by Calvin and other Reformers, in which all become brothers by becoming equally others. Nelson's emphasis on the "genealogy of ideas" and the encounters of "the Brother" and "the Other" anticipated current intellectual concerns.

In a series of essays, Nelson went beyond Weber's ideas about religion and rationalization. He focused on the roles of mediatorial elites, especially "priests" and "prophets," in developing systems of spiritual direction in the histories of civilizations. He emphasized that rationalizing and universalizing movements occurred in medieval sociocultural life, especially in theology, after the twelfth century. He argued that the quest for subjective certitude in religion and objective certainty in knowledge later led Luther, Galileo, and others in the Reformation and scientific revolution to attack the Medieval system of conscience, moral casuistry, and cure of souls. Since this crucial period, new religious ideals and technocultures have emerged, including linkages of science to Protestant values, the antinomian transmoral conscience, and new rationalizations of conduct (e.g., Taylorism, cost-benefit analysis).

Nelson consistently opposed theoretical and practical "uniformitarianism" in favor of studying varied cultural "histories." His later work consequently emphasized the study of civilizational complexes and encounters, including, especially, comparisons between China and the West.

Active in many professional organizations, Nelson helped found the Society for the Scientific Study of Religion, serving as its Vice President from 1976 until his death. He also was President of the International Society for the Comparative Study of Civilizations from 1971 until his death.

—*Donald A. Nielsen*

REFERENCES

B. Nelson, "The Future of Illusions," *Psychoanalysis* 2, 4(1954):16-37; B. Nelson, "Scholastic Rationales of 'Conscience', Early Modern Crises of Credibility, and the Scientific-Technocultural Revolutions of the 17th and 20th Centuries," *Journal for the Scientific Study of Religion* 7(1968):157-177; B. Nelson, "Max Weber's 'Author's Introduction' (1920)," *Sociological Inquiry* 44(1974):269-278; B. Nelson, "Max Weber, Ernst Troeltsch, and Georg Jellinek as Comparative Historical Sociologists," *Sociological Analysis*

36(1975):229-240; B. Nelson, "On Orient and Occident in Max Weber," *Social Research* 43(1976):114-129; B. Nelson, *On the Roads to Modernity* (Totowa, N.J.: Rowman & Littlefield, 1981).

NEW CHRISTIAN RIGHT *see* Christian Right, Evangelicalism, Fundamentalism, Politics, Televangelism

NEW RELIGIOUS MOVEMENTS   The term *new religious movements* (NRMs, sometimes referred to as alternative religious movements, marginal religious movements, or cults) identifies an important but difficult-to-demarcate set of religious entities. Although some NRMs indeed are of recent origin, many others constitute contemporary rediscoveries or recombinations of cultural themes explored by predecessor groups. Likewise, many NRMs are not religious in the traditional sense. The admixture of contemporary forms of technological innovation, therapy and medicine, economic enterprise, and global organization has given some NRMs a decidedly anomalous profile. In contrast to movements in earlier eras, contemporary NRMs are much more likely to make conscious decisions about whether to define and present themselves as religious and whether to seek administrative/legal legitimation as religious bodies. Finally, a great number of NRMs are cultural transplants, most often of Asian origin, new in the sense only that they are new to the West. Such groups may manifest social movement characteristics in their societies of destination but are likely to have a much more institutional form in their societies of origin.

The available evidence strongly indicates that there has been a long history of nontraditional religious groups in the United States and that these groups have maintained a strong minority presence (Moore 1985). Since a high proportion of these NRMs have survived, the overall number has continued to rise. Through the 1950s, the religious triumvirate—Protestantism, Catholicism, Judaism—dominated the American religious landscape. The erosion of the cultural dominance of these established traditions along with the rapid influx of NRMs has enhanced awareness of religious diversity and of the minority traditions that historically have maintained a more subterranean presence. The period beginning in 1965 was one of exceptional growth in NRMs, particularly of groups of Asian origin, as a result of a relaxation in immigration statutes. According to Melton (1995), currently there are over 1,500 religious groups in the United States, and about half of those are "nonconventional" (a label that excludes various mainstream groups, sectarian offshoots of these groups, and immigrant churches). Despite these impressive numbers, the vast majority of NRMs, of course, are small and are likely to have more impact as a set than individually.

When the term *NRM* is employed, then, the characteristics that the designated groups share in varying degrees are that they are part of a very large number of movements that appeared in Western societies or experienced rapid growth since the mid-1960s, are nontraditional and nonimmigrant religious groups, began with first-generation converts as their primary membership base, attracted among their converts higher status young adults, manifest social movement characteristics and may present an anomalous profile with respect to traditional, mainstream religious organization and belief, and proclaim themselves to be in search of spiritual enlightenment, personal development, or contact with immanent/transcendent forces, entities, or knowledge.

The extraordinary diversity of NRMs is captured by the number of traditions represented in their ranks. These traditions include the Jesus People Movement (The Family [Children of God], Jesus People U.S.A., Alamo Foundation, Church of Bible Understanding) and other Christian-related groups (Holy Spirit Association for the Unification of World Christianity [Moonies], Crossroads Movement [Boston Church of Christ], The Way International); Sufism (Gurdjieff Foundation, Subud); Hinduism (Dawn Horse Communion, Divine Light Mission [Elan Vital], International Society for Krishna Consciousness, International Meditation Society [Transcendental Meditation], Ananda Marga Yoga Society, the Bhagwan movement of Shree Rajneesh, Brahma Kumaris); Buddhism (Nichiren Shoshu of America [Soka Gakki]); Sikhism (Healthy, Happy, Holy Organization); New Age and Human Potential Movement groups (Arica, The Farm, Findhorn, est [The Forum], Insight/MSIA, Primal Therapy, Psychosynthesis); Dianic and Neopagan witchcraft groups; ritual magic groups (Ordo Templi Orientis); satanic churches (Church of Satan, Temple of Set); and UFO groups (Raelians).

Types of Movements   Most scholars studying NRMs have recognized that there is a complex of factors associated with the surge in the number of NRMs and converts' interest in them. One of the most important ways that social scientists have sought to offer theoretical interpretations for NRMs, while dealing with their obvious diversity, has been to create typologies through which theoretically linked explanations for different forms of movement ideology and organization can be fashioned. A substantial number of typologies have been created, with differing objectives and perspectives—type of meaning system, form of movement organization and adherent-movement relationship, and relationship between movement and larger society.

Working from the premise that NRMs constitute responses to pervasive moral ambiguity, several typologies categorize movements in terms of the kinds of meaning they offer or individuals seek. Anthony and Robbins (1982) have distinguished between *monistic* and *dualistic* NRMs and also have developed a number of additional subtypes. Movements with a monistic perspective proclaim meaning systems that are relativistic and subjectivistic, and are likely to conceive of the sacred as immanent. Dualistic movements affirm moral absolutism and tend to conceive of the sacred as transcendent. Monism-dualism most sharply distinguishes Eastern and quasi-religious therapies, which are more likely to be monistic, from Western religions (particularly conservative Christianity), which are more likely to be dualistic. This distinction is roughly paralleled by Westley's (1983) division of NRMs into those that locate the sacred lying inside versus outside the human individual. Hargrove (1978) divides NRMs and individual seekers into two types, *integrative* and *transformative*, based on the kind of meaning that individuals are seeking and that movements offer. Alienation is a problem for liberal personalities, and therefore they are likely to search out transformative NRMs in search of personal growth and new experiences; conservative personalities experiencing a breakdown in moral codes are likely to seek integrative NRMs that provide greater community.

Other typologies focus on the form of movement organization and the nature of the relationship between organization and adherents. Lofland and Richardson (1984) define "elemental forms" of NRM organization based on the extent of their corporateness, that is, the extent to which individuals create a shared collective life: the clinic, congregation, work collective, household collective, corps, and colony. Stark and Bainbridge (1985) distinguish three types of cults, which identify levels of organizational and client involvement: (1) audience cults, which exhibit virtually no formal organization because there is no significant commitment from participants/consumers; (2) client cults, in which spiritual service providers are relatively organized in contrast to their clients, who are linked into moderate commitment social networks through which valued goods and services are exchanged; and (3) cult movements, which seek to provide services that meet all of adherents' spiritual needs, although they vary consider-

ably in the degree to which they mobilize adherents' time, energy, and commitment. Finally, Bird (1979) develops a tripartite typology based on the relationship between adherents and movement. In *devotee* groups, adherents submit themselves to a spiritual master or transcendent truth; in *discipleship* groups, adherents strive for mastery of spiritual disciplines in pursuit of spiritual enlightenment; and in *apprenticeship* groups, adherents work to acquire a variety of skills that will allow them to unleash spiritual powers that reside within them.

Finally, NRMs have been categorized on the basis of their relationship to the prevailing structure of social relations. Wallis (1984) distinguishes between *world-affirming* and *world-rejecting* movements. The former affirms conventional norms and values and offers a means for adherents to realize untapped individual potential with minimal distancing from conventional society; the latter is antagonistic to conventional society and requires that adherents distance themselves from mainstream social life, which is deemed irreparably corrupted and doomed to destruction. Bromley (1997) makes a similar distinction, between *adaptive* and *transformative* movements. However, he roots the distinction in the form of social relations each type of movement seeks to authorize and empower. Adaptive movements distance less from conventional society because they are more compatible with the dominant contractual form of social relations (authorized by state/economy), while transformative movements that reassert covenantal forms of social relations (authorized by family, religion, community) are inherently involved in conflict with the organizational mode of dominant institutions.

Interpretations of NRMs Among scholars studying NRMs, there have been a number of explanations for their appearance and significance. Some social scientists regard NRMs as evidence of the fallacy of a linear evolutionary model of secularization or have offered alternative models, such as the Stark and Bainbridge (1985) cyclical model of periodic resurgence of new religious movements, with NRMs appearing and gaining adherents as mainline religious bodies secularize. Others take the emergence of NRMs as evidence of secularization. Wilson (1982), for example, argues that Western societies have become highly secularized, and religion has become one component of consumer-determined lifestyle choices; NRMs are simply among the more exotic choices available in the contemporary spiritual supermarket. Bell (1977) contends that ongoing secularization motivates individuals to search for new forms of religion as secular alternatives and traditional religions fail to offer meaningful religious understandings.

One of the most common explanations for the emergence of NRMs links them directly to the ferment of the 1960s and 1970s, which was punctuated by the Vietnam War, the Watergate political scandal, and countercultural rebellion. Robert Bellah (1976), for example, argues that American civil religion provided a master narrative merging the values of biblical religion and utilitarian individualism, but that the latter became the dominant element in contemporary society, precipitating a crisis of meaning. He identifies NRMs as successor movements to the countercultural movements of the 1960s. Working from this perspective, Tipton (1982) studied several different types of NRMs that constituted different responses to the failure of mainline religious traditions to provide a meaningful moral context for everyday life and offered alternative routes for their adherents to get "saved from the sixties." These explanations tend to focus on demand for new forms of religion by individuals in search of meaning. A strong case has been made that supply-related rather than demand-related factors are central to explaining religious change (Finke and Iannaccone 1993).

NRM Continuity and Discontinuity with Conventional Society   There has been considerable reflection by social scientists on the degree of continuity/discontinuity between NRMs and the prevailing social order. Explanations for NRM emergence emphasizing factors such as the erosion of moral order, expansion of contractual social relations, or the tumult surrounding the youth counterculture have tended to emphasize the discontinuities, because social movements of any kind are by definition organizations engaged in protest. At the same time, typologies such as those of Wallis (1984) and Bromley (1997) have distinguished between degrees of movement distancing, noting that some movements maintain adherents' positions in conventional society while others isolate and encapsulate them. Various other lines of research have concluded that the continuity-discontinuity relationship between movement and society can be quite complex. It seems clear that a number of NRMs appear to have functioned not only as ways out of conventional society but also as ways back in as they essentially become halfway houses between countercultural and conventional lifestyles. Robbins et al. (1975) delineated four processes through which NRMs have facilitated the social reintegration of adherents: (1) *inculcation* of values or behavioral patterns congruent with societal norms, (2) *combination* of countercultural and conventional values, (3) *compensation* in spiritual form for alienating attributes of

conventional society, and (4) *redirection* of deviant behavior into more conventional channels.

From this perspective, individuals may acquire orientations and skills commensurate with conventional society even if they currently can be acquired and rehearsed in a deviant social context. Further, there can be a variable degree of coincidence between organizational and adherent interests in NRMs. While movements as organizations have been prone to develop commitment-enhancing and commitment-maintaining mechanisms, individual adherents have been equally prone to adopt an experimental posture with respect to NRM affiliation (Robbins and Bromley 1992). Similarly, even in the most intensive periods of mobilization, research has indicated that NRM membership has tended to be composed of a relatively small core of highly committed adherents surrounded by a much larger band of less committed affiliates. As NRMs have passed this point of mobilization, they have elaborated membership categories so as to include affiliates with lower or declining levels of involvement. Finally, NRMs often have rejected some elements of the conventional order while adopting others, perhaps even becoming models that more conventional religious groups may adopt once distanced from their controversial origins. For example, NRMs in essence have nominated new modes of integrating religion and technology (e.g., televangelism), new relationships between religion and healing (quasi-religious therapies), and new ways of financing religious organization (e.g., global corporate holding companies). At an individual level, NRMs may offer adherents a means for recombination of the situational-expressive ethic of the counterculture with various elements of the dominant social order (Tipton 1982). At both structural and individual levels, then, NRMs combine conformity and resistance to conventional social patterns.

Research on Affiliation/Conversion and Organization/Change   The most active area of research on NRMs has been the process of affiliation/conversion and, more recently, defection. Beyond the simple assertion that conversion involves radical personal change, there is great debate over how to specify that change. A variety of causal factors have been proposed to account for variation in the propensity for and probability of conversion, which Machalek and Snow (1993) divide into individual attributes (physical, psychological, social status) and contextual influences (temporal, sociocultural). Positions on type and degree of change vary from simple membership change to a qualitative shift in identity or orientation, from a unique form of change to simply another type of socialization (Long and Hadden 1983), from change in symbolic behavior to change in role behavior (Bromley and Shupe 1986). Some research has proposed causal process models (Lofland and Stark 1965, Bromley and Shupe 1986), while other research has attempted to delineate different types of conversion. In the latter cases, these typologies have differentiated degree of adherent involvement/commitment or types of conversion. For example, Lofland and Skonovd (1981) identify five conversion types based on degree of pressure, temporal duration, affective arousal, af-fective content, and belief-participation ordering; Lofland and Richardson (1984) delineate four major types and eleven subtypes of conversion organized by level of analysis and degree of individual agency. Most of the categories of conversion contained in these typologies presume a substantial measure of convert voluntarism. Although some scholars have proposed much more manipulative, coercive models of NRM conversions (Singer with Lalich 1995), these largely have been rejected by social scientists as adequate explanations for NRM affiliation (Barker 1984, Bromley and Richardson 1983, Shupe and Bromley 1994).

After the initial wave of theorizing and research on conversion/affiliation, the agenda on conversion-related issues has gradually expanded. Two of the most important of these issues are defection from NRMs and gender differences in NRM involvement. As it became clear that most NRM careers were relatively short-lived, research began to focus on the defection process. Scholars working in this area have encountered similar definitional problems and have developed similar models, usually either linking defection to changes in movement structure or examining defection at a social psychological level through a causal process model (Wright and Ebaugh 1993). As yet there have been only a few attempts to develop models that incorporate both conversion and defection (Bromley 1997). In the case of research on gender and NRMs, feminist scholars have effectively advanced the argument that generic theories offering explanations for the emergence of NRMs or of conversions to them fail to take into account significant gender differences. To the extent that sociocultural patterns are patriarchal, then the response of men and women to both stability and change in these patterns may differ substantially. With respect to the latter issue, Davidman (1991) suggests that conversion motives of newly Orthodox Jewish women may be distinctive, and Jacobs (1989) finds gender-specific reasons for NRM disaffiliation. Recently, there has been more research on specifically feminist forms of spirituality, such as witchcraft (Neitz 1994), that explores forms of religious expression by women in specific social locations (Palmer 1994).

There are far fewer theoretical or empirical works on leadership and organization of NRMs than on conversion. The existing corpus of theory and research addresses the issues of (1) attributes of the prophetic leaders who founded NRMs, with movement toward normalizing rather than stigmatizing models; (2) the way in which charismatic authority is exercised and yields to more institutionalized leadership; (3) the implications for NRMs of leadership succession upon the death of the prophetic founder, suggesting surprisingly little organizational disruption; (4) the dynamics of charismatic leadership, documenting the capacity of these leaders to sense and identify cultural contradictions and mobilize adherents, as well as instability and abuse of charismatic authority; (5) factors associated with movement success and failure, indicating a very mixed record and uncertain prospects for most current NRMs; (6) the variety of means through which NRMs finance themselves, describing new ways of combining economic, technological, organizational, and religious forms; and (7) the way in which control agencies and oppositional movements have influenced NRM organizations and development, suggesting that opposition has significant impact on NRMs but does not typically determine their developmental trajectories.

New Religious Movements as an Area of Study
There has been a long-standing interest in marginal groups in the sociology of religion, primarily in the form of theory and research on sects and on the relationship between churches and sects. With the recent proliferation of NRMs and growing awareness of the extent of religious diversity, NRMs have developed rapidly as an area of study. The maturation of NRM research as a semiautonomous area has led to a number of problems in developing an integrated corpus of knowledge. First, there has been disproportionate focus on some of the largest and most controversial of the NRMs while the vast majority of the small, more fluid New Age and feminist spirituality groups, by contrast, remain unstudied. Second, even among the more extensively studied groups, research usually has consisted of single-occasion studies that have not been followed up. Given the rapidity with which NRMs have changed during the early phases of their histories, findings become dated rapidly and developmental histories difficult to compile. Third, in the absence of theoretical/methodological protocols, limited baseline information is available across movements. Fourth, only a narrow range of issues has been researched in depth. The vast majority of research has been social psychological in nature, which in substantial measure reflects the origination of NRM research in the controversy over how and why young adults came to affiliate

with these movements. Fifth, virtually all of the research on NRMs has been conducted in North America and western Europe. The experiences and impact of globally deployed NRMs have received considerably less scrutiny. In addition, virtually none of the very large number of NRMs outside of the West has been studied systematically, severely limiting the capacity for cross-culturally based theoretical development. Sixth, there is only a slightly better track record with respect to historical comparison. While social scientists are extremely aware of parallels in the development of and reaction to religious groups such as the Catholics and Mormons, Christian Scientists and Jehovah's Witnesses, historical-comparative work remains a largely undeveloped area.

In addition to research by individual scholars, research units and advocacy groups of various types have been created specifically directed at collecting and disseminating data on new religions. Among the most active of these have been the Center for the Study of New Religious Movements at the Graduate Theological Union in Berkeley, California; the Institution for the Study of American Religion at the University of California at Santa Barbara; the Information Network Focus on Religious Movements (INFORM) at the London School of Economics in London, England; the Center for Studies on New Religions (CESNUR) in Torino, Italy. Most prominent among the advocacy groups are oppositional groups such as the Cult Awareness Network (CAN) headquartered in Chicago, Illinois; FAIR in the United Kingdom; and the Association for the Defense of the Family and the Individual (ADFI) in France.

There is also a network of Christian organizations that oppose NRMs on theological grounds, and civil libertarian organizations, often funded by the targeted groups, that advocate religious liberty. A few scholarly journals have been established as forums for theory and research on NRMs. These include *Syzygy* in the United States, *Update* in Denmark, and the *Journal of Contemporary Religion* in England. A number of recent publications on NRMs contain comprehensive information on scholarly issues, specific groups, and evaluations of movement organization and practices. These include Melton's *Encyclopedia of American Religions* (Gale 1992), Bromley and Hadden's *The Handbook on Cults and Sects in America* (JAI 1994), Miller's *America's Alternative Religions* (SUNY Press 1995), Robbins's *Cults, Converts, and Charisma* (Sage 1988), Saliba's two bibliographic books, *Psychiatry and the Cults* (Garland 1987) and *Social Science and the Cults* (Garland 1990), and Galanter's *Cults and New Religious Movements* (American Psychiatric Association 1989).

See also Anti-Cult Movement, Brainwashing, Charisma, Civil Religion, Cult

—*David G. Bromley*

REFERENCES

D. Anthony and T. Robbins, "Spiritual Innovation and the Crisis of American Civil Religion," in *Religion in America,* ed. M. Douglas and S. Tipton (Boston: Beacon, 1982): 229-248; E. Barker, *The Making of a "Moonie"* (Oxford: Blackwell, 1984); D. Bell, "The Return of the Sacred," *British Journal of Sociology* 28(1977):419-449; R. Bellah, "New Religious Consciousness and the Crisis in Modernity," in *The New Religious Consciousness,* ed. C. Glock and R. Bellah (Berkeley: University of California Press, 1976): 333-352; F. Bird, "The Pursuit of Innocence," *Sociological Analysis* 40(1979):335-346; D. G. Bromley, "A Sociological Narrative of Crisis Episodes, Collective Action, Culture Workers, and Countermovements," *Sociology of Religion* 58(1997):105-140; D. G. Bromley and J. K. Hadden (eds.), *Handbook on Cults and Sects in America* (Greenwich, Conn.: JAI, 1993); D. G. Bromley and J. T. Richardson (eds.), *The Brainwashing/Deprogramming Controversy* (Lewiston, N.Y.: Mellen, 1983); D. Bromley and A. Shupe, "Affiliation and Disaffiliation," *Thought* 61(1986):192-211; L. Davidman, *Tradition in a Rootless World* (Berkeley: University of California Press, 1991); R. Finke and L. Iannaccone, "Supply-Side Explanations for Religious Change," *Annals* 527(1993):27-39; B. Hargrove, "Integrative and Transformative Religions," in *Understanding the New Religions,* ed. J. Needleman and G. Baker (New York: Seabury, 1978): 257-266; J. Jacobs, *Divine Disenchantment* (Bloomington: Indiana University Press, 1989); J. Lofland and J. T. Richardson, "Religious Movement Organizations," in *Research in Social Movements, Conflicts and Change,* ed. L. Kriesberg (Greenwich, Conn.: JAI, 1984): 29-51; J. Lofland and L. Skonovd, "Conversion Motifs," *Journal for the Scientific Study of Religion* 20(1981):373-385; J. Lofland and R. Stark, "Becoming a World-Saver," *American Sociological Review* 30(1965):862-875; T. Long and J. K. Hadden, "Religious Conversion and the Concept of Socialization," *Journal for the Scientific Study of Religion* 22(1983):1-14; R. Machalek and D. Snow, "Conversion to New Religious Movements," in Bromley and Hadden, *q.v.,* Vol. B (1993): 53-74; J. G. Melton, "The Changing Scene of New Religious Movements," *Social Compass* 42(1995):265-276; L. Moore, *Religious Outsiders and the Making of Americans* (New York: Oxford University Press, 1985); M. J. Neitz, "Quasi-Religions and Cultural Movements," in *Between Sacred and Secular,* ed. A. Greil and T. Robbins (Greenwich, Conn.: JAI, 1994): 127-150; S. Palmer, *Moon Sisters* (Syracuse, N.Y.: Syracuse University Press, 1994); T. Robbins and D. Bromley, "Social Experimentation and the Significance of American New Religions," *Research in the Social Scientific Study of Religion,* Vol. 4 (Greenwich, Conn: JAI, 1992): 1-28; T. Robbins et al., "Youth Culture Religious Movements," *Sociological Quarterly* 16(1975):48-64; A. Shupe and D. G. Bromley (eds.), *Anti-Cult Movements in Cross-Cultural Perspective* (New York: Garland, 1994); M. T. Singer with J.

Lalich, *Cults in Our Midst* (San Francisco: Jossey-Bass, 1995); R. Stark, "Normal Revelations," in *Religion and the Social Order,* ed. D. G. Bromley (Greenwich, Conn.: JAI, 1991): 239-252; R. Stark and W. S. Bainbridge, *The Future of Religion* (Berkeley: University of California Press, 1985); S. Tipton, *Getting Saved from the Sixties* (Berkeley: University of California Press, 1982); R. Wallis, *Elementary Forms of the New Religious Life* (London: Routledge, 1984); F. Westley, *The Complex Forms of the New Religious Life* (Chico, Calif.: Scholars Press, 1983); B. Wilson, *Religion in Sociological Perspective* (Oxford: Oxford University Press, 1982); S. Wright and H. R. Ebaugh, "Leaving New Religions," in Bromley and Hadden, *q.v.,* Vol. B (1993): 117-138.

NEW TESTAMENT   *see* Biblical Studies

NIEBUHR, H(ELMUT) RICHARD (1894-1962)

American theologian and ethicist, born in Wright City, Missouri; younger brother of Reinhold Niebuhr.

Richard Niebuhr graduated from Elmhurst College (1912) and Eden Theological Seminary (1915), Washington University (M.A., 1917), and Yale University Divinity School (B.D., 1923; Ph.D., 1924). In the interim, Niebuhr was ordained in the Evangelical and Reformed Church (1916) and for a short time was a pastor in St. Louis. He taught (1919-1922 and 1927-1931) at Eden Theological Seminary and served as President of Elmhurst College (1924-1927). In 1931, he joined the faculty of Yale Divinity School and, in 1954, was named Sterling Professor of Theology and Christian Ethics at Yale, a post he held until his death.

H. Richard Niebuhr was a complex theologian whom his brother described as the more philosophical of the two famous siblings. Whereas Reinhold leaned toward Luther's theological stance, Richard was more inclined toward Augustinian, Calvinistic approaches to the realm of theological and ethical discourse. Kierkegaard and Barth as well as MacIntosh and Royce informed his early theological reflections, but he was also deeply influenced by Ernst Troeltsch and the whole liberal German tradition that Troeltsch represented. Niebuhr's first major book, *The Social Sources of Denominationalism* (Holt 1929), evidenced the fiery indignation of a young man concerned with the unity of the church. Although often considered Niebuhr's most sociological essay because he used, while modifying, the notions of "church" and "sect" derived from Troeltsch, the theoretical infrastructure of his argument was more readily influenced by the American progressive historians, especially Beard and Turner, rather than Troeltsch. Moreover, his argument was mildly Marxist in that it stressed the causative influence of material factors—class, race, region, immigrant status, and so forth—in accounting for divisions in the church. Niebuhr's second book, *The Kingdom of God in America* (Harper 1937), took the opposite tack and offered an ideational account of the development of American Protestant thought. The tension in the Niebuhrian corpus between material and ideational factors in these volumes written back-to-back was somewhat resolved in *Christ and Culture* (Harper 1951), wherein a five-part typology was constructed for understanding the options by which faith and secular culture, ideal and material forces, could be interrelated.

A bold new departure in Niebuhr's thinking was introduced in *The Meaning of Revelation* (Macmillan 1941), when the social theory of George Herbert Mead was appropriated to provide the infrastructure to Niebuhr's theological reflection. Socialization into a faith orientation of a community of selves became for Niebuhr the inner history of belief from which the meaning of revelation derived. Henceforth Niebuhr constructed his theological-ethical reflection around a tripartite structure and "trialectical" process among self-community-God. This pattern is manifested most clearly in *The Responsible Self* (Harper 1963), although it also appears in somewhat underdeveloped form in *Radical Monotheism and Western Culture* (Harper 1960) and the posthumous volume *Faith on Earth* (Yale University Press 1989).

Niebuhr was one of the few theologians who could successfully integrate social theory with theological construction. He ranks alongside Jonathan Edwards as one of the truly creative American theologians.

See also Church-Sect Theory

—*William R. Garrett*

REFERENCES

J. W. Fowler, *To See the Kingdom* (Nashville: Abingdon, 1974); W. R. Garrett, "The Sociological Theology of H. Richard Niebuhr," in W. H. Swatos, Jr. (ed.), *Religious Sociology* (Westport, Conn.: Greenwood, 1987): 41-55; P. Ramsay, *Faith and Ethics* (New York: Harper, 1957).

NIEBUHR, REINHOLD (1892-1971)

Neo-orthodox theologian and social ethicist; older brother of H. Richard Niebuhr.

A graduate of Yale Divinity School (B.D., 1914; M.A., 1915), Niebuhr served (1915-1928) as pastor of Bethel Evangelical Church in Detroit, where be became deeply involved in industrial social problems, especially labor union affairs, and disillusioned by Social Gospel optimism. He began teaching at Union Theological Seminary of New York in 1928 and was appointed Professor of Applied Christianity in 1930, a post he held until retirement in 1960. Niebuhr's break with the naïveté of liberal Protestant theology was signaled by the publication of *Moral Man and Immoral Society* (Scribner 1932), in which he argued that only human beings can act morally; *justice* is the most one can expect from social groups. His approach to politics was described as "political realism," a stance consistent with his ethical thought. Niebuhr exercised considerable influence over theologians, governmental leaders, and social scientists.

—*William R. Garrett*

REFERENCES

R. W. Fox, *Reinhold Niebuhr* (San Francisco: Harper, 1985); G. Harland, *The Thought of Reinhold Niebuhr* (New York: Oxford University Press, 1960); R. Niebuhr, *The Nature and Destiny of Man*, 2 vols. (New York: Scribner, 1941-1943); R. Niebuhr, *Faith and History* (New York: Scribner, 1949); R. Niebuhr, *Man's Nature and His Communities* (New York: Scribner, 1965).

NIETZSCHE, FRIEDRICH (1844-1900)

German philosopher and psychologist; became Professor of Classical Philology at the University of Basel at age 26. Nietzsche's first book traced the birth of Greek tragedy to religious ritual, the combination of the ecstatic cult of the reborn Dionysios with the Apollonian emphasis on harmonious form. Frequently ill, he resigned in 1879 and wrote his main works on morality as an independent intellectual.

Nietzsche saw Christianity as a slave revolt in morals, fueled by *ressentiment* and the desire for priestly power, which effected a transvaluation of ancient noble values. Christianity helped create the "last man" of modernity, who values happiness, and also promoted nihilism, first by denying life and later by embracing all modern secular values. Nietzsche opposed "progress" with the eternal recurrence of all events, a Dionysian theodicy requiring the "overman," who creatively transcends repeated sufferings. Nietzsche collapsed into insanity in 1889, living another decade under the care of his mother and sister.

—*Donald A. Nielsen*

REFERENCES

R. J. Hollingdale, *Nietzsche* (Baton Rouge: Louisiana State University Press, 1965); W. Kaufmann, *Nietzsche,* 3rd ed. (Princeton, N.J.: Princeton University Press, 1968).

NONOFFICIAL RELIGION   Assumes a background of "official religion." Just as "religion" is now widely seen as a distinctively Western concept, and the articular "religions" as typological concepts, so "religion" itself begins to look like a typological concept, a particular *form* of "commitment."

Eighteenth-century philosophers and subsequent scholars may have derived "religion" from classical Latin, but its ordinary usage in Western languages follows medieval Latin. It then referred not so much to "joining together" either people, or people and divinities, as to the whole (holistic) way of life *religio,* of those who lived according to a Rule *(regula).*

In the first instance, the Rule was that of St. Benedict (480-c. 550). This was gradually extended to include, first, "returns" to that Rule, then, "reforms" of the Rule, and finally confessedly new Rules, such as those of the Friars. However, with the gradual secularization and dissolution of monasteries, and the development of a universal, organized church, which was first centralized and then nationalized, the focus of meaning shifted from the canonically "religious" (i.e., monastic) orders to the ecclesiastical (or canonically "secular") hierarchy. In recent times, the continuing, popular meaning of "religion" (epitomized in its medieval reference) has resurfaced: whatever is both conscientious and "habitual" (e.g., "I answer all my correspondence religiously").

Against this background, what is sometimes called nonofficial religion includes all those phenomena that are considered to be "religious" (i.e., as expressing the core within all intentionality) but that are not incorporated within "official religion." The precise boundaries of official (or real, proper, true, recognized, or canonical) religion vary in accordance with the religion, denomination, religious status, culture, and person. Thus Icelandic Christians may take for granted, as part of their faith, "spiritist" concerns, which other churches, or their own Lutheran denomination in other countries, may consider beyond the pale, either of the Christian faith or of human reason. (The extent of such variations is seldom welcomed or realized.)

At the opposite end of the spectrum to official religion is sometimes placed the "heresy" and "sect," or "blasphemy" and "sacrilege," which official religion recognizes as constituting a rival to itself. However, these are better described as the truly profane: as opposing forms of similar sanctities. The alternative to "official religion," therefore, consists of those expressions of a sacred intentionality that official religion tends to call "pagan" (Latin, *pagus*, rural, that is, outside "a" [named] religion), or "irreligious" (in the sense of a-religious, nonreligious) or "secular" (of this age and therefore not of fundamental religious significance), or "apathetic" (without [the capacity for] suffering [including action]) or "uncommitted" (i.e., not committed in ways that official religion recognizes as being religious).

Thus between the two ends of this spectrum lie all those ways in which official religion is related to (or "exploits") human concerns, such as anxiety or changes in status (superstition, magic, or popular religion) plus all those ways in which people relate to (or "exploit") religious facilities, such as canonical symbols or the *rites de passage* (civil religion or folk religion), and all those self-chosen philanthropic ways in which religious people put their faith into practice—and the nonreligious likewise put their (nonreligious) faith into practice.

In practical life, religious discrimination is as necessary as, for instance, medical or educational discrimination. However, the empirical study of religion (or of humanity) is incomplete if restricted by the official normative definitions of its subject matter. Indeed, the official institutions will themselves be impoverished, and alienated, if they neglect their roots, in popular religion, medicine, education, and so on. For the specialist institutions of highly differentiated cultures are either the dramatic expositions (typologizations) of aspects of ordinary life or else they are "unreal."

See also Implicit Religion, Popular Religion, Secular Religion

—*Edward I. Bailey*

REFERENCES

J. Baillie, *The Roots of Religion in the Human Soul* (London: Hodder and Stoughton, 1926); E. H. Erikson, "Ontology of Ritualization in Man," *Journal of the Royal Anthropological Institute* 251(1966):337-349; A. Gallus, "A Biofunctional Theory of Religion," *Current Anthropology* 13(1972):543-568; R. Horton, "African Traditional Thought & Western Science," *Africa* 37(1967):50-71, 155-187; L. Moore, Jr., "From Profane to Sacred America," *Journal of the American Academy of Religion* 39(1971):321-338; C. J. Sommerville, *The Secularization of Early Modern England* (New York: Oxford University Press, 1992).

NONRATIONAL EXPERIENCE

A category of perception termed *nonrational* because it seems outside of logical reasoning.

Certain types of religious experiences, such as those described by William James, are neither rational nor irrational yet have impact on religious belief. Otto (1923) contended that the experience of the *holy* is beyond rational or ethical conception. Both Otto and O'Dea (1966) suggest that all religiosity is generated from nonrational religious experience. McClenon (1994) found that various unusual experiences (extrasensory perceptions, out-of-body and near-death experiences, apparitions, night paralysis, and contacts with the dead) have universal features that appear to contribute to commonalities in religious conceptions of spirits, souls, life after death, and wondrous human capacities.

See also William James, Thomas F. O'Dea, Rudolf Otto

—*James McClenon*

REFERENCES

W. James, *Varieties of Religious Experience* (New York: New American Library, 1958 [1902]); J. McClenon, *Wondrous Events* (Philadelphia: University of Pennsylvania Press, 1994); T. O'Dea, *Sociology of Religion* (Englewood Cliffs, N.J.: Prentice Hall, 1966); R. Otto, *The Idea of the Holy* (London: Oxford University Press, 1923).

NOYES, JOHN HUMPHREY (1811-1886)

Founder of the Oneida Community; born in Vermont to upper-class parents, educated at Dartmouth and apprenticed as a lawyer. He underwent religious conversion in the 1830s, and attended Andover and Yale theological seminaries, but his license to preach was revoked due to his unorthodox views, especially the idea that mankind was without sin.

He and his wife, Harriet Holton, formed a Perfectionist community in Putney, Vermont, but were forced to leave under threat of prosecution for adultery. After five of their six children were stillborn, Noyes developed the method of *coitus reservatus,* later employed successfully at Oneida, allowing sexual intercourse without pregnancy. Driven out for their unusual (and then illegal) practices, the small group formed a flourishing community in Oneida, New York.

Their practices included democratic discussion, but decisions by Noyes (as God's representative) and a small, educated, male leadership; economic communism, combined ultimately with enterprises such as trap manufacturing and, later, silver making; free love (or "complex marriage") and a form of eugenics through Noyes's determination of marriage partners ("stirpiculture"); communal child rearing; mutual criticism of moral flaws, especially excessive egoism. Internal controversy and threats of legal prosecution forced Noyes and a few friends to leave the community for Canada 1879, where he died in 1886. The community disbanded in 1881 but continued as a joint-stock company (Oneida, Ltd.) around their successful businesses. Noyes's community was one of the most forward-looking religious experiments of its time, and their beliefs and practices remain of interest today.

—*Donald A. Nielsen*

REFERENCES

M. L. Carden, *Oneida* (Baltimore: Johns Hopkins University Press, 1969); W. M. Kephart, *Extraordinary Groups* (New York: St. Martin's, 1987).

NRM, NRMs   *see* New Religious Movements

NUESSE, C. JOSEPH (1913–)   B.E. from Central State Teachers College, Wisconsin; M.A., Northwestern University, Illinois; Ph.D. in sociology at Catholic University of America. He spent most of his academic career at Catholic University of America (1945-1981) as a member, and later chair, of the sociology department, as Dean of the School of Social Science, as Executive Vice President, and as Provost. President, American Catholic Sociological Society, 1954.

Nuesse has been a member of numerous national and international professional committees and has been appointed to public office in several spheres of service, including UNESCO and the Commissioners of the District of Columbia. His published works have ranged over education, history, international relations, religion, and sociology of religion. One of his books, *The Sociology of the Parish* coedited with Thomas J. Harte, C.Ss.R. (Bruce 1951), was one of the earliest on the sociology of American Catholicism published by a member of the American Catholic Sociological Society. In its Introduction, Samuel Cardinal Stritch of Chicago voiced the prevailing concern of many members of the American hierarchy: "The fault in much of sociological studies of our times is a failure to grasp the importance of religion in society. . . . The purpose and the end of all sociological studies is the betterment of society" (p. ix).

Nuesse's ACSS presidential address reflected his concerns about the lack of "a genuine corporate concern on the part of American Catholic agencies and institutions for the support of social research." He called upon graduate departments of sociology to enhance their efforts and upgrade their demands in academic and research achievements.

—*Loretta M. Morris*

OCCUPATIONS   The location of a person in the social structure of a society affects the person's religious orientations. In industrial societies, occupation is an important social location variable.

The fundamental insights about the effect of occupation on religion were stated by Max Weber (1978 [1920]: 468 ff.). He argues that religion is affected by the conditions of a person's life. Occupation can affect an individual's religious orientations, religious interests, beliefs, and practices.

Weber offers several examples to show how this works. Warrior nobles face death and the irrationalities of human destiny. They want a religion to help them cope with their life situation by assigning preeminent value to courage, self-sacrifice, and a sense of honor. Warriors do not need a rational religious ethic. On the other hand, merchants whose lives are devoted to the use of capital that is continuously and rationally used in productive enterprise for profit will seek out ethical and rational religions.

The religion of peasants will glorify agriculture. Only a life devoted to agriculture is pleasing to God. Artisans, by contrast, are less connected to nature than peasants. They are less exposed than peasants to the irrational forces of nature and therefore do not need to use magic to control irrational forces. These artisans cope with calculable risks and must develop a capacity for purposive manipulation of their world. So artisans will seek out rational ethical religions. Such religions

teach that honesty is the best policy and that faithful work will be rewarded.

Occupation affects religious choices for four different units of analysis: individual people, local churches, religious movements, and subcategories of occupations.

Much research is available to show how *individuals* seek religious ideas and groups that speak to the situation of their lives. Steven Tipton (1982) describes Erhard Seminars Training (est) as an orientation to life that is useful to lower-middle-class office workers whose jobs require that they develop skills in dealing with people. Erhard teaches that each person creates his world. The mind is the real shaper of reality. The world just is; right and wrong are meaningless concepts. This is excellent training for middle-level white-collar workers whose work involves manipulation of people. Similarly, Max Stackhouse (1983) observed that conversion to Christianity in Southeast Asia has an occupational aspect. Christianity is linked to technology and pietism. Such a religion appeals to engineers and entrepreneurs.

Occupation also affects *local churches*. Douglass and Brunner (1935) showed that the occupational background and other social characteristics of modal church members has a powerful effect on church programs. Churches where the modal member is a white-collar worker provide worship, educational programs, evangelism, social action, and other programs that fit this way of life. Churches where the modal member is a factory worker offer programs that meet the needs of their congregants. A recent study of Connecticut churches shows the same patterns (Roozen et al. 1984).

Large *religious movements* also have been influenced by occupation. Darian (1977) argues that one reason for the growth of Buddhism was that it satisfied the economic and status needs of merchants, who in turn benefitted from imperial expansion in India.

Particular occupations that are not homogeneous have members with different involvements with religion. The professorate is an occupation that has been extensively studied (Anderson 1968, Lehman and Shriver 1968). Professors are less involved with religion than comparable middle-class Americans. The usual explanation for this is that an academic discipline and life on campus can provide a way of life that substitutes for organized religion. Professors in different fields differ systematically in their involvement with religion. Professors in engineering, science, and professional schools are more involved with religion than professors in the core liberal arts fields. Here again, professors in the core liberal arts fields find it easier than colleagues in professional schools and in the "hands-on" disciplines to avoid ordinary middle-class lifestyles.

See also Stratification

—*William Silverman*

REFERENCES

C. Anderson, "The Intellectual Subsociety Hypothesis," *Sociological Quarterly* 9(1968):210-227; J. C. Darian, "Social and Economic Factors in the Rise of Buddhism," *Sociological Analysis* 38(1977):226-238; H. P. Douglass and E. deS. Brunner, *The Protestant Church as a Social Institution* (New York: Harper, 1935); E. C. Lehman, Jr., and D. W. Shriver, Jr., "Academic Discipline as Predictive of Family Religiosity," *Social Forces* 47(1968):171-182; D. A. Roozen et al., *Varieties of Religious Presence* (New York: Pilgrim, 1984); M. L. Stackhouse, "Faiths and Politics in South East Asia," *This World* 4(1983):20-48; S. M. Tipton, *Getting Saved from the Sixties* (Berkeley: University of California Press, 1982); M. Weber, *Economy and Society* (Berkeley: University of California Press, 1978 [1920]).

O'DEA, THOMAS F. (1915-1974)   Sociologist of religion; Ph.D., Harvard University. Author of numerous publications regarding religion, Roman Catholic thought and life, and social issues. Leading participant in the American Catholic Sociological Society and its successor, the Association for the Sociology of Religion.

O'Dea's sociological analysis is noteworthy for his attention to the institutional parameters of religious belief and practice within modern societies, the dilemmas facing these institutions, and the implications of secularization for religions and individual believers. Much of his writing also reflects the systematic understanding of historical processes and trends that he typically brought to bear in his work as a sociologist. He was firmly convinced of the benefits of drawing upon interdisciplinary sources. These insights, he believed, should contribute to the construction of sociological perspectives characterized by strong linkages among research, interpretation, and theory. Although his attention as a scholar was directed for the most part at religious life in the United States, he also demonstrated a thorough knowledge of developments occurring elsewhere.

Early Directions: Studies in Catholicism and Mormonism   This catholicity in his thought was no doubt due in large measure to a personal and professional background marked by a rich diversity of influences and experiences. Born in Amesbury, Massachusetts, to a working-class, Irish Catholic family, O'Dea reached maturity during the Great Depression. The economic and social hardships he witnessed, coupled with his strong political idealism, moved O'Dea to become an activist in the Young Communist League during the 1930s. This role would lead to serious confrontations with congressional authorities at the time of the anticommunist witch-hunts and would have ongoing implications throughout his academic career. During World War II, O'Dea served with distinction in the U.S. Army Air Force and was stationed in China, India, and the South Pacific. These experiences with other cultures would later lend a global perspective to O'Dea's work on religion and comparative cultures.

When he enrolled in Harvard following the war, O'Dea quickly distinguished himself through his insight into religious matters. A student of Talcott Parsons, O'Dea began entering into the dialogue with functionalist theory that would shape much of his scholarly work. Through various case studies and explorations into sociological theory, he examined the possibilities and limitations of the functionalist approach for understanding the content of religious experience, as well as the ambiguities and tensions inherent in religion's functions for societies, groups, and individuals. Of special interest were the processes by which, through historical and situational developments, religion's functions may subsequently turn dysfunctional for a religion.

His first major study, completed as an undergraduate honors thesis in 1949, examined the conflicts then building between St. Benedict's Center in Cambridge, Massachusetts, and Roman Catholic authorities in what became known as the "Boston Heresy Case." Extending Troeltsch's church-sect typology, O'Dea demonstrated how sects may emerge not only as a form of ethical protest against church policy or practice but also as a defensive response to situational "strains" or "tensions." For complex historical and sociocultural reasons, the church may experience extreme difficulties, as it did in this case, in defusing or containing these sectarian developments, thereby leading to a crisis "resolved" by excommunication. This study proved to be not only highly prescient (O'Dea had, in effect, applied sociological concepts and content analysis to predict the eventual outcome of the conflict), it also clearly identified his research preferences and direction. Even at this early stage in his career, O'Dea revealed his fascination with the historical and sociological sources of dissent within religious institutions as well as church leaders' responses to these challenges to ecclesiastical authority.

When, as a graduate student, he participated in the Harvard research project, the Comparative Study of Values in Five Cultures, during the early 1950s, O'Dea began what became a lifelong study of the Mormons. With his later expanded book-length treatment of the subject in *The Mormons* (University of Chicago Press 1957), he had produced one of the first and best sociological analyses of the Mormons while continuing to build upon his critique of Troeltsch's typology. More than a mid-twentieth-century snapshot of Mormonism in the United States, this work was also an attempt to understand the historical, political, cultural, and theological factors that had shaped this religious movement's success as a distinctively, if peculiarly, American and quasi-ethnic phenomenon (especially in the Southwest). Characteristically, O'Dea identified the tensions then facing the Mormon Church in its multifaceted encounters with modern or "mainstream" beliefs and institutions.

During this period, O'Dea raised similar questions and themes within his ongoing studies of contemporary Roman Catholic life. In *American Catholic Dilemma* (Sheed & Ward 1958), he provided a timely assessment of Catholicism's minority status as a religion in the United States (appealing mainly to specific immigrant groups), the apparent anti-intellectualism evident within Catholic circles, and the likely prospects for changes in this situation. O'Dea took the position that the American Catholic Church was at a major turning point. Essentially, the institution was faced with the dilemma of responding to a modern, rapidly changing sociocultural context that, by placing a high value on innovation as well as intellectual and critical inquiry, questioned traditional church authority and religious certitude. The historical church emphasis on formalism, authoritarianism, clericalism, moralism, and cultural defensiveness, while functional for protecting a traditional Catholic worldview, nevertheless left the church and its individual members poorly prepared to meet the religious and sociocultural expectations and needs of the modern age. Without the proper institutional supports, Catholic voices would continue to be absent not only from American intellectual discourse but also from involvement in the decisions shaping the future of the United States as a global power.

The Dilemmas of Institutionalization In later works, particularly his widely read *The Sociology of Religion* (Prentice Hall 1966), O'Dea expanded his initial analysis of institutional dilemmas within the Catholic Church by developing a more general explanation of the phenomena. By building upon and extending, among other influences, Troeltsch's study of church and sect, Weber's insights into the routinization of charisma, and Parsons's discussion of deinstitutionalization, O'Dea created a conceptual scheme for understanding the factors contributing to the functioning of, and change processes within, religious movements and organizations. In an example of middle-range sociological theory, O'Dea identified five dilemmas that were "structurally inherent" to religious institutionalization:

(1) Dilemma of mixed motivation. Over time, institutionalization tends to produce specialized offices and other roles. The originally religious goals, values, and motives of those involved in the organization, whether at the leadership or laity levels, may become more worldly. The organization is faced with the question of whether, and how, to adapt to this divergence in, and widening of, members' motives.

(2) Symbolic dilemma: Objectification versus alienation. The original sacred experience of transcendence must, if it is to be socially shared within a cohesive group, find expression through a collection of objectified symbols. With institutionalization, the sense of awe and power associated with sacred symbols and rituals may become routinized and the symbols themselves may become alienated from the believer.

(3) Dilemma of administrative order: Elaboration and alienation. Institutionalization tends to generate new demands that are usually met most efficiently through bureaucratic offices. Expansion of the bureaucracy typically follows, as does the potential for detachment or alienation of both the offices and the office-holders from the laity.

(4) Dilemma of delimitation: Concrete definition versus substitution of the letter for the spirit. In communicating and protecting the spirit of its religious insights, the organization is typically driven toward dogmatism, fundamentalism, and the establishment of specialized interpretive structures and processes. The scope and depth of the original religious message may become further reduced as a result of attempts to maintain its relevance for believers or through efforts aimed at attracting converts.

(5) Dilemma of power: Conversion versus coercion. During the early history of a religious movement or organization, individual believers usually demonstrate their faith and commitment to the emerging religion through an act of conversion. Through time, the institution, to maintain and even strengthen its status, tends to become more closely aligned with secular authorities and may draw upon the power of the state to support its goals. Doing so, however, raises the likelihood that membership in the religious body will be seen as mandatory, and increases the risk that protest groups may arise in response. The stronger ties to secular institutions may also foster cynicism and secularization among both the religious leadership and the laity.

Sociologists of various stripes have applied O'Dea's analysis of these structural dilemmas fairly widely to the study of religion but less so to research on secular movements or organizations. O'Dea himself believed that this conceptual scheme was a significant contribution to the sociology of religion as well as to sociology generally. Some theorists of modern complex organizations have recognized the potential in further extending the initial framework to examine not only internal processes but also the dilemmas found in an institution's relationships with its external sociopolitical environments (Yinger 1970:236). While appreciating the value of the framework, other scholars have raised criticisms regarding O'Dea's assumptions that the dilemmas are structurally inherent (Mathisen 1987:316) and that social movements institutionalize as a result of deliberate choices (McGuire 1981:135). O'Dea also failed to develop in a systematic fashion the dilemmas of deinstitutionalization (Brown 1977:142).

New Directions: Secularization and Comparative Religions   O'Dea's interest in institutional tensions or dilemmas, especially those taking place within American Catholicism (a community whose diversity was becoming increasingly problematic to the church leadership), continued to hold his attention during the final stages of his career. In *The Catholic Crisis* (Beacon 1968), he wrote an insightful commentary on Vatican II and its historical antecedents that systematically probed the dilemmas and challenges that modern culture raised for the church's identity, unity, and authority. In 1969, he, along with many other prominent scholars, participated in the International Symposium on the Culture of Unbelief held in Rome, focusing on the stresses or tensions facing religious organizations as a result of secularization.

For O'Dea, the attempt to examine and come to terms with modern institutional dilemmas and their implications for individuals was not simply an academic exercise. It was also part of a highly personal, lifelong quest to understand his own perceived marginality to American society that was coupled, at times, with the feeling that he did not truly belong in the Catholic community either. His life was marked by a series of difficult and often painful struggles to reconcile his spirituality with recurring doubts about his Catholic identity. As a sociologist and intellectual who knew better than most how the "working out" of institutional dilemmas may contribute to the doubts of individual believers, he was nevertheless remarkably successful in maintaining his integrity and methodological detachment as a scholar when studying religion and, specifically, the tensions within Catholicism. At the same time, he never failed to take with utmost seriousness the capacity of faith to satisfy the extraordinary needs of all individuals, including himself, for deeper meanings and a sense of purpose.

Toward the end of his life, O'Dea was becoming increasingly interested in pursuing comparative studies among Christianity, Judaism, and Islam. He had traveled to Israel in the early 1970s as a visiting professor of sociology at Hebrew University (Jerusalem), an experience that affected him profoundly and led to the beginnings of his collaborations with other scholars on research into these religious traditions. At about this time, a debilitating and ultimately fatal illness prevented O'Dea from participating further.

O'Dea's papers are housed in the archives at Brigham Young University in Provo, Utah.

—*Bruce Karlenzig*

REFERENCES

D. Brown, "Dilemmas of Deinstitutionalization," *Sociological Analysis* 38(1977):140-144; D. Dohen, "Tensions of the Believer as Sociologist of Religion," *Sociological Analysis* 38(1977):131-136; J. P. Fitzpatrick, "The Sociologist as Catholic," *America* 132(Jan. 1975):7-9; J. A. Mathisen, "Thomas O'Dea's Dilemmas of Institutionalization," *Sociological Analysis* 47(1987):302-318; M. B. McGuire, *Religion*, 2nd ed. (Belmont, Calif.: Wadsworth, 1981); R. S. Michaelsen, "Enigmas in Interpreting Mormonism," *Sociological Analysis* 38(1977):145-153; T. F. O'Dea, *Alienation, Atheism, and the Religious Crisis* (New York: Sheed and Ward, 1969);

T. F. O'Dea, *Sociology and the Study of Religion* (New York: Basic Books, 1970); T. F. O'Dea et al., *Religion and Man* (New York: Harper, 1972); T. Parsons, "The Institutionalization of Belief," *Sociological Analysis* 38(1977):137-139; J. M. Yinger, *The Scientific Study of Religion* (London: Macmillan, 1970).

OLD TESTAMENT   *see* Biblical Studies

ORDERS   Generally a group of either men or women (although some mixed-sex orders have been tried), particularly but not exclusively, in Christianity or Buddhism, who voluntarily take vows to live under more stringent religious standards than are required for the modal or average member of their religious tradition; a form of *virtuoso religiosity*. In Christianity, religious orders are almost entirely restricted to the liturgical traditions of Orthodoxy, Anglicanism, European Lutheranism, and Roman Catholicism, and it is in the Catholic context that they have had the greatest impact upon Western civilization.

Religious orders of men and women in the Roman Catholic Church are part of the official church structure and are coordinated by the Congregation for Religious Institutes of Consecrated Life (CICL). Individuals in these orders take vows of celibacy, poverty, and obedience as well as a commitment to live by the constitutions of their particular religious order. These constitutions are approved by the Congregation for Religious Institutes, a Vatican office that also oversees compliance with the guidelines and spirit of the constitutions.

Statistics on the numbers of religious show that there are approximately 1,190,272 members of religious orders throughout the world, of whom 229,181 are men (including 156,191 clerics and 73,090 lay) and 960,991 women (Schneiders 1987). There are therefore nearly four female Catholic religious for every male religious in the world.

Throughout history, and continuing today, there are three basic forms of the religious life that correlate with three types of orders: contemplative, semicontemplative, and active orders (Neal 1990). Contemplative orders give primacy to prayer in a monastery or convent setting with almost total exclusion of nonmembers. The majority of orders in the early medieval church of Europe and North Africa were contemplative in nature. Women in these contemplative orders were called nuns, and men were known as monks. Contemplative religious orders followed the routine of daily singing or reciting of the Divine Office, daily meditation, attendance at Mass and other required communal prayers,

periodic gatherings for meals, instruction, and the physical labor required for the economic sustenance of the convent. Semicontemplative orders combined the doing of good works and the performance of traditional prayer forms, which characterized monastery and convent living from the seventeenth century to the beginning of the Second Vatican Council in the early l960s. Active orders, which date to the founding of the Daughters of Charity in 1633, gave up the idea of monastic life so as to respond to the needs of the sick and the poor in the emerging cities in Europe. With active orders, the physical structures and monastic life of isolation and solemn prayer were relaxed to provide services to the poor, uneducated, sick, and needy. Men in active orders are either priestly clerics or lay brothers, and women are known as Catholic sisters. (In popular usage, however, terms such as *nun* and *sister* are often conflated.)

Christian religious orders are almost as old as the church itself. In the early centuries of the church, the two clearly defined roles for women in the church were virgins and widows who committed themselves to a celibate way of life "for the sake of the Kingdom" (1 Tim. 5:3-17). As the period of persecutions came to an end and the church began to be officially recognized and accepted in the Roman Empire, a clearly recognizable religious order began to emerge in the form of the holy ascetic who escaped to the desert to pray and do penance. Both men and women were attracted to desert asceticism. By the fifth century, in the West, Roman civilization began to weaken with the onslaught of barbarian tribes. Monasteries and convents became refuge cloisters where the treasures of civilizations were protected (Cada et al. 1979).

The *Age of Monasticism* (500-1200 C.E.) can be dated to St. Benedict's founding of the monastery Monte Cassino in 529. As the West was moving into a system of feudal kingdoms organized around lords and serfs, Benedict established a parallel structure in his monasteries, with the abbot or abbess serving as the feudal lord who protects, cares for, and guides his or her servants. Benedict's conception of the religious community as a family has remained powerful throughout the continuing history of religious orders (Cada et al. 1979).

In reaction to the laxities that crept into monastic life in the latter part of the medieval era, primarily as a result of accumulated wealth, the next era of religious orders was characterized by a commitment to live in poverty as Christ had done. Many monks left their monasteries and wandered among the people to witness to gospel poverty. Most mendicant orders were exclusively male because it was considered improper for women to live in abject poverty and wander about seeking alms. However, mendicant orders of men had parallel communities for women called "second orders," in which women shared the values of celibacy and poverty but remained in their convents.

The far-reaching changes that were transforming Europe by the middle of the fifteenth century (e.g., new humanism of the Renaissance, printing, geographic discoveries of "new worlds," and eventually the Protestant Reformation) led to the founding of the Jesuits for religious men and the Ursulines for women. Both groups had the goal of providing an elite corps of dedicated servants ready to aid the church in its new apostolic needs, and valued a high level of personal holiness that would enable the religious members to face the new task of the church without the protections of the monastery. The evolution of the teaching orders in Europe in the late 1700s and throughout the 1800s were part of the new apostolic thrust for religious women. About 600 new religious orders were founded in Europe during the nineteenth century (Neal 1990). These orders were dedicated to building and staffing parochial institutions such as schools, hospitals, and agencies to assist the poor. It was from these teaching orders that many American bishops and priests recruited sisters to come to the United States to tend the needs of immigrant Catholics.

Throughout the nineteenth and early twentieth centuries, the number of American sisters continued to grow, reaching their highest number in 1965 when there were 179,954 Catholic sisters in the United States (*Official Catholic Directory* 1965). However, in the late 1960s that trend began to reverse itself as increasing numbers of sisters left their religious orders to return to a lay life and decreasing numbers of young Catholic women entered convents. The decline in numbers of religious women has continued and has created alarm both within religious orders themselves and within the church, which depends on religious personnel as service providers. Between 1965-1990, religious orders of women suffered a 43% decrease in membership with a drop to 103,269 by 1990. While the exodus from religious orders has dwindled, few women are entering. The fact that many of the departees were younger sisters and that few young women were entering has resulted in a very high median age for American sisters, estimated at 66 years. The decline in numbers of American sisters raises many questions regarding the viability and future forms that religious life may assume in the United States (Ebaugh 1993a, Neal 1990, Nygren and Ukeritis 1993, Wittberg 1994). Many religious orders of men are facing similar problems in regard to both defections and declining recruits, although the decline in membership has not been as drastic for religious males (an 18% decrease in members from 1962-1992 compared with the 43% decrease for women; Nygren and Ukeritis 1993).

Of interest, while the numbers of Catholic sisters are declining significantly in the Western world, in developing countries numbers of religious women are growing or remaining constant in relationship to the Catholic population (Ebaugh 1993b, Ebaugh et al. 1996). There is indication that social factors related to development and industrialization may affect growth and decline patterns of Catholic religious orders.

—*Helen Rose Ebaugh*

REFERENCES

L. Cada et al., *Shaping the Coming Age of Religious Life* (New York: Seabury, 1979); H. R. Ebaugh, "The Growth and Decline of Catholic Religious Orders of Women Worldwide," *Journal for the Scientific Study of Religion* 32(1993a):68-75; H. R. Ebaugh, *Women in the Vanishing Cloister* (New Brunswick, N.J.: Rutgers University Press, 1993b); H. R. Ebaugh et al., "The Growth and Decline of the Population of Catholic Nuns Cross-Nationally," *Journal for the Scientific Study of Religion* 35(1996):171-183; M. Hill, *The Religious Order* (London: Heinemann, 1973); J. A. M. McNamara, *Sisters in Arms* (Cambridge: Harvard University Press, 1996); M. A. Neal, *From Nuns to Sisters* (Mystic, Conn.: Twenty-Third Publications, 1990); D. Nygren and M. Ukeritis, *The Future of Religious Orders in the United States* (Westport, Conn.: Praeger, 1993) S. M. Schneiders, "Reflections on the History of Religious Life and Contemporary Developments," in *Turning Points in Religious Life*, ed. C. Tingley (Wilmington, Del.: Glazier, 1987): 13-60; P. Wittberg, *The Rise and Decline of Catholic Religious Orders* (Albany: SUNY, 1994).

ORDINATION   Representing a professional status in most religious organizations, ordination normally involves seminary training, internship, examination, and a vocational commitment or "calling." Religious organizations with a congregational polity typically have had a single ordination rite in which a commission comes from the local membership, with additional requirements or ratification necessary for denominationwide recognition. Organizations with an episcopal polity normally ordain clergy twice, first to a preparatory status, which normally is the diaconate, and second to a final status as presbyter, elder, or priest, allowing full pastoral, preaching, and sacramental activity and eligibility for consecration as a bishop. Several religious organizations recently have developed multiple ordination tracks that facilitate specialized ministries.

Although ordination is emphasized as a sacrament in Roman Catholic, Orthodox, and Anglican traditions, Protestant denominations have used ordination as a means to set apart clergy for certain leadership functions while affirming, to use Luther's emphasis, the "priesthood of all believers." Some religious groups have shunned ordination altogether, although officers or leaders may be commissioned or otherwise formally designated. The Jewish rabbinate, an ordained status formally accorded those who have mastered the rabbinical literature and are considered capable of deciding matters of Jewish law following years of formal training, also emphasizes educational, pastoral, worship, and community leadership functions. Although Muslims do not formally ordain religious leaders, the *imām* serves as a spiritual leader and religious authority. The imām in Shī'ite tradition is directly descended from Muhammad, while in Sunni tradition the imām is a leader of worship in the mosque and an adviser on Islamic law, or Sharia. In Buddhist traditions, those formally admitted into the monastery, or Sangha, have been considered ordained. Monks, called priests where they perform community worship ritual functions, also have been leaders in education and political activism. Roles and responsibilities of ordained monks or priests vary by sect and host culture.

All religions ordaining clergy at some point in their development have limited ordination to men either by normative assumption or by explicit injunction, which not only has marginalized women from leadership opportunities but resulted in men controlling religious doctrine, scriptural interpretation, worship ritual, and governance. Although some evidence exists that women were ordained in a few Christian communities as late as the eleventh century, women have been ordained to the same office with the same denominational status and privileges as men only since the mid-nineteenth century. Neither the Roman Catholic Church nor any Orthodox tradition ordains women; some Anglican dioceses and conservative Protestant churches also do not ordain women.

Controversy surrounding women's ordination persists to the present day. Arguments for excluding women in conservative Protestant traditions have relied on scriptural justification (e.g., 1 Cor. 14:34-36, 1 Tim. 2:12). Roman Catholic exclusion has argued that the priest sacramentally represents the person of Jesus Christ, who was male. Male denominational leaders, including bishops, and male and female laity consistently have been more supportive of women's ordination than have rank-and-file male clergy, who have blocked or delayed women's ordination in several denominations or have generated backlash movements restricting opportunities for women's ordination and

deployment. Examples of denominations where these strategies have been employed include the Southern Baptist Convention, the Episcopal Church, the Church of England, and the Evangelical Lutheran Church of Latvia. Bishops in the Episcopal Synod of America refuse to recognize the priestly and episcopal acts of the denomination's ordained women, including allowing them to function in ESA dioceses, while numerous "continuing" churches have separated from the Episcopal Church over the issue.

Ordination controversies since the 1970s also have centered on sexual orientation. Some denominations restrict ordination to heterosexuals, while others require celibacy of all but legally married clergy. Only the Metropolitan Community Church, the United Church of Christ, the Unitarian Universalist, and the Reform Jewish traditions ordain nonheterosexual clergy without mandating celibacy.

—*Paula D. Nesbitt*

REFERENCES

K. E. Børresen, "Women's Ordination," *Theology Digest* 40 (1993):15-19; M. Chaves, *Ordaining Women* (Cambridge: Harvard University Press, 1997); *The Perennial Dictionary of World Religions* (San Francisco: Harper, 1989); E. G. Hinson, "Ordination in Christian History," *Review and Expositor* 78(1981):485-496; J. G. Melton, *The Church Speaks On* (Detroit: Gale Research, 1991); A. Swidler (ed.), *Homosexuality and World Religions* (Valley Forge, Pa.: Trinity, 1993); M. Warkentin, *Ordination* (Grand Rapids, Mich.: Eerdmans, 1982); B. B. Zikmund, "Winning Ordination for Women in Mainstream Protestant Churches," in *Women and Religion in America,* ed. R. R. Ruether and R. S. Keller (San Francisco: Harper, 1986): 339-383.

ORGANIZATION THEORY AND RELIGIOUS ORGANIZATION

An organization is a social formation in which the parts appear to belong more to each other than to something outside; that is, an organization has a *boundary* around it more or less. Organizing happens whenever some want to do or carry out something. Organizing is ancient and probably first emerged to carry out hunting or military campaigns. The first organizations were clans or clusters of families and were probably organized according to principles of seniority and gender (oldest males first), what today we term *patriarchalism*. This "clan" principle still dominates in many societies, in both political and religious sectors, and is frequently conducive to "corruption," nepotism, and lack of fairness to women and children.

The ancient Romans perfected the bureaucratic military model, and when the Roman Empire ceased, the emerging Roman Catholic Church borrowed much of its organization and nomenclature from Rome, converting caesar into pope, senators into cardinals, and so on down to converting plebeians into lay folk. Up until the Second Vatican Council, the RCC officially consisted of only the pope, cardinals, bishops, and clergy, but now the "faithful" too are included as essential.

Modern Organization Theory Modern organizing began with the rise of the European nation-states out of the combining of regional principalities in the seventeenth to nineteenth centuries. England and France led, followed much later by Germany and Italy. Central kings became powerful and needed to secure their boundaries by more permanent military forces, which in turn required central treasuries, new forms of taxation, and civil organization separate from the king's household.

In the nineteenth century, many attempted to codify thoughts and rules of organizing. Theorizing in Europe tended to start with the society as a whole and to work down to the civil unit or specific organization (civil agency); whereas, in the United States, theorists started with the lowest level, the "small (work) group," and worked their way up to the organization unit (the factory, union, congregation), but seldom dealt with the wider external environment.

Individual social theorists tended to conceptualize organizations and organizing as they wanted to see them. Adam Smith, for example, saw organization as somewhat flat and inchoate with firms or partnerships competing opportunistically to form unstable *markets*. Decisions are made purely in terms of rational cost-benefit analysis. Émile Durkheim, in trying to characterize religious organization, went back to nonliterate, tribal *clans* as the prototypical, feelings-based model for religious group solidarity, and argued that the solidarity of society itself was based on religious feelings. Max Weber was impressed with nineteenth-century German civil service—*bureaucracy*—typifying this form by its use of hierarchy and rational rules for managing complex social tasks with efficiency and fairness. He thought bureaucracy had overcome the evils of patriarchalism and nepotism.

Weber also was aware of the existence and power of "mission" movement organizations whose leaders were endowed with *charisma,* although he thought such organizations would eventually be "routinized" into either patriarchal or rational-legal bureaucratic forms. Alexis de Tocqueville, in his early nineteenth-century tour of the United States, was impressed with the prominence of the mutual-benefit *voluntary associa-tion* as the organizing principle for communal, religious organization on the American frontier. The decentralized, sociopolitical environment of the United States thus contributed another organizational form.

Each of these observers, then, discovered a *portion* of the truth, but a fuller measure of truth lies in seeing markets, bureaucracies, clans, missions, and voluntary associations as *complementary* to each other and perhaps even as sequential. That is, it will be most helpful if we try to see how individual organizations can embody bits and pieces of *all* types simultaneously. Historically, religious organizations have tended to be clanlike and to be fused with common ethnicity and/or nationality. Even today, in some American denominations (which we may term *European transplants,* such as Catholics, Lutherans), the members predominantly are not adult converts but have been "born" into the faith and so descend from certain characteristic, territorial ethnic ancestries. The denomination is the truly American form of religion, and because of American church-state separation and "nonestablishment," all religious organizations in the new society are definitionally voluntary associations, as Tocqueville noted. To the extent that congregations (and denominations) are fully "voluntary," to that extent they are "coalitions," meaning that the members are free to leave at any time (although they normally don't). We may term a council of churches a *federation* (an organization of organizations) with member units also free to leave at any point.

Through time, some American denominations have had to become somewhat centralized and to develop central bureaucratic departments to organize evangelization and new congregation formation, publication, ministerial education, and overseas ministries more effectively. Although the central offices underwent some bureaucratization, the congregations still remained rather flat in structure with much mainly volunteer participation. Harrison (1959) notes, with reference to American Baptists, that while official ideology was antihierarchic, Baptists have had to develop the functional equivalent of bishops (a hierarchy) to pursue their tasks of evangelizing and congregation building. In recent decades, however, more and more "megacongregations" have been developed with thousands of members, which tend to look and behave more and more like religious crowds or "markets" with the turnover, "shopping," and loose ties associated with modern shopping malls and TV audiences. Mission forms will tend to be exceptional, short-lived, and dominated by charismatic or quasi-charismatic personalities. If enduring and institutionalized as parts of denominations, missions will be supplemental and devoted to specific tasks (e.g., Catholic religious orders). If freestanding, mission forms will come and go as parts of wider societal social movements, some acting defensively (e.g., "right to life") and others liberatingly (e.g., Amnesty International). They all will be voluntary and supported by the gifts and volunteer efforts of members. Some missions will even self-destruct because of internal rivalry and a preponderance of "evil" outcomes.

"Open Systems" Theory More recently, organization theorists have been concerned to explicate two dimensions of organizational structure and functioning. On the one hand, there is a new awareness of how individual organizations are no longer isolated from events around them and how they are affected by other organizations, religious and secular, by the sociocultural environment, and especially by the state (including the courts, legislatures, and executive) and its regulatory powers. In the United States, at least, the interorganizational situation of the nineteenth century seems primitive compared with the complex organizational, environmental "fields" of today. Few relationships are very "closed," and everything seems "open" to everything else. This is the meaning of *open systems*. It is interesting that recent research on congregations reveals that those congregations that are most "open" to the "outside" (i.e., participate in providing shelter for the homeless, have members of differing ethnic backgrounds, and so on) appear to grow the most compared with more "closed" congregations.

On the other hand, nineteenth-century organization theory seemed to place a premium on rationality, with early theory seeing the organization (or its subunits) as utilitarian, as means to an end. With liberal optimism, managers saw themselves in control of their situations and as able to marshal people and group components efficiently in accord with the mangers' biddings. Frederick Taylor, the founder of "scientific management" in the late nineteenth century, thought there was "one best way" to do everything. Today, we realize that, while not just "any way" will do either, there are many contingencies in the situation that make it impossible to develop only "one best way" for all situations. The alternative to "rational" systems is the notion of "natural" systems. That is, many organizations should be viewed as being based on feelings and as having "lives of their own." The uniqueness and "naturalness" of an organization comes not only from the human traits of the member-employees (which they bring with them when they enter the organization) but also from what today is called the "organizational culture"—the traditions, memories, and symbols of the organization itself as it develops in its own life history. Thus an organization

may have very rational aims, but it doesn't necessarily always behave in a rational manner.

A "systems" or process view of organizations thus sees the organization as existing within an environment—a "network" of other organizations that can be its sister units (e.g., other congregations) in the same denomination or its competitors, rivals, or allies outside (e.g., other denominations or faiths). "Systems," furthermore, means that one must view organizations as *processes*. That is, organizations must (1) mobilize resources, personnel, funds, reputation, ideology, and so on (inputs); (2) seek to transform these resources by doing something with them (throughputs); and, finally, (3) exchange these products with other organizations or the community at large (outputs). Organizations, in turn, exchange their own outputs for other organizations' resources or inputs.

Religious organizations are not only *like* other organizations—unions, corporations, stores, armies—they are also unique or *different*. Like other organizations, especially other voluntary associations, congregations must assemble resources, educate and enthuse the members to do the will of God, and, they hope, motivate the members to bear witness to their faith in their families and in their external occupations and communities. On the other hand, religious associations as "normative" organizations are unique in having transcendent resources—God, the "Holy Spirit," sacramental acts and rites, prayer—that provide them with far superior motivations and loyalties in comparison with secular "utilitarian" organizations, which employ people mainly for money. The far antithesis to "normative" organizations (like churches) are "coercive" organizations (like prisons) that tend to alienate the more they coerce. Like other voluntary associations (unions, political parties, professional associations), religious organizations can suffer what Michels called the "iron law of oligarchy," whereby a few leaders can become entrenched, undemocratic, and distant from the rank and file, perpetuating themselves in leadership to the detriment of the organization and its members.

Voluntarism a Mixed Blessing? Societies with "multicultural pluralism" such as the United States offer both possibilities and limits for religious organizations. On the one hand, pluralistic-democratic societies such as America have kept their religious organizations from making war on each other by declaring that religious preference—from the community's standpoint—is officially a *private* matter. The typical American church form, the denomination, thus can only maintain a policy of "intolerance with*in* but tolerance with*out*." That is, American religious groups may adopt strict codes for their members within but have to agree to an "agree to disagree" policy with those outside. This situation, together with religion's general exemption from having to pay income taxes to the state, tends to make denominationalism as a system rather bland and nondecisive vis-à-vis external "power" and authority. That is, there is a trade-off, which in general has been benign for religion and religious organizations but that also has demanded a price, the possibility of total privatization and social irrelevance for the religious enterprise. But as James R. Wood shows (1981), religious privatization in the face of the external community's common problems and divisions can be overcome with time, education, and skilled and dedicated church leadership.

See also Charisma, Church-and-State Issues, Denominationalism, Leadership

—*Ross P. Scherer*

REFERENCES

A. Etzioni, *Modern Organizations* (Englewood Cliffs, N.J.: Prentice Hall, 1964); P. Harrison, *Authority and Power in the Free Church Tradition* (Carbondale: Southern Illinois University Press, 1959); J. F. McCann, *Church and Organization* (Scranton, Pa.: Scranton University Press, 1993); R. P. Scherer, "The Church as a Formal Voluntary Organization," in *Voluntary Action Research,* ed. D. Smith (Lexington, Mass.: Lexington/Heath, 1972): 81-108; R. P. Scherer, *American Denominational Organization* (Pasadena, Calif.: William Carey Library, 1980); R. P. Scherer, "A New Typology for Organizations," *Journal for the Scientific Study of Religion* 27(1988):475-498; W. R. Scott, *Organizations* (Englewood Cliffs, N.J.: Prentice Hall, 1981); M. Weber, *Economy and Society* (Berkeley: University of California Press, 1978); J. R. Wood, *Leadership in Voluntary Organizations* (New Brunswick, N.J.: Rutgers University Press, 1981).

ORTHODOX CHRISTIANITY *see* Eastern Orthodoxy

ORTHODOX JUDAISM *see* Judaism

ORTHODOXY (BELIEF ORTHODOXY)

Orthodoxy in the generic sense means intellectual assent to prescribed religious doctrines. Its opposite, *heterodoxy,* refers to holding beliefs that deviate to a greater or lesser degree from prescribed doctrines. Orthodoxy in a religious tradition implies at a minimum the presence of specialists with the authority to determine the correctness of beliefs and to safeguard doctrine from contaminating influences and interpreta-

tions. The religious cultures of most preliterate, simple societies showed little tendency toward the development of orthodoxy. It was the rise of agrarian societies and universal religions that created an appropriate arena for the appearance of orthodox religious cultures and, in their wake, campaigns to eliminate heresy. We also see, in this connection, a link between orthodoxy and intolerance toward others who hold different religious beliefs. This was the subject of an important study in the United States by Glock and Stark (1966), which showed that belief in orthodox Christian doctrines was associated with anti-Semitism.

The historical lineaments of orthodoxy were classically set forth by Max Weber (1978). According to him, a universalistic-congregational church with an organized priesthood having responsibility for instructing laity as well as novitiates, religious texts in need of collection, systematization, exegesis, and ethical prophecy, are the historical ingredients required for the development of religious orthodoxy in its most extreme form. Weber considered these ingredients to have been most fully operative in the history of Western Christianity, where the concern for doctrinal correctness reached an apogee. Orthodoxy was never as prominent an issue in Islam, Buddhism, and the other historical religions because one or more of the basic ingredients were either missing or weak.

Current developments within Islam provide evidence that Weber's insights are still pertinent. Under premodern conditions, the Muslim *'ulamā'* (religious officials) were a tiny minority headquartered in major cities and had only a limited influence on the population as a whole. Among the vast majority of Muslims, religious belief was eclectic, syncretistic, and heterodox. There was widespread belief in the mediation of Muslim saints, in Sufi mysticism, in pious lore concerning the Prophet Muhammad and other heroes of the faith, and in magical prophylaxis and healing. The Qurān and the orthodox ritual requirements of Islam were respected but were not practical foci of worship among illiterate peasants and herders. Many of the beliefs associated with rural religious traditions were pre-Islamic and non-Islamic in origin and were condemned by the 'ulamā' but to little avail. Orthodoxy may have been fervently desired by the 'ulamā', but it was not achievable (Hodgson 1974).

The picture has changed dramatically in the last century. An Islamic revival that militantly promotes orthodoxy is on the rise (Esposito 1990). This development is usually explained by reference to the revival being antisecular and anti-Western. While not an inaccurate characterization, this explanation neglects to take notice of important changes in religious demography as they relate to this newfound emphasis on orthodoxy.

Urban populations in Muslim countries have been exploding for decades, a result of relentless rural-urban migration as much as the high birthrate. An enormous increase in the number of mosques and religious officials to staff them has come about to meet the requirements of these growing urban populations. In addition to being places of worship, the mosques are community centers and meeting places where migrants can make connections to find housing and jobs. Knowledge of orthodox Islam is often lacking in the rural areas, but it is prestigious in the cities and towns, where literacy is greater. The supply of trained religious officials has increased concomitantly with the population's's demand for instruction in correct religious principles, a demand that increases with the spread of literacy and being able to read religious literature rather than using religious exemplars (such as saints and Sufi mentors) as intermediaries with God. Thus several of the same underlying factors that Weber mentioned are active in the revivalist push for a wider acceptance of orthodox beliefs in contemporary Islam as well as in other putative orthodoxies.

The link between orthodoxy and religious revival brings to our attention a feature of religious discourse as prominent in the past as it is today: Campaigns for orthodoxy are about stamping out religious deviance and promoting moral renewal (for an interesting historical case study, see Erikson 1966). This is true of Islamic revivalism today (Kepel 1986) but is equally noteworthy in the conservative Christian political coalition that has risen to national prominence in the United States in recent decades. In both cases, orthodox doctrines are used as litmus tests for the correctness of government policies and to assail the moral rectitude of political leaders. Orthodoxy also has a bearing on understanding exclusion of deviance at the level of local congregations and religious communes, where the promulgation of literalist doctrines, stigmatizing beliefs, and high levels of religious conformity and participation reinforces the homogeneity of the members by eliminating those who are less committed (Iannaccone 1992, 1994).

See also Dogmatism, Islam, Christian Right

—*Edward B. Reeves*

REFERENCES

K. T. Erikson, *Wayward Puritans* (New York: Wiley, 1966); J. L. Esposito, *Islam* (New York: Oxford University Press, 1990); C. Y. Glock and R. Stark, *American Piety and Anti-Semitism* (New York: Harper, 1966); M. G. S. Hodgson, *The Venture of Islam*, 3 vols. (Chicago: University of Chicago Press, 1974); L. Iannaccone, "Sacrifice and Stigma," *Journal of Political Economy* 100(1992):271-291; L. Iannaccone, "Why Strict Churches Are Strong," *American Journal of Sociology* 99(1994):1180-1211; G. Kepel, *Muslim Extremism in Egypt* (Berkeley: University of California Press, 1986); M. Weber, *Economy and Society* (Berkeley: University of California Press, 1978).

ORTHOPRAXY In contemporary Christian usage, actions and lifestyle rooted in emulation of Christ's solidarity with the poor and oppressed. In a broader usage, *orthopraxy* (right practice) is also basic to Orthodox Judaism and many forms of Islam, as well as Christian (Eastern) Orthodoxy, and refers to the proper performance of religious duties, largely ritual in character.

A cornerstone of more political forms of theology, especially liberation theology, orthopraxy in the former sense combines adherence to Christian principles, as found in the Bible, with an understanding of social injustice and oppression rooted in Marxism. The ultimate goal is to act in favor of the poor through the conversion of both individual practice and unjust social structures. A key mechanism or method may be seen in the principle of "see-judge-act." According to this principle, individuals observe unjust social situations, analyze their root causes, and then act to resolve injustice.

See also Preferential Option for the Poor

—*W. E. Hewitt*

OSHO *see* Rajneesh Movement

OTHER-WORLDLY A principal polar soteriological concept in Max Weber's sociology of religion, contrasting with *inner-worldly*. Both concepts refer to the locus of salvation orientation: That is, is salvation primarily determined by activities oriented to a world beyond the empirical realm (e.g., heaven), or is salvation primarily determined by deeds done within a this-worldly economy of salvation (e.g., ethical righteousness)? Because polar types are ideal-typical, purely inner- or other-worldly systems of action are rare, and the actual deeds performed by a believer may appear identical in some cases. Nevertheless, the *meaning system* of the believer orients the action differently: Is the action being done to "get into heaven" or "bring the kingdom of heaven on earth"? Medieval Western Christianity and classical Hinduism represent other-worldly forms, whereas prophetic Judaism, Calvinist Protestantism, and much contemporary Pentecostalism are inner-worldly.

—*William H. Swatos, Jr.*

OTTO, RUDOLF (1869-1937) German Protestant theologian and philosopher. Born in Peine (Hanover), he achieved the rank of Privatdozent in Systematic Theology (1897) and Ausserordentlicher Professor (1904) at Göttingen and was appointed to an official Chair at Breslau (1914). He spent much of his career as Professor of Systematic Theology at Marburg-on-the-Lahn (1917-1937).

Otto's *Das Heilige,* published in 1917 and translated as *The Idea of the Holy,* was immediately successful. His *Mysticism East and West,* published in 1932, contains the collected lectures he gave in 1924 at Oberlin College comparing Eastern and Western mysticism.

The Idea of the Holy is Otto's main achievement. It fit the needs of disillusioned, thoughtful, religious Christians following World War I. Otto devised the term *numinous* to represent a special, irreducible quality that he felt provided the basis for religious experience. Numinous "creature-consciousness" or "creature-feeling" reflects an overpowering, inexpressible might that must be experienced to be understood. The feeling, objective and outside the self, was labeled *mysterium tremendum.* Conceptually, *mysterium* denotes that which is hidden and esoteric, beyond conception and understanding, extraordinary and unfamiliar. *Mysterium tremendum* has the characteristics of awfulness (inspiring fearful awe), overpoweringness, energy or urgency, being "wholly other," and arousing fascination.

Otto portrayed the numinous as responsible for the evolution of religious sentiment. In its crude, primitive form, it manifests as "eerie," or "weird," granting ghosts and demons their culturally universal qualities. "This crudely naive and primordial emotional disturbance, and the fantastic images to which it gives rise, are later overborne and ousted by more highly developed forms of the numinous emotion, with all its mysteriously impelling power" (*The Idea of the Holy,* p. 16). Demons, ghosts, and specters are "a link in the chain of development which religious consciousness has undergone." Modern religious sentiment is the result of a "growth to maturity" parallel to that of the development of the taste for refined music (pp. 72 f.).

The concept of "the holy" or "sacred" consists of the numinous, which is nonrational, and other elements reflecting rationality, purpose, personality, and morality. There exists a "predisposition" of the human spirit for religiosity, which "awakens when aroused by divers excitations" (p. 115). The numinous, a universal feature quickening this arousal, is a

> primal element of our psychical nature that needs to be grasped purely in its uniqueness and cannot itself be explained from anything else. Like all other primal psychical elements, it *emerges* in due course in the developing life of human mind and spirit and is henceforward simply present. (p. 124)

Otto believed that the numinous manifests in its fullest form within the Christian faith (p. 178). Although modern researchers find that most reported religious experiences do not contain the fearful awe that Otto considered so important, the universal features within mystical accounts could be regarded as supporting modified versions of his orientation.

See also Experience, Mysticism

—*James McClenon*

REFERENCES

R. Otto, *The Idea of the Holy* (New York: Oxford University Press, 1958); R. Otto, *Mysticism East and West* (New York: Collier, 1962).

PAPACY A form of rule based on the authority of the Bishop of Rome as head on earth of the (Roman) Catholic Church. Its history is one of succession, decay, and reform in a lineage traced to the apostles. The authority of the pope ranges from the infallible to the advisory and is expressed in and through councils, letters, and encyclicals. The role of the pope exemplifies a tension between charisma and bureaucracy, although it is little mentioned in Weber's writings. The current pope, John Paul II, has made notable efforts to engage with the social sciences in their dealings with culture. His pilgrimages, approaches to liberation theology, and encyclicals have attracted a notable sociological literature in France and the United States especially. (The term *pope* is also used in some small ancient churches, such as the Coptic, for their supreme human authority.)

See also Encyclicals, Vatican II

—*Kieran Flanagan*

REFERENCES

F. Houtart, "In Favour of a Sociology of the Papacy," *Social Compass* 37(1990):195-197; G. Zizola, "A Bibliography on the Sociology of the Papacy," *Social Compass* 36(1989):355-373.

PARAPSYCHOLOGY The scientific study of psychic phenomena.

The term was first popularized by J. B. Rhine at Duke University. During the 1930s, Rhine standardized the nomenclature and techniques within the field of parapsychology by having subjects guess at symbols on a specially designed deck of cards and statistically analyzing the results. Later, Rhine verified to his satisfaction that some humans could mentally influence physical events, such as dice scores, a phenomenon termed *psychokinesis*. Although other researchers replicated Rhine's results, it became apparent that psychic phenomena were not easy to elicit. After decades of research, Rhine and other parapsychologists concluded that psychic phenomena were real, that certain internal statistical variations were associated with their occurrence, and that various attitudes and personality traits were related to their detection. Although controversy surrounds these conclusions, the Parapsychological Association, established in 1957, was admitted as an affiliate to the American Association for the Advancement of Science in 1969. Modern parapsychologists use sophisticated computerized methods to ensure randomization of extrasensory targets and to reduce the possibility of fraud.

—*James McClenon*

REFERENCES

R. S. Broughton, *Parapsychology* (New York: Ballantine, 1991); J. McClenon, *Deviant Science* (Philadelphia: University of Pennsylvania Press, 1984).

PARISH   *Parish, congregation,* and *local church, synagogue/temple* or *masjid/mosque* are often used interchangeably to refer to the dominant institutional form of the world's major lived religious traditions in which adherents come together for worship and other religious activities.

Parish usually implies a geographic division of a larger religious or social entity into smaller, more manageable parts. Such subdivisions were common in England prior to the Reformation. The Council of Trent (1545-1563) of the Roman Catholic Counterreformation provided for the subdivision of cities, each under the authority of a priest, although this practice was not universally followed. The 1918 code of canon law attempted to make such subdivision an absolute law for Roman Catholics. In *Southern Parish* (University of Chicago Press 1951), Joseph Fichter shows that the Roman Catholic parish is a humanly devised institution developed for practical purposes of administration and maintained as an operative area within the total social structure of the church. The parish is not a voluntary association of laity but the product of a formal decision by the local bishop. It has four elements: (1) an appointed pastor, (2) a church building and parsonage (rectory, manse), (3) territorial limits, and (4) a designated group of persons ("members"). It functions as the ecclesiastical microcosm, "the church in miniature."

For much of American history, parish understandings of local religious communities predominated. In seventeenth- and eighteenth-century New England, the creation of new towns followed legislative approval for the gathering of a new parish. For Roman Catholics in nineteenth-century urban America, one's parish was often a critical component of one's identity, and for Orthodox Jews, restrictions on sabbath travel formed a powerful link between neighborhood residence and religious participation.

By the twentieth century, with improved transportation, increased religious competition, and widespread cultural insistence on freedom of choice in religious matters, churches, synagogues, and mosques have become more voluntaristic in character. In Roman Catholicism, for example, while the geographic parish remains the formal means by which dioceses are organized, laity feel free to choose a parish based on personal preference. An understanding of churches, synagogues, and mosques as congregations has become more prevalent.

The historian E. Brooks Holifield (in Wind and Lewis 1994:23-53) has identified four major periods in the social role of Christian congregations in America. *Comprehensive congregations* (1607-1789) comprehended or included the community as a whole. In most of the colonies, there was one congregation for the community and its exclusive claim was protected by government. Congregations were simple organizations with a focus on worship, which usually was understood as the responsibility of the entire community. *Devotional congregations* (1789-1870) were a product of social diversity. Holifield notes that the number of congregations increased from fewer than 3,000 in 1780 to about 54,000 in 1860. Life had become more segmented, and congregations began to serve particular slices of the population. Worship too became segmented and focused on diverse forms of religious devotion, and new subdivisions were evident within religious traditions. *Social congregations* (1870-1950) reflect a willingness of congregations to transform their practices to become social centers. Holifield notes the emergence of the church parlor and the church picnic as new institutional forms, as well as new attention to the congregation's social and educational role. Congregations were becoming "busy" places. Finally, *participatory congregations* (1950-1990+) emphasize member involvement and shared involvement in congregational governance and leadership. Meaning and belonging are important themes, and congregations that take these themes seriously seem most likely to flourish. Some congregations seem to embody the comprehensive ideals of colonial groups by providing a total environment for committed members.

American congregations tend to be quite small, most averaging fewer than 200 in weekend worship. Roman Catholic congregations, which for the most part remain geographically based parishes, are larger than those of Protestant Christians, Jews, and Muslims. It is impossible to know how many individuals and families are members of congregations. Denominations and faith traditions vary in their understanding of membership and in record keeping. Some national denominations gather detailed data on their members and congregations; others lack even an address list of their member units. The U.S. government collects little information on religious organizations and no data on religious affiliation out of sensitivity to the separation of church and state. Each year, the National Council of Churches of Christ in the USA publishes the *Yearbook of American and Canadian Churches,* which reports aggregated membership and financial statistics supplied by national religious bodies. The 1991 *Yearbook* reported a total of over 350,000 congregations. Another voluntary effort to develop data on congregations is an informal coalition organized by the Association of Statisticians of American Religious Bodies to produce a decennial report known as the *Churches and Church Membership* series. County-level counts of congregations and members have been produced for the years 1971, 1980, and 1990 based on data provided by most of the larger national denominations. Unfortunately, both the *Yearbook* and the *Churches and Church Membership* series underreport immigrant, non-Christian, and racial-ethnic populations as well as independent congregations.

The rise of independent congregations is an important development in the past quarter century. Through most of American history, congregations were usually affiliated with denominational bodies who supplied resources in the form of theological training for clergy, discipline for congregations and their leaders, opportunities for missionary work in this country and abroad, and books, hymnals, and educational materials. Most congregations remain part of denominational structures, but increasing numbers have chosen to become independent and freestanding. Others maintain an official denominational connection to a traditional denomination but function as independents. Some of these congregations—known popularly as *megachurches* or *seeker churches*—are quite large, attracting thousands of persons each week to worship services and ancillary programs (see Truehart 1996).

Scholarly attention to local churches, synagogues, and mosques has undergone several shifts in the twentieth century. In the early years of American sociology, the social sciences and religious communities were often viewed as partners, with the shared goal of social and moral reform. Ecological approaches to the study of urban and rural communities were well suited to parish understandings of religious communities and influenced pioneers in religious research such as H. Paul Douglass. The Institute of Social and Religious Research, founded by Douglass, sponsored dozens of community studies in the 1930s and stimulated hundreds of others. By the 1960s, this social ecology emphasis shifted somewhat with the rise of the human potential movement and organization development as an academic discipline. Published work on congregations took on a more critical tone as authors probed their weaknesses, particularly what many authors saw as an unwillingness on the part of laity to engage the social issues of the time. A new genre of "church renewal" literature was popular among Protestant Christians of various denominations. When, by the late 1960s and early 1970s, it had become apparent that after several decades of steady growth, many congregations were beginning to lose members each year, scholars and popular authors began to give attention to the dynamics of church growth and decline. Especially notable was the publication in 1979 of *Understanding Church Growth and Decline,* edited by Dean R. Hoge and David A. Roozen (Pilgrim). The new attention to church growth helped to popularize the missiological writings of Donald McGavran, C. Peter Wagner, and others associated with Fuller Theological Seminary.

One can trace shifts in the study of congregations by examining the career history of the influential Protestant church consultant Lyle Schaller, who began his long career as an urban planner but by the 1980s had come to focus on dynamics of interpersonal and institutional relationships as more important than community dynamics or denominational factors. Schaller's recent work has focused on church planning and growth with attention to small, midsized, large, and megachurches.

The work of James F. Hopewell, published posthumously in the book *Congregation* (Fortress 1987), signaled a change in parish or congregational studies. Hopewell, who was trained in the history of religions and anthropology, turned his attention to congregational story or narrative, drawing not on ecological or organizational methodologies but on literary theory as a means of understanding congregations. With others, Hopewell approached congregations not to improve their operations or to enlist them in the service of larger social and religious ends but because they are intrinsically interesting as human communities.

If the emphasis of H. Paul Douglass was on identifying commonalities among congregations in their community context, the new wave of congregational studies in the 1980s and 1990s has been on congregational uniqueness. This has brought attention to *congregational culture* as a research focus.

The Lilly Endowment, an Indianapolis-based family foundation, has been an important factor in bringing congregations to the attention of scholars and the public. It has supported several large-scale research projects that led to publication of the multivolume collections, *The American Catholic Parish,* edited by Jay P. Dolan (Paulist Press 1987), and *American Congregations,* edited by James P. Wind and James A. Lewis (University of Chicago Press 1994). Lilly has also supported the work of the Project Team for Congregational Studies, an informal coalition of individuals and organizations committed to the scholarly study of congregations and producers of the book *Building Effective Ministries* edited by Carl S. Dudley (Harper 1983) and the *Handbook for Congregational Studies* edited by Jackson W.

Carroll, Carl S. Dudley, and William McKinney (Abingdon 1987).

Paralleling the renewed interest in congregations in academic circles has been the creation since the 1960s of organizations that serve congregations through programs of research, education, consulting, and publication. Some are independent ecumenical nonprofit organizations, often associated with an a charismatic individual; examples include the Alban Institute (Loren Mead), the Yokefellows Institute (Lyle Schaller), National Evangelistic Association (Herb Miller), and the Center for Parish Development (Paul Dietterich). Others are affiliated with universities or theological schools such as the Cushwa Center for American Catholicism at Notre Dame, the Cohen Center for Modern Jewish Studies at Brandeis, the Ormond Center at Duke, the Institute for Church Growth at Fuller Theological Seminary, and Hartford Seminary's Center for Social and Religious Research. Most of these organizations are supported by sale of services to individuals and congregations and by grants from foundations.

Much of the research on congregations is a- or pretheoretical and centered on problems faced by contemporary congregations. Systems theory informs much of this work, sometimes implicitly—as in the *Handbook for Congregational Studies* and many of the publications of the Alban Institute—and sometimes explicitly—as in the work of the Center for Parish Development. The *Handbook,* which is widely used in theological seminaries, suggests a framework for understanding congregations that attends to the congregation's social context, identity, process, and program. Edwin Friedman uses family systems theory in his influential book *Generation to Generation* (Guilford 1985).

Although few propose a theory of the congregation, middle-range theories abound. Hoge and Roozen examined a variety of theories accounting for church growth. Their sorting of theories into national versus local, and contextual versus institutional, explanations has influenced subsequent research on this issue. Similarly, the work of Speed B. Leas on church conflict, Douglas Walrath on social context typologies, Lyle Schaller and Arlin Routhage on congregational size, Carl Dudley on small church dynamics, and Jackson Carroll, David Roozen, and William McKinney on congregation-community interaction has contributed to theory development in the field.

While congregational participation is for most believers the main organizational expression of their religious commitments, congregations receive surprisingly little attention from theologians. This may be changing as a result of renewed interest in the theological subdis-

cipline of practical theology stimulated by the work of Don S. Browning, David Kelsey, and others. Liberation theologians have shown a good deal of interest in *comunidades de base* in Latin America but tend to be very ambivalent about traditional congregations in North America. In biblical studies, the work of Wayne Meeks and Howard Kee on New Testament congregations has attracted a good deal of attention and reflects new interest in this field in the application of social scientific methods.

The past decade has seen the publication of several book-length studies of individual congregations of varying backgrounds; many of these reports are quite sophisticated methodologically. Nancy Ammerman's *Bible Believers* (Rutgers University Press 1987), R. Stephen Warner's *New Wine in Old Wineskins* (University of California Press 1988), Melvin Williams's *Community in a Black Pentecostal Church* (Waveland 1984), and Samuel Heilman's *Synagogue Life* (University of Chicago Press 1976) provide readers with a window on the heretofore private life of Baptist fundamentalist, evangelical Presbyterian, African American Pentecostal, and Orthodox Jewish congregations. In the case of each of these books, the impact of broader religious developments is seen in microcosm. Congregations also have received attention from journalists in the 1990s with the publication of *Upon This Rock* by Samuel Friedman (Harper 1993), *Congregation* by Gary Dorsey (Viking 1995), and *And They Shall Be My People* by Paul Wilkes (Atlantic Monthly Press 1994).

—*William McKinney*

REFERENCES

J. H. Fichter, *Urban Parish* (Chicago: University of Chicago Press, 1954); C. Truehart, "Welcome to the New Church," *Atlantic Monthly* (August 1996): 37-58; J. P. Wind and J. W. Lewis, *American Congregations,* Vol. 2 (Chicago: University of Chicago Press, 1994).

PARSONS, TALCOTT (1902-1979)   Leading American sociological theorist and student of religion; "a somewhat backsliding Protestant of Congregationalist background" (1978:233) who spent most of his career as Professor of Sociology at Harvard University; President, American Sociological Association, 1949; Chairman of the Committee for the Scientific Study of Religion (CSSR, the nascent SSSR), 1952-1953.

Parsons developed a general, voluntaristic theory of action, based on influential, imaginative readings of the sociological classics, which he applied to a wide variety of sociological problems. He played an important role as an early translator of major European studies, most notably Max Weber's *Protestant Ethic and the Spirit of Capitalism* (Scribner 1930). An active figure in his discipline, Parsons was prominent in numerous professional organizations and cofounded the Society for the Scientific Study of Religion. Parsons trained and influenced many acclaimed scholars, notably specialists in the study of religion such as Robert Bellah, Clifford Geertz, and Benton Johnson. Although he had a direct impact on the work of such scholars, Parsons's ideas, long the subject of extensive debates in sociology, currently have a more limited and diffuse influence than they did during his career.

Parsons's Synthesis   Religion played an integral part in Parsons's work from beginning to end. His overall project can be described as an effort to refute a Weberian view of modernity with Durkheimian means. Theoretically, he regarded religion as a source of general images of order and specific societal values, crucial to maintaining minimal coherence in any society. Historically, Parsons interpreted American society as successfully institutionalizing certain values rooted in individualistic, ascetic Protestantism under conditions of social differentiation and cultural pluralism. America represented a phase in the Christianization of the world. Parsons's own progressive view of religious evolution in the West actually sharpened his attention to continuing tensions between religious meaning and potentially destructive aspects of worldly human experience. He also analyzed social and cultural movements that opposed (he thought ineffectively) the complex-but-viable framework of America as an open-but-religious society.

Parsons's first and last publications (1928-1929, 1979)—on Weber's and Sombart's view of capitalism and on economic and religious symbolism in the West, respectively—display the strong Weberian thrust in all his work. Like Weber, Parsons was interested in the religious roots of modern culture, which he sought in the implications of the Protestant Reformation. Similarly, Parsons thought of Christianity, especially in its ascetic Protestant incarnation, as giving special significance to such "worldly" domains as the economic and erotic while at the same time introducing a special tension between worldly motives and transcendent religious aspirations. But whereas Weber thought that Protestantism was bound to lose its social influence in a rationalized society, Parsons claimed that the Protestant worldview remained significant in modern times. Specifically, he considered dominant American values, described as instrumental activism and institu-

tionalized individualism, to be new, generalized versions of Christian universalism, individualism, and world mastery. The institutional form of American religion, denominational pluralism, similarly reflected Protestant notions of faith as a matter of individual choice, and organization as a matter of voluntary allegiance. Even American citizenship, aiming for maximum inclusion of all persons irrespective of ascriptive features, appeared meaningfully linked to Protestantism's eminently democratic "priesthood of all believers."

For Weber, the modern world increasingly became disenchanted; for Parsons, a liberalized version of Christian culture continued to shape American society in the mid-twentieth century. For Weber, differentiation meant that gods proliferated, and individuals were left to their own devices; for Parsons, differentiation was matched by new modes of integration, and individual choice was guided by shared normative standards. In this sense, Parsons attempted to refute Weber. Yet until the end, he also adhered to the Weberian insight that Christian ambivalence toward "the world" could not be resolved. The tension between religious culture and economic action could not be eliminated. In this respect, he actually extended a Weberian idea. In the West, Parsons argued, religion maintained a crucial cultural role precisely in counteracting the potential dominance of economic thought and action. Were such tension to disappear, one may infer, Western history would come to an end.

Durkheim came to provide the analytical tools for Parsons's ambivalent struggle with Weber. In *The Structure of Social Action* (McGraw-Hill 1937), Parsons had been skeptical of positivist elements in Durkheim's sociology, which seemingly denied the autonomy of cultural categories by treating them as epiphenomenal effects of basic social processes. He also continued to question Durkheim's equation of church and society, because it denied the possibility of differentiating a religious and a distinctly social sphere. Still, Parsons's view of action and order owed much to Durkheim. Without shared normative regulation, rational action remains rudderless—little more than the idle individual pursuit of random ends. Without general normative regulation of its institutional framework that inspires binding commitments on the part of members, a society cannot cohere for long. Such regulation selects possibilities of action, but to be effective requires the operation of many other components of a social structure. Parsons's treatment of the normative is anti-idealist in principle; institutionalization of values is always a contingent process. Yet the normative pattern that provides a society its identity is the single most important functional facet that Parsons emphasizes throughout. The

Durkheimian influence is evident. Whatever else it is, a society must be a moral community; those who belong to it necessarily share a religion in some sense—and vice versa (1978:250).

Parsons on American Religion and Society   American society, Parsons claimed, in fact functioned as a moral community bound by a civil religion that consisted of very general but transcendent values. The secret to America's success as a viable, complex modern society was that it had transformed its sacred canopy in a manner that made highly differentiated social action and allegiance to many different worldviews possible. Out of Weberian components, America had fashioned a Durkheimian solution to the problems of modernity.

Parsons used his evolutionary interpretation of Christian history (1968) to bolster this view of America. Although Christ was divine and human, Christianity preserved God's transcendence while crucially breaking His special bond with the "Chosen People." Belonging to the Christian church was a matter of belief, available to all, in principle. At the same time, the early Christian church dramatically differentiated itself from the secular society of its time, which both facilitated its long-term survival and its later ability to reshape secular society according to its norms. In spite of fluctuations over time, the Western church's autonomy and theology inspired a mission for the world, a long-term effort to build the kingdom of God on Earth. This was intensified in the Western, ascetic branch of Protestantism, which maintained the radical dualism between the transcendental and the "world," and thereby stressed the importance of human agency in creating a holy community. Individuals, all with equal religious obligations and capacities, were to participate in building the kingdom, as members of the invisible church in the world.

The visible church "had" to become a voluntary association, a religious development only firmly institutionalized after the formal separation of church and state in America. Because of the importance of associational involvement and the religious legitimation of individual achievement, American individualism was by no means "anarchic" but effectively helped to build a large-scale society that left considerable free space to individuals. The basic framework of American ascetic Protestantism was also flexible enough to allow the inclusion of non-Protestant groups in the national community, still a "nation under God." In short, Christian history, mined with Weber's help, provided many of the materials needed to construct a new culture, true to core Christian principles yet upgraded to support a large-scale, highly differentiated society.

Thus, in Parsons's view, American society constituted an evolutionary breakthrough; it displayed a higher level of organized complexity than any other. This advance was made possible by its distinctive adaptation of Christian values and its elaboration of denominational pluralism. At the leading edge of social evolution, America was both the most secular and the most religious of modern societies. By the problems it faced and the answers it found, it showed a path toward modernity for others to follow. Yet Parsons did not think of evolutionary change in a unilinear manner. America was a beacon, but not a model to the world; in different religious traditions, different kinds of adaptations would have to be developed. Even the Christian tradition, after all, had become internally differentiated; only one branch happened to contribute to and "fit" with the main pattern of modernizing change. But in the system of modern societies, everyone must confront the same basic realities. The fundamental question, to Parsons, was whether a society had the cultural resources to respond to modern predicaments by legitimating differentiation and pluralism, economic growth, and social inclusion.

Even within the United States, Parsons had pointed out, fundamentalists resisted the thrust of evolutionary change by harking back to the security of sectarian values as the basis of a simple communal life. As his wartime essays on Germany showed (1954), when societies experience traumatic change in a basically illiberal culture, a violently romantic movement may result. Some movements, notably Marxist ones, could adopt the economic factor that seemed to usher in the modern era in the first place as a guiding principle. Their eschatological and utopian view, holding out the prospect of ultimate emancipation and undifferentiated community, is itself a quasi-religious response to problems of meaning posed by economic change. Marxism was part of the "*religious* drama over the significance of things economic" (1979:24)—plausible mainly in countries that had not been through the Reformation. But its attempt to base a new form of solidarity on economic factors alone must fail: It ignored many critical dimensions of action and could not do justice to the actual complexity of modern social systems. Thus even the most powerful and coherent absolutist response to the modern predicament could not succeed. Modernity defeats absolutisms absolutely. But this is not to say that antimodern reactions will simply disappear. Modernity allows for considerable pluralism; culture and society function in relative autonomy. Thus there are ample sources of critical reaction to the direction of change, even in societies like America, where a minimal societal religion obtains, according to Parsons.

Assessment Many aspects of Parsons's work are subject to criticism. Neither he nor his students ever offered a full-fledged analysis of religion as an institution or an "action complex" in the technical terms of his theory. The very foundations of that theory have been called into question, including Parsons's claim that it embodies a synthetic convergence in the views of classic predecessors. Parsons's own applications of his theory appear to betray an idealist bias, stressing the dominant integrative role of religiously derived values. The historical analysis of Christianity was deliberately selective; in a presentist manner, Parsons searched for those elements that bolster his view of contemporary American society; almost every single historical claim of his requires the most critical scrutiny. Those who think of secularization as the inexorable decline of religion's social significance would challenge Parsons's view of America as an essentially (Judeo-)Christian society. Scholars might similarly question the extent to which American civil religion provided America with a base for normative integration, or the extent to which the remnants of ascetic Protestantism continue to infuse America's social system with creative tension. Parsons's belief in the leading role of America as a cultural innovator, rather than as an economic power, would necessarily encounter considerable resistance in contemporary global debates. Yet Parsons is one twentieth-century scholar whose very ambitions continue to inspire and whose mistakes continue to be fruitful. As a religiously attuned, confidently liberal interpreter of American culture in his time, if not as an empirical sociologist in the conventional sense, Parsons will serve as a benchmark in the social scientific study of modern religion well into the twenty-first century.

—*Frank J. Lechner*

REFERENCES

R. Bellah, "Religious Evolution," *American Sociological Review* 29(1964):358-374; C. Geertz, "Religion as a Cultural System," in *The Interpretation of Cultures* (New York: Basic Books, 1973): 87-125; T. Parsons, " 'Capitalism' in Recent German literature," *Journal of Political Economy* 36-37(1928-1929):641-661, 31-51; T. Parsons, "The Place of Ultimate Values in Sociological Theory," *International Journal of Ethics* 45(1935):282-316; T. Parsons, *Essays in Sociological Theory* (New York: Free Press, 1954); T. Parsons, *Sociological Theory and Modern Society* (New York: Free Press, 1967); T. Parsons, "Christianity," in *International Encyclopedia of the Social Sciences* 2(1968):425-447; T. Parsons, *Action Theory and the Human Condition* (New York: Free Press, 1978); T. Parsons, "Religious and Economic Symbolism in the Western World," *Sociological Inquiry* 49 (1979):1-48; R. Robertson et al., "Talcott Parsons on Religion," special issue, *Sociological Analysis* 43, 4(1982): papers by V. Lidz, R. Robertson (which influenced this article), R. Baum, and E. Tiryakian, and an extensive bibliography by Robertson and M. Cavanaugh.

PARTICULARISM The concept of religious particularism connotes a belief in the exclusive authenticity of one's own religious tradition. Religious particularists are likely to believe that salvation is confined to rather narrowly defined groups of believers.

First developed by Glock and Stark, particularism has been shown to have a strong relationship with doctrinal orthodoxy. Several recent analysts have suggested that religious particularism was a strong inhibition on the political influence of the Christian Right in the 1980s. Jerry Falwell seemed unable to expand beyond a base of Protestant fundamentalists, while support for Pat Robertson's presidential bid in 1988 appears to have been confined to Pentecostalists and charismatics. Similarly, the antiabortion movement may have been hampered by mutual dislike between Roman Catholics and evangelical Protestants. Recent proponents of religious political mobilization (such as the Christian Coalition) have emphasized the importance of ecumenism, in part to avert the fragmenting effects of particularism.

—*Ted G. Jelen*

REFERENCES

C. Y. Glock and R. Stark, *Christian Beliefs and Anti-Semitism* (Westport, Conn: Greenwood, 1966); J. C. Green, "Pat Robertson and the Latest Crusade," *Social Science Quarterly* 74(1993):157-168; T. G. Jelen, *The Political Mobilization of Religious Beliefs* (New York: Praeger, 1991); R. Reed, *Politically Incorrect* (Dallas: Word, 1994); R. Stark and C. Y. Glock, *American Piety* (Berkeley: University of California Press, 1968); C. Wilcox, *God's Warriors* (Baltimore: Johns Hopkins University Press, 1992).

PAUL OF TARSUS (ST.) *see* Biblical Studies

PEACE The idea that human beings should exist in a state of harmony with each other.

Formally at least, social peace has long been a goal of organized religion. Religious principle, however, historically has failed to ensure the absence of societal conflict. The tendency to war in particular has been a noteworthy feature of most societies, despite the fact that most forms of religious teaching are vehemently at odds with the taking of human life. This seeming contradiction results from the tension that exists between religion and culture. While religion may eschew violence and promote peace, societal conditions, national pride, or political exigency may call for conflict, directed toward either the members of the society or the nation itself (civil war or political repression) or directed against "outsiders" (e.g., citizens of other societies or nations).

In the face of this conflict, whole religions, or simply elements within religious organizations, have adopted various positions. Some have remained steadfastly pacifist, vocally decrying all forms of violence. Such is the case with many Protestant sects, such as the Quakers. Others have accepted the inevitability of conflict, working instead to moderate its effects. For example, armies have long enjoyed the presence of religious figures (chaplains) of military rank who provide religious services for those suffering under the strains of battle. Religious groups also have become involved in helping to set the rules of war. Such was the case in the Middle Ages in Europe, where the rules of combat were regulated by the code of "chivalry." More recently, organized religion has worked to limit the ability of nations to use weapons of mass destruction during wartime, such as deadly gases or nuclear weapons.

At the other extreme, religion has sometimes openly embraced conflict as a means to religious ends. Such was the case during the Crusades of the early Middle Ages, when Christian armies left Europe to conquer the souls of the "heathen" in the Mediterranean region. In the twentieth century, some sects within Islam also have embraced the concept in the form of the *jihād,* or holy war. The seven-year war between Iran and Iraq, for example, was viewed in these terms by some Iranian clerics. As a result, Iranian soldiers were promised instant martyrdom should their lives be taken during the conflict.

During the late twentieth century, there have been growing calls within most major religious organizations for adherence to purely pacifist principles. Within Christianity, for example, individuals and groups have vocally supported a more active role for the churches in ending societal conflict of all varieties. Such advocacy was clearly manifest in the United States in the strong religious presence in both the anti-Vietnam War and the antinuclear movements of the 1960s and 1970s. There also has been a strong linkage between advocacy for church involvement in the peace movement and advocacy for involvement in movements designed to foster a more humane world through the promotion of social justice.

—*W. E. Hewitt*

REFERENCE

J. Kelsay and J. T. Johnson (eds.), *Just War and Jihad* (New York: Greenwood, 1991).

PEAK EXPERIENCE   Abraham Maslow's main contribution to the study of religion, this category encompasses those profound experiences considered religious as well as phenomenologically similar experiences not interpreted through a theological framework.

Maslow found that among "self-actualized" individuals he studied, it was fairly common to find reports of mystical-type experiences. A lifelong atheist, Maslow wanted to distinguish mystical experiences from traditional religious experiences and to emphasize their natural origin, so he gave them a theologically neutral label. Although surveys suggest the experience is fairly common (as Maslow hypothesized), an empirical connection between self-actualization and peak experience has never been definitively established.

See also Experience, Mysticism

—*David Yamane*

REFERENCES

A. Maslow, *Toward a Psychology of Being* (New York: Van Nostrand, 1962); A. Maslow, *Religions, Values, and Peak Experiences* (New York: Penguin, 1964).

PEMBERTON, PRENTISS L. (1909-1987)
Earned a bachelor's degree from Ottawa University in 1932, a Bachelor of Divinity degree from then Andover-Newton Theological School in 1935, and an M.A. and Ph.D. from Harvard University in, respectively, 1938 and 1950. Chairman of the Committee for the Scientific Study of Religion (the nascent SSSR), 1954-1955.

After service in the parish ministry and with the Y.M.C.A., he was Associate Professor, Andover-Newton from 1945 to 1958; Assistant Director, Danforth Foundation, 1954-1958; and Arthur Gosnell Professor of Social Ethics and the Sociology of Religion, Colgate

Rochester Divinity School, 1958-1974. One of the founding members of the Society for the Scientific Study of Religion, he was the first editor of its journal, serving in that capacity from 1961 to 1965. Pemberton was the author of five books and numerous articles; his last book was *Toward a Christian Social Ethic* (Winston 1985).

—Charles Y. Glock

PENTECOSTALISM A religious movement that has spawned a denominational family within the doctrinally conservative ("evangelical") wing of Protestant Christianity. The movement takes its name from the experience of Jesus's disciples on the day of Pentecost, described in the New Testament book of the Acts of the Apostles (2:4), when "they were all filled with the Holy Spirit and began to speak in other tongues, as the Spirit gave them utterance."

Pentecostalism has grown dramatically worldwide throughout the twentieth century, making it arguably the most important recent development in Christianity. Although there are many readily identifiable pentecostal *denominations*—the Assemblies of God being the largest—precise figures on the size of the pentecostal *movement* are more difficult to obtain both because smaller, independent pentecostal churches tend to elude religious censuses and because it is impossible to quantify the influence of pentecostalism in non-pentecostal denominations. Estimates, however, range from 10 million to 29 million followers in the United States alone. What most clearly distinguishes pentecostalism and identifies it as a coherent religious family is the belief in and experience of "baptism of the Spirit" as evidenced by speaking in tongues *(glossolalia)*.

History Pentecostalism germinated from the fertile soil of nineteenth-century American revivalism, specifically the Holiness movement in Methodism. The Holiness movement was actually brought into Methodism through the influence of other "Methodized" Protestants—such as Oberlin evangelist Charles Finney—who had discovered John Wesley's writings on Christian perfection. In addition to the emphasis on perfectionism, Holiness theology professed the doctrine of entire sanctification, whereby a dramatic "second blessing" (sanctification) ratifies a person's holiness subsequent to the born-again experience of conversion (justification). Increasingly, that event was described in the Holiness movement as "baptism of the Holy Spirit," and soon speaking in tongues was seen as an outward sign of that baptism, and hence of sanctification. Benjamin Hardin Irwin's Fire-Baptized Holiness Association further set the stage for pentecostalism by maintaining that "baptism with the Holy Ghost and fire" was a "third blessing." These principles and practices were directly carried over into pentecostalism. The pentecostal movement's novel contribution to Holiness revivalism was rendering glossolalia *normative,* an *essential* sign of "Spirit baptism." Although not all who have experienced baptism of the Spirit also claim to have spoken in tongues, and vice versa, the percentages of Pentecostalists who have experienced both is very high (67% in Poloma's [1989] study of the Assemblies of God).

The precise origin of pentecostalism is traced to Charles Parham and his Bethel Bible College in Topeka, Kansas. In 1901, after being instructed by Parham to read the biblical book of Acts, student Agnes Ozman received baptism of the Spirit and spoke in tongues. When others at the school had a similar experience, Parham concluded that glossolalia was evidence of Spirit baptism. He then embarked on a series of revival meetings in Missouri and Kansas, establishing loosely organized "Apostolic Faith Missions," although his most important encounter was in Houston, where he evangelized an African American Holiness preacher, William Seymour. Seymour took Parham's campaign to Los Angeles, where his Azusa Street Mission became the center of pentecostalism in the United States and the springboard for its worldwide expansion.

From its inception, pentecostalism has included a diverse assortment of churches and associations. In an effort to develop some measure of doctrinal uniformity and cooperation between various independent pentecostal churches, a "General Convention of Pentecostal Saints and Churches of God in Christ" was called for April 1914 in Hot Springs, Arkansas. A creed was issued, and an organization called the Assemblies of God was formed, along with a general council to oversee it. This moment is historically significant because it inaugurated pentecostal denominationalism.

Schisms Pentecostalism, true to its Protestant heritage, has coupled growth with splintering. Conservative estimates suggest there are some 300 pentecostal denominations and organizations in the United States. While pentecostalists were officially opposed to "dogma," with its stultifying Catholic and mainline Protestant overtones, issues of correct interpretation of the Bible have been the source of considerable dissension within the movement. Although all adhere to a biblically conservative theology, two major disputes have divided pentecostalists.

One of the main cleavages in the pentecostal movement was between those who adhered to a Wesleyan Holiness view of the doctrine of sanctification and those who adopted a non-Wesleyan ("Reformed") position. Early pentecostalists working within the Holiness tradition as modified in the Fire-Baptized Holiness Movement saw baptism of the Spirit as the third step in the Wesleyan formula of justification—sanctification. Reformed Pentecostalists, in contrast, came to see salvation as sufficient, as "a finished work of grace" that frees the believer from the *guilt* of sin. Sanctification, which flows from conversion, is an ongoing process that frees the believer from the *power* of sin. Spirit baptism, in this view, is not dependent upon a "second blessing" assuring sanctification.

The second major cleavage within pentecostalism materialized at a 1913 camp meeting during which a "Jesus only" theology was proposed. This Jesus Unitarian doctrine held that there is only one person in the Godhead, and to baptize in the name of the "Father, Son and Holy Ghost" is simply to recognize the three titles of the one God: Jesus. Dispute over this "Oneness" doctrine gave rise to an enduring division in the pentecostal movement and was a major reason that a Statement of Fundamental Truths was issued by the Assemblies of God in 1916 definitively endorsing Trinitarianism.

Three major groupings of pentecostal denominations are formed by these divisions: (1) Holiness Pentecostals, (2) Reformed or "Finished Work" Pentecostals, and (3) "Oneness" Pentecostals. *Holiness Pentecostals* include the largest historically African American Pentecostal denomination, the Church of God in Christ (COGIC in Memphis, Tennessee) as well as historically white denominations such as the Church of God (Cleveland, Tennessee), the Church of God in Christ-International, and the Pentecostal Holiness Church. *Reformed Pentecostals* include the Assemblies of God (the largest historically white Pentecostal denomination), International Church of the Foursquare Gospel, and Pentecostal Church of God. *Oneness Pentecostals* include two major denominations—the Pentecostal Assemblies of the World (African American) and the United Pentecostal Church (white)—which formed from a racial split within the Pentecostal Assemblies of the World.

Secularization Theory: Old and New The rapid growth of Holiness and Pentecostal churches in the most advanced industrial society in the world poses an empirical challenge to mechanistic theories of "secularization," particularly those informed by Max Weber's idea that societal rationalization would lead to the "disenchantment" of the world. Rodney Stark and his colleagues have offered an alternative "economic approach" to religion, which accounts for the persistence of religion in the modern world by maintaining that secularization is a self-limiting process. As mainline churches become worldly and mundane (secularized), more vital sectarian movements arise that seek to restore the "potency" of religious traditions. These less worldly sects are better able to compete in the religious economy and therefore experience substantial growth.

In Finke and Stark's view, the emergence of the Holiness-Pentecostal churches from Methodism and their subsequent growth is paradigmatic of the history of *The Churching of America* (Rutgers University Press 1992). While the sectarian Church of the Nazarene and Assemblies of God *gained* 42% and 371%, respectively, in market share between 1940 and 1985, the United Methodist Church *lost* 48% over the same period (p. 248). In the nineteenth century, when Methodism grew in numbers to be the largest church in America, its laity became more economically prosperous and its clergy more educated and professionalized. As a consequence, its focus on outward holiness was compromised, and in accommodating to the world, its sectlike vigor was transformed into churchlike tedium. The emergence of the Holiness revivals in the nineteenth century was a reaction to the increasing "worldliness" of this and other mainstream Protestant denominations.

Although the Holiness movement began as a revitalization movement *within* Methodism, by the late nineteenth century, ecclesiastical officials had shown themselves to be resistant to change, and the Church of God (Anderson, Indiana) became the first independent Holiness church. The Holiness movement has followed the American pattern of denominationalism since, producing churches such as the Salvation Army, Wesleyan Methodists, and Free Methodists. The largest Holiness denomination, the Church of the Nazarene, has seen dramatic growth since its official founding in 1908 as the result of a series of mergers between several small, independent Holiness congregations. In 1906, there were 6,657 Nazarenes, or 0.08 members per 1,000 population; by 1986, there were 530,912, or 2.20 members per 1,000, an increase in market share of 2,750% (p. 165).

As remarkable as the case of the Church of the Nazarene is, its growth has been more modest than that of the Assemblies of God, which is not only the largest pentecostal denomination but is the twelfth largest of all Protestant denominations in the United States today.

In the past four-score years, its market share has grown even more significantly.

Growth and Institutional Dilemmas The remarkable growth experienced by denominations such as the Assemblies of God raises certain organizational challenges—notably, how to balance the need for institutionalization with the desire to keep spontaneous charismata at the center of religious practice. Poloma (1989) analyzes this situation in terms of O'Dea's five "dilemmas of institutionalization," and finds that the Assemblies of God has managed to keep these dilemmas alive, not allowing institutionalization to routinize completely the church's spirit of charisma. It has done this in part by combining congregational and presbyterian governance and thereby facilitating heterogeneity (e.g., in staffing, in ritual style) within the denomination. The dilemmas of institutionalization, however, are ever present, and the fallen teleministries of Jim Bakker and Jimmy Swaggart exemplify the powerful forces of accommodation that bear on successful churches. Indeed, as the Assemblies of God becomes more suburban, more educated, and more middle class, the specter is raised of a schism within the church as it becomes more worldly, more compromised—in a word, more secularized.

The Social Sources of Pentecostalism Sectarian religious movements have long been seen as the religion of "the disinherited." In his historical study, Anderson (1979:240) locates pentecostalism among those on the margins of the new, urban, bureaucratic industrial social order—the working poor, blacks, immigrants, marginal farmers. But even if social dislocation and economic deprivation create a *pool* of candidates, they cannot explain *who* among the disinherited actually become involved in sects. Anderson concludes that the social sources of Pentecostal membership were the combination of deprivation *and* coming from a revivalistic Protestant or superstitious Catholic background.

As pentecostal denominations have grown, they resemble less their disinherited forebears. Poloma (1989) compared a sample of 1,275 Assemblies of God members with a national sample of Protestants and found that members had slightly higher than average earnings and were more likely to be college graduates. More generally, however, although the gap between upstart sects and mainline Protestants in the United States has narrowed considerably over the course of the twentieth century, members of Holiness-Pentecostal churches are still below national averages

in education, income, and occupational prestige (Roof and McKinney 1987).

Moral, Social, and Political Views When scholars classify religious groups according to ideology, pentecostal denominations are routinely counted among the "conservative" churches. This conservatism is not only theological, it also can be seen in the moral attitudes, social views, and political beliefs of pentecostals. Compared with Americans generally, pentecostals are very traditional on moral issues such as abortion, sex education in schools, premarital and extramarital sex, and homosexuality. On social issues, pentecostals routinely take conservative positions on the role of women in society, the death penalty, and corporal punishment. They are far less favorable than the average American to the granting of atheists, communists, and homosexuals such civil liberties as the right to speak in public, and are also less supportive of racial justice (e.g., laws against miscegenation) than Americans generally (Roof and McKinney 1987). One exception to this consistently conservative outlook is that Pentecostals are surprisingly liberal on the economic issue of welfare spending, probably a reflection of their class position.

In general, Pentecostal churches tend to uphold strict codes of behavior, proscribing social dancing, gambling, and the use of tobacco or alcohol, and prescribing self-control and individual achievement. According to Johnson (1961), this orientation is a variant of what Weber has called the ethic of inner-worldly asceticism, a latent function of which is the socialization of adherents in the dominant values of American society.

As theologically conservative Christians, pentecostals are typically grouped with fundamentalists and other evangelicals in the "New Christian Right" (NCR), which gained considerable notoriety for its political activities in the 1980s. More subtle analyses of NCR politics, however, have revealed diverse social and political attitudes. In *God's Warriors* (Johns Hopkins University Press 1992), Clyde Wilcox shows that a major divide in the 1988 Republican presidential primaries was between pentecostals, who gave the candidacy of charismatic Baptist televangelist Pat Robertson the strongest and most consistent support, and fundamentalists, who followed Jerry Falwell and the Moral Majority in supporting George Bush.

—*David Yamane*

REFERENCES

R. M. Anderson, *Vision of the Disinherited* (New York: Oxford University Press, 1979); B. Johnson, "Do Holiness Sects Socialize in Dominant Values?" *Social Forces* 40(1961):309-316; M. M. Poloma, *The Assemblies of God at the Crossroads* (Knoxville: University of Tennessee Press, 1989); W. C. Roof and W. McKinney, *American Mainline Religion* (New Brunswick, N.J.: Rutgers University Press, 1987).

PEOPLES TEMPLE The Peoples Temple is most well known for the tragedy at Jonestown, Guyana, that took the lives of over 900 Americans in 1978. Started by the Rev. Jim Jones in the mid-1950s, the People's Temple migrated from Indiana to Ukiah, a small town north of San Francisco in the mid-1960s, and a few years later established a larger church in San Francisco. The Peoples Temple was unusual in that, even when it began in the still-segregated 1950s, it actively and successfully encouraged integration in its congregation. In the mid-1970s, spurred by conflicts with local government officials and concerned relatives of members, a group from the church formed a settlement in the jungle of the Northwest District of Guyana that was soon after known as Jonestown.

The membership of the Peoples Temple differed from that of most new religious movements of the 1960s and 1970s in several key ways. During this period in the United States, most members of new religious movements were young, white, middle class, and relatively well educated. The origins of the Peoples Temple were in the Christian Church, mainly in Pentecostalism. Its membership was predominantly black and working- and lower-class white. It included a number of elderly members and had a middle-class, educated, white elite. The Peoples Temple provided a wide range of social services for its needy members and tried to promote sweeping social reform, then decided to withdraw from U.S. society when it was clear that reform was not working (Weightman 1989).

The tragedy at Jonestown was apparently precipitated by a visit from Congressman Leo Ryan of California and an entourage of news media who came to investigate complaints lodged against the Peoples Temple by concerned relatives of church members. On November 18, 1978, after a visit that did not go well for Jones and the Peoples Temple, several members were sent to the nearby airstrip to intercept Congressman Ryan and his party. Five of the Ryan party were shot down while trying to leave, including Ryan. After the attack, Jones, apparently feeling that the Peoples Temple could not escape persecution even by moving to the jungles of South America, gathered the members of the Peoples Temple for mass suicide.

An estimated 911 Jonestown community members died in the tragedy, in addition to those of Congressman Ryan's party who were killed. More than 200 children were murdered. Most members, including Jim Jones and other leaders of the Jonestown community, voluntarily committed suicide by drinking a mixture of potassium cyanide and tranquilizers. There are indications from an audiotape made at the scene and other evidence that 50 to 100 members did not voluntarily commit suicide but were coerced into drinking the poison or were shot by Peoples Temple guards (Moore and McGehee 1989).

The press and the U.S. public tended to interpret the events at Jonestown in purely psychological or psychiatric terms, and certainly as an event that was bizarre and inexplicable. Jim Jones was often portrayed as being insane, motivated by a mad quest for power, or as pathologically authoritarian. Peoples Temple members were commonly depicted as insane or victims of brainwashing. Additionally, there was a tendency in media coverage of the tragedy to suggest or imply that the Peoples Temple was similar to other new religious movements in the United States at that time in ways that posed a danger of similar tragedies connected with these new movements (see Richardson 1980). These trends were encouraged by those in the anti-cult movement. The incident at Jonestown was used to point to the supposed dangers of involvement in religious "cults." Some anti-cult members suggested that Jonestown was the first of such tragedies among new religious movements or "cults" and that similar events would become much more common. Jonestown did produce short-lived support for key items on the anti-cult agenda, such as increased support for restrictions on new religious movements. However, much of that support waned with the absence of any wave of mass suicides and with the decline or partial assimilation of many new religious movements (see Shupe et al. 1989).

Unlike most views presented in the mass media, social scientific examinations of the Peoples Temple and the Jonestown tragedy have tended to regard the Jonestown events, while to some extent unusual and extreme, as explicable and not unprecedented. Richardson (1980) and Weightman (1989) point to key differences between the Peoples Temple and other new religious movements in the United States, suggesting that similarities between the Peoples Temple and other new religious movements have been overstated. Robbins (1989) states that Jonestown is not unprecedented and compares Jonestown suicides with those in the Old Believers of Russia in the late seventeenth century and with those in the Circumcellion group of the Donatist "Church of Martyrs" in North Africa during late Antiquity. Hall (1981) analyzes the Peoples Temple as an other-worldly sect with characteristics similar to other other-worldly sects, but with special characteristics and circumstances that made the mass suicide option more likely and perhaps more attractive. Recent events such as the tragedy at the Branch Davidian compound in Waco, Texas, and the mass suicide of the Heaven's Gate members in the United States, along with instances of religiously motivated mass suicide or murder in Switzerland and Japan, have rekindled scholarly interest in the connection between religion and violence.

See also Deviance, Violence

—*Edward F. Breschel*

REFERENCES

J. Hall, "The Apocalypse at Jonestown," in *In Gods We Trust*, ed. T. Robbins and D. Anthony (New Brunswick, N.J.: Transaction, 1981); J. Hall, *Gone from the Promised Land* (New Brunswick, N.J.: Transaction, 1987); K. Levi (ed.), *Violence and Religious Commitment* (University Park: Penn State University Press, 1982); R. Moore and R. McGehee III (eds.), *New Religious Movements, Mass Suicide, and People's Temple* (Lewiston, N.Y.: Mellen, 1989); J. T. Richardson, "People's Temple and Jonestown," *Journal for the Scientific Study of Religion* 19(1980):239-255; T. Robbins, "The Historical Antecedents of Jonestown," in Moore and McGehee, *q.v.* (1989): 51-76; A. Shupe et al., "The Peoples Temple, the Apocalypse at Jonestown, and the Anti-Cult Movement," in Moore and McGehee, *q.v.* (1989): 153-178; R. Weightman, "The Peoples Temple as a Continuation and an Interruption of Religious Marginality in America," in Moore and McGehee, *q.v.* (1989): 5-24.

PERRY, EVERETT L. (1911–) From 1945 until retirement in 1977, Perry served in various capacities on the staff of the United Presbyterian Church, U.S.A., including coordinating research and survey efforts of the Board of National Missions. He received a Ph.D. from the University of Chicago with Samuel Kincheloe and served on project staffs with H. Paul Douglass.

The author of numerous survey and planning reports, book chapters, and journal articles, Perry has more than 80 reports included in the H. Paul Douglass collection. He is a founding member of the Religious Research Association and has served the association in many capacities.

—*Jackson W. Carroll*

PERSONALITY Became a specialty of American psychology in reaction to the failure of psychology to study the whole person.

Most personality theorists agree that the study of personality ought to be holistic and to seek to identify commonalities within an individual over time as well as differences among individuals. In addition, most personality psychologists study relatively normal functioning in adults. In 1937, Gordon W. Allport published the first textbook in personality, *Personality: A Psychological Interpretation* (Holt), which literally created this specialty. He championed idiographic studies, or the study of individual lives, in opposition to the search for general principles or laws across individuals. In the contemporary psychology of religion, personality theory and research is dominated by psychoanalytic, object relations, and Jungian theorists. Many use case study methods. These orientations often focus upon the reconstruction of infantile experiences and their presumed effects on current adult actions, thoughts, and feelings. Religious experiences typically are seen as rooted in these early infantile states.

Empirically oriented personality psychologists of religion focus upon measurement studies, typically assessing various traits and using them to predict religious variables. Empirical personality researchers focus upon adult characteristics that can be measured. Most seek nomothetic, or general, laws; few continue to champion Allport's original emphasis on the study of the single individual. One area of study linking empirical psychologists and those of a more dynamic persuasion is that of authoritarianism. Conceived as a personality construct, the authoritarian personality has been a continuous focus of theory development and research since the early 1950s. It is generally seen by both dynamic and empirical theorists to be a major factor in accounting for the appeal of more dysfunctional forms of religiosity and is one of the few areas of empirical research linked to the testing of theories heavily influenced by psychoanalytic thought.

—*Ralph W. Hood, Jr.*

REFERENCES

T. W. Adorno, *The Authoritarian Personality* (New York: Harper, 1950); C. Capps and W. H. Capps (eds.), *The Religious Personality* (Belmont, Calif.: Wadsworth, 1970); A. van Kaam, *Religion and Personality* (Englewood Cliffs, N.J.: Prentice Hall, 1964).

PHENOMENOLOGY A mode of inquiry common in Continental philosophy and North American sociology.

Edmund Husserl (1859-1938) conceived of phenomenology as a description of ways objects are present to consciousness and conscious acts make objects of ideas and sensations. What is available to an inquirer, according to Husserl, what is empirical in a strict sense, is the act of being conscious of something *("intentionalität"),* not some external object. Husserl observed that there are different modes of intentionality and that describing the physical world in mathematical terms is only one such mode within science. A mode that is particularly relevant to the social sciences is the creation or "constitution" of shared life-worlds with distinct provinces of meaning.

Alfred Schutz (1899-1959) approached sociology as an effort to correlate such life-worlds or "multiple realities" with typical activities. In the study of religion, phenomenology has been used to describe the religious mentality (Otto 1923), to develop a philosophical anthropology upon which theoretical statements have been predicated (Luckmann 1967, Berger 1967), and to conceptualize meditative states (Damrell 1977) and ritual (Blasi 1985, Flanagan 1991, Spickard 1991). Phenomenologists have criticized a natural science-like approach to human conduct, wherein scientists' theories neglect finding any grounding in social actors' consciousnesses; such critiques (Garrett 1974, Blasi 1985) have addressed the study of religion.

—*Anthony J. Blasi*

REFERENCES

P. L. Berger, *The Sacred Canopy* (Garden City, N.Y.: Doubleday, 1967); A. J. Blasi, *A Phenomenological Transformation of the Social Scientific Study of Religion* (New York: Peter Lang, 1985); J. Damrell, *Seeking Spiritual Meaning* (Beverly Hills, Calif.: Sage, 1977); K. Flanagan, *Sociology and Liturgy* (New York: St. Martin's, 1991); W. R. Garrett, "Troublesome Transcendence," *Sociological Analysis* 35(1974):167-180; T. Luckmann, *The Invisible Religion* (New York: Macmillan, 1967); R. Otto, *The Idea of the Holy* (London: Oxford University Press, 1923); J. V. Spickard, "Experiencing Religious Rituals," *Sociological Analysis* 52(1991):191-204.

PIAGET, JEAN (1896-1980)   Widely recognized Swiss developmental psychologist. His stage theory of intellectual development has indirectly influenced the psychology of religion via those theorists who have proposed theories of moral and faith development. However, early in his career as Director of Studies at the Rosseu Institute in Geneva, Piaget helped found a research group directly involved in the empirical study of religion. It included other members of the Student Christian Association of French Switzerland. He used a typology based upon contradictory qualities attributed to God: immanence and transcendence. Anticipating much of the image of God research in contemporary psychology, Piaget correlated these types with early parental relations. Piaget's direct contributions to the psychology of religion are restricted to his work as part of this early French eclectic tradition. Unfortunately, his early writings, focused directly on research in psychology of religion, remain untranslated into English. That work did have some influence on American sociology through Guy Swanson's use of immanence and transcendence in *Religion and Regime* (University of Michigan Press 1967) and various articles published since that time.

—*Ralph W. Hood, Jr.*

REFERENCES

J. Piaget and J. de la Harpe, *Deux types d'attitude religiuese* (Geneva: Labor, 1928); M. Vander Goot, *Piaget as a Visionary Thinker* (Bristol, Ind.: Wyndham Hall, 1985); D. M. Wulff, "A French Eclectic Tradition," in *Psychology of Religion* (New York: Wiley, 1991): 26-31.

PILGRIMAGE/TOURISM   The word *tourism* derives from the verb *tour* meaning "travel." Travelers, whether alone or in a group, date back to ancient times—the sign, perhaps, of an innate need in man. In ancient Greece, for example, people would travel to attend the Olympic Games or to worship the gods in particularly important temples.

In pre-Christian times, the oracle at Delphi played an especially important role in ancient Greece. The panhellenic religious feasts held at Olympia every four years and at Delphi led to the two sites becoming famous outside Greece. The oracle at Delphi, in particular, exercised a strong attraction, drawing a large number of pilgrims.

Latin literature in its turn often mentions the *otia*, the periods of free time that the upper classes devoted to activities other than work. The *horae subsicivae* of the Romans, for example, were given over to leisure activities as a well-earned rest after work. During their otia, the Romans used to visit cities with particular climatic conditions, such as Pompeii.

The Middle Ages are marked by journeys and pilgrimages to holy places. This is the period in which "religious tourism" became popular with its interdependent means of transport, accommodation for pilgrims, and stops along the route at which peddlers would sell "relics." The most common destinations of the period were Santiago de Compostela, Czestochowa, and Rome.

In the Middle Ages, pilgrimages were a collective phenomenon that was an integral part of the Christian world. Pilgrims were considered to be extremely spiritual and were held in high regard by society. Pilgrims were "the initiated" who sought to free themselves from the structures surrounding them and to ascend to a new level of existence. To go on a pilgrimage meant leaving behind the worldly aspects of life so as to concentrate on the purity of one's faith. When they returned home, pilgrims were greeted with admiration and were aware of having taken a further step toward spirituality.

In Medieval times, the ecclesiastically legitimated pilgrimage represented elements of a very precise nature: the "movement" of the journey, the religious "motivation," and the "destination," which had to be a place that was considered holy. In general, pilgrimages arose from the search for salvation and, sometimes, the need to be physically healed. Medieval travelers undertook their journeys for a purpose—to increase their spirituality—and in this sense pilgrims in the Middle Ages were clearly different from those who traveled to satisfy their curiosity.

In the seventeenth century, those traveling for the purposes of tourism emphasized the search for truth, but the real change in the nature of tourism came about in the following century. With the reduction in working hours, more leisure time became available, and cultural tourism, with the accent on art and poetry, became popular. The major change dates to 1828, the year in which George Stephenson invented the steam locomotive. This was also the period of the "grand tour of Europe" of the English aristocracy and the no less famous "Journey to Italy" of the German nobles, intellectuals, and artists who were treading in the footsteps of Goethe. This was soon followed by visits to spa towns.

As time passed, "tourism" came to mean the opportunities available to the increasing mass of individuals who felt attracted by these offers of excursions for pleasure. The growing demand led to the birth of travel agencies; the first was founded in Leicester in 1841 by Thomas Cook. He went on to become famous because, in 1866, he organized the first tour of the United States and, in 1872, the first round-the-world tour.

At the beginning of this century, tourism was turning into a business, although it slackened in the first half of the century, owing to the two world wars. After these difficulties, tourism came to signify the personal transfer from one place to another of income for the purposes of consumerism as the result of economic well-being and technological progress.

Tourism has led to the creation of new habits and different behavior and life models as well as a different conception of time. It has generated a movement of culture that encourages travelers to see and understand social, cultural, and environmental differences: The *homo turisticus* has become the symbol of an evolved society.

Today, the old pilgrimage sites have begun again to attract masses of pilgrims, the difference now being that the pilgrims also come across tourists on holiday. What does this mass movement signify? A search for salvation or a return to the roots of the past as a form of resistance against the rationality of modern times? Without a doubt, the tourist industry and the media are offering pilgrimages as consumerism. Given that tourists share the same attitudes as pilgrims—in other words, the search for authenticity at different levels of depth and involvement—it could be said that pilgrims are partly tourists and that tourists are partly pilgrims. Thus they complement one another; the promotion of "religious" tourism today, seen as both devotional and cultural, is proof of the existence of this common "search."

The rediscovery of pilgrimages also shows that religious values, doctrines, and institutions have lost nothing of their status in, and their influence over, everyday behavior. This means that the modern individual is seeking transcendental values to overcome the fragments, the discontinuity, of modern society and that he or she is the "pilgrim tourist" of modern times.

—*Luigi Tomasi*

REFERENCES

R. Barresi, *Lo sviluppo del turismo* (Naples: Liguori, 1984); M. Boyer, *Le tourisme* (Paris: Seuil, 1982); E. Cohen, "Toward a Sociology of International Tourism," in *Social Research* 1(1972):164-182; N. Costa, *Sociologia del turismo* (Milan: Iulm, 1989); N. Costa, "Il Pellegrino ed il turista," in *Politica del turismo* 3-4(1991):54-60; N. Doiron, *L'art de voyager* (Sainte-foy, Québec: Les Presses de l'Université Laval, 1995); D. MacCannel, *The Tourist* (New York: Schocken, 1976); M. L. Nolan, *Christian Pilgrimage in Modern Western Europe* (Chapel Hill: University of North Carolina Press, 1989); D. Pearce, *Tourism Today* (London: Longman, 1987); "Pilgrimage and Modernity," *Social Compass* 2(1989):138-245; A. Savelli, *Sociologia del turismo* (Milan: Angeli, 1989); S. L. J. Smith, *Tourism Analysis* (Harlow, U.K.: Longman, 1989); J. Sumption, *Pilgrimage* (Totowa, N.J.: Rowman & Littlefield, 1976); V. Turner and E. Turner, *Image and Pilgrimage in Christian Culture* (New York: Columbia University

Press, 1978); E. Vauchez, *La spiritualité du Moyen-Age Occidental* (Paris: Puf, 1975).

PILLARIZATION The structuring of society into organizational complexes that promote social functions and activities on a religious or ideological basis. The core of a pillar may be a church or a political party. Such subsystems strive toward autarky by providing their members with all possible services—unions, insurance, banking, mass media, schools, hospitals, old people's homes, youth and adult movements. They emerged in the nineteenth century to protect their membership in a secularizing society or to emancipate the lower classes. In the twentieth century, they disintegrated under the impact of internal secularization or survived by generalizing their particular values.

—*Karel Dobbelaere*

REFERENCES

K. Dobbelaere and L. Voyé, "From Pillar to Postmodernity," *Sociological Analysis* 51(1990):S1-S13; S. Rokkan, "Towards a Generalized Concept of 'Verzuiling,' " *Political Studies* 25(1977):563-570; M. P. C. M. Van Schendelen (ed.), *Consociationalism, Pillarization and Conflict-Management in the Low Countries* (Meppel, Neth.: Boom, 1984).

PLAUSIBILITY The *believability* of religious and/or secular meanings.

Within the social scientific study of religion, the problem of plausibility usually revolves around the question of why and how individuals regard their beliefs as real or true. Although some psychological explanations have interpreted plausibility as an almost purely subjective phenomenon, many social scientists focus not only on the content of meaning systems but also on the dialectical relationship between meanings and the broader sociocultural context within which these meanings "make sense" or are plausible.

Any beliefs held by individuals and groups are sustained through sociocultural institutions and processes. But the metaempirical or transcendent nature of religious beliefs makes their plausibility especially problematic. Believers require social support, usually in the form of a religious community or congregation, to authenticate and reaffirm the typically extraordinary truth claims of their faith. Members of the community will likely use a somewhat specialized language and participate in sacred rituals as important means for expressing, sharing, and internalizing their beliefs. For the religion to survive beyond the current generation, believers also must develop appropriate socialization processes to ensure that new and future members accept their faith as plausible.

Some sociologists refer to the concept of "plausibility structure" when describing the sociocultural context or "base" for meaning systems. Societywide structures were likely the norm in earlier historical periods. But in a modern, pluralistic society characterized by rapid social change, many diverse groups, each with its own somewhat distinctive plausibility structure, are forced to coexist. For religious groups especially, the very presence of other denominations, sects, and cults carries with it the implication that alternative truth claims are now available to members. As the relativization of meaning systems continues, each group's confidence in the plausibility or certainty of its shared beliefs may become weakened.

Sociological research into this phenomenon, particularly among scholars interested in the development and career stages of new religious movements, has examined the factors influencing the strength or relative "firmness" of a given religious plausibility structure (see Snow 1982). Some studies have directed attention to the strategies employed by specific religions in protecting the plausibility of their meaning system from the effects of pluralism and social change. Researchers also have applied the concept to theory construction regarding conversion and defection dynamics as well as the process by which some defectors from religious communities become reintegrated within other groups.

—*Bruce Karlenzig*

REFERENCES

P. L. Berger, *The Sacred Canopy* (Garden City, N.Y.: Doubleday, 1967); C. Geertz, "Religion as a Cultural System," in *Anthropological Approaches to the Study of Religion*, ed. M. Banton (London: Tavistock, 1966): 1-46; F. Musgrove, *Margins of the Mind* (London: Methuen, 1977); D. Snow, "On the Presumed Fragility of Unconventional Beliefs," *Journal for the Scientific Study of Religion* 21(1982):15-26; S. A. Wright, *Leaving Cults* (Washington, D.C.: Society for the Scientific Study of Religion, 1987).

PLURALISM Mutual accommodation among the different religious, regional, occupational, and professional groups in a society that have had diverse cultural and historical origins. Pluralism often has been treated as a principal effect of globalization and cause of secularization, although these causal directions may be disputed. It is probably best to see pluralism as part of an expanding circle of processes that characterize the development of the modern world system. Partly this entry refers to general characteristics of pluralism and partly to India as a specific case. India may be taken as paradigmatic of both the virtues and the vices of pluralism.

The Political Economics of Pluralism All nation-states, old and new, are pluralistic in the sense that they contain within their ambit many ethnic groups. Nationally, the modern state rests on the principle of equidistance; all groups have equal access to it. However, there are two obstacles to this goal: First, in nearly all the nation-states, some groups that are in a majority dominate others who are in a minority. Second, in the new nation-states of Asia and Africa, primordial loyalties (based on kinship, religion, ethnicity, region, and so on) often create impediments in the working of a civil society built on democratic values. Nevertheless, many of these new states have provided constitutional guarantees for the equitable treatment of their citizens. In recent years, the Indian judiciary, for example, has made an exemplary effort to uphold citizens' rights by revoking arbitrary acts of government.

In Western nations, pluralism has evolved through a capitalistic economic system. Here, political ideologies—right, center, and left—have tended to define pluralism through different perspectives, thereby bringing to the fore certain tensions and conflicts. In contrast, J. S. Furnivall (e.g., 1977 [1934]), who served in the Asian colonial administration, defined it in terms of the *market* principle. Referring to such societies as Burma and Indonesia during the colonial era, he noted that their indigenous people shared economic ties with immigrants from China, India, and so on, but the indigenous/immigrant groups were not united with each other in cultural terms. These societies were politically subordinated to the colonial rulers who also controlled the market transactions.

R. K. Jain (1994), a commentator on the overseas Indian communities, has pointed out that the Furnivallian model is more strictly applicable to settlement societies such as Trinidad and Tobago, Fiji, and Mauritius than such civilizations as India, China, and Europe. In the former, there is a short history, a colonial background, and a culturally disparate population. In the latter, a long duration of tradition and cultural unity are conspicuous. Jain notes that Indian civilization has evolved through a diachronic interaction between the

Great Tradition (derived from Sanskritic heritage) and the Little Tradition (derived from regional diversities in language and ethnicity). In addition to these, the indigenous bhakti (devotional) movements, the influx of Christianity in the colonial era, and the struggle for independence also contributed to Indian pluralism. Insofar as the settlement societies are concerned, Jain states that in the postcolonial era, there is a need for a replacement of the previous research model of acculturation—which implied the domination of one group over the other—by an intercultural model based on reciprocity among ethnic groups.

Structural Dimensions of Pluralism in India Through centuries of interactions between different religions and ethnic groups, Indian society has developed a composite culture. Its ethnic groups include the many castes that operate within the framework of Hinduism as well as the non-Hindu groups such as Muslims, Christians, and Sikhs. Encounters among these groups have led to the emergence of a symbiotic, rather than consensual, society in which structural tensions persist.

Although hierarchically organized, the Hindu caste system provided some scope for interdependence. The upper castes consisting of intellectual and landowning castes were dependent on lower servicing castes in economic as well as ritual terms. In addition, there was an implicit scope for mobility in the caste system; the bhakti movement opened up channels of upward mobility. Also, a few enterprising individuals could rise to be the rulers of the land through military prowess in spite of their previous low status. In recent decades, the process called Sanskritization (see Srinivas 1966) has enabled low-status groups to adopt rituals and norms of the higher groups to acquire a better status. Hence, despite the apparent rigidity, the Indian caste system has provided for pluralistic accommodation. However, the rising demands of different groups for higher status have created social tensions.

In the post-Independence period, Indian pluralism based on cultural unity has been under great strain. Not only the religious minorities but also the castes are scrambling for power and privilege. Although their aspirations may be timely and legitimate, the competition among them is often marked by distrust or hostility. In the words of G. S. Ghurye (1969), India seems to be heading toward a "Furnivallian" pluralism, with its market orientation rather than a cultural orientation. In this respect, it mirrors a general pattern of Western societies, which have been characterized, at least since Peter Berger (1967), as having a *marketplace* orientation marked by *competition*. Political parties in India are likewise often pursuing populist policies that use ad hoc measures to cater to minorities and weaker sections. India has achieved progress in many respects, but social discontent has also proportionately increased.

Historically, secularism in India has not meant a sharp break with religious traditions. Hindu, Buddhist, or Jain rulers allowed different faiths to exist in their realms. The development of secular occupations was not in conflict with religion. Max Weber (1958) noted that India had made progress in the *preindustrial* economy through its numerous crafts and arts, which were organized into guilds. But the social barriers among different castes placed obstacles in India's transition to an industrial economy. However, secularism as a political ideology became a topical issue only in more recent times. India's exposure to the rest of the world during the colonial state and thereafter has been an important factor in this development.

The 1950 Indian constitution defined secularism as the freedom to pursue different religions. At the same time, the constitution enjoins citizens to avoid interference in others' religious affairs. The policy of the government of India is not atheistic. Also, the Indian constitution recognizes only one kind of minority, the *non-Hindu* religious minority. Buddhism, Jainism, and Hinduism are regarded as one for juridical purposes, such as inheritance of property.

Secularism thus needs to be understood in the context of the overwhelming religiosity of the Indian people. No village or town in India is devoid of a religious monument, temple, mosque, or church. Excepting a few elites, for most people, religious obligations have remained a ubiquitous part of their lives. Many of the schools and colleges are still operated by religious organizations. These centers also have provided education to the students belonging to other religious groups. They do not insist that outsiders should follow particular religious tenets. In sum, except where religion has been used for political or antisocial purposes, it has not been an obstacle to the secular development of Indian society.

See also American Religion, Peter L. Berger, Secularization

—*C. N. Venugopal*

REFERENCES

P. L. Berger, *The Sacred Canopy* (Garden City, N.Y.: Doubleday, 1967); J. S. Furnivall, *Studies in the Social and Economic Development of the Netherlands East Indies* (New York: AMS, 1977 [1934]); G. S. Ghurye, *Caste and Race in India* (Bombay: Popular, 1969); R. K. Jain, "Civilization and Settlement Societies," *Eastern Anthropologist* 47(1994):1-14; D. Mandelbaum, *Society in India* (Bombay: Popular, 1984); M. N. Srinivas, *Social Change in Modern India* (Berkeley: University of California Press, 1966); M. Weber, *The Religion of India* (Glencoe, Ill.: Free Press, 1958).

POLITICS Intermittently throughout American history, religious belief and practice have been an important source of political conflict. The occasional, and occasionally intense, nature of religious politics in the United States may be attributable to the unique role that religion plays in the life of the American nation. On one hand, religious belief and observance are quite widespread in the United States; relative to other industrialized nations, the U.S. population is highly religious. On the other hand, as a constitutional principle, religion is regarded as a separate sphere of activity from politics and government. Although the exact nature of church-state separation is a frequent topic of debate, few would dispute the principle itself.

Some scholars have suggested that these two characteristics of religion in the United States are not unrelated. Because religion (either singularly or collectively) is not accorded public support, religious denominations must compete for lay "consumers." In contrast to nations with established churches (which are regarded as similar to industrial monopolies), a competitive religious "market" encourages churches to attend to the needs and preferences of potential members. The laity is thought to respond to the efforts of the clergy by increased religious observance and devotion.

What this may mean is that, in many periods of American history, religion is an important personal matter for most citizens, but one with a very tenuous place in public discourse. The lack of public affirmations of specific religious principles may allow the perception that there exists a religious-moral consensus in American political culture. Observers from Alexis de Tocqueville to A. James Reichley and Richard Neuhaus have noted the widespread American adherence to "Christianity," or a "Judeo-Christian tradition." Because religious observance (church attendance and so on) is relegated to a private sphere, it may well be that most Americans are unaware of significant doctrinal or theological differences, or regard such distinctions as unimportant. In a religiously "consensual" polity, religion is not considered a direct source of political values but provides a context within which the political life of the nation can be conducted. Consensual religion is thought to provide boundaries on the range of permissible public policies rather than providing specific policy guidance.

Religious Mobilization Historically, religious values cease to be a background characteristic of American politics and become a source of political mobilization when a group falling outside the prevailing "consensus" assumes a highly visible public role. In such a situation, religious values often are reafffirmed in public discourse as a means of defending a "lifestyle" that suddenly may seem threatened. Religiously orthodox citizens may use interest group activity, organize political parties, or form factions within the major parties in response to the perceived threat to the cultural hegemony of consensual religion.

On several occasions, religious beliefs have been mobilized politically in response to waves of immigration. In the 1850s, the "Know-Nothing" Party was formed in response to a large influx of Irish-Catholic immigrants. This movement was explicitly nativist and anti-Catholic, and served as one of the groups contributing to the rise of the Republican Party. Paul Kleppner (1987) has argued that, outside the South, the party system was divided on ethnoreligious grounds, with "ritualists" (Roman Catholics and "high church" Protestants) forming a constituency for the Democratic Party and "pietists" (experientially and evangelically oriented "low church" Protestants) tending to identify with the Republican Party.

Similarly, the Prohibition movement of the early twentieth century is often regarded as a reaction to another wave of Catholic immigration following World War I. Indeed, the Prohibition issue empowered a strong, "nativist" coalition of "mainline" Protestants and "fundamentalists." The former group was committed to the "Social Gospel," or a reinterpretation of Scripture as a response to modernity. The Social Gospel involved an emphasis on the ethical message of Christianity, an analysis of social problems in structural terms, and a corresponding deemphasis on doctrinal orthodoxy. By contrast, "fundamentalists" sought to reaffirm the doctrinal "fundamentals" of Christianity, including the inerrancy of Scripture and the importance of individual conversion (as opposed to social reform). These divergent theological perspectives converged around the issue of alcohol. Proponents of the Social Gospel were able to portray alcohol as one of the most pernicious evils of modern, urban life, while fundamentalists were able to invoke specific scriptural injunctions against "demon rum."

Occasionally, publicly visible "out-groups" may not involve questions of immigration. In the 1950s, the specter of communism (both international and domestic) occasioned the formation of several interest groups, such as the Christian Anti-Communist Crusade and the John Birch Society. In these groups, and in other circles, the cold war between the United States and the Soviet Union was often interpreted in apocalyptic terms, with international events viewed through the theological prism of the Book of Revelation. "Atheistic" communism was often perceived as literally diabolical by citizens on the theological and political right.

In the 1960s and 1970s, conservative religious sentiment was mobilized by issues of lifestyle concern. In response to "countercultural" issues such as drug use, sexual permissiveness, feminism, abortion, and gay rights, doctrinally conservative Christians mobilized sporadically throughout the period. The 1972 election is thought to be particularly critical in this regard, as the Democratic candidate, George McGovern, was widely perceived to represent groups opposed to traditional morality. Richard Nixon's appeal to the more traditionalist "Silent Majority," as well as the characterization of McGovern as the candidate of "Acid, Amnesty, and Abortion," may have attracted many previously apolitical or Democratic evangelical Christians to the Republican camp. Indeed, the McGovern candidacy was an important negative symbol for Republican candidates as recently as the off-year elections of 1994.

The candidacy and presidency of Jimmy Carter is an important watershed in the recent political mobilization of evangelical Christians. Although Carter's evangelical roots seem to have interrupted the realignment of white evangelicals to the Republican Party, the attraction of an explicitly evangelical candidate generated a strong increase in the turnout of doctrinally conservative Christians. Many evangelical Protestants had previously adopted an attitude of religious "separatism," which inhibited participation in political affairs. The Carter candidacy appears to have legitimized electoral participation for a large number of these people. However, the apparent liberalism on lifestyle issues that characterized the Carter administration proved disappointing to many conservative religious leaders. A White House Conference on Families, in which the Carter administration appeared sympathetic to alternative forms of family living (including cohabitation outside of marriage and homosexual couples), was regarded by many as a catalyst for another mobilization of the theological right.

In response to the renewed visibility of cultural, "lifestyle" minorities (the gay rights movement seemed particularly salient during this period), a number of conservative religious interest groups were formed. These included Christian Voice, Religious Roundtable, and Moral Majority. The latter group was formed in 1979 by the Rev. Jerry Falwell, a Virginia Baptist minister. Falwell also produced a television program called *The Old Time Gospel Hour,* which, along with Pat Robertson's *700 Club,* Jim and Tammy Bakker's *PTL*

Club, and Jimmy Swaggart's televised ministry, was the most visible manifestation of a phenomenon that came to be known as "televangelism." The message of conservative Christianity, which was sometimes quite politically charged, was broadcast into millions of homes.

While stopping short of an outright endorsement, Falwell actively promoted the presidential candidacy of Ronald Reagan in 1980 and claimed a large share of the credit for Reagan's eventual victory. While the contribution of evangelical Christians to the outcome of the presidential election has been disputed, Falwell's attempts to mobilize conservative Christians (including voter registration drives) were widely credited with altering the results of several U.S. Senate elections. The 1980 election resulted in the defeat of several venerable Senate liberals, including John Culver of Iowa, Frank Church of Idaho, and (perhaps inevitably) George McGovern of South Dakota. Since the 1980 election, white evangelicals have been a reliable component of the Republican coalition, providing strong support for Reagan as well as for (Episcopalian) George Bush.

Religious Demobilization It is important to note that religiously mobilized political activity is not a permanent feature of American politics. While religiously based political movements appear to arise as the result of a perceived threat to the cultural hegemony of traditional values, such movements appear to have finite, limited life spans. At least three processes appear to account for the political demobilization of religious beliefs.

Perhaps the simplest process of demobilization comes about as the result of issue displacement. Issues of lifestyle, gender roles, or "values" may give way to other matters and lose their prominent place on the political agenda. For example, the ethnoreligious party coalitions of the 1850s appear to have been displaced by economic depression in the 1890s. Indeed, Paul Kleppner (1987) has characterized the realignment begun in the 1896 election as the "secularization of politics." Similarly, issues of Prohibition and nativism that were salient in the 1920s may well have been displaced by the Great Depression of 1929. More recently, the oft-quoted internal slogan of Bill Clinton's 1992 presidential campaign, "It's the economy, stupid!" reflects a conviction that economic issues may have a priority on the political agenda and that concerns about "lifestyle" issues may require a certain level of economic prosperity to assume a prominent role in political debate. However, noneconomic matters may also play a role in the process of issue displacement. It may well be that the religious anticommunist movement of the 1950s became less

urgent with the election of Dwight Eisenhower and the death of Senator Joseph McCarthy in 1957. It is also possible that the anticommunist issue was displaced in part by the civil rights movement, with its strong religious overtones.

A second process contributing to the political demobilization of religion may involve the countermobilization of other groups. For example, the presidential candidacy of Catholic Al Smith in 1928 seems to have had the effect of encouraging recent Catholic immigrants to enter the electoral arena. The alliance between urban, immigrant Catholics and the Democratic Party was cemented by Roosevelt's New Deal in the next presidential election. More recently, popular reaction to the Supreme Court's 1989 decision in *Webster v. Missouri Reproductive Services* on the issue of abortion appears to have mobilized pro-choice sentiment in a number of states. The *Webster* decision, which was widely interpreted as allowing state governments increased discretion in regulating the delivery of abortion services, seems to have repoliticized the abortion issue, which was credited for Democratic victories in a number of states in 1989 and 1990. Perhaps in response to these results, the Republican Party (staunchly pro-life in its party platforms since 1980) has sought to deemphasize the abortion issue in recent years. Party spokespersons have argued that it is more important to "change attitudes" than to pass restrictive abortion laws, or that the Republican Party is a "big tent," capable of accommodating a variety of positions on the abortion issue. The general point is that it is often politically costly for a political party to accommodate religiously based values, and "pragmatic" party activists may seek to suppress such issues on the political agenda.

Finally, religious particularism may contribute to the political demobilization of religion. The political mobilization of religious values entails the articulation of religious principles. It may be that, as previously implicit religious beliefs become explicit, the fragile nature of the American religious-moral "consensus" becomes apparent. Theological differences, which might not have been perceived or taken seriously, may well produce cleavages between "traditionalist" or "orthodox" Christians. Faced with such differences, potentially formidable political coalitions may fragment and splinter.

To illustrate, it has been argued that the nativist, Protestant coalition of mainline Protestants and fundamentalists were able to submerge their modern-antimodern differences over the issue of Prohibition. Each side was able to find congenial theological reasons for a common position. However, issues of science and public education (culminating in the Scopes trial) exacerbated those very doctrinal differences. Adherents of the Social Gospel were quite willing to modify their understanding of Scripture to accommodate the insights of modern science, while the fundamentalists were moved to defend the inerrancy of the Bible.

More recently, organizations associated with what has been termed the "New Christian Right" have been weakened by the effects of religious particularism. Despite Falwell's claim that Moral Majority was an ecumenical, political organization rather than a religious one, the membership of Moral Majority never extended far beyond the bounds of Independent Baptist congregations. Support for Moral Majority was quite weak, even among those citizens sympathetic to the organization's religious and political positions. Similarly, the 1988 presidential campaign of Marion "Pat" Robertson was quite unsuccessful, in large part because of Robertson's inability to expand his base of Pentecostal Christians. Indeed, fundamentalist Jerry Falwell's early endorsement of George Bush's candidacy, and his expressed skepticism regarding spiritual gifts such as glossolalia, no doubt inhibited the formation of a potentially powerful coalition of fundamentalists, Pentecostalists, and charismatics. Finally, several observers have suggested that the political effectiveness of various antiabortion organizations has been diluted by mutual antipathy between evangelical Protestants and Roman Catholics. Despite a common "pro-life" stance, theological differences between these two traditions have made political cooperation unusually difficult. The general point here is that agreement on political issues can be rendered politically irrelevant by disagreement on matters of doctrine or theology.

Toward the Future   In the early part of the 1990s, various attempts have been made to remobilize religious conservatives while avoiding the divisive effects of religious particularism. Such mobilization may have been made easier by the Clinton administration, which began by raising the controversial issue of the suitability of gays for military service. This issue, along with allegations of draft evasion, drug usage, and marital infidelity, may have made the urgency of defending "traditional" values more salient to doctrinally conservative Christians.

Perhaps the most impressive attempt at religious remobilization has been made by an organization called the Christian Coalition. Although nominally led by Pat Robertson, the most visible spokesperson for the Christian Coalition has been former executive director Ralph Reed. Prior to Reed's resignation in 1997, Reed had consistently taken the position that specifically doctrinal values are private matters and are not appropriate for public discussion. Instead, Reed has emphasized the

importance of a "new ecumenism" in which people of different religious traditions will work together to achieve public policies designed to protect and enhance "family values." Thus the emphasis of the Christian Coalition is on the application of religiously based ethics, and not on religious beliefs themselves. Some preliminary evidence among political activists has suggested that, unlike Falwell or Robertson, the Christian Coalition has an ecumenical appeal among religiously observant and orthodox people across different denominations. It seems quite clear that the leaders of Christian Coalition have recognized the divisive effects of religious particularism and are responding to the challenge posed by the persistence of religious prejudice.

—*Ted G. Jelen*

REFERENCES

K. Andersen, *The Creation of a Democratic Majority* (Chicago: University of Chicago Press, 1979); E. A. Cook et al., *Between Two Absolutes* (Boulder, Colo.: Westview, 1992); J. Falwell, *Listen, America!* (Garden City, N.Y.: Doubleday, 1980); R. Finke and R. Stark, *The Churching of America* (New Brunswick, N.J.: Rutgers University Press, 1992); J. C. Green, "Pat Robertson and the Latest Crusade," *Social Science Quarterly* 74(1993):157-168; J. D. Hunter, *Culture Wars* (New York: Basic Books, 1991); L. R. Iannaccone, "Why Strict Churches Are Strong," *American Journal of Sociology* 99(1994):1180-1211; T. G. Jelen, "The Effects of Religious Separatism on White Protestants in the 1984 Presidential Election," *Sociological Analysis* 48(1987):30-45; T. G. Jelen, *The Political Mobilization of Religious Beliefs* (New York: Praeger, 1991); T. G. Jelen, "The Political Consequences of Religious Group Attitudes," *Journal of Politics* 55(1993):178-190; L. A. Kellstedt, "Evangelicals and Political Realignment," in *Contemporary Evangelical Political Involvement*, ed. C. Smidt (New York: University Press of America, 1989): 99-117; L. A. Kellstedt et al., "Religious Voting Blocs in the 1992 Election," in *The Rapture of Politics*, ed. S. Bruce et al. (New Brunswick, N.J.: Transaction, 1994): 85-104; P. Kleppner, *The Cross of Culture* (New York: Free Press, 1970); P. Kleppner, *Continuity and Change in Electoral Politics* (New York: Greenwood, 1987); H. Lindsey, *The Late Great Planet Earth* (New York: Bantam, 1970); S. M. Lipset and E. Raab, "The Election and the Evangelicals," *Commentary* 71(1981):25-31; P. Lopatto, *Religion and the Presidential Election* (New York: Praeger, 1980); R. J. Neuhaus, *The Naked Public Square* (Grand Rapids, Mich.: Eerdmans, 1984); R. Reed, *Politically Incorrect* (Dallas: Word, 1994); A. J. Reichley, *Religion in American Public Life* (Washington, D.C.: Brookings Institution, 1985); A. de Tocqueville, *Democracy in America* (New York: Vintage, 1945 [1835]); K. D. Wald, *Religion and Politics in the United States*, 2nd ed. (Washington, D.C.: CQ Press, 1992); C. Wilcox, "The New Christian Right and the Mobilization of the Evangelicals," in *Religion and Political Behavior in the United States*, ed. T. G. Jelen

(New York: Praeger, 1989): 139-156; C. Wilcox, *God's Warriors* (Baltimore: Johns Hopkins University Press, 1992); G. Wills, *Under God* (New York: Simon & Schuster, 1990).

POPE　*see* Papacy

POPE, LISTON (1909-1974)　Born in Thomasville, North Carolina; B.A., B.D., Duke University; Ph.D. in sociology, Yale University, 1940. Ordained to the ministry of the Congregational Church. In 1938, appointed lecturer in Social Ethics at Yale Divinity School, where he remained on the faculty until 1973; Dean of the Divinity School, 1949-1962.

Pope's most important contribution to the social scientific study of religion is his book *Millhands and Preachers: A Study of Gastonia* (Yale University Press 1942). This book describes a strike by workers in a cotton mill in Gastonia, North Carolina, in 1929. The striking union was led by communists. The story of the strike is placed in the historical context of the development of the town, the pattern of social stratification in the town, and changes in the textile industry. Pope is especially concerned to show how the churches of Gaston County reacted to the strike. Clergy in middle-class ("Uptown") churches were less likely than clergy of working-class ("Mill") churches to favor the strikers, but all the churches were controlled by people sympathetic to the mill owners. Pope uses this case study to draw conclusions about the difficulties faced by churches that try to become involved in economic affairs. (In 1976, an attempt by Earle et al. to restudy Gastonia using survey research techniques was published under the title *Spindles and Spires* by Knox.)

—*William Silverman*

POPULAR RELIGION　Usually refers to customs of an overtly religious character that are practiced, with predominantly lay momentum, at particular places and times, in relatively densely populated areas (urban or rural). Examples include the "official birthday" (to use a monarchical term) of saints in Sicily or gods in India. It represents an "incomplete" social differentiation of religion from other facets of culture, such as the arts, entertainment, and commerce.

Tailor-made for touristic photography, it is typified in open-air festivals with Third World warmth, both climatic and cultural. Thus it is sometimes seen as a "survival." However, popular religion should no more

be isolated in the abstract, from its context in the rest of popular life and culture, than it is on the ground. So popular religion, like popular music, survives, and indeed thrives, in contemporary societies and culture, albeit in new ways. Examples include the liturgical appearances of Billy Graham or Pope John Paul II, the fan-ship of Cliff Richard or Mother Teresa, the "commercialization of Christmas" or the tabloid publication of prayers and "obituaries." To these examples of the popular appeal of explicit religious phenomena might be added that religiosity that is to be found *within* secular life (as suggested by the Network for the Study of Implicit Religion).

Today, its creators are more likely to be named (as "stars"). Its production, or reproduction, is not merely planned but more likely to be costed, massified, and profitable to its originators. Its consumption tends to be indoor (whether domestic, communal, or crowd), private, and subjective. The width and depth of its appeal, however, continues to be underestimated, by both students and leaders of both society and religion.

See also Folk Religion, Implicit Religion

—*Edward I. Bailey*

REFERENCES

E. Bailey, *Implicit Religion in Contemporary Society* (Kampen, Neth.: Kok Pharos, 1997); C. Booth, *Life and Labour of the People in London*, vols. 7 and 9 (London: Macmillan, 1903); W. A. Christian, *Local Religion in Sixteenth-Century Spain* (Princeton, N.J.: Princeton University Press, 1981); S. Cohen, *Folk Devils and Moral Panics* (London: MacGibbon & Kee, 1972); C. Lippy, *Modern American Popular Religion* (Westport, Conn.: Greenwood, 1996); P. A. Vrijhof and J. Waardenburg (eds.), *Official and Popular Religion* (The Hague: Mouton, 1979); W. L. Warner, *The Family of God* (New Haven: Yale University Press, 1961); P. Williams, *Popular Religion in America* (Englewood Cliffs: Prentice-Hall, 1980).

POSITIVISM

A term associated with the work of French social theorists and prophets of the post-Revolutionary era. Saint-Simon's (1760-1825) shifting theories criticized the religious, political, and legal hierarchy of the old regime in the name of a technocratic rule by the "producers" (i.e., industrialists, scientists, engineers). His emphasis on the role of knowledge elites did not prevent him from later envisioning a "New Christianity" that would replace the parasitic Roman hierarchy with a moral-religious community based on brotherly love. A brilliant, but poorly organized thinker, unfamiliar with scientific and technical matters, Saint-Simon enlisted the Polytechnic-trained Auguste Comte as his secretary, but disagreements over authorship and Comte's desire for intellectual autonomy led to a rupture in their relationship. The Saint-Simonian movement was influential in France and elsewhere.

Auguste Comte (1798-1857) made the word *positivism* central to his theoretical and practical aims. *The Cours de Philosophie Positive* developed his "law of the three stages," which saw human culture passing through theological, metaphysical, and positive phases. The theological stage involved spiritual explanations of reality and is further divided into fetishism, polytheism, and monotheism. The metaphysical stage is transitional and replaces the gods of the higher theological phase with philosophical abstractions, such as Being, Substance, and so forth. Positive thought includes all the sciences, which emerge in determinate order from their prescientific forms (i.e., mathematics, astronomy, physics, chemistry, biology, and sociology). *Sociology* (Comte's original coinage), the most synthetic form of knowledge, occupies the role of "queen of the sciences" once played by medieval theology. Sociology synthesizes the knowledge needed for proper social planning. In Comte's words, knowledge leads to prediction, which in turn leads to control.

An idealistic love affair with Clothilde de Vaux, her death, and his subsequent mental collapse led Comte, upon recovery, to supplement his rationalist faith with the idea that human community can be achieved only through *altruism* (another Comtean linguistic invention), love, and their practical offspring, the Religion of Humanity. This cult worships the Great Being through the best examples of humanity, those "saints" from all over the globe who contributed most to morality, the sciences, and the arts. It included a revised calendar, with days and rites devoted to such individuals, and featured Comte himself as high priest. The grand sweep of Comte's historical law holds little appeal today and its roots in European history seem provincial, yet his thought has been influential. Echoes can be heard in the Durkheim school, Lévi-Strauss, Teillard de Chardin, and others. His positivist religion succeeded most in Roman Catholic countries, where a new form of religious integration was desired, yet traditional rites and beliefs seemed incongruent with modernity. The Brazilian flag still carries the Comtean motto, "Order and Progress." Although Comte's Religion of Humanity may now seem a fanciful "cult," its calendar for the worship of humanity's "heroes" is strikingly contemporary and appears as the harbinger of an "international civil religion" yet to be created.

In the twentieth century, positivism has been elaborated in various forms and become widely influential in the social sciences. It also has been the subject of extensive criticism and played an important role in debates over the study of religion. Critical engagement with the early phase of positivism already appeared in the work of Dilthey, Simmel, Weber, Troeltsch, and even Durkheim and was continued in various ways by later figures such as Mannheim, Schutz, and Parsons. The new phase of positivism in early-twentieth-century philosophy emphasized language clarification, falsification of empirical statements, precise measurement, the unity of the sciences, and distinction between theoretical-factual and axiological systems. It led to suspicion of all linguistically "meaningless" and "unverifiable" concepts, including those of metaphysics and theology, as well as some of the methods used in the investigation of religion and culture.

In turn, such positivistic assumptions were criticized as unduly restrictive by proponents of historical-cultural sociology, phenomenology, interpretive theories of social action, and critical theory. Examples include the encounter between George Lundberg and Paul Hanly Furfey over positivism in the study of religion, and the conflict over method between Karl Popper and various critical social theorists. Concurrently, however, *positivism* has become a rather omnibus term, with its meaning inflated by its opponents to include those committed in any way to the development of analytical and systematic perspectives in the study of culture and society. This has given the discussion considerable indeterminacy. In this way, for example, positivist residues have been discovered in Marx's theories, and thinkers such as Weber and Parsons have been labeled positivists. The debate over the meaning of "science" in the social sciences has been especially acute and wide ranging once again since the 1960s. More recently, feminists, representatives of multiculturalist perspectives, and postmodernist thinkers all have subjected positivism, in the term's most general sense, to new critiques from their own special standpoints. While the tenacious grip of positivism within the social sciences has loosened considerably as a result of these discussions, analytical theory, quantitative evidence, and a general posture of "methodological agnosticism" toward the claims of believers continue to play a central role in the scientific study of religion.

—*Donald A. Nielsen*

REFERENCES

T. W. Adorno et al., *The Positivist Dispute in German Sociology* (New York: Harper, 1976); P. H. Furfey, *The Scope and Method of Sociology* (New York: Harper, 1953); G. Lenzer (ed.), *Auguste Comte and Positivism* (New York: Harper, 1975); G. A. Lundberg, "The Natural Science Trend in Sociology," *American Journal of Sociology* 61(1955):191-202; G.

A. Lundberg, *Foundations of Sociology,* 2nd ed. (New York: McKay, 1964 [1939]); G. A. Lundberg and P. H. Furfey, "Letters and Rejoinders," *American Catholic Sociological Review* 7(1946):203-204, 8(1947):47-48; F. E. Manuel, *The Prophets of Paris* (Cambridge: Harvard University Press, 1962); F. M. H. Markham (ed.), *Saint-Simon* (Oxford: Oxford University Press, 1952).

POSTMILLENNIALISM   *see* Premillennialism

POSTMODERNISM   While the term has gained currency in academia only in the past two decades, evidence of its use prior to that time can be found. For example, C. Wright Mills (1959:166) proclaimed, without further elaboration, that "the Modern Age is being succeeded by a post-modern period." In its brief and highly contested history, postmodernism has had a pronounced impact in certain disciplines, particularly in literature and cultural studies. Postmodernism has filtered into the social sciences, although with less impact than in some other fields of inquiry (Kivisto 1994, Gottdiener 1993).

There are a number of interpretive difficulties that are encountered in coming to terms with the idea of postmodernism. First, postmodernist theorists often disagree with one another about what the precise parameters of postmodernism actually are. Norman Denzin (1991:vii), for example, has contended that the term is "undefinable." Second, postmodernists frequently write in an impenetrable jargon, and, as such, their ideas sometimes appear—like a latter-day gnosticism—to be comprehensible only to those who are initiates into the mysteries associated with such concepts as antifoundationalism, logocentrism, hyperreality, and simulacra. A third reason has something to do with the French intellectual origins of postmodernism, where there is a tendency to accentuate the novelty of claims that are being made and the positions that are being staked out—a phenomenon resulting from the peculiar intellectual fashion-consciousness of the French.

One common thread linking various manifestations of postmodernist theory is a conviction that grand narratives have proved to be intellectually exhausted. Grand narratives, in postmodernist discourse, refer to large panoramic accounts or explanations of current social circumstances and future trends: Marx on the logic of capitalist development, Weber on rationalization, Durkheim on the development of organic solidarity, and Parsons on processes of universalization. However different these theories might be, they share the Enlightenment conviction that we have the ability to make sweeping generalizations about the directions of social change, and with that the capacity to translate knowledge into praxis (Best and Kellner 1991).

Postmodernists cast suspicion on these convictions. Jacques Derrida, for example, sees the construction of grand narratives as the product of "logocentrism," by which he means modes of thinking that refer truth claims to universally truthful propositions. The postmodernist position articulated by Derrida (1976, 1978) calls for a repudiation of logocentrism and the embracing of an antifoundational stance toward truth claims. In its most extreme versions, postmodernism constitutes a profound repudiation of the entire Western philosophical tradition and represents an extreme form of relativism.

Critics have argued that postmodernism is a contemporary form of nihilism, characterized by a loss of meaning and a loss of faith in our ability to translate theory into practice. The Enlightenment belief that a more rational world would lead to a more humane world is abandoned. Given this orientation, critics contend that postmodernism can be seen either as encouraging escapism and political passivism or as promoting an irrationality that can easily lead to reactionary political stances (O'Neill 1995, Callinicos 1989).

In relation to religion, Ernest Gellner (1992) has suggested that postmodernism constitutes one of the three main contestants in shaping collective visions about contemporary social life. The other two are religious fundamentalism and Enlightenment rationalism (which he also refers to as "rational fundamentalism"). In his estimation, while the salutary effect of postmodernist relativism is to force a more critical account of both religion and reason, this is all it can do. It cannot, in the last instance, serve as a substitute for either.

—*Peter Kivisto*

REFERENCES

S. Best and D. Kellner, *Postmodern Theory* (New York: Guilford, 1991); A. Callinicos, *Against Postmodernism* (Cambridge: Polity, 1989); N. Denzin, *Images of Postmodern Society* (Newbury Park, Calif.: Sage, 1991); J. Derrida, *Of Grammatology* (Baltimore, Md.: Johns Hopkins University Press, 1976); J. Derrida, *Writing and Difference* (Chicago: University of Chicago Press, 1978); K. Flanagan and P. Jupp (eds.), *Postmodernity, Sociology and Religion* (London: Macmillan, 1996); E. Gellner, *Postmodernism, Reason and Religion* (London: Routledge, 1992); M. Gottdiener, "Ideology, Foundationalism and Sociological Theory," *Sociological Quarterly* 34(1993):653-671; P. Kivisto, "Toward a Relevant but Antifoundational Sociology," *Sociological Quarterly*

34(1994):723-728; J. O'Neill, *The Poverty of Postmodernism* (London: Routledge, 1995).

POVERTY Condition affecting those who do not possess the means to ensure an adequate quality of life by local societal standards. Poverty is thus a societally relative conception. In the developing world, the poor may include those who are able only (or not able in some cases) to ensure their physical survival. In the developed countries, where survival needs may be met through social welfare provisions, poverty may be measured in terms of the proportion of income spent to obtain the necessities of life (e.g., food, clothing, shelter).

Poverty has been viewed in several different ways by theologians and religious leaders. On the one hand, as in traditional Catholicism, it may be viewed as a natural condition, as God's will. Poverty, in this conception, is one's "lot in life," something to be endured, but something that will eventually give way—at least for the truly believing—to the reward of an eternity in heaven. The poor are to be treated with compassion, and it becomes the moral duty of the more affluent to provide support to the poor through alms or other works of charity.

Another view, which arose concurrently with some brands of Protestantism, sees poverty as something to be disdained, avoided at all costs. In fact, stemming from the doctrines of John Calvin, the early Protestants came to equate poverty with lack of favor in the eyes of God. Calvin's teaching promoted hard work as a moral duty and as means to alleviate the anxiety caused by not knowing one's fate in the afterlife. Those who took Calvin's advice and devoted themselves to their worldly tasks often achieved success in terms of material possessions. In time, this became seen as a sign that one was indeed saved, a sign all believers were anxious to acquire. The legacy of this thinking is incorporated in the modern-day conception of poverty as the result of individual failing, as something to be avoided, or escaped from, by one's own hand.

A more recent religious conception sees poverty as a primarily secular evil, one perpetuated by human greed and thus to be actively opposed and eliminated. Such a view finds its most salient expression since the 1960s in the writings of Catholic theologians supportive of liberation theology. Liberation theologians have argued that poverty is systemic, and that owing to the political domination of elites, the means for its escape are not readily available to the poor. As a result, they advocate an organizational alliance with the poor and oppressed to help them find active ways to oppose those structures that ensure their subjugation. Thus liberation theologians were active in the formation of social movements and agencies within the structure of the Catholic Church in countries such as Brazil, or the Philippines, designed to give voice to the aspirations of the common people and to organize the poor as a political force against the forces of economic and social oppression.

—*W. E. Hewitt*

REFERENCES

V. Elizondo and N. Greinacher (eds.), *Church and Peace* (New York: Seabury, 1983); M. K. Nealen, *The Poor in the Ecclesiology of Juan Luis Segundo* (New York: Peter Lang, 1991).

PRACTICE Émile Durkheim combined both belief and practice in his definition of religion, but others have stressed their separation, arguing the priority of one over the other. The *lex orandi, lex credendi* phrase dear to many high church Anglicans gives obvious priority to practice. To complicate matters further, practice takes on different connotations in different settings. Christian liberationists stress the importance of doing right deeds in the world, while Eastern Orthodox equate practice with strict obedience to ritual requirements.

An important (still unresolved) question for the social sciences that goes back at least to Robertson Smith (1889) is this: Which is more fundamental to religious experience—belief or practice? Although it is difficult to imagine how to go about identifying religion in the first place without taking belief into account, social scientists who have studied religion through field research have been moved to speculate on whether religious practice is actually not more central than belief after all. Let us see how this might occur.

Field researchers are often confronted with a disconcerting gap when they attempt to question informants about their understandings of religious practices. The informants are unable to supply much information. Faced with a really persistent researcher, informants may become irritated, confused, and embarrassed. They may state that they cannot say what the practices actually mean but they do them because it is a custom that they feel obligated to follow. Even when an informant can supply an interpretation of religious practices, this may strike the researcher as halfhearted and less than genuine. Perhaps the informant doesn't seem convinced by his or her own explanation but says it out of a desire to avoid appearing foolish or merely to bring the researcher's exasperating questions to a halt. Sometimes an informant can provide an extensive analysis, but unless the informant is a religious specialist, this is atypical. Most people appear content to practice their religious traditions without inquiring very deeply about their meaning and without being able to give an extensive account of what their practices signify.

Another disconcerting finding of field research has been that the participants in religious practices often have little shared understanding of what these practices mean. A classic study in this respect is the anthropologist James Fernandez's (1965) work on the Fang cult of the Bwiti in West Africa. In analyzing Fang ritual, Fernandez was led to distinguish between social consensus and cultural consensus. By *social consensus,* he meant general agreement about the appropriateness of certain practices in particular circumstances. By *cultural consensus,* he meant agreement among the people on the meaning of these practices. Fernandez concluded that it is social consensus that holds the Fang cult together, and not cultural consensus. Extrapolated as a general principle, such a position assigns priority to people's consensus about practice, net of an absence of consensus in their religious beliefs. This position poses a challenge to social scientists in the Weberian tradition who regard cultural meanings to be the hallmark of religion.

It should not be surprising then that social scientists often have accepted the distinction between belief and practice, and in some instances have been inclined to give greater weight to practice. The dichotomy may well be a misleading one, however, made to seem appropriate because of deep-seated Western philosophical premises in which thought and action are held to be separate. Some recent fieldwork (Bachnick 1995) attacks the dichotomy on these terms, arguing that the meaning of religious traditions should not be treated as distinct from practice. The gist of the argument is that any attempt by the field researcher to elicit an exegesis from informants presupposes a false distinction between belief and practice that violates informants' own experience of their religious traditions. Particularly when familiarization with religious practices occurs in early childhood, the practices may never acquire the sort of elaborate exegesis that field researchers delight in finding (see, for example, Reeves 1990:110 f).

—*Edward B. Reeves*

REFERENCES

J. M. Bachnick, "Orchestrated Reciprocity," in *Ceremony and Ritual in Japan,* ed. J. Van Breman and D. P. Martinez (London: Routledge, 1995): 108–145; J. W. Fernandez, "Symbolic Consensus in a Fang Reformative Cult," *American Anthropologist* 67(1965):902–929; E. B. Reeves, *The Hidden Government* (Salt Lake City: University of Utah Press, 1990); W. R. Smith, *Lectures on the Religion of the Semites,* 2nd ed. (London: Black, 1889).

PREACHERS *see* Clergy

PREFERENTIAL OPTION FOR THE POOR

Shift of emphasis within Latin American Christianity, particularly Roman Catholicism, from a definition of charity as almsgiving to an advocacy of social justice through the empowerment of disadvantaged classes. Its intellectual articulation is found in the theology of liberation and its most concrete application in base ecclesial communities.

The *option for the poor* originated in the 1950s in the actions of bishops and priests who were concerned about the growth of socialist movements and Protestant sects, which they saw as threats to the influence of the Catholic Church. To counter these trends, the bishops encouraged pastoral innovations, such as lay leadership and Bible study in small groups, as well as activism toward social reform. The option for the poor was institutionalized in 1968 at the Second General Conference of the Latin American Bishops in Medellín, Colombia. At this conference, the Catholic bishops signed documents that would eventually place them in opposition to the military governments that were in the process of taking over almost all of the continent. During the years of the military dictatorships, when many sources of opposition were suppressed, the church provided a space for dissent. Although it is likely that some of the bishops who signed the Medellín documents were not aware of their radical implications, both for the church and for the larger society, these documents would provide an inspiration for the actions of many priests, sisters, and laypeople as well as legitimation for liberation theology.

The *theology of liberation* may be defined as the articulation of the belief that one's eternal salvation is inseparable from the struggle toward social justice. Among its major writers are the Catholic theologians Gustavo Gutiérrez, Leonardo and Clodovis Boff, Clara Maria Bingemer, José Comblin, Carlos Mesters, Alejandro Cussianovich, and Ivone Gebarra and the Protestants Rubem Alves and José Miguez Bonino. Although critics have accused liberation theologians of Marxism, these theologians indicate that their beliefs are rooted in Scripture. It is likely that there is truth in both positions. On the one hand, there is evidence of sociological insight in liberation theology, and Latin American sociologists tend to draw heavily on Marx's theory of social class. On the other hand, it also could be argued that the writings of both liberation theologians and Marx were influenced by a common source, that is, the socially critical Judaic tradition, seen especially in the prophetic books of the Hebrew Bible.

Base ecclesial communities (CEBs), also called base Christian communities, are small groups of laypeople who gather to study the Bible and to discuss its implications for their everyday lives. The priests, sisters, and lay workers who organize these groups give particular encouragement to their formation among the poor. As a result, the discussion of everyday life results in a critical analysis of the conditions in which these people live. The relating of their experiences to the biblical themes of love and justice frequently leads base community members to engage in social activism. In urban areas, base communities have become involved in organized labor, women's issues, and mobilization around housing, health care, and sanitation. In the countryside, they have been active in mobilization for agrarian reform. It is estimated that there are more than 100,000 base communities in Latin America.

In recent years, there has been evidence that the Roman Catholic Church is withdrawing from the more radical implications of the "preferential option for the poor." After the Medellín conference, conservative forces within the church began to mobilize to reverse its effects, and they found allies in the Vatican. The main strategies of the Vatican have been to silence liberation theologians and to replace progressive bishops, who retire or die, with conservative ones. As a result of the latter strategy, the anti-liberation theology forces were in control of the Fourth General Conference of the Latin American Bishops, held in Santo Domingo in 1992. In contrast to the Medellín documents, and those of the Puebla conference in 1979, which advocated the transformation of society and encouraged the formation of base communities, the Santo Domingo documents emphasized personal holiness and traditional middle-class lay movements. Base communities were scarcely mentioned. These developments have led some observers to speculate that the option for the poor will die out. However, others have argued that the lay dynamic that it unleashed cannot easily be reined in.

Although the base communities have never represented more than a minority of Latin American Catholics, they are an active and vocal minority who have become accustomed to lay initiative. In addition, they are supported by priests and sisters who remain progressive, despite the changes in bishops. Finally, not all of the bishops oppose the option for the poor. There are progressive bishops who are still alive and not ready to retire. Furthermore, the Vatican's strategy of appointing conservative bishops does not always work. Some of the bishops who did not have a previous record of supporting social activism and lay leadership have changed their view when confronted with the harsh social realities in their dioceses. A realistic prediction for the future of Latin American Catholicism would not include the disappearance of the preferential option for the poor but, instead, increasing conflict over lay leadership and the relationship of the church to social justice.

See also Social Justice, Third World

—*Madeleine R. Cousineau*

REFERENCES

M. Adriance, *Opting for the Poor* (Kansas City, Mo.: Sheed & Ward, 1986); L. Boff, *Jesus Christ Liberator* (Maryknoll, N.Y.: Orbis, 1978); G. Gutiérrez, *A Theology of Liberation* (Maryknoll, N.Y.: Orbis, 1973); D. H. Levine, *Popular Voices in Latin American Catholicism* (Princeton, N.J.: Princeton University Press, 1992); S. Mainwaring, *The Catholic Church and Politics in Brazil* (Stanford, Calif.: Stanford University Press, 1986); M. A. Neal, *The Just Demands of the Poor* (New York: Paulist Press, 1987); M. Peña, *Theologies and Liberation in Peru* (Philadelphia: Temple University Press, 1995).

PREJUDICE *see* Authoritarianism, Emory S. Bogardus, Intrinsic-Extrinsic Religiosity, Racism, Milton Rokeach

PREMILLENNIALISM The Christian theological view that Jesus will return before the biblical thousand-year reign of the Kingdom of God on earth. Although premillennialism dates back to the early church, a twentieth-century revision known as dispensational premillennialism has become the dominant paradigm within American fundamentalism. This version of premillennialism anticipates an imminent, miraculous removal of Christians from the world (rapture) and a cataclysmic end to the existing world (Armageddon). Initially popularized by the Scofield Reference Bible, dispensational premillennialism has become widely accepted in fundamentalist circles through widespread distribution of Hal Lindsey's book, *The Late Great Planet Earth* (Bantam 1970).

As an alternative view, postmillennialism, teaches that Jesus will return at the end of (an often figurative) thousand-year reign of the Kingdom of God. Postmillennialism had been the eschatology embraced by some Puritans, Jonathan Edwards, and the nineteenth-century evangelicals and Social Gospelers. But by the second half of the twentieth century, postmillennialism was embraced and promoted by an influential but little-known group of fundamentalist Presbyterians: Christian Reconstructionists. As part of the religious right's rise to power in the 1970s and 1980s, premillennialist fundamentalists incorporated aspects of postmillennialism in their theology despite its seeming contradictions.

The social implications of these views vary widely. Some premillennial fundamentalists avoid any activism other than evangelism, believing it is futile to attempt to redeem human institutions, while others are influenced by reconstructionist postmillennialists to build a "Christian America" in apparent contradiction to their premillennialist eschatology. The postmillennialists, on the other hand, are intent on social activism and see it as their Christian duty to work to "usher in the Kingdom of God" on earth through such activism.

See also Apocalyptic, Eschatology

—*Julie Ingersoll*

REFERENCE

T. R. Weber, *Living in the Shadow of the Second Coming* (Chicago: University of Chicago Press, 1987).

PRESBYTERIANISM   Presbyterians have their roots in the Reformed Protestant tradition of sixteenth-century Europe; for Presbyterians, the key figure is John Calvin. His *Institutes of the Christian Religion* (1559) is a cornerstone of Reformed faith and life. John Knox, the Scottish divine of the sixteenth century, contributed to Presbyterianism by establishing a Presbyterian polity in Scotland as the national church (Balmer and Fitzmier 1993, Leith 1977). Another building block of the tradition is English Presbyterianism. The British Parliament of the Great Rebellion, during which the episcopacy of the Church of England was temporarily abolished, called the Westminster Assembly of Divines together in 1643. The *Westminster Confession of Faith, Shorter and Larger Catechism* came from this assembly.

The Scots, Scots-Irish, and English Presbyterians came to the New World and established the first Presbyterian stronghold in the Middle Colonies. Francis Makemie, the "father of American Presbyterianism," helped to plant churches in Newark, Elizabeth, Fairfield, and Philadelphia in the second half of the seventeenth century. In 1706, Makemie created the first North American presbytery (regional ruling body of preaching ministers and representative congregational officers—"elders"), known as "The General Presbytery." The Scots-Irish and the New England aggregations of Presbyterians developed tensions early in the eighteenth century. The Scots-Irish remained loyal to a dogmatic understanding of the Westminster Confession, while the New England Presbyterians emphasized the importance of religious piety and the centrality of the Bible. In the midst of the Great Awakening, the two sides reached a compromise with the Adopting Act of 1729. The act distinguished between the essential and the nonessential standards of the Westminster Confession. This debate foreshadowed the pattern of conflict over Presbyterian doctrines in the eighteenth and nineteenth centuries. Schisms broke out between the New Side and Old Side Presbyterians in 1741, and between the Old School and New School factions in 1837. In each case, sides were taken in response to the revivalism that was sweeping the countryside. The traditional camps moved toward a more scholastic, legalist view of Calvinism and the Westminster doctrines, while the so-called New School Presbyterians were anxious to adopt the warmhearted piety of the evangelical movement, represented by George Whitefield and Jonathan Edwards.

As the Civil War broke out, the schisms between the Old and New School Presbyterians came to a head over the slavery issue. In 1861, the Presbyterian Church in the United States of America (PCUSA) passed the Spring Resolution, affirming support of the federal union. In reaction, the Presbyterian Church in the Confederate States of America (PCCSA) was formed by Southern Old School Presbyterians. In 1864, the PCCSA merged with the United Synod of the South to form the Presbyterian Church in the United States (PCUS).

Modernism   The battle over modernism was joined with the publication of Charles Darwin's *Origin of Species* in 1859 and the growing historical/critical methodology in the interpretation of Scripture. Charles Hodge, the Princeton Theological Seminary Old School theologian, argued against Darwinism in his *What Is Darwinism* (1874). Not all Presbyterians agreed with Hodge. Charles Briggs of Union Theological Seminary in New York asserted that the Bible contained error that could not readily be explained. He was brought to ecclesiastical trial and the charges against him were sustained, leading to the suspension of his ordination in 1893. In response to these proceedings, the PCUSA General Assembly in 1892 declared that the original manuscripts of the Bible were "without error." The reaction to modernism continued in 1910 with the adoption of the "five points" of fundamentalism (the five fundamentals): the inerrancy of the Bible, the virgin birth of Christ, his substitutional atonement, Christ's bodily resurrection, and the authenticity of miracles. On May 21, 1922, Harry Emerson Fosdick preached "Shall the Fundamentalists Win?" from the pulpit of First Presbyterian Church of New York City. This sermon, in part, brought on the fundamentalist-modernist conflict.

J. Gresham Machen of Princeton Seminary led the counterattack of the conservatives by claiming that liberal Christianity was not a form of authentic Christian faith but a new religion. Moderates in the denomination gathered and signed the "Auburn Affirmation" in 1924. This document affirmed the "five points" but allowed for alternative formulae for explaining these doctrines, and it called for toleration in the denomination. Over the next several annual General Assemblies, Machen's contentions were repudiated, and he was denied an appointment at Princeton Seminary. Machen left Princeton to form Westminster Seminary in Philadelphia in 1929. Southern Presbyterians were less affected by the controversy, because liberal opinions on Scripture and doctrines were rare in their ranks (Loetscher 1954, Longfield 1991).

The final act in closing the fundamentalist-modernist controversy came with the commission to study mission in the Protestant Church, led by William Ernest Hocking, a professor at Harvard University. The commission issued a one-volume summary of its work called *Rethinking Missions* (Harper 1932). The project was funded by John D. Rockefeller, Jr., the benefactor behind Fosdick's Riverside Church. The report urged greater sensitivity to the integrity of other religions and called for a more stringent standard in the selection of missionary candidates, criticizing missionaries for their "rigidity." The report received an ambivalent response; it solidified conservative rejection of modernism but, over the next half century, became the basis for much of contemporary mission work in the Presbyterian church.

Social Science and Presbyterianism The social scientific study of American Presbyterianism began in earnest with H. Richard Niebuhr's classic *The Social Sources of Denominationalism* (Holt 1929). Niebuhr dissected the class basis for denominations. In 1951,

Niebuhr published *Christ and Culture* (Harper), identifying the Reformed movement and its Presbyterian forms as an effort that seeks to transform culture. Other midcentury figures included Gibson Winter (1961) and Peter Berger (1961); they critiqued the church and attained intellectual respectability, but as R. Laurence Moore has commented, this respectability "encouraged them to jettison those things that social scientists now suggest are essential to the survival of religion in human cultures" (1989:251).

More contemporary figures in the social scientific study of religion have continued the analysis of Protestantism in American religion and, in particular, the Presbyterian denomination. R. Stephen Warner's study of a small Presbyterian church in Mendocino, California (1988), analyzed the vicissitudes of a church struggling with conflict between liberals and conservatives. Warner makes it clear that conservatives are more committed to the local church and give the church greater vitality. Liberals tend to be issue oriented and less able to commit to a local institution. An encyclopedic panorama of Presbyterian life in the twentieth century is provided by the six-volume work published between 1990 and 1992, edited by Milton J Coalter, John M. Mulder, and Louis B. Weeks, titled *The Presbyterian Presence: The Twentieth-Century Experience* (Westminster).

Dean Hoge, Benton Johnson, and Donald Luidens's study *Vanishing Boundaries* (Westminster 1994) outlines the religious practice of baby-boomer young adults and the reasons for their disaffiliation from the Presbyterian church. This study promotes understanding of the rapid decline of the Presbyterian church in the last 30 years. In 1958, through the merger of PCUSA and the United Presbyterian Church of North America, the United Presbyterian Church in the United States of America (UPCUSA) was formed. At its height, the church's membership reached 4.2 million in 1965. In 1996, even after the historic reunion of the UPCUSA with the PCUS in 1983, membership hovered around 2.7 million—a drop in membership of more than 30% over 30 years (see also Thompson et al. 1993). *Vanishing Boundaries* concludes the Presbyterian Church has declined not because of a liberal church hierarchy or the counterculture of the 1960s but because of changing religious beliefs of its members, brought on in part by the liberal theology of Presbyterian theologians, and because of the steep decline in birthrates in the babyboomer generation. The new theology is more inclusive, open to alternative religions, more focused on the social and political issues of the day. These factors helped to eventuate a rapid decrease in rates of baptism and confirmation that began in the 1960s and continues into the 1990s. These new theological perspectives tend to decrease the loyalty of individuals to churches in particular and to Christianity in general. Benton Johnson in "On Dropping the Subject: Presbyterians and Sabbath Observance in the Twentieth Century" (1992) shows how the church during this century stopped emphasizing Sabbath observance, family devotions, and other forms of personal piety to the point that spiritual practices as a normative part of religion have disappeared from contemporary Presbyterian theological discourse. Robert Wuthnow also uses the Presbyterian church as a case study to understand the decline of American Protestantism. He comes to the conclusion that the church has lost its ability to witness to any positive religious beliefs; that is, "too often, the strident voices of special purpose groups have become the church's primary witness to the wider world" (1989:92).

Nonetheless, the Presbyterian Church (USA) denomination has continued to work on defining its theological identity. The *Confession of 1967* was a significant theological statement, focusing the witness of the gospel on important social issues of the day. Moreover, in leading up to the reunion with the PCUS (or "Southern Church"), the church collected its major confessional documents in the *Book of Confession*. Following the 1983 reunion, the PC(USA) adopted *A Brief Statement of Faith* that stated the essentials of the theological tradition in an elegant, concise, and contemporary fashion.

Presbyterians have remained committed to a belief in a sovereign God who is both transcendent over creation, yet intimately and personally involved in the redemption of creation. Presbyterians have consistently supported a representative ecclesiastical government and have continued their struggle to remain united in their witness to the Scripture and to its creeds in the midst of a diverse culture and a history of internecine church conflict. Thus Presbyterians take into an uncertain future a bulwark of long-standing beliefs and ecclesiastical policies.

See also Calvinism, Protestant Ethic Thesis

—*James K. Wellman, Jr.*

REFERENCES

R. Balmer and J. R. Fitzmier, *The Presbyterians* (Westport, Conn.: Greenwood, 1993); P. L. Berger, *The Noise of Solemn Assemblies* (Garden City, N.Y.: Doubleday, 1961); B. Johnson, "From Old to New Agendas," in *The Confessional Mosaic,* ed. M. J Coalter et al. (Louisville: Westminster, 1990): 208-235; B. Johnson, "On Dropping the Subject," in *The Presbyterian Predicament,* ed. M. J Coalter et al. (Louisville: Westminster, 1992); D. R. Hoge and D. A. Roozen (eds.), *Understanding Church Growth and Decline* (New York: Pilgrim, 1979); J. H. Leith, *Introduction to the Reformed Tradi-*tion (Atlanta: Knox, 1977); L. A. Loetscher, *The Broadening Church* (Philadelphia: University of Pennsylvania Press, 1954); B. J. Longfield, *The Presbyterian Controversy* (New York: Oxford University Press, 1991); R. L. Moore, "Secularization," in *Between the Times,* ed. W. R. Hutchison (Cambridge: Cambridge University Press, 1989); W. L. Thompson et al., "Growth or Decline in Presbyterian Congregations," *Church & Denominational Growth,* ed. D. A. Roozen and C. K. Hadaway (Nashville: Abingdon, 1993); R. S. Warner, *New Wine in Old Wineskins* (Berkeley: University of California Press, 1988); G. Winter, *The Suburban Captivity of the Churches* (Garden City, N.Y.: Doubleday, 1961); R. Wuthnow, *The Struggle for America's Soul* (Grand Rapids, Mich.: Eerdmans, 1989).

PRIESTS　　*see* Clergy

PROFANE　　*see* Sacred

PROGRESSIVISM　　A social and political reform movement, generally placed in American politics from the turn of the twentieth century to the U.S. entry into World War I. Large-scale immigration, urbanization, and industrialization had generated concerns about the future and the character of the nation. The populist movement of the 1890s was one response to these changes, based in the threats to midwestern and southern agricultural groups. A nativist, nostalgic retreat was another response, symbolized by groups such as the American Protective Association and the Ku Klux Klan. In contrast, progressivism called upon liberal religion's Social Gospel and the newly emerging social sciences (particularly sociology; see Vidich and Lyman 1985) to fashion an optimistic forward-looking vision of a brighter future. There was confidence in progress and faith in enlightenment (Fox 1993).

Progressivism emerged from institutions outside the polity. Churches, parachurch groups, women's associations, and newly formed graduate divisions of universities (many of them church related) were the organizational bases for progressivism's reformist ideas. In that sense, progressivism was anti-institutional, focusing its attacks on the established order of turn-of-the-century society: monopolistic business corporations, urban ethnic political machines, traditional church hierarchies, and the established political parties. It saw the political partisanship of the parties and the theological partisanship of the established churches as problematic. Solutions were sought in political and educational reforms, informed by social ethics, social science, and a civil religious "religion of America" (Eisenach 1994) that fostered faith in democracy, as conceived by professional and managerial reformers. Policy programs included breaking up business monopolies ("trust busting"), deracinating the new immigrants from southern and eastern Europe (e.g., Hull House), sponsoring ecumenical religious organizations (such as the Federal Council of Churches of Christ, founded in 1908), and putting a new emphasis on public schools as the fundamental institutions of the American democratic system.

The carriers of progressivist ideas were an emergent professional class of academic reformers and social workers, northern liberal evangelical clergy, and middle-class women connected to moral reform associations. Jane Addams, Ralph Bourne, Herbert Croly, John Dewey, Franklin Giddings, Charlotte Perkins Gilman, Washington Gladden, and Walter Rauschenbusch were key progressivist thinkers. Progressivism merged traditional national-millennial themes of creating the Kingdom of God on earth with a social evolutionist perspective on "progress" (Eisenach 1994, Handy 1984). It was a "theology of the fulfillment of America as a historic nation" (Eisenach 1994:66) wherein democracy became a national faith, undergirded by a social ethic drawn from a new covenant based on public theology.

In this sense, progressivism was both a secularization of Protestant theology and a sacralization of sociology and public philosophy (Fox 1993, Lasch 1991, Vidich and Lyman 1985). It was an indirect hegemonic conquest of public discourse by a merger of modernized Protestant evangelical theology and the new social sciences. And, of course, this merger help set the context for the modernist-fundamentalist split Protestantism experienced in the next decade.

—Rhys H. Williams

REFERENCES

E. J. Eisenach, *The Lost Promise of Progressivism* (Lawrence: University of Kansas Press, 1994); R. W. Fox, "The Culture of Liberal Protestant Progressivism," *Journal of Interdisciplinary History* 23(1993):639-660; R. T. Handy, *A Christian America*, 2nd ed. (New York: Oxford University Press, 1984); C. Lasch, "Religious Contributions to Social Movements," *Journal of Religious Ethics* 18(1991):7-25; A. J. Vidich and S. M. Lyman, *American Sociology* (New Haven, Conn.: Yale University Press, 1985).

PROTESTANT ETHIC THESIS Formulated by Max Weber in a series of essays first published in 1904-1906, hence also known as "the Weber thesis," the PE argument, although in Gordon Marshall's words "unambiguous and breathtakingly simple" (1982:70), has been one of the most important and controversial topics in the sociology of religion.

Weber argues that Protestantism was part of the causal chain that led to the development of world-system dominance by Anglo-American capitalism. Specifically, Calvin's doctrine of predestination—namely, that a person's eternal fate as elect to heaven or damned to hell was determined by God before the person's birth and could not be altered by any act the person performed while on earth—when superimposed upon Luther's radical alteration of "vocation" *(beruf)* to refer to one's daily occupation in the world (rather than a monastic withdrawal from the world), dynamically interacted with the social psychological condition of *salvation anxiety* to create conditions whereby people sought to determine whether or not they were among those elected to eternal life. Weber argued that among the English Puritans, epitomized by Richard Baxter, the tension of Calvin's austere doctrine was resolved by a belief (based principally on the Old Testament book of Proverbs) that God would reward in this life those whom he had elected to eternal glory, who lived according to his laws. Thus the "rising parvenus" of the English middle classes were told that if they strictly followed biblical teachings for the conduct of life (as interpreted by the Puritans) and they succeeded in their businesses, this would be a sign of their election—*but only* if they also used the fruits of their labors properly. Specifically, they were to *invest* all their income beyond the necessities of a frugal lifestyle, in so doing making even more money, to invest similarly all the days of their life. This is the connection between the Protestant "work ethic" and capitalism, not merely as an economic philosophy but a lifestyle.

Origins *The Protestant Ethic and the Spirit of Capitalism* in its present, generally used English translation by Talcott Parsons (Weber 1930, but see Collins 1996) is a 1920 revision by Weber of two essays he first published in 1904-1905. To these are prefixed the introduction (written c. 1920) to his entire world religions corpus, which was the context for his revision. When combined with Weber's 1909-1910 reaction (translated 1978) to criticisms of the original essays by Felix Rachfahl, this introduction is extremely important for understanding what it was Weber thought he was (and was not) doing in his work. There is also a third Protestant ethic essay, related to his observations on the Protestant ethic in America, that appeared in 1906 and is translated separately in both its revised 1920 version (1946) and the original (1985).

In spite of occasional claims to the contrary, the work is accurately titled. It is an enthymematic argument about a religious way of *acting* and an economic world-view. Religious *beliefs,* as Gianfranco Poggi has aptly noted (1983:56), are "upstream" of Weber's thesis; the thesis is not about belief but about practices that a specific social strata derived from those beliefs and how those in turn affected economics. The original context for Weber's writing was his acceptance of the coeditor-ship of the journal *Archiv für Sozialwissenschaft und Sozialpolitik,* on the one hand, and his frustration, on the other, at finding a political solution to what he perceived to be a German national identity crisis. The "Protestant" in *The Protestant Ethic* properly contrasts to "Lutheran," not Catholic (see Liebersohn 1988, Maurer 1924); although by the time of the 1920 revision this was altered, and a universal-historical dimension seeking to discern the *impediments to the capitalist ethos* in the action systems of the world religions was added. The essay remains basically historical in charac-ter, however, and offers an intentionally one-sided ar-gument (1930:27) that the breakthrough to modern rational capitalism as a life-encompassing social system was facilitated by Protestant morality (the "work ethic"). It does *not* argue that Protestantism as a specific set of Christian dogmas was either necessary or suffi-cient to "cause" modern rational capitalism to appear, but that Protestantism, especially at the hands of late sixteenth- and early seventeenth-century English Puri-tans, did create a system of meaningful action that functioned historically as the "last intensification" (Col-lins 1986:93) in a causal chain that led to modern capitalism, "the most fateful force in our modern life" (1930:17).

This historical point is all Weber needed to carry on not only a "dialogue with the ghost of Karl Marx," as Albert Salomon phrased it (1945:596), but also with other theorists in the social sciences as well as Weber's German political allies and adversaries. What Weber lamented in Germany and in himself (see Jaspers 1989:169) was "the fact that our nation has never experienced the school of hard asceticism in *any* form." On this cultural critique he lay tremendous weight as an explanation for the failure of Germany to attain the international political-economic stature of Anglo-America. This historical logic can be seen, for example, in a somewhat exasperated comment in Weber's re-sponse to Rachfahl's criticisms of Weber's thesis when Weber writes that "the great centers of the Middle Ages such as Florence, . . . were, God knows, capitalistically developed to quite another degree than . . . the Ameri-can colonies with their largely subsistence economy," yet Anglo-America became the cultural center of the *spirit* of capitalism, while the centers of capitalism's origin paled (1978:1119).

Extensions and Critiques   The PE thesis has gener-ated several kinds of extensions (see the literature re-views in Fischoff 1944, Kivisto and Swatos 1988, Little 1969, Nelson 1973). Among the most fruitful is Robert Merton's work (1970 [1938]) on religion and science in seventeenth-century England, where he applies a Weber-like analysis to British scientific acumen; this argument, now often simply referred to as "the Merton thesis," has been so significant as to have generated a literature all its own.

Another line of research has been the search for PE "analogies" in favorable developmental contexts else-where in the world—particularly the new nations of Africa and Asia (see, e.g., Bellah 1957, 1970). The theoretical strategy of this approach is to find in the PE a constellation of action orientations that enhance the disposition toward capitalism; although it can overex-tend itself, the value of this type of study is to reinforce the crucial Weberian principle that the PE is *not* a specific theological doctrine but a generalizable system of action that can occur without any theological refer-ent at all (as Weber himself pointed out in the somewhat apocalyptic conclusion to the 1920 revision of the 1905 essay).

A third valuable line of extension has been to use a PE-like analysis to assess other historical associations between action models and economic orientations in Western civilization; the most finely nuanced example of this approach is Colin Campbell's work *The Ro-mantic Ethic and the Spirit of Modern Consumerism* (1987).

Other critiques, which began with that of Rachfahl to which Weber himself replied, have been more mis-guided, hence far less helpful. In general, these critiques make either or both of two errors based on misreading Weber's text: (1) They attempt to study theology rather than practice—for example, suggesting that Puritanism is a corruption of "pure" Calvinism (e.g., Hudson 1961, George and George 1955)—ignoring the fact that not theology, but the working out of theology in practical action, is Weber's concern. This is why Weber can lump together such theologically diverse groups as Presbyte-rianism of the Westminster Confession, the Inde-pendents, Baptist sects, some Continental pietists, Men-nonites, Quakers, and Methodists under the single rubric of the PE (see 1930:95-154, 217). (2) They fail to differentiate among types of capitalism, again ignor-ing Weber's careful distinction of the character of "modern rational" capitalism (1930:17-27) and ignor-ing Weber's reply to Rachfahl, which shows that Weber was well aware of the origins of capitalist thought and its varying historical appearances.

Early forms of this critique were those of Werner Sombart (1915), who associated capitalism with the

Jews, to whom Weber himself replied, and H. M. Robertson (1933), who attempted to identify capitalism with the Jesuits (refuted by Broderick 1934). A more current, tendentious critique is that of Kurt Samuelsson (1961, reprinted 1993), which commits both of the errors noted here; as David Little notes, "Samuelsson's book demands attention not because of its contribution to the general literature (which is negligible), but because it is the most recent expression of so many of the typical and wildly inadequate rejections of Weber's thesis" (1969:228). A reader lacking historical sophistication in either religion or economics can, however, be greatly misled by the Samuelsson text.

Perhaps the strongest advocate for Weber's thesis against these critics is an unwitting one, namely, the Spanish author Jaime Balmes, who wrote well prior to Weber. In *El Protestantismo*, Balmes, who died in 1848, makes precisely the case that Weber does, that Protestantism is the principal engine of modern rational capitalism and all it entails, not least its peculiar work discipline. (The difference between Weber and Balmes is that Balmes bemoans the triumph of capitalism, while Weber generally celebrates it; Balmes's book appeared in an English translation in the United States by 1850, *European Civilization*.)

Another line of extension and critique that has proved relatively valueless has been to study contemporary Protestants and Catholics (and others) for evidence of the presence or absence of the PE, usually using some form of survey research procedure. Weber himself indicates that this is not at all the context in which the thesis is to be applied (see 1978:1120), and that in fact the PE has been transvalued into a *secular* work ethic quite apart from, and perhaps even antithetical to, any religious considerations. Weber specifically points to Benjamin Franklin's *Poor Richard's Almanac* as early evidence of this process. The unproductivity of this line of research in the 1960s led Andrew Greeley (1964) to suggest a "moratorium" on further PE research in contemporary American society, although he later (1989) would offer his own comparative differentiation between current Protestant and Catholic life orientations.

A final, more difficult set of issues surrounds the phenomenon of Puritanism itself. Beginning with Michael Walzer's work (e.g., 1966) specifically, there has been increasing concern to assess the complexity of Puritanism. David Zaret (e.g., 1985) also has made contributions in this area, and each has drawn responses (e.g., Little 1966). With regard to any historical actions, the process of discerning and labeling a "movement" is a secondary objectivation of meaning; in Weber's case, this involves some form of typification. In other words, the PE comes to symbolize a collection of action orientations that only occasionally, if ever, coalesce in concrete cases. The PE thesis ultimately rests on making a convincing *comparative* case that one "type" of life orientation differs sufficiently from another type of life orientation that an "either this or that" argument may be drawn. In Weber's cases, for example, the role of holy days is particularly instructive; a quite clear line can be drawn between those groups in Western Christianity that historically observed the principal Christian holy days and those that did not. The groups Weber identifies with the PE did not. (This is connected, in turn, to the larger question of work discipline.) The treatment of Sunday as festival or Sabbath similarly separates these groups, as does the role of the sermon in worship. In general, then, one can identify two *types* of Western life orientation, promulgated in the name of Christianity, that began to divide from each other in the sixteenth century, and suggest that these divisions had consequences beyond a narrowly "religious" realm; perhaps the finest small-scale illustration of this dynamic is Stephen Kent's study (1990) of the impact of the "fixed-price" policy of Quakers on all of subsequent economic history.

—William H. Swatos, Jr.

REFERENCES

J. Balmes, *El Protestantismo comprado con el catolicismo* (Madrid: Biblioteca de Autores Cristianos, 1968 [1842]); R. Bellah, *Tokugawa Religion* (Glencoe, Ill.: Free Press, 1957); R. Bellah, "Reflections on the Protestant Ethic Analogy in Asia," in *Beyond Belief* (New York: Harper, 1970): 53-63; J. Broderick, *The Economic Morals of the Jesuits* (London: Oxford University Press, 1934); C. Campbell, *The Romantic Ethic and the Spirit of Modern Consumerism* (Oxford: Blackwell, 1987); R. Collins, *Max Weber* (Beverly Hills, Calif.: Sage, 1986); R. Collins, "Introduction," in *The Protestant Ethic and the Spirit of Capitalism* (Los Angeles: Roxbury, 1996): vii-xxxix; E. Fischoff, "The Protestant Ethic and the Spirit of Capitalism," *Social Research* 2(1944):53-77; C. H. George and K. George, "The Weber Thesis," in *The Protestant Mind of the English Reformation* (Princeton, N.J.: Princeton University Press, 1955): 144-149; A. M. Greeley, "The Protestant Ethic," *Sociological Analysis* 25(1964):20-33; A. M. Greeley, "Protestant and Catholic," *American Sociological Review* 54(1989):385-402; W. Hudson, "The Weber Thesis Reexamined," *Church History* 30(1961):88-99; K. Jaspers, *On Max Weber* (New York: Paragon House, 1989); S. Kent, "The Quaker Ethic and the Fixed Price Policy," in *Time, Place, and Circumstance*, ed. W. H. Swatos, Jr. (New York: Greenwood, 1990): 139-150; P. Kivisto and W. H. Swatos, Jr., *Max Weber* (New York: Greenwood, 1988); H. Liebersohn, *Fate and Utopia in German Sociology* (Cambridge: MIT Press, 1988); D. Little, "Max Weber Revisited," *Harvard Theological Review* 59(1966):415-428; D. Little, *Religion, Order, and Law* (New York: Harper, 1969); G. Marshall, *In Search of the Spirit of Capitalism* (New York: Columbia University Press, 1982); H. Maurer, "Studies in the Sociology of Religion I," *American Journal of Sociology* 30(1924):257-286; R. K. Merton, *Science, Technology and Society in Seventeenth Century England* (New York: Harper, 1970 [1938]); B. Nelson, "Weber's Protestant Ethic," in *Beyond the Classics?* ed. C. Y. Glock and P. E. Hammond (New York: Harper, 1973): 71-130; G. Poggi, *Calvinism and the Capitalist Spirit* (Amherst: University of Massachusetts Press, 1983); H. M. Robertson, *Aspects of the Rise of Economic Individualism* (Clifton, N.J.: Kelley, 1933); A. Salomon, "German Sociology," in *Twentieth Century Sociology*, ed. G. Gurvitch and W. E. Moore (New York: Philosophical Library, 1945): 586-614; K. Samuelsson, *Religion and Economic Action* (New York: Basic Books, 1961 [1993 reprint, University of Toronto Press]); W. Sombart, *The Quintessence of Capitalism* (London: Unwin, 1915); M. Walzer, *Revolution of the Saints* (London: Weidenfeld and Nicolson, 1966); M. Weber, "Die Protestantische Ethik und der 'Geist' des Kapitlismus," *Archiv für Sozialwissenschaft und Sozialpolitik* 20(1904):1-54, 21(1905):1-110; " 'Kirchen' und 'Sekten' in Nordamerika," *Die christliche Welt*, 24-25(1906):558-562, 577-583; "Antikritisches Schlusswort zum 'Geist' des Kapitalismus," *Archiv für Sozialwissenschaft und Sozialpolitik* 30(1910):176-202; "Vorbemerkung," *Gesammelte Aufsätze zu Religionssoziologie* (Tübingen: Mohr, 1920): 1-16; *The Protestant Ethic and the Spirit of Capitalism* (New York: Scribner, 1930); "The Protestant Sects and the Spirit of Capitalism," in *From Max Weber* (New York: Oxford University Press, 1946): 302-322; "Anticritical Last Word on *The Spirit of Capitalism*," *American Journal of Sociology* 83(1978): 1105-1131; " 'Churches' and 'Sects' in North America," *Sociological Theory* 3(1985):1-13; *The Protestant Ethic and the Spirit of Capitalism* (Los Angeles: Roxbury, 1996); D. Zaret, *The Heavenly Contract* (Chicago: University of Chicago Press, 1985).

PROTESTANTISM, PROTESTANTS

Christians belonging to denominations that reformed themselves in the sixteenth century, seceded from already established Protestant denominations, or founded new denominations on the basis of reformation principles.

Denominational Distribution It is surprising how few reformed denominations have *Protestant* in their official titles. Designations such as Evangelisch, Lutheran, Reformed, Methodist, Baptist, Pentecostal, and so on are preferred, or the names of states that reformed themselves, or both (e.g., De Nederlandse Hervormde Kerk; the Church of Scotland). The word *Protestant* was coined in 1529 to denote those German princes and reformed cities that lodged a *protestatio* (protestation) at the Diet of Speyer (1529) after the repudiation of toleration in Catholic areas of the Holy Roman Empire. It is anachronistic to refer to earlier social movements that strove to reform the Catholic Church (the follow-

ers of Wycliffe, 1329?-1384, in England and Huss, 1369?-1415, in Prague) as "Protestants." Although *Protestant* is often construed in a negative sense (i.e., "anti-Catholic"), the original meaning of *protestatio* (a legal term) was much closer to a declaration "on behalf of" or "in favor of" something *(pro)*.

According to Barrett (1990), there were 324.2 million Protestants in 1990, and 53.8 million Anglicans (a separate category despite the fact that the Church of England was also reformed in the sixteenth century). Other major "ecclesiastical blocs" are Roman Catholics (962.6 million), Eastern Orthodox (179.5), and "Nonwhite indigenous Christians" (143.8). Although Protestants are found in almost every country, they are still concentrated in the traditional heartlands of the Reformation: northern Germany; the northern and western cantons of Switzerland; the northern provinces of the Netherlands; Scandinavia; Bohemia and Moravia; England, Wales, Scotland, and Northern Ireland; Alsace and the Massif Central in France; and other parts of the world that were colonized and/or settled by the British, Dutch, French, and Germans (including the United States, where they are the majority religion). In most of France, Italy, the Iberian Peninsula, the southern German *Lände*, the southern parts of the Netherlands, Belgium, Austria, and Poland, Protestantism was decimated or eradicated by Catholic princes during the Counterreformation that followed the Council of Trent (1545-1563). Calvinism survived in Hungary because it fell under the hegemony of the Turks. In the Orthodox heartlands of Eastern Europe, Protestants are not found in large numbers. Protestantism was introduced there by migrants (mostly Germans) during the *Drang nach Osten* in the nineteenth century. Pentecostalists established congregations in Russia before 1917. The fastest growing Protestant congregations (Pentecostalist and Reformed) are in South Korea. Evangelical and Pentecostalist missions are now making increasingly large numbers of converts in Latin America (Martin 1990).

The faith of Protestants is traditionally defined in terms of (1) *sola gratia* (by grace alone), (2) *sola fide* (justification by faith alone), and (3) *sola scriptura* (by scripture alone). This has been termed by Paul Tillich the "Protestant Principle." Radical Protestants rejected the classical creeds (the Apostles' Creed and the Creed of Nicea-Constantinople) and refused to define their faith in authoritative documents. Many classical Protestant denominations did produce confessional statements, such as the Confession of Augsburg (Lutheran), the Heidelberg Confession, the Confessio Belgica, the Westminster Confession (Calvinistic), the Savoy Declaration (Congregationalist), the "Articles" of the Church of England, and the "standards" of the Methodists (all collected by Philip Schaff [1877] in three volumes)—hence the distinctions between "confessional families" of Protestants.

Variations and Cleavages   Protestants not only differ on doctrines, they also differ on church order or "ecclesiastical polity," one of the most difficult problems in the Ecumenical Movement. Having rejected the hierarchical system of Rome, some (e.g., the Church of England, the Lutheran state churches in Scandinavia, Hungarian Calvinists) adopted an episcopal church order (without the Primacy of the Bishop of Rome). Presbyterians opted for church councils (consisting of teaching and ruling "elders") whose representatives meet "in presbytery" (or "classis") and "in synod." Congregationalists rejected both the "bishop" and the "classis." In New England, they insisted at least upon the right to rebuke another congregation for heresy or backsliding (see documents in Walker 1960 [1893]). Methodists organized local "classes" and "bands," which were then organized into "circuits" (a territory originally supervised by one itinerant minister on horseback). After the death of John Wesley (1791) and the separation of Methodists from the Church of England, the Methodist Conference began to assume a central role.

Another cleavage is the difference between pacifist denominations whose members usually refuse military service (e.g., Mennonites, Quakers, most of the other Anabaptists [Littell 1958], and Jehovah's Witnesses) and the nonpacifist majority. Quakers, Mennonites, and most Anabaptists also refused to take the oath and declined election to the office of civil magistrate, but Anglicans and Calvinists are usually well represented among the magistrates. (Dutch preachers still wear the same black gown—*toga*—and "bands"—*bef*—worn by magistrates and judges.) Lutherans, Calvinists, and Zwinglians fought against Catholics during the wars of religion, before the Peace of Westphalia (1648) terminated the Thirty Year's War (Germany) and the Eighty Year's War (The Netherlands), and established that the prince is entitled to determine the religion of his territory in accordance with the principle *cuius regio, eius religio.*

Zwingli died on the battlefield in 1531, while 10% of adult males in England perished between 1642 and 1660 in battles between monarchistic Episcopalians ("Cavaliers") and republican Presbyterians ("Roundheads") after Oliver Cromwell raised the New Model Army in opposition to the reign of King Charles I. In Bohemia, Holland, and Germany, Protestants such as John Ziska, John of Leyden, and Thomas Münzer led revolutionary movements, while Cromwell's Revolu-

tion was overtaken by radical religious movements such as the Fifth Monarchy Men, Levellers, and Diggers (Lewy 1974). These have been interpreted as "millenarian movements" (e.g., Cohn 1957), the precursors of Marxist revolution, or as the "radical" Reformation (Williams 1962). Williams's distinction between the "radicals" and the rest is not always helpful, because it relegates both revolutionaries and pacifists (especially Anabaptists) to the same category.

There is also a distinction between "established" denominations (official state churches) and nonestablished or no-longer established denominations (Littell 1962), and denominations established in one country but not in another. There are also "ethnic" versions of several Protestant traditions: such as German and Swedish versions of Lutheranism, and Dutch, English, Scottish, and Afrikaaner versions of Calvinism. Such differences can persist (e.g., in America or Australia) even when language is no longer problematic.

Given the wide range of distinctions among them (Marty 1976) and the almost infinite permutations of creed, church order, nationality, and political status, it is not surprising that the number of Protestant denominations is now determined to be 8,196 (1985 projections in Barrett 1982:792 f). The differences within Protestantism were also sharpened by the English and German Enlightenment (e.g., Locke, the English Deists, Lessing, Kant, and Schleiermacher), biblical and historical criticism (e.g., F. C. Bauer, D. F. Strauss, and A. Ritschl and their disciples), and Darwin's theory of evolution (which divided Liberals and Modernists from the Orthodox, Evangelicals, and Fundamentalists). Protestant (and other Christian) denominations have been systematically catalogued by the practitioners of *Symbolik* (Symbolics), *Konfessionskunde,* and *Kirchenkunde.* Such typically German disciplines obviously influenced American works such as those of Schaff and Piepkorn (see examples in the references at the end of the entry).

The Sociology of Protestantism   How do historical sociologists treat the Protestants? Durkheim (whose background was Jewish) did not deal with Protestantism as a discrete phenomenon. Pickering (in Pickering and Martin 1994:435-439) doubts "whether he really understood it," but Weber did devote considerable attention to Protestantism, especially in his highly controversial "Protestant ethic thesis." Both Weber (1922) and Troeltsch (1912) developed the *church-sect typology.*

Troeltsch defined *sect* as "a voluntary society" whose members have experienced "the new birth" who live "apart from the world" in "small groups." The term *church* (defined by Troeltsch as "an institution which . . . is able to receive the masses, and to adjust itself to the world, because, to a certain extent it can afford to ignore the need for subjective holiness for the sake of the objective treasures of grace and of redemption") is applicable to the Church of England, but Methodists reintroduced "subjective holiness" and the experience of "spiritual regeneration" into the Church of England, while the Catholic Revival (1833) of Keble, Newman, and Pusey reemphasized the "objective treasures of grace and of redemption" (although the Methodist and Catholic Revivals did not always influence the same segments of the Church of England).

Troeltsch added "mysticism" as a third element. It transformed formal worship and rigid doctrines "into a purely personal and inward experience" in such a way that it "leads to the formation of groups on a purely personal basis, with no permanent form, which also tend to weaken the significance of forms of worship, doctrine, and the historical element." (Such a definition is at least applicable to the Quakers.) Although the typology of Troeltsch and Weber is not a perfect instrument (hence attempts to refine it by Niebuhr 1929, Brewer 1952, Wilson 1959), it enabled Troeltsch to organize his description of the Protestants when he wrote *The Social Teachings of the Christian Churches*.

Troeltsch also challenged the claim that the advent of Protestantism marks the transition to the Modern World (1911)—hence his distinction between early Protestantism (Lutheranism and Calvinism) and modern/later Protestantism (1911 [1958]: 44 f), which he dates from the end of the seventeenth century. The basis of his distinction is that the Early Reformation "claims [the right] to regulate State and society, science and education, law, commerce and industry" and treats Natural Law "as being identical with the Law of God." This debate raises many fundamental questions such as the following: What do we mean by "modernity"? When did it first arise? (Troeltsch dated it from the Enlightenment.) Is Protestantism the "cause" of modernity, or is modernity the "cause" of Protestantism?

Although Troeltsch's arguments are not always clear (and on occasion little more than sweeping statements), it might be possible to establish this distinction (and the caesura at the end of the seventeenth century) on the basis of more convincing arguments. It can be argued that at least some Protestants continued to theologize until well into the seventeenth century in the same terms and categories as the medieval Scholastics, but their arguments led to Protestant (rather than Catholic) conclusions. Reist (1966:95-97) recognizes the importance of Troeltsch's claim that the Lutheran Reformation was "from within," because "Luther's reform of Catholicism is . . . only a

reconstruction of the Catholic formulation of the question, to which there comes a new answer." The ethic of early Protestantism presupposes the same foundations "on which medieval Catholicism had built." To the extent that this is the case, the presence or the absence of explicitly Thomistic or Aristotelian features ultimately differentiates between Troeltsch's "Two Protestantisms" (see McGrath 1993).

Troeltsch influenced both Richard Niebuhr (1929) and Dietrich Bonhoeffer, whose dissertation (1930) is an attempt to rewrite "ecclesiology" in the light of the sociological insights of Troeltsch, Simmel, and Weber, and Tönnies's distinction between *Gesellschaft* and *Gemeinschaft*. Troeltsch and Weber stressed that Protestants are characterized by individual autonomy (if human beings have a will that is actually free, which is denied by some of the Calvinists), the "voluntary principle" (noted by Baird as early as 1856), and "this-worldliness" *(innerweltlichkeit)* or "this-worldly asceticism" *(innerweltliche Askese)*. They are pivotal concepts in the Protestant ethic thesis together with "vocation" *(Beruf)*.

The Halévy Thesis   The touchstone of Troeltsch's distinction between early and late Protestantism is seventeenth-century Methodism, which also brings us to the Halévy thesis. By no stretch of the imagination could it be claimed that John Wesley thought in explicitly Aristotelian or Scholastic categories. The English Reformation was strongly influenced by the Platonism of Colet, Fisher, More, and Hooker, and there was a revival of Platonism in Cambridge in the seventeenth century (Cragg 1968). Wesley "openly claimed his heritage of Christian Platonism" (Wesley 1984:54) but accepted the Thomist dictum that "there is nothing in the mind not previously in the senses." Because he was an empiricist in an age of empiricism, we are not entitled to assume that Wesley swallowed Scholasticism hook, line, and sinker! (He could have quoted Locke to make the same point.) On this score, he cannot be treated as an example of early Protestantism.

Semmel (1973:19) goes further: "Wesley extended the 'modern' values introduced by Calvinism in a decidedly liberal direction" (which suggests that Calvinism is more "modern" than Troeltsch assumed). Semmel took four of the five items from the formal scheme used by Parsons and Shils to explain the transition from "traditional" to "modern" (1962:77-91) and applied it to Calvinists and Methodists (omitting the "division of labor") and concludes that Methodism is "modern" on all four counts: (1) affectivity to affective neutrality, (2) collectivity orientation to self-orientation, (3) particularism versus universalism, and (4) achievement rather than ascription. Calvinism is "modern" on (1) and (2) but not on (3) and (4), because Calvinists assumed that grace is "bestowed"—rather than "earned"—and reserved salvation for the "elect" in accordance with the doctrine of predestination (Semmel 1973:18). This is yet another fundamental cleavage in Protestantism, because Methodists believed in conditional universal election; that is, Christ died for *all* (provided one accepts the Gospel) rather than for the "elect." Many American Calvinists adopted this doctrine from the Methodists: hence the distinction between the "generals" and the "particulars" that became common currency in the eighteenth century.

Michael Hill notes that Weber's work generated considerable sociological and historical research, but "the important insight of Halévy has been almost totally ignored" (1973:183). By this he means the attempt of Halévy (a French historian) to explain the "extraordinary stability" that England experienced when confronted by revolutions in America and in France. Having systematically eliminated all of the other possible variables ("We have sought in vain to find the explanation by an analysis of her political institutions and economic organization"), Halévy concluded that it must have been the revival of the Methodists and the Evangelicals that prevented violent revolution during this particularly turbulent period (1924:339, 371).

But how did they do it? Socialist and Marxist historians (e.g., the Hammonds, Hobsbawm, Thompson) treated Methodism as a reactionary religion that crushed the spirit of the new proletariat, but Semmel came to the conclusion that it was ultimately a revolutionary movement "aimed at countering the destructive spiritual consequences of certain of the illiberal, traditional doctrines preached by the Reformation." In short, Methodist enthusiasm

> transformed men, summoning them to assert rational control over their own lives, while providing in its system of mutual discipline the psychological security necessary for autonomous conscience and liberal ideals to become internalized, an integrated part of the 'new men' . . . regenerated by Wesleyan preaching. (1973:3, 198)

The Methodist Revolution thesis (the Halévy thesis) is both controversial and disputed, as is Weber's Protestant ethic thesis. It could be treated as an application of Weber's thesis to the Methodists were it not for the fact that Halévy published contemporaneously, but independently of association, with Weber, and Halévy's work was based on the work of predecessors such as Taine, Guizot, and Lecky—a different intellectual tradition from Weber's. John Wesley himself had already noted that many Methodists became successful entrepreneurs (Wesley 1987, Vol. 7:95 f). Having become rich, many Methodists left the society, and some switched to the Church of England. (Because Methodism rejected gambling and alcohol, the eradication of "secondary poverty" at least enabled Methodists on good wages to accumulate capital.)

Michael Hill (1973:185) claims that the Methodist Revolution "filled both a social *and* an ideological vacuum" in English society, thus "opening up the channels of social and ideological mobility [the "escalator thesis"] . . . which worked against the polarization of English society into rigid social classes." It "worked" by influencing first "the dissenting sects [the transition from 'particulars' to 'generals'], then the establishment, finally secular opinion" (Halévy 1924:339). This explains how a relatively small number of Methodists (little more than 90,000 in 1800) exerted this kind of effect on English society; to which one could add that, during the first half of the nineteenth century, "Methodists" were not always the same people (if the "escalator thesis" is valid and many did indeed switch to the Church of England). Methodism cannot be treated as a totally reactionary phenomenon because the Kilhamites (expelled in 1796) did advocate violent revolution. Paradoxically, Methodism seems to have been a viable alternative to radical politics and violent revolution, but (on occasion) it was quite capable of going in the opposite direction.

English Methodism was an antirevolutionary movement that succeeded (to the extent that it did) because it was a revolution of a radically different kind (Semmel 1973). It also was capable of generating considerable social change (M. Hill 1973). Methodism, however, is no more paradoxical than Puritan Piety and German *Pietismus*. Christopher Hill (1940, 1958, 1966) and Michael Waltzer (1974) each treat English Puritanism as a "revolutionary ideology," but Fulbrook (1983) argues that Pietists adopted an aggressively antiabsolutist stance in England, a passive antiabsolutist stance in Württemberg, and an absolutist stance in Prussia.

Protestantism and State Formation Fulbrook, Skocpol (1979), and Tilly and his disciples (Tilly 1975, 1978) exploited all the resources of historical sociology to explain (among other things) the important part played by Protestants in the processes of "state formation." Van Beek et al. treated Purity as a "greedy ideology" in a cross-cultural perspective that includes Geneva, Holland, and New England and the "Quest for Purity" in non-Christian religions; Staples (van Beek 1988:75) stressed the transition from "external coercion" to "internal discipline" (e.g., the abolition of auricular confession and the practice of self-scrutiny in the form of spiritual diaries). External coercion (exercised by godly elders and magistrates) was reimposed if internal discipline failed. Gorski (1993) goes even further: "Calvinism was unique in employing surveillance as a technique of mass political organization" and "provided the channel through which the discipline of the monastery entered the political world," thus enabling highly disciplined movements to obtain political power. This means that both the presence and the absence of "disciplinary revolution" and the "level of economic development" are important variables in the processes of state formation.

The main difference between the disciplinary revolutions in Prussia and Holland is that the former was a state-led revolution "from above" (rather than a revolution "from below") in which a "quasi-monastic discipline" was codified "in written rules and regulations." But one should not lose sight of the theological variables (McGrath 1993). The Lutheran doctrine of the Two Kingdoms (the separation of the ecclesiastical competence of the Church and the political competence of the State, legitimated by Rom. 13) could help to explain why Pietism was passive in Württemberg and absolutist in Prussia, but neither in Holland nor in England—because neither Dutch nor English Protestants accepted the separation of powers advocated by Luther. Martin (1978) has also argued that different permutations of Catholicism and various kinds of Protestantism can explain differential rates of "secularization" in Europe.

In short, Protestantism is a highly pluriform phenomenon that is capable of generating substantial social changes of many different kinds from the local to the political and economic level. But the pluriformity of Protestantism does not always manifest itself in the form of homogeneous denominations. Some Protestant denominations are characterized by substantial levels of internal pluriformity. Having been influenced by Puritan, Methodist, Evangelical, and Catholic revivals, the Church of England consists of two vertical "pillars" (one Catholic and the other Evangelical) with the "Broad Church" in between. All three pillars are now horizontally divided into "progressive" and "conservative" layers: a new cleavage that now runs through the whole of the Protestant constituency (Staples 1981, compare with Glock et al. 1967). The pluriformity of the Netherlands Reformed Church (Conservatives *[Gereformeerde Bonders]*, Confessionals [influenced by the neo-orthodox theologian Karl Barth], Ethicals *[Ethischen]*, and Liberals) is described by Haitjema (1953). High church movements are not unknown in Scandinavian and German Lutheranism (e.g., the disciples of Söderblom and

Heiler) and in the Netherlands Reformed Church (especially among the Ethicals; see Staples 1981, 1985). So sociologists should also consider the possibility that discrete segments in Protestant denominations might ultimately be "sects" within "churches" or "churches" within "churches" (as defined by Troeltsch and Weber).

—*Peter Staples*

REFERENCES

R. Baird, *Religion in America* (New York: Harper, 1856); D. B. Barrett (ed.), *World Christian Encyclopedia* (Nairobi: Oxford University Press, 1982); D. B. Barrett, "Status of Global Mission," *International Bulletin of Missionary Research,* January 1990, p. 27; W. van Beek (ed.), *The Quest for Purity* (Berlin: de Gruyter, 1988); D. Bonhoeffer, *Sanctorum Communio* (München: Kaiser, 1930); E. D. C. Brewer, "Sect and Church in Methodism," *Social Forces* 30(1952):400-408; N. Cohn, *The Pursuit of the Millennium* (London: Seker & Warburg, 1957); G. R. Cragg (ed.), *The Cambridge Platonists* (New York: Oxford University Press, 1968); M. Fulbrook, *Piety and Politics* (Cambridge: Cambridge University Press, 1983); C. Y. Glock et al., *To Comfort and to Challenge* (Berkeley: University of California Press, 1967); P. S. Gorski, "The Protestant Ethic Revisited," *American Journal of Sociology* 99(1993):265-316; T. L Haitjema, *De richtingen in de Nederlandse Hervormde Kerk* (Wageningen: Veenman & Zonen, 1953); É. Halévy, *A History of the English People in 1815* (London: Fisher Unwin, 1924); É. Halévy, *A History of the English People 1830-1841* (London: Fisher Unwin, 1927); C. Hill, *The English Revolution* (London: Lawrence & Wishart, 1940); C. Hill, *Puritanism and Revolution* (London: Secker & Warburg, 1958); C. Hill, *The Century of Revolution* (New York: Norton, 1966); M. Hill, *A Sociology of Religion* (London: Heinemann, 1973); C. N. Impeta, *Kaart van kerkelijk Nederland* (Kok: Kampen, 1972); G. Lewy, *Religion and Revolution* (New York: Oxford University Press, 1974); F. H. Littell, *The Anabaptist View of the Church* (Boston: Beacon, 1958); F. H. Littell, *From State Church to Pluralism* (Garden City, N.Y.: Doubleday, 1962); D. Martin, *A General Theory of Secularization* (Oxford: Blackwell, 1978); D. Martin, *Tongues of Fire* (Oxford: Blackwell, 1990); M. E. Marty, *A Nation of Behavers* (Chicago: University of Chicago Press, 1976); A. McGrath, *The Intellectual Origins of the European Reformation* (Oxford: Blackwell, 1993); R. Mehl, *The Sociology of Protestantism* (London: SCM, 1970); R. Mehl, "Protestantism," in *Dictionary of the Ecumenical Movement,* ed. N. Lossky (Grand Rapids, Mich.: Eerdmans, 1991): 830-838; E. Molland, *Christendom* (London: Mowbray, 1961); H. R. Niebuhr, *The Social Sources of Denominationalism* (New York: Holt, 1929); T. Parsons and E. A. Shils, *Toward a General Theory of Action* (Cambridge: Harvard University Press, 1962); W. S. F. Pickering and H. Martin (eds.), *Debating Durkheim* (London: Routledge, 1994); A. C. Piepkorn, *Profiles of Belief,* vols. 2 and 3 (New York: Harper, 1978-1979); B. A. Reist, *Towards a Theology of Involvement* (London: SCM, 1966); P. Schaff, *The Creeds of Christendom* (Grand

Rapids, Mich.: Baker, 1966 [1877]); B. Semmel, *The Methodist Revolution* (New York: Basic Books, 1973); T. Skocpol, *States and Social Revolutions* (Cambridge: Cambridge University Press, 1979); P. Staples, *The Church of England: 1961-1980* (Utrecht/Leiden: IIMO, 1981); P. Staples, *The Liturgical Movement in the Netherlands Reformed Church: 1911-1955* (Utrecht/Leiden: IIMO, 1985); C. Tilly (ed.), *The Formation of National States in Western Europe* (Princeton, N.J.: Princeton University Press, 1975); C. Tilly, *From Mobilization to Revolution* (Reading, Mass.: Addison-Wesley, 1978); E. Troeltsch, *Protestantism and Progress* (Boston: Beacon, 1958 [1911]); E. Troeltsch, *The Social Teaching of the Christian Churches* (New York: Macmillan, 1931 [1912]); W. Walker, *The Creeds and Platforms of Congregationalism* (Boston: Pilgrim, 1960 [1893]); M. Waltzer, *The Revolution of the Saints* (New York: Atheneum, 1974); M. Weber, *Economy and Society* (Berkeley: University of California Press, 1978 [1922]); J. Wesley, *The Works of John Wesley*, vols. 1 and 4 (Nashville: Abingdon, 1984, 1987); G. H. Williams, *The Radical Reformation* (Philadelphia: Westminster, 1962); B. R. Wilson, "An Analysis of Sect Development," *American Sociological Review* 24(1959):3-15. Series: *Die Kirchen der Welt* (Stuttgart: Evangelischen Verlagswerk, 1959–); *Denominations in America* (New York: Greenwood, 1985–).

PROTESTANT REFORMATION   see Reformation

PROUDFOOT, WAYNE (1939–)   Professor of Religion at Columbia University who, with Phillip Shaver (1975), introduced the insights of psychology's *attribution theory* into the study of religion.

Attribution theory is concerned with people's explanations of the causes of experiences or behaviors. Proudfoot and Shaver argue that "religious experiences" can be explained as diffuse emotional states or ambiguous states of physiological arousal that are interpreted through a religious meaning-belief system. Advocates of the attributional approach have sought to go beyond Proudfoot and Shaver's *emotion-attribution theory* and articulate a *general attribution theory*, which sees religion as a broad-scale meaning-belief system that potentially supports causal attributions in many spheres of life. The explanatory task is to determine the factors that make a religious interpretation seem appropriate for a given event or experience.

In his American Academy of Religion award-winning book *Religious Experience* (University of California Press 1985), Proudfoot further applies attribution theory to religious experience in the context of a more philosophical and critical investigation of the idea of religious experience as it has developed through the past 200 years. He pays particular attention to the work

of the theologian Friedrich Schleiermacher and to William James. Drawing on philosophy of mind and language in addition to cognitive psychology, Proudfoot concludes that religious experience cannot be independent of but instead assumes religious beliefs and practices as well as linguistic practices and grammatical rules for labeling experiences.

See also Attribution Theory, Mysticism

—*David Yamane*

REFERENCE

W. Proudfoot and Phillip Shaver, "Attribution Theory and the Psychology of Religion," *Journal for the Scientific Study of Religion* 14(1975):317-330.

PRUYSER, PAUL W. (1916-1987)   Director of the Interdisciplinary Studies Program and Emeritus Henry March Pfeiffer Professor of Research and Education in Psychiatry at the Menninger Foundation. President of the Society for the Scientific Study of Religion (1974-1975); recipient of the William C. Bier award (1986) by Division 36 of the American Psychological Association for outstanding and sustained scholarly study of the psychology of religion.

Pruyser was a prominent clinician, active in encouraging the valid role of mature, nonanthropomorphic religion in psychological health. Psychoanalytic in orientation, he opposed the positivistic underpinnings that dominate the contemporary empirical psychology of religion. Influenced by object relations theory, he developed an analysis of religion based upon illusion that rescued it from the pejorative connotations it had acquired in Freudian theory. Religion, conceived as shared illusion, occupies a world between internal fantasy and external reality. Shared illusion is involved not only in religion but also in play, creativity, and art. Illusion is a product of a tutored imagination, fundamental to culture. As a major domain for the expression of this imagination, religion is fated to continue to play a dominant role in culture.

—*Ralph W. Hood, Jr.*

REFERENCES

P. W. Pruyser, *A Dynamic Psychology of Religion* (New York: Harper, 1968); P. W. Pruyser, *Between Belief and Unbelief* (New York: Harper, 1974); P. W. Pruyser, *The Minister as Diagnostician* (Philadelphia: Westminster, 1976); P. W. Pruyser, *The Play of the Imagination* (New York: International Universities Press, 1983); P. W. Pruyser, "The Tutored Imagination in Religion," in *Changing Views of the Human Condition* (Macon, Ga.: Mercer University Press, 1987).

PSYCHIC PHENOMENA (PSI)   Events thought to exceed the limits of what is deemed physically possible based on current scientific assumptions.

The term *psi* is a general one used either as a noun or adjective to identify ESP or PK. *Extrasensory perception* (ESP) is defined as paranormal cognition: the acquisition of information about an external event, object, or influence (mental or physical, past, present, or future) in some way other than through any of the known sensory channels. *Psychokinesis* (PK) is paranormal action: the influence of mind on a physical system that cannot be entirely accounted for by the mediation of any known physical energy. Scientists who investigate psi are known as parapsychologists. J. B. Rhine, a researcher at Duke University who published statistical studies of ESP in 1934, is generally considered to be the father of modern parapsychology.

Edgar Cayce (1877-1945) was the center of the largest lay organization in the United States focusing attention on psychic phenomena. Cayce was a photographer who diagnosed illness and uttered prophecies while in trance. His followers founded the Association for Research and Enlightenment (ARE) in 1934. After Cayce's death, the ARE sorted and indexed some 15,000 transcripts of his statements, all of which are available to visitors at the ARE's headquarters in Virginia Beach. The ARE is a forerunner of the American holistic health movement.

—*James McClenon*

REFERENCES

R. S. Broughton, *Parapsychology* (New York: Ballantine, 1991); J. McClenon, *Deviant Science* (Philadelphia: University of Pennsylvania Press, 1984); J. McClenon, *Wondrous Events* (Philadelphia: University of Pennsylvania Press, 1994); J. B. Rhine, *Extra-Sensory Perception* (Boston: Boston Society for Psychic Research, 1934).

PSYCHOANALYSIS   *see* Sigmund Freud

PSYCHOLOGY OF RELIGION   Takes religious phenomena as objects of inquiry either to be described or to be explained by principles of psychology. Relationships between psychology and religion are complicated by the fact that little consensus exists on the meaning of either of these terms. Psychology is less a single science than a generic discipline defined by the methods and procedures that, when consensually shared, identify the various schools of psychology. These schools have produced largely distinct literatures and research traditions that collectively constitute the current psychology of religion. Each school is itself heterogeneous so that even in identifying a particular school it is best to refer to it in the plural.

Across schools of psychology, religion is approached substantively or functionally. Substantive approaches define religion by its content or by its specific practices, focusing upon such phenomena as belief in God, conversion, or prayer. Functional approaches define religion by specific processes that explain how religion operates in individual's lives. Debates continue as to whether or not there are unique contents or processes in the psychology of religion. Religious psychology argues for the latter while psychology of religion assumes that processes in religion are not different from in other areas of investigation.

Research in the psychology of religion is best understood within particular schools, which define both the area and the relevant methodological criteria for evaluation. Across schools, criteria are often incommensurate.

Schools of Psychology and Their Research Traditions   *Psychoanalytical schools* are heavily rooted in the classical work of Sigmund Freud. They have unique methodologies, aimed ultimately at uncovering the unconscious basis of religious beliefs, emotions, and practices. Many of the powerful reductive explanations of psychoanalysis, demanding a naturalistic explanation of all transcendent phenomena, have been themselves challenged within psychoanalysis. The Oedipus complex, central to much of classical psychoanalysis, has been challenged as a form of orthodoxy. However, efforts to test classical psychoanalytic theories by more positivistic methodologies remain controversial, both within psychoanalysis and among those who doubt that theories derived from radically different schools of psychology can be tested by a single set of methodological criteria. It is now widely recognized that illusional processes operating in religion, motivated by both conscious and unconscious desires, cannot be used to justify the ultimately ontological claim that religion is delusional.

This has made psychoanalysis more hospitable to religious phenomena. Many contemporary psychoanalysts have even provided explanations of religious phenomena compatible with religious faith. Hence psychoanalysis is no longer seen as necessarily hostile to religion or capable of giving an exhaustive naturalistic interpretation of religious phenomena. The major methodological approach remains the clinical case study. Biographical analyses of historical religious personages are also common. Psychoanalytic literature remains the most dominant literature in the psychology of religion and no doubt has the greatest cultural impact of any school.

Analytical schools, rooted in the work of Carl Jung, continue to produce an impressive literature. Their orientation tends to be hermeneutical and interpretative rather than causal and explanatory. Focusing upon individual case studies, dream interpretation, and analyses of literature, Jung's rich descriptive vocabulary is used to provide interpretative analysis of religious phenomena particularly appealing to clinical and counseling psychologists. Consistent with Jung's own view, analytical psychology employs a powerful descriptive language that incorporates much of the content of religious traditions in a manner that often provides a novel hermeneutic when combined with interpretations based upon Jungian archetypes. However, many empirical psychologists see such efforts as more akin to literary criticism than legitimate science. Few research scientists have tried to test analytic theories empirically. It is not clear that such tests would be meaningful given the radical discrepancies in the ontological assumptions of measurement and Jungian schools of psychology.

Object relations schools continue the psychoanalytical tradition of interest in religious experience. Like psychoanalysts, they find much to illuminate in religious experience by the reconstruction of early infant states. However, their focus is upon pre-Oedipal states. This has shifted the focus to maternal influences and spawned a large descriptive literature that, like Jung's psychology, has heavily influenced feminist thought. Their methods are primarily clinical case studies of adult subjects. The concept of illusion as an intermediate world between that of private fantasy and objective reality has been deemed to be particularly appropriate to the description of religious phenomena in particular and cultural phenomena in general.

Transpersonal schools explicitly confront spiritual realities in a nonreductive manner. They employ an eclectic mixture of scientific and spiritual methodologies in which the focus is upon transcendent experiences and the conceptual systems that both legitimate and define their reality. Most transpersonal psychologists explicitly assume the ontological reality of a spiritual realm that can be investigated by appropriate methodologies. This has led some to perceive them primarily as a religious psychology and not as a psychology of religion. For more than a quarter of a century, transpersonal psychologists have published a highly successful

journal, the *Journal of Transpersonal Psychology.* Transpersonal psychologies are close to measurement schools insofar as they have spawned a large literature that is both empirically based and of interest to clinicians, counselors, and theoreticians.

Phenomenological schools eschew experimentation and analysis in favor of essentially descriptive approaches to religious experience. Emphasizing the necessity for a critical reflexive awareness of the assumptions, presuppositions, and prejudices that affect what appears to consciousness, phenomenological schools have produced a literature rich in description but with little consensual validation. Their descriptive approach attempts to transcend individual variations in religious experience in favor of uncovering the essence of religious phenomena. Several phenomenologists have attempted to formulate appropriate methodologies by which a more consistent phenomenological database can be obtained. Yet to date there is less consensus on appropriate phenomenological methodologies than upon methodologies accepted by measurement schools of psychology.

Measurement schools dominate the academic investigation of religion in psychology departments that primarily identify psychology as a science within the naturalistic tradition. Having little in common other than a commitment to operationally defining variables in a fashion that permits their measurement, this school provides the essential database for the empirical psychology of religion. For many psychologists, only theories developed with reference to this database are legitimately scientific. Much of the empirical research within measurement schools is essentially correlational, making causal relationships difficult to establish. Multivariate procedures are now beginning to dominate the field. However, hypothesis-testing procedures that employ either quasi- or true experimental procedures are preferred and employed by the more rigorous researchers. No credence is given to the development of a religious psychology; rather, psychology of religion is seen as a specialty within mainstream psychology, most often social psychology. Many investigators would accept the independence of religion and psychology, and not necessarily demand that measurement psychology aim to provide a naturalistic reductive explanation of religious phenomena.

Major Content Areas in the Psychology of Religion
Since its American reemergence in 1960, the measurement-based schools of the psychology of religion have been characterized by their focus upon a limited number of content areas. While having no specialty journal of their own, they have relied upon interdisciplinary journals such as the *Journal for the Scientific Study of*

Religion and the *Review of Religious Research.* To a lesser extent, they have used specialty journals in mainstream psychology to publish their research. More recently, the *International Journal for the Psychology of Religion* and the *Journal for the Psychology of Religion* have begun publication. Both are devoted exclusively to the psychology of religion, the latter emphasizing qualitative studies. However, quantitative studies define what most measurement schools will accept as a valid empirical psychology of religion.

Scale construction: Psychometric research has successfully produced a plethora of scales to measure a wide variety of religious phenomena including attitudes, beliefs, and values. It is widely recognized that religion is best measured as a multidimensional construct. Most research has focused upon indices of intrinsic (religion as an end), extrinsic (religion as a means), and quest (religion as a search) dimensions of religiosity. A variety of multidimensional scales also are available to assess images of God, fear of death, religious experience, and prayer. Among general dimensions frequently assessed are religious orthodoxy and liberalism-conservatism. Scales to measure religious constructs have good reliabilities and validities matching those in other areas of mainstream psychology. It is unlikely that a scale to measure any major construct of interest to researchers is not already readily available.

Intrinsic-extrinsic-quest religiosity: Early findings that religion tended to correlate positively with prejudice were a major impetus for psychologists of religion to develop more sophisticated measures of religious orientation. Starting with the seminal work of Gordon W. Allport, studies of intrinsic-extrinsic religiosity have dominated the psychology of religion. Initially focused upon unraveling the nature of the religion-prejudice relationship, extrinsic religiosity—that is, using religion for ulterior ends—generally has been found to be that aspect of religion not only related to prejudice but to a host of other undesirable social and psychological characteristics as well. On the other hand, not only has intrinsic religiosity (accepting religion as an end) most often been seen to be unrelated or negatively related to prejudice, it also has been related positively to a wide variety of desirable social and psychological characteristics. Hence, for many researchers, much of the complex nature of religiosity has been felt to be resolved with intrinsic and extrinsic religiosity clarifying the more functional and dysfunctional effects of religion.

However, a challenge to this established body of research came from the assessment of another dimension of religiosity, that is, quest, or religion as an open-ended search. In terms of prejudice research, quest religiosity, and not intrinsic religiosity, has been found to be largely unrelated to prejudice. It is argued that intrinsic religiosity is only apparently unrelated to prejudice. Instead, it may mask a socially desirable tendency merely to wish to appear unprejudiced. Extrinsic religiosity remains generally positively related to prejudice. Quest religiosity also has been generally found to relate to other desirable social psychological characteristics such as more complex thinking, open-minded attitudes, and a willingness to be appropriately altruistic. Despite numerous criticisms of both the measurement and the research traditions associated with intrinsic-extrinsic religiosity and quest religiosity, these have dominated, and are likely to continue to dominate, the empirical research literature for years to come.

Coping and psychopathology: Perhaps most overlapping with the interests of other schools of psychology, measurement psychologists have explored the complex relationships between religion, coping, and psychopathology. Long past accepting by fiat definitional claims that equate religion and psychopathology, it has been found that religion can differentially function in a number of ways relevant to psychopathology: as an expression of disorder, as a suppressing or socializing device, as a heaven, as therapy, as a hazard. Likewise, religion may aid or foster either problem solving or emotion focused coping. Much of the difficulty of summarizing the massive research literature in these areas is that neither psychological health nor effective coping are definable in neutral terms. Hence measurements are inherently value laden and reflect the implicit or explicit ideological basis of research in the psychology of religion. Much of the research literature finds a positive role for religion in the establishment of a subjective sense of well-being even when objective health factors are not affected.

Religious development: Developmental psychologists often postulated developmental sequences or stages for a variety of phenomena. Psychologists of religion have focused upon these theories to assess both the relevance of stages of intellectual development of the acceptance of religious beliefs and the relevance of stages of moral development relevant to religious faith. Unique to the psychology of religion are theories of faith development. While operationalized and capable of adequate measurement, relationships between various stages of development and religious variables are confounded by complex evaluations unlikely to be empirically resolved. Inevitably, some religious traditions are seen as fostering unhealthy development or unduly attracting those at lower stages of development. Religious fundamentalism has been particularly scrutinized and found deficient within most developmental theories of intellectual, moral, or faith development.

Among those developmental theories that do not postulate stages, increasing attention is given to attachment theory in religious development. Newer developments in attachment theory link it more explicitly to evolutionary psychology, a newly emerging paradigm in mainstream psychology.

Conversion, glossolalia, and religious experience: Long a focus of concern by psychologists, researchers continue to investigate religious experiences such as conversion, glossolalia, and mysticism. Much of this research has fostered the movement of the psychology of religion into mainstream psychology. For instance, role theory from social psychology has been used to illuminate both glossolalia and conversion, while attribution theory has been used to make useful theoretical predictions regarding the conditions under which experiences are meaningfully interpreted as religious. The commonality of religious experiences has been repeatedly documented, substantiating that they are part of normal psychology and need not be assumed to be pathological. Mysticism has been a focus of significant empirical research in survey, laboratory, and naturalistic studies. Factors that facilitate the report of religious experience have been identified and include language, psychedelic drugs, and set/setting conditions. Renewed emphasis has been focused on perhaps the most universal of religious practices, prayer.

Religion and death: Given that the fear of death often has been postulated as a major factor in the origin of religion, it is not surprising that researchers have studied religion and attitudes toward death. A pervasive death anxiety has not been substantiated or found related to religion. Attitude toward death is multidimensional. Perspectives such as death as pain, as an afterlife reward, as courage, as unknown, or simply as an end have been found to vary in complex ways in relation to aspects of religion. Perhaps the most robust finding is that fear and negative perspectives on death and dying are mitigated by belief in a benevolent afterlife, a feature common to many religious traditions. Closely paralleling this is the robust finding that religious participation serves to give social and emotional support to survivors and to keep people integrated with each other in the face of death.

Religion and psychotherapy: The hostility of some schools of psychology (such as classical psychoanalysis) to religion is mitigated by new approaches within all schools of psychology that give validity to religion. Some schools, such as transpersonal psychology, are explicitly spiritual psychologies. Even within mainstream psychology, the scientist-practitioner model has yielded to awareness of the crucial role of values at every level in the therapeutic enterprise. In addition, contemporary philosophy of science has lessened the uniqueness of science as a form of knowing and made sharp demarcations between science and religion less defensible. Hence the explicit recognition of the possible value and use of religion in therapy is no longer a province only of the religious psychologies. Psychology schools can no longer take a hostile or noninteractive stance toward religion. At a minimum, the demand that clinical and counseling psychologies be sensitive to religious beliefs as part of the recognition of their training in multiculturalism assures that the psychology of religion will no longer be seen as irrelevant to the training of clinical and counseling practitioners.

—Ralph W. Hood, Jr.

REFERENCES

C. D. Batson et al., *Religion and the Individual* (New York: Oxford University Press, 1993); R. L. Gorsuch, "The Psychology of Religion," *Annual Review of Psychology* 39 (1988):201-221; R. W. Hood, Jr., *Handbook of Religious Experience* (Birmingham, Ala.: Religious Education Press, 1995); R. W. Hood et al., *The Psychology of Religion*, 2nd ed. (New York: Guilford, 1996); S. L. Jones, "A Constructive Relationship for Religion with the Science and Profession of Psychology," *American Psychologist* 49(1994):184-199; J. McDargh, *Psychoanalytic Objects Relation Theory and the Study of Religion* (Lanham, Md.: University Press of America, 1983); W. W. Meissner, *Psychoanalysis and Religious Experience* (New Haven, Conn.: Yale University Press, 1984); R. F. Paloutzian and L. A. Kirkpatrick (eds.), "Religious Influences on Personal and Societal Well-Being," *Journal of Social Issues* 51, 2(1995); K. Pargament, *The Psychology of Religion and Coping* (New York: Guilford, 1997); J. F. Schumaker (ed.), *Religion and Mental Health* (New York: Oxford University Press, 1992); E. P. Shafranske, *Religion and the Clinical Practice of Psychology* (New York: American Psychological Association, 1995); B. Spilka and D. N. McIntosh (eds.), *The Psychology of Religion* (Boulder, Colo.: Westview, 1997); C. T. Tart (ed.), *Transpersonal Psychologies* (New York: Harper, 1975); D. M. Wulff (ed.), *Psychology of Religion* (New York: Wiley, 1991).

PUBLIC OPINION POLLING Since the 1980s, interest in the public role of religion has increased in both the journalistic and the scholarly communities. Because of this rise in the visibility of religious phenomena, there has been a corresponding increase in the attention paid to religion by analysts of public opinion.

Any discussion of public opinion polling must begin with the Gallup Organization, which is perhaps the best-known polling entity in the United States. Indeed, the Gallup Poll has long been a leader in the measurement of religious phenomena among the mass public. For approximately four decades, George Gallup, Jr., has evinced a strong interest in religion in the United States. The Gallup polls have consistently contained items relating to religious belief and practice, and Gallup has frequently conducted special surveys for religious organizations. The result of this sustained attention to American religion is an extensive set of longitudinal data, which has enabled researchers to track elements of stability and change in religion in the United States.

During the period in which Gallup has been studying American religion, certain continuities have stood out. Americans, by and large, are a very religious people who have held a number of consistent beliefs throughout the latter half of the twentieth century. For example, Gallup reports that large majorities of the American public believe in a personal, "heavenly father" God, in the divinity of Jesus Christ, in life after death, and in the existence of a literal heaven. Comparably large majorities of Americans regard religion as personally very important and have high levels of confidence in the clergy. Over time, a bare majority has expressed a belief in a literal hell. Thus Gallup has recorded something of a consensus in the United States concerning what might be considered the minimal doctrinal essentials of Christianity. Despite major social changes, the past three decades have witnessed little change in the distribution of these core beliefs. In terms of religious practice, the frequency of church attendance and personal prayer has been quite stable and consistently higher in the United States than elsewhere.

In the midst of this overall level of stability, Gallup also has recorded some important changes in American religion. Due to a number of processes, which include differential fertility rates, changes in immigration rates, and denomination switching, American denominational affiliation has become generally less Protestant, and affiliation with mainline denominations (e.g., Methodist, Episcopalian, Presbyterian) has declined. Increases have occurred in fundamentalist or pentecostal churches, and among the ranks of the unchurched (although most people without formal denominational affiliations remain "believers" in the sense described above). Another important change is that Americans are progressively less inclined to accept religious authority: Over time, Gallup has shown that Americans increasingly believe that religious leaders should pay more attention to the opinions of the laity, and that church decisions should be made in consultation between the pulpit and the pew. Americans expect religious denominations to provide spiritual services, and most of these relate to the "comforting" function of religion. While

Gallup reports that the trend away from the acceptance of religious authority is strongest among the "unchurched," the tendency toward individualized religious beliefs and practices is increasingly frequent among all denominations and all levels of religious observance. Even actively practicing Catholics (from a denomination that consistently has asserted its teaching authority), majorities reject church teachings in such areas as personal morality, abortion, or birth control. In response to declining commitments to institutionalized religious authority, Americans are increasingly supplementing their religious practice with more intimate, informal, religious observances such as Bible-reading groups, prayer meetings, and the like (Poloma and Gallup 1991).

Despite the importance of religion to the American public, Gallup has shown that many Americans are not particularly knowledgeable about religion. For example, the *Christianity Today* survey (1979) showed that fewer than half of Gallup's respondents could name five of the Ten Commandments, and fewer than one-third could identify the scriptural context of the quote, "Ye must be born again."

In recent years, Gallup has shown a great interest in the rise of American evangelicalism. Perhaps in response to the general weakening of denominational ties, Gallup has emphasized doctrinal and experiential criteria in operationalizing "evangelicalism." For example, in the *Christianity Today* survey, Gallup distinguished between "orthodox" and "conversionalist" evangelicals. The former are characterized by a belief in the divinity of Jesus Christ, a belief that salvation is only possible through Jesus Christ, and a conviction that the Bible is inerrant. To be considered orthodox evangelicals, respondents also had to report monthly (or more frequent) church attendance and Bible reading. A "conversionalist" evangelical is a person who reads the Bible, attends religious services at least monthly, and reports a powerful religious experience that remains personally important. This experience is understood as a religious conversion, in which Jesus Christ becomes one's personal savior. Gallup reports considerable, but by no means complete, overlap between the two groups.

Other survey organizations also have made important contributions to the measurement of religious phenomena. Under the guidance of Andrew Greeley (1981, 1982), several versions of the General Social Surveys (conducted by the National Opinion Research Center at the University of Chicago) have included items measuring personal images of God. Using both adjective ratings and semantic differentials, respondents are asked (for example) to characterize God as male or female, as interventionist or passive, and as judgmental or forgiving. These image items have added a cognitive dimension to some of the doctrinal questions that the Gallup organization has made standard.

More recently, the American National Election Studies (conducted out of the University of Michigan) also have incorporated religious items into their national surveys. Based on a pilot study conducted in 1989, recent versions of the ANES have included relatively sophisticated and precise measures of denominational affiliation as well as batteries of items measuring religious individualism or communalism, religious self-identifications, and various aspects of religious salience. In general, the ANES have advanced our understanding of the political role of religion by measuring aspects of religion as social group membership rather than as a set of individualized beliefs or values (see Leege and Kellstedt 1993).

Finally, numerous scholars have conducted specialized surveys for the purpose of investigating specific religious topics in greater depth than the typical national survey might allow. For example, Marler and Hadaway (1993) have conducted a four-state telephone survey, supplemented by intensive, face-to-face interviews, to examine the phenomenon of religious marginality. Based on these quantitative and qualitative data, Marler and Hadaway were able to produce a fourfold typology of persons who are nominally affiliated with Protestant denominations but who are religiously inactive. Similarly, James Davison Hunter (1990) conducted a survey for the Williamsburg Charter organization in 1987 to provide detailed information about public attitudes toward church-state relations in the United States. These data were analyzed by Jelen and Wilcox (1995), who supplemented the Williamsburg data with their own telephone survey of attitudes toward church-state relations in the Washington, D.C., area. The analyses of these data have generally suggested that public disagreement about the political role of religion is not simply a matter of disagreement about the value of religion per se. Rather, many devout citizens oppose religious involvement in politics for theological, rather than political, reasons. Although studies such as these are often limited in geographic scope or in the range of topics considered, they can provide detailed insight into particular questions regarding the sociology of religion. Such studies also can offer research innovations, which can then be incorporated into larger scale surveys of the mass public.

See also Church-and-State Issues, Evangelicalism, Andrew M. Greeley, Particularism, Politics

—*Ted G. Jelen*

REFERENCES

G. Gallup, Jr., *The Unchurched American* (Princeton, N.J.: Princeton Religious Research Center, 1978); G. Gallup, Jr., "The *Christianity Today*-Gallup Poll," *Christianity Today* 23(1979):1663-1673; G. Gallup, Jr., *Religion in America* (Princeton, N.J.: Princeton Religious Research Center, 1982); G. Gallup, Jr., and J. Castelli, *The American Catholic People* (Garden City, N.Y.: Doubleday, 1987); G. Gallup, Jr., and J. Castelli, *The People's Religion* (New York: Macmillan, 1989); G. Gallup, Jr., and D. Poling, *The Search for America's Faith* (Nashville: Abingdon, 1980); A. M. Greeley, *The Religious Imagination* (New York: Sadlier, 1981); A. M. Greeley, *Religion* (New York: Free Press, 1982); J. D. Hunter, "The Williamsburg Charter Survey," *Journal of Law and Religion* 8(1990):257-271; T. G. Jelen and C. Wilcox, *Public Attitudes Toward Church and State* (Armonk, N.Y.: Sharpe, 1995); D. C. Leege and L. A. Kellstedt (eds.), *Rediscovering the Impact of Religion on Political Behavior* (Armonk, N.Y.: Sharpe, 1993); P. L. Marler and C. K. Hadaway, "Toward a Typology of 'Marginal Member'," *Review of Religious Research* 35(1993):34-54; M. M. Poloma and G. Gallup, Jr., *Varieties of Prayer* (Philadelphia: Trinity, 1991).

PUBLIC RELIGION   Refers both to a form of civic faith within a republic and to public expressions of religious faith in cultures where religion is more familiarly categorized as a private affair.

In respect to civic faith, the term derives from a phrase by Benjamin Franklin. In 1749, the American founder made "proposals" for an educational academy in Philadelphia. When discussing the study of "history," he argued that it would "afford frequent Opportunities of showing the Necessity of a *Publick Religion*," arguing "from its Usefulness to the Publick; the Advantages of a Religious Character among private Persons," and the like.

In recent decades, as portrayed by Princeton historian John Wilson, "public religion" has come to be seen as a parallel or alternative to "civil religion" as a societal expression. Robert N. Bellah's notable essay (1967) describing and cautiously promoting "civil religion," inspired in part as it was by reference to collectivities in the schemes of Jean-Jacques Rousseau and Émile Durkheim, struck many as representing a kind of "top-down" governmental development.

In contrast to this, the Franklinian tradition of public religion was, in a way, seen as a "from-the-bottom-up" proposal. That is, Franklin and most other of the nation's founders were concerned about public morality and virtue, reasoning that without these the U.S. Constitution that they were drafting would be ineffective for republican life. They looked out on 13 colonies in which varieties of churches and other spiritual and moral forces were at work. Each had a peculiarity that gave it sectarian life, but almost all promoted the common good—and this endeavor was to be part of the public religion, to be discerned in education and voluntary acts of citizens.

Public religion, second, refers to expressions of religious belief and behavior generated by private individuals or in the subcommunities, communities, and associations in the voluntary sector but having direct bearings on public order. As such, the term serves to refer to one side of the familiar private-public dichotomy.

In a liberal society such as that of the United States, there is a long tradition of wariness voiced by those who have seen religious and tribal warfare elsewhere and the threat of the same domestically. In part because of such concerns, this tradition lends support to the folk distinction that religion is "a private affair." It has an honored place in the heart and the home, or in the religious institution and voluntary agencies with specific faith-based purposes. But, in part because of the volatile potential when religion goes public in a pluralist society, the publicness was discouraged.

Those who point to and even celebrate public religion, however, argue that religion will inevitably find outlets and will make intrusions in the public realm, and that it is better to recognize this and make such religion a subject of citizen observation and debate than to keep it covert and leave it unacknowledged. By "public," such advocates never mean that it does or should displace the private forms. Nor, they are quick to insist, does "public" mean always and only "political." The place of religion in politics particularly is related to its place in the public generically. The public includes all the spheres and zones where the different individuals and groups come out of privacy and seclusion into settings and occasions where citizens meet "the other," those who are not of one's own group, whether this group is religious, racial, ethnic, ideological, or whatever.

Those who both observe and advance public religion contend that faith is a major element in world and national history, and has its place in curricula; that it plays such a large part in life that it cannot fairly or safely be overlooked by mass communicators; that it is too vital to go uncriticized as it only can be criticized when it is subject to public view; that it can play its part not only in repressing dissent and variety but, more

positively, in encouraging the development of virtue and contributing to ethical judgments.

Public religion thrives in many forms, but not, in the eyes of many who see hope in its category, as an official, legal, governmentally monitored phenomenon. Instead, it prospers when individuals and groups resort not to coercion but to persuasion and example, by dialogue and argument and voluntary action. Only in the eyes of a few is it seen as a rival or potential replacement for the nonpublic or less public forms of faith and religious institutions. Rather, most would say that public religion depends upon the cultivation that goes on in the more private expressions, because it does not aspire to satisfy many of the needs of the souls as citizens give voice to them.

See also Civil Religion

—*Martin E. Marty*

REFERENCES

R. N. Bellah, "Civil Religion in America," *Daedalus* 96 (1967):1-21; J. Casanova, *Public Religions in the Modern World* (Chicago: University of Chicago Press, 1994); M. E. Marty, *Religion and the Republic* (Boston: Beacon, 1987); J. F. Wilson, *Public Religion in American Culture* (Philadelphia: Temple University Press, 1979).

PURITANISM   *see* Protestant Ethic Thesis

PURITY   Perfection, genuineness, faultlessness, innocence, cleanness.

Many, but not all, religions associate purity with holiness. They see it as sacred and oppose it to pollution, contamination, and so on, which they see as profane. Religious virtuosi in these traditions seek purity, either by self-abnegation or by separating themselves from the profane things of the world. Mary Douglas (e.g., in *Purity and Danger,* Routledge 1966) notes that ideas about what is pure vary from society to society; one religion's purity is another's abomination. Similarly, some religions seek holiness ascetically, while others seek it in the midst of sensual life. In any case, the search for purity often results in a separation from outsiders, because believers think that relationships with them are unclean.

—*James V. Spickard*

QUAKERS Also known as the Religious Society of Friends, the Quakers are a Christian-based religious movement that began in the apocalyptic and politically charged period after the English Civil War (c. 1650). Aligned with radical parliamentary positions that were suspect when monarchial rule resumed in 1660, Quakerism (under direction of its most influential early figure, George Fox) quickly adopted a pacifist position toward war. The persecution that Quakers suffered (largely from tithe resistance and refusal to swear oaths) prior to the establishment of limited religious toleration in 1689 contributed to the group's introversion, which continued until the end of the nineteenth century. Quakerism's basic theological claim of "indwelling divinity within all persons," in combination with its formal anticlericalism (at least during its early days), placed it at the far left of Puritanism.

People hold memberships in Quakerism through Monthly Meetings, which gather regularly for worship and meet monthly to conduct business. Monthly Meetings in the same geographic area that share similar beliefs join to form Yearly Meetings. The structure and operations of Yearly Meetings vary, but all of them follow procedures outlined in church government doctrines that they agree upon independently through consensus decision making (see Hare 1973). Historic schisms led to five main strains of Quakerism, to which Yearly Meetings may affiliate themselves: Conservative (those who adhere to practices and beliefs rooted in previous centuries); Evangelical (with pastors leading programmed, Christocentric meetings); Friends General Conference (whose members are Christian humanists and universalists); Friends United Meeting (conservative Christians, including some pastored meetings); and United (sharing equal affiliations with Friends General Conference and Friends United Meeting). Worldwide membership stands around 300,000, with people in approximately 55 countries (concentrated in the United States, Great Britain, and Kenya).

Historically, the group distinguished itself by its members' contributions to slavery abolition, prison reform, women's rights, and peace work (often through Friends Service Committees). Quakers see these undertakings as outward manifestations of what they call "the peace testimony" (which renounces war and decries conditions that foster violence), and in turn the peace testimony stems from the group's core tenet that there is "that of God in every person."

Members' belief in the reality of continuous revelation translates into a series of inspirational "advices and queries" that Yearly Meetings either produce themselves or borrow, and that are designed to orient people toward values of lifestyle simplicity, contemplation, and social action. In what Quakers call "unprogrammed" meetings for worship, people sit in silence, which anyone may interrupt to deliver a statement that he or she feels is divinely inspired and worthy of sharing.

Researchers have produced extensive studies of Quakerism. Kent (1990 [1983]) highlighted the importance of early Quakerism's "fixed price" policy in the development of Max Weber's "Protestant ethic" thesis. He also argued that development of the doctrine partly reflected feelings of deep social resentment (along lines previously identified by Nietzsche and Marxist revisionist Eduard Bernstein) rather than apolitical or antipolitical Puritan spirituality as Weber claimed. Baltzell (1979) discussed how the egalitarian and antiauthoritarian Quaker ethos of Philadelphia (founded by Quaker William Penn and settled by fellow Friends) prevented its citizens from achieving social, judicial, or civic prominence. Kent and Spickard (1994) replied, however, that Quaker theology and ethics contributed heavily to a "sectarian civil religion" that consistently protested against social and political injustices. Mullett (1984) showed that the historical complexity of Quakerism's evolving activities and beliefs makes it exceedingly difficult to place the group within sociological "sect" or "denomination" typologies.

Addressing other issues, a linguistic study (Bauman 1983) examined how seventeenth-century Quaker "plain speech" and silence served as vehicles through which Friends both conceptualized their message of spiritual and social egalitarianism and took that message into the world of social relations. Despite its pacifistic stance, Quaker families in one Yearly Meeting reported higher levels of particular types of family violence than did families in an American national study (Brutz and Ingoldsby 1984). Further studies explored Quakerism's "considerable influence on the overall development of British managerial thought" in industrial relations (Child 1964). One historian discussed Quakerism's instrumental role in British and American peace movements (Kennedy 1984), while others have documented the religion's international reconciliation efforts during crises such as the India-Pakistan War of 1965 and the Nigerian Civil War from 1967 to 1970 (Yarrow 1978). Finally, discussions exist of the group's war relief programs throughout Europe in the nineteenth century (e.g., Germany, Greece, Ireland, the Balkans, and Russia) and elsewhere into the twentieth century (South Africa, post civil-war Spain, World War I ambulance services and postwar relief, and various refuge efforts; Greenwood 1975).

See also Church-Sect Theory, Church-and-State Issues, Protestant Ethic Thesis, Max Weber

—*Stephen A. Kent*

REFERENCES

E. D. Baltzell, *Puritan Boston and Quaker Philadelphia* (New York: Free Press, 1979); R. Bauman, *Let Your Words Be Few* (Prospect Heights, Ill.: Waveland, 1983); J. L. Brutz and B. B. Ingoldsby, "Conflict Resolution in Quaker Families, *Journal of Marriage and the Family* 46(1984):21-26; J. Child, "Quaker Employers and Industrial Relations," *Sociological Review* 12(1964):293-315; P. J. Collins, " 'Plaining,' " *Journal of Contemporary Religion* 11(1996):277-288; J. O. Greenwood, *Quaker Encounters*, Vol. 1 (York, U.K.: Sessions, 1975); T. D. Hamm, *The Transformation of American Quakerism* (Bloomington: Indiana University Press, 1988); A. P. Hare, "Group Decision by Consensus," *Sociological Inquiry* 43(1973):75-84; L. Ingle, *First Among Friends* (Oxford: Oxford University Press, 1994); T. C. Kennedy, "The Quaker Renaissance and the Origins of the Modern British Peace Movement," *Albion* 16(1984):243-272; S. A. Kent, "The Quaker Ethic and the Fixed Price Policy," *Sociological Inquiry* 53(1983):16-32, revised reprint in *Time, Place, and Circumstance*, ed. W. H. Swatos, Jr. (New York: Greenwood, 1990): 139-150; S. A. Kent and J. V. Spickard, "The 'Other' Civil Religion and the Tradition of Radical Quaker Politics," *Journal of Church and State* 36(1994):373-387; M. Mullett, "From Sect to Denomination?" *Journal of Religious History* 13 (1984):168-191; C. H. M. Yarrow, *Quaker Experiences in International Conciliation* (New Haven, Conn.: Yale University Press, 1978).

QUASI-RELIGIONS   Concept developed in the sociological study of religion by Arthur L. Greil (Alfred University) to encompass activities and groups that deal with the sacred but are anomalous in the context of American folk definitions of "religion."

Many of the phenomena that Greil would classify as quasi-religions probably would qualify as religions under standard sociological definitions but either do not see themselves or are not seen by others as unambiguously religious. Quasi-religions straddle the line between *sacred* and *secular*, as these terms are commonly applied. Examples would include New Age and holistic health groups, spiritualist groups, witchcraft, Alcoholics Anonymous, and some excoriated "cults." With David Rudy, Greil developed the concept of the *Identity Transformation Organization (ITO)* and has argued that all organizations that try to "change" people have certain organizational features in common, whether or not the organizations are explicitly "religious."

—*Thomas Robbins*

REFERENCES

A. L. Greil, "Explorations Along the Sacred Frontier," in *Handbook of Cults and Sects in America,* Vol. A, ed. D. G. Bromley and J. K. Hadden (Greenwich, Conn.: JAI, 1993): 153-172; A. L. Greil and T. Robbins (eds.), *Between the Sacred and the Secular* (Greenwich, Conn.: JAI, 1994); A. L. Greil and D. R. Rudy, "Social Cocoons," *Sociological Inquiry* 54(1984):260-278.

RACISM An ideology that begins with the idea that humans can be divided into distinct categories or groups based on perceived physical differences, which in turn are seen as being intrinsically related to differences regarding intellectual abilities, moral character, personality traits, and cultural values. These differences are used to depict some groups as being inherently superior and others inherently inferior, thereby serving as a rationale for systems of racial stratification and domination (Banton 1987, Shibutani and Kwan 1965).

Prior to the nineteenth century, religion was the primary vehicle used in the articulation and propagation of racist ideas. Modern thinking about racial divisions arose at the time that Europeans began to explore and colonize vast part of the globe. The impetus for such thinking revolved around the question of what kinds of policies Europeans ought to enact in establishing relations with the indigenous peoples they encountered. This was clearly an important matter in the Americas. It was unclear to the earlier colonial powers whether the proper course of action was to attempt to incorporate or assimilate these peoples, establish some form of pluralism, or engage in exclusionist policies.

These questions were apparent in the famous sixteenth-century debate in Spain between Bartolome de las Casas and Juan Gines de Sepulveda. The latter, using Aristotle's description of the "natural slave," argued that the domination by Spaniards of the indigenous peoples of the Americas was just because of the sins of those peoples (especially important to him was the sin of idolatry). Subjugation was considered necessary as a precursor to efforts aimed at converting the natives to Christianity. In short, Sepulveda offered a philosophical and theological justification for the colonial domination and enslavement of the Indian population.

Las Casas countered this conclusion by arguing, first, that the Indians were fully human and therefore the equals of the Spaniards. Although he did not disagree with the proselytizing work of Catholic missionaries, he forcefully challenged what he took to be the unwarranted arrogance of those who failed to realize that nobody is born enlightened. Las Casas argued that every human must be nurtured and instructed, and that this must be done in all instances with a sense of humility and compassion. In short, his understanding of Christian theology provided him with a basis for challenging the racist doctrine advanced by his opponent. Although some observers at the debate found Las Casas to be the more persuasive of the two, subsequent historical events clearly indicate that Sepulveda's views prevailed in practice, as the Spanish initiated a ruthless campaign of subjugation (Hanke 1970).

Similar views were held by other European colonizers and were clearly evident throughout the nineteenth century. In the United States, for example, an ideological justification for the policy of Indian removal from their ancestral lands was contained in the Manifest Destiny doctrine. This doctrine reflected a conviction that the white settler nation was destined to control the continent from the Atlantic to the Pacific. Underpinning the concept was the religious belief held since the Puritan period that the United States had a providential mission to tame the continent and Christianize it (Dinnerstein et al. 1990:87 ff.).

According to Roy Harvey Pearce (1967), the American Indian was seen as religiously and morally incomplete and as an impediment to civilization. Although some Europeans—Catholics earlier than Protestants—saw it as their duty to convert these nonbelievers, others were less sanguine about the prospects of "civilizing" them and sought to remove or otherwise eliminate the American Indians from their midst.

However, during the nineteenth century, two developments emerged that reshaped the role of religion in the formulation and perpetuation of racist discourses. The first development involved the supplanting of religion by science in providing an ideological grounding for racialist thought. This shift was evident, for example, in Arthur de Gobineau's *The Inequality of Human Races,* which first appeared in the middle of the nineteenth century. De Gobineau offered a quasi-scientific, rather than religious, justification for the European colonization of much of the rest of the world. Such scientific racism also was evident in the nativist attacks on mass immigration in the early twentieth century. By this time, Darwinism and eugenics had become the dominant conceptual undergirdings of racist thought. Although such thinking has increasingly come under attack, particularly after World War II, those ideologues who still attempt to advance racist ideas generally do so by turning to science rather than religion, as the most recent example of such thinking, Herrnstein and Murray's *The Bell Curve* (Free Press 1994), attests.

The second change occurred at the same time that science replaced religion in legitimating racist discourses. Increasingly from the nineteenth century onward, religion was used as a vehicle for attacking racism. The abolitionist movement, generally rooted in Protestant churches, became the focal point of opposition to slavery. Abolitionists, despite their desire to abolish what historian Kenneth Stampp referred to as "the peculiar institution" in a book with that title (Knopf 1956), often shared with proponents of slavery a belief in the inherent inferiority of blacks. But they understood that presumed inferiority, not by recourse to religious discourse about the children of light and the children of darkness, but to biology, and later to cultural explanations that were not generally infused with theological arguments.

Religion performed a crucial role in structuring a distinctive worldview within the African American community. Beginning during the antebellum era, as historian Eugene Genovese (1972) has shown, the world the slaves made was shaped by a Christianity that had been transformed from the version promoted by the slaveholders, with its emphasis on quiescence and acceptance of slavery, to one in which Christianity became the primary ideological basis for resisting oppression and for seeking liberation from slavery. After emancipation, with the emergence of a distinct African American community, the church proved to be a center of resistance to the oppressive conditions of the new racial order that emerged after the failure of Reconstruction. With the beginning of the civil rights movement in the 1950s, the church proved to be an important resource insofar as it supplied the movement with leaders, a mobilized mass, and an ideological rationale for nonviolent confrontation. The singular importance of the Southern Christian Leadership Conference (SCLC) in the campaign to end segregation in the American South is evidence of the important role religion played in resistance to racism (Lincoln and Mamiya 1990).

The white Christian churches were divided. Many liberal Protestant denominations and liberal Catholics—the clergy often before the laity—embraced and often actively took part in the civil rights movement. While some conservative religious bodies expressed vocal opposition to the civil rights movement, many churches simply remained silent on the issue. However, by the end of the 1960s, racism was rather roundly repudiated by religious bodies across the political spectrum. Thus the New Christian Right publicly condemns racism and argues on behalf of racial equality.

At the beginning of the twenty-first century, the religious center has become an important component of antiracist discourses. Only at the periphery—and one can look on the one hand at the Christian Identity movement and on the other at the Nation of Islam—can one find religion being used to legitimate racist thought.

—*Peter Kivisto*

REFERENCES

M. Banton, *Racial Theories* (Cambridge: Cambridge University Press, 1987); L. Dinnerstein et al., *Ethnic Americans* (New York: Oxford University Press, 1990); E. Genovese, *Roll, Jordan, Roll* (New York: Pantheon, 1972); A. de Gobineau, *The Inequality of Human Races* (London: Heinemann, 1915 [1853-1855]); L. Hanke, *Aristotle and the American Indians* (Bloomington: University of Indiana Press, 1970); C. E. Lincoln and L. H. Mamiya, *The Black Church in the African American Experience* (Durham, N.C.: Duke University Press, 1990); R. H. Pearce, *Savagism and Civilization* (Baltimore: Johns Hopkins University Press, 1967); T. Shibutani and K. M. Kwan, *Ethnic Stratification* (New York: Macmillan, 1965).

RADCLIFFE-BROWN, A(LFRED) R(EGINALD) (1881-1945)

Cambridge-educated British social anthropologist closely associated with the theory of structural-functionalism.

Radcliffe-Brown was an indefatigable field-worker who conducted research in the Adaman Islands (1906-1908), Australia (1910-1912), and South Africa. His theoretical contributions gained far more attention than his careful ethnographic work. He taught at the University of Chicago from 1931 to 1937 and had tremendous influence on a generation of American anthropologists. Radcliffe-Brown's theoretical model draws heavily on analogies between the workings of social institutions and the workings of biological organisms. Throughout his career, he emphasized that social institutions—like biological organisms—possess readily discernible structures, and that each feature of social life has a "function" that contributes to the coherence and perpetuation of society as a whole. The major function of religion, according to Radcliffe-Brown, is to affirm and strengthen sentiments necessary for a society to continue. In his most cited work, *The Adaman Islanders* (Free Press 1964), he argues that Adaman myth and ritual are essential to Adaman society because they express sentiments upon which Adaman culture ultimately depends.

See also Functionalism

—*Stephen D. Glazier*

REFERENCE

A. H. Radcliffe-Brown, *Structure and Function in Primitive Society* (London: Cohen & West, 1952).

RADICALISM Two theories, Marxism and functionalism, have stressed religion's contribution to status quo maintenance. But empirical studies abound that document religion's contribution to the formation, mobilization, and justification of political radicalism.

In Western Europe, organized religion resisted, first, liberal bourgeois revolutions and then socialist labor movements. However, in other parts of the world, liberal-left political movements have had religious sym-

bolism as ideology and religious groups as constituent members.

In the United States, religion often has been associated with political change movements, including abolitionism (McKivigan 1984), populism (Williams and Alexander 1994), labor (Billings 1990), feminism (Porterfield 1987), and contemporary direct action (Epstein 1991).

In Latin America, liberation theology has been the most celebrated marriage of religion and radicalism (e.g., Adriance 1994, Smith 1991). In other parts of the Third World, there has been extensive political involvement by religious "fundamentalisms" (Marty and Appleby 1993). While these movements are "conservative" in areas such as gender relations, many of them are militantly anti-imperialist, calling for the radical restructuring of society on explicitly anti-Western principles (Juergensmeyer 1993).

Many of these studies draw on the work of neo-Marxist Antonio Gramsci, who directly theorized the need for ideological work to combat dominant political hegemony, a need ably filled by religion (e.g., Billings 1990, Fulton 1987, Maduro 1982).

—*Rhys H. Williams*

REFERENCES

M. Adriance, "Base Communities and Rural Mobilization in Northern Brazil," *Sociology of Religion* 55(1994):163-178; D. B. Billings, "Religion as Opposition," *American Journal of Sociology* 96(1990):1-31; B. Epstein, *Political Protest and Cultural Revolution* (Berkeley: University of California Press, 1991); J. Fulton, "Religion and Politics in Gramsci," *Sociological Analysis* 48(1987):197-216; M. Juergensmeyer, *The New Cold War?* (Berkeley: University of California Press, 1993); O. Maduro, *Religion and Social Conflicts* (Maryknoll, N.Y.: Orbis, 1982); M. E. Marty and R. S. Appleby (eds.), *Fundamentalisms and the State* (Chicago: University of Chicago Press, 1993); J. R. McKivigan, *The War Against Proslavery Religion* (Ithaca, N.Y.: Cornell University Press, 1984); A. Porterfield, "Feminist Theology as a Revitalization Movement," *Sociological Analysis* 48(1987):234-244; C. Smith, *The Emergence of Liberation Theology* (Chicago: University of Chicago Press, 1991); R. H. Williams and S. M. Alexander, "Religious Rhetoric in American Populism," *Journal for the Scientific Study of Religion* 33(1994):1-15.

RAJNEESH MOVEMENT The Rajneesh Movement, currently titled the Osho Commune International, is a new religious movement that grew out of the daily discourses of the Jain-born Marxist critic of religion and former philosophy professor, Mohan Chandra Rajneesh (1931-1990).

Titled Bhagwan Shree Rajneesh (often "the Bhagwan") once he revealed his status as an enlightened master, Rajneesh established an ashram in Poona, India, that was a center in the mid-1970s for avant-garde therapies emerging from the human potential movement. Thousands of Westerners were initiated into "neo-sannyas," attracted by this master's original, eclectic philosophy that combined oriental mysticism with Western psychological models. In 1981, Rajneesh and his red-garbed disciples bought a ranch in Oregon and built the city of Rajneeshpuram based on utopian principles of communalism, free love, absolute birth control, work as "worship," ecological harmony, and women's rule. Rajneesh also became famous for his collection of 93 Rolls Royces, bestowed upon him as gifts.

In 1985, a series of criminal charges and scandals resulting from both external pressures and internal rivalries and corruption led to the disbanding of Rajneeshpuram, and Rajneesh returned to Poona, was renamed "Osho," and died in 1990. This international movement, numbering around 20,000 core disciples at its peak, persists on an informal level. Neo-sannyasins have renounced the commune, wearing red and the *mala* bearing Rajneesh's photograph, but they tend to live and work in co-ops; they tend to remain childless and to meditate and party together. The Poona ashram continues to attract visitors to its meditation-therapy workshops and to initiate new disciples.

Studies on Rajneesh/Rajneeshees have focused on the rise and fall of Rajneeshpuram and the city's conflicts with Oregon's secular authorities (Fitzgerald 1986, Gordon 1987, Carter 1990, Mann 1991), women's roles (Palmer 1994, Puttick 1995), appeal for and experiences of disciples (Palmer and Sharma 1993), and apostates' memoirs (Strelley 1987).

—*Susan J. Palmer*

REFERENCES

L. F. Carter, *Charisma and Control in Rajneeshpuram* (Cambridge: Cambridge University Press, 1990); F. Fitzgerald, *Cities on a Hill* (New York: Simon & Schuster, 1986); J. S. Gordon, *The Golden Guru* (Lexington, Mass.: Stephen Greene, 1987); W. E. Mann, *The Quest for Total Bliss* (Toronto: Canadian Scholars Press, 1991); S. J. Palmer, *Moon Sisters, Krishna Mothers, Rajneesh Lovers* (Syracuse, N.Y.: Syracuse University Press, 1994); S. J. Palmer and A. Sharma (eds.), *The Rajneesh Papers* (New Delhi: Motilal Banarsidass, 1993); K. Strelley, *The Ultimate Game* (New York: Harper, 1987).

RASTAFARIANISM   *see* Caribbean Religions

RATIONAL CHOICE THEORY   Adam Smith (1723-1790) is generally acknowledged as the forefather of the modern theory on utilitarian individualism or rational choice theory. In this connection, in particular, his essay *On the Wealth of Nations* (1776) is often cited.

The U.S. sociologists George C. Homans and Peter Blau are seen by many as the instigators of rational choice theory in the social sciences during the 1960s. However, Homans's insights are sometimes referred to by "orthodox" members of the rational choice community in sociology as being psychological. This, because he filled his model of man with learning theory. Peter Blau grew severely disappointed with rational choice theory and returned to structuralist theory of some sort. Nevertheless, since the 1970s, such a community can clearly be discerned, as rational choice theory has made great inroads into the social sciences both in North America and in western Europe. The community must be characterized as an oddly assorted group: It consists of economists (e.g., the Chicago economist and Nobel prize winner Gary Becker developed a "new household economic" reasoning, a name by which rational choice theory also has become known), psychologists, sociologists, game theorists, and students of collective action and of public choice.

When it appeared, Mancur Olson's *The Logic of Collective Action* (Harvard University Press 1965), nowadays hailed as one of the milestones of the approach, was not recognized by most sociologists as a major advance in theorizing. Psychologists, on the other hand, easily assessed it as a new and fruitful innovation—partly because of the great attention paid in their discipline to social dilemmas and partly because of the different image of man they used in their theories. Since 1989, the rational choice community boasts of a scientific journal of its own: *Rationality and Society*. And apart from being a medium to promote the application of rational choice theory, its editors state that they hope to restore the connections with the fields of sociology, moral philosophy, economics, political science, cognitive psychology, and game theory. The appearance of James S. Coleman's *The Foundations of Social Theory* (Harvard University Press 1990) must be seen as a major step in the further development of the rational choice paradigm for the social sciences: It gave the community its first handbook. Its contents form a demonstration of the application of rational choice theory to sociological problems and of how empirical macroproblems must theoretically be resolved at the micro level.

Rational choice theory is a (microeconomic) theory of human behavior, and rational choice adherents all subscribe to the Popperian dictum of methodological individualism: Scientific (macro)problems have to be solved at the level of individuals (acting purposively). The hard core consists of an empirical generalization—some would say axiom—stating that individuals choose the most efficient means as they perceive them for the attainment of their goals. Individuals, because of human nature, make a rational trade-off between costs and profits. Costs and rewards are both material and immaterial, and also are personal and situational.

These assumptions are elegantly represented by the *RREEMM* acronym:

These letters stand for: Resourceful: man can search for and find possibilities, he can learn and be inventive; Restricted: man is confronted with scarcity and must substitute (choose); Expecting: man attaches subjective probabilities to (future) events; Evaluating: man has ordered preferences and evaluates (future) events; Maximizing: man maximizes (expected) utility when choosing a course of action; Man. (Lindenberg 1985b:100)

The assumptions thus worded are not at all in contradiction to Becker's (1975) assumptions of "maximizing behavior, market equilibrium and stable preferences" but are more sociologically and less economistically worded. The *explanandum* is seen as the result of purposive actions of individuals with preferences, who are embedded within a sociocultural context that both structures and restricts their actions. To be precise, the purposive actions consist of a striving for physical well-being (e.g., good health, leisure) and social approval; the latter can be distinguished into status, positive affection (to be loved), and confirmation of behavior (to behave oneself in the eyes of relevant others).

The rational choice approach to the "scientific" study of religion has been stimulated by a great number of individual contributions of both a theoretical and an empirical nature but especially by the appearance of *A Theory of Religion* (Lang 1987) by Rodney Stark and William Sims Bainbridge. In the book, they provide an elegant deductive and comprehensive theory on "religious" people acting purposively. Stark and Bainbridge's efforts must be assessed as a major breakthrough in the sociology of religion in the fields of both theorizing and theory-guided empirical research. (Religious) people want rewards against low costs, and if rewards are scarce or not there at all, they will take compensators or IOUs for rewards.

The "validity" and usefulness of the axiom of a purposive rational actor who tries to avoid costs to maximize gains is a contested issue not only for those studying the sociology of religion but for many other sociologists as well. Apart from these, debated issues in the study of religion with regard to rational choice theory are the "market" theory of religion and "secularization" theory (Stark 1994). For decades, for example, it has been assumed that religious pluralism leads to a low degree of religious commitment. Both theoretically and empirically, however, market theorists have shown that the more enterprises that are operating on the (religious) market, the more they will specialize and compete with each other; similarly, the higher the competition among the churches, the higher the religious participation of the "buyers" will be. An empirical study in the United States in which this argument is falsified (Breault 1989) has not been accepted by the protagonists of the market theory. The reason is that it cannot be replicated by others because the data sets are destroyed. Yet serious doubts may be raised that if the market theory is applied under sociocultural conditions other than the United States (e.g., in western Europe), similar outcomes as in the United States would be reached (see Hak and Sanders 1996).

Recently, a critical assessment of the use of rational choice theory in the sociology of religion was made in a special issue of the *Journal for the Scientific Study of Religion* (1995). The outcome of the debate was that critics of rational choice theory were less convincing in their arguments than its defenders. Nevertheless, one of the criticisms seems to be sustained: In rational choice theory, room must be made for changing personal preferences to account for individual choices. Traditional microeconomic theory is based on the assumption that individuals' preferences are stable; the new model would suggest that preferences vary from person to person and time to time, and that these variations are shaped by the embeddedness of individuals within social contexts. While some rational choice theorists will probably begin to include preferences, other sociologically based theorists of the rational choice community will still argue that they can do without personal preferences because the sociocultural restrictions can explain individual choice.

See also Compensators, George C. Homans, Investments, Rodney Stark

—*Durk H. Hak*

REFERENCES

G. S. Becker, *The Economic Approach to Human Behavior* (Chicago: University of Chicago Press, 1976); K. D. Breault,

"New Evidence on Religious Pluralism, Urbanism, and Religious Participation," *American Sociological Review* 54 (1989):1048-1053; D. H. Hak and K. Sanders, "Kerkvorming en ontkerkelijking in de negentiende eeuw in Friesland," *Mens en Maatschappij* 96(1996):220-237; S. Lindenberg, "Rational Choice and Sociological Theory," *Zeitschrift für die gesamte Staatswissenschaft* 141(1985a):244-255; S. Lindenberg, "An Assessment of the New Political Economy," *Sociological Theory* 3(1985b):99-114; R. Stark, "Rational Choice Theories of Religion," *Agora* 2(1994):1.

RAUSCHENBUSH, WALTER   *see* Social Gospel

REDFIELD, ROBERT (1897-1958)   American anthropologist who studied and taught at the University of Chicago and pioneered the anthropological study of peasant communities and urbanization.

Best known for his extensive fieldwork among Mexican peasants, Redfield worked diligently to broaden the focus of anthropology from the exclusive study of tribal peoples to the comparative study of advanced civilizations, epitomized in his "folk-urban continuum." He made a distinction between the "moral order" of "folk society" of indigenous societies and peasant communities in complex societies, and the "technical order" of civilization. Whereas the moral order is based on human sentiments as to what is right, the technical order bases social relationships upon expediency and sometimes coercion. With respect to humanity's relationship with the supernatural, the former manifests itself in the "Little Tradition" of folk religion and the latter in the "Great Tradition" of world religions.

While these categorizations inspired—and continue to inspire—considerable debate among anthropologists of religion, they have had a profound influence on the study of religious change and processes of modernization.

—*Hans A. Baer and Stephen D. Glazier*

REFERENCES

R. Redfield, *The Primitive World and Its Transformations* (Ithaca, N.Y.: Cornell University Press, 1953); R. Redfield, *Peasant Society and Culture* (Chicago: University of Chicago Press, 1956).

REDUCTIONISM   Reductionism has been stigmatized by Gilbert Ryle as "nothing but-ery": Religion is "nothing but" longing for a lost parent; love is "nothing but" sex; sex is "nothing but" body chemistry; body chemistry is "nothing but" a dance of fundamental particles; and so on. The most notorious kind of reductionism, that of the thoughts of rational agents to chemical processes within their bodies, is in fact self-refuting; to take chemists seriously is to imply that they say and write what they do because they have good reasons for doing so, which is not compatible with complete physical determination.

—*Hugo Meynell*

REFERENCE

I. A. Idinopulos and E. A. Yonan (eds.), *Religion and Reductionism* (Leiden: Brill, 1994); C. Taylor, *The Explanation of Behavior* (New York: Humanities Press, 1964).

REFORMATION   A period in Western Christian history, usually dated as beginning in the early sixteenth century and extending to the mid-seventeenth, that yielded the theologies and organizations now known as *Protestant* but also altered the Western religious landscape and the character of Western Christianity to yield *Roman Catholicism* as that phrase is currently employed (i.e., strictly speaking, Christianity in western Europe should be referred to as *Western Christianity* prior to the Reformation).

Two questions precipitated the Reformation: (1) What is the relationship between church and state? (2) What assures life after death?

Central to the question of church-state relations was an ongoing dispute over control of land claimed by the Holy Roman Empire in the German nation. The papacy in the early sixteenth century struggled to maintain control. One form of mediation between political and religious uncertainty involved the sale of indulgences. In 1506, Pope Julius II announced an opportunity for penitents to purchase a new form of indulgence, the proceeds from which were earmarked to construct St. Peter's Basilica in Rome. This opportunity became the catalyst for a theological response that triggered social and political change.

On October 31, 1517, the eve of the feast of All Saints, Martin Luther, cleric and academic at the University of Wittenburg, posted his 95 theses on the door of Castle Church. By attacking the sale of indulgences, he not only threatened a source of revenue for the church, he also attacked the rationale for purchasing such writs in the first place. Salvation was granted, he declared, "by faith alone." He based his position, furthermore, on his reading of the Bible (particularly Paul's Epistle to the Romans) rather than any reference to a church authority.

The effect of this theological and political rejoinder to the status quo generated essentially three strands of allegiance. Lutherans and Anglicans adopted a theology of "grace" and maintained most ritual and liturgical traditions. Followers of John Calvin and Ulrich Zwingli minimized the importance of ritual and stressed scholarship and prudence. Finally, the Counterreformation restored Roman Catholicism in a reinvigorated form to much of western Europe by the end of the Thirty-Years War (1618-1648).

Guy E. Swanson in *Religion and Regime* (University of Michigan Press 1967) argues that the political and social persistence of these theological traditions depended on the nature of ruling regimes. Catholicism reemerged and persisted in "commensual" or centrist regimes (France, Ireland, Poland). Lutheran-Anglican traditions formed in "limited centralist states" (Denmark, England, Sweden). Calvinist-Zwinglian traditions emerged under "hetrarchic and balanced" governments (Bohemia, Scotland, Switzerland).

In addition to these territorial and political changes, the concurrent invention of the printing press and Luther's translation of the Bible into German created a cultural reformation. Social distance between clergy and laity, at least in Protestant circles, was drastically reduced as people learned to study scripture, articulate theology, and practice their faith in common worship.

—*Jerry Koch*

REFERENCE

H. J. Grimm, *The Reformation Era* (New York: Macmillan, 1954).

ues in Catholic education. Editor of *Sociological Analysis,* 1961-1968; President, American Catholic Sociological Society, 1970.

Reiss's presidential address to the ACSS was primarily concerned with a sociological analysis of the ACSS. Examining the 29 extant (of 32) presidential addresses prior to his presidency, Reiss diagnosed five trends that he thought manifested a "definite evolution in the thinking of the members of the Society particularly around the issue of sociology and Catholicism." The five trends were (1) assertions of a Catholic sociology; (2) explanations of the relationship of sociology to theology, social philosophy, or social action; (3) explanations of and/or exhortations to scientific sociology; (4) studies of an aspect of the sociology of Catholicism; (5) examinations of the character of the ACSS. He saw 1963 as the year in which annual meetings began to focus on the sociology of religion. (It was not, however, until the tenure of Reiss's successor as president—Ralph Lane, 1971—that the ACSS changed its name to the Association for the Sociology of Religion.) As Reiss saw it,

Not only is there no such thing as a Catholic sociology as claimed in phase one, but there is also no need for an organization of Catholic sociologists as implied in phases two and three. The focus of phase four on the sociology of Catholicism also does not provide adequate rationale, as this sociology has become an integral part of religion. (*Sociological Analysis* 31[1970]: 119 f)

He correctly predicted that phase five would promote the evolution of ACSS into a more specialized association focusing on the sociology of religion.

—*Loretta M. Morris*

REFORM JUDAISM *see* Judaism

REISS, PAUL J. (1930–) Having earned a B.S., magna cum laude, from Holy Cross College, an M.A. from Fordham University, and a Ph.D. from Harvard, Reiss taught at Marquette University (1957-1963) and then at Fordham (1963-1985). From 1969 until he left Fordham to become President of Saint Michael's College, Colchester, Vermont (from which he retired as President Emeritus in 1996), he worked in administration as Dean, Vice President, and Executive Vice President. His published works in sociology are primarily concerned with family, kinship, education, and val-

RELIGION *see* Definition of Religion

RELIGION This quarterly now subtitles itself *An International Journal*. When originally founded at the end of the 1960s, however, its subtitle was *Journal of Religion and the Religions*. Describing its provenance as the "Northern British Universities," it was part of the movement (particularly associated with Ninian Smart) to extend theology to religious studies, to expand such study from the ancient British universities to the new, and to include current experience as well as historical texts. Thus, although thoroughly international now, its editors and editorial board still maintain a notable input particularly from the University of Lancaster. (Publisher: Academic Press, 24-28 Oval Road, London NW1 7DX.)

—*Edward Bailey*

RELIGIOSITY   In social scientific use, a generic term for religious commitment ("religiousness") as potentially measurable along more than a single dimension.

Two related, but separable, problems for the study of religion concern definition. One is that of the subject matter itself—that is, the "definition-of-religion" problematic. The other is to determine what it "means" to describe someone as "religious." The latter manifests itself particularly in questions of measurement.

At least from the work of Joseph Fichter (e.g., 1954) forward, there has been general agreement among social scientists that religious involvement and/or commitment varies among people who may nevertheless denominate themselves identically, hence that a simple denominational measure (e.g., "Baptist," "Catholic," "Jew") is extremely weak as an indicator of involvement/commitment. In fact, a denominational measure actually may obfuscate the effect of religious involvement/commitment upon other aspects of a person's life-world. (For example, the position of a highly involved Baptist with regard to premarital sexual relations actually may be more like that of a highly involved Catholic than a minimally involved Baptist; hence to inquire about denominational affiliation on the one hand and relate it to premarital sex on the other may lead to mistaken conclusions about the relationship between religiosity and sexuality.)

The most extensive elaboration of the religiosity problematic occurred under the leadership of Charles Glock (see, esp., Glock and Stark 1965: chap. 2), although the beginnings of this approach should probably be traced to Yoshio Fukuyama (1961). Glock and his colleagues developed and tested what became known as the "5-D" approach to religiosity. This was a *multidimensional* approach to religious involvement/commitment encompassing five areas: (1) *ritual* activities (including, but not only, "church" attendance); (2) *ideology* or adherence to the principal beliefs of the religion; (3) *experience* or the "feeling" aspect of religion; (4) the *intellectual* side of religion, which involved religious "knowledge" and was frequently measured by such activities as reading religious publications (including, but not only, sacred texts); (5) the *consequential* dimension, which attempted to measure the "effect" of an individual's religion in its other

dimensions upon his or her "life" (see Faulkner and DeJong 1966). According to the 5-D thesis, these five dimensions could be related, but they also could vary at least semi-independently. (For example, a person might believe [ideological dimension] the core doctrines of the Baptist faith but not attend church [ritual] very often—or vice versa. A person might believe [ideology] the Bible to be "inerrant" but not actually ever read the Bible [intellectual]—or vice versa.)

The dimensions-of-religiosity approach fit particularly well with a *functionalist* view of religion, inasmuch as it suggested that religion fulfills different functional "needs" for different people; this also correlated with a *deprivation* theory of religion, which suggested that people "turned" to the "supernatural" comforts and/or challenges of religion to meet needs that they did not find being adequately met in the natural realm. Critics, on the other hand, noted a strongly American Protestant bias. For example, Roman Catholic ideology stresses Mass attendance; to be a Jew is not to "believe" anything in the ideological sense but to be observant of the law; and so on. A death blow of sorts was dealt to the *multi*dimensionality thesis in an article by Richard Clayton, "5-D or 1?" (1971), where he used a factor analytic approach to demonstrate that a belief factor underlies all the others; this approach to belief, however, broadens the concept to include beliefs about what Glock would later (1988) term "the ways the world works" rather than simply religious dogma itself. No theory yet accounts for how individuals develop different belief systems about the ways the world works, some of which appear to "demand" supernatural referents, while others do not—nor why some supernaturalistic belief systems demand public expression ("going to church"), while others do not.

Currently, social scientists are in general agreement that religious commitment varies across all religions, and that religious commitment may manifest itself in different ways within the same religious tradition. Good research attempts to "triangulate" belief, practice, and self-perception in determining the relative effect of "religiosity" on behavioral and attitudinal measures.

See also Commitment

—*William H. Swatos, Jr.*

REFERENCES

R. R. Clayton, "5-D or 1?" *Journal for the Scientific Study of Religion* 10(1971):37-40; G. Davie, "Believing Without Belonging," *Social Compass* 37(1990):455-469; J. Faulkner and G. DeJong, "Religiosity in 5-D," *Social Forces* 45(1966): 246-255; J. H. Fichter, *Social Relations in the Urban Parish* (Chicago: University of Chicago Press, 1954); Y. Fukuyama, "The Major Dimensions of Church Membership," *Review of*

Religious Research 2(1961):154-161; C. Y. Glock, "The Ways the World Works," *Sociological Analysis* 49(1988):93-103; C. Y. Glock and R. Stark, *Religion and Society in Tension* (Chicago: Rand McNally, 1965); A. J. Weigert and D. L. Thomas, "Religiosity in 5-D," *Social Forces* 48(1969):260-263.

RELIGIOUS EDUCATION

RELIGIOUS EDUCATION   The close association of religion with education can be seen in the Swahili word *dini*. Unfamiliar with either religion or education as separate activities, before the arrival of Moslem traders and Christian missionaries in the second half of the nineteenth century, the Swahili word for these "religions (of the Book)" also meant "reading." Certainly, the ability to read sacred literature has commonly accompanied the training of a qualified workforce in motivating the spread of modern education.

The separate institutionalization of education, following that of religion, however, makes a conflict inevitable, especially in religious education. For both religion and education are forms of socialization on the one hand, while, on the other hand, each at times wishes to question, prophetlike, the values of society. When, in addition, society is itself unsure of its own values, and the religious and educational systems are differentiated and yet interface, conflict is likely to be endemic. To convert the constitutional separation of church and state into a chimeric dichotomy between religion and society fails even to shelve, let alone solve, the issues involved.

The Home and Church   The bulk of the world's religious education has been communicated through what came to be institutionalized in the apprenticeship system. Children learned about life (and Life) as they learned about the world of work or the family: through watching older relations (parents, grandparents, siblings, and other family members), through listening to their philosophies of life, and through consideration of their and their peers' experience against this background. Although difficult to operationalize, the regular lip service that is paid to the continuing importance of education, and not least to religious education, in these contexts and by these means, is paid with sincerity. The Jesuit maxim, "Give us a child until [s]he's seven, and [s]he's ours forever," has been quoted until it is a cliché, but that is because experience seems to suggest it is true.

Thereafter, as people move out of the "small-scale society" of the nuclear family, into the "historical" type of society, in which individual names ("John," "Mary") replace attitudinal forms of address ("Dear," "You!"), religious education likewise begins to take on specialized forms. The Christian catechumenate, originally intended for adult inquirers, has long been used primarily as a follow-up for children who have been baptized in infancy. However, the recent increase in adult inquirers, whether baptized in infancy or not, has led to the development of forms appropriate for adult catechumens, again.

Non-Roman parallels to the catechumenate have tended to prepare the baptized for confirmation. As a moment both of personal decision and of personal reception of what was done in infancy, such confirmation preparation has been seen as facilitating both an informed decision, to follow Christ, and a proper appreciation of the sacraments (Baptism and Communion) instituted by him.

The criteria of suitability for confirmation are a perennial problem. The Roman Catholic and Orthodox Churches emphasize the divine blessing bestowed in the sacraments, and the human response subsequently. The "Reformed Churches" generally emphasize the human choice required to receive the sacraments, and the blessings received by faith afterward. Lutherans, Baptists, Methodists, Pentecostalists, and others have variously judged readiness for confirmation by age, or willingness to confess Jesus as Lord, or a personal testimony to grace, or particular gifts of the Spirit. It seems unlikely, however, that any foolproof criterion can be achieved in religion any more than in the rest of life.

Confirmation (and the reception of Communion) is generally administered at a later age in the reformed churches than in the Roman Catholic Church, where First Communion is often at 7 years of age. The gap between the family, as the cradle of religious education, and the church, at the time of confirmation, is often bridged therefore by Sunday school. Robert Raikes of Gloucester is usually credited with its initiation, but that is largely because the friendly editor of the local newspaper brought his work to public attention. As usual, with new and successful innovations whose "time has come," Sunday schools had numerous independent points of simultaneous origin.

Sunday and Weekday Schools   Before the development of nationwide schools, in the second half of the nineteenth century, Sunday schools were held on Sunday, not simply because they were religious but because that was the only day when the children were free from paid work. Similarly, although the motivation was religious, the activities were educational in a broader sense. They were concerned with literacy and numeracy and social education as well as with the Bible or the church or morality.

Even after the development of church, national, and board schools in Britain, the number of children attending Sunday school continued to rise, in keeping with the population, until the beginning of the twentieth century. Many Nonconformist churches also held Sunday schools for adults, as did (and do) churches in North America. Thus, although their enrollment has been falling throughout the present century (first, relative to the increasing population, but then absolutely), the numbers involved, as the century draws to a close, are still significant. Indeed, it may be suggested that, if evangelicalism and industry lie at the heart of nineteenth-century British society, so the "public" (independent) schools and Sunday schools lay at the heart of "Victorian" culture in Britain from roughly 1850 to 1950.

Just as Sunday schools originally taught technical skills such as reading and writing, so day schools in Britain held a daily assembly and taught what has been successively called Scripture, Religious Instruction, or Religious Education. Criticized by the clergy for their lack of contact with a worshiping community, criticized by the teachers for pretending that they and the pupils both possessed a knowledge and a commitment that they lacked, and criticized by the "literati" for attempting indoctrination (which was as hypothetical as it was impossible)—the assembly and lessons were, nevertheless, what most parents wanted. For, with the exception of a few Barthian clergy or agnostic teachers or humanist "literati," the British did not distinguish between the moral and the religious, or between religious education and worship. In the sphere of religion, they preferred the unitary worldview of small-scale living to the differentiated specialisms of historical (let alone, mass) society. This view was common across most of Europe and likewise, at the local level, in much of North America.

Christian "Formation"   Religious education does not, however, concern only the teaching of the faith, or education more generally, for the benefit of adult inquirers or of children in church or school. It also embraces the "further education" of those who identify themselves as Christians, the formation of candidates for the various roles (full-time or part-time) within the tradition, and (especially during this last half-century of diminishing participation in worship) assisting with programs of religious studies for students of all ages, backgrounds, and motives. Just as such activities are not confined to any one global region, neither are they confined to any one global religion. Thus, to take a single, small segment of the total range of religious-education activity, the number of "Bible schools" around the world is nothing less than "legion," as the Rockefeller Foundation discovered in the 1960s.

Education, old style or new style, has indeed long been something of a self-authenticating imperative or divinity for the religious. It has been easily justified in terms of loving God with the mind, with the Platonic absolute of truth. In recent years, however, religious, as other, education has been sufficiently instrumentalized to become the subject of census and research. This cannot produce "perfect" (i.e., mechanistic, magical) programs or methods, but it is leading to a knowledge and wisdom that can illumine the traditional tasks of spiritual discrimination (and spiritual discernment).

See also Christian School Movement, Faith Development

—*Edward I. Bailey*

REFERENCES

J. Fowler, *Stages of Faith* (San Francisco: Harper, 1981); R. Goldman, *Religious Thinking from Childhood to Adolescence* (London: Routledge, 1964); M. Grimmitt, *Religious Education and Human Development* (Great Wavering, U.K.: McCrimmon, 1987); H. Loukes, *New Ground in Christian Education* (London: SCM, 1965); N. Smart, *Secular Education and the Logic of Religion* (London: Faber, 1968).

RELIGIOUS EVOLUTION   *see* Evolution of Religion

RELIGIOUS RESEARCH ASSOCIATION (RRA)   Formally organized as the Religious Research Fellowship on June 21, 1951, the group traces its heritage to the work of H. Paul Douglass, originally under the auspices of the Institute of Social and Religious Research in association with the Federal Council of Churches, extending back to the 1920s.

The earliest members were Protestant denominational researchers and/or seminary faculty. The decision to organize formally in 1951, however, was taken to create a clear institutional separation between these persons, who had been meeting under various styles, and the Central Department of Research and Survey of the National Council of Churches, which came to supplant the Federal Council at that time. Catholic and Jewish researchers, as well as nonaffiliated academics, came into membership by the mid-1950s. Since the early 1970s, the RRA has met annually with the Society for the Scientific Study of Religion; a major feature of these meetings has been the RRA-sponsored H. Paul Douglass lecture, which began in the early 1960s. Since 1959, the RRA has published the *Review of Religious Research,* which circulates to approximately 500 individual members and 500 libraries. The RRA also supports original applied and basic research through the Constant H. Jacquet awards.

The current goals of the RRA are (1) to increase understanding of the function of religion in persons and society through application of social scientific and other scholarly methods; (2) to promote the circulation, interpretation, and use of the findings of religious research among religious bodies and other interested groups; (3) to cooperate with other professional societies, groups, and individuals interested in the study of religion; and (4) to aid in the professional development of religious researchers. As American denominations have generally reduced the size or eliminated "in-house" staffs, an increasing proportion of RRA members are drawn from the academic social scientists of religion; however, the applied perspective of the founders along with strong respect for faith traditions remain hallmarks of the RRA.

—*William H. Swatos, Jr.*

RELIGIOUS STUDIES Defined most straightforwardly, the term refers to a subject matter. By this definition, *religious studies* is confined to no specific discipline and encompasses the contributions of psychologists, sociologists, anthropologists, economists, literary critics, art historians, and philosophers. *Religious studies* so defined is an area studies. It is the subject area of a library card catalog.

When religious studies is defined this broadly, the distinctive contribution of members of departments of religious studies—scholars of religion—is limited. Their task is merely to amass and classify data about religions and to leave to psychologists, sociologists, and others the analysis of the data. Just as the role of a subject librarian is to assemble the books for others to read, so here the role of scholars of religion is to assemble the data for others to analyze. A library is judged by how many books it has collected on a subject, not by what the subject librarian thinks of the subject. The categorization of books as "religious" is the responsibility of the subject librarian, but even the chief subject librarian of the Library of Congress ordinarily defers to the author. A book by a psychologist purportedly ana-

lyzing religion psychologically would get categorized under religion, even if also cross-catalogued under psychology.

A second, slightly bolder way of defining *religious studies* is to entrust scholars of religion with not merely gathering data but also presenting them from the worshiper's point of view. Scholars of religion here record the actor's point of view, but they do not assess it. They present the worshiper's view of the origin, function, and meaning of religion, but they leave to psychologists, sociologists, and others the determination of the "actual" origin, function, and even meaning of religion.

The third, far bolder way of defining *religious studies* is to grant it the status of a discipline and not merely a subject matter. Defined this way, *religious studies* is the distinctive prerogative of scholars of religion. To study religion is now to study a distinctively, or "irreducibly," religious subject. Some scholars of religion bar others from studying religion on the grounds that what others study is by definition psychology or sociology *rather than* religion. Most scholars of religion allow others to participate in the study of religion, but they still demarcate one aspect of the subject as irreducibly religious. Psychologists and sociologists, it is granted, decipher the psychological and sociological aspects of religion, but there remains an irreducibly religious aspect. Scholars of religion who insist on an irreducibly religious aspect of religion are sometimes called "religionists."

What *is* this irreducibly religious aspect of religion? Most often, it is claimed to be the *object* of religious worship: *god, divinity,* or, to use the preferred term, the *sacred.* Religious studies alone, argue religionists, can grasp the sacred, precisely because the sacred is unlike anything else. To study the sacred is to study something that by nature is not psychological, sociological, or otherwise nonreligious.

The other aspect that is claimed to be distinctively religious is the *origin and function* of religion. Religionists assert that persons become and remain religious to satisfy an irreducibly religious need. To be irreducibly religious, that need cannot be merely one satisfied by religion, as might be said of the need for food, health, victory in battle, explanation of the world, or purpose in life. The need must itself be irreducibly religious. It is the need to *experience the sacred.* Many religionists deem this need universal, even if it goes unfulfilled in some persons. The function of religion is exactly to provide opportunities for experiencing the sacred.

Criticisms Criticisms of religious studies defined in any of these ways abound. As commendable as the ecumenism of the definition of religious studies as a subject area is, religious studies is thereby demoted to a mere repository of data for full-fledged disciplines to scrutinize. Taking this consequence as a criticism is, of course, to beg the question about the real nature of religious studies. At the same time, religious studies defined meekly as a mere subject area does not possess even the limited autonomy of other area studies. For religious studies seen in this way harbors only a provisional subject matter, one awaiting translation into the terms of whichever disciplines turn to it. For example, the psychology of religion translates religious phenomena into psychological ones. Worshipers may think that they are praying to their god, but from a Freudian point of view, they are praying to their fathers. The subject matter becomes psychology rather than religion. Books currently catalogued under "religion" get recatalogued under "psychology."

Religious studies credited with at least presenting the worshiper's point of view is one step beyond religious studies restricted to a mere subject area, but here too religious studies constitutes less than a discipline and is permitted to take no stand on the actual origin, function, and meaning of religion. Religious studies defined this way does not presume to say why human beings are in fact religious, only why they think they are.

Religious studies defined as an outright discipline has all the virtues that religious studies defined as anything less lacks. It is entitled to make its own claims about the origin, function, and meaning of religion. It is on par with other disciplines that do the same. The question here, however, is whether religious studies can justify itself as an independent discipline. Too often the justification offered for an irreducibly religious approach to religion is simply an appeal to the worshiper's point of view. But other disciplines do not deny the worshiper's point of view. Rather, they seek to account for it. For psychologists, sociologists, and others, the analysis of religion *begins* with the worshiper's point of view but does not *end* there. For religionists to invoke the worshiper's point of view against psychologists, sociologists, and others—as if religionists alone take that point of view into account—is to invoke a straw man (see Segal 1989:1-36, 1992:35-49).

Origin of the Discipline of Religious Studies: Müller and Otto

The chief figure in the establishment of religious studies as a discipline and not merely a subject matter was the Indologist Friedrich Max Müller. According to Müller, everyone is religious: "Wherever there is human life, there is religion" (1910:7). Religion originates in the experience of the sacred, which he calls the "Infinite." Because the experience of the Infinite is spontaneous, Müller postulates no religious need. Human beings experience the Infinite not directly but through nature—most of all through celestial phenomena, especially the sun:

> What position the sun must have occupied in the thoughts of the early dwellers on earth, we shall never be able to fully understand. Not even the most recent scientific discoveries described in Tyndall's genuine eloquence, which teach us how we live, and move, and have our being in the sun, how we burn it, how we breathe it, how we feed on it—give us any idea of what this source of light and life . . . was to the awakening consciousness of mankind. (1910:200)

The object of worship is not, however, the sun itself but the Infinite, which transcends the natural world through which it manifests itself. The Infinite is experienced through the senses but lies beyond the senses.

This distinctive subject matter requires a distinctive discipline to study it. Hence the autonomy of religious studies: It alone studies the true object of worship, which is beyond the ken of other disciplines. Books on religion currently cross-listed under "psychology" and other disciplines are recatalogued under "religion" exclusively.

The theologian Rudolf Otto (1923) went even further than Müller in isolating the sacred, which Otto prefers to call the "Holy." For Müller, the sacred, while distinct from the profane, is manifested through it and is therefore akin to it. For Otto, the sacred is the opposite of the profane and must be experienced directly. While Otto's concern is not disciplinary, his emphasis on the radical other-ness of the sacred only reinforced the call for a separate discipline to comprehend it.

Wach and Eliade

Whereas Müller wanted to encompass all of religious studies in a single "science of religion," his successors more often have sought to extricate individual strands within it. The strands most commonly singled out have been the phenomenology of religion, which is equivalent to comparative religion, and the history of religions, which focuses on individual religions. Some scholars have pitted phenomenology against history (see van der Leeuw 1963: 686); others have sought to reconcile the two (see Pettazzoni 1954:215-219, Bleeker 1963:1-15).

It was above all the historian Joachim Wach (1944, 1958, 1968, 1989a, 1989b) who strove to establish the autonomy of the history of religions. According to

Wach, the history of religions leaves to theology and philosophy the determination of both the essence and the truth of religion, and leaves to the social sciences the determination of the origin and function of religion. The distinctive issue left for the history of religions is for Wach the "meaning" of religion, or its significance for the worshipers themselves:

> No one will deny that bracketing [the question of truth] makes it possible to study the philosophical systems of all peoples and times and to value them as expressions of world views. . . . Those who study the arts are familiar with this procedure. Their discipline attempts to understand a work of art by attempting to draw out its "meaning"; it does not raise the question of "truth." (1989a:25)

Far more enamored of sociology than of psychology, Wach grants that sociology can account for both the origin and the function of religion: "A wide field is open for the sociologist of religion in the examination of the sociological roots and functions of myths, doctrines and dogmas, of cultures and association in general and in particular (hic et nunc)." Sociology can even account for the particular form a religion takes: "To what extent are the different types of the expression of religious experience in different societies and cultures socially conditioned (technological, moral, cultural level)?" (1989b:100).

Yet Wach is still prepared to pronounce the essence of religion irreducibly religious: "A religious manifestation must be understood as a religious manifestation" (1989a:162). The heart of religion is, as for Müller and Otto, the experience of the sacred. Sociology can account for the *form* religion takes, but it can never grasp the common pristine experience expressed through that form: "There can be no doubt that it is characteristic of religious experience to transcend cultural conditions" (1989b:135). The origin and intended function of religion turn out to be irreducibly religious, and even sociology can tackle only the *unintended* functions of religion: "We have tried to show that social integration is not the 'aim' or 'purpose' of religion. Religion is sound and true to its nature only as long as it has no aim or purpose except the worship of God" (1944:381). Wach, like Müller, assumes religion to be both universal and spontaneous, and thereby more easily seen as self-explanatory.

Following Wach, the historian of religions Mircea Eliade (1958, 1959, 1968a, 1968b, 1969) strove to distinguish the history of religions from at once theology and the social sciences. Like Wach, Eliade declares religion universal, deems the core of religion the expe-

rience of the sacred, and castigates the reduction of religion to something nonreligious. Acknowledging that the social sciences can identify the historical context of religion, he seems to be granting them the determination of the origin and function of religion. But, in fact, he confines them to only the *preconditions* of religion. The direct origin and function of religion remain, as for Wach, irreducibly religious:

> Few religious phenomena are more directly and more obviously connected with sociopolitical circumstances than the modern messianic and millenarian movements among colonial peoples (cargo-cults, etc.). Yet identifying and analyzing the conditions that prepared and made possible such messianic movements form only a part of the work of the historian of religions. For these movements are equally creations of the human spirit, in the sense that they have become what they are—*religious movements,* and not merely gestures of protest and revolt—through a creative act of the spirit. (1969:6)

As for Wach, so for Eliade, the social sciences can, moreover, say nothing of the meaning of religion: "Like it or not, the scholar has not finished his work when he has reconstructed the history of a religious form or brought out its sociological, economic, or political contexts. In addition, he must understand its meaning" (1969:2). Unlike Wach, Eliade accords no special place to sociology or to any other social science. The egalitarian Eliade abhors all social sciences equally.

Whereas Müller and Otto stress the spontaneous encounter with the sacred, Eliade emphasizes the actual need for the sacred and sees religion as the fulfillment of that need. Myths and rituals are the prime ways in which religion provides contact with the sacred. Myths return one to the time when the sacred was near. Rituals open one up to the continuing presence of the sacred. Because Eliade postulates a panhuman need for the sacred, he is eager to show how self-professed atheists and agnostics are really religious at heart: "The majority of the 'irreligious' still behave religiously, even though they are not aware of the fact. . . . [T]he modern man who feels and claims that he is nonreligious still retains a large stock of camouflaged myths and degenerated rituals" (1968b:204 f). Venturing far beyond his predecessors, Eliade seeks to show that all humans are actually, not merely potentially, religious. He gleefully uncovers the religious dimension in seemingly profane activities such as reading novels, seeing movies, celebrating holidays, and moving house. Religious studies thus is no longer confined to explicit cases of religion but now encroaches on secular domains and disciplines. The disciplinary tables have turned. (On the history of religious studies, see Jastrow 1901, Jordan 1905, Kita- gawa 1985, Preus 1987, Rudolph 1985, Sharpe 1986.)

The legacy of the tradition from Müller to Eliade has been the isolation of the discipline of religious studies from other disciplines, which are seen as threatening to the autonomy of religious studies. While the field of religious studies is indisputably ever more and more open to interdisciplinary approaches, the fear of a hostile takeover by, above all, the social sciences remains. It is not coincidental that in the United States the social scientific study of religion occupies a minor place in the American Academy of Religion, the umbrella organization for scholars of religious studies, and is instead carried out by separate organizations such as the Society for the Scientific Study of Religion, the Association for the Sociology of Religion, and the Religious Research Association.

—*Robert A. Segal*

REFERENCES

C. J. Bleeker, *The Sacred Bridge* (Leiden: Brill, 1963); M. Eliade *Patterns in Comparative Religion* (Cleveland, Ohio: Meridian, 1958); M. Eliade, *Cosmos and History* (New York: Harper, 1959); M. Eliade, *Myth and Reality* (New York: Harper, 1968a); M. Eliade, *The Sacred and the Profane* (New York: Harvest, 1968b); M. Eliade, *The Quest* (Chicago: University of Chicago Press, 1969); M. Jastrow, Jr., *The Study of Religion* (London: Scott, 1901); L. H. Jordan, *Comparative Religion* (Edinburgh: Clark, 1905); J. M. Kitagawa (ed.), *The History of Religions* (New York: Macmillan, 1985); G. van der Leeuw, *Religion in Essence and Manifestation* (New York: Harper, 1963 [1933]); F. E. Manuel, *The Eighteenth Century Confronts the Gods* (Cambridge: Harvard University Press, 1959); F. M. Müller, *Chips from a German Workshop* (Oxford: Oxford University Press, 1867-1875); F. M. Müller, *Lectures on the Origin and Growth of Religion* (New York: Scribner, 1910); R. Otto, *The Idea of the Holy* (London: Oxford University Press, 1923); R. Pettazzoni, *Essays on the History of Religions* (Leiden: Brill, 1954); J. S. Preus, *Explaining Religion* (New Haven, Conn.: Yale University Press, 1987); K. Rudolph, *Historical Fundamentals and the Study of Religions* (New York: Macmillan, 1985); W. Schmidt, *The Origin and Growth of Religion* (London: Methuen, 1931); R. A. Segal, *Religion and the Social Sciences* (Atlanta: Scholars Press, 1989); R. A. Segal, *Explaining and Interpreting Religion* (New York: Lang, 1992); E. J. Sharpe, *Comparative Religion,* 2nd ed. (LaSalle, Ill.: Open Court, 1986); J. Wach, *Sociology of Religion* (Chicago: University of Chicago Press, 1944); J. Wach, *The Comparative Study of Religions* (New York: Columbia University Press, 1958); J. Wach, *Understanding and Believing* (New York: Harper, 1968); J. Wach, *Introduction to the History of Religions* (New York: Macmillan, 1989a); J. Wach, *Essays in the History of Religions* (New York: Macmillan, 1989b).

RESEARCH COMMITTEE 22   With the title "Sociology of Religion," this is one of the major networks linking scholars in this field at the international level. It was among the earliest research committees established in the context of the International Sociological Association, which was founded at a meeting held in Oslo, September 5-11, 1949.

Over the years, RC22 has organized various academic-scientific activities; these also have kept pace with the association's statutory development, which saw significant modifications in the quadrennia from 1970 to the present. It has organized various thematic sessions during World Congresses of Sociology (with a maximum of 16 at Bielefeld in 1994). The committee also organizes its own international conferences; among others should be noted the conference in Sofia, Bulgaria, August 2-7, 1992, on the subject "Nation-Building: Yesterday, Today, and Tomorrow," and in Rome, July 12-16, 1993, on the theme "Religions sans frontières? Present and Future Trends of Migration, Culture, and Communication."

The committee has had its own annual bulletin since 1986, *Sociology of Religion: Newsletter of I.S.A. Research Committee 22.* It contains information on forthcoming conferences, grants and awards, research funding, new publications, reports of meetings and activities, and other news and announcements. Editors have been Roberto Cipriani (1986-1990) and Raymond Lemieux (1990-1994). The editor for the period 1994-1998 is William E. Biernatzki.

The committee was established with the intent of opening a broader range of opportunities for participation in activities in the field of the sociology of religion. To this end, the committee undertakes measures to develop personal and institutional contacts, to encourage the international dissemination and exchange of information, and to promote international, cross-cultural research. The board of RC22 consists of a president, three vice-presidents, a secretary-treasurer, ten members, and three *ex officio* members (representatives of the Association for the Sociology of Religion, the International Society for the Sociology of Religion, and the Society for the Scientific Study of Religion). Every four years, at least half the board must be renewed. To enhance equitable representation of the various regions of the world, members of the board are elected from different continental areas: Africa, Asia, Australia, Europe, Latin America, North America. The committee convenes every four years, during the World Congress of Sociology.

The most recent presidents of the Committee are Johannis (Hans) Mol (1974-1978), originally from the Netherlands; Karel Dobbelaere (1978-1982), from Belgium; James A. Beckford (1982-1986), from Great Britain; Nikos Kokosalakis (1986-1990), originally from Greece; Roberto Cipriani (1990-1994), from Italy; Raymond Lemieux (1994-1998), from Canada.

—*Roberto Cipriani*

REFERENCE

R. Cipriani, *Religions sans frontières?* (Rome: Presidenza del Consiglio dei Ministri, 1994).

RESEARCH METHODS The principal basis for advancing knowledge in the social scientific study of religion is observation of the empirical world. How to conduct these observations in ways that will give good information is the task of the methodologist. The research methodologist is concerned not so much with whether to look at the causes or the consequences of religious actions, characteristics, and orientations but with *how* to look at them. Within the social sciences, various techniques have been developed to study virtually any aspect of empirical reality—in and out of the domain of religion. These techniques and how to employ them are the heart of research methods.

The social scientific study of religion began in France during a time when the principles of natural science were being applied wholesale to the study of society. The guiding philosophy of this period was *positivism,* a system of thought founded by Auguste Comte (1798-1857), which held that societies demonstrate regularities just the way that organisms do and that these regularities can be understood through empirical study. A number of assumptions operated behind the scenes in the creation of positivistic science. Among these are three important ones: a belief in the fundamental reality of being, the possibility of knowing the empirical world at all, and the separateness of the knower from that which is to be known. Each of these assumptions has been assailed by philosophers offering views of ontology, epistemology, and objectivity that differ from the views of positivists such as Comte.

Empirical Inquiry in the Social Scientific Study of Religion The application of scientific principles derived from these assumptions was assumed to be the best way to understand reality. In fact, this model became so well entrenched in social science that it was considered by many the only way to do science. Thus the method of positivism has been construed as *the* scientific method; the assumptions behind the method, the guiding principles for the conduct of empirical research.

This scientific method includes a series of steps that will be familiar to any student of physical or social science: theoretical understanding of the object or process under study, development of hypotheses that guide one's study, direct observation of relevant aspects of the world, and derivation of empirical generalizations that lead to the refinement of theory. Science operates through the logical processes of deduction and induction to generate our understanding of the world and how it works (Wallace 1971). It is clear to sociologists today, however, in ways that were not clear to Auguste Comte, that there is no single or unitary scientific method. The Nobel prize winning physicist P. W. Bridgman denied the very existence of a special *scientific* method of inquiry. Philosopher Paul Feyerabend (1993:14) put it this way: "The only principle that does not inhibit progress is: *anything goes.*"

Positivistic social science, which once dominated the conduct of inquiry in the sociology of religion, now faces a number of competing paradigms, based upon competing assumptions. Among the critics of positivism are a number of alternative schools of thought. These include *postpositivism, critical theory,* and *constructivism* (Guba 1990). These alternative paradigms make different assumptions about the unity of science, about the universality of human experience, about the nature of knowledge, about the possibility and even the desirability of so-called objectivity (see Weber 1949). Consequently, they dictate alternative principles for the conduct of inquiry.

The thing that unites all these approaches, however—including traditional positivism—is a common desire to understand the social world. Understanding was and remains the major reason for doing research in the first place; but irrespective of how one proceeds in the conduct of inquiry, there are certain dilemmas that must be faced, certain questions that must be answered. It is the business of the research methodologist to help answer these questions.

The methodologist Joel Smith (1991) helps to cut through the competing assumptions offered by these and other schools of thought. He observes that regardless of which philosophical assumptions one adopts, the researcher's experience of the empirical world will always be partial, always be influenced to a great extent by whatever conceptions the researcher adopts. This fact suggests a series of dilemmas that must be resolved for research to go forward. Smith expresses his insight as a series of questions. Building upon his approach, I suggest addressing the following questions as the main tasks of methodology:

1. What do you want to know?
2. Why do you want to know it?
3. What will you observe so as to know it?
4. Which specific objects will you observe?
5. How many objects will you observe?
6. Within what time frame will you observe them?
7. How will the objects be observed?
8. How will the answers be decided?
9. What should you do?
10. To whom/what are you accountable?

These questions provide a useful framework for understanding the challenge before empirical researchers in all fields—including the social scientific study of religion.

What Do You Want to Know? Conceptualization

The first challenge for any researcher is to be clear about the focus of the study: to know what the research is to investigate. In the absence of an articulate research question, it is virtually impossible to conduct useful empirical inquiry. It is also important to realize that the ideas in the mind of the researcher are essentially conceptual. It is in the researcher's mind, first of all, that a coherent picture of the world develops. This means that, in a very real sense, what one wants to study does not exist apart from the mind of the researcher. It is in the researcher's mind that order emerges and systematic empirical inquiry becomes possible. Jacob Bronowski, the noted mathematician and philosopher of science, made the following observation about order in the empirical world:

> Order does not display itself of itself; if it can be said to be there at all, it is not there for the mere looking. There is no way of pointing a finger or a camera at it; order must be discovered and, in a deep sense, it must be created. What we see, as we see it, is mere disorder. (1956:13 f)

The order that the researcher sees in the world is a product of an ordering of reality that begins with the development of concepts. Concepts are mental devices for ordering the world. Let us take religiosity as an example.

The question of why it is that some people are more religious than others has fascinated sociologists since the time of Émile Durkheim (1858-1917). It has been recognized for some time that there are different dimensions of religiosity. Charles Glock and Rodney Stark (1965) identified five dimensions: the experiential, ideological, ritualistic, intellectual, and consequential. Are there really five dimensions? Could religiosity not be seen to have more or fewer dimensions? Durkheim thought there were two. Such questions are essentially conceptual. The development of concepts and the identification of the dimensions that constitute them is a fundamental activity of the research process.

Why Do You Want to Know It? The Goals of Research

A second question is closely related to this first one. The researcher must be clear about why she or he is interested in the research question. This is another way of asking what the goals of the research are. Generally speaking, one conducts empirical research for one or more of three reasons: *to explain* a possibly causal relationship, *to describe* something that is of interest, or *to explore* possible relationships among variables. Choice about one's reasons for conducting research will facilitate responses to other questions one must ask as well, such as how to observe and how to analyze data.

In their study of racial differences in religiosity, Jacobson et al. (1990) sought *to explain* differences in the kinds of piety that characterize black and white Americans. Data for their study were derived from questionnaires administered to several hundred respondents sampled at two different points in time from the population of a well-known midwestern city. Their conclusion that the differences observed "may stem from basic differences in the functions that religion serves in the two communities" was based on the application of powerful statistical techniques (factor analysis and linear structural relationships analysis) to the quantitative data they examined. Their form of data collection, research design, sample, and analytical techniques all were determined in large measure by the researchers' intent to *explain* what they were examining. Had their goal been different, their approach also could have been different.

Consider, for example, the conduct of ethnographic research. One of the main purposes of ethnography often is *to describe* the social world. This sort of research operates in very different ways from the quantitative work exemplified by Jacobson and his colleagues. This is so in large part because the goals of qualitative research are frequently different from the goals of quantitative research. David Preston's study (1988) of two Southern California Zen communities may be taken as an example. The first few chapters of this ethnographic work constitute thick descriptions of various aspects of Zen practice: the social characteristics of members, the role of the Zen teacher and his interactions with his students, how and what one learns as a new practitioner, and so on. Preston's goal in these chapters was to achieve what Max Weber (1864-1920) called *Verstehen,* or understanding derived from the point of view of the other. Good description is essential to developing this sort of first-person understanding.

At the same time, while understanding is the goal of all research, in some cases it is not possible to know precisely how best to acquire understanding. Nor is it always possible at the outset of a study to know exactly what one should be looking for. Thus some research legitimately has *exploration* as a goal. My own research on Northern Ireland may be used as an example. I went to Antrim and Londonderry Counties as a field researcher with the intention of studying sermons in different Protestant and Catholic denominations, reasoning that if the conflict in Northern Ireland were about religion to any significant degree, I would hear about politics from the pulpits. I quickly discovered that politics is rarely mentioned in explicit terms in the churches.

I attended a number of church services for several weeks before becoming aware that the sermons should not be the main point of interest. Prayers, hymns, and announcements, along with theology, ecclesiology, and church history, were much more important indicators of the politico-religious intersection. This field research showed the importance of being open to the empirical world, the significance of exploration. One sometimes comes away from the field understanding that the less one knows about a subject, the more appropriate exploration is as a research goal.

What Will You Observe to Know It? Measurement
Once it is clear what th focus of the research is to be, the researcher must decide on what actions, characteristics, beliefs, and/or attitudes he or she will examine to locate indicators of the concepts that are of primary interest. As noted above, concepts exist in the mind of the researcher but the empirical world provides innumerable ways of operationalizing these concepts so that the empirical relationships anticipated from theory may be assessed for accuracy. Researchers must examine the world to test and develop their ideas.

It has been argued that anything that exists can be measured. At the same time, not every measurement of a concept is equally valid. Sociologists use the term *validity* to describe a concept that actually is measured by the researcher's attempt to do so. Let us consider the case of religiosity again. It may be argued that regular attendance at religious services is a valid measure of religiosity. Surely, most people would agree that it is a more valid measure than whether one was baptized at some point in one's life. At the same time, ritual attendance, while it may be one dimension of religiosity, would not be so valid a measure of religiosity as would a composite measure that incorporated several of the previously mentioned dimensions of religiosity.

What the researcher wants in the measurement of any concept of interest is as complete a sampling as possible of all dimensions that make up the concept. Adequate sampling of the content of the concept is a first step in the creation of valid measurement tools. These measurements eventually will involve such things as questions on a survey instrument, observations in a field setting, public records in an archive, or other empirical items that make visible the concepts in which the researcher is actually interested. Measurements are always approximations of the concepts. They can be good (valid) approximations that are manifested in a consistent manner through repeated measurement— that is, they are *reliable*—or they can be poor approximations. Once it has been determined what parts of the empirical world one will examine, and what parts of it one will ignore, then one must decide how many of the objects in the world one will examine. This is the next question to be decided.

Which Specific Objects Will You Observe? Units of Analysis Most sociological studies focus on individuals as the source of their information. Through one or more of the data collection strategies used in the social sciences, information can be gathered about *people* (e.g., individual members of a congregation), *social groups* (e.g., Presbyterian and Episcopal clergy), *organizations* (e.g., Catholic parishes), and *artifacts* (e.g., hymnals). The phrase *unit of analysis* is widely used to identify the individuals, groups, organizations, and artifacts that supply the data for the study. The questions here are from whom or from what is the information to be collected? And about whom or what will the research be able to say anything?

One could, for example, research the same question using different units of analysis. Suppose, for example, that one is interested in the question of whether Jews or Catholics are more likely to marry someone outside their own religions. One could select a population of *individuals* from representative congregations to investigate the question. Or one could study marriage records (artifacts) in various communities to answer the question. Alternatively, if one were interested in divorce and remarriage among clergy, one could study *individual* rabbis, ministers, and priests, or one could look at the ways in which different religious *organizations* handle the question as a matter of policy. In any case, once it has been determined what will be observed, the next problem will be to decide how many observations will be sufficient. Will a study of one parish teach me about all parishes? Am I interested in all parishes? This suggests the problem of sampling.

How Many Cases Will You Examine? Sampling   In a totally homogeneous population, a sample as small as one case will yield an accurate representation of the population. But human populations are never totally homogeneous, and in religious matters the diversity of human expression is vast. This does not mean that a study of a single case cannot prove useful. This depends upon the purposes for which one is undertaking the research in the first place.

The key issue here is how many cases there should be and how these cases should be selected. The size of a sample should be dictated not by the size of the population in which one is interested but in the diversity of the elements making up the population. Two broad sets of techniques are available for selecting the sample. These are nonprobability and probability designs. In a probability sample (e.g., a *simple random sample;* see Shepherd and Shepherd 1986), one knows with certainty how likely it is that any element in the population will be selected for inclusion, while in a nonprobability sample (e.g., a *snowball sample;* see Kaufman 1991) this knowledge is unavailable, sometimes because the actual size of the population is unknown or even unknowable.

Thus one might readily conduct a probability sample of the members of a particular parish because official membership lists are generally available for such populations. On the other hand, one would be hard pressed to select a probability sample from the population of clergy who have committed crimes. One could study clergy accused or convicted of such actions, but the total size of the population is unknown, thereby defeating an attempt to draw a full probability sample.

Within What Time Frame Will You Observe? Research Design   Some research questions—especially questions that implicitly or explicitly concern social change—call for a *longitudinal* dimension. This means that data must be collected minimally at two points in time to answer such questions. If, for example, one wants to investigate changes in religious commitment over time, as Smidt and Penning (1982) did, then data should represent at least two points in time. This sort of design is like a moving picture compared with a still photograph. For some research questions, a still photo is quite adequate. This sort of study, in contrast to a longitudinal study, is known as a *cross-sectional* study.

Once it has been decided how, how many, and when cases are to be examined, the next problem is to determine how the data for the empirical study actually will be gathered. Answers to this question often rely on a series of standard methods of inquiry, but new methods are constantly being developed. In general, there are four principal techniques in wide use. These are experiments, surveys, participant observation, and the use of existing records. Other techniques such as focus groups, depth interviews, unobtrusive measures, and content analysis are best considered within the context of these major approaches.

How Will You Examine the Cases? Observation   There are many different ways that one could design a study to answer a particular question. This entry focuses on four traditional techniques—some of which result in quantitative (or *hard*) data and some of which result in qualitative (or *soft*) data.

Experiments: Experimental and quasi-experimental designs are not the most common approaches to the empirical social world, but the logic underlying them informs many of the other approaches one sees more often. The logic of experimental designs is essentially the logic of positivism. It assumes a rational world in which everything that is has a prior cause. It assumes too that research can be designed that will make it possible to determine the contribution that each putative cause makes to the outcome. In such a model, factors either are *independent* variables that effect an outcome or they are *dependent* variables that are determined in some sense by these independent variables. The logic behind this model is pervasive in traditional science. It is shown in the following formula:

$$Y = (f)X$$

where Y is the dependent variable and X is the independent variable. Given this relationship, it may be possible to manipulate the condition of X to observe the effect that this manipulation has upon the dependent variable Y. Manipulation of the independent variable is at the heart of all experimental designs.

One way to manipulate a variable is through the use of experimental and control groups. Weldon T. Johnson (1971) used this approach to investigate whether exposure to religious revivalism would produce religious change in those attending. He selected two experimental groups and one control group comprising students. The first group was instructed about how to play an active role at a Billy Graham crusade meeting. The second experimental group was instructed to participate passively at the revival. The third group did not attend the revival but was a control or nontreatment group. The "religious commitment" of individuals in all three groups was assessed before the revival meeting and twice after at three-week intervals. The question for Johnson was whether attendance at the revival would affect students' level of religious commitment. Johnson concluded that attendance at the Graham meeting was ineffectual in changing beliefs, behaviors, or self-concepts. This technique of using experimental designs—even field experiments—is rare in the social scientific study of religion compared with the next type.

Survey research: Interviews and surveys are much more common approaches to the social world than are experiments. This technique may be implemented in a number of different ways: telephone interviews, mailed questionnaires, depth interviews, face-to-face interviews, and so on. At the heart of them all is the asking and answering of questions. Debra Kaufman, in her study of women who became Orthodox Jews, conducted long, semistructured interviews that allowed the 150 subjects of her study to "speak in their own voices" (Kaufman 1991). Other studies have relied upon more traditionally structured interviews for gathering the data for their studies. Kosmin and Lachman (1993) used a computer-generated sample of 113,000 people to conduct their National Survey of Religious Identification in 1990. The numbers of respondents they sought clearly militated against any sort of in-depth or unstructured interviews.

In any case, the questions in an interview constitute the operational definitions of the concepts in the study. Questions may be *closed-ended* or *open-ended* depending upon the nature of the research under investigation. The former refers to questions that present a fixed set of choices as responses, while the latter refers to questions that permit free responses to the questions asked. The type of questions asked, the way the questions are worded, whether others are present to focus the attention of the respondents, the amount of latitude the respondents have to answer the questions as asked, are up to the survey researcher. It is important to remember, however, that the interview is reflective of a relationship between the interviewer and the interviewees. As such, a sense of reciprocity is in order. Rapport with the respondents will almost always enhance the quality of the data collected. Rapport is always important in social research but nowhere more so than in the qualitative technique discussed next.

Participant observation: There are a number of different names for the next sort of observational approach; *field research* and *qualitative research* are two of the more prominent ones, but the most common

name for it probably is *participant observation* (PO for short). As the name suggests, the researcher using this approach is both a participant and an observer. It quite literally may involve a detached form of "observation" of subjects with or without their explicit knowledge that they are being observed. It may involve a pattern of engaged interaction with the persons being observed. Babbie (1995) suggests a continuum of roles for the researcher to play, ranging from the complete participant at one end of the spectrum to the complete observer at the other end. Most of this research involves a mix of participation and observation.

A number of interesting research projects have been undertaken in the sociology of religion using PO techniques: a Billy Graham crusade, charismatic Catholics, the Cursillo movement, Quakers, the Divine Light Mission, Hasidism, meditation, Mennonites, Rajneeshpuram, Scientology, Synanon, the Unification Church, Yoga and Zen, as well as countless other groups, movements, and belief systems. PO has proved to be an indispensable technique for developing *Verstehen* (understanding).

Existing records: Public documents provide a rich source of empirical observations for the social scientist prepared to use them. They have the distinct advantage of virtually ruling out researcher-subject contamination and are therefore considered "unobtrusive" measures. In fact, such records are only part of the wealth of information that exists for social science use. Tombstones, court records, maps, manuscript census records, and many other sources have provided data for social scientists interested in historical and comparative research. Of course, the use of records and documents has been the métier of historians as long as there has been historical research, but sociologists also have come to appreciate the wealth that exists in archival data.

Sociological use of such data may be considered in two intersecting traditions: *historical* and *comparative* research. Numerous examples of each of these exist in the social scientific study of religion. Working in the historical tradition, Rodney Stark and Roger Finke developed a detailed statistical portrait of America for 1776. Their work depended in part upon an atlas of colonial maps resulting from "an effort to identify and locate every church congregation in America for the period January 1, 1775 to July 4, 1776" (Stark and Finke 1988:40).

Rosabeth Kanter used a comparative and historical approach in her 1972 book *Commitment and Community.* This work relies on archival data to study the characteristics of nineteenth-century communes and utopian communities. Her purpose was to see how those movements that endured differed from those that failed. Her research produced a theoretical framework for understanding the mechanisms of attachment and detachment that separate successful and unsuccessful communitarian movements.

Another way in which existing data have come to inform sociological research is through the technique known as *content analysis,* which may be applied to virtually any form of communication: written or oral, on film, tape, or video. Magazine articles, newspaper columns, popular songs, photographs, published speeches, every form of communication lends itself to content analysis. Shepherd and Shepherd (1986) used this technique to study modes of leadership within the Mormon community. They examined a 600-speech sample of between 9,000 and 12,000 addresses made to General Conferences during a 150-year span of Mormon history (1830-1979). They then classified the speeches according to their principal themes and analyzed their data to understand better the evolution of official rhetoric within Mormonism.

In an increasing number of cases, researchers are using multiple methods to develop a broader understanding of the phenomena they are studying. Michael Ducey used multiple approaches in his study of religious ritual in four churches in a Chicago neighborhood. In one parish where he conducted classic field research, he was known as "an inquisitive participant doing research on religious ritual." But he also used "interviews conducted with the pastors of all the churches and with many members of the congregations." In addition, he used documents "to construct a history of each church and of the community and to verify some of the information obtained in interviews" (1977:5). This multiplicity of methods for purposes of verification is known as *triangulation.*

How Will You Know? Analysis Once the data are collected, one must decide what to make of them. What do the data tell the researcher? Contrary to the hackneyed expression, data never "speak for themselves." A crucial job of the researcher is to interpret what he or she has collected and analyzed. On the quantitative side, this may involve rudimentary comparison of numerical summaries and elementary descriptive statistics (as in Kosmin and Lachman 1993), or it may involve the use of powerful statistical techniques (as in Jacobson et al. 1990). Quantitative data most often are processed using one or more statistical and computational packages such as SPSS, MicroCase, or SAS. These tools of analysis allow the researcher to create graphs, construct tables, and conduct statistical analyses of quantitative data.

In terms of qualitative data, interpretation may not involve numerical analysis at all (Preston 1988, Kaufman 1991). Nonetheless, even in these cases, the use of computers for recording and analyzing data is becoming more common. Software has moved from standard word processors to text retrievers, text base managers, and even code-based theory builders such as ATLAS/ti, Hyper-Research, and NUDIST. The availability of code-and-retrieve capabilities promises to change the face of qualitative analysis.

It is at the point of analysis, of course, that the final product of inquiry—understanding—can emerge. In every case, quantitative as well as qualitative, there will be a necessary tentativeness in what we can say. Knowledge of the world is always tentative knowledge because our understanding of the world is, as Smith (1991) points out, always partial and mediated.

What Should You Do? Research Ethics All the above considerations are essentially technical matters addressing questions of how to proceed. But there is another set of questions that also needs to be asked; this is the domain of right behavior—ethics. These issues address the more thorny questions of what the researcher should and should not do in the conduct of inquiry. There is hardly a more fundamental question for social science than that of right behavior.

Professional associations (e.g., the American Sociological Association) have developed comprehensive codes of conduct for their members. In the social scientific study of religion, as in other disciplines, these would normally revolve around concerns for the protection of human subjects. Concerns about human subjects generally are manifested in four domains: (1) harm, (2) consent, (3) privacy, and (4) deception. It is the first and foremost moral duty of any researcher to ensure that subjects will not be physically, psychologically, or emotionally endangered as a result of their participation in a study. This is best done by assuring that their informed consent to participate in the study at all is freely given. Insofar as possible, subjects must know what they are getting into when they agree to be studied.

Researchers also must be sure that their research is not overly intrusive, or at least that it will not reveal anything about the subjects that might cause them harm. The right to privacy of the subjects must be protected at all times. This protection of privacy is sometimes manifested as a confidentiality screen. Just as journalists are sworn to protect confidential sources, so too researchers must protect their subjects from unwanted exposure. In some cases, it is possible to collect the data without the researcher even knowing the identity of the respondents, so that the protection of respondents' confidentiality can be guaranteed—although this has the drawback of making follow-up studies impossible. Even when this is not feasible, there are ways to assure that subjects will remain anonymous to all but one or two key researchers working on a project.

Finally, subjects in research studies have the right not to be deceived. This last point is somewhat controversial because there may be good reasons that a researcher would not reveal details about the reasons for doing the research. Further, in some social psychological research, a degree of deception may be essential. In these cases, researchers must be careful to debrief subjects and be sure that no harm has been done to them.

To Whom/What Are You Accountable? Uses of Research These issues do not fully exhaust the ethical concerns. Ethicists are interested in the question, "What should I do?" but they are also interested in the question of accountability. Feminist researchers have made a strong argument for the accountability of the researcher back to the respondents and the communities from which they come (Reinharz 1992). Many people have argued that one should feed back the findings of the study to the respondents not only as a matter of validity checking but also as a matter of reciprocity and social exchange.

The question of what happens with the findings of a study must be considered in the context of the researcher's values. At one point, people advocated "value-freeness" for social science, but that position is no longer tenable. Social scientists cannot simply hand over the results of their research and presume that policymakers will "do the right thing." The consequences of doing this in the physical sciences are plain. Alvin Gouldner (1963) reminds us that before Hiroshima, physicists used to talk about value-free science but that many of them are no longer so sure. The question of *ethical neutrality,* raised by Max Weber as long ago as 1917, remains a controversial issue today (see Weber 1949). How involved and how detached should the social scientist be?

Conclusion In the social scientific study of religion, the role of social scientists as advocates for religious points of view has been one area of controversy; however, as Bryan Wilson has pointed out, to understand a religious group may require empathy, but "empathy need not lead to advocacy" (1983:184). The danger that awaits the empirical researcher—perhaps especially the participant observer—is that of *going native.* The researcher who goes native in essence becomes a member of the group he or she is studying and thereby loses whatever objectivity he or she might have had—assuming, as noted above, that objectivity is a genuine possibility.

Not everyone would see this as a bad thing, just as not everyone accepts objectivity as either real or desirable. Some researchers argue that advocacy is a very appropriate role for sociologists, noting that we are expressing our values whenever we decide what to study and what not to study. Our decisions on what is more and less important are expressions of our personal values—points about which we should be clear and explicit. Whether this should go so far as advocacy of a particular religious viewpoint is a question that has divided the discipline (see Horowitz 1983, Wilson 1983). How should the sociologist act in conducting empirical research?

The theologian Dietrich Bonhoeffer argued from his Nazi prison cell that it was the obligation of the modern believer to act *etsi deus non daretur* (as if there were no God). Such "atheism" is just the sort of position that sociologists of religion need to adopt. Peter Berger used the term *methodological atheism* to signify the sociological understanding of religion, an understanding that religion should be perceived "as a human projection, grounded in specific infrastructures of human history" (1967:180). The implication of this is that sociologists should treat religious ideas as they would treat any other ideas; that the subject concerns religion or God is irrelevant to the social and methodological issues involved. Others have used the expression *methodological agnosticism* to suggest that the existence of God should remain an open question to social research—neither true nor false but simply not subject to verification by social science. What, then, is the place of values in the study of religion? Berger thought personal valuations should be "kept strictly apart from the theoretical analysis of religion." Others would disagree, saying that it is important for the methodologist to be clear about her or his own values, to be explicit about them, and to act in accord with them.

This was the position advocated by former president of the Association for the Sociology of Religion, David Moberg. In his 1977 presidential address, Moberg argued that "making explicit the value commitments under which we operate can be very constructive for ourselves and for our discipline" (1978:2). The virtues he recommended at the time were integrity, humility, love, justice, vision, and transcendence. Any methodologist whose work takes cognizance of virtues such as these would likely advance the progress of the sociology of religion in particular and would likely advance empirical social science generally. Such progress is a suitable task for sociology as well as for methodology.

—*Ronald J. McAllister*

REFERENCES

E. Babbie, *The Practice of Social Research,* 7th ed. (Belmont, Calif.: Wadsworth, 1995); P. L. Berger, *The Sacred Canopy* (Garden City, N.Y.: Doubleday, 1967); D. Bonhoeffer, *Letters and Papers from Prison* (New York: Macmillan, 1967); J. Bronowski, *Science and Human Values* (New York: Harper, 1956); M. H. Ducey, *Sunday Morning* (New York: Free Press, 1977); P. Feyerabend, *Against Method,* 3rd ed. (Verso: London, 1993); C. Y. Glock and R. Stark, *Religion and Society in Tension* (Chicago: Rand McNally, 1965); A. Gouldner, "Anti-Minotaur," in *Sociology on Trial,* ed. M. Stein and A. Vidich (Englewood Cliffs, N.J.: Prentice Hall, 1963): 35-52; E. C. Guba, "The Alternative Paradigm Dialogue," in *The Paradigm Dialogue* (Newbury Park, Calif.: Sage, 1990): 17-27; I. L. Horowitz, "Universal Standards, Not Uniform Beliefs," *Sociological Analysis* 44(1983):179-182; C. K. Jacobson et al., "Black-White Differences in Religiosity," *Sociological Analysis* 51(1990):257-270; W. T. Johnson, "The Religious Crusade," *American Journal of Sociology* 76 (1971):873-890; R. M. Kanter, *Commitment and Community* (Cambridge: Harvard University Press, 1972); D. Kaufman, *Rachel's Daughters* (New Brunswick, N.J.: Rutgers University Press, 1991); B. A. Kosmin and S. P. Lachman, *One Nation Under God* (New York: Harmony, 1993); D. Moberg, "Virtues for the Sociology of Religion," *Sociological Analysis* 39(1978):1-18: D. L. Preston, *The Social Organization of Zen Practice* (Cambridge: Cambridge University Press, 1988); S. Reinharz, *Feminist Methods in Social Research* (New York: Oxford University Press, 1992); G. Shepherd and G. Shepherd, "Modes of Leader Rhetoric in the Institutional Development of Mormonism," *Sociological Analysis* 47(1986):125-136; C. Smidt and J. M. Penning, "Religious Commitment, Political Conservatism, and Political Social Tolerance in the United States," *Sociological Analysis* 43(1982):231-246; J. Smith, "A Methodology for Twenty-First Century Sociology," *Social Forces* 70(1991):1-17; R. Stark and R. Finke, "American Religion in 1776," *Sociological Analysis* 49(1988):39-51; W. L. Wallace, *The Logic of Science in Sociology* (Chicago: Aldine-Atherton, 1971); M. Weber, *The Methodology of the Social Sciences* (New York: Free Press, 1949); B. R. Wilson, "Sympathetic Detachment and Disinterested Involvement," *Sociological Analysis* 44 (1983):183-188.

RESOURCE MOBILIZATION (RM) A theoretical perspective that discounts the effect of underlying social strain or deprivation in social movement genesis in favor of rational strategic and political considerations. There are two principal versions: (1) the *political organizer* model, which stresses the role of external elite sponsors in providing financing, organization, and strategic/tactical leadership, and (2) the *political process* model, which emphasizes the provision of critical movement resources by the indigenous grassroots.

The work of Mayer Zald, professor of sociology at the University of Michigan, has been crucial to RM theory. In the 1960s, Zald (1970) undertook a seminal study that detailed the organizational transformation of the YMCA from evangelism to social service. A decade later, he expanded this organization-environment model to the field of social movements in the form of the "resource mobilization" paradigm (McCarthy and Zald 1977). In 1981, he delivered the H. Paul Douglass lecture to the Religious Research Association in which he called for a marriage of RM theory with Robert Wuthnow's version of world systems, and therein applied the model to denominational schisms. Among Zald's doctoral students at Vanderbilt University who subsequently have made significant contributions to the social scientific study of religion were O. Kendall White, Kenneth Westhues, Hart Nelsen, and James R. Wood.

In related work, both McAdam (1982) and Morris (1984) have recognized the historic importance of black community churches in supplying money, meeting space, and leadership to the U.S. civil rights movement in the 1950s and 1960s. Sociologists have applied the resource mobilization perspective to a variety of other religious contexts including new religious movements (Bromley and Shupe 1976, Khalsa 1986) and evangelistic crusades (Johnson et al. 1984).

—*John Hannigan*

REFERENCES

D. G. Bromley and A. D. Shupe, *The Moonies in America* (Beverly Hills, Calif.: Sage, 1976); N. Johnson et al., "Attendance at a Billy Graham Crusade," *Sociological Analysis* 45(1984):383-392; K. Khalsa, "New Religious Movements Turn to Worldly Success," *Journal for the Social Scientific Study of Religion* 25(1986):233-247; D. McAdam, *Political Process and the Development of Black Insurgency* (Chicago: University of Chicago Press, 1982); J. D. McCarthy and M. N. Zald, "Resource Mobilization and Social Movements," *American Journal of Sociology* 82(1977):1212-1239; A. Morris, *The Origins of the Civil Rights Movement* (New York: Free Press, 1984); M. Zald, *Organizational Change* (Chicago: University of Chicago Press, 1970); M. N. Zald, "Theological Crucibles," *Review of Religious Research* 23(1982):317-336.

REVELATION, BOOK OF *see* Apocalyptic

REVIEW OF RELIGIOUS RESEARCH

Interdisciplinary journal, published four times a year by the Religious Research Association, devoted to the social scientific study of religion. The journal was initiated in 1959 with Frederick Shippey as first editor. Subsequent editors include W. Widick Schroeder, David O. Moberg, Richard D. Knudten, James D. Davidson, Hart M. Nelsen, Edward C. Lehman, and D. Paul Johnson. The journal emphasizes research articles that advance knowledge of the role of religion in society and has practical implications for church-based researchers. It also includes reviews of recent books in the field. The subscription list of approximately 1,200 includes major university libraries.

—Doyle Paul Johnson

REVITALIZATION MOVEMENTS A term first proposed in 1956 by Anthony F. C. Wallace of the University of Pennsylvania to encompass such variously labeled social movements as nativistic movements, millenarian movements, reformative movements, and cargo cults because, he suggested, all possess a similar processual structure.

All these movements constitute deliberate, organized attempts by some members of society to create a more satisfying culture. All seek to undermine existing institutions with the intention of bringing about a new and meaningful integration through manipulation of the world. Wallace asserted that all religions come into existence as parts of revitalization movements and that whenever conditions of individual or social stress exist, a prophet emerges with a new cultural paradigm that, if accepted, becomes the basis for a new social reality or new social order. He delineated the sequence of development in revitalization movements as follows: (1) a steady state of culture, (2) a period of individual stress, (3) a period of cultural distortion, (4) a revitalization, and (5) the establishment of a new steady state of culture.

—Stephen D. Glazier

REFERENCE

A. F. C. Wallace, "Revitalization Movements," *American Anthropologist* 58(1956):264-281.

REVIVALISM *see* Evangelicalism, Charles G. Finney, Billy Graham, Televangelism

REVOLUTION An extensive, significant change in the ordering of human social relationships, which may be sudden and usually carries a political aspect. The concept is also applied retrospectively, often in connection with technological change—for example, the print revolution, the industrial revolution, the atomic revolution, the communication revolution, or, within religions, specifically, the Cluniac Revolution. Revolutions may or may not be characterized by violence; violent overthrow of government leaders without change in the structuring of social relationships does not, strictly speaking, constitute revolution in the social scientific sense.

In the work of Max Weber, particularly, revolution is associated with charismatic leadership, which often presents an explicitly religious aspect. Weber also, however, takes account of the possibility of traditionalist revolution bearing a religious character. In so doing, he highlights the internal dialectic in religion between creating new futures and restoring putative pasts. In both cases, as well as that of system maintenance, the potential political role of religion becomes clear. The relationships between religion and revolution have been treated in detail particularly by Lewy (1974) and Berman (1983). Specific political revolutions that have been studied for their religious aspects include Engels's treatment of the Peasants' Revolt in sixteenth-century Germany (see Marx and Engels 1975) and the traditionalist revolution led by the Ayatollah Khomeini in the late 1970s in Iran (see Kimmel 1990). Others have looked at the relationship between religion and broad cultural movements, usually termed *revolutions,* such as the relationship between Methodism and the industrial revolution in England (the Halévy thesis, subsequently adapted by E. P. Thompson) or Protestantism and the rise of science in seventeenth-century England (the Merton thesis).

—William H. Swatos, Jr.

REFERENCES

H. Berman, *Law and Revolution* (Cambridge: Harvard University Press, 1983); E. Halévy, *The Birth of Methodism in England* (Chicago: University of Chicago Press, 1971 [1915]); M. Kimmel, *Revolution* (Philadelphia: Temple University Press, 1990); G. Lewy, *Religion and Revolution* (New York: Oxford University Press, 1974); K. Marx and F. Engels, *On Religion* (Moscow: Progress, 1975); R. Merton, *Science, Technology, and Society in Seventeenth-Century England* (New York: Harper, 1970 [1937]); E. P. Thompson, *The Making of the English Working Class* (New York: Pantheon, 1963);

M. Weber, *Economy and Society* (Berkeley: University of California Press, 1978).

RHETORIC   Rhetoric, or the art of speech, was developed by the ancient Greeks (traditionally discovered by the Sicilians Corax and Tisias) in the context of city-state debate and court procedure. As a comprehensive program of "liberal education," rhetoric is associated with the Isocratean school in Athens. By the end of the fourth century B.C.E., however, it was construed more narrowly as the art of "sophistical disputation" or the use of verbal strategies to win an argument irrespective of issues of truth and falsity. The Platonic critique of rhetoric continues to inform the modern use of the term (as in "mere rhetoric"). Throughout the Middle Ages, these two understandings coexisted—the general art of discourse and the technique of false reasoning.

The link between classical and modern rhetoric lies in the work of Augustine of Hippo (354-430), whose thought straddles the Hellenic culture of philosophy and rhetoric, and the concerns and practices of Christian faith. With Augustine and the Augustinian tradition, classical rhetoric is redirected into the more practical concerns of Christian teaching, the composition of sermons, and related doctrinal practices. It is important to note that many of the classical techniques and tropes of Greco-Latin rhetorical education were redeployed in the training and instruction of priests. Rhetoric thus witnessed something of a new lease on life both in the oral culture of everyday sermonizing and casuistry and in the increasing importance of persuasive literacy that became a marked feature of the spread of Christianity during the so-called Dark Ages.

During the early modern period, rhetoric experienced a rapid decline as a serious discipline and only recently has it shown signs of revival through the influence of modern linguistics, literary criticism, postanalytical philosophy, and various kinds of text theory and cultural theory. Today, however, the field of rhetoric, communication, and language has reemerged, through the impact of writers such as Kenneth Burke, Chaim Perelman, Hayden White, Paul Ricoeur, Jacques Derrida, Paul de Man, and others. The overlapping field of "discourse analysis" and "rhetorical theory" raises a range of fundamental questions for all disciplines concerned with meaning, understanding, and interpretation.

—*Barry Sandywell*

REFERENCES

Aristotle, *Rhetoric*; K. Burke, *A Rhetoric of Motives* (Berkeley: University of California, 1969 [1950]); Cicero, *De inventione*; T. M. Conley, *Rhetoric in the European Tradition* (Chicago: University of Chicago Press, 1990); J. Derrida, *Of Grammatology* (Baltimore: Johns Hopkins University Press, 1976 [1967]); P. de Man, *The Rhetoric of Romanticism* (New York: Columbia University Press, 1984); Plato, *Gorgias*; Quintilian, *De institutione oratoria*; H. White, *Metahistory* (Baltimore: Johns Hopkins University Press, 1973).

RHINE, J. B.   *see* Psychic Phenomena

RICHARDSON, JAMES T. (1941–)   Professor of Sociology and Judicial Studies and Director of the Center for Judicial Studies, University of Nevada at Reno. Ph.D., sociology, Washington State University, 1968; J.D., Nevada School of Law, Old College, Reno, 1986; admitted to Nevada Bar, 1986. B.A., M.A., sociology, Texas Tech University, 1964, 1965. President, Association for the Sociology of Religion, 1986. Richardson has traveled widely abroad and has held visiting appointments at the Department of Sociology at the London School of Economics (1974-1975); the Department of Psychology of Culture and Religion at the University of Nijmegen, the Netherlands (Fulbright Fellow, 1981); and the University of Queensland, Sydney University, and University of Melbourne (1993-1994). Active in Nevada politics, Richardson served as a delegate to the Democratic National Convention in 1992.

James T. Richardson has been an outstanding figure in American sociology of religion for more than two decades. He was practically the first sociologist of religion to become involved in the study of the "new religions" that were attracting young people at the end of the 1960s. Over the years, Richardson has made pioneering contributions to a number of interrelated subareas of contemporary sociology of religion; these include the development of "youth culture fundamentalist" sects out of the diffuse "Jesus Movement" of the very early 1970s (Richardson et al. 1979), revision of received "sect-church" models to accommodate recent alternative religions (1978), extension of received "movement organization" models to identify the distinctive features and varieties of "religious movement organizations" (RMOs), development and politicization of the contemporary concept of "cult," conversion and commitment processes in religious movements (1985a), economic problems and adaptations of new and marginal religious movements (1988a, 1988b), social and legal conflicts surrounding recent unconventional religious movements (Bromley and Richardson 1983), distinctive patterns of exiting and disaffiliation from contemporary religious movements (Richardson et al. 1986), processes of stereotyping and opinion formation regarding "cults," and the demystification of recent agitation over alleged omnipresent Satanist conspiracies and the posited explosion of Satanic ritual abuse (Richardson et al. 1991).

What is distinctive and particularly valuable about Richardson's work is its tendency to link different areas and disciplines, such as law and social psychology, law and economics, sociology and clinical psychology, the sociology of conversion and the sociology of occupations. In this latter context, Richardson's concept of "conversion careers" pinpointed patterns of religious "serial monogamy" among young "seekers" in the 1970s (Richardson and Stewart 1978). Although Richardson has not been explicitly associated with new microeconomic "rational choice" models of religion, he appears to have anticipated the insight, subsequently formulated by Rodney Stark and others, that the (often unpredictably) shifting policies of the Internal Revenue Service represent the most salient environmental factor affecting the adaptive evolution of new religious movements and shaping their transformative patterns of institutionalization (Richardson 1985b).

The interface of psychology and sociology also has been prominently featured in Richardson's work. A notable critic of typifications of conversion processes in unconventional religions in terms of pathological "brainwashing" (1993), Richardson has been the author (and coauthor) of several important reviews of psychiatric and psychological studies that bear upon the mental health of members of controversial movements. Richardson has published a number of articles in psychology journals, most notably a seminal piece, with Brock Kilbourne, that analyzed the latent functional equivalence and general relationship between religious movements and professional psychotherapists. As a result of their roles as competitive healers, continuous tension between them is more or less institutionalized (Kilbourne and Richardson 1984). Kilbourne and Richardson have published several sociological analyses of healing movements.

Although some of the publications of Richardson referred to here have not received the attention that in retrospect they seem to have warranted, some of his works have been enormously influential. Richardson's article "The Active and the Passive Convert" (1985a) encoded the fundamental duality that discriminates divergent contemporary models of religious conversion and underlies controversies over alleged cultic "mind control."

Richardson has been a committed fighter for religious freedom and the rights of religious minorities. He has served as either an expert witness or a consultant in several court cases, and he collaborated in writing an *amicus* brief submitted by the Society for the Scientific Study of Religion that influenced an important appellate decision involving the Hare Krishna movement. Richardson's concern with religious freedom is broadly cosmopolitan and reflects his frequent travels and experiences as a visiting scholar abroad. A number of his recent articles analyze legal developments in Europe and Australia.

—*Thomas Robbins*

REFERENCES

D. G. Bromley and J. T. Richardson (eds.), *The Brainwashing-Deprogramming Controversy* (Toronto: Mellen, 1983); B. Kilbourne and J. T. Richardson, "Psychotherapy and New Religions in a Pluralistic Society," *American Psychologist* 39(1984):237-251; J. T. Richardson, "An Oppositional and General Conceptualization of Cult," *Annual Review of the Social Sciences of Religion* 2(1978):29-52; J. T. Richardson, "The Active vs. Passive Convert," *Journal for the Scientific Study of Religion* 24(1985a):163-179; J. T. Richardson, "The 'Deformation' of New Religions," in *Cults, Culture and the Law,* ed. T. Robbins et al. (Chico, Calif.: Scholars Press, 1985b); J. T. Richardson, "Changing Times," *Sociological Analysis* 49S(1988a):1-14; J. T. Richardson (ed.), *Money and Power in the New Religions* (Toronto: Mellen, 1988b); J. T. Richardson, "A Social Psychological Critique of 'Brainwashing' Claims About Recruitment to New Religions," in *The Handbook of Cults and Sects in America,* Vol. B, ed. D. G. Bromley and J. K. Hadden (Greenwich, Conn.: JAI, 1993): 75-98; J. T. Richardson and M. Stewart, "Conversion Process Models and the Jesus Movement," in *Conversion Careers,* ed. J. T. Richardson (Beverly Hills, Calif.: Sage, 1978): 24-42; J. T. Richardson et al., *Organized Miracles* (New Brunswick, N.J.: Transaction, 1979); J. T. Richardson et al., "Leaving and Labeling," *Research in Social Movements* 9(1986):97-126; J. T. Richardson et al. (eds.), *The Satanism Scare* (New York: Aldine, 1991).

RITES OF PASSAGE Rituals that symbolize and bring about a transition in social status. The concept is strongly associated with the French folklorist Arnold van Gennep (1873-1957), who was among the first to document it as an analytical category in 1908.

Gennep used the phrase very loosely and provided a plethora of examples of acts that bring about a transition within calendrical cycles, across spatial boundaries, and/or from one social status to another. Examples of rites of passage in contemporary American society might include baptisms, pilgrimages to Graceland, graduation ceremonies, marriage, and funerals. Through Gennep's efforts, rites of passage have been recognized as a unique and important category of ritual, especially in the work of anthropologists Victor Turner and Mary Douglas.

A central theme of Gennep's work is the identification of a threefold sequence that he believed characterizes rites of passage in every culture: separation (preliminal), transition (liminal), and reintegration (postliminal). Gennep borrowed the term *liminal* from the Latin word *limen* meaning a boundary or threshold (1908:21). An individual undergoing a rite of passage is first separated from his or her old identity and surroundings. At that point, the individual is outside of the social structure. He or she is betwixt and between social categories and expectations. Finally, the individual is reintegrated in a new group or given a new social status.

Mary Douglas and Victor Turner have focused their studies on the liminal stage of rites of passage. Douglas (1966), for example, has argued that all social transition is perceived as dangerous. Because their status is temporarily undefined, persons experiencing transition have no place in society. Turner and his students took this argument one step further by suggesting that the liminal period represents the possibility of an unstructured, egalitarian social world termed *communitas* (1967), which, for Turner, is the building block of utopian fiction, experimental communes, and millenarian movements.

—*Stephen D. Glazier*

REFERENCES

M. Douglas, *Purity and Danger* (Harmondsworth, U.K.: Penguin, 1966); A. van Gennep, *The Rites of Passage* (Chicago: University of Chicago Press, 1960 [1908]); V. Turner, *The Forest of Symbols* (Ithaca, N.Y.: Cornell University Press, 1967).

RITUAL In the social scientific study of religion, refers to symbolic actions, the customary ceremonies, the prescribed forms of rite that manifest belief in the Divine through patterned and closely regulated social means. (In older usage, *ritual* refers to the words involved in such events—both words spoken and written directions—while *ceremony* refers to the actions.)

Religious rituals have manifold functions of propitiation, of rendering worship, and of the conferral of powers and delegations. Rituals operate with a hierarchical order and proclaim a power to reconstitute the social and the physical. Religious rituals can be classified according to their stipulated functions and the elaborate or simple nature of their ceremonial forms.

Some forms of ritual have instrumental properties, hence are magical in their explanatory functions and the causal reconstitution of what they effect. But religious rituals, especially those of Christianity, operate in a more indirect and indeterminate manner in relation to the powers that transcend their basis. They display an absence of concern with tangible ends that lends a disinterested, objective quality to their rites. In their ritual actions, the actors give witness to a gift beyond their discretion to invoke, hence the proper distinction between religious rituals on the one hand and magic on the other.

The Paradox of Ritual Religious rituals have a property of danger where powers of the unknown are confronted in forms of petition. Sacrifice in ritual manifests a gift destroyed to secure that which cannot be realized solely through social means. These elements point to a crucial function of religious rituals, of providing social means of domesticating fear of the unknown. These capacities give them a mysterious power of transformation and representation that invokes faith in the symbolic and hidden basis of the transactions. Somehow they manage to implicate the definiteness of their form into the indefiniteness of that which they signify. As settled social procedures drawn from tradition and custom, these rites also serve to handle routinely transitions in life cycles in the setting of religious belief. They contribute to social and spiritual notions of health in their capacity to domesticate fractious issues in a harmonizing manner where otherwise the social fabric might be rent. Religious rituals embody cultural values that relate both to the secular and to the sacred. Civic and traditional properties merge with those of the sacerdotal, especially in English society. Religious rites relate to values of national pride and are vehicles for sentiment, such as mourning. They give condensed expression to national sensibilities of grief or celebration such as royal funerals and weddings. They also have a dual collective function of ameliorating egoism and at the same time affirming the necessity of belief in the transcendent and the mysterious. These dual spiritual and social functions have led to divisions of understanding within sociology and anthropology.

Like other ritual forms, religious rites dignify transactions that risk sliding into the trivial. The ceremonial resources of rite, its stylized actions, its formalized gestures, elaborate clothing and speech serve as artificial means of providing a protective mantle to theological propositions that might otherwise slip into trivia, into presumption, and into insignificance. Religious rituals operate in a series of paradoxes that are routinely overcome: The tradition that makes them seem unoriginal endows them with the authority of servicing a lineage of collective memory (Hervieu-Léger 1993) and making rites anew in the present; the fixed order of enactment that diminishes discretion permits the routine handling of dangerous emotions and that which might evaporate into ephemeral enthusiasms; and despite a tangible social apparatus that represents the unutterable, they manage to re-present utterances that belong to the Divine in a mysterious manner. The fixedness of ritual form contrasts with the unfixed properties they routinely handle, of death, marriage, and initiation. This fixedness proclaims a security, a witness to a mysterious capacity for inexhaustible repetition.

The multitude of functions of religious rites and readings that can be derived from their stereotypical social facades generates a sociological fascination as to their ritual style and order, their symbols and procedures for handling routinely the unknown. But this management of antinomies and ambiguities in a credible manner marks a limit to sociological understandings of the social basis of rite.

There is a dramatic quality to the facility of rites to service often contradictory ends. Religious rituals can be understood as forms of theater (Turner 1982). As social transactions, these rites can be characterized as forms of play or games that give them a significance in a culture of postmodernity (Flanagan 1991, Gadamer 1979, Huizinga 1949). Music, silence, awe, terror, and joy are some of the experiential properties so released that also form the characterizing phenomena of rite. The numinous and mysterious properties of being acted on by forces beyond human manufacture provide a fascination for the actors so engaged in this holy hunt.

Religious ritual forms are microcosms of social and cultural values. In a Durkheimian understanding, rituals sacralize the social, affirm the collectivity, and provide indispensable means of harnessing the social to heal fragmentation (Durkheim 1915). Even in civic and secular cultures, religious rituals have powerful legitimizing powers that rulers invoke through symbols to secure recognition of their right to rule (Bloch 1992, Cannadine 1983, Cannadine and Price 1987).

This overlap between polity and theodicy draws attention to wider issues of ambiguity that sociology faces in striving to arbitrate between the social form of rite (its describable ceremonial rules and procedures), which is literally *not* what it is about to its adherents,

and the content, of the mysterious, the intangible and transcendent properties it signifies and sometimes evokes, which lies outside sociological accountability but that is central to its theological language of purpose.

Sociological Interpretations of Ritual Sociology faces a dilemma of interpretation of religious rituals, of either providing reductionist explanatory accounts of the social mechanisms that overturn the sensibilities and the self-understandings of the actors involved in the reproduction of rite, or of bracketing suspicion and trying to understand the link between the theology proclaimed and the ritual so enacted, which the actors strive to fuse together if the action is to be credible to themselves.

Sociologists might wish to confirm suspicions of the Enlightenment that these rites are inherently deluding, that they service the irrational, the superstitious, and that Feuerbach, Marx, Frazer, Freud, and Durkheim were right, that they simply mirror the social and, in intensified use, are ceremonial neuroses, rites of delusion for their adherents. But this reductionist tradition has been overturned since the early 1970s, with acceptance of the notion of performative utterances, that doing is a form of saying (Austin 1979), that there is an internal relationship between action and context (Winch 1963), and that culture is a form of text (Geertz 1988), thus action has a hermeneutic dimension (Ricoeur 1981). These shifts have led to changes of expectation over how religious rituals are to be authentically understood. Rituals are read increasingly in sociological and anthropological terms as openings, as operative and performative ceremonies (Lewis 1980, Skorupski 1976, Tambiah 1979). Rites have their own language, and their actors play their enactments by the book (Grainger 1974).

In these approaches, symbols are to be deciphered (Geertz 1968), tacit meanings in action are to be read for what is unstated, and sociology has to find a grammar for reading religious rituals in terms of their own criteria of authenticity and self-recognition. The move from reductionist functionalist accounts to those that seek to amplify the meanings rituals make manifest has facilitated a link between sociology and hermeneutics that has wider implications for debate on sociology and culture. Religious rituals, especially those of Catholicism, combine the ingredients of hermeneutic debate, action, symbol, text in a way that merges perspectives of Gadamer and Ricoeur with sociological considerations (Flanagan 1991).

As these rites are to be deciphered in the fullness of meanings they amplify, interest moves to understanding how actors convert the determinate into the indeterminate. But if rites are indeterminate in effect, the scope for deceptions becomes enormous, as "lies are the bastard offspring of symbols" (Rappaport 1979). Sociological questions emerge about the impression management of religious rituals that suggest that they are paradigms for understanding the sacredness of all social transactions.

Rituals provide a tale in their ceremonial orders, the reading of which tells much about a society, its cultural heritage, what it values and what it believes. In Catholicism, the link can be understood in the term *inculturation*, the imperative to reflect the cultural genius of a people in ritual styles (Chupungco 1982).

Using symbols and formalized actions, religious rituals convey a power for dealing with the mysterious through social means that has wider sociological implications. This sacramental power was understood by Max Weber and is central to the understanding of recent approaches to the sociology of culture (Bourdieu 1987).

Christian Rituals and Sociology   There are structural reasons within sociology for the neglect of Christian religious rituals that have so shaped the culture of advanced industrialized secular societies, and whose metaphors still haunt the sociological imagination. The issue of ritual seemed to belong to anthropology and ethnography. Apart from Durkheim's seminal contribution, the issue of religious ritual seemed not a sociological question. It belonged to the nonrational principles of efficacy and intervention of magic, and to accounts of the structure of primitive society. Neither did it belong to sociology of religion. Of late, sociology of religion concentrated on debates on secularization and on sects, the fringes of the main Christian tradition, all of which confirmed the notion that its religious rituals were incredible and had failed. Ironically, in turn, sociology of religion was marginalized from the main theoretical concerns of sociology.

But as the issue of culture is becoming of central concern in sociology, the importance of religious rituals as fields for theoretical reflection can only expand. For instance, the issues of time, space, and structuration of Giddens have been fruitfully explored in relation to the liturgies of the medieval parish church (Graves 1989); the term *habitus*, central to Bourdieu's approach to sociology and culture, derives from an appreciation of the link between disposition, belief systems, and architecture (Bourdieu 1977); and the notion of the liminal for understanding ritual and structure has clear implications for approaches to culture (Holmes 1973, Turner 1969).

Little sociological attention has been given to understanding the liturgies of Catholicism and Anglicanism, their public stipulated forms of worship whose ritual order abides by ecclesiastical authority (Martimort 1987). These rites exemplify an important link of praxis between theology and sociology, where grace mingles with the social. Sacraments can be understood in liturgical contexts as rites of initiation (Gennep 1960, Smolarski 1994). Sociological comments on liturgy tend to be traditionalist and critical of the confusion between renewal and modernization since Vatican II. Thus one finds unexpected anthropological appreciations of the Tridentine Mass (Turner 1976), the use of sacramental metaphors to understand culture, and a sympathetic understanding of the estrangement felt by those whose memory of rite was obliterated in the face of the havoc wrought after Vatican II (Bourdieu 1991).

Flanagan's study of liturgy (1991) was an attempt to understand its ritual basis from within the assumptions and expectations of sociology. The methodological difficulties of studying these rites in relation to theology and sociology were explored. To uncover their possible social assumptions, the study concentrated on the precariousness of their ceremonial social mechanism in their realization of the liminal and the numinous. The focus of the study was on the minor liturgical actors, the choirboys and the altar servers, those marginal to the rite but who exemplified its basis. They seemed obvious complements to the playful, the angelic, and the antinomic properties characterizing liturgical operations. These rites are instruments of the enchantment being sought in a culture of postmodernity (Flanagan 1996a).

The Wider Sociological Significance of Ritual   One of the interesting movements in contemporary sociology in relation to the debate on postmodernism is the rehabilitation and reappreciation of rituals. With growing concern with New Age religions and new religious movements, the issue of ritual practices has come to the fore in debates on postmodernity. These movements against secularization, that seek to reenchant, should not distract attention from the study of the more traditional rituals of the main religions that are still undertheorized.

Ritual operates as a form of solace for the self in late modernity, where it marks the return of the repressed (Giddens 1991). Even in the consumer culture characterizing postmodernism, ritual services a need for some form of sacred symbols in a secular society (Featherstone 1991). This broadening of the use and significance of ritual relates to the enduring significance of Durkheim but also to debates on civil religion (Bellah 1967). Far from postmodernism marking the demise of ritual, it seems to have accentuated its significance (Gellner 1992).

Debate on ritual is likely to center on the effects of internal secularization on the autonomy of rites in traditional Christian theologies. The fundamentalism that marks a revolt against modernity signifies a re-evaluation of the sacred and ritual in the context of postmodernity. Second, as the self is connected to understandings of ritual (Flanagan 1996b), issues of authenticity will emerge in terms of the politics of representation of the sacred in the marketplace and the degree to which postmodernity facilitates, if at all, experimentation in forms of rite. Issues of authenticity and credibility will enhance the quest for under-standings between theology and sociology in dealings with culture. Finally, as the implications of virtue ethics are being subject to sociological appreciation, the inter-nal cultural characteristics of ritual are likely to increase in significance, especially in terms of the actor's ac-count, a tale of rite that qualitative sociology is well fitted to articulate.

—*Kieran Flanagan*

REFERENCES

J. L. Austin, "Performative Utterances," in *Philosophical Papers*, ed. J. O. Urmson and G. J. Warnock (Oxford: Oxford University Press, 1979): 233-252; R. N. Bellah, "Civil Religion in America," *Daedalus* 96(1967):1-21; M. Bloch, *Prey into Hunter* (Cambridge: Cambridge University Press, 1992); P. Bourdieu, *Outline of a Theory of Practice* (Cambridge: Cambridge University Press, 1977); P. Bourdieu, "Legitima-tion and Structured Interests in Weber's Sociology of Reli-gion," in *Max Weber, Rationality and Modernity*, ed. S. Lash and S. Whimster (London: Allen & Unwin, 1987): 119-136; P. Bourdieu, *Language and Symbolic Power* (Cambridge: Pol-ity, 1991); D. Cannadine, "The Context, Performance and Meaning of Ritual," in *The Invention of Tradition*, ed. E. Hobsbawm and T. Ranger (Cambridge: Cambridge Univer-sity Press, 1983): 101-164; D. Cannadine and S. Price (eds.), *Rituals of Royalty* (Cambridge: Cambridge University Press, 1987); A. J. Chupungco, *Cultural Adaptation of the Liturgy* (Ramsey, N.J.: Paulist Press, 1982); É. Durkheim, *The Ele-mentary Forms of the Religious Life* (London: Allen & Unwin, 1915); M. Featherstone, *Consumer Culture and Postmod-ernism* (London: Sage, 1991); K. Flanagan, *Sociology and Liturgy* (New York: St. Martin, 1991); K. Flanagan, *The En-chantment of Sociology* (New York: St. Martin, 1996a); K. Flanagan, "Postmodernity and Culture," in *Postmodernity, So-ciology and Religion*, ed. K. Flanagan and P. Jupp (London: Macmillan, 1996b): 152-173; H. Gadamer, *Truth and Method* (London: Sheed & Ward, 1979); C. Geertz, "Religion as a Cultural System," in *The Religious Situation*, ed. D. R. Culter (Boston: Beacon, 1968): 639-688; C. Geertz, *Works and Lives* (Cambridge: Polity, 1988); E. Gellner, *Postmodernism, Reason and Religion* (London: Routledge, 1992); A. van Gen-nep, *The Rites of Passage* (London: Routledge, 1960); A. Gid-dens, *Modernity and Self-Identity* (Cambridge: Polity, 1991); R. Grainger, *The Language of the Rite* (London: Darton, Longman & Todd, 1974); C. P. Graves, "Social Space in the English Medieval Parish Church," *Economy and Society* 18(1989):296-322; D. Hervieu-Léger, *La religion pour mémoire* (Paris: Cerf, 1993); U. T. Holmes, "Liminality and Liturgy," *Worship* 47(1973):386-397; J. Huizinga, *Homo Ludens* (London: Routledge, 1949); G. Lewis, *Day of Shining Red* (Cambridge: Cambridge University Press, 1980); A. G. Martimort, *The Church at Prayer*, Vol. 2 (London: Chapman, 1987); R. Rappaport, *Ecology, Meaning and Religion* (Rich-mond, Calif.: North Atlantic, 1979); P. Ricoeur, *Hermeneutics and the Human Sciences* (Cambridge: Cambridge University Press, 1981); J. Skorupski, *Symbol and Theory* (Cambridge: Cambridge University Press, 1976); D. C. Smolarski, *Sacred Mysteries* (New York: Paulist Press, 1994); S. J. Tambiah, *A Performative Approach to Ritual* (Oxford: Oxford University Press, 1979); V. Turner, *The Ritual Process* (London: Rout-ledge, 1969); V. Turner, "Ritual, Tribal and Catholic," *Worship* 50(1976):504-526; V. Turner, *From Ritual to Theatre* (New York: Performing Arts Journal Publications, 1982); P. Winch, *The Idea of a Social Science and Its Relation to Phi-losophy* (London: Routledge, 1963).

ROBBINS, THOMAS (1943–) Independent scholar affiliated with the Santa Barbara Centre for Humanistic Studies; B.A., government, Harvard Uni-versity, 1965; Ph.D., sociology, University of North Carolina at Chapel Hill, 1973. Subsequent teaching or research appointments at Queens College (CUNY), the New School for Social Research, Yale University, and the Graduate Theological Union.

As a sociologist of religion, Robbins has specialized in the study of new, marginal, and deviant religious movements. Over a several-decade period, he has been one of the leading contributors to the social scientific literature in this area. His early work was significantly informed by functionalism, and his later work by social constructionism and deviance theory. Three central themes run through Robbins's work on new religious groups: exploring the range and diversity of current religious expression, comparing historical episodes that parallel present developments, and analyzing the inter-action of legal, policy, and cultural issues surrounding contemporary groups.

Throughout Robbins's career, he has attempted to capture and convey in his writing the extraordinary variety of forms in which contemporary religiosity is manifested. He has conceptualized this variety in terms of religious "innovation" and "experimentation" (Rob-bins and Bromley 1992). His concern for the relation-ship between the growth of culturally innovative spiri-tual movements and the evolution of American society at the end of the twentieth century is evident in *In Gods We Trust: New Patterns of Religious Pluralism in Amer-*

ica (with Dick Anthony, Transaction 1981). The broadening of his interests is reflected in the second edition of this volume (Transaction 1990), which highlights the current surge of evangelical and fundamentalist Christianity as well as the changing and contested role of women in American religion. In other work, Robbins has explored comparisons between historical and contemporary events. Most notable are his studies of mass suicides among the Russian Old Believers as compared with those at Jonestown in 1979 (Robbins 1986) and a comparative analysis of current agitation against "cults" with early-nineteenth-century controversies over Catholics, Mormons, and Freemasons (Robbins and Anthony 1979). A further development in exploring the diversity of contemporary religious forms is *Between the Sacred and the Secular: Research and Theory on Quasi-Religion* (JAI 1994), coedited with Arthur L. Greil. In this volume, Robbins and Greil bring together a number of scholars who examine the increasingly ambiguous and contested "boundary" of religion and the consequent enhanced salience for the sociology of religion of the study of how "religious" designations are produced and negotiated in modern society. Robbins also has attempted to synthesize the large and rapidly growing literature on new religious movements. His most notable work of this kind is *Cults, Converts and Charisma* (Sage 1988), which is the most comprehensive integration of the sociological literature on the growth of new religions in North America and Europe for the two-decade period beginning in the late 1960s.

Beginning in the mid-1980s, Robbins became increasingly interested in the legal and church-state issues being raised by contemporary religious movements. In particular, he developed a corpus of work on the interface of legal and social science issues in controversies over the alleged use of "mind control" by religious and therapeutic "cults." Robbins initially pursued these interests by assembling interdisciplinary essays addressing a range of church-state issues in *Cults, Culture and the Law* (Scholars Press 1985, with William Shepherd and James McBride) and in *Church-State Relations* (Transaction 1987, with Roland Robertson). Following these books, Robbins produced a series of seminal articles on related issues, most notably "Law, Social Science and the 'Brainwashing' Exception to the First Amendment" (Anthony and Robbins 1992). In much of this work, Robbins collaborated with other scholars sharing his interests, including Dick Anthony, James Beckford, and David Bromley.

Robbins's concern with issues arising from the controversies and conflicts surrounding new movements sensitized him to the increasingly problematic quality of "objectivity" in the contemporary study of religion. As a result, he has explored the tendency of scholars to "become part of their data," which ultimately raises the question of "whether a value-neutral 'scientific' study of religion can remain viable in a period of religious tumult" (Robbins and Robertson 1991).

Robbins's most recent stream of work extends his interest in religious diversity to an analysis of apocalypticism. This line of work began with two book chapters in 1995: the first, "Sects and Violence," deals with the interaction of "exogenous" and "endogenous" factors in precipitating violent confrontations between religious officials and state authorities; the second, "Religious Totalism, Violence and Exemplary Dualism," employs insights from depth psychology to explore the volatility and the potential for violence in apocalyptic and millennial sects. His most recent project, *Millennium, Messiahs and Mayhem* (with Susan J. Palmer, Routledge 1997), brings together an array of scholars concerned with apocalypticism to explore various facets and manifestations of contemporary apocalyptic movements.

—*David G. Bromley*

REFERENCES

D. Anthony and T. Robbins, "Law, Social Science and the 'Brainwashing' Exception to the First Amendment," *Behavioral Sciences and the Law* 10(1992):5-30; D. Anthony and T. Robbins, "Religious Totalism, Violence, and Exemplary Dualism," in *Terrorism and Political Violence* 7(1995):10-50; T. Robbins, "Religious Mass Suicide Before Jonestown," *Sociological Analysis* 41(1986):1-20; T. Robbins and D. Anthony, "Cults, Brainwashing and Counter-Subversion," *Annals* 446(1979):78-90; T. Robbins and D. Anthony, "Sects and Violence," in *Armageddon at Waco*, ed. S. A. Wright (Chicago: University of Chicago Press, 1995): 236-259; T. Robbins and D. Bromley, "Social Experimentation and the Significance of American New Religions," *Research in the Social Scientific Study of Religion*, Vol. 4 (Greenwich, Conn.: JAI, 1992): 1-29; T. Robbins and R. Robertson, "Studying Religion Today," *Religion* 21(1991):319-339.

—*David G. Bromley*

ROBERTS, (GRANVILLE) ORAL   *see* Televangelism

ROBERTSON, (MARION G.) PAT (1930–)

Evangelical Christian and entrepreneur; son of U.S. Senator Absalom W. Robertson; graduated magna cum laude from Washington and Lee (1950); graduate of Yale Law School but failed bar examinations; graduate of the Bible Seminary of New York (renamed New York

Theological Seminary). Introduced to and became interested in Pentecostalism in 1957; leader in the modern charismatic movement, a fervent evangelical reaching an interdenominational Christian audience. Ordained minister Southern Baptist Church. Bought Christian television (UHF) station, Channel 27, Portsmouth, VA (1959); in 1976 purchased 142 acres in Virginia Beach as the future site of Regent University and the Family Channel.

Robertson established the Christian Broadcasting Network (CBN) in the Tidewater area of Virginia, first broadcasting on radio, then establishing Christian television station WHAH-TV, October 1961. Robertson later distanced himself from religious broadcasting (although he still hosts the *700 Club*) to become a Christian educator, entrepreneur, and political advocate. Still engaging in advocacy journalism using *700 Club* as a vehicle for political analyses of the news, he briefly stepped down as host to run as a candidate for the Republican presidential nomination in 1988. When his bid for the presidency ended early in the campaign, he founded the Christian Coalition and became its President, with Ralph Reed as Executive Director. Robertson is still President of CC, which has an estimated membership of 1.7 million (Regan and Dunham 1995). The coalition has actively influenced the Republican platform in the last two presidential elections and is committed to involvement in the grassroots as well as national political levels on issues such as abortion, prayer in public schools, and school choice.

His financial success with CBN enabled him to establish Regent University (formerly CBN University), which provides only graduate-level courses, and a number of political action groups such as the American Center for Law and Justice (National Legal Foundation). The International Family Entertainment Corporation (IFE), which he and his son Tim acquired in 1990, is a holding company that owns the Family Channel, formerly CBN Cable Network. In this transition to a publicly traded corporation, a block of IFE shares were given to the *700 Club* and Regent University. Under Tim Robertson's leadership, IFE has bought the Mary Tyler Moore (MTM) company, the producers of *Hill Street Blues*, *The Bob Newhart Show*, and *Evening Shade*, among others, through its acquisition of British Broadcaster RVS, the parent company of MTM.

The financial and organizational growth of IFE is impressive. In its 1993 annual report to stockholders, IFE reported total revenues of $43.8 million for the second quarter, a 37% increase over the comparable quarter in 1992, and its total operating revenues for 1993 increased 56% to $208.2 million; however, the value of stock declined from $0.70 to 0.49 per share.

See also Christian Right, Televangelism

—*Razelle Frankl*

REFERENCES

R. Frankl, *Televangelism* (Carbondale: Southern Illinois University Press, 1987); J. K. Hadden and A. D. Shupe, *Televangelism* (New York: Holt, 1988); D. Harrell, Jr., *Pat Robertson* (San Francisco: Harper, 1987); S. M. Hoover, *Mass Media Religion* (Beverly Hills, Calif.: Sage, 1988); International Family Entertainment, Inc., *Report to Stockholders*, 1994; J. Peck, *The Gods of Televangelism* (Cresskill, N.J.: Hampton, 1993); M. Regan and R. Dunham, "Gimme That Old-Time Marketing," *Business Week* (Nov. 6, 1995): 76-78.

ROBERTSON, ROLAND (1938–)   Professor of Sociology at the University of Pittsburgh, born and educated in England; President, Association for the Sociology of Religion, 1988.

Throughout his career, Robertson's interest in the study of religion, initially inspired by the work of his teacher Bryan Wilson, has focused on religion as that domain of modern culture in which rival conceptions of order and identity clash most fatefully. Challenging conventional views of religion that portray it as epiphenomenal, privatized, or bound-to-be-secularized, Robertson regards religion as a significant object of intercivilizational encounters, and indeed as a force shaping a newly emergent, heterogeneous global culture. While Robertson has been an influential interpreter of Weber, Durkheim, and Simmel, he has drawn much of his own theoretical inspiration from the work of Talcott Parsons as well.

Apart from essays on the Salvation Army and Parsonian theory, Robertson's early work focused on issues of international development. With J. P. Nettl (1968), he criticized analyses of socioeconomic development that portrayed the process as requiring universal preconditions, leading to similar goals across the globe. Instead, he interpreted development as deliberate efforts by elites focused on extrinsic goals, measuring the performance of their societies against yardsticks set by others and the changes achieved by competitors in an international ranking system. All "local" development was therefore part of a global system; all societal policies were inherently related to transsocietal standards and reference groups. Robertson was among the first to conceptualize an international stratification system. The relativity of change implied by this new view of the global system has remained a theme in his thinking.

Robertson's first major study in the sociology of religion (1970) not only served as an authoritative introduction but also outlined desirable modes and problems of inquiry for the field. Robertson defended a strongly substantive view of religion, urged a distinction between social and cultural aspects of religion, outlined different dimensions of secularization, and emphasized the distinctive contribution of a reflexive sociology in the study of religion. In each respect, Robertson proposed a resolution of old conundrums. Throughout the book, he interpreted distinctive features of American religious culture and organization with analytical tools partly derived from the classical European tradition. For instance, he interpreted the tendency of scholars such as Parsons and Bellah to attribute special spiritual significance to the actual historical tradition of their society as a typically American form of secularizing immanentism.

After spending some years reinterpreting the classical figures in sociology (1978, Robertson and Holzner 1980), Robertson gradually merged his interests in the cultural role of religion with his thinking about the emerging system of societies. He proposed that the world as a whole was undergoing massive changes that were turning it into one relatively integrated sociocultural system, one "place." Actors around the world were increasingly conscious of this process, but due to their various locations and traditions, all such actors, notably religious leaders, offered radically different views of desirable global change. Religion was an integral part of the process of globalization and a crucial domain in which conflicts over alternative directions were played out. By concentrating on the religious aspect of global change, Robertson also intended to challenge conventional views of the world system as caused by economic forces and made up of economic structures. At the same time, Robertson did not intend to substitute an idealist picture of the world as shaped by religion for an older materialist version. The main processes of globalization can be described, he argued, in terms of the relationships between four increasingly differentiated units: individual selves, humankind, national societies, and the system of societies.

This shift in perspective has had important implications for Robertson (1992). First, while much of sociology has been concerned with the dynamics of culturally bounded national societies, he argues that individual and societal identities are increasingly relativized in the new global setting. National cultures are called into question just as the need to declare one's identity under global pressure increased. Church-state tensions around the world illustrate the process at work. Second, in response to unsettling global changes, religious groups and movements may urge a return to fundamentals, not simply as a way to root individual selves in the religious culture of a nation but also as a way to reshape world order as such. The ambitions of Islamic fundamentalism are a case in point. Third, while religious groups and institutions may have lost some of their historic social significance, the secularization of Western countries should not obscure their central role in offering new images of world order. Indeed, religions and their representatives are participants in a global debate about the direction of global change. "The world," no longer just an abstract theological notion, now presents concrete problems of meaning. However, given the complexity and pluralism of the world scene, it is unlikely that any one actor can claim special success in addressing them. Fourth, the study of religion has something to offer world-system analysis. Specifically, it focuses attention on the way in which new global actors are created and legitimated and on the way in which new rules of global interaction and discourse are set. On this score, Robertson regards the decades before and after 1900 as crucial. Fifth, studying world conflict from this sociology of religion perspective debunks conventional forms of economic or political reductionism. According to Robertson, to accentuate the point, all world politics is cultural.

In this way, Robertson has begun to reconsider many classic issues in the sociology of religion from a distinctive global point of view. He wants to move beyond traditional debates about societal secularization, about religion as a source of identity, or about fundamentalism as localized antimodern movements. In many ways, however, his later work proposes a research agenda rather than a finished project. While this reflects the fluidity of the very changes he aims to capture in his writings, it leaves questions about the origins and prime movers of his cultural globalization still unanswered. Similarly, his work has an interpretive character and often shies away from making firm causal claims. As a critique of reductionism in world-system analysis, it has been quite effective, yet readers may detect a compensatory idealism in Robertson's own thinking. New categories of thought, new interpretations of the global scene, often appear to shape that scene most effectively. Still, Robertson has already had an impact on the agenda of the sociology of religion. His writings not only have stimulated a new way of thinking about the world but also have made sociologists of religion rethink the premises of their own enterprise. As he would put it, they are now trying to make sense of a new form of global complexity, of a world of reflexive interlocutors in which they themselves intervene through their interpretations of religious action and change.

—Frank J. Lechner

REFERENCES

P. Beyer, *Religion and Globalization* (London: Sage, 1994); F. J. Lechner (ed.), "The Sociology of Roland Robertson," *Journal for the Scientific Study of Religion* 31(1992):294-323; T. Robbins and R. Robertson (eds.), *Church-State Relations* (New Brunswick, N.J.: Transaction, 1986); R. Robertson, *The Sociological Interpretation of Religion* (Oxford: Blackwell, 1970); R. Robertson, *Meaning and Change* (Oxford: Blackwell, 1978); R. Robertson, *Globalization* (London: Sage, 1992); R. Robertson and B. Holzner (eds.), *Identity and Authority* (Oxford: Blackwell, 1980); R. Robertson and J. P. Nettl, *International Systems and the Modernization of Societies* (New York: Basic Books, 1968).

ROBINSON, LEO (1899-1968)   Jesuit priest; Ph.D., St. Louis University (1934) from which he was assigned to Gonzaga University (Spokane, Washington) as President, Rector of the Jesuit community, and Professor of Sociology until 1942. He was then chosen to lead the Jesuit Oregon Province as Provincial, its chief administrator, a position he held until 1948. President, American Catholic Sociological Society, 1947.

While teaching at Seattle University, Robinson was diagnosed with multiple sclerosis and returned to Gonzaga for the remainder of his life. He worked to advance the cause of coeducation at Gonzaga, supported the transition from Eurocentric to Amerocentric approaches to Jesuit education, and advocated the development of the social sciences model as distinct from the humanities.

—David A. Kingma

ROKEACH, MILTON (1918-1988)   Social psychologist most noted for research on attitudes, beliefs, and values.

Rokeach's influential theory of *dogmatism* was developed in response to perceived inadequacies in the authoritarian personality research tradition. In particular, Rokeach argues that the process of belief is more a determinant of prejudice than the content of belief. His dogmatism construct and the widely used scale to assess it, the *Dogmatism Scale,* purports to be an ideological and content-free measure of closed-mindedness. It has been used widely in studies of religion and prejudice.

In 1969, Rokeach delivered the H. Paul Douglass lecture to the Religious Research Association in which he proposed the *Rokeach Value Survey,* a way to rank-measure instrumental and terminal values. Generally, he proposed that the religious are less socially compassionate than others, a finding that continues to stimulate debate and research in the contemporary empirical psychology of religion.

—Ralph W. Hood, Jr.

REFERENCES

M. Rokeach, "Political and Religious Dogmatism," *Psychological Monographs* 425(1956); M. Rokeach, *The Open and Closed Mind* (New York: Basic Books, 1960); M. Rokeach, *Beliefs, Attitudes, and Values* (San Francisco: Jossey-Bass, 1968); M. Rokeach, "The H. Paul Douglass Lectures for 1969," *Review of Religious Research* 11(1969):1-39.

ROLES   Comprehensive patterns of behavior and attitudes, constituting a strategy for coping with a recurrent set of situations (Turner 1990). A social role is played by different individuals and supplies a major basis for identifying and placing persons in a group, organization, or society. Roles consist of rights, duties, and expected behavior and give stability and structure to social situations.

Turner delineates four types of roles: (1) basic roles —such as gender and age roles—that are located in society rather than particular organizations; (2) structural status roles—such as occupational, family, minister, nun—that are attached to office or status in particular organizations; (3) functional group roles— such as mediator, leader, challenger—that are not formally designated or attached to group positions or offices but are recognized in the group culture; and (4) value roles— such as hero, traitor, heretic, saint—that embody values of the group. Each type of role involves expectations of behavior associated with individuals in the particular role.

Roles are not static entities; rather, role change is one characteristic on which roles vary. Role change is defined as change in the shared conception and operationalization of typical role performance and role boundaries. Roles can change in several ways. A new role can be created or an existing role can be dissolved; a role can change quantitatively by the addition or subtraction of duties, rights, or prestige associated with the role;

and a role can change qualitatively by a change in the interpretation of its meaning. Because roles always have relational meaning to one or more other roles, change in one role always has repercussions on related roles; for example, change in the expectations for church ministers involves change in the roles of laity.

While role change deals with changes in the expectations associated with the role itself, role exit occurs when individuals who occupy given roles abandon them for new roles. Most of the social science literature on roles focuses upon socialization into new roles; however, beginning with Ebaugh's (1988) work on role exit, recent studies are taking into account both entry into roles and the process of leaving them. Role exit is the process of disengagement from a role that is central to one's self-identity and the reestablishment of an identity in a new role that takes into account one's ex-role. Being an "ex" is unique sociologically in that the expectations, norms, and identity of an ex-role relate not to what one is currently doing but to social expectations associated with the previous role. Because of "role residual," that is, elements of role identity that an individual carries over into a new role as well as memories and associations that significant others have of one's previous role identity, being an ex constitutes a unique role in itself.

In the past several decades, religious roles, both ministerial and lay, have changed significantly within many churches. The profound changes occurring within the clergy and religious orders of women in the Roman Catholic Church are one example of the impact of role change on religious institutions. In fact, the quantitative and qualitative changes in role expectations of Catholic priests have led to a severe clergy shortage (Schoenherr and Young 1993, Hoge et al. 1988) due to increased role exits of priests and fewer Catholic men entering seminaries. Likewise, the dramatic decline in numbers of young women entering Catholic convents, along with the numerous exits of Catholic nuns in the late 1960s and early 1970s, has led some researchers to predict substantial organizational changes (Neal 1990, Wittberg 1994, Nygren and Ukeritis 1993) and even the organizational demise (Ebaugh 1993) of women's religious orders.

Because social roles are part of the structural features of every organization, substantial role change affects and defines the health, viability, and future of all organizations. Analysis of religious organizations therefore inevitably involves the study of the stability and change in social roles of those who constitute the organization.

—*Helen Rose Ebaugh*

REFERENCES

H. R. Ebaugh, *Becoming an Ex* (Chicago: University of Chicago Press, 1988); H. R. Ebaugh, *Women in the Vanishing Cloister* (New Brunswick, N.J.: Rutgers University Press, 1993); D. R. Hoge et al., "Changing Age Distribution and Theological Attitudes of Catholic Priests," *Sociological Analysis* 49(1988):264-280; M. A. Neal, *From Nuns to Sisters* (Mystic, Conn.: Twenty-Third Publications, 1990); D. Nygren and M. Ukeritis, *The Future of Religious Orders in the United States* (Westport, Conn.: Praeger, 1993); R. A. Schoenherr and L. A. Young, *Full Pews and Empty Altars* (Madison: University of Wisconsin Press, 1993); R. H. Turner, "Role," in *International Encyclopedia of the Social Sciences* 13(1968):552-557; R. H. Turner, "Role Change," *Annual Review of Sociology* 16(1990):87-110; P. Wittberg, *The Rise and Fall of Catholic Religious Orders* (Albany: SUNY Press, 1994).

ROMAN CATHOLICISM   Social scientific study of Roman Catholicism varies over time, as international or domestic events make religion, and Roman Catholicism specifically, seem connected or unconnected to significant shapings of the world and of human behaviors. Conceptions of sociological theory and practice also make a difference. Here too the eye of the beholder importantly affects, first, what is seen, and then what is judged as significant. Sociologists are currently, although unevenly, retrieving a sense of the great importance of culture and the construction of meaning for adequately understanding human behavior, especially personal and shared identities, and this "hermeneutical" turn significantly makes them more attentive to the interpretative power and social consequences of the Catholic religious imagination and its dense and worldwide institutionalization.

Background   If we roughly date the emergence of a self-conscious social *science* with the era following Comte (d. 1857), then we can say that classical social science treated religion, and especially Catholicism, in the Enlightenment fashion as a form of premodern thought producing and sustaining authoritarian regimes destined for replacement through scientific and moral progress. The Marxian revolutionist version of this "projectionist false consciousness" was merely the least equivocal and most assured rendering of this broad Enlightenment thesis. Although many qualifications need making, in social science, this Enlightenment premise was fashioned into "secularization" theory. Again with many qualifications, no small part of the early moral energy of social science derived from the expectation that an applied social science would replace religiously derived ethics in the guidance of society and the legitimation of its organizing principles and outcomes.

Because of its hierarchical organization, its anchoring ritual, and its premodern doctrines, especially its defense of sacramental reality, Roman Catholicism represented to social science intellectuals the most vivid example of the Enlightenment premise that at bottom there was no metaphysical distinction between religion and magic that might require any serious application of the terms *true* or *false*. In his early essay on religious evolution, Bellah (1970:32 ff.) more benignly but firmly located Catholicism within the "historic religions" strata, which he contrasted with the "early modern" represented by Reformation Protestantism and especially its valorization of individual conscience. Itself ironically mirroring Enlightenment-inspired secularization theory, a highly defensive post-Reformation Catholicism could promise to reward empirical inquiry and (especially) evolutionary schema, with few initiatives or historical surprises beyond what some might regard as an interesting genius for survival.

Although there were some conspicuous exceptions, especially in the immediate post-World War II era (Thomas O'Dea, Werner Stark, and Joseph Fichter being among the most obvious), for the first part of the twentieth century the term *residual* would have satisfactorily categorized any of these lingering empirical interests in Roman Catholicism for all but those few who came to be associated with the American Catholic Sociological Society (1938-1967). In fairness, it should be noted that these explicitly Catholic sociologists did not consider their rejection of a "value-free sociology" as apologetics but, in anticipation of postmodernist sentiment, as intellectually honest and necessary for the advancement of a critical sociology that, for them, was aligned with the tradition of Catholic social thought. (On the desire to make social science capable of social criticism, see Furfey 1946; for some of the tensions between social science and its Catholic context, see Fichter 1973; for the continuing appeal of this explicit "integralist" linking of social science with Catholic social thought, consider the Society of Catholic Social Scientists, formed in 1992.)

The Contemporary Setting Today, as the varieties of positivistic social science yield intellectual terrain to the pluralisms of the postmodern, and Roman Catholicism shaped by the Second Vatican Council (1962-1965) struggles to achieve more ecumenical, interfaith, and world-engaging spiritualities, a changed social science finds more of interest in a changed Roman Catholicism—and vice versa. Catholicism appears as an important actor in and influence on those world events (Johnston and Sampson 1994), from the Philippines to Poland, connected with the demise of world communism and, closer to home, in those "boundary disputes" concerning law and morality lately labeled "culture wars." On most of these issues, world Catholicism is found to align itself with the defense of human rights, indigenous culture, and the advancement of a human solidarity no longer plausibly carried by Marxist and Enlightenment ideologies.

Varieties of liberation theology, the "preferential option for the poor," are only the most explicit signaling of this uneven but explicit institutional effort to change from a nineteenth-century psychology of defensive maintenance to one of critical but dialogic engagement. Bellah (1970:251) aptly characterized the classical era (especially Durkheim and Freud) of social science's more sophisticated treatment of religion as either "symbolic reductionism," whereby religion's emotional truths are categorized as prescientific thought, or as "consequential reductionism," whereby its social force is explained by (and reduced to) its replaceable social functions. In contemporary social science, there are challenging possibilities for a less reductionistic and more open-minded interest in the reciprocal influences of Catholicism, culture, society, and politics. The methodologies are as varied as the questions asked.

Survey research: Contemporary surveys on Catholic beliefs, attitudes, and the varieties of church participation are made by sociologists, church staff, and pollsters. Greeley has summarized (1977, 1989) decades of survey research about Catholicism (often rhetorically marshaled to debunk what he calls stereotypes of things Catholic) dealing with myriad topics such as Catholics and social class, religious beliefs, attendance rates, institutional loyalty, political attitudes, acceptance of church moral teachings, and the performance of parochial schools. Although as recently as the mid-1960s, half the Catholic adult population was still either first- or second-generation American, post-World War II educational and employment opportunities led to the "mid classification" of white American Catholics. By the 1970s, Catholics exceeded the national average in educational and income levels. Inspecting apostasy rates (between 14% and 20%), Mass attendance (more than 70% are likely to say at least twice a month), support for Catholic schools (high), acceptance of church leadership ("selective loyalty" whereby laity readily affirm core doctrines while in effect following the "Protestant principle" of individual judgment on moral teachings), and satisfaction with local parish life (high), Greeley concludes that Catholics in America are "acculturated but not assimilated."

Later studies (Seidler and Meyer 1989, D'Antonio et al. 1989) corroborate this broad assessment. In a longitudinal case study of a Catholic high school, adeptly titled *Conscience First, Tradition Second,* Patrick McNamara (SUNY Press 1992) reports a receptivity toward the peace and justice themes of Vatican II and the 1980 pastoral letters (*The Challenge of Peace* and *Economic Justice for All*) of the National Conference of Catholic Bishops, a broad-based agreement that they should listen to the church's teaching but then make up their own minds, and only about 12% who years later characterized themselves as alienated from the church.

Empirical studies of Catholicism tend to discourage any single-variable explanations of the decline or increase of specific Catholic behaviors during any given period of time. For example, although Greeley initially argued that the reduced level of Catholic institutional conformity was largely due to the 1968 encyclical of Pope Paul VI titled *Humanae Vitae,* which affirmed the traditional teaching that every conjugal act (save those during naturally infecund periods) had to be open to the possibility of conception, other studies were not able to corroborate this confidently. The fact that church attendance during the same period declined in liberal Protestant denominations, where there were no controversies about contraception, minimally suggested more complexity. More recently, Greeley found that only 10% of those who rejected the ban on artificial contraception and said they had little confidence in Catholic officials had completely abandoned church attendance (1989:50). In practice, church hierarchies are likely to interpret the ban as a matter of idealism, while local clergy are likely to ignore it. The same sorts of complex mix of continuity, accommodation, and subtle reinterpretation are found in other areas. Indeed, devising the appropriate wording for questionnaire items represents a constant challenge for the sociological imagination.

Studies about marriage stability among Catholics have not yet attempted to incorporate the distinction important in Catholic teaching between "annulment" and divorce. But the evidence shows increased acceptance for both among Catholics. Past studies reported that Catholics were far less likely than Protestants to end their marriages in courts of law, but these differences have declined. The Notre Dame study of registered Catholics (1987) found that 64% thought "the church should liberalize its position on divorce." American Catholicism seems to be handling this issue in historic Catholic ways of viewing law as expressing an ideal often failed and then rectified by pastoral accommodation and canon law, and in this way seeking to preserve the principle while reinterpreting its application. Marriage tribunals petitioned for annulment increasingly rely on psychological factors for determining whether a marriage was initially "sacramentally valid," declaring valid only those unions formed by the free consent of partners, which, in turn, requires the maturity to make such a commitment.

It is ideologically important to Roman Catholicism to present all changes in teaching and practice in a framework of continuity that purports to show that core doctrines and teachings have been more deeply understood, that is, "developed," rather than displaced by new doctrines. The legitimation of its magisterial teaching and hierarchical authority is highly dependent on such theological reconstruction. But so too is its considerable power for social critique. For example, the American Bishops' widely discussed 1983 pastoral letter *The Challenge of Peace,* which condemned the use of nuclear weapons and even the threat to use them, relied heavily on the principle they had also enunciated in their opposition to abortion, namely, that innocent human life cannot directly be killed. Among other dimensions of ecclesial social psychology that need noting in an ecumenical era is that one result of the Reformation seems to be an unplanned division of labor within Christianity whereby classical Protestantism tended to understand itself as representing individual conscience and cultural flexibility while Catholicism in opposition defined itself as the primary locus of Christian memory and moral tradition (Kelly 1984).

Americanization While the Catholic magisterium emphasizes moral traditionalism and Catholic behavior evinces a more individualized approach to these moral norms, in terms of "culture war" issues, neither Catholic laity nor hierarchical teaching fit into the conventional "liberal" versus "conservative" labels routinely employed in journalism. The standard media presentation of polls showing the "Americanization" of Catholic attitudes toward reproductive and "lifestyle" issues frames lay tolerance against a deepening magisterium rigidity in a tone suggesting "gathering storms" of revolt. But the data suggest considerably more complexity, and it's not always a simple matter to represent succinctly Catholic reactions to "culture war" issues. On both the federal and the local levels, depending on the issue, Catholics are as likely to form coalitions with mainstream Protestants as with evangelical Protestants. The frequently found generalization is that Catholic leaders and much of the laity will be conservative on moral issues and liberal on "peace and justice" ones, but, even here, there are nuances that need noting. Catholics on any level rarely involve themselves in disputes about prayer in the schools or the teaching of creationism. Catholic leadership vigorously rejects welfare reform that penalizes unmarried mothers by providing no additional funds to children born on welfare, anticipating that this frugality assumes reliance on Medicaid-funded abortion.

Indeed, the institutional Catholic position on legal abortion especially separates the "moral conservatism" of the Catholic tradition from the "fiscal conservatism" found in antiabortion Republican politics since the 1980 presidential campaign of Ronald Reagan. Although publicly identified with opposition to legal abortion, the position of the American Catholic bishops is that abortion opposition should reflect a "consistent ethic of life." This "consistent ethic" not only supports social services for pregnant women otherwise economically driven to consider abortion—both the voluntary efforts of groups such as "Birthright" and "Alternatives to Abortion International" and government social services—it also opposes capital punishment, the arms race, and the militarization of national security. Even when they support some legalization of abortion, American Catholics reject "abortion on demand" and reject the categorization of abortion simply as a form of birth control (Gremillion and Castelli 1987). One of the most admired Catholic politicians by right-to-life groups is Pennsylvania's Governor William Casey, whose state abortion regulations, found constitutional by the U.S. Supreme Court in 1992 (Kelly 1995), are modeled on a "woman's right to know" and the provision of state resources to encourage childbirth. While the role of Roman Catholics in the abortion controversy has received some scholarly attention (Byrnes and Segers 1992), research on its role in opposing "assisted suicide" legislation is only in its beginning stages.

Although the common journalistic "Catholic" story highlights the gap between lay attitudes and hierarchical teaching, even the term *quiet schism* does not fit the survey data showing the discrepancy between lay opinion and magisterium teaching. For example, polls report the vast majority of American Catholics say they admire Pope John Paul II; the majority say he is "infallible" with regard to core beliefs of faith but less than half will say he is "infallible" when he teaches about morals. It's not easy for interpreters to state definitively what such findings mean, because by the norms of Catholic theology itself, pre-Vatican II beliefs can be said to express an "overbelief" rather than essential teaching. In addition, throughout many centuries, Catholic political ethics, in the tradition of "prudence" or practical reason, has acknowledged (although not always practiced) that disagreement over a political application of a moral principle does not necessarily mean disagreement over the moral principle itself. Because so much of Catholic social and moral teaching about the family and reproductive ethics assumes a supporting community and a political authority responsive to the redistributionist ethics of *subsidiarity,* there are dynamic interconnections, often missed, among the magisterium's moral traditionalism, the local churches' organizational vitality, and the increasingly critical public policy positions of Catholic teaching. All dioceses, for example, have extensive programs in "natural family planning," "pre-Cana" marriage preparation programs for those thinking of marriage, and "Cana" for engaged Catholics. Only about a fifth of all American parishes have explicit ministries for the divorced and separated, but Catholic Family Ministry officials note that most divorcing Catholics prefer help and support groups from a parish where they are not personally known.

Except for the conventional construction of abortion politics, the positions taken by the American bishops on questions of economic justice and national security are well to the "left" of American political discourse. The church's very moral traditionalism about the centrality of families is itself a strong ideological and organizational propellant toward a critique of market-driven political economies. Catholic documents now routinely judge the economy in terms of how it affects the poor and routinely criticize military spending and the militarization of foreign aid. Although these criticisms rarely penetrate in much detail to the parish level, American Catholics, when compared with the generic Protestant, remain more likely to support government intervention to aid those adversely affected by market forces and to be critical of both isolationist and hegemonic tendencies in foreign policies (Gallup and Castelli 1987). Perhaps missing the connection between Catholicism's moral conservatism and critical social teaching, D'Antonio et al. (1989) were surprised to find that the more orthodox the respondents, the more likely they were to say they read and approved of the pastoral letters *The Challenge of Peace* and *Economic Justice for All.* Despite their upward mobility, Catholics are still more likely to identify as Democrats than Republicans, and Catholic college graduates are more than twice as likely as Protestant college graduates to believe that government should do more to improve society (Kosmin and Lachman 1993).

When compared with the generic Protestant, Catholics have been found more tolerant of homosexuals (Gallup and Castelli 1987, Greeley 1990). Hierarchical responses to gay rights have been supportive of homosexual claims and concerns when they can be interpreted as a matter of general respect for the human person—such as the right to employment, nondiscrimination, health care, protection against intolerance—and oppositional to policies or politics that explicitly suggest a public definition of homosexuality as a sexual lifestyle morally equal to marriage between heterosexuals.

Declining Number of Clergy and Religious Although Catholics generally approve of church leadership and at least mildly reflect in their political positions the broad priorities of Catholic social thought, soon after Vatican II there were far fewer clerical and publicly vowed leadership left of whom to approve. Hoge (1987) and Schoenherr and Young (1993) document the large decline in the numbers of seminarians and priests in the post-Vatican years. The decline in the number of American sisters was even steeper (Wittberg 1994). In 1967, there were 59,892 priests and 7,972 seminarians. By 1985, there were 57,313 priests and 4,063 seminarians. At their peak in 1965, Roman Catholic religious communities in this country included 181,421 women; in 1994, there were about 94,000, and their median age was over 65.

While vocations have greatly increased in non-Western cultures, they have not revived in the West. There are more than 19,000 Catholic parishes in America. By the early 1990s, Wallace (1992) was able to study women parish administrators among the several hundred parishes without a resident priest. Murnion et al. (1992) estimate that 0.8% of American parishes lack resident priests and that about two-thirds of all parishes have only one priest serving full-time.

The Notre Dame study of registered Catholics (Castelli and Gremillion 1987) found that 63% would accept married clergy but were less likely (38%) to approve of the ordination of women. Data show that laity are more likely to *accept* these changes than to *approve* of them, but recent polls show incremental increases in approval of both a married clergy and the ordination of women. No doubt, future research will show a deepening conflict in the area of eligibility criteria for ordained ministry.

Declining Professional Class, Ascending Laity Although not compensating for the decline in the numbers of ordained and of vowed religious, there has been a great growth in newer forms of ministry. There are now over 10,000 American men in the restored order of the diaconate and a proliferation of lay ministries. Not counting school and maintenance staff, there are now about 10,000 paid lay pastoral ministers, mostly women and mostly married, engaged in parish roles formerly performed by priests and sisters, such as pastoral administrator, director of religious education, catechumenate director, liturgy director, youth minis-

ter, business manager, and so on (Murnion et al. 1992). Increasingly there are suggestions that women be ordained to the diaconate, which has clearer New Testament precedents than their ordination to the priesthood.

Historic Catholicism resists sectarianism and seeks to interpenetrate cultures and societies. Representing this "church" ethos, as well as the needs of its early American immigrant past, there are some 232 church-related colleges and universities enrolling over 550,000 students. Greeley (1990) has pronounced the undergraduate colleges to be "decent" and the graduate schools to be "mediocre." The vast Catholic grammar and secondary school systems (7,174 Catholic elementary schools in 1993) are recognized as the equal of most of the public school system in middle-class areas, superior to those in poorer areas, and especially highly regarded for their relatively high success rate with minority students. Just about 9% of blacks are Catholic, but they are more likely to be college graduates than other Americans and 40% more likely than other black Americans (Kosmin and Lachman 1993). There are about 640 Catholic hospitals serving 41 million patients as well as more than 1,000 long-term-care facilities and many other health services. There is also a large "Catholic charity" network providing social work services in each Catholic diocese. Issues of church-state relationship and Catholic "identity" are increasingly discussed by elites in this dense network of institutional presences, but social science research is surprisingly sparse. Other topics need more attention as well.

National surveys do not always obtain reliable data on nonwhite Catholics. Although there is currently considerable anxious speculation about, for example, the retention rate of Catholics of Hispanic backgrounds, the few systematic studies available (Fitzpatrick 1971, Gonzalez and LaVelle 1985) reported some loss but mostly relative stability. More recent reports (Suro 1989), however, find "perhaps more than four million of the 20 million Hispanic Americans now practice some form of Protestant Christianity." Future studies will address the complex methodological issues of relating present identification with religion of origin, because the vitality of Protestantism in Latin American cultures makes untenable the older assumption that Hispanic culture itself produced Catholic allegiance on some level. Also complicating survey research is the oft-reported finding that many Hispanics practice a noninstitutionally based religion focused on cultural identity and family.

It is worth noting that academically based scholars interested in non-Caucasian Catholics and multiculturalism should not overlook studies done by scholars working within church institutional settings, such as the more than 60 diocesan offices of Pastoral Research and Planning and the research done by the National Conference of Catholic Education dealing with Hispanic, black, and Asian Catholics. Perhaps of particular interest are the emerging studies of Hispanic Catholicism by sociologists of Hispanic backgrounds themselves (for example, Diaz-Stevens 1993).

Applied and Institutionally Based Research Although applied research has been institutionalized to some extent in American Protestantism since the early 1900s, it was not until the post-Vatican 1960s that sponsored research offices started in Roman Catholicism. Before that time, there were individual and even university-based collaborative efforts (for example, at Catholic University, Loyola University of Chicago, and Fordham University) that applied current research methods to administrative concerns, such as improving parish life or evangelization. But these were ad hoc and only implicitly focused on institutional use. The first studies (e.g., Buchofen 1926, Bustanagel 1930, Schnepp 1942, see Doyle 1995) could generously be described as applied and interdisciplinary in that they employed specific questions and orientations derived from canon law and studied topics such as parish administration and rates of defection.

By the 1950s, this long-standing interest in parish life went beyond administrative needs, and sociologists associated with recently formed departments of sociology at Catholic universities developed more sophisticated surveys and typologies (e.g., Fichter 1954; other contributors to parish research were Joseph H. Scheuer, John P. Donovan, and Joseph F. Schuyler, S.J.). This period of informal overlap of church and university research interests ended by the mid-1960s. *The American Catholic Sociological Review,* which started in 1939 as the journal of the American Catholic Sociological Society, became *Sociological Analysis* in 1964, signifying both the professionalization of sociology among Catholics and the loss of the earlier sense that Catholic social thought was such a distinctly privileged source of social critique that in itself it could lay claim to an aligned applied empirical method. Still, both applied (Sweetser 1983) and university-based research (Gremillion and Castelli 1987) on parish life continued.

Since the 1960s, centers of applied research also emerged outside academia under church auspices. The Second Vatican Council sanctioned a more collaborative style of decision making, which, along with the adoption of contemporary models of data-based managerial styles, led to the institutionalization of data gathering offices in most Catholic dioceses. The first office

of Pastoral Research opened in 1966 in the Archdiocese of Baltimore, and by the end of the 1980s about half of all Catholic dioceses had such offices. The research done by these offices covers a wide range of topics and contains data useful for sociologists of religion: profiles of dioceses and parishes derived from census data and diocesan censuses; evaluation of diocesan programs; attitudes, beliefs, and practices of Catholics; reception of sacraments; diocesan and parish need assessment; studies of Hispanic, black, and Asian Catholics. Doyle (1995) provides a history of the first empirical studies of Catholic parish life and the formation of the research offices connected with Catholic dioceses.

Since 1969, the Lilly Endowment has funded many research projects on American Roman Catholicism (see Kelly 1988, 1989). Other important sources of empirical data about Catholic life generated by nonacademic sources include the National Catholic Educational Association, Washington, D.C.; the National Pastoral Life Center, 299 Elizabeth Street, New York City 10012; and the Center for Applied Research in the Apostolate, located at Georgetown University, Washington, D.C.

World Catholicism The empirical and ideological complexity of Catholicism, it bears repeating, deflates any confident air of generalization. For example, in critical tone and revolutionary aim, the post-Vatican II, Latin American-initiated "liberation theology"—wedding an adapted Marxist vocabulary to Christian discipleship in a critique of capitalism—is worlds apart from the "managerial" North American applied research just described. Although any summary of the range and importance of liberation theology, and its varying ecclesiastical controversies and sociopolitical impacts, cannot be attempted here, it should at least be noted that its "liberationist" focus on "praxis" (action) and equality has already influenced North American thought on such topics as feminism, the nature of the church, the role of "small groups" in the formation of disciples, and the moral challenges of globalization. This influence is likely to increase, although always as greatly shaped by the force of North American culture.

Obviously, research on international Catholicism resists summarization even more than research within a nation-state. Less than one-quarter of the world's population is Christian, but about half of that is Catholic. The rough comparative statistics (see Gannon 1988) show a continuing "de-Europeanization" of Catholicism, with Latin America containing more Catholics than Europe and North America combined. The fastest growing Catholic churches are in Africa and Asia. Throughout Europe, the subcultural institutions that sheltered a Catholic identity have been largely dismantled, but a diffuse attachment, fitting neither the models of secularization nor of classical ecclesiology, remains. Seidler's (see Seidler and Mayer 1989) term *contested accommodation* captures well enough the broad pattern of hierarchical responses to modern Western political and cultural development. But finding the apt term to characterize the complex lay responses is more difficult.

Depending on their own appraisal, sociologists describe this "diffuse, more than residual but less than committed" attachment to Catholicism that remains in highly secularized Europe in various ways, ranging from Greeley's rather sanguine phrase *communal Catholic* to Martin's more skeptical *apolitical and doctrineless* attachment (1988). For example, while 52% of French Catholics typically describe themselves as "nonpracticing," polls find that 83% continue to identify themselves as "Catholic," 75% believe that baptism is important, and 61% say religious education is valuable. Hornsby-Smith (in Gannon 1988) reports that Catholic institutions in Britain are attenuated but that Catholic beliefs are widely disseminated "albeit in a somewhat amorphous manner." The greater and more intense role of Catholicism in Ireland and Poland is explained by noting the "civil religion" functions that still pertain there but not elsewhere. But nowhere can it safely be said that Catholicism no longer matters in understanding behaviors or events.

In a secondary analysis of the 1985-1986 *International Social Survey Project,* Greeley (1989), guided by the classic analyses of Weber and Durkheim, found in a half-dozen European states small but statistically significant differences between Catholics and generic Protestants on "pre-capitalist" and "mechanical solidarity" types of measures such as valuing equality more than merit-based distributions, favoring more equal distribution of incomes, approving of more government ownership of industry, and affirming more "immanent" and benevolent images of God. Martin (1985) agrees on the different "styles" of being Catholic and Protestant but focuses on the institutional "density" of Catholicism instead of on beliefs and attitudes: Where Catholicism is also the carrier of national symbols of resistance or defiance (Poland, Ireland), differentiation between church and state has not yet led to a comparable thinning of institutional presence.

In non-Western areas, where Catholics are a minority, the Catholic blend of theological conservatism and political liberalism supports a vital social presence and a sharp reminder that Roman Catholicism intends to be, and often is, experienced as far more than a federation of regional or national churches. Casanova's (1994) study of the public dimensions of religion describes Catholicism especially as being transformed from a "state-oriented" kind of civil religion to a "society-oriented" institution that, ironically, carries the Enlightenment project of achieving human freedom and moral progress into the post-Enlightenment era.

Not to be lost among "geopolitical" investigations are the more qualitative and ethnographic studies loosely called studies of "folk Catholicisms" that exist not only in nonindustrial regions but also in highly urbanized areas where often defiant supporters of "Marian" apparitions can be found as well as stubbornly and often antagonistic forms of pre-Vatican II Catholicism (see the studies by Carroll, Hynes, and Dinges in O'Toole 1990). These phenomena, perhaps more dramatically than what is construed as "normal" religiosity, remind the sociologist that the critical and illuminating power of classical treatments of religion should not be abandoned even as their reductionism is no longer epistemologically privileged.

Social scientists especially interested in scholarship that contributes to a deeper understanding of the conditions of world justice will be most interested in the study of Roman Catholicism's Vatican II commitment to ecumenical and interfaith dialogue and, since Pope John XXIII's papacy, the significance of the use by all succeeding popes of an explicit appeal to "all men and women of good will" in all their encyclicals dealing with broadly human concerns.

—*James R. Kelly*

REFERENCES

R. N. Bellah, *Beyond Belief* (New York: Harper, 1970); C. A. Buchofen, *The Canonical and Civil Status of Catholic Parishes in the United States* (St. Louis: Herder, 1926); C. V. Bustanagel, *The Appointment of Parochial Adjuncts and Assistants* (Washington, D.C.: Catholic University of America Press, 1930); T. A. Byrnes and M. C. Segers, *The Catholic Church and the Politics of Abortion* (Boulder, Colo.: Westview, 1992); J. Casanova, *Public Religions in the Modern World* (Chicago: University of Chicago Press, 1994); W. V. D'Antonio et al., *American Catholic Laity* (Kansas City, Mo.: Sheed & Ward, 1989); A. M. Diaz-Stevens, *Oxcart Catholicism on Fifth Avenue* (Notre Dame, Ind.: University of Notre Dame Press, 1993); R. N. Doyle, *Diocesan Planning and Research,* Doctoral dissertation, Fordham University, 1995; J. H. Fichter, *Southern Parish* (Chicago: University of Chicago Press, 1954); J. H. Fichter, *One Man Research* (New York: Wiley, 1973); J. P. Fitzpatrick, *Puerto Rican Americans* (Englewood Cliffs, N.J.: Prentice Hall, 1971); P. H. Furfey, "Value Judgments in Sociology," *American Catholic Sociological Review* 7(1946):83-95; G. Gallup, Jr., and J. Castelli, *The American Catholic People* (Garden City, N.Y.: Doubleday, 1987); T. M. Gannon (ed.), *World Catholicism in Transition* (New York:

Macmillan, 1988); R. O. Gonzalez and M. LaVelle, *The Hispanic Catholic in the United States* (New York: Northeast Catholic Pastoral Center for Hispanics, 1985); A. M. Greeley, *The American Catholic* (New York: Basic Books, 1977); A. M. Greeley, "Protestant and Catholic," *American Sociological Review* 54(1989):485-502; A. M. Greeley et al., *Catholic Schools in a Declining Church* (Kansas City, Mo.: Sheed & Ward, 1976); J. Gremillion and J. Castelli, *The Emerging Parish* (San Francisco, Calif.: Harper, 1987); D. R. Hoge, *Future of Catholic Leadership* (Kansas City, Mo.: Sheed & Ward, 1987); D. Johnston and C. Sampson, *Religion: The Missing Dimension of Statecraft* (New York: Oxford University Press, 1994); J. R. Kelly, "Catholicism and Modern Memory," *Sociological Analysis* 45(1984):131-144; J. R. Kelly, *The First Decade of Grant Making for the Study of Roman Catholicism* (Indianapolis: Lilly Foundation, 1988); J. R. Kelly, "Data and Mystery," *America* (Nov. 1989): 345-350; J. R. Kelly, "Beyond Compromise," in *Abortion Politics in American States*, ed. M. C. Segars and T. A. Byrnes (Armonk, N.Y.: Sharpe, 1995): 205-224; B. Kosmin and S. P. Lachman, *One Nation Under God* (New York: Harmony, 1993); D. Martin, "Religion and Public Values," *Review of Religious Research* 26(1985):313-331; D. Martin, "Catholicism in Transition," in T. M. Gannon (1988), *q.v.*: 3-35; P. J. Murnion et al., *New Parish Ministries* (New York: National Pastoral Life Center, 1992); R. O'Toole (ed.), *Sociological Studies in Roman Catholicism* (Lewiston, N.Y.: Mellen, 1990); G. J. Schnepp, *Leakage from a Catholic Parish* (Washington, D.C.: Catholic University of America Press, 1942); R. A. Schoenherr and L. A. Young, *Full Pews and Empty Altars* (Madison: University of Wisconsin Press, 1993); J. Seidler and K. Meyer, *Conflict and Change in the Catholic Church* (New Brunswick, N.J.: Rutgers University Press, 1989); R. Suro, "Switch by Hispanic Catholics Changes Face of U.S. Religion," *New York Times* (Mar. 14, 1989): 1; T. P. Sweetser, *Successful Parishes* (New York: Harper, 1983); R. Wallace, *They Call Her Pastor* (Albany: SUNY Press, 1992); P. Wittberg, *The Rise and Fall of Catholic Religious Orders* (Albany: SUNY, 1994).

ROOF, WADE CLARK (1939-) J. F. Rowny Professor of Religion and Society and Director, Center for the Study of Religion, Department of Religious Studies, University of California, Santa Barbara. President, Religious Research Association, 1991-1992; Society for the Scientific Study of Religion, 1996-1997.

A native of Columbia, South Carolina, Wade Clark Roof graduated from Wofford College and Yale Divinity School before completing a Ph.D. in sociology at the University of North Carolina, where he worked with Gerhard Lenski and others. Following his doctoral studies, Roof joined the faculty of the University of Massachusetts at Amherst, which named him a full

Professor of Sociology in 1979. In 1990, he left Massachusetts for his current position at UCSB.

Author of 11 books and dozens of journal articles, Roof has been an active participant in professional societies in the social sciences and religion. In addition to his organizational presidencies, he served as Vice President of the Association for the Sociology of Religion. He also served as Executive Secretary of SSSR from 1978 to 1983 and has been a member of the Council of the Société Internationale de Sociologie des Religions.

Roof's research may be seen as encompassing several broad themes. His early contributions centered on research methods for studying religion. Here his UNC doctoral dissertation, published as *Community and Commitment: Religious Plausibility in a Liberal Protestant Church* (Elsevier 1978), reflects his interest in theoretical and methodological issues. *Community and Commitment* explored "localism" and "cosmopolitanism" in North Carolina Episcopal churches and inspired other efforts to examine worldviews in congregational settings. While Roof's more recent work has been more topical in character, his interest and contributions to theory and methodology are never far from the surface. Particularly notable was his 1992 RRA Presidential Address in which he called for practitioners in the social sciences to explore the possibilities of religious narrative in their research.

A second theme in Roof's research has been the scholar's role in interpreting change in American religion. As editor of the *Annals*' 1985 and 1993 volumes on religion in America, Roof has commissioned important essays that help define the U.S. "religious situation." *American Mainline Religion* (with William McKinney, Rutgers University Press 1987), and two edited collections, *Liberal Protestantism: Its Changing Shape and Future* (with Robert Michaelson, Pilgrim 1986) and *Beyond Establishment: Mainline Traditions in Transition* (with Jackson Carroll, Westminster 1993), serve a similar function. On the one hand, these books present solid new research on issues facing religious communities in America; on the other hand, they assist scholars, religious leaders, and the public in understanding the place of religion more broadly in American culture. This role as a "public intellectual" has led Roof to be recognized as a respected commentator on religious issues by the media and government agencies.

American Mainline Religion's principal theme is the emergence of what the authors call a "new voluntarism" in American religious life. The new voluntarism reflects a post-1960s emphasis on the theme of choice in American religion. Looking back at H. Richard Niebuhr's classic 1929 book, *The Social Sources of Denomination-alism* (Holt), Roof and McKinney point to evidence that Niebuhr's social sources of religious belonging (ethnicity, region, social class, sectionalism, and, to a lesser extent, race) seem less important in the late twentieth century. People are freer to opt for religious commitments different from those of their parents—or to withdraw from religious participation altogether. The new voluntarism is felt by religious communities across the spectrum but has presented special challenges for the older Protestant communions whose traditional clientele has had higher exposure to the social forces that have given rise to the new voluntarism (education, mobility, and so on).

The book also explores the demographic characteristics and social views of members of various religious groups, points to the emergence of several broad religious "families" (liberal, moderate, black, and conservative Protestants; Roman Catholics; Jews; and the religiously unaffiliated), and explores their current status and future prospects.

A third theme in Roof's research is a persistent interest in religion's relationship to other social institutions. This is most apparent with respect to religion and race, which has been a continuing concern, and, more recently, religion and family.

With financial support from the Lilly Endowment, in 1988 Roof began a major study of "baby boomers and religion" that resulted in the 1993 book *A Generation of Seekers* (Harper). This multipart project looked at persons born in the postwar period and living in four states: California, Ohio, Massachusetts, and North Carolina. Boomers, the book concluded, are unexpectedly interested in spirituality but not terribly interested in religion. The book combined statistical analysis based on survey data with narrative case studies based on lengthy in-person interviews, reflecting its author's new interest in narrative methods in studying religion.

Roof's 1990 relocation to Southern California provided him with opportunities to explore questions of race, ethnicity, and religion in new ways. Following civil disturbances in Los Angeles in the early 1990s, Roof began a collaboration with Donald Miller and John Orr to explore religion and public life in that city. Early reports from that study suggest the emergence of new constellations of relationships across denominational, theological, ideological, and racial-ethnic lines in what the researchers identify as a new "politics of the spirit."

—*William McKinney*

ROSS, EVA JENNY (1903-1970)   Born in Belfast, Northern Ireland, Ross earned her undergraduate degree at Bedford College, University of London. She came to the United States in 1930 and received an M.A. from St. Louis University and a Ph.D. in sociology from Yale University. She headed the Department of Sociology at Trinity College, Washington, D.C., from the time of her arrival on its faculty in 1940 to her retirement in 1969.

Elected President of the American Catholic Sociological Society in 1943, Ross was the first woman in the United States to hold presidential office in a professional organization of sociologists, national or regional. She was unable to give a presidential address, however, because her term came in the midst of World War II when the ACSS, like many professional groups, had suspended its annual national meetings. She was a member of the ACSS Executive Council for several years and a member of the editorial board of *American Catholic Sociological Review* from 1940 to 1950. Ross claimed to be the only Catholic at that time with a Ph.D. from a "non-Catholic" university—mistakenly, however, because her contemporary, Franz Mueller, had a degree from a "non-Catholic" university in Germany.

While disagreeing with the concept of "Catholic sociology," she firmly insisted that there was a role for the Catholic *sociologist* as one able to bring a value-oriented approach to sociological research, yet without slanting empirical data. She was vocal in her objections to the prevailing intellectual climate in professional sociological organizations that proclaimed the dogma of value neutrality, looked askance at anyone who seemed value oriented, and anathematized those who confessed a religious belief system. Although her primary research was in the sociology of cooperatives, she wielded considerable influence in the early formation of the ACSS. When the society changed its focus to the sociological study of Catholicism and renamed its journal, she felt that this duplicated the work of the mainly European Société Internationale de Sociologie des Religions and the *Journal for the Scientific Study of Religion*. In the light of this, and having attended every meeting of the ACSS (except for the 1938 organizational meeting at Loyola University), Ross decided in 1970 not to renew her membership.

—*Loretta M. Morris*

ROUSSEAU, JEAN-JACQUES (1712-1778)
Sociopolitical theorist; a major figure of the Enlightenment.

Jean-Jacques Rousseau regarded true religion as natural to humanity, unless corrupted by society. Christianity as described in the Gospels was regarded as true, simple, and sublime. However, according to Rousseau, Christianity severed the connection between religious and political authority. To provide a transcendent basis for political authority, Rousseau advocated "civil religion," which would not make specific theological claims but would provide the moral basis for citizenship. Private religions that did not contradict the demands of civil religion could be tolerated, but religions that provided for competing allegiances between God and temporal sovereignty "ought to be driven from the State."

—Ted G. Jelen

REFERENCES

J. J. Rousseau, *Émile, or Education* (London: Dent, 1911 [1762]); J. J. Rousseau, *The Social Contract and Discourses* (London: Dent, 1973 [1755, 1762]).

ROUTINIZATION In Max Weber's sociology, particularly, the process whereby charisma is stabilized into ongoing authority structures. According to Weber, all legitimate social authority is rooted in charisma, but because charisma is founded on a personal relationship between a followership and a leader, charismatic authority is inherently unstable; that is, it cannot directly survive the loss of the leader. If the social organization is to survive, some form of *routinization* must take place; an orderly (or routine) determination of who legitimately wields power must be determined. According to Weber, the two principal types of routinization are traditional and rational-legal. In the traditional structure, a person is understood to inherit charisma in some way, often with mystical sanction (e.g., kingship). In rational-legal authority structures, a set of laws or rules serves this purpose. Real-world authority structures are usually of mixed character. Perhaps the most important routinization form for the social scientific study of religion itself is *office charisma*, a traditionalist structure wherein the "office" to which a functionary is usually "ordained" is considered to be sacred (e.g., "Holy Orders") and to convey sanctity in turn upon the occupant's acts, without regard to his or her moral character generally.

See also Charisma

—William H. Swatos, Jr.

REFERENCE

M. Weber, *Economy and Society* (Berkeley: University of California, 1978).

RRA *see* Religious Research Association

RRR *see* Review of Religious Research

RYAN, JOHN A. (1869-1945) A native of Iowa and a priest, Ryan spent most of his life in Washington, D.C. He received a Ph.D. degree in moral theology from the Catholic University of America in 1906.

Ryan's lectures and publications, including his Ph.D. dissertation, were focused on political, economic, and ethical considerations concerning the just wage, labor unions, and the minimum wage for women. He was a strong supporter of Roosevelt and the New Deal, and is considered to have been directly involved in shaping these policies. His most important published work, *Distributive Justice* (Macmillan 1916), was an analysis of the ethical obligations of all parties in a modern industrial society. "His special role was to show Catholic America that these [New Deal] progressive reforms were essential for achieving the social justice to which their religion beckoned them" (Broderick 1963:277 f). The influence of Ryan was extensive and is still evident in older Catholic labor relations writers such as Msgr. George A. Higgins.

See also Christian Social Thought

—Loretta M. Morris

REFERENCE

F. L. Broderick, *Right Reverend New Dealer* (New York: Macmillan, 1963).

SACRED Probably the key concept in the study of religion. Indeed, to define *religion* as "that which has to do with the sacred" has become almost a tautology. Yet the sacred, as a phenomenon, is far wider than religion—at least as that has often been understood by students (in contrast to practitioners) of religion.

The sacred, as a phenomenon of experience, is generally recognized, by witnesses both direct and indirect, as possessing four characteristics. In experience, it is special, even unique; in value, it is important, even all-demanding; in consciousness, it is fundamental, even primordial; in communication, it is dynamic, yet ineffable.

All these characteristics issue in a single consequence that is easily described but is less a separate quality than an aspect or by-product of them all: It imposes "taboos," restrictions. Ultimately, these are beyond rationality. This is necessarily the case, in view of its own character, such as being prior to reasoning. The Levitical prohibitions, for instance, regularly defeat well-meaning attempts at rationalizing them, yet they *make sense*—if they are understood as the "data" (gifts) of a "personalizing" deity. As a lover (or a Messiah) might say, "Do this (for my sake), in remembrance of me (because I want you to): That's the way I am."

The sacred can be, and has been, presented as the object of esoteric experience. In the 1960s, during the Indian summer (or the swan song) of the secularization thesis, students of religion or society would be intro-duced to the concept as referring to an experience that was peculiar to earlier societies but unknown in industrial society. Investigation has shown this view to have been based on ignorance.

In 1969, for instance, a hundred individuals in England (somewhat weighted toward urban teenagers) were asked, "Is there anything you might be prepared to use the word 'sacred' of?" The three replies that best represented the total spectrum (in descending order of popularity) are as follows: "Each person's own beliefs"; "To me, Jesus is a sacred. Our Lord is sacred—he's the most sacred thing in my life"; and "People talk about sacred places, but I wouldn't use it ['sacred'] at all." The interviewees were then asked, "What do you mean or understand by 'sacred'?" The three replies that best represented all the strands present (not necessarily from the same three respondents) are as follows:

Something which is personal, which should be cherished, and which you alone have got. . . .

It's a belief in something that is almost untouchable, or something that has got to be revered in some way.

Those aspects of life which directly or indirectly relate to God. (Bailey 1997:73)

It is this kind of finding that was echoed, for instance, by the Religious Experience Research Unit (now, the

443

Alister Hardy Centre) in the 1970s. When the person-on-the-street (literally) was asked whether she or he had ever had a religious experience, one-third answered in the affirmative—and a further one-third felt too unsure to say no.

Such findings received theoretical recognition, for instance, in Phillip Hammond's "Introduction" to *The Sacred in a Secular Age* (University of California Press 1985:5):

> We seem to have mistaken religion and the sacred. In any era, therefore, when religion, at least as commonly understood, is receding, vitality of the sacred may come as a surprise. The present era would seem to fit such a description, and we find ourselves unable to comprehend the sacred. The past accretions that transformed the sacred into religion—accretions which in many instances have been corroded by secularization—keep us from the re-focussing necessary if we are to study the sacred in a secular age . . . unless we can revise our thinking about secularization.

The first step that is necessary, so that a secular age can understand the sacred both in its own day and at other times, is to consider the possible ubiquity of the experience.

Émile Durkheim's point (1912)—that the sacred is part of the structure of consciousness, and indeed the continuing sine qua non of all its development, rather than an early stage that can be left behind—may have validity. The second step is the recognition that the experience it embraces is "both wider and narrower" than the one that early modern society meant by "religion."

The third step is probably to distinguish the sacred from the "holy." The 1969 interviewer, expecting respondents to be nonplussed by such esoteric addenda to the main interview, followed the question about the meaning of "sacred," by asking, "What would you mean or understand by 'holy'?" Again, it was understood—and was distinguished from sacred:

> The "sacred" isn't religious, but "holy" does mean "religious" to me. I could apply it to everybody's religious symbols. But it's not a word I've clarified yet—it just carries overtones of incense.

> It's very close to "sacred," but again I would understand it in other people's terms. I am impressed by people who are able to see something as holy, such as people who draw strength from a grave. I approve—although my approval is irrelevant, of course—of a personally-felt holiness.

> "God-fearing"—you can't be a 'holy' man, apart from religion; it's an attitude. (Bailey 1997:73)

Durkheim and Rudolf Otto (and their English translators), in choosing *sacred* and *holy,* respectively, for their accounts of religious experience, were therefore tapping into popular understandings of each term. They were in fact describing the type of religious experience to be found in different kinds of societies. In small-scale societies, it may be described as a "sense of the sacred"; in historical societies, as "an encounter with a holy."

The next steps in refocusing the meaning of *sacred,* and its various relations with society, may involve the recognition that the small-scale type of society and historical type of society survive within contemporary society; that individuals, as well as societies, progress through these stages, as they pass from mother's knee to first school to concrete jungle; that psychic health seems to require continuing movement between all three types of setting; and that three (at least) varying types of religious experience may be anticipated, in these different contexts. Thus the form it takes in contemporary society is the particular concern expressed in the concept of "implicit religion."

See also Émile Durkheim, Implicit Religion, Religious Studies, Rudolf Otto

—*Edward Bailey*

REFERENCES

S. S. Acquaviva, *The Decline of the Sacred in Industrial Society* (Oxford: Blackwell, 1979); É. Durkheim, *The Elementary Forms of the Religious Life* (Glencoe, Ill.: Free Press, 1947); P. E. Hammond (ed.), *The Sacred in a Secular Age* (Berkeley: University of California Press, 1985); J. C. Livingston, *Anatomy of the Sacred* (New York: Macmillan, 1989); R. Otto, *The Idea of the Holy* (Harmondsworth, U.K.: Penguin, 1959 [1917]); R. Wuthnow, *Rediscovering the Sacred* (Grand Rapids, Mich.: Eerdmans, 1992).

SACRIFICE The ritual slaying of a living creature (human or nonhuman) and the dedication of the corpse to the realm of the sacred or divine. Alternatively, bloodless sacrifices may substitute vegetables or cultural products.

Every sacrificial act includes at least four essential elements: the individual who offers the sacrifice (the sacrificer), the object sacrificed (the material of oblation), a rite or method of sacrifice, and a specific time and place in which sacrifice should take place. Sacrifice has been variously interpreted as a gift, as an attempt to establish reciprocity between humans and nonhumans, as an offering, as a means of establishing a link between humans and the realm of the sacred, or as some combination of these (Hubert and Mauss 1899). It has also been interpreted as a form of expiation or as a reenactment of an earlier, primordial event (Girard 1977).

Sacrifice is a dominant ritual in many tribal religions, early Judaism, Aztec religion, Chinese religion, and the Vedic (pre-Hindu) tradition of India. Although rites of sacrifice have no place in orthodox Islam, they continue to play a part in popular piety. Christianity has its formative character established through a sacrificial interpretation of the crucifixion of Jesus along Judaic lines; Jesus's death on the cross is believed to be the perfect and ultimate sacrifice (atonement) that rendered all previous sacrifices and all alternative sacrificial systems superfluous. However, there are sharp disagreements within Christianity concerning the present character of the crucifixion. While Roman Catholic doctrine stresses the celebration of the Eucharist as a real and present sacrifice, Protestant theology downplays the sacrificial dimension of the Eucharist and stresses its commemorative functions. For Catholics, the Mass constitutes a continual representation of Jesus's sacrifice until the end of time, while Protestants stress the "once and for all" character of the atonement.

See also W. Robertson Smith

—*Stephen D. Glazier*

REFERENCES

R. Girard, *Violence and the Sacred* (Baltimore: Johns Hopkins University Press, 1977); H. Hubert and M. Mauss, *Sacrifice* (Chicago: University of Chicago Press, 1964 [1899]).

SAINT-SIMON, AUGUSTE   *see* Positivism

SALIENCE   One way that social scientists measure *religiosity* (or degree of religious commitment).

Salience is a subjective indicator of importance of religion to a person. The measurement of salience typically involves asking a survey respondent a question, for example, "How important would you say that religion is to you? Extremely important, quite important, fairly important, not too important, or not important at all." It is rather highly correlated to several other measures of religiosity, such as frequency of prayer and regularity of attendance at worship services.

See also Commitment, Religiosity

—*Keith A. Roberts*

SALVATION ARMY   Founded by William Booth (1829-1912) in the 1860s as the Christian Mission for Evangelistic, Social and Rescue Work in the slums of London's East End, the name Salvation Army was adopted in 1878.

The Salvation Army now has missions in nearly 100 countries with 25,000 full-time officers and is well known for its charitable work for the homeless and in tracking down the whereabouts of lost persons. The Salvation Army, however, is also a religious organization, with a specific doctrinal statement of its beliefs and practices. The movement is organized as a military bureaucracy with a general at its apex; members wear a familiar uniform, with the women still donning traditional bonnets. Meetings are frequently held on street corners and other public places to the accompaniment of a brass band.

Roland Robertson (1967) provides a social scientific account of the Salvation Army's development using a church-sect model.

—*Eileen Barker*

REFERENCES

F. Coutts, *No Discharge in This War,* 6 vols. (London: Nelson, 1947-1968); E. H. MacKinley, *Marching to Glory* (San Francisco: Harper, 1984); R. Robertson, "The Salvation Army," in *Patterns of Sectarianism,* ed. B. Wilson (London: Heinemann, 1967): 49-105.

SANTERIA   *see* Caribbean Religions

SAPIR, EDWARD (1884-1939)   Anthropologist, best known for his pioneering essays on the relationship between language and thought, and for initiating a seminar on this topic with insurance executive Benjamin Lee Whorf, which yielded the *Sapir-Whorf hypothesis*—that language exercises a determinative influence on how people think.

Sapir emigrated to the United States with his parents from Germany when he was 5 years old. He won scholarships to attend the Horace Mann School in New York City and was later awarded a Pulitzer fellowship to study anthropology at Columbia University under Franz Boas and Morris Swadesh. At Columbia, Sapir began his intensive research on American Indian languages and cultures. Following appointments at the University of California, Berkeley, the University of Pennsylvania, the Canadian National Museum in Toronto, and the University of Chicago, he joined the faculty of Yale University as Sterling Professor of Anthropology and Linguistics.

Sapir's writings on religion have not received as much attention as his work on language. This is unfortunate. His 1928 essay "The Meaning of Religion" (*American Mercury* 15:72-79) anticipates many of the arguments of Clifford Geertz and Melford Spiro and makes a useful distinction between "a religion" and "religion," which offers a satisfactory solution to the Great Tradition-Little Tradition debate in the anthropology of religion raised later in the works of Robert Redfield.

—*Stephen D. Glazier*

REFERENCE

R. Darnell, *Edward Sapir* (Berkeley: University of California Press, 1990).

SATANISM   Satanism has been a recurrent demonological theme in Western society virtually since the beginnings of Christianity, although details such as the "Black Mass" are relatively new inventions. As Stevens notes (1991:30), "The function of demonologies is that they can detract people from immediate yet daunting social problems." Thus we have seen interest in satanism ebb and flow over time, with there being considerable interest developing in it in the recent past history of a number of Western societies, including particularly the United States.

There has been a huge interest in the past decade or so in satanism, with an outpouring of books, many by Christian fundamentalists, claiming that Satan is alive and well in the United States. Related claims are that satanic groups have organized a major national or even international conspiracy, taking over selected institutional structures in society (such as children's day care) and operating hundreds if not thousands of "satanic cults" that abuse people and engage in all sorts of despicable acts. Virtually all scholarly examinations of these claims have resulted in little or no evidence being found for such claims (Carlson and Larue 1989, Richardson et al. 1991, Hicks 1991,

Jenkins 1992, La Fontaine 1994, Richardson 1997). But proving a negative has been difficult, and the claims persist.

The application of a "social constructionist" perspective to the persistence of current claims about satanism suggests that interest in satanism seems to result from the confluence of a number of different and ostensibly independent movements or factors. Included are (1) the growth of interest in fundamentalist Christianity, with its specific focus on a real and personalized Satan; (2) the development of a few small, yet well-publicized satanic churches, initially established by Anton LaVey in San Francisco; (3) the development of a virulent "anti-cult" movement focused on control of "new religions" (often referred to as "cults"); (4) growth of the "child saver" movement made up of social workers, therapists, and others focused on protection of children from harm; (5) the emergence of the "adult survivor" movement made up of people (mostly women) who claim to have been sexually abused when young children, often in allegedly satanic rituals; (6) the evolution of the feminist movement, with its great concern for the welfare of females, including children; (7) the development of satellite and cable electronic media capabilities, which creates a great demand for programming, with "talk TV and radio" formats becoming popular; and (8) the development of popular "satanism seminars" for professionals such as social workers, police, and therapists who must gain "continuing education" credits to remain certified.

Those involved in these movements and other developments have discovered common interests in promoting the idea of Satan or satanism within a given society. Fundamentalists promote the idea of Satan as a key part of their belief system and are ready to agree with others who claim to see the hand of Satan at work, such as in allegations of child care centers being used by satanists to gain access to children. The minuscule satanic churches take solace from any who want to accept their anti-Christian beliefs, even as they disavow any involvement in such things as child sex abuse. The anti-cult movement has made great use of the "satanic cult" idea as a weapon in the battle against newer religious groups. Those in the child saver movement, including many social workers in burgeoning child welfare bureaucracies, find it easy to accept that satanists might have become involved in some child care operations as a way to gain access to children. Adult occult survivors promote satanism because the presence of a strong satanism movement lends credence to claims that they were molested in ritual abuse situations while young children. A few in the feminist movement may give credence to claims of satanic activity because to do so seems supportive of women making claims as adult survivors. Hosts on TV talk shows may look to satanism as a popular topic that attracts listeners, thus giving a forum to anyone willing to make such claims. And social workers, police, and other professionals such as therapists may learn of the work of Satan through seminars and workshops organized to make professionals aware of the growing menace of satanism.

The "strange bedfellows" of satanism have led to the development of a typology of those involved in promoting satanism (even as they ironically claim to be fighting it). Richardson (1997) defines three types of "objectivists" who promote satanism either directly or indirectly, with the types depending on the degree to which the person accepts the objective reality of Satan. *Strict objectivists* such as fundamentalist Christians believe in an actual Satan that is active in human affairs, promoting evil at every opportunity. *Secular objectivists* may not believe in a real Satan, but they are willing to entertain the idea of a "satanic conspiracy" operating in our society, say in child care centers or the government. This may occur in particular if accepting the idea of satanism promotes other interests they may have, such as the development of a larger welfare bureaucracy or the spread of feminist ideas of female exploitation. *Opportunistic objectivists* are those, perhaps including some media talk show personalities (as well as others), who do not believe in Satan or the idea of a satanic conspiracy but who nonetheless are willing to promote the idea for their own purposes.

Satanism has become defined as an international social problem of late, with outbreaks of considerable concern in a number of other Western countries, including the United Kingdom, Australia, and New Zealand (Jenkins 1992, La Fontaine 1994, Richardson 1997). These newer international developments seem to derive almost totally from the work of American "anti-Satan missionaries" distributing materials developed in the United States to religious, child care worker, police, and therapy groups in other countries. The focus of these materials often has been on the alleged sexual abuse of children in satanic rituals in families and in child care facilities.

Whether satanism continues to attract so much attention remains to be seen. There does appear to be an ebbing of attention to satanism in the United States at this time, probably caused in large part by the failure to convince many, including some juries and judges, that satanism has in fact infiltrated major segments of the child care industry. Also, there has been increased scholarly attention on the issue of satanism, and that attention has been nearly totally unanimous in reporting that there is no satanic conspiracy operating within American society.

—*James T. Richardson*

REFERENCES

S. Carlson and G. Larue, *Satanism in America* (El Cerrito, Calif.: Gaia, 1989); R. Hicks, *Pursuit of Satan* (Buffalo, N.Y.: Prometheus, 1991); P. Jenkins, *Intimate Enemies* (Hawthorne, N.Y.: Aldine, 1992); J. La Fontaine, *The Nature and Extent of Organized and Ritual Abuse* (London: HMSO, 1994); A. LaVey, *The Satanic Bible* (New York: Avon, 1969); A. H. Randall, "The Church of Satan," in *The New Religious Consciousness*, ed. C. Y. Glock and R. N. Bellah (Berkeley: University of California Press, 1976): 180-202; J. T. Richardson, "The Social Construction of Satanism," *Australian Journal of Social Issues* 32(1997):61-85; J. T. Richardson et al. (eds.), *The Satanism Scare* (Hawthorne, N.Y.: Gruyter, 1991); J. Russell, *The Prince of Darkness* (Ithaca, N.Y.: Cornell University Press, 1988); P. Stevens, "The Demonology of Satanism," in J. T. Richardson et al., *q.v.* (1991): 21-40; J. Victor, *Satanic Panic* (Chicago: Open Court, 1993).

***

SCHALLER, LYLE   *see* Parish

SCHERER, ROSS P. (1922–)

Emeritus Professor of Sociology, Loyola University Chicago. Scherer was educated in Lutheran schools and ordained a Lutheran pastor in 1950. He completed the Ph.D. at the University of Chicago in 1963, where he studied with Ernest Burgess, Samuel Kinchloe, and Joachim Wach. In the 1960s, he was on the staff of the National Council of Churches of Christ and contributed to the NCC's large and influential research program in that era. From 1966 to 1990, he taught at Loyola University Chicago, which named him Emeritus Professor in 1990. President, Religious Research Association, 1976-1977.

Scherer's research focus began with an interest in congregations and evolved to encompass the sociology of occupations and organizations. His 1980 edited collection, *American Denominational Organization* (William Carey Press 1980), reflects these interests. In more recent years, he has given attention to religion and medicine as well.

Scherer is a founding member of both the Society for the Scientific Study of Religion and the Religious Research Association.

—*William McKinney*

SCHNEIDER, LOUIS (1915-1978)   Sociologist of religion. As a student at Columbia University, he found Robert K. Merton's references to manifest and latent functions suggestive for studying nonlogical action. His dissertation under Merton compared Sigmund Freud's and Thorstein Veblen's theories. Later disowning the Freudian model, Schneider's line of inquiry led nevertheless to studies of practical psychologies behind economic conduct (e.g., deferred gratification) and their unanticipated consequences (as depicted by the Scottish moralists).

Schneider was a functionalist in Merton's middle-range, ad hoc manner rather than in Parsons's system approach. With Sanford Dornbusch, he studied nonlogical religious conduct in an analysis of inspirational books. Over time, this literature spoke less of pain and sacrifice, and more of serenity and success: Could its latent function be achieved if it became manifest (i.e., transparent)? He began to see religion as a major nonrational aspect of culture. Given that ironic consequences rather than beliefs were focal, he advocated wide rather than narrow definitions of religion, including nonchurch quests and political ideologies. He observed nonreligious styles of action entering religious contexts, such as secular protest modalities in a dispute among Catholic clerics.

Schneider's reader, *Religion, Culture, and Society* (Wiley 1964), influenced a generation of scholars in the sociology of religion; his *Sociological Approach to Religion* (Wiley 1970) promoted functionalism in an era in which younger sociologists found that functionalism legitimated the status quo in a way that Schneider himself, ironically, would not have wished. His students in the sociology of religion include Richard Machalek, Donald A. Nielsen, and Anthony J. Blasi.

—*Anthony J. Blasi*

REFERENCES

L. Schneider, *The Freudian Psychology and Veblen's Social Theory* (New York: King's Crown, 1948); L. Schneider (ed.), *The Scottish Moralists on Human Nature and Society* (Chicago: University of Chicago Press, 1967); L. Schneider, "Ideological Conflict Between Clergy and Laity," *Social Science Quarterly* 49(1969):925-927; L. Schneider, "The Sociology of Religion," *Sociological Analysis* 31(1970):131-144; L. Schneider, "Dialectical Orientation and the Sociology of Religion," *Sociological Inquiry* 49(1974a):49-73; L. Schneider, "The Scope of the 'Religious Factor' and the Sociology of Religion," *Social Research* 41(1974b):340-361; L. Schneider, *The Grammar of Social Relations* (New Brunswick, N.J.: Transaction, 1984); L. Schneider and S. M. Dornbusch, *Popular Religion* (Chicago: University of Chicago Press, 1958); L. Schneider and S. Lysgaard, "The Deferred Gratification Pattern," *American Sociological Review* 18(1953):142-159; L. Schneider and L. Zurcher, Jr., "Toward Understanding the Catholic Crisis," *Journal for the Scientific Study of Religion* 9 (1970):197-207.

SCHNEPP, GERALD J. (1908-1985)   A member of the Society of Mary (Marianists), Schnepp held a B.A. from the University of Dayton and both an M.A. and a Ph.D. from Catholic University of America. He spent a number of years as a faculty member at St. Mary's University and at St. Louis University before being elected Treasurer General of his order, headquartered in Rome, a post he held from 1960 to 1976. President, American Catholic Sociological Society, 1945; President, Association for the Scientific Study of Religion-Southwest, 1985.

Brother Schnepp's publications in the sociology of religion included *Leakage from a Catholic Parish* (Catholic University of America Press 1942) and a chapter in *Parish Sociology* edited by Nuesse and Harte (Bruce 1951). He wrote for a wide variety of journals and publications on the family, Catholic education, economics, sociological theory, and social justice issues.

—*Loretta Morris*

SCHOENHERR, RICHARD A. (1935-1996)   Member of the sociology faculty, University of Wisconsin from 1971 until his death; Associate Dean of Letters and Sciences, 1979-1988; Ph.D., University of Chicago, 1970.

A former Roman Catholic priest, Schoenherr continued to study organizational change in that body, particularly in the United States. With Lawrence A. Young, he published *Full Pews and Empty Altars* (University of Wisconsin Press 1993), the definitive quantitative study documenting the inability of the Roman Catholic Church to provide adequate numbers of priests for its lay membership ("priest shortage"). This work received the Society for the Scientific Study of Religion distinguished book award in 1996. He was also an outspoken critic of the Catholic policy of priestly celibacy, particularly evidenced in the title of the book on which he was working at the time of his death, *Goodbye Father: Celibacy and Patriarchy in the Catholic Church.*

—*William H. Swatos, Jr.*

SCHOOL PRAYER Refers to the current public policy issue in the United States on whether children should be allowed to engage in organized prayer in public schools. Proponents argue that it is a beneficial affirmation of religious values, consistent with our nation's heritage, while opponents say that it is a hollow ritual that offends the rights and sensibilities of children from minority religions or from no religion at all.

The issue of prayer in schools was catapulted onto the national agenda when the Supreme Court ruled in *Engel v. Vitale* (370 U.S. 421, 1962) that the State of New York's provision for a voluntary, nonsectarian prayer led by school officials violated the "establishment clause" of the First Amendment. The prayer read: "Almighty God, we acknowledge our dependence upon Thee, and we beg Thy blessings upon us, our parents, our teachers, and our country." The Supreme Court stated that its voluntary and nondenominational aspects did not "free it from the limitations of the Establishment Clause" because the government was placing its power and moral authority behind "a particular religious belief."

The school prayer decision spearheaded opposition to the Supreme Court in the 1960s (Grossman and Wells 1980) and became an object of legislative attempts to overturn it. Many members of Congress introduced constitutional amendments over the years to overturn the decision directly; the high-water mark of those efforts came in 1984, when the U.S. Senate defeated an amendment drafted by the Reagan administration to overturn *Engel* on a 56-44 vote, 11 votes short of the required two-thirds margin for passage (Moen 1989).

Legislators tried other tactics to reinstitute prayer in schools. They introduced measures restricting the ability of the courts to hear school prayer cases; those "court stripping" bills never gained much support, however, because they tried to restrict the constitutional jurisdiction of the Supreme Court by statute. Legislators fared better with "equal access" legislation, which guaranteed student religious groups access to secondary public school facilities on the same basis as other voluntary student groups (Hertzke 1988). Congress passed the "equal access" bill in the 98th Congress (1983-1984), and the Supreme Court upheld its constitutionality in *Board of Education of Westside Community Schools v. Mergens* (1990). It allows voluntary student religious groups to engage in religious activities after the school day is over, such as vocal prayer, if other voluntary student groups also are allowed to use the school's facilities.

An additional permutation of prayer in schools has met with failure. Proponents have advocated a "moment of silence" at the start of the school day, during which time students could pray silently if they wished. That practice was ruled an unconstitutional establishment of religion by the Supreme Court in *Wallace v. Jaffree* (1985), which judged it an attempt to reinstitute formal prayer in schools.

In recent years, proponents have placed greater emphasis on the rights of students to pray so long as they initiate it (thereby undercutting the issue of state endorsement). In the meantime, the constitutional prohibition against prayer in schools is often cited as one of the more often violated Supreme Court rulings. The school prayer issue has resonated strongly as a symbolic affirmation of tradition and religiosity, especially among conservative Protestants.

Social scientists traditionally have studied the reasoning of the Supreme Court's prayer decisions, the symbolic importance of the issue to religious conservatives, and the degree of congruence between public opinion and elite action on this issue. Prayer in schools remains a topic of discussion, but its saliency has been decreasing over time.

—*Matthew C. Moen and Julie Ingersoll*

REFERENCES

K. M. Dolbeare and P. E. Hammond, *The School Prayer Decisions* (Chicago: University of Chicago Press, 1971); J. B. Grossman and R. S. Wells, *Constitutional Law and Judicial Policymaking* (New York: Wiley, 1980); A. D. Hertzke, *Representing God in Washington* (Knoxville: University of Tennessee Press, 1988); M. C. Moen, *The Christian Right and Congress* (Tuscaloosa: University of Alabama Press, 1989).

SCHULLER, ROBERT *see* Televangelism

SCIENCE AND RELIGION If *science* is defined as that body of knowledge about man and the universe that is based on observation, experiment, and measurement, while *religion* embodies teachings that are based on faith, then it follows that these two domains are bound to come into conflict with one another if they are treated as epistemological equivalents.

One reason this is inevitable is that most religions contain both a cosmology and a biology, that is, they include an account of the origin of the universe and of life on the planet. In this sense, most religious teachings include scientific claims. However, as it took many centuries for science to emerge as a distinct and organized human activity, this conflict did not become apparent in the West until the sixteenth and seventeenth centuries. The "warfare" that developed at that time between an emergent science and religion is epitomized by Galileo's epic struggle with the Catholic Church over the Copernican heliocentric theory of the heavens. Although eventually forced to recant by the Inquisition, Galileo was influential in developing the rational scientific method by his refusal to accept without question statements that were not based on direct evidence but that merely derived their authority from others.

This warfare has continued to the present day, reaching something of a climax in the nineteenth century in the battle between creationism and the Darwinian theory of human evolution. It should be noted, however that, although science could not emerge until intellectual inquiry was freed from the dogmatic constraints of an ecclesiastically imposed theology, it was developments in religious thought that eventually gave birth to modern science. For, as Robert Merton (1938) has suggested, following Max Weber's lead, it was developments in Protestantism that led to the emergence in seventeenth-century England of a culture of individualistic rationalism conducive to scientific modes of thought.

In the contemporary world, it is science and not religion that tends to possess the greater cultural status and significance. One index of this is the extent to which new religious movements, such as Christian Science and Scientology, try to appropriate this prestige to themselves by incorporating the word *science* into their titles. However, it cannot be assumed that science is complete master of the battlefield. Although the set-piece battles of the nineteenth century may have been won by science, skirmishes continue. Indeed, some have claimed that a fresh round of fighting is about to begin, following the growing popular disenchantment with science and technology that marked the decades of the 1960s and 1970s as well as the more recent crisis of confidence in secular thought represented by the "turn to postmodernism."

Certainly the 1980s and 1990s have seen a spate of books that purport to demonstrate that modern scientific thought, and especially modern cosmological thinking, is consonant with, if not actually supportive of, a religious position. This movement began in 1984 when Paul Davies, professor of mathematical physics at the University of Adelaide, published *God and the New Physics* (Cambridge University Press 1984), only to receive a further (and unintended) boost from the sensational success of Stephen Hawking's *A Brief History of Time* (Oxford University Press 1988), a book that ends with the sentence, "If we find the answer [to the problem of a complete theory of the universe] . . . it would be the ultimate triumph of human reason—for then we would truly know the mind of God." It was this comment that prompted Paul Davies to write *The Mind of God* (Heinemann 1992) in which he tries to prove logically and scientifically that God, or some sort of supreme being, must exist. Other writers have followed Davies's lead and tried to show that it might be scientifically possible for a God to intervene in the universe without breaking the laws of nature, while more recently Frank Tipler, in *The Physics of Mortality: Modern Cosmology, God and the Resurrection of the Dead* (Macmillan 1995), has tried to argue that the universe was created so that we could be here to observe it, and consequently that theology should be conceived as a branch of physics.

Against these attempts to incorporate scientific cosmology into a religious worldview, and in a manner somewhat reminiscent of T. H. Huxley's defense of Darwinian evolutionary theory, the biologist Richard Dawkins has sprung to the defense of an atheistic science. Dawkins, in *The Blind Watchmaker* (Longman 1986) and *The Selfish Gene* (Oxford University Press 1989) observes that the term *God,* used in this sophisticated, physicist's sense, bears no relation to the God of the Bible or of any other religion. If a physicist says God is another name for Planck's constant, or God is a superstring, we should take it as a picturesque metaphorical way of saying that the nature of superstrings or the value of Planck's constant is a profound mystery. As Dawkins observes, the God hypothesis explains nothing; rather, it amounts to postulating what one is trying to explain, which is complexity. Science has been very successful in explaining complexity, whereas "God" is merely an improbably complex hypothesis invoked in an attempt to explain the complex.

It is too early to say whether this most recent attempt to represent science as supportive of theism constitutes a serious and lasting movement or is simply a publishing phenomenon, one in which theological references serve as little more than a marketing ploy, with the word *God* being employed by scientists and God apologists alike simply as a means of drawing attention to their work. It is also possible that the flirtation by cosmologists with the god hypothesis tells us more about the increasingly speculative nature of their theorizing than it does about the relationship between religion and science in general. In any event, these books provide little comfort for the supporters of any particular religious tradition. They support no specific religious claim and provide no comfort for hard-pressed clergy confronted with the hostility and indifference of a secular world.

See also Social Science and Religion

—*Colin Campbell*

REFERENCE

R. K. Merton, *Science, Technology and Society in Seventeenth Century England* (New York: Harper 1970 [1938]).

SCIENTOLOGY   One of the more controversial of the so-called new religions. Begun by science fiction writer L. Ron Hubbard initially under the term *Dianetics,* the Church of Scientology is now a worldwide new religion of significance.

Hubbard began developing his ideas concerning Dianetics as a way to heal the mind in the late 1940s in science fiction publications. His promotion of a lay psychotherapy in *Dianetics,* published in 1950, was supposed to offer relief from psychosomatic and psychological symptoms. The book, which became an immediate best-seller, had a large appeal, and informal groups sprang up around the United States to put Hubbard's ideas into practice. A few years later, Hubbard broke with those leading the Dianetics movement, apparently over issues of his authoritarian control, and established Scientology. The new movement incorporated ideas from Dianetics but also added a number of new elements, which, according to Hubbard, gave the new movement much more of a spiritual dimension. In 1956, Hubbard officially established the Founding Church of Scientology.

A key idea from Dianetics was that of *engrams,* which are defined as "psychic scars" deriving from past traumatic events. These engrams preclude a person developing his or her full potential unless *cleared* through processes known only to Scientology. Some of the processes developed within Scientology use a device called an "E-meter," which is based on the principle of galvanic skin response. Use of this device was banned at one time by the Food and Drug Administration over claims being made by Scientology that its use could cure many ills.

Scientology has been in a continual controversy with the psychiatric profession over some techniques, such as shock therapy, used within the mental health profession. Scientology also has a reputation of being the most litigious of all the new religions, as it quite frequently engages in legal battles with governments and with other detractors. It also has been the target of civil and criminal actions as well as of government bans in some countries. Scientology has overcome many of the legal hurdles it has faced over the years, and some of the cases have become major freedom-of-religion cases. For instance, the leading case in Australia on the issue of defining religion and establishing legal guarantees for minority religions derived from a battle won by Scientology to define itself as a tax-exempt religion. Recently in the United States, the Internal Revenue Service announced that it was giving up its decades-long battle with Scientology over the tax-exempt status of payments for Scientology courses designed to achieve various levels of the "clear" status. The U.S. State Department also has officially expressed its concern to Germany over German repression of Scientology.

Scientology has recently joined a number of other minority and new religions in moving into former Soviet Union and Eastern and Central European countries following the fall of communism. It has established organizational outposts in those countries and is expending significant resources to spread its message.

—*James T. Richardson*

REFERENCES

W. S. Bainbridge and R. Stark, "Scientology," *Sociological Analysis* 41(1980):128-136; G. Malko, *Scientology* (New York: Dell, 1970); R. Wallis, *The Road to Total Freedom* (London: Heinemann, 1976).

SECONDARY ANXIETY   Anxiety created by religious rituals or belief. Secondary anxiety is defined in relation to primary anxiety, the naturally occurring apprehensions that are often relieved by a religious ritual. Homans (1941:171) described secondary anxiety as follows:

> When a man has followed the technical procedures at his command and performed the traditional rituals at his command, his primary anxiety remains latent. We say that the rites give him confidence. Under these circumstances, he will feel anxiety only when the rites themselves are not properly performed. In fact this attitude becomes generalized and anxiety is felt whenever any one of the traditions of society is not observed. This anxiety may be called secondary or displaced anxiety.

Secondary anxiety also may result from the fact that religious rituals remind individuals of the link between moral behavior and physical/spiritual well-being. Nature and morality are thought to be mutually dependent, and unintentional transgressions may be punished.

—*James McClenon*

REFERENCES

G. Homans, "Anxiety and Ritual," *American Anthropologist* 43(1941):164-172; K. A. Roberts, *Religion in Sociological Perspective* (Belmont, Calif.: Wadsworth, 1995).

SECOND VATICAN COUNCIL　*see* Vatican II

SECTARIANISM　*see* Church-Sect Theory, Bryan R. Wilson

SECULARIZATION　A controversial concept because of its distinct use in different disciplines, such as philosophy, social sciences, theology, canon law (Lübbe 1975). Even in the social sciences, various levels of analysis of the religious situation result in different definitions and divergent evaluations of the situation. If the founding fathers rarely used the term, concepts and views related to theories of *secularization* were already present, such as generalization and differentiation (Durkheim). Weber used the term— but to typify the way in which, in the United States, membership in distinguished clubs and fraternal societies replaced membership in Protestant sects, in guaranteeing moral rectitude and credit worthiness (1920:212). Later generations of sociologists continued to employ the term but attached different meanings to it (Shiner 1967). Not until the 1960s were several theories of secularization developed, most prominently by Peter Berger, Thomas Luckmann, and Bryan Wilson. These theories subsequently led to discussion concerning the existence and validity of such a "theory" (Hammond 1985, Hadden 1987, Lechner 1991, Bruce 1992).

Other sociologists have systematically analyzed existing theories because some discussions failed to scrutinize the ideas, levels of analysis, and arguments of those being criticized. Tschannen has suggested treating secularization theories as a paradigm (1992), and Dobbelaere has stressed the need to differentiate between levels of analysis (1981), suggesting convergences and divergences between theories (1984).

The current treatment is dependent upon Tschannen's "exemplars" of the secularization paradigm and refers to authors who have extensively written about them, without suggesting, however, that they were the only ones to do so. The exemplars are ordered according to the levels of analysis (macro, or societal, level; meso, or subsystem, level; and micro, or individual, level). Some exemplars are renamed, and one is added: institutional differentiation or segmentation (Luckmann 1967), autonomization (Berger 1967), ratio-nalization (Berger 1967, Wilson 1982), societalization (Wilson 1976), disenchantment of the world (Weber 1920, Berger 1967), privatization (Berger 1967, Luckmann 1967), generalization (Bellah 1967, Parsons 1967), pluralization (Martin 1978), relativization (Berger 1967), this-worldliness (Luckmann 1990), individualization (Bellah et al. 1985), *bricolage* (Luckmann 1979), unbelief (Berger 1967), decline of church religiosity (Martin 1978).

According to Tschannen, three exemplars are central to the secularization paradigm: differentiation, rationalization, and this-worldliness. The other exemplars are related to these. Beginning with the macro level, it seems possible, using Luhmann's conceptual distinction between three types of differentiation (1982:262-265), to come to a more well-integrated perspective of the processes related to secularization.

The Societal Level　Because modern societies are primarily differentiated along functional lines, subsystems developed different functional domains (e.g., economy, polity, science, family). Each subsystem's communication is based on its own medium (money, power, truth, love) and each developed its own values (success, separation of powers, reliability and validity, primacy of love) and norms. Regarding religion, they claim autonomy and reject religiously prescribed rules—such as the emancipation of education from ecclesiastical authority, the separation of church and state, the rejection of church prescriptions about birth control and abortion, the decline of religious content in literature and arts, and the development of science as an autonomous secular perspective.

Diagnosing the loss of religion's influence in the so-called secular world, members of the religious subsystem were the first to talk about secularization. In this context, Luhmann speaks about secularization in the sense of a specifically religious conception of society as the environment of the religious system (1977:225-232). Denominations, most crucially the Roman Catholic Church, reacted with a counteroffensive, stimulating among other things a process of pillarization and the organization of Catholic Action and calling for a second evangelization of Europe. Consequently, secularization expresses a description and an interpretation of an experience: It is not a causal concept. The sociological explanation starts with the process of functional differentiation. Secularization is situated on the societal level and should be seen as resulting from the processes of functional differentiation and the autonomization of the societal subsystems. Consequently, we state forcefully, with Wilson, that secularization "maintains no more than that religion ceases to be significant in the working of the social system" (1982:150). This says nothing about the religious consciousness of individuals, although it may affect it. This conception of the process of secularization allowed Chaves to state that secularization refers to the declining scope of religious authority (1994:754).

Declining religious authority allowed the development of functional rationality. The economy lost its religious ethos (Weber 1920:163-206). Consequently, the political subsystem also had to rationalize, and little room was left for traditional and charismatic authority. Political authority became rational. Economic production and distribution developed large-scale economic organizations, and modern states extended their administration. These structures needed more and more people trained in science and rational techniques. Consequently, in education, a scientific approach to the world and the teaching of technical knowledge increasingly replaced a religious-literary formation. The development of scientific techniques had their impact also on the life-world: Domestic tasks became increasingly mechanized, and even the most intimate, sexual relationships and their "consequences" were considered to be calculable and controllable. Not only could one better control the consequences, but in modern "handbooks" the sexual act itself is also presented as "technically improvable." The consequences of these developments are the disenchantment of the world and the societalization of the subsystem.

Indeed, the world is increasingly considered to be calculable and man-made, the result of controlled planning. Such a world has engendered not only new roles, but new, basically rational and critical, attitudes and a new cognition. According to Acquaviva (1979), this new cognition has eliminated prelogical and thus religious concepts and has been objectified in a new language that has changed the image of reality. The media, using this new language, have radicalized the process and made it a social phenomenon. This suggests a possible impact of the macro on the micro level, that is, the consciousness of the individual.

Subsystems are also *gesellschaftlich,* or societalized. The organized world is "based on impersonal roles, relationships, the coordination of skills, and essentially formal and contractual patterns of behaviour, in which personal virtue, as distinguished from role obligations, is of small consequence" (Wilson 1982:155). In such systems, Wilson goes on, control is no longer based on morals and religion, it has become impersonal, a matter of routine techniques and unknown officials—legal, technical, mechanized, computerized, and electronic. Thus religion has lost one of its important latent functions; as long as control was interpersonal, it was based on religiously based mores and substantive values.

Berger and Luckmann stressed another consequence of the process of functional differentiation and the autonomization of the secular spheres, that is, the privatization of religion. According to Luckmann (1967:94-106), the validity of religious norms became restricted to its "proper" sphere, that is, that of private life, and Berger (1967:133) stressed the "functionality" of this "for the maintenance of the highly rationalized order of modern economic and political institutions," that is, the public sphere. This dichotomy, private-public, carries with it at least two shortcomings (Dobbelaere 1981:79-84). It suggests that secularization was limited to the "public" sphere, which is incorrect; family life was also secularized. Second, it is the adoption in sociological discourse of ideological concepts used by liberals and socialists in the nineteenth century to legitimate functional differentiation and the autonomization of "secular" institutions: "Religion is a private matter." Later, these concepts were used by workers to defend their political, religious, or family options against possible sanctions and eventual dismissal by the management of Christian organizations (e.g., schools or hospitals) if they failed to behave according to ecclesiastical rules in matters of family life, politics, or religion. They defended their "private" options, their "private" life, in what managers of ecclesiastical organizations called the "public" sphere.

Clearly, the dichotomy "private-public" is not a structural aspect of society but a legitimizing conceptualization of the world, an ideological pair used in conflicts by participants. Sociologists might, of course, study the use of this dichotomy in social discourse and conflicts, but it is not a sociological conceptualization. It should be replaced by Habermas's conceptual dichotomy—system versus life-world, used here in a purely descriptive sense. It is in the systemic interactions that societalization occurs: Relationships became basically secondary, segmented, utilitarian, and formal. By contrast, in the life-world—the family, groups of friends, social networks, the neighborhood—interaction is communal. Primary relations are the binding forces of such groups; relationships are total, trustful, considerate, sympathetic, and personal (see Wilson 1976, 1982). The trend toward societalization is very clear in the distribution and the banking sector—such as the replacement of neighborhood stores by large department stores where the interactions between shopper and seller are limited to a money exchange for goods. Beyond the life-world, interactions became societalized.

Relationship Between the Macro and Meso Levels

According to Parsons (1967), pluralization, or the segmentary differentiation of the subsystem religion, was

possible only after the Christian ethic was institutionalized in the so-called secular world, in other words, once
the Christian ethic became generalized. Consequently,
pluralization was not to be considered an indicator of
secularization, quite the contrary (for a critique, see
Lechner 1991:1109 f); however, the relationship is not
causal, it is functional. Pluralization will indeed aug-
ment the necessity of generalization. Together with
Bellah (1967), Parsons stressed the need for a civil
religion that overarches conventional religions to legitimate the system. One may also consider the need for
laws, overarching religiously inspired mores. Martin
suggests that when religion adapts to every status group
"through every variety of pullulating sectarianism,"
then there is a need to preserve the unity of the nation
"by a national myth which represents a common denominator of all faiths: one nation under God"
(1978:36). Indeed, civil religion generalizes the different notions of God present in the various denominations: the God of Jews, Catholics, Unitarians, Calvinists, and so on. The national myth sacralizes its
prophets, martyrs, and historical places, has its ritualistic expressions, and also may use biblical archetypes
(Bellah 1967:18).

Such myths, such legitimations, are not always
religious: Civil religion is one possibility; there are
also secular myths, such as the French myth based on
the laïcité, which legitimates the French state, its
schools, and its laws. What explains the emergence of
a "religious" rather than a "secular" myth, or vice
versa? And, more generally, what explains how such
a myth—religious or secular—emerges? Fenn suggests
that this is possible only when a society conceives of
itself as a "nation," as "really 'real' "—typical examples are the United States, Japan, and France. On the
other hand, the myth instead is seen as a cultural
"fiction," according to Fenn, to the extent that a
society sees itself as an arena for conflicting and
cooperative activities of various classes, groups, corporations, and organizations (1978:41-53). Another
issue for inquiry is how and to what extent in certain
countries a conventional religion may function as a
civil religion in a religiously pluralistic society—such
as Anglicanism in England and Calvinism in the Netherlands. What degree of pluralism is incongruent with
a church fulfilling the role of civil religion?

The Meso Level   On the meso level, pluralization
has resulted in a religious market, where different
religions either compete for the souls of the people or
make agreements not to proselytize, as the Anglican
Church has agreed with the Catholic Church in Belgium. Religious pluralism and competition augments
the relativity of their respective religious message, or in
Berger's terms "it relativizes their religious contents,"
their religious message is "de-objectivated," and, more
generally, "the pluralistic situation . . . ipso facto
plunges religion into a crisis of credibility" (1967:150
f).

The emergence of new religious movements (NRMs)
is related to the process of secularization. The "Christian collective consciousness" of the West was disintegrating. Pluralism had undermined its "objectivity," and
the slowly perceived useless character of Christian religions on the societal level, accompanied by a loss of
status and power, allowed exotic religions to improve
their position on the religious market. Some, such as
the Unification Church, The Family, or ISKCON
(Krishna Consciousness) wanted to resacralize the
world and its institutions by bringing God back in, such
as in the family, the economy, even the polity. Wallis
(1984) designates them "world-rejecting new religions." The vast majority, however, are of another type;
they are "world affirming." They offer members esoteric means of attaining immediate and automatic success, recovery, heightened spiritual powers, assertive-
ness, and a clearer mind. Mahikari provides an
omitama, or amulet; TM, a personal mantra; Scientology, auditing and the E-meter; the Human Potential
Movements offer therapies, encounter groups, or alternative health and spiritual centers; Nichiren Shoshu
promotes chanting of an invocation before a mandala,
while Elan Vital offers the Knowledge revealed by
Maharaji or one of his appointed instructors.

Luckmann suggests that the level of transcendence
in many religions was lowered; religions became "this-
worldly" or mundane (1990). The historical religions
are examples of "great transcendences," referring to
something other than everyday reality. Many new
religions, especially the world-affirming religions, appear to reach only the level of "intermediate transcendences." They bridge time and space, promote intersubjective communion, but remain at the immanent
level of everyday reality. Consequently, some (e.g.,
TM) claim to be spiritual rather than religious movements.

If one employed a substantive definition of religion,
referring to transcendent beliefs and practices, the supernatural or the sacred, many NRMs would not be
considered religions. They would not qualify as religions even according to some functional definitions.
Luhmann, for example, might not call some of them
religion because they do not relate "to the problem of
simultaneity of indefiniteness and certainty" (1977:46),
the typical function of religion. Indeed, these world-affirming religions are not concerned with the problems
of simultaneity of transcendence and immanence because they focus only on the immanent, the everyday

life. Stark and Bainbridge (1987) miss this point when they criticize secularization theory when referring to changes on the meso level. Moreover, their argument, that the newly emerging "spiritual movements" prove that secularization is a self-limiting process, backfires because these so-called new religious movements are adaptations to a secularized world.

This mundane orientation of religion is not new; Berger and Luckmann have suggested that the higher attendances in American churches compared with European churches might be explained by the mundane orientation of religion in America. Luckmann called it internal secularization: "a radical inner change in American church religion . . . . [T]oday the secular ideas of the American Dream pervade church religion" (Luckmann 1967:36 f.). In asserting that American churches were "becoming highly secularized themselves" (Berger 1967:108), these authors sought to reconcile data at the level of the individual that conflicted with secularization theories. However, they missed the point; church attendance is not an indicator of the process of secularization, which is a societal process. This does not imply that people's religious consciousness and their behavioral practices may not be influenced by the societal situation, but that the explanation of individual behavior is more complex.

The Micro Level   These arguments bring us to the individual, or micro, level and the exemplars individualization, unbelief, bricolage, and decline in church religiosity, that is, the unchurching of individuals and their lower church involvement. The individualization of religion has been related to its becoming part of the "private sphere." The church is the local congregation but also a "chosen community," "a loving community in which individuals can experience the joy of belonging," consequently "the ultimate meaning of the church is an expressive-individualistic one," and love is shared within the community, not with the world at large (Bellah et al. 1985:219-237). The church is considered to be part of the life-world.

How did individualization come about in the life-world? First, although the social system and the subsystems are still "an objective reality," a given, functional differentiation can only "work" if the independence of the subsystem is maintained. However, this cannot be enforced on the micro level, the level of individual motives, where interferences may occur. Luhmann suggests that a structural equivalent of enforcement is found in the "individualization of decisions," which may produce a statistical neutralization of these individually motivated choices (1977:233-242; Beyer 1990:374 ff). Functional dif-

ferentiation has stimulated an individualization of choices, and this has had its impact on the life-world. It was made possible by the detraditionalization of the life-world: Ascriptive roles were becoming less pressing; cars allowed people to escape the control of family and neighborhood; traditions were relativized; TV carried conflicting visions, messages, ideas, and values into the living room; women were liberated from their ascriptive, biological roles particularly by oral contraceptives; and the educational level rose. The "golden sixties" were not only an economic boom, giving people more freedom, more choices, less constraint, but they made possible similar claims in religious matters. The rejection of the encyclical on birth control by an overwhelming majority of Catholics—that is, criticism of an imposing, "infallible" religious authority, and the rejection of its rules and legitimations—was symptomatic, as was the National Pastoral Council in the Netherlands and the Underground Church in America. In fact, Descartes's *Cogito ergo sum* was now being understood as "I think and I choose," not only my networks, my friends, my dress patterns but also the beliefs, norms, and practices that express my religious feelings.

Had secularization anything to do with this? First, secularization and individualization are produced by functional differentiation; they are two sides of one coin. Secularization meant not only that religious authority was undermined; the denominations also lost status and power, subverting the religious collective consciousness of society, which facilitated individualization, as Durkheim had already indicated. The foregoing arguments make clear that the religious situation at the individual level cannot be explained exclusively by the secularization of the social system; other factors were also at work, consequently the religiousness of individuals is not a valid indicator in evaluating the process of secularization.

The loss of church authority, and the rise of religious pluralism and individualization, have led to a religious bricolage, an individual patchwork or recomposition. The religious menu of a denomination was not accepted; rather, "a religion à la carte" was individually constructed. Referring to postmodernity, Voyé suggests that individual religiosity is characterized by the "end of Great Narratives," a "mixing of codes," and a certain

> re-enchantment of the World. . . . The mixing of codes . . . is reflected in the religious field in a threefold manner: references and practices blending the institutional and the popular; occasional borrowings from scientific discourses as well as from religious ones; and inspiration sought in

diverse religions, notably, oriental religions. (1995:201)

Whereas functional differentiation stimulated instrumental individualism, the individualism of the life-world is more expressive, and this type of individualism is not accommodated in the churches.

Empirical research records growing unbelief and unchurching as well as decline in church attendance and the religious involvement of church members (see Halman and de Moor 1993). This may be explained by relating it to changes on the societal level, referring to functional rationality and societalization in the steps of sociologists and anthropologists who have shown that people develop a concept of personified supernatural beings directly from the model that their society provides (see Dobbelaere 1995:177-181). Functional rationality promoted an attitude in people that they themselves or specialists could solve their problems, which removed God from the world and stimulated unbelief. However, if some people still believe in God, then they conceive Him rather as a general power and not as "a person," because people experience fewer and fewer "personal relationships" in their social lives. If they can no longer believe in "God as a person," they drop out of Christian rituals because these are centered on a relationship with God as a person.

The relationship is not one-sided because the processes discussed are manifestly or latently set in motion by people. Consequently, we may expect that growing unbelief and distancing from the denominations might lead to growing secularization on the societal level, even if the hard religious core and some fundamentalist denominations may do everything possible to prevent this.

Conclusion Analysis of secularization theories, distinguishing levels of analysis and reordering the concepts employed, has made it possible to link processes and consequences, to suggest relationships between different levels of analysis, and to reformulate general theoretical propositions. This facilitates the deduction of hypotheses to be tested in empirical research. It was shown that the relationships are not causal but functional, such as the relationship between processes on the macro and the micro level and between generalization and pluralism. Many of these hypotheses and relations can be tested only on the basis of comparative research, and such research in the sociology of religion is rare. Such a general theoretical framework and international research should facilitate the construction of a theory of secularization rather than a paradigm.

—*Karel Dobbelaere*

REFERENCES

S. S. Acquaviva, *The Decline of the Sacred in Industrial Society* (Oxford: Blackwell, 1979); R. N. Bellah, "Civil Religion in America," *Daedalus* 96(1967):1-21; R. N. Bellah et al., *Habits of the Heart* (Berkeley: University of California Press, 1985); P. L. Berger, *The Sacred Canopy* (Garden City, N.Y.: Doubleday, 1967); P. F. Beyer, "Privatization and the Global Influence of Religion in Global Society," in *Global Culture*, ed. M. Featherstone (London: Sage, 1990): 373-395; S. Bruce (ed.), *Religion and Modernization* (New York: Oxford University Press, 1992); M. Chaves, "Secularization as Declining Religious Authority," *Social Forces* 72(1994):749-774; K. Dobbelaere, *Secularization* (London: Sage, 1981); K. Dobbelaere, "Secularization Theories and Sociological Paradigms," *Social Compass* 31(1984):199-219; K. Dobbelaere, "The Surviving Dominant Catholic Church in Belgium," in *The Post-War Generation and Establishment Religion*, ed. W. C. Roof et al. (Boulder, Colo.: Westview, 1995): 171-190; R. K. Fenn, *Toward a Theory of Secularization* (Storrs, Conn.: Society for the Scientific Study of Religion, 1978); J. K. Hadden, "Toward Desacralizing Secularization Theory," *Social Forces* 65(1987):587-611; L. Halman and R. de Moor, "Religion, Churches and Moral Values," in *The Individualizing Society*, ed. P. Ester et al. (Tilburg, Neth.: Tilburg University Press, 1993): 37-65; P. E. Hammond (ed.), *The Sacred in a Secular Age* (Berkeley: University of California Press, 1985); F. J. Lechner, "The Case Against Secularization," *Social Forces* 69(1991):1103-1119; H. Lübbe, *Säkularisierung* (Freiburg: Alber, 1975); T. Luckmann, *The Invisible Religion* (New York: Macmillan, 1967); T. Luckmann, "The Structural Conditions of Religious Consciousness in Modern Societies," *Japanese Journal of Religious Studies* 6(1979):121-137; T. Luckmann, "Shrinking Transcendence, Expanding Religion?" *Sociological Analysis* 50(1990):127-138; N. Luhmann, *Funktion der Religion* (Frankfurt: Suhrkamp, 1977); N. Luhmann, *The Differentiation of Society* (New York: Columbia University Press, 1982); D. A. Martin, *A General Theory of Secularization* (Oxford: Blackwell, 1978); T. Parsons, "Christianity and Modern Industrial Society," *Sociological Theory, Values and Sociocultural Change*, ed. E. A. Tiryakian (New York: Harper, 1967): 33-70; L. Shiner, "The Concept of Secularization in Empirical Research," in *Journal for the Scientific Study of Religion* 6(1967):207-220; R. Stark and W. S. Bainbridge, *A Theory of Religion* (New York: Lang, 1987); O. Tschannen, *Les théories de la sécularisation* (Geneva: Librairie Droz, 1992); L. Voyé, "From Institutional Catholicism to 'Christian Inspiration,' " in *The Post-War Generation and Establishment Religion*, ed. W. C. Roof et al. (Boulder, Colo.: Westview, 1995): 191-204; R. Wallis, *The Elementary Forms of the New Religious Life* (London: Routledge, 1984); M. Weber, *Gesammelte Aufsätze zur Religionssoziologie* (Tübingen: Mohr, 1920); B. R. Wilson, "Aspects of Secularization in the West," in *Japanese Journal of Religious Studies* 3(1976):259-276; B. R. Wilson, *Religion in Sociological Perspective* (Oxford: Oxford University Press, 1982).

SECULAR RELIGION Momentarily, *secular religion* may seem to be paradoxical or even an outright contradiction in terms. Does not *secular* mean the opposite, or absence, of religion? (Is that, indeed, not confirmed by its incorrigibly adjectival status—even when converted into cultural *secularity* or ideological *secularism*?) Is not the phrase, at best, eschatological: looking forward to the day when, either the whole of "the earth is the Lord's" and there will be "no [need of a] temple in the city [of God]"; or else when religion is abolished and secularity rules the world?

Yet this is based upon, if not an ethnocentric then a "temperocentric" view of religion: that of the "early modern" period. True, *secular* can be defined with remarkable ease: as the opposite of religion (whatever that is, in any particular situation). Thus *religion* refers to a whole way of life, in small-scale societies (before that way is spelled out, for voluntary groups, in a religious Rule). Subsequently, in historical societies it refers to that willed program of commitment that is, ideally, expressed in the whole of life. When that program no longer takes the form of a traditional religion (as, for instance, in the case of humanism), then the program itself may be described as a "secular religion."

"Secular religion" is, therefore, a natural way of describing ordinary human life: either as that way of life that is expressed in religion, or as that way of life in which religion is expressed. The conceptual need to reestablish the secular ramifications of what appertains to a religious order, or to a hierarchical church, or to a transcendent sacred, only proves the symbiotic relationship of the religious and the secular. Thus even a "secular" form of religion will still need its "extramural" forms of expression—if it is to be called a religion at all.

The choice of examples of "secular religions" will depend upon the observer's estimate of actors' motivations. The invention, or the use, of religious look-alikes for ends that were authentic to the initiators, as in Comtism or Freemasonry, is one thing. Their use for purposes of manipulation, as in political religions, is another.

—*Edward I. Bailey*

REFERENCES

A. Bergesen, *The Sacred and the Subversive* (Storrs, Conn.: Society for the Scientific Study of Religion, 1984); A. Bergesen, "Beyond the Dichotomy of Secularity and Religion," *Journal of Oriental Studies* 26, 1(1987); J. G. Davies, *Every Day God* (London: SCM, 1973); H. Fingarette, *Confucius* (New York: Harper, 1972); P. Nathanson, *Over the Rainbow* (Albany: SUNY Press, 1991); M. Rousseau and C. Gallagher, *Sex Is Holy* (Shaftesbury, U.K.: Element, 1986); H. W. Turner, "A Model for the Structural Analysis of Religions in Relation to the Secular," *Cahiers des Religions Africaines* 3(1969):173-197; P. C. Vitz, *Psychology as Religion* (Grand Rapids, Mich.: Eerdmans, 1977); M. Zeldin, "The Religious Nature of Russian Marxism," *Journal for the Scientific Study of Religion* 8(1969):100-111.

SELF-DENIAL Many historical religions, both ancient and modern, have pursued an ethic of self-denial as a path of salvation. In both Eastern and Western faiths, the strict control of the body, affective and sexual abstinence, and an ascetic worldview have been prescribed as essential preconditions of spirituality and wisdom. Self-denial is frequently understood as a process of renunciation to enable the soul to escape the prison of the flesh. In the Greek tradition, the motif of corporeal transcendence can be traced from the Pythagorean sects of the late sixth and fifth centuries B.C.E. Orphism, to the ambivalent figure of Socrates and the Socratic sects, and on to Platonism and Neoplatonism; in Latin culture, its practice is often associated with the mystery religions and, on a more public plane, the philosophy of the Stoics, the term *stoicism* still being in use today as a synonym particularly for emotional self-denial. As a powerful doctrinal element in early Christianity, asceticism or the "mortification of the flesh" was supported by both the Eastern and the Western branches of the church, evolving into the asceticism of the monk's path, institutionalized in the medieval monastic system.

After Max Weber's famous work *The Protestant Ethic and the Spirit of Capitalism* (Scribner 1930 [1904-1905]), we now view the individualist, this-worldly ascetic ethic of the Protestant sects as one of the important cultural preconditions for the rise of capitalism and the modern world order. The pervasive presence of the dualist cosmology of matter and spirit—body and soul—in modern culture is no doubt one of the products of ancient asceticism.

See also Asceticism

—*Barry Sandywell*

SEMINARIES AND SEMINARIANS

"Seminary" (from the Latin *seminarium,* meaning "seed plot") was adopted by Roman Catholic Church fathers at the Council of Trent (sixteenth century) as the designation for settings where candidates for the priesthood could be nourished and formed in their vocations apart from distracting "worldly" influences. In the United States, "theological seminary" is now used as one of several names for institutions that provide postbaccalaureate training for men and women for various ministries in churches and synagogues. Other designations include "school of theology" and "divinity school," the latter generally referring to schools attached to a university. For most of their history, the primary purpose of these institutions has been the education of persons intending to become ordained ministers or rabbis. That purpose has been broadened in recent years.

Until the early nineteenth century, most Protestant clergy received a liberal arts education in colleges such as Harvard, Yale, or Princeton, followed by an apprenticeship of six months to a year during which one "read divinity" with an ordained clergyman. Concern for the adequacy of such preparation led Massachusetts Congregationalists to found Andover Theological Seminary in 1808. Other theological schools were established shortly thereafter. The shift away from the older liberal-arts-*cum*-apprenticeship pattern of education was an important step in the professionalization of Protestant clergy. Roman Catholics had founded their first U.S. seminary, St. Mary's in Baltimore, 17 years earlier in 1791. American Jews founded Hebrew Union College in Cincinnati in 1875 as the first Jewish institution to train rabbis. Over the years, most theological schools, excepting Roman Catholics, followed the trends of professionalization that Protestant schools early adopted and that many other occupations also pursued (Bledstein 1978). For Catholics, however, it was only after Vatican II that seminaries shifted their focus substantially from moral and spiritual formation to preparation for professional ministry, with a renewed emphasis on the study of scriptures and increased practical training (Hemrick and Hoge 1986).

A fairly recent development is the establishment by several large evangelical seminaries of substantial extension programs offering degrees to part-time students. Several of these programs use satellite and computer technologies for course delivery (Morgan 1994). Recently, there has been considerable discussion of the character and purpose of theological education, with a particular concern over the dominance of the professional model of ministry (see Gilpin [1988] for a bibliography).

In 1994, the Association of Theological Schools in the United States and Canada (ATS), the accrediting agency for theological education, listed 189 fully accredited theological schools (165 in the United States and 32 in Canada). Another 30 schools are listed as candidates for accreditation or associate schools, for a total of 219 (*Fact Book* 1993-1994:3). The 219 schools represent various Protestant denominations as well as the Roman Catholic and Orthodox churches. Of the total, 130 are affiliated with one or more Protestant or Orthodox denominations, 52 are Roman Catholic, and 37 are interdenominational or nondenominational. Four accredited schools provide rabbinical training for the Reform, Conservative, Reconstructionist, and Orthodox branches of Judaism. Some Roman Catholic seminaries have chosen not to affiliate with the ATS. A number of Jewish schools also are not members. A number of Bible colleges and institutes also provide ministerial training for churches that do not require postbaccalaureate training for their clergy. They may be accredited by the Accrediting Association of Bible Colleges.

Most theological schools, regardless of religious affiliation, are small when compared with other institutions of higher education. Enrollment in the largest school in 1993-1994 was 3,458 students, which translates to a full-time equivalent (FTE) enrollment of 2,656 students. The smallest school had 16 students (13 FTE). Overall, 23 schools had a total enrollment of 75 or less, and 34 had more than 500. The modal school has a total student enrollment of between 151 and 300 students.

Theological schools vary in structure and governance. A large majority of Protestant schools are free-standing institutions. Most, but not all, are affiliated with a denomination and governed by a self-perpetuating or denominationally elected board of trustees. A smaller number are divinity schools related to a university and subject to the university's governing board. Most, although not all, university-related schools are interdenominational or ecumenical in character. The Roman Catholic Church also has free-standing as well as some university-related seminaries. Some are under the control of dioceses; others are controlled by religious orders. Jewish seminaries typically have close ties to a university but are governed by independent boards of trustees. Funding patterns vary. Some sponsoring denominations—for example, Southern Baptists, Lutherans, and United Methodists—supply substantial annual funding for their schools. Roman Catholic dioceses and religious congregations also contribute to the schools they sponsor, and often contribute the services of priests and members of the religious order as faculty members and administrators. Most schools rely on endowment earnings, annual fund-raising efforts, and tuitions for much of their income.

That many theological schools have a formal denominational relationship makes their environment considerably different from most other professional schools and creates a multiple-accountability structure: to governing boards, accrediting agencies, and the denomination. While denomination-seminary relationships are often strained, they can become exceedingly difficult, as recent events within the Southern Baptist Convention have illustrated. Fundamentalist Southern Baptist denominational leaders have led a "purge" of their seminaries, removing trustees, administrators, and faculty who hold moderate or liberal theological positions.

Typical seminary faculty size is small. Protestant faculties range from 3 to 106 with an average of 17; Roman Catholic faculties range from 4 to 36 and average 14; Jewish faculties range from 10 to 40 in size (Wheeler et al. 1992). The composition of theological faculties is changing slowly to reflect gender and ethnic diversity.

Total enrollment in theological schools grew substantially between 1972 and 1987, up approximately 60% when all degree programs are taken into account. Between 1987 and 1993, total enrollment grew by 14%. Enrollment in master of divinity (M.Div.) programs (the major program leading to ordination) has remained relatively flat since the mid-1980s. The increase in total enrollment has come mostly through the expansion of other degree programs: such as the doctor of ministry (D.Min.), an advanced degree for ordained clergy, and specialized master's programs for students interested in careers other than ordained ministry (e.g., youth ministry, religious education, or counseling).

During the 20-year period 1973-1993, the enrollment of women in ATS schools grew from approximately 10% to more than 30%. In mainline Protestant and ecumenical schools, women constitute more than half of the student body. Protestant schools with an evangelical orientation enroll considerably fewer women (approximately 14% in 1986). Women students enrolled in M.Div. programs are considerably less likely than men to be planning a career in pastoral ministry and are more likely to seek employment as counselors or chaplains (O'Neill and Grandy 1994).

From 1972 to 1993, the enrollment of African Americans in all theological schools went from 3% to 8% of the total number of students. Hispanics increased from 1% to 3%. The number of Asian students grew from 1% in 1981 to almost 6% in 1993.

Focusing only on overall enrollment trends masks considerable variation by type of schools. The largest increases since the early 1970s came in Protestant schools with an evangelical orientation. Mainline Protestant schools also grew during this period, but less so than evangelical schools. Roman Catholic seminaries experienced overall declines, especially in the number of candidates preparing for the priesthood (Carroll 1989). These declines have reached crisis proportions in recent years, even as total U.S. Catholic membership is growing (Schoenherr and Young 1993).

Age changes among students have been important. The mean age of entering seminarians in 1962 was 25.4 years. By 1988, it was 31 (Larsen and Shopshire 1988). In 1993, the ATS reported the modal age of male students as between 30 and 39 years. The age for women was bimodal, almost equally divided between the 30-39 and 40-49 age groups (*Fact Book* 1993-1994:83). The overall trend to older students, while often salutary in terms of the maturity and life experience, means a substantial decrease in service years in ordained ministry per student graduate. It also substantially increases the average cost of educating a stable supply of clergy.

The cost to individual students of theological education is low in comparison with other professional schools (1993 tuition ranged between $1,200 and $13,000), reflecting both the relatively low earnings potential of many graduates and the efforts by some denominations to subsidize their students' education. Nevertheless, rising educational costs have led to an increasingly heavy debt load for many students (Ruger and Wheeler 1994).

Seminary leaders worry not only about the number of student enrollments but also about the quality of students when compared with entrants into other professions or with previous cohorts of seminary students. Comparative data are inadequate to substantiate these worries. Limited evidence suggests that entering seminarians have slightly lower grade point averages than students entering medicine and law. Additionally, analysis of GRE scores indicates that women students planning to pursue an M.Div. degree have higher average scores than their male counterparts, but that both men and women score somewhat higher than those pursuing master's degrees in other helping professions—such as counseling, social work, and nursing (Grandy and Greiner 1990:8 f). Recent entering seminarians are less likely to have been in undergraduate leadership positions as seminarians in the past (O'Neill and Murphy 1991).

—*Jackson W. Carroll*

REFERENCES

B. J. Bledstein, *The Culture of Professionalism* (New York: Norton, 1978); J. W. Carroll, "The State of the Art," *Christianity and Crisis* 49(1989):106-110; *Fact Book on Theological Education* (Pittsburgh: Association of Theological Schools, 1993-1994); G. Gilpin, "Basic Issues in Theological Education," *Theological Education* 25(1988):115-121; J. Grandy and M. Greiner, "Academic Preparation of Master of Divinity Candidates," in *Ministry Research Notes* (Princeton, N.J.: Educational Testing Service, 1990); E. F. Hemrick and D. R.

Hoge, *Seminarians in Theology* (Washington, D.C.: U.S. Catholic Conference, 1986); E. L. Larsen and J. M. Shopshire, "A Profile of Contemporary Seminarians," *Theological Education* 24(1988):1-136; T. C. Morgan, "Re-engineering the Seminary," *Christianity Today* 38, 12(1994): 74-79; J. P. O'Neill and J. Grandy, "The Image of Ministry," in *Ministry Research Notes* (Princeton, N.J.: Educational Testing Service, 1994); J. P. O'Neill and R. T. Murphy, "Changing Age and Gender Profiles Among Entering Seminary Students," in *Ministry Research Notes* (Princeton, N.J.: Educational Testing Service, 1991); A. Ruger and B. G. Wheeler, "Deeper in Debt," *Christian Century* 111(1994): 100-103; R. A. Schoenherr and L. A. Young, *Full Pews and Empty Altars* (Madison: University of Wisconsin Press, 1993); B. G. Wheeler et al., "Theological Education," in *Encyclopedia of Educational Research*, Vol. 4 (New York: Macmillan, 1992): 1422-1427.

SEXISM   Millions of believers gather regularly in churches, synagogues, and other "holy" places to worship a higher power, learn the doctrines and principles of their faith, socialize with other followers, and celebrate a particular form of "family life." Commensurate with the faith messages are admonitions concerning the rights and responsibilities of men, women, and children within the general life of the faith community, the wider society, and, most important, the family unit. The relationship between religion and gender involves a complicated web of social interactions and teachings on the supernatural, human sexuality, gender relations, spiritual vocations, and weekly routine of life in the faith tradition. However, within the last 30 years, much of what was once taken for granted has come under criticism—and significant voices of challenge are feminist in their orientation.

The Challenge to Reevaluate the "Inspired Truths"
Through both feminist theological scholarship and discontent among women in the pew has come the impetus to reconsider religious truths particularly as they pertain to the role and status of women. Confusion and controversy characterize the debate on the biblical record and women. Theological teaching has been used to justify the exclusion of women from positions of church leadership and from ordination to the priesthood or full-time religious office. Those who argue for a restrictive role for women base their position on Old Testament laws, Eve's beguilement by a serpent, and the Pauline instructions contained in the pastoral epistles of the New Testament. Other scholars conclude their search of the Christian Scriptures by justifying an expanded role for women; they base their conclusions on the equality of men and women in the creation narrative and the numerous examples of women who transcended traditional roles in ancient Israel, interpret Jesus's treatment of women as revolutionary, and consider the openness of the Apostle Paul to equal and free participation for all people within the early Christian movement. Feminist scholars both within and beyond faith communities have concluded that much of the misogynist treatment of women is not an integral part of the original "holy" and inspired manuscripts but is an introduction by male clerics and others eager to extinguish the early fires of egalitarianism among women and men, slave and free, or Jew and Gentile.

More than 20 years ago, Mary Daly argued that women of faith need to look beyond the concept of God the Father—the all-knowing, all-powerful male. "A woman's asking for equality in the church would be comparable to a black person's demanding equality in the Ku Klux Klan," she wrote (1975:6). Other feminist theologians, however, disagreed with this position. Phyllis Trible, Elizabeth Schüssler Fiorenza, and Rosemary Radford Ruether, to name but a few, claim that biblical faith can have a liberating potential. Within their perspectives, the essential elements of the Judeo-Christian faith are not captured in the sanctity of patriarchy but in a sense of relatedness to God. Themes such as the exodus of the children of Israel, the plea for justice by the prophets, and Jesus's own words and concern about the poor fuel the optimism of feminist theologians. The task of the feminist "herstorian," according to Fiorenza, is to recapture the theme of liberation in the Jewish-Christian tradition and to assist people's spiritual journeys by providing a context for both renewal and conversion.

In the Western world, there is ample evidence that women are more faithful church attenders than men and that they cling more fully to the teachings of their faith communities (Bibby 1987, McGuire 1992). Despite admonitions by some feminist writers that women en masse leave their churches and patriarchal faith communities, researchers have found that women are "defecting in place," challenging the institution from within, and supplementing their faith journey by contact with women's spirituality groups (Winter et al. 1994). Moreover, women from various spiritual and doctrinal positions are "reclaiming" and "rediscovering" the place of women within the pages of their sacred books. As a result, many lay people are no longer content to equate present church or faith practices with "unchanging truths." Many pew warmers and activists alike echo Pontius Pilate's question, "What is truth?"

The Challenge to Rethink the Image of the Religious Leader The issue of women and ordained ministry remains contentious, even within those faith traditions that formally recognize women's ordination. Although the struggle for admission into the ordained ministry has received the most attention, the career path of clergywomen tends to be laden with obstacles and inequities as they seek placement and other career opportunities (Lehman 1985, Carroll et al. 1983). Yet the evidence suggests that women clergy bring no measurable disadvantage to the local congregation and, in fact, several advantages (Royle 1987).

Several common features characterize the struggle for women's ordination (Nason-Clark 1993). In the early stages of the debate, theological issues appear in the forefront, although there is little evidence to show that theology accounts for the resistance. Sociologists who have considered the resistance to the ordained ministry of women agree that religious beliefs alone are unable to account for the opposition to women clergy (Lehman 1987, Chaves 1997). In a British sample of clergymen in the 1980s, those opposed to the ordination of women to the priesthood in the Church of England were more restrictive in their views on women's role in society and in the family (Nason-Clark 1987b). They were more likely to believe that a woman's place was in the home, reported less support for equality between men and women in the workplace, and were less supportive of women choosing to combine motherhood and careers. A study of these same clergymen in the 1990s (nine years later) revealed that such factors as working with a clergywoman, or fathering a daughter, or having a wife who works full-time for pay were related to changes in their attitudes toward women and ordained ministry.

Once denominations have exhausted the debate in theological terms, the second stage of resistance centers on appropriate timing. At this phase of resistance, practical issues take precedence: the geographic mobility of married clergywomen; the possibility of temporary vacancies due to pregnancy leave; the acceptance of younger, never-married clergywomen by parishioners; problems of placement; and opportunities for career advancement. Such discussions prolong the decision about women's ordination, under the guise that practical details present insurmountable problems for the religious organization.

After official recognition as ordained elders is granted, the next stage of controversy centers on placement issues and the persistent finding that women appear to be frequently passed over in the selection process (Lehman 1985) and overrepresented in junior positions (Nesbitt 1993). An obstacle faced by all clergywomen is continued resistance to their ministry by their clerical colleagues (Nason-Clark 1987a). Although contact between clergywomen and clergymen plays a role in reducing the resistance (Lehman 1985), these men have few opportunities to work with female ministerial colleagues, and as a result changes in their gender role ideology occur at a slower pace.

The Challenge to Rethink Lay Leadership Although it is critical to highlight women's struggle for official recognition in ordained ministries, it is important to realize that women do not participate on an equal footing with men even as lay members of local congregations. Rather, a gendered division of labor characterizes most churches, such that women perform a multitude of sex-typed tasks in a supportive role to men, not unlike the responsibilities women traditionally have performed in the home. The challenge in the contemporary Christian church is to prevail over sex-typing and to recognize and incorporate the differences among women and men by offering tasks based on talent rather than gender.

What would a church look like if it took the responsibilities of Christian men and women to be equal as partners in sharing their faith and in leadership (Nason-Clark 1993:230 f)? The gender breakdown of the local church governing council would be comparable to the nursery roster; the proportion of women on the platform would approximate the number in the pew; the language and liturgy of worship and instruction would reflect the diversity among believers; the full expanse of the church's ministry would include men and women serving as partners, on the basis of talent, willingness, and spiritual maturity; and the programs offered to the congregation and the local community would be inclusive of the full range of needs and experiences of ordinary people, male and female. The inclusion and copartnership of men and women in active lay service can only be realized by rethinking the power and prestige conferred by ordination.

The Challenge to Rethink Clerical Power and Privilege Sexual scandals involving clergy bring to center stage the vulnerability of churches and parishioners when clerical trust has been violated. Although it would be clearly erroneous and misleading to suggest that all ordained priests and ministers wield unleashed power over others, sexual scandals provide a case study of the power of the "clerical collar." In part, crimes of clergy malfeasance continue because of the awe, respect, and reverence attributed to the priesthood. Churches fail to respond quickly and decisively to curtail the abuse and support the victims partly because of their desire to protect the priesthood and the office of the parish minister (Nason-Clark 1997). Within new religious movements also, spiritual leaders and advisers are reported to take sexual advantage of women and children (Jacobs 1989). Yet several factors have begun to erode the power of clergy in the Western world: the shortage of male priests (Hoge 1987), nonordained women performing clerical tasks (Wallace 1992), the presence of women clergy (Lehman 1987) and the changes they have introduced (Ice 1987), declining church attendance (Bibby 1993), increased education among the general church-attending populace, the pluralism of modern religious life together with the proliferation of secular professionals in the helping professions, and a generalized growing intolerance of unchecked power in any sphere of contemporary society.

The Counterchallenge—Fundamentalism and Gender   Controversies about gender, and by extension the social, reproductive, and economic status of women, occupy center stage in the social/political agenda of religious fundamentalists. Fundamentalist religion worldwide idealizes woman as the self-sacrificing wife and mother, content to run the home rather than be occupied with the business or external world (Hawley 1994). Antimodern religious groups—whether they draw their followers from American fundamentalism, Indian Islam, Hinduism, or Japanese new religions—preach a powerful message of solid, changeless familial relationships. In fact, fundamentalist religions have responded to the uncertainty of modernity by firming up the boundaries having to do with women. Such a process has been labeled *gender inerrancy* (Nason-Clark 1995), referring to the nonnegotiable ideas about gender roles, gender expectations, and performance standards. The contemporary gender challenge to fundamentalism is profound at the point where feminism asserts that a woman's deepest sense of identity may be found in something other than her family connections.

For contemporary American fundamentalists, the gender struggle—celebrated most vociferously in the pro-choice/pro-life abortion war—is rooted in a nostalgia for a bygone era: an idealized version of family and community in rural nineteenth-century America. The sacred texts of Christianity, Hinduism, Islam, and Japanese new religions differ, but the message for women is much the same: "Know thy place." In knowing her place, the American fundamentalist woman is accepting an ideal that flourished in the postindustrial small-town United States, ignoring that such a traditional concept of femininity itself was a nineteenth-century construct made possible only by the advances of modernity (Balmer 1994). In knowing her place, the Hindu fundamentalist woman defends her "right" to choose whether or not to cast her living

body on the burning pyre of a dead husband (Hawley 1994). In knowing the place of women, Islamic fundamentalists decry any move to liberalize divorce laws or to grant women economic security once divorced (Awn 1994). And in knowing the place of woman, Japanese female leaders of new religious movements define women's salvation in relation to their domestic choices (Hardacre 1994).

According to McGuire (1992), there is impressive historical evidence that nonofficial religion continues to be a vehicle for women asserting an expanded religious role, with examples ranging from healing cults (Csordas 1994) to contemporary witchcraft (Neitz 1990). Yet there is also evidence of pushing the boundaries within official religious institutions, for Catholic women pastors serving in priest-less parishes (Wallace 1992), small-group female or shared leadership in evangelical and charismatic churches (Wuthnow 1994), not to mention the long-standing role of women as pentecostal itinerant preachers or missionaries in "foreign" contexts.

Despite the rhetoric, however, there is far more latitude in the way conservative Protestant men and women interpret and operationalize these gender messages than one might think (Ammerman 1987, Heaton and Cornwall 1986).

Religion and Gender Roles   Gender is a social construct, involving three interrelated dimensions: differentiation, traits, and hierarchy (MacKie 1987). As differentiation, gender implies a biological distinction upon which an elaborate set of meanings have been built. Gender as traits refers to societal norms identifying what men and women should be, feel, and do to exhibit masculinity or femininity. The third aspect, hierarchy, involves the ranking of males and females in such a way that there is a cultural devaluation of female characteristics and activities.

The content of gender socialization, including gender scripts, is learned during our childhood, first and foremost from parents and then through the influence of teachers, peers, the media, and religious institutions. Gender role attitudes constitute one part of the gender script that is learned in childhood. These attitudes include consensual beliefs about the differing characteristics of men and women, coupled with a tendency to ascribe greater social value to masculine, rather than feminine, behaviors. Despite the fact that the Western world is changing its gender text and a noticeable shift can be observed in attitudes toward the rights and responsibilities of women in modern society (Thornton et al. 1983), large differences in gender attitudes still exist depending on sex, age, educational attainment, characteristics of one's mother, employment history, and religious affiliation and practice (McMurray 1978, Molm 1978, Porter and Albert 1977).

Religious participation offers a socializing group atmosphere where values and beliefs are learned and transmitted. The opposition to the Equal Rights Amendment (ERA) in the United States maintained by many Christian women belonging to conservative Protestant denominations attests to this influence (Brady and Tedin 1976). Conversely, feminists are less likely to engage in religious behavior or to hold religious beliefs than nonfeminists (McClain 1979).

Porter and Albert argue that specific types of religious orientations persist and that religious subcultures are affected by the secular value system of the country in which they are located. They claim that if many women in one's religious reference group are actually involved in paid employment, this may mitigate or modify the effects of religious ideology, even for those women who do not work outside the home. Porter and Albert consider their data to suggest the persistence of religious subcultural ideologies in modern industrial societies. They also argue that religious orientations are "clearly shaped and modified to some extent by other cultural and structural factors" (1977:358).

In her study of Jewish women who return to orthodoxy, Lynn Davidman (1991) found that there was an attraction to the restrictive gender script; for some women, narrow proscribed roles and responsibilities provide a sense of stability in what is perceived to be a changing, "rootless" world. Other data corroborate the finding that religious orientations are influenced and molded by nonreligious cultural and structural factors. In a study of the gender role orientation of English clergy, it was found that within denominations, personal, familial, and educational characteristics could be understood to shape and modify particular gender role attitudes (Nason-Clark 1993). The *etiology* of a traditional view on the rights and responsibilities of women may well be fostered by personal and familial variables through the process of socialization, but it is *maintained* by structural constraints, including those religious in nature, that reinforce patterns of behavior and associated attitudes.

Summary The evidence suggests that there are numerous challenges to the patriarchal bias of religion in the contemporary Western world, involving reevaluating "spiritual truth" and the religious elite who proclaim it. Yet a strong countercurrent remains. There is an undeniable link between religious fundamentalism and a restrictive gender role ideology. Why do some people of faith adopt egalitarian gender role attitudes and others cling to restrictive interpretations of the

female role? One's understanding of the Christian paradigm is dynamically interrelated with personal background characteristics.

—*Nancy Nason-Clark*

REFERENCES

N. Ammerman, *Bible Believers* (New Brunswick, N.J.: Rutgers University Press, 1987); P. Awn, "Indian Islam," in Hawley, *q.v.* (1994): 63-78; R. Balmer, "American Fundamentalism," in Hawley, *q.v.* (1994): 47-62; R. Bibby, *Fragmented Gods* (Toronto: Irwin, 1987); R. Bibby, *Unknown Gods* (Toronto: Stoddart, 1993); D. Brady and K. Tedin, "Ladies in Pink," *Social Science Quarterly* 56(1976):564-574; J. Carroll et al., *Women of the Cloth* (San Francisco: Harper, 1983); M. Chaves, *Ordaining Women* (Cambridge: Harvard University Press, 1997); T. Csordas, *The Sacred Self* (Berkeley: University of California Press, 1994); M. Daly, *The Church and the Second Sex* (New York: Harper, 1975); L. Davidman, *Tradition in a Rootless World* (Berkeley: University of California Press, 1991); E. S. Fiorenza, *But She Said* (Boston: Beacon, 1992); H. Hardacre, "Japanese New Religions," in Hawley, *q.v.* (1994): 111-136; J. S. Hawley (ed.), *Fundamentalism and Gender* (New York: Oxford University Press, 1994); T. Heaton and M. Cornwall, "Religious Group Variation in the Socioeconomic Status of Family Behavior of Women," *Journal for the Scientific Study of Religion* 28(1986):283-299; D. R. Hoge, *The Future of Catholic Leadership* (Kansas City, Mo.: Sheed & Ward, 1987); M. Ice, *Clergywomen and Their Worldviews* (New York: Praeger, 1987); J. Jacobs, *Divine Disenchantment* (Bloomington: Indiana University Press, 1989); E. C. Lehman, Jr., *Women Clergy* (New Brunswick, N.J.: Transaction, 1985); E. C. Lehman, Jr., *Women Clergy in England* (Lewiston, N.Y.: Mellen, 1987); M. MacKie, *Constructing Men and Women* (Toronto: Holt, 1987); E. McClain, "Religious Orientation the Key to Psychodynamic Differences Between Feminists and Nonfeminists," *Journal for the Scientific Study of Religion* 18(1979):40-45; M. McGuire, *Religion*, 3rd ed. (Belmont, Calif.: Wadsworth, 1992); M. McMurray, "Religion and Women's Sex Role Traditionalism," *Sociological Focus* 1(1978):81-95; L. Molm, "Sex Role Attitudes and the Employment of Married Women," *Sociological Quarterly* 19(1978):522-533; N. Nason-Clark, "Are Women Changing the Image of Ministry?" *Review of Religious Research* 28(1987a):330-340; N. Nason-Clark, "Ordaining Women as Priests vs. Sexist Explanations for Clerical Attitudes," *Sociological Analysis* 48(1987b):259-273; N. Nason-Clark, "Gender Relations in Contemporary Christian Organizations," in *The Sociology of Religion*, ed. W. E. Hewitt (Toronto: Butterworth, 1993): 215-234; N. Nason-Clark, "Conservative Protestants and Violence Against Women," *Sex, Lies and Sanctity*, ed. M. Goldman and M. J. Neitz (Storrs, Conn.: JAI, 1995): 109-130; N. Nason-Clark, "Abuses of Clergy Trust," in *Wolves Among the Fold*, ed. A. D. Shupe (New Brunswick, N.J.: Rutgers University Press, 1997); M. J. Neitz, *Charisma and Community* (New Brunswick, N.J.: Transaction, 1987); M. J. Neitz, "In Goddess We Trust," in *In Gods We Trust*, 2nd ed., ed. T. Robbins and D.

Anthony (New Brunswick, N.J.: Transaction, 1990); P. Nesbitt, "Dual Ordination Tracks," *Sociology of Religion* 54 (1993):13-30; J. Porter and A. Albert, "Subculture or Assimilation?" *Journal for the Scientific Study of Religion* 16(1977):345-359; M. Royle, "Using Bifocals to Overcome Blindspots," *Review of Religious Research* 28(1987):341-350; A. Thornton et al., "Causes and Consequences of Sex-Role Attitudes and Attitude Change," *American Sociological Review* 48(1983):211-227; R. Wallace, *They Call Her Pastor* (Albany: SUNY Press, 1992); M. Warner, *Alone of All Her Sex* (London: Picador, 1985); T. Winter et al., *Defecting in Place* (New York: Crossroad, 1994); R. Wuthnow, *I Come Away Stronger* (Grand Rapids, Mich.: Eerdmans, 1994).

SEXUALITY AND FERTILITY   Religion and sexuality are cohabitors in history and across cultures (see Weber 1946:343-350). Sexuality and sexual practice are regulated by religious belief and doctrine; religious ritual may prescribe sexual activity including intercourse with gods or their earthly representatives; gods may be seen in myths as engaging in sexual work leading to the creation of the world or a particular people. The fecundity of the earth and the sexual fertility of humans are linked in cultic prostitution and orgies; other times and places understand the higher worship of god or gods to be possible only by celibate virgins. The parameters differ, but the underlying relationship remains; it is the human experience that the mystery of human sexuality demands religious response.

Sex and the Sacred   Sexuality plays a role in the explanation of deity, divinity, and sacredness in much of what the world terms *religion*. Consider, for example, the creation myth of Japanese Shinto, which teaches that Japan, the sacred land of a sacred people (in Shinto), was created by the sexual union of two kami, Izangi (male) and Izanami (female). Their intercourse produces all other gods, including Amaterasu, the great sun goddess whose descendants are the emperors of Japan. The births, deaths, and sexual activity of the early Japanese deities suggest that cultic worship practices concerned with food and sex abounded in the islands' ancient past (see Reader 1991). Sexuality is an integral component in the sacred standing of these deities.

The absence of sexuality and sexual activity also can be important in asserting divine privilege and power. We need look no farther than the Christian assertion of the virgin birth to understand more fully the insistence on purity, celibacy, and chastity. The sacred scriptures of Christians, and the earliest creeds of Christianity, known as the Apostles and Nicene, assert that Jesus's mother, Mary, "had not lain with a man" and that Jesus was "born of a virgin." While claims of virgin births were not restricted to Christians in the first century B.C.E., the scripture passage that Joseph "knew her not until after" the birth of Jesus (Matt. 1:25) had, by the Middle Ages, become understood in popularized Christianity to mean that Jesus passed through the birth canal without destroying Mary's physical virginity—nor did Mary ever, in fact, engage in sexual relations at any time. In the nineteenth century, this led to the Roman Catholic pronouncement that blessed Mary was "ever virgin" (the "perpetual virginity") and herself conceived "immaculately" (Warner 1983). Contrast this image with that of the biblical Eve, the seductress who is sexually insatiable.

Religion and the Practice of Sex   Today, religious teachings of all sorts officially pronounce and proscribe many beliefs about sexuality and sexual practices. The Church of Jesus Christ of Latter-day Saints, the Mormons, for example, believes that sexuality belongs correctly within marriage, that sexual intercourse must be free to bring another spirit being, waiting in another place, to physical birth in this world. Large families are the norm but are the decision of the couple. Artificial birth control is rare, but not completely banned, as in official Roman Catholic teaching. Roman Catholics are to engage in intercourse if conception is possible; sexual practices among heterosexual couples such as mutual masturbation and oral and anal intercourse, which are not procreative by nature, were once prohibited and even now are discouraged. Many of the more conservative branches of Judaism, and most of Islam's sects, ban nonprocreative sexual practices.

All of these groups, of course, find homosexuality and its sexual practices incompatible with religious teaching. Gay and lesbian believers, on the other hand, often express dissatisfaction with equating moralistic or cultural values with religious commandments. Religious teachings in each of these Western, monotheistic traditions are used today to condemn and affirm, prohibit and bless, homosexual activity, orientations, and unions.

Sexuality can be dictated, studied, and even suggested by religious teachings and institutions. Cults and communes of the 1960s and 1970s, too numerous to name or classify, often practiced group sex to bind together members or to bind women followers to a male leader. The nineteenth-century Oneida Community practiced a marriage of all believers in such a way that all were available sexual partners to all opposite sex members of the group. In practice, the founder and leader, John Humphrey Noyes, seems to have regulated who engaged in sexual union with whom and, it has been suggested, even engaged in an early form of eugenic breeding in his planned couplings (see DeMaria 1978). The Shakers, on the other hand, lived a celibate lifestyle but incorporated such energetic ritualized dancing in their worship as to be suggestive of orgiastic frenzy.

Sex can be understood by religion as necessary but evil, as among the people of Inis Beag, a small island off the coast of Ireland. These people shroud sexuality in ignorance and guilt, discuss sex rarely and never joke about it, discourage nudity, proscribe sex until after marriage, practice quick intercourse, in private and without much expectation for women to achieve orgasm, and believe that for men, the sex act drains the body's natural energies. Inis Beag is heavily Roman Catholic. Among the Mangaia people located in the Polynesian chain, by contrast, sexuality is active, vigorous, and of lengthy duration, and partners are committed to mutually pleasurable experience. Young people are encouraged to masturbate; more experienced partners educate and provide practice for youth in sexual pleasuring. These people live in small huts, and sexual intercourse takes place in the presence of the young woman's family, who politely ignore the couple. Male prowess is much discussed and compared among the women of Mangaia. Affection and love are thought to develop from satisfactory sexual relations. Human sexuality and pleasure are connected to the fertility of the island surrounding the community, and religious ritual can include sexually charged events, including the younger people before marriage (see, for both cases, Gagnon 1977).

Sex and Procreation in the Religious View Religious involvement in defining appropriate sexuality can extend to modern medicine's ability to achieve procreative goals without intercourse. The Roman Catholic Church, for example, prohibits artificial insemination when a couple cannot naturally conceive because it is an "unnatural act," and terms the use of donor sperm in a controlled medical setting an act of adultery. Such sexually charged language can hardly be accurate when describing a medical procedure, in a clinical setting, where the sperm is deposited by a syringe guided by gloved medical hands into a woman's vagina. Nevertheless, a pregnancy occurring after a rape is considered "natural."

Until the end of the eighteenth century, virtually all sexual practices in Western societies were governed by religious values. "Sex was an impulse of the flesh [and]

it came to represent a fall from grace." Sex's one purpose was procreation, and often celibacy held higher religious value even among Protestants. In Victorian London, there were 40,000 prostitutes, but "good" women were only the infrequent sexual partners of their "proper" husbands (Blumenfeld and Raymond 1993). Protestant missionaries in the nineteenth century, confronted by sexual practice in many Pacific regions where rear vaginal entry of the female by the male was preferred, condemned such activity as against God, who prefers, they taught, what became known as the "missionary" position of the male lying atop and facing his female partner (a name that has stayed with this position to the present day, completely outside that religious context).

Religious teaching preaches an image of sexuality when speaking on creation, marriage, fertility, divinity, and the sacred order. It is difficult, if not impossible, to separate an understanding of humanity's sexual nature as either good or evil from religious roots in many, if not all, traditions. Appropriately, the study of sexuality in its cultural context requires an understanding of religion and religious practices to provide full meaning to the prevalent sexual behaviors and attitudes in any culture.

—*Barbara J. Denison*

REFERENCES

W. J. Blumenfeld and D. Raymond, *Looking at Gay and Lesbian Life* (Boston: Beacon, 1993); R. DeMaria, *Communal Love at Oneida* (Lewiston, N.Y.: Mellen, 1978); J. H. Gagnon, *Human Sexualities* (Glenview, Ill.: Scott Foresman, 1977); G. Parrender, *Sex in the World's Religions* (New York: Oxford University Press, 1980); *A Profile of Faith* [video] (Salt Lake City: Church of Jesus Christ of Latter-day Saints, 1993); I. Reader, *Religion in Contemporary Japan* (Honolulu: University of Hawaii Press, 1991); M. Warner, *Alone of All Her Sex* (New York: Random House, 1983); M. Weber, *From Max Weber* (New York: Oxford University Press, 1946).

SHAKERS Originally known as the "Shaking Quakers," the United Society of Believers in Christ's Second Appearing are more commonly called "Shakers." The name comes from the uncontrolled ecstatic motions of the Shaking Quakers, which, in turn, became ritualized, stylized movements bringing the believer into union with one another and an ambisexual God, in whom paradise was foretold.

Already a member of an ecstatic breakaway group of Quakers, the illiterate British founder of the Shakers was "Mother" Ann Lee. Marriage and the death of her four children in infancy convinced Mother Ann that the root of evil was in sexual intercourse. After receiving a vision in 1770 depicting the Original Sin in Eden, Mother Ann preached celibacy. She ultimately led her followers to America in 1774.

After Mother Ann's death in 1784, the Shakers became a communitarian body, living celibately as a family. All property was shared in common; male and female living quarters were maintained separately. Given that humans existed in male and female images of God's being, God must therefore be ambisexual, or the equivalent of both genders. On earth, Jesus Christ embodied the fullest male expression of God; Mother Ann the fullest expression of the female.

The Shaker ritual, the organized reenactment of the sacred story of community and the dawn of the new millennium in God, was perfected in the nineteenth century. Shakers danced separately, male and female, but in harmony as parts of a whole. Their stylized movements became uncontrolled ecstasy.

Ambisexual God and celibacy aside, by the mid-nineteenth century the Shakers were prosperous farmers, craftspeople, and artisans. Shaker creations in furniture, art, woodwork, and household items depicted the perfect, simple harmony and functional efficiency of Shaker belief. Austere, communal living in pastoral and agricultural settings created businesses in seeds and pharmaceuticals. Neighbors recognized the Shakers for their pragmatic farming know-how.

More than 6,000 people flocked to the 18 Shaker communities in New York and New England, Kentucky, Ohio, and Indiana. Men and women were equal among the Shakers; in the community (unlike in much of the outside world of the nineteenth century), women held leadership positions. Entire families with parents and multiple children joined, the children becoming responsibilities of the community. The menfolk often left soon after, leaving behind the rest of the family. Widows and abandoned women with families also joined, and the Shakers (even though declining in recruits and total numbers by this time) took in hundreds of orphans after the Civil War. With no procreation to bring about their own "replacement" members, conversion and the rearing of others' children in the community were the only means of new membership.

Today one community remains at Sabbath Day Lake, Maine, with less than a dozen adherents. Their faith remains. In a documentary made several years ago, one survivor put it thus: Mother Ann arrived in America with nine followers; we could once again number in the thousands.

—Barbara J. Denison

REFERENCES

E. Andrews, *The People Called Shakers* (New York: Dover, 1963); P. Brewer, *Shaker Communities, Shaker Lives* (Hanover, N.H.: University Press of New England, 1986); H. Desroche, *American Shakers* (Amherst: University of Massachusetts Press, 1974 [1955]).

SHINTO   Religious beliefs and observances native to and preeminently practiced in Japan. Shinto beliefs and practices are found in a variety of forms. Shrine Shinto (Jinja Shinto), previously associated with the state, has a priesthood associated with Shinto shrines. Sect Shinto (Kyoha Shinto) refers to several sects in the Shinto tradition that arose in the nineteenth century. What might be termed Folk Shinto (Minzoku Shinto) refers to a host of beliefs and practices with no formal structure associated with Shinto tradition. Shinto has no formal doctrine but is composed of an assortment of beliefs and practices, including veneration of ancestors and spirits.

Early Japanese religious practice was not called Shinto until Buddhism was introduced to Japan (officially in 552 C.E.). The name *Shinto* means way of the *kami,* as distinguished from *Butsudo,* or the way of the Buddha. *Kami,* loosely translated, refers to one of an assortment of spirits that range from deities to deified clan founders, warriors, leaders, and forces of nature. Early Buddhist, Confucian, and Taoist thought had considerable influence on Shinto practice. However, the precise extent of this influence on native Japanese belief and practice is unclear, as no known record of Shinto beliefs antedates the introduction of writing by the Chinese. Two early recordings of Shinto myths, the *Kijiki* (Record of Ancient Matters, dating from around 712) and the *Nihonshoki Chronicles of Japan,* dating from about 720, while not delineating dogma, are considered somewhat sacred texts in Shinto.

Shinto practice fell out of official favor during the Tokugawa period (1603-1868; see Bellah 1985). During this time, Buddhism and neo-Confucianism were adopted by the Tokugawa regime as guiding ideologies. With the Meiji Restoration in 1868, Buddhism was disestablished. In the 1880s, religious freedom was guaranteed by the government, but Shrine Shinto was established as a nominally secular institution used by the state to transform Shinto shrines into foci of loyalty to the state.

Currently, most Japanese practice a combination of Shinto and Buddhism. Special Shinto observances are common for such important life events and rites of passage as births, weddings, and attainment of adulthood. While most Japanese participate in Shinto rituals for these events, only about 10% perform Shinto funerals, most preferring Buddhist rites. Shinto rites are performed for other important events, such as the dedication of building sites or launching of ships. There are Shinto rites for spring and harvest festivals and for other special days and times through the year.

Social scientific interest in Shinto goes back at least as far as Max Weber (1958, 1978), who examined the importance of the institution of nineteenth-century Shinto as the state religion, with its legitimation of the emperor after 1868, and as an example of a religion with a priesthood but no doctrine in the Western sense. Current social science literature has emphasized the relationship of Shinto to the state or has examined details of religious belief in Japan (e.g., Takayama 1988, Kaneko 1990).

—*Edward F. Breschel*

REFERENCES

R. N. Bellah, *Tokugawa Religion* (New York: Free Press, 1985 [1957]); S. Kaneko, "Dimensions of Religiosity Among Believers in Japanese Folk Religion," *Journal for the Scientific Study of Religion* 29(1990):1-18; K. P. Takayama, "Revitalization Movement of Modern Japanese Civil Religion," *Sociological Analysis* 48(1988):328-341; M. Weber, *The Religion of India* (Glencoe, Ill.: Free Press, 1958); M. Weber, *Economy and Society* (Berkeley: University of California Press, 1978).

SHIPPEY, FREDERICK A. (1909-1994)   James Pearsall Professor of the Sociology of Religion, Drew University, where he taught from 1950 to 1975. First editor of the *Review of Religious Research* (1959-1964). United Methodist minister, member of the staff of the home division of the board of missions of that body from 1944 to 1953, where he established a department of research and surveys. Known for his work in church planning and location and the relationship between community dynamics and religious life, epitomized in his books *Church Work in the City* (Abingdon 1952) and *Protestantism in Suburban Life* (Abingdon 1964). His work is archived at Drew, where the Shippey Lectureship in the Sociology of Christianity is given in his honor.

—*William H. Swatos, Jr.*

SHRIVER, PEGGY L. (1931–)   Professional church leadership administrator (since 1990; research, 1976-1988), National Council of Churches. Previous positions: Presbyterian Church, U.S. (research, 1973-1975) and Union Theological Seminary (development, 1987-1991). President, Religious Research Association, 1993-1994. Lecturer and author. Born in Iowa; awarded B.A., 1953, and honorary doctorate in humanities, 1979, Central College (Pella, Iowa); married (since 1953) to Donald W. Shriver, Jr., President Emeritus of Union Theological Seminary; awarded Union Medal, 1991.

—*Doyle Paul Johnson*

REFERENCES

P. L. Shriver, *The Bible Vote* (New York: Pilgrim, 1981); P. L. Shriver, *Having Gifts That Differ* (New York: Friendship, 1989); P. L. Shriver, *Pinches of Salt* (Louisville: Westminster, 1990).

SHUPE, ANSON D., JR. (1948–)   Professor of Sociology, joint campus of Indiana University-Purdue University (Fort Wayne).

Shupe completed his doctorate in political sociology at Indiana University in 1975 under the direction of Lawrence E. Hazelrigg, a sociologist in the Weberian tradition who worked in the areas of theory and stratification. Shupe's research and teaching both continued to reflect a strong Weberian influence. During the late 1970s, he began combining his interests in religion, politics, and deviance, publishing more than half a dozen books and numerous articles in professional journals, analyzing the post-World War II cohort of new religious movements and the countermovements that arose in opposition to them.

Conducting fieldwork among several new religious movements, most notably the Unification Church, as well as their organized opponents in the anti-cult movement, Shupe played a key role in constructing the social science understanding of the phenomena. He incorporated a historical viewpoint of such movements into his writings, drawing parallels with earlier cohorts of religious movements, and contributed a number of concepts—"apostate," "atrocity story," and "anti-cultism"—that were widely employed in analyzing the controversy surrounding new religious movements. Among his most notable books on new religions and countermovement are *Moonies in America: Cult, Church and Crusade* (with David Bromley, Sage 1979), *The New Vigilantes: Anti-Cultists, Deprogrammers and the New Religions* (with David Bromley, Sage 1980), and *Strange Gods: The Great American Cult Scare* (with David Bromley, Beacon 1981).

Shupe subsequently diversified his research to include a separate, but related, set of religious groups and movements—the New Christian Right, religious broadcasting, and the role of fundamentalist religious traditions in the global resurgence of political revolution—that yielded more than a half-dozen books.

Continuing his interest in deviance, Shupe also produced another body of research on violent and abusive practices within families, most notably *The Family Secret* (with William Stacey, Beacon 1983) and *The Violent Couple* (with William Stacey and Lawrence Hazelwood, Praeger 1994). He combined his research interest in family violence and his prior work on religion in a new line on violation of trust by clergy, most notably *In the Name of All That's Holy: A Theory of Clergy Malfeasance* (Praeger 1995). Exploring in deductive fashion the dynamics of instances when clergy violate their fiduciary responsibilities and exploit their institutional trustees, this work constitutes a contribution to a rapidly developing interdisciplinary area of study in religion and deviance.

Throughout his career, Shupe frequently employed a collaborative research style. He worked with a number of other scholars in the sociology of religion, including David G. Bromley and Jeffrey K. Hadden. Based on his active scholarship, Shupe was elected to office in several professional associations, including the Society for the Scientific Study of Religion and the Association for the Sociology of Religion. He also became an articulate advocate, through his writing for both popular and professional audiences, for religious libertarianism.

—*David G. Bromley*

SIKHISM　Guru Nanak, who founded Sikhism in Punjab in the early part of the sixteenth century, based his new doctrine on simple living, piety, monotheism, opposition to idolatry and magic, and equality of all believers—men and women—before the transcendent god. He was succeeded by nine more gurus, the last of whom was Govind Singh, who founded the Sikh *Khalsa* (community of the elect) in 1708.

The objectives of the Khalsa were to respond militarily to the capricious Muslim and Hindu rulers of the north, to propagate the values and ideals of Sikhism, and to make way for a distinctive sociopolitical order among the Sikhs. The five external symbols of the Sikh

men are (1) uncut hair, (2) the comb, (3) the dagger, (4) the steel bangle, and (5) a pair of shorts. The possession of these symbols denoted not only the steadfastness of the Sikhs but also their readiness to fight for the cause of Khalsa.

The sacred text of the Sikhs is *Adi Granth,* which has a composite character; it has drawn from the literary compositions of Hindu, Muslim, and Sikh saints. Devotion was the common factor among these saints. Sufi Islam has left an indelible imprint not only on the Hindus of north India but also on the Sikhs.

In spite of the founding of Khalsa in 1708, until the last quarter of the nineteenth century, most Sikhs lived in peaceful coexistence with the non-Sikhs of Punjab. They often participated in the religious functions of Hindus and Muslims. Many also believed in the worship of deceased ancestors, spirits, sorcery, astrology, and so on. It was then that elitist Sikhs made a determined effort to eliminate non-Sikh liturgical elements not only in the domestic circles but also in the places of worship *(Gurdwaras).* In free India, a number of Sikhs have been drawn to a separatist ideology that is centered on the establishment of a Khalsa state in Punjab. This has resulted in clashes with Indian governmental authorities, civil strife, and, particularly, the assassination of prime minister Indira Gandhi.

Although the Hindu and Sikh religious identities are separate, most Sikhs at the folk level follow heterogenous rituals in performing life-crisis ceremonies (e.g., birth, marriage, death); these rites are often drawn from non-Sikh sources. Their social life varies according to local, regional, or specific historical circumstances. They also retain some notions of caste hierarchy and belief in *karma* (rebirth)

—*C. N. Venugopal*

REFERENCES

H. Oberoi, *The Construction of Religious Boundaries* (Delhi: Oxford University Press, 1994); J. P. S. Oberoi, "Five Symbols of Sikh Identity," in *Religion in India,* ed. T. N. Madan (Delhi: Oxford University Press, 1991): 320-333; T. K. Oommen, "Religious Nationalism and Democratic Polity," *Sociology of Religion* 55(1994):455-479.

SILVA MIND CONTROL　A quasi-religious human potential movement founded by José Silva in the late 1960s. The movement's goal is to turn its members into active psychics who are able to conduct psychic healing sessions.

Healing and other psychic abilities are considered part of natural human potential rather than being supernatural in origin. In Silva Mind Control, certain types of learned behavior and mental habits such as "negativity" are seen as blocks to natural psychic ability. Local instructors hold week-long training sessions to teach Silva's techniques to interested students for a fee. At the end of that week, students are expected to successfully complete a healing ritual that involves identifying and healing illnesses in persons whom the students have never seen. Silva Mind Control is seen by Westley (1978) as an example of a religious form predicted by Durkheim that would locate the sacred within individuals. Bird (1979) suggests that Silva Mind Control, like other similar apprenticeship groups, encourages a reduced sense of moral accountability.

—*Edward F. Breschel*

REFERENCES

F. Bird, "The Pursuit of Innocence," *Sociological Analysis* 40(1979):335-346; A. M. Powers, *Silva Mind Control* (New York: Garland, 1992); J. Silva, *The Silva Mind Control Method of Mental Dynamics* (London: Grafton, 1990); F. R. Westley, " 'Cult of Man': Durkheim's Predictions and NRMs," *Sociological Analysis* 39(1978):135-145.

SIMMEL, GEORG (1858-1918)

German-Jewish philosopher and sociologist who spent much of his career as *Privatdozent* at the University of Berlin, largely due to anti-Semitism, and only gained a regular appointment at the University of Strasbourg in 1914.

Simmel contributed an original formal sociology and a distinctive interpretation of modernity. Religion played a relatively minor role in his work, but his ideas on it were characteristically insightful. In his main essay on religion, Simmel (1959 [1906]) portrayed it as one form in which manifold social experiences can be organized, distinguished by its transcendent dimension and claim to totality. Like Durkheim, Simmel offered a kind of sociological projection theory. Religion emerges in social relations of special intensity. In his relation with God, the individual repeats and transcends his relation to the collectivity. The unity of the group is expressed in religious terms; the deity is the name for that unity.

The tension between unifying and differentiating forces in social life is also reflected in religious terms, for example, in the Christian notions of equality before God and individual salvation. But religion is not mere reflection or projection. Even tensions within religious thought are part of a symbolic whole that integrates experience in a manner transcending any other. The social origins of religion thus do not fully account for its nature and function. Simmel's ideas, justified by a broader program, have had relatively little impact in the sociology of religion, due to lack of understanding of that program and Simmel's abstract mode of exposition.

—*Frank J. Lechner*

REFERENCES

M. Kaern (ed.), *Georg Simmel and Contemporary Sociology* (Dordrecht, Neth.: Kluwer, 1990); D. Levine (ed.), *Georg Simmel on Individuality and Social Forms* (Chicago: University of Chicago Press, 1971); G. Simmel, *Sociology of Religion* (New York: Philosophical Library, 1959 [*Die Religion*, 1906]); G. Simmel, *The Philosophy of Money* (London: Routledge, 1978); G. Simmel, *Essays on Religion* (New Haven, Conn.: Yale University Press, 1997).

SIMPSON, JOHN H. (1936–)   After completing his Th.M. under Samuel W. Blizzard at Princeton Theological Seminary and his Ph.D. under John W. Meyer at Stanford University, he was appointed in 1970 to the Department of Sociology, University of Toronto, where he subsequently served as department head until returning to teaching in 1996. President, Association for the Sociology of Religion, 1995.

Simpson collaborated with James N. Lapsley on some of the earliest research on the phenomenon of glossolalia in the mainline Protestant churches of the early 1960s. He was the first researcher to publish a measurement model estimating the strength in the American population of attitudes toward sociomoral issues politicized in the late 1970s and early 1980s by the New Christian Right. Other publications focus on high gods in the context of Guy Swanson's work as well as theoretical and comparative aspects of religion and politics. His more recent work centers on the relation between community and self in the global context, and the status and role of the body as unit of action in postmodernity.

—*Peter F. Beyer*

REFERENCES

J. N. Lapsley and J. H. Simpson, "Speaking in Tongues," *Pastoral Psychology* 15(1964):48-55; J. H. Simpson, "Sovereign

Groups, Subsistence Activities, and the Presence of a High God in Primitive Societies," in *The Religious Dimension,* ed. R. Wuthnow (New York: Academic Press, 1979): 299-310; J. H. Simpson, "Moral Issues and Status Politics," in *The New Christian Right,* ed. R. C. Liebman and R. Wuthnow (New York: Aldine, 1983): 188-205; J. H. Simpson, "Toward a Theory of America," in *Secularization and Fundamentalism Reconsidered,* ed. J. K. Hadden and A. Shupe (New York: Paragon, 1989): 78-90; J. H. Simpson, "Globalization and Religion," *Religion and Global Order,* ed. R. Robertson and W. R. Garrett (New York: Paragon, 1991): 1-18; J. H. Simpson, "The Body in Late Capitalism," in *Abortion Politics in the United States and Canada,* ed. T. G. Jelen and M. A. Chandler (Westport, Conn.: Praeger, 1994): 1-13.

SISR   *see* Société Internationale de Sociologie des Religions

SISTERS   *see* Communal Groups, Orders

SKLARE, MARSHALL (1921-1992)   Founder of the Cohen Center for Modern Jewish Studies at Brandeis University, the first research center devoted to social scientific study of contemporary American Jewry, and the acknowledged "dean" of American Jewish sociology. President of the Association for the Social Scientific Study of Jewry, 1973-1975, which now gives the Marshall Sklare award annually for outstanding scholarship in this field, in his memory.

Born in Chicago, Sklare graduated from both Northwestern University and Chicago's College of Jewish Studies in 1943; M.A., University of Chicago (1948). His Columbia University (1953) doctoral dissertation, *Conservative Judaism: An American Religious Movement* (Free Press 1955, 1972, 1985), is his best known work and remains a classic, as does his *Jewish Identity on the Suburban Frontier: A Study of Survival in an Open Society,* with coauthor Joseph Greenblum (Basic Books 1967, 1979). His anthologies—*The Jews: Social Patterns of an American Group* (Free Press 1958) and *The Jew in American Society* and *The Jewish Community in America* (both Behrman 1974)—and the widely used text, *America's Jews* (Random House 1971), still define the sociology of contemporary Jewish life. Throughout, insights from history and Jewish studies informed his study of religious practices, American Zionism, and Jewish primary and secondary group life.

Sklare served as Study Director for the American Jewish Committee from 1954 to 1966, conducting many survey studies. He was Professor of Sociology at Yeshiva University from 1966 to 1970, before going to Brandeis (1970-1990). He also lectured at Hebrew University (Jerusalem) and Princeton Theological Seminary.

—*J. Alan Winter and M. Herbert Danzger*

SLAVERY   A mode of labor articulation wherein one human being (the *slave*) is "owned" by another (the *master,* although in some cases the owner may be an institution; the term *mistress* is sometimes used for the wife of a master, but many cultures, including the U.S. slave South, prohibit ownership of property, hence slaves, by women).

Actual slave systems vary significantly in the ways in which the two parties stand in relationship to each other, but in general the condition is characterized by the inability of the slave "freely" to cease his or her relationship with the owner. Slave systems have existed throughout most of history around the world. Among the best known today are those of ancient Rome and of the colonial and early U.S. South. The latter was relatively unique for its *racism* and the increasing inability for a slave to be *manumitted* ("freed") under any conditions.

The phrase *wage slavery* was applied by Karl Marx to capitalist industrial enterprise, particularly in Great Britain, to mean that the worker had to work in the factories or die of starvation. The argument has been made by Orlando Patterson (1982, 1991), the preeminent contemporary social scientist of slavery, that New Testament Christianity cannot be understood apart from Roman slave codes. Max Weber has argued that slavery was responsible for the fall of Rome, although that argument now is generally discredited.

Slavery in colonial North America began when a Dutch ship intended for the Caribbean ran adrift at Jamestown, Virginia, in 1619 and had only a small number of African slaves left to trade for badly needed supplies. The slaves could be adopted into southern agriculture and culture because Tudor poor laws in England already provided for slavery as a method for dealing with the British poor themselves. It was not until the 1690s that the racist system of slavery that came to characterize the U.S. South developed that form.

—*William H. Swatos, Jr.*

REFERENCES

O. Patterson, *Slavery and Social Death* (Cambridge: Harvard University Press, 1982); O. Patterson, *Freedom* (New York: Basic Books, 1991); W. H. Swatos, Jr., *Mediating Capitalism and Slavery* (Tampa, Fla.: USF Monographs in Religion and Public Policy, 1987).

SMITH, JOSEPH, JR. (1805-1844)   Founding prophet of the Church of Jesus Christ of Latter-day Saints (Mormons) and of derivative schismatic groups, the most important being the Reorganized Church of Jesus Christ of Latter-day Saints, which arose around his son, Joseph Smith III (after the main Mormon body had migrated to Utah under Brigham Young).

Smith was born in Sharon, Vermont, in a large family that always lived in poverty. In 1816, the family moved to Palmyra, near Rochester, New York, an area included in the "burned over district" of the Second Great Awakening. In 1820, young Smith sought and experienced an epiphany with deity, followed in the next few years by several visionary encounters with angels (in some of which he was joined by selected disciples). The Book of Mormon was one of the ultimate products of these encounters. Smith led his persecuted but growing band of Mormons from place to place until his assassination in 1844 near Nauvoo, Illinois, a city of some 10,000, which he had established five years earlier.

Only since the mid-twentieth century has a serious scholarly literature on Smith emerged that is neither devotional nor debunking, much of it in the form of articles in scholarly journals. The first book-length work of modern times was by Fawn Brodie, *No Man Knows My History: The Life of Joseph Smith, the Mormon Prophet* (Knopf 1945), a somewhat sympathetic treatment that still portrayed Smith essentially as a talented fraud and psychopath. While thus remaining rather in the debunking tradition, Brodie's study was nevertheless a sophisticated piece of psychohistory. More evenhanded treatments will be found in Richard Bushman's analysis of Smith's formative years, *Joseph Smith and the Beginnings of Mormonism* (University of Illinois Press 1984) and in Donna Hill's comprehensive, one-volume biography, *Joseph Smith, the First Mormon* (Doubleday 1977). All three of these authors have Mormon origins but are sophisticated professional scholars. Several other works on American religion more generally have devoted major portions to Smith and his career, placing them in a broader historical context, both Christian and gnostic (see, e.g., D. Michael Quinn, *Early Mormonism and the Magic World View,* Signature 1987, and John L. Brooke, *The Refiner's Fire: The Making of Mormon Cosmology, 1644-1844,* Cambridge University Press 1994). Perhaps the most incisive of these, however, are Jan Shipps's *Mormonism: The Story of a New Religious Tradition* (University of Illinois Press 1985) and Harold Bloom's *Yale Review* essay, "The Religion-Making Imagination of Joseph Smith," (80[1992]:26-42), both of which reflect the emerging scholarly consensus that Smith was neither fraud nor divine instrument but an authentic religious genius with enormous charisma.

—*Armand L. Mauss*

SMITH, WILFRED CANTWELL (1916–)   A Canadian by birth, Smith is a member of the American Academy of Arts and Sciences and was awarded the Chaveau Medal of the Royal Society of Canada in 1974.

A specialist in Islamic studies, Smith is among the most distinguished of those scholars who have sought to establish common ground between apparently diverse religious traditions. According to him, it is a mistake to envisage each "religion"—for example, "Christianity" or "Islam"—as an entity distinct from other "religions." Rather, we should envisage humanity as involved in a single religious history, wherein individuals and social groups relate to the transcendent each in their own terms. He distinguishes between "faith," or personal relation to the transcendent, and "cumulative traditions," consisting of the scriptures, temples, rituals, doctrinal systems, dances, and so on through which such faith has been transmitted and expressed.

—*Hugo Meynell*

REFERENCES

W. C. Smith, *The Meaning and End of Religion* (London: SPCK, 1978); W. C. Smith, *Towards a World Theology* (Philadelphia: Westminster, 1981).

SMITH, W(ILLIAM) ROBERTSON (1846-1894)   Scots philologist, physicist, archaeologist, and biblical critic controversial for his applications of "objective" scientific analysis to the Hebrews of the Old Testament. He sought to document what he saw as the pagan origin of ancient Hebrew rituals.

Smith was a major figure in the development of the functionalist view of religion and society, being among the first theorists to suggest that religious rites are primarily social in nature and have the primary function of strengthening group solidarity. His ideas had a profound impact on Émile Durkheim and Sigmund Freud. Smith also attained notoriety for his attempts to document aspects of totemic belief in early Semitic ritual; particularly in Hebrew rites of sacrifice. In consuming the totemic animal, he contended, members of a tribal group dramatize their unity with their God. He suggested that symbols of divinity are ultimately drawn from earth symbols and/or "natural symbols," thereby anticipating the arguments of Mary Douglas (1970).

See also Functionalism

—*Stephen D. Glazier*

REFERENCES

M. Douglas, *Natural Symbols* (New York: Random House, 1970); W. R. Smith, *The Religion of the Semites* (New York: Schocken, 1972 [1889]).

SNAKE-HANDLING SECTS   Folk-religious Protestant groups, unique to America, that originated when George Hensley first handled serpents at the turn of the twentieth century in the rural South.

Snake-handling was normative for some time in the Church of God (of Cleveland, Tennessee) but later abandoned. Today the practice is restricted primarily to Holiness churches in Appalachia. The practice is justified as one of the signs specified in Mark (16:17-18), which also includes the casting out of demons, speaking in tongues, healing, and the drinking of poisons. Most serpent-handling sects practice all of these five signs. No firm data on the number of serpent-handling sects are available, but active sects continue to be identified in many southeastern states despite the fact that the practice has been outlawed in some.

Despite numerous bites, there are fewer than 80 documented cases of death by serpent bite. Both bites and death are relatively rare given the frequency with which snakes are handled. Members differ on whether they seek medical treatment if bitten and on whether handling is to be done by faith or only when one experiences an anointing. Despite continual predictions of their disappearance, these sects continue to survive their obituaries.

—*Ralph W. Hood, Jr.*

REFERENCES

T. Burton, *Serpent-Handling Believers* (Knoxville: University of Tennessee Press, 1993); D. L. Kimbrough, *Park Saylor and the Eastern Kentucky Snake Handlers* (Chapel Hill: University of North Carolina Press, 1995); W. LaBarre, *They Shall Take Up Serpents* (Minneapolis: University of Minnesota Press, 1962).

SOCIAL ACTION   In common parlance, action designed to promote social justice, taken on behalf or in support of the disadvantaged in society. The term also has a more technical meaning, originating in the work of Max Weber, who used it to describe action that is socially directed, that is, resulting from the presence of others.

Weberian Action Theory   In Weber's sociology, social action is behavior to which human beings attach a specific meaning or set of meanings. It is also behavior that is guided by or takes account of the behavior of other human beings (either as individuals or as a group). Such behavior may be overt and obvious to others, or inward and subjective. Moreover, it may be both active and passive. Thus it may take the form of positive intervention, or of refraining from intervention. Meaningful social behavior—social action—thus contrasts with nonsocial or reactive behavior, undertaken more or less automatically in response to some stimulus. Nevertheless, Weber recognized that the line demarcating the two types is blurred at best; in fact, he argues, "a very considerable part of all sociologically relevant behavior . . . is marginal between the two."

Social action thus conceived forms the basis for Weber's sociology. Just as human beings are seen as acting on the basis of meaning, the sociological enterprise seeks to understand the source of these meanings and thus the motivation behind human social behavior. The bases of social action, Weber argues, are revealed using *Verstehen*. The simple translation of this term is "understanding." Weber, however, uses *Verstehen* to mean a method of analysis (putting oneself in the other's shoes, so to speak), whereby the motivations of human social behavior may be fruitfully revealed to the observer.

Weber delimits four basic types of social action. These are (1) action oriented by expectations of the behavior of both objects and other individuals in the surrounding milieu (according to Weber, individuals "make use of these expectations as 'conditions' or 'means' for the successful attainment of the actor's own rationally chosen ends"); (2) action oriented to some absolute value as embodied in some ethical, aesthetic, or perhaps religious code, in other words, action which is morally guided, and not undertaken simply for one's own gain; (3) action guided by emotive response to or feelings about the surrounding milieu; and (4) actions performed as part of long-standing societal tradition.

Of these four types, the last two lie closest to the borderline of what Weber refers to as nonsocial behavior. By contrast, because they are more likely to involve subjective assessment, and result from the process of rationalization, the first two types are inherently more social forms of human action. Moreover, Weber points out, it is unlikely that any of these types operates independently of one another in the human individual. Typically, social action is guided by some combination of motivations, including both rational (1 and 2) and nonrational elements (3 and 4).

Weber examined the concept of social action within a number of sociological fields, from class behavior, to politics, to religion. The best-known example of Weber's study of social action, however, is contained in his now famous work *The Protestant Ethic and the Spirit of Capitalism* (Scribner 1930). In this work, Weber examines the motivation behind social action in the economic sphere. Specifically, he suggests that the spirit that drives modern capitalistic enterprise is motivated by the ethical doctrine of Protestantism.

In opening his study, Weber notes a relationship between the zeal for business profit and membership in specific Protestant denominations in post-Reformation Europe. Of interest, he observes, this attitude toward moneymaking is embraced not only by the so-called captains of industry but by ordinary workers and peasants. For Weber, this suggests the existence of a new mentality or attitude toward work, one in which the pursuit of gain (living to labor) has gained supremacy over the more traditional view that sees work simply as necessary for survival (laboring to live).

At base, this new way of thinking—which Weber dubs the "spirit of capitalism"—appears concurrently with basic changes in religious thinking brought about by the Reformation. Two developments figure most prominently in this regard. The first was the notion of the "calling" introduced by the Roman Catholic monk, Martin Luther. Luther taught that working in the service of God was the moral duty of all Christians, not just those called to serve the church in the clergy or Holy Orders. Where work was traditionally viewed simply as a means to worldly ends (i.e., survival), Luther argued that individuals must treat their labor as a gift to God. Thus, claims Weber, Luther brought the "monastery into the world," motivating ordinary believers, whatever their worldly occupation, to work hard in the service of God.

The other theological pillar of the new capitalist mentality, Weber argued, was the notion of predestination formulated by John Calvin, a French-Swiss reformer. Calvin taught that salvation was unattainable by the individual alone. Only God had the power to save, and the knowledge of who would enter the Kingdom of Heaven and who would not was His alone. Thus one was born either "saved" or "damned," and there was nothing the individual could do to change his or her fate. Recognizing the fact that such a doctrine would create considerable anxiety among the faithful as they pondered their ultimate fate, Calvin promoted hard work as a means of therapy. Indeed, he claimed, it was a Christian duty always to work hard, to please God. This prescription was combined with a ban on frivolous and/or immoral pleasures (drinking, dancing, sex for purposes other than procreation, and so on), which were seen as displeasing to God.

What both Luther's and Calvin's teachings contributed was the emergence of a new type of Christian who valued work as a moral duty, lived an ascetic lifestyle, and as a result achieved considerable success in material terms. This in turn came to be viewed as a sign of God's favor—that one was indeed saved. The possibility existed, Weber argued, for religious prescription (especially relating to predestination) to lead to fatalism. The fact is, however, that it did not; most believers wanted to work hard in their calling and to achieve material success, if only to show others they were indeed touched by divine grace. In any case, as Protestantism evolved, Weber points out, its harsher elements were softened. The notion of predestination, in particular, eventually lost favor, and it became generally accepted that salvation was attainable, but only through a life of "good works."

Ultimately, claims Weber, the legacy of early Protestantism, in terms of the way in which it motivated capitalistic economic behavior, became widespread in the Western world. At the same time, Weber claims in the closing paragraphs of his classic work that individuals largely have come to reject the religious roots of the spirit of capitalism and have become increasingly consumed instead by the secular passion for profit and the acquisition of material goods.

Social Action and Social Welfare Aside from the usage promoted by Weber's work, social action also has come to acquire meaning as a concrete expression of social justice. In North America, early involvement in justice-related matters arose with the spread of the Social Gospel movement (1865-1915), which saw a number of Protestant organizations and their members concern themselves with the welfare of the weakest members of society: farmers, factory workers, the poor, the sick and infirm. Not only did many Protestant churches and their members assist these groups directly, they spoke out publicly on their behalf. In Canada, the Social Gospel is credited with forming a major plank in the platform of the continent's first viable socialist political party, the Cooperative Commonwealth Federation (CCF), later the New Democratic Party (NDP), which has formed the government in several Canadian provinces since 1930.

In the Roman Catholic tradition, various social action strategies, oriented to diverse ends, also have emerged over the past century. Early Catholic involvement in social action was seen as a way for the church as an organization to operate more directly in the world and to reach sectors of the modern society seen as vulnerable to Protestantism and various secular value movements. Such was the case in turn-of-the-century Europe. While the church retained a strong following in rural areas, its hold on the growing numbers of working people in urban areas became increasingly tenuous. In response, the church moved to enter these milieux and expand its base through involvement in working-class movements. Catholic labor unions emerged as a primary social action strategy around this time. On the political front, Catholic political parties also began to form with the aim of promoting Catholic values at the level of the state.

Later in the twentieth century, efforts on this front gave way to a more formal thrust in the form of Catholic Action, which achieved some measure of success in both Europe and some parts of the developing world, especially Latin America. Spearheaded by clerics, nuns, and activist laypersons, Catholic Action groups were formed to enhance the presence of the church where people lived and worked: in schools and universities, factories, fields, and among the urban and rural poor. Some of these groups eventually moved to espouse not just religious but radical social ends, calling for an end to socioeconomic or political repression within their respective milieux of operation. In Latin America, such groups were seen as the forerunners of base ecclesial communities, which during the 1970s and 1980s emerged as a potent church-based force for popular resistance to dictatorship and economic hardship.

In Latin America and elsewhere in the developing world, social action within the Catholic Church has taken on other forms as well. Since the late 1960s, regional bishops conferences have produced documents condemning the plight of the "poor and oppressed" and calling for a radical restructuring of local or global economies away from capitalistic principles. At the national level, some churches have established bodies and organizations to act on behalf of the poor. In the 1970s in Brazil, for example, the church established a number of agencies and commissions, operating at both the national and the local levels, to speak on behalf of political prisoners, small landholders, native people, and human rights generally. The Brazilian episcopate

also regularly published and distributed documents condemning the military government of the time and promoting the creation of a more just social order. Even in developed countries, such as Canada, social action has been vigorously pursued through encouragement of local "social action offices." Run by individual dioceses, such offices have served as a means to disseminate information on social injustice and sometimes to coordinate local protest.

These efforts at promoting social justice achieved some measure of success in a number of countries. In the Philippines, for example, church intervention was seen as critical to the success of the "people power" movement that eventually ended the Marcos dictatorship. In Brazil, social action initiatives made the citizenry more aware of the military regime's arbitrary abuses and also put forth political, social, and economic alternatives to the models that the regime blindly pursued. This in turn helped to facilitate the eventual transition from military to civilian government during the mid-1980s.

By the 1990s, the emphasis on social action within the global Catholic Church, however, began to fade. In its place, the church has begun to focus more diligently on the devotional side of Catholicism, and movements designed to tap spiritual yearning effectively—such as Opus Dei and the Catholic charismatic movement—have begun to flourish. At the same time, elements within the Catholic Church continue to work toward social justice, joined by many within the Protestant community. Quakers, Unitarians, and Mennonites, in particular, have long histories of devotion to working to improve the conditions of the disadvantaged.

—*W. E. Hewitt*

REFERENCES

C. Campbell, *The Myth of Social Action* (Cambridge: Cambridge University Press, 1996); M. Weber, *The Protestant Ethic and the Spirit of Capitalism* (New York: Scribner, 1930 [1904-1905]); M. Weber, *Economy and Society* (Berkeley: University of California Press, 1978 [1922]).

SOCIAL CLASS   *see* Status, Stratification

SOCIAL COMPASS   International journal of sociology of religion was founded in the Hague in 1953 by G. Zeegers, director of the Katholiek Sociaal Kerkelijk Instituut (KASKI), to publish studies of sociology applied to the pastoral work of the Roman Catholic Church.

Since 1959, *Social Compass* has been produced by the Socio-Religious Center (Catholic University of Louvain) for the International Federation of Socio-Religious Institutes. The journal stresses a scientific approach to religion. Each issue is thematic, often concentrating on a specific country. Since 1991, this quarterly review has been published by Sage, and each year the first issue is devoted to papers presented at SISR conferences.

—Karel Dobbelaere

SOCIAL CONFLICT see Conflict

SOCIAL CONTROL All the material and symbolic resources, including religious resources, available to a society to ensure that the behavior of its members complies with certain prescribed and sanctioned rules. It is related to the problem of social order.

Social control concerns the requirements of social living; it is the result of people's actions directed at themselves and their surroundings to achieve such conditions of life as the aspirations, needs, and requirements of human nature can create, through a scaling down of egoistic and heterodestructive impulses. In other words, social control is the problem, with regard to social relations, of how to limit and direct people's attitudes. In contemporary sociology, the concept is primarily encountered in the analysis of deviant behavior, where it is an aspect of labeling theory.

—Luigi Tomasi

REFERENCES

L. L. Bernard, *Social Control in Its Sociological Aspects* (New York: Macmillan, 1939); G. Gurvitch, "Social Control," in *Twentieth Century Sociology,* ed. G. Gurvitch and W. E. Moore (New York: Philosophical Library, 1945): 267-296.

SOCIAL DARWINISM see Science and
Religion, Herbert Spencer

SOCIAL DISTANCE see Emory S. Bogardus

SOCIAL GOSPEL A movement principally within liberal Protestantism during the late nineteenth and early twentieth centuries that sought to apply the principles of "real Christianity" or "the religion of Jesus" to ameliorate the problems of the poor and working classes, particularly as a result of industrialization and urbanization.

Although the precise connections are complex, this movement had a direct impact on the development of sociology; it also had connections to Christian socialism, particularly in Europe. American leaders included Washington Gladden and Walter Rauschenbusch. In academic settings, Social Gospel principles were taught under such headings as "Applied Christianity," "Practical Christianity," and "Christian Sociology." In the United States, the principles of the movement tended to be adopted in secularized form in both the organized labor movement and New Deal legislation. In Europe, Max Weber initially worked with the Evangelical Social Movement, as it was called there, but withdrew as the movement increasingly became a political party.

In terms of the development of American religious history, the Social Gospel movement in many ways inherited the mantle of abolitionism as the "conscience of the nation" but now focused its attention primarily on the rapidly industrializing North. Factory working conditions and the treatment of immigrants, particularly with regard to housing and sanitation, became major concerns. These were sometimes aligned with, other times set in contrast to, the rising temperance movement, but as a whole were a part of the progressivist agenda. Over time, the Social Gospel agenda became a major factor in the division between conservatives and liberals in U.S. Protestantism particularly, and to some extent this is still so. A major shift occurred beginning in the 1970s, however, as conservatives, who previously eschewed involvement in "politics" as being in conflict with their core mission of the redemption of individual "souls," developed a social agenda of their own, focused especially on opposition to abortion and advocacy of school prayer.

See also Christian Sociology, Progressivism

—William H. Swatos, Jr.

REFERENCES

P. Kivisto and W. H. Swatos, Jr., "Max Weber as 'Christian Sociologist,'" *Journal for the Scientific Study of Religion* 30(1991):347-362; W. Rauschenbusch, "The Ideals of Social Reformers," *American Journal of Sociology* 2(1896):202-219; W. H. Swatos, Jr., *Faith of the Fathers* (Bristol, Ind.: Wyndham Hall Press, 1984).

SOCIAL INTEGRATION Referring primarily to how the parts of a society operate as a whole, the notion of integration has a long sociological pedigree, but one fraught with imprecision. *Social integration* generally refers to the way shared cultural goods receive normative expression, and also to the functional interdependence of the parts of a social system as in a division of labor.

The concept has its roots in early modern and modern European thought in which the question of social order became salient in light of the great changes that society was undergoing. Classic expressions of the role of religion in social integration are to be found in Marx and Durkheim, both of whom saw it as critical, although less so for future society. Parsons tried to clarify the issue by locating religion's role more clearly in the area of cultural integration, assigning social integration more to other institutions such as law. Religion's periodic role in social conflicts does not necessarily contradict its integrative role. The religious pluralism of most modern societies, by contrast, has presented a more thorough challenge, as is evidenced in the work of Berger and Luckmann. Parsons and Bellah, however, have reassigned this integrative role to a putative "civil religion," thereby circumventing factual religious pluralism. Overall, the concept and religion's role in it are subject to a wide variety of interpretations. Some doubt its continued usefulness for sociological understanding; others still find it an important construct for analyses of religion.

—*Peter Beyer*

REFERENCES

R. Bellah, "Civil Religion in America," *Daedalus* 96(1967):1-21; É. Durkheim, *The Elementary Forms of the Religious Life* (London: Allen & Unwin, 1915); T. Parsons, *The Social System* (Glencoe, Ill.: Free Press, 1951); J. Rousseau, *On the Social Contract* (Indianapolis: Hackett, 1987 [1762]).

SOCIALIZATION   The process by which values, norms, attitudes, and behavior, shared by the subjects who belong to a particular group, are transmitted to a new member. It is the process whereby people learn to conform to social norms, a process that makes possible an enduring society and the transmission of its culture and religion between generations.

Socialization therefore is the action by which a person becomes the member of a society, through a mechanism of interaction. It is a learning process whose purpose is to prepare individuals for the range of roles that they will interpret in the future. The primary stage involves the socialization of the young child in the family, the secondary stage involves the school, and the third stage is adult socialization. In the process of socialization, the attitudes and values of adult roles are acquired. Correct socialization is a normal operation by the social system designed to prevent any deviant behavior.

See also Religious Education

—*Luigi Tomasi*

REFERENCES

D. A. Goslin (ed.), *Handbook of Socialization Theory and Research* (Chicago: Rand McNally, 1969); A. Kerckhoff, *Socialization and Social Class* (Englewood Cliffs, N.J.: Prentice Hall, 1972).

SOCIAL JUSTICE   Has a long history in Western religious writings in relation to the concept of the distribution of a society's resources according to people's needs. It has roots in the Bible, particularly in the prophets and in Leviticus, and in the works of early Christian writers. Within the past hundred years, it has found renewed expression in the Protestant Social Gospel, in the encyclicals of Roman Catholic popes, and in documents on social action produced by the Union of American Hebrew Congregations.

The essence of the contemporary religious view of justice is that a society should redistribute wealth not only because poor people need it, but because it is rightfully theirs. This contrasts with the notion of charity as almsgiving. Thus the poor are perceived not as requiring alms because they are lacking in basic necessities but as deserving their rightful share of the resources produced by their labor. Peasants have a right to land because they work it, and factory workers have a right to good wages and other benefits because their labor produces the wealth of industrial societies.

In the Christian denominations, there is a potential tension between social justice and pastoral care, although these need not be separate in principle. Christianity emphasizes eternal salvation, which results in a concern of the clergy for ministering to the spiritual needs of the laity. This individual pastoral outreach is not always easy to combine with a prophetic demand for justice. There are laypeople who complain, and even leave a congregation, when the priest or minister preaches about social problems. On the other hand, there are those who claim that one cannot address spiritual concerns without dealing with people's serious material deprivation.

The religious view of social justice has found its most radical expression in liberation theology, which articulates the belief that sin and salvation are not exclusively individual but are also social. In the context of this theology, people's eternal salvation is understood to be inseparable from their involvement in the struggle to build a just society.

See also Preferential Option for the Poor, Social Action

—*Madeleine R. Cousineau*

REFERENCES

G. Gutiérrez, *A Theology of Liberation* (Maryknoll, N.Y.: Orbis, 1973); R. T. Handy (ed.), *The Social Gospel in America* (New York: Oxford University Press, 1966); D. Hollenbach, *Justice, Peace, and Human Rights* (New York: Crossroad, 1990); A. Vorspan and E. J. Lipman, *Justice and Judaism* (New York: Union of American Hebrew Congregations, 1956).

SOCIAL MOBILITY   *see* Mobility

SOCIAL MOVEMENTS   Network-configured collectivities that seek to promote or resist political and/or cultural change on the basis of shared group identity. As Stanford Lyman (1995:397) has observed, "In virtually all their various manifestations in the United States, social movements have proclaimed a salvational message, each has sought to cure the soul of either the nation, a sodality within society or the individual."

To the nineteenth-century European pioneers of sociological thought, religion and social movements were closely intertwined and central to the discussion of social change. Thus the crowd psychologist Scipio Sighele (1898) viewed the sect as the "nucleus" of a new social order, while Max Weber's analysis (1978) of the relationship between charisma and routinization stressed the importance of the "prophet" in shaking up and reshaping the legitimate order.

Upon reaching the United States, however, the scholarly treatment of social and religious movements took a different turn. Preoccupied with reforming and reconstructing an urban society fractured, they believed, by rapid industrialization and massive immigration, Robert Park and other second-generation pioneers of American sociology identified social movements as forms of collective behavior that were marginal to the thrust of social progress. This was especially so for religious movements, which appeared exotic, expressive, and retreatist. Furthermore, such movements were

dismissed as constituting the "religion of the lower orders," a designation that was reified by Liston Pope's classic contrast (1942) between southern churches, whose members were drawn from respectable elites, and sects, whose followers came disproportionately from the ranks of the blue-collar mill hands. In a world that was seen as rapidly secularizing, religious movements appeared as colorful but largely irrelevant throwbacks to the revivalist era of the past. This view predominated for nearly half a century, being evident, for example, in the early 1960s in Neil Smelser's seminal treatise, *Theory of Collective Behavior* (Free Press 1962).

Smelser's "value-added" theory of collective behavior isolates six determining factors or conditions that must be present for collective behavior to occur: structural conduciveness, structural strain, generalized beliefs, precipitating factors, mobilization for action, and the operation of social control. The most controversial of these is the third—the formation of generalized beliefs. Critics pointed to Smelser's notion that such beliefs "short-circuit" reality as being misleading, because this suggests, for example, that social movement activists prefer to rely on "magical" rather than straightforward, rational thinking. Religious movements seemed to be especially vulnerable to the emergence of generalized beliefs because they dealt in an otherworldly currency, which was assumed to be largely irrational.

In the late 1960s and 1970s, researchers detected the upsurge of a "new religious consciousness" that arose out of the social and political ferment bubbling in the youth counterculture. Sociologists of religion attempted to plumb the impact and meaning of these "new religious movements" (NRMs) with varying results. Did these religious experimenters represent, Bellah (1976a) pondered, a "bellwether" of things to come or a "backwater" whose effects were only temporary? Among the groups that received considerable scholarly attention were the Hare Krishna, Scientology, the Divine Light Mission, the Unification Church ("Moonies"), the Rajneesh commune, and Nichiren Shoshu.

Sociological commentators approached NRMs from several different directions. Some employed a "cultural historical" style through which the analyst attempted to interpret the "deepest meaning" of the new religious consciousness in the context of modern American history (Bellah 1976b). This resulted in a number of "crisis" or "modernization" theories that pinpointed an "acute and distinctively modern dislocation which is said to be producing some mode of alienation, anomie or deprivation" (Robbins 1988). Among others, the source of this dislocation was identified as being one or more of the following: the pervasive moral ambiguity of American culture, domination by inhuman bureaucratic megastructures, generational angst, the deinstitutionalization of the private realm, and the relentless forward march of secularization.

Other researchers employed a more quantitative-empirical style, seeking answers to the rise of NRMs in microinteractional models of religious attraction, choice, recruitment, and conversion. Sociological profiles were constructed of the "world-saver" (Lofland and Stark 1965) and the "convert" (Snow and Machalek 1983). Friendship and kinship networks were discovered to be important avenues through which NRM recruitment takes place, although these "networks of faith" (Stark and Bainbridge 1980) appeared less important in the case of social isolates who were said to be more "structurally available" for recruitment precisely because they were free of countervailing attachments. Conversion was conceptualized as an episode in "biographical reconstruction" (Snow and Machalek 1983) that followed an identifiable career (Richardson and Stewart 1977). Devotees of NRMs were found to share common social attributes: They were typically young, single, middle class, well educated, from stable family environments, and relatively free from competing occupational ties (Snow and Machalek 1983).

Finally, a handful of religious researchers borrowed from the "resource mobilization" paradigm in the social movements field, analyzing the rise of NRMs in terms of leadership, finances, and other organizational factors.

After nearly a quarter of a century of intensive study, NRM research began to slow by the early 1990s. While some researchers switched their energies to other varieties of contemporary spiritual movements (Wiccans, New Agers, ecofeminists), there was simultaneously an effort to reach out beyond the confines of religion and directly engage a wider body of social and cultural theory. Several sociological commentators (John Hannigan 1991, James Beckford 1990, 1991) looked to the largely European-based "new social movement" (NSM) theory, which attempted to relate environmentalism, feminism, antinuclearism, peace activism, and other "global" movements to large-scale structural and cultural changes. They not only identified religious analogues of these movements but claimed to detect strong spiritual currents running through the ideologies of ecology, feminism, and other NSMs. This new spirituality characteristically favors "synoptic, holistic and global perspectives on issues transcending the privatizing self and the individual state" (Beckford 1990:9).

More recently, some sociologists of religion, notably Rhys Williams, have attempted to plug religion into the accelerating dialogue between cultural sociology and social movement theory. Williams (1995) argues for the usefulness of approaching social movement ideology as a set of cultural resources that are both contextual and public. Taking the rhetoric about the "public good" as one example of a cultural resource important to social movements, he presents three ideal types: the "covenant" model derived from the traditional U.S. religious conception of the "moral community"; the "contractual" model, which uses the language of "rights"; and the "stewardship" model that flourishes in many U.S. churches and denominations, which employs a language of communal duties. In similar fashion, Williams and Alexander (1994) examine the "civil religious" themes in American political rhetoric through an analysis of the religious rhetoric in late-nineteenth-century American populism.

Building on earlier attempts to develop a rational, market-based model of religion and religious movements (Iannaccone 1990, Stark and Bainbridge 1985), R. Stephen Warner has proposed a new paradigm that is organizational, rather than social psychological or cultural, and visualizes the rise of new religious organizations taking place within a wider, open marketplace of religious choice. In this rational choice model, religious adherents are conceptualized as "investors" who may hedge their strategies by assembling "religious portfolios," that is, dabbling in a variety of different religions from mainstream churches to more "risky" sectarian and cultic movements (Iannaccone 1995).

Finally, the social psychological concept of "collective identity" has recently advanced into the foreground of research on social and religious movements. Collective identity is constructed out of the continual interplay of interaction, negotiation, and conflict that characterizes small-group activity within the boundaries of the movement. Collective identity building of this type has been conceptualized as an attributional or claims-making process. Such attributions or claims cluster around three "identity fields" (Hunt et al. 1994): protagonists (advocates of movement causes such as leaders, prophets, and martyrs), antagonists (opponents including social control agents, countermovements, star adversaries), and audiences (allied social movement organizations, media, powerful elites, marginal supporters, sympathizers, bystander publics).

Focusing on collective identity provides a necessary counterweight to the economistic and strategic emphasis of models of religion and religious movements such as those proposed by Iannaccone, Stark and Bainbridge, and Warner. At the same time, collective identity is a moving target that is difficult to pin down empirically. Emergent and in a constant state of flux, collective identity is primarily shaped in the course of interaction within the collectivity itself (Johnston et al. 1994).

Social scientific commentators on religion have yet to conceptualize religious movements explicitly in these terms, but there would seem to be a rich vein of opportunity here from case analyses of dramatic events such as the confrontation between federal agents and the Branch Davidians at Waco, Texas, to longer term relations between religious movements and the wider society. This approach would be further enriched and broadened if it were to be fused with the cultural resource model proposed by Williams and others.

See also New Religious Movements, Resource Mobilization

—*John Hannigan*

REFERENCES

J. A. Beckford, "The Sociology of Religion and Social Problems," *Sociological Analysis* 51(1990):1-14; J. A. Beckford, *Religion and Advanced Industrial Society* (London: Unwin Hyman, 1991); R. N. Bellah, (a) "The New Religions in Social Context," and (b) "New Religious Consciousness and the Crisis in Modernity," in *The New Religious Consciousness*, ed. C. Y. Glock and R. N. Bellah (Berkeley: University of California Press, 1976): 267-293, 333-352; J. A. Hannigan, "Social Movement Theory and the Sociology of Religion," *Sociological Analysis* 52(1991):311-331; S. A. Hunt et al., "Identity Fields," in *New Social Movements*, ed. E. Larana et al. (Philadelphia: Temple University Press, 1994): 185-208; L. R. Iannaccone, "Religious Practice," *Journal for the Scientific Study of Religion* 29(1990):297-314; L. R. Iannaccone, "Voodoo Economics?" *Journal for the Scientific Study of Religion* 34(1995):76-89; H. Johnston et al., "Identities, Grievances and New Social Movements," in *New Social Movements*, ed. E. Larana et al. (Philadelphia: Temple University Press, 1994): 3-35; J. Lofland and R. Stark, "Becoming a World-Saver," *American Sociological Review* 30(1965):862-874; S. M. Lyman (ed.), *Social Movements* (Basingstoke, U.K.: Macmillan, 1995); L. Pope, *Millhands and Preachers* (New Haven, Conn.: Yale University Press, 1942); J. T. Richardson and M. Stewart, "Conversion Process Models and the Jesus Movement," *American Behavioral Scientist* 20(1977):819-838; T. Robbins, *Cults, Converts and Charisma* (London: Sage, 1988); S. Sighele, *Psychologie des sects* (Paris: Giard et Briere, 1898); D. A. Snow, "The Sociology of Conversion," *Annual Review of Sociology* 10 (1984):167-190; D. A. Snow and R. Machalek, "The Convert as a Social Type," *Sociological Theory* 1(1983):259-289; R. Stark and W. S. Bainbridge, "Networks of Faith," *American Journal of Sociology* 85(1980):1376-1395; R. Stark and W. S. Bainbridge, *The Future of Religion* (Berkeley: University of California Press, 1985); R. S. Warner, "Work in Progress Toward a New Paradigm for the Sociological Study of Religion in the United States," *American Journal of Sociology* 98(1993):1044-1093; M. Weber, *Economy and Society* (Berkeley: University of California Press, 1978); R. H. Williams, "Constructing the Public Good," *Social Problems* 42(1995):124-144; R. H. Williams and S. M. Alexander, "Religious Rhetoric in American Populism," *Journal for the Scientific Study of Religion* 33(1994):1-15.

SOCIAL PSYCHOLOGY   A subdiscipline of both sociology and psychology, yet much of the two major disciplines is actually social psychology. If sociology deals with social categories or groups and if psychology deals with individuals, social psychology involves the intersection of the social and the individual where the individual is influenced by the social and, in turn, interacts with the social and influences it as well.

Another way of looking at the turf of social psychology is that it is the study of how micro- and macrosocial phenomena—the individual and society—interact. Social psychology tries to answer such questions as the following: How does an individual develop his or her self-concept or personality? Or, how do social situations influence the way an individual thinks or acts?

Two of the many perspectives in social psychological thought are symbolic interaction and social exchange. Symbolic interaction began with early, twentieth-century social theorists Charles Horton Cooley and George Herbert Mead. Social psychology later was developed by theorists such as Herbert Blumer, and it continues to develop and grow popular today through such social psychologists as Norman Denzin, Sheldon Stryker, and Victor Gecas.

Symbolic interaction explains how individuals are socialized through social interactions with others. In the process of developing a self, language and other symbols and values become meaningful through social interaction with significant others, primary groups, reference groups, and generalized others. Through this process of interactions, individuals also learn roles that they play as they act in their social groups and in the larger society.

Social psychology's social exchange perspective complements symbolic interaction but emphasizes the exchanges that link individuals with each other and with groups. The social exchange perspective has been influenced by many including B. F. Skinner, George Homans, Peter Blau, John Thibaut, and Harold Kelly. Social exchange concepts include value, punishment, sanctions, cost, profit, reward, and behavior.

From social scientific theory and research, George Homans developed several propositions on success, stimuli, value, satiation, and aggression that explain how social exchange works at the individual level. Peter Blau describes how individual exchanges emerge from social attractions into personal exchanges and power, and into more general, macroexchanges involving group authority and opposition.

To meet needs and fulfill desires, individuals—especially in a society with many, highly specialized, social roles—must interact with others in a process of social exchanges. For example, very few people produce the food they eat, but obtain it in exchange for goods, services, and money they provide through a network of others in roles and organizations that specialize in one or another aspect of food production and distribution. Without these complex, interdependent social exchanges, most of us would starve. From the symbolic interaction and social exchange perspectives in social psychology, one might say that individuals are able to interact—and indeed must interact with each other as individuals and as members of social groups—through shared meanings and values that they learn. They also play various social roles in a process of social exchanges with others to meet their basic needs and to fulfill many of their desires.

Other important social psychological concepts include attitudes, beliefs, and other types of dispositions as well as norms, leadership, collective behavior, and commitment. Religion is one set of symbolic meanings that individuals more or less derive from their experiences with their social groups. Religion provides cultural values that underlie many exchanges that are rewarding to individuals in a society, and these shared, personal meanings and values give rise to both order and change in societies.

—*Ronald C. Wimberley*

REFERENCES

P. Blau, *Exchange and Power in Social Life* (New York: Wiley, 1964); K. S. Cook et al. (eds.), *Sociological Perspectives on Social Psychology* (Boston: Allyn & Bacon, 1995); N. K. Denzin (ed.), *Studies in Symbolic Interaction* 19 (Greenwich, Conn.: JAI, 1995); G. C. Homans, *Social Behavior*, rev. ed. (New York: Harcourt, 1974); J. A. Wiggins et al., *Social Psychology*, 5th ed. (New York: McGraw Hill, 1994).

SOCIAL SCIENCE AND RELIGION Modern social science emerged when scholars began to emancipate themselves from normative thinking, that is, when their aim became to arrive at knowledge of human society and human beings free from value judgments or value prescriptions. In Western Europe in the nineteenth century, a number of scholars no longer wanted to make blueprints of a future society but instead wanted to intervene in the actual operation of society to improve the quality of life of its participants. This development did not come out of the blue but was prepared by various philosophers, among whom the most well known are David Hume, Adam Smith, Adam Ferguson, Condorcet, and Montesquieu. In Scotland and in France in the previous century, these philosophers had made a successful breakaway from older, "natural law" thinking. The new thinking was more or less empiricist, that is, based on human experience, and positivist, that is, based on what was given by the senses. Consequently, the relationship between social science and religion was from its inception a precarious one. This is well reflected in the ideas of the French thinker Auguste Comte. According to him, progress in human knowledge knew of three stages: the theological stage, the metaphysical, and, finally, the positive stage, in which knowledge had become free of norms.

The pioneers of young social sciences such as ethnology, sociology, and psychology not only studied human religion, some also combated it. Evolutionism was the main paradigm to study culture and religion in early-nineteenth-century ethnology or anthropology. One of its pioneers, Lewis Henry Morgan, thought religion too irrational to subject it to an evolutionary scheme. For Edward Tylor, the origin of religion was to be found in the belief in spirits of early man, which he called animism, and from there on it had developed further till monotheism. Herbert Spencer had more or less similar ideas as Tylor. In the thinking of Karl Marx, religion was only a marginal issue, and as he grew older it became even more marginal. For him, religion was a reflection of the particular, historical phase of the structure of society. The religious mind was a product of society; it was self-alienation. Quite contrary to Marx's ideas, religion was prominently present in Sigmund Freud's writings. To the founder of psychoanalysis, religion was nothing but a projection. It was the worship of an *erhöhter Vater*, and it had its roots in an infantile need for protection, hence a yearning for the (mythical) ancient father. It could persist only because of human helplessness.

It was Émile Durkheim's conviction that religion not only stabilized society but also gave direction to it. In the end, society celebrated itself in religion through its rituals and beliefs. The more consensus was achieved on religious dogmas, the more they steered human actions in society and the more morality was to be found in religion. Later on in life, Durkheim thought religious persuasions to be part of the collective consciousness. The stronger they are found to be in society and met by the individual, the more they will be practiced. According to Durkheim, religion enabled societal order, but how is order possible in a "disenchanted" world, that is, a world robbed of its divine shine by science? To Max Weber, religion formed a human answer to everything irrational in life. Only religion could render life meaningful by giving not only norms for everyday life but also answers to existential questions.

These various positions continue to be found among social scientists. There are some who proclaim the end of religion in their scientific writings, while others observe in their research on religion a kind of "methodological agnosticism." Finally, there are also scientists who mix religious persuasions and scientific insights.

—*Durk H. Hak*

REFERENCES

É. Durkheim, *Suicide* (New York: Free Press, 1951 [1897]); É. Durkheim, *The Elementary Forms of the Religious Life* (London: Allan & Unwin, 1952 [1912]); E. E. Evans-Pritchard, *Theories of Primitive Religion* (Oxford: Oxford University Press, 1966); H. H. Gerth and C. W. Mills (eds.), *From Max Weber* (New York: Oxford University Press, 1946); S. Freud, *Totem and Taboo* (New York: Random House, 1946 [1913]); S. Freud, *The Future of Illusion* (Garden City, N.Y.: Doubleday, 1961 [1928]); M. Weber, *Economy and Society* (Berkeley: University of California Press, 1978 [1922]).

SOCIÉTÉ INTERNATIONALE DE SOCIOLOGIE DES RELIGIONS (SISR/ISSR)

The International Society for the Sociology of Religion—as it has been called since the twentieth conference of the society in 1989 Helsinki, Finland—was founded in 1948 in Leuven, Belgium, on the initiative of Jacques Leclercq as the Conférence Internationale de Sociologie Religieuse (CISR)/International Conference of Religious Sociology. Initially, it was an international gathering of university professors and researchers who compared the results of their sociological studies and aimed at improving their research methods. The name "religious sociology" clearly expressed their commitments; *sociology* was to be understood as a study of empirical facts, and *religious* referred both to its function of providing insights into the social conditions of belief and practices (specifically to inform those in charge of evangeliza-

tion) and to the modes of analysis to be used. This approach was enlightened by the faith of the researchers and their religious commitment.

At the third conference, in Breda, Holland, clerics who lacked any sociological background also attended. This brought a pastoral and Catholic "flavor" to the conference. The denominational character was institutionalized by a change of statutes against the will of its founder, who defended its original nondenominational character. At the fourth conference, in La Tourette, France, in 1953, Gabriel Le Bras came to the conclusion that CISR had become "a pastoral and confessional, i.e., Catholic, organization." From then on, clerics and researchers had divergent expectations of the CISR: the former being interested only in the results of the studies and their pastoral implications, whereas the latter focused their attention on methodological and theoretical issues. This uneasy cohabitation continued for five further conferences.

At the tenth conference in Rome (1969), the General Assembly decided to eliminate all confessional references from the statutes of the society. To mark this openness, the next conference was to take place in Yugoslavia (1971) with the central theme, "Religion and Religiosity, Atheism and Non-belief in Industrial and Urban Society." In the new statutes, which were proposed by Jacques Verscheure and adopted in Opatija, article 4 stated the purely scientific purpose of CISR: "to advance sociology and related sciences in the analysis and interpretation of religions and related phenomena." To fulfill this purpose, the society has promoted international contacts and has organized biennial conferences in different European and North American countries.

The Executive Committee, which comprises university professors of sociology from all over the world, invites speakers to address a central theme in plenary sessions at each conference. These sessions are augmented by thematic sessions, linguistic discussion groups, free papers, and reports of working groups initiated by members. English and French are the official languages of the conference, and plenary sessions are simultaneously translated. From the ninth conference to the nineteenth in 1987, the General Secretariat published the conference proceedings. Since the twentieth conference, a selection of free papers in addition to papers delivered in plenary sessions have been published in subsequent issues of *Social Compass*.

See also Jean Labbens, Jacques Leclercq, Jacques Verscheure

—*Karel Dobbelaere*

REFERENCES

K. Dobbelaere, "CISR: An Alternative Approach to Sociology of Religion in Europe," *Sociological Analysis* 50(1989): 377-387; *Social Compass* 37, 1(1990).

SOCIETY FOR THE SCIENTIFIC STUDY OF RELIGION (SSSR)

Created in 1949 as the Committee for the Scientific Study of Religion, the SSSR name was adopted by the mid-1950s and by the early 1960s the society had its *Journal for the Scientific Study of Religion*. The CSSR was initiated by discussion between J. Paul Williams, Mount Holyoke College, and Walter H. Clark, Middlebury College. According to William M. Newman, who has written the definitive article about the early history of this organization, other early participants included Gordon Allport, Allan Eister, Horace Kallen, Prentiss L. Pemberton, James Luther Adams, Paul Tillich, Pitirim Sorokin, and Talcott Parsons. Over the years, the society has continued to have the involvement of the leading figures in the social and behavioral scientific study of religion.

In the early years, meetings occurred on college and university campuses on the East Coast, and organizational matters were arranged informally. As the organization grew, becoming a national society (with an increasing number of international members), the office of the executive secretary became more important. In those developmental years especially, William V. D'Antonio as executive secretary and Lorraine D'Antonio as business manager were prominent in this office. Annual meetings are now held in major cities in North America.

The first issue of the *JSSR* states that the aim of the members in joining together is

> (1) To encourage the study of religion through the media of their respective sciences, (2) To facilitate cooperation between groups and individuals engaging in such studies, (3) To make known . . . the nature, progress and findings of their diverse inquiries, (4) To stimulate free and friendly intercommunication between students in the field . . . , (5) To publish a Journal which . . . will further free inquiry, knowledge and understanding among religions.

These statements and other material from this issue reflect a membership drawn not only from social psychology and sociology but also from religious studies, religion, and philosophy. Some members had strong interest and training in the "hard sciences" as well.

Sometimes over the years the organizational question was raised on whether the SSSR should stand alone or, instead, be affiliated with either the American Psychological Association or the American Sociological Association. On occasion, the question of merging the SSSR and RRA was raised by various members and officers. However, as Jeffrey Hadden wrote, "The fact that SSSR members by and large insisted that the roles of faith and science were independent and that RRA members insisted on seeing the two as integral seemed to reinforce the gap between the two groups." There was also a third group, the Association for the Sociology of Religion (formerly the American Catholic Sociological Society). The SSSR and RRA typically hold a joint meeting in late October, and the ASR meets in August just prior to the meeting of the American Sociological Association. The diversity of disciplines represented among SSSR members discouraged mergers and affiliation with either the ASA or the APA. In recent years, sociologists have come to predominate in the SSSR; even so, the continuing interdisciplinary nature of this organization adds to the intellectual stimulation of its annual meeting.

The society has about 1,600 members and its journal is subscribed to by the major research libraries and perhaps as many as two-thirds of college and university libraries in the United States. An important part of this journal is its book reviews. A research fund is created yearly from general revenues and dues, and members can apply for funding. Awards are given annually for the outstanding book and the outstanding article published by a social scientist on religion as well as for the outstanding student paper given at the annual meeting. Current addresses can be found in recent issues of the *JSSR*.

—*Hart M. Nelsen*

REFERENCES

J. K. Hadden, "A Brief History of the Religious Research Association," *Review of Religious Research* 15(1974):128-136; W. M. Newman, "The Society for the Scientific Study of Religion," *Review of Religious Research* 15(1974):137-151.

SOCIETY OF FRIENDS   see Quakers

SOCIOECONOMIC STATUS   see Status, Stratification

SOCIOLOGICAL ANALYSIS see *Sociology of Religion: A Quarterly Review*

SOCIOLOGY OF RELIGION A recently published British textbook describes the task of the sociology of religion in three ways: first, to further the understanding of the role of religion in society; second, to analyze its significance in and impact upon human history; and, third, to understand the social forces and influences that in turn shape religion (Hamilton 1994). A single assumption is, however, embedded in all three statements: The sociologist of religion is concerned with religion *only insofar as it relates to the context in which it inevitably exists*. It is this relational quality that distinguishes the strictly sociological from a wide variety of other disciplines that have interests in this area (McGuire 1987).

Such a statement narrows the field a little, but not much, for both contexts and religions are infinitely varied. How then does the sociologist of religion go about the tasks outlined above? Answers to this question reflect the evolution of the subdiscipline from its earliest days to the modern period. They also are conditioned not only by widely differing cultural and academic traditions but by institutional settings. Different conditions provoke different lines of thinking.

The Founders The tension inherent in the concept of the transcendent embodied in earthly forms has engaged the attention of philosophers from the beginning of time. The sociology of religion as such, however, is inseparable from the beginnings of sociology as a distinctive discipline. Its early and distinguished practitioners were the founding fathers of sociology itself: Marx, Weber, and Durkheim. Each of these writers was reacting to the economic and social upheavals of the late nineteenth and early twentieth centuries, prompted more often than not by the devastating consequences that rapid industrialization had inflicted on the populations of which they were part. The study of religion could hardly be avoided within this framework, for religion was seen as an integral part of the society that appeared to be mutating beyond recognition. Each writer, however, tackled the subject from a different perspective (O'Toole 1984).

Karl Marx (1818-1883) predates the others by at least a generation. There are two essential elements in the Marxist perspective on religion; the first is descriptive, the second evaluative. Marx *described* religion as a dependent variable; in other words, its form and nature were dependent on social and above all economic relations, which formed the bedrock of social analysis. Nothing could be understood apart from the economic order and the relationship of the capital-

ist/worker to the means of production. The second aspect follows from this but contains an *evaluative* element. Religion is a form of alienation; it is a symptom of social malformation that will disappear with the advent of a classless society. Religion cannot therefore be understood apart from the world of which it is part, a crucial dimension of sociological thinking.

Max Weber's (1864-1920) contribution to the sociology of religion spreads into every corner of the discipline. Central to his understanding is the conviction that religion can be constituted as something other than, or separate from, society. Three points follow from this (Beckford 1989:32): that the relationship between religion and "the world" is contingent and variable, that this relationship can only be examined in its historical and sociocultural specificity, and, third, that the relationship tends to develop in a determinate direction. These three assumptions underpin Weber's magnum opus in the field, his comparative study of the major world faiths and their impact on everyday behavior in different parts of the world. Everyday behavior, moreover, becomes cumulative—hence the social consequences of religious decisions. The precise effect of such decisions is, however, a matter for empirical investigation, not a priori assumption, for religion may legitimate or challenge the prevailing order. A further point follows from this. Religion may *cease* to have the effects that it previously had, opening the possibility of the decline of religious influence within any given society, the process known as secularization.

Émile Durkheim (1858-1917)—the exact contemporary of Weber—began from a very different position. Working outward from his study of totemic religion among Australian Aborigines, he became convinced of the binding qualities of religion: "Religion celebrates, and thereby, reinforces, the fact that people can form societies" (Beckford 1989:25). What then will happen when time-honored forms of society begin to mutate so rapidly that traditional forms of religion inevitably collapse? Durkheim responded as follows: The religious aspects of society should also be allowed to evolve, so that the symbols of solidarity appropriate to the developing social order (in this case, incipient industrial society) may emerge. The theoretical position runs parallel: Religion as such will always be present for it performs a necessary *function*. The precise nature of that religion will, however, differ not only over time but between one society and another.

Despite their differences, the founding fathers acknowledged the centrality of religion to human endeavor. Motivated by the shift from preindustrial to industrial society, they wrestled with the place of religion in the changing social order. The sociology of religion was off to an excellent start—an excellence, however, that was difficult to maintain.

American Initiatives   Indeed, almost half a century passed before a second wave of activity took place. It came, moreover, from a very different quarter, from within the churches themselves. Such activity took different forms on different sides of the Atlantic. In the United States, where religious institutions remained relatively buoyant and where religious practice continued to grow, sociologists of religion in the early twentieth century were, very largely, motivated by and concerned with the Social Gospel. A second theme ran parallel, one in which religion became increasingly associated with the social divisions of American society. H. Richard Niebuhr's *The Social Sources of Denominationalism* (Holt 1929) and rather later Jay Demerath's *Social Class in American Protestantism* (Rand McNally 1965) are titles that represent this trend.

By the 1950s and 1960s, however, the principal focus of American sociology lay in the normative functionalism of Talcott Parsons, who stressed above everything the integrative role of religion. Religion—a functional prerequisite—was central to the complex models of social systems and social action elaborated by Parsons. His influence was lasting; it can be seen in subsequent generations of American scholars, notably Robert Bellah. The relationship with American society is also important. The functionalism of Parsons emerged from a social order entirely different from the turbulence that motivated the founding fathers; postwar America symbolized a settled period of industrialism in which consensus appeared not only desirable but possible. The assumption that the social order should be underpinned by religious values was widespread.

Such optimism did not last. As the 1960s gave way to a far less confident decade, the sociology of religion shifted once again—this time to the social construction of meaning systems epitomized by the work of Berger and Luckmann. The Parsonian model is inverted; social order exists but it is constructed from below. The later 1970s merge into the modern period, a world in which conflict—including religious conflict—rather than consensus dominates the agenda (Beckford 1989:8-13). Religion has become increasingly contentious.

From *Sociologie Religieuse* to the Sociology of Religion   In Western Europe, the sociology of religion was evolving along very different lines. Religious institutions on the European side of the Atlantic were far from buoyant, a situation displayed in the titles published in France in the early years of the war. The most celebrated of these, Godin and Daniel's *La France, pays de mission*

(Cerf 1943), illustrates the mood of a growing group within French Catholicism who were increasingly worried by the weakening position of the church in French society. Anxiety proved, however, a powerful motivator. So that the situation might be remedied, accurate information was essential; hence a whole series of inquiries began under the direction of Gabriel Le Bras with the intention of discovering what exactly characterized the religion of the people, or "lived religion" *(la religion vécue)* as it became known.

Accurate information acquired a momentum of its own, however, which led to certain tensions. There were those, in France and elsewhere, whose work remained motivated by pastoral concern; there were others who felt that knowledge was valuable for its own sake and resented the ties to the Catholic Church. What emerged in due course was an independent section within the Centre National de la Recherche Scientifique, the Groupe de Sociologie des Religions. The change in title was significant. There was, however, continuity as well as change. The initial enthusiasm for mapping, for example, which began with Boulard and Le Bras on rural Catholicism (1947), and continued through the work of Boulard and Rémy on urban France (1968), culminated in the magnificent *Atlas de la pratique religieuse des catholiques en France* by Isambert and Terrenoire (FNSP-CNRS 1980). Alongside such cartographic successes developed explanations for the geographic differences that emerged. These explanations were primarily historical; their sources lay deep within regional cultures. There was nothing superficial about this analysis that could, quite clearly, be applied to religions other than Catholicism.

Willaime (1995:37-57) tells this primarily French (or more accurately francophone) story in more detail: that is, the emergence of accurate and careful documentation motivated primarily by pastoral concerns, the establishment of the Groupe de Sociologie des Religions in Paris in 1954, the gradual extension of the subject matter beyond Catholicism, the development of a distinctive sociology of Protestantism, the methodological problems encountered along the way, and finally the emergence of an international organization and the *déconfessionalisation* of the sociology of religion. The evolution of the Conférence International de Sociologie Religieuse, founded in Leuven in 1948, through the Conférence Internationale de Sociologie des Religions (1981) to the present Société Internationale de Sociologie des Religions (1989) epitomizes this story. It marks a shift from a group primarily motivated by religion to one that is motivated by science. It is, however, a story that emerges—and could only emerge—from a particular part of the world, Catholic Europe. Such initiatives have been crucial to the development of the sociology of religion; they lead, however, to preoccupations that are not always shared by scholars from other parts of the world.

Themes and Perspectives

Summarizing the issues that predominate within the sociology of religion is a difficult task, for it is almost impossible to do justice to the diversity within the discipline. The increasing and welcome internationalization of the sociology of religion in the last two decades simply makes the task more difficult. The following sections should be seen as representative rather than exhaustive, and each may be explored in greater detail separately within this encyclopedia.

Definitions: Definitions of religion are both crucial and infinitely problematic. There are two aspects to this question. First, what do we mean by *religion*? And, it inevitably follows, how do we limit the sociology of religion to anything approximating a commonly agreed agenda?

The debate goes back to the founding fathers, to, that is, the primarily Weberian emphasis on the substantive definition (what religion is) versus a primarily Durkheimian functionalism (what religion does). It is a debate that continues today. The most recent attempt to square the circle can be found in the work of Hervieu-Léger (1993), who endeavors to integrate the best of both emphases through the concept of religious memory. The specificity of religion lies in a particular mode of believing, in which the idea of a *chain* of memory is crucial. Religion becomes therefore "the ideological, symbolic and social device by which the individual and collective awareness of belonging to a particular lineage of believers is created, maintained, developed and controlled" (in Davie 1996:110). The aim is to include more than the beliefs and practices of universally acknowledged world faiths but to avoid widening the agenda so far that it is difficult to distinguish the specifically religious from any other meaning system.

Secularization: The links between definitions of religion and the ongoing debate about secularization are obvious. Those who see religion primarily in substantive terms are more likely to argue that Western society is becoming increasingly secular, for what they perceive as religion is diminishing in a way that can be convincingly measured. Bruce (1995a) is a formidable exponent of this approach. Those, on the other hand, who see religion in functional terms will be less convinced, for they will want to include within the definition a set of phenomena that at the very least meet the Durkheimian description of the sacred; these

show a far greater degree of resilience. One point is immediately clear. Secularization is a debate by Western scholars about *Western* society. A second assumption very frequently follows, namely, that the tendencies that characterize Western (and more often than not European) societies today will, necessarily, occur in other parts of the world tomorrow. Such a view is increasingly challenged. A further limitation is historical rather than geographical; secularization almost always has been explored in relation to the rapid industrialization and urbanization of the nineteenth and early twentieth centuries (hence, among other things, the interest of the founding fathers in this question). The debate about advanced industrial society is only just beginning.

Secularization is sometimes referred to as a theory. It is probably more accurate to describe it as an organizing principle. As such, it has, no doubt, provided an effective way forward, a framework in which to consider a wide range of ideas and information about religion in modern societies. Wallis and Bruce (1989), for example, use this theme to order their review of the British contribution to the sociology of religion. In so doing, they are right to recall the exacting nature of the task; secularization is a complex, nuanced, and at times contradictory field of study (Martin 1978, Wilson 1982). At its best, it is highly illuminating; at its worst, it becomes an ill-disguised cover for ideological secularism.

Dimensions of religiosity: A related discussion—admirably illustrated by the work of Dobbelaere (1981) and Casanova (1994)—concerns the different dimensions of religiosity. The idea of secularization is inevitably complicated by the fact that some aspects of religious life may prosper while others decline. The indicators do not necessarily move in the same direction. At this point, the comparison between Europe and the United States provides an important illustration, for the rigorously secular nature of the American Constitution contrasts with the church-state connections still dominant—although considerably more muted than they were historically—in Europe. Conversely, religious activity is far more evident in the United States than in almost all European societies. How evident is disputed (Hadaway et al. 1993), but the contrasts with Europe remain whatever the case.

In Europe, the discussion relating to dimensions of religiosity takes a different form. The principal feature of the late twentieth century appears to be the persistence of the softer indicators of religious life (i.e., those concerned with feelings, experience, and the more numinous religious beliefs) alongside the undeniable and at times dramatic drop in the hard indicators (those that measure religious orthodoxy, ritual participation, and institutional attachment). These are the findings of the European Values Study, an invaluable source of empirical information for a growing number of societies (Barker et al. 1993).

Civil religion: The debate about civil religion is associated above all with the work of Robert Bellah. "Civil Religion in America" (1967) became a seminal article that drew attention to the peculiar mix of transcendental religion and national preoccupations that characterized the belief systems of most Americans. The British equivalent takes a different form; it is epitomized in the sacredness that surrounds the royal family (a sacredness somewhat tarnished by the younger generation of royals, but still intact). The French case has evolved rather differently; it is a version of civil religion in which the concept of *laïcité* replaces the transcendent. The transfer of power from one French president to another is a strictly godless ceremony.

An interesting development of this thinking can be found in the evolution of European identity. If Europe is to function effectively as a unit, it will—it can be argued—require its own civil religion, complete with flag, anthem, and belief system. It is paradoxical that a continent that has, very largely, ceased to practice its historic faith, appeals to this heritage once again to define its borders.

New religious movements and the New Age: There remains a persistent paradox within the material available to the sociology of religion, for we know, sociologically at least, considerably more about new religious movements than we do about the beliefs and practices of the great majority within many populations. Or, to put the same point in a more positive way, there is an important and growing body of material on sects, cults, and new religious movements carried by some of the most distinguished writers scholars in the field (Barker, Beckford, Dobbelaere, Richardson, Wallis, and Wilson, to name but the most obvious). The contribution of Japanese sociologists in this area also should be noted. Material on new religious movements has frequently dominated the journals. This is surprising in view of the relatively small numbers of people involved in such movements but less surprising in view of the issues raised by the presence of new religions in contemporary society, notably the question of religious toleration. It is worth noting that the legal aspects of these issues very often return to problems of definition; disputes about what precisely constitutes a "real" religion are as intractable in court as they are in sociological debate.

One form of new religious life has acquired the title "New Age." New Age religion constitutes a rich amalgam of philosophies and practices from both Eastern and Western traditions. Its significance lies in its affirmation of the sacred in contemporary society but in far from conventional forms. It is often associated with the approach of a new millennium (Heelas 1996).

Fundamentalisms: Strikingly different and at last an aspect of sociology less dominated by the West, the emergence of fundamentalisms worldwide has demanded sociological attention. The interest has been considerable, epitomized in the massively financed Fundamentalism Project at the University of Chicago, from which, eventually, six volumes will appear, covering not only diverse aspects of fundamentalism itself but detailed empirical studies from every world faith and almost every part of the globe. "The project tests the hypothesis that there are 'family resemblances' among disparate movements of religiously inspired reaction to global processes of modernization and secularization in the 20th century" (Marty and Appleby 1993:2). In other words, it looks for the common features in widely diverse fundamentalist movements. One way forward in this enterprise lies in constructing a Weberian ideal-type, a methodological influence from the founding fathers that still resonates. In terms of content, the agenda, once again, is being driven by the impact of world events, notably the spread of fundamentalist movements in recent decades. Explanations are sought, very frequently, in discussions of globalization and in the nature of late capitalism. Wider discussions of the globalization theme can be found in Roland Robertson's (1992) and Peter Beyer's (1994) work.

Religion and the everyday: An alternative and much more recent focus draws from a different line of sociological thinking. It concerns the significance of religion in everyday life, not least its impact upon the basics of human existence and the relationship of humanity to the environment. All religions have something to say about the body and about nature—diet, sex, sexuality, health, healing, death, even martyrdom (to name but some features of this debate) all lie within the remit of religious control and religious teaching. In opening up this debate, the 23rd Conference of the SISR (Québec 1995) significantly enlarged the agenda of the sociology of religion, not least in encouraging a new set of links with related branches of sociology. At the same time, the conference reaffirmed the importance of anthropological contributions to the sociology of religion (Turner 1974, Douglas 1973, 1978).

One aspect of a renewed emphasis on the importance of religion in everyday life can be found in work on *gender* and religion. A crucial question, for example, surrounds the issue of whether women are more religious than men because of what they *are* or because of what they *do*. Within the Western context, there is persuasive evidence that women display a greater degree of religiousness than men—in practice, in strength of belief, and in what they believe. Why this is so and whether the situation is likely to alter has become the subject of considerable sociological debate—the more so in view of the history of the Western church as a profoundly patriarchal institution within which women have been systematically excluded from positions of responsibility. A second question follows: As women become increasingly involved in the leadership of at least the Protestant churches, is their presence likely to influence not only the institutions themselves but the nature of the message that they are called to proclaim?

Current Dilemmas

Imbalances: Imbalances prosper within the sociology of religion. One of these has already been mentioned. Sociologists know far more about the exotic edges of religious life than they do about the beliefs of ordinary people. Or, to put the same point in a different way, the edges of the religious jigsaw are far more adequately defined than the picture in the middle, which at times remains alarmingly blurred. Nobody would deny that the edges throw up interesting questions—maybe the most interesting—but the lack of information about the center is hardly reassuring. Explanations for this lack derive, at least in part, from a preoccupation with secularization. Sociologists have assumed that the picture in the middle of the puzzle is blurred because it is fading away. It is true that certain aspects of religious life show a marked decline in Western societies; we need to know why this is so. Other aspects, however, do not, and why not is an equally important question. Non-Western societies, moreover, demonstrate markedly different religious evolutions.

The imbalance needs therefore to be tackled in two ways. On the one hand, there is a need to refocus attention on the middle of the Western picture, following, for example, the work of Roof (1993) and Roof and McKinney (1987). At the same time, the subdiscipline needs to escape from the assumption that the West is necessarily leading the way. Why, for example, do we look from Latin Europe toward Latin America and not the other way around? The following citation from Martin (1996:41 f) makes precisely this point with admirable clarity:

Initially, about a quarter of a century ago, I asked myself why the voluntary denominations of Anglo-American cultures had not taken off in Latin America as they had in the U.S.A., and concluded

that Latin America must be too similar to Latin Europe for that to happen. But I am now inclined to reverse the question and ask why the burgeoning denominations of Latin America have not taken off in Latin Europe. After all, the conditions which gave both Latin America and Latin Europe their specific character over the last two centuries have largely disappeared, and the old emplacements of "fortress Catholicism" or militant secularity are not what they were. There are new spaces being cleared in which a competitive denominational culture can emerge.

Isolation and insulation from mainstream sociology: Beckford (1989) has underlined both the insulation and the isolation of the sociology of religion from the parent discipline. Both partners have been impoverished as a result. The sociology of religion has lost the stimulus of theoretical developments within sociology; mainline sociologists continue to assume that religion is of marginal interest in contemporary society. Is it possible to escape from this dilemma? The following are tentative suggestions.

Theoretical possibilities: The sociology of religion has, very largely, become trapped in the discussions that concern the shift from preindustrial to industrial societies. The debate needs to move on. Building on to the best of the contributions concerning the nature and forms of modernity (Giddens, Beck, Baumann, and so on), those with appropriate skills need to offer alternative analyses that integrate rather than marginalize the role of religion in the modern world (Beckford 1996). Hervieu-Léger (1986, 1993) has made a significant start in this direction, recognizing that the nature and forms of religion at the turn of a new century depend significantly on the nature of modernity itself. Contemporary religion is a product of, not a reaction to, modernity.

A second possibility might pursue an idea already suggested by Beckford: the proposition that religion should be seen as a cultural resource, not as a social institution. The deregulation of religion presents a fresh set of opportunities, for the religious sphere itself *and* for those who study it.

A third and entirely different opening lies in the exploration of rational choice theory. Stark and Bainbridge, Iannaccone, Pettersson, and Hamburg have presented a supply-side model of religion. Bruce (1995b) summarizes this debate. The model supposes, first, that a free market is more efficient than a monopoly and, second, that this is as true for the production and consumption of religion as it is for anything else. It follows that European religion would flourish if the free market were allowed to operate as it does in the United

States. Others, notably Bruce himself, have rebutted this argument strongly.

The focus on new religious movements has, at times, led to extreme forms of marginalization within the sociology of religion. Paradoxically, it can also provide a route back into the discipline—the more so since the upsurge of sociological interest in social movement analysis. Not all those interested in this field are necessarily aware of the religious dimension. The links, however, should be pursued by those who are, for social movements prosper in the late twentieth century. Equally related to the developments of secular society are the separate evolutions of religious belief and religious belonging (Davie 1994), a divergence evident in multiple aspects of social life. It can be exemplified in the decline of large-scale political parties, in the demise of trade unions, and in the mutation of leisure activities. Changes in religious life should be seen against this background. Explanations may lie in societal rather than religious change. *All* belief systems, after all, present similar problems of credibility. In a celebrated essay on the environment, the anthropologist Mary Douglas (1975) makes precisely this point.

Substantive suggestions: A second set of possibilities can be discovered in the evolving subject matter of sociology. Three examples are given here.

First is the rapidly developing interest in the sociology of health. Traditional constructions of the history of medical care have emphasized its growing separation from the influence of religion in modern, technological society. Postmodern emphases—and here the controversial term is entirely appropriate—reintegrate the two, minimizing the boundaries between body, mind, and soul, for health is a reflection of wholeness rather than fragmentation.

A second example can be found in the sociology of law as the legal rights of religious minorities begin to assert themselves in increasingly pluralist societies. Here comparative analysis is essential to display the influence of context on these interrelationships. To which court, for example, is a case about toleration brought? This will vary from country to country. On what grounds is the case argued? By whom? In which court is the final judgment made? The final question is particularly apposite in Europe, or indeed in any federal framework, as national and supranational interests stake out their relative positions. The work of Richardson (qualified in both law and sociology) makes an excellent start in this area.

A third overlap involves political science. It is true that the conventional patterns of religio-political allegiance have diminished, particularly in Europe. It is not true, however, that religion is no longer a political issue.

Indeed, its potency is asserting itself on a global scale, at times associated with extreme violence. Political divisions can become dangerous confrontations when reinforced by religious ideologies. Attempts to understand them better require the cooperation of scholars from a diversity of disciplines.

A demanding agenda awaits the sociologist of religion at the turn of the twenty-first century. Drawing on the widest possible range of sources, theoretical as well as empirical, he or she must rise to the challenge. Religion must become once more an integral part of the discipline of sociology.

Organizations and Journals The International Society for the Sociology of Religion has already been mentioned. It evolved from Conférence Internationale de Sociologie Religieuse. Its origins lie in the *sociologie religieuse* of Catholic Europe. Bit by bit, however, it has shed such emphases to become a truly global society encouraging a diversity of trends within the sociology of religion (see *Social Compass,* 1990, No. 1). It mails regularly to up to 700 individuals in more than 40 countries. Approximately 300 scholars attended the 1995 meeting in Québec.

Research Committee 22 of the International Sociological Association provides a second international forum, an excellent launching pad for establishing creative links with mainline sociology.

National organizations for the sociology of religion exist in a number of countries; the three American groups are the largest, each supporting an independent journal. (The Association for the Sociology of Religion publishes *Sociology of Religion,* formerly *Sociological Analysis;* the Religious Research Association publishes the *Review of Religious Research;* and the Society for the Scientific Study of Religion publishes the *Journal for the Scientific Study of Religion.*)

There are two European journals. *Social Compass,* which grew from Dutch origins, is now edited in Louvain-la-Neuve. Since 1989, it has been published by Sage; it has developed close links with the SISR, who provide material for the first issue of each year. *Archives de sciences sociales des religions* is edited in Paris. It too has changed its name in the course of its history. It is a production of the Centre National de la Recherche Scientifique, currently edited jointly with the École des Hautes Études en Sciences Sociales.

—*Grace Davie*

REFERENCES

D. Barker et al., *The European Values Study 1981-1990* (London: European Values Study, 1993); J. Beckford, *Religion and Advanced Industrial Society* (London: Unwin-Hyman, 1989);

J. Beckford, "Post-Modernity, High-Modernity and New-Modernity," in *Postmodernity, Sociology and Religion,* ed. K. Flanagan and P. Jupp (London: Macmillan, 1996): 30-47; R. Bellah, "Civil Religion in America," *Daedalus* 96(1967):1-21; P. Beyer, *Religion and Globalization* (London: Sage, 1994); R. Boulard and G. Le Bras, *Carte religieuse de la France rurale* (Paris: Aux cahiers du clergé rural, 1947); R. Boulard and J. Rémy, *Pratique religieuse urbaine et régions culturelles* (Paris: Ed. ouvrières-Economie et Humanisme, 1968); S. Bruce, *From Cathedrals to Cults* (Oxford: Oxford University Press, 1995a); S. Bruce, "The Truth About Religion in Britain," *Journal for the Scientific Study of Religion* 34(1995b):417-430; J. Casanova, *Public Religions in the Modern World* (Chicago: University of Chicago Press, 1994); G. Davie, *Religion in Britain Since 1945* (Oxford: Blackwell, 1994); G. Davie, "Religion and Modernity," in *Postmodernity, Sociology and Religion,* ed. K. Flanagan and P. Jupp (London: Macmillan, 1996): 101-117; K. Dobbelaere, *Secularization* (London: Sage, 1981); M. Douglas, *Natural Symbols* (London: Barrie and Jenkins, 1973); M. Douglas, *Implicit Meanings* (London: Routledge, 1975); M. Douglas, *Purity and Danger* (London: Routledge, 1978); C. K. Hadaway et al., "What the Polls Don't Show," *American Sociological Review* 58(1993):741-752; M. Hamilton, *The Sociology of Religion* (London: Routledge, 1994); P. Heelas, *The New Age* (Oxford: Blackwell, 1996); D. Hervieu-Léger, *Vers un nouveau christianisme?* (Paris: Cerf, 1986); D. Hervieu-Léger, *La religion pour mémoire* (Paris: Cerf, 1993); D. Martin, *A General Theory of Secularization* (Oxford: Blackwell, 1978); D. Martin, "Remise en question de la théorie de la sécularisation," in *Identités religieuses en Europe,* ed. G. Davie and D. Hervieu-Léger (Paris: La Découverte, 1996); M. Marty and R. S. Appleby, *Fundamentalisms and Society* (Chicago: University of Chicago Press, 1993); M. McGuire, *Religion* (Belmont, Calif.: Wadsworth, 1987); R. O'Toole, *Religion* (Toronto: McGraw-Hill, Ryerson, 1984); R. Robert- son, *Globalization* (London: Sage, 1992); W. C. Roof, *A Generation of Seekers* (San Francisco: Harper, 1993); W. C. Roof and W. McKinney, *American Mainline Religion* (New Brunswick, N.J.: Rutgers University Press, 1987); V. Turner, *The Ritual Process* (Harmondsworth, U.K.: Penguin, 1974); R. Wallis and S. Bruce, "Religion," *British Journal of Sociology* 40(1989):493-519; J. Willaime, *Sociologie des Religions* (Paris: Presses Universitaires de France, 1995); B. R. Wilson, *Religion in Sociological Perspective* (Oxford: Oxford University Press, 1982).

SOCIOLOGY OF RELIGION: A QUARTERLY REVIEW Originally titled the *American Catholic Sociological Review,* the official journal of the American Catholic Sociological Society, which was founded in 1938. The *Review* first appeared in 1940 and included articles on all subjects of concern to Catholic sociologists. In 1964, the journal's name was changed to *Sociological Analysis,* and it began more and more to include only material relevant to the sociology of religion. The journal no longer was expected to have a Catholic slant. In 1970, the American Catholic Sociological Society became the Association for the Sociology of Religion. The journal was titled *Sociology of Religion* in 1993; it is the official publication of the Association for the Sociology of Religion.

—*Joseph B. Tamney*

SOKA GAKKAI A lay organization of the Nichiren Shoshu (after Nichiren, a thirteenth-century Buddhist evangelist), a sect within Japanese Buddhism. Soka Gakkai was founded in the 1930s by a schoolteacher, Tsunesaburo Makiguchi. After World War II, the movement expanded dramatically and quickly became the largest of the new Japanese faiths. In Japan, Soka Gakkai has been associated with the conservative Komeito, or the "Clean Government" party, and with Japanese nationalism. Religious practice, both in Japan and in the United States, emphasizes chanting (diamoku) and intensive efforts directed toward the conversion of new members (shakubuku). Soka Gakkai is evangelistic and its main goal is *kosen rufu,* or the spreading of Nichiren Shoshu Buddhism to promote peace and happiness for all.

In the mid-1960s, Soka Gakkai and its U.S. organization, Nichiren Shoshu of America, began to recruit non-Japanese Americans. The organization has since built a significant non-Japanese segment of its membership. Like many new religious movements in the United States in the late 1960s and 1970s, Soka Gakkai initially was able to recruit a fairly large membership, which later declined (Hashimoto and McPherson 1976). Scholarly interest in Soka Gakkai in Japan has focused on its response to a values crisis in Japan after World War II and its political impact (e.g., Solomon 1977). Soka Gakkai in the United States has been examined as one of many new religious movements that arose in the 1960s and 1970s (e.g., Hurst 1992, Hashimoto and McPherson 1976). Of particular note is the Snow and Phillips (1980) study examining the adequacy of the Lofland-Stark conversion model in relation to Soka Gakkai in the United States.

See also Buddhism, New Religious Movements

—*Edward F. Breschel*

REFERENCES

H. Hashimoto and W. McPherson, "Rise and Decline of Sokagakkai in Japan and the United States," *Review of Religious Research* 17(1976):82-92; J. Hurst, *Nichiren-Shoshu Bud-*

dhism and the Soka-Gakkai in America (New York: Garland, 1992); D. A. Snow and C. L. Phillips, "The Lofland-Stark Conversion Model," *Social Problems* 27(1980):430-447; T. J. Solomon, "Response of Three New Religions to the Crisis of the Japanese Value System," *Journal for the Scientific Study of Religion* 16(1977):1-14.

SOUTHERN BAPTISTS   *see* Baptists

SOUTHERNIZATION   The process whereby the distinctive cultural forms associated with the American South spread to other geographic regions of the United States.

Scholarly attention in the 1970s to the disappearance of regional distinctiveness in the United States—the homogenization of American culture—included examination of how the South was becoming more like the rest of the nation (i.e., more urban, more industrial, more secular, and so on). The South, it was argued, was being absorbed into mainstream American culture. In his book, *The Americanization of Dixie* (Harper 1974), southern journalist John Egerton also explored the reciprocal influence of southern culture on the rest of the nation, a process he called "the Southernization of America." Egerton suggested that religion was one of the elements of southern culture having a discernable impact on the wider society. He wrote, for example, that Billy Graham "has taken the old-time religion of his native South out into the nation and the world. . . . In doing so, he has firmly established himself as the single most influential figure in what can fairly be called the Southernization of American religion" (p. 195).

In his article "The Southernization of America Religion: Testing a Hypothesis" (*Sociological Analysis* 1991), Mark A. Shibley undertook a systematic, empirical examination of the Egerton thesis. Using church membership data from the Glenmary Research Center and population and migration data from the U.S. Census, he showed that virtually all the membership growth in evangelical churches during the 1970s could be attributed to growth in historically southern evangelical churches. Moreover, Shibley found that the growth of southern-style religion was especially marked outside the South and corresponds with regions that experienced high levels of in-migration from the South during the same period. Shibley's book, *Resurgent Evangelicalism in the United States* (University of South Carolina Press 1996), showed that the pattern held through the 1980s, but this more thoroughgoing examination of the southernization thesis, which includes fieldwork in

southern churches outside the South, concludes that while southern religion has changed the face of American culture in recent decades, it has itself been fundamentally changed in the process. Ultimately, the southernization concept proved useful in helping to explain the contemporary resurgence of evangelicalism in the United States.

—*Mark A. Shibley*

SPENCER, ANTHONY (1928–)   Working in the tradition of *sociologie religieuse,* Spencer aimed to establish an accurate demographic profile of the Catholic community in England and Wales. With this in mind, he set up the Newman Demographic Survey (1953) with the particular intention of providing the Catholic Education Council with accurate statistical information. In the 1960s, he created the Pastoral Research Centre. Spencer taught first at the Cavendish Square Graduate College (1964-1969), then at Queen's University, Belfast (1970-1987). He was elected President of the International Conference for the Sociology of Religion in 1963 and 1965, and was active in the International Federation of Institutes of Social and Socio-Religious Research.

—*Grace Davie*

SPENCER, HERBERT (1820-1903)   British philosopher and sociologist; influential source of "social Darwinism" in the late nineteenth century. Nurtured by the middle-class radicalism and dissenting religion of Joseph Priestly, William Godwin, and others, he creatively synthesized the varied intellectual currents of his time. His early evolutionism anticipated Charles Darwin's *Origin of Species* (1859) but emphasized uniformitarian continuity between the organic and "superorganic" (i.e., cultural) realms and rested on Larmarckism. Everything developed from homogeneity to heterogeneity, including society, whose social differentiation increased as it changed from a centrally coordinated "military" type to an "industrial" one marked by individual freedom of contract. If unimpeded by government intervention, industrial society's progress would achieve a complete adaptation of mankind to its social state. Because all ills result from the maladaptation of constitution to conditions, the "evanescence of evil" would result.

Spencer saw "the unknowable" element in reality as the root of religion. It was unlikely that scientific advance would eliminate religion because the sense of mystery formerly attributed to the world by religious thought would continue to operate at the point where scientific explanations ended. The third volume of his *Principles of Sociology* (1876-1896, part of his 10-volume *Synthetic Philosophy*) presented a mass of evidence connected with "Ecclesiastical Institutions" in accordance with his evolutionary theory. Included were analyses of religious roles (e.g., medicine men, priests), organizations (church, sect), the conservatism of religious institutions, the differentiation of church and state, and religious elites as forerunners of the modern professions. The second volume of *Principles* also dealt with "Ceremonial Institutions," and contained an extensive amount of material on religion. Spencer's later writings (e.g., *The Man Versus the State* [1884]) showed increased pessimism concerning further progress of society and a fear of the return to a "military"-type regime.

—*Donald A. Nielsen*

REFERENCES

J. D. Y. Peel (ed.), *Herbert Spencer on Social Evolution* (Chicago: University of Chicago Press, 1984); J. Rumney, *Herbert Spencer's Sociology* (New York: Atherton, 1966 [1937]); J. H. Turner, *Herbert Spencer* (Newbury Park, Calif.: Sage, 1985).

SPILKA, BERNARD (1926–)

Professor of Psychology at the University of Denver and a core faculty member of the Joint University of Denver-Iliff School of Theology, Religion and Psychological Studies program. President of Division 36 of the American Psychological Association (1985-1986) and a recipient of its William James award for outstanding and sustained contribution to the empirical psychology of religion (1982); Vice-President (1977-1979) of the Society for the Scientific Study of Religion.

Spilka is a coauthor of an authoritative textbook on the empirical psychology of religion. He is widely recognized for his contributions to measurement in a variety of areas in the psychology of religion including refinements of the intrinsic-extrinsic dimensions and the construction of scales to measure attitudes toward death. He continues to be influential in testing a variety of hypotheses in the empirical psychology of

religion associated with research on images of God, mysticism, religious experience, and fear of death. He also is involved in research relating religion to mental health issues, coping, and physical disease (especially cancer). He has been influential in documenting the minimal treatment of the psychology of religion in introductory psychology textbooks. His major theoretical contribution continues to be his pioneering application of general attribution theory to the study of religion.

—*Ralph W. Hood, Jr.*

REFERENCES

R. A. Bridges and B. Spilka, "Religion and the Mental Health of Women," in *Religion and Mental Health,* ed. J. Schumaker (London: Oxford University Press, 1992); B. Spilka, "Religion in the Introductory Psychology Textbook," *Journal for the Scientific Study of Religion* 28(1989):366-371; B. Spilka and D. N. McIntosh, "Attribution Theory and Religious Experience," in *Handbook of Religious Experience,* ed. R. W. Hood, Jr. (Birmingham, Ala.: Religious Education Press, 1995); B. Spilka et al., *The Psychology of Religion* (Englewood Cliffs, N.J.: Prentice Hall, 1985a); B. Spilka et al., "A General Attribution Theory for the Psychology of Religion," *Journal for the Scientific Study of Religion* 24(1985b):1-20.

SPIRITUAL FRONTIERS FELLOWSHIP INTERNATIONAL (SFFI)

Interfaith, nonprofit organization founded in 1956 by a group of religious leaders, writers, businesspeople, and professionals to foster "spiritual unfoldment within the individual through the exploration of both old and new dimensions of human experience leading to a unity of body, mind and spirit."

The early leaders of SFFI were deeply interested in paranormal phenomena as they relate to spiritual experience and transformative consciousness. They selected three areas for major concentration: mystical prayer and meditation, spiritual healing, and the survival of consciousness beyond bodily death. More recently, SFFI has also been concerned with planetary stewardship, global awareness, and various aspects of consciousness research. The SFFI mails out a bimonthly newsletter, publishes a journal, and sponsors retreats, conferences, and seminars. Members have access to a lending library through the mails of 15,000 volumes, an on-premise research library of 5,000 volumes, a prayer healing ministry, and a bookshop. The SFFI had approximately 2,500 active members in 1994. The Academy of Religion and Psychical Research is its academic affiliate (address: P.O. Box 7868, Philadelphia, PA, 19101).

—James McClenon

SPIRITUALISM   Religious and social movement based on the belief that it is possible to communicate with the deceased after their bodily death.

Although mediumship exists in many societies, the American Spiritualist Movement was launched in 1848 with mysterious knockings in a house in Hydesville, New York. The phenomena, thought to be caused by spirits, attracted much publicity and stimulated similar phenomena in other locations. Spiritualists demonstrated mediumship, table tipping, and a wide variety of extrasensory and psychokinetic phenomena. Although many mediums were revealed as frauds, some caused scientific investigators to believe in paranormal phenomena. The Society for Psychical Research in England and the American Society for Psychical Research were founded to investigate paranormal claims. By the turn of the century, spiritualist phenomena became less prevalent and the movement declined. Theosophy can be regarded as a combination of spiritualism, Western mysticism, and Asian religious doctrines. Of the 500-600 cults listed in J. Gordon Melton's *Encyclopedia of American Religions* (Gale 1989), there are over 100 theosophical and spiritualist groups.

A significant contribution to social scientific research on the Spiritualist Movement has been made by Geoffrey Nelson in *Spiritualism and Society* (Schocken 1969). He surveyed members of a central-England district of the British Spiritualist National Union in 1968. He found that they wished to understand "psychic gifts," are dissatisfied with Christianity, are influenced by parents and friends, and seek healing and comfort. They tend to be middle class, occupationally mobile, and widowed. Further studies examined the role of the medium and the ideology of modern spiritualism. Other contributions that may be mentioned are Loggie Barrow's *Independent Spirits* (Routledge 1986) and Swatos and Gissurarson's *Icelandic Spiritualism* (Transaction 1996).

The Spiritualist Movement, which lasted into the early 1900s, may be viewed as a Western manifestation of the physiological propensity for humans to perceive that they can communicate with spirits through a standardized set of procedures (rapping, table tipping, trance, and so on). Throughout history and all over the world, humans have found that a small percentage of those within their group seemingly have anomalous capacities. The demonstration of these talents leads to belief in spirits, souls, and life after death (see McClenon 1994).

—James McClenon

REFERENCES

R. S. Broughton, *Parapsychology* (New York: Ballantine, 1991); A. Gauld, *The Founders of Psychical Research* (New York: Schocken, 1968); A. Gauld, *Mediumship and Survival* (London: Heinemann, 1982); J. McClenon, *Wondrous Events* (Philadelphia: University of Pennsylvania Press, 1994); F. Podmore, *Mediums of the Nineteenth Century* (New Hyde Park, N.Y.: University Books, 1963, originally published as *Modern Spiritualism*, 1902).

SPIRITUALITY   Frequently used, but ill-defined, term in the social sciences of religion; most generally understood as a quality of an individual whose inner life is oriented toward God, the supernatural, or the sacred. Recalling William James's distinction between personal experience and inherited tradition, it is increasingly common to contrast "spirituality" with "religion."

Spirituality is considered primary, more pure, more directly related to the soul in its relation to the divine, while religion is secondary, dogmatic and stifling, often distorted by oppressive sociopolitical and socioeconomic forces. In *A Generation of Seekers* (Harper 1993), Wade Clark Roof found that American baby boomers frequently rejected organized "religion" in favor of individual "spirituality." The return to or recovery of spirituality was central to the cultural ferment of the 1960s in America, and the term *spirituality* is therefore often modified by adjectives associated with some of the major cultural movements of the 1960s and post-1960s era, including *New Age spirituality*, *postmodern spirituality*, and most notably, *feminist spirituality*.

—David Yamane

REFERENCE

C. Eller, *Living in the Lap of the Goddess* (New York: Crossroad, 1993).

SPIRITUAL WELL-BEING   *see* Well-Being

SPIRO, MELFORD (ELLIOT) (1920–)   Founding member of the Department of Anthropology at the

University of California, San Diego, where he serves as an emeritus professor.

His research stresses the need to consider both psychoanalytic and cultural forces in attempting to understand human behavior. Spiro conducted fieldwork in Micronesia, Burma, and Israel (focusing on sex roles in the kibbutzim). Human nature, he contends, is grounded in individual needs. He cogently argues that religion is a projective system rooted in family experiences. Spiro's major contributions to the study of religion examine the articulation of personality systems, belief systems, and social structures. His first book-length treatment of a religious system, *Burmese Supernaturalism* (Transaction 1996 [1978]), looks at folk religion and demonstrates how different types of religious beliefs can coexist and function to serve the emotional needs of group members. Another important contribution, *Buddhism and Society* (University of California Press 1982), examines discrepancies between observed ritual practice and the official doctrines of Buddhism. Supernaturalism, Spiro concludes, offers alternate explanations for suffering and thereby meets existential needs. His seminal essay "Religion: Problems of Definition and Explanation" (1966) reviews major definitions of religion, followed by his own attempt at a definition. For Spiro, religion is "an institution consisting of culturally patterned interaction with culturally postulated super-human beings." The remainder of his essay astutely analyzes manifest and latent functions of religion and assesses "causal" as distinct from "functional" explanations for religious belief.

—Stephen D. Glazier

REFERENCE

M. Spiro, "Religion," in *Anthropological Approaches to the Study of Religion*, ed. M. Banton (London: Tavistock, 1966): 85-126.

SPITZER, ALLEN (1909-1967) President of the American Catholic Sociological Society in 1957 and professor at St. Louis University.

Spitzer used an anthropological, typological approach to discuss the organization, beliefs, and practices of mainstream North American, Mexican, and Montana Blackfeet Catholics. He portrayed Catholicism as a continuum that includes formal, nominal, cultural, and folk categories. Formal Catholicism is represented by the official church. Nominal Catholicism involves membership and membership allegiance.

Cultural Catholicism represents such elements as national, artistic, aesthetic, and social life. Folk Catholicism represents popular Catholic expressions within indigenous cults, pagan elements, and superstitions. All these elements appear in the groups Spitzer analyzed.

—James McClenon

REFERENCES

A. Spitzer, "The Culture Organization of Catholicism," *American Catholic Sociological Review* 19(1958):2-12; A. Spitzer, "Religious Structure in Mexico," *Alpha Kappa Delta* 37(1960):54-58; A. Spitzer and M. L. Spitzer, "Religious Reorganization Among the Montana Blackfoot," *Review of Religious Research* 2(1960):19-34.

SSSR *see* Society for the Scientific Study of Religion

STARK, RODNEY (1934–) Professor of Sociology and Comparative Religion, University of Washington. President, Association for the Sociology of Religion, 1983; ASA Sociology of Religion Section, 1997.

Having begun his life's work as a journalist working for the *Oakland Tribune* from 1959 to 1961, Stark entered graduate school at the University of California, Berkeley, in 1961 and earned his M.A. (1965) and Ph.D. (1971) there. He has twice received the Distinguished Book Award from the Society for the Scientific Study of Religion (SSSR), in 1986 for *The Future of Religion: Secularization, Revival, and Cult Formation* (with William Sims Bainbridge, University of California Press 1985) and in 1993 for *The Churching of America 1776-1990* (with Roger Finke, Rutgers University Press 1992).

Stark's early work on religion was done with Charles Glock, with whom he wrote several books. One of these joint efforts is *American Piety: The Nature of Religious Commitment* (University of California Press 1968). This book dealt with the issue of the dimensionality of religiosity/religious commitment, a topic that was being addressed by numerous social scientists at that time. In their collaborative work, Stark and Glock explored the use of a *multidimensional* approach to religiosity that included beliefs, ritual practices, knowledge, personal experiences, and sociomoral consequences.

Of greater significance was Glock and Stark's earlier work *Religion and Society in Tension* (Rand McNally 1965). This work set the stage for their other books by defining religion from a sociological perspective (including a taxonomy of religious experiences), describing the new denominationalism in American society by focusing on what people believe in the various churches, and elaborating the role of religion in the integration of society and in promoting (or discouraging) social change. The chapter on religion and radicalism remains relevant, for example, to the 1990s situation in American politics concerning the religious right strongly pushing the Republican Party toward conservative stances on sociomoral issues. Many of the patterns being discussed today were already evident in the late 1950s and early 1960s, even though the players then were different.

While the importance of his early empirical work should not be overlooked, Stark's most influential writings are theoretical in nature. This includes a large number of articles and books written in collaboration with William Sims Bainbridge in the late 1970s to mid-1980s, and with Roger Finke (among others) from the mid-1990s to the present time. His work with Bainbridge began the development of a new theoretical perspective on religion, one that is derived in part from social exchange theory. Stark and Bainbridge began to propose this theory by stating a number of axioms, definitions, and propositions. According to the authors, "the concept of compensators is key to the theory of religion which follows" (1980:121). A *compensator* is the promise of a future reward that cannot be tested by empirical means. A major proposition is that when humans cannot achieve a desired reward, they will accept a compensator instead, and will even treat the compensator as if it were a tangible reward.

This new theoretical approach was later expanded with the publication by Stark and Bainbridge of *A Theory of Religion* (Lang 1987), a seminal work with 344 propositions, beginning with those proposed in the article cited above, and moving on to apply this theoretical approach to a macrosociological analysis of the role of religion in society as well as to the impact of society on religion. Perhaps of greatest importance was the idea that secularization could be self-limiting because the increased secularization of a church could, and often did, lead to the starting of a new sect as a splinter group from that denomination. Thus the new theory contributed to church-sect theory, which Stark described as being like a "stagnant pool wherein participants, like algae, are content to add encrustation to a sunken ship." The new theory added to the old by offering a process model for how sects came to break away from churches, describing how the increased secularization through accommodation with society would lead people to leave a church to form a new religious body. In addition, impetus was given to "shifting the scope of church-sect theory from religious organiza-

tions per se to whole societies" (1985:139 f). This in turn led to the next new development: the religious economies (or rational choice) perspective.

The religious economies perspective is being developed through the writings of Stark, Bainbridge, Roger Finke, Laurence Iannaccone, R. Stephen Warner, and others. Stark employs as a basic principle that the religious mind is rational, that "it makes sense to model religion as the behavior of rational, well-informed actors who choose to 'consume' secular commodities" (1994:2). Thus the choice of religious affiliation is made in a rational way, with the potential member weighing costs and benefits of each possible choice before choosing the one that maximizes rewards (although not necessarily the one that minimizes costs). As such, it challenges the conventional thought that the religious mind is either irrational or, at least, nonrational.

Also challenged by this new perspective is the contention that religious pluralism "weakens faith by calling all faiths into question" (1994:1). The traditional thought was that only a religious monopoly could enhance the spread of faith within a society. The religious economies perspective argues the opposite, that "to the degree that a religious economy is competitive and pluralistic, overall levels of religious participation will tend to be high" (1994:3). Finke and Stark provide empirical support for this proposition in their analysis of the impact of religious pluralism on religious participation in American cities, using data from the U.S. Census on religious bodies collected in 1906. Their findings indicated that religious adherence is higher in urban environments than in rural areas, and that this is due in large part to the greater availability of religious options in the city. "Thus, a natural consequence of an open religious economy is a religious pluralism that forces each religious body to appeal successfully to some segment of the religious market, or to slide into oblivion" (1988: 47). With religious bodies specializing, it becomes easier for religious "consumers" to find the best product for them.

A third point of contention between traditional thought and the new perspective relates to the view of secularization. The traditional approach argued that a decline in religious demand was caused by modernity, in essence that the increased emphasis on science and rationality would lead people away from supernatural explanations. They cite the low rates of religious adherence in northern Europe as evidence of this process of secularization. Again, proponents of the religious economies perspective disagree. "We argue," Stark says, that the religious condition of northern Europe is largely a supply-side problem rather than a lack of demand. That is, lack of religious participation in much of Europe reflects highly regulated [religious] economies dominated by state supported churches and that these are lazy, inefficient firms who do nothing to create demand. (1994:4)

Stark also notes that it is only church attendance that is low in Europe, with many people still believing in God, few describing themselves as atheists, and a majority being critical of the state churches.

Much of Stark's recent writing has been a reexamination of American religious history from a religious economies perspective, primarily in collaboration with Roger Finke. Their primary emphasis has been on clearing up a variety of misconceptions about religious life in America, beginning with the colonial era. *The Churching of America, 1776-1990* (Rutgers University Press 1992) is the culmination of these efforts. In it they note such popular myths as the high religiosity of colonial New England (their estimates are that only 17% of colonialists had a religious affiliation), that mainline churches (Episcopal, Congregational, Presbyterian, and so on) began to decline in the 1960s (they find it started in the mid-1800s), and that the 1960s and 1970s were characterized by religious "eruptions" such as cult formation, Eastern religions making inroads, and the New Age (which they state are all exaggerated).

Stark and Finke go on to provide evidence for a different view of American religious history, one in which the colonial era is seen as a time of low religious fervor. They note that this did not change until the colonies became more interdependent economically, forcing colonies to be more tolerant of religious traditions not financially supported by them. Eventually the U.S. Constitution opened up the religious marketplace, making it easier for new religious groups to flourish. Through several chapters, they indicate the impact this religious freedom had on the rising fortunes of such groups as Baptists, Methodists, and Catholics, as well as the subsequent decline of the Methodists.

The final chapter presents an excellent synthesis of the religious economies perspective with church-sect theory. Ultimately, they argue that they

do not believe that the church-sect process has the blind inevitability of Marx's dialectic or even the wheel of karma . . . The sect-church process appears so unstoppable because humans seems [sic] to have rather mixed motives when they make choices about religion.

They also argue that secularization is not an inevitable aspect of this process. As they indicate, "sudden shifts do occur in our religious economy, but these involve the rising and falling of religious firms, not the rise and fall of religion per se" (1992:274 f).

Stark continues to work in the area of theory and religious history. He provides a fascinating autobiographical account of the process by which he came to the rational choice perspective, as well as a summons to bring theory back into the research process (1997). In 1996, Stark completed *The Rise of Christianity: A Sociologist Reconsiders History* (Princeton University Press), a book on the early Christian church and Greco-Roman times that extended his interest in theory and history in yet another direction, presaged by several articles during the first half of the 1990s.

See also Church-Sect Theory, Compensators, Rational Choice Theory

—*André Nauta*

REFERENCES

R. Finke and R. Stark, "Religious Economies and Sacred Canopies," *American Sociological Review* 53(1988):41-49; R. Stark, "Church and Sect," in *The Sacred in a Secular Age*, ed. P. E. Hammond (Berkeley: University of California Press, 1985): 139-149; R. Stark, "Rational Choice Theories of Religion," *Agora* 2, 1(1994):1-5; R. Stark, "Bringing Theory Back In," in *Rational Choice Theory and Religion*, ed. L. A. Young (New York: Routledge, 1997): 3-23; R. Stark and W. S. Bainbridge, "Towards a Theory of Religion," *Journal for the Scientific Study of Religion* 19(1980):114-128.

STARK, WERNER (1909-1985)   Born in Marienbad, Czechoslovakia, and educated at the universities of Hamburg, Prague, and Geneva and at the London School of Economics, Stark's training and scholarship encompassed history, philosophy, political science, law, economics, literature, art, music, and sociology. He held doctorates both in law and in political science. The rise of Nazism resulted in his leaving Germany for Prague in 1934, where he became a lecturer at the Prague School of Political Science. In 1939, when the invading Nazis closed the university, Stark left for England, where he served in the military. After the war, he taught at major British universities, including Cambridge, Edinburgh, and Manchester, until his acceptance in 1963 of a professorship at Fordham University. He stayed at Fordham until his mandatory retirement in 1975, when he returned to Europe, holding an honorary professorship at the University of Salzburg until his death.

Stark was internationally recognized for work in the sociology of religion, social theory, and sociology of knowledge. His scholarship was consistently multidisciplinary, his research constantly nourishing his teaching. A convert to Catholicism from Judaism, his adopted religion became an important influence in his life. Stark was distressed by what he considered religion's erosion in the modern world, strongly believing that religion provides guidelines for individual action that neither custom nor law can give. As he saw it, excessive individualism lay at the root of Christianity's contemporary crisis. He believed that modern intellectuals had been strongly affected by post-Renaissance rationalism, resulting in "a super-rationalism which tends to blind them towards many non-rational values, for instance, those of tradition, of religion, and even of art" (*The Sociology of Knowledge,* Routledge 1958).

In the sociology of religion, Stark considered Weber's work a challenge of great importance, although he thought Weber lacked necessary insight into "true religiosity" (*The Sociology of Religion,* 5 volumes, Fordham University Press 1966-1972). His international reputation was both reflected and built by translations of many of his works into Japanese, Italian, German, and Spanish. *The Social Bond* (6 volumes, Fordham University Press 1976-1987) is considered by some critics to be definitive in establishing his intellectual legacy, embedding "two keys to Stark's work: the cultural-sociological approach, and his faith in Catholicism" (Leonard et al. 1993:13)

—*Loretta M. Morris*

REFERENCE

E. Leonard et al., *In Search of Community* (New York: Fordham University Press 1993).

STATUS Of considerable significance for social scientific investigations of the origins, development, and decline of a wide variety of religious ideologies, movements, and institutions. Like other concepts that seek to impose *sociological* rigor on familiar *societal* terminology, *status* is subject to a number of distinct (although overlapping) usages that sometimes generate confusion.

The Legal Context In its origins in social and political philosophy, *status* is used in a predominantly *legal* sense as a crucial element in the analysis of power, authority, individual rights, and social order. It denotes a legal capacity (or limitations on such capacity) to exert rights or enforce obligations within an organized and established social framework of superordination and subordination. The high-water mark of such usage was initiated by Henry Sumner Maine's influential 1861 depiction of the *shift from status to contract* in the evolution of human societies. Although the legal aspects of status no doubt retain relevance in a number of contexts, social scientific literature has rarely employed the concept in this restricted sense since the early decades of the present century.

The Structural Context Displacement of such pioneering usage was the accomplishment of the American anthropologist Ralph Linton's structural interpretation of the concept. Appropriated by textbook sociology after World War II, it attained almost universal currency in social scientific circles, most notably in the heyday of the "structural functionalism" inspired by the writings of the Harvard sociologist Talcott Parsons. Constituting the basic analytic unit in a social system and denoting simply a *position* in a particular structure or pattern of reciprocal behavior, a status entails specifically institutionalized rights and duties. The invocation and enactment of these expectations and obligations (i.e., the pattern of appropriate behavior) is designated by the inextricably related concept of *role*. In this dramaturgical depiction, a role involves performance of a socially assigned part and thus represents the dynamic aspect of status.

Although often thought to be Parsonian in origin, the widely used *distinction between status ascription and status achievement* is an integral part of Linton's original formulation. In his founding version of this dichotomy (clearly influenced by Maine), ascribed statuses are those assigned to individuals irrespective of their innate abilities or unique personal qualities. They are occupied as a matter of inherent destiny and hereditary right on the basis of criteria ascertainable at birth, and are thereby biologically determined to a significant degree. Age, sex (gender), and kinship are the crucial and largely irrevocable determinants of status ascription. By contrast, achieved statuses are those filled on the basis of specific qualities, knowledge, or skills through individual effort and competition. In terms of a crude dichotomy between "traditional" and "modern" social types, ascription (communally embedded in custom and inheritance) is inevitably linked to the former, while achievement (generated by individual ability and mobility) is intimately associated with the latter. For a time, indeed, the term *Achieving Society* with its instant evocation of individual aspiration, ambition, and initiative served as a potent inspirational slogan among advocates of economic, political, and social modernization.

Although later proponents of a social structural conception of status introduce numerous variations to its main themes, their indebtedness to Linton's original composition is manifest. The ascription-achievement distinction has long raised theoretical and empirical questions, but in a postmodernist climate, critical of both received categories and social inequities, its assumptions may be regarded as highly problematic and provocative in some scholarly quarters.

The Hierarchical Context A hint of the hierarchical aspect of status may be inferred from Linton's acknowledgment that the term sometimes implies the sum total of an individual's statuses; that is, in this sense, it denotes an overall position in a total society. However, social scientific discussion of status as a central element in systems of hierarchy and social *stratification* had already begun a generation earlier in the writings of the pioneering German sociologist Max Weber (1864-1920). As employed by Weber, the term *status* (the usual translation of the German *Stand*) possesses precise referents intended to distinguish it clearly from the related concept of *class.* Although both class and status are aspects of the distribution of power within communities, *class is determined by the economic order and class situation is ultimately a market situation.* Although not communities in themselves, classes represent possible and frequent bases for communal action. By contrast, status is governed by the social order, that is, the way in which social honor is distributed among the various groups or segments within a community. *Status situation thus denotes* every typical component of individuals' life-fate, which is a function of a specific (positive or negative) *social estimation of honor.* Unlike classes, status groups are normally communities, although often of an amorphous kind. These express their collective sense of standing, honor, or prestige through a distinctive *style of life* that imposes various kinds and degrees of restriction on social intercourse with outsiders (e.g., endogamy). Such status distinctions and exclusions may rest purely on convention or, in a more rigid form, involve formal legal privileges and penalties. In its most extreme manifestation, status differentiation solidifies into a hermetic hierarchy of *castes* whose boundaries, duties, and privileges are prescribed by sacred rituals. Religious notions of impurity, stigma, and pollution are thus crucial to the legitimation and survival of this specific system of stratified segregation.

Grounded in a collective sense of "belonging together" and a profound hostility to the impersonal rationality of market forces, status (whether the outcome of ascription or achievement) is fundamentally different from class. Nonetheless, mutual and complex interaction of economic and social orders means that class and status distinctions are frequently interwoven even in avowedly egalitarian societies. Thus class is by no means the only significant element in modern social stratification systems, while status is in no way restricted to traditional social contexts. Use of the term *status* along essentially Weberian lines is a permanent feature of contemporary social scientific studies of stratification as well as of less rigorous characterizations of the social scene. It is a key ingredient in the more comprehensive category of *social class,* which has had wide currency among social scientists since the pioneering American investigations of W. Lloyd Warner and August B. Hollingshead.

Religion and Status In any of the usages outlined above, the concept of status may be applied in diverse religious contexts. Of broadest analytic relevance in its structural sense and most restricted in its legal application, it is most provocative when defined and employed as a component in systems of social stratification. In this respect, Weber's subtle investigation of the Hindu caste system continues to provide a paradigmatic demonstration of its utility in religiously charged situations, despite eloquent complaints that Western social scientific conceptions of stratification are entirely inadequate to the analysis of hierarchy in an Indian setting.

The recurrent role of religion in legitimating, maintaining, and perpetuating existing status hierarchies has long been rightly acknowledged in a wide range of scholarship. This vague variant on Marx's "opium of the people" thesis has, however, been increasingly complemented by a necessary recognition of the religious factor as a potentially radical threat to social order and the status quo. Likewise, although its impact is often extremely difficult to distinguish from that of class, status (as a prime ingredient of stratification) independently exerts an obvious influence on both the static and the dynamic aspects of religion. The significance of status (as either cause or effect) is so evident in such a broad comparative-historical range of religious phenomena that it has become an unquestioned assumption of contemporary social scientific investigations of topics as varied as priesthood, conversion, defection, millenarianism, sectarianism, fundamentalism, secularization, religious mobility, rites of passage, popular religiosity, and early Christianity.

The establishment of status so firmly on the modern scholarly agenda is, in no small part, the legacy of Max Weber, whose preoccupation with class, status, and other aspects of social stratification is directly related to his classic blueprint for research in the sociology of religion. By discerning the genesis of certain status distinctions within shared religious ideas and perceiving the source of various religious propensities in the situation of specific status groups, he demonstrates vital connections between religious affiliation and social stratification. His rich comparative-historical accounts of the religious tendencies of such (privileged and unprivileged) social strata as nobles, peasants, merchants, artisans, and intellectuals blend with his efforts to identify those status groups sensitive to the appeals of (ethical and exemplary) prophecy and thereby disposed to embrace novel forms of salvation religion. In tracing the elective affinities between status groups and religious orientations in specific instances, Weber underlines the reciprocity, complexity, and indeterminism of such links. That religious ideas are never a simple reflection of the social position of their proponents anymore than social statuses are ever the pure product of religious ideology is a truth that, fortunately, now constitutes part of the creed of the social scientific study of religion.

See also Karl Marx, Marxism, Roles, Stratification, Max Weber

—*Roger O'Toole*

REFERENCES

L. Dumont, *Homo Hierarchicus* (Chicago: University of Chicago Press, 1970); R. Linton, *The Study of Man* (New York: Appleton, 1936); H. S. Maine, *Ancient Law* (London: Dent, 1960 [1861]); D. C. McClelland, *The Achieving Society* (New York: Free Press, 1961); M. Milner, *Status and Sacredness* (New York: Oxford University Press, 1994); T. Parsons, *The Social System* (Glencoe, Ill.: Free Press, 1951); M. Weber, *The Religion of India* (New York: Free Press, 1958); M. Weber, *Economy and Society* (Berkeley: University of California Press, 1978).

STOICISM   *see* Self-Denial

STRATIFICATION   A structure of social inequality in which individuals and groups have an unequal share in the distribution of power, privilege, and prestige in society. Over the years, social scientists have investigated the relationship between religion and social inequality. Researchers have focused on issues such as the impact of inequality on religion, the effect of religion on inequality, and the relationship between religion and socioeconomic status.

Inequality's Effect on Religion   Research on religion and inequality has highlighted the extent to which denominations can be ranked along a status hierarchy. H. Richard Niebuhr's *The Social Sources of Denominationalism* (Holt 1929) emphasized the primacy of social rather than religious factors as the basis for the formation of religious groups. Niebuhr stressed that a group's sectlike or churchlike character was influenced by its social class standing. Sectarian groups—elective associations characterized by doctrinal purity, an emphasis on the priesthood of all believers, ethical austerity, and a high degree of tension with the dominant society—have a special appeal for the lower classes. Churchlike groups—inclusive organizations characterized by a bureaucratic organizational structure, a professional clergy, and a low degree of tension with the secular world—are preferred by the middle and upper classes.

Religious theodicies: Weber suggested that members of different social classes adopt different belief systems, or theodicies, to explain their social situation. The affluent embrace good fortune theodicies, which emphasize that prosperity is a blessing of God. Good fortune theodicies allow the successful to believe that their success is deserved and that the less fortunate also experience their due. Theodicies of misfortune, on the other hand, appeal to the poor and present a less sanguine picture of worldly success. Theodicies of misfortune emphasize that affluence is a sign of evil and that suffering in this world will be rewarded in the next. Weber suggested that this type of transvaluational orientation has been a characteristic feature of lower class worship.

Social class and religious practice: Rich and poor express their religion in different ways. The lower classes are more likely than affluent groups to pray in private, believe in the doctrines of their faith, and have intense religious experiences (Demerath 1965, Davidson 1977); the middle and upper classes are more likely to attend worship services and take part in church organizations and activities. Stark (1972) suggests that the poor show greater religiousness in those aspects of faith that serve as relief for suffering; the middle and upper classes participate in religious activities that help confirm the legitimacy of their claim to high status.

Religion and the new class: Some research suggests that transformation of the economy in the post-World War II period has facilitated a restructuring of the class basis for religion. Berger (1981) has argued that conservative-liberal religious divisions reflect a larger class conflict between two elites in America struggling for power and privilege. The old elite made up of the business class is involved in industrial production and business enterprise. The suggestion is that conservative theology tends to justify the self-interests of the business elite. A new elite made up of intellectuals, educators, social planners, and bureaucrats manages the production of ideas. Mainline theology reflects the interests of this new class (see Hargrove 1986). Berger claims that the upsurge of evangelical Protestantism is a reaction against the power grab of the new class.

Religion's Impact on Inequality A good deal of research has investigated the relationship between religion and worldly success. Following in the spirit of Weber's Protestant ethic thesis, researchers have looked at the influence of religion in promoting social mobility. Benton Johnson (1961) argued that Holiness sects socialize their adherents to dominant values of sobriety, self-reliance, and hard work, which works to improve the members' socioeconomic standing. A number of studies have looked at the effect of Catholic or Protestant affiliation on economic achievement. Gerhard Lenski's *The Religious Factor* (Doubleday 1961) indicated that Protestants were more likely than Catholics to rise in the economic system, especially at the upper-middle-class level. Other research, however, suggests a Protestant-Catholic convergence on socioeconomic indicators (Glenn and Hyland 1967). Andrew Greeley (1981) has argued that Catholics rank above Episcopalians and Presbyterians in income, although W. Clark Roof (1979) has disputed this claim. The consensus is that Protestant-Catholic socioeconomic differences have largely vanished (Roof and McKinney 1987).

Legitimating function of religion: Both Karl Marx and Max Weber emphasized that religion performs a legitimating function for members of the dominant class, whereas it provides a means of escape for members of subordinate classes. Weber's discussion of theodicies of good fortune and misfortune indicated how religion can sanctify the status quo and mollify those at the bottom of the social structure. Marx argued that religion serves to reinforce the power of ruling groups by providing heavenly sanction for existing social conditions. A Marxist perspective stresses that those with wealth and power can do much to control the belief system of the society, and they appropriate religious ideas that legitimate current forms of inequality (Howe 1981). Each ruling class constructs an ideological expression of its outlook on life. Marx believed that Protestant theology, which served the interests of the bourgeoisie, discouraged workers from efforts at social, political, and economic change. He claimed that for the proletariat, religion is a narcotic that dulls their understanding of their life experiences.

Liston Pope's study of a mill town in North Carolina, *Millhands and Preachers* (Yale University Press 1942), vividly illustrated how religion can serve to legitimate current forms of inequality. Pope described how uptown churches validated prevailing economic arrangements, whereas mill churches provided workers with a form of escape from the harshness of life. Gary Marx (1967), looking at religiosity and militancy among blacks, found that high levels of religious involvement for blacks were associated with low levels of militancy on civil rights issues. His study also indicated that an other-worldly emphasis was negatively related to race protest.

Researchers have looked at the degree to which religious beliefs sanctify inequality by promoting harsh attitudes toward the poor. Weber (1958 [1904-1905]) argued that a Calvinist doctrine of predestination served as legitimation for inequality by advocating the view that success was a sign of divine favor and poverty an indication of moral failing. Feagin (1975) has suggested that Calvinist views served as inspiration and legitimation for a judgmental stance toward the poor. Rokeach (1969) has argued that Christian values are associated with austere attitudes toward the impoverished, and Tropman (1986) suggests that a Protestant ethic has encouraged condemnation of those who require public assistance.

Prophetic function of religion: Religion is not just a force that perpetuates the status quo. Religion also can serve a prophetic function, promoting social action to redress society's ills. Clergy involvement in the civil rights movement in the United States (Morris 1984) and in liberation theology in Latin America (Adriance 1986, Neal 1987) illustrates the degree to which religion can play an important role in supporting social change movements.

Prophetic action often takes place in the context of autonomy; when groups experience a degree of autonomy from dominant institutions, they are able to critique the larger structure and promote strategies for system reform (Demerath and Hammond 1969). Burns (1992) notes that Catholic clergy adopted liberal social teachings when separated from the papal state. Davidson (1985) has suggested that advocacy groups, such as the Lafayette Urban Ministry, that draw resources mainly from churches and not the state are able to propose reform measures and social programs at odds with conservative state policies.

When clergy are not dependent on elites for their livelihood, they have greater opportunities to mobilize for social transformation. Billings's (1990) analysis of union activity among Appalachian miners showed that clergy who were dependent upon coal operators for their employment were ready to preach about the evils of unionism. Autonomous miner-ministers, however, rejected the doctrines espoused in company churches and played a leadership role in promoting union activity. When clergy have a measure of job security and are not dependent on a local congregation for their employment, they have greater opportunities to speak prophetically. Because of their tenured status, Catholic bishops can issue progressive social pronouncements, such as their 1986 pastoral letter on economic justice, that are somewhat critical of dominant institutions and policies. The anonymity that Protestant officials enjoy allows them to take progressive stands on social policy issues.

At times, religion is associated with a tendency for some laypeople to adopt egalitarian views and champion the cause of the poor. Tropman (1986) has suggested that a Catholic ethic, unlike a Protestant ethic, promotes a sense of compassion for the poor and instills support for social welfare activities. Pyle (1993) found that members of Pentecostal-Holiness groups were more likely than mainline Protestants to support governmental efforts to help the poor and reduce income inequality. Mock (1988) has suggested that theodicies of social justice can work to eradicate poverty.

Religion and Socioeconomic Status　Religious groups can be differentiated according to the socioeconomic standing of their members. The first comprehensive studies of denominational socioeconomic rankings were conducted in the 1940s (Cantril 1943, Pope 1948). These early studies showed that colonial mainline Protestants (Episcopalians, Presbyterians, and Congregationalists), Jews, and Unitarians were located in the upper socioeconomic ranks; moderate Protestants (such as Methodists and Lutherans) were located in the middle; and Catholics and evangelical Protestants occupied the bottom ranks. With a few exceptions, this relative ranking persists today. Groups representative of the colonial mainline continue to rank at the upper levels in terms of education, income, and occupational prestige, whereas sectarian bodies such as the Churches of God rank much lower on socioeconomic indicators (Roof and McKinney 1987).

However, there has been some change in denominational socioeconomic rankings in the last 50 years. The greatest status change has occurred among Roman Catholics, who moved from the bottom socioeconomic levels to the middle ranks during the post-World War II era. Catholics in the 1940s ranked below Protestants on socioeconomic indicators (Cantril 1943), but by the 1960s Catholic-Protestant socioeconomic differences were negligible (Glenn and Hyland 1967). Jews, well positioned during the 1940s, have improved their socioeconomic standing during the post-World War II years and now rank at the top in terms of socioeconomic status. Mormons also have experienced social and economic gains. Over the long term, Methodists have shown the most dramatic gains, rising from sectarian origins in the nineteenth century to middle-class status by the twentieth (Finke and Stark 1992).

Religion among America's elite:　Researchers have analyzed the religious affiliation of American leaders to ascertain the degree to which an older Protestant Establishment has given way to a more representative ordering of religious groups among the elite. Studies of the religious preferences of individuals listed in *Who's Who* during the 1930-1992 period indicate that the rankings of religious groups among the elite largely reflect the status rankings of religious groups among the general population (Davidson et al. 1995). From the depression era until the present, colonial mainline groups have been overrepresented among Americans listed in *Who's Who,* but Catholics and Jews have made substantial gains since 1930. Baptists and sectarians, however, remain underrepresented among American elites. The colonial mainline is especially overrepresented among elites in business-political spheres, and Jews are especially prominent among elites in cultural-intellectual realms (Pyle 1996).

Research looking at the differential representation of religious groups among the elite suggests that religion exerts an influence in three areas that affect movement to the leadership ranks: educational admissions, occupational selection, and career mobility (Pyle 1996). Although religious quotas at prestigious private colleges have been eliminated, mainline Protestants (and now Jews) are highly overrepresented among elites reporting degrees from Ivy League schools. Legacy admissions at elite colleges (preferential admissions given to children of alumni) work to perpetuate the advantages of historically dominant religious groups. Some studies indicate that religion continues to play a role in job selection and promotion at the upper levels of the business-legal hierarchy. There is evidence of a lingering Gentile-Jewish divide in big business and commercial banking (Korman 1988). Persisting religious discrimination in admissions at exclusive private clubs limits non-WASPs' participation in important areas of social interplay that affect career mobility. Insider-outsider distinctions based on religion continue to play a role in perpetuating denominational differences among the elite.

Research on stratification and religion is guided by contradictory theoretical perspectives, but studies consistently highlight the degree to which religion influences and is influenced by social inequality. The consensus is that social factors play an important role in perpetuating America's religious mosaic.

See also Mobility, Preferential Option for the Poor, Status

—*Ralph E. Pyle and James D. Davidson*

REFERENCES

M. Adriance, *Opting for the Poor* (Kansas City, Mo.: Sheed & Ward, 1986); P. L. Berger, "The Class Struggle in American Religion," *Christian Century* 98(1981):194-199; D. B. Billings, "Religion as Opposition," *American Journal of Sociology* 96(1990):1-31; G. Burns, *The Frontiers of Catholicism* (Berkeley: University of California Press, 1992); H. Cantril, "Educational and Economic Composition of Religious Groups," *American Journal of Sociology* 47(1943):574-579; J. D. Davidson, "Socio-Economic Status and Ten Dimensions of Religious Commitment," *Sociology and Social Research* 61(1977):462-485; J. D. Davidson, *Mobilizing Social Movement Organizations* (Storrs, Conn.: Society for the Scientific Study of Religion, 1985); J. D. Davidson, "Religion Among America's Elite," *Sociology of Religion* 55(1994):419-440; J. D. Davidson et al., "Persistence and Change in the Protestant Establishment," *Social Forces* 74(1995):157-175; N. J. Demerath III, *Social Class in American Protestantism* (Chicago: Rand McNally, 1965); N. J. Demerath III and P. E. Hammond, *Religion in Social Context* (New York: Random House, 1969); J. R. Feagin, *Subordinating the Poor* (Englewood Cliffs, N.J.: Prentice Hall, 1975); R. Finke and R. Stark, *The Churching of America* (New Brunswick, N.J.: Rutgers University Press, 1992); N. D. Glenn and R. Hyland, "Religious Preference and Worldly Success," *American Sociological Review* 32(1967):73-85; A. M. Greeley, "Catholics and the Upper Middle Class," *Social Forces* 59(1981):824-830; B. W. Hargrove, *The Emerging New Class* (New York: Pilgrim, 1986); G. N. Howe, "The Political Economy of American Religion," in *Political Economy,* ed. S. McNall (Glenview, Ill.: Scott, Foresman, 1981): 110-137; B. Johnson, "Do Holiness Sects Socialize in Dominant Values?" *Social Forces* 39(1961):309-316; A. K. Korman, *The Outsiders* (Lexington, Mass.: Lexington, 1988); G. T. Marx, "Religion," *American Sociological Review* 32(1967):64-72; A. K. Mock, *Social Differentiation and Individual Belief,* Doctoral dissertation, Purdue University, 1988; A. D. Morris, *The Origins of the Civil Rights Movement* (New York: Free Press, 1984); M. A. Neal, *The Just Demands of the Poor* (New York: Paulist Press, 1987); L. Pope, "Religion and the Class Structure," *Annals* 256(1948):84-91; R. E. Pyle, "Faith and Commitment to the Poor," *Sociology of Religion* 54(1993): 385-401; R. E. Pyle, *Persistence and Change in the Protestant Establishment* (Westport, Conn.: Praeger, 1996); M. Rokeach, "Religious Values and Social Compassion," *Review of Religious Research* 11(1969):24-39; W. C. Roof, "Socioeconomic Differentials Among White Socioreligious Groups in the United States," *Social Forces* 58(1979):280-289; W. C. Roof and W. McKinney, *American Mainline Religion* (New Brunswick, N.J.: Rutgers University Press, 1987); R. Stark, "The Economics of Piety," in *Issues in Social Inequality,* ed. G. Thielbar and S. Feldman (Boston: Little Brown, 1972): 483-503; J. E. Tropman, "The 'Catholic Ethic' versus the 'Protestant Ethic' " *Social Thought* 12(1986):13-22; M. Weber, *The Protestant Ethic and the Spirit of Capitalism* (New York: Scribner, 1958 [1904-1905]).

STRUCTURAL FUNCTIONALISM *see* Functionalism, Robert K. Merton

SUBSIDIARITY Although now one of the core terms in Catholic social thought, to expect for the term *subsidiarity* any substantive content or any specific rule for its application would be a case of misplaced concreteness. The term captures the aspiration that polities and administrations have responsibilities for "distributive justice" in ways that promote "social" or "participatory" justice.

Subsidiarity is used when critiquing statist solutions to the distribution of social goods because they absorb the "mediating" institutions and groups that ensure the human scale required for pluralism and local initiative. In turn, unregulated market solutions to the distribution of social goods are criticized for their monopolistic outcomes and tendency to convert market control into political monopoly. In practice, Catholic teaching employs the term pragmatically to critique whatever tendency distortive of the common good—collectivist statism or economistic laissez faire—predominates in a particular political-economic period. In the present era, the principle of subsidiarity is most often used to critique the failure of polities in market-driven economies sufficiently to help regional or local losers and the tendencies of Western liberal democracies, not always intentionally, to extract subordination as the price paid for their foreign aid.

Subsidiarity has clear affinities with all those social science conceptions that self-consciously consider themselves "communitarian." Its core meaning involves the moral duty for centralized authorities to intervene in nonhegemonic ways that preserve and even enhance the pluralisms of civil society and the culture of individual initiative. This core meaning is analogously applied along the continuum of micro-macro organizational life, from family to geopolitics. Since its first explicit appearance in Pius XI's encyclical *Quadragesimo Anno* (1931), subsidiarity has been employed in most of the significant social justice documents produced by the Roman Catholic hierarchy in the remainder of the twentieth century.

With the term, Pius XI crystallized the cluster of moral judgments emerging in Catholic social thought dialectically seeking to conjoin the individual liberty prized by liberal capitalism with the concern for social justice animating Marxist communism:

> Just as it is gravely wrong to take from individuals what they can accomplish by their own initiative and industry and give it to the community, so also it is an injustice and at the same time a grave evil and disturbance of right order to assign to a greater or higher association what lesser and subordinate organizations can do. For every social activity ought of its very nature to furnish help to the members of the body social, and never destroy and absorb them.

Some recent critical applications of the term *subsidiarity* can be found in the American bishops' proposals for economic reform in their 1986 pastoral letter *Economic Justice for All* and in the March 16, 1995, critique by the Administrative Board of the U.S. Catholic Conference of the "Contract with America" Republican 1995 welfare reforms, which, although couched in a "subsidiaritylike" language of block grants, violate the principle of subsidiarity because they dissolve federal responsibility for ensuring a minimum level of economic rights and offer no increased likelihood of making the poor participants in and contributors to the social order.

In addition to being an appreciative explication of the principle and its historical context, Bellah (1991) shows the affinities between *subsidiarity* and cognate terms in social science, such as the more familiar terms *populism* and *federalism,* and some of the more academic ones, such as the Habermasian project of *discourse ethics* aimed at preserving *life-worlds* found in *social orders* from the *colonization* inherent in *social systems.*

—*James R. Kelly*

REFERENCES

M. E. Allsopp, "Principle of Subsidiarity," in *The New Dictionary of Catholic Social Thought,* ed. J. A. Dwyer (Collegeville, Minn.: Liturgical Press, 1994): 927-929; R. N. Bellah, "The Importance of Catholic Social Teaching for Envisioning the Good Society," *New Oxford Review* (Nov. 1991): 8-16; F. H. Mueller, "The Principle of Subsidiarity in the Christian Tradition," *American Catholic Sociological Review* 4(1943):144-157.

SUBSTANTIVE DEFINITIONS　　　*see* Definition of Religion

SUFISM　　*see* Islam

SUPERNATURAL　　A certain type of theology (or atheism) will identify the supernatural with divinity; in ordinary speech, especially since the 1960s, it means the "mysterious." David Martin (1969) pointed out the coincidence of a particular understanding of "religion" and of assumptions regarding the inevitability of "secularization": This understanding assumed the universality of dichotomies, such as that between the natural and the supernatural, which were peculiarly associated with the Platonic strand within the Western form of the Christian religion.

Thus the attention given to, and the meaning attributed to, the "supernatural," by the (ideological and/or academic) exponent of secularism has tended to be culture-specific, if not eccentric, from the point of view of the "ordinary person," whether in the pew or not. For most people, religion has been and is, on the whole, both natural and normal.

The definition of *super-natural* inevitably begs the question of the meaning of *natural.* A mechanistic worldview will impute to it "personal tinkering." A less dichotomized worldview will see it as "focused significance." Just as "religion is not so much different from the rest of life, but life at its most intense" (Cook 1918), so "there is nothing so natural as the supernatural" (Oman 1931).

Between these two understandings of religion and the supernatural lies the current popular meaning of the latter: those puzzling but rather secular happenings that mundane science cannot explain.

—*Edward I. Bailey*

REFERENCES

S. A. Cook, "Religion," in *Encyclopaedia of Religion and Ethics* (Edinburgh: Clark, 1918): 667-693; D. A. Martin, *The Religious and the Secular* (London: SCM, 1969); J. Oman, *The Natural and the Supernatural* (Cambridge: Cambridge University Press, 1931).

SURROGATES FOR RELIGION　　Attempts to define *religion* have usually discussed the inclusion/exclusion of marginal phenomena. Examples commonly include a sport or the stars of entertainment (baseball or Elvis Presley in the United States, football or the monarchy in the United Kingdom) and various political and/or philosophical systems, such as the "isms" (communism following World War II, then nationalism), and an atheistic or nontheistic system that is already generally recognized as religious (Hinayana or Southern Buddhism). Such examples tend to be grouped together as "surrogate religions," "quasi-religions," "pseudo-religions"— or, rather more circumspectly, as "functional alternatives to religion."

Contrary, perhaps, to expectation, social scientists, on the one hand, and historians or phenomenologists of religion, on the other hand, do not neatly divide, by profession, into inclusivists and exclusivists. Social scientists sometimes fear "calling everything religious, since 'religious' would then be meaningless," and historians of religion sometimes speak of "false religions." However, "straw opponents" do not advance any discussion. The inclusivist suggests "any"-thing "may" be (not, "every"-thing "is") religious, and the exclusivist insists on the necessity of recognizing the irreducibility of the sacred—to recognize the depths that are experienced within reality, both religious and secular.

—*Edward I. Bailey*

REFERENCES

U. Bianchi, *The History of Religions* (Leiden: Brill, 1975); M. L. Bringle, *The God of Thinness* (Nashville: Abingdon, 1992); S. Brown, *Secular Alternatives to Religion* (Milton Keynes, U.K.: Open University Press, 1978); J. E. Smith, *Quasi-Religions* (New York: St Martin's, 1994); J. M. Yinger, *The Scientific Study of Religion* (New York, Macmillan, 1970).

SWAGGART, JIMMY   *see* Televangelism

SWANSON, GUY E. (1922-1995)   Sociologist of religion and social psychologist who spent most of his career at the University of Michigan and then the University of California, Berkeley.

Swanson investigated how different types of social relations affect the formation of ultimate values and personal development. He combined Émile Durkheim's emphasis on representational parallelism with Max Weber's emphasis on forms of power/authority (*Herrschaft*) to account for variations in beliefs and practices. With the book *The Birth of the Gods: The Origin of Primitive Beliefs* (University of Michigan Press 1967), involving the rise of belief in the supernatural, he argued in Durkheimian fashion that belief in spirits represents experiences with the constitutional structure of sovereign groups. Using data on premodern societies, he demonstrated relations between types of constitutional structure and varieties of belief. He found that high gods appear where a government coordinates other kinds of organization: "Monotheism is positively related to the presence of a hierarchy of three or more sovereign groups in a society."

In *Religion and Regime: A Sociological Account of the Reformation* (University of Michigan Press 1968), Swanson attempted to explain why only some European societies adopted Protestantism in the sixteenth century. He argued that Catholics think God is immanent in the world. He considered regimes "immanent" if they implement their own distinctive purposes rather than serve private interests. His finding was that immanent European regimes tended to remain Catholic; the more constituent bodies of a community had a role in governing (thus making its regime "transcendent"), the more likely a regime was to adopt Protestantism and its more transcendent God.

Swanson thought that ultimate values arise in the experiences of human beings with each other and their society. Such values vary according to whether a society operates like a system or like an association. As societies secularize, specialized religious communities lose influence in formulating ultimate values but previously secular institutions take on greater roles in a sacred order.

—*Frank J. Lechner*

REFERENCES

G. E. Swanson, "Modern Secularity," in *The Religious Situation,* ed. D. Cutler (Boston: Beacon, 1968): 801-834; G. E. Swanson, "Life with God," *Journal for the Scientific Study of Religion* 10(1971):169-199; G. E. Swanson, "Immanence and Transcendence," *Sociological Analysis* 47(1986):189-213; "Symposium on the Work of Guy E. Swanson," *Sociological Analysis* 45(1984):177-222.

SYMBOLIC REALISM   A framework for analyzing and understanding the role of religion in human life. Originally put forward by Robert Bellah (1970), this framework has informed much work within the study of religion, although the term itself has not been broadly used.

Symbolic realism provides a counterpoint to what Bellah calls the "symbolic reductionism" of some social scientific study of religion. Rooted in a cognitivist bias of some strands of Western intellectual culture, symbolic reductionists understand religious symbols as myth-ridden attempts to express truths that science can better express and substantiate. Such reductionism often reveals itself when social science strives to model itself narrowly on the natural sciences, rather than understanding its position as a middle ground between the humanities and the natural sciences. Examples of such reductionism include a materialist understanding of religion as simply a reflection of economic contradictions and social struggles, or a psychoanalytic view of religious striving as simply projected psychological tensions.

Symbolic realism counters this reductionist view by drawing on Alfred Schutz's (1962) understanding of the multiple realities in which human beings live, some of which transcend the everyday, objective realities. Symbolic realism sees religious symbolism as expressing a dimension of human experience that does not so much contradict everyday life or objectivist analysis as transcend them; religious symbols simply cannot be analyzed in those terms. It insists that religious symbols express a truth of their own regarding the ultimate grounds of human existence or, as many human communities have come to conceive of those grounds, regarding God.

—*Richard L. Wood*

REFERENCES

R. N. Bellah, *Beyond Belief* (New York: Harper, 1970); G. A. Lindbeck, *The Nature of Doctrine* (Philadelphia: Westminster, 1984); A. Schutz, *Collected Papers*, Vol. 1 (The Hague, Neth.: Nijhoff, 1962).

SYMBOLS   A signifier or thing that represents something else. As cultural beings, humans are symbol-using creatures. This reality has prompted many anthropologists and sociologists to recognize the relationship between religion and symbols. The social scientific study of religion tends to concern itself with symbols of a nonempirical world, notably those present in cosmologies and rituals. Religious symbols entail both intellectual and emotional significance to the people who hold them. Religion is made up either of symbols or of activities that are mediated by symbols.

E. E. Evans-Pritchard (1902-1973) rejected the positivist orientation of British social anthropology with his emphasis on symbolic analysis. In his monographs on two Sudanese populations—the Azande and the Nuer—he explored the symbolic coherence of various religious beliefs. In *Nuer Religion* (Clarendon 1956), Evans-Pritchard insists that the Nuer distinguish clearly between the natural and the supernatural. For example, a particular individual or group may symbolically refer to a crocodile or some other animal as Spirit to conceptualize their respective association with the Spirit. The Nuer, however, do not believe that animals are Spirits.

Like Evans-Pritchard, the anthropologist Clifford Geertz eschews grand theory. He believes it is the task of the anthropologist to interpret the web of significances within which humans find themselves embedded as cultural creatures. The process of "thick description" will reveal the fact that any aspect of human behavior has more than one meaning. In a seminal article, Geertz regards religion as part of a cultural system. He defines "culture" as "historically transmitted patterns of meanings embodied in symbols—a system of inherited conceptions expressed in symbolic forms" (1966:3). He defines "religion" as

(1) a system of symbols which acts to (2) establish powerful, pervasive, and long-lasting moods and motivations in men by (3) formulating conceptions of a general order of existence and (4) clothing these conceptions with such an aura of factuality that (5) the moods and motivations seem uniquely realistic.

In other words, religion defines the cosmos in such a manner that people know how to respond to it. As a symbolic system, religion orders the universe, thereby eliminating chaos, ambiguity, and helplessness. Religion provides an ultimate answer as it explains the otherwise incomprehensible. According to Geertz, religious symbols fuse multiple referents, thus enabling believers to accept or affirm their existence even when their experiences contradict one another. In *Islam Observed* (University of Chicago Press 1968), he interprets the lives and symbolic representations of two religious leaders, one from Morocco and another from Indonesia.

The anthropologist Victor Turner (1920-1983) significantly contributed to the study of ritual symbols. He analyzed the healing rituals of the Ndembu of northern Zambia (1961). Turner defines a symbol as a "storage unit," the basic unit or "molecule" of ritual behavior. Ritual symbols contain the property of "condensation" in that they allow for the ready relation of emotional tension in various ways. Ritual symbols also are "multivocal" in that they may represent many things. Multivocality endows ceremonies, even those of the simplest form, with multiple levels of meaning, with referents from cosmology to social relations. Turner essentially portrays ritual as a set of symbolic actions and displays of symbolic objects that represent the premises, core values, and norms of a particular culture. In his books *The Ritual Process* (Aldine 1969) and

Dramas, Fields, and Metaphors (Cornell University Press 1974), Turner maintains that humans alternate between socially structured behavior and situations of liminality or nonstructure. Symbols of liminality serve to reinforce rather than to challenge structure. According to Turner (1969:95), the liminal phase exhibits "an unstructured or rudimentarily structured and relatively undifferentiated comitatus, community, or even communion of equal individuals who submit together to the general authority of the ritual elders." Liminality and communitas entail a merging of the symbols of the self and symbols of the sacred other.

In *Purity and Danger: An Analysis of Concepts of Pollution and Taboo* (Routledge 1966), the anthropologist Mary Douglas examines the relation of particular ritual acts to the symbolic meanings of different parts of the human body emphasized in the actions. She regards pollution beliefs as metaphorical statements about the natural and social order. By attaching efficacy to symbols and forms of behavior, pollution beliefs with their accompanying taboos and purification rites manifest a magical attitude. Like her mentor, E. E. Evans-Pritchard, Douglas fears that anthropology as an endeavor of demystification may destroy the rich meaning of religious symbolism. In *Natural Symbols* (Pantheon 1970), she argues that symbols in both indigenous and civilized societies assume salience in groups that possess rigid social boundaries. Conversely, symbols are diffuse in groups where social boundaries are weak.

The anthropologist Edmund Leach (1972) views rituals as "storage systems" that carry powerful symbols and transmit a worldview and ethos. In a somewhat similar vein, Peter Berger, a phenomenological sociologist, maintains in *The Sacred Canopy* (Doubleday 1967, p. 22) that people "are congenitally compelled to impose a meaningful order upon reality." He argues that religious symbols and systems offer explanations and rationales for the maintenance of the cultural order that include explanations of suffering with different types of theodicy such as karma and millenarianism. Berger portrays religion as a protective cover for the cultural construction and maintenance of reality. Thomas Luckmann, a close associate of Berger, uses an approach to religion that also emphasizes meaning. In *The Invisible Religion* (Macmillan 1967), Luckmann asserts that religions constitute the institutionalization of the general process by which a "symbolic universe" is socially constructed and related to everyday social life. Symbolic universes function as systems of meaning that bring social reality into relation with a transcendent reality.

Whereas most studies of religious symbols have adopted an interpretive or phenomenological orientation, prior to the heyday of symbolic anthropology, Eric Wolf, a leading proponent of a political economic perspective within anthropology, attempted to situate the symbolism of the Virgin of Guadalupe into the context of the Mexican nation-state. He refers to the Virgin of Guadalupe as a "master symbol" that "seems to enshrine the major hopes and aspirations of an entire society" (1958:34). Wolf posits connections between the Guadalupe symbol and several sets of social relationships. At the familial level, for example, the Guadalupe symbol is associated with a desire to return to the comfort that a Mexican mother provides to her offspring. For Mexicans of Indian descent, the Guadalupe symbol validates their right to legal rights, citizenship, supernatural salvation as well as salvation from social oppression. According to Wolf (p. 38), "The Guadalupe symbol thus links together family, politics and religion: colonial past and independent present; Indian and Mexican. . . . It provides a cultural idiom through which the tenor and emotions of these relationships can be expressed."

In her ethnography of a specific indigenous group in Mexico, Barbara G. Myerhoff analyzes the deer-maize-peyote symbol complex in her book *Peyote Hunt: The Sacred Journal of the Huichol Indians* (Cornell University Press 1974). She argues that the deer symbolizes an earlier foraging stage among the Huichol while maize symbolism concerns their present efforts to function as agriculturalists within the Mexican economy. Peyote symbolically resolves the dialectic between foraging and agrarian modes of subsistence by allowing the Huichol to return to their aboriginal homeland and culture during the annual Peyote Hunt, a symbolic recreation of their primordial past when humans and the gods, plants and animals, the natural and the supernatural, and men and women coexisted in harmony. During the peyote pilgrimage, humans become gods and the social distinctions of age, gender, ritual status, and family are eradicated.

In his book *Kwaio Religion* (Columbia University Press 1982), about the religious system of a Melanesian horticultural society, Roger Keesing provides a sobering critique of symbolic anthropological studies of religion. He maintains that symbolic anthropologists tend to adopt an essentialist view when they impute meanings to a culture when any population exhibits differential understandings. Keesing asserts that "ritual symbols, like other cultural symbols, *evoke* meanings, which may depend on who individuals are, what they have experienced, and what they know" (p. 185). In the case of Kwaio society, he observes that whereas religious specialists often exhibit extensive knowledge of the grammar of religious symbolism, "most Kwaio see only segments and elements" (p. 207). Conversely, a ritual specialist may demonstrate detailed knowledge of how to conduct a ritual without fully comprehending its symbolism. Keesing maintains that the view that ritual constitutes a system of communication predisposes anthropologists to seek meanings when in reality the natives of a particular culture engage in ritual primarily as a mode of action directed at specific social ends. He criticizes symbolic anthropologists for their common failure to recognize the fact that indigenous religions and societies have histories that are embedded in political-economic realities, including ones shaped by an ever-expanding capitalist world system. According to Keesing,

> Religious systems like that of the Kwaio do not simply infuse human life with meaning. Like other ideological systems they serve political ends as well: maintaining relations of dominance and submission, power and privilege. Ideologies of women's pollution and men's control of sacred knowledge may serve, as in many New Guinean societies, to sustain male subordination and exploitation. Ideologies in New Guinea that semen is necessary for growth sustain male homosexual cults in which seniors dominate, brutalize, and sexually exploit juniors. . . . A symbolist anthropology is necessary; but we cannot let it blind us to earthly political and economic relationships by a wave of the analytical wand, telling ourselves that meanings are shared. (p. 245)

—*Hans A. Baer*

REFERENCES

C. Geertz, "Religion as a Cultural System," in *Anthropological Approaches to the Study of Religion*, ed. M. Banton (London: Tavistock, 1966): 1-46; E. Leach, "Ritualization in Man in Relation to Conceptual and Social Development," in *Reader in Comparative Religion*, 3rd ed., ed. W. A. Lessa and E. Z. Vogt (New York: Harper, 1972): 333-337; V. Turner, *Ndembu Divination* (Manchester: Manchester University Press, 1961); E. Wolf, "The Virgin of Guadalupe," *Journal of American Folklore* 46(1958):34-39.

SYNCRETISM   Syncretism combines heterogeneous beliefs, usually uncritically. The term was first used by Plutarch (*De fraterno amore,* 19) for the fusion of religious cults that was common in the ancient world—as in gnosticism and the Hermetic literature. Theosophy exemplifies the same tendency in modern times, although it is probably found everywhere there is contact between different religions. For example, to claim to be at once Muslim and Buddhist is to forget that Muslims believe passionately in God, whereas Buddhists are indifferently agnostic about the matter. However, apparently contradictory beliefs need not actually be so; "God does not exist," meaning there is no white-bearded gentleman in the sky, does not contradict "God exists" in the sense that there is that than which none greater can be conceived. Christians who learn from Confucianists or Marxists about, for example, the moral implications of their own beliefs should not necessarily be stigmatized as syncretist in an abusive sense.

—*Hugo Meynell*

REFERENCES

J. D. Gort et al. (eds.), *Dialogue and Syncretism* (Grand Rapids, Mich.: Eerdmans, 1989); J. Hick, *God and the Universe of Faiths* (London: Macmillan, 1988).

SYSTEMS THEORY   The concept of system as a boundary-maintaining set of elements in interdependent relationships can be applied to various levels of social life (Buckley 1967). One example is structural-functional theory, dominant in the United States during the 1950s and early 1960s, which emphasized the function of religion as a basic institution that helps contribute to social integration through fulfilling the need for shared values (Parsons 1971). This consensual model has proved to be inadequate. Although the role of religion may vary for different segments of society, religion as a framework of ultimate meaning that helps provide structure for collective life is still recognized (Luhmann 1984). Moreover, religious organizations themselves may be analyzed as systems—each congregation, for example, being regarded as a system that is part of an even larger system (Scherer 1980). The systems theory emphasis on varying degrees and forms of interdependence also may be used in analyzing the role of religion in the emerging global order (Robertson 1991).

—*Doyle Paul Johnson*

REFERENCES

W. Buckley, *Sociology and Modern Systems Theory* (Englewood Cliffs, N.J.: Prentice Hall, 1967); N. Luhmann, *Religious Dogmatics and the Evolution of Societies* (Lewiston, N.Y.: Mellen, 1984); T. Parsons, *The System of Modern Societies* (Englewood Cliffs, N.J.: Prentice Hall, 1971); R. Robertson, *Religion and Global Order* (New York: International Religious Foundation, 1991); R. P. Scherer, *American Denominational Organization* (Pasadena, Calif.: William Carey Library, 1980).

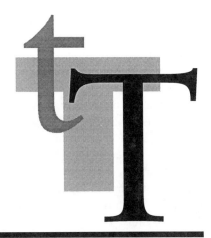

TABOO Also *tabu, tapu, kapu;* a prohibition of acts and/or contacts dangerous to the doer and his or her group.

Captain James Cook first heard the word in 1777 at Tonga and found the idea of taboo even more prevalent on the Sandwich Islands. Cook discovered that the term had wide usage among various groups in the South Pacific, signifying that a thing is forbidden. Violation of some taboos was punishable by death. When social scientists began the study of religions, the term was used to indicate the cautions set up by groups to guard against behavior or objects thought to be spiritually dangerous.

Taboo stands for all fear-inspired inhibitions proceeding from religious beliefs. The social scientific meaning focuses on supernatural penalties and reduces emphasis on human sanctions. Violation of group codes or contact with sources of infection is considered to be an immediate threat to the individual. He or she acquires a contagion that might spread to the whole group. Groups tend to be more concerned with purification rather than punishment. Coming into contact with a certain object or situation requires special rituals in order for the individual to be safe for social relations.

Many taboos are associated with blood and death. In many societies, corpses are thought to have contagious qualities that require destruction or abandonment of objects that touched them. Relatives and mourners may require purification rituals before normal life can resume. Blood from menstruation or childbirth is often taboo, requiring isolation and purification rituals for those in contact.

R. R. Marett conducted a psychological study of taboos in *The Threshold of Religion* (Methuen 1909). J. G. Frazer included a volume, *Taboo and the Perils of the Soul,* in Part II of *The Golden Bough* (St. Martin's 1990 [1913]). Sigmund Freud, stimulated in part by Frazer's work, attempted to relate primitive taboos to psychoneurosis in *Totem and Taboo* (Moffat 1919). Although Freud's efforts were naive from an anthropological vantage point, his theories had profound impacts on his followers.

Taboos often function to support status hierarchies. For example, women may be prohibited from eating certain foods or touching certain objects. Those who might violate a prohibition are placed in a weakened position because they might unknowingly be bringing bad fortune to the group.

Modern anthropologists such as Marvin Harris (1993) note that taboos diminish dissent, compel conformity, and resolve ambiguities. These qualities allow taboos to fulfill both social and ecological functions. The incest taboo, which prohibits sexual relationships within culturally proscribed kin relationships, prevents people from succumbing to temptations that would bring short-term satisfaction but long-term negative consequences. Because of the incest taboo, family members are prohibited from dysfunctional activities and directed toward mating behaviors that establish beneficial relationships with outside groups. The taboo's religious quality removes doubts and ambiguities that might otherwise occur. Incest taboos do not stop all prohibited behavior, but they bring doubts and psychological conflicts under more effective social control.

Harris argues that prohibitions against eating pork or beef fulfill similar positive functions. In areas where deforestation has occurred, such as in the Middle East, the raising of pigs became ecologically unsound. As a consequence, the ancient Israelites prohibited the consumption of pork, removing the temptation to engage in that ecologically damaging activity. Once in existence, the prohibition against eating pork (and other foods) became a means of demarcating Jewish from non-Jewish groups and of establishing group identity and solidarity. Taboos against eating beef in India fulfill similar functions. By using cows only for traction power and as a source of fertilizer, the land could be used more efficiently for raising grain fed mainly to humans.

In summary, the word *taboo* has a variety of connotations. The South Pacific word was redefined by social scientists. The term also has acquired a broader definition within general language to mean "forbidden by traditional or general usage."

—*James McClenon*

REFERENCES

J. Cook, *A Voyage to the Pacific Ocean* (London: Nicol and Cadell, 1784); M. Harris, *Culture, People, Nature*, 6th ed. (New York: Harper, 1993).

TAMNEY, JOSEPH B(ERNARD PAUL) (1933–)
Professor of Sociology, Ball State University (Muncie, Indiana); editor *Sociology of Religion*, 1995-2000.

Tamney's research in the sociology of religion has focused on the reasons for religiosity and on religious change. His publications emphasize a cross-cultural approach that is equally amenable to both quantitative and qualitative data. He works comfortably in the study of contemporary Christianity and in East Asian traditions. His major book-length studies are *The Resilience of Christianity in the Modern World* (SUNY Press 1992), an account of the persistence of Christian belief and practice in contradistinction to predictions of secularization theories, and *American Society in the Buddhist Mirror* (Garland 1992), an assessment of the appeal of Buddhism in the United States.

Tamney has published extensively in the major journals in the social scientific study of religion. His articles on religion in the United States emphasize religion-and-politics issues—the religious right generally and abortion-related topics specifically. Because Muncie is the locale of the historic "Middletown" studies conducted by the Lynds in the 1920s and 1930s, a significant portion of his research has used that site as a database. In non-U.S. settings, Tamney is a recognized authority on the sociology of Islam in Indonesia, the most populous Islamic country. He has also written on Confucianism, Taoism, and Buddhism in East Asia generally and in Singapore specifically. Tamney has traveled extensively in Singapore, Malaysia, and Indonesia. He was a member of the faculty of the University of Singapore from 1968 to 1971, prior to coming to his present position. He was chair of the Sociology Department at Marquette University from 1963 to 1967.

Especially after working in Singapore, Tamney has used modernization theory to understand religious change. In *The Struggle over Singapore's Soul: Western Modernization and Asian Culture* (de Gruyter 1996), Tamney describes the conflict among a capitalist dominant ideology, the state's "Asian" civil morality, and the response of oppositional groups espousing a counterculture that includes religious and humanist values. Tamney's work emphasizes the continual need for religion to change, as society changes, to remain popular.

—*William H. Swatos, Jr.*

TAOISM Religious and philosophical tradition of China founded on the philosophy of mystic Lao Tzu (or Tze), a contemporary of Confucius (although some doubt exists regarding his historicity, the name simply meaning Old One or Old Master). A central concept of Taoism is the *Tao,* or the Way, which involves a state of acceptance or accommodation to the world.

Lao Tzu suggested that aggressive action brings about reaction according to the *yin-yang* principle; hence gentle noninterference or keeping within the natural Tao or rhythms is recommended. Such habits as correct hygiene and proper cultivation of the Tao are required for adaptation of one's vital rhythms to those of the universe. The concepts of yin and yang represent the fundamental duality of the Tao or natural order. This duality is expressed in such pairs of characteristics or themes as masculine and feminine, hot and cold, shady and luminous, and heaven and earth. Taoism was first organized as a religious movement in northern Szechwan province in the second century C.E. with the advent of the Way of the Celestial Masters (T'ien-shih Tao). This movement was led by the first and most famous celestial master, Chang Tao-lin, considered by many to be the founder of Taoism as a religion. Taoist thought and practice over the centuries has influenced neighboring philosophical and religious traditions. Notably, Taoist thought exercised considerable influence on early Shinto beliefs, when strong Chinese influence began in Japan in the seventh century. Ch'an, a variety of Buddhism with strong Taoist elements, became the Zen Buddhist tradition in Japan. Strands of Taoist thought are to be found in the two Chinese Zen schools of Lin-chi (Rinzai) and Ts'ao-tung (Soto) introduced to Japan in the twelfth and thirteenth centuries.

As Max Weber (1951) points out, Taoism as a religion traditionally has been associated with Chinese peasants—in contrast to Confucianism, which has traditionally been more of a religion or philosophy of cultured intellectuals. Taoism over the centuries acquired elements of traditional Chinese "superstitions" and other traditional beliefs that did not originate with Lao Tzu. Popular aspects of Taoism in the United States include Tai Chi Chuan, a movement discipline asso- ciated with Taoism led by Master Lee that is similar to some forms of Yoga; the *Tao te Ching* (Book of Changes); and a number of books (e.g., *The Tao of Pooh* and *The Tao of Physics*) popularizing aspects of Taoist philosophical thought. In the twentieth century, the principal refuge of Taoism has been Taiwan. This resulted largely from emigration from Fukien province on the Mainland in the seventeenth and eighteenth centuries, and from the exodus of the 63rd celestial master, Chang En-pu, to Taiwan in 1949.

Western social scientific interest in Taoism goes back not only to Weber (1951) but also to Marcel Mauss (1973 [1934]), who discusses Taoism in reference to socially taught ways of movement, breathing, and aspects of body awareness. More recent social scientific research has analyzed the structure of consciousness produced by Taoism (Freiberg 1975), local Taoist practices in the People's Republic of China (Dean 1993), and moral accountability in new religious movements and quasi-religions in the United States (Bird 1979).

—*Edward F. Breschel*

REFERENCES

F. Bird, "The Pursuit of Innocence," *Sociological Analysis* 40(1979):335-346; K. Dean, *Taoist Ritual and Popular Cults of South-East China* (Princeton, N.J.: Princeton University Press, 1993); J. W. Freiberg, "The Taoist Mind," *Sociological Analysis* 36(1975):304-322; M. Mauss, "Techniques of the Body," *Economy and Society* 2(1973 [1934]):70-88; M. Weber, *The Religion of China* (Glencoe, Ill.: Free Press, 1951).

TAWNEY, R(ICHARD) H(ENRY) (1880-1962)

British historian; argued in *Religion and the Rise of Capitalism* (Harcourt 1926 [2nd ed., 1937]) that changing religious ideas were the consequence as well as the cause of capitalist development.

Late Medieval business practices, agrarian transformations, expansion to the Americas, new state structures, Renaissance political and economic theories, including political arithmetic, and other factors were central to the development of modern capitalism. Protestantism did express the economic individualism of the British commercial classes, but Weber's original "Protestant ethic thesis" had overemphasized changing religious motives, simplified Calvinism's complex development, and neglected the impact of other intellectual changes. Religious and moral casuistry, including the debates over usury, were especially central for Tawney, who had edited Thomas Wilson's *Discourse upon Usury* (Harcourt 1925 [1572]). The second edition of Tawney's book reproduced his main argument but presented a tempered view of Weber's limitations, based on a fuller study of his main writings.

—*Donald A. Nielsen*

TECHNOLOGY   Application of science to the solution of human problems.

The use of technology traditionally has been viewed as somewhat problematic by theologians and religious leaders. On the one hand, technology brings forth new practices and procedures that pose ethical dilemmas. Such is the case with the development of effective artificial birth control methods, which official Roman Catholicism has condemned as contrary to natural law. The use of fetal tissue to aid Parkinson's patients, medical abortion, freezing of human embryos, and artificial insemination are also the subject of ethical concern and controversy within a number of faiths. On the other hand, technology is seen as providing an alternative meaning system to traditional religion. In part, the secularization thesis in fact argues that as people come to place their faith in society's ability to gain mastery over the natural world using scientific means, religion becomes a less meaningful force. In this regard, technology also might be seen as an alternative to magic and superstition.

In 1979, the World Council of Churches—a body that represents a majority of the world's Christian faith organizations—met to consider the question of the relation between faith and technology. Among the concerns addressed were the problems to which technology should be properly applied, ethical concerns arising from present and future use of technology, the equitable sharing of technology and science so as to ensure a just world distribution of resources, and new expressions of Christian thought and action on the subject of technology as the pathway to an equitable, sustainable society.

Despite the obvious tension between technology and religion, there is growing evidence of increasing reliance on technology in the everyday affairs of religious organizations. Religious radio and television programming—the so-called electronic church—is now an established feature of North American broadcasting. In both Canada and the United States, religious organizations, either individually or in cooperation with one another, have established commercially viable television stations. Religious organizations, such as the Church of Jesus Christ of Latter-day Saints (Mormons), rely heavily on satellite technology for internal communication. Many churches also now maintain a presence on the Internet.

—W. E. Hewitt

REFERENCE

R. L. Shinn (ed.), *Faith and Justice in an Unjust World* (Philadelphia: Fortress, 1980).

TELEVANGELISM   Term first used by Jeffrey K. Hadden and Charles E. Swann in *Prime Time Preachers: The Rising Power of Televangelism* (Addison-Wesley 1981) to describe a new form of religious broadcasting combining television and evangelism. Televangelism also is referred to as "the electric church" by religious broadcasters, especially Ben Armstrong (*The Electric Church,* Nelson 1979), or "the electronic church" by mainline Christian critics. As described by Armstrong, the term *electric church* encompasses all religious broadcasters with an evangelical Christian message, including radio and television programming. *Electronic church* was used pejoratively to describe members of the

clergy who went on the air to raise money for their own use instead of emphasizing spiritual messages in the traditional denominational sense. The term *televangelism* gained widespread usage when scandals involving several of its most prominent personalities turned mass media attention on television evangelists (televangelists) and their multimillion-dollar organizations. In general usage, *televangelism* refers to evangelical religious television programming that depends upon viewers for direct financial support.

Televangelists are independent, entrepreneurial evangelists who use television marketing to build their ministries. In general, three beliefs are shared by these evangelicals: biblical inerrancy, acceptance of the Holy Spirit, and personal born-again redemption. The specific form and content of televangelists' ministries (teleministries), however, are grounded in their own personal interpretation of their calling.

History of the Medium   The early radio evangelists focused on saving souls. With the addition of television as a means of delivery, the emphasis and interpretations of individual callings were modified due to the need to develop financial and audience support. In general, appeals to individuals to become Christians ("born-again" experiences), to reinforce Christian lifestyles, and to join in support of a particular evangelist's ministry have marked all televangelists. Individual programs showed a wide range of formats, from televised preaching to talk shows. Within these various formats, the televangelists' messages ranged from inspirational with little theology (Schuller, Roberts, Bakker) to overtly sociopolitical (Falwell and Robertson, for example).

Television as a mass media tool was introduced in the 1950s and, along with other electronic media, was used for evangelism and constituency building. By the 1980s, there were 1,370 religious radio stations and more than 220 religious television stations. Three Christian networks broadcast 24 hours a day to nationwide audiences. The Golden Age of televangelism, from approximately 1980 to 1987, brought religious broadcasting to national attention. During this period, Nielson and Arbitron rating services measured audience size. According to the results of the rating services, Oral Roberts lost the number one position to Robert Schuller (the *Hour of Power*) and Jimmy Swaggart Ministries, who vied for the top rating. There were eight individual teleministries that began developing stable and large audiences and built complex organizations that became both part of the ministry and a rationale for viewer financial support. These organizations reflected different interests; however, the major televangelists had educational components, many of which continue to operate: Oral Roberts University, Liberty University, Jimmy Swaggart Bible College, and Regent University (formerly Christian Broadcasting Network University). These educational projects varied with the interests and the finances of the evangelist.

Social and Structural Origins of Televangelism
Televangelism is a hybrid institution derived from urban revivalism and television (see Frankl 1984, 1987). Urban revivalism assumes that the clergy influence an individual's choice of salvation, which previously rested only with God, and is responsible for the establishment of a message suitable for mass consumption. Both the high cost of paid airtime and the newly acquired ability of broadcasters to sell public service time determined religious broadcasting's organizational structure, contributed to its prevalence, and stimulated its popularity. The true impact of urban revivalism on religious practice can best be seen in an examination of the legacies of three great urban revivalists: Charles Grandison Finney, Dwight Moody, and Billy Sunday.

Charles Finney (1792-1875) articulated the ethos of urban revivalism upon which contemporary televangelism is based. Finney's 1860 *Lectures: On Revivals of Religion* explained to the clergy how to conduct revivals or, given the primary calling of the revivalists, how to win souls. Part of Finney's legacy was his preaching style, which relied on a sales strategy and the use of plain talk to appeal to audiences. Finney embedded biblical literalism into the revivalists' preaching style, a tradition that continues today among the evangelical-fundamentalist preachers. Finney favored the direct biblical words rather than sophisticated theological doctrines, just as he favored the grammar and rhetoric of plain people. *Lectures* provided the ideological justification for making revivalism a planned event instead of a mystical, spirit-filled happening. Furthermore, Finney exhorted ministers to use "any means" to produce powerful excitement and to play an active role as an agent of God.

Under Finney's tutelage, the work and social relationships of the revivalist preacher were changed, as the preacher functioned as gatekeeper in the heavenly hierarchy. He became God's subcontractor, his tools being the Bible, a hymnal, and unique techniques to excite religious fervor. When Oral Roberts "speaks to God" and urges his viewers to contact him so that he can pray for them, for example, he is following Finney's precepts for being the "wise minister" whose special task is to kindle interest and enthusiasm for Jesus among sinners.

Whereas Finney profoundly altered the ethos, preaching style, and content of revivalism, Dwight Moody (1837-1899) rationalized and routinized the organization of revivalism and some of its rituals about 30 years later. Overall, Moody's major contribution to urban revivalism was to introduce a businesslike organizational structure into the religious realm and to institute managerial techniques to improve the operation and effectiveness of revivals. Moody also contributed to the social milieu of revivalism through the creation of an infrastructure for Bible schools and institutes. These schools, in particular the Moody Bible Institute in Chicago, continue to educate and train students to carry on the work of Moody and other revivalists. When fundamentalism evolved as a social movement, some of these Bible schools became part of that movement. These Christian schools are major building blocks for many televangelists (Oral Roberts, Pat Robertson, and Jerry Falwell in particular). They also serve as successful vehicles for fund-raising.

Billy Sunday (1862-1935) characterized himself as a "businessman for the Lord." According to Weisberger (1958) and McLoughlin (1955), Sunday transformed urban revivals into "professional amusements" by his showmanship and commercialism and played down much of the religious connotation associated with revival meetings. In his emphasis on large-scale entertainment and his streamlining of Moody's churches, schools, and missions into one single-minded revivalist corporation, Sunday developed urban revivalism into an ideal organizational structure for entering into the business of broadcast programming at the dawn of radio and television (Frankl 1984).

Overview of the Largest Teleministries Starting in Akron, Ohio, *Rex Humbard* was one of the first evangelists (1952) to build a ministry that incorporated radio and television programming. Humbard's *Cathedral of Tomorrow*, a church and weekly program by the same name, was designed specifically to accommodate television equipment, crew, and chorus as well as seating for 5,000 people (Armstrong 1979:83 ff.).

Humbard's programs consisted of popular and personalized religious messages; any personal attacks on social institutions or social morality were either nonspecific or not politically directed. His program format was entertainment—inspirational singing, with a strong family emphasis—he avoided taking political positions on the air (Liebman and Wuthnow 1983:41). He was aware of the effect his television ministry might have on local churches and worked together with local pastors to get recent converts involved in their local churches.

Humbard was the third-ranked televangelist in 1981 (Nielsen) and continued broadcasting with the 14 members of his family (including wife Maude Aimée) until 1988, when the televangelism scandals, in which his ministry was not directly involved, resulted in a serious reduction in viewer donations, forcing him to reduce broadcasting. The facilities were sold to Ernst Angley's healing ministry, while the Humbard program continued to air for several years from another site. The Humbard family no longer produces programs.

Granville *Oral Roberts* made the transition from tent crusader as the "King of Faith Healers" into radio and television broadcasting. His radio audience was larger than any other faith healer (Morris 1973). By 1955, Roberts was the national leader of paid religious television (Frankl 1987:74).

With the success of television, Roberts expanded his "Healing Waters" ministry into the Oral Roberts Evangelical Association (OREA) and purchased 175 acres of land in Tulsa, Oklahoma. A major component of OREA was Oral Roberts University (ORU) (1963), which included schools of arts and sciences, law, medicine, theology and missions, and the School for Lifelong Education (a correspondence school). ORU is a fully accredited "charismatic university" based on "God's authority and on the Holy Spirit." The City of Faith (COF) Hospital and Research Center were added to integrate medical science and religious healing (Harrell 1985:448). Roberts later closed the City of Faith, including the medical school. The law school and library holdings were donated to then CBN (now Regent) University when donations fell as a result of the televangelism scandals.

Set apart from many fundamentalist revivalists by his tolerance for theological diversity, Roberts has been willing to work with a wide range of Christians, thus separating himself from doctrinaire fundamentalists (Harrell 1985:442 ff). Roberts accepted biblical inerrancy as a living revelation perceived by experience; he believes in direct intervention of God (see *Miracle of Seed Faith,* Revell 1970). He abandoned the Pentecostal Holiness Church in the 1960s for the more inclusive Methodist Church. Friends with Billy Graham (who dedicated ORU in 1967) and Pat Robertson, he avoided involvement with the Moral Majority movement, eschewing the mixing of politics and religion. His upbeat message of hope was combined with promises of health, happiness, and prosperity. His son Richard shares the pulpit with him and is second president of ORU and the OREA.

Robert Schuller received his Bachelor of Divinity from Western Theological Seminary (Holland, Michigan) and was ordained by the Dutch Reformed Church of America. Schuller is the only televangelist from a mainline denomination. In 1955, with his wife Arvella (née DeHaan), he established a congregation in Garden Grove, California. From the snack bar roof of the Orange drive-in theater, he conducted Sunday Services.

Schuller's *Hour of Power* (1970) is derived from Norman Vincent Peale's "Power of Positive Thinking" and shares his positive theology of "possibility thinking" (i.e., management of ideas, lessening negative self-talk, and exploring ideas for the possibilities they present). Schuller (1983:109-124) has a "Ten Commandments of Possibility Thinking" addressed to individual Christians to change their lives. In 1980, the Crystal Cathedral, an all-glass church, was dedicated and fully paid for at a cost of $16 million by the viewers of *The Hour of Power.* During the 1980s, Schuller vied with Oral Roberts for the position of most watched televangelist. In 1994, Arbitron rated *Hour of Power* the most watched religious program in the United States. It is also seen in 44 foreign countries by an estimated 20 million viewers of special foreign-language versions. As part of his ministry, he founded the Institute for Successful Church Leadership (1970), which has more than 20,000 graduates; New Hope, a Christian 24-hour counseling center (1970); and the International School of Christian Communication, specializing in the art of preaching (1992). Schuller is the author of more than 30 books.

Jerry Falwell graduated from Baptist Bible College, Springfield, Michigan. In 1956, Falwell founded the Thomas Road Baptist Church of Lynchburg, Virginia, which has a current membership of 22,000. From this church, Falwell broadcasts the *Old-Time Gospel Hour,* his television outreach program, and *Listen America Radio,* three minutes of radio news and commentary with conservative leaders addressing political issues. Falwell is the author of 12 books and founder of the Moral Majority (1979-1989), renamed Liberty Federation.

The Moral Majority and the Christian Voice, both established in 1979, were the principal umbrella organizations for the New Christian Right. The Moral Majority had "access to a national network of fundamentalists united by a common fellowship, a commitment to building great churches and Christian Schools" (Liebman and Wuthnow 1983:7, see Bromley and Shupe 1984:36). Preaching to congregations across the nation and establishing lengthy mailing lists for direct mail campaigns, Falwell registered thousands of voters united by the Moral Majority against abortion, pornography, the ERA, homosexuality, and the decline of moral and familial values. Through lobbying and distributing mass petitions to bring attention to conservative positions, Falwell saw the Moral Majority "as a means to a much broader social movement" (Hadden and Shupe 1988). The Christian Voice, although smaller than the Moral Majority, did campaign for conservative Christian viewpoints against homosexuality and pornography.

The Religious Roundtable, formed in 1979 by Ed McAteer under the umbrella of Moral Majority and Christian Voice, provided a forum for conservative political discussions. Falwell was seen as a spokesperson for the Religious Roundtable, which in 1980 held a large conference in Dallas with New Christian Right leaders, televangelists, and Ronald Reagan in attendance. Roundtable forums urged audiences to lobby for conservative issues, such as supporting prayer in schools and the teaching of creationism, through mass mail campaigns to Congress. In 1980, Falwell focused his message on the social and moral aspects of politics in his revivalist "I Love America" rallies held on steps of state capitol buildings across the nation. During these rallies, Christian ministers were invited to speak, as were politicians sympathetic to Falwell's message. In his book *Listen, America!* (Doubleday 1980:244), Falwell states his political objective: to "rally together the people of this country who still believe in decency, the home, the family, morality, the free enterprise system."

During the 1980 presidential elections, the New Christian Right supported Ronald Reagan. Political action committees, such as the Christian Voice's Moral Government Fund, set up the "Christians for Reagan" group, which sent endorsement letters to members of clergy during the presidential primaries. After the 1980 elections, Falwell took credit for helping to elect President Reagan and conservative members of Congress. Although the exact number of new voters who were registered through the Moral Majority's influence has been disputed, a reasonable estimate is nearly 2 million people registered (Liebman and Wuthnow 1983).

In 1986, Falwell dissolved the Moral Majority and created the Liberty Federation, "a new political arm." According to Hadden and Shupe (1988), Moral Majority needed to be dissolved as it had received much negative attention and was not as powerful as Falwell had stated. The 2 to 3 million following was disproved; the claim that the Moral Majority was a large grassroots group and suggestions that it had a religiously diverse following were disproved as well. His Moral Majority members were mostly southern Baptists (Wilcox 1986).

Falwell started the Lynchburg Christian Academy in 1967, with kindergarten through 12th grade. He is founder and Chancellor of Liberty University, formerly Liberty Baptist College (1971), with an enrollment of over 11,000 students from all 50 states and 48 countries in 1993-1994. Described as a comprehensive university, accredited by the Southern Association of Colleges and Schools, it includes a College of Arts and Sciences, a School of Business and Government, School of Communications, School of Education, School of General Studies, School of Religion, and School of Life Long Learning, which uses videotapes for its innovative distance learning program. Falwell is founder and Chancellor of Liberty Baptist Theological Seminary (1973) and the Liberty Home Bible Institute (1976).

Falwell played a brief role in the PTL bankruptcy scandal when Jim and Tammy Bakker left their ministry to be run by Falwell. He attempted to reform and stabilize the sinking PTL and Heritage Village, but his efforts were criticized by pentecostals who disapproved of his noncharismatic, fundamentalist Baptist message. When the Bakkers wished to return to PTL, Falwell refused them, fired Bakker's close associates within the ministry, and kept his fundamentalist board of directors while assuring that the ministry would be ecumenical (Hadden and Shupe 1988).

Jimmy Lee Swaggart was ordained in the Assemblies of God (AOG), a pentecostal denomination. Swaggart rose from poverty to lead one of the largest teleministries in the United States, with an estimated $141 million worldwide organization and 8 million viewers per week. The World Ministry Center in Baton Rouge, Louisiana, includes dormitories and a 7,500-seat Family Worship Center. Swaggart reached the pinnacle of his power in 1986-1988. Swaggart's open criticism of mainline denominations, especially Roman Catholicism, put him at odds with both leaders in the denomination and other, more tolerant television evangelists. At the height of his career, he was a leading figure in the AOG as a political benefactor, generous financial contributor, and media star (Poloma 1989:222).

Swaggart lost considerable credibility among his followers when it was revealed in 1987 that he regularly visited a prostitute. This led to Swaggart's public confession of sins and ultimate defrocking as an Assemblies of God minister because he would not submit to the AOG's recommendation to abstain from preaching for a year and to participate in a rehabilitation program. Swaggart returned to his own pulpit as an independent minister, decreasing his airtime and emphasizing his international evangelical activities. Swaggart is the author of *Rape of the Nation*, published in 1985 (Jimmy Swaggart Ministries), a treatise on what he saw as the moral decay of the United States.

Swaggart's television ministry is known for its exuberant, emotional preaching and singing service, which is attributed to his family and geographic upbringing in Ferriday, Louisiana. Cousin to Mickey Gilley of country music fame and Jerry Lee Lewis, rock music pioneer, Swaggart has 12 gold records of gospel music to his credit (Schaffer and Todd 1987:135).

Jim Bakker, prominent televangelist with his wife, Tammy Faye (née LaValley), developed the PTL (Praise the Lord or People That Love) Club into a multimillion-dollar television ministry composed of a cable network and a real estate venture known as Heritage USA.

The Bakkers began their careers as itinerant revivalists, ordained by Assemblies of God. In 1965, Bakker joined the Christian Broadcasting Network (CBN) in Portsmouth, Virginia. Bakker is credited with originating the *700 Club* talk-show format and was the first host. Bakker is also credited with creating the most successful on-air fund-raising shows, the proceeds of which established CBN as a well-financed entity. Bakker left CBN in November 1972 to join Paul Crouch at the Trinity Broadcasting System (TBS), where he started the *Praise the Lord Show*. Bakker resigned in 1973 as president of TBS. His interpretation of pentecostalism was described as the "gospel of prosperity" (Poloma 1989:219) because he claimed that material prosperity was a sign of God's love. Tammy Faye was an advocate for the right of Christian women to dress as they pleased without incurring disapproval from their congregations (Barnhart 1988:33). The Bakkers' personal lifestyle of extravagant spending, including multiple homes, expensive cars, and frequent home renovations, made them stereotypical targets in the secular popular media. The Bakkers' messages and appeals were ecumenical and interracial.

The Bakkers were not known for their involvement in politics and kept their political leanings to themselves. Jim Bakker did lend his name as a sponsor to the 1980 "One Nation Under God" rally in Washington, an ostensibly apolitical gathering that nonetheless had political pretensions (Hadden and Swann 1981:128).

Heritage USA, the Bakkers' "Christian Disneyland" in Fort Mill, South Carolina, included family vacation facilities, a Christian theme park, and the Heritage Grand Hotel. In March 1987, Bakker was accused of sexual misconduct with former church secretary Jessica Hahn and convicted in 1989 on federal wire and mail fraud charges in an attempt to finance Heritage USA, selling more time-shares in the hotel than were available to fund other building projects. He was subsequently defrocked by the Assemblies of God. His properties were taken in bankruptcy proceedings. While Jim was in prison, the Bakkers divorced and Tammy subsequently remarried. This scandal had major consequences for television ministries and televangelism. It led to a reduction in financial support for all televangelists and to major changes in televangelism as a whole.

At the present time, *Pat Robertson* has become the preeminent televangelist by transforming his early radio and television network into a major, publicly traded cable and satellite network known primarily for the Family Channel, which is owned by International Family Entertainment, Inc.

Televangelism Scandals of 1987-1988   The scandals involving Jim and Tammy Bakker, Marvin Gorman, and Jimmy Swaggart have roots in pentecostalism, its interpretations among practitioners, and the competition brought about by the growth of teleministries. The Bakkers and Marvin Gorman represent a more modern interpretation of charisma that accommodates materialism, while Swaggart represents the traditional charisma that shuns modernism and self-aggrandizement (at least for the laity).

According to Poloma (1989), the beginning of the fall of the televangelism stars in the Assemblies of God (all of the above-mentioned ministers belong to the denomination) came in 1986 when it was revealed by Swaggart that Marvin Gorman had been having extramarital affairs. Swaggart saw Gorman's small but growing ministry as a threat to his own and made Gorman's indiscretions public. This led to Gorman's downfall and subsequent defrocking by the Assemblies. Swaggart then turned his wrath on the Bakkers, whom he perceived to be his biggest rivals and who represented a threat in the form of "modernism." Whereas Swaggart was literal, the Bakkers were interpretive; whereas Swaggart adhered to the practices of speaking in tongues and the altar call, the Bakkers relied on personal testimonials in faith, particularly ones that spoke of financial triumphs in a talk-show format. Bakker was brought down when it was revealed that he had an extramarital affair with a church secretary, Jessica Hahn (although there were also financial mismanagement charges).

Swaggart, who initiated the complaints against Gorman, had the favor returned when Gorman hired a private detective to follow Swaggart and caught him on film leaving a cheap motel with a prostitute outside of New Orleans. Although the Assemblies of God voted to put him in therapy and relieve him of his ministry for one year, Swaggart refused this directive and demonstrated his staying power by continuing his ministry, claiming to retain his international audiences as well. Bakker spent five years in prison before being released in 1995. Although Gorman, Bakker, and Swaggart were defrocked by the Assemblies, Bakker alone remained without a pulpit by 1996.

The Regulatory Environment   While religious broadcasting has developed along with the radio and television industries, access for the evangelical Christians was limited for many years by the mainline denominations, who had a "gentlemen's agreement" with the networks, in effect, to select only mainline broadcasters. It was not until stations were able to sell their public service times (required for licensing renewals) that the evangelicals could purchase airtime (Frankl 1987). The National Religious Broadcasters (NRB) was founded in response to the evangelicals' limited access, and it is for this reason that the National Religious Broadcasters is critical for these broadcasters in protecting access to the airways. As stated in their membership guide,

> NRB was founded to safeguard free and complete access to the broadcast media for religious broadcasting. NRB supports the rights to purchase airtime and to use sustaining time on radio and television by retaining a former Federal Communications Commissioner as their counsel and maintaining close relationships with the FCC through lobbying activities.

The NRB is an important professional organization, publishing *Religious Broadcasting,* a trade periodical that reflects the policy and philosophy of the NRB Board of Trustees. Annual and regional meetings, which educate members and showcase the latest technology and Christian support services, are important social and political events for these broadcasters. Membership in the NRB means that the broadcasters have agreed to standards of financial accountability (enforced after the 1987 scandals) that are essential to retaining legitimacy in the broadcasting industry.

Audiences In the 1980s, eight televangelists, according to Nielsen and Arbitron audience data, were watched by 85% of the total national religious television audience. These televangelists were Robert Schuller, Jimmy Swaggart, Oral Roberts, Rex Humbard, Jerry Falwell, Jim Bakker, Pat Robertson, and James Robison. During this period, these televangelists competed with each other for larger shares of the religious market. Serious disagreement ensued between the televangelists and the mainstream religious broadcasters regarding the exact number of viewers and who these viewers were. A historic research collaboration, funded by both the evangelicals and the mainline federation, was commissioned to answer these questions. The results did not settle the argument. The evangelical broadcasters preferred the Gallup data, which claimed that "approximately one in three adults (60 million) had watched religious television in the past 30 days," while the mainline opponents argued for the more conservative Arbitron figures of "between 7.3 and 9.2 million persons." It should be noted that these figures are based on radically different research methods and

therefore cannot be compared (see Frankl and Hadden 1987).

The scandals in spring 1987 ended this debate. As the funding for the major teleministries dropped substantially, they were all forced to scale back their organizations and the amount of airtime they purchased.

Religion and Politics From the beginning, documenting and understanding the financial and political linkages between the growth of the religious right and the growth of the televangelists have involved debate. Not all observers of televangelism have understood that there is a link between televangelism and the development of the religious right. Hadden, Frankl, and Shupe, to name a few, believe that the televangelists were part of a new social movement, with mass media, especially television, used as a critical resource to mobilize financial and political support for conservative politics.

By far the implications of the rise of televangelism transcend concerns of interdenominational competition. The use of mass broadcasting, the altering of the religious message to popularize and sell religion, and the link between the religious right and the resurgence of neoconservatism, although initially discredited, now seem clear.

See also Christian Right, Pat Robertson

—*Razelle Frankl*

REFERENCES

J. Barnhart, *Jim and Tammy* (Buffalo, N.Y.: Prometheus, 1988); D. G. Bromley and A. D. Shupe, *New Christian Politics* (Macon, Ga.: Mercer University Press, 1984); R. Frankl, "Television and Popular Religion," in Bromley and Shupe, *q.v.* (1984): 129-138; R. Frankl, *Televangelism* (Carbondale: Southern Illinois University Press, 1987); R. Frankl, "Transformation of Televangelism," in *Culture, Media and the Religious Right,* ed. J. Lesage and L. Kintz (Minneapolis: University of Minnesota Press, 1997); R. Frankl and J. K. Hadden, "A Critical Review of the Religion and Television Research Report," *Review of Religious Research* 29(1987): 111-124; J. K. Hadden and A. D. Shupe, *Televangelism* (New York: Holt, 1988); D. Harrell, Jr., *Oral Roberts* (San Francisco: Harper, 1985); D. Harrell, Jr., *Pat Robertson* (San Francisco: Harper, 1987); R. Liebman and R. Wuthnow, *The New Christian Right* (New York: Aldine, 1983); W. McLoughlin, *Billy Sunday Was His Real Name* (Chicago: University of Chicago, 1955); J. Morris, *The Preachers* (New York: St. Martin's, 1973); J. Peck, *The Gods of Televangelism* (Cresskill, N.J.: Hampton, 1993); M. Poloma, *The Assemblies of God at the Crossroads* (Knoxville: University of Tennessee Press, 1989); J. Schaffer and C. Todd, *Christian Wives* (Garden City, N.Y.: Doubleday, 1987); R. Schuller, *Tough Times Never Last, But Tough People Do!* (Nashville: Nelson 1983); C. Shepard, *Forgiven* (New York: Atlantic Monthly Press, 1989); B. Weisberger, *They Gathered at the River* (Boston: Little, Brown, 1958); C. Wilcox, "Evangelicals and Fundamentalists in the New Christian Right," *Journal for the Scientific Study of Religion* 25(1986):355-363.

TERESA, MOTHER (1910-1997)   Born Agnes Gonxhua Bojaxhiu in Albania; former member of the Sisters of Loretto; founder (1950) of the Roman Catholic Congregation of the Missionaries of Charity. A teacher by training, Mother Teresa has worked in India since 1928, after 1946 exclusively in the service of the poor, providing hospital care to the sick and infirm. After 1965, these efforts took on a global dimension, and to date the Missionaries of Charity have opened 443 relief centers in 95 countries. In 1979, Mother Teresa was awarded the Nobel peace prize. Despite her achievements, she has sometimes been criticized for treating the symptoms of poverty as opposed to attacking its root cause in inegalitarian social structures.

—*W. E. Hewitt*

REFERENCE

F. Zambonini, *Teresa of Calcutta* (New York: Alba, 1993).

THEODICY   One of several terms originating in natural theology that have now come to have a special significance within the sociology of religion. As with that even more famous term to have undergone a similar fate, *charisma,* Max Weber is the person principally responsible for this transition. The word had featured in the title of an influential work by the German philosopher and mathematician Gottfried Wilhelm Leibniz, published in 1710, in which he attempted to respond to the mounting rationalist attack on revealed religion by demonstrating that belief in a benevolent and omnipotent god was consistent with believing that this same god was the creator of an imperfect world. Leibniz was endeavoring to resolve what Weber referred to as "the problem of theodicy," that is, if a wise and just God exists, why is there evil in the world? It is this issue, together with the manner of its resolution, which Turner (1981:148) suggests is "central to Weber's sociology of religion."

Certainly in the religions of the West, the conception of the divine as transcendental, unchangeable, omnipo-

tent, and omniscient focused attention upon the problem of how the power and goodness of such a god can be reconciled with the imperfections of that world that he created (see Weber 1978:518-526). Yet even in the East, a conception of the divine as impersonal and supertheistic still raises the issue of accounting for the world's imperfections. Hence, in one form or another, this problem exists in all religions, and Weber outlined what he considered to be the three "various theoretically pure types" of solution that emerged. The first possibility he considers is that involving messianic eschatologies and the belief in a coming revolution that will bring the world into accord with God's nature, that is, the establishment of a Kingdom of God on earth.

Weber goes on to show how this view is likely to develop into a belief in predestination, as more and more emphasis is placed upon the chasm between a totally transcendent and inscrutable God and human beings enmeshed in the coils of sin: "God's sovereign, completely inexplicable, voluntary, and antecedently established (a consequence of omniscience) determination has decreed not only human fate on earth but also human destiny after death." This, as Weber notes, is less a solution to the problem of theodicy than a way of defining it out of existence. In addition to predestination, Weber specifies two other religious outlooks that he suggests provide "systematically conceptualized" treatments of the problem of the world's imperfections. The first of these is dualism, the view that the universe is governed by the two, roughly equal, powers of good and evil, represented mainly by Zoroastrianism and Manichaeism. The second outlook is the Indian doctrine of *karma.* The latter Weber describes as "the most complete formal solution of the problem of theodicy" because the world is regarded as a completely connected and self-contained cosmos of ethical retribution in which each individual forges his or her own destiny, with guilt and merit in this world unfailingly compensated in a succeeding incarnation.

Weber makes it clear that these are ideal-type "solutions" to the problem of theodicy and that in reality religions of salvation combined ingredients from these three types together in various mixes, with the consequence that "the differences among various religious theories of god's relation to the world and to man must be measured by their degree of approximation to one or another of these pure types." It must be doubted, however, whether the full complexity of Greek thought—whether Platonic, Epicurean, or Stoic—can be successfully incorporated into Weber's triadic scheme, while it is also difficult to see where one would place what John Hick (1966) has called the Irenaean type of theodicy, which is the theory that God deliberately created imperfect beings, exposing them to a morally mixed environment to help bring them to a state of perfection. For this reason, there must be some doubt about Weber's claim that all theodicies can be understood in terms of the types that he outlines, as there also must be over the suggestion that they represent a form of treatment of the problem of the world's imperfections that is more especially "systematically conceptualized" than those he omits from discussion.

Calvin's theodicy of predestinarian determinism would not appear to be either the logical or the historical end point of Western theological endeavors to resolve the problem of theodicy, for the thinkers who came after him cannot be considered to have done more than elaborate or refine his views or, alternatively, to have rejected religion entirely. On the contrary, a succession of seventeenth- and early eighteenth- century philosophers, including such eminent figures as Pascal, Spinoza, Leibniz, Kant, and Hegel, devoted considerable effort to the construction of a philosophical theology that would serve in place of an increasingly discredited Calvinism; moreover, Campbell (1987) has proposed that Romanticism should be seen as Calvinism's true theodical successor.

In the contemporary world, widespread interest in theodicies appears to have waned as secularization has progressed. However, there is evidence that many people still seek for answers to the fundamental problem of evil, and that popular theodicies exist to meet this need (Towler 1984).

—*Colin Campbell*

REFERENCES

C. Campbell, *The Romantic Ethic and the Spirit of Modern Consumerism* (Oxford: Blackwell, 1987); J. Hick, *Evil and the Love of God* (London: Macmillan, 1966); R. Towler, *The Need for Certainty* (London: Routledge, 1984); B. S. Turner, *For Weber* (London: Routledge, 1981); M. Weber, *Economy and Society* (Berkeley: University of California Press, 1978).

THEOLOGY   The scholarly and critical study of religious beliefs.

There has been an increasing use of the social sciences within academic theology during the twentieth century. Traditionally, theologians have related to the dominant philosophies of many ages and cultures and, at least since the nineteenth century, to academic historical and textual scholarship. However, during the last two decades, the social sciences increasingly have been seen as directly relevant to theology. This can be traced in four distinct areas: in the writings of some of the classical sociologists, in biblical studies, in systematic theology, and in applied theology.

Among classical sociologists, Max Weber showed a profound interest in theology. Influenced by the theologian/historian Ernst Troeltsch, Weber exhibited this interest in a number of ways. Most obviously, his work *The Protestant Ethic and the Spirit of Capitalism* (Scribner 1930 [1904-1905]) advanced the possibility that theological differences may have been socially significant. He argued that notions within popular Calvinism may have been important in developing the culture in northwestern Europe that assisted the rise of rational capitalism. Unlike Karl Marx, who tended to see theology either as epiphenomenal or as a dependent social variable, Weber argued that theology also might become an independent variable within society. His later work showed other theological interests—notably in charismatic prophecy—and demonstrated a considerable knowledge of contemporary biblical scholarship.

Weber's writings had a major influence upon several theologians in the first half of the twentieth century. In America, H. Richard Niebuhr's *The Social Sources of Denominationalism* (Holt 1929) was influenced by both Weber and Troeltsch. In Germany, the young Dietrich Bonhoeffer's *Sanctorum Communio* (SCM 1963 [1930]) was similarly influenced. Paul Tillich, a German emigré to the United States, was also a part of this trend. However, the growing dominance of theologians such as Karl Barth—with his radical stress upon revelation and the "Word of God"—strictly limited this influence. Sociology came to be seen as dangerously "secular" and a force for relativization.

In biblical studies, these fears may have delayed the use of the social sciences, although there were always some biblical scholars who used them. Radical biblical critics such as Rudolf Bultmann used ideas with many affinities to the social sciences—especially in his development of form criticism, which tried to identify the ways that particular communities shaped stories and sayings that eventually appeared in the Gospels. However, biblical scholars tended to make little direct use of social theory. Even Weber was often treated as an amateur by Old Testament scholars. Textual, historical, and exegetical issues tended to predominate.

During the last two decades, on the other hand, there has been a radical change in biblical scholarship. A new focus upon social origins and another upon hermeneutics have raised sociological questions more directly. For example, John Gager's *Kingdom and Community* (Prentice Hall 1975) made direct use of cognitive dissonance theory to understand better the millennial expectations in parts of the New Testament. He argued that this theory, drawn from social psychology, helped to understand the drive toward mission among the earliest Christians, despite the death of Jesus and the nonarrival of the Parousia. Richer still in sociological nuance is Wayne Meeks's *The First Urban Christians* (Yale University Press 1983). In this highly influential book, Meeks made considerable use of anthropological and sociological theory to understand the shift between the rural world of Jesus and the urban world of Paul. Finally, in Germany, the New Testament scholar Gerd Theissen's work has made extensive use of sociology and psychology.

In recent systematic theology, there also has been increasing use of the social sciences. Liberation theology has been a major influence upon this. Gustavo Guttiérrez's seminal book *A Theology of Liberation* (Orbis 1973) argued against an understanding of theology as being concerned with timeless "orthodoxy." Instead, he argued for a notion of "orthopraxis," stressing that the way Christians behave and whether they argue for the rich and powerful, or assert the "preferential option for the poor," should be central theological concerns. This understanding of theology has frequently seen Marxism as an ally rather than as a foe. Within modern theology, the social sciences' influence has now extended into feminist theology and into postmodern theology. All of these tend to give the social sciences a dominant role both in identifying more accurately the nature of modern culture and in understanding theology as a social reality within that culture. Within feminist theology, for example, the social sciences often are used to understand the ways that patriarchy has shaped both theology and the culture within which theology is set.

The increasing emphasis upon social context and praxis within modern theology have tended to blur a traditional distinction between systematic and moral theology. For Karl Barth, systematic or dogmatic theology attempted to establish the doctrinal framework within which ethical decision making could then be done. Within many forms of liberation and post-liberation theology, by contrast, ethics and belief constantly interact; therefore, a rigid distinction between theology and ethics seems no longer viable. Influential Christian ethicists such as Stanley Hauerwas have championed, instead, a stress upon the formation of Christian character. Theological ethics attempts to identify the ways that Christian living is distinctive in a "secular" world. For many Christian ethicists, such identification involves an extensive use of the social sciences. Heavily influenced by Alasdair MacIntyre's *After Virtue* (Duckworth 1981), they, like him, often make extensive use of sociology as well as philosophy in attempting to identify theological virtues.

Within applied theology generally, there also has been increasing use of the social sciences. The study of church structures and strategies has proved particularly open to this influence. For example, the Dutch theologian Mady Thung's *The Precarious Organization* (Mouton 1976) made extensive use of both the sociology of knowledge and the sociology of organizations to understand the "mission" of churches. Other works, such as E. Mansell Pattison's *Pastor and Parish* (Fortress 1977), have used systems theory to understand the social dimensions of pastoral ministry. Management theory is similarly increasingly used by churches, and in many parts of the Western world, theories of church growth have made extensive use of descriptive forms of sociology—especially in membership and attendance statistics. Worship and liturgy also have become a focus of sociological interest, as in Kieran Flanagan's *Sociology and Liturgy* (St. Martin's 1991), and symbolic interactionist/constructionist approaches have been applied to pastoral care in George Furniss's *The Social Context of Pastoral Care* (Westminster 1994).

—*Robin Gill*

REFERENCES

G. Baum, *Religion and Alienation* (New York: Paulist Press, 1975); R. Gill, *The Social Context of Theology* (Oxford: Mowbray, 1975); R. Gill, *Theology and Sociology* (London: Cassell, 1996); D. Martin et al. (eds.), *Sociology and Theology* (Sussex: Harvester, 1980); J. Milbank, *Theology and Social Theory* (Oxford: Blackwell, 1990).

THEORY   The attempt to explain or account for religion and its role in society as well as in individual experience; systematic social scientific theories begin primarily in the nineteenth and early twentieth century with such writers as Marx, Weber, Durkheim and his school, Freud, Troeltsch, James, and others. Although more recent work builds on these earlier efforts to comprehend religion's role in history and human experience, contemporary thinkers also have constructed special theories analyzing a variety of phenomena. In doing so, they often have uncoupled the empirical and theoretical study of religion's many facets from the grand historical narratives, philosophical assumptions, and theological concerns of the earlier pioneers.

One persistent strand of theorizing has emphasized the general idea that religion is largely ideological or compensatory in character. This orientation tends also toward the reduction of religion to nonreligious social or psychological forces. Marx's emphasis on the social-class origins of religion (religion as the "opium of the masses") expresses this view, as does Nietzsche's psychological diagnosis of resentment as a source of early Christianity. Freud's view of religion as infantile wish projection or a rationalization of conduct rooted in more primary processes such as aggression, ambivalence, and guilt has much the same quality. The Stark-Bainbridge theory of religion as a system of compensators represents a recent, more empirically oriented extension of this general theoretical style.

These explanations can be distinguished from ones that focus on the functions of religion without committing themselves to religion's ontological "reality." Durkheim's idea that religious beliefs and practices concerning the sacred sustain social integration and form the matrix for our central categories of thinking, as well as Malinowski's emphasis on the defensive functions of religion against the threat posed to society and the individual by death, fall into this category.

Although these two styles of theorizing have much in common, they have distinctive emphases. Durkheim's additional claim to have discovered the origin of religion in the experience of society itself moves him closer to the aforementioned type of perspective. Swanson's more recent analysis of the social roots of transcendent and immanent religious experience has a similar thrust. However, Durkheim's emphasis on religious rituals and collective effervescence has provided a basis for diverse theoretical approaches, not only (for example) Bellah's integrative concept of "civil religion" but also his emphasis on "symbolic realism" and the role of collective religious processes in transfiguring social reality.

Max Weber's theory of religion largely departs from the above standpoints in its emphasis on the autonomous role of religious ideas. His work faces in two different directions: (1) the development of a systematic sociology of religion and (2) the study of the relationships between the world religions and the emergence of modernity. Both efforts are carried through in similar comparative, historical scope and depth. They are not unrelated, but the latter project takes precedence over the attempt to provide a truly general theory of religion (in contrast, for example, to Joachim Wach's systematic *Sociology of Religion,* University of Chicago Press 1947). Weber's systematic sociology develops the central concepts and typologies that have sustained much sociology of religion since his time: charisma, the roles of prophets and priests, asceticism and mysticism, church versus sect types, the interrelationships among religious ethics and worldly activities in the spheres of economics,

politics, the family and sexuality, the sciences and arts, and so forth. Many of these analyses are carried over in his comparative study of religions and civilizations, especially in his examination of the economic ethics of the world's religions and his attempt to account for the role played by religion in the rise of capitalism and modernity. Studies in theory and history by Troeltsch on church, sect, and mysticism in European Christianity, and by Niebuhr on the denomination in America, develop ideas closely related to Weber's work.

Weber separates the question of religion's truth claims from his scientific analysis and avoids the reductionistic implications of Marxian, Freudian, and even Durkheimian theories. For instance, his key concept of charisma locates legitimation of the religious leader's extraordinary gifts in a complex relationship among leader, followers, and cultural context but remains silent on the ultimate validity of these gifts. Weber's version of the sociologist's calling was combined with a high regard for genuine religious commitment. This uneasy resolution of the problem paved the way for current "methodological agnosticism" in the study of religion.

The problem of "religious experience" suggests another form of theorizing about religion. William James's focus on the individual, rather than on the institutional element of religion, and his analysis of mystical experience is a landmark for this approach. Rudolf Otto's discussion of the numinous experience, the *mysterium tremendum,* helped lay the foundation for a phenomenology of religion. Comparative-historical studies from this general standpoint have been developed by van der Leeuw and Eliade. Such approaches are decidedly antireductionistic, are favorably disposed toward religion, and generally avoid any attempt at "explanations" of religion, even functional ones. Rather, the focus is on a study of the varied manifestations of religion's most universal characteristics in the hope of thereby identifying its essence. Berger's theory of meaning systems, plausibility structures, and legitimations represents one of the most fully developed efforts to combine the phenomenology of religious experience and meaning with sociological concepts.

The sociology of religion today is marked by a wide range of theories. They include analyses of phenomena such as conversion (Lofland), commitment (Kanter), privatization (Luckmann), globalization of religion (Robertson), civil religion (Bellah), millenarianism (Worsley, Burridge), and religion and modernization (Wuthnow), to mention only a few. Some extend the classical theorists' insights to current social changes, while others probe in greater detail specific theoretical problems less thoroughly examined by earlier writers.

See also Experience, Karl Marx, H. Richard Niebuhr, Ernst Troeltsch, Joachim Wach, Max Weber

—*Donald A. Nielsen*

REFERENCES

R. N. Bellah, *Beyond Belief* (New York: Harper, 1970); K. Burridge, *New Heaven, New Earth* (New York: Schocken, 1969); C. Y. Glock and P. Hammond (eds.), *Beyond the Classics?* (New York: Harper, 1973); R. M. Kanter, *Commitment and Community* (Cambridge: Harvard University Press, 1972); J. Lofland, *Doomsday Cult* (New York: Irvington, 1977); T. Luckmann, *The Invisible Religion* (New York: Macmillan, 1967); R. O'Toole, *Religion* (Toronto: McGraw-Hill-Ryerson, 1984); R. Robertson, *The Sociological Interpretation of Religion* (New York: Schocken, 1970); R. Robertson, *Globalization* (London: Sage, 1992); P. Worsley, *The Trumpet Shall Sound*, 2nd ed. (New York: Schocken, 1968); R. Wuthnow, *Communities of Discourse* (Cambridge: Harvard University Press).

THEOSOPHY   Philosophical doctrine used as one source of inspiration by Mme. Helene Petrova Blavatsky (1831-1891), who founded the Theosophical Society in 1875. Theosophy has connections to Hinduism, Buddhism, and Jainism and is intrinsically related to Indian thought. As originally defined, theosophy is the common philosophical element within Eastern religions.

Early theosophical doctrines were essentially intellectual, constituting a way of thinking about religious questions. Mme. Blavatsky, a psychic and medium, gave the term a special connotation. In 1873, she met Henry Steel Olcott, who was captivated by her mediumistic performances and talk of occult knowledge. Blavatsky transmitted letters to Olcott from various unseen mystical adepts beginning in 1875 and, in that year, she, Olcott, and Charles Sotheran, a noted journalist and socialist, founded the Theosophical Society. Blavatsky's erudition, charisma, and alleged psychokinetic and extrasensory abilities attracted many followers and enabled her to overcome challenges regarding her leadership from Olcott and others.

Blavatsky's miraculous performances were revealed to be fraudulent by Dr. Richard Hodgson of the Society for Psychical Research. Although this debunking damaged the Theosophical Society, most of Mme. Blavatsky's core followers remained faithful, and she attracted new converts through her writings. After Blavatsky's death, Annie Besant and William Q. Judge, whom Blavatsky had appointed co-heads of the Eastern School of Theosophy, joined forces against Olcott and succeeded in obtaining his resignation. Society members accept the notions of reincarnation, karma, and transmigration; encourage the study of comparative religion; and advocate the investigation of the unexplained laws of nature and the powers latent in man. Esoteric doctrines include emphasis on hidden traditions that evolved from the magic of medieval Europe, the Knights Templar, Freemasonry, and a postulated secret society called the Great White Brotherhood. These doctrines have had important impacts on many modern mystical belief systems.

—*James McClenon*

REFERENCES

H. P. Blavatsky, *The Secret Doctrine* (Point Loma, Calif.: Aryan Theosophical Press, 1909); S. Cranston, *HBP* (New York: Putnam, 1993); F. E. Garrett, *Isis Very Much Unveiled*, 4th ed. (London: Westminster Gazette, 1895); K. P. Johnson, *Initiates of Theosophical Masters* (Albany: SUNY Press, 1995); J. B. Tamney, *American Society in the Buddhist Mirror* (New York: Garland, 1992).

THIRD WORLD   A term that was created to refer to poor, formerly colonial countries, in contrast to the dominant capitalist-industrial *First World* and the communist *Second World*. *Third World* became the preferred term of scholars and activists who resisted using the word *underdeveloped* because they believed it implied (1) that the poorer countries were inferior and (2) that they could become "developed" simply by imitating the wealthier countries.

In recent years, some writers have used *Third World* to refer to disadvantaged groups within the First World, including people of color and those whose ethnic origin is in the Third World.

—*Madeleine R. Cousineau*

THOMAS, JOHN L. (1910-1991)   In addition to degrees in theology and philosophy, Thomas held an M.A. in both English and French literature from the University of Montréal and a Ph.D. in sociology from the University of Chicago (1949). A Jesuit, he began his teaching and sociological scholarship at St. Louis University (1949-1953) and helped inaugurate the Institute of Social Order, a national Jesuit Research Institute in

Social Sciences, at St. Louis (1949-1965). The institute subsequently moved to Cambridge, Massachusetts, and then to Georgetown, where Thomas worked until 1986. In that year, he moved to Marquette University, where he lived until his death. Thomas was the only person to become president of both the American Catholic Sociological Society (1960) and its successor, the Association for the Sociology of Religion (1976).

Thomas was primarily noted for his scholarship, writings, and lectures on marriage and family, producing at least nine books, numerous articles, and a series of weekly columns carried in 48 Catholic publications (1957-1963). His ACSS presidential address, titled "The Sociological Implications of Catholic Thought," urged the membership to focus on Catholicism itself as an object of sociological research.

—*Loretta M. Morris*

TILLICH, PAUL (1886-1965)

TILLICH, PAUL (1886-1965)   German-born Protestant theologian known for his theology of culture, his political theology, and a theological method of sociocultural analysis. Tillich received his Ph.D. from Breslau (1911) and licentiate in theology from Halle (1912).

After serving as a chaplain in World War I, Tillich grew increasingly interested in political theory and the cultural situation in the Weimar Republic. He soon became an active part of the Independent Social Democrats, the more radical of the socialist forums. In 1923, his essay "Basic Principles of Religious Socialism" (Grundinien des religiosen Sozialismus) became foundational for the growing religious socialist movement. *The Religious Situation* (Die religiose Lage der Gegenwart) in 1926 (Holt 1932), drawing heavily on Max Weber and Ernst Troeltsch, pointed out the estrangement prevalent in European society. While teaching at the University of Frankfurt, he was a member of the Institut für Sozialforschung, which was dedicated to social research and the development of a critical theory of society. His work in Germany culminated in *The Socialist Decision* (University Press of America 1983 [1932]), a religious socialist manifesto. Tillich emigrated to America to escape the Nazi threat in 1933 and joined Reinhold Niebuhr at Union Theological Seminary.

Tillich's method changed the way the relationship between religion and culture was considered in theological studies. The method defined "theology" as the reflection of answers to questions of ultimate concern raised out of the human experience (the religious di-

mension), and "culture" as the practical reflection of the religious dimension of a people. He developed this method further in such works as *Theology of Culture* (Oxford University Press 1959), a theological analysis of culture using the method to define the religion-culture relationship in integrative terms ("religion is the substance of culture, culture is the form of religion"); *Dynamics of Faith* (Harper 1957), a phenomenological study of religious faith as the universal human experience of being ultimately concerned; and the three volumes of *Systematic Theology* (University of Chicago Press 1951, 1957, 1963). Following his death in 1965, he was the focus of his friend Rollo May's psychoanalysis in *Paulus: Reminiscences of a Friendship* (Harper 1973) and his wife Hannah's personal account of life with Tillich, *From Time to Time* (Stein and Day 1973).

—*Gary Mann*

REFERENCES

R. H. Stone, *Paul Tillich's Radical Social Thought* (Atlanta: Knox, 1980); P. Tillich, "The Church and Communism," *Religion in Life* 6(1937):347-357; P. Tillich, "Protestantism in the Present World Situation," *American Journal of Sociology* 43(1938):236-248; P. Tillich, "Man and Society in Religious Socialism," *Christianity and Society* 8, 4(1943):10-21; P. Tillich, *Love, Power, and Justice* (London: Oxford University Press, 1954); P. Tillich, "The Philosophy of Social Work," *Social Science Review* 36(1962):13-16.

TIMASHEFF, NICHOLAS S. (1886-1970)

TIMASHEFF, NICHOLAS S. (1886-1970) Born in St. Petersburg, Russia, the son of the minister of trade under the last czarist regime, Timasheff was educated at the University of St. Petersburg, receiving both master's and doctoral degrees. Together with later Harvard sociologist Pitirim Sorokin, he studied under L. J. Petrazhitsky, who introduced him to the systematic study of society through law. He taught sociological jurisprudence and was Dean of the Polytechnic Institute of St. Petersburg before he had to flee the country in 1932.

Timasheff first taught at the University of Prague and at the Sorbonne before coming to the United States in 1936, where, at Sorokin's invitation, he lectured in sociology at Harvard University until 1939. He joined the Sociology Department at Fordham University in 1940, where he remained until his retirement in 1957. Timasheff continued to teach at Marymount College in Manhattan until 1963. Although almost immobilized with arthritis and in a wheelchair, he still continued his scholarly work. He published *War and Revolution*

(Sheed & Ward) in 1965, revised his book *Sociological Theory* (Random House 1967), and at the time of his death was preparing a revised edition of *Sociology of Law* (Harvard University Press 1939). He is considered one of the founders of the sociology of law. One of his early works was *Religion in Soviet Russia 1917-42* (Greenwood 1980 [1942]).

Timasheff was a scholar and a deeply religious man, recognized as a theologian of the Russian Orthodox Church. In a memorial note, Joseph P. Fitzpatrick wrote,

> He faced continuously the problem of relating his religious beliefs to his scholarly activities and consistently stated that he found no serious dilemma in this area. This was largely due to his firm insistence that the canons of scientific evidence and a scientific methodology be strictly followed in sociology. He would have been deeply troubled by the obscuring of the lines between science and ideology. (*Sociological Analysis* 1970:56).

—*Loretta M. Morris*

TIRYAKIAN, EDWARD A. (1929–) American sociologist; educated at Princeton and Harvard, where his teachers included Jacques Maritain, Talcott Parsons, and P. A. Sorokin; he taught at both these institutions before moving in 1967 to his present position at Duke University.

Tiryakian's *Sociologism and Existentialism* (Prentice Hall 1961) analyzed the similarities and differences in the study of the individual and society between Émile Durkheim and a group of "existentialist" philosophers, including Søren Kierkegaard, Martin Heidegger, Jean-Paul Sartre, and others. Tiryakian raised related questions concerning the relationship between sociology and philosophy in his important essay, "Existential Phenomenology and the Sociological Tradition." In these and many other writings about Durkheim, he opened important new horizons for sociology by removing the discussion of Durkheim's work from the positivistic setting in which it frequently had been found.

In several collective volumes, Tiryakian combined with other colleagues to focus attention on the sociological study of phenomena such as esoteric culture, global crises, and the role of the new nationalisms in modern Western societies. His various writings on the place of symbolic rebellion in societal change have made a particularly strong case for the study of religious

heterodoxy, occult practices, sexual experimentation, stylistic rebellions, and other phenomena "on the margin of the visible" as important harbingers of wider political revolutions and social changes. The result has been not only an advance in the sociological study of neglected cultural phenomena but a theoretical clarification of processes connected with what Parsons called the "latency" and "pattern maintenance" structures of societies.

A valued mentor, Tiryakian has encouraged a variety of younger scholars, in part through a series of National Endowment for the Humanities Summer Seminars that he hosted on five different occasions at Duke between 1978 and 1991. He also served as President of the North American Society for the Study of Religion from 1981 to 1984, and has been awarded an honorary doctorate from the Université René Descartes in Paris.

—*Donald A. Nielsen*

REFERENCES

E. A. Tiryakian, "Existential Phenomenology and the Sociological Tradition," *American Sociological Review* 30(1965): 674-688; E. A. Tiryakian (ed.), *On the Margins of the Visible* (New York: Wiley, 1974).

TOCQUEVILLE, ALEXIS DE (1805-1859)

French social theorist and politician; the outstanding classical interpreter of religion's role in modern American democracy and prerevolutionary France. The son of an aristocratic and monarchist family, Tocqueville's travels in America, England, and Ireland led him to a reformist political stance in support of democratic institutions.

Before traveling to America and after experiencing the social chaos and despotism in early-nineteenth-century France, Tocqueville suspected that democracy led inevitably to "a debased taste for equality, which leads the weak to want to drag the strong down to their level and which induces men to prefer equality in servitude to inequality in freedom" (1969 [1835-1840]: 49). He feared that this servile egalitarianism would lead to despotism by leaving people defenseless against public opinion.

In contrast, Tocqueville encountered in America a "legitimate passion for equality which rouses in all men a desire to be strong and respected" (p. 49). He traced this legitimate egalitarianism to the pervasive influence of American democratic institutions and saw it at work most extensively in the American propensity to form "voluntary associations" to address myriad shared needs. Tocqueville observed and chronicled religion's role in sustaining this voluntarist ethos and providing the social space in which much reformist organizing occurs. He traced the way that religion in America accepts self-interest as a prime motivation in people's lives, yet so revitalizes engagement in common endeavors that people come to appreciate and commit themselves to social institutions that transcend their private worlds. This "enlightened self-interest" represents for Tocqueville the key for understanding the flourishing of American democracy.

Yet Tocqueville cautioned that the American self-reliance also could lead people to pursue only their own private interests, and he coined a new term, *individualism,* for this tendency. He cautioned that individualism ultimately could lead to such an erosion of common concern that it would undermine democratic life.

—*Richard L. Wood*

REFERENCES

S. Drescher, *Tocqueville and England* (Cambridge: Harvard University Press, 1964); S. A. Hadari, *Theory in Practice* (Stanford, Calif.: Stanford University Press, 1989); R. Herr, *Tocqueville and the Old Regime* (Princeton, N.J.: Princeton University Press, 1962); J. C. Koritansky, *Alexis de Tocqueville and the New Science of Politics* (Durham: Carolina Academic Press, 1986); J. Lively, *The Social and Political Thought of Alexis de Tocqueville* (Oxford: Clarendon, 1965); J. P. Mayer, *Alexis de Tocqueville* (New York: Viking, 1966); A. de Tocqueville, *The Old Regime and the French Revolution* (Garden City, N.Y.: Doubleday, 1955 [1856]); A. de Tocqueville, *Democracy in America* (New York: Doubleday, 1969 [1835-1840]); A. de Tocqueville, *Recollections* (London: MacDonald, 1970 [1893]); A. de Tocqueville, *Selected Letters on Politics and Society* (Berkeley: University of California Press, 1985); I. M. Zeitlin, *Liberty, Equality, and Revolution in Alexis de Tocqueville* (New York: Little, Brown, 1971); M. Zetterbaum, *Tocqueville and the Problem of Democracy* (Stanford, Calif.: Stanford University Press, 1967).

TOTEMISM   Primitive system of religious and social organization. Totemism is exemplified in various North American and Australian tribes characterized as clans or bands united by kinship. The clan is distinguished by the name of an animal, plant, or, more rarely, natural phenomenon. The object is usually the subject of religious emotion. Within this system, those within the clan group are given protection but cannot marry or have sexual intercourse within the clan. Émile Durkheim argued that the totemic principle—defined as belief in a mystical relationship between a group and an animal, plant, or other object, which served as their emblem—was the basis for the distinction between the sacred and the profane.

See also Émile Durkheim, Sigmund Freud

—*James McClenon*

REFERENCES

É. Durkheim, *The Elementary Forms of the Religious Life* (New York: Free Press, 1965 [1912]); J. G. Frazer, *Totemism and Exogamy* (London: Macmillan, 1910); D. P. Johnson, *Sociological Theory* (New York: Macmillan, 1986); A. Lang, *Myth, Ritual and Religion* (London: Longmans, Green, 1899); A. Lang, *Social Origins* (London: Longmans, 1903); A. Lang, *The Secret of the Totem* (London: Longmans, 1905).

TOURISM   *see* Pilgrimage

TRANSCENDENTAL MEDITATION (TM)

Maharishi Mahesh Yogi came to the United States from India in 1959 and established a nonprofit corporation named Spiritual Regeneration Foundation, the first of many such organizations designed to help spread his message of "transcendental meditation."

The Maharishi previously had obtained a degree in physics from a university in India, but he had abandoned a life based on science and instead became a hermit, living in caves and walking through the forests of India for some 13 years before becoming a missionary pledged to sharing his ideas with all of humankind. Maharishi Yogi developed a form of meditation he called Transcendental Meditation or TM (a copyrighted symbol), which involves silently meditating for two 20-minute periods each day using an individual secret Sanskrit mantra given to the meditator. The technique became quite popular in the 1960s and 1970s, and some well-known media people became adherents of the Maharishi Yogi, including the internationally popular Beatles singing group and actresses Jane Fonda and Mia Farrow. Tens of thousands of people have practiced TM techniques over the years since its inception in the United States, and most major cities continue to have TM centers open to the public.

TM received a major boost in attention and credibility in 1970, ironically from science itself. An article was published in the most prestigious scientific journal in the world—*Science*—presenting results of a scientific study comparing meditators with nonmeditators. The meditators were all trained to use TM meditating techniques. Quite significant differences on a number of physiological measures were found between the two categories, with TM receiving the credit. This and many other studies that followed helped establish TM as a technique with positive consequences and led to its being accepted by many people and in many different organizations, from schools to prisons and large corporations.

However, TM has since come under considerable attack from those who think of it as a religion and others who question findings of some of the earlier research. Indeed, TM lost a major court case in 1978 in which it sought to defend the claim that it was not a religion but was instead simply a technique of meditation. Losing this case made it easier for foes of TM to have it removed from organizational settings in which it had been accepted, and contributed to its dramatic decline in popularity and number of adherents. Claims that TM techniques could be used for levitation also undermined positive views of this movement.

—*James T. Richardson*

REFERENCES

D. Cohen, *The New Believers* (New York: Ballantine, 1975); H. Johnston, "The Marketed Social Movement," in *Money and Power in the New Religions,* ed. J. T. Richardson (Lewiston, N.Y.: Mellen, 1988): 163-183; R. K. Wallace, "Physiological Effects of Transcendental Meditation," *Science* (Mar. 27, 1970): 1751-1754.

TRANSCENDENTALISM   A philosophical orientation stressing spirituality defined in a variety of ways. The philosopher Kant argued that God and religious forces cannot be objects of scientific knowledge and were therefore transcendent, or outside the limits of possible knowledge. For the poet Coleridge, transcendentalism was an emphasis on the spiritual side of human nature. *New England transcendentalism* refers to doctrines of a philosophical and literary group based in Concord, Massachusetts (c. 1836-1860), which included Ralph Waldo Emerson, Henry David Thoreau, and Margaret Fuller. The orientation was eclectic, having Platonic, Oriental, and Kantian influences. It argued that there were two ways of knowing, through the senses and through intuition, and asserted that intuition was transcendent.

—*James McClenon*

REFERENCES

W. T. Mott, *Encyclopedia of Transcendentalism* (Westport, Conn.: Greenwood, 1996); A. Versluis, *American Transcendentalism and Asian Religions* (New York: Oxford University Press, 1993).

TROELTSCH, ERNST (1865-1923)   German theologian and philosopher; was appointed Professor of Theology at Heidelberg 1894, but in 1915 became Professor of Philosophy at Berlin. Although Albert Ritschl was his early mentor, Troeltsch continually absorbed new intellectual influences, including the ideas of Wilhelm Dilthey and, later, the philosophy of the southwest German Kantian school (especially Heinrich Rickert) and the sociology of Max Weber, among others.

Troeltsch sought to understand the varied relationships between Christianity and culture, especially modernity. He pursued this aim through the study of Christianity's development in all its main historical phases. His pioneering work *The Social Teachings of the Christian Churches* (Macmillan 1931 [1912]), influenced in part by Max Weber's sociology, embodies Troeltsch's own historical and sociological method. Troeltsch distinguished between church, sect, and mysticism as primary types of religious life. The church is more peremptorily inclusive and achieves greater accommodation to worldly institutions. The sect demands voluntary commitment from its members, is more perfectionistic in its aims, and often adopts a critical stance toward existing social arrangements. Mysticism's individualistic and spiritualistic religiosity, to which Troeltsch himself was strongly attracted, is an ever present historical possibility, but it forges especially strong links with sect organizations and has a diffuse appeal under modern social conditions. These concepts have since become central to the sociological study of religious processes and have been variously adapted by more recent thinkers (e.g., H. Richard Niebuhr and Liston Pope).

Despite many points of agreement with Weber, Troeltsch's method and sense of historical-developmental periodization were distinctive. His use of concepts is historical and dialectical. He shows the ways in which sects and forms of mysticism emerge out of conflicts within church structures over reappropriation of the common religious traditions and civilization. The typological analysis is suffused with detail drawn from the early and medieval churches, Luther, Calvin and Protestant sects, and later developments. In his book *Prot-*

estantism and Progress (Putnam 1912), Troeltsch examined the relationship of Protestant teachings to the entire range of modernity (i.e., politics, economic life, social classes, culture, and so on). Troeltsch saw modernity emerging with the Enlightenment and, unlike Weber, thought the ideas of both Luther and Calvin remained largely medieval in cast.

Troeltsch also was interested in the role of natural law doctrines in the development of Christianity. With the waning of early Christian apocalyptic expectations, the church absorbed Stoic natural law theories, as well as other elements of ancient philosophy, and adapted them to Christianity's increasing involvement in Roman society. The result was a twofold development. On the one hand, Stoic-Christian natural law allowed Christianity to accommodate its teachings to the systems of patriarchal family authority, imperial law and political organization, economic life (including slavery), and other social practices of late Antiquity, while at the same time tempering these practices in the name of Christian principles. Christianity could thus elaborate church doctrines suited to its seemingly permanent existence in a fallen world. On the other hand, the idea of a natural law of the prelapsarian state allowed for the repeated emergence of communities that aimed at mimetically recapturing primitive perfection or re-creating the apostolic life. The rationales provided by Stoic-Christian natural law thereby aided the development of both church and sect types of religiosity (Troeltsch 1991).

Troeltsch's theological commitments made it difficult for him to dispense entirely with Christianity's universal truth claims, and he grappled throughout his life with the problem of Christianity's historical relativity. This problem was related to his early interest in the history-of-religions school. His posthumously published work on historicism and its problems was a full study of these perspectives and their relationship to his theological concerns. Although he came increasingly to accept the historical relativity of Christianity, it is not clear that he ever fully resolved the tensions between a thoroughgoing relativism in the comparative-historical study of religion and the idea of Christianity as a universally valid salvation religion whose essence was, in some sense, always present despite its varied manifestations under differing historical circumstances (Troeltsch 1972). However, few authors have confronted these issues so directly and effectively as Troeltsch, and his work remains a cornerstone in the edifice of the sociology of religion.

See also James Luther Adams, Church-Sect Theory, H. Richard Niebuhr, Max Weber

—*Donald A. Nielsen*

REFERENCES

H. Drescher, *Ernst Troeltsch* (London: SCM, 1992); E. Troeltsch, *The Absoluteness of Christianity and the History of Religions* (London: SCM Press, 1972); E. Troeltsch, *Religion in History* (Minneapolis: Fortress, 1991).

TURNER, VICTOR W(ITTER) (1920-1983)

Scots-born social anthropologist who studied at University College, London, and took his Ph.D. under Max Gluckman at the University of Manchester. From 1950 to 1954, Turner was a research officer at the Rhodes-Livingston Institute in Zambia, where he began what was to be a lifelong study of Ndembu village life, ritual, and symbolism. He taught at the University of Manchester from 1955 to 1963, when he moved to the United States. Turner served as Professor of Anthropology at Cornell University, 1964-1968. From 1968 to 1977, he was Professor of Anthropology and Social Thought at the University of Chicago, and then until the time of his death he was William R. Kenan Professor of Anthropology and Religion at the University of Virginia.

Turner ultimately broke with Gluckman's functional analysis in favor of a more processual model of cultural systems. Turner's first major book, *Schism and Continuity in an African Society* (Manchester University Press 1957), documented ways in which ritual performances play an important role in resolving village conflict. He was a leading proponent of the "case study" approach in ethnographic research and is noted for his scrupulous attention to ethnographic detail.

Although Turner considered his approach to be a radical departure from his functionalist contemporaries (like Gluckman), he shared much with functional theorists of his day, including a focus on ritual and ceremonial performance in the perpetuation of society. Perhaps Turner's greatest contributions lie in his keen recognition that rituals serve not only to maintain the social order but have the potential to create new social possibilities as well. Building on the work of Arnold van Gennep (1909), Turner was especially fascinated by the "liminal" stage in rites of passage. He suggested that rituals offer "decisive keys to the understanding of how people think and feel about relationships and about the natural and social environments in which they operate" (1969:6).

The bulk of Turner's work has been an attempt to understand the general characteristics of ritual, in particular its fusion of ideological content, emotional power, and efficacy. But his influence extends beyond his own writings. Turner also served as general editor of the acclaimed "Symbol, Myth, and Ritual" series for Cornell University Press, which provided for the dissemination of the ideas of Frank Manning, Barbara Babcock, Ronald Grimes, Raymond Firth, Barbara Meyerhoff, and others. With his wife, Edith L. B. Turner, he also conducted extensive ethnographic research on pilgrimages and pilgrimage sites in Europe and the Americas. Their findings were published in a seminal work, *Image and Pilgrimage in Christian Culture* (Columbia University Press 1995 [1978]).

See also Rites of Passage

—*Stephen D. Glazier*

REFERENCES

A. van Gennep, *The Rites of Passage* (London: Routledge, 1960 [1909]); V. W. Turner, *The Forest of Symbols* (Ithaca, N.Y.: Cornell University Press, 1967); V. W. Turner, *The Ritual Process* (Chicago: Aldine, 1969); V. W. Turner, *On the Edge of the Bush* (Tucson: University of Arizona Press, 1985).

TWO-PARTY THESIS   Originated by Jean Miller Schmidt, popularized by Martin Marty in *Righteous Empire* (Dial 1970); an interpretation of the historical development of American Protestantism based on analogy to U.S. politics (Democrats and Republicans).

Protestants are identified as either progressive, reform oriented (often currently termed *liberal*) or pietistic and personalistic (now, in shorthand, either *conservative* or *evangelical*). Although the thesis provides a convenient heuristic device for addressing major trends in the dominant, white, Protestant traditions, it also misses many nuances and tends to ignore minority traditions. It rightly signals, however, the ironically close connection between religious and political developments in a nation that pioneered the formal "separation of church and state." Robert Wuthnow's *The Restructuring of American Religion* (Princeton University Press 1987) represents perhaps the best example of both the strengths and the weaknesses of this type of analysis in the current case. Taken to an extreme, from which Marty himself has dissented, this view can be said to be a precursor to the *Culture Wars* model of James Davison Hunter (Basic Books 1991).

—*William H. Swatos, Jr.*

REFERENCE

J. M. Schmidt, *Souls or the Social Order* (Brooklyn, N.Y.: Carlson, 1991).

TYLOR, EDWARD B(URNETT) (1832-1917)

Founder of British anthropology. Tylor was the son of a Quaker brass-founder. The most complete presentation of Tylor's concepts is found in his work *Primitive Culture* (1871), reprinted as *Religion in Primitive Culture* (Harper 1958). He published many major articles as well as the first general anthropology textbook (1881).

Tylor gradually gained recognition for his work, received an honorary doctorate from the University of Oxford in 1875, became keeper of the Oxford University Museum in 1883, reader in anthropology in 1884, and was knighted in 1912. Tylor's major contribution was his theory that all religions are based on *animism*. Although his evolutionary orientation appears ethnocentric to modern readers, he had a major impact on the development of anthropological thought with regard to religion.

Tylor defined religion as "the belief in spiritual beings" and argued that this belief exists in all known societies. Although Tylor did not invent the concept of animism, he gave it added scope. He defined animism as having two parts: belief in the human soul that survives bodily death and belief in other spirits, including deities. Tylor hypothesized that animism was the foundation of all religions.

Tylor argued that the development of belief in souls was a natural result of attempts to explain such phenomena as dreams, trances, apparitions, visions, shadows, reflections, loss of consciousness, and death. He provided many example cases from a wide variety of societies exemplifying the forms of behavior and faith associated with acceptance of souls. The hypothesis that belief in souls evolved from naturally occurring phenomena explains the fact that all known societies have conceived of the notion that humans have souls.

Tylor suggested that belief in spirits and deities was an outgrowth of belief in souls. He cited many accounts of beliefs regarding soul travel, souls lingering about the deceased, restless souls of the dead whose objectives during life have not been accomplished, and a wide variety of funeral rites. The souls of departed relatives are a target for propitiation and worship. Spirits may take over a living body, creating shamanic possession, a phenomenon prevalent in many societies. Numerous societies believed that the souls of the dead could associate themselves with objects and, consequently, these objects came to represent spiritual entities. This led to the doctrine of fetishism: veneration paid to animals, trees, fish, plants, idols, pebbles, claws of beasts, sticks, and so forth.

According to Tylor, this concept was extended to veneration of specific spirits and gods less attached to objects. As a consequence, primitive people devised the concepts of gods, demons, spirits, devils, ghosts, fairies, gnomes, elves, and angels. A further development is the association of gods with the concept of good and evil, a duality leading to belief in highly powerful deities. An alternate pathway to development of powerful deities is the seeking of "first causes" for reality. Such questions, coupled with fusion of lesser deities, may result in the concept of a Supreme Being. Tylor argued that "Animism has its distinct and consistent outcome, and Polytheism its distinct and consistent completion, in the doctrine of a Supreme Deity" (1958:422).

Tylor felt that "savage animism is almost devoid of that ethical element which to the educated modern mind is the very mainspring of practical religion. . . . The lower animism is not immoral, it is unmoral" (1958:446). The practices of prayer, sacrifice, fasting, "artificial ecstasy," and purification rituals were associated with consideration of moral issues.

Later anthropologists took issue with many of Tylor's arguments. Robert Marett (1936 [1914]) argued that not all primitive people felt that the spirits in inanimate objects were equivalent to souls; he hypothesized that supernatural forces probably had a variety of origins other than the concept of the human soul. Andrew Lang argued validly that supposedly "low" races of humans had belief in "high" gods that were neither ghosts nor spirits. Modern anthropologists criticize Tylor for ignoring the many economic, political, and psychological functions that religions fulfill. Tylor's work is often regarded as naively evolutionistic and overly intellectual.

David Hufford (1982) and James McClenon (1994) provide a theory that is parallel to some of Tylor's arguments. They suggest that certain primary elements within some anomalous experiences (for example, sleep paralysis and near-death experience) support and, in some cases, produce belief in souls, spirits, life after death, and anomalous abilities. Although Tylor's orientation viewed primitive people as unable to distinguish objective from subjective perceptions, Hufford's and McClenon's orientations portray the development of religious sentiment as a rational process. Within this theory, extrasensory perceptions, apparitions, out-of-body experiences, sleep paralysis, and contacts with the dead had effects on primitive people similar to the effects they have on modern individuals; experiences lead to belief in spiritual forces. This perspective coincides with Tylor's theory in seeking to understand the religious repercussions of people's anomalous perceptions.

See also Animism

—*James McClenon*

REFERENCES

J. W. Burrow, *Evolution and Society* (London: Cambridge University Press, 1966); D. J. Hufford, *The Terror That Comes in the Night* (Philadelphia: University of Pennsylvania Press, 1982); R. R. Marett, *Tylor* (New York: Wiley, 1936 [1914]); J. McClenon, *Wondrous Events* (Philadelphia: University of Pennsylvania Press, 1994); E. J. Sharpe, *Comparative Religion* (New York: Scribner, 1975).

UFO/FLYING SAUCER CULTS

Although UFO (unidentified flying object) sightings occurred in the 1880s, modern accounts of UFO phenomena began after World War II. In 1947, pilot Kenneth Arnold reported sighting (what came to be known as) "flying saucers" near Mount Rainier, and many people insist that a few weeks later an alien craft crashed near Roswell, New Mexico. Speculation persists that the U.S. military keeps the Roswell debris at a top-secret military base in Nevada (popularly called Area 51), and UFO believers reject the U.S. government's official explanation that the downed object was a balloon (with radar and instruments) being tested secretly as a low pressure wave detector for monitoring Soviet nuclear weapons explosions. Consequently, UFO believers harbor deep distrust of government.

Flying saucer cults began in the 1950s after people disseminated tales of their alleged contacts with intelligent extraterrestrial life forms. To their alleged encounters, "contactees" such as George Adamski and Orfeo Angelucci attached religious meaning, which often incorporated spiritualist and theosophical principles with apocalyptic and millennialist themes. These themes reflected growing American cultural fears of communism and nuclear destruction, combined with faith in the salvific nature of technology. Masonic and Rosicrucian ideals and rituals also appeared within some of the early groups and, most recently, in the Order of the Solar Temple. Contemporary UFO groups additionally borrow from "New Age" and Christian doctrines (as

did Heaven's Gate) as well as from the general science fiction milieu. The range of beliefs among these groups is quite wide, including people who claim to have seen UFOs, alleged contactees, alleged contactees who have visited ships or other worlds, reputed victims of alien experimentation, and alleged aliens who live among humans.

Two of the oldest and most studied flying saucer groups are the Aetherius Society (founded by George King) and the Unarius Foundation (founded by the late Ruth Norman). The founders of these groups were "mystagogues" (to use Weber's term), who attempted to mesh theosophical and millenarian principles with modern scientific thought and technology. This sort of "technoanimism" is magical thinking that employs "space" rather than nature imagery amidst faith in the salvific nature of alien technology. A less studied French group, the Raelian movement, operates around the teachings of its charismatic leader, Rael, who preaches salvation through science and alien technology, in the context of the divine nature of human sexuality. Followers seek communion with the divine through sensual meditation, and embrace sexual experimentation that transgresses the boundaries of conventional sexuality (such as homosexuality and transvestism).

The most controversial groups combining UFO belief with variations of contactee assertions are the Order of the Solar Temple and Heaven's Gate. Both groups are distinctly apocalyptic, and they believe that suicide would provide them with immortality in the (literal) heavens through their contact with space beings. Often groups alleging contact with aliens who impart wisdom shade into the popular theosophical/New Age phenomenon of reputedly channeling messages from higher, more advanced entities. Likewise, Christian-based UFO groups believe that UFOs manifest angels and other spiritual guides that will help believers battle the Antichrist and survive the apocalypse. In contrast, some fundamentalist Christians see UFO phenomena as a precursor to the apocalypse.

Melodie Campbell and Stephen A. Kent

REFERENCES

R. Balch, "Looking Behind the Scenes in a Religious Cult," *Sociological Analysis* 41(1980):137-143; C. D. B. Bryan, *Close Encounters of the Fourth Kind* (New York: Knopf, 1995); D. Curan, *In Advance of the Landing* (New York: Abbeville, 1985); R. S. Ellwood, "Spiritualism and UFO Religion in New Zealand," *Syzygy* 1(1992):323-393; L. Festinger et al., *When Prophecy Fails* (Minneapolis: University of Minnesota Press, 1956); M. Introvigne, "Ordeal by Fire," *Religion* 25(1995):267-283; R. G. Kirkpatrick and D. Tumminia, "California Space Goddess," in *Twentieth-Century World Religious Movements in Neo-Weberian Perspective*, ed. W. H. Swatos, Jr. (Lewiston, N.Y.: Mellen, 1992): 299-311; J. Lewis (ed.), *The Gods Have Landed* (Albany: SUNY Press, 1995); T. Miller, *America's Alternative Religions* (Albany: SUNY Press, 1995).

ULTIMACY   The academic (and legal and political) problems with the concept of "religion," which arise from its context of origin, are epitomized (although less often mentioned) in the particular case of the concept of "God." The adoption of such paraphrases as *the sacred* or *the holy* probably owed as much, in the early stages of religious studies, to a desire to avoid appearing theological as it did to their empirical appropriateness. Indeed, there is still a dearth of comparative studies of both the overlap and the individual distinctiveness of the meanings popularly given to the concepts of *God," "sacred," and "holy,"* or of *"gods,"* the *"supernatural," "divine,"* and so on.

Among these paraphrases, *ultimacy* has an honorable pedigree but has been underused. Theologian Paul Tillich's description of all religion (both official and otherwise) as "ultimate concern" echoed both Luther's description of gods and Jesus's of devotion. It had the distinct advantage, for ministers or academics who deal empirically with religion, of returning divinity to experience. That it fell out of fashion following Tillich's

death may have been due partly to the absence of any tradition that operationalized it, in those terms, and partly to the fear (among both believers and nonbelievers) that it was intended to be an exact synonym for God. J. Milton Yinger (1973) also attempted within social science to construct an inclusive functionalist definition of religion based on "ultimate concern," which generated initial interest but, similarly, appears to have had little continuing impact.

The Institute for the Study of Human Ideas of Ultimate Reality and Meaning (URAM) has, however, more recently taken up and developed the expression. The articles in its quarterly journal, *Ultimate Reality and Meaning: Inter-Disciplinary Studies in the Philosophy of "Understanding"* (University of Toronto Press) are intended to build up an encyclopedia of that name. Its editors, Tibor Horvath and John F. Perry, describe its purpose as publishing

> studies dealing with those facts, things, ideas, axioms, persons and values which people throughout history have considered ultimate (i.e., that to which the human mind reduces and relates everything and that which one does not reduce and relate to anything else) or as horizons (i.e., world views in the light of which humans understand whatever they understand) or as supreme value (i.e., for which someone would sacrifice everything and which one would not lose for anything). [The hope is that t]he analytical and critical description of all that the human mind ever thought about the ultimate reality and meaning of human existence is expected to initiate systematic and structural studies of the most universal dynamics that have driven human consciousness from its dawn until the present day.

Edward I. Bailey

REFERENCES

P. Tillich, *Ultimate Concern* (London: SCM, 1965); J. M. Yinger, *The Scientific Study of Religion* (New York: Macmillan, 1973); T. H. Zock, *A Psychology of Ultimate Concern* (Amsterdam: Rodopi, 1990).

UNIFICATION CHURCH   New religious movement, known under a number of names including, in particular, officially, the Holy Spirit Association for the Unification of World Christianity and, in common parlance, the Moonies.

Origins The movement has its roots in the Korea of the 1940s. The founder, Sun Myung Moon (1920–), was born in a rural part of what is now North Korea to parents who had converted to a Presbyterian version of Christianity when he was 10 years old. On Easter in 1936, it is claimed that Moon received a message from Jesus telling him that he had been chosen to fulfill the special mission of establishing God's Kingdom of Heaven on earth. During the next nine years, Moon is said to have received further revelations through prayer, study, and a number of conversations with important religious leaders such as Moses and Buddha and, indeed, with God. The teachings, which came to be known as the *Divine Principle,* were eventually written down by Moon's followers, the first version in Korean in 1957. They were later translated into English and other languages in a number of different editions (e.g., Kwak 1980).

Moon enrolled as an electrical engineering student in Japan in 1941. Two years later, he returned to Korea and found work as an electrician but was arrested by the Japanese police for alleged involvement in underground political activities in support of Korean independence. Later he was to be arrested more than once by the communists on a variety of counts, including "teaching heretical doctrines." There are several accounts of the torture to which he was subjected and about the time he spent in a labor camp during the Korean War. Released by the U.N. forces in 1950, Moon made his way to Pusan and then, with a small group of followers, moved to Seoul. His problems with the authorities continued, but the movement started to attract a growing membership and began sending missionaries to other parts of the world. In 1959, an erstwhile college professor, Dr. Young Oon Kim, took the teachings to the United States, and it was the small group that she set up on the West Coast that was the subject of John Lofland's *Doomsday Cult,* first published in 1966 (Irvington 1977).

Official Beliefs The *Divine Principle,* which is based on Moon's interpretation of the Old and New Testaments, is one of the more comprehensive and systematic of the belief systems to be found among contemporary new religious movements. It teaches that God created Adam and Eve intending that they would marry and, with their children, establish a God-centered family. Moon's special interpretation of the Fall is that, before Adam and Eve had matured sufficiently to be blessed in marriage, the Archangel Lucifer, jealous of God's love for Adam, developed a relationship with Eve that culminated in an illicit (spiritual) sexual relationship. Eve then tempted Adam to have a (physical) sexual relationship with her. The consequences were that the family arising from this union, instead of being God-centered, was Lucifer-centered, and that "Fallen Nature" (a Unification concept with some similarities to that of original sin) has been passed down from generation to generation. Thus not merely disobedience but the misuse of love, the most powerful of all forces, was and has continued to be responsible for the evil to be found throughout the world.

According to the *Divine Principle,* the whole of history can be interpreted as God's attempts to work with key figures to restore the Kingdom of Heaven on earth. Ultimately this is possible only through a Messiah faithfully playing the role that Adam failed to perform—to establish a God-centered family. This was the mission of Jesus, but partly because John the Baptist did not encourage the people to follow him, Jesus was murdered before he had the opportunity to marry. A Unification reading of subsequent history reveals remarkable parallels between the time of Jesus and the past 2000 years. It encourages us, furthermore, to recognize that the Lord of the Second Advent was born in Korea between 1917 and 1930. Unificationists believe Moon is that Messiah and that he laid the foundation for the restoration of God's Kingdom when he married his present wife in 1960.

There is a further elaboration of Unification beliefs not contained in the *Divine Principle* but to be found in the speeches that Moon has delivered to his followers throughout the years. These beliefs center on the person of Moon and his family, and explain the important role that they have played and continue to play. Moon and many of his followers have always had a close association with spiritualist beliefs and mediumship, and after the death of one of Moon's sons, Heung Jin Nim, a number of people reported having received messages from him from the spirit world; then, for some months, a young member from Zimbabwe conducted what appeared to be a revivalist movement within the church and was widely accredited as being a "second self Heung Jin Nim." Eventually, however, the young man's authority and statements showed signs of conflicting with those of Moon, and the young man returned to Africa, where he set up a schismatic movement.

Life in the Movement In the early 1970s, Moon moved to the United States. Within a few years, his had become a household name, and the "Moonies," as they became known, developed a highly visible profile, selling candles, literature, and other goods in public places and inviting thousands to attend public rallies and residential Unification seminars where potential converts could learn about the movement. New members in those days typically lived in a Unification center or with a mobile fund-raising team, working full time for the movement either fund-raising or "witnessing" to potential members.

After having been in the movement for some time, members may be "matched" to a partner chosen by Moon, whom they might never have met before—who might not even speak the same language. Although they can reject Moon's suggestion (and several have done so), the majority have gone on to what is probably the most important Unification ritual, the Holy Wine Ceremony, when the members believe their blood lineage is purified, followed by a mass wedding ceremony, known as the Blessing, with as many as several thousand other couples. It is believed that the children born into these families are without Fallen Nature.

Although Unificationism does not practice as many rituals as some of the other new religions, its members do perform a short "Pledge" ceremony at 5 a.m. on the movement's holy days and on the first day of each week and month. There are special ceremonies that a couple will go through when they consummate their marriage and when their children are born, and there are also a number of practices including the use of holy salt and the establishment of a number of holy places throughout the world.

There have been literally hundreds of organizations associated, often through overlapping membership, with the Unification Church. Among the better known of these are the student arm of the movement CARP (Collegiate Association for Research into Principles), several political organizations (such as CAUSA and, in the early days, the Freedom Leadership Foundation), the International Religious Foundation, the International Cultural Foundation, and various projects connected with the arts such as the Korean Folk Ballet. Another project is the building of an international highway around the world, starting with a tunnel between Korea and Japan. On the academic side, there are the Little Angels school and a new university in Korea, the Unification Theological Seminary in upstate New York, ICUS (the International Conference on the Unity of the Sciences), the Professors World Peace Academy, and the Washington Institute.

Controversies   As in Korea and Japan, a number of voices in the West have been raised against Moon and his followers. In the 1970s, disquiet was expressed about various political activities arising out of Moon's stridently anticommunist stance, these ranging from his support of Nixon's continuing presidency at the time of the Watergate affair to the movement's coming under the scrutiny of the Fraser Committee's Investigation of Korean-American Relations (1979). More recently, Moon had widely publicized meetings with Soviet president Gorbachev and with Kim Il Sung, the late president of North Korea. Questions also have been raised about the vast sums of money that the movement has seemed to have at its disposal and the number of properties that it has bought in the United States, South America, and elsewhere. Unification businesses, such as an extensive fishing industry and the Il Hwa Pharmaceutical Company, have seemed to be prospering, and the organization appeared to be extending its influence through extravagant dinners and conferences to which influential persons have been invited and such ventures as the *Washington Times* and the Paragon House Press.

In the early 1970s, incomprehension and fear were expressed about the numbers of disproportionately middle-class, well-educated youth who were giving up college and careers to work for as many as 18 hours a day on the streets collecting money for the movement. Several anxious and angry parents began to organize, and a number of "anti-cult" groups came into existence throughout the West. Accusations of deceptive and exploitative practices and the use of brainwashing and mind control techniques being used to recruit helpless victims became widely reported in the media, and the illegal, but frequently condoned, practice of deprogramming (forcibly kidnapping members from the movement) became a not uncommon occurrence.

The influence that the Unification Church has wielded over potential and actual members has not, however, ever been close to as effective as its opponents have claimed—or even as its members might have wanted. The overwhelming majority of those subjected to the so-called brainwashing techniques have not joined the movement, and most of those who have joined have not only been capable of leaving but have left it of their own free will within a couple of years (Barker 1984, Galanter 1980, Levine 1984). By the mid-1990s, the movement had no more than a few hundred full-time members in any Western society, and at most a few tens of thousands worldwide. There is, however, a greater number of persons (but probably no more than a hundred thousand) who feel some allegiance to the movement while leading "normal" lives, living in their own homes and working in non-Unification jobs.

Changes   The movement has undergone a number of changes throughout the past few decades. Demographically, it is no longer predominantly comprised of youthful idealists with few responsibilities, eager to travel around the world at a moment's notice and to work for long hours with little or no remuneration to bring about the imminent restoration of the Kingdom of Heaven on earth. By the late 1990s, a sizable proportion of the membership has been born into the movement, and the young converts of the 1970s and 1980s are middle-aged and frequently facing financial and other responsibilities. Many, having sacrificed educational qualifications and careers for the movement, are, at least according to socioeconomic criteria, in a considerably lower position than their parents.

As with any new religion moving into a phase of second- and even third-generation membership, initial enthusiasms have waned, expectations have been disappointed, and several long-term rank-and-file members have become disillusioned with the leadership and less certain about several aspects of the belief system. Years of negative publicity and a number of court cases—including Moon's conviction in 1982 by a U.S. federal court jury of conspiracy to evade taxes and his subsequent imprisonment—have had their toll on the movement in North America and Europe. Moreover, by the late 1990s, there have been several indications that many of the movement's business ventures have been facing substantial difficulties.

The Future Inevitably questions are asked about what will happen to the movement in the future. Moon's wife and children have been playing an increasingly important role since the 1990s, but none of them has his charismatic authority, and the behavior of some has given rise to alarm among even committed Unificationists. In addition, there always have been potential factions among the Korean leadership. It is possible that there will be a number of schisms once the Unification Messiah is no longer here on earth to provide a unifying focus for the movement. It is, however, also likely that the Unification Church will continue, albeit in a somewhat different form, well into the twenty-first century.

See also Doomsday Cult, New Religious Movements

Eileen Barker

REFERENCES

E. Barker, *The Making of a Moonie* (Oxford: Blackwell, 1984); D. G. Bromley and A. Shupe, *"Moonies" in America* (Beverly Hills, Calif.: Sage, 1979); D. G. Bromley and J. T. Richardson (eds.), *The Brainwashing/Deprogramming Controversy* (Lewiston, N.Y.: Mellen, 1983); M. Galanter, "Psychological Induction into the Large Group," *American Journal of Psychiatry* 137(1980):1574-1579; C. H. Kwak, *Outline of the Principle* (New York: Holy Spirit Association for the Unification of World Christianity, 1980); S. Levine, *Radical Departures* (San Diego: Harcourt, 1984); M. L. Mickler, *A History of the Unification Church in the Bay Area*, Master's thesis, University of California, Berkeley, Graduate Theological Union, 1980; H. Richardson (ed.), *The New Religions and Mental Health* (New York: Mellen, 1980); F.

Sontag, *Sun Myung Moon and the Unification Church* (Nashville: Abingdon, 1977); B. R. Wilson (ed.), *The Social Impact of New Religious Movements* (New York: Rose of Sharon, 1981).

UNITARIANISM Rooted in Christianity, Unitarianism represents both a theological position and a religious organization.

Strictly speaking, theological unitarianism means denying the orthodox Christian doctrine of the Trinity, that God is *"three-in-one:* Father, Son, and Holy Spirit." Classical unitarianism taught the Fatherhood of God alone, and the humanity of Jesus of Nazareth. As a theological position, Unitarianism can be dated to the fourth-century Christological controversies. It was revived during the Reformation, principally by Socinius.

The Unitarian Church in the United States dates from the nineteenth century; although there were multiple wellsprings of unitarianism, including the transcendentalism emanating from Harvard University, an ordination sermon William Ellery Channing delivered in Baltimore in 1819 is normally cited as the formal beginning of the organized movement, sometimes called "liberal Christianity." Organizationally, American Unitarianism may be seen as a division from founding New England Congregationalism; it represents the organizational culmination of late eighteenth-century deist ideology. The American Unitarian Association was founded in 1825. For some years, there was a competition of sorts between the AUA and the Western Unitarian Conference, headquartered in Chicago, the WUC being considered more radical. In 1961, the AUA and the Universalists merged to form the Unitarian Universalist Association (UUA), still headquartered in Boston. Although there had been debate about the "Christianity" of Unitarianism since the late nineteenth century, from the 1960s on there has been a more marked tendency in the UUA to distance itself from Christianity and to embrace a wider variety of spiritualities.

Sociologically, Unitarian Universalists are dramatically well educated in comparison with the general population and similarly overrepresented among socioeconomic elites. The UUA has significant difficulties in holding its membership, which numbers about 250,000, cross-generationally. Its major institutions are the Harvard Divinity School, Meadville-Lombard (Chicago), and Starr King (Berkeley, California).

William H. Swatos, Jr.

REFERENCES

R. W. Lee, "Strained Bedfellows," *Sociology of Religion* 56(1995):379-396; D. Robinson, *The Unitarians and the Universalists* (Westport, Conn.: Greenwood, 1985); R. Tapp, *Religion Among the Unitarian Universalists* (New York: Seminar Press, 1973).

UNITED CHURCH OF CHRIST   *see* Congregationalism

UNIVERSALISM   The theological position, principally within Christianity, that everyone shall be "saved" or, correspondingly, that no one shall be eternally "damned."

The most frequent supporting rationale is that *eternal* damnation demeans both the goodness and the power of God. This view often draws particular inspiration from the First Letter (of Paul) to the Corinthians in the New Testament and has woven in and out of Christianity since the earliest times. Many official church councils, by contrast, condemned universalism.

In nineteenth-century America, the Universalist Church was founded as a separate denomination; it has since merged with the Unitarians into the Unitarian Universalist Association (UUA), headquartered in Boston.

William H. Swatos, Jr.

VALUES A value is a normative proposition; it meets a need that seeks to satisfy or that finds its meaning in a universal truth, accepted by the subject. At the same time, it is made up either of an object of particular importance for the subject agent or of a higher truth; it has a prescriptive nature, and a person is subject to a continuous effort to assert the value in which he or she believes.

A value is subordinated to the existential context, and it is always verified by social events. It is the sphere of existence that founds and circumscribes that of values. As an orientation toward a person's actions with respect to an end, a value also can be a reference point for several norms, even as one norm may constitute the reference for a plurality of values.

In sociology, the concept of the value acquired importance in the twentieth century in a cultural context of reaction against the preceding culture. According to Luciano Gallino (1988:722-724), in this period the independent emergence of the term *value* was characterized by a high level of generalization. It marked the manifestation of a profound change in modern culture that occurred in particular on the social side. It was in this period that the concept of the value became an object of analysis by sociologists who offered various interpretations.

Values in Sociological Interpretation In American sociology, the cultural change of the twentieth century led to the decline of the instinctual categories of behav-

ior that encouraged social scholars to consider instincts, interests, and needs as the causes of behavior. It began to be accepted that the organic factor was not the cause of behavior in its rough form but only in the form that it assumes as the product of experience.

The first systematic discussion of the concept of values appeared in "Methodological Note" in the book by William I. Thomas and Florian Znaniecki, *The Polish Peasant in Europe and America* (University of Chicago Press 1918-1920). Here values were defined in connection with the psychological concept of "attitude." According to Thomas and Znaniecki, while "the value" is an object that has an accessible content and meaning for the members of the social group, "the attitude" is a subjective orientation of the members of the group toward values.

These authors intended the definition of *value* and *attitude* only to be a starting point for the development of social theory. Roles are objects and not part of the orientation of the actors; social roles do not only refer to attitudes, they also express them. In Thomas and Znaniecki's opinion, the scientific value of an event depends on its connection to other events and, in this connection, the most common factors are precisely those that have the greatest value.

By *social value,* Thomas and Znaniecki meant each datum that has an empirical content that is accessible to the members of a social group and a meaning in reference to which it is or it can be the object of activity. Social values contrast with natural things; they have no meaning for human activity and they are treated as valueless: When natural things assume a meaning, they become social values.

This interpretation by Thomas and Znaniecki acted as a spur to further studies and theories that have continued up until the present day. An important contribution was made by Clyde Kluckhohn in his article "Values and Value-Orientations in the Theory of Action" (1951), where he stated that "a value is a conception, explicit or implicit, distinctive of an individual or characteristic of a group, of the desirable which influences the selection from available modes, means and ends of action." Here the cognitive element is the decisive criterion between the values and the subjective quantities such as feelings, emotions, attitudes, and needs as well as values and preferences.

In Kluckhohn's opinion, a value is expressed in the long term and becomes desirable when it is interiorized by the subject and integrated into his or her personality system. The action is thus motivated by the "needs-orientations," which are the objective conditions, and by the "values-orientations," which correspond to the choices made by the person on the basis of interiorized values.

Values explain their prescriptive nature, by fixing limits within which the example of the affective faculty is admitted; they depend on the hierarchy and configuration of the ends of the personality and on the situation and requirements of the cultural system. The integration of values in an evaluative system that contributes to a large extent to identifying individual cultures is a condition for the integration of motivations in a certain system that identifies individual personalities.

Other important American approaches include Pitirim Sorokin's *Society, Culture and Personality* (Harper 1947) and Paul Hanly Furfey's *The Scope and Method of Sociology* (Harper 1953). Sorokin defined a *value* as follows: "Any meaning in a narrow sense is a value. Any value presupposes a norm of conduct with reference to its realization or rejection." Furfey's definition is also useful: "The quality of recognized desirability founded on goodness."

Howard Paul Becker, in his work *Through Values to Social Interpretation* (Duke University Press 1950), stated that a value is "any object of any need." Intrinsic to his work is the theory that values must be discovered in phenomena as well as in the object itself; a value is created in the object when it becomes the result of necessity or desire. In other words, as Franz Adler stated in "The Value Concept of Sociology" (1956), "a value is what is valued." Ideally, this approach should move from static considerations of definitional abstractions to research on the *process* of valuing.

A further definition sees values as placed in humans and deriving from their biological necessities or from their "mind." The following is, for example, the definition of a value that Kimball Young gave in *Sociology: A Study of Society and Culture* (American Book Company 1949): "A combination of ideas and attitudes which gives a scale of preference or priority to motives and goals as well as to a course of action from motive to goal."

The theories of Robert E. Park, William E. Burgess, Ellsworth Faris, and George Herbert Mead are also of note. The definition given by Park and Burgess in *Introduction to the Science of Sociology* (University of Chicago Press 1924)—"anything capable of being appreciated (wished for) is a 'value' "—considers values as things that arise in the object where and when desire or need call upon it. Faris and G. H. Mead can be considered two sociologists who formulated a new conceptualization of values as elements of the personality.

Faris, in his two essays "Social Attitudes" and "The Concept of Social Attitudes" in *The Nature of Human Nature* (McGraw-Hill 1937), stated that values have an objective dimension toward which actors can direct their attitudes and actions and an attitudinal dimension that constitutes an element of orientation. Mead, in *Mind, Self and Society* (University of Chicago Press 1934), formulated principles according to which normative attitudes become the central part of the human personality.

Also worthy of mention is the interpretation of a value given by Milton Rokeach in his book *The Nature of Human Values* (Free Press 1973):

> A value is an enduring belief that a specific mode of conduct or end-state of existence is personally or socially preferable to an opposite or converse mode of conduct or end-state of existence. A value system is an enduring organization of beliefs concerning desirable modes of conduct or end-states of existence along a continuum of relative importance.

The 1930s saw the return of the European theorists, in particular Max Weber and Émile Durkheim, and a wealth of theoretical and methodological concepts were published concerning, among others, the concept of values. It can be said that the relaunch of the notion of values in contemporary sociology can be attributed to Talcott Parsons's work *The Social System* (Free Press 1951), which is perhaps the most complete expression of the structural-functionalist current of thought. It is a work that starts from the presupposition of the rejection of the positivistic conception of conduct as predetermined by the situation.

—*Luigi Tomasi*

REFERENCES

F. Adler, "The Value Concept in Sociology," *American Journal of Sociology* 27(1956):272-279; L. Gallino, *Dizionario di Sociologia* (Turin: Utet, 1988); C. Kluckhohn, "Values and Value-Orientations in the Theory of Action," in *Towards a General Theory of Action,* ed. T. Parsons and E. Shils (Cambridge: Harvard University Press, 1951): 388-433.

VATICAN II

The Second Vatican Council in Roman Catholicism, 1962-1965, which was the first "ecumenical" church council of Roman Catholics since Vatican I in 1869-1870, was convened by Pope John XXIII with the explicit purpose of *aggiornamento,* that is, updating the church to function in modern society.

According to Roman Catholic teaching, an ecumenical council consists of all cardinals and bishops assembled to consider church affairs and who are institutionally empowered to affect the teaching, pastoral policy, and self-organization of the church. The mandate given by Pope John XXIII to the council fathers was to adapt church structures to the needs and methods of our times.

The 16 conciliar decrees that resulted from the four council sessions created major changes in the theology and practices of the Catholic Church worldwide. These changes are summarized by Dulles (1988) as follows: (1) *aggiornamento,* that is, updating, modernization, or adaptation of the church to the mid-twentieth century; (2) reformability of the church, that is, the admission that the church has committed errors in the past, accepts responsibility, and is intent on reformation; (3) renewed attention to the Word of God, focus upon the Scriptures, and liturgy in the vernacular so that people can understand the message of God; (4) collegiality, that is, the view of the pope as head of the college of bishops with each bishop governing his diocese in consultation with his priests, religious, and laity; (5) religious freedom, or the approval of civil tolerance for all faiths and the rejection of any coercion in the sphere of belief; (6) active role of the laity, that is, expansion of roles for the laity in divine worship, in pastoral councils, and in the mission of the church; (7) regional and local variety, or the recognition that diversity of customs, language, and observances enhances the richness of the church; (8) ecumenism, or reverence for the heritage of other Christian churches; (9) dialogue with other religions, both Christian and non-Christian alike, that establishes

dynamic tension between dialogue and the need for mission activities so that Christ may be acknowledged among all peoples; (10) social mission of the church, establishing the apostolate of peace and social justice as a continuation of Christ's compassion on the poor and oppressed.

While many Catholics lauded the changes effected by Vatican II, there also arose a reactionary movement whose members accused the church of succumbing to the heresy of modernism. The conflict between the liberals and conservatives in the postconciliar church remains unsettled. However, there is widespread agreement among both Catholics and non-Catholics that the post-Vatican II Catholic Church is very different from the church that existed prior to the Second Vatican Council.

—*Helen Rose Ebaugh*

REFERENCES

G. Burns, *The Frontiers of Catholicism* (Berkeley: University of California Press, 1992); A. Dulles, *The Reshaping of Catholicism* (San Francisco: Harper, 1988); H. R. Ebaugh (ed.), *Vatican II and U.S. Catholicism* (Greenwich, Conn.: JAI, 1991); W. McSweeney, *Roman Catholicism* (New York: St. Martin's, 1980).

VERBIT, MERVIN F. (1936–)

Received his bachelor's degree from the University of Pennsylvania (1958), and master's (1961) and doctorate (1968) from Columbia University. Founding President (1971-1973) of the Association for the Sociological (now Social Scientific) Study of Jewry, and served later (1977-1980) as Chairman of the Editorial Board of its journal, *Contemporary Jewry.* From 1977 to 1979, he was a contributing editor for *Review of Religious Research,* and since 1990, a member of the Wilstein Institute for Jewish Policy Studies' Advisory Board.

His writings focus on contemporary Jewish life, with special emphasis on the structure and substance of Jewish identity, particularly among American university students.

—*J. Alan Winter*

VERSCHEURE, JACQUES (1913-1987)

Deputy Director of the Social Secretariat of the Diocese of Lille (France) in which capacity he stimulated socioreligious research; this resulted in the establishment in 1959 of a regional Center of Socioreligious Research, which he chaired.

In 1969, at a crucial moment in the history of the International Society for the Sociology of Religion (then CISR, now SISR), he became Secretary General. In this capacity, he organized eight international conferences and made the transition from a socioreligious society toward a scientific organization acceptable to members involved in pastoral research. The successive presidents—Acquaviva, Wilson, Martin, and Dobbelaere—whom he seconded organizationally, were in charge of its scientific policy.

—*Karel Dobbelaere*

VIOLENCE   The (usually intentional) use of harmful force; studies involving religion include examinations of international religious violence (e.g., Indian and Pakistani tensions), violence between groups and society (e.g., the Sikh nationalist movement), violence among groups (e.g., Protestants versus Catholics in Northern Ireland), violence among members (e.g., members' murders of other Jonestown followers), and violence against self (e.g., religious suicide).

Because religion provides reputedly divine justification for activities, history is replete with examples of groups or members invoking the supernatural to sanctify their violent actions (e.g., abortion clinic bombings). While some explanations focus upon the pathogenic nature of the participants, others address the social contexts in which violence occurs.

A number of studies examine the processes by which some groups demonize and dehumanize nonmembers in a manner that facilitates violence. In extreme cases, demonization and dehumanization can lead to acts of religious terrorism (i.e., Islamic fundamentalist sectarianism fostering the World Trade Center bombing). Additional studies examine how various religions use violence, force, and coercion to control or punish their own members (including children) through extreme hardships, corporal punishment, injury, or death. During periods of tension, violence often increases as class, ethnic, and nationalist loyalties interweave with religion.

On the level of imagery and meaning, many religiously related symbols highlight violent tendencies in various traditions. Patriarchal symbols, myths, and teachings, for example, facilitate gender imbalances that often translate into male violence against women. Sacrificial imagery (as in Christianity) has led to reli-

gious models for personal and collective acts of martyrdom and self-violence. Christian scriptures also formed the basis for anti-Semitic violence. Likewise, apocalyptic and messianic imagery involving divine judgments of evil translate into messianically violent tendencies in some traditions of Judaism, Christianity, Islam, and folk Buddhism.

Violent religious persecution is likely to occur either when the state is unable to control rising tensions among competing groups (e.g., in the former Yugoslavia) or when the state itself feels offended or threatened by religiously motivated behavior (e.g., the Iranian attacks against Baha'is).

—*Stephen A. Kent*

REFERENCES

M. Barkun, *Religion and the Racist Right* (Chapel Hill: University of North Carolina Press, 1995); D. A. Blanchard and T. J. Prewitt, *Religious Violence and Abortion* (Gainesville: University Press of Florida, 1993); R. Cartwright and S. Kent, "Social Control in Alternative Religions," *Sociological Analysis* 53(1992):345-361; N. Cohn, *Pursuit of the Millennium* (New York: Oxford University Press, 1976); L. Collins and D. LaPierre, *Freedom at Midnight* (New York: Simon & Schuster, 1975); A. J. Droge and J. D. Tabor, *A Noble Death* (San Francisco: Harper, 1992); S. Ganguly, *The Origins of War in South Asia* (Boulder, Colo.: Westview, 1986); R. Girard, *Violence and the Sacred* (Baltimore: Johns Hopkins University Press, 1977); P. Greven, *Spare the Child* (New York: Knopf, 1991); J. H. Hall, *Gone from the Promised Land* (New Brunswick, N.J.: Transaction, 1987); D. Hiro, *Holy Wars* (New York: Routledge, 1989); A. L. Horton and J. A. Williamson (eds.), *Abuse and Religion* (Toronto: Lexington, 1988); R. Kapur, *Sikh Separatism* (London: Allen & Unwin, 1986); K. Levi (ed.), *Violence and Religious Commitment* (University Park: Pennsylvania State University Press, 1982); D. L. Overmyer, *Folk Buddhist Religion* (Cambridge: Harvard University Press, 1976); R. Wallis, "Sex, Violence, and Religion," *Update* 7, 4(1983):3-11.

VIRGINITY   A state of purity, particularly a body not yet defiled by sexual activity.

The early church fathers held that sexual union corrupted men; it took their minds off God and caused them to be preoccupied with their lower nature. Rosemary Radford Ruether (1974:150-183) studied the rationale for Christian virginity and found that the virgin state allowed women to *rise above* their sinful nature and enabled men to *fulfill* their good nature. Historically, a vow of chastity was a woman's only path to holiness. The Virgin Mary encompasses the mystery and honor accorded the celibate state. In the words of Marina Warner (1985), she represents a central theme in the history of Western attitudes to women.

See also Purity

—*Nancy Nason-Clark*

REFERENCES

R. R. Ruether (ed.), *Religion and Sexism* (New York: Simon & Schuster, 1974); M. Warner, *Alone of All Her Sex* (London: Picador, 1985).

VIRGIN MARY   Title generally applied to the birth mother of Jesus of Nazareth.

Christian scholars are not united in their understanding of the role and status accorded to the birth mother of Jesus. Within the Roman Catholic tradition, Mary has been venerated and indeed Mariology introduces a major female character into Christian doctrine and worship. Protestants, on the other hand, have downplayed Mary's role, implying that too much emphasis on Mary constitutes idolatry.

Luke's infancy narrative, the most detailed scriptural account of the circumstances surrounding the birth of Jesus, portrays Mary as an "active, personal agent in the drama of God's incarnation." Rosemary Radford Ruether (1979) argues that Luke's gospel narrative transforms Mary from being the historic mother of Jesus into an independent agent cooperating with God in the redemption of all men and women. Her humble obedience to the angelic messenger is recorded in these well-known words: "Behold I am the handmaid of the Lord; let it be to me according to your word" (Luke 1:38). Through "Mary's song," the Magnificat (Luke 1:46-53), she proclaims herself as the embodiment of Israel. Through her God-ordained role, she becomes a key figure in the unfolding drama of the entrance of God into human history.

Mary can be understood as symbolizing the new Eve, as Jesus her son represents the second Adam. The concept of Mary as a perpetual virgin traces back to the early church fathers Ambrose and Jerome and their belief that the power and mystery of the sexual drive was associated with evil. By the late fourth century, churches were being dedicated to Mary on or near the site of a former temple belonging to a goddess. At this stage, Ruether argues, Marian devotion was appearing on two levels: Mary the virgin who was docilely obedient to the divine will, and Mary of the people, an earth Mother venerated for power in coping with natural crises.

By the fifth century, debate had arisen over the application of the title "Mother of God" *(theotokos)* to Mary. From Egypt also emerged the belief in Mary's bodily assumption, which became papal decree in 1950. Ruether argues that in medieval theology Mary had become representative of redeemed humanity, and from the twelfth through to the fifteenth century, her veneration increased in inverse proportion to the downgrading of ordinary women. In 1854, the doctrine of the immaculate conception was declared Roman Catholic dogma, although the belief that Mary had been preserved from all actual sin is Augustinian in origin.

Three aspects help to account for the obscurity of Marian devotion in Protestant thought: strong emphasis on the Bible; the abolition of monasticism by the Reformers, together with the consequent rejection of virginity as the highest expression of Christian devotion; and a diminished emphasis on the "feminine" as a symbol of the church in relation to God (Ruether 1979).

The Virgin Mary encompasses the mystery and honor accorded the celibate state. In the words of Marina Warner (1985), she represents a central place in the history of Western attitudes to women. In fact, the sinfulness of Eve and the sinlessness of Mary are two prevalent themes illustrating attitudes toward women as the early church became institutionalized. A similar message was conveyed by the evil of sexual intercourse and the purity of celibacy. Spirituality and natural womanliness, throughout most periods of Christian church history, have been considered incompatible. Women who wished to embark on a spiritual journey needed to leave behind their sexuality. Virginity became the criterion for female spirituality in much the same way circumcision had been the sign of God's elect in the Old Testament. A cloistered environment offered women a "world that suggested and symbolized spiritual equivalence" (Nason-Clark 1993).

> She . . . had no peer
> Either in our first mother or in all women
> Who were to come. But alone of all her sex
> She pleased the Lord
> *Caelius Sedulius*   (quoted in Warner 1985:xxv)

—*Nancy Nason-Clark*

REFERENCES

N. Nason-Clark, "Gender Relations in Contemporary Christian Organizations," in *The Sociology of Religion,* ed. W. E.

Hewitt (Toronto: Butterworth, 1993): 215-234; R. R. Ruether, *Mary* (London: SCM, 1979); M. Warner, *Alone of All Her Sex* (London: Picador, 1985).

VIRTUOSO   Introduced in the work of Max Weber, the concept of the religious virtuoso is that of someone who strives for perfection *within* an existing religious tradition. The virtuoso strives to fulfill to the utmost the demands of his or her religion. Strictly speaking, virtuoso religiosity is the polar opposite of charismatic religiosity, in that the charismatic introduces a "new thing" or a distinctive "gift," while the virtuoso is set on a course toward embodying the received traditions of a faith community. In practice, the virtuoso may at times go to such extremes that she or he unwittingly becomes a charismatic leader, particularly if the constituted authorities of his or her tradition reject the virtuoso's claims to legitimacy. In Western Christianity, Catholic virtuosity often has resulted in the founding of new religious *orders,* whereas in Protestantism it has created schisms, hence sects. The most recent comprehensive contribution to the study of religious virtuosity is Patricia Wittberg's *The Rise and Fall of Catholic Religious Orders* (SUNY Press 1994).

See also Asceticism, Charisma, Max Weber

—*William H. Swatos, Jr.*

REFERENCES

M. Hill, *The Religious Order* (London: Heinemann, 1973); M. Weber, *Economy and Society* (Berkeley: University of California Press, 1978).

VOCATION, DOCTRINE OF   *see* Protestant Ethic Thesis

VODUN   *see* Voodoo

VOLUNTEERISM   Volunteering is the main mode by which religious and service agencies in pluralistic societies staff the so-called independent, voluntary sector and implement its basic programs and goals with a maximum of part-time, unpaid, nonprofessional "volunteers" (even though many might be former, retired professionals). Tocqueville noted that the "New World" adopted a pattern of denominational pluralism with the

"voluntary church" as its mode of organizing. This mode inspired the historic development of a gamut of voluntary and service agencies (Wuthnow's "special purpose groups") as adjuncts of denominations and congregations as well as community organizations parallel to the churches. The growth of religious and community volunteering has been assisted by the development of interest groups based upon the lines of gender, age, ethnicity, class, political identification, feelings of "relative deprivation" and discrimination, as well as by greater leisure and longevity in retirement, greater affluence, and government support and programming.

Recent national polls reveal that over 60% of Americans "volunteer," with the most active ones in middle age; 40% of the "young-old" (aged 65-75) and 29% of those beyond 75 report an overall average of six hours weekly. Much of volunteering is informal and probably underreported.

Recent religious history has been studded with religious special purpose groups. These are involved in providing services to the needy, evangelization, advocacy for "causes" (e.g., women's ordination, curbing abortions or teenage sexuality). But since World War II, many more have become interdenominational or "secular" in orientation. Often such groups have redirected or revitalized denominational policy. On the other hand, associated with the proliferation of volunteerism can be faction formation, community cleavage, the development of oligarchy, and the phenomenon of the "professional layperson" career.

See also Organization Theory

—*Ross P. Scherer*

REFERENCES

D. E. Driver, *The Good Heart Book* (Chicago: Noble, 1989); M. K. Kouri, *Volunteerism and Older Adults* (Santa Barbara, Calif.: ABC-CLIO, 1990); R. Wuthnow, *The Restructuring of American Religion* (Princeton, N.J.: Princeton University Press, 1988).

VOODOO   Haitian Afro-Catholic folk religion.

African dances were performed by slaves in the western part of Hispaniola as early as the seventeenth century, but the period from 1730 to 1790, when African slaves were imported in increasing numbers, is usually interpreted as voodoo's formative period. It was during this time that religious beliefs and practices of Dahomeans, Sengalese, Congolese, Yoruba, and African tribal groups combined with selected ideas concerning the Catholic saints to form the complex religious system now known as "voodoo."

A central focus of voodoo is devotion to the *Ioa* or *Iwa* (deities). All-important members of the pantheon are said to be from Africa, as is reflected in their names: Dambellah, Ezurlie, Legba, Ogun, Shango, and so on. One can find variants of voodoo throughout urban centers in the United States, Europe, and the Caribbean. Many North American practitioners are non-Haitians (see Brown 1991). Voodoo is among the fastest growing religions in North America. One of the most significant and understudied religious movements in the United States over the past 20 years has been the large-scale transfer of Haitian voodoo to urban centers in New York, Miami, Los Angeles, and Toronto.

—*Steven D. Glazier*

REFERENCES

K. M. Brown, *Mama Lola* (Berkeley: University of California Press, 1991); L. G. Desmangles, *The Faces of the Gods* (Chapel Hill: University of North Carolina Press, 1992).

VOYÉ, LILIANE (1938–)   Professor at the Catholic University at Louvain, Belgium; President, International Society for the Sociology of Religion, 1995-1999.

She has studied religious practice in Belgium, which is influenced by regional differences but also by the phenomena of migration and linguistic borders, which have an impact on cultural reproduction. In *Sociologie du geste religieux* (Vie Ouvrière 1973), she demonstrates that Sunday church attendance is a gesture that structures the rhythm of everyday life and is self-reproducing. She is particularly sensitive to Belgium's historico-geographic variables, and hence to the necessary distinctions between Walloons and Flemish, the Catholic "pillar" and the socialist one, and is concerned principally to analyze the coexistence of the Catholic Church with modernity (in Dobbelaere et al., *La Belgique et ses Dieux,* Cabay 1985), identifying the spread of a religious *bricolage* and a situational ethic (in Bawin-Legros et al., *Belges, heureux et satisfaits,* De Boeck Université 1992).

—*Roberto Cipriani*

WACH, JOACHIM (1898-1955)

WACH, JOACHIM (1898-1955)   Historian of religions. Studied at the universities of Leipzig, Munich, and Berlin, and received his Ph.D. from Leipzig in 1922. He taught at Leipzig from 1924 until he was dismissed by the Nazi-dominated Saxony government in 1935. He came to the United States, where he taught at Brown University and, from 1945 to 1955, at the Divinity School of the University of Chicago.

Wach was primarily a specialist in the history of religion. His major contribution to the social scientific study of religion is his textbook *Sociology of Religion* (University of Chicago Press 1944). This book provides an erudite, historically well-informed discussion of major issues in the field. (A short essay in which some of Wach's major ideas about the sociology of religion are presented was published in 1945.) In a 1951 essay about church, sect, and denomination, he defines these concepts and provides a wide range of historical cases as illustrations.

See also Religious Studies

—*William Silverman*

REFERENCES

J. M. Kitagawa, "Joachim Wach," *Encyclopedia of Religion* 15(1987):311-313; J. Wach, "Sociology of Religion," in *Twentieth Century Sociology*, ed. G. Gurvitch and W. E. Moore (New York: Philosophical Library, 1945): 406-437; J. Wach, "Church, Denomination and Sect," in *Types of Religious Experience* (Chicago: University of Chicago Press, 1951): 187-208.

WALLACE, ANTHONY F. C. (1923–)

WALLACE, ANTHONY F. C. (1923–)
Professor of Anthropology, University of Pennsylvania.

A leading figure in the study of culture and personality as well as the anthropology of religion, Wallace conducted fieldwork among the Tuscarora, Iroquois, and Seneca Indians of New York and also in a Pennsylvania mental hospital. He first introduced the concept of *mazeway* to refer to cognitive maps. This concept was further elaborated in his discussions of religion, social change, and revitalization movements.

Wallace's text *Religion: An Anthropological View* (Random House 1966) has become a classic overview of the field. Religion, he contended, is "a set of rituals, rationalized by myth, which mobilizes supernatural powers for the purpose of achieving or preventing transformation of state in man and nature." He also argued—somewhat less effectively—that religious specialists (like shamans) tend to be highly neurotic individuals and that religious orientations are intimately connected with the cure of identity disorders.

—*Stephen D. Glazier*

REFERENCES

A. F. C. Wallace, "Revitalization Movements," *American Anthropologist* 59(1956):264-281; A. F. C. Wallace, *Culture and Personality* (New York: Random House, 1970a); A. F. C. Wallace, *Death and Rebirth of the Seneca* (New York: Knopf, 1970b).

WALLACE, RUTH A. (1932–)   Professor of Sociology, George Washington University. B.A., Immaculate Heart College, Los Angeles; M.A., University of Notre Dame; Ph.D., University of California, Berkeley. Wallace taught for two years at Immaculate Heart College before taking up an appointment at GWU in 1970. President, Association for the Sociology of Religion, 1975; Society for the Scientific Study of Religion, 1994-1995; American Sociological Association Sociology of Religion Section, 1998.

Her areas of interest and scholarly publications are in theory, gender, and religion. Her scholarly research in the field of religion began with a Ph.D. dissertation on social determinants of change of religious affiliation. She has been coauthor with William D'Antonio, James Davidson, and Dean Hoge: *American Catholic Laity in a Changing Church* and *Laity: American and Catholic* (Sheed & Ward 1989, 1996). Her groundbreaking study of women pastors of Catholic churches, *They Call Her Pastor* (SUNY 1992), centered primarily on American Catholic parishes in rural or small town areas. A continuation of this study focused on women pastors in urban areas. Wallace has presented papers on the priest shortage as a major force for gender equality in the Catholic Church, democratic participation in the Roman Catholic Church, feminist spirituality in a Catholic context, legitimation rituals and role transition for women pastors, and women's roles in religion.

—*Loretta M. Morris*

WALLIS, ROY (1945-1990)   Sociologist of religion. Wallis's career took him from a junior lectureship in 1977 at the University of Stirling, Scotland, to the established chair of sociology at the Queen's University of Belfast, where he became Dean of the Faculty of Social Sciences and then Pro-Vice-Chancellor in 1989. Despite this move into university management and his untimely death, he made significant contributions to the sociology of religion and social movements.

Wallis was one of an impressive generation of students of Bryan Wilson at Oxford. In his doctoral thesis on Scientology, subsequently published as *The Road to Total Freedom* (Heinemann 1976), he first displayed characteristic skill in assimilating and simplifying a large amount of diverse material into a parsimonious reworking of the classic church-sect typology that also included a denomination-cult dimension. He argued that the bulk of what interested us in such differentiation could be traced to two simple principles: the extent to which the ideology saw itself as uniquely (rather than pluralistically) legitimate, and the extent to which the ideology was viewed as respectable (rather than deviant) by the surrounding society.

His interest in new religious movements led to a general study, *The Elementary Forms of the New Religious Life* (Routledge 1984), which again showed his skill at going to the heart of the matter in categorizing new religious movements as world-affirming, world-rejecting, and world-accommodating.

Wallis also produced a theory of factionalism and schism in *Salvation and Protest* (Pinter 1979), a theory of charisma in his edited collection *Millennialism and Charisma* (Queen's University of Belfast 1982), and a series of robust defenses of the secularization thesis, usually presented as criticisms of the Stark and Bainbridge theory of religion. Less well known is his interest in the dividing lines between science, religion, and medicine. He edited or coedited three collections of essays in this area, to which he made important original contributions: *Marginal Medicine* (with Peter Morley, Owen 1976), *Culture and Curing* (with Peter Morley, Owen 1978), and *On the Margins of Science* (Sociological Review Monographs 1979).

—*Steve Bruce*

WARNER, R. STEPHEN (1941–)   Professor of Sociology and Director of the New Ethnic and Immigrant Congregations Project, University of Illinois at Chicago; Ph.D., University of California, Berkeley. President, Association for the Sociology of Religion, 1997.

Early in his career, Warner made a number of significant contributions in social theory, but he is best known in the study of religion for his more recent works. He received the SSSR Distinguished Book Award in 1989 for his book *New Wine in Old Wineskins: Evangelicals and Liberals in a Small-Town Church* (University of California Press 1988). The book addresses the struggles between conservative and liberal members of a single congregation, raising the issue of whether one can judge an individual's religious stance by the church that she or he attends. He received the SSSR Distinguished Article Award in 1994 for an article in the *American Journal of Sociology* (1993) that addresses the rational choice-religious economies perspective, noting both the strengths and the weaknesses of this new approach to the study of religion.

Warner's most recent efforts have focused on the role of the religious congregation in the United States (Warner 1994). In particular, through the New Ethnic and Immigrant Congregations Project, jointly funded by the Pew Trust and Lilly Endowment, he is focusing on the role congregations play in the assimilation process of new immigrants and ethnic groups by providing a bridge between the ethnic subculture and the larger American culture.

—*André Nauta*

REFERENCES

R. S. Warner, "Work in Progress Toward a New Paradigm for the Sociological Study of Religion in the United States," *American Journal of Sociology* 98(1993):1044-1093; R. S. Warner, "The Place of the Congregation in the American Religious Configuration," in *American Congregations*, Vol. 2, ed. J. P. Wind and J. W. Lewis (Chicago: University of Chicago Press, 1994): 54-99.

WAXMAN, CHAIM I. (1941–)   Earned his B.A. (1963) and master's of Hebrew Literature (1966) from Yeshiva University, and his master's (1965) and doctorate (1974) in sociology from the New School for Social Research; President, Association for the Social Scientific Study of Jewry, 1979-1981.

Waxman has conducted sociological studies of Jews in the United States (Waxman 1983) and Israel (Waxman 1994) and of immigrants from the United States to Israel (Waxman 1989). He has written on both religious and ethnic aspects of Jewish identity as well as on Jewish family life. He has served as editor (1993–) of *Israel Studies Bulletin* and on the editorial boards (1991–) of the *Journal of Israel Studies* and *Contemporary Jewry* (1987–).

—*J. Alan Winter*

REFERENCES

C. I. Waxman, *America's Jews in Transition* (Philadelphia: Temple University Press, 1983); C. I. Waxman, *American Aliya* (Detroit: Wayne State University Press, 1989); C. I. Waxman (ed.), *Israel as a Religious Reality* (Northvale, N.J.: Aronson, 1994).

WEBER, MAX (1864-1920)   German political economist and sociologist, originally trained in jurisprudence. Faculty member, for most of his life adjunct, at the University of Heidelberg, and from 1904 editorial director of the *Archiv für Sozialwissenschaft und Sozialpolitik*. Author of a prodigious corpus, including the essays *The Protestant Ethic and the Spirit of Capitalism*, originally published in 1904-1905 (Scribner 1930).

The main source of information on Weber's life is a biography by his widow, Marianne Schnitger Weber, written the year after his death and published in 1926 as *Max Weber, ein Lebensbild*. This work has been translated and edited in a 1975 English edition by Harry Zohn, *Max Weber: A Biography* (Transaction). Because Zohn has systematically researched many of Marianne's ellipses and euphemisms, it is in many ways superior to either the original German edition or its subsequent German edition. Although Marianne Weber was a scholar in her own right, the *Biography* is hardly all today's researcher might want. It is richly laced with Max Weber's own letters and notes, as well as ones Marianne wrote, but it also displays both the fidelity of a devoted widow to her husband's greatness and the Victorian tendency to say many things indirectly. Yet, we concur with Zohn when he says that there is "no comparable 'Life and Works' of Max Weber on the international book market" to equal the *Biography*.

Marianne's biography, however, is not the only source we have from contemporaries. In English, Paul Honigsheim, a student and friend of the Webers, has provided a valuable contribution in his *On Max Weber* (Free Press 1968). This work has the advantage of setting Weber somewhat more into the intellectual activity of the time. Also available in English are some personal recollections by Karl Loewenstein appended to his *Max Weber's Political Ideas in the Perspective of Our Time* (University of Massachusetts Press 1966). Additional personal recollections are available only in German. These include essays published along with Honigsheim's original piece in the *Kölner Zeitschrift für*

Soziologie und Sozialpsychologie in 1963 and Eduard Baumgarten's book *Max Weber: Werk und Person* published in 1964.

To these accounts should be added the outstanding intellectual biographies by Reinhard Bendix, *Max Weber: An Intellectual Portrait* (Doubleday 1960), and by Julian Freund, *The Sociology of Max Weber* (Pantheon 1968). Although both of these works were published in the 1960s, few additions of significance have been made to the outlines they present. A more recent collection that tries to place Weber more clearly in juxtaposition to the intellectual currents of his own time is Wolfgang Mommsen and Jürgen Osterhammel's *Max Weber and his Contemporaries* (Allen & Unwin 1987). Also of importance for one slice of Weber's life is Mommsen's *Max Weber and German Politics* (University of Chicago Press 1984).

Finally should be mentioned Arthur Mitzman's *The Iron Cage: An Historical Interpretation of Max Weber* (Knopf 1970), a basically Freudian psychohistorical account of Weber's life and work. In keeping with this genre, Mitzman places heavy emphasis upon Weber's relationships with his mother and father, and subsequently his sexual relationship to his wife, as being critical to Weber's personality development. Beyond this, Mitzman also argues that this personality permeates—indeed, that it practically determines—Weber's theoretical structure and intellectual development. In this context, Mitzman also sees strong influences upon Weber's work by the thought of Friedrich Nietzsche. (Kivisto and Swatos, 1988:14-18, have indicated elsewhere the historiographic flaws of Mitzman's approach.)

Weber and Religion   Weber's self-description as religiously "unmusical" has become a catchphrase for many commentators. Like Marx's "opium of the people," however, this phrase is more often quoted than understood. Although probably only Weber could explain exactly what he meant by the term *unmusical*—which he used in a variety of circumstances, not only with regard to religion—the quote can be at least given in full and placed in context, namely, a letter of February 9, 1909: "It is true that I am absolutely unmusical religiously and have no need or ability to erect any psychic edifices of a religious character within me. But a thorough self-examination has told me that I am neither antireligious *nor irreligious*." It is those last words, emphasized in the original, that seem often ignored. Marianne, by contrast, tells us that Weber "always preserved a profound reverence for the Gospel and genuine Christian religiosity," and scattered references in his discourse throughout the *Biography* show a vocabulary and *mentalité* steeped in religion. Just as

Weber's applied sociology has been given short shrift by most later interpreters, so his Christianity is almost entirely ignored (see Swatos and Kivisto 1991a, 1991b). Several points from this aspect of his life bear noting.

First, Weber's extended family had strong, although temperamentally different, religious convictions. Weber was reared as a Christian in his mother's liberal, nondogmatic mode. He was confirmed in his teen years, and it is clear from his letters, both at the time and after, that this was an important experience for him.

Second, while Weber was always uncomfortable with Lutheran orthodoxy, he gave much of his time in the 1890s to the work of the Evangelical-Social Congress. In association with his cousin Otto Baumgarten, and such German "social gospel" leaders as Friedrich Naumann, Paul Göhre, Martin Rade, and others, Weber wrote and spoke for a whole series of sociopolitical agenda items. Contrary to claims of great differentiation between Weber and early American sociologists, Weber can be considered as involved in and committed to an applied social gospel as were his American colleagues. A careful reading of the *Biography* shows that much of Weber's strength in the 1890s up to his breakdown in 1898 was spent in speaking and writing projects, particularly at Naumann's behest, all over the country, for what in the United States would have been called projects of "Christian sociology." It was only when Naumann attempted to form a political party that Weber began to withdraw from these activities.

This involvement did not end with the conclusion of the acute phase of Weber's illness. Although his activity level diminished, he continued to attend Evangelical-Social Congresses at least as late as 1907. Almost immediately upon the Webers' return from their trip to the United States in 1905, Weber became a part of a newly founded theological discussion group (the "Eranos") at Heidelberg. Weber also was drawn to the mystical elements in Roman Catholicism and Eastern Orthodoxy, and had respect for "real religiousness." At one point, for example, he told Honigsheim (1968:100), after making something of a joke about one theologian's "proof" for the existence of God: "This should not be taken to mean that it is not very essential to me to stand in the right relationship to that Lord."

It is in this total life context, then, that the Protestant ethic essays, along with the rest of Weber's studies in world religions (inter alia *The Religion of China, The Religion of India, Ancient Judaism,* Free Press 1951, 1952, 1958), must be viewed. Weber did not take up *The Protestant Ethic and the Spirit of Capitalism* whimsically but because the *Archiv* itself had as its scope "a scholarly investigation of the conditions created by modern capitalism," which Weber chose to expand to include "the historical and theoretical recognition *of the general cultural significance of the capitalistic development.*" One part of this was the Protestant ethic, as he himself makes clear in several places. Likewise, his industrial sociology was precisely intended to take up "the other side of the problems that are at the center of the treatise on the spirit of capitalism."

Marianne best summarizes the whole Weber-and-religion complex in these lines (1975:335):

Unprejudiced investigation had taught Weber early on that every phenomenon of cultural life is *also* economically determined, but that none is *only* so determined. As early as 1892-93, when as a young scholar he inquired into reasons for the flight of farmers from rural regions in eastern Germany, he was struck by the insight that ideological impulses were just as decisive as the "bread-and-butter questions." And when he undertook his second inquiry into the situation of farm workers, together with the theologian Göhre, it was from the outset his intention to investigate, in addition to the economic situation of the rural population, the moral and religious situation as well as the interaction of the various factors. Evidently he concerned himself at an early age with the question of the world-shaping significance of ideal forces. Perhaps this tendency of his quest for knowledge—*a permanent concern with religion*—was the form in which the genuine religiosity of his maternal family lived on in him.

Weber's Sociology of Religion   At the outset of his study of religion, Weber notes that his point is not to seek "the essence of religion" but "to study the conditions and effects of a particular type of social action." For Weber, "action" includes not only overt behavior but, most important, the understanding, meaning, or significance of an act to the person engaged in it. With respect to religion, specifically, he writes,

The external courses of religious behavior are so diverse that an understanding of the behavior can be achieved only from the viewpoint of the subjective experiences, ideas, and purposes of the individuals concerned—in short, from the viewpoint of the religious behavior's "meaning" *(Sinn).* (1978:399)

The scholar of religions confronts religious constructions of reality as sociologically *real* constructions of reality to be studied objectively through the subjective accounts of the participants. "Not ethical and theological theories but the practical impulses toward action that derive from religion," Marianne writes, were the foci of Weber's studies in world religions. Yet, in his studies of religion, Weber chose aspects of the religious experience as selective foci for his research. Although he did not label the dimensions upon which he focused "the essences of religion," by the act of choosing them he gave high priority to them as important elements to understanding religions. Why and how did he take this approach?

The "why" can be answered, at least partially, in terms of the question he is asking: What can be learned about religions as a broad range of actions in relationship to the whole array of social actions? Despite his initial point of departure, Weber was not interested in interaction among a few individuals. At the core of Weber's sociology is the idea of *Verstehen,* understanding the meaning of social action. Weber was able to perceive new relationships from the reading and studying—both historical and contemporary—he had done. These implications were not a "personal experience" but were placed in the eye of the public for analytical testing. The critical questions concern the objectivity of his work and the usefulness of his analyses. Weber's analyses of religions sometimes take the form of sets of categories, sometimes of dimensions. For simplicity, we will treat them all as dimensions and consider them in a twofold aspect: (1) the dimension of *social relationships,* which involves the meaning of relationships of the leadership and of the laity of a religious group to a "concealed being," and (2) the *ethical* dimension, which Weber sees as peculiarly manifested in the problems of theodicy and soteriology.

Unlike Émile Durkheim, who was philosophically oriented and thus asked such questions as those surrounding the origins of different kinds of ideas of gods, Weber, in his "practical" historical orientation, accepted the idea that people believed in and acted upon the existence of them. For the participants involved in a religious action system, the evidence is "relatively rational" as "it follows the rules of experience" that a supernatural existence rests in the "extraordinary powers," the "charisma," present in those entities so endowed. The existence of charismatic units also implies the existence of a system of relationships between "certain beings," the "charismatically endowed," and some person or persons. General patterns of social relationships, based upon "symbolic activity," emerge that can be studied through the types of leaders within different religious organizational types. Finally, through the concept of "elective affinity," Weber focuses sharply and uniquely upon the meanings imparted to religion by the *laity,* inasmuch as any pattern of relationships is derived from the meanings of all the actors involved in the system of action. Thus Weber delineates a dimension of social relationships that can be termed *religious* as follows: (1) a belief in one or several of a wide-ranging variety of *supernatural powers* (2) that are evidenced in a variety of *charismatic manifestations* (3) articulated through *symbolic expressions,* (4) responded to in a *variety of forms,* (5) under the guidance of *various types of leaders,* (6) in a variety of patterns of relationships significantly determined by the *patterned behavior of the lay people* of the community.

For Weber, as was true of the social relationship dimension, *ethics* came in a wide variety of forms that changed with historical circumstances. As Weber analyzed religiously oriented behavior over time, he certainly saw an increasing prominence of ethics as part of the pattern, but he seems to say that in the earliest forms there was also an element of ethics present. This primitive form of ethics is most clearly manifested in the *taboo.* He argues that societies made increasing ethical demands upon the gods with the development of increased political organization, increased intellectual comprehension of an external cosmos, and increased complexity in social relationships—with an attendant necessity for oral or written contracts. The need for order intensified the need for a more orderly ethic, rather than the highly situational one found in the earlier magical period of religious development. It was the hiatus between the frequency of unethical human conduct and of uneven justice, whether humanly distributed or from external natural events, that led to perceptions of an ever "higher" god, hence to an enhancement of the ethical problem and its increased significance to religious behavior within limits set by human variance. Thus we come to the problems of *theodicy* and *soteriology.*

Weber's discussion of theodicy is brief, serving as the bridge to his discussion of salvation. *Theodicy* is defined as "the problem of how the extraordinary power of such a god may be reconciled with the imperfection of the world that he has created and rules over." This problem is particularly acute for those who understand their god as "a transcendental unitary god who is universal," but it is not found only there. He finds it in ancient Egypt, in Aeschylus, in Hinduism, in ancient China, and elsewhere; indeed, he writes, "this problem belongs everywhere among the factors determining religious evolution and the need for salvation." As to the variety of forms that the answers to this problem take, and thus to the variety of forms that religion itself takes, Weber denotes five: messianic eschatology, trans-

migration of the soul, a universal day of judgment, predestination, and dualism.

The second manifestation of the ethical dimension to which Weber turned was the problem of soteriology: salvation and how to achieve it. This problem occupies considerably more space in his work than theodicy. Nowhere does Weber specifically define salvation, but in speaking of such things as wealth and long life, he comments that "the crassest utilitarian expectations frequently replace anything we are accustomed to term 'salvation.' " By implication, then, salvation is to be perceived broadly; in any case, as social scientists, he writes, "our concern is essentially with the quest for salvation, whatever its form, insofar as it produced certain consequences for practical behavior in the world." There is ample evidence that Weber sees the problem of soteriology to have existed in the earliest forms of religion. In speaking of the first of his five major forms of the road to salvation—that is, ritualism—he notes the possibility of the superiority of magical relations. In speaking of his second—good works and attendant self-perfection—he mentions the importance of rebirth in "animistic" religion; in the third form, ecstasy, he acknowledges historically early activities. The other forms of soteriology he discusses are asceticism and mysticism, both this-worldly (innerworldly) and other-worldly.

Thus for Weber ethics is a variable to be confronted at all times and in all places when studying religion, especially in its two problematic circumstances, theodicy and soteriology. Furthermore, ethics as a variable generates many potential religious forms. We can thus say, very briefly, that for Weber *religion is a patterning of social relationships around a belief in supernatural powers, creating ethical considerations.* Weber thus pioneers among classical sociological theorists a *substantive* definition of religion (as distinct from Durkheim's functional definition based on social integration).

Weber's Reception   One puzzle that surrounds Max Weber's life is the waxing and waning of his popularity among different audiences (see, e.g., Mommsen 1984, Parsons 1980, Glassman 1983). How is it that this famous German of the 1890s and again of the period immediately after World War I seemed to become a relative "unknown" to be "rediscovered" by the American Talcott Parsons in the 1930s, then "returned" to Germany in the 1950s, to be the subject of a "renaissance" in the 1980s in the West as a whole?

Although Weber was invited to, attended, and spoke at the 1904 Congress of Arts and Sciences in St. Louis (on his East Elban research), his impact on sociology in the United States prior to the 1930s was almost nil. Although the early Protestant ethic essays must have been completed by the time of his visit—which he used to write the last major piece in that series—they seem to have had no part in his presentation to the Congress nor to have been taken up by American sociology during his lifetime (as were, by contrast, the contributions of Simmel and others, who are comparably ignored today).

The most important reasons that Weber was ignored have to do with the incompatibility between his understanding of the discipline and the conception of the science of society harbored by scholars in the United States. In the first place, Weber was not a system-builder, at a time when many American sociologists were intent on building a grand disciplinary system. Second, Weber's interdisciplinary proclivities did not resonate well with those concerned to establish a distinct niche in the academy for sociology. Third, perhaps of greatest weight, Weber was decidedly antievolutionary at a time when evolutionary thinking cast a spell over many prominent sociologists. Finally, the pessimism that colored Weber's work simply did not resonate with intellectuals participating in the optimism of the "American century."

As the "Chicago School" began to consolidate itself as the most important center for the discipline, the lack of interest in Weber was exacerbated. Their ahistorical tendencies were compounded with atheoretical and empiricist biases. Beyond this, the empirical concerns that preoccupied the Chicago School—the dynamics of the contemporary city and race relations—were not central to Weber. By contrast, the Weberian preoccupation with politics and religion did not strike a responsive chord with Chicago sociologist Robert Park and his colleagues—or his students. The Chicago School was remarkably apolitical, seen clearly in its ecological analyses of the metropolis. In terms of religion, Chicago-trained sociologists did not enter into the Protestant ethic debate, although other American theologians and historians were doing so just a few years after the initial German publication of Weber's thesis.

This situation changed by the 1930s. In part this was abetted by growing access to English translations of Weber's work, beginning with economist Frank Knight's production of the *General Economic History* in 1927 (Free Press) and then Talcott Parsons's translation of *The Protestant Ethic and the Spirit of Capitalism* in 1930. Another reason for an evolving interest in Weber was the fact that Americans continued to study in Germany; although Weber was already dead, these students nonetheless came under the influence of his thought. Two notable instances are Howard Becker and Talcott Parsons. The former would return and produce

a number of publications devoted to explicating the ideal-type and historical sociology; the latter would, in his watershed publication *The Structure of Social Action* (McGraw-Hill 1937), treat Weber as of paramount importance in Parsons's own effort to construct his grand theoretical synthesis.

If these were the only contributing figures, a distinctly American variant of Weberian sociology might have emerged. However, the ascendance of Hitler to power in 1933 resulted in the exodus of numerous German intellectuals to the United States. Collective settlements of these emigré scholars were established at the New School for Social Research and, to a lesser extent, at Columbia University. In terms of Weber scholarship, names of importance included, at the former institution, Emil Lederer, Adolph Loew, Karl Mayer, Albert Salomon, Alfred Schutz, and Hans Speier, and at the latter, Theodor Adorno, Max Horkheimer, Paul Lazarsfeld, and Herbert Marcuse. Other figures who found academic homes throughout the country included Theodore Abel, Reinhard Bendix, Carl Friedrich, Hans Gerth, Paul Honigsheim, and Alexander von Schelting. The influence of some of these scholars was largely limited to the students they taught, while for others it extended well beyond their exilic institutions to the discipline at large.

Due to the multiplicity of interpretations of Weberian thought, no one assessment came to dominate American sociology's understanding of Weber. In addition, because the translation of Weber into English occurred slowly, also in fits and starts, it is not surprising that Weberian sociology is less identified with a specific American "school" than, for example, Durkheim is with functionalism. What is clear is that aspects of his work began to be used during the 1950s and 1960s, and indeed, a rapidly expanding body of literature devoted to Weberian themes was produced. The three topics that received by far the most attention were bureaucracy, charismatic authority, and the Protestant ethic thesis. In each instance, however, but perhaps most evidently in the last, much of this research was conducted in an ahistorical manner quite at variance with the thrust of Weber's own work on these themes. Ironically, the hegemony achieved in American sociology by Parsonian functionalism both advanced and retarded Weber scholarship, despite efforts by such figures as Bendix and C. Wright Mills to offer an alternative view. The publication of a complete translation of Weber's *Economy and Society* in 1968 (University of California Press 1978) began a major rethinking as well as a flurry of new scholarship (see Kivisto and Swatos 1988).

Recovering Weber: Interpretive Conflicts and Quandaries Whatever critique may be made of Parsons and his use(es) of Weber, it is nevertheless true that Weber's *General Economic History* was available in English in the United States several years before Parsons's translation of *The Protestant Ethic and the Spirit of Capitalism* and a full decade before Parsons's own *Structure of Social Action*. A number of scholars in the 1980s—encouraged by an admirable effort by Randall Collins to systematize Weber's argument on the appearance of Western rational capitalism—have attempted to make the case that the *General Economic History*, which was compiled posthumously by his students and his wife from Weber's scribbled notes, and which in his lifetime he termed "an improvisation with a thousand defects," is to be given intellectual priority over *The Protestant Ethic and the Spirit of Capitalism*.

Because the Protestant ethic essays are one of the core texts of the sociology of religion, this thesis needs careful examination and encounters several problems: First, Weber himself revised the final version of the Protestant ethic essays from which Parsons made his translation. The "Author's Introduction" to the collection of Weber's essays on religion as a whole that Parsons placed at the front of the English translation of the *PE* essays provides quite explicitly the interpretive context that Weber intends for them. This may well have been the last thing Weber wrote and saw to almost final form in 1920. Should this material about which he was most satisfied be relegated to a secondary position vis-à-vis that of which he was most critical?

Second, the *General Economic History* received little attention in Anglo-America compared with that accorded *The Protestant Ethic and the Spirit of Capitalism*. If the *General Economic History* is actually better than the Protestant ethic essays, why was it not more well received earlier or offered later in criticism of Parsons's subsequent use of the Protestant ethic essays? Surely its temporal priority should work in its favor rather than against it, and at the time, its translator, University of Chicago economics professor Frank H. Knight, had far more prestige than the young Parsons.

Third, it is now clear that Parsons misrepresented the Protestant ethic essays in tracing his evolutionary functionalism back to them. As a result, the *General Economic History* may well provide welcome relief from the many misinterpretations that have been heaped upon *The Protestant Ethic and the Spirit of Capitalism* over the years—by both friends and enemies, so to speak. Nevertheless, caution needs to be exercised in regard to the claim that the *General Economic History* represents "more accurately" the "real Max Weber"

than the last words that Max Weber himself brought to publication.

Fourth, in view of the lack of prior attention to the *General Economic History*, careful consideration must be given to the possibility that the *General Economic History* permits a conflict-theoretical, quasi-Marxist reading of Weber more consistent with the left-liberal predilections of one current of contemporary Anglo-American sociological theory than is warranted by Weber's corpus as a whole. Such an approach would warp Weber no less seriously than that which Talcott Parsons has been accused of doing in *The Structure of Social Action*.

See also Talcott Parsons, Protestant Ethic Thesis

—*William H. Swatos, Jr.,*
Peter Kivisto, and
Paul M. Gustafson

REFERENCES

R. Collins, *Max Weber* (Beverly Hills, Calif.: Sage, 1986); R. M. Glassman, "The Weber Renaissance," *Current Perspectives in Social Theory* 4(1983):239-251; P. Kivisto and W. H. Swatos, Jr., *Max Weber* (New York: Greenwood, 1988); W. Mommsen, *Max Weber and German Politics* (Chicago: University of Chicago Press, 1984); T. Parsons, "The Circumstances of My Encounter with Max Weber," *Sociological Traditions from Generation to Generation*, ed. R. K. Merton (Norwood, N.J.: Ablex, 1980): 31-43; W. H. Swatos, Jr., and P. Kivisto, "Beyond *Wertfreiheit*," *Sociological Focus* 24 (1991a):117-128; W. H. Swatos, Jr., and P. Kivisto, "Max Weber as 'Christian Sociologist,'" *Journal for the Scientific Study of Religion* 30(1991b):347-362.

WEIGERT, ANDREW J. (1934–) American sociologist. Initial interests at St. Louis University were epistemology and economics (M.A.). Teaching in a bicultural Jesuit high school in Puerto Rico convinced him that culture was foundational to human action. He studied theology at Woodstock College and some anthropology at Columbia University. In the sociology doctoral program at the University of Minnesota, Murray Strauss's and Reuben Hill's family studies, Don Martindale's theoretical frameworks, and Gregory Stone's symbolic interactionist interpretation of George H. Mead attracted him. Peter Berger and Thomas Luckmann's *Social Construction of Reality* (Doubleday 1966) grounded his perspective and led him to the works of Alfred Schutz.

His 1968 dissertation, under Strauss, served as the core of a vast and theoretically relevant empirical literature on family socialization into religion (e.g., Weigert et al., 1974). To develop family theory further, he later wrote phenomenological articles with his Notre Dame University graduate students.

Weigert early criticized "immoral scientific rhetoric" in sociology—the highlighting of themes and procedures for disciplinary funding and prestige—and explored the thought of Schutz, Mead, and Ortega y Gasset (e.g., Weigert 1983). Schutz offered culture-based sensitizing concepts for the interpretive analysis of solitary action, interaction, and typical actions. Mead, from a pragmatist foundation, and Ortega, from a phenomenological one, presented the prospect of proceeding from an indubitable valued reality—human life processes. In his own thought, Weigert pursued such themes as time and trust in everyday life. The complexity of contemporary everyday experience led to a book on ambivalence as a social experience (*Mixed Emotion: Certain Steps Toward Understanding Ambivalence,* SUNY Press 1991). The place of the individual in such a world was also a concern, as expressed in essays on the substantival self, identity, and identity loss (see Weigert et al., 1986) and a synthetic text in social psychology.

Most of the themes found in his studies in family and theory characterize his sociology of religion. A critique of a study of the dimensions of religiosity focuses on what respondents to questionnaire items mean by their responses (Weigert and Thomas 1969). A review of changes occasioned by the introduction of secular studies into the training of Jesuits led to the issue of hyphenated professional identities (Weigert 1971). Another hyphenated-identity study focused on Protestantism in the assimilation of Mexican Americans. In general, Weigert argues against approaches that ignore the centrality of lived experience and the social definitions emergent in social life, and that posit some universal religious need or function. Thus he criticized Luckmann's "invisible religion" thesis, despite its grounding in phenomenology, and argued that any definition of religion should be based on social actors' definitions (Weigert 1974). These concerns took the form of methodological suggestions in a programmatic essay (Weigert and Blasi 1976). Openness to social actors' definitions suggested framing the Catholic charismatic movement as an emergent "faithstyle" rather than an order, sect, or cult (Weigert and Johnson 1978), focusing on the cognitive organizing of experiences evident in texts of pseudoconfessions (Weigert and Johnson 1980) and developing an observational procedure for the comparative study of liturgies (Weigert and Hesser 1980). He used ambivalence, identity, and time as dimensions of experience in his interpretation of resur-gent Christian fundamentalist eschatology (Weigert 1988, 1989).

—*Anthony J. Blasi*

REFERENCES

A. J. Weigert, "An Emerging Intellectual Group Within a Religious Organization," *Social Compass* 18(1971):101-115; A. J. Weigert, "Functional, Substantive, or Political?" *Journal for the Scientific Study of Religion* 13(1974):483-486; A. J. Weigert, *Sociology of Everyday Life* (New York: Longman, 1981); A. J. Weigert, *Life and Society* (New York: Irvington, 1983); A. J. Weigert, "Christian Eschatological Identities and the Nuclear Context," *Journal for the Scientific Study of Religion* 27(1988):175-191; A. J. Weigert, "Joyful Disaster," *Sociological Analysis* 50(1989):73-88; A. J. Weigert and A. J. Blasi, "Towards a Sociology of Religion," *Sociological Analysis* 37(1976):189-204; A. J. Weigert and G. Hesser, "Comparative Dimensions of Liturgy," *Sociological Analysis* 41 (1980):215-229; A. J. Weigert and C. L. Johnson, "An Emerging Faithstyle," *Sociological Analysis* 39(1978):165-172; A. J. Weigert and C. L. Johnson, "Frames in Confession," *Journal for the Scientific Study of Religion* 19(1980): 368-381; A. J. Weigert and D. L. Thomas, "Religiosity in 5-D," *Social Forces* 48(1969):260-263; A. J. Weigert et al., *Family Socialization and Adolescents* (Boston: Lexington, 1974); A. J. Weigert et al., *Society and Identity* (New York: Cambridge University Press, 1986).

WELL-BEING   Overall life conditions that enable the optimal level of individual functioning in all aspects of life and that promote general feelings of satisfaction with one's life.

Many factors are related to a person's sense of well-being, including objective conditions such as health, economic resources, and social relations plus subjective assessment of one's specific circumstances and overall life satisfaction. Although some studies do not emphasize religion explicitly (Andrews and Withey 1976), religious or spiritual well-being may be regarded as a distinct dimension of well-being in its own right (Moberg 1979). Overall, the critical question is whether religion contributes significantly to subjective well-being. The weight of the evidence indicates an affirmative answer for persons with a strong personal (intrinsic) faith and/or high levels of involvement in their religious group (Petersen and Roy 1985, Witter et al. 1985). Although the evidence is not entirely consistent and depends in part on how religiosity is measured, some studies suggest that religious faith, experience, and practice may be positively related to good physical and/or mental health (Ferraro and Albrecht-Jensen 1991, Kass et al. 1991).

See also Life Satisfaction, Mental Health

—*Doyle Paul Johnson*

REFERENCES

F. M. Andrews and S. B. Withey, *Social Indicators of Well-Being* (New York: Plenum, 1976); K. F. Ferraro and C. M. Albrecht-Jensen, "Does Religion Influence Adult Health?" *Journal for the Scientific Study of Religion* 30(1991):193-202; J. D. Kass et al., "Health Outcomes and a New Index of Spiritual Experience," *Journal for the Scientific Study of Religion* 30(1991):203-211; D. O. Moberg (ed.), *Spiritual Well-Being* (Washington, D.C.: University Press of America, 1979); L. R. Petersen and A. Roy, "Religiosity, Anxiety, and Meaning and Purpose," *Review of Religious Research* 27(1985):49-62; R. A. Witter et al., "Religion and Subjective Well-Being in Adulthood," *Review of Religious Research* 26(1985):332-342.

WELLNESS The healing arts and religion have experienced ambivalent and, at times, conflicting relationships. The ancient Greeks were aware that the whole/"well" person was a balance of different "temperaments" and was simultaneously influenced by several internal and external sources—ecology, lifestyle (including diet), drugs and herbs, and the body's internal fluids—"the four humors." The individual was in optimal health when these humors were in balance. The Christian world also adopted Greek medicine. More spiritually, however, Jesus and the New Testament authors saw physical and spiritual wellness as so intertwined that, for optimal healthiness, individuals had to have right intentions and relations toward both God and their fellows ("neighbors"). Although bodily ills might come, right intentions and relations could produce divinely given "healing"—alleviation of disease, forgiveness for cleansing of the soul, and sometimes miraculous cures of body and mind. Communitywide disease, however, was often viewed punitively, with clergy eventually leading liturgies for alleviation. Much later and at different times, an "angelic connection," whereby selected clergy practiced both pastoral and medical arts in tandem, emerged and was viewed as positive.

Body-Mind/Soul Split Through the centuries, medicine became professionalized and secularized, especially during the period from the seventeenth to nineteenth centuries. As Western Christendom divided into warring factions and monopolies during the Reformation and its aftermath, medicine went its way, developing separate biomechanical insights and specific technologies in various European regions to form the foundations of "modern scientific medicine." The final shakedown in the last half of the nineteenth century involved the discovery of aseptic technique, germ theory and "magic bullets," anesthesia, X rays, modern surgery, and recognition of the futility of sectarian and cultlike medical wars, which led to government recognition and regulation, medical monopoly, and the rise of hospital-based clinical training.

Lying behind all of these, however, was a landmark dictum pronounced in the mid-seventeenth century by the French philosopher-mathematician-physician René Descartes to the effect that "the body is a machine" and should be investigated solely by natural science methods without attention to mind and soul. Some allege that with this dictum, medicine, now unobstructed, could dissect the "body" while the church could keep the "soul." Perhaps in the short run, this "deal" was positive for freer medical investigation of the body. In the long view, however, this split of body from mind/soul tended to institutionalize mind-body dualism, to ignore the holistic interactions of body-in-environment, and to be too reductionist in explaining the symbolic-cultural in terms solely of biomechanical origins (genes and brain functions). In short, body, mind, (social) role, and soul were no longer seen as mutually interacting and influencing each other. This body-mind split became woven into the warp and woof of modern medicine.

Biomedicine Not the Whole Truth While biomedicine continued to advance as the final paradigm for medical truth, voices arose to point to its incompleteness and inability to interpret all of the human person. In the nineteenth century, Freud, Jung, and the psychoanalysts began to observe the recurring connections between mind and body in the unconscious, to found the subprofession of psychiatry, and to write of "psychosomatic" medicine. Selye in the mid-twentieth century wrote of "stress" and the ways persons were pushed and pulled from within and without. Challenges to "mainstream" medicine also came from "alternative" forms from the developing world and from Asia and the Far East. Cartesian or mainstream medicine could no longer remain just "medicine" or even "allopathic medicine" but increasingly came to be referred to as *biomedicine,* mainly dominant but actually only one paradigm of medicine.

Public health technologies, improved sanitation, "miracle drugs," immunizations, and disease control vastly reduced the toll of mortality at the turn of the nineteenth century and beginning of the twentieth. All this resulted in a vast reduction of mortality from contagious and infant diseases. The result was that human populations began to age, and the focus of medicine began to shift from acute to chronic conditions (e.g., alcoholism, diabetes, arthritis, lung cancer). Today, many of these ills are termed *lifestyle* or *civilization* diseases, the alleviations or preventions of which more and more have to be put into the hands of the sick persons themselves. This means that the victims' social outlooks, intentions, support networks, peer relations, and personal philosophies—all psychosocial factors—become crucial to living with or slowing the progress of such conditions.

In the 1970s, George Engel came up with the proposal for a new, more holistic medical paradigm he termed *biopsychosocial* medicine, implying that the reigning and existing paradigm of biomedicine needed to be complemented by an alternate paradigm known as *psychosocial* medicine. Neither paradigm would replace the other, but the psychosocial, while accepting biomechanical foundations in the body, would see the person-in-body as embedded in varying social group situations, life histories, and symbolic-cultural environments including the individual's spiritual identity.

Rhetorical Shift from "Disease" to Health and "Wellness"   Aaron Antonovsky has perhaps done the most to couple expansion of the biomedical paradigm into a biopsychosocial one with a whole new rhetoric for the health care enterprise. He says the concern must be *not* with "disease care" but with "ease care" or wellness, with *salutogenesis* or health origination. Antonovsky proposes a type of open-systems notion of health. He emphasizes immunology and the whole person's natural defenses against threats to health both from within and from the physical and social environments. The study of the mind/brain's ability to enhance or suppress one's immunity to disease (psychoneuroimmunology) became a new research frontier. In Antonovsky's system of health, major psychosocial factors—generalized resistance resources—intervene between persons and their stressors and assist persons in coping. Included in these resources is the person's "sense of coherence" (SOC). One's SOC includes one's meaning or value system, "philosophy of life," personal theodicy, and concept of religious faith. The SOC provides an interpretive basis for comprehending the near and ultimate meanings of stressful situations. Wellness does not mean attaining "perfect health" but accommodating to a particular point on a continuum between perfect un-health and perfect health. Further, many of life's stresses need to be viewed positively (eustress) as well as negatively (distress). Unfortunately, there is mounting evidence that modern psychiatric literature seldom deals with religious variables as it seeks to probe what holds people together or pulls them apart. Even much less is biomedicine concerned with a person's biopsychosocial "coherence."

Placebo Effect: A Window into Biomedicine?
The placebo effect (PE) is a phenomenon that modern medicine, from the mid-twentieth century onward, has attempted to deal with as "interference" with the allegedly positive medical applications of its drugs, procedures, and manipulations. The PE refers to the increments of healing that result *naturally* and apart from any specific, medical treatments. That is, some of the remissions of disease appear to result from trust by the patient in the authority of the caregiver and his or her ministrations on behalf of the patient. Biomedically, then, physicians *should* feel that medicine has failed if the patient gets well not from the physician's ministrations but because of trust and a will to live (or, conversely, gets worse, despite medicine's ministrations, because of lack of trust or a will to die). The PE is a bit of "secret" medical knowledge. Probably most caregivers are fairly aware of the bonus effects that PE-related acts of kindness, pleasantness, and truthfulness produce that caregivers can direct to anxious patients. In fact, survey evidence shows that up to half of the favorable outcomes in health care are believed by caregivers to result from these very PEs. Thus caregivers are already practicing biopsychosocial medicine, although the literature does not officially recognize this.

Religious Faith as Psychosocial?   Most theologies frown on advocating "faith healings" as a substitute for professional medicine. Yet scientific evidence is mounting that religious affiliation, practice, and related life-styles are conducive to greater longevity, reduced disease, better health, and greater life satisfaction. The Protestant reformers concluded that medical "miracles" ceased with the apostolic age. They feared that the promise of "miracle" cures would compromise the idea of genuine "faith" and smack of magic, whereby a medical outcome of "no cure" would be deemed to be due to no, little, or weak faith. Contemporary hospital chaplains have to be careful in this area and so are personally inclined to follow a "two-track" approach, advocating both modern medicine (including PEs) but also religious faith, prayer, and sacraments promising divine "healing" but not necessarily physical "curing" (along with a secret prayer wish for a "miracle" or two).

There is also evidence that contemporary hospital caregivers see religious support and ministering as special, even unique, and not just as an extension of the "psychosocial" (whole-person interaction, social support, doctor-patient equality, mind-over-body). Caregivers may be ambivalent about the healing power of faith, but they do not seem to wish to reduce it to merely human, natural forces either. A recent survey of caregivers in three suburban American hospitals indicates that almost three-fourths prefer a Judaic-Christian, religio-philosophical view that holds that "God suffers with us" and works through human healing agents but does not necessarily promise miracle cures. The remaining caregiver segments embrace humanistic, "New Age," or miraculous "faith healing" views.

The Park Ridge Center is a research and consulting institute in Chicago, founded by Martin Marty and others, to study the relations between health, faith, and ethics. It once produced a journal and a newsletter and sponsored a series of outstanding publications, some of which have dealt with the historical relations of religion and health, such as Numbers and Amundsen, *Caring and Curing* (Macmillan 1986). Other volumes have featured various denominations' and various world religions' individual approaches to health and medicine.

—*Ross P. Scherer*

REFERENCES

A. Antonovsky, *Health, Stress, and Coping* (San Francisco: Jossey-Bass, 1979); A. Antonovsky, *Unraveling the Mystery of Health* (San Francisco: Jossey-Bass, 1987); G. Engel, "The Need for a New Medical Model," *Science* 196(1977):129-136; L. Foss, "The Challenge of Biomedicine," *Journal of Medicine and Philosophy* 14(1989):165-191; D. Goleman and J. Guerin (eds.), *Mind-Body Medicine* (Yonkers, N.Y.: Consumer Reports Books, 1993); M. T. Kelsey, *Psychology, Medicine, and Christian Healing,* 2nd ed. (San Francisco: Harper, 1988); D. B. Larson and S. S. Larson, "Religious Commitment and Health, Valuing the Relationship," *Second Opinion* 17(1991):27-40; R. P. Scherer, "Hospital Caregivers' Own Religion in Relation to Their Perceptions of Psychosocial Emphases in Health and Healing," *Review of Religious Research* 37(1996):302-324; H. Selye, *The Stress of Life* (New York: McGraw-Hill, 1956); J. A. Turner et al., "The Importance of Placebo Effects in Pain Treatment and Research," *Journal of the American Medical Association* 271(1994):1609-1614.

WE-THEY BOUNDARIES We-they boundaries serve as a source both of in-group solidarity and of prejudice between religious groups. A sense of group identification and loyalty among members is important for a group's survival, but this sense of "we" also can become the basis for ethnocentrism and bigotry toward outsiders. Sociological research indicates that the sense of belonging to a reference group of close associates is an especially potent influence on the behaviors and attitudes of religious group members. Research also suggests that people will often develop antipathy toward anyone who appears "different" from in-group members.

The development of religiously based we-they prejudice is especially likely in situations where racial boundaries and religious boundaries are coextensive. If members of another religious group also look different, speak a different language, are of a different social class, and/or belong to a different political party, the exclusionary tendencies are reinforced and hardened. If the lines of differentiation are crosscutting, so that members of different religious groups are together in a class or political party conflict, then "we" and "they" categories become temporal, and members of groups are less likely to reify the differentiations.

—*Keith A. Roberts*

WHITMAN, LAURIS B. (1909-1983)   B.D., Andover-Newton; Ph.D., Penn State. First president, Religious Research Association (1959-1961).

Whitman's career bridged religion and the social sciences: pastorates, sociology professor, most of 1955-1969 employed by the National Council of Churches as Research Department Director, where he drew upon the expertise of consultant sociologists for in-house and interdenominational research planning. He also employed a psychologist for a landmark Christian education study. As first president of the church-oriented Religious Research Association, he performed a liaison function with the academically oriented Society for the Scientific Study of Religion. In his 1966 RRA H. Paul Douglass lecture, "Religion and Social Science: Two Worlds or One?" (in the *Review of Religious Research* 1968), he described desirable collaboration between religion and the social sciences.

—*Everett L. Perry*

WILLIAMS, J. PAUL (1900-1973)   A native of New York City, Williams earned his doctorate at Columbia University and, in 1956, received an honorary degree from Baker University, Kansas. Williams joined the faculty of Mt. Holyoke College in 1939, became a full Professor of Religion in 1945, and retired as Professor Emeritus in 1966.

Along with Walter Houston Clark, Williams was a prime mover in the establishment and early management of the Society for the Scientific Study of Religion. He is the author of several books including *What Americans Believe and How They Worship* (Harper 1952, revised 1962).

—*Charles Y. Glock*

WILLIGAN, WALTER L(UKE) (1908-1974)

Receiving M.A. (1930) and Ph.D. (1934) degrees in history from Fordham University, Willigan became a member of the faculty of social sciences at St. John's University, Jamaica, New York, until his retirement in 1973 as Professor of American History. President, American Catholic Sociological Society, 1942.

Willigan was coauthor of two textbooks concerned with the field of sociology, *Sociology* and *Social Order* (both with John J. O'Connor, Longmans 1940, 1941), was also coauthor of *The Concept of Freedom* (Regnery 1959), and contributed chapters extensively to books in history. His principal area was social and intellectual history, especially with reference to the twentieth century. There is no record of an ACSS presidential address, although a national meeting of ACSS was held in Cleveland during his term of office.

—*Loretta M. Morris*

WILMORE, GAYRAUD S. (1921–)

Professor at Interdenominational Theological Center of the Atlanta University Center; accepted position in 1960 on the faculty at Pittsburgh Theological Seminary, went to Boston University in 1972, then Colgate Rochester Divinity School/Crozer Theological Seminary in 1974, and New York Theological Seminary in 1983; ordained minister of the Presbyterian Church (U.S.A.).

Wilmore is one of the leading figures in the scholarly study of African American religion in the United States as well as an early proponent of Black Theology. His experiences in the Italian campaign during World War II prompted him to become a minister as a means to address human cruelty. Wilmore has conducted extensive research on social ethics, African Americans in the Presbyterian church, and ecumenism. His first book was *The Secular Relevance of the Church* (Westminster 1962). In his now-classic *Black Religion and Black Radicalism: An Interpretation of the Religious History of Afro-American People* (Orbis, second edition, 1983), Wilmore explores the historical struggle for freedom in African American religion during the antebellum and post-Civil War eras, the "deradicalization" of the black church during the first half of the twentieth century, and the rejuvenation of social activism in African American religion as part of the civil rights and Black Power movements. His book provides a moving chronicle, celebration, and critique of black religion in its variegated forms. According to Wilmore, African American religion exhibits a paradoxical nature in that "it is at once the most reactionary and most radical of black institutions; the most imbued with the mythology and values of white America, and yet the most proud, the most independent and indigenous collectivity in the black community" (p. x).

When *Black Religion and Black Radicalism* first appeared in 1972, relatively little scholarly attention had been given to African American religion. This book served as a seminal work in stimulating a renaissance in the scholarly study of black religion in the United States. As a committed social activist, Wilmore personally became acquainted with many of the progressive voices in the "black church" who were involved in the civil rights movement and the Black Power movement of the 1960s. He and James H. Cone, another renowned historian-theologian-activist, edited two anthologies titled *Black Theology: A Documentary History, 1966-1979* (Orbis 1979) and *Black Theology: A Documentary History, 1980-1992* (Orbis 1993).

In *Black and Presbyterian: The Heritage of Hope* (Geneva 1983), Wilmore explores the status of blacks and race relations in his own denomination. He observes that "no church was more high-sounding and profound in its Biblical analysis of slavery and did less about it" (p. 62). With Wilmore's input, black Presbyterians organized into new caucuses in 1963 with the creation of the Concerned Presbyterians group and in 1968 with the creation of the Black Presbyterians United. He also has served as the editor of *Afro-American Religious Studies: An Interdisciplinary Anthology* (Duke University Press 1989).

—*Hans A. Baer*

WILSON, BRYAN R. (1926–)

Reader (senior academic post, other than professorial chair) in Sociology at Oxford University, 1962-1992; President of the International Society for the Sociology of Religion (SISR), 1971-1975, Honorary President 1991–.

Bryan Wilson has exercised a formative influence on the sociology of religion in Britain, not only directly through his many publications but also through the generations of graduate students he has supervised with great generosity. He has made a decisive contribution to the sociology of religion in the areas of sectarian religion and secularization; in the latter respect, particularly, he has largely set the research agenda for sociology of religion throughout the world.

His pioneering 1959 article "An Analysis of Sect Development" in the *American Sociological Review* and his book *Sects and Society* (Heinemann 1961)—a study of the Elim Pentecostal Church, the Christadelphians, and Christian Science (based on his doctoral thesis at the London School of Economics, under the supervision of Donald MacRae)—shaped a paradigm for subsequent sociological studies of sectarian religion, many of which have been conducted by his own students. His typologies and classifications of sects were further expounded in *Patterns of Sectarianism* (Heinemann 1967) and presented in a more popular form in *Religious Sects* (Weidenfeld and Nicholson 1971). Wilson's interests later shifted from Christian-inspired sectarian groups to new religious movements, reflected in a collection of essays he edited, *The Social Impact of New Religious Movements* (Rose of Sharon Press 1981), and his own essays *The Social Dimensions of Sectarianism: Sects and New Religious Movements in Contemporary Society* (Oxford University Press 1990).

In *Religion in Secular Society* (Penguin 1969 [1966]), Wilson defined *secularization* as "the process whereby religious thinking, practice and institutions lose social significance," and argued persuasively not only that this process has been dominant in Europe, along with the well-charted decline in church attendance, but also in the United States, "a country in which instrumental values, rational procedures and technical methods have gone furthest and a country in which the sense of the sacred, the sense of the sanctity of life and deep religiosity are most conspicuously absent." With this book, Wilson set the terms of the debate on secularization—a thesis much challenged in the 1960s but later adopted in part by many of its critics. He returned to the theme a decade later in *Contemporary Transformations of Religion* (Oxford University Press 1976) and again in *Religion in Sociological Perspective* (Oxford University Press 1982).

Wilson's work always has been characterized by objectivity and value neutrality, eschewing consideration of metaphysical and theological concepts of ultimate truth but guided by the Weberian concept of the rationalization of culture. He edited a collection of influential essays by philosophers and anthropologists:

Rationality (Blackwell 1970). Wilson's attention has increasingly shifted to non-Christian and non-European religion. This general theme was explored in *Magic and the Millennium* (Heinemann 1973), a wide-ranging analysis of the collision between preindustrial societies and modern Western modes of life and thought, and later in *The Noble Savages: The Primitive Origins of Charisma and Its Contemporary Survival* (University of California Press 1975). Wilson has made an extensive study of new religious movements in Japan, and *A Time to Chant* (Oxford University Press 1994), written with Karel Dobbelaere, is a study of the progress of one such movement, the Soka Gakkai Buddhists, in Britain. His most recent research has focused on the relationship between minority religious groups, the state, and the law.

—*Peter Gee*

REFERENCE

E. Barker et al. (eds.), *Secularization, Rationalism and Sectarianism* (Oxford: Oxford University Press, 1993).

WIMBERLEY, RONALD C. (1942–)   Professor and sometime Chair of Sociology, North Carolina State University. President, Rural Sociological Society, 1991-1992.

The principal contribution of Ronald Wimberley to the sociology of religion was a series of quantitative empirical studies from the mid-1970s to the early 1980s, about half of which were done in collaboration with James Christenson, seeking to measure and evaluate the nature of the concept of "civil religion" revived by Robert Bellah from the French school, dating to Rousseau. He also has collaborated on research on Billy Graham crusades, studied clergy career mobility patterns, and written generally on the nature of "commitment."

Wimberley's research was designed to test Bellah's model of a transcendent universal American "civil religion" at the level of the individual believer. Wimberley's findings, using factor and cluster analysis, demonstrated the existence of a "civil religion" variable separate from either denominational religious belief, on the one hand, or political commitment, on the other. A study focused on the 1972 U.S. presidential election (Richard Nixon), for example, found that civil religion was a better predictor of political choice than such more standard variables as denomination, general political orientation, or socioeconomic status. A further study showed higher intercorrelation between civil religiosity and religio-political conservatism but also broad support for civil religious tenets among a majority of Americans. Wimberley's measurement items are tabulated most succinctly in Gail Gehrig's monograph *American Civil Religion* (1979:88).

In more recent years, Wimberley has distinguished himself as a sociologist of the southern "Black Belt." In 1997, Wimberley was awarded a William Neal Reynolds Professorship, the first of such professorships awarded to a social scientist at NCSU since 1961.

—*William H. Swatos, Jr.*

REFERENCES

J. A. Christenson and R. C. Wimberley, "Who Is Civil Religious?" *Sociological Analysis* 39(1978):77-83; G. Gehrig, *American Civil Religion* (Storrs, Conn.: Society for the Scientific Study of Religion, 1979); R. C. Wimberley, "Testing the Civil Religion Hypothesis," *Sociological Analysis* 37 (1976):341-352; R. C. Wimberley, "Dimensions of Commitment," *Journal for the Scientific Study of Religion* 17(1978): 225-240; R. C. Wimberley, "Civil Religion and the Choice for Nixon in 1972," *Social Forces* 59(1980):44-61; R. C. Wimberley and J. A. Christenson, "Civil Religion and Other Religious Identities," *Sociological Analysis* 42(1981): 91-100; R. C. Wimberley et al., "The Civil Religious Dimension," *Social Forces* 54(1976):890-900.

WINTER, JERRY ALAN (1937–) Professor of Sociology, Connecticut College. After receiving his Ph.D. from the University of Michigan in social psychology in 1964, Winter taught at Michigan, Rutgers, and Temple before moving to Connecticut College in 1970, where he has enjoyed a long and distinguished career.

While Winter has taught and conducted research in a wide variety of fields in sociology, his main focus has been on the sociology of religion and Judaic studies. He has published in and served in editorial capacities for major journals in the field. His books include *Continuities in the Sociology of Religion* (Harper 1977), the monograph *Clergy in Action Training* (North American IDOC 1971), and *Jewish Choices: American Jewish Denominationalism* (with coauthors Bernard Lazerwitz, Arnold Dashefsky, and Ephraim Tabory, SUNY 1997). Editor, *Contemporary Jewry,* the official journal of the Association for the Social Scientific Study of Jewry, 1992-1997; Treasurer, ASSJ 1990-1992.

—*Arnold M. Dashefsky*

WITCHCRAFT, WITCHES (WICCA)   Witches and witchcraft are associated with some of the most horrifying episodes in western European and American history. Some historians estimate that upward of one million people were put to death for allegedly being witches during several centuries in Europe, with the major persecutions occurring in the sixteenth and seventeeth centuries (Johnson 1990). The Salem witch trials episode that took place in colonial America was a tragic although small example of the strength of such beliefs about witchcraft (Erikson 1966). It is of note that most of those accused and put to death as witches were women, leading some scholars to suggest that the witch craze was in part a way to control women and to take their property on behalf of the dominant religion (Catholicism) and other authorities in European society. A number of major figures in Christianity—including Luther, Calvin, Wesley, and St. Thomas Aquinas—offered theological justifications for the persecution of alleged witches.

Witchcraft and witches have attained a new level of visibility recently in American society, in part because of the growing interest in paganism and more specifically in "goddess religions," a significant aspect of some "New Age" religions (York 1995). Johnson (1990) suggests that as many as 100,000 people, mostly women, are involved in witchcraft, which has gained considerable attention for this movement by the media. Some see the growth of interest in witchcraft as partially a reaction to the perception of the extremely patriarchal nature of Christianity. Witchcraft is practiced under the rubric of "Wicca" today and is also sometimes referred to as "the Craft." Practitioners often are associated with "covens," which is the usual name for the small groups of witches that meet to practice Wiccan rituals.

Typical practitioners of Wicca believe in the sacredness of the Earth, revere living things, and assume that the Divine is not just a male personage. They observe cycles of nature, with special celebrations (called "sabats") associated with the changing of seasons. They make use of magical powers, typically to achieve self-development and to help others with some personal difficulty. These beliefs are not typical of traditional religious groups in Western society, which means that practitioners often experience difficulty being accepted by authority figures, including religious leaders, and receiving the typical protections of freedom of religion laws (Hume 1995). Sometimes associated mistakenly with satanism, Wicca has managed to receive somewhat better treatment in the media than representations of satanism (Rowe and Cavender 1991). This may be the case because of current ties that exist between Wicca and feminism.

—*James T. Richardson*

REFERENCES

M. Adler, *Drawing Down the Moon* (New York: Viking, 1979); K. Erikson, *Wayward Puritans* (New York: Wiley, 1966); L. Hume, "Witchcraft and the Law in Australia," *Journal of Church and State* 37(1995):135-150; P. J. Johnson, "Witchcraft," in J. Patton (eds.), *Dictionary of Pastoral Care and Counseling,* ed. R. Hunter (Nashville: Abingdon, 1990): 1328-1329; L. Rowe and G. Cavender, "Cauldrons Bubble, Satan's Trouble, But Witches Are Okay," in *The Satanism Scare,* ed. J. T. Richardson et al. (Hawthorne, N.Y.: Aldine, 1991): 263-275; Starhawk, *The Spiral Dance* (San Francisco: Harper, 1979); M. York, *The Emerging Network* (Lanham, Md.: Rowman and Littlefield, 1995).

WOMEN AND RELIGION   see Feminist Research and Theory, Feminist Theology, Feminization Thesis, Gender, Sexism

WOOD, JAMES R. (1933–)   James R. Wood was born to pious Methodist parents and has remained loyal but not uncritical toward his religious background. He attended Yale Divinity School, where he was influenced by H. Richard Niebuhr and James Gustafson in ethics. He obtained his Ph.D. in sociology at Vanderbilt in 1967 under Mayer Zald. He was ordained into the Methodist ministry in which he served in the late 1950s and early 1960s. He has spent his entire academic career, from 1967, at Indiana University, where he rose from Assistant Professor to Professor of Sociology, also serving as Associate Dean and Acting Dean of Liberal Arts and Chair of Sociology. Wood has served as board member of the Association of Voluntary Action Scholars, Secretary and also board member of the Religious Research Association, Editor of the monograph series and also Chair of the Article Awards Committee for the Society for the Scientific Study of Religion, and Chair of Finance and also Vice President for the Association for the Sociology of Religion. He delivered the ASR's Furfey lecture in 1983.

Wood has employed all methodological forms in his research, including the sample survey. From early in his career, he has been interested in applying open-systems organizational models to the study of religious organizations. He has been especially interested in seeing how religious leaders can implement controversial (civil rights) social policies within their denominations and the civil sector. He has hypothesized that local congregations' official stances can "transcend" (i.e., be more liberal than) individual member attitudes and vary directly with their overhead denominations' official policies and control structures. This is evidenced particularly in his book *Leadership in Voluntary Organizations* (Rutgers University Press 1981), a work that has affected not only the scientific study of religion but also the sociology of organizations more generally.

More recently, Wood has been exploring the religious sector's relations with other voluntary and non-profit organizations, toward explaining the distinctive influences of religion upon volunteering and the extent of the church's role as a "private legislature" for public policies. He is also studying how nonprofits often serve as alternatives to religious organizations.

See also Organization Theory, Volunteerism

—*Ross P. Scherer*

REFERENCES

J. R. Wood, "Authority and Controversial Policy," *American Sociological Review* 25(1970):1057-1069; J. R. Wood, "Unanticipated Consequences of Organizational Coalitions," *Social Forces* 50(1972):512-521; J. R. Wood, "Legitimate Control and 'Organizational Transcendence,' " *Social Forces* 54(1975):199-211; J. R. Wood, "Leaders, Values, and Societal Change," *Sociological Analysis* 45(1984):1-9; J. R. Wood, "Liberal Protestant Social Action in a Period of Decline," in *Faith and Philanthropy in America,* ed. R. Wuthnow and V. Hodgkinson (San Francisco: Jossey Bass, 1990); J. R. Wood and J. Bloch, "The Role of Church Assemblies in Building a Civil Society," *Sociology of Religion* 56(1995):121-136.

WOODS, FRANCES JEROME (1913-1992)
A member of the Congregation of the Sisters of Divine Providence (C.D.P.) order, Sister Frances Jerome Woods spent 44 years in teaching and administration at Our Lady of the Lake University in San Antonio, Texas. President, American Catholic Sociological Society, 1962.

At a time when the Catholic Church was somewhat suspicious of empirical research, Woods committed her career to "value-free" investigation of the social world, the topic of her ACSS presidential address. For 30 years, she studied a 10-generation Southern Creole family, research reported in *Marginality and Identity: A Colored Creole Family Through Ten Generations* (Louisiana State University Press 1972) and *Value Retention Among Young Creoles* (Mellen 1989). She wrote an introductory sociology text, one on the American family, and a third on American ethnic groups, in addition to numerous scholarly articles.

—*Helen Rose Ebaugh*

WORKERS' MOVEMENTS

WORKERS' MOVEMENTS Social movements initiated by, or on behalf of, wage laborers to press demands for better pay and/or improvements in working conditions. Although such linkages are less in evidence today, in the past workers' movements often have counted on the direct assistance or sponsorship of religious organizations. For example, prior to World War I, the Catholic Church helped to form a number of working-class organizations in Italy and France. At the same time, leading elements of the Protestant-based Social Gospel movement in the United States were involved with formation of the revolutionary I.W.W. (Industrial Workers of the World). In French Canada, Catholic labor unions were common prior to the 1970s.

—*W. E. Hewitt*

REFERENCES

R. Camp, *The Papal Ideology of Social Reform* (Leiden: Brill, 1969); D. E. Winters, Jr., *The Soul of the Wobblies* (Westport, Conn.: Greenwood, 1985).

WORLD CHRISTIAN ENCYCLOPEDIA

WORLD CHRISTIAN ENCYCLOPEDIA Data source, edited by David B. Barrett (Oxford University Press 1982). The core of this work is a country-by-country analysis of religions, not limited to Christianity, around the world. Each country section includes a chart detailing the distribution of religious affiliation and practice as well as affiliational trends through time. An essay about each nation contains sections on the state of Christianity, non-Christian religions, church-state relations, interdenominational organizations, and religious broadcasting. The work also contains several global tables, a religious dictionary, an atlas (in which a number of religious variables are depicted in graphic form), a "Who's Who in the Christian World," and an annotated listing of religious organizations. Also included is an essay on the growth of world Christianity in the twentieth century.

—*Ted G. Jelen*

WORLD-SYSTEM THEORY

WORLD-SYSTEM THEORY Developed above all by Immanuel Wallerstein and several collaborators, this Marxist-inspired theory conceives a globally extended world capitalist economy as constitutive of a single world-system. It treats religion as secondary and derivative. Countries or regions participate in the system as part of a dominant core, an exploited periphery, or a hybrid semiperiphery that functions to keep the periphery at bay. Within countries, socioeconomic classes are the primary divisions. By viewing the economy as primary, the theory regards other aspects ultimately as derivative: States are the tools of national bourgeoisie; culture, including religion, nationalisms, racism, and sexism express economic relations, even though cultural identities especially may in fact provide the immediate rationales of action for antisystemic movements. Having its historical origins in sixteenth-century Europe, the world capitalist economy has undergone successive cycles of expansion and contraction that will eventuate in the future collapse of the system, yielding to the formation of a single world-socialist state.

See also Globalization

—*Peter F. Beyer*

REFERENCE

I. Wallerstein, *The Modern World-System*, 3 vols. (New York: Academic Press, 1974-1989).

WUTHNOW, ROBERT (1946–)

WUTHNOW, ROBERT (1946–) Andlinger Professor of Social Sciences and Director of the Center for the Study of American Religion at Princeton, Wuthnow studied under both Robert Bellah and Charles Glock at the University of California, Berkeley, where he received his Ph.D. in 1975. Chair, Section on Sociology of Religion, American Sociological Association, 1995; Chair, Section on Sociology of Culture, American Sociological Association, 1996; Executive Council, Association for the Sociology of Religion, 1987-1990; Executive Council, Society for the Scientific Study of Religion, 1978-1981.

Wuthnow's intellectual pedigree is acknowledged by his dedicating to Bellah and Glock his book *Meaning and Moral Order* (University of California Press 1987), which establishes Wuthnow as a leading sociologist not only of religion but also of culture and theory. A central concern of this work is to understand cultural change in terms of the social ecology of ideologies: their production, competition, selection, and institutionalization. He applies this perspective in *Communities of*

Discourse (Harvard University Press 1989), the Society for the Scientific Study of Religion's Distinguished Book of 1990. The book consists of historical studies of the social structural conditions that favored the institutionalization of the ideologies of the Reformation, the Enlightenment, and European socialism. In these studies, Wuthnow addresses the "problem of articulation": the reality that ideas must articulate closely enough with their social settings to be taken seriously, but not so closely that they appear parochial. The problem of articulation is solved only in concrete living-and-breathing communities in which discourse is produced and becomes meaningful. Notable for their theoretical breadth and empirical richness, these works bring Wuthnow's interest in religion to a broader audience of sociologists.

Wuthnow's specifically religious research bears the marks of Glock's quantitative orientation and Bellah's cultural-interpretive approach as he regularly embeds statistical analysis of survey data in broad cultural arguments without regard to polemics about their incompatibility. Although his work ranges widely, his main concern has been to understand the overall forms and structure of postwar American religion. A recurrent theme is that religion has neither beat a wholesale retreat nor persisted unchanged in modern society. While it is impossible to summarize his entire corpus, three major variations on this theme can be highlighted.

The New Religious Consciousness Wuthnow's early work grew out of the "New Religious Consciousness" project directed by Glock and Bellah. In *The Consciousness Reformation* (University of California Press 1976), Wuthnow argues against "structural" explanations of the counterculture, suggesting instead that a long-range cultural shift created a context conducive to social experimentation in the 1960s and 1970s. He uses data from a San Francisco Bay Area survey to argue for the existence of four distinct meaning systems (distinguished by what is identified as the primary force governing life): theistic (God), individualistic (the individual), social scientific (social forces), and mystical (unintelligible forces). Wuthnow finds that attitudes toward experimentation vary with adherence to different meaning systems and concludes that the general cultural drift in American society has been from theistic and individualistic to scientific and mystical meaning systems. *Experimentation in American Religion* (University of California Press 1978) takes up in greater detail the specifically religious experimentation that seemed so prominent a part of the cultural ferment of the time. Again using the Bay Area survey, Wuthnow dissects the factors for selec-

tion into and the consequences of membership in "new religious movements." Although he stops short of arguing that people leave churches specifically to join new religious movements, Wuthnow sees the advance of the youth counterculture and the retreat of mainline religion in the 1960s and 1970s as mutually reinforcing patterns.

Restructuring American Religion The second major cluster of Wuthnow's works takes up the concern with the religious mainstream more centrally. In *The Restructuring of American Religion* (Princeton University Press 1988), Wuthnow investigates the overall structure of the religious field. By *structure* he means "an identifiable pattern in the symbolic-expressive dimension of social life." Such cultural structures can be identified by "looking for symbolic boundaries that divide up the social world and by looking at the categories created by these boundaries." Thus Wuthnow is concerned to understand the patterns of religious boundaries and how they shift with changes in the broader social environment (he highlights especially the state-sponsored expansion of higher education as a motor of change). Wuthnow's major claim is that postwar America has witnessed a concurrent decline in the significance of denominationalism and an increase in the significance of special purpose groups organized around extradenominational interests. Historic denominational divisions are "restructured" in contemporary society into a division between religious liberals and conservatives engaged in what Wuthnow has called *The Struggle for America's Soul* (Eerdmans 1989).

Religion in the Voluntary Sector From the structure of the religious sphere, Wuthnow turns his attention to the social location of religious groups and organizations among the many thousands of other voluntary associations that are central to the societal sphere alternatively called "civil society" or the "voluntary sector." This third cluster of studies is motivated by Wuthnow's belief that a strong voluntary sector, especially religious institutions, is vital to foster the caring and compassion that are needed for a good society. In *Acts of Compassion* (Princeton University Press 1991), Wuthnow focuses on Americans' voluntary caring behavior and finds religious people more compassionate, especially when they have ties to organized religious communities (as opposed to an individualized spirituality). An increasingly prominent form in which religious communities manifest themselves is the small support group, and it is here that Wuthnow finds much of the caring in an increasingly anomic society. He explores this phenomenon in *Sharing the Journey* (Free Press 1994), arguing that the cultivation of compassionate relationships in these small groups is effecting a redefinition of the sacred itself. God becomes more an internal presence than a transcendent authority, a comforting intimate rather than a judging lord.

While Wuthnow recognizes the benefits of small groups, he also fears that their excessive focus on comforting people to the exclusion of challenging them will have negative effects, especially for the role of religion in the public sphere. This same concern surfaces in Wuthnow's study of the relationship between religion and economics, *God and Mammon in America* (Free Press 1994). He argues that in general religion has too little effect on individuals' economic lives and materialistic attitudes, evidence that "churches do a better job of comforting the afflicted than they do of afflicting the comfortable." Wuthnow has most recently considered volunteering in the teenage years, which he sees as a key transition from the primary caring of childhood to the institutional kindness of adulthood. In *Learning to Care* (Oxford University Press 1995), he argues that virtue—"the habitual practice of courage and compassion"—must be instilled in society's youth because it is the key to responsible citizenship in a good society.

Overall, Wuthnow's story about the voluntary sector is optimistically cautious. Americans do care about others and are committed to communities despite an individualistic culture, but that same individualism also renders caring and commitment precarious. Religion plays an important role in civil society by making the provision of *charity* (broadly understood) a more stable part of the institutional structure of America and the character structure of Americans.

Conclusion While Wuthnow's accomplishments distinguish him as a consummate academician, his vocation is in no sense narrowly academic. On the editorial board of both the mainline *Christian Century* and the evangelical *Books and Culture,* Wuthnow is a public intellectual to mainline Protestants, evangelicals, and participants in the voluntary sector. His success in addressing a wide audience is reflected in the fact that *Acts of Compassion* was nominated for both the Pulitzer prize and the National Book Award.

—*David Yamane*

YINGER, J(OHN) MILTON (1916–)

YINGER, J(OHN) MILTON (1916–) The son of a minister and a writer, Yinger received his Ph.D. from the University of Wisconsin, Madison, in 1942 and is now Emeritus Professor of Sociology at Oberlin College. President, American Sociological Association, 1976-1977.

Yinger has written extensively on religion, race and ethnic relations, education, social theory, and the sociology of contracultures, with some of his works being translated into Italian, French, Spanish, Oriya, and Portuguese. It was he who first coined the idea of a counterculture (although he used the term *contraculture*) in 1960. The concept has a good deal of relevance for the study of sects and new religious movements. Yinger's widely used text of the 1950s, *Religion, Society, and the Individual* (Macmillan 1957), was significantly overhauled into *The Scientific Study of Religion* (Macmillan 1970). Although intended as a textbook, the latter was also a classic summary of the field of sociology of religion at the time, and offered several innovative approaches to concepts and theories. Yinger is perhaps best known among religious scholars for his functional definition of religion and his contribution to the study of "invisible religion," for his sect-church model, and for his field theory of religion.

Definition of Religion and Invisible Religions

Milton Yinger was among the first to set forth an inclusive "functional definition" of religion. He suggests that religion be defined not in terms of what it essentially *is* but on what it *does*. He proposes that a social phenomenon be identified as religious if it fulfills the manifest function of religion: the provision of purpose in life and meaning in the face of death, suffering, evil, and injustice. Religion helps individuals cope by providing a strategy to overcome despair, hopelessness, and futility.

Using this type of definition, a wide range of phenomena become relevant as forms of religion. Yinger insists that nontheistic and even nonsupernatural systems of belief and practice can be appropriate foci for the student of religion. Religion is manifest wherever one sees a closing of the gap between fact and hope, or a leap of faith that allows a person to believe that suffering and evil will someday be defeated. A secular faith that science and technology will ultimately solve all our problems or a deep faith in the ultimate value of the nation or of capitalism becomes religious in nature. The functional definition of religion asks what *new forms* religion is taking rather than *whether* people are religious.

Yinger's definition of religion, then, is as follows:

Where one finds awareness of and interest in the continuing, recurrent, *permanent* problems of human existence—the human condition itself, as contrasted with specific problems; where one finds rites and shared beliefs relevant to that awareness, which define the strategy of an ultimate victory; and where one has groups organized to heighten that awareness and to teach and maintain those rites and beliefs—there one has religion. (1970:33)

Yinger suggested that in rapidly changing societies, religion itself may be changing and may "look different." New forms of religion may be emerging—forms that are not measured by traditional questions. Rather than starting with traditional concepts of religiosity and trying to assess its effect on everyday life, functional definitions begin with the consequential dimension.

Using such a functional definition of religion, Yinger operationalizes his research in a very different way. Rather than asking about one's *religion* (a term that brings to mind traditional concepts of ritual, prayer, and orthodoxy for most people), Yinger tries to elicit the level of agreement—on a five-point, strongly agree to strongly disagree scale—with various statements aimed at identifying one's "ultimate concern":

- Suffering, injustice, and finally death are the lot of humanity; but they need not be negative experiences; their significance and effects can be shaped by our beliefs.
- Somehow, I cannot get very interested in the talk about "the basic human condition" and "humanity's ultimate problems."
- A person's most difficult and destructive experiences are often the source of increased understanding and powers of endurance.
- Despite the often chaotic conditions of human life, I believe that there is an order and pattern to existence that someday we will come to understand.

Depending on how respondents answer these questions, Yinger feels one has an indication of the basic religiosity of the individual. He then seeks to determine what it is that serves as an ultimate concern for those religious persons by asking an open-ended question:

In your most reflective moments, when you are thinking beyond the immediate issues of the day—however important—beyond headlines, beyond the temporary, what do you consider the most important issue humanity has to face? Or, to put the question another way, what do you see as the basic, permanent question for humankind? (1969:93)

Because Yinger also believes that religion is essentially a social phenomenon that takes on its most sig-

nificant aspects in social contexts, he also seeks to discover in what groups the individual may be participating that support the emphasis on this ultimate concern and that develop a strategy to address it. His follow-up question is this:

Are you a participant or member of some group, whether large or small, for which the "basic, permanent question" and the beliefs connected with it are the focus of attention and the most important reasons for its existence? If so, please characterize the group briefly. (1969:93)

Yinger uses an inductive method, seeking to discover what concerns people ultimately and what provides people with a sense of meaning and hope. This approach is not very conducive to quantitative research and analysis, but his model has generated a good deal of work on "invisible religion" in a society; it is also very compatible with etic approaches to the study of religion in society.

Yinger's Church-Sect Model   Yinger also developed a church-sect model that tried to avoid cumbersome typologies (with their odd combinations of both social and theological variables). He opted instead for a model emphasizing three variables, and he stressed the dynamic evolution of groups over time rather than a stable typology. His three variables are as follows:

1. The degree to which the membership policy of the group is exclusive and selective or open and inclusive.
2. The extent to which the group accepts or rejects the secular values and structures of society.
3. The extent to which, as an organization, the group integrates a number of local units into one national structure, develops professional staffs, and creates a bureaucracy. (1970:257)

Yinger acknowledged that the first two variables are closely correlated: groups rejecting secular values are likely to be exclusive and selective in their membership policies. He also pointed out that institutionalization may occur independently from membership policy and acceptance of secular values.

Using membership policy and attitude toward societal values as one axis of variation and the extent of institutionalization as the other, Yinger developed a model that illuminates a multilinear evolution of groups from sectlike to churchlike. This model invited analysis of the external social pressures and internal characteristics that cause groups to change along each of these

Inclusiveness of the religious structures
Extent of alienation from societal values

	High			Low
High	Institutional ecclesia	Institutional denomination	rare	null
Extent of organization, complexity, and distinctiveness of the religious structures.*	Diffused ecclesia	Diffused denomination	Established sect	null
	rare	rare	Estabished lay sect	Sect movement
Low	null	null	null	Charismatic sect

*Measurement of degree of complexity of religious structures:

	Are religious units integrated?	Are there religious professionals?	Is there a bureaucratic structure?
4. Most complex	yes	yes	yes
3.	yes	yes	no
2.	yes	no	no
1. Least complex	no	no	no

Figure Y.1. Yinger's Schema: Types of Religious Organizations

two axes. It also allows recognition that a group may stabilize at a particular position or type along the way because of internal or external factors. For example, sects whose primary concern is social evils and injustices are more likely to become established sects and may never become ecclesiastical or denominational bodies. Economic recessions also may slow a group's assimilation to the values of the larger society. His model (Figure Y.1) makes social characteristics the defining factors; theological orientations become variables that

may influence the rate or the direction of the group's evolution.

A Field Theory of Religion   In *The Scientific Study of Religion*, Yinger made an attempt to synthesize insights of conflict, functional, and structural-functional theories into a "field theory" of religion. Objecting to the tautology of some functional reasoning and to the oft-made assumption by functionalists of "system normalcy," Yinger tried to depict systems *simultaneously*

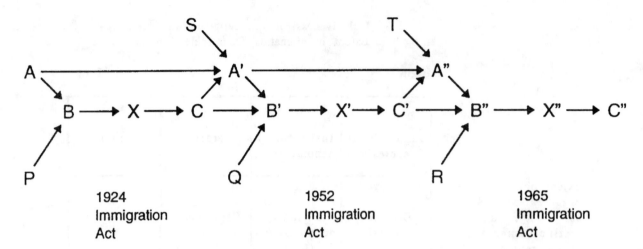

Figure Y.2. Yinger's Field Theory

as integrated and coercive, as evolutionary (changing) and relatively stable, as protecting the vested interests of those with power and meeting needs of individuals and of the larger system.

The first problem of functional models that had to be addressed was the idea of a feedback loop, because consequences clearly cannot go back in time to influence their antecedents. His model is therefore diachronic, indicating ongoing change of individuals and of systems. In his model (see Figure Y.2), structural forces (A) influence individual or "character" factors (B), which result in some specified action, policy, or law (X). For example, church leaders vote on immigration law based on structural needs and pressures (e.g., competent leadership) and on personal attitudes and biases. That action in turn has consequences, and the consequences influence both individuals and the system. But because both the individual and the system have changed, they become A_1 and B_1. The modified society with different structural forces (A_1) influences individuals (B_1) whose values and attitudes may have changed over time. These changed individuals—perhaps decades later—pass new immigration laws, which become X_1, and those laws influence individuals and the social system, becoming A_2 and B_2. This conceptualization avoids the confusing idea in functional feedback models that consequences influence their causes, and also moves beyond the ahistoricism of classical functional models.

The model is also an open field model in recognizing that an outside force—a process external to the system (P, Q, R, S, T)—may have an effect on the structure and on individual character within the system. No subsystem or institution is autonomous—as the functionalist feedback loop implies. Examples of outside influences on immigration policy might include a war, changes in birthrates within the country resulting in a need for more workers, conflicts or alliances of ethnic groups within the country, changes in educational level of the public, and globalization of technology and of the economy. These factors originate outside the normal loop of action regarding immigration law but may enter the field of action at some point. Yinger suggests that religion must be seen as a dynamic, changing process through time (as conflict theorists point out) but as having consequences that may satisfy needs within the system (as functionalists insist).

Yinger's field theory remains one of the more interesting efforts to synthesize elements of functional and conflict analysis.

See also Church-Sect Theory, Definition of Religion, Ethnicity, Functionalism, Invisible Religion, Racism, Paul Tillich

—*Keith A. Roberts*

REFERENCES

J. M. Yinger, *Religion in the Struggle for Power* (Durham, N.C.: Duke University Press, 1946); "Contraculture and Subculture," *American Sociological Review* 25(1960):625-635; *Sociology Looks at Religion* (New York: Macmillan, 1963); *Toward a Field Theory of Religion* (New York: McGraw-Hill, 1965); "A Structural Examination of Religion," *Journal for the Scientific Study of Religion* 8(1969):88-100; "A Comparative Study of the Substructure of Religion," *Journal for the Scientific Study of Religion* 16(1977):67-86.

YOGA Beliefs and practices originating in Indian religion that operate on different levels. An ancient Sanskrit text called *Yoga Sutra* is attributed to Patanjali (second century B.C.E.). Hinduism, Buddhism, and Jainism each have incorporated elements of yoga. On the religious plane, its basic objective is to make the aspirant fit in mind and body so that she or he can receive illumination.

According to yogic belief, in the human body there are seven *chakras* (or nerve centers) that, when awakened, lead to spiritual ascent. These centers are located in the body in an ascending order. The three lower centers are found in the pelvic region, and their functions relate to alimentation, procreation, and the instinct to survive. The four higher centers are found in the suprapelvic region (heart, base of neck, pineal region, and upper part of the skull); their functions relate, respectively, to awakening of compassion, transcendence of gender differences, acquisition of paranormal powers, and attainment of supreme consciousness. The paranormal powers include telepathy, precognition, clairvoyance, and so on.

The main reason for the use of yogic techniques is the enforcement of religious discipline. Usually these techniques are taught by a master to his disciples. The training can be prolonged and difficult. In Indian religions, intellectual understanding of religion is not regarded as sufficient. Religion must be experienced by the mind-body set so that the aspirant undergoes a holistic development. Transcendental Meditation (TM) is a modern yoga popular in the West with demonstrated physiological benefits.

See also Hinduism, Wellness

—C. N. Venugopal

REFERENCES

H. Benson and M. Z. Klipper, *The Relaxation Response* (New York: Avon, 1976); J. Campbell, *The Power of Myth* (Garden City, N.Y.: Doubleday, 1968); D. Chattopadhyaya, *Indian Philosophy* (New Delhi: People's Publishing House, 1982).

YOUNG, BRIGHAM (1801-1877)   Successor to the founder of Mormonism, Joseph Smith, and, like him, born in Vermont. In many ways, Young was the more important to the survival and spread of Mormonism, not only in America but in England as well. Young's mission to England in 1840-1841 contributed greatly to the conversion of thousands there and to their orderly mass migration to Mormon settlements in America.

Following the assassination of Joseph Smith in 1844, Young almost single-handedly guided the fractious and traumatized Mormon community through the succession crisis and eventually led them, Moses-like, to the mountains of Utah in the single longest and most dramatic wilderness trek in American history. Beginning in 1847 with the founding of Salt Lake City, Young established hundreds of Mormon colonies between the Rockies and the Sierra Nevada. During most of the 1850s, Young was the Territorial Governor of Utah and simultaneously Superintendent of Indian Affairs there. These historic secular accomplishments, along with his towering spiritual presence as the Mormon prophet, have tended to be overshadowed by salacious popular treatments of his polygynous household, when in reality early Mormon polygyny was rather an austere institution.

Most of the scholarly literature on Young over the years has appeared in numerous journal articles (e.g., *Pacific Historical Review* and *Utah Historical Quarterly*) but in only a few books. The most thorough of these are *Brigham Young: American Moses* (Knopf 1985) and *Great Basin Kingdom: An Economic History of the Latter-day Saints* (Harvard University Press 1958), both by the distinguished western historian Leonard J. Arrington and based on key collections of primary sources. Much shorter but also very useful is Newell G. Bringhurst's *Brigham Young and the Expanding American Frontier* (Little Brown 1986).

—Armand L. Mauss

YOUTH CULTURE   *see* Adolescence

ZAHN, GORDON C. (1918–) Ph.D. Catholic University, 1952; Professor of Sociology, Loyola University of Chicago, 1953-1967; University of Massachusetts at Boston, 1967-1980. President, American Catholic Sociological Society, 1968.

A quintessential organic intellectual, Zahn critically extended the conceptualizations found in the general sociological literature on social control to the historical issues of the accommodation of religions (focusing on his own Roman Catholic tradition) to national security ideologies. His studies of German Catholics during World War II (magnified by his role as a founder of *Pax Christi*, America) have been major sources for Catholic peace activists and the Austrian national reflection on the loss of conscience during the Nazi era.

—*James R. Kelly*

REFERENCES

G. Zahn, *German Catholics and Hitler's Wars* (Notre Dame, Ind.: University of Notre Dame Press, 1989 [1962]); G. Zahn, *What Is Society?#* (New York: Hawthorn, 1964); G. Zahn, *In Solitary Witness* (Springfield, Ill.: Templegate, 1986 [1964]); G. Zahn, *Another Part of the War* (Amherst: University of Massachusetts Press, 1979).

ZOROASTRIANISM (ZOROASTER) An ancient religion founded in pre-Islamic Persia (now Iran) in the early part of the first millennium B.C.E. When Moslem Arabs conquered Persia, many Zoroastrians fled to India.

Founded by Zarathustra (or Zoroaster), the faith's primary innovation was monotheism, combined with a radical dualism of good and evil. The Judeo-Christian idea of the Devil was borrowed from Zoroastrianism at the time of the Babylonian exile. Also, a strong emphasis on individual responsibility for moral choices was an early defining characteristic of Zoroastrianism, whose key symbol is fire. European philosophers, from Voltaire to Nietzsche, have drawn on the work of Zarathustra. There are an estimated 6,000 adherents in North America, almost entirely of Iranian, Indian, or Pakistani descent. These groups have some doctrinal differences, and each has some doctrinal conflict with the orthodox centers in Bombay, India, and Iran. As of the mid-1990s, Zoroastrian associations ("churches") are located in cities around the globe, with perhaps two dozen in North America. Zoroastrianism is also sometimes called Mazdaism, after their god's name, Mazda. Particularly in India, Zoroastrians are also known as Parsis or Parsees, from their Persian origin.

—*Keith A. Roberts*

REFERENCES

M. Boyce, *A History of Zoroastrianism* (Leiden: Brill, 1975); M. Boyce, *Zoroastrians* (London: Routledge, 1979); Center for Zoroastrian Research, 3270 E. Robinson Road, Bloomington, Ind. 47401-9301.

Index

B

I

J

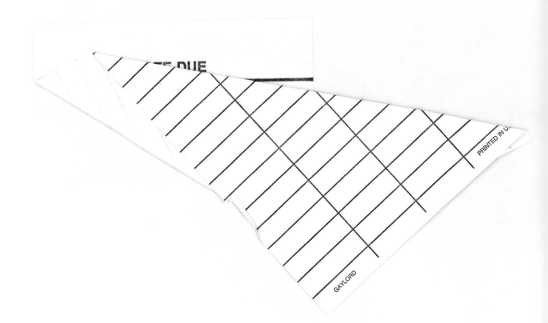

DUE

PRINTED IN U.

GAYLORD